Pam Owens
949 5749
452 59 MM

Cases
in
Constitutional Law

Robert F. Cushman

with

Susan P. Koniak

Cases
in
Constitutional Law

Seventh Edition

PRENTICE HALL
Englewood Cliffs, New Jersey 07632

Library of Congress Cataloging-in-Publication Data

Cushman, Robert Fairchild, (Date)
  Cases in constitutional law.

   1. United States--Constitutional law--Cases.
I. Title.
KF4549.C8 1989   342.73   88-12544
                  347.302

Editorial/production supervision: Linda Zuk
Cover design: Edsal Enterprises
Manufacturing buyer: Peter Havens

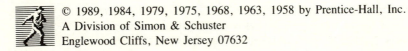

© 1989, 1984, 1979, 1975, 1968, 1963, 1958 by Prentice-Hall, Inc.
A Division of Simon & Schuster
Englewood Cliffs, New Jersey 07632

Printed in the United States of America
10 9 8 7 6 5 4 3 2 1

ISBN 0-13-118316-8

Prentice-Hall International (UK) Limited, *London*
Prentice-Hall of Australia Pty. Limited, *Sydney*
Prentice-Hall Canada Inc., *Toronto*
Prentice-Hall Hispanoamericana, S.A., *Mexico*
Prentice-Hall of India Private Limited, *New Delhi*
Prentice-Hall of Japan, Inc., *Tokyo*
Simon & Schuster Asia Pte. Ltd., *Singapore*
Editora Prentice-Hall do Brasil, Ltda., *Rio de Janeiro*

For my brother, John F. Cushman
1922–1988

Contents

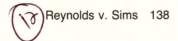

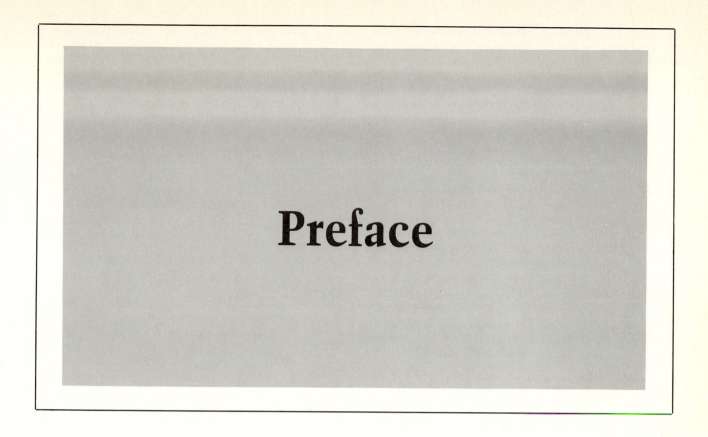

Preface

The aim of this book is to assemble a body of basic material that will be adequate for a full-year upper-class college course in American constitutional law or a first-year course in a law school. The book is divided into two substantially equal parts, the first dealing with the basic structure of the United States government and the second with the rights of individuals against government. Each of these subdivisions is designed to provide text material for one term or semester. However, a one-term course could be built upon a judicious selection of material from both parts.

Many college and university courses in constitutional law are taught in institutions in which access to the United States Supreme Court Reports is not readily available to undergraduates. With this in mind, the book is designed to be self-contained in the sense that its utility and effectiveness do not depend upon supplementary and often inaccessible materials. It is, however, a book designed for a case study of the Constitution and no effort has been made to duplicate the ground covered by the many excellent books on judicial behavior, the politics of the Supreme Court, or the structure of the judicial system.

The Supreme Court does not work in a vacuum and each of the excerpts from the Court's opinion is preceded by introductory notes designed to place that opinion in its social, economic, or political context. Although the Court does work in a social environment, it is engaged in interpreting and applying the Constitution to the decision of cases before it. For this reason it works under rules that prevent it from responding overtly to the kinds of pressures to which the political branches respond. It has taken upon itself an obligation to listen to rational argument and to provide a reasoned explanation for its decisions—to explain, within the context of the case before it, what the Constitution means and why.

The meaning of the Constitution is not a static thing and buried within the Court's opinions are the explanations of how the changes in this meaning take place. The note material is designed to make clear the evolution of these meanings in past cases and to tempt the reader to be critical of the way the Court handles its obligation to be rational in their development. A democratic people with such an oligarchic institution in their midst should form some idea of the role that institution plays and the rules by which it plays it. By occasionally providing more than one case on a subject or a spirited dissent, the editor assumes that the give and take of classroom analysis is not only good mental discipline, but can be an intellectually stimulating and an enjoyable thing, worth doing for that reason alone.

The need to keep the book about the same size as the previous edition means dropping some cases and replacing them with more recent ones. In the present edition Watkins v. United States was dropped from Chapter 2 and its essence incorporated into the Barenblatt note. Bowsher v. Synar holding void part of the Graham-Rudman-Hollings act has been added to Chapter 3, while Chapter 5 now includes Garcia v. San Antonio Metro. which overruled the Usery case. Usery, however, was kept to provide both sides of the argument. In Chapter 6 McCray v. United States—an old classic—was dropped to make room for South Dakota v. Dole holding valid congressional use of the tax power to set a national minimum drinking age.

Three cases in the Establishment of Religion area—Allen, Abington and Nyquist—are now mentioned in other notes, while two new cases replace them. These are Edwards v. Aguillard, holding void Louisiana's law requiring the teaching of "creation science," and Lynch v. Donnelly upholding the right of a town to include a crèche and other religious symbols in a town-supported Christmas display. Under race discrimination, Norris v. Alabama gave way to Batson v. Kentucky, holding void a long-standing method of selecting juries which virtually assured an all-white jury in those cases where the prosecutor wanted one.

Three new cases have been added from the 1987-88 term of the Court: Morrison v. Olson, which holds valid the appointment by the judiciary of a special prosecutor; Thompson v. Oklahoma, which holds that a 15-year-old boy convicted of murder cannot be executed; and Arizona v. Roberson which holds that a suspect who has invoked his Miranda rights as to one crime cannot be questioned about another, unrelated crime.

While every effort has been made to have the final version of the cases conform to one of the printed versions of the reports, case citations and page references, statute citation and footnotes have been omitted without ellipsis. Footnotes appear with increasing frequency in the more recent cases as the justices elect to put their most cogent and intelligible arguments there rather than in the text of the opinion itself.

Special thanks are extended to Mead Data Central, Inc., for permitting access to LEXIS. With this edition, for the first time, a limited number of cases have been added at the end of the book to update it through the 1987-1988 term of Court. The last-minute decisions regarding the choice of these cases owes much of it effectiveness to LEXIS. My deepest gratitude goes also to Professor Nancy Kassop of the State University of New York at New Paltz, an acknowledged authority on presidential power, for her help with the note to Morrison v. Olson.

1

The Supreme Court and the Nature of the Constitution

AMENDING THE CONSTITUTION

HAWKE v. SMITH

253 U. S. 221; 40 S. Ct. 495; 64 L. Ed. 871(1920)

In prescribing how the Constitution shall be amended, Article V states that once adopted an amendment becomes ''to all intents and purposes'' a part of the Constitution. Article V, however, is subject to interpretation by the Supreme Court in exactly the same way as other constitutional provisions. Those who have felt themselves aggrieved by a new amendment have not hesitated to challenge its validity in court.

The first such challenge was to the Eleventh Amendment in the case of Hollingsworth v. Virginia (1798). That amendment barred suits in the federal courts brought against a state by citizens of other states, or of a foreign country. It was argued, first, that if the amendment annulled suits started before its adoption, it was ex post facto and therefore invalid. The Supreme Court held unanimously that the amendment went into effect immediately upon ratification and that this removed the Court's jurisdiction to decide any case, past or future, to which the amendment applied. It was further argued that the amendment was invalidly adopted because the resolution of Congress proposing it had not been submitted to the President for approval or veto. The Court rejected this argument on the ground that the

President's veto applies only to ordinary legislation and not to the amending process.

In its decision in the National Prohibition Cases (1920) the Court, without opinion, stated a number of propositions, one of which was that the two-thirds vote required to pass a resolution proposing an amendment in Congress was two-thirds of those present and voting, and not two-thirds of the entire membership of the two houses.

In attacks on the Eighteenth and Nineteenth Amendments it was urged that there are limits upon the purposes for which amendments may be adopted and that prohibition and woman's suffrage lay outside those limits. In the National Prohibition Cases the Court stated that ''the prohibition of the manufacture, sale, transportation, importation and exportation of intoxicating liquors for beverage purposes, as embodied in the 18th Amendment, is within the power to amend reserved by Article 5 of the Constitution.'' In Leser v. Garnett (1922) the Court sustained the Nineteenth Amendment against the charge that ''so great an addition to the electorate, if made without the state's consent, destroys its autonomy as a political body.'' The Court rejected the argument and pointed out that the Nineteenth Amendment was phrased like, and made no more fundamental changes in the electorate than, the Fifteenth, which had been considered valid and enforced by the Court for fifty years. It seems safe to conclude that a constitutional amendment will not be held invalid because of what it does.

In United States v. Sprague (1931) it was argued

that the Eighteenth Amendment was void because it was ratified by state legislatures rather than by state ratifying conventions; while minor constitutional changes might properly be ratified by state legislatures, amendments conferring on the United States new direct powers over individuals should be ratified by conventions. The Supreme Court rejected the argument and held that Congress has an absolutely free choice between the two methods. All amendments adopted prior to 1931 had been ratified by state legislatures, and many had made changes quite as fundamental as that of the Eighteenth.

Can the states by their constitutions and laws so control the ratification process as to provide a popular statewide referendum in cases where Congress has selected the method of legislative ratification? This was the major issue in the present case. Two years later, in its brief opinion in Leser v. Garnett, the Court said explicitly that the function of a state legislature in ratifying an amendment is "a Federal function, derived from the Federal Constitution; and it transcends any limitations sought to be imposed by the people of a state." The Court referred specifically to Tennessee, whose legislature had ratified the Nineteenth Amendment without waiting for an intervening state election as required by the state constitution. The Tennessee legislature did not need to wait.

The lack of popular consent involved in having state legislatures ratify amendments was pointed up in efforts to undo by amendment the one man-one vote rulings of the Supreme Court. In a rather cynical race against time, opponents of the rule, led by Senator Dirksen of Illinois, tried to get their proposal before the state legislatures before enough of them had been reapportioned to make ratification unlikely. The proposal, which would have allowed states to apportion one house on a basis other than population, was defeated in the Senate in both 1964 and 1965.

Only four cases have been reversed by constitutional amendment: Chisolm v. Georgia (1793) was nullified by the Eleventh Amendment; the ruling of the Dred Scott case (1857) that blacks could not be citizens was nullified by the Fourteenth Amendment; the Sixteenth Amendment reversed the Income Tax Cases (1895), while the Twenty-sixth reversed the holding in Oregon v. Mitchell (1970) that 18-year-olds had no constitutional right to vote in a state election. In recent years efforts have been made to reverse Supreme Court decisions prohibiting prayers in the public schools and forbidding states to outlaw abortions. Since most proposed amendments that actually go to the states are ratified, the real stumbling block to their passage is the need for a two-thirds vote in Congress itself. In 1981 the Senate made an effort to avoid this difficulty by proposing a statute (which requires only a majority vote of both houses) declaring that a fetus was a person within the meaning of the Fourteenth Amendment. The effect would be to reverse the Court's interpretation of that amendment in Roe v. Wade without invoking the amending process.

Over the years efforts have been made to invoke an unused part of the amending machinery which requires Congress to call a constitutional convention at the request of two-thirds of the states. Among the best known of these was the effort to have such a convention propose an amendment limiting income taxes to 25 percent—a result Congress itself could achieve by simply amending the income tax laws. In 1963 state legislatures began quietly to petition Congress to invoke this machinery (1) to eliminate federal control over state legislative apportionment, (2) to create a Court of the Union made up of the 50 state chief justices to review Supreme Court decisions, and (3) to provide machinery whereby the states could initiate amendments. Sixteen states had signed one or more of these petitions when the move was discovered, and the ensuing public opposition brought it to a halt. Following the defeat of the "Dirksen Amendment," states again began to petition Congress to invoke the machinery, this time to submit the defeated proposal to the states. By March of 1967 all but two of the necessary 38 state legislatures had adopted such petitions.

While Congress would probably call such a convention, assuming the technical requirements were met, it is not at all clear that such a convention would feel itself limited to the subjects mentioned in the petitions, or even bound to deal with them. Certainly experience with the last such convention—in 1789—does not encourage the belief that it would feel itself restricted in any way.

If you are a student with no previous exposure to court cases you will find yourself confronted with a whole new language. Since this is the language of the law, it is worth the trouble to translate, for practice, some of the most difficult paragraphs into English you can understand, just as though it were an assignment in Latin. Use a dictionary where necessary. In one sentence, state the issue in this case.

Mr. Justice **Day** delivered the opinion of the Court, saying in part:

Plaintiff in error (plaintiff below) filed a petition for an injunction in the court of common pleas of Franklin county, Ohio, seeking to enjoin the secretary of state of Ohio from spending the public money in preparing and printing forms of ballot for submission of a referendum to the electors of that state on the question of the ratification which the general assembly had made of the proposed 18th Amendment to the Federal Constitution. . . .

A joint resolution proposing to the states this Amendment to the Constitution of the United States was adopted on the 3rd day of December, 1917. . . . The senate and house of representatives of the state of Ohio adopted a resolution ratifying the proposed Amendment by the general assembly of the state of Ohio, and ordered that certified copies of the joint resolution of ratification be forwarded by the governor to the Secretary of State at Washington and to the presiding officer of each House of Congress. This resolution was adopted on January 7, 1919; on January 27, 1919, the governor of Ohio complied with the resolution. On January 29, 1919, the Secretary of State of the United States proclaimed the ratification of the Amendment, naming thirty-six states as having ratified the same, among them the state of Ohio.

The question for our consideration is: Whether the provision of the Ohio Constitution, adopted at the general election, November, 1918, extending the referendum to the ratification by the general assembly of proposed amendments to the Federal Constitution, is in conflict with article 5 of the Constitution of the United States. . . .

The framers of the Constitution realized that it might, in the progress of time and the development of new conditions, require changes, and they intended to provide an orderly manner in which these could be accomplished; to that end they adopted the 5th article.

This article makes provision for the proposal of amendments either by two thirds of both Houses of Congress, or on application of the legislatures of two thirds of the states; thus securing deliberation and consideration before any change can be proposed. The proposed change can only become effective by the ratification of the legislatures of three fourths of the states, or by conventions in a like number of states. The method of ratification is left to the choice of Congress. Both methods of ratification, by legislatures or conventions, call for action by deliberative assemblages representative of the people, which it was assumed would voice the will of the people.

The 5th article is a grant of authority by the people to Congress. The determination of the method of ratification is the exercise of a national power specifically granted by the Constitution; that power is conferred upon Congress, and is limited to two methods: by action of the legislatures of three fourths of the states, or conventions in a like number of states. Dodge v. Woolsey [1856]. The framers of the Constitution might have adopted a different method. Ratification might have been left to a vote of the people, or to some authority of government other than that selected. The language of the article is plain, and admits of no doubt in its interpretation. It is not the function of courts or legislative bodies, national or state, to alter the method which the Constitution has fixed.

All of the amendments to the Constitution have been submitted with a requirement for legislative ratification; by this method all of them have been adopted.

The only question really for determination is: What did the framers of the Constitution mean in requiring ratification by ''*legislatures?*'' That was not a term of uncertain meaning when incorporated into the Constitution. What it meant when adopted it still means for the purpose of interpretation. A legislature was then the representative body which made the laws of the people. The term is often used in the Constitution with this evident meaning. Article 1, § 2, prescribes the qualifications of electors of Congressmen as ''those requisite for electors of the most numerous branch of the state legislature.'' Article 1, § 3, provided that Senators shall be chosen in each state by the legislature thereof, and this was the method of choosing Senators until the adoption of the 17th Amendment, which made provision for the

election of Senators by vote of the people, the electors to have the qualifications requisite for electors of the most numerous branch of the state legislature. That Congress and the states understood that this election by the people was entirely distinct from legislative action is shown by the provision of the Amendment giving the legislature of any state the power to authorize the executive to make temporary appointments until the people shall fill the vacancies by election. It was never suggested, so far as we are aware, that the purpose of making the office of Senator elective by the people could be accomplished by a referendum vote. The necessity of the Amendment to accomplish the purpose of popular election is shown in the adoption of the Amendment. In article 4 the United States is required to protect every state against domestic violence upon application of the legislature, or of the executive when the legislature cannot be convened. Article 6 requires the members of the several legislatures to be bound by oath or affirmation, to support the Constitution of the United States. By article 1, § 8, Congress is given exclusive jurisdiction over all places purchased by the consent of the legislature of the state in which the same shall be. Article 4, § 3, provides that no new states shall be carved out of old states without the consent of the legislatures of the states concerned.

There can be no question that the framers of the Constitution clearly understood and carefully used the terms in which that instrument referred to the action of the legislatures of the states. When they intended that direct action by the people should be had they were no less accurate in the use of apt phraseology to carry out such purpose. The members of the House of Representatives were required to be chosen by the people of the several states. Article 1, § 2.

The Constitution of Ohio in its present form, although making provisions for a referendum, vests the legislative power primarily in a general assembly consisting of a senate and house of representatives. Article 2, § 1, provides:

''The legislative power of the state shall be vested in a general assembly consisting of a senate and house of representatives, but the people reserve to themselves the power to propose to the general assembly laws and amendments to the Constitution, and to adopt or reject the same at the polls on a referendum vote as hereinafter provided.''

The argument to support the power of the state to require the approval by the people of the state of the ratification of amendments to the Federal Constitution through the medium of a referendum rests upon the proposition that the Federal Constitution requires ratification by the legislative action of the states through the medium provided at the time of the proposed approval of an amendment. This argument is fallacious in this,—ratification by a state of a constitutional amendment is not an act of legislation within the proper sense of the word. It is but the expression of the assent of the state to a proposed amendment.

At an early day this court settled that the submission of a constitutional amendment did not require the action of the President. The question arose over the adoption of the 11th Amendment. Hollingsworth v. Virginia [1798]. . . .

It is true that the power to legislate in the enactment of the laws of a state is derived from the people of the state. But the power to ratify a proposed amendment to the Federal Constitution has its source in the Federal Constitution. The act of ratification by the state derives its authority from the Federal Constitution to which the state and its people have alike assented.

This view of the amendment is confirmed in the history of its adoption found in 2 Watson on the Constitution, 1301 et seq. Any other view might lead to endless confusion in the manner of ratification of Federal amendments. The choice of means of ratification was wisely withheld from conflicting action in the several states. . . .

It follows that the court erred in holding that the state had authority to require the submission of the ratification to a referendum under the state Constitution, and its judgment is reversed and the cause remanded for further proceedings not inconsistent with this opinion.

Reversed.

COLEMAN v. MILLER

307 U. S. 433; 59 S. Ct. 972; 83 L. Ed. 1385
(1939)

The cases just discussed left unanswered several important questions about the federal amending process.

First, can a state which has ratified an amendment withdraw that ratification later? New Jersey, Ohio, and Oregon sought to withdraw their ratifications of the Fourteenth Amendment in 1868. The Secretary of State, acting on instructions from Congress embodied in a concurrent resolution, counted the ratifications as binding and proclaimed the amendment in force. New York tried to withdraw her ratification of the Fifteenth Amendment, and Tennessee sought to withdraw ratification of the Nineteenth Amendment. The Secretary of State counted both states as having ratified and Congress left the decision undisturbed. The General Services Administration is now authorized by Congress to keep the score and certify the ratification.

Second, can a state whose legislature has formally rejected a federal amendment later ratify it?

Third, do proposed federal amendments die of old age, as it were, by remaining before the states unratified for too long a time? In Dillon v. Gloss (1921) the Supreme Court held that "the fair inference or implication from Article 5 is that the ratification must be within some reasonable time after the proposal." The Eighteenth Amendment was not void because Congress in submitting it to the states stipulated that it should be inoperative unless ratified within seven years; Congress could place a reasonable time limit on the period of ratification, and seven years was a reasonable limit. But

in most cases Congress has set no time limit. Does this mean that there is no time limit? Two amendments proposed as part of the Bill of Rights in 1789, one proposed in 1810, and another proposed in 1861 have never been ratified by enough states.

In 1923, three years after the Nineteenth Amendment was adopted granting women the right to vote, the Equal Rights Amendment [ERA] was first introduced in Congress. The ERA would prohibit the states and the federal government from denying equal rights on the basis of sex. In 1971 the House of Representatives voted 354 to 24 to propose that the states ratify the ERA and in 1972 the Senate agreed with a vote of 84 to 8. In proposing the Amendment, Congress provided that the states had seven years in which to ratify it. If three fourths of the states had not ratified by that time, the amendment would lapse. As the prescribed deadline drew near, only thirty-five states had ratified the amendment, three short of the number needed for adoption. To prevent the amendment's imminent demise Congress, with a simple majority vote, extended the deadline by three years and three months—until June 30, 1982.

As 1981 drew to a close and the new deadline drew closer, the ERA was still three states short of the necessary thirty-eight and five of the 35 ratifying states had voted to rescind their ratification. While supporters and opponents of the ERA were still arguing the need for and possible effects of the amendment, there was almost universal agreement that its future was bleak.

Then on December 23, 1981, a federal district court in Boise, Idaho, issued an opinion which seemed to sound the death knell of the amendment. The court held that Congress had no power to extend the ratification deadline (hence the extension was unconstitutional) and even if it could extend it, it certainly could not do it by simple majority vote when the original proposal required two-thirds. The Court also held that the states could rescind their ratifications if they wished, since the idea of the amending power was to reflect the contemporaneous approval of three-fourths of the states.

Reaction to the decision was strong and immediate. Opponents of the amendment cheered while its supporters appealed to the Supreme Court for an expedited review. In an unexpected move the Supreme Court stayed the district court ruling (unexpected, since there was no court order to stay) but refused to expedite review. Whatever symbolic force the district court opinion might have had was blunted by the Court's action, but although the case was still technically on the docket at the end of the Court's term, the June 30 deadline passed without the necessary 38 states having ratified and the constitutional issues posed by the case became moot.

Query: Could states which had not ratified an amendment proposed in 1789 now proceed to do so and thus bring the amendment into effect? What would the requisite number of states be in the case of an amendment proposed in 1789? Supposing a state ratified shortly after the time limit set by Con-

gress had expired, could Congress count the ratification? Who would decide these issues if they arose?

Chief Justice **Hughes** wrote the opinion of the Court, saying in part:

In June, 1924, the Congress proposed an amendment to the Constitution, known as the Child Labor Amendment. In January, 1925, the Legislature of Kansas adopted a resolution rejecting the proposed amendment and a certified copy of the resolution was sent to the Secretary of State of the United States. In January, 1937, a resolution . . . was introduced in the Senate of Kansas ratifying the proposed amendment. There were forty senators. When the resolution came up for consideration, twenty senators voted in favor of its adoption and twenty voted against it. The Lieutenant Governor, the presiding officer of the Senate, then cast his vote in favor of the resolution. The resolution was later adopted by the House of Representatives on the vote of a majority of its members.

This original proceeding in mandamus was then brought in the Supreme Court of Kansas by twenty-one members of the Senate [Coleman, et al.], including the twenty senators who had voted against the resolution, and three members of the House of Representatives, to compel the Secretary of the Senate [Miller] to erase an endorsement on the resolution to the effect that it had been adopted by the Senate and to endorse thereon the words "was not passed," and to restrain the officers of the Senate and House of Representatives from signing the resolution and the Secretary of State of Kansas from authenticating it and delivering it to the Governor. The petition challenged the right of the Lieutenant Governor to cast the deciding vote in the Senate. The petition also set forth the prior rejection of the proposed amendment and alleged that in the period from June, 1924, to March, 1927, the amendment had been rejected by both houses of the legislatures of twenty-six states, and had been ratified in only five states, and that by reason of that rejection and the failure of ratification within a reasonable time the proposed amendment had lost its vitality. . . .

[The Court first considered whether the petitioners had sufficient standing in the way of direct interest to invoke the jurisdiction of the Court, and held they had. Secondly, by a vote of four to four, it affirmed, without considering the merits, the decision of the state supreme court that the lieutenant governor had authority to break a tie in the state senate.]

Third.—The effect of the previous rejection of the amendment and of the lapse of time since its submission.

1. The state court adopted the view expressed by text-writers that a state legislature which has rejected an amendment proposed by the Congress may later ratify. The argument in support of that view is that Article V says nothing of rejection but speaks only of ratification and provides that a proposed amendment shall be valid as part of the Constitution when ratified by three-fourths of the States; that the power to ratify is thus conferred upon the State by the Constitution and, as a ratifying power, persists despite a previous rejection. The opposing view proceeds on an assumption that if ratification by "Conventions" were prescribed by the Congress, a convention could not reject and, having adjourned sine die, be reassembled and ratify. It is also premised, in accordance with the views expressed by text-writers, that ratification if once given cannot afterwards be rescinded and the amendment rejected, and it is urged that the same effect in the exhaustion of the State's power to act should be ascribed to rejection; that a State can act "but once, either by convention or through its legislature."

Historic instances are cited. In [December 18] 1865, the Thirteenth Amendment was rejected by the legislature of New Jersey which subsequently ratified it, but the question did not become important as ratification by the requisite number of States had already been proclaimed. The question did arise in connection with the adoption of the Fourteenth Amendment. The legislatures of Georgia, North Carolina and South Carolina had rejected the amendment in November and December, 1866. New governments were erected in those States (and in others) under the direction of Congress. The new legislatures ratified the amendment, that of North Carolina on July 4, 1868, that of South Carolina on July 9, 1868, and that of Georgia on July 21, 1868. Ohio and New Jersey first ratified and then passed resolutions withdrawing their consent. As there were then thirty-seven States, twenty-eight were needed to constitute the requisite three-fourths. On July 9, 1868, the Congress adopted a resolution requesting the Secretary of State to communicate "a list of the States of the Union whose legislatures have ratified the fourteenth article of amendment," and in Secretary Seward's report attention was called to the action of Ohio and New Jersey. On July 20th Secretary Seward issued a proclamation reciting the ratification by twenty-eight States, including North Carolina, South Carolina, Ohio and New Jersey, and stating that it appeared that Ohio and New Jersey had since passed resolutions withdrawing their consent and that "it is deemed a matter of doubt and uncertainty whether such resolutions are not irregular, invalid and therefore ineffectual." The Secretary certified that if the ratifying resolutions of Ohio and New Jersey were still in full force and effect, notwithstanding the attempted withdrawal, the amendment had become a part of the Constitution. On the following day the Congress adopted a concurrent resolution which, reciting that three-fourths of the States having ratified (the list including North Carolina, South Carolina, Ohio and New Jersey), declared the Fourteenth Amendment to be a part of the Constitution and that it should be duly promulgated as such by the Secretary of State. Accordingly, Secretary Seward, on July 28th, issued his proclamation embracing the States mentioned in the congressional resolution and adding Georgia.

Thus the political departments of the Government dealt with the effect both of previous rejection and of attempted withdrawal and determined that both were ineffectual in the presence of an actual ratification. . . . This decision by the political departments of the Government as to the validity of the adoption of the Fourteenth Amendment has been accepted.

We think that in accordance with this historic precedent the question of the efficacy of ratifications by state legislatures, in the light of previous rejection or attempted withdrawal, should be regarded as a political question pertaining to the political departments, with the ultimate authority in the Congress in the exercise of its control over the promulgation of the adoption of the amendment.

The precise question as now raised is whether, when the legislature of the State, as we have found, has actually ratified the proposed amendment, the Court should restrain the state officers from certifying the ratification to the Secretary of State, because of an earlier rejection, and thus prevent the question from coming before the political departments. We find no basis in either Constitution or statute for such judicial action. Article V, speaking solely of ratification, contains no provision as to rejection. Nor has the Congress enacted a statute relating to rejections. . . .

The statute [relating to the promulgation of constitutional amendments] presupposes official notice to the Secretary of State when a state legislature has adopted a resolution of ratification. We see no warrant for judicial interference with the performance of that duty. . . .

2. The more serious question is whether the proposal by the Congress of the amendment had lost its vitality through lapse of time and hence it could not be ratified by the Kansas legislature in 1937. The argument of petitioners stresses the fact that nearly thirteen years elapsed between the proposal in 1924 and the ratification in question. It is said that when the amendment was proposed there was a definitely adverse popular sentiment and that at the end of 1925 there had been rejection by both houses of the legislatures of sixteen States and ratification by only four States, and that it was not until about 1933 that an aggressive campaign was started in favor of the amendment. In reply, it is urged that Congress did not fix a limit of time for ratification and that an unreasonably long time had not elapsed since the submission; that the conditions which gave rise to the amendment had not been eliminated; that the prevalence of child labor, the diversity of state laws and the disparity in their administration, with the resulting competitive inequalities, continued to exist. Reference is also made to the fact that a number of the States have treated the amendment as still pending and that in the proceedings of the national government there have been indications of the same view. It is said that there were fourteen ratifications in 1933, four in 1935, one in 1936, and three in 1937.

We have held that the Congress in proposing an amendment may fix a reasonable time for ratification. Dillon v. Gloss [1921]. There we sustained the action of the Congress in providing in the proposed Eighteenth

Amendment that it should be inoperative unless ratified within seven years. No limitation of time for ratification is provided in the instant case either in the proposed amendment or in the resolution of submission. But petitioners contend that, in the absence of a limitation by the Congress, the Court can and should decide what is a reasonable period within which ratification may be had. We are unable to agree with that contention.

It is true that in Dillon v. Gloss the Court said that nothing was found in Article V which suggested that an amendment once proposed was to be open to ratification for all time, or that ratification in some States might be separated from that in others by many years and yet be effective; that there was a strong suggestion to the contrary in that proposal and ratification were but succeeding steps in a single endeavor; that as amendments were deemed to be prompted by necessity, they should be considered and disposed of presently; and that there is a fair implication that ratification must be sufficiently contemporaneous in the required number of States to reflect the will of the people in all sections at relatively the same period; and hence that ratification must be within some reasonable time after the proposal. These considerations were cogent reasons for the decision in Dillon v. Gloss, that the Congress had the power to fix a reasonable time for ratification. But it does not follow that, whenever Congress has not exercised that power, the Court should take upon itself the responsibility of deciding what constitutes a reasonable time and determine accordingly the validity of ratifications. That question was not involved in Dillon v. Gloss and, in accordance with familiar principle, what was there said must be read in the light of the point decided.

Where are to be found the criteria for such a judicial determination? None are to be found in Constitution or statute. In their endeavor to answer this question petitioners' counsel have suggested that at least two years should be allowed; that six years would not seem to be unreasonably long; that seven years had been used by the Congress as a reasonable period; that one year, six months and thirteen days was the average time used in passing upon amendments which have been ratified since the first ten amendments; that three years, six months and twenty-five days has been the longest time used in ratifying. To this list of variables, counsel add that "the nature and extent of publicity and the activity of the public and of the legislatures of the several States in relation to any particular proposal should be taken into consideration." That statement is pertinent, but there are additional matters to be examined and weighed. When a proposed amendment springs from a conception of economic needs, it would be necessary, in determining whether a reasonable time had elapsed since its submission, to consider the economic conditions prevailing in the country, whether these had so far changed since the submission as to make the proposal no longer responsive to the conception which inspired it or whether conditions were such as to intensify the feeling of need and the appropriateness of the proposed remedial action. In short, the question of a reasonable time in many cases would involve, as in this case it does involve, an appraisal of a great variety of relevant conditions, political, social and economic, which can hardly be said to be within the appropriate range of evidence receivable in a court of justice and as to which it would be an extravagant extension of judicial authority to assert judicial notice as the basis of deciding a controversy with respect to the validity of an amendment actually ratified. On the other hand, these conditions are appropriate for the consideration of the political departments of the Government. The questions they involve are essentially political and not justiciable. They can be decided by the Congress with the full knowledge and appreciation ascribed to the national legislature of the political, social and economic conditions which have prevailed during the period since the submission of the amendment.

Our decision that the Congress has the power under Article V to fix a reasonable limit of time for ratification in proposing an amendment proceeds upon the assumption that the question, what is a reasonable time, lies within the congressional province. If it be deemed that such a question is an open one when the limit has not been fixed in advance, we think that it should be regarded as an open one for the consideration of the Congress when, in the presence of certified ratifications by three-fourths of the States, the time arrives for the promulgation of the adoption of the amendment. The decision by the Congress, in its control of the action of the Secretary of State, of the question whether the amendment had been adopted within a reasonable time would not be subject to review by the courts. . . .

For the reasons we have stated . . . we think that the Congress in controlling the promulgation of the adoption of a constitutional amendment has the final determination of the question whether by lapse of time its proposal of the amendment had lost its vitality prior to the required ratifications. The state officials should not be restrained from certifying to the Secretary of State the adoption by the legislature of Kansas of the resolution of ratification.

As we find no reason for disturbing the decision of the Supreme Court of Kansas in denying the mandamus sought by petitioners, its judgment is affirmed but upon the grounds stated in this opinion.

Affirmed.

Concurring opinion by Mr. Justice **Black**, in which Mr. Justice **Roberts**, Mr. Justice **Frankfurter**, and Mr. Justice **Douglas** join, stated in part:

Since Congress has sole and complete control over the amending process, subject to no judicial review, the views of any court upon this process cannot be binding upon Congress, and in so far as Dillon v. Gloss attempts judicially to impose a limitation upon the right of Congress to determine final adoption of an amendment, it should be disapproved. . . .

Mr. Justice **Frankfurter** wrote a separate concurring opinion in which Justices **Roberts, Black**, and **Douglas** joined.

Mr. Justice **Butler**, with whom Mr. Justice **McReynolds** joined, dissented, saying in part:

In Dillon v. Gloss . . . we definitely held that Article 5 impliedly requires amendments submitted to be ratified within a reasonable time after proposal; that Congress may fix a reasonable time for ratification, and that the period of seven years fixed by the Congress was reasonable. . . .

. . . I would hold that more than a reasonable time had elapsed and that the judgment of the Kansas supreme court should be reversed.

The point, that the question—whether more than a reasonable time had elapsed—is not justiciable but one for Congress after attempted ratification by the requisite number of States, was not raised by the parties or by the United States appearing as amicus curiae; it was not suggested by us when ordering reargument. As the Court, in the Dillon Case, did directly decide upon the reasonableness of the seven years fixed by the Congress, it ought not now, without hearing argument upon the point, hold itself to lack power to decide whether more than 13 years between proposal by Congress and attempted ratification by Kansas is reasonable.

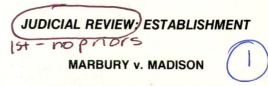

JUDICIAL REVIEW: ESTABLISHMENT

1st - no priors

MARBURY v. MADISON

1 Cranch 137; 2 L. Ed. 60 (1803)

Although the election in the autumn of 1800 brought to the Federalists a defeat from which they never recovered, President Adams and his Federalist associates did not retire from office until March, 1801. The Federalists had been for some time considering plans to reform the federal courts by remodeling the Judiciary Act of 1789, and now in the eleventh hour they boldly set themselves to the task with renewed energy in order, undoubtedly, to insure a fortress for Federalist principles which would not easily be broken down. Accordingly they passed the Judiciary Act of February 13, 1801, which relieved the Supreme Court justices of circuit court duty, reduced the size of the Supreme Court from six to five, and created six new circuit courts with 16 new judgeships. Two weeks later Congress passed an act providing that the President might appoint for the District of Columbia for five-year terms as many justices of the peace as he thought necessary. President Adams proceeded during the last sixteen days of his administration to fill these newly created vacancies (fifty-eight in all) with loyal Federalists; and the task of signing their commissions occupied him until well into the night before the inauguration of Jefferson on March 4, 1801. Among the judicial appointments made by Adams in the closing weeks of his administration was that of John Marshall, a staunch Federalist, to be Chief Justice of the United States.

The federal courts had already incurred the bitter animosity of the Jeffersonians, largely because of the vigor with which they had enforced the obnoxious Alien and Sedition Acts of 1798; and the Republicans were enraged beyond measure at what they deemed the effrontery of the Federalists in enacting the Judiciary Act of 1801. The judiciary was caustically referred to by Randolph as a "hospital for decayed politicians," while Jefferson wrote to a friend, "The Federalists have retired into the judiciary as a stronghold . . . and from that battery all the works of republicanism are to be beaten down and erased." One of the first efforts of the Republican administration was to repeal the Judiciary Act of 1801, and after a long and acrimonious debate this was accomplished, March 8, 1802. The repealing act restored the Supreme Court justices to circuit court duty, restored the size of the Supreme Court to six, and abolished the new circuit judgeships which had been created. The Federalists in Congress bitterly assailed the repealing statute as unconstitutional. Marshall himself apparently adhered to that view, and probably would have held the law void if it had come before him immediately in his judicial capacity. In order to prevent this, however, the repealing act had so altered the sessions of the Supreme Court that it did not convene again for fourteen months, by which time acquiescence in the act by the judges affected made a decision of unconstitutionality impracticable.

However, when the Court convened in February, 1803, the case of Marbury v. Madison was on the docket. Marbury was one of those whom President Adams had appointed to a five-year justiceship of the peace in the District of Columbia. His commission, signed and sealed on March 3, was among four that had not been delivered when Jefferson had taken office on March 4. It was, in fact, Marshall, then serving as Secretary of State as well as Chief Justice, who had sealed but had not delivered Marbury's commission. Jefferson immediately ordered his new Secretary of State, James Madison, to withhold the commission; and Marbury filed suit asking the Supreme Court in the exercise of its original jurisdiction to issue a writ of mandamus to compel Madison to give him his commission. The right to issue such a writ had been conferred upon the Court by a provision of the Judiciary Act of 1789, and jurisdiction thereunder had been exercised by the Court twice before Marshall's accession to the bench. When the case came on for argument, it assumed very largely the aspect of a quarrel between the President and the judiciary. Marbury's own interest in it was small, since Jefferson made it fairly clear that he had no intention of giving Marbury his commission even if the Court ordered him to do so. The Republicans seem to have expected that the Court would issue the mandamus asked for, and there were open threats that Marshall and his colleagues would be impeached if that occurred.

Marshall's decision that the Constitution forbade the Court to issue the writ of mandamus asked for by Marbury might have placated the Republicans had he not in their judgment gratuitously gone beyond the necessities of the case. While holding that the Court could not take jurisdiction and decide the case, inasmuch as the statute authorizing it was unconstitutional, he nonetheless pointed out that Marbury was entitled to his commission; that a writ of mandamus was the proper remedy; and that the executive was properly subject to mandamus if the case were started in the proper court. In addition he scolded the administration for not delivering the commission. In the storm of criticism thereby engendered, the judicial review aspect of the case seems largely to have escaped attack; and when, six months later, a circuit court held unconstitutional another act of Congress abolishing fees granted by an earlier law to justices of the peace in the District of Columbia, it evoked no criticism of any kind. The case, not in any official report, is noted by Charles Warren, The Supreme Court in United States History, Vol. I, 255.

No more vehement argument has ever raged in the field of constitutional law and theory than that over the genesis of the power of judicial review. Did the framers of the Constitution intend to grant the power as part of the checks and balances system in the first three articles? Or did Chief Justice Marshall "usurp" this power for the judiciary in his decision in Marbury v. Madison? Scholars still disagree, and the real intention of the framers will probably never be known. But a number of things are certain. It is certain that this was the first case in which the Supreme Court openly and clearly held unconstitutional an act of Congress. It is equally certain that the idea of judicial review did not originate with Marshall. Most of the arguments which he used in his famous opinion had been presented again and again in the debates in Congress on the Repeal Act of 1802, and the basic theory had been advanced by Hamilton in Number 78 of The Federalist. Moreover, the lower federal courts, without exciting opposition, had held invalid the act of Congress making them, in effect, claims commissioners for pension claims (a fact pointed out by Marshall in his opinion); and a number of earlier state cases have been considered as embodying the principle; see Bayard v. Singleton (1787). That Marshall cited no precedents to bolster his interpretation of judicial power is not particularly surprising. As a jurist he relied heavily on deductive reasoning, and in neither Gibbons v. Ogden (1824) nor McCulloch v. Maryland (1819), two of his most famous opinions, did he cite a single case as precedent.

There is evidence that public opinion tended to look upon the power of judicial review as one of the normal incidents of judicial power. The Court considered the constitutionality of the carriage tax in Hylton v. United States (1796); and its refusal to declare it unconstitutional, as well as the refusal of the lower federal courts to hold unconstitutional the Alien and Sedition Acts and the United States Bank Charter, was bitterly condemned by the Republicans, who seemed to feel that the courts were neglecting their duty in not sustaining the Constitution against legislative usurpation of power. That Congress itself recognized the power is perhaps evidenced by their alteration of the term of the Supreme Court to prevent the Repeal Act of 1802 from coming to the Court for review for more than a year after its enactment. Nor was the Court hesitant to review the validity of state action which allegedly violated the Constitution. Shortly after the Carriage Tax Case the Court held that a Connecticut law revising a judicial decision was not ex post facto in violation of Article I, Sec. 9.

The case of Marbury v. Madison has a certain strategic significance which should not be left out of account. The next case in which an act of Congress was invalidated by the Supreme Court was the famous Dred Scott case, decided in 1857. By that time nearly seventy years had elapsed from the time of the formation of our constitutional system, and the Court was composed of men holding nationalistic views far less strong than those of Marshall and his associates. Moreover, Marbury v. Madison involved the use of judicial power to protect the Court itself against interference by the legislature, a use reasonably easy to justify in view of the separation of powers; while the Dred Scott case involved the use of congressional power in quite another field. Had the power of judicial review not been exercised and the doctrine established in the case of Marbury v. Madison, one may well conjecture whether our constitutional development would have been the same.

As Marshall makes clear in the case below, the Court interprets the provisions of the Constitution in the course of deciding cases and in the context of the problems presented by those cases. The best way to learn what is involved in such interpretation is to assume a hypothetical set of facts and put yourself in the position of the Court trying to make a decision. An effort to find logical reasons for whatever decision you reach will give you some feel for the work of the Court and the nature of constitutional interpretation.

Query: How would you decide the following constitutional questions? Would the Court decide these questions?

Assume Congress proposes to the states the following Constitutional amendment:

"The judicial power of the United States shall not be construed to authorize any court to declare invalid any statute of Congress or to refuse to enforce such statute in any matter before it.

"This amendment shall be deemed to have been ratified if approved by a majority of those voting at a national referendum to be called for such purpose."

Following the adoption of the amendment in the manner provided, a person is found guilty of a newly enacted federal crime of performing an abortion and claims in his defense that the criminal statute is unconstitutional. He appeals to the Supreme Court, claiming that the act is void because it is based upon an unconstitutional amendment and that the amendment is void (1) because the amending power does not extend to abolishing the Court's power of judicial review and (2) even if it did, the amendment was not properly ratified.

Mr. Chief Justice **Marshall** delivered the opinion of the Court, saying in part:

In the order in which the court has viewed this subject, the following questions have been considered and decided.

1st. Has the applicant a right to the commission he demands? [The Court finds that he has.]

2d. If he has a right, and that right has been violated, do the laws of his country afford him a remedy? [The Court finds that they do.]

3d. If they do afford him a remedy, is it a mandamus issuing from this court? . . .

This, then, is a plain case for a mandamus, either to deliver the commission, or a copy of it from the record; and it only remains to be inquired,

Whether it can issue from this court.

The act to establish the judicial courts of the United States authorizes the Supreme Court "to issue writs of mandamus in cases warranted by the principles and usages of law, to any courts appointed, or persons holding office, under the authority of the United States."

The Secretary of State, being a person holding an office under the authority of the United States, is precisely within the letter of the description, and if this court is not authorized to issue a writ of mandamus to such an officer, it must be because the law is unconstitutional, and therefore absolutely incapable of conferring the authority, and assigning the duties which its words purport to confer and assign.

The constitution vests the whole judicial power of the United States in one Supreme Court, and such inferior courts as congress shall, from time to time, ordain and establish. . . .

In the distribution of this power it is declared that "the Supreme Court shall have original jurisdiction in all cases affecting ambassadors, other public ministers and consuls, and those in which a state shall be a party. In all other cases, the Supreme Court shall have appellate jurisdiction." . . .

If it had been intended to leave it in the discretion of the legislature to apportion the judicial power between the supreme and inferior courts according to the will of that body, it would certainly have been useless to have proceeded further than to have defined the judicial power, and the tribunals in which it should be vested. The subsequent part of the section is mere surplusage, is entirely without meaning, . . . the distribution of jurisdiction, made in the constitution, is form without substance. . . .

It cannot be presumed that any clause in the constitution is intended to be without effect; and, therefore, such a construction is inadmissible, unless the words require it. . . .

To enable this court, then, to issue a mandamus, it must be shown to be an exercise of appellate jurisdiction, or to be necessary to enable them to exercise appellate jurisdiction. . . .

It is the essential criterion of appellate jurisdiction, that it revises and corrects the proceedings in a cause already instituted, and does not create that cause. Although, therefore, a mandamus may be directed to courts, yet to issue such a writ to an officer for the delivery of a paper, is in effect the same as to sustain an original action for that paper, and, therefore, seems not to belong to appellate, but to original jurisdiction. Neither is it necessary in such a case as this, to enable the court to exercise its appellate jurisdiction.

The authority, therefore, given to the Supreme Court, by the act establishing the judicial courts of the United States, to issue writs of mandamus to public officers, appears not to be warranted by the constitution; and it becomes necessary to inquire whether a jurisdiction so conferred can be exercised.

The question, whether an act, repugnant to the constitution, can become the law of the land, is a question deeply interesting to the United States; but, happily, not of an intricacy proportioned to its interest. It seems only necessary to recognize certain principles, supposed to have been long and well established, to decide it.

That the people have an original right to establish, for their future government, such principles, as, in their opinion, shall most conduce to their own happiness is the basis on which the whole American fabric has been erected. The exercise of this original right is a very great exertion; nor can it, nor ought it, to be frequently repeated. The principles, therefore, so established, are deemed fundamental. And as the authority from which they proceed is supreme, and can seldom act, they are designed to be permanent.

This original and supreme will organizes the government, and assigns to different departments their respective powers. It may either stop here, or establish certain limits not to be transcended by those departments.

The government of the United States is of the latter description. The powers of the legislature are defined and limited; and that those limits may not be mistaken, or forgotten, the constitution is written. To what purpose are powers limited, and to what purpose is that limitation committed to writing, if these limits may, at any time, be passed by those intended to be restrained? The distinction between a government with limited and unlimited powers is abolished, if those limits do not confine the persons on whom they are imposed, and if acts prohibited and acts allowed, are of equal obligation. It is a proposition too plain to be contested, that the constitution controls any legislative act repugnant to it; or, that the legislature may alter the constitution by an ordinary act.

Between these alternatives there is no middle ground. The constitution is either a superior paramount law, unchangeable by ordinary means, or it is on a level with ordinary legislative acts, and, like other acts, is alterable when the legislature shall please to alter it.

If the former part of the alternative be true, then a legislative act contrary to the constitution is not law: if the latter part be true, then written constitutions are absurd attempts, on the part of the people, to limit a power in its own nature illimitable.

Certainly all those who have framed written constitutions contemplate them as forming the fundamental and paramount law of the nation, and, consequently, the theory of every such government must be, that an act of the Legislature, repugnant to the constitution, is void.

This theory is essentially attached to a written constitution, and, is consequently, to be considered, by this court, as one of the fundamental principles of our society. It is not therefore to be lost sight of in the further consideration of this subject.

If an act of the Legislature, repugnant to the constitution, is void, does it, notwithstanding its invalidity, bind the courts, and oblige them to give it effect? Or, in other words, though it be not law, does it constitute a rule as operative as if it was a law? This would be to overthrow in fact what was established in theory; and would seem, at first view, an absurdity too gross to be insisted on. It shall, however, receive a more attentive consideration.

It is emphatically the province and duty of the judicial department to say what the law is. Those who apply the rule to particular cases, must of necessity expound and interpret that rule. If two laws conflict with each other, the courts must decide on the operation of each.

So if a law be in opposition to the constitution; if both the law and the constitution apply to a particular case, so that the court must either decide that case conformably to the law, disregarding the constitution; or conformably to the constitution, disregarding the law; the court must determine which of these conflicting rules governs the case. This is of the very essence of judicial duty.

If, then, the courts are to regard the constitution, and the constitution is superior to any ordinary act of the Legislature, the constitution, and not such ordinary act, must govern the case to which they both apply.

Those then, who controvert the principle that the constitution is to be considered, in court, as a paramount law, are reduced to the necessity of maintaining that courts must close their eyes on the constitution, and see only the law.

This doctrine would subvert the very foundation of all written constitutions. It would declare that an act which, according to the principles and theory of our government, is entirely void, is yet, in practice, completely obligatory. It would declare that if the legislature shall do what is expressly forbidden, such act, notwithstanding the express prohibition, is in reality effectual. It would be giving to the legislature a practical and real omnipotence, with the same breath which professes to restrict their powers within narrow limits. It is prescribing limits, and declaring that those limits may be passed at pleasure.

That it thus reduces to nothing what we have deemed the greatest improvement on political institutions, a written constitution, would of itself be sufficient, in America, where written constitutions have been viewed with so much reverence, for rejecting the construction. But the peculiar expressions of the constitution of the United States furnish additional arguments in favor of its rejection.

The judicial power of the United States is extended to all cases arising under the constitution.

Could it be the intention of those who gave this power, to say that in using it the constitution should not be looked into? That a case arising under the constitution should be decided without examining the instrument under which it arises?

This is too extravagant to be maintained.

In some cases, then, the constitution must be looked into by the judges. And if they can open it at all, what part of it are they forbidden to read or to obey?

There are many other parts of the constitution which serve to illustrate this subject.

It is declared that "no tax or duty shall be laid on articles exported from any State." Suppose a duty on the export of cotton, of tobacco, or of flour; and a suit instituted to recover it. Ought judgment to be rendered in such a case? Ought the judges to close their eyes on the constitution, and only see the law?

The constitution declares "that no bill of attainder or ex post facto law shall be passed."

If, however, such a bill should be passed, and a person should be prosecuted under it; must the court condemn to death those victims whom the constitution endeavors to preserve?

"No person," says the constitution, "shall be convicted of treason unless on the testimony of two witnesses to the same overt act, or on confession in open court."

Here the language of the constitution is addressed especially to the courts. It prescribes, directly for them, a rule of evidence not to be departed from. If the legislature should change that rule, and declare one witness, or a confession out of court, sufficient for conviction, must the constitutional principle yield to the legislative act?

From these, and many other selections which might be made, it is apparent, that the framers of the constitution contemplated that instrument as a rule for the government of courts, as well as of the legislature.

Why otherwise does it direct the judges to take an oath to support it? This oath certainly applies in an especial manner, to their conduct in their official character. How immoral to impose it on them, if they were to be used as the instruments, and the knowing instruments, for violating what they swear to support!

The oath of office, too, imposed by the legislature, is completely demonstrative of the legislative opinion on this subject. It is in these words: "I do solemnly swear that I will administer justice without respect to persons, and do equal right to the poor and to the rich; and that I will faithfully and impartially discharge all the duties incumbent on me as ———, according to the best of my abilities and understanding agreeably to the constitution and laws of the United States."

Why does a judge swear to discharge his duties agreeably to the constitution of the United States, if that constitution forms no rule for his government? if it is closed upon him, and cannot be inspected by him?

If such be the real state of things, this is worse than solemn mockery. To prescribe, or to take this oath, becomes equally a crime.

It is also not entirely unworthy of observation, that in declaring what shall be the supreme law of the land, the constitution itself is first mentioned; and not the laws of the United States generally, but those only which shall be made in pursuance of the constitution, have that rank.

Thus, the particular phraseology of the constitution of the United States confirms and strengthens the principle, supposed to be essential to all written constitutions, that a law repugnant to the constitution is void; and that courts, as well as other departments, are bound by that instrument.

The rule must be discharged.

EAKIN v. RAUB

12 Sergeant and Rawle (Pennsylvania Supreme
Court) 330 (1825)

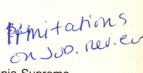

So accustomed are we to the Supreme Court's exercise of the power of judicial review, and so impressive is Marshall's defense of the practice, that we forget there is nothing inevitable about it. In most of the countries of the world, including England, a constitution is viewed not as a law to be enforced by the courts, but as a compact between the sovereign and the people regarding the rights and powers of each. Thus, when the English nobility cornered King John I at Runnymede and forced him to sign the Magna Charta assuring them freedom from certain misuses of royal power, there was no thought that violations of this charter could be challenged in court. John did not always live up to his agreements, just as our government does not always behave constitutionally, but Magna Charta and other documents like it are the English constitution. There may be differences of opinion over what certain rights mean but it is not vital that these differences be decided by a court and an Englishman does not expect that they will be. It is the nature of constitutional government that the agencies of political power try to live up to the spirit of the constitutional restrictions upon them and observe the rights of the people. If they do not do so, then a country does not have a constitutional government and no power of judicial review by a court is going to alter that fact. Jefferson, Marshall's most bitter personal and political adversary, never admitted the paramount authority of the Supreme Court to determine the validity of an act of Congress, but held that each of the three departments of the national government, being equal and separate, was equally empowered "to decide on the validity of an act according to its own judgment and uncontrolled by the opinions of any other department."

The Supreme Court has always had its critics, and following particularly unpopular decisions invalidating acts of Congress the attacks have been exceedingly bitter. Such decisions as the Dred Scott case, the Income Tax case, and a whole series of cases prior to 1937 which invalidated social legislation stirred up opposition which reduced the prestige of the Court and which endured until either a constitutional amendment or the Court itself changed the effect of the ruling. Recognizing the wide latitude left to the judges in interpreting the Constitution, and the manifest political and economic character of many of their decisions a number of critics have attacked the power of judicial review as an undemocratic instrument of government in an increasingly democratic society, and from time to time some of the justices on the Court itself (usually, it may be said, in dissenting opinions) have appeared to share this view. Against this background, it is interesting to note that at no time in our history has the power of judicial review been seriously endangered. Despite attacks on the Court's decisions, on its personnel and even on the procedures by which review is exercised, no major political party has ever urged the complete abolition of the power of review itself. The resounding defeat in Congress of the so-called Court Packing Plan, suggested by President Franklin D. Roosevelt at the height of his popularity, indicates that popular dissatisfaction with the use of the power of judicial review does not necessarily imply a feeling that the Court should be dominated by the political branches of the government.

Undaunted by the experiences of the Roosevelt era Attorney General Edwin Meese 3rd, speaking for the administration of Ronald Reagan, in 1985 launched an all-out campaign to effect dramatic changes in constitutional law and underlying doctrine. He announced that in his opinion the only valid interpretation of the Constitution was one which reflected the values of the original framers and established a policy that no person would be nominated for a federal judgeship who did not subscribe to this point of view.

While the ''intent of the framers'' is one of the earliest techniques of constitutional interpretation, it tends to produce extremely conservative results by today's standards and has largely given way to techniques which more closely reflect the current needs of a modern society. Moreover, assuming it was the intent of the framers to have the document interpreted by the courts at all, it may fairly be argued that they did not intend it to be interpreted with the rigidity of a statute. As Justice Marshall emphasized in McCulloch v. Maryland (1819), ''we must never forget that it is a constitution we are expounding.'' Also, it is worth noting that even in the opinion below, Marshall does not rely on the intent of the framers for support. Pushed far enough, an interpretation based exclusively on ''original intent'' would virtually emasculate the due process clauses of the Fifth and Fourteenth Amendments and could conceivably result in abandoning judicial review entirely.

The response of the Court was unprecedented. Two justices publicly attacked the government's position, one of them naming Meese by name, and even Jus-

tice (now Chief Justice) Rehnquist, the Court's most conservative member, urged him to take a more moderate tone.

Perhaps the most lucid and carefully reasoned answer to Marshall's argument in Marbury v. Madison is to be found in the following excerpts from a dissenting opinion written by Justice Gibson of the supreme court of Pennsylvania in 1825. The case itself is of no intrinsic interest or importance, but it raised the question of the power of a state supreme court to invalidate a statute, and Justice Gibson took occasion to express his views upon this point, although a majority of his brethren did not agree with him. It is interesting to note that twenty years later a lawyer in pleading his case cited to the court this opinion, whereupon Justice Gibson replied to the lawyer, ''I have changed that opinion, for two reasons. The late convention [which had framed the Pennsylvania constitution of 1838], by their silence, sanctioned the pretensions of the court to deal freely with the act of the legislature; and from experience of the necessity of the case.'' See Norris v. Clymer, 2 Pa. St. 277, 281 (1845).

Mr. Justice **Gibson**, dissenting, said in part:

. . . I am aware, that a right to declare all unconstitutional acts void, without distinction as to either constitution, is generally held as a professional dogma; but, I apprehend, rather as a matter of faith than of reason. I admit that I once embraced the same doctrine, but without examination, and I shall therefore state the arguments that impelled me to abandon it, with great respect for those by whom it is still maintained. But I may premise, that it is not a little remarkable, that although the right in question has all along been claimed by the judiciary, no judge has ventured to discuss it, except Chief Justice Marshall (in Marbury v. Madison [1803]''), and if the argument of a jurist so distinguished for the strength of his ratiocinative powers be found inconclusive, it may fairly be set down to the weakness of the position which he attempts to defend. . . .

The Constitution and the *right* of the legislature to pass the act, may be in collision. But is that a legitimate subject for judicial determination? If it be, the judiciary must be a peculiar organ, to revise the proceedings of the legislature, and to correct its mistakes; and in what part of the Constitution are we to look for this proud preeminence? Viewing the matter in the opposite direction, what would be thought of an act of assembly in which it should be declared that the Supreme Court had, in a particular case, put a wrong construction on the Constitution of the United States, and that the judgment should therefore be reversed? It would doubtless be thought a usurpation of judicial power. But it is by no means clear, that to declare a law void which has been enacted according to the forms prescribed in the Constitution, is not a usurpation of legislative power. It is an act of sovereignty; and sovereignty and legislative power are said by Sir William Blackstone to be convertible terms. It is the business of the judiciary to interpret the laws, not scan the authority of the lawgiver; and without the latter, it cannot take cognizance of a collision between a law and the Constitution. So that to affirm that the judiciary has a right to judge of the existence of such collision, is to take for granted the very thing to be proved. And, that a very cogent argument may be made in this way, I am not disposed to deny; for no conclusions are so strong as those that are drawn from the petitio principii.

But it has been said to be emphatically the business of the judiciary, to ascertain and pronounce what the law is; and that this necessarily involves a consideration of the Constitution. It does so; but how far? If the judiciary will inquire into anything besides the form of enactment, where shall it stop? There must be some point of limitation to such an inquiry; for no one will pretend that a judge would be justifiable in calling for the election returns, or scrutinizing the qualifications of those who composed the legislature. . . .

Every one knows how seldom men think exactly alike on ordinary subjects; and a government constructed on the principle of assent by all its parts, would be inadequate to the most simple operations. The notion of a complication of counter checks has been carried to an extent in theory, of which the framers of the Constitution never dreamt. When the entire sovereignty was separated into its elementary parts, and distributed to the appropriate branches, all things incident to the exercise of its powers were committed to each branch exclusively. The negative which each part of the legislature may exercise, in regard to the acts of the other, was thought sufficient to prevent material infractions of the restraints which were put on the power of the whole; for, had it been intended to interpose the judiciary as an additional barrier, the matter would surely not have been left in doubt. The judges would not have been left to stand on the insecure and ever-shifting ground of public opinion as to constructive powers; they would have been placed on the impregnable ground of an express grant. . . .

But the judges are sworn to support the Constitution, and are they not bound by it as the law of the land? In some respects they are. In the very few cases in which the judiciary, and not the legislature, is the immediate organ to execute its provisions, they are bound by it in preference to any act of assembly to the contrary. In such cases, the Constitution is a rule to the courts. But what I have in view in this inquiry, is the supposed right of the judiciary to interfere, in cases where the Constitution is to be carried into effect through the instrumentality of the legislature, and where that organ must necessarily first decide on the constitutionality of its own act. The oath to support the Constitution is not peculiar to the judges, but is taken indiscriminately by every officer of the government, and is designed rather as a test of the political principles of the man, than to bind the officer in the discharge of his duty: otherwise it were difficult to determine what operation it is to have in the case of a recorder of deeds, for instance, who, in the execution of his office, has nothing to do with the Constitution. But granting it to relate to the official conduct of the judge, as well as every other officer, and not to his political principles, still it must be understood in reference to supporting the Constitution, *only as far as that may be involved in his official duty*; and, consequently, if his official duty does not comprehend an inquiry into the authority of the legislature, neither does his oath.

It is worthy of remark here, that the foundation of every argument in favor of the right of the judiciary, is found at last to be an assumption of the whole ground in dispute. Granting that the object of the oath is to secure a support of the Constitution in the discharge of official duty, its terms may be satisfied by restraining it to official duty in the exercise of the *ordinary* judicial powers. Thus, the Constitution may furnish a rule of construction, where a particular interpretation of a law would conflict with some constitutional principle; and such interpretation where it may is always to be avoided. But the oath was more probably designed to secure the powers of each of the different branches from being usurped by any of the rest: for instance, to prevent the House of Representatives from erecting itself into a court of judicature, or the Supreme Court from attempting to control the legislature; and, in this view, the oath furnishes an argument, equally plausible *against* the right of the judiciary. But if it require a support of the Constitution in anything beside official duty, it is in fact an oath of allegiance to a particular form of government; and, considered as such, it is not easy to see why it should not be taken by the citizens at large, as well as by the officers of the government. It has never been thought that an officer is under greater restraint as to measures which have for their avowed end a total change of the Constitution, than a citizen who has taken no oath at all. The official oath, then, relates only to the official conduct of the officer, and does not prove that he ought to stray from the path of his ordinary business to search for violations of duty in the business of others; nor does it, as supposed, define the powers of the officer.

But do not the judges do a *positive act* in violation of the Constitution, when they give effect to an unconstitutional law? Not if the law has been passed according to the forms established in the Constitution. The fallacy of the question is, in supposing that the judiciary adopts the acts of the legislature as its own; whereas the enactment of a law and the interpretation of it are not concurrent acts, and as the judiciary is not required to concur in the enactment, neither is it in the breach of the Constitution which may be the consequence of the enactment. The fault is imputable to the legislature, and on it the responsibility exclusively rests. In this respect, the judges are in the predicament of jurors who are bound to serve in capital cases, although unable, under any circumstances, to reconcile it to their duty to deprive a human being of life. To one of these, who applied to be discharged from the panel, I once heard it remarked, by an eminent and humane judge: "*You* do not deprive a prisoner of life by finding him guilty of a capital crime; you but pronounce his case to be within the law, and it is, therefore, those who declare the law, and not you, who deprive him of life.''

Limitations on Jud. review

CASES AND CONTROVERSIES

MUSKRAT v. UNITED STATES

219 U. S. 346; 31 S. Ct. 250; 55 L. Ed. 246
(1911)

Second only to the power of judicial review itself is the power to decide which constitutional issues will come before the Supreme Court and which will not. There are always persons standing in the wings ready to challenge every governmental action on constitutional grounds, and the Court has articulated rules to determine who may bring such challenges and who may not. How these rules are interpreted and applied determines in large measure both the course of constitutional development and the role which the Court itself will play in the constitutional system.

In his opinion in Marbury v. Madison (1803) Marshall grounded his constitutional argument for judicial review upon the language of Article III, which extends to the Supreme Court (and inferior courts) judicial power to be exercised in ''all cases, in law and equity, arising under this Constitution. . . .'' In short, the reason why the Court occasionally declares an act of Congress unconstitutional is that, according to Marshall, it has to do so in deciding the ''cases and controversies'' coming before it in the exercise of its ''judicial powers.'' Thus Marshall permanently tied judicial review to ''cases and controversies.'' This has meant, over the years, that only when one of the parties in an actual ''case'' relies for his rights upon a statute will the Court undertake to decide whether or not that statute violates the Constitution; furthermore, it will do so only when such a decision is essential to the disposal of the case. Since Article III also extends judicial power to ''such inferior courts as the Congress may from time to time ordain and establish,'' these lower courts also exercise the power of judicial review. Under the statutes, however, such lower court decisions striking down laws as unconstitutional are subject to review by the Supreme Court, and almost invariably they are so reviewed. The Supreme Court has the last word.

But what is a ''case'' or ''controversy'' within the meaning of Article III? An essential requirement is that there be actual litigants with conflicting interests of such a nature that they are subject to judicial determination. Thus the Court held in United States v. Evans (1909) that it would not hear an appeal by the government on a point of law taken from a trial court case in which the defendant had been acquitted, despite an act of Congress giving the government ''the same right of appeal as is given to the defendant'' but with the proviso that ''a verdict in
favor of the defendant shall not be set aside.'' Evans had been tried for murder in the District of Columbia and acquitted, and the government objected to the exclusion by the trial judge of certain evidence. The Court ruled that the acquittal of Evans, in view of the prohibition against double jeopardy, had removed one of the parties to the suit. To decide the question of law involved, since there were no longer two litigants and therefore no case, would be to render an advisory opinion.

An important effect of the Evans decision is to make impossible a Supreme Court review of the constitutionality of a federal penal statute in a case where the lower court acquits the defendant by holding invalid the act under which he was prosecuted. To overcome this difficulty the trial judge is often persuaded to rule on the constitutionality of the indictment, and to quash it if he concludes that it is brought under an invalid criminal statute. Since indicting a person does not put him in jeopardy in terms of the double jeopardy provision of the Fifth Amendment, the lower court's ruling on the constitutional issues can be appealed directly to the Supreme Court without abridging the rights of the accused. United States v. Classic (1941), testing the constitutionality of federal control of primary elections, was carried to the Supreme Court in this way.

The requirement that there be adverse parties if there is to be a case or controversy rules out friendly or collusive suits; see Chicago & Grand Trunk Ry. Co. v. Wellman (1892). In this case the railroad claimed that rates set by Michigan law were so low as to be confiscatory and hence a denial of due process of law. On the day the rates went into effect, Wellman was refused a ticket at the new low rate and brought suit for damages. The parties, Wellman and the railroad, presented an agreed statement of facts concerning the cost of operating the railroad, its earnings, etc., in the preparation of which the state was not represented. Therefore there was no representative for the point of view that the railroad could make money at the new rate. The Court refused to upset the rate statute on this ground: that the agreed statement might have kept out of the record information tending to show that the railroad could make money under the new rate. Since the facts necessary to decide the constitutional issue were confined to the ones agreed to by the parties, the Court felt it was being handed the decision along with the case. ''The theory,'' the Court observed, ''upon which, apparently, this suit was brought is that parties have an appeal from the legislature to the courts, and that the latter are given an immediate and general supervision of the constitutionality of the acts of the former. Such is not true. Whenever, in the pursuance of an honest and antagonistic assertion of rights by one individual against another, there is presented a question involving the validity of any act of any legislature, state or federal, and the decision necessarily rests on the competency of the legislature to so enact, the court must, in the exercise of its solemn duties, determine whether the act be constitutional or not; but such an exercise of power is the ultimate and supreme func-

tion of courts. It is legitimate only in the last resort, and as a necessity in the determination of real, earnest, and vital controversy between the individuals. It never was thought that, by means of a friendly suit, a party beaten in the legislature could transfer to the courts an inquiry as to the constitutionality of the legislative act.''

While the Court will not hear collusive suits such as the one just described, this does not mean that there must be animosity between the litigants. ''Friendly'' suits may be brought to test the validity of a statute if it can be shown that the legal claims of the parties under the act are in conflict. For instance, the famous Income Tax Case of 1895 was a suit brought by a stockholder to enjoin the Farmers' Loan and Trust Co. from paying what was thought to be an unconstitutional tax, although the idea that the bank wished to pay the tax is somewhat ludicrous. The statute, however, required the bank to do so. In cases of this kind it is customary for the Attorney General to enter the case as amicus curiae to represent the public interest. This was done in the Income Tax Case, and in 1937 such representation was formally provided for by statute.

Occasionally, where the actual facts are not essential to a decision of the constitutional issue involved, the Court will admit an agreed statement of facts which has been carefully worked out so as to provide jurisdiction and present the legal or constitutional point in its clearest terms. An extreme example of this is found in Hylton v. United States (1796), in which it was stipulated by both parties that the defendant owned ''one hundred and twenty-five chariots . . . for the defendant's own private use, and not to be let out to hire. . . .'' In Ex parte Young (1908) the Court held that due process of law was denied by a statute placing so severe a penalty on violation of a railroad rate law as to make a test case of the law virtually impossible. A ticket agent faced a $5000 fine and five years in jail for every ticket he sold at higher than the legal rate, and it had proved impossible to obtain a sufficiently courageous ticket agent to secure a violation of the law. The case was brought into court by a petition to enjoin the attorney general (Young) of the state from enforcing the new rate law. The state urged that such an action was barred by the Eleventh Amendment, but the Court rejected this view.

In the present case a congressional statute explicitly authorized judicial review of the constitutionality of certain statutes. Following the admission to citizenship of the Cherokee Indians, Congress had by law altered the original distribution of tribal property. Since this had the effect of reducing the amount of lands and funds to which certain Indians were entitled, its constitutionality was seriously questioned. To settle the matter Congress passed an act specifically providing that David Muskrat and others might bring suits in the court of claims, with a right of appeal to the Supreme Court, to test the constitutionality of the redistribution statutes. The courts involved were ordered to give preference to these suits; the Attorney General was ordered to defend them; and if Muskrat et al. won, the government was to pay their at-

And others

torney's fees. Justice Day's opinion is notable for its historical summary of the limits of judicial power.

Mr. Justice **Day** delivered the opinion of the Court, saying in part:

The first question in these cases, as in others, involves the jurisdiction of this court to entertain the proceeding, and that depends upon whether the jurisdiction conferred is within the power of Congress, having in view the limitations of the judicial power, as established by the Constitution of the United States. . . .

It will serve to elucidate the nature and extent of the judicial power thus conferred by the Constitution [Sections 1 and 2 of Article III] to note certain instances in which this court has had occasion to examine and define the same. As early as 1792 an act of Congress was brought to the attention of this court, which undertook to provide for the settlement of claims of widows and orphans, barred by the limitations theretofore established regulating claims to invalid pensions. The act was not construed by this court, but came under consideration before the then chief justice and another justice of this court and the district judge, and their conclusions are given in the margin of the report of Hayburn's Case [1792]. The act undertook to devolve upon the circuit court of the United States the duty of examining proofs, of determining what amount of the monthly pay would be equivalent to the disability ascertained, and to certify the same to the Secretary of War, who was to place the names of the applicants on the pension list of the United States in conformity thereto, unless he had cause to suspect imposition or mistake, in which event he might withhold the name of the applicant and report the same to Congress.

In the note to the report of the case it appeared that Chief Justice Jay, Mr. Justice Cushing, and District Judge Duane unanimously agreed:

''That by the Constitution of the United States, the government thereof is divided into three distinct and independent branches, and that it is the duty of each to abstain from, and to oppose, encroachments on either.

''That neither the legislative nor the executive branches can constitutionally assign to the judicial any duties but such as are properly judicial, and to be performed in a judicial manner.

''That the duties assigned to the circuit courts by this act are not of that description, and that the act itself does not appear to contemplate them as such; inasmuch as it subjects the decisions of these courts, made pursuant to those duties, first to the consideration and suspension of the Secretary of War, and then to the revision of the legislature; whereas by the Constitution, neither the Secretary of War, nor any other executive officer, nor even the legislature, are authorized to sit as a court of errors on the judicial acts or opinions of this court.'' . . .

In 1793, by direction of the President, Secretary of State Jefferson addressed to the justices of the Supreme Court a communication soliciting their views upon the question whether their advice to the Executive would be available in the solution of important questions of the construction of treaties, laws of nations and laws of the land, which the Secretary said were often presented under circumstances which "*do not give a cognizance of them to the tribunals of the country.*" The answer to the question was postponed until the subsequent sitting of the Supreme Court, when Chief Justice Jay and his associates answered to President Washington that in consideration of the lines of separation drawn by the Constitution between the three departments of government, and being judges of a court of last resort, afforded strong arguments against the propriety of extrajudicially deciding the questions alluded to, and expressing the view that the power given by the Constitution to the President, of calling on heads of departments for opinions, "seems to have been purposely, as well as expressly, united to the executive departments." Correspondence & Public Papers of John Jay, Vol. 3, p. 486.

The subject underwent a complete examination in the case of Gordon v. United States [1865], reported in an appendix to 117 U.S. 697, in which the opinion of Mr. Chief Justice Taney, prepared by him and placed in the hands of the clerk, is published in full. It is said to have been his last judicial utterance, and the whole subject of the nature and extent of the judicial power conferred by the Constitution is treated with great learning and fullness. In that case an act of Congress was held invalid which undertook to confer jurisdiction upon the court of claims and thence by appeal to this court, the judgment, however, not to be paid until an appropriation had been estimated therefor by the Secretary of the Treasury; and, as was said by the chief justice, the result was that neither court could enforce its judgment by any process, and whether it was to be paid or not depended on the future action of the Secretary of the Treasury and of Congress. "The Supreme Court," says the Chief Justice, "does not owe its existence or its powers to the legislative department of the government. It is created by the Constitution, and represents one of the three great divisions of power in the government of the United States, to each of which the Constitution has assigned its appropriate duties and powers, and made each independent of the other in performing its appropriate functions. The power conferred on this court is exclusively judicial, and it cannot be required or authorized to exercise any other." . . .

At the last term of the court, in the case of Baltimore & O. R. Co. v. Interstate Commerce Commission [1909], this court declined to take jurisdiction of a case which undertook to extend its appellate power to the consideration of a case in which there was no judgment in the court below. In that case former cases were reviewed by Mr. Chief Justice Fuller, who spoke for the court, and the requirement that this court adhere strictly to the jurisdiction, original and appellate, conferred upon it by the Constitution, was emphasized and enforced. It is therefore apparent that from its earliest history this court has consistently declined to exercise any powers other than those which are strictly judicial in their nature.

It therefore becomes necessary to inquire what is meant by the judicial power thus conferred by the Constitution upon this court, and with the aid of appropriate legislation, upon the inferior courts of the United States. "Judicial power," says Mr. Justice Miller, in his work on the Constitution, "is the power of a court to decide and pronounce a judgment and carry it into effect between persons and parties who bring a case before it for decision." . . .

As we have already seen, by the express terms of the Constitution, the exercise of the judicial power is limited to "cases" and "controversies." Beyond this it does not extend, and unless it is asserted in a case or controversy within the meaning of the Constitution, the power to exercise it is nowhere conferred.

What, then, does the Constitution mean in conferring this judicial power with the right to determine "cases" and "controversies." A "case" was defined by Mr. Chief Justice Marshall as early as the leading case of Marbury v. Madison to be a suit instituted according to the regular course of judicial procedure. And what more, if anything, is meant in the use of the term "controversy?" That question was dealt with by Mr. Justice Field, at the circuit, in the case of Re Pacific Railway Commission, 32 Fed. 241 [1887]. Of these terms that learned justice said:

"The judicial article of the Constitution mentions cases and controversies. The term 'controversies,' if distinguishable at all from 'cases,' is so in that it is less comprehensive than the latter, and includes only suits of a civil nature. Chisholm v. Georgia [1793]. By cases and controversies are intended the claims of litigants brought before the courts for determination by such regular proceedings as are established by law or custom for the protection or enforcement of rights, or the prevention, redress, or punishment of wrongs. Whenever the claim of a party under the Constitution, laws, or treaties of the United States takes such a form that the judicial power is capable of acting upon it, then it has become a case. The term implies the existence of present or possible adverse parties, whose contentions are submitted to the court for adjudication."

The power being thus limited to require an application of the judicial power to cases and controversies, Is the act which undertook to authorize the present suits to determine the constitutional validity of certain legislation within the constitutional authority of the court? This inquiry in the case before us includes the broader question, When may this court, in the exercise of the judicial power, pass upon the constitutional validity of an act of Congress? That question has been settled from the early history of the court, the leading case on the subject being Marbury v. Madison [1803].

In that case Chief Justice Marshall, who spoke for the court, was careful to point out that the right to declare an act of Congress unconstitutional could only be exercised when a proper case between opposing parties was submitted for judicial determination; that there was no general veto power in the court upon the legislation of Congress; and that the authority to declare an act uncon-

Describes Marb. v Mad. at a pnd proceeding

stitutional sprang from the requirement that the court, in administering the law and pronouncing judgment between the parties to a case, and choosing between the requirements of the fundamental law established by the people and embodied in the Constitution and an act of the agents of the people, acting under authority of the Constitution, should enforce the Constitution as the supreme law of the land. The Chief Justice demonstrated, in a manner which has been regarded as settling the question, that with the choice thus given between a constitutional requirement and a conflicting statutory enactment, the plain duty of the court was to follow and enforce the Constitution as the supreme law established by the people. And the court recognized, in Marbury v. Madison and subsequent cases, that the exercise of this great power could only be invoked in cases which came regularly before the courts for determination, for, said the chief justice, in Osborn v. Bank of United States [1824], speaking of the third article of the Constitution, conferring judicial power:

"This clause enables the judicial department to receive jurisdiction to the full extent of the Constitution, laws, and treaties of the United States, when any question respecting them shall assume such a form that the judicial power is capable of acting on it. That power is capable of acting only when the subject is submitted to it by a party who asserts his rights in the form prescribed by law. It then becomes a case, and the Constitution declares that the judicial power shall extend to all cases arising under the Constitution, laws, and treaties of the United States.''

Again, in the case of Cohens v. Virginia [1821], Chief Justice Marshall, amplifying and reasserting the doctrine of Marbury v. Madison, recognized the limitations upon the right of this court to declare an act of Congress unconstitutional. . . .

. . . ''The article does not extend the judicial power to every violation of the Constitution which may possibly take place, but to 'a case in law or equity' in which a right under such law is asserted in a court of justice. If the question cannot be brought into a court, then there is no case in law or equity, and no jurisdiction is given by the words of the article. But if, in any controversy depending in a court, the cause should depend on the validity of such a law, that would be a case arising under the Constitution, to which the judicial power of the United States would extend. . . .''

See also in this connection Chicago & G. T. R. Co. v. Wellman [1892]. . . .

Applying the principles thus long settled by the decisions of this court to the act of Congress undertaking to confer jurisdiction in this case, we find that [David Muskrat et al.] . . . are authorized and empowered to institute suits in the court of claims to determine the validity of acts of Congress passed since the act of July 1, 1902, in so far as the same attempt to increase or extend the restrictions upon alienation, encumbrance, or the right to lease the allotments of lands of Cherokee citizens, or to increase the number of persons entitled to share in the final distribution of lands and funds of the Cherokees beyond those enrolled for allotment as of September 1, 1902, and provided for in the said act of July 1, 1902.

The jurisdiction was given for that purpose first to the court of claims, and then upon appeal to this court. That is, the object and purpose of the suit is wholly comprised in the determination of the constitutional validity of certain acts of Congress; and furthermore, in the last paragraph of the section, should a judgment be rendered in the court of claims or this court, denying the constitutional validity of such acts, then the amount of compensation to be paid to attorneys employed for the purpose of testing the constitutionality of the law is to be paid out of funds in the Treasury of the United States belonging to the beneficiaries, the act having previously provided that the United States should be made a party, and the Attorney General be charged with the defense of the suits.

It is therefore evident that there is neither more nor less in this procedure than an attempt to provide for a judicial determination, final in this court, of the constitutional validity of an act of Congress. Is such a determination within the judicial power conferred by the Constitution, as the same has been interpreted and defined in the authoritative decisions to which we have referred? We think it is not. That judicial power, as we have seen, is the right to determine actual controversies arising between adverse litigants, duly instituted in courts of proper jurisdiction. The right to declare a law unconstitutional arises because an act of Congress relied upon by one or the other of such parties in determining their rights is in conflict with the fundamental law. The exercise of this, the most important and delicate duty of this court, is not given to it as a body with revisory power over the action of Congress, but because the rights of the litigants in justiciable controversies require the court to choose between the fundamental law and a law purporting to be enacted within constitutional authority, but in fact beyond the power delegated to the legislative branch of the government. This attempt to obtain a judicial declaration of the validity of the act of Congress is not presented in a ''case'' or ''controversy,'' to which, under the Constitution of the United States, the judicial power alone extends. It is true the United States is made a defendant to this action, but it has no interest adverse to the claimants. The object is not to assert a property right as against the government, or to demand compensation for alleged wrongs because of action upon its part. The whole purpose of the law is to determine the constitutional validity of this class of legislation, in a suit not arising between parties concerning a property right necessarily involved in the decision in question, but in a proceeding against the government in its sovereign capacity, and concerning which the only judgment required is to settle the doubtful character of the legislation in question. Such judgment will not conclude private parties, when actual litigation brings to the court the question of the constitutionality of such legislation. In a legal sense the judgment could not be executed, and amounts in fact to no more than an expression of opinion upon the validity of the acts in question. Confining the jurisdiction of this court within the limitations conferred by the Constitution, which the court has hitherto been careful to observe, and whose boundaries it has refused to transcend, we think the Congress, in the act of March 1, 1907, exceeded the limitations of legislative authority, so far as it required of this court action not judicial in its nature within the meaning of the Constitution.

. . . If such actions as are here attempted, to determine the validity of legislation, are sustained, the result will be that this court, instead of keeping within the limits of judicial power, and deciding cases or controversies arising between opposing parties, as the Constitution intended it should, will be required to give opinions in the nature of advice concerning legislative action,—a function never conferred upon it by the Constitution, and against the exercise of which this court has steadily set its face from the beginning.

The questions involved in this proceeding as to the validity of the legislation may arise in suits between individuals, and when they do and are properly brought before this court for consideration they, of course, must be determined in the exercise of its judicial functions. For the reasons we have stated, we are constrained to hold that these actions present no justiciable controversy within the authority of the court, acting within the limitations of the Constitution under which it was created. . . .

The judgments will be reversed and the cases remanded to the Court of Claims, with directions to dismiss the petitions for want of jurisdiction.

LUTHER v. BORDEN

7 Howard 1; 12 L. Ed. 581 (1849)

As the Court made apparent in Coleman v. Miller (1939), one other important corollary of its refusal to exercise nonjudicial powers is the doctrine of "political questions." Very early in the exercise of its power of judicial review the Court pointed out that certain powers are vested in the legislative or executive departments of the government to be exercised in a purely discretionary manner, and that whether they have been constitutionally exercised or not is a "political question" which the Court will not undertake to decide. One of the early and very striking instances of this type of question was that which was raised in the famous case of Luther v. Borden.

This case arose out of the following facts: the original constitution of Rhode Island, which was merely the colonial charter with a few minor adaptations, provided for a very restricted suffrage based upon the possession of property; and the right to vote continued to be thus limited long after universal male suffrage had been rather generally adopted throughout the country. Many efforts were made to have the constitution amended so as to put the franchise upon a more democratic basis, but all such attempts were defeated by the relatively small group of legal voters. In 1841 the popular feeling re-

garding the situation ran even higher than before; mass meetings were held throughout the state, and without any semblance of constitutional sanction the citizens were directed to choose, by universal male suffrage, delegates to a constitutional convention. The convention thus formed duly met and drafted a new state constitution, which established adult male suffrage and made many other changes. A popular referendum was conducted in which all the adult male citizens of the state were permitted to vote, and the new constitution was approved by a majority of the votes cast. The leader of the whole movement was a young lawyer, Thomas W. Dorr, who was elected governor under the new constitution and immediately attempted to put the new government into operation. The regular charter government, of course, did not recognize the validity of any of these acts. It called out the state militia, declared martial law, and finally appealed to President Tyler to send federal troops to aid in putting down the insurrection. The President took steps to comply with this request and the "Dorr Rebellion" collapsed. Dorr himself was captured, tried for treason, and finally sentenced to life imprisonment. He was later pardoned.

He naturally had managed to arouse a good deal of sympathy for his cause outside the state, particularly among the Democrats, and it was felt that it would be desirable to present to the Supreme Court of the United States the question of the legality of the new constitution and the acts done under it. This was tried first by Dorr himself by attempting to sue out a writ of habeas corpus in the Supreme Court, but that tribunal dismissed the petition for want of jurisdiction; see Ex parte Dorr (1845). Under the assumption that the same issue could be raised collaterally, the civil controversy between Luther and Borden, relatively unimportant in itself, was pushed through to the Supreme Court. Luther had been a supporter of the Dorr movement; and in an effort to arrest him, Borden and others who were enrolled as members of the militia under the charter government broke into Luther's house. This act they justified upon the ground that martial law had been declared and that they were acting under the orders of their superior officers. Luther, however, sued Borden for trespass, claiming that the act of the legislature establishing martial law was void inasmuch as the Dorr government, elected by the people of the state, was the lawful government. (It should be noted that in January, 1842, the charter government had called a constitutional convention and drafted a new constitution, which was ratified by the people in due form and went into effect in 1843. Thus the Dorr movement did not entirely fail in its purposes.)

There are, of course, numerous other questions which have been held by the courts to be "political" in character. Such is the question whether there is a sufficient emergency to justify the President, acting under the authority of an act of Congress, in calling out the militia to repel invasion or to put down insurrection; see Martin v. Mott (1827). Such, also, are many of the questions which arise for determination in the course of conducting foreign relations; as, for instance, the recogni-

tion of a foreign government, the acquisition of territory, the determination of boundaries, the existence or termination of a treaty, and the like. The early case of Foster v. Neilson (1829), raising the question as to the title to certain territory which was the subject of international dispute, emphasized the unwillingness of the Court to attempt to settle this type of question. The question whether or not a state of the Union has a republican form of government within the meaning of that clause of the Constitution guaranteeing such form of government was squarely raised in 1912 in the case of Pacific States Telephone & Telegraph Co. v. Oregon. In 1902 Oregon had amended its state constitution to establish the initiative and referendum. In 1906 a law was proposed by popular initiative and duly enacted by the people which imposed certain taxes on corporations. The plaintiff corporation resisted the payment of the tax on the ground that the incorporation of the initiative and referendum into the constitutional system of the state destroyed the republican character of its government and thus robbed it of lawful authority. The argument was that republican government means representative government and that representative government is destroyed by the system of direct legislation. The Supreme Court refused to pass on the question whether Oregon had a republican form of government or not and pointed out that that question was political in character and had been determined by Congress in admitting senators and representatives of the state to their seats in Congress.

Mr. Chief Justice **Taney** delivered the opinion of the Court, saying in part:

Certainly, the question which the plaintiff proposed to raise by the testimony he offered has not heretofore been recognized as a judicial one in any of the State courts. . . .

Moreover, the Constitution of the United States, as far as it has provided for an emergency of this kind, and authorized the general government to interfere in the domestic concerns of a State, has treated the subject as political in its nature, and placed the power in the hands of that department.

The fourth section of the fourth article of the Constitution of the United States provides that the United States shall guarantee to every State in the Union a republican form of government, and shall protect each of them against invasion; and on the application of the Legislature or of the executive (when the Legislature cannot be convened) against domestic violence.

Under this article of the Constitution it rests with Congress to decide what government is the established one in a State. For as the United States guarantee to each State a republican government, Congress must necessarily decide what government is established in the State before it can determine whether it is republican or not. And when the senators and representatives of a State are admitted into the councils of the Union, the authority of the government under which they are appointed, as well as its republican character, is recognized by the proper con-

stitutional authority. And its decision is binding on every other department of the government, and could not be questioned in a judicial tribunal. It is true that the contest in this case did not last long enough to bring the matter to this issue; and as no senators or representatives were elected under the authority of the government of which Mr. Dorr was the head, Congress was not called upon to decide the controversy. Yet the right to decide is placed there, and not in the courts.

So, too, as relates to the clause in the above mentioned article of the Constitution, providing for cases of domestic violence. It rested with Congress, too, to determine upon the means proper to be adopted to fulfill this guarantee. They might, if they had deemed it most advisable to do so, have placed it in the power of a court to decide when the contingency had happened which required the federal government to interfere. But Congress thought otherwise, and no doubt wisely; and by the Act of February 28, 1795, provided, that, "in case of any insurrection in any State against the government thereof it shall be lawful for the President of the United States, on application of the Legislature of such State or of the executive (when the Legislature cannot be convened), to call forth such number of the militia of any other State or States, as may be applied for, as he may judge sufficient to suppress such insurrection."

By this act, the power of deciding whether the exigency had arisen upon which the government of the United States is bound to interfere, is given to the President. He is to act upon the application of the Legislature or of the executive, and consequently he must determine what body of men constitute the Legislature, and who is the governor, before he can act. The fact that both parties claim the right to the government cannot alter the case, for both cannot be entitled to it. If there is an armed conflict, like the one of which we are speaking, it is a case of domestic violence, and one of the parties must be in insurrection against the lawful government. And the President must, of necessity, decide which is the government, and which party is unlawfully arrayed against it, before he can perform the duty imposed upon him by the act of Congress.

After the President has acted and called out the militia, is a circuit court of the United States authorized to inquire whether his decision was right? Could the court, while the parties were actually contending in arms for the possession of the government, call witnesses before it and inquire which party represented a majority of the people? If it could, then it would become the duty of the court (provided it came to the conclusion that the President had decided incorrectly) to discharge those who were arrested or detained by the troops in the service of the United States or the government, which the President was endeavoring to maintain. If the judicial power extends so far, the guarantee contained in the Constitution of the United States is a guarantee of anarchy, and not of order. Yet if this right does not reside in the courts when the conflict is raging, if the judicial power is at that time, bound to follow the decision of the political, it must be equally bound when the contest is over. It cannot, when peace is restored, punish as offenses and crimes the acts which it before recognized, and was bound to recognize, as lawful.

It is true that in this case the militia were not called out by the President. But upon the application of the governor under the charter government, the President recognized him as the executive power of the State, and took measures to call out the militia to support his authority if it should be found necessary for the general government to interfere; and it is admitted in the argument, that it was the knowledge of this decision that put an end to the armed opposition to the charter government, and prevented any further efforts to establish by force the proposed constitution. The interference of the President, therefore, by announcing his determination, was as effectual as if the militia had been assembled under his orders. And it should be equally authoritative. For certainly no court of the United States, with a knowledge of this decision, would have been justified in recognizing the opposing party as the lawful government; or in treating as wrong-doers or insurgents the officers of the government which the President had recognized, and was prepared to support by an armed force. In the case of foreign nations, the government acknowledged by the President is always recognized in the courts of justice. And this principle has been applied by the act of Congress to the sovereign States of the Union.

It is said that this power in the President is dangerous to liberty, and may be abused. All power may be abused if placed in unworthy hands. But it would be difficult, we think, to point out any other hands in which this power would be more safe, and at the same time equally effectual. When citizens of the same State are in arms against each other, and the constituted authorities unable to execute the laws, the interposition of the United States must be prompt, or it is of little value. The ordinary course of proceedings in courts of justice would be utterly unfit for the crisis. And the elevated office of the President, chosen as he is by the people of the United States, and the high responsibility he could not fail to feel when acting in a case of so much moment, appear to furnish as strong safeguards against a wilful abuse of power as human prudence and foresight could well provide. At all events, it is conferred upon him by the Constitution and laws of the United States, and must therefore, be respected and enforced in its judicial tribunals.

. . . Undoubtedly, if the President, in exercising this power, shall fall into error, or invade the rights of the people of the State, it would be in the power of Congress to apply the proper remedy. But the courts must administer the law as they find it. . . .

Much of the argument on the part of the plaintiff turned upon political rights and political questions, upon which the court has been urged to express an opinion. We decline doing so. The high power has been conferred on this court of passing judgment upon the acts of the State sovereignties, and of the legislative and executive branches of the federal government, and of determining whether they are beyond the limits of power marked out

for them respectively by the Constitution of the United States. This tribunal, therefore, should be the last to overstep the boundaries which limit its own jurisdiction. And while it should always be ready to meet any question confided to it by the Constitution, it is equally its duty not to pass beyond its appropriate sphere of action, and to take care not to involve itself in discussions which properly belong to other forums. No one, we believe, has ever doubted the proposition, that, according to the institutions of this country, the sovereignty in every State resides in the people of the State, and that they may alter and change their form of government at their own pleasure. But whether they have changed it or not by abolishing an old government, and establishing a new one in its place, is a question to be settled by the political power. And when that power has decided, the courts are bound to take notice of its decision, and to follow it.

The judgment of the Circuit Court [upholding the validity of the charter government and its acts] must therefore be affirmed.

COLEGROVE v. GREEN

328 U.S. 549; 66 S. Ct. 1198; 90 L. Ed. 1432 (1946)

One of the anomalous by-products of our system of representative government is the fact that voters are not equally represented in the legislature. This is true because the districts from which representatives are elected vary in population, with the result that the influence of one voter in electing his representative may be much greater than the influence of another voter in another district. Also the boundaries of legislative districts are drawn by state legislatures; and astute politicians, by the skillful juggling of these district lines, have achieved wonderful feats of inflating or deflating party voting strength by what is called the "gerrymander." (For a diagram and history of the first gerrymander in 1812, see Webster's Eighth Collegiate Dictionary.) Quite as important, however, has been the effect of what is known as the "silent gerrymander," the underrepresentation of cities and overrepresentation of rural areas achieved simply by a failure over the years to redraw district lines to keep pace with the movement of the population from the farm to the city.

Both the state and federal legislatures had long felt the oppressive effect of the "silent gerrymander" in Illinois. The Illinois constitution of 1870 provided that the state should be divided into fifty-one state senatorial districts, from each of which one state senator and three state representatives should be chosen. The legislature, after each census, was to redraw the lines of these districts to meet changes in population. By the turn of the century it was obvious that more than half the population of the state would shortly be concentrated in the metropolitan area of Chicago. Legislators from the down-state rural districts, enjoying a comfortable legislative majority, felt no inclination to yield their political control by reapportioning the state to give the growing metropolis the proportion of the fifty-one districts to which its population clearly entitled it. The political bitterness created by this inequitable situation had made it impossible for the Illinois legislature to agree upon a revision of its legislative districts since the apportionment of 1901. Attempts were made to invoke court action, but the supreme court of Illinois, itself applying the doctrine of "political questions," held that it had no power to compel the legislature to pass a new and fair redistricting law.

This all bears on the problem of congressional apportionment posed in Colegrove v. Green. When Congress after each census reapportions seats in the House of Representatives among the states, it becomes the duty of each state legislature to carve out such new congressional districts as the new allotments may require. But the Illinois legislature was no more willing to give the Chicago metropolitan area its fair share of seats in Congress than in the state legislature itself. At the time the present case arose, it had not reapportioned congressional seats since 1901. Rank inequalities had resulted. One congressional district in Chicago had a population of 914,053, while another in southern Illinois had a population of 112,116. The Court was asked to enjoin the appropriate Illinois state officials from conducting an election in November, 1946, under the provisions of the old congressional apportionment act of 1901. Such an injunction would have compelled the state to elect all of its congressmen on one general ballot, instead of by districts; and this would have given full effect to the political strength of the populous urban areas. Justice Frankfurter, speaking for himself and Justices Reed and Burton, held this to be a political question which the Court could not decide. This opinion was widely construed as the ruling of the case, although Justice Rutledge concurred on different grounds.

Mr. Justice **Frankfurter** announced the judgment of the Court and an opinion in which Mr. Justice **Reed**, and Mr. Justice **Burton** concurred, saying in part:

. . . Appellants are three qualified voters in Illinois districts which have much larger populations than other Illinois Congressional districts. They brought this suit against the Governor, the Secretary of State, and the Auditor of the State of Illinois, as members ex officio of the Illinois Primary Certifying Board, to restrain them, in effect, from taking proceedings for an election in November 1946, under the provisions of Illinois law governing Congressional districts. . . . Formally, the appellants asked for a decree, with its incidental relief, . . . declaring these provisions to be invalid because they violated various provisions of the United States Constitution and § 3 of the Reapportionment Act of August 8, 1911, . . . in that by reason of subsequent changes in population the Congressional districts for the election of Representatives in the Congress created by the Illinois Laws of 1901 . . . lacked compactness of territory and approximate equality of population. The District Court . . . dismissed the complaint. . . .

We are of opinion that the petitioners ask of this Court what is beyond its competence to grant. This is one of those demands on judicial power which cannot be met by verbal fencing about "jurisdiction." It must be resolved by considerations on the basis of which this Court, from time to time, has refused to intervene in controversies. It has refused to do so because due regard for the effective working of our government revealed this issue to be of a peculiarly political nature and therefore not meet for judicial determination.

This is not an action to recover for damage because of the discriminatory exclusion of a plaintiff from rights enjoyed by other citizens. The basis for the suit is not a private wrong, but a wrong suffered by Illinois as a polity. . . . In effect this is an appeal to the federal courts to reconstruct the electoral process of Illinois in order that it may be adequately represented in the councils of the Nation. Because the Illinois Legislature has failed to revise its Congressional Representative districts in order to reflect great changes, during more than a generation, in the distribution of its population, we are asked to do this, as it were, for Illinois.

Of course no court can affirmatively re-map the Illinois districts so as to bring them more in conformity with the standards of fairness for a representative system. At best we could only declare the existing electoral system invalid. The result would be to leave Illinois undistricted and to bring into operation, if the Illinois legislature chose not to act, the choice of members for the House of Representatives on a state-wide ticket. The last stage may be worse than the first. The upshot of judicial action may defeat the vital political principle which led Congress, more than a hundred years ago, to require districting. This requirement, in the language of Chancellor Kent, "was recommended by the wisdom and justice of giving, as far as possible, to the local subdivisions of the people of each state, a due influence in the choice of representatives, so as not to leave the aggregate minority of the people in a state, though approaching perhaps to a majority, to be wholly overpowered by the combined action of the numerical majority, without any voice whatever in the national councils." . . . Assuming acquiescence on the part of the authorities of Illinois in the selection of its Representatives by a mode that defies the direction of Congress for selection by districts, the House of Representatives may not acquiesce. In the exercise of its power to judge the qualifications of its own members, the House may reject a delegation of Representatives-at-large. Article 1, § 5, cl. 1. . . . Nothing is clearer than that this controversy concerns matters that bring courts into immediate and active relations with party contests. From the determination of such issues this Court has traditionally held aloof. It is hostile to a democratic system to involve the judiciary in the politics of the people. And it is not less pernicious if such judicial intervention in an essentially political contest be dressed up in the abstract phrases of the law.

The petitioners urge with great zeal that the conditions of which they complain are grave evils and offend public morality. The Constitution of the United States gives ample power to provide against these evils. But due regard for the Constitution as a viable system precludes judicial correction. Authority for dealing with such problems resides elsewhere. Article 1, § 4 of the Constitution provides that "The Times, Places and Manner of holding Elections for . . . Representatives, shall be prescribed in each State by the Legislature thereof; but the Congress may at any time by Law make or alter such Regulations. . . ." The short of it is that the Constitution has conferred upon Congress exclusive authority to secure fair representation by the States in the popular House and left to that House determination whether States have fulfilled their responsibility. If Congress failed in exercising its powers, whereby standards of fairness are offended, the remedy ultimately lies with the people. Whether Congress faithfully discharges its duty or not, the subject has been committed to the exclusive control of Congress. An aspect of government from which the judiciary, in view of what is involved, has been excluded by the clear intention of the Constitution cannot be entered by the federal courts because Congress may have been in default in exacting from States obedience to its mandate. . . .

To sustain this action would cut very deep into the very being of Congress. Courts ought not to enter this political thicket. The remedy for unfairness in districting is to secure State legislatures that will apportion properly, or to invoke the ample powers of Congress. The Constitution has many commands that are not enforceable by courts because they clearly fall outside the conditions and purposes that circumscribe judicial action. Thus, "on demand of the executive authority," Art. IV, § 2, of a State it is the duty of a sister State to deliver up a fugitive from justice. But the fulfillment of this duty cannot be judicially enforced. Kentucky v. Dennison [1861]. The duty to see to it that the laws are faithfully executed cannot be brought under legal compulsion, Mississippi v. Johnson [1867]. Violation of the great guaranty of a republican form of government in States cannot be challenged in the courts. Pacific Teleph. & Teleg. Co. v. Oregon [1912]. The Constitution has left the performance of many duties in our governmental scheme to depend on the fidelity of the executive and legislative action and, ultimately, on the vigilance of the people in exercising their political rights.

Dismissal of the complaint is affirmed.

Mr. Justice **Rutledge** concurred on the ground that the Court should decline to exercise its equity jurisdiction.

Mr. Justice **Black** dissented in an opinion concurred in by Justices **Douglas** and **Murphy**.

Mr. Justice **Jackson** did not sit in this case.

BAKER v. CARR

369 U. S. 186; 82 S. Ct. 691; 7 L. Ed. 2d 663
(1962)

In the years following Colegrove v. Green (1946), the Court continued to adhere to its stand that state political districting could not be upset by the federal courts. In MacDougall v. Green (1948) the efforts of the Progressive party to get on the ballot in Illinois were defeated by their inability to get petition signatures in the rural counties. While the Court conceded that the "requirement of two hundred signatures from at least fifty counties gives to the voters of less populous counties . . . the power completely to block the nomination . . ." it held that neither due process nor equal protection "deny a State the power to assure a proper diffusion of political initiative." In South v. Peters (1950) the Court refused to interfere with the "County Unit System" in Georgia, a scheme which assigned to each county from two to six electoral votes which went to the candidate receiving the most votes in the county. Despite the fact that this discriminated heavily against the urban black voter, the Court refused to review the case, noting that "federal courts consistently refuse to exercise their equity powers in cases posing political issues arising from a state's geographical distribution of electoral strength among its political subdivisions."

The first break in the Court's attitude came in 1960 in the case of Gomillion v. Lightfoot. There the Court, without passing upon the truth of the alleged discrimination, unanimously rejected the idea that legislative apportionment could never be the subject for judicial review. The issue raised was unique. An Alabama statute of 1957 had redefined the boundaries of the city of Tuskeegee, within which is the well-known Tuskeegee Institute. The city, which had been square in shape, was transformed "into a strangely irregular twenty-eight sided figure," with the intention and result of removing from the city "all save four or five of its 400 black voters while not removing a single white voter or resident." The blacks thus excluded could not, as a result, vote in municipal elections. The lower federal courts, relying in part upon Colegrove v. Green, had dismissed the complaint attacking the validity of the statute. In an opinion by Justice Frankfurter, eight justices agreed that the plaintiffs had a right to have a court decide whether the weird apportionment denied them the right to vote, in violation of the Fifteenth Amendment. Justice Whittaker, denying that the right to vote was involved "inasmuch as no one has the right to vote in . . . an area in which he does not reside," argued that the discrimination violated both the equal protection and due process clauses of the Fourteenth Amendment.

Baker v. Carr is a landmark in constitutional law and in American government and politics. In most states since the turn of the century the rural areas lost population to the cities as an agrarian way of life gave way to the demands of industry. In recent decades another trend has complicated the picture as the inner city population has moved into increasingly densely populated suburban areas. Under Colegrove v. Green only the state legislatures could provide relief for these underrepresented populations and this they had no inclination to do. Nor could reform be achieved through state constitutional amendment since the amending process was under the control of the existing malapportioned legislatures. Baker v. Carr broke the political log jam to which there was no apparent political solution by opening to judicial scrutiny the fairness of legislative apportionment. Since no state could afford to ignore a court order to reapportion for fear of having its election held void, respect for judicial intervention has been uniformly high. The case stands in sharp contrast to Luther v. Borden where one of the reasons behind the "political question" argument was the fear that judicial power would be ineffective if pitted against the political. In 1964 two bills introduced in Congress limiting federal jurisdiction in apportionment cases reached the conference committee stage but failed to become law.

The political question doctrine came before the Court again in 1969 in Powell v. McCormack. There the Court held that whether or not a congressman is qualified to take his seat is not a political question despite the constitutional provision that "each house shall be the judge of the . . . qualifications of its own members." Congress had long assumed that it had complete discretion in such matters. See the note to McGrain v. Daugherty.

Query: The opinion below describes as "significant" the distinction between "jurisdiction" and "justiciability." What is the difference and why is it significant? How had the Court handled the matter in Luther, Coleman and Colegrove?

Mr. Justice **Brennan** delivered the opinion of the Court, saying in part:

This civil action was brought . . . to redress the alleged deprivation of federal constitutional rights. The complaint, alleging that by means of a 1901 statute of Tennessee apportioning the members of the General Assembly among the State's 95 counties, "these plaintiffs and others similarly situated, are denied the equal protection of the laws accorded them by the Fourteenth Amendment to the Constitution of the United States by virtue of the debasement of their votes," was dismissed by a three-judge court. . . . We hold that the dismissal was error, and remand the cause to the District Court for trial and further proceedings consistent with this opinion.

The General Assembly of Tennessee consists of the Senate with 33 members and the House of Representatives with 99 members. The Tennessee Constitution provides in Art. II as follows: . . . [The text of sections 3–6 follows.]

Thus, Tennessee's standard for allocating legislative representation among her counties is the total number of qualified voters resident in the respective counties, subject only to minor qualifications. . . . In 1901 the General Assembly abandoned separate enumeration in favor of reliance upon the Federal Census and passed the Apportionment Act here in controversy. In the more than 60 years since that action, all proposals in both Houses of the General Assembly for reapportionment have failed to pass.

Between 1901 and 1961, Tennessee has experienced substantial growth and redistribution of her population. In 1901 the population was 2,020,616, of whom 487,380 were eligible to vote. The 1960 Federal Census reports the State's population at 3,567,089, of whom 2,092,891 are eligible to vote. The relative standings of the counties in terms of qualified voters have changed significantly. It is primarily the continued application of the 1901 Apportionment Act to this shifted and enlarged voting population which gives rise to the present controversy.

Indeed, the complaint alleges that the 1901 statute, even as of the time of its passage, "made no apportionment of Representatives and Senators in accordance with the constitutional formula . . . , but instead arbitrarily and capriciously apportioned representatives in the Senate and House without reference . . . to any logical or reasonable formula whatever." It is further alleged that "because of the population changes since 1900, and the failure of the Legislature to reapportion itself since 1901," the 1901 statute became "unconstitutional and obsolete." Appellants also argue that, because of the composition of the legislature effected by the 1901 Apportionment Act, redress in the form of a state constitutional amendment to change the entire mechanism for reapportioning, or any other change short of that, is difficult or impossible. The complaint concludes that "these plaintiffs and others similarly situated, are denied the equal protection of the laws accorded them by the Fourteenth Amendment to the Constitution of the United States by virtue of the debasement of their votes." They seek a declaration that the 1901 statute is unconstitutional and an injunction restraining the appellees from acting to conduct any further elections under it. They also pray that unless and until the General Assembly enacts a valid reapportionment, the District Court should either decree a reapportionment by mathematical application of the Tennessee constitutional formulae to the most recent Federal Census figures, or direct the appellees to conduct legislative elections, primary and general, at large. They also pray for such other and further relief as may be appropriate.

I. The District Court's Opinion and Order of Dismissal.

[Here summarized.]

In light of the District Court's treatment of the case, we hold today only (a) that the court possessed jurisdiction of the subject matter; (b) that a justiciable cause of action is stated upon which appellants would be entitled to appropriate relief; and (c) because appellees raise the issue before this Court, that the appellants have standing to challenge the Tennessee apportionment statutes. Beyond noting that we have no cause at this stage to doubt the District Court will be able to fashion relief if violations of constitutional rights are found, it is improper now to consider what remedy would be most appropriate if appellants prevail at the trial.

II. Jurisdiction of the Subject Matter.

The District Court was uncertain whether our cases withholding federal judicial relief rested upon a lack of federal jurisdiction or upon the inappropriateness of the subject matter for judicial consideration—what we have designated "nonjusticiability." The distinction between the two grounds is significant. In the instance of nonjusticiability, consideration of the cause is not wholly and immediately foreclosed; rather, the Court's inquiry necessarily proceeds to the point of deciding whether the duty asserted can be judicially identified and its breach judicially determined, and whether protection for the right asserted can be judicially molded. In the instance of lack of jurisdiction the cause either does not "arise under" the Federal Constitution, laws or treaties (or fall within one of the other enumerated categories of Art. III § 2), or is not a "case or controversy" within the meaning of that section; or the cause is not one described by any jurisdictional statute. Our conclusion that this cause presents no nonjusticiable "political question" settles the only possible doubt that it is a case or controversy. Under the present heading of "Jurisdiction of the Subject Matter" we hold only that the matter set forth in the complaint does arise under the Constitution. . . .

Article III § 2, of the Federal Constitution provides that "The judicial Power shall extend to all Cases, in Law and Equity, arising under this Constitution, the Laws of the United States, and Treaties made, or which shall be made, under their Authority. . . ." It is clear that the cause of action is one which "arises under" the Federal Constitution. The complaint alleges that the 1901 statute effects an apportionment that deprives the appellants of the equal protection of the laws in violation of the Fourteenth Amendment. Dismissal of the complaint upon the ground of lack of jurisdiction of the subject matter would, therefore, be justified only if that claim were "so attenuated and unsubstantial as to be absolutely devoid of merit." . . . Since the District Court obviously and correctly did not deem the asserted federal constitutional claim unsubstantial and frivolous, it should not have dismissed the complaint for want of jurisdiction of the subject matter. And of course no further consideration of the merits of the claim is relevant to a determination of the court's jurisdiction of the subject matter. . . .

An unbroken line of our precedents sustains the federal courts' jurisdiction of the subject matter of federal constitutional claims of this nature. The first cases involved the redistricting of States for the purpose of

electing Representatives to the Federal Congress. When the Ohio Supreme Court sustained Ohio legislation against an attack for repugnancy to Art. I § 4, of the Federal Constitution, we affirmed on the merits and expressly refused to dismiss for want of jurisdiction "in view . . . of the subject-matter of the controversy and the Federal characteristics which inhere in it. . . ." Ohio ex rel. Davis v. Hildebrant [1916]. When the Minnesota Supreme Court affirmed the dismissal of a suit to enjoin the Secretary of State of Minnesota from acting under Minnesota redistricting legislation, we reviewed the constitutional merits of the legislation and reversed the State Supreme Court. Smiley v. Holm [1932]. . . .

The appellees refer to Colegrove v. Green [1946], as authority that the District Court lacked jurisdiction of the subject matter. Appellees misconceive the holding of that case. The holding was precisely contrary to their reading of it. Seven members of the Court participated in the decision. Unlike many other cases in this field which have assumed without discussion that there was jurisdiction, all three opinions filed in Colegrove discussed the question. Two of the opinions expressing the views of four of the Justices, a majority, flatly held that there was jurisdiction of the subject matter. Mr. Justice Black joined by Mr. Justice Douglas and Mr. Justice Murphy stated: "It is my judgment that the District Court had jurisdiction. . . ." Mr. Justice Rutledge, writing separately, expressed agreement with this conclusion. . . .

We hold that the District Court has jurisdiction of the subject matter of the federal constitutional claim asserted in the complaint.

III. Standing.

A federal court cannot "pronounce any statute, either of a State or of the United States, void, because irreconcilable with the Constitution, except as it is called upon to adjudge the legal rights of litigants in actual controversies." . . . Have the appellants alleged such a personal stake in the outcome of the controversy as to assure that concrete adverseness which sharpens the presentation of issues upon which the court so largely depends for illumination of difficult constitutional questions? This is the gist of the question of standing. It is, of course, a question of federal law. . . .

We hold that the appellants do have standing to maintain this suit. Our decisions plainly support this conclusion. Many of the cases have assumed rather than articulated the premise in deciding the merits of similar claims. And Colegrove v. Green squarely held that voters who allege facts showing disadvantage to themselves as individuals have standing to sue. . . .

These appellants seek relief in order to protect or vindicate an interest of their own, and of those similarly situated. Their constitutional claim is, in substance, that the 1901 statute constitutes arbitrary and capricious state action, offensive to the Fourteenth Amendment in its irrational disregard of the standard of apportionment prescribed by the State's Constitution or of any standard, effecting a gross disproportion of representation to voting population. The injury which appellants assert is that this classification disfavors the voters in the counties in which they reside, placing them in a position of constitutionally unjustifiable inequality vis-à-vis voters in irrationally favored counties. A citizen's right to a vote free of arbitrary impairment by state action has been judicially recognized as a right secured by the Constitution, when such impairment resulted from dilution by a false tally, cf. United States v. Classic [1941], or by a refusal to count votes from arbitrarily selected precincts, . . . or by a stuffing of the ballot box, cf. Ex parte Siebold [1880]. . . .

It would not be necessary to decide whether appellants' allegations of impairment of their votes by the 1901 apportionment will, ultimately, entitle them to any relief, in order to hold that they have standing to seek it. If such impairment does produce a legally cognizable injury, they are among those who have sustained it. They are asserting "a plain, direct and adequate interest in maintaining the effectiveness of their votes," . . . not merely a claim of "the right, possessed by every citizen, to require that the Government be administered according to law. . . ." Fairchild v. Hughes [1922]. . . . They are entitled to a hearing and to the District Court's decision on their claims. "The very essence of civil liberty certainly consists in the right of every individual to claim the protection of the laws, whenever he receives an injury." Marbury v. Madison.

IV. Justiciability.

In holding that the subject matter of this suit was not justiciable, the District Court relied on Colegrove v. Green, and subsequent per curiam cases. The court stated: "From a review of these decisions there can be no doubt that the federal rule . . . is that the federal courts . . . will not intervene in cases of this type to compel legislative reapportionment." We understand the District Court to have read the cited cases as compelling the conclusion that since the appellants sought to have a legislative apportionment held unconstitutional, their suit presented a "political question" and was therefore nonjusticiable. We hold that this challenge to an apportionment presents no nonjusticiable "political question." The cited cases do not hold the contrary.

Of course the mere fact that the suit seeks protection of a political right does not mean it presents a political question. Such an objection "is little more than a play upon words." . . . Rather, it is argued that apportionment cases, whatever the actual wording of the complaint, can involve no federal constitutional right except one resting on the guaranty of a republican form of government, and that complaints based on that clause have been held to present political questions which are nonjusticiable.

We hold that the claim pleaded here neither rests upon nor implicates the Guaranty Clause and that its justiciability is therefore not foreclosed by our decisions of cases involving that clause. The District Court misinterpreted Colegrove v. Green and other decisions of this Court on which it relied. Appellants' claim that they are being denied equal protection is justiciable, and if "discrimination is sufficiently shown, the right to relief under the equal protection clause is not diminished by the fact that the discrimination relates to political rights." . . . To show why we reject the argument based on the Guaranty Clause, we must examine the authorities under it. But because there appears to be some uncertainty as to why those cases did present political questions, and specifically as to whether this apportionment case is like those cases, we deem it necessary first to consider the contours of the "political question" doctrine.

Our discussion, even at the price of extending this opinion, requires review of a number of political question cases, in order to expose the attributes of the doctrine—attributes which, in various settings, diverge, combine, appear, and disappear in seeming disorderliness. Since that review is undertaken solely to demonstrate that neither singly nor collectively do these cases support a conclusion that this apportionment case is nonjusticiable, we of course do not explore their implications in other contexts. That review reveals that in the Guaranty Clause cases and in the other "political question" cases, it is the relationship between the judiciary and the coordinate branches of the Federal Government, and not the federal judiciary's relationship to the States, which gives rise to the "political question."

We have said that "In determining whether a question falls within [the political question] category, the appropriateness under our system of government of attributing finality to the action of the political departments and also the lack of satisfactory criteria for a judicial determination are dominant considerations." Coleman v. Miller [1939]. The nonjusticiability of a political question is primarily a function of the separation of powers. Much confusion results from the capacity of the "political question" label to obscure the need for case-by-case inquiry. Deciding whether a matter has in any measure been committed by the Constitution to another branch of government, or whether the action of that branch exceeds whatever authority has been committed, is itself a delicate exercise in constitutional interpretation, and is a responsibility of this Court as ultimate interpreter of the Constitution. To demonstrate this requires no less than to analyze representative cases and to infer from them the analytical threads that make up the political question doctrine. We shall then show that none of those threads catches this case. . . .

[Here follows a long summary of cases involving the political question doctrine as they have arisen in the fields of (1) foreign relations, (2) dates of duration of hostilities, (3) validity of enactments, (4) status of Indian tribes, and (5) republican form of government.]

We come, finally, to the ultimate inquiry whether our precedents as to what constitutes a nonjusticiable "political question" bring the case before us under the umbrella of that doctrine. A natural beginning is to note whether any of the common characteristics which we have been able to identify and label descriptively are present. We find none: The question here is the consistency of state action with the Federal Constitution. We have no question decided, or to be decided, by a political branch of government coequal with this Court. Nor do we risk embarrassment of our government abroad, or grave disturbance at home if we take issue with Tennessee as to the constitutionality of her action here challenged. Nor need the appellants, in order to succeed in this action, ask the Court to enter upon policy determinations for which judicially manageable standards are lacking. Judicial standards under the Equal Protection Clause are well developed and familiar, and it has been open to courts since the enactment of the Fourteenth Amendment to determine, if on the particular facts they must, that a discrimination reflects *no* policy, but simply arbitrary and capricious action. . . .

We conclude that the complaint's allegations of a denial of equal protection present a justiciable constitutional cause of action upon which appellants are entitled to a trial and a decision. The right asserted is within the reach of judicial protection under the Fourteenth Amendment.

The judgment of the District Court is reversed and the cause is remanded for further proceedings consistent with this opinion.

Reversed and remanded.

Mr. Justice **Whittaker** did not participate in the decision of this case.

Mr. Justice **Douglas**, concurring, said in part:

While I join the opinion of the Court and, like the Court, do not reach the merits, a word of explanation is necessary. I put to one side the problems of "political" questions involving the distribution of power between this Court, the Congress, and the Chief Executive. We have here a phase of the recurring problem of the relation of the federal courts to state agencies. More particularly, the question is the extent to which a State may weight one person's vote more heavily than it does another's. . . .

I agree with my Brother Clark that if the allegations in the complaint can be sustained a case for relief is established. We are told that a single vote in Moore County, Tennessee, is worth 19 votes in Hamilton County, that one vote in Stewart or in Chester County is worth nearly eight times a single vote in Shelby or Knox County. The opportunity to prove that an "invidious discrimination" exists should therefore be given the appellants. . . .

With the exceptions of Colegrove v. Green, MacDougall v. Green [1948], South v. Peters [1950], and the decisions they spawned, the Court has never thought that protection of voting rights was beyond judicial cognizance. Today's treatment of those cases removes the only impediment to judicial cognizance of the claims stated in the present complaint. . . .

Mr. Justice **Clark**, concurring, said in part:

One emerging from the rash of opinions with their accompanying clashing of views may well find himself suffering a mental blindness. The Court holds that the appellants have alleged a cause of action. However, it refuses to award relief here—although the facts are undisputed—and fails to give the District Court any guidance whatever. One dissenting opinion, bursting with words that go through so much and conclude with so little, contemns the majority action as "a massive repudiation of the experience of our whole past." Another describes the complaint as merely asserting conclusory allegations that Tennessee's apportionment is "incorrect," "arbitrary," "obsolete," and "unconstitutional." I believe it can be shown that this case is distinguishable from earlier cases dealing with the distribution of political power by a State, that a patent violation of the Equal Protection Clause of the United States Constitution has been shown, and that an appropriate remedy may be formulated.

I. . . .

. . . The widely heralded case of Colegrove v. Green was one not only in which the Court was bobtailed but in which there was no majority opinion. Indeed, even the "political question" point in Mr. Justice Frankfurter's opinion was no more than an alternative ground. Moreover, the appellants did not present an equal protection argument. While it has served as a Mother Hubbard to most of the subsequent cases, I feel it was in that respect ill-cast and for all of these reasons put it to one side. . . .

II.

The controlling facts cannot be disputed. . . .
. . . The frequency and magnitude of the inequalities in the present districting admit of no policy whatever. . . . It leaves but one conclusion, namely that Tennessee's apportionment is a crazy quilt without rational basis. . . .
[Examples are given of the inequalities in apportionment in Tennessee.]
The truth is that—although this case has been here for two years and has had over six hours' argument (three times the ordinary case) and has been most carefully considered over and over again by us in Conference and individually—no one, not even the State nor the dissenters, has come up with any rational basis for Tennessee's apportionment statute.
. . . Like the District Court, I conclude that appellants have met the burden of showing "Tennessee is guilty of a clear violation of the state constitution and of the [federal] rights of the plaintiffs. . . ."

III.

Although I find the Tennessee apportionment statute offends the Equal Protection Clause, I would not consider intervention by this Court into so delicate a field if there were any other relief available to the people of Tennessee. But the majority of the people of Tennessee have no "practical opportunities for exerting their political weight at the polls" to correct the existing "invidious discrimination." Tennessee has no initiative and referendum. I have searched diligently for other "practical opportunities" present under the law. I find none other than through the federal courts. . . .

IV. . . .

As John Rutledge (later Chief Justice) said 175 years ago in the course of the Constitutional Convention, a chief function of the Court is to secure the national rights. Its decision today supports the proposition for which our forebears fought and many died, namely, that to be fully conformable to the principle of right, the form of government must be representative. That is the keystone upon which our government was founded and lacking which no republic can survive. It is well for this Court to practice self-restraint and discipline in constitutional adjudication, but never in its history have those principles received sanction where the national rights of so many have been so clearly infringed for so long a time. National respect for the courts is more enhanced through the forthright enforcement of those rights rather than by rendering them nugatory through the interposition of subterfuges. In my view the ultimate decision today is in the greatest tradition of this Court.

Mr. Justice **Stewart** wrote a brief concurring opinion.

Mr. Justice **Frankfurter**, whom Mr. Justice **Harlan** joins, dissenting, said in part:

The Court today reverses a uniform course of decision established by a dozen cases, including one by which the very claim now sustained was unanimously rejected only five years ago. The impressive body of rulings thus cast aside reflected the equally uniform course of our political history regarding the relationship between population and legislative representation—a wholly different matter from denial of the franchise to individuals because of race, color, religion or sex. Such a massive repudiation of the experience of our whole past in asserting destructively novel judicial power demands a detailed analysis of the role of this Court in our constitutional scheme. Disregard of inherent limits in the effective exercise of the Court's "judicial Power" not only presages the futility of judicial intervention in the essentially political conflict of forces by which the relation between population and representation has time out of mind been and now is determined. It may well impair the Court's position as the ultimate organ of "the supreme Law of the Land" in that vast range of legal problems, often strongly entangled in popular feeling, on which this Court must pronounce. The Court's authority—possessed of neither the purse nor the sword—ultimately rests on sustained public confidence in its moral sanction. Such feeling must be nourished by the Court's complete detachment, in fact and in appearance, from political entanglements and by abstention from injecting itself into the clash of political forces in political settlements. . . .

. . . The Framers carefully and with deliberate forethought refused so to enthrone the judiciary. In this situation, as in others of like nature, appeal for relief does not belong here. Appeal must be to an informed, civically militant electorate. In a democratic society like ours, relief must come through an aroused popular conscience that sears the conscience of the people's representatives. In any event there is nothing judicially more unseemly nor more self-defeating than for this Court to make in terrorem pronouncements, to indulge in merely empty rhetoric, sounding a word of promise to the ear, sure to be disappointing to the hope. . . .

[Mr. Justice Frankfurter continued in a long and heavily documented opinion to support the position he had taken in Colegrove v. Green.]

Mr. Justice **Harlan** wrote a dissenting opinion in which Mr. Justice **Frankfurter** joined.

FROTHINGHAM v. MELLON

262 U. S. 447; 43 S. Ct. 597; 67 L. Ed. 1078
(1923)

The Supreme Court's insistence that parties to a case must have adverse interests raised the question of how slight this adverse interest may be. The Court has ruled that the interest of the parties must be "substantial." Just what constitutes a substantial interest is a matter to be decided as cases arise. But the Court has made it clear that the person who brings a suit to challenge the validity of a statute must have an interest at least greater than that shared with all his fellow citizens in having the government behave in a constitutional manner. Thus in Fairchild v. Hughes (1922) the Court dismissed a suit brought to enjoin the Secretary of State from proclaiming the Nineteenth Amendment and the Attorney General from carrying out an enforcement act then being debated in Congress. It was argued that the amendment would be void and that its proclamation would mislead election officers in a number of states. The Court observed: "Plaintiff has only the right, possessed by every citizen, to require that the government be administered according to law, and that the public moneys be not wasted. Obviously this general right does not entitle a private citizen to institute in the Federal courts a suit to secure by indirection a determination whether a statute, if passed, or a constitutional Amendment about to be adopted, will be valid."

In Ex parte Levitt (1937) a suit was brought to challenge the right of Justice Black to take his seat on the

Supreme Court, on the ground that he was ineligible and that there was no vacancy. In a per curiam opinion the Court said, "the motion papers disclose no interest upon the part of the petitioner other than that of a citizen and a member of the bar of this Court. That is insufficient. It is an established principle that to entitle a private individual to invoke the judicial power to determine the validity of executive or legislative action he *must show that he has sustained or is immediately in danger of sustaining a direct injury as the result of that action and it is not sufficient that he has merely a general interest common to all members of the public."*

The present case combines two suits, *Massachusetts v. Mellon* and *Frothingham v. Mellon,* each of which raises a different aspect of the question of who has an interest to sue to challenge the constitutionality of a statute. *Massachusetts v. Mellon poses the issue whether a state which considers its sovereignty impaired by an act of Congress has sustained the kind of injury which would enable it to sue. The Court dismissed the case "for want of jurisdiction,"* noting that "in the last analysis, the complaint of the plaintiff state is brought to the naked contention that Congress has usurped the reserved powers of the several states by the mere enactment of the statute, though nothing has been done and nothing is to be done without their consent; and it is plain that the question, as it is thus presented, is political, and not judicial, in character, and therefore is not a matter which admits of the exercise of the judicial power."

In the Frothingham case, *Mrs. Frothingham, a wealthy Massachusetts woman, sued as a taxpayer to prevent the spending of federal funds under the statute* involved in the Massachusetts case to "reduce maternal and infant mortality and protect the health of mothers and infants," a cause of which she disapproved.

Mr. Justice **Sutherland** delivered the opinion of the Court, saying in part:

Second. The attack upon the statute in the Frothingham Case is, generally, the same, but this plaintiff alleges, in addition, that she is a taxpayer of the United States; and her contention, though not clear, seems to be that the effect of the appropriations complained of will be to increase the burden of future taxation and thereby take her property without due process of law. The right of a taxpayer to enjoin the execution of a Federal appropriation act, on the ground that it is invalid and will result in taxation for illegal purposes, has never been passed upon by this court. In cases where it was presented, the question has either been allowed to pass sub silentio, or the determination of it expressly withheld. . . . Bradfield v. Roberts [1899]. The case last cited came here from the court of appeals of the District of Columbia, and that court sustained the right of the plaintiff to sue by treating the case as one directed against the District of Columbia, and therefore subject to the rule frequently stated by this court, that resident taxpayers may sue to enjoin an illegal use of the moneys of a municipal corporation. . . . The interest of a taxpayer of a municipality in the application of its moneys is direct and immediate, and the remedy by injunction to prevent their misuse is not inappropriate. It is upheld by a large number of state cases and is the rule of this court. . . . Nevertheless, there are decisions to the contrary. . . . The reasons which support the extension of the equitable remedy to a single taxpayer in such cases are based upon the peculiar relation of the corporate taxpayer to the corporation, which is not without some resemblance to that subsisting between stockholder and private corporation. . . . But the relation of a taxpayer of the United States to the Federal government is very different. His interest in the moneys of the Treasury—partly realized from taxation and partly from other sources—is shared with millions of others; is comparatively minute and indeterminable; and the effect upon future taxation of any payment out of the funds so remote, fluctuating, and uncertain that no basis is afforded for an appeal to the preventive powers of a court of equity.

The administration of any statute likely to produce additional taxation to be imposed upon a vast number of taxpayers, the extent of whose several liability is indefinite and constantly changing, is essentially a matter of public, and not of individual, concern. If one taxpayer may champion and litigate such a cause, then every other taxpayer may do the same, not only in respect to the statute here under review, but also in respect of every other appropriation act and statute whose administration requires the outlay of public money, and whose validity may be questioned. The bare suggestion of such a result, with its attendant inconveniences, goes far to sustain the conclusion which we have reached, that a suit of this character cannot be maintained. It is of much significance that no precedent sustaining the right to maintain suits like this has been called to our attention, although, since the formation of the government, as an examination of the acts of Congress will disclose, a large number of statutes appropriating or involving the expenditure of moneys for nonFederal purposes have been enacted and carried into effect.

The functions of government under our system are apportioned. To the legislative department has been committed the duty of making laws; to the executive the duty of executing them; and to the judiciary, the duty of interpreting and applying them in cases properly brought before the courts. The general rule is that neither department may invade the province of the other, and neither may control, direct, or restrain the action of the other. We are not now speaking of the merely ministerial duties of officials. . . . We have no power per se to review and annul acts of Congress on the ground that they are unconstitutional. That question may be considered only when the justification for some direct injury suffered or threatened, presenting a justiciable issue, is made to rest upon such an act. Then the power exercised is that of ascertaining and declaring the law applicable to the controversy. It amounts to little more than the negative power to disregard an unconstitutional enactment, which otherwise would stand in the way of the enforcement of a legal right. The party who invokes the power must be able to show not only that the statute is invalid, but that he has sustained or is immediately in danger of sustaining some direct injury as the result of its enforcement, and not merely that he suffers in some indefinite way in common with people generally. If a case for preventive relief be presented, the court enjoins, in effect, not the execution of the statute, but the acts of the official, the statute notwithstanding. Here the parties plaintiff have no such case. Looking through forms of words to the substance of their complaint, it is merely that officials of the executive department of the government are executing and will execute an act of Congress asserted to be unconstitutional; and this we are asked to prevent. To do so would be not to decide a judicial controversy, but to assume a position of authority over the governmental acts of another and coequal department,—an authority which plainly we do not possess.

[The suit brought by Massachusetts was dismissed; the decision of the lower court dismissing the suit brought by Mrs. Frothingham was affirmed.]

FLAST v. COHEN

392 U. S. 83; 88 S. Ct. 1942; 20 L. Ed. 2d 947 (1968)

The result of the Frothingham decision was to render almost completely immune to constitutional attack the vast system of grants-in-aid by which the federal government supports and supervises a wide variety of public service activities conducted by the states, as well as other far-flung federal spending programs. It should be noted that the taxpayer's suit forbidden by Frothingham v. Mellon (1923) is not the suit brought by a taxpayer to contest the amount of the tax bill or the constitutionality of the tax itself. A taxpayer who is asked to pay too much, or pay a tax forbidden by the Constitution, clearly has standing to contest such exaction. What is forbidden is a suit challenging a tax on the ground that the money raised will be spent for some unconstitutional purpose. To permit such suits would be to permit any federal taxpayer to challenge the validity of any governmental action, and it seems clear that the specter of such a wholesale attack influenced the Court in Frothingham v. Mellon.

While the Court has adhered to Frothingham where suits against the federal government were concerned, it has not entirely ruled out taxpayer suits where a municipal corporation was involved. In Everson v. Board of Education (1947) the Court reviewed and found valid the expenditure of tax money to transport pupils to religious schools, holding that the aid was being given to the child and not his religion. In Doremus v. Board of Education (1952), on the other hand, it refused to review a taxpayer's complaint that the Bible was being read in the public school, noting that "there is no allegation that this activity is supported by any separate tax or paid for from any particular appropriation or that it adds any sum whatever to the cost of conducting the school. No information is given as to what kind of taxes are paid by

appellants and there is no averment that the Bible reading increases any tax they do pay or that as taxpayers they are, will, or possibly can be out of pocket because of it." In Everson there had been a "measurable appropriation or disbursement of school-district funds."

The present case arose as a challenge to the validity of the Education Act of 1965, under which Congress had spent about $1 billion in 1966, some $60 million of which was channeled through public school systems into religious schools. If such expenditures are not subject to challenge by taxpayer's suits, there is serious doubt whether they are subject to judicial review at all.

Mr. Chief Justice **Warren** delivered the opinion of the Court, saying in part:

In Frothingham v. Mellon (1923), this Court ruled that a federal taxpayer is without standing to challenge the constitutionality of a federal statute. That ruling has stood for 45 years as an impenetrable barrier to suits against Acts of Congress brought by individuals who can assert only the interest of federal taxpayers. In this case, we must decide whether the Frothingham barrier should be lowered when a taxpayer attacks a federal statute on the ground that it violates the Establishment and Free Exercise Clauses of the First Amendment.

Appellants filed suit in the United States District Court for the Southern District of New York to enjoin the allegedly unconstitutional expenditure of federal funds under Titles I and II of the Elementary and Secondary Education Act of 1965. The complaint alleged that the seven appellants had as a common attribute that "each pay[s] income taxes of the United States," and it is clear from the complaint that the appellants were resting their standing to maintain the action solely on their status as federal taxpayers. The appellees, who are charged by Congress with administering the Elementary and Secondary Education Act of 1965, were sued in their official capacities. . . .

The gravamen of the appellants' complaint was that federal funds appropriated under the Act were being used to finance instruction in reading, arithmetic, and other subjects in religious schools, and to purchase textbooks and other instructional materials for use in such schools. Such expenditures were alleged to be in contravention of the Establishment and Free Exercise Clauses of the First Amendment. . . .

The Government moved to dismiss the complaint on the ground that appellants lacked standing to maintain the action. . . .

II.

This Court first faced squarely the question whether a litigant asserting only his status as a taxpayer has standing to maintain a suit in a federal court in Frothingham v. Mellon, and that decision must be the starting point for analysis in this case. The taxpayer in Frothingham attacked as unconstitutional the Maternity Act of 1921 which established a federal program of grants to those States which would undertake programs to reduce maternal and infant mortality. The taxpayer alleged that Congress, in enacting the challenged statute, had exceeded the powers delegated to it under Article I of the Constitution and had invaded the legislative province reserved to the several States by the Tenth Amendment. The taxpayer complained that the result of the allegedly unconstitutional enactment would be to increase her future federal tax liability and "thereby take her property without due process of law." The Court noted that a federal taxpayer's "interest in the moneys of the Treasury . . . is comparatively minute and indeterminable" and that "the effect upon future taxation, of any payment out of the [Treasury's] funds, . . . [is] remote, fluctuating and uncertain." As a result, the Court ruled that the taxpayer had failed to allege the type of "direct injury" necessary to confer standing.

Although the barrier Frothingham erected against federal taxpayer suits has never been breached, the decision has been the source of some confusion and the object of considerable criticism. The confusion has developed as commentators have tried to determine whether Frothingham establishes a constitutional bar to taxpayer suits or whether the Court was simply imposing a rule of self-restraint which was not constitutionally compelled. The conflicting viewpoints are reflected in the arguments made to this Court by the parties in this case. The Government has pressed upon us the view that Frothingham announced a constitutional rule, compelled by the Article III limitations on federal court jurisdiction and grounded in considerations of the doctrine of separation of powers. Appellants, however, insist that Frothingham expressed no more than a policy of judicial self-restraint which can be disregarded when compelling reasons for assuming jurisdiction over a taxpayer's suit exist. The opinion delivered in Frothingham can be read to support either position. The concluding sentence of the opinion states that, to take jurisdiction of the taxpayer's suit, "would be not to decide a judicial controversy, but to assume a position of authority over the governmental acts of another and coequal department, an authority which plainly we do not possess." Yet the concrete reasons given for denying standing to a federal taxpayer suggest that the Court's holding rests on something less than a constitutional foundation. For example, the Court conceded that standing had previously been conferred on municipal taxpayers to sue in that capacity. However, the Court viewed the interest of a federal taxpayer in total federal tax revenues as "comparatively minute and indeterminable" when measured against a municipal taxpayer's interest in a smaller city treasury. This suggests that the petitioner in Frothingham was denied standing not because she was a taxpayer but because her tax bill was not large enough. . . .

To the extent that Frothingham has been viewed as resting on policy considerations, it has been criticized as depending on assumptions not consistent with modern conditions. For example, some commentators have pointed out that a number of corporate taxpayers today have a federal tax liability running into hundreds of millions of dollars, and such taxpayers have a far greater monetary stake in the Federal Treasury than they do in any municipal treasury. . . . Whatever the merits of the current debate over Frothingham, its very existence suggests that we should undertake a fresh examination of the limitations upon standing to sue in a federal court and the application of those limitations to taxpayer suits.

III.

The jurisdiction of federal courts is defined and limited by Article III of the Constitution. In terms relevant to the question for decision in this case, the judicial power of federal courts is constitutionally restricted to "cases" and "controversies." As is so often the situation in constitutional adjudication, those two words have an iceberg quality, containing beneath their surface simplicity submerged complexities which go to the very heart of our constitutional form of government. Embodied in the words "cases" and "controversies" are two complementary but somewhat different limitations. In part those words limit the business of federal courts to questions presented in an adversary context and in a form historically viewed as capable of resolution through the judicial process. And in part those words define the role assigned to the judiciary in a tripartite allocation of power to assure that the federal courts will not intrude into areas committed to the other branches of government. Justiciability is the term of art employed to give expression to this dual limitation placed upon federal courts by the case-and-controversy doctrine.

Justiciability is itself a concept of uncertain meaning and scope. Its reach is illustrated by the various grounds upon which questions sought to be adjudicated in federal courts have been held not to be justiciable. Thus, no justiciable controversy is presented when the parties seek adjudication of only a political question, when the parties are asking for an advisory opinion, when the question sought to be adjudicated has been mooted by subsequent developments, and when there is no standing to maintain the action. Yet it remains true that "[j]usticiability is . . . not a legal concept with a fixed content or susceptible of scientific verification. Its utilization is the resultant of many subtle pressures. . . ." Poe v. Ullman (1961). . . .

Additional uncertainty exists in the doctrine of justiciability because that doctrine has become a blend of constitutional requirements and policy considerations. And a policy limitation is "not always clearly distinguished from the constitutional limitation." . . .

It is in this context that the standing question presented by this case must be viewed and that the Government's argument on that question must be evaluated. As we understand it, the Government's position is that the constitutional scheme of separation of powers, and the deference owed by the federal judiciary to the other two branches of government within that scheme, present an absolute bar to taxpayer suits challenging the validity of

Gov't position

federal spending programs. The Government views such suits as involving no more than the mere disagreement by the taxpayer "with the uses to which tax money is put." According to the Government, the resolution of such disagreements is committed to other branches of the Federal Government and not to the judiciary. Consequently, the Government contends that, under no circumstances, should standing be conferred on federal taxpayers to challenge a federal taxing or spending program. An analysis of the function served by standing limitations compels a rejection of the Government's position.

Standing is an aspect of justiciability and, as such, the problem of standing is surrounded by the same complexities and vagaries that inhere in justiciability. . . .

Despite the complexities and uncertainties, some meaningful form can be given to the jurisdictional limitations placed on federal court power by the concept of standing. The fundamental aspect of standing is that it focuses on the party seeking to get his complaint before a federal court and not on the issues he wishes to have adjudicated. The "gist of the question of standing" is whether the party seeking relief has "alleged such a personal stake in the outcome of the controversy as to assure that concrete adverseness which sharpens the presentation of issues upon which the court so largely depends for illumination of difficult constitutional questions." Baker v. Carr (1962). In other words, when standing is placed in issue in a case, the question is whether the person whose standing is challenged is a proper party to request an adjudication of a particular issue and not whether the issue itself is justiciable. Thus, a party may have standing in a particular case, but the federal court may nevertheless decline to pass on the merits of the case because, for example, it presents a political question. . . .

When the emphasis in the standing problem is placed on whether the person invoking a federal court's jurisdiction is a proper party to maintain the action, the weakness of the Government's argument in this case becomes apparent. The question whether a particular person is a proper party to maintain the action does not, by its own force, raise separation of powers problems related to improper judicial interference in areas committed to other branches of the Federal Government. Such problems arise, if at all, only from the substantive issues the individual seeks to have adjudicated. Thus, in terms of Article III limitations on federal court jurisdiction, the question of standing is related only to whether the dispute sought to be adjudicated will be presented in an adversary context and in a form historically viewed as capable of judicial resolution. It is for that reason that the emphasis in standing problems is on whether the party invoking federal court jurisdiction has "a personal stake in the outcome of the controversy," Baker v. Carr. . . . A taxpayer may or may not have the requisite personal stake in the outcome, depending upon the circumstances of the particular case. Therefore, we find no absolute bar in Article III to suits by federal taxpayers challenging allegedly unconstitutional federal taxing and spending programs. . . .

IV.

. . . We have noted that, in deciding the question of standing, it is not relevant that the substantive issues in the litigation might be nonjusticiable. However, our decisions establish that, in ruling on standing, it is both appropriate and necessary to look to the substantive issues for another purpose, namely, to determine whether there is a logical nexus between the status asserted and the claim sought to be adjudicated. . . .

The nexus demanded of federal taxpayers has two aspects to it. First, the taxpayer must establish a logical link between that status and the type of legislative enactment attacked. Thus, a taxpayer will be a proper party to allege the unconstitutionality only of exercises of congressional power under the taxing and spending clause of Art. I, § 8, of the Constitution. It will not be sufficient to allege an incidental expenditure of tax funds in the administration of an essentially regulatory statute. . . . Secondly, the taxpayer must establish a nexus between that status and the precise nature of the constitutional infringement alleged. Under this requirement, the taxpayer must show that the challenged enactment exceeds specific constitutional limitations imposed upon the exercise of the congressional taxing and spending power and not simply that the enactment is generally beyond the powers delegated to Congress by Art. I, § 8. When both nexuses are established, the litigant will have shown a taxpayer's stake in the outcome of the controversy and will be a proper and appropriate party to invoke a federal court's jurisdiction.

The taxpayer-appellants in this case have satisfied both nexuses to support their claim of standing under the test we announce today. Their constitutional challenge is made to an exercise by Congress of its power under Art. I, § 8, to spend for the general welfare, and the challenged program involves a substantial expenditure of federal tax funds. In addition, appellants have alleged that the challenged expenditures violate the Establishment and Free Exercise Clauses of the First Amendment. Our history vividly illustrates that one of the specific evils feared by those who drafted the Establishment Clause and fought for its adoption was that the taxing and spending power would be used to favor one religion over another or to support religion in general. . . . The Establishment Clause was designed as a specific bulwark against such potential abuses of governmental power, and that clause of the First Amendment operates as a specific constitutional limitation upon the exercise by Congress of the taxing and spending power conferred by Art. I, § 8.

The allegations of the taxpayer in Frothingham v. Mellon, were quite different from those made in this case, and the result in Frothingham is consistent with the test of taxpayer standing announced today. The taxpayer in Frothingham attacked a federal spending program and she, therefore, established the first nexus required. However, she lacked standing because her constitutional attack was not based on an allegation that Congress, in enacting the Maternity Act of 1921, had breached a specific limitation upon its taxing and spending power. The taxpayer in Frothingham alleged essentially that Congress, by enacting the challenged statute, had exceeded the general powers delegated to it by Art. I, § 8, and that Congress had thereby invaded the legislative province reserved to the States by the Tenth Amendment. To be sure, Mrs. Frothingham made the additional allegation that her tax liability would be increased as a result of the allegedly unconstitutional enactment, and she framed that allegation in terms of a deprivation of property without due process of law. However, the Due Process Clause of the Fifth Amendment does not protect taxpayers against increases in tax liability, and the taxpayer in Frothingham failed to make any additional claim that the harm she alleged resulted from a breach by Congress of the specific constitutional limitations imposed upon an exercise of the taxing and spending power. In essence, Mrs. Frothingham was attempting to assert the States' interest in their legislative prerogatives and not a federal taxpayer's interest in being free of taxing and spending in contravention of specific constitutional limitations imposed upon Congress' taxing and spending power.

We have noted that the Establishment Clause of the First Amendment does specifically limit the taxing and spending power conferred by Art. I, § 8. Whether the Constitution contains other specific limitations can be determined only in the context of future cases. However, whenever such specific limitations are found, we believe a taxpayer will have a clear stake as a taxpayer in assuring that they are not breached by Congress. Consequently, we hold that a taxpayer will have standing consistent with Article III to invoke federal judicial power when he alleges that congressional action under the taxing and spending clause is in derogation of those constitutional provisions which operate to restrict the exercise of the taxing and spending power. The taxpayer's allegation in such cases would be that his tax money is being extracted and spent in violation of specific constitutional protections against such abuses of legislative power. Such an injury is appropriate for judicial redress, and the taxpayer has established the necessary nexus between his status and the nature of the allegedly unconstitutional action to support his claim of standing to secure judicial review. Under such circumstances, we feel confident that the questions will be framed with the necessary specificity, that the issues will be contested with the necessary adverseness and that the litigation will be pursued with the necessary vigor to assure that the constitutional challenge will be made in a form traditionally thought to be capable of judicial resolution. We lack that confidence in cases such as Frothingham where a taxpayer seeks to employ a federal court as a forum in which to air his generalized grievances about the conduct of government or the allocation of power in the Federal System.

While we express no view at all on the merits of appellants' claims in this case, their complaint contains sufficient allegations under the criteria we have outlined to give them standing to invoke a federal court's jurisdiction for an adjudication on the merits.

Reversed.

Mr. Justice **Douglas** joined the opinion of the Court and wrote a concurring opinion urging the abandonment of Frothingham v. Mellon.

Mr. Justice **Stewart** joined the opinion of the Court and wrote a brief concurring opinion.

Mr. Justice **Fortas,** concurring, rejected the implication that any other than the Establishment Clause could serve as the basis of a taxpayer suit.

Mr. Justice **Harlan,** dissenting, said in part:

The problems presented by this case are narrow and relatively abstract, but the principles by which they must be resolved involve nothing less than the proper functioning of the federal courts, and so run to the roots of our constitutional system. The nub of my view is that the end result of Frothingham v. Mellon was correct, even though, like others, I do not subscribe to all of its reasoning and premises. Although I therefore agree with certain of the conclusions reached today by the Court, I cannot accept the standing doctrine that it substitutes for Frothingham, for it seems to me that this new doctrine rests on premises that do not withstand analysis. Accordingly I respectfully dissent. . . .

II. . . .

The Court's analysis consists principally of the observation that the requirements of standing are met if a taxpayer has the "requisite personal stake in the outcome" of his suit. This does not, of course, resolve the standing problem; it merely restates it. The Court implements this standard with the declaration that taxpayers will be "deemed" to have the necessary personal interest if their suits satisfy two criteria: *first,* the challenged expenditure must form part of a federal spending program, and not merely be "incidental" to a regulatory program; and *second,* the constitutional provision under which the plaintiff claims must be a "specific limitation" upon Congress' spending powers. The difficulties with these criteria are many and severe, but it is enough for the moment to emphasize that they are not in any sense a measurement of any plaintiff's interest in the outcome of any suit. As even a cursory examination of the criteria will show, the Court's standard for the determination of standing and its criteria for the satisfaction of that standard are entirely unrelated.

It is surely clear that a plaintiff's interest in the outcome of a suit in which he challenges the constitutionality of a federal expenditure is not made greater or smaller by the unconnected fact that the expenditure is, or is not, "incidental" to an "essentially regulatory" program. An example will illustrate the point. Assume that two independent federal programs are authorized by Congress, that the first is designed to encourage a specified religious group by the provision to it of direct grants-in-aid, and that the second is designed to discourage all other religious groups by the imposition of various forms of discriminatory regulation. Equal amounts are appropriated by Congress for the two programs. If a taxpayer challenges their constitutionality in separate suits, are we to suppose, as evidently does the Court, that his "personal stake" in the suit involving the second is necessarily smaller than it is in the suit involving the first, and that he should therefore have standing in one but not the other?

Presumably the Court does not believe that regulatory programs are necessarily less destructive of First Amendment rights, or that regulatory programs are necessarily less prodigal of public funds than are grants-in-aid, for both these general propositions are demonstrably false. The Court's disregard of regulatory expenditures is not even a logical consequence of its apparent assumption that taxpayer-plaintiffs assert essentially monetary interests, for it surely cannot matter to a taxpayer qua taxpayer whether an unconstitutional expenditure is used to hire the services of regulatory personnel or is distributed among private and local governmental agencies as grants-in-aid. His interest as taxpayer arises, if at all, from the fact of an unlawful expenditure, and not as a consequence of the expenditure's form. Apparently the Court has repudiated the emphasis in Frothingham upon the amount of the plaintiff's tax bill, only to substitute an equally irrelevant emphasis upon the form of the challenged expenditure.

The Court's second criterion is similarly unrelated to its standard for the determination of standing. The intensity of a plaintiff's interest in a suit is not measured, even obliquely, by the fact that the constitutional provision under which he claims is, or is not, a "specific limitation" upon Congress' spending powers. Thus, among the claims in Frothingham was the assertion that the Maternity Act deprived the petitioner of property without due process of law. The Court has evidently concluded that this claim did not confer standing because the Due Process Clause of the Fifth Amendment is not a specific limitation upon the spending powers. Disregarding for the moment the formidable obscurity of the Court's categories, how can it be said that Mrs. Frothingham's interests in her suit were, as a consequence of her choice of a constitutional claim, necessarily less intense than those, for example, of the present appellants? I am quite unable to understand how, if a taxpayer believes that a given public expenditure is unconstitutional, and if he seeks to vindicate that belief in a federal court, his interest in the suit can be said necessarily to vary according to the constitutional provision under which he states his claim.

VALLEY FORGE CHRISTIAN COLLEGE v. AMERICANS UNITED

454 U. S. 464; 102 S. Ct. 752; 70 L. Ed. 2d 700 (1982)

The importance of these seemingly technical legal questions regarding standing cannot be overemphasized, for it is in the decision of these issues that the Court establishes the role it will play in the governmental process; see note to Muskrat v. United States. For example, it is not hard to imagine that the Court could reasonably have found that Mrs. Frothingham had suffered sufficient injury to warrant relief, thus opening up to judicial review all the things the government does with its money. And by deciding in Baker v. Carr (1962) that a person was "injured" by malapportionment and thus had standing to sue, the Court extended to the judiciary control over this long-standing and seemingly insoluble problem. The extent to which the Court should play an "activist" role, moving aggressively into new areas to solve difficult social problems, or exercise "judicial self-restraint" and stay out of them, is a matter on which members of the Court over the years have been sharply and often bitterly divided. It is an area, too, in which the political branches attempt to exert influence upon the Court; in Senate hearings on the confirmation of Justice O'Connor she was sharply questioned on her attitude about the role of the Court.

In the years following Flast v. Cohen (1968) the Court dealt with the problem of standing largely in terms of a person's right to complain about the actions of government agencies that affected him or her adversely. The essential test under Article III was whether the individual had alleged sufficient injury to provide a case or controversy, and in a series of cases the Court found injury in such widely varied allegations as: (1) The Comptroller of the Currency was permitting injurious business competition by letting banks sell data processing services (Data Processing Service v. Camp, 1970); (2) the Secretary of Agriculture had changed the agricultural subsidy rules to make a tenant farmer more dependent on his landlord (Barlow v. Collins, 1970); and (3) the ICC was raising railroad rates, thus discouraging the use of recyclable materials and damaging the environment (United States v. SCRAP, 1973). All of these cases rested on a provision of the Administrative Procedure Act authorizing judicial review where a person is "adversely affected or aggrieved by agency action," and in each case the petitioners alleged personal injury.

Only in Sierra Club v. Morton (1972) did the Court fail to find injury. There the well-known nature club had sought to enjoin the building of a ski resort in Mineral King Valley and Sequoia National Park, but unlike those involved in the SCRAP case, it had failed to claim that it or any of its members used the park and would suffer actual injury as a result of injury to the environment. It is interesting to note that the decisive alle-

gations of injury in SCRAP were no more than that SCRAP members "suffered economic, recreational and aesthetic harm directly as a result of the adverse environmental impact of the railroad freight structure" which would "discourage the use of 'recyclable' materials, and promote the use of new raw materials that compete with scrap, thereby adversely affecting the environment."

In distinguishing the SCRAP case from Sierra, decided the year before, the Court made clear that the only test was the threat of actual personal injury. "Unlike the specific and geographically limited federal action of which the petitioner complained in Sierra Club, the challenged agency action in this case is applicable to substantially all the Nation's railroads, and thus allegedly has an adverse environmental impact on all the natural resources of the country. Rather than a limited group of persons who used a picturesque valley in California, all persons who utilize the scenic resources of the country, and indeed all who breathe its air, could claim harm similar to that alleged by the environmental groups here. But we have already made it clear that standing is not to be denied simply because many people suffer the same injury. . . . To deny standing to persons who are in fact injured simply because many others are also injured, would mean that the most injurious and widespread Government actions could be questioned by nobody. We cannot accept that conclusion."

While it is essential to "standing" that a person allege personal injury, the "personalness" of the injury must itself meet certain tests. In Schlesinger v. Reservists to Stop the War (1974) members of the group brought a class action on behalf of themselves and all others who wanted to stop the war in Vietnam by the process of persuading Congress to take action. They pointed out that Article I, § 6, cl. 2, provides that no person "holding office under the United States, shall be a member of either house" of Congress and challenged the membership of congressmen in the military reserves on the ground that they were personally injured by such membership both as citizens and as taxpayers. Such membership in the military, they argued, denied them representatives who could approach the Vietnam War question impartially.

The Court rejected their right to sue as citizens on the ground that they had failed to allege actual injury, since the failure of congressmen to observe the Incompatibility Clause "would adversely affect only the generalized interest of all citizens in constitutional governance, and that is an abstract injury. . . . To permit a complainant who has no concrete injury to require a court to rule on important constitutional issues in the abstract would create the potential for abuse of the judicial process, distort the role of the Judiciary in its relationship to the Executive and the Legislature and open the Judiciary to an arguable charge of providing " 'government by injunction.' " The Court distinguished the Data Processing and SCRAP cases, noting that they provide "the setting for a focused consideration of a concrete injury," while in the present case "it can be only a matter of speculation whether the claimed violation has caused concrete injury to the particular complainant." Nor could they sue as taxpayers, since the Incompatibility Clause was not a limit on the spending power and thus failed part of the "logical nexus" test of Flast v. Cohen.

In United States v. Richardson, decided the same day as Schlesinger, the Court rejected a taxpayer suit brought to compel Congress to make public the expenditures of the Central Intelligence Agency. This agency had by statute been exempted from the constitutional requirement of Article I, Sec. 9, Cl. 8 that "no money shall be drawn from the treasury, but in consequence of appropriations made by law; and a regular statement and account of the receipts and expenditures of all public money shall be published from time to time." The taxpayer's claim failed the test of Flast v. Cohen since "there is no 'logical nexus' between the asserted status of taxpayer and the claimed failure of the Congress to require the Executive to supply a more detailed report of the expenditures of that agency." Justice Douglas, in dissent, pointed out that the purpose of the clause was to let a taxpayer see how his money was being spent.

Justice **Rehnquist** delivered the opinion of the Court, saying in part:

I.

Article IV, § 3, Cl. 2, of the Constitution vests Congress with the "Power to dispose of and make all needful Rules and Regulations respecting the . . . Property belonging to the United States." Shortly after the termination of hostilities in the Second World War, Congress enacted the Federal Property and Administrative Services Act of 1949. The Act was designed, in part, to provide "an economical and efficient system for . . . the disposal of surplus property." In furtherance of this policy, federal agencies are directed to maintain adequate inventories of the property under their control and to identify excess property for transfer to other agencies able to use it. Property that has outlived its usefulness to the federal government is declared "surplus" and may be transferred to private or other public entities.

The Act authorizes the Secretary of Health, Education, and Welfare (now the Secretary of Education) to assume responsibility for disposing of surplus real property "for school, classroom, or other educational use." Subject to the disapproval of the Administrator of General Services, the Secretary may sell or lease the property to nonprofit, tax exempt educational institutions for consideration that takes into account "any benefit which has accrued or may accrue to the United States" from the transferee's use of the property. By regulation, the Secretary has provided for the computation of a "public benefit allowance," which discounts the transfer price of the property "on the basis of benefits to the United States from the use of such property for educational purposes."

The property which spawned this litigation was acquired by the Department of the Army in 1942, as part of a larger tract of approximately 181 acres of land northwest of Philadelphia. The Army built on that land the Valley Forge General Hospital, and for 30 years thereafter, that hospital provided medical care for members of the Armed Forces. In April 1973, as part of a plan to reduce the number of military installations in the United States, the Secretary of Defense proposed to close the hospital, and the General Services Administration declared it to be "surplus property."

The Department of Health, Education, and Welfare (HEW) eventually assumed responsibility for disposing of portions of the property, and in August 1976, it conveyed a 77-acre tract to petitioner, the Valley Forge Christian College. The appraised value of the property at the time of conveyance was $577,500. This appraised value was discounted, however, by the Secretary's computation of a 100 percent public benefit allowance, which permitted petitioner to acquire the property without making any financial payment for it. The deed from HEW conveyed the land in fee simple with certain conditions subsequent, which required petitioner to use the property for 30 years solely for the educational purposes described in petitioner's application. In that description, petitioner stated its intention to conduct "a program of education . . . meeting the accrediting standards of the State of Pennsylvania, The American Association of Bible Colleges, the Division of Education of the General Council of the Assemblies of God and the Veterans Administration."

Petitioner is a nonprofit educational institution operating under the supervision of a religious order known as the Assemblies of God. By its own description, petitioner's purpose is "to offer systematic training on the collegiate level to men and women for Christian service as either ministers or laymen." . . .

In September 1976, respondents Americans United for Separation of Church and State, Inc. (Americans United), and four of its employees, learned of the conveyance through a news release. Two months later, they brought suit in the United States District Court for the District of Columbia, later transferred to the Eastern District of Pennsylvania to challenge the conveyance on the ground that it violated the Establishment Clause of the First Amendment. In its amended complaint, Americans United described itself as a nonprofit organization composed of 90,000 "taxpayer members." The complaint asserted that each member "would be deprived of the fair and constitutional use of his (her) tax dollar for constitutional purposes in violation of his (her) rights under the First Amendment of the United States Constitution." Respondents sought a declaration that the conveyance was null and void, and an order compelling petitioner to transfer the property back to the United States. . . .

II.

Article III of the Constitution limits the "judicial power" of the United States to the resolution of "cases" and "controversies." The constitutional power of federal courts cannot be defined, and indeed has no substance, without reference to the necessity "to adjudge

the legal rights of litigants in actual controversies." . . . The requirements of Art. III are not satisfied merely because a party requests a court of the United States to declare its legal rights, and has couched that request for forms of relief historically associated with courts of law in terms that have a familiar ring to those trained in the legal process. The judicial power of the United States defined by Art. III is not an unconditioned authority to determine the constitutionality of legislative or executive acts. The power to declare the rights of individuals and to measure the authority of governments, this Court said 90 years ago, "is legitimate only in the last resort, and as a necessity in the determination of real, earnest and vital controversy." Chicago & Grand Trunk R. Co. v. Wellman (1892). Otherwise, the power "is not judicial . . . in the sense in which judicial power is granted by the Constitution to the courts of the United States." . . .

As an incident to the elaboration of this bedrock requirement, this Court has always required that a litigant have "standing" to challenge the action sought to be adjudicated in the lawsuit. The term "standing" subsumes a blend of constitutional requirements and prudential considerations . . . and it has not always been clear in the opinions of this Court whether particular features of the "standing" requirement have been required by Art. III ex proprio vigore, or whether they are requirements that the Court itself has erected and which were not compelled by the language of the Constitution. . . .

A recent line of decisions, however, has resolved that ambiguity, at least to the following extent: at an irreducible minimum, Art. III requires the party who invokes the court's authority to "show that he personally has suffered some actual or threatened injury as a result of the putatively illegal conduct of the defendant," Gladstone, Realtors v. Village of Bellwood (1979), and that the injury "fairly can be traced to the challenged action" and "is likely to be redressed by a favorable decision," Simon v. Eastern Kentucky Welfare Rights Org. (1976). In this manner does Art. III limit the federal judicial power "to those disputes which confine federal courts to a role consistent with a system of separated powers and which are traditionally thought to be capable of resolution through the judicial process." Flast v. Cohen [1968].

The requirement of "actual injury redressable by the court," Simon, serves several of the "implicit policies embodied in Art. III," Flast. It tends to assure that the legal questions presented to the court will be resolved, not in the rarified atmosphere of a debating society, but in a concrete factual context conducive to a realistic appreciation of the consequences of judicial action. . . .

The Art. III aspect of standing also reflects a due regard for the autonomy of those persons likely to be most directly affected by a judicial order. The federal courts have abjured appeals to their authority which would convert the judicial process into "no more than a vehicle for the vindication of the value interests of concerned bystanders." United States v. SCRAP (1973). Were the federal courts merely publicly funded forums for the ventilation of public grievances or the refinement of jurisprudential understanding, the concept of "standing" would be quite unnecessary. But the "cases and controversies" language of Art. III forecloses the conversion of courts of the United States into judicial versions of college debating forums. . . . The exercise of judicial power, which can so profoundly affect the lives, liberty, and property of those to whom it extends, is therefore restricted to litigants who can show "injury in fact" resulting from the action which they seek to have the Court adjudicate.

The exercise of the judicial power also affects relationships between the coequal arms of the National Government. The effect is, of course, most vivid when a federal court declares unconstitutional an act of the Legislative or Executive branch. While the exercise of that "ultimate and supreme function" . . . is a formidable means of vindicating individual rights, when employed unwisely or unnecessarily it is also the ultimate threat to the continued effectiveness of the federal courts in performing that role. While the propriety of such action by a federal court has been recognized since Marbury v. Madison (1803), it has been recognized as a tool of last resort on the part of the federal judiciary throughout its nearly 200 years of existence. . . . Proper regard for the complex nature of our constitutional structure requires neither that the Judicial Branch shrink from a confrontation with the other two coequal branches of the Federal government, nor that it hospitably accept for adjudication claims of constitutional violation by other branches of government where the claimant has not suffered cognizable injury. Thus, this Court has "refrain[ed] from passing upon the constitutionality of an act [of the representative branches] unless obliged to do so in the proper performance of our judicial function, when the question is raised by a party whose interests entitle him to raise it." Blair v. United States (1919). The importance of this precondition should not be underestimated as a means of "defin[ing] the role assigned to the judiciary in a tripartite allocation of power." Flast v. Cohen.

Beyond the constitutional requirements, the federal judiciary has also adhered to a set of prudential principles that bear on the question of standing. Thus, this Court has held that "the plaintiff generally must assert his own legal rights and interests, and cannot rest his claim to relief on the legal rights or interests of third parties." . . . In addition, even when the plaintiff has alleged redressable injury sufficient to meet the requirements of Art. III, the Court has refrained from adjudicating "abstract questions of wide public significance" which amount to "generalized grievances," pervasively shared and most appropriately addressed in the representative branches. Finally, the Court has required that the plaintiff's complaint fall within "the zone of interests to be protected or regulated by the statute or constitutional guarantee in question." [Data Processing Service] v. Camp (1970). . . .

We need not mince words when we say that the concept of "Article III standing" has not been defined with complete consistency in all of the various cases decided by this Court which have discussed it, nor when we say that this very fact is probably proof that the concept cannot be reduced to a one-sentence or one-paragraph definition. But of one thing we may be sure: Those who do not possess Art. III standing may not litigate as suitors in the courts of the United States.* Article III, which is every bit as important in its circumscription of the judicial power of the United States as in its granting of that power, is not merely a troublesome hurdle to be overcome if possible so as to reach the "merits" of a lawsuit which a party desires to have adjudicated; it is a part of the basic charter promulgated by the Framers of the Constitution at Philadelphia in 1787, a charter which created a general government, provided for the interaction between that government and the governments of the several States, and was later amended so as to either enhance or limit its authority with respect to both States and individuals.

III.

The injury alleged by respondents in their amended complaint is the "depriv[ation] of the fair and constitutional use of [their] tax dollar." As a result, our discussion must begin with Frothingham v. Mellon (1923). . . .

[The Court here summarizes both Frothingham v. Mellon and Doremus v. Board of Education (1952), showing that both turned on the failure to show direct pecuniary injury.]

The Court again visited the problem of taxpayer standing in Flast v. Cohen (1968). The taxpayer plaintiffs in Flast sought to enjoin the expenditure of federal funds under the Elementary and Secondary Education Act of 1965, which they alleged were being used to support religious schools in violation of the Establishment Clause. The Court developed a two-part test to determine whether the plaintiffs had standing to sue. First, because a taxpayer alleges injury only by virtue of his liability for taxes, the Court held that "a taxpayer will be a proper party to allege the unconstitutionality only of exercises of congressional power under the taxing and spending clause of Art. I, § 8, of the Constitution." Second, the Court required the taxpayer to "show that the challenged enactment exceeds specific constitutional limitations upon the exercise of the taxing and spending power and not simply that the enactment is generally beyond the powers delegated to Congress by Art. I, § 8."

---

*Justice Brennan's dissent takes us to task for "tend[ing] merely to obfuscate, rather than inform, our understanding of the meaning of rights under the law." Were this court constituted to operate a national classroom on "the meaning of rights" for the benefit of interested litigants, this criticism would carry weight. The teaching of Art. III, however, is that constitutional adjudication is available only on terms prescribed by the Constitution, among which is the requirement of a plaintiff with standing to sue. The dissent asserts that this requirement "overrides no other provision of the Constitution." . . . Art. III obligates a federal court to act only when it is assured of the power to do so, that is, when it is called upon to resolve an actual case or controversy. Then, and only then, may it turn its attention to other constitutional provisions and presume to provide a forum for the adjudication of rights. . . .

The plaintiffs in Flast satisfied this test because "[t]heir constitutional challenge [was] made to an exercise by Congress of its power under Art. I, § 8, to spend for the general welfare," and because the Establishment Clause, on which plaintiffs' complaint rested, "operates as a specific constitutional limitation upon the exercise by Congress of the taxing and spending power conferred by Art. I, § 8." The Court distinguished Frothingham v. Mellon on the ground that Mrs. Frothingham had relied, not on a specific limitation on the power to tax and spend, but on a more general claim based on the Due Process Clause. Thus, the Court reaffirmed that the "case or controversy" aspect of standing is unsatisfied "where a taxpayer seeks to employ a federal court as a forum in which to air his generalized grievances about the conduct of government or the allocation of power in the Federal System."

Unlike the plaintiffs in Flast, respondents fail the first prong of the test for taxpayer standing. Their claim is deficient in two respects. First, the source of their complaint is not a congressional action, but a decision by HEW to transfer a parcel of federal property. Flast limited taxpayer standing to challenges directed "only [at] exercises of congressional power." See Schlesinger v. Reservists Committee to Stop the War [1974] (denying standing because the taxpayer plaintiffs "did not challenge an enactment under Art. I, § 8, but rather the action of the Executive Branch").

Second, and perhaps redundantly, the property transfer about which respondents complain was not an exercise of authority conferred by the Taxing and Spending Clause of Art. I, § 8. The authorizing legislation, the Federal Property and Administrative Services Act of 1949, was an evident exercise of Congress' power under the Property Clause, Art. IV, § 3, cl. 2. Respondents do not dispute this conclusion, and it is decisive of any claim of taxpayer standing under the Flast precedent.*
. . .

IV. . . .

The complaint in this case shares a common deficiency with those in Schlesinger and [United States v.] Richardson. Although they claim that the Constitution has been violated, they claim nothing else. They fail to identify any personal injury suffered by the plaintiffs *as a consequence* of the alleged constitutional error, other than the psychological consequence presumably produced by observation of conduct with which one disagrees. That is not an injury sufficient to confer standing under Art. III, even though the disagreement is phrased in constitutional terms. It is evident that respondents are firmly committed to the constitutional principle of separation of church and State, but standing is not measured by the intensity of the litigant's interest or the fervor of his advocacy. "[T]hat concrete adverseness which sharpens the presentation of issues," Baker v. Carr, is the anticipated consequence of proceedings commenced by one who has been injured in fact; it is not a permissible substitute for the showing of injury itself.

In reaching this conclusion, we do not retreat from our earlier holdings that standing may be predicated on noneconomic injury. See, e.g., United States v. SCRAP; [Data Processing Service] v. Camp. We simply cannot see that respondents have alleged an *injury of any* kind, economic or otherwise, sufficient to confer standing. Respondents complain of a transfer of property located in Chester County, Pa. The named plaintiffs reside in Maryland and Virginia; their organizational headquarters are located in Washington, D.C. They learned of the transfer through a news release. Their claim that the Government has violated the Establishment Clause does not provide a special license to roam the country in search of governmental wrongdoing and to reveal their discoveries in federal court. The federal courts were simply not constituted as ombudsmen of the general welfare.

V. . . .

. . . Respondents' claim of standing implicitly rests on the presumption that violations of the Establishment Clause typically will not cause injury sufficient to confer standing under the "traditional" view of Art. III. But "[t]he assumption that if respondents have no standing to sue, no one would have standing, is not a reason to find standing." Schlesinger v. Reservists Committee to Stop the War. This view would convert standing into a requirement that must be observed only when satisfied. Moreover, we are unwilling to assume that injured parties are nonexistent simply because they have not joined respondents in their suit. . . .

Were we to accept respondents' claim of standing in this case, there would be no principled basis for confining our exception to litigants relying on the Establishment Clause. Ultimately, that exception derives from the idea that the judicial power requires nothing more for its invocation than important issues and able litigants. The existence of injured parties who might not wish to bring suit becomes irrelevant. Because we are unwilling to countenance such a departure from the limits on judicial power contained in Art. III, the judgment of the Court of Appeals is reversed.

It is so ordered.

Justice **Brennan,** with whom Justice **Marshall** and Justice **Blackmun** join, dissenting, said in part:

A plaintiff's standing is a jurisdictional matter for Art. III courts, and thus a "threshold question" to be resolved before turning attention to more "substantive" is-

---

*Although not necessary to our decision, we note that any connection between the challenged property transfer and respondents' tax burden is at best speculative and at worst nonexistent. . . . In fact, respondents' only objection is that the Government did not receive adequate consideration for the transfer, because petitioner's use of the property will not confer a public benefit. Assuming, arguendo, that this proposition is true, an assumption by no means clear, there is no basis for believing that a transfer to a different purchaser would have added to Government receipts. As the Government argues, "the ultimate purchaser would, in all likelihood, have been another non-profit institution or local school district rather than a purchaser for cash." . . .

sues. . . . But in consequence there is an impulse to decide difficult questions of substantive law obliquely in the course of opinions purporting to do nothing more than determine what the Court labels ''standing''; this accounts for the phenomenon of opinions, such as the one today, that tend merely to obfuscate, rather than inform, our understanding of the meaning of rights under the law. The serious by-product of that practice is that the Court disregards its constitutional responsibility when, by failing to acknowledge the protections afforded by the Constitution, it uses ''standing to slam the courthouse door against plaintiffs who are entitled to full consideration of their claims on the merits.'' . . .

I. . . .

. . . The Court makes a fundamental mistake when it determines that a plaintiff has failed to satisfy the two-pronged ''injury-in-fact'' test, or indeed any other test of ''standing,'' without first determining whether the Constitution or a statute defines injury, and creates a cause of action for redress of that injury, in precisely the circumstance presented to the Court. . . .

The ''case and controversy'' limitation of Art. III overrides no other provision of the Constitution.* To construe that Article to deny standing '' 'to the class for whose sake [a] constitutional protection is given,' '' . . . simply turns the Constitution on its head. . . .

II. . . .

B.

In 1947, nine Justices of this Court recognized that the Establishment Clause does impose a very definite restriction on the power to tax. The Court held in Everson v. Board of Education that the '' 'establishment of religion' clause of the First Amendment means at least this:''

''No tax in any amount, large or small, can be levied to support any religious activities or institutions, whatever they may be called, or whatever form they may adopt, to teach or practice religion.''

The members of the Court could not have been more explicit. ''One of our basic rights is to be free of taxation to support a transgression of the constitutional command that the authorities 'shall make no law respecting an establishment of religion, or prohibiting the free exercise thereof.' '' (Jackson, J., dissenting). ''[A]part from efforts to inject religious training or exercises and sectarian issues into the public schools, the only serious threat to maintaining that complete and permanent separation of religion and civil power which the First Amendment commands is through the use of the taxing power to support religion, religious establishments, or establishments having a religious foundation whatever their form

---

*When the Constitution makes it clear that a particular person is to be protected from a particular form of government action, then that person has a ''right'' to be free of that action; when that right is infringed, then there is injury, and a personal stake, within the meaning of Article III.

or special religious function. . . . [M]oney taken by taxation from one is not to be used or given to support another's religious training or belief, or indeed one's own.'' (Rutledge, J., dissenting). . . .

[Justice Brennan here reviews the history of the adoption of the establishment clause.]

It is clear in the light of this history, that one of the primary purposes of the Establishment Clause was to prevent the use of tax monies for religious purposes. *The taxpayer was the direct and intended beneficiary of the prohibition on financial aid to religion.* This basic understanding of the meaning of the Establishment Clause explains why the Court in Everson, while rejecting appellant's claim on the merits, perceived the issue presented there as it did. The appellant sued ''in his capacity as a district taxpayer,'' challenging the actions of the Board of Education in passing a resolution providing reimbursement to parents for the cost of transporting their children to parochial schools, and seeking to have that resolution ''set aside.'' Appellant's Establishment Clause claim was precisely that the ''statute . . . forced inhabitants to pay taxes to help support and maintain'' church schools. It seems obvious that all the Justices who participated in Everson would have agreed with Justice Jackson's succinct statement of the question presented: ''Is it constitutional to tax this complainant to pay the cost of carrying pupils to Church schools of one specified denomination?'' (Jackson, J., dissenting). Given this view of the issues, could it fairly be doubted that this taxpayer alleged injury in precisely the form that the Establishment Clause sought to make actionable?

C.

In Flast v. Cohen (1968), federal taxpayers sought to challenge the Department of Health, Education, and Welfare's administration of the Elementary and Secondary Education Act of 1965: specifically the Department's practice of allowing funds distributed under that Act to be used to finance instruction in religious schools. Appellants urged that the use of federal funds for such a purpose violated the Establishment and Free Exercise Clauses of the First Amendment, and sought a declaration that this use of federal funds was not authorized by the Act, or that to the extent the use was authorized, the Act was ''unconstitutional and void.'' . . . The Frothingham rule stood as a seemingly absolute barrier to the maintenance of the claim. The Court held, however, the Frothingham barrier could be overcome by any claim that met both requirements of a two part ''nexus'' test.

The Justices who participated in Flast were not unaware of the Court's continued recognition of a federally cognizable ''case or controversy'' when a *local* taxpayer seeks to challenge as unconstitutional the use of a *municipality's* funds—the propriety of which had, of course, gone unquestioned in Everson. The Court was aware as well of the rule stated in Doremus v. Board of Education (1952) that the interest of a taxpayer, even one raising an Establishment Clause claim, was limited to the actions of a government involving the expenditure of funds. But in reaching its holding, it is also quite clear that the Court was responding, not only to Everson's continued acceptance of municipal taxpayer actions but also to Everson's exposition of the history and meaning of the Establishment Clause. See Flast.

It is at once apparent that the test of standing formulated by the Court in Flast sought to reconcile the developing doctrine of taxpayer "standing" with the Court's historical understanding that the Establishment Clause was intended to prohibit the Federal Government from using tax funds for the advancement of religion, and thus the constitutional imperative of taxpayer standing in certain cases brought pursuant to the Establishment Clause. The two-pronged "nexus" test offered by the Court, despite its general language, is best understood as "a determinant of standing of plaintiffs alleging only injury as taxpayers who challenge alleged violations of the Establishment and Free Exercise Clauses of the First Amendment," and not as a general statement of standing principles. . . . The test explains what forms of governmental action may be attacked by someone alleging only taxpayer status, and, without ruling out the possibility that history might reveal another similarly founded provision, explains why an Establishment Clause claim is treated differently from any other assertion that the Federal Government has exceeded the bounds of the law in allocating its largesse. Thus, consistent with Doremus, Flast required, as the first prong of its test, that the taxpayer demonstrate a logical connection between his taxpayer status and the type of legislation attacked. Appellants' challenge to a program of grants to educational institutions clearly satisfied this first requirement. As the second prong, consistent with the prohibition of taxpayer claims of the kind advanced in Frothingham, appellants were required to show a connection between their status and the precise nature of the infringement alleged. They had no difficulty meeting this requirement: the Court agreed that the Establishment Clause jealously protects taxpayers from diversion of their funds to the support of religion through the offices of the Federal Government. . . .

It may be that Congress can tax for *almost* any reason, or for no reason at all. There is, so far as I have been able to discern, but one constitutionally imposed limit on that authority. Congress cannot use tax money to support a church, or to encourage religion. That is "*the* forbidden exaction." Everson v. Board of Education (Rutledge, J., dissenting) (emphasis added). In absolute terms the history of the Establishment Clause of the First Amendment makes this clear. History also makes it clear that the federal taxpayer is a singularly "proper and appropriate party to invoke a federal court's jurisdiction" to challenge a federal bestowal of largesse as a violation of the Establishment Clause. Each, and indeed every, federal taxpayer suffers precisely the injury that the Establishment Clause guards against when the Federal Government directs that funds be taken from the pocketbooks of the citizenry and placed into the coffers of the ministry.

A taxpayer cannot be asked to raise his objection

to such use of his funds at the time he pays his tax. Apart from the unlikely circumstance in which the Government announced in advance that a particular levy would be used for religious subsidies, taxpayers could hardly assert that they were being injured until the Government actually lent its support to a religious venture. . . . Surely, then, a taxpayer must have standing at the time that he learns of the Government's alleged Establishment Clause violation to seek equitable relief in order to halt the continuing and intolerable burden on his pocketbook, his conscience, and his constitutional rights.

III.

Blind to history, the Court attempts to distinguish this case from Flast by wrenching snippets of language from our opinions, and by perfunctorily applying that language under color of the first prong of Flast's two-part nexus test. The tortuous distinctions thus produced are specious, at best: at worst, they are pernicious to our constitutional heritage.

First, the Court finds this case different from Flast because here the "source of [plaintiff's] complaint is not a *congressional* action, but a decision by HEW to transfer a parcel of federal property." This attempt at distinction cannot withstand scrutiny. Flast involved a challenge to the actions of the Commissioner of Education, and other officials of HEW, in disbursing funds under the Elementary and Secondary Education Act of 1965 to "religious and sectarian" schools. . . . In the present case, respondents challenge HEW's grant of property pursuant to the Federal Property and Administrative Services Act of 1949, seeking to enjoin HEW "from making a grant of this and other property to the [defendant] so long as such a grant will violate the Establishment Clause." . . .

More fundamentally, no clear division can be drawn in this context between actions of the Legislative Branch and those of the Executive Branch. To be sure, the First Amendment is phrased as a restriction on Congress' legislative authority; this is only natural since the Constitution assigns the authority to legislate and appropriate only to the Congress. But it is difficult to conceive of an expenditure for which the last governmental actor, either implementing directly the legislative will, or acting within the scope of legislatively delegated authority, is not an Executive Branch official. The First Amendment binds the Government as a whole, regardless of which branch is at work in a particular instance.

The Court's second purported distinction between this case and Flast is equally unavailing. The majority finds it "decisive" that the Federal Property and Administrative Services Act of 1949 'was an evident exercise of Congress' power under the Property Clause, Art. IV, § 3, cl. 2," while the Government action in Flast was taken under Art. I, § 8. The Court relies on United States v. Richardson (1974) and Schlesinger v. Reservists Committee to Stop the War (1974) to support the distinction between the two Clauses, noting that those cases involved alleged deviations from the requirements of Art.

I, § 9, cl. 7 and Art. I, § 6, cl. 2, respectively. The standing defect in each case was *not*, however, the failure to allege a violation of the Spending Clause; rather, the taxpayers in those cases had not complained of the distribution of Government largesse, and thus failed to meet the essential requirement of taxpayer standing recognized in Doremus.

It can make no constitutional difference in the case before us whether the donation to the petitioner here was in the form of a cash grant to build a facility, see Tilton v. Richardson (1971), or in the nature of a gift of property including a facility already built. That this is a meaningless distinction is illustrated by Tilton. In that case, taxpayers were afforded standing to object to the fact that the Government had not received adequate assurance that if the property that it financed for use as an educational facility was later converted to religious uses, it would receive full value for the property, as the Constitution requires. The complaint here is precisely that, although the property at issue is actually being used for a sectarian purpose, the Government has not received, nor demanded, full value payment. Whether undertaken pursuant to the Property Clause or the Spending Clause, the breach of the Establishment Clause, and the relationship of the taxpayer to that breach, is precisely the same. . . .

Justice **Stevens,** dissenting, said in part:

In Parts I, II, and III of his dissenting opinion, Justice Brennan demonstrates that respondent taxpayers have standing to mount an Establishment Clause challenge against the Federal Government's transfer of property worth $1,300,000 to the Assemblies of God. For the Court to hold that plaintiffs' standing depends on whether the Government's transfer was an exercise of its power to spend money, on the one hand, or its power to dispose of tangible property, on the other, is to trivialize the standing doctrine.

One cannot read the Court's opinion and the concurring opinions of Justice Stewart and Justice Fortas in Flast v. Cohen without forming the firm conclusion that the plaintiffs' invocation of the Establishment Clause was of decisive importance in resolving the standing issue in that case. Justice Fortas made this point directly:
. . .

''Perhaps the vital interest of a citizen in the establishment issue, without reference to his taxpayer's status, would be acceptable as a basis for this challenge. We need not decide this. But certainly, I believe, we must recognize that our principle of judicial scrutiny of legislative acts which raise important constitutional questions requires that the issue here presented—the separation of state and church—which the Founding Fathers regarded as fundamental to our constitutional system—should be subjected to judicial testing. This is not a question which we, if we are to be faithful to our trust, should consign to limbo, unacknowledged, unresolved, and undecided. . . .''

Today the Court holds, in effect, that the Judiciary has no greater role in enforcing the Establishment Clause than in enforcing other ''norm[s] of conduct which the Federal Government is bound to honor'' such as the Accounts Clause . . . and the Incompatibility Clause. . . . Ironically, however, its decision rests on the premise that the difference between a disposition of funds pursuant to the Spending Clause and a disposition of realty pursuant to the Property Clause is of fundamental jurisprudential significance. With all due respect, I am persuaded that the essential holding of Flast v. Cohen attaches special importance to the Establishment Clause and does not permit the drawing of a tenuous distinction between the Spending Clause and the Property Clause.

For this reason, and for the reasons stated in Parts I, II, and III of Justice Brennan's opinion, I would affirm the judgment of the Court of Appeals.

2

The Legislative Branch

CONGRESSIONAL CONTROL OVER THE COURT

EX PARTE McCARDLE

7 Wallace 506; 19 L. Ed. 264 (1869)

The men who drafted the Constitution were men of practical political experience, and it was as a practical political expedient that they adopted the principle of the separation of powers. But they did not intend to adopt, nor did they feel that Montesquieu's celebrated doctrine called for, a complete and air-tight separation. They wanted to avoid such concentration of governing power in any one department of government as would enable that department to become despotic. This end could best be achieved, not by a theoretically pure separation of legislative, executive, and judicial power, but by a judicious blending and overlapping which would permit each branch to check and balance the tyrannical tendencies of the others. In what has become known as a system of checks and balances, the classic American statement of this position is made by Madison in No. 47 of The Federalist. *According to Madison, when Montesquieu said, " 'There can be no liberty where the legislative and executive powers are united in the same person, or body of magistrates,' or, 'if the power of judging be not separated from the legislative and executive powers,' he did not mean that these departments ought to have no partial agency in, or no control over, the acts of each other. His meaning, as his own words import, and still*

more conclusively as illustrated by the example in his eye [the British constitution], can amount to no more than this, that where the whole power of one department is exercised by the same hands which possess the whole power of another department, the fundamental principles of a free constitution are subverted."

Those charged with the efficient administration of government in a twentieth-century society are often tempted to feel that the doctrine of the separation of powers makes real governmental efficiency impossible by scattering power and responsibility among the three departments of government. They may be entirely right. They may solace themselves, if possible, by reading the words of Justice Brandeis, dissenting in Myers v. United States (1926), who said: "The doctrine of the separation of powers was adopted by the Convention of 1787 not to promote efficiency but to preclude the exercise of arbitrary power. The purpose was not to avoid friction, but, by means of the inevitable friction incident to the distribution of the governmental powers among three departments, to save the people from autocracy."

But while it is clear that the framers never in fact intended a pure separation of powers, there are statements in The Federalist *from which one can infer that they had a fairly clear idea as to exactly what constituted legislative, executive, and judicial powers; and had they wanted to divide them clearly, they could have done so. As Madison observed in paper No. 48, "After discriminating, therefore, in theory, the several classes of power, as they may in their nature be legislative, executive, or judiciary, the next and most difficult task is to provide some practical security for each. . . ." Cer-*

tainly the Supreme Court has upon occasion felt competent to distinguish these various kinds of power, despite the fact that since 1789 enough new government machinery has been invented to cast doubt upon the value of the traditional historical divisions.

Two things should be noted with regard to the separation of powers. First, although the words tend to be used casually even by the Supreme Court, it is not a concept specified in the words of the Constitution. Rather, it is implied from the so-called distributing clauses—the first clauses of Articles I, II, and III which allocate the powers of government to the three branches. Hence, to show that an action violates the separation of powers, it is necessary to show that it violates one of these clauses or some other grant of power to a specific branch, rather than to allege merely that the principle has been violated. The separation of powers doctrine takes its content from the specific clauses of the Constitution, not the other way around.

Second, quite apart from the specific checks on each branch specified in the Constitution, the separation of powers doctrine is not interpreted as encompassing rigid categories. In a famous dissent in an otherwise insignificant territorial case (Springer v. Philippine Islands, 1928) Justice Holmes expressed what is conceded to be the classic theory:

"The great ordinances of the Constitution do not establish and divide fields of black and white. Even the more specific of them are found to terminate in a penumbra shading gradually from one extreme to the other. Property must not be taken without compensation, but with the help of a phrase (the police power) some property may be taken or destroyed for public use without paying for it, if you do not take too much. When we come to the fundamental distinctions it is still more obvious that they must be received with a certain latitude or our government could not go on.

"To make a rule of conduct applicable to an individual who but for such action would be free from it is to legislate—yet it is what the judges do whenever they determine which of two competing principles of policy shall prevail. At an early date it was held that Congress could delegate to the courts the power to regulate process, which certainly is lawmaking so far as it goes. Wayman v. Southard [1825]; Bank of the United States v. Halstead [1825]. With regard to the Executive, Congress has delegated to it or to some branch of it the power to impose penalties, Oceanic Steam Navigation Co. v. Stranahan [1909]; . . . to make regulations as to forest reserves, United States v. Grimaud [1911], and other powers not needing to be stated in further detail. . . . Congress has authorized the President to suspend the operation of a statute, even one suspending commercial intercourse with another country, Field v. Clark [1892], and very recently it has been decided that the President might be given power to change the tariff. J. W. Hampton, Jr. & Co. v. United States [1928]. It is said that the powers of Congress cannot be delegated, yet Congress has established the Interstate Commerce Commission, which does legislative, judicial and executive acts, only softened by a quasi; makes regulations,

Intermountain Rate Cases [1914], issues reparation orders, and performs executive functions in connection with Safety Appliance Acts, Boiler Inspection Acts, etc. Congress also has made effective excursions in the other direction. It has withdrawn jurisdiction of a case after it has been argued. Ex parte McCardle [1869]. It has granted an amnesty, notwithstanding the grant to the President of the power to pardon. Brown v. Walker [1896]. A territorial legislature has granted a divorce. Maynard v. Hill [1888]. Congress has declared lawful an obstruction to navigation that this Court has declared unlawful. Pennsylvania v. Wheeling & Belmont Bridge Co. [1856]. Parallel to the case before us Congress long ago established the Smithsonian Institution to question which would be to lay hands on the Ark of the Covenant; not to speak of later similar exercises of power hitherto unquestioned, so far as I know.

"It does not seem to need argument to show that however we may disguise it by veiling words we do not and cannot carry out the distinction between legislative and executive action with mathematical precision and divide the branches into watertight compartments, were it ever so desirable to do so, which I am far from believing that it is, or that the Constitution requires." . . .

A court, in order to be a court and behave like one, must possess two kinds of authority. The first is jurisdiction, which is the power of the court to bring parties before it for the purpose of deciding the kinds of disputes in which those parties are involved. What the court can do about a dispute properly before it depends upon its possession of judicial power. Both jurisdiction and judicial power are provided for the federal courts in Article III of the Constitution.

Article III provides that "the judicial power shall extend to all cases . . . ." and then proceeds to enumerate two classes of cases to which federal jurisdiction extends. One class of cases comes to the courts because of their subject matter. These are cases in which so-called "federal questions" are raised, i.e., questions of the interpretation of the Constitution, laws or treaties of the United States. A second category is based on the nature of the parties to the suit and includes generally cases where the state courts might not be impartial. Here are the cases between states and between citizens of different states.

Since lower federal courts are invested with judicial power by Article III, does the phrase "judicial power shall extend" mean that any federal court, as soon as it is created by Congress, is fully invested with both kinds of jurisdiction? The answer is no, despite the urging of Federalists who favored a strong independent judiciary. The wording of the Judiciary Act of 1789 creating the courts and the circumstances surrounding its passage both indicate a legislative acceptance of the idea that Congress has complete control over the jurisdiction of the lower federal courts; ten years later, in Turner v. Bank of North America (1799), the Supreme Court approved that interpretation. Congress had specifically denied the courts a portion of the jurisdiction based upon diversity of citizenship; and the bank argued that since diversity jurisdiction was given by Article III,

Congress had no power to take it away. The Court upheld the congressional limitation and refused to take jurisdiction. Congress has made free use of its power to grant, withhold, or distribute the jurisdiction of the lower federal courts as it has thought wise. Some of the jurisdiction mentioned in Article III, such as diversity jurisdiction in cases involving small sums, has never been conferred on the federal courts at all. It was not until 1875 that the lower federal courts were given jurisdiction over cases involving federal questions.

The Constitution, in providing for the Supreme Court, distinguishes between its original jurisdiction to decide cases which start in the Supreme Court and its appellate jurisdiction to decide cases which come to it on appeal, or by other procedure, from some other court. Article III provides that "in all cases affecting ambassadors, other public ministers, and consuls, and those in which a State shall be a party, the Supreme Court shall have original jurisdiction. In all the other cases before mentioned, the Supreme Court shall have appellate jurisdiction, both as to law and fact, with such exceptions, and under such regulations as the Congress shall make." The Supreme Court held in Marbury v. Madison (1803) that Congress cannot validly enlarge the original jurisdiction of the Court. That portion of the Judiciary Act of 1789 which purported to enlarge the original jurisdiction of the Court to include the power to issue writs of mandamus was held unconstitutional.

But to what extent and by what means may Congress control the appellate jurisdiction of the Supreme Court? The present case was one of a series of attempts by the Southern states to get from the Supreme Court a clear decision on the validity of the military reconstruction program set up by Congress after the Civil War. The behavior of the Court must to some extent be judged in the light of the bitterness which this conflict engendered. McCardle, a Southern newspaper editor, was arrested for sedition and tried and convicted by a federal military commission. When his petition to the circuit court for a writ of habeas corpus was denied, he appealed directly to the Supreme Court under a statute designed, ironically, to provide quick access to the Supreme Court for blacks and federal officers in the South. The Court unanimously agreed that the statute gave it jurisdiction in McCardle's case; and in view of its denunciation of military commissions in Ex parte Milligan three years before (1866), there was a widespread expectation that the Court would hold the Reconstruction Acts unconstitutional because of their establishment of military government throughout much of the South.

To prevent possible judicial sabotage of its reconstruction program, the House had already passed a bill providing that the Court could invalidate acts of Congress only by a two-thirds vote, but the Senate had not concurred. Then, with argument in the McCardle case already concluded, Congress undertook to block a decision of the Court by repealing the law by which jurisdiction to hear McCardle's appeal had been conferred. Despite impeachment proceedings against him, the President vetoed the act; but it was repassed over his veto. The Court, which had waited to see whether the repealing statute would pass, put off until the following term the question of the effect of this repeal on its jurisdiction in the McCardle case. Justices Grier and Field bitterly excoriated their brethren for what they regarded as a shameful and cowardly delay in deciding the case.

Four years later the Court again faced a confrontation with Congress over an attempt to withdraw jurisdiction and this time it did not back down. Klein, a former supporter of the Confederacy, had been granted a pardon by President Johnson. Johnson granted pardons and reinstatements of their confiscated property to persons such as Klein on condition they took an oath to support the United States. Title to confiscated property had always remained with the owners, but to get it or its value back from the Treasury they had to sue in the Court of Claims. Although the Supreme Court had previously upheld the binding nature of such conditional pardons, Congress, liking neither the pardons nor the return of the property to former rebels, by statute ordered the Court of Claims (or the Supreme Court on appeal) to consider the acceptance of the pardon by the individual as conclusive evidence of disloyalty and ordered the suits dismissed for lack of jurisdiction.

The Supreme Court in United States v. Klein (1872) held the act invalid. It conceded that Congress had complete control over the organization and jurisdiction of the Court of Claims and could confer or withhold the right of appeal from its decisions, adding "and if this act did nothing more, it would be our duty to give it effect. . . .

"But the language of the proviso shows plainly that it does not intend to withhold appellate jurisdiction except as a means to an end. Its great and controlling purpose is to deny to pardons granted by the President the effect which this court had adjudged them to have. . . .

"It seems to us that this is not an exercise of the acknowledged power of Congress to make exceptions and prescribe regulations to the appellate power.

"The court is required to ascertain the existence of certain facts and thereupon to declare that its jurisdiction on appeal has ceased. . . . What is this but to prescribe a rule for the decision of a cause in a particular way? . . .

"Congress has already provided that the Supreme Court shall have jurisdiction of the judgments of the court of claims on appeal. Can it prescribe a rule in conformity with which the court must deny to itself the jurisdiction thus conferred, because and only because its decision, in accordance with settled law, must be adverse to the government and favorable to the suitor? This question seems to us to answer itself."

The Court noted that "to the Executive alone is intrusted the power of pardon; and it is granted without limit." Clearly it included the right to remove the guilt which had justified the confiscation, and Congress, by using the pardon to prove guilt, was denying the pardon its legal effect. Without any allusion whatever to Ex parte McCardle the Court simply concluded that the provision had been "inserted in the appropriation bill through inadvertence" and declined to enforce it.

In 1982 over 30 bills were introduced in Congress that would strip the Supreme Court and lower federal courts of jurisdiction in certain constitutional cases or the power to grant certain remedies in those cases. The issues involved included abortion, prayer in the public schools and busing as a means to desegregate schools. These bills were defeated, in large measure because of the lobbying efforts against them by organized groups concerned with the substantive issues involved, e.g., pro-abortion. In 1983 a new crop of bills to limit the jurisdiction of the federal courts surfaced. In an effort to avoid the attention of the organized issue groups and enhance the chance that these new bills would be passed, they were drafted in procedural terms. The 1983 bills make no mention of abortion, busing or prayer in schools; instead, they speak of curtailing "federal-question" jurisdiction, revising judicial appropriation procedures, overseeing the conduct of federal judges and overturning the "incorporation doctrine"—the constitutional rule by which courts apply the Bill of Rights to the states. The language of these bills may be stripped of all the emotionally-charged words contained in the 1982 bills, but to date none of them has been successful. In September 1985 the Senate rejected by a vote of sixty-two to thirty-six a bill introduced by Senator Jesse Helms of North Carolina to withdraw court jurisdiction over school prayer cases. In a related but quite different approach, the anti-abortion forces got into the 1984 Republican national platform a provision pledging the appointment of judges committed to their position.

In the last analysis, if Congress finds itself in conflict with the Supreme Court on constitutional issues, it may always seek to employ the direct and orderly process of constitutional amendment to accomplish its ends. It has done this in three cases. Chisolm v. Georgia (1793) was nullified by the Eleventh Amendment; the Dred Scott case (1857), ruling on the nature and source of citizenship, was nullified by the first section of the Fourteenth Amendment; while the Sixteenth Amendment reversed at least part of the Court's ruling in the Income Tax Cases (1895). Such changes are not easy to accomplish, however, and most efforts to alter or nullify controversial Court decisions have been unsuccessful. Moreover, as the history of both the Fourteenth Amendment and the Income Tax Amendment makes clear, the meaning of an amendment is subject to the interpretation of the Supreme Court just as was the original constitutional provision.

While the Constitution explicitly defines the outer limits of federal jurisdiction by listing the types of cases to which federal judicial power extends, it does not, in similar detail, state what this judicial power is. Judicial power, like legislative and executive power, derives its meaning from the pages of history. The framers did not feel that precise definition was necessary. One obvious component of judicial power, noted in the Muskrat case (1911), is "the power of a court to decide and pronounce a judgment and carry it into effect between persons and parties who bring a case before it for a decision." Another aspect is the power to pass upon the constitutionality of congressional and executive acts.

More difficult is the question whether this judicial power is vested directly in the courts by the Constitution, and to what (if any) extent it is thereby rendered immune from control by Congress. Article III provides that "the judicial power of the United States, shall be vested in one Supreme Court, and in such inferior courts as the Congress may from time to time ordain and establish." A comparison of this with the grants of power in Articles I and II suggest that judicial power, like legislative and executive power, is given to the courts directly by the Constitution. The judicial branch is no more dependent upon Congress for its judicial power than the President is for his executive power. Thus, while jurisdiction can be granted or withheld by Congress in accordance with the language of Article III, judicial power is inherent in the courts. An apt metaphor in a circuit court of appeals case (Michaelson v. United States, 1923) describes it thus: "Viewing the inferior courts and also the Supreme Court as an appellate tribunal, we see that Congress, the agency to exercise the legislative power of the United States, can, as a potter, shape the vessel of jurisdiction, the capacity to receive; but, the vessel having been made, the judicial power of the United States is poured into the vessel, large or small, not by Congress, but by the Constitution."

Two kinds of cases have, in the past, brought efforts by Congress to curb judicial power: (1) the use of the inherent judicial power to punish for contempt newspaper comment critical of a court and (2) the use of the judicial power to issue injunctions (whose violations were punishable as contempt) to prevent or stop labor strikes. In a number of cases challenging both these efforts at control the Supreme Court, while reiterating "that the power to punish for contempt is inherent in all courts, has been many times decided and may be regarded as settled law," found that the particular regulations involved were not an interference with the courts' inherent judicial power.

While the Court's willingness to accept certain limits on its contempt power may be viewed as a denial of the existence of such power, the Court has made clear that the power does exist and is inherent. In United States v. Shipp (1906) a sheriff was cited for contempt for turning a prisoner in his charge over to a lynch mob after the Supreme Court had said he was entitled to a writ of habeas corpus in a federal court. Although there was serious doubt about the federal jurisdiction, the Court made clear that "even if the circuit court had no jurisdiction to entertain Johnson's petition, and if this court had no jurisdiction of the appeal, this court, and this court alone, could decide that such was the law." The Court reaffirmed this rule in United States v. United Mine Workers (1947) where a district court had enjoined the union from calling a strike despite language in the Clayton Act and the Norris-LaGuardia Act seeming to forbid this use of the injunction. "The District Court unquestionably had the power to issue a restraining order *for the purpose of preserving existing conditions pending a decision upon its own jurisdiction.''*

Not only is the power of the lower federal courts to punish for criminal contempt subject to the ''reasonable'' control of Congress, it is also subject to the pardoning power of the President. While the power to pardon ordinary federal prisoners is undisputed, the right to pardon contempts of the legislative and judicial branches of the government has been challenged as an interference with the exercise by those branches of their own authority and consequently a violation of the separation of powers. The power to pardon contempts of Congress has never been tested in the courts. In Ex parte Grossman (1925) the Court held valid the presidential pardon of a man who had been committed to jail by a United States district court for criminal contempt. The lower court argued that such a power was an interference by the executive with an inherent judicial power to enforce its decrees. The Supreme Court replied that such contempts were offenses against the United States, not merely against the court involved, and as such were subject to the pardoning power. Whatever the source or extent of the contempt power, the specific grant to the President of the power to pardon made it irrelevant whether it was a limit on the power of the court or not. Although criminal contempts have been considered crimes at least since Grossman, it was not until 1966 that the Court overruled a century of precedent and announced that in the future criminal contempts involving sentences exceeding six months had to be tried by a jury; see Cheff v. Schnackenberg (1966).

> *Query: Could Congress abolish the appellate jurisdiction of the Supreme Court? Could Congress have withdrawn from the Supreme Court jurisdiction to pass on the validity of the Reconstruction Acts? Can Congress forbid the courts of the United States to decide any cases involving the constitutional right to abortion? Could Congress forbid the federal courts to issue temporary injunctions in labor disputes? How would the Court handle such a law?*

Mr. Chief Justice **Chase** delivered the opinion of the Court, saying in part:

The first question necessarily is that of jurisdiction; for, if the Act of March, 1868, takes away the jurisdiction defined by the Act of February, 1867, it is useless, if not improper, to enter into any discussion of other questions.

It is quite true, as was argued by the counsel for the petitioner, that the appellate jurisdiction of this court is not derived from Acts of Congress. It is, strictly speaking, conferred by the Constitution. But it is conferred ''with such exceptions and under such regulations as Congress shall make.''

It is unnecessary to consider whether, if Congress had made no exceptions and no regulations, this court might not have exercised general appellate jurisdiction under rules prescribed by itself. From among the earliest Acts of the first Congress, at its first session, was the Act of September 24th, 1789, to establish the judicial courts of the United States. That Act provided for the organization of this court, and prescribed regulations for the exercise of its jurisdiction.

The source of that jurisdiction, and the limitations of it by the Constitution and by statute, have been on several occasions subjects of consideration here. In the case of Durousseau v. U. S. [1810]; Wiscart v. Dauchy [1796], particularly, the whole matter was carefully examined, and the court held, that while ''the appellate powers of this court are not given by the Judicial Act, but are given by the Constitution;'' they are, nevertheless, ''limited and regulated by that Act, and by such other Acts as have been passed on the subject.'' The court said, further, that the Judicial Act was an exercise of the power given by the Constitution to Congress ''of making exceptions to the appellate jurisdiction of the Supreme Court.''

''They have described affirmatively,'' said the court, ''its jurisdiction, and this affirmative description has been understood to imply a negation of the exercise of such appellate power as is not comprehended within it.''

The principle that the affirmation of appellate jurisdiction implies the negation of all such jurisdiction not affirmed having been thus established, it was an almost necessary consequence that Acts of Congress, providing for the exercise of jurisdiction, should come to be spoken of as Acts granting jurisdiction, and not as Acts making exceptions to the constitutional grant of it.

The exception to appellate jurisdiction in the case before us, however, is not an inference from the affirmation of other appellate jurisdiction. It is made in terms. The provision of the Act of 1867, affirming the appellate jurisdiction of this court in cases of habeas corpus, is expressly repealed. It is hardly possible to imagine a plainer instance of positive exception.

We are not at liberty to inquire into the motives of the Legislature. We can only examine into its power under the Constitution; and the power to make exceptions to the appellate jurisdiction of this court is given by express words.

What, then, is the effect of the repealing Act upon the case before us? We cannot doubt as to this. Without jurisdiction the court cannot proceed at all in any cause. Jurisdiction is power to declare the law, and when it ceases to exist, the only function remaining to the court is that of announcing the fact and dismissing the cause. And this is not less clear upon authority than upon principle.

Several cases were cited by the counsel for the petitioner in support of the position that jurisdiction of this case is not affected by the repealing Act. But none of them, in our judgment, afford any support to it. . . .

On the other hand, the general rule, supported by the best elementary writers . . . is, that ''when an Act of the Legislature is repealed, it must be considered, except as to transactions past and closed, as if it never existed.'' And the effect of repealing Acts upon suits under Acts repealed, has been determined by the adjudications of this court. The subject was fully considered in Norris v. Crocker [1852], and more recently in [Insurance Company] v. Ritchie [1867]. In both of these cases it was held that no judgment could be rendered in a suit after the repeal of the Act under which it was brought and prosecuted.

It is quite clear, therefore, that this court cannot proceed to pronounce judgment in this case, for it has no longer jurisdiction of the appeal; and judicial duty is not less fitly performed by declining ungranted jurisdiction than in exercising firmly that which the Constitution and the laws confer.

Counsel seem to have supposed, if effect be given to the repealing Act in question, that the whole appellate power of the court, in cases of habeas corpus, is denied. But this is in error. The Act of 1868 does not except from that jurisdiction any cases but appeals from circuit courts under the Act of 1867. It does not affect the jurisdiction which was previously exercised. . . .

The appeal of the petitioner in this case must be dismissed for want of jurisdiction.

LEGISLATIVE INVESTIGATIONS

McGRAIN v. DAUGHERTY

273 U. S. 135; 47 S. Ct. 319; 71 L. Ed. 580
(1927)

The nonprofessional thinks of the Supreme Court as the guardian of the Constitution and the protector of individual rights against abridgment by the political branches. It may seem plausible, then, that the Court should use its judicial power to restrain the passage of unconstitutional legislation. But the power to pass laws is a legislative power, committed under our system to the legislative branch of the government; it is no part of the judicial power either to legislate or to supervise the exercise by the legislature of its own inherent power. Thus in New Orleans Waterworks Co. v. New Orleans (1896) the Supreme Court refused to enjoin a city council from passing an ordinance which threatened the monopoly enjoyed by the waterworks. The Court pointed out that "the courts will pass the line that separates judicial from legislative authority if by any order or in any mode they assume to control the discretion with which municipal assemblies are invested, when deliberating upon the adoption or rejection of ordinances proposed for their adoption." The Court made it clear, however, that "if an ordinance be passed and is invalid, the jurisdiction of the courts may then be invoked for the protection of private rights that may be violated by its enforcement."

Nor will the courts undertake to compel the legislature to pass laws which they are constitutionally obliged to pass. The Constitution imposes a clear mandate on Congress to reapportion the House of Representatives every ten years. Because of political conflict Congress was unable to pass an apportionment act after the census of 1920, and for the succeeding ten years Congress failed to perform this constitutional duty. It is obvious that the Supreme Court, bound by the doctrine of the separation of powers, could not have compelled Congress to pass the statute required by the Constitution; and no one suggested any such judicial action.

Where a law is in existence whose provisions infringe individual rights, however, the courts have authority to enjoin the operations of the act. Thus, [I]n the years since Reynolds v. Sims (1964) the federal courts have forbidden the conduct of elections under discriminatory apportionment schemes, and following traditional equity procedures, have on occasion fashioned temporary apportionment schemes to protect the rights of voters who would otherwise have been disfranchised. The courts can also order local officials to carry out policies required of them by either the law or the Constitution, even though it calls for legislative action. Ten years after Brown v. Board of Education of Topeka (1954) a United States district court ordered the Prince Edward County board of supervisors to reestablish its public school system on a desegregated basis and levy taxes for its support. After failing to discover what the penalty would be for noncompliance, the board did as it was told. See Griffin v. School Board of Prince Edward County (1964).

In Ex parte United States (1916) the Court held that the lower courts had no power to suspend a criminal sentence without statutory authority. The power to establish the sentence is a legislative power, while the power to relieve a person of a legal sentence belongs to the executive; therefore the suspension of sentence by the court was an exercise of legislative and executive powers forbidden by the separation of powers.

So accustomed are we to thinking of ours as a written constitution, with the Supreme Court as ultimate interpreter, that we overlook how large a part of our fundamental law is, like the British constitution, unwritten. One can always argue, of course, whether any particular law is fundamental enough to be considered as "constitution," but such things as the right to vote for presidential electors, the national party nominating conventions, or the civil service merit system would seem clearly to fit this description. Any move to abolish them would be considered a truly fundamental change. Into this category, too, falls much of the structure and workings of Congress. The party organization, the seniority system, the insistence that a representative be a resident of his or her district, are all virtually untouchable but enjoy this status through the weight of tradition, not because the Constitution itself or the Supreme Court has said so.

One aspect of this is the right of each house of Congress to control who shall be seated as a member. True, the Constitution specified the qualifications a rep-

resentative should have, but it also stated that "each house shall be the judge of the . . . qualifications of its own members," and Congress had on several occasions used this power to exclude members it felt were unfit. Following the Civil War a number of Southern members were excluded for their part in the rebellion. In 1900, Brigham H. Roberts of Utah was refused a seat on the grounds that he was a polygamist, and in 1919 the House refused to seat Victor L. Berger of Milwaukee, who had been convicted in federal court of sedition. He was reelected and again refused his seat, but after a third election, his conviction having been reversed by the Supreme Court, he was finally seated. Following the primary elections of 1926, the Senate refused to seat William S. Vare of Pennsylvania and Frank Smith of Illinois because of the enormous amounts of money they had spent getting nominated. Although Newberry v. United States (1921) had held the Corrupt Practices Act did not apply to primaries, the Senate felt its provisions morally binding and proceeded to enforce it. While the constitutionality of each of these exclusions was bitterly contested in Congress, the decision to exclude in each case added weight to the tradition in favor of the power.

In 1967 the House refused to seat Adam Clayton Powell, Jr., of New York on the ground that he had refused to pay a judgment against him in the New York courts and had misappropriated House funds. By a vote of nearly two to one, the House voted to exclude Powell and declared his seat vacant. In Powell v. McCormack (1965) the Supreme Court held that Powell had been wrongly excluded, and while the ninetieth Congress was long a thing of the past so he could not get his seat back, he did have standing to sue for his back pay. The Court rejected the House claim that the right to judge "the qualifications of its own members" was a "textually demonstrable constitutional commitment" of the matter to Congress which would make it a political question. On the basis of a long historical analysis the Court concluded that the right granted was the right to judge the existence of those qualifications spelled out in the Constitution itself—age, residency, and citizenship—and there was no commitment to pass on the general desirability of those whom a state chose to send as its representatives. The framers, moreover, distinguished sharply between exclusion and expulsion, and while Congress could clearly have removed Powell by a two-thirds vote to expel him, the vote in this case was merely a vote to exclude, and the size of the actual vote was immaterial.

Following his victory in the Supreme Court the district court ruled that Powell would have to prove he had "clean hands"—that he had not misappropriated federal funds . . . before he could recover the $55,000 in back pay. Powell then asked the Supreme Court for a mandamus ordering the House to restore his seniority, give him his back pay, and remit the fine. This the Court declined to do. See Powell v. Hart (1970).

The legislative power of Congress is the power to pass laws, and the actual process of lawmaking is not subject to judicial control. The extent to which Congress can, by making laws, enlarge or diminish the powers of the judiciary and executive is discussed in connection with those branches. But may Congress, as a means of performing its own delegated functions, use the powers usually thought of as belonging to another branch? The power to subpoena witnesses and punish them for contempt by fine and imprisonment if they do not appear and testify is a vital and inherent judicial power. No court is really a court without it. As the opinion below indicates, the Court has long held that the houses of Congress may make use of this judicial power, in aid of their legislative duties, without violating the separation doctrine. The power may also be used by Congress to facilitate its exercise of nonlegislative congressional powers. In the case of Barry v. United States ex rel. Cunningham (1929) the Court upheld the power of a Senate committee investigating senatorial campaign expenditures in Pennsylvania to punish for contempt a witness who refused to answer relevant questions. There can be no doubt of the similar right of a committee of the House of Representatives to punish recalcitrant witnesses in a hearing on the question of bringing impeachment charges against an officer of the government.

There are two ways in which either house of Congress may exercise its power to punish stubborn witnesses for contempt. First, it may pass a resolution holding them in contempt and punishing them summarily. They may be fined, or they may be sent at once to prison. In Anderson v. Dunn (1821) the Supreme Court held that such imprisonment could not, however, extend beyond the adjournment of Congress. While Congress still enjoys this power of direct and summary punishment for contempt, experience early proved it unsatisfactory in a number of ways. Accordingly, in 1857 Congress provided a second method for dealing with the problem. It passed a statute making it a crime for a person to refuse to testify or answer questions before either house of Congress or any congressional committee when subpoenaed to do so. The maximum penalty is a fine of $1000 or a year in prison. The statute is summarized in the opinion in the present case. The procedure under this statute is as follows: if a witness refuses to testify before a congressional investigating committee, the committee reports this refusal to the House (or Senate) and that body, usually as a matter of routine, passes a resolution declaring the witness to be in contempt of the House or Senate. This resolution is then sent to the United States Attorney in the District of Columbia, who presents the matter to a grand jury for indictment under the statute. If thus indicted, the witness is tried in the federal district court, and at trial presents any legal or constitutional defenses he or she may have. Punishment is, of course, imposed by the court.

The Supreme Court has said that executive and administrative agencies of government cannot be given the power to punish anyone for contempt; see Interstate Commerce Commission v. Brimson (1894). To allow them to exercise this power of punishment would be a denial of due process of law. At the same time some of these officers and agencies must be able to compel testi-

mony in order to carry on their work. Congress, therefore, has made this possible in the following way: the agency (say, the Interstate Commerce Commission) is given by law the power to subpoena witnesses and question them. If a witness refuses to testify, the commission takes the witness before the nearest federal district court. If the judge, after hearing the case, decides that the commission could lawfully require the witness to answer the questions, he orders him or her to do so. If he or she again refuses to answer, the witness is in contempt of the court, not the commission, and may be punished accordingly. This procedure, now followed by a substantial number of government agencies, has the advantage of submitting all the legal issues in a contempt action, including the rights of the witness, to judicial scrutiny and decision before *the witness is actually in contempt and liable to punishment.*

The present case arose out of a spectacular political situation. Harry M. Daugherty had managed Harding's campaign for the presidency in 1921. He became Attorney General, holding office until March, 1924, when he resigned. During that period scandals in connection with the naval oil leases and in the Veterans Bureau were exposed without aid from the Department of Justice. Mr. Daugherty was widely and harshly criticized for not prosecuting the lawbreakers as well as for failure to enforce effectively the antitrust acts and other federal laws. The Senate took the matter up and appointed a special committee to investigate the Department of Justice and the activities and inactivities of Mr. Daugherty, which were believed to amount to misconduct in office and the prevention of proper law enforcement. In the course of the investigation the committee subpoenaed Mally S. Daugherty, brother of the Attorney General, to appear before it and testify. This he failed to do. The Senate then issued a warrant ordering the sergeant-at-arms to arrest Mally Daugherty and bring him before the Senate to testify. McGrain, a deputy sergeant-at-arms, thereupon made the arrest in Ohio. Daugherty at once applied to a federal district court for a writ of habeas corpus and, upon hearing, the court discharged him from custody on the ground that the Senate in ordering the investigation and the arrest had exceeded its powers under the Constitution.

Mr. Justice **Van Devanter** delivered the opinion of the Court, saying in part:

This is an appeal from the final order in a proceeding in habeas corpus discharging a recusant witness held in custody under process of attachment issued from the United States Senate in the course of an investigation which it was making of the administration of the Department of Justice. . . .

The first of the principal questions—the one which the witness particularly presses on our attention—is, as before shown, whether the Senate—or the House of Representatives, both being on the same plane in this regard—has power, through its own process, to compel a private individual to appear before it or one of its com-

mittees and give testimony needed to enable it efficiently to exercise a legislative function belonging to it under the Constitution.

The Constitution provides for a Congress consisting of a Senate and House of Representatives and invests it with ''all legislative powers'' granted to the United States, and with power ''to make all laws which shall be necessary and proper'' for carrying into execution these powers and ''all other powers'' vested by the Constitution in the United States or in any department or officer thereof. Art. I, §§ 1, 8. . . . But there is no provision expressly investing either house with power to make investigations and exact testimony to the end that it may exercise its legislative function advisedly and effectively. So the question arises whether this power is so far incidental to the legislative function as to be implied.

In actual legislative practice power to secure needed information by such means has long been treated as an attribute of the power to legislate. It was so regarded in the British Parliament and in the colonial legislatures before the American Revolution; and a like view has prevailed and been carried into effect in both houses of Congress and in most of the state legislatures.

This power was both asserted and exerted by the House of Representatives in 1792, when it appointed a select committee to inquire into the St. Clair expedition and authorized the committee to send for necessary persons, papers and records. Mr. Madison, who had taken an important part in framing the Constitution only five years before, and four of his associates in that work, were members of the House of Representatives at the time, and all voted for the inquiry. . . . Other exertions of the power by the House of Representatives, as also by the Senate, are shown in the citations already made. Among those by the Senate, the inquiry ordered in 1859 respecting the raid by John Brown and his adherents on the armory and arsenal of the United States at Harper's Ferry is of special significance. The resolution directing the inquiry authorized the committee to send for persons and papers, to inquire into the facts pertaining to the raid and the means by which it was organized and supported, and to report what legislation, if any, was necessary to preserve the peace of the country and protect the public property. The resolution was briefly discussed and adopted without opposition. . . . Later on the committee reported that Thaddeus Hyatt, although subpoenaed to appear as a witness, had refused to do so; whereupon the Senate ordered that he be attached and brought before it to answer for his refusal. When he was brought in he answered by challenging the power of the Senate to direct the inquiry and exact testimony to aid it in exercising its legislative function. The question of power thus presented was thoroughly discussed by several senators—Mr. Sumner of Massachusetts taking the lead in denying the power, and Mr. Fessenden of Maine in supporting it. Sectional and party lines were put aside and the question was debated and determined with special regard to principle and precedent. The vote was taken on a resolution pronouncing the witness's answer insufficient and directing that he be committed until he should signify that he was ready and willing to testify. The resolution was adopted—forty-four senators voting for it and ten against. . . .

The deliberate solution of the question on that occasion has been accepted and followed on other occasions by both houses of Congress, and never has been rejected or questioned by either.

The state courts quite generally have held that the power to legislate carries with it by necessary implication ample authority to obtain information needed in the rightful exercise of that power, and to employ compulsory process for the purpose. . . .

We have referred to the practice of the two houses of Congress; and we now shall notice some significant congressional enactments. . . .

[The Court here reviews the congressional statutes leading up to the passage of the Compulsory Testimony Act of 1857.]

. . . They show very plainly that Congress intended thereby (a) to recognize the power of either house to institute inquiries and exact evidence touching subjects within its jurisdiction and on which it was disposed to act; (b) to recognize that such inquiries may be conducted through committees; (c) to subject defaulting and contumacious witnesses to indictment and punishment in the courts, and thereby to enable either house to exert the power of inquiry "more effectually;" and (d) to open the way for obtaining evidence in such an inquiry, which otherwise could not be obtained, by exempting witnesses required to give evidence therein from criminal and penal prosecutions in respect of matters disclosed by their evidence.

Four decisions of this court are cited and more or less relied on, and we now turn to them.

The first decision was in Anderson v. Dunn [1821]. The question there was whether, under the Constitution, the House of Representatives has power to attach and punish a person other than a member for contempt of its authority—in fact, an attempt to bribe one of its members. The court regarded the power as essential to the effective exertion of other powers expressly granted, and therefore as implied. . . .

The next decision was in Kilbourn v. Thompson [1881]. The question there was whether the House of Representatives had exceeded its power in directing one of its committees to make a particular investigation. The decision was that it had. The principles announced and applied in the case are—that neither house of Congress possesses a "general power of making inquiry into the private affairs of the citizen;" that the power actually possessed is limited to inquiries relating to matters of which the particular house "has jurisdiction," and in respect of which it rightfully may take other actions; that if the inquiry relates to "a matter wherein relief or redress could be had only by a judicial proceeding" it is not within the range of this power, but must be left to the courts, conformably to the constitutional separation of governmental powers; and that for the purpose of determining the essential character of the inquiry recourse may be had to the resolution or order under which it is

made. The court examined the resolution which was the basis of the particular inquiry, and ascertained therefrom that the inquiry related to a private real-estate pool or partnership in the District of Columbia. Jay Cook & Company had had an interest in the pool, but had become bankrupts, and their estate was in course of administration in a federal bankruptcy court in Pennsylvania. The United States was one of their creditors. The trustee in the bankruptcy proceeding had effected a settlement of the bankrupts' interest in the pool, and of course his action was subject to examination and approval or disapproval by the bankruptcy court. Some of the creditors, including the United States, were dissatisfied with the settlement. In these circumstances, disclosed in the preamble, the resolution directed the committee "to inquire into the matter and history of said real-estate pool and the character of said settlement, with the amount of property involved in which Jay Cook & Company were interested, and the amount paid or to be paid in said settlement, with power to send for persons and papers and report to the House." The court pointed out that the resolution contained no suggestion of contemplated legislation; that the matter was one in respect to which no valid legislation could be had; that the bankrupts' estate and the trustee's settlement were still pending in the bankruptcy court; and that the United States and other creditors were free to press their claims in that proceeding. And on these grounds the court held that in undertaking the investigation "the House of Representatives not only exceeded the limit of its own authority, but assumed power which could only be properly exercised by another branch of the government, because it was in its nature clearly judicial." . . .

[The Court also reviewed In re Chapman (1897) and Marshall v. Gordon (1917), involving the power to compel testimony and punish for contempt.]

While these cases are not decisive of the question we are considering, they definitely settle two propositions which we recognize as entirely sound and having a bearing on its solution: One, that the two houses of Congress, in their separate relations, possess not only such powers as are expressly granted to them by the Constitution, but such auxiliary powers as are necessary and appropriate to make the express powers effective; and, the other, that neither house is invested with "general" power to inquire into private affairs and compel disclosures, but only with such limited power of inquiry as is shown to exist when the rule of constitutional interpretation just stated is rightly applied. . . .

With this review of the legislative practice, congressional enactments and court decisions, we proceed to a statement of our conclusions on the question.

We are of opinion that the power of inquiry—with process to enforce it—is an essential and appropriate auxiliary to the legislative function. It was so regarded and employed in American legislatures before the Constitution was framed and ratified. Both Houses of Congress took this view of it early in their history—the House of Representatives with the approving votes of Mr. Madison and other members whose service in the convention which framed the Constitution gives special significance to their action—and both houses have employed the power accordingly up to the present time. The Acts of 1798 and 1857, judged by their comprehensive terms, were intended to recognize the existence of this power in both houses and to enable them to employ it "more effectually" than before. So, when their practice in the matter is appraised according to the circumstances in which it was begun and to those in which it has been continued, it falls nothing short of a practical construction, long continued, of the constitutional provisions respecting their powers, and therefore should be taken as fixing the meaning of those provisions, if otherwise doubtful.

We are further of opinion that the provisions are not of doubtful meaning, but, as was held by this court in the cases we have reviewed, are intended to be effectively exercised, and therefore to carry with them such auxiliary powers as are necessary and appropriate to that end. While the power to exact information in aid of the legislative function was not involved in those cases, the rule of interpretation applied there is applicable here. A legislative body cannot legislate wisely or effectively in the absence of information respecting the conditions which the legislation is intended to affect or change; and where the legislative body does not itself possess the requisite information—which not infrequently is true—recourse must be had to others who do possess it. Experience has taught that mere requests for such information often are unavailing, and also that information which is volunteered is not always accurate or complete; so some means of compulsion are essential to obtain what is needed. . . .

The contention is earnestly made on behalf of the witness that this power of inquiry, if sustained, may be abusively and oppressively exerted. If this be so, it affords no ground for denying the power. . . . And it is a necessary deduction from the decisions in Kilbourn v. Thompson and Re Chapman that a witness rightfully may refuse to answer where the bounds of the power are exceeded or the questions are not pertinent to the matter under inquiry.

We come now to the question whether it sufficiently appears that the purpose for which the witness's testimony was sought was to obtain information in aid of the legislative function. The court below answered the question in the negative, and put its decision largely on this ground, as is shown by the following excerpts from its opinion:

"It will be noted that in the second resolution the Senate has expressly avowed that the investigation is in aid of other action than legislation. Its purpose is to 'obtain information necessary as a basis for such legislative and other action as the Senate may deem necessary and proper.' This indicates that the Senate is contemplating the taking of action other than legislative, as the outcome of the investigation, at least the possibility of so doing. The extreme personal cast of the original resolutions; the spirit of hostility towards the then Attorney General which they breathe; that it was not avowed that legislative action was had in view until after the action of the Senate had been challenged; and that the avowal then was coupled with an avowal that other action was had in view—are calculated to create the impression that the idea of legislative action being in contemplation was an afterthought. . . .

"That the Senate has in contemplation the possibility of taking action other than legislation as an outcome of the investigation, as thus expressly avowed, would seem of itself to invalidate the entire proceeding. But, whether so or not, the Senate's action is invalid and absolutely void, in that, in ordering and conducting the investigation, it is exercising the judicial function, and power to exercise that function, in such a case as we have here, has not been conferred upon it expressly or by fair implication. What it is proposing to do is to determine the guilt of the Attorney General of the shortcomings and wrongdoings set forth in the resolutions. It is 'to hear, adjudge, and condemn.' In so doing it is exercising the judicial function. . . .

"What the Senate is engaged in doing is not investigating the Attorney General's office; it is investigating the former Attorney General. What it has done is to put him on trial before it. In so doing it is exercising the judicial function. This it has no power to do."

We are of opinion that the court's ruling on this question was wrong, and that it sufficiently appears, when the proceedings are rightly interpreted, that the object of the investigation and of the effort to secure the witness's testimony was to obtain information for legislative purposes.

It is quite true that the resolution directing the investigation does not in terms avow that it is intended to be in aid of legislation; but it does show that the subject to be investigated was the administration of the Department of Justice—whether its functions were being properly discharged or were being neglected or misdirected, and particularly whether the Attorney General and his assistants were performing or neglecting their duties in respect of the institution and prosecution of proceedings to punish crimes and enforce appropriate remedies against the wrongdoers—specific instances of alleged neglect being recited. Plainly the subject was one on which legislation could be had and would be materially aided by the information which the investigation was calculated to elicit. This becomes manifest when it is reflected that the functions of the Department of Justice, the powers and duties of the Attorney General and the duties of his assistants, are all subject to regulation by congressional legislation, and that the department is maintained and its activities are carried on under such appropriations as in the judgment of Congress are needed from year to year.

The only legitimate object the Senate could have in ordering the investigation was to aid it in legislating; and we think the subject-matter was such that the presumption should be indulged that this was the real object. An express avowal of the object would have been better; but in view of the particular subject-matter was not indispensable. . . .

We conclude that the investigation was ordered for

a legitimate object; that the witness wrongfully refused to appear and testify before the committee and was lawfully attached; that the Senate is entitled to have him give testimony pertinent to the inquiry, either at its bar or before the committee; and that the district court erred in discharging him from custody under the attachment. . . .

Final order reversed.

Mr. Justice **Stone** did not participate in the case.

BARENBLATT v. UNITED STATES

360 U. S. 109; 79 S. Ct. 1081; 3 L. Ed. 2d 1115 (1959)

When, in 1967, the Supreme Court in Watkins v. United States held void a conviction for contempt of HUAC, it understandably came as a profound and unwelcome shock to those who regarded our congressional committees on subversive activities as the most useful defenders of our national security and as enjoying unrestricted authority in their investigations. Apparently striking at the very core of the committee, the Court made clear that "there is no congressional power to expose for the sake of exposure," and "investigations conducted solely for the personal aggrandizement of the investigators or to 'punish' those investigated are indefensible." Moreover, questions asked of a witness had to be pertinent to the matter under inquiry, and the vagueness of the term "unAmerican" and the "excessively broad charter" of HUAC, coupled with the failure of the committee itself to define the "question under inquiry," made it impossible for the witness to judge whether or not the committee had the right to insist that he answer. "Fundamental fairness," said the Court, "demands that no witness be compelled to make such a determination with so little guidance."

The decision in the Barenblatt case, printed below, came as a blow to those who had welcomed the Watkins decision and as a relief to its critics. Not only did the Court not strike dead the HUAC, but it seemed to back away from Chief Justice Warren's statement in Watkins that the Committee could not "expose for the sake of exposure." But the impression that Barenblatt had in effect overruled Watkins proved to be unwarranted, and in subsequent cases the Supreme Court both sustained and struck down convictions for contempt of congressional committees. In Braden v. United States and Wilkinson v. United States the Court in 1961 upheld by five-to-four votes the contempt convictions of the defendants who refused to testify before the HUAC. Although the Committee's investigation was apparently sparked by the opposition these men had expressed to the work of the Committee, the Court held that this did not alter the validity of what, on the basis of Barenblatt, was an otherwise valid investigation. In Deutsch v. United States (1961), on the other hand, the Court held that questions regarding Communist activity at Cornell University were not pertinent to an investigation of Communism in the Albany, New York, labor movement. In the 1970's Congress abolished its committees on "un-American activities" but in 1981 the Senate established within its judiciary committee a subcommittee on "security and terrorism."

The decision of the cases just discussed turned on whether the legislative committee was authorized to investigate a particular activity, and if it was, whether the question asked of the witness was pertinent to such investigation. In 1962 the Court added a new dimension to this last problem. In Russell v. United States, it held that a prosecution for contempt was void unless the indictment by which the charge was brought stated explicitly the purpose of the investigation. The indictment in question had listed as a separate count each question the witness had refused to answer, but had stated merely that they were pertinent without stating what the subject of the inquiry was. This, said the Court, not only made it impossible to make an independent judgment of pertinency on appeal but did not sufficiently clearly indicate to the defendant the exact crime for which he was being tried. A new indictment was subsequently obtained stating that "the subject of these hearings was Communist Party activities within the field of labor. . . ." The Court again held the indictment void, this time because "the subject of the inquiry was never specified or authorized by the Committee, as required by its own rules, nor was there a lawful delegation of authority to the Subcommittee to conduct the investigation." See Gojack v. United States (1966).

For twenty-five years the Supreme Court has been asked to hold that there was a constitutional "right to silence" flowing from the First Amendment which would justify a person in refusing to testify before a legislative committee. The Court has never conceded such a right, but in 1963 in Gibson v. Florida Investigation Committee it upheld for the first time against a legislative committee the closely related claim of "associational privacy." The Florida committee, in the course of investigating Communist infiltration of the civil rights movement, subpoenaed the membership lists of the Miami chapter of the NAACP. The Court sustained the chapter's refusal to produce them. Conceding the right of the state to inform itself, the Court held that absent any tie in, or "nexus," between the NAACP and subversion, there was no showing of "an overriding and compelling state interest" sufficient to override the right of association. A similar result was reached in De Gregory v. Attorney General (1966), where the New Hampshire attorney general sought to inquire into De Gregory's Communist activities of a decade earlier. Since the record was "devoid of any evidence that there is any communist movement in New Hampshire," there was no such " 'overriding and compelling state interest' . . . that would warrant intrusion into the realm of political and associational privacy. . . ." Justices Harlan, Stewart, and Clark dissented on the ground that the purpose of the inquiry was to find out if there were such a "movement."

In the summer of 1987 the nation was treated to a first-hand view of a congressional investigating committee at work. Two, and sometimes three, major television networks cancelled their regular programs while the nation watched a joint House and Senate committee question witnesses in an effort to find out: (1) whether the sale of arms to Iran was in fact an "arms for hostages" deal; (2) whether the extra money made on the arms sale went to aid the Nicaraguan contras; and (3) what the President of the United States had known about these things and how much he had approved or authorized. Two key witnesses, Admiral John Poindexter, the President's national security advisor, and his aide, Lt. Col. Oliver North, testified under a limited grant of immunity from prosecution. Both had pleaded the Fifth Amendment on the ground that an independent counsel appointed by Congress was investigating their roles in the affair with the possibility they might face criminal charges. In late July, confronted with much conflicting testimony and questions about the veracity of some witnesses, the committee adjourned to write its report.

Query: *Could Congress investigate the editorial policies of newspapers in view of the First Amendment guarantee of a free press? Are there powers other than the power to legislate which Congress could invoke to support such an investigation?*

Mr. Justice **Harlan** delivered the opinion of the Court, saying in part:

Once more the Court is required to resolve the conflicting constitutional claims of congressional power and of an individual's right to resist its exercise. The congressional power in question concerns the internal process of Congress in moving within its legislative domain; it involves the utilization of its committees to secure "testimony needed to enable it efficiently to exercise a legislative function belonging to it under the Constitution." McGrain v. Daugherty [1927]. The power of inquiry has been employed by Congress throughout our history, over the whole range of the national interests concerning which Congress might legislate or decide upon due investigation not to legislate; it has similarly been utilized in determining what to appropriate from the national purse, or whether to appropriate. The scope of the power of inquiry, in short, is as penetrating and far-reaching as the potential power to enact and appropriate under the Constitution.

Broad as it is, the power is not, however, without limitations. Since Congress may only investigate into those areas in which it may potentially legislate or appropriate, it cannot inquire into matters which are within the exclusive province of one of the other branches of the Government. Lacking the judicial power given to the Judiciary, it cannot inquire into matters that are exclusively the concern of the Judiciary. Neither can it supplant the Executive in what exclusively belongs to the Executive. And the Congress, in common with all branches of the Government, must exercise its powers subject to the lim-

itations placed by the Constitution on governmental action, more particularly in the context of this case the relevant limitations of the Bill of Rights.

The congressional power of inquiry, its range and scope, and an individual's duty in relation to it, must be viewed in proper perspective. . . . The power and the right of resistance to it are to be judged in the concrete, not on the basis of abstractions. In the present case congressional efforts to learn the extent of a nationwide, indeed world wide, problem have brought one of its investigating committees into the field of education. Of course, broadly viewed, inquiries cannot be made into the teaching that is pursued in any of our educational institutions. When academic teaching-freedom and its corollary learning-freedom, so essential to the well-being of the Nation, are claimed, this Court will always be on the alert against intrusion by Congress into this constitutionally protected domain. But this does not mean that the Congress is precluded from interrogating a witness merely because he is a teacher. An educational institution is not a constitutional sanctuary from inquiry into matters that may otherwise be within the constitutional legislative domain merely for the reason that inquiry is made of someone within its walls.

In the setting of this framework of constitutional history, practice and legal precedents, we turn to the particularities of this case.

We here review petitioner's conviction for contempt of Congress, arising from his refusal to answer certain questions put to him by a Subcommittee of the House Committee on Un-American Activities during the course of an inquiry concerning alleged Communist infiltration into the field of education. . . .

Petitioner's various contentions resolve themselves into three propositions: First, the compelling of testimony by the Subcommittee was neither legislatively authorized nor constitutionally permissible because of the vagueness of Rule XI of the House of Representatives, Eighty-third Congress, the charter of authority of the parent Committee. Second, petitioner was not adequately apprised of the pertinency of the Subcommittee's questions to the subject matter of the inquiry. Third, the questions petitioner refused to answer infringed rights protected by the First Amendment.

Subcommittee's Authority to Compel Testimony

At the outset it should be noted that Rule XI authorized this Subcommittee to compel testimony within the framework of the investigative authority conferred on the Un-American Activities Committee. Petitioner contends that Watkins v. United States [1957] nevertheless held the grant of this power in all circumstances ineffective because of the vagueness of Rule XI in delineating the Committee jurisdiction to which its exercise was to be appurtenant. This view of Watkins was accepted by two of the dissenting judges below.

The Watkins Case cannot properly be read as standing for such a proposition. A principal contention in Watkins was that the refusals to answer were justified because the requirement of 2 USC § 192 that the questions asked be "pertinent to the question under inquiry" had not been satisfied. This Court reversed the conviction solely on that ground, holding that Watkins had not been adequately apprised of the subject matter of the Subcommittee's investigation or the pertinency thereto of the questions he refused to answer. In so deciding the Court drew upon Rule XI only as one of the facets in the total mise en scène in its search for the "question under inquiry" in that particular investigation. The Court, in other words, was not dealing with Rule XI at large, and indeed in effect stated that no such issue was before it. That the vagueness of Rule XI was not alone determinative is also shown by the Court's further statement that aside from the Rule "the remarks of the chairman or members of the Committee, or even the nature of the proceedings themselves, might sometimes make the topic [under inquiry] clear." In short, while Watkins was critical of Rule XI, it did not involve the broad and inflexible holding petitioner now attributes to it.

Petitioner also contends, independently of Watkins, that the vagueness of Rule XI deprived the Subcommittee of the right to compel testimony in this investigation into Communist activity. We cannot agree with this contention, which in its furthest reach would mean that the House Un-American Activities Committee under its existing authority has no right to compel testimony in any circumstances. Granting the vagueness of the Rule, we may not read it in isolation from its long history in the House of Representatives. Just as legislation is often given meaning by the gloss of legislative reports, administrative interpretation, and long usage, so the proper meaning of an authorization to a congressional committee is not to be derived alone from its abstract terms unrelated to the definite content furnished them by the course of congressional actions. The Rule comes to us with a "persuasive gloss of legislative history," which shows beyond doubt that in pursuance of its legislative concerns in the domain of "national security" the House has clothed the Un-American Activities Committee with pervasive authority to investigate Communist activities in this country. . . .

[The Court here summarizes the history of the Committee, showing the wide range of areas in which it had pursued its search for Communists.]

In the context of these unremitting pursuits, the House has steadily continued the life of the Committee at the commencement of each new Congress; it has never narrowed the powers of the Committee, whose authority has remained throughout identical with that contained in Rule XI; and it has continuingly supported the Committee's activities with substantial appropriations. Beyond this, the Committee was raised to the level of a standing committee of the House in 1945, it having been but a special committee prior to that time.

In light of this long and illuminating history it can hardly be seriously argued that the investigation of Communist activities generally, and the attendant use of compulsory process, was beyond the purview of the Committee's intended authority under Rule XI.

We are urged, however, to construe Rule XI so as at least to exclude the field of education from the Committee's compulsory authority. . . .

[The Court finds Congress was aware of and did not disapprove previous investigations in this field.]

In this framework of the Committee's history we must conclude that its legislative authority to conduct the inquiry presently under consideration is unassailable, and that independently of whatever bearing the broad scope of Rule XI may have on the issue of "pertinency" in a given investigation into Communist activities, as in Watkins, the Rule cannot be said to be constitutionally infirm on the score of vagueness. The constitutional permissibility of that authority otherwise is a matter to be discussed later.

Pertinency Claim

Undeniably a conviction for contempt under 2 USC § 192 cannot stand unless the questions asked are pertinent to the subject matter of the investigation. Watkins v. United States. But the factors which led us to rest decision on this ground in Watkins were very different from those involved here.

In Watkins the petitioner had made specific objection to the Subcommittee's questions on the ground of pertinency; the question under inquiry had not been disclosed in any illuminating manner; and the questions asked the petitioner were not only amorphous on their face, but in some instances clearly foreign to the alleged subject matter of the investigation—"Communism in labor."

In contrast, petitioner in the case before us raised no objections on the ground of pertinency at the time any of the questions were put to him. . . .

We need not, however, rest decision on petitioner's failure to object on this score, for here "pertinency" was made to appear "with undisputable clarity." First of all, it goes without saying that the scope of the Committee's authority was for the House, not a witness, to determine, subject to the ultimate reviewing responsibility of this Court. What we deal with here is whether petitioner was sufficiently apprised of "the topic under inquiry" thus authorized "and the connective reasoning whereby the precise questions asked relate[d] to it." In light of his prepared memorandum of constitutional objections there can be no doubt that this petitioner was well aware of the Subcommittee's authority and purpose to question him as it did. In addition the other sources of this information which we recognized in Watkins leave no room for a "pertinency" objection on this record. The subject matter of the inquiry had been identified at the commencement of the investigation as Communist infiltration into the field of education. Just prior to petitioner's appearance before the Subcommittee, the scope of the day's hearings had been announced as "in the main communism in education and the experiences and background in the party by Francis X. T. Crowley. It will deal with activities in Michigan, Boston, and in some small degree, New York." Petitioner had heard the Subcommittee interrogate the witness Crowley along the same lines as he, petitioner, was evidently to be questioned, and had listened to Crowley's testimony identifying him as a former member of an alleged Communist student organization at the University of Michigan while they both were in attendance there. Further, petitioner had stood mute in the face of the Chairman's statement as to why he had been called as a witness by the Subcommittee. And, lastly, unlike Watkins, petitioner refused to answer questions as to his own Communist Party affiliations, whose pertinency of course was clear beyond doubt.

Petitioner's contentions on this aspect of the case cannot be sustained.

Constitutional Contentions

Our function, at this point, is purely one of constitutional adjudication in the particular case and upon the particular record before us, not to pass judgment upon the general wisdom or efficacy of the activities of this Committee in a vexing and complicated field.

The precise constitutional issue confronting us is whether the Subcommittee's inquiry into petitioner's past or present membership in the Communist Party transgressed the provisions of the First Amendment, which of course reach and limit congressional investigations. Watkins.

The Court's past cases establish sure guides to decision. Undeniably, the First Amendment in some circumstances protects an individual from being compelled to disclose his associational relationships. However, the protections of the First Amendment, unlike a proper claim of the privilege against self-incrimination under the Fifth Amendment, do not afford a witness the right to resist inquiry in all circumstances. Where First Amendment rights are asserted to bar governmental interrogation resolution of the issue always involves a balancing by the courts of the competing private and public interests at stake in the particular circumstances shown. These principles were recognized in the Watkins Case. . . .

The first question is whether this investigation was related to a valid legislative purpose, for Congress may not constitutionally require an individual to disclose his political relationships or other private affairs except in relation to such a purpose. See Watkins v. United States.

That Congress has wide power to legislate in the field of Communist activity in this Country, and to conduct appropriate investigations in aid thereof, is hardly debatable. The existence of such power has never been questioned by this Court, and it is sufficient to say, without particularization, that Congress has enacted or considered in this field a wide range of legislative measures, not a few of which have stemmed from recommendations of the very Committee whose actions have been drawn in question here. In the last analysis this power rests on the right of self-preservation, "the ultimate value of any society," Dennis v. United States [1951]. Justification for its exercise in turn rests on the long and widely accepted view that the tenets of the Communist Party include the ultimate overthrow of the Government of the United States by force and violence, a view which has been given formal expression by the Congress. . . .

. . . To suggest that because the Communist Party may also sponsor peaceable political reforms the constitutional issues before us should now be judged as if that Party were just an ordinary political party from the standpoint of national security, is to ask this Court to blind itself to world affairs which have determined the whole course of our national policy since the close of World War II, . . . and to the vast burdens which these conditions have entailed for the entire Nation.

We think that investigatory power in this domain is not to be denied Congress solely because the field of education is involved. Nothing in the prevailing opinions in Sweezy v. New Hampshire [1957] stands for a contrary view. The vice existing there was that the questioning of Sweezy, who had not been shown ever to have been connected with the Communist Party, as to the contents of a lecture he had given at the University of New Hampshire, and as to his connections with the Progressive Party, then on the ballot as a normal political party in some 26 States, was too far removed from the premises on which the constitutionality of the State's investigation had to depend to withstand attack under the Fourteenth Amendment. This is a very different thing from inquiring into the extent to which the Communist Party has succeeded in infiltrating into our universities, or elsewhere, persons and groups committed to furthering the objective of overthrow. Indeed we do not understand petitioner here to suggest that Congress in no circumstances may inquire into Communist activity in the field of education. Rather, his position is in effect that this particular investigation was aimed not at the revolutionary aspects but at the theoretical classroom discussion of communism.

In our opinion this position rests on a too constricted view of the nature of the investigatory process, and is not supported by a fair assessment of the record before us. An investigation of advocacy of or preparation for overthrow certainly embraces the right to identify a witness as a member of the Communist Party, and to inquire into the various manifestations of the Party's tenets. The strict requirements of a prosecution under the Smith Act, see Dennis v. United States [1951] and Yates v. United States [1957], are not the measure of the permissible scope of a congressional investigation into "overthrow," for of necessity the investigatory process must proceed step by step. Nor can it fairly be concluded that this investigation was directed at controlling what is being taught at our universities rather than at overthrow. The statement of the Subcommittee Chairman at the opening of the investigation evinces no such intention, and so far as this record reveals nothing thereafter transpired which would justify our holding that the thrust of the investigation later changed. The record discloses considerable testimony concerning the foreign domination and revolutionary purposes and efforts of the Communist Party. That there was also testimony on the abstract philosophical level does not detract from the dominant theme of this investigation—Communist infiltration furthering the alleged ultimate purpose of overthrow. And certainly the conclusion would not be justified that the questioning of petitioner would have exceeded permissible bounds had he not shut off the Subcommittee at the threshold.

Nor can we accept the further contention that this investigation should not be deemed to have been in furtherance of a legislative purpose because the true objective of the Committee and of the Congress was purely "exposure." So long as Congress acts in pursuance of its constitutional power, the Judiciary lacks authority to intervene on the basis of the motives which spurred the exercise of that power. "It is, of course, true," as was said in McCray v. United States [1904], "that if there be no authority in the judiciary to restrain a lawful exercise of power by another department of the government, where a wrong motive or purpose has impelled to the exertion of the power, that abuses of a power conferred may be temporarily effectual. The remedy for this, however, lies, not in the abuse by the judicial authority of its functions, but in the people, upon whom, after all, under our institutions, reliance must be placed for the correction of abuses committed in the exercise of a lawful power." These principles of course apply as well to committee investigations into the need for legislation as to the enactments which such investigations may produce. Thus, in stating in the Watkins Case that "there is no congressional power to expose for the sake of exposure," we at the same time declined to inquire into the "motives of committee members," and recognized that their "motives alone would not vitiate an investigation which had been instituted by a House of Congress if that assembly's legislative purpose is being served." Having scrutinized this record we cannot say that the unanimous panel of the Court of Appeals which first considered this case was wrong in concluding that "the primary purposes of the inquiry were in aid of legislative processes." Certainly this is not a case like Kilbourn v. Thompson [1881], where "the House of Representatives not only exceeded the limit of its own authority, but assumed a power which could only be properly exercised by another branch of the government, because it was in its nature clearly judicial." The constitutional legislative power of Congress in this instance is beyond question.

Finally, the record is barren of other factors which in themselves might sometimes lead to the conclusion that the individual interests at stake were not subordinate to those of the state. There is no indication in this record that the Subcommittee was attempting to pillory witnesses. Nor did petitioner's appearance as a witness follow from indiscriminate dragnet procedures, lacking in probable cause for belief that he possessed information which might be helpful to the Subcommittee. And the relevancy of the questions put to him by the Subcommittee is not open to doubt.

We conclude that the balance between the individual and the governmental interests here at stake must be struck in favor of the latter, and that therefore the provisions of the First Amendment have not been offended.

We hold that petitioner's conviction for contempt of Congress discloses no infirmity and that the judgment of the Court of Appeals must be
Affirmed.

Mr. Justice **Black,** with whom Chief Justice **Warren** and Mr. Justice **Douglas** concurred, dissented on grounds that (1) the term "un-American" was so vague as to make the Committee's mandate void for vagueness under the due process clause; (2) the Court's "balancing test" is not the way to determine the scope of freedom of speech, and if it were, the Court should have balanced the interest of society in "being able to join organizations, advocate causes and make political 'mistakes' "against the government's limited interest in making laws in the area of free speech—an interest which cannot reasonably be equated with "self-preservation"; (3) the chief aim of the HUAC is to "try witnesses and punish them because they are or have been Communists," which constitutes a bill of attainder.

Mr. Justice **Brennan** dissented, saying in part:

I would reverse this conviction. It is sufficient that I state my complete agreement with my Brother Black that no purpose for the investigation of Barenblatt is revealed by the record except exposure purely for the sake of exposure. This is not a purpose to which Barenblatt's rights under the First Amendment can validly be subordinated. An investigation in which the processes of lawmaking and law-evaluating are submerged entirely in exposure of individual behavior—in adjudication, of a sort, through the exposure process—is outside the constitutional pale of congressional inquiry. Watkins v. United States.

THE DELEGATION OF LEGISLATIVE POWER

SCHECHTER POULTRY CORPORATION v. UNITED STATES

295 U. S. 495; 55 S. Ct. 837; 79 L. Ed. 1570 (1935)

Like the other powers granted to the three great branches of the government, the legislative power of Congress is nowhere defined in the Constitution. Clearly it includes the power to pass statutes, and the words "powers herein granted" suggest that it is limited in scope to the matters listed in Article I, Sec. 8. But whether the words were intended to vest all the government's rule making power in Congress is nowhere made clear. Whatever "the legislative power" is, however, it is given to Congress and not to the other branches of government and by inference is not to be exercised by those branches even if Congress wanted to delegate it to them.

The relatively small size and simplicity of the early administrative structure kept the problem of the delegation of legislative power a fairly simple one, and when the Supreme Court first confronted the problem in the case of Brig Aurora v. United States (1813) it had no difficulty devising a theory that would allow some *rule making* by the administration. The case involved the Non-Intercourse Acts of 1809 against France and England. Congress had provided that the President, if he found either nation had ceased preying on our neutral shipping, could so proclaim and the embargo would come into force against the remaining offender. The President found that France had agreed to cease her depredations and proclaimed the act in force against England. In sustaining the validity of this action the Court pointed out that Congress could make the act apply conditionally if it chose. It was Congress which had made the policy; the President had merely *found the fact* upon which Congress had conditioned the application of the act; and the putting of the act into force was not an exercise of legislative power. In other words, Congress had not delegated its legislative power when it gave to the President the power to put the law into effect when he found *that certain conditions, defined by Congress, had come into existence.* The fact that Congress itself could have done what it directed the President to do did not make the delegation invalid.

In Field v. Clark (1892) the constitutionality of a provision of the Tariff Act of 1890 was challenged as an invalid delegation of power. The act set up a comprehensive list of tariff rates, but provided that certain agricultural articles might be admitted without paying the listed tariff. If, however, the country shipping the articles placed a tariff on our agricultural goods which, in view of the free entry of their goods, the President found to be "reciprocally unequal," he was directed to suspend the free entry "for such time as he shall deem just." Acting under this provision the President suspended the free entry of certain cloth goods, and the listed tariffs on them went into effect. The Court found the role of the President, as in the Brig Aurora case, to be merely that of fact-finder. He had no discretion except as to the duration of the suspension, and "that related only to the enforcement of the policy established by Congress. As the suspension was absolutely required when the President ascertained the existence of a particular fact, it cannot be said that in ascertaining that fact and in issuing his proclamation, in obedience to the legislative will, he exercised the function of making laws."

While in the Field case the Court may have stretched the concept of "fact-finding" in using it to describe the nice judgment involved in equating two countries' tariff systems and fixing the "duration" of suspension, here at least the law described exactly what was to happen when these facts were found: a predetermined tariff rate was to go into effect.

In *J.W. Hampton, Jr. & Co. v. United States* (1928), however, *it was apparent that too much discretion was being given to the President to permit describing his role as mere "fact-finding."* Unlike the Field case, a "*flexible tariff*" provision required the President (with the advice of a Tariff Commission) to determine the cost of production of imports which competed with domestic products, compare such cost with the cost of producing the product locally, and adjust the tariff on the imports to compensate for the difference. Chief Justice Taft, who brought to the Court the experience of having been President, recognized that a more flexible theory of delegation would have to be devised if the policies of Congress were to be effectively carried out. In upholding the delegation in Hampton he noted that "in determining what [Congress] may do in seeking assistance from another branch, the extent and character of that assistance must be fixed according to common sense" and announced the following rule: "If Congress shall lay down by legislative action an intelligible principle to which the person or body authorized to fix such rates is directed to conform, such legislative action is not a forbidden delegation of legislative power."

The distinction between an unrestrained legislative power which cannot be delegated and a limited one, usually called "quasi-legislative" or "rule-making," which can is not new. Marshall, a confirmed constitutional pragmatist, spelled it out in Wayman v. Southard (1825). In a case involving the delegation by Congress to the courts of the power to make rules of procedure, he said: "It will not be contended that Congress can delegate to the courts, or to any other tribunals, powers which are strictly and exclusively legislative. But Congress may certainly delegate to others, powers which the legislature may rightfully exercise itself. . . . The line has not been exactly drawn which separates those important subjects, which must be entirely regulated by the legislature itself, from those of less interest, in which a general provision may be made, and power given to those who are to act under such general provisions to fill up the details." Over the years the Supreme Court dealt so generously with the power of Congress to delegate some of its power to others that a distinguished scholar was led to observe in 1934 that "Congress is enabled to delegate its powers whenever it is necessary and proper to do so in order to exercise them effectively." See E.S. Corwin, Twilight of the Supreme Court, p. 145.

The most spectacular phase of the New Deal recovery program was the NRA, the enormous administrative organization set up under the authority of the National Industrial Recovery Act. It sought to stimulate the volume of business and improve working conditions by raising wages, reducing hours, and eliminating child labor; to drive out unfair and destructive competitive practices; to conserve natural resources in certain basic commodities; and to relieve unemployment. These salutary results were to be accomplished by the establishment of "codes of fair competition" in the industries brought under the act. These codes were to be drawn up by representatives of the industries in co-operation with government officials and were to be approved by the President, who was charged by the law with seeing that certain minimum standards with respect to working conditions and freedom from monopoly were observed.

Should an industry be unable to formulate a code for itself, the President might impose a code upon it. Within 18 months codes were established in more than 700 industries. These codes were mandatory upon all those engaged in the industry, whether they had participated in their formulation or not; and the provisions were enforceable both by criminal prosecution and by civil process. It was not until the National Industrial Recovery Act was almost on the point of expiring by limitation on June 16, 1935, that a decision on the constitutionality of the statute was handed down by the Supreme Court. The government chose the Schechter case, arising under the poultry code, as the one on which to stake the constitutional fortunes of the NRA. The act was held void both as an invalid delegation of legislative power to the President and as an invalid exercise by Congress of its power to regulate interstate commerce.

In January 1935 the Court in Panama Refining Co. v. Ryan invalidated the oil control provisions of the NRA on the ground that they delegated legislative power to the President. This section of the act had given the President power to forbid the transportation in interstate commerce of "hot oil" (oil produced or withdrawn from storage in violation of state law) but, as the Court pointed out, the statute did not tell when or under what circumstances the transportation was to be permitted or prohibited. "It establishes no criterion to govern the President's course. It does not require any finding by the President as a condition of his action. The Congress . . . thus declares no policy as to the transportation of the excess production. So far as this section is concerned, it gives the President an unlimited authority to determine the policy and to lay down the prohibition, or not to lay it down, as it may see fit." Justice Cardozo alone dissented on the ground that the President's discretion was sufficiently limited by the broad statement of purposes contained in the statute. The net result of the "Hot Oil Case," together with the Schechter case, seems to be that while very broad powers of administrative rulemaking may be delegated to the President, there must still be a legislative statement of policy sufficiently definite to prevent the exercise upon his part of pure discretion.

No statutes have been found invalid on the ground they invalidly delegated legislative power since the Court crisis of 1937, although sustaining certain wartime measures called for an exceedingly liberal interpretation of the rules. The Emergency Price Control Act of 1942 conferred broad powers on an Office of Price Administration (OPA) to set prices and ration goods. It spelled out in detail the purposes of the act and directed the OPA to fix prices that would tend to achieve these purposes and which would be "fair and equitable." Also, it was ordered "so far as practicable" to "give due consideration to the prices prevailing between October 1 and October 15, 1941." In Yakus v. United States (1944) the Court, besides finding the act valid on other grounds, held that it did not invalidly delegate legislative power to the OPA.

In Lichter v. United States (1948) the Court held valid the broad delegation provisions of the War Contracts Renegotiation Act of 1942. The necessity of getting war production started without delay had resulted in the letting of contracts for war materials with little or no knowledge of what the costs of production would be. The Renegotiation Act authorized the heads of the various services to renegotiate these initial contracts on the basis of experience in order to prevent "excessive profits." Furthermore, they were authorized to recover from the contractors "excessive profits," which had already been made. Although the act did not define "excessive profits," the Court held that, in view of the background and purposes of the act and the fact that it was an exercise of the war powers, the term was not so vague a standard as to result in a delegation by Congress of its own legislative power. The Court also noted that the War Department had developed a detailed set of administrative practices under the act and that Congress, in amending the act without altering these practices, had given approval to them. The fact that the standard of conduct set out in the statute had produced the kind of practices Congress desired showed that the standard was not too vague.

Query: Could Congress validly delegate to the President the power to cut the federal budget, giving him in effect a line item veto?

Mr. Chief Justice **Hughes** delivered the opinion of the Court, saying in part:

Petitioners . . . were convicted in the District Court of the United States for the Eastern District of New York on eighteen counts of an indictment charging violations of what is known as the "Live Poultry Code," and on an additional count for conspiracy to commit such violations. . . .

New York City is the largest live-poultry market in the United States. Ninety-six per cent of the live poultry there marketed comes from other States. Three-fourths of this amount arrives by rail and is consigned to commission men or receivers. . . . The commission men transact by far the greater part of the business on a commission basis. . . . They sell to slaughterhouse operators who are also called marketmen.

The defendants are slaughterhouse operators of the latter class. . . . Defendants ordinarily purchase their live poultry from commission men at the West Washington Market in New York City or at the railroad terminals serving the city, but occasionally they purchase from commission men in Philadelphia. They buy the poultry for slaughter and resale. After the poultry is trucked to their slaughter-house markets in Brooklyn, it is there sold, usually within twenty-fours hours, to retail poultry dealers and butchers who sell directly to consumers. The poultry purchased from defendants is immediately slaughtered, prior to delivery, by shochtim in defendant's employ. Defendants do not sell poultry in interstate commerce.

The "Live Poultry Code" was promulgated under

§ 3 of the National Industrial Recovery Act. That section . . . authorizes the President to approve "codes of fair competition." . . .

The "Live Poultry Code" was approved by the President on April 13, 1934. . . .

. . . The Code is established as "a code for fair competition for the live poultry industry of the metropolitan area in and about the City of New York." . . .

The Code fixes the number of hours for workdays. It provides that no employe, with certain exceptions, shall be permitted to work in excess of forty (40) hours in any one week, and that no employe, save as stated, "shall be paid in any pay period less than at the rate of fifty (50) cents per hour." The article containing "general labor provisions" prohibits the employment of any person under sixteen years of age, and declares that employes shall have the right of "collective bargaining" and freedom of choice with respect to labor organizations, in the terms of § 7(a) of the act. The minimum number of employes who shall be employed by slaughterhouse operators is fixed, the numbers being graduated according to the average volume of weekly sales. . . .

The seventh article, containing "trade practice provisions," prohibits various practices which are said to constitute "unfair methods of competition." . . .

The President approved the code by an executive order. . . .

Of the eighteen counts of the indictment upon which the defendants were convicted, aside from the count for conspiracy, two counts charged violation of the minimum wage and maximum hour provisions of the code, and ten counts were for violation of the requirement (found in the "trade practice provisions") of "straight killing." This requirement was really one of "straight" selling. The term "straight killing" was defined in the code as "the practice of requiring persons purchasing poultry for resale to accept the run of any half coop, coop, or coops, as purchased by slaughter-house operators, except for culls." The charges in the ten counts, respectively, were that the defendants in selling to retail dealers and butchers had permitted "selections of individual chickens taken from particular coops and half coops."

Of the other six counts, one charged the sale to a butcher of an unfit chicken; two counts charged the making of sales without having the poultry inspected or approved in accordance with regulations or ordinances of the City of New York; two counts charged the making of false reports or the failure to make reports relating to the range of daily prices and volume of sales for certain periods; and the remaining count was for sales to slaughterers or dealers who were without licenses required by the ordinances and regulations of the City of New York. . . .

Second. The question of the delegation of legislative power. . . . The Constitution provides that "all legislative powers herein granted shall be vested in a Congress of the United States, which shall consist of a Senate and House of Representatives." Art. 1, § 1. And the Congress is authorized "to make all laws which shall be necessary and proper for carrying into execution" its general power. Art. 1, § 8, par. 18. The Congress is not permitted to abdicate or to transfer to others the essential legislative functions with which it is thus vested. We have repeatedly recognized the necessity of adapting legislation to complex conditions involving a host of details with which the national Legislature cannot deal directly. We pointed out in the Panama Ref. Co. case that the Constitution has never been regarded as denying to Congress the necessary resources of flexibility and practicality, which will enable it to perform its function in laying down policies and establishing standards, while leaving to selected instrumentalities the making of subordinate rules within prescribed limits and the determination of facts to which the policy as declared by the Legislature is to apply. But we said that the constant recognition of the necessity and validity of such provisions, and the wide range of administrative authority which has been developed by means of them, cannot be allowed to obscure the limitations of the authority to delegate, if our constitutional system is to be maintained.

Accordingly we look to the statute to see whether Congress has overstepped these limitations,—whether Congress in authorizing "Codes of Fair Competition" has itself established the standards of legal obligation, thus performing its essential legislative function, or, by the failure to enact such standards, has attempted to transfer that function to others. . . .

What is meant by "fair competition" as the term is used in the act? Does it refer to a category established in the law, and is the authority to make codes limited accordingly? Or is it used as a convenient designation for whatever set of laws the formulators of a code for a particular trade or industry may propose and the President may approve (subject to certain restrictions), or the President may himself prescribe, as being wise and beneficent provisions for the government of the trade or industry in order to accomplish the broad purposes of rehabilitation, correction and expansion which are stated in the first section of Title I?

The act does not define "fair competition." "Unfair competition" as known to the common law is a limited concept. Primarily, and strictly, it relates to the palming off of one's goods as those of a rival trader. . . . In recent years its scope has been extended. It has been held to apply to misappropriation as well as misrepresentation, to the selling of another's goods as one's own—to misappropriation of what equitably belongs to a competitor. . . . Unfairness in competition has been predicated of acts which lie outside the ordinary course of business and are tainted by fraud, or coercion, or conduct otherwise prohibited by law. But it is evident that in its widest range "unfair competition," as it has been understood in the law, does not reach the objectives of the codes which are authorized by the National Industrial Recovery Act. The codes may, indeed, cover conduct which existing law condemns, but they are not limited to conduct of that sort. The Government does not contend that the act contemplates such a limitation. It would be opposed both to the declared purposes of the act and to its administrative construction. . . . [Here follows an analysis of the term "unfair methods of competition" used in the Federal Trade Commission Act as construed by judicial decisions.]

. . . We cannot regard the "fair competition" of the codes as antithetical to the "unfair methods of competition" of the Federal Trade Commission Act. The "fair competition" of the codes has a much broader range and a new significance. . . .

For a statement of the authorized objectives and content of the "codes of fair competition" we are referred repeatedly to the "declaration of policy" in § 1 of Title I of the Recovery Act. Thus, the approval of a code by the President is conditioned on his finding that it "will tend to effectuate the policy of this title." Section 3 (a). The President is authorized to impose such conditions "for the protection of consumers, competitors, employes and others, and in furtherance of the public interest, and may provide such exceptions to and exemptions from the provisions of such code as the President in his discretion deems necessary to effectuate the policy herein declared." The "policy herein declared" is manifestly that set forth in § 1. That declaration embraces a broad range of objectives. Among them we find the elimination of "unfair competitive practices." But even if this clause were to be taken to relate to practices which fall under the ban of existing law, either common law or statute, it is still only one of the authorized aims described in § 1. It is there declared to be "the policy of Congress"—"to remove obstructions to the free flow of interstate and foreign commerce which tend to diminish the amount thereof; and to provide for the general welfare by promoting the organization of industry for the purpose of co-operative action among trade groups, to induce and maintain united action of labor and management under adequate governmental sanctions and supervision, to eliminate unfair competitive practices, to promote the fullest possible utilization of the present productive capacity of industries, to avoid undue restriction of production (except as may be temporarily required), to increase the consumption of industrial and agricultural products by increasing purchasing power, to reduce and relieve unemployment, to improve standards of labor, and otherwise to rehabilitate industry and to conserve natural resources."

Under § 3, whatever "may tend to effectuate" these general purposes may be included in the "codes of fair competition." We think the conclusion is inescapable that the authority sought to be conferred by § 3 was not merely to deal with "unfair competitive practices" which offend against existing law, and could be the subject of judicial condemnation without further legislation, or to create administrative machinery for the application of established principles of law to particular instances of violation. Rather, the purpose is clearly disclosed to authorize new and controlling prohibitions through codes of laws which would embrace what the formulators would propose, and what the President would approve, or prescribe, as wise and beneficent measures for the government of trades and industries in order to bring about their rehabilitation, correction and development,

according to the general declaration of policy in § 1. . . .

The Government urges that the code will "consist of rules of competition deemed fair for each industry—by representative members of that industry, by the persons most vitally concerned and most familiar with its problems." Instances are cited in which Congress has availed itself of such assistance: as e.g., in the exercise of its authority over the public domain, with respect to the recognition of local customs or rules of miners as to mining claims or in matters of a more or less technical nature, as in designating the standard height of drawbars. But would it be seriously contended that Congress could delegate its legislative authority to trade or industrial associations or groups so as to empower them to enact the laws they deem to be wise and beneficent for the rehabilitation and expansion of their trade or industries? Could trade or industrial associations or groups be constituted legislative bodies for that purpose because such associations or groups are familiar with the problems of their enterprises? And, could an effort of that sort be made valid by such a preface of generalities as to permissible aims as we find in § 1 of Title I? The answer is obvious. Such a delegation of legislative power is unknown to our law and is utterly inconsistent with the constitutional prerogatives and duties of Congress.

The question, then, turns upon the authority which § 3 of the Recovery Act vests in the President to approve or prescribe. If the codes have standing as penal statutes, this must be due to the effect of the executive action. But Congress cannot delegate legislative power to the President to exercise an unfettered discretion to make whatever laws he thinks may be needed or advisable for the rehabilitation and expansion of trade or industry. . . .

Accordingly we turn to the Recovery Act to ascertain what limits have been set to the exercise of the President's discretion. *First*, the President, as a condition of approval, is required to find that the trade or industrial associations or groups which propose a code "impose no inequitable restrictions on admission to membership" and are "truly representative." That condition, however, relates only to the status of the initiators of the new laws and not to the permissible scope of such laws. *Second*, the President is required to find that the code is not "designed to promote monopolies or to eliminate or oppress small enterprises and will not operate to discriminate against them." And to this is added a proviso that the code "shall not permit monopolies or monopolistic practices." But these restrictions leave virtually untouched the field of policy envisaged by § 1, and in that wide field of legislative possibilities the proponents of a code, refraining from monopolistic designs, may roam at will and the President may approve or disapprove their proposals as he may see fit. . . .

To summarize and conclude upon this point: § 3 of the Recovery Act is without precedent. It supplies no standards for any trade, industry or activity. It does not undertake to prescribe rules of conduct to be applied to particular states of fact determined by appropriate administrative procedure. Instead of prescribing rules of conduct, it authorizes the making of codes to prescribe them. For that legislative undertaking, § 3 sets up no standards, aside from the statement of the general aims of rehabilitation, correction and expansion described in § 1. In view of the scope of that broad declaration, and of the nature of the few restrictions that are imposed, the discretion of the President in approving or prescribing codes, and thus enacting laws for the government of trade and industry throughout the country, is virtually unfettered. We think that the code-making authority thus conferred is an unconstitutional delegation of legislative power. . . .

[The section of the Schechter case dealing with the commerce power is printed in the section on interstate commerce.]

UNITED STATES v. CURTISS-WRIGHT EXPORT CORPORATION

299 U. S. 304; 57 S. Ct. 216; 81 L. Ed. 255 (1936)

While the United States in its domestic affairs is closely governed by the constitutional requirements of the federal system, in its dealing with other nations it must be in a position to speak and act as a nation among other nations. Thus, while it may exercise only its delegated powers in the field of internal affairs, these delegations of power do not mark the limit of its authority to cope with international problems; see Fong Yue Ting v. United States (1893). But if the national government is the only government which can deal with foreign nations and has the power to do so on terms of equality, does this alter the fact that it is a government made up of three branches, each with its defined powers? Is the power of Congress to deal with international affairs still a legislative power which cannot be delegated to the President?

In 1934 Congress passed a joint resolution providing that if the President finds that an embargo on the sale of arms and munitions in the United States to countries at war in the Chaco (Bolivia and Paraguay) "may contribute to the reestablishment of peace between those countries," he may, after consultation with other American republics, establish such an embargo by proclamation. Violation of such an embargo was made a crime. The joint resolution did not restrict or direct the President's discretion in setting up the embargo. It clearly delegated legislative power without any of the standards which the Court in the Schechter case (1935) had held to be vital if the delegation were to be held valid. The President proclaimed the embargo and the defendant company, indicted for selling guns to Bolivia, challenged the constitutionality of the resolution.

Nearly half a century later, in a vastly different political climate, Congress passed the Arms Export Control Act sharply limiting and regulating the sale of arms to foreign countries. Congressional investigation and testimony at the Iran-Contra hearings in the summer of

1987 suggested that the transfer of arms to Iran had been made by the government in violation of this law.

Query: Could the President, without any resolution by Congress, have issued the embargo proclamation? Congress has by statute required the President to make findings and inform certain congressional committees before conducting covert operations abroad. Is such a restriction constitutional?

Mr. Justice **Sutherland** delivered the opinion of the Court, saying in part:

On January 27, 1936, an indictment was returned in the court below, the first count of which charges that appellees, beginning with the 29th day of May, 1934, conspired to sell in the United States certain arms of war, namely, fifteen machine guns, to Bolivia, a country then engaged in armed conflict in the Chaco, in violation of the Joint Resolution of Congress approved May 28, 1934, and the provisions of a proclamation issued on the same day by the President of the United States pursuant to authority conferred by § 1 of the resolution. In pursuance of the conspiracy, the commission of certain overt acts was alleged, details of which need not be stated. The Joint Resolution follows:

"*Resolved by the Senate and House of Representatives of the United States of America in Congress assembled*, That if the President finds that the prohibition of the sale of arms and munitions of war in the United States to those countries now engaged in armed conflict in the Chaco may contribute to the reestablishment of peace between those countries, and if after consultation with the governments of other American Republics and with their cooperation, as well as that of such other governments as he may deem necessary, he makes proclamation to that effect, it shall be unlawful to sell, except under such limitations and exceptions as the President prescribes, any arms or munitions of war in any place in the United States to the countries now engaged in that armed conflict, or to any person, company, or association acting in the interest of either country, until otherwise ordered by the President or by Congress.

"Sec. 2. Whoever sells any arms or munitions of war in violation of section 1 shall, on conviction, be punished by a fine not exceeding $10,000 or by imprisonment not exceeding two years, or both." . . .

Appellees severally demurred to the first count of the indictment on the grounds (1) that it did not charge facts sufficient to show the commission by appellees of any offense against any law of the United States. . . . The points urged in support of the demurrers were, first, that the joint resolution effects an invalid delegation of legislative power to the Executive; second, that the joint resolution never became effective because of the failure of the President to find essential jurisdictional facts. . . .

The court below sustained the demurrers upon the first point, but overruled them on the second and third points. The government appealed to this court under the provisions of the Criminal Appeals Act of March 2, 1907. . . . That act authorizes the United States to appeal from a district court direct to this court in criminal cases where, among other things, the decision sustaining a demurrer to the indictment or any count thereof is based upon the invalidity or construction of the statute upon which the indictment is founded.

First. It is contended that by the Joint Resolution, the going into effect and continued operation of the resolution was conditioned (a) upon the President's judgment as to its beneficial effect upon the reestablishment of peace between the countries engaged in armed conflict in the Chaco; (b) upon the making of a proclamation, which was left to his unfettered discretion, thus constituting an attempted substitution of the President's will for that of Congress; (c) upon the making of a proclamation putting an end to the operation of the resolution, which again was left to the President's unfettered discretion; and (d) further, that the extent of its operation in particular cases was subject to limitation and exception by the President, controlled by no standard. In each of these particulars, appellees urge that Congress abdicated its essential functions and delegated them to the Executive.

Whether, if the Joint Resolution had related solely to internal affairs it would be open to the challenge that it constituted an unlawful delegation of legislative power to the Executive, we find it unnecessary to determine. The whole aim of the resolution is to affect a situation entirely external to the United States, and falling within the category of foreign affairs. The determination which we are called to make, therefore, is whether the Joint Resolution, as applied to that situation, is vulnerable to attack under the rule that forbids a delegation of the law-making power. In other words, assuming (but not deciding) that the challenged delegation, if it were confined to internal affairs, would be invalid, may it nevertheless be sustained on the ground that its exclusive aim is to afford a remedy for a hurtful condition within foreign territory?

It will contribute to the elucidation of the question if we first consider the differences between the powers of the Federal government in respect of foreign or external affairs and those in respect of domestic or internal affairs. That there are differences between them, and that these differences are fundamental, may not be doubted.

The two classes of powers are different, both in respect of their origin and their nature. The broad statement that the Federal government can exercise no powers except those specifically enumerated in the Constitution, and such implied powers as are necessary and proper to carry into effect the enumerated powers, is categorically true only in respect of our internal affairs. In that field, the primary purpose of the Constitution was to carve from the general mass of legislative powers *then possessed by the states* such portions as it was thought desirable to vest in the Federal government, leaving those not included in the enumeration still in the states. Carter v. Carter Coal Co. [1936]. That this doctrine applies only to powers which the states had is self-evident. And since the states severally never possessed international powers, such powers could not have been carved from the mass of state powers but obviously were transmitted to the United States from some other source. During the colonial period, those powers were possessed exclusively by and were entirely under the control of the Crown. By the Declaration of Independence, "the Representatives of the United States of America" declared the United [not the several] Colonies to be free and independent states, and as such to have "full Power to levy War, conclude Peace, contract Alliances, establish Commerce and to do all other Acts and Things which Independent States may of right do."

As a result of the separation from Great Britain by the colonies, acting as a unit, the powers of external sovereignty passed from the Crown not to the colonies severally, but to the colonies in their collective and corporate capacity as the United States of America. Even before the Declaration, the colonies were a unit in foreign affairs, acting through a common agency—namely the Continental Congress, composed of delegates from the thirteen colonies. That agency exercised the powers of war and peace, raised an army, created a navy, and finally adopted the Declaration of Independence. Rulers come and go; governments end and forms of government change; but sovereignty survives. A political society cannot endure without a supreme will somewhere. Sovereignty is never held in suspense. When, therefore, the external sovereignty of Great Britain in respect of the colonies ceased, it immediately passed to the Union. . . . That fact was given practical application almost at once. The treaty of peace, made on September 3, 1783, was concluded between his Britannic Majesty and the "United States of America." . . .

The Union existed before the Constitution, which was ordained and established among other things to form "a more perfect Union." Prior to that event it is clear that the Union, declared by the Articles of Confederation to be "perpetual," was the sole possessor of external sovereignty and in the Union it remained without change save in so far as the Constitution in express terms qualified its exercise. . . .

It results that the investment of the Federal government with the powers of external sovereignty did not depend upon the affirmative grants of the Constitution. The powers to declare and wage war, to conclude peace, to make treaties, to maintain diplomatic relations with other sovereignties, if they had never been mentioned in the Constitution, would have vested in the Federal government as necessary concomitants of nationality. Neither the Constitution nor the laws passed in pursuance of it have any force in foreign territory unless in respect of our own citizens . . . ; and operations of the nation in such territory must be governed by treaties, international understandings and compacts, and the principles of international law. As a member of the family of nations, the right and power of the United States in that field are equal to the right and power of the other members of the international family. Otherwise, the United States is not completely sovereign. The power to acquire territory by discovery and occupation (Jones v. United States [1890]), the power to expel undesirable aliens (Fong Yue Ting v. United States [1893]), the power to make such international agreements as do not constitute treaties in the constitutional sense (Altman & Co. v. United States [1912] . . .), none of which is expressly affirmed by the Constitution, nevertheless exist as inherently inseparable from the conception of nationality. This the court recognized, and in each of the cases cited found the warrant for its conclusions not in the provisions of the Constitution, but in the law of nations. . . .

Not only, as we have shown, is the Federal power over external affairs in origin and essential character different from that over internal affairs, but participation in the exercise of the power is significantly limited. In this vast external realm, with its important, complicated, delicate and manifold problems, the President alone has the power to speak or listen as a representative of the nation. He *makes* treaties with the advice and consent of the Senate; but he alone negotiates. Into the field of negotiation the Senate cannot intrude; and Congress itself is powerless to invade it. . . .

It is important to bear in mind that we are here dealing not alone with an authority vested in the President by an exertion of legislative power, but with such an authority plus the very delicate, plenary and exclusive power of the President as the sole organ of the Federal government in the field of international relations—a power which does not require as a basis for its exercise an act of Congress, but which, of course, like every other governmental power, must be exercised in subordination to the applicable provisions of the Constitution. It is quite apparent that if, in the maintenance of our international relations, embarrassment—perhaps serious embarrassment—is to be avoided and success for our aims achieved, congressional legislation which is to be made effective through negotiation and inquiry within the international field must often accord to the President a degree of discretion and freedom from statutory restriction which would not be admissible were domestic affairs alone involved. Moreover, he, not Congress, has the better opportunity of knowing the conditions which prevail in foreign countries, and especially is this true in time of war. He has his confidential sources of information. He has his agents in the form of diplomatic, consular and other officials. Secrecy in respect of information gathered by them may be highly necessary, and the premature disclosure of it productive of harmful results. Indeed, so clearly is this true that the first President refused to accede to a request to lay before the House of Representatives the instructions, correspondence and documents relating to the negotiation of the Jay Treaty—a refusal the wisdom of which was recognized by the House itself and has never since been doubted. In his reply to the request, President Washington said:

"The nature of foreign negotiations requires caution, and their success must often depend on secrecy; and even when brought to a conclusion a full disclosure of all the measures, demands, or eventual concessions which

may have been proposed or contemplated would be extremely impolitic; for this might have a pernicious influence on future negotiations, or produce immediate inconveniences, perhaps danger and mischief, in relation to other powers. The necessity of such caution and secrecy was one cogent reason for vesting the power of making treaties in the President, with the advice and consent of the Senate, the principle on which that body was formed confining it to a small number of members. To admit, then a right in the House of Representatives to demand and to have as a matter of course all the papers respecting a negotiation with a foreign power would be to establish a dangerous precedent." 1 Messages and Papers of the Presidents, p. 194.

The marked difference between foreign affairs and domestic affairs in this respect is recognized by both houses of Congress in the very form of their requisitions for information from the executive departments. In the case of every department except the Department of State, the resolution *directs* the official to furnish the information. In the case of the State Department, dealing with foreign affairs, the President is requested to furnish the information "if not incompatible with the public interest." A statement that to furnish the information is not compatible with the public interest rarely, if ever, is questioned.

When the President is to be authorized by legislation to act in respect of a matter intended to affect a situation in foreign territory, the legislator properly bears in mind the important consideration that the form of the President's action—or, indeed, whether he shall act at all—may well depend, among other things, upon the nature of the confidential information which he has or may thereafter receive, or upon the effect which his action may have upon our foreign relations. This consideration, in connection with what we have already said on the subject, discloses the unwisdom of requiring Congress in this field of governmental power to lay down narrowly definite standards by which the President is to be governed. As this court said in Mackenzie v. Hare (1915), "As a government, the United States is invested with all the attributes of sovereignty. As it has the character of nationality it has the powers of nationality, especially those which concern its relations and intercourse with other countries. *We should hesitate long before limiting or embarrassing such powers.*" (Italics supplied.)

In the light of the foregoing observations, it is evident that this court should not be in haste to apply a general rule which will have the effect of condemning legislation like that under review as constituting an unlawful delegation of legislative power. The principles which justify such legislation find overwhelming support in the unbroken legislative practice which has prevailed almost from the inception of the national government to the present day. . . .

Practically every volume of the United States Statutes contains one or more acts or joint resolutions of Congress authorizing action by the President in respect of subjects affecting foreign relations, which either leave the exercise of the power to his unrestricted judgment, or provide a standard far more general than that which has always been considered requisite with regard to domestic affairs. . . .

. . . A legislative practice such as we have here, evidenced not by only occasional instances, but marked by the movement of a steady stream for a century and a half of time, goes a long way in the direction of proving the presence of unassailable ground for the constitutionality of the practice, to be found in the origin and history of the power involved, or in its nature, or in both combined. . . .

We deem it unnecessary to consider, seriatim, the several clauses which are said to evidence the unconstitutionality of the Joint Resolution as involving an unlawful delegation of legislative power. It is enough to summarize by saying that, both upon principle and in accordance with precedent, we conclude there is sufficient warrant for the broad discretion vested in the President to determine whether the enforcement of the statute will have a beneficial effect upon the reestablishment of peace in the affected countries; whether he shall make proclamation to bring the resolution into operation; whether and when the resolution shall cease to operate and to make proclamation accordingly; and to prescribe limitations and exceptions to which the enforcement of the resolution shall be subject.

Second. The second point raised by the demurrer was that the Joint Resolution never became effective because the President failed to find essential jurisdictional facts. . . .

1. The Executive proclamation recites, ''I have found that the prohibition of the sale of arms and munitions of war in the United States to those countries now engaged in armed conflict in the Chaco may contribute to the re-establishment of peace between those countries, and that I have consulted with the governments of other American Republics *and have been assured of the cooperation of such governments as I have deemed necessary as contemplated by the said joint resolution.*'' This finding satisfies every requirement of the Joint Resolution. There is no suggestion that the resolution is fatally uncertain or indefinite; and a finding which follows its language, as this finding does, cannot well be challenged as insufficient. . . .

The judgment of the court below must be reversed and the cause remanded for further proceedings in accordance with the foregoing opinion.

Reversed.

Mr. Justice **McReynolds** does not agree. He is of opinion that the court below reached the right conclusion and its judgment ought to be affirmed.

Mr. Justice **Stone** took no part in the consideration or decision of this case.

(Should have attached stress
to it)

under this Am. war to Vietnam
lead to the War powers act.

3

The Executive Branch

CONSTITUTIONAL POWERS OF THE PRESIDENT

EX PARTE MILLIGAN

4 Wallace 2; 18 L. Ed. 281 (1866)

It is one of the evils of war that there seems frequently to be a certain incompatibility between the demands of military necessity and a punctilious regard for the civil rights of the individual. Certainly in war emergencies the citizen finds his liberty curtailed and his rights abridged in ways that in times of peace would seem intolerable. There is plenty of evidence that President Lincoln, largely supported by public opinion, definitely proceeded during the Civil War upon the theory that questions of constitutional power were to be dealt with in the light of the great objective of preserving the Union. No President has ever invaded private constitutional rights more flagrantly, or from worthier motives, than he. This may be illustrated by the famous case of Ex parte Merryman (1861). Merryman was a Southern agitator residing in Maryland who persisted during the early days of the war in conduct and utterances which in the judgment of the military authorities hindered the success of the Northern cause. He was thereupon arrested and locked up in the military prison at Fort McHenry. Merryman promptly petitioned Chief Justice Taney for a writ of habeas corpus. Taney issued the writ, directed to the general in command of the fort. The general did not honor the writ, replying that he was authorized by the President to suspend the writ of habeas corpus, but would seek further instructions; and he declined to obey the writ further. Taney thereupon issued a writ of contempt against the general and sent the United States marshal to serve it. The marshal reported that he had not been allowed to enter the outer gate of the fort, although he had sent in his card, and that he had not been able to serve the writ. Taney, while protesting that the marshal had a perfect right to summon a posse comitatus and storm the fort, excused him from that duty. Rather, he contented himself with writing a full account of the entire case which he addressed to President Lincoln and which concluded with the observation that it now remained for the President, acting in fulfillment of his solemn oath of office, to enforce the laws, execute the judgment of the court, and release the prisoner. Lincoln made no answer whatever to this document, but Merryman was later released from military confinement and turned over to the civil authorities.

No case of this kind came to the Supreme Court while the war was in progress, although in 1864 an attempt was made to bring before that tribunal on a writ of habeas corpus the validity of the arrest of the notorious agitator, Vallandigham. The Court held that it was without jurisdiction and dismissed the case; see Ex parte Vallandigham (1864). It is interesting to speculate what the results might have been had the Supreme Court locked horns with the President in such a case; if, for example, the Milligan case had come up for decision during the early part of the war instead of in 1866.

The facts in the Milligan case were as follows: Milligan, a civilian, was arrested by order of General Hovey, who commanded the military district of Indiana; was tried in October, 1864, by a military commission which had been established under presidential authority; was found guilty of initiating insurrection and of various treasonable and disloyal practices; and was sentenced to be hanged on May 19, 1865. This sentence was approved by President Johnson. On May 10, 1865, Milligan sued out a writ of habeas corpus to the United States circuit court in Indiana, alleging the unconstitutional character of the proceedings under which he had been convicted and claiming the right of trial by jury as guaranteed by the Constitution. Thus, for the first time, the Supreme Court faced the question of the right of the President to suspend the writ of habeas corpus and to substitute trial by military authority for trial in the ordinary civil courts in districts outside the actual field of military operations.

The Supreme Court itself found difficulty in agreeing upon the important questions presented. They all held that a military commission set up by the President under such circumstances and without special authority from Congress was unlawful and without any power whatsoever. Five of the judges took the view that neither Congress nor the President had the power to set up military tribunals except in the actual theater of war where the civil courts were no longer functioning. Four judges, while denying such power to the President, held that it could be exercised by Congress. The Court decided, however, that Milligan had been unlawfully convicted and he was released.

The subsequent story of the case is not without interest. Milligan's sentence had been commuted to life imprisonment by the President in June, 1865, and he had been imprisoned by General Hovey in the Ohio penitentiary until his final release on April 10, 1866, as a result of the decision of the Supreme Court. On March 13, 1868, he brought an action of damages against General Hovey for unlawful imprisonment. The case was tried in the federal circuit court and the jury rendered a verdict for Milligan, but awarded only nominal damages inasmuch as the two-year statute of limitations allowed him to recover damages only for his imprisonment between March 13 and April 10, 1866.

The fact that the decision in the Milligan case set up a powerful judicial protection against military and executive invasion of individual constitutional rights was not sufficient to distract contemporary attention from the vital political consequences of the rule regarding congressional power which was laid down. Congress was in the midst of the important work of reconstruction. The radical leaders of the Republican party were committed to a policy of reconstruction which should keep the Southern states under the control of federal military forces until conditions seemed to warrant the adoption of a less drastic policy. But the doctrine of the Milligan case, by condemning military government in peaceful sections where the civil courts were open, was obviously incompatible with any such form of military reconstruction. It looked as though the Court was trying to prevent the carrying out of the congressional policy, and the decision was received with an outburst of anger by the congressional leaders. There was some talk of impeaching the judges; Congress went forward with its plans for military government in the South in contemptuous disregard for the decision, and utterances from prominent men were not lacking to the effect that the Court would come off the loser in any combat over the validity of the reconstruction plan adopted. It is an interesting fact that the constitutionality of these reconstruction acts was never passed upon by the Supreme Court.

The spectacular case of the Nazi saboteurs, Ex parte Quirin (1942), appeared at first to reopen the major issue settled by the Milligan case. In June 1942, eight saboteurs landed in this country from a German submarine. They brought with them explosives, incendiaries, fuses, detonators, timing devices, and acids. They had about $175,000 in American money for expenses and bribes, and they carried elaborate lists of American factories, railroad centers, bridges, power plants, and other key war facilities. They were all born in Germany, had previously lived in this country, and had, upon returning to Germany, been trained in a special school for saboteurs.

About ten days after they landed, they were arrested by the FBI. Thereupon President Roosevelt issued two proclamations. The first denied to enemies who enter this country to commit sabotage or other hostile acts the right of access to the civil courts and directed that they be tried by military tribunals in accordance with the law of war. The second created a military commission of eight army officers to try the saboteurs, ordered the Attorney General and the Judge Advocate General to prosecute them, and designated two army officers to act as defense counsel. Four charges were filed against the saboteurs, all stating offenses under the law of war. At the outset of the trial, defense counsel attacked the constitutionality of the President's proclamation and the jurisdiction of the military commission, but the trial proceeded. Late in July the country was startled by the announcement that the Supreme Court (then in summer recess) would reconvene in two days to permit the filing of petitions for writs of habeas corpus on behalf of the prisoners. After proceedings that lasted two days, the Court denied the petitions and adjourned. The trial continued and the saboteurs were convicted. Six were executed and two imprisoned.

In October, the Court handed down its opinion in the case. It held that the President had the authority to establish the military commission by virtue of statutes passed by Congress, and that the offenses charged were offenses against the law of war. It held that the grand jury indictment and the jury trial provisions of the Fifth and Sixth Amendments are not applicable to trials before military tribunals for crimes against the law of war. The Court then commented upon the Milligan case; it pointed out that Milligan was a citizen and resident of Indiana, had never lived in a rebellious state, was not an enemy belligerent, and was therefore not subject to the law of war. The Court said: "We construe the Court's statement as to the applicability of the law of war to Milligan's case as having particular reference to the facts before it." The most important point about the case is that the Supreme Court did examine into the right of the military authorities to try the saboteurs. It upheld the military tribunal, but not until it satisfied itself that the tribunal had jurisdiction and was proceeding according to law.

The issues raised by Ex parte Milligan came before the Court again in 1946 in Duncan v. Kahanamoku, a case arising out of the declaration of martial law in the Hawaiian Islands. The day following the Japanese attack on Pearl Harbor the Army established military government and took over legislative, executive, and judicial functions. The administration of criminal justice by the civil courts was completely blacked out. Courtrooms and offices were taken over by the Army; grand jury proceedings, trial by jury, the subpoenaing of witnesses, and the issuance of writs of habeas corpus were all forbidden; and criminal cases of every description were handled by summary military procedure. This continued until March, 1943, when a partial restoration of authority to the civil officers was ordered, mainly with respect to civil matters. Most classes of civilian crimes were still tried by the Army. Martial law was finally abolished in the islands by a presidential proclamation in October, 1944.

To responsible military leaders this drastic subordination of civilian affairs to Army control undoubtedly seemed imperative, but to the civil officers of the territory it seemed a wanton and unnecessary denial of constitutionally protected civil liberties. It was urged that any active danger of the invasion of the islands was ended by the Battle of Midway in June, 1942. It was also pointed out that there were no known acts of sabotage, espionage, or other disloyal conduct by any of the Japanese in Hawaii either on or after the day of the Pearl Harbor attack. The civil courts of the territory were ready at all times to perform their normal functions had they been allowed to do so, and experienced federal judges testified that there was no good reason why any of the civilian criminal cases handled by Army courts could not just as well have been handled by the courts of the territory. The bitter resentment engendered by this military suppression of civil government finally came to a climax in a dramatic struggle between federal district judge Delbert E. Metzger and Lieutenant General Robert C. Richardson, Commanding General of the Central Pacific Area.

Judge Metzger issued a writ of habeas corpus in the case of two German-American citizens who had been interned by summary military action. General Richardson replied with an order forbidding any judge in the territory to issue a writ of habeas corpus. The judge countered by fining General Richardson $5000 for contempt of court. To break this deadlock an emissary was sent from the Department of Justice in Washington, and a compromise was reached by which the President remitted the fine imposed on General Richardson and the general withdrew his order against Judge Metzger. It was agreed that writs of habeas corpus might be issued, but that prisoners would not be released unless higher courts on appeal so ordered. While in the Duncan case the Court held invalid the military government of the islands, a majority of the Court did not rest their decision on constitutional grounds. They dealt rather with the question whether Congress, in passing the Hawaiian organic act of 1900 under the authority of which military rule in Hawaii had been set up, intended to authorize this complete supplanting of civil government by martial law. In reaching its conclusion that Congress did not so intend, the Court plainly implies, in the final paragraphs of its opinion and particularly in its reference to the Milligan case, that if the organic act did authorize such military domination of civilian life it would be unconstitutional.

Query: Does the Milligan opinion make clear how the writ of habeas corpus is to be suspended, and by whom?

Mr. Justice **Davis** delivered the opinion of the Court, saying in part:

The importance of the main question presented by this record cannot be overstated, for it involves the very framework of the government and the fundamental principles of American liberty.

During the late wicked Rebellion, the temper of the times did not allow that calmness in deliberation and discussion so necessary to a correct conclusion of a purely judicial question. Then, considerations of safety were mingled with the exercise of power, and feelings and interests prevailed which are happily terminated. Now that the public safety is assured, this question, as well as all others, can be discussed and decided without passion or the admixture of any element not required to form a legal judgment. We approach the investigation of this case fully sensible of the magnitude of the inquiry and the necessity of full and cautious deliberation. . . .

The controlling question in the case is this: Upon the facts stated in Milligan's petition, and the exhibits filed, had the Military Commission mentioned in it jurisdiction, legally, to try and sentence him? Milligan, not a resident of one of the rebellious states, or a prisoner of war, but a citizen of Indiana for twenty years past, and never in the military or naval service, is, while at his home, arrested by the military power of the United States, imprisoned and, on certain criminal charges preferred against him, tried, convicted, and sentenced to be hanged by a military commission, organized under the direction of the military commander of the military district of Indiana. Had this tribunal the legal power and authority to try and punish this man?

No graver question was ever considered by this court, nor one which more nearly concerns the rights of the whole people; for it is the birthright of every American citizen when charged with crime, to be tried and punished according to law. The power of punishment is alone through the means which the laws have provided for that purpose, and if they are ineffectual, there is an immunity from punishment, no matter how great an offender the individual may be, or how much his crimes may have shocked the sense of justice of the country, or endangered its safety. By the protection of the law human rights are secured; withdraw that protection, and they are at the mercy of wicked rulers, or the clamor of an excited people. If there was law to justify this military trial, it is not our province to interfere; if there was not, it is our duty to declare the nullity of the whole proceedings. The decision of this question does not depend on argument or judicial precedents, numerous and highly illustrative as they are. These precedents inform us of the extent of the struggle to preserve liberty and to relieve those in civil life from military trials. The founders of our government were familiar with the history of that struggle; and secured in a written Constitution every right which the people had wrested from power during a contest of ages. By that Constitution and the laws authorized by it, this question must be determined. The provisions of that instrument on the administration of criminal justice are too plain and direct to leave room for misconstruction or doubt of their true meaning. Those applicable to this case are found in that clause of the original Constitution which says ''that the trial of all crimes, except in case of impeachment, shall be by jury;'' and in the fourth, fifth, and sixth articles of the amendments. . . .

Time has proven the discernment of our ancestors; for even these provisions, expressed in such plain English words, that it would seem the ingenuity of man could not evade them, are now, after the lapse of more than seventy years, sought to be avoided. Those great and good men foresaw that troublous times would arise, when rulers and people would become restive under restraint, and seek by sharp and decisive measures to accomplish ends deemed just and proper; and that the principles of constitutional liberty would be in peril, unless established by irrepealable law. The history of the world had taught them that what was done in the past might be attempted in the future. The Constitution of the United States is a law for rulers and people, equally in war and in peace, and covers with the shield of its protection all classes of men, at all times, and under all circumstances. No doctrine, involving more pernicious consequences, was ever invented by the wit of man than that any of its provisions can be suspended during any of the great exigencies of government. Such a doctrine leads directly to anarchy or despotism, but the theory of necessity on which it is based is false; for the government, within the Constitution, has all the powers granted to it which are necessary to preserve its existence, as has been happily proved by the result of the great effort to throw off its just authority.

Have any of the rights guaranteed by the Constitution been violated in the case of Milligan? and if so, what are they?

Every trial involves the exercise of judicial power; and from what source did the Military Commission that tried him derive their authority? Certainly no part of the judicial power of the country was conferred on them; because the Constitution expressly vests it ''in one Supreme Court and such inferior courts as the Congress may from time to time ordain and establish,'' and it is not pretended that the commission was a court ordained and established by Congress. They cannot justify on the mandate of the President; because he is controlled by law, and has his appropriate sphere of duty, which is to execute, not to make, the laws; and there is ''no unwritten criminal code to which resort can be had as a source of jurisdiction.''

But it is said that the jurisdiction is complete under the ''laws and usages of war.''

It can serve no useful purpose to inquire what those laws and usages are, whence they originated, where found, and on whom they operate; they can never be applied to citizens in states which have upheld the authority of the government, and where the courts are open and their process unobstructed. This court has judicial knowledge that in Indiana the Federal authority was always unopposed, and its courts always open to hear criminal accusations and redress grievances; and no usage of war could sanction a military trial there for any offense whatever of a citizen in civil life, in nowise connected with the military service. Congress could grant no such power; and to the honor of our national legislature be it said, it has never been provoked by the state of the country even to attempt its exercise. One of the plainest constitutional provisions was, therefore, infringed when Milligan was tried by a court not ordained and established by Congress, and not composed of judges appointed during good behavior.

Why was he not delivered to the circuit court of Indiana to be proceeded against according to law? No reason of necessity could be urged against it; because Congress had declared penalties against the offenses charged, provided for their punishment, and directed that court to hear and determine them. And soon after this military tribunal was ended, the circuit court met, peacefully transacted its business, and adjourned. It needed no bayonets to protect it, and required no military aid to execute its judgments. It was held in a state, eminently distinguished for patriotism, by judges commissioned during the Rebellion, who were provided with juries, upright, intelligent, and selected by a marshal appointed by the President. The government had no right to conclude that Milligan, if guilty, would not receive in that court merited punishment; for its records disclose that it was constantly engaged in the trial of similar offenses, and was never interrupted in its administration of criminal justice. If it was dangerous, in the distracted condition of affairs, to leave Milligan unrestrained of his liberty, because he ''conspired against the government, afforded aid and comfort to rebels, and incited the people to insurrection," the law said arrest him, confine him closely, render him powerless to do further mischief; and then present his case to the grand jury of the district, with proofs of his guilt and, if indicted, try him according to the course of the common law. If this had been done, the Constitution would have been vindicated, the law of 1863 enforced, and the securities for personal liberty preserved and defended.

Another guarantee of freedom was broken when Milligan was denied a trial by jury. The great minds of the country have differed on the correct interpretation to be given to various provisions of the Federal Constitution; and judicial decision has been often invoked to settle their true meaning; but until recently no one ever doubted that the right of trial by jury was fortified in the organic law against the power of attack. It is now assailed; but if ideas can be expressed in words, and language has any meaning, this right—one of the most valuable in a free country—is preserved to every one accused of crime who is not attached to the Army, or Navy, or Militia in actual service. The sixth Amendment affirms that "in all criminal prosecutions the accused shall enjoy the right to a speedy and public trial by an impartial jury," language broad enough to embrace all persons and cases; but the fifth, recognizing the necessity of an indictment, or presentment, before any one can be held to answer for high crimes, "excepts cases arising in the land or naval forces, or in the militia, when in actual service, in time of war or public danger;" and the framers of the Constitution, doubtless, meant to limit the right to trial by jury, in the Sixth Amendment, to those persons who were subject to indictment or presentment in the Fifth.

The discipline necessary to the efficiency of the army and navy required other and swifter modes of trial than are furnished by the common law courts; and, in pursuance of the power conferred by the Constitution, Congress has declared the kinds of trial and the manner in which they shall be conducted, for offenses committed while the party is in the military or naval service. Every one connected with these branches of public service is amenable to the jurisdiction which Congress has created for their government, and, while thus serving, surrenders his right to be tried by the civil courts. All other persons, citizens of states where the courts are open, if charged with crime, are guaranteed the inestimable privilege of trial by jury. . . .

It is claimed that martial law covers with its broad mantle the proceedings of this military commission. The proposition is this: That in a time of war the commander of an armed force (if in his opinion the exigencies of the country demand it, and of which he is to judge) has the power, within the lines of his military district, to suspend all civil rights and their remedies, and subject citizens as well as soldiers to the rule of his will; and in the exercise of his lawful authority cannot be restrained, except by his superior officer or the President of the United States.

If this position is sound to the extent claimed, then when war exists, foreign or domestic, and the country is subdivided into military departments for mere convenience, the commander of one of them can, if he chooses, within the limits, on the plea of necessity, with the approval of the Executive, substitute military force for and to the exclusion of the laws, and punish all persons, as he thinks right and proper, without fixed or certain rules.

The statement of this proposition shows its importance; for, if true, republican government is a failure, and there is an end of liberty regulated by law. Martial law, established on such a basis, destroys every guarantee of the Constitution, and effectually renders the "military independent of and superior to the civil power"—the attempt to do which by the King of Great Britain was deemed by our fathers such an offense, that they assigned it to the world as one of the causes which impelled them to declare their independence. Civil liberty and this kind of martial law cannot endure together; the antagonism is irreconcilable and, in the conflict, one or the other must perish.

This nation, as experience has proved, cannot always remain at peace, and has no right to expect that it will always have wise and humane rulers, sincerely attached to the principles of the Constitution. Wicked men, ambitious of power, with hatred of liberty and contempt of law, may fill the place once occupied by Washington and Lincoln; and if this right is conceded, and the calamities of war again befall us, the dangers to human liberty are frightful to contemplate. If our fathers had failed to provide for just such a contingency, they would have been false to the trust reposed in them. They knew—the history of the world told them—the nation they were founding, be its existence short or long, would be involved in war; how often or how long continued, human foresight could not tell; and that unlimited power, wherever lodged at such a time, was especially hazardous to freemen. For this, and other equally weighty reasons, they secured the inheritance they had fought to maintain, by incorporating in a written Constitution the safeguards which time had proved were essential to its preservation. Not one of these safeguards can the President or Congress or the Judiciary disturb, except the one concerning the writ of habeas corpus.

It is essential to the safety of every government that, in a great crisis, like the one we have just passed through, there should be a power somewhere of suspending the writ of habeas corpus. In every war, there are men of previously good character, wicked enough to counsel their fellow citizens to resist the measures deemed necessary by a good government to sustain its just authority and overthrow its enemies; and their influence may lead to dangerous combinations. In the emergency of the times, an immediate public investigation according to law may not be possible; and yet, the peril to the country may be too imminent to suffer such persons to go at large. Unquestionably, there is then an exigency which demands that the government, if it should see fit, in the exercise of a proper discretion, to make arrests, should not be required to produce the person arrested in answer to a writ of habeas corpus. The Constitution goes no further. It does not say after a writ of habeas corpus is denied a citizen, that he shall be tried otherwise than by the course of common law. If it had intended this result, it was easy by the use of direct words to have accomplished it. The illustrious men who framed that instrument were guarding the foundations of civil liberty against the abuses of unlimited power; they were full of wisdom, and the lessons of history informed them that a trial by an established court, assisted by an impartial jury, was the only sure way of protecting the citizen against oppression and wrong. Knowing this, they limited the suspension to one great right, and left the rest to remain forever inviolable. But it is insisted that the safety of the country in time of war demands that this broad claim for martial law shall be sustained. If this were true, it could be well said that a country, preserved at the sacrifice of all the cardinal principles of liberty, is not worth the cost of preservation. Happily, it is not so.

It will be borne in mind that this is not a question of the power to proclaim martial law, when war exists in a community and the courts and civil authorities are overthrown. Nor is it a question what rule a military commander, at the head of his army, can impose on States in rebellion to cripple their resources and quell the insurrection. The jurisdiction claimed is much more extensive. The necessities of the service, during the late Rebellion, required that the loyal states should be placed within the limits of certain military districts and commanders appointed in them; and, it is urged, that this, in a military sense, constituted them the theatre of military operations; and, as in this case, Indiana had been and was again threatened with invasion by the enemy, the occasion was furnished to establish martial law. The conclusion does not follow from the premises. If armies were collected in Indiana, they were to be employed in another locality, where the laws were obstructed and the national authority disputed. On her soil there was no hostile foot; if once invaded, that invasion was at an end, and with it all pretext for martial law. Martial law cannot arise from a threatened invasion. The necessity must be actual and present; the invasion real, such as effectually closes the courts and deposes the civil administration.

It is difficult to see how the safety of the country required martial law in Indiana. If any of her citizens were plotting treason, the power of arrest could secure them, until the government was prepared for their trial, when the courts were open and ready to try them. It was as easy to protect witnesses before a civil as a military tribunal; and as there could be no wish to convict, except on sufficient legal evidence, surely an ordained and established court were better able to judge of this than a military tribunal composed of gentlemen not trained to the profession of the law.

It follows, from what has been said on this subject, that there are occasions when martial rule can be properly applied. If, in foreign invasion or civil war, the courts are actually closed, and it is impossible to administer criminal justice according to law, then, on the theatre of active military operations, where war really prevails, there is a necessity to furnish a substitute for the civil authority, thus overthrown, to preserve the safety of the army and society; and as no power is left but the military, it is allowed to govern by martial rule until the laws can have their free course. As necessity creates the rule, so it limits its duration; for, if this government is continued after the courts are reinstated, it is a gross usurpation of power. Martial rule can never exist where the courts are open, and in the proper and unobstructed exercise of their jurisdiction. It is also confined to the locality of actual war. Because, during the late Rebellion it could have been enforced in Virginia, where the national authority was overturned and the courts driven out, it does not follow that it should obtain in Indiana, where that authority was never disputed, and justice was always administered. And so in the case of a foreign invasion, martial rule may become a necessity in one state, when, in another, it would be "mere lawless violence." . . .

The two remaining questions in this case must be answered in the affirmative. The suspension of the privilege of the writ of habeas corpus does not suspend the writ itself. The writ issues as a matter of course; and on the return made to it the court decides whether the party applying is denied the right of proceeding any further with it.

If the military trial of Milligan was contrary to law, then he was entitled, on the facts stated in his petition, to be discharged from custody by the terms of the act of Congress of March 3d, 1863. The provisions of this law having been considered in a previous part of this opinion, we will not restate the views there presented. Milligan avers he was a citizen of Indiana, not in the military or naval service, and was detained in close confinement, by order of the President, from the 5th day of October, 1864, until the 2d day of January, 1865, when the circuit court for the district of Indiana, with a grand jury, convened in session at Indianapolis; and afterwards, on the 27th day of the same month, adjourned without finding an indictment or presentment against him. If these averments were true (and their truth is conceded for the purposes of this case), the court was required to liberate him on taking certain oaths prescribed by the law, and entering into recognizance for his good behavior.

But it is insisted that Milligan was a prisoner of war, and, therefore, excluded from the privileges of the statute. It is not easy to see how he can be treated as a prisoner of war, when he lived in Indiana for the past twenty years, was arrested there, and had not been, during the late troubles, a resident of any of the states in rebellion. If in Indiana he conspired with bad men to assist the enemy, he is punishable for it in the courts of Indiana; but, when tried for the offense, he cannot plead the rights of war; for he was not engaged in legal acts of hostility against the government, and only such persons, when captured, are prisoners of war. If he cannot enjoy the immunities attaching to the character of a prisoner of war, how can he be subject to their pains and penalties? . . .

Mr. Chief Justice **Chase,** for himself and Mr. Justice **Wayne,** Mr. Justice **Swayne,** and Mr. Justice **Miller,** delivered an opinion in which he differed from the Court in several important points, but concurred in the judgment in the case.

IN RE NEAGLE

135 U.S. 1; 10 S. Ct. 658; 34 L. Ed. 55 (1890)

The constitutional grants of power over foreign affairs and as Commander in Chief have always been interpreted as being independent grants to the President to make important policy decisions in these two fields, and whatever power Congress has in these areas can be delegated to the President virtually without limit. In contrast to this his duty to "take care that the laws be faithfully executed" seems a requirement that he carry out the laws of Congress. The effect of the present case is to interpret this clause, too, as a grant of policy-making authority. The laws are not merely the laws of Congress, but include independent acts of the President himself. There is, moreover, a peace of the United States, and the President, as chief executive, is protector of that peace, with power to prevent violations. It was on the President's power to "take care that the laws be faithfully executed" that Chief Justice Vinson relied in his dissent in the Steel Seizure Case (1952), but the majority of the Court gave the power a much narrower construction. The decision in the Neagle case also applies the doctrine of the supremacy of national law, discussed in McCulloch v. Maryland (1819).

The case arose out of an extraordinary set of circumstances. A long and bitter legal battle involving title to more than a million dollars had culminated in the United States circuit court in California at a time when Justice Field of the United States Supreme Court was sitting as circuit justice. The disappointed contestant was represented by her husband, a lawyer named Terry, who had once been chief justice of the California supreme court. At the close of the case Mrs. Terry accused Justice Field of selling justice, and the United States marshal was ordered to quiet her. A fight ensued and Terry and his wife went to prison for six months for contempt of court. Upon their release they threatened to kill Justice Field if he ever came back to California. Since the law at that time required Supreme Court justices to ride circuit, the matter was laid before the Attorney General; and when Field again returned to California, Neagle, a deputy marshal, was detailed to serve as a bodyguard. Terry, following up his threat, tried to make a murderous attack upon the Justice in a railroad restaurant where the Justice had stopped while traveling on circuit duty. He was about to draw his knife when Neagle shot and killed him. Neagle was promptly arrested by the local authorities and held for murder. He was released from the custody of the state court upon a writ of habeas corpus by the federal circuit court on the ground that he was held in custody for "an act done in pursuance of a law of the United States" within the meaning of the federal statute providing for the issuance of the writ in such cases.

The most significant feature of the case is that the "law of the United States" in pursuance of which Neagle acted was not an act of Congress, but merely an executive order issued by authority of the President. In sustaining Neagle's release the Court holds that the President in the exercise of the duty imposed upon him to see that the laws are faithfully executed may, without special statutory authority, appoint an officer to protect the life of a federal judge.

Mr. Justice **Miller** delivered the opinion of the Court, saying in part:

. . . Without a more minute discussion of this testimony, it produces upon us the conviction of a settled purpose on the part of Terry and his wife, amounting to a conspiracy, to murder Justice Field. And we are quite sure that if Neagle had been merely a brother or a friend of Judge Field, traveling with him, and aware of all the previous relations of Terry to the judge,—as he was,—of his bitter animosity, his declared purpose to have revenge even to the point of killing him, he would have been justified in what he did in defense of Mr. Justice Field's life, and possibly of his own.

But such a justification would be a proper subject for consideration on a trial of the case for murder in the courts of the State of California, and there exists no authority in the courts of the United States to discharge the prisoner while held in custody by the State authorities for this offense, unless there be found in aid of the defense of the prisoner some element of power and authority asserted under the government of the United States.

This element is said to be found in the facts that Mr. Justice Field, when attacked, was in the immediate discharge of his duty as judge of the circuit courts of the United States within California; that the assault upon him grew out of the animosity of Terry and wife, arising out of the previous discharge of his duty as circuit justice in the case for which they were committed for contempt of court; and that the deputy marshal of the United States, who killed Terry in defense of Field's life, was charged with a duty under the law of the United States to protect Field from the violence which Terry was inflicting, and which was intended to lead to Field's death.

To the inquiry whether this proposition is sustained by law and the facts which we have recited, we now address ourselves. . . .

We have no doubt that Mr. Justice Field when attacked by Terry was engaged in the discharge of his duties as circuit justice of the Ninth Circuit, and was entitled to all the protection under those circumstances which the law could give him.

It is urged, however, that there exists no statute authorizing any such protection as that which Neagle was instructed to give Judge Field in the present case, and indeed no protection whatever against a vindictive or malicious assault growing out of the faithful discharge of his official duties; and that the language of section 753 of the Revised Statutes, that the party seeking the benefit of the writ of habeas corpus must in this connection show that he is "in custody for an act done or omitted in pursuance of a law of the United States," makes it necessary that upon this occasion it should be shown that the act for which Neagle is imprisoned was done by virtue of an Act of Congress. It is not supposed that any special Act of Congress exists which authorizes the marshals or deputy marshals of the United States in express terms to accompany the judges of the supreme court through their circuits and act as a body-guard to them to defend them against malicious assaults against their persons. But we are of opinion that this view of the Statute is an unwarranted restriction of the meaning of a law designed to extend in a liberal manner the benefit of the writ of habeas corpus to persons imprisoned for the performance of their duty. And we are satisfied that if it was the duty of Neagle, under the circumstances, a duty which could only arise under the laws of the United States, to defend Mr. Justice Field from a murderous attack upon him, he brings himself within the meaning of the section we have recited. This view of the subject is confirmed by the alternative provision, that he must be in custody "for an act done or omitted in pursuance of a law of the United States or of an order, process or decree of a court or judge thereof, or is in custody in violation of the Constitution or of a law or treaty of the United States."

In the view we take of the Constitution of the United States, any obligation fairly and properly inferable from that instrument, or any duty of the marshal to be derived from the general scope of his duties under the laws of the United States, is "a law" within the meaning of this phrase. It would be a great reproach to the system of government of the United States, declared to be within its sphere sovereign and supreme, if there is to be found within the domain of its powers no means of protecting the judges, in the conscientious and faithful discharge of their duties, from the malice and hatred of those upon whom their judgments may operate unfavorably. . . .

Where, then, are we to look for the protection which we have shown Judge Field was entitled to when engaged in the discharge of his official duties? Not to the courts of the United States; because, as has been more than once said in this court, in the division of the powers of government between the three great departments, executive, legislative and judicial, the judicial is the weakest for the purposes of self-protection and for the enforcement of the powers which it exercises. The ministerial officers through whom its commands must be executed are marshals of the United States, and belong emphatically to the Executive Department of the government. They are appointed by the President, with the advice and consent of the Senate. They are removable from office at his pleasure. They are subjected by Act of Congress to the supervision and control of the Department of Justice, in the hands of one of the cabinet officers of the President, and their compensation is provided by Acts of Congress. The same may be said of the district attorneys of the United States, who prosecute and defend the claims of the government in the courts.

The legislative branch of the government can only protect the judicial officers by the enactment of laws for that purpose, and the argument we are now combating assumes that no such law has been passed by Congress.

If we turn to the Executive Department of the government, we find a very different condition of affairs. The Constitution, section 3, article 2, declares that the President "shall take care that the laws be faithfully executed," and he is provided with the means of fulfilling this obligation by his authority to commission all the officers of the United States, and, by and with the advice and consent of the Senate, to appoint the most important of them and to fill vacancies. He is declared to be commander-in-chief of the army and navy of the United States. The duties which are thus imposed upon him he is further enabled to perform by the recognition in the Constitution, and the creation by Acts of Congress, of executive departments, which have varied in number from four or five to seven or eight, the heads of which are familiarly called cabinet ministers. These aid him in the performance of the great duties of his office and represent him in a thousand acts to which it can hardly be supposed his personal attention is called, and thus he is enabled to fulfill the duty of his great department, expressed in the phrase that "he shall take care that the laws be faithfully executed."

Is this duty limited to the enforcement of Acts of Congress or of treaties of the United States according to their *express terms*, or does it include the rights, duties and obligations growing out of the Constitution itself, our international relations, and all the protection implied by the nature of the government under the Constitution? . . .

We cannot doubt the power of the President to take measures for the protection of a judge of one of the courts of the United States, who, while in the discharge of the duties of his office, is threatened with a personal attack which may probably result in his death, and we think it clear that where this protection is to be afforded through the civil power, the Department of Justice is the proper one to set in motion the necessary means of protection. The correspondence already recited in this opinion between the marshal of the Northern District of California, and the Attorney-General, and the district attorney of the United States for that district, although prescribing no very specific mode of affording this protection by the Attorney-General, is sufficient, we think, to warrant the marshal in taking the steps which he did take, in making the provisions which he did make, for the protection and defense of Mr. Justice Field.

But there is positive law investing the marshals and their deputies with powers which not only justify what Marshal Neagle did in this matter, but which imposed it upon him as a duty. In chapter fourteen of the Revised Statutes of the United States, which is devoted to the appointment and duties of the district attorneys, marshals and clerks of the courts of the United States, section 788 declares:

"The marshals and their deputies shall have, in each State, the same powers, in executing the laws of the United States, as the sheriffs and their deputies in such State may have, by law, in executing the laws thereof."

If, therefore, a sheriff of the State of California was authorized to do in regard to the laws of California what Neagle did, that is, if he was authorized to keep the peace, to protect a judge from assault and murder, then Neagle was authorized to do the same thing in reference to the laws of the United States. . . .

That there is a peace of the United States; that a man assaulting a judge of the United States while in the discharge of his duties violates that peace; that in such case the marshal of the United States stands in the same relation to the peace of the United States which the sheriff of the county does to the peace of the State of California; are questions too clear to need argument to prove them. That it would be the duty of a sheriff, if one had been present at this assault by Terry upon Judge Field, to prevent this breach of the peace, to prevent this assault, to prevent the murder which was contemplated by it, cannot be doubted. And if, in performing this duty, it became necessary for the protection of Judge Field, or of himself, to kill Terry, in a case where, like this, it was evidently a question of the choice of who should be killed, the assailant and violator of the law and disturber of the peace, or the unoffending man who was in his power, there can be no question of the authority of the sheriff to have killed Terry. So the marshal of the United States, charged with the duty of protecting and guarding the judge of the United States court against this special assault upon his person and his life, being present at the critical moment, when prompt action was necessary, found it to be his duty, a duty which he had no liberty to refuse to perform, to take the steps which resulted in Terry's death. This duty was imposed on him by the section of the Revised Statutes which we have recited, in connection with the powers conferred by the State of California upon its peace officers, which become, by this statute, in proper cases, transferred as duties to the marshals of the United States. . . .

The result at which we have arrived upon this examination is, that in the protection of the person and the life of Mr. Justice Field while in the discharge of his official duties, Neagle was authorized to resist the attack of Terry upon him; that Neagle was correct in the belief that without prompt action on his part the assault of Terry upon the judge would have ended in the death of the latter; that such being his well-founded belief, he was justified in taking the life of Terry, as the only means of preventing the death of the man who was intended to be his victim; that in taking the life of Terry, under the circumstances, he was acting under the authority of the law of the United States, and was justified in so doing; and that he is not liable to answer in the courts of California on account of his part in that transaction.

We therefore affirm the judgment of the Circuit Court authorizing his discharge from the custody of the sheriff of San Joaquin County.

Mr. Justice **Lamar** delivered a dissenting opinion in which Mr. Chief Justice **Fuller** concurred. Mr. Justice **Field** did not sit in this case.

YOUNGSTOWN SHEET & TUBE COMPANY v. SAWYER

343 U. S. 579; 72 S. Ct. 863; 96 L. Ed. 1153 (1952)

The President exercises the bulk of his policy-making powers under delegations of authority made to him by Congress. But there are important areas in which he enjoys powers granted not by Congress but by the Constitution itself. One such grant is found in Article II which makes the President the Commander in Chief of the Army and Navy. This is clearly not a power merely to command the disposition of the armed forces. But if it is more than that, how much more? A democratic distrust of executive power cannot alter the fact that in times of war a near-dictatorship may be necessary to preserve the nation. In such times Congress has wisely delegated vast areas of authority to the President. But where Congress has not done so, and the President has felt that the emergency justified it, he has often acted on his own authority. The fact that Congress usually gives belated approval to such executive acts hardly obscures the fact that the crucial policy decisions are made by the executive.

The Constitution gives Congress the power to declare war; but may the President on his own authority decide that a state of war exists, and on the strength of this decision take action affecting the lives and property of American citizens? Following the firing upon Fort Sumter in 1861, President Lincoln declared the existence of a state of insurrection and called out the militia. Authority to do this had been given him by Congress, and the Court had held in Martin v. Mott (1827) that vesting of this discretion in the President was valid. But a week after Sumter the President, acting wholly on his own authority, declared a naval blockade of the Confederate ports. Pursuant to this proclamation four blockade runners were captured and condemned. The Court sustained this action in the Prize Cases (1863), pointing out that "if a war be made by invasion of a foreign nation, the President is not only authorized but bound to resist force, by force. He does not initiate the war, but is bound to accept the challenge without waiting for any special legislative authority. And whether the hostile party be a foreign invader, or States organized in rebellion, it is none the less a war. . . ." The proclamation of a blockade was held "itself, official and conclusive evidence to the court that a state of war existed which demanded and authorized a recourse to such a measure, under the circumstances peculiar to the case."

Even the most drastic and dictatorial exercises of power by the President acting under his authority as Commander in Chief have usually not resulted in clarifying or determining the actual constitutional scope of pure executive power. This is because Congress in nearly all such cases has hastened to shore up the President's authority by legislative ratification of what he has done. Thus when Congress came into session on July 4, 1861, it underwrote the President's blockade of Southern ports by passing an act "approving, legalizing and making valid all the acts, proclamations, and orders of the President, & c., as if they had been issued and done under the previous express authority and direction of the Congress. . . ." In 1944, following the issue of the executive order creating military districts from which persons of Japanese ancestry were excluded (see Korematsu v. United States, 1944), Congress made it a crime to "enter, remain in, leave, or commit any act in any military area . . . prescribed [by executive order] . . . contrary to the order of the Secretary of War or any such military commander. . . ."

In September 1940, the President, by executive agreement with Great Britain, traded fifty old destroyers for the right to build air bases on certain British islands in the Caribbean. The constitutionality of this move was widely argued, since it is Congress which possesses the power to dispose of the property of the United States. The action was never challenged in the courts, as indeed it scarcely could have been since no one was "injured," and Congress gave its silent approval by appropriating money to build the air bases. While it is clear that presidential discretion alone initiated the agreement, the implied ratification of the agreement by Congress tends to provide a measure of delegated authority and thus prevents a clear test of inherent presidential power. It was the extent of this inherent power that was tested in the Steel Seizure Case printed below.

This case climaxed a long dispute between the steel companies and the steel workers. On December 18, 1951, the United Steel Workers of America, CIO, gave notice that it would strike on December 31. The Federal Mediation and Conciliation Service failed to effect a settlement. The Federal Wage Stabilization Board, to which President Truman referred the dispute on December 22, also failed. The President did not invoke the provisions of the Taft-Hartley Act, which would have set up a "period of waiting" before a strike. On April 4, 1952, the union announced that it would call a nationwide strike on April 9. A few hours before the strike was to begin the President directed Secretary of Commerce Sawyer to seize and operate most of the country's steel mills. The Secretary issued the appropriate orders. The President reported the seizure to Congress on April 9, and again on April 21, but Congress took no action. The steel companies complied under protest with the seizure order, but sought a temporary injunction to restrain the government's action. On April 30, the district court of the District of Columbia issued a preliminary injunction, which was stayed on the same day by the court of appeals. On May 3, the Supreme Court, bypassing the court of appeals, brought the case to its docket by certiorari. It heard argument on May 12, and decided the case on June 2. These dates indicate the celerity with which the Supreme Court can act when the national interest requires speed.

The difficulty and complexity of the case is shown by the fact that the Court divided six to three, and that seven justices wrote separate opinions, totaling 128 pages. The Court did not face here the naked question of the President's power to seize the steel plants in the absence of any congressional enactments or expressions of policy. Congress had provided limited powers of seizure in the Selective Service Act of 1948 and in the Defense Production Act of 1950. Furthermore, in its debates on the Taft-Hartley Act of 1947 Congress had considered an amendment authorizing seizure of plants by the President in case of a strike, and had rejected it. In fact, over a period of years, Congress had made it clear that the seizure of private property in time of emergency was a problem to be controlled by congressional policy. For a variety of reasons, the majority of the Court found that this legislative occupation of the field made untenable the President's claim of authority to seize the plants as an exercise of inherent executive power or as Commander in Chief. Congress had set up various procedures for the President to follow in such cases, and he had not followed them.

On November 4, 1979, Iranian radicals, demanding the return of the deposed Shah, took hostage fifty-three members of the American embassy in Tehran. President Carter refused to return the Shah, ordered frozen all Iranian assets in the United States, and nullified all claims against such assets including some still in the process of litigation. Fourteen months later the hostages were released in exchange for the return of the assets to Iran. In Dames & Moore v. Regan (1981) the Court upheld the presidential seizure. It distinguished the Youngstown case, noting that "from the history of acquiescence in executive claims settlement—we conclude that the President was authorized to suspend pending claims. . . ."

Mr. Justice **Black** delivered the opinion of the Court, saying in part:

We are asked to decide whether the President was acting within his constitutional power when he issued an order directing the Secretary of Commerce to take possession of and operate most of the Nation's steel mills. The mill owners argue that the President's order amounts to lawmaking, a legislative function which the Constitution has expressly confided to the Congress and not to the President. The Government's position is that the order was made on findings of the President that his action was necessary to avert a national catastrophe which would inevitably result from a stoppage of steel production, and that in meeting this grave emergency the President was acting within the aggregate of his constitutional powers as the Nation's Chief Executive and the Commander in Chief of the Armed Forces of the United States. . . .

The President's power, if any, to issue the order must stem either from an act of Congress or from the Constitution itself. There is no statute that expressly authorizes the President to take possession of property as he did here. Nor is there any act of Congress to which our attention has been directed from which such a power can fairly be implied. Indeed, we do not understand the Government to rely on statutory authorization for this seizure. There are two statutes which do authorize the President to take both personal and real property under certain conditions. [The Selective Service Act of 1948 and the Defense Production Act of 1950.] However, the Government admits that these conditions were not met and that the President's order was not rooted in either of the statutes. The Government refers to the seizure provisions of one of these statutes (§ 201 (b) of the Defense Production Act) as "much too cumbersome, involved, and time-consuming for the crisis which was at hand."

Moreover, the use of the seizure technique to solve labor disputes in order to prevent work stoppages was not only unauthorized by any congressional enactment; prior to this controversy, Congress had refused to adopt that method of settling labor disputes. When the Taft-Hartley Act was under consideration in 1947, Congress rejected an amendment which would have authorized such governmental seizures in cases of emergency. Apparently it was thought that the technique of seizure, like that of compulsory arbitration, would interfere with the process of collective bargaining. Consequently, the plan Congress adopted in that Act did not provide for seizure under any circumstances. Instead, the plan sought to bring about settlements by use of the customary devices of mediation, conciliation, investigation by boards of inquiry, and public reports. In some instances temporary injunctions were authorized to provide cooling-off periods. All this failing, unions were left free to strike after a secret vote by employees as to whether they wished to accept their employers' final settlement offer.

It is clear that if the President had authority to issue the order he did, it must be found in some provisions of the Constitution. And it is not claimed that express constitutional language grants this power to the President. The contention is that presidential power should be implied from the aggregate of his powers under the Constitution. Particular reliance is placed on provisions in Article II which say that "The executive Power shall be vested in a President . . ."; that "he shall take Care that the Laws be faithfully executed;" and that he "shall be Commander in Chief of the Army and Navy of the United States."

The order cannot properly be sustained as an exercise of the President's military power as Commander in Chief of the Armed Forces. The Government attempts to do so by citing a number of cases upholding broad powers in military commanders engaged in day-to-day fighting in a theater of war. Such cases need not concern us here. Even though "theater of war" be an expanding concept, we cannot with faithfulness to our constitutional system hold that the Commander in Chief of the Armed Forces has the ultimate power as such to take possession of private property in order to keep labor disputes from stopping production. This is a job for the Nation's lawmakers, not for its military authorities.

Nor can the seizure order be sustained because of the several constitutional provisions that grant executive power to the President. In the framework of our Constitution the President's power to see that the laws are faithfully executed refutes the idea that he is to be a lawmaker. The Constitution limits his functions in the lawmaking process to the recommending of laws he thinks wise and the vetoing of laws he thinks bad. And the Constitution is neither silent nor equivocal about who shall make laws which the President is to execute. The first section of the first article says that "All legislative Powers herein granted shall be vested in a Congress of the United States." . . .

The President's order does not direct that a congressional policy be executed in a manner prescribed by Congress—it directs that a presidential policy be executed in a manner prescribed by the President. The preamble of the order itself, like that of many statutes, sets out reasons why the President believes certain policies should be adopted, proclaims these policies as rules of conduct to be followed, and again, like a statute, authorizes a government official to promulgate additional rules and regulations consistent with the policy proclaimed and needed to carry that policy into execution. The power of Congress to adopt such public policies as those proclaimed by the order is beyond question. It can authorize the taking of private property for public use. It can make laws regulating the relationships between employers and employees, prescribing rules designed to settle labor disputes, and fixing wages and working conditions in certain fields of our economy. The Constitution did not subject this lawmaking power of Congress to presidential or military supervision or control.

It is said that other Presidents without congressional authority have taken possession of private business enterprises in order to settle labor disputes. But even if this be true, Congress has not thereby lost its exclusive constitutional authority to make laws necessary and proper to carry out the powers vested by the Constitution "in the Government of the United States, or any Department or Officer thereof."

The Founders of this Nation entrusted the lawmaking power to the Congress alone in both good and bad times. It would do no good to recall the historical events, the fears of power and the hopes for freedom that lay behind their choice. Such a review would but confirm our holding that this seizure order cannot stand.

The judgment of the District Court is
Affirmed.

Mr. Justice **Frankfurter,** concurring with the judgment and opinion of the Court, said in part:

Apart from his vast share of responsibility for the conduct of our foreign relations, the embracing function of the President is that "he shall take Care that the Laws be faithfully executed. . . ." Art. II, § 3. The nature of that authority has for me been comprehensively indicated by Mr. Justice Holmes. "The duty of the President to see that the laws be executed is a duty that does not go beyond the laws or require him to achieve more than Congress sees fit to leave within his power." Myers v.

United States [1926]. The powers of the President are not as particularized as are those of Congress. But unenumerated powers do not mean undefined powers. The separation of powers built into our Constitution gives essential content to undefined provisions in the frame of our government. . . .

A scheme of government like ours no doubt at times feels the lack of power to act with complete, all-embracing, swiftly moving authority. No doubt a government with distributed authority, subject to be challenged in the courts of law, at least long enough to consider and adjudicate the challenge, labors under restrictions from which other governments are free. It has not been our tradition to envy such governments. In any event our government was designed to have such restrictions. The price was deemed not too high in view of the safeguards which these restrictions afford. . . .

Mr. Justice **Douglas,** concurring with the judgment and opinion of the Court, said in part:

There can be no doubt that the emergency which caused the President to seize these steel plants was one that bore heavily on the country. But the emergency did not create power; it merely marked an occasion when power should be exercised. And the fact that it was necessary that measures be taken to keep steel in production does not mean that the President, rather than the Congress, had the constitutional authority to act. The Congress, as well as the President, is trustee of the national welfare. The President can act more quickly than the Congress. The President with the armed services at his disposal can move with force as well as with speed. All executive power—from the reign of ancient kings to the rule of modern dictators—has the outward appearance of efficiency.

Legislative power, by contrast, is slower to exercise. There must be delay while the ponderous machinery of committees, hearings, and debates is put into motion. That takes time; and while the Congress slowly moves into action, the emergency may take its toll in wages, consumer goods, war production, the standard of living of the people, and perhaps even lives. Legislative action may indeed often be cumbersome, time-consuming, and apparently inefficient. But as Mr. Justice Brandeis stated in his dissent in Myers v. United States:

"The doctrine of the separation of powers was adopted by the Convention of 1787, not to promote efficiency but to preclude the exercise of arbitrary power. The purpose was, not to avoid friction, but, by means of the inevitable friction incident to the distribution of the governmental powers among three departments, to save the people from autocracy."

We therefore cannot decide this case by determining which branch of government can deal most expeditiously with the present crisis. The answer must depend on the allocation of powers under the Constitution. That in turn requires an analysis of the conditions giving rise to the seizure and of the seizure itself. . . .

The great office of President is not a weak and powerless one. The President represents the people and is their spokesman in domestic and foreign affairs. The office is respected more than any other in the land. It gives a position of leadership that is unique. The power to formulate policies and mould opinion inheres in the Presidency and conditions our national life. The impact of the man and the philosophy he represents may at times be thwarted by the Congress. Stalemates may occur when emergencies mount and the Nation suffers for lack of harmonious, reciprocal action between the White House and Capitol Hill. That is a risk inherent in our system of separation of powers. The tragedy of such stalemates might be avoided by allowing the President the use of some legislative authority. The Framers with memories of the tyrannies produced by a blending of executive and legislative power rejected that political arrangement. Some future generation may, however, deem it so urgent that the President have legislative authority that the Constitution will be amended. We could not sanction the seizure and condemnations of the steel plants in this case without reading Article 2 as giving the President not only the power to execute the laws but to make some. Such a step would most assuredly alter the pattern of the Constitution.

We pay a price for our system of checks and balances, for the distribution of power among the three branches of government. It is a price that today may seem exorbitant to many. Today a kindly President uses the seizure power to effect a wage increase and to keep the steel furnaces in production. Yet tomorrow another President might use the same power to prevent a wage increase, to curb trade-unionists, to regiment labor as oppressively as industry thinks it has been regimented by this seizure.

Mr. Justice **Jackson,** concurring in the judgment and opinion of the Court, said in part:

That seems to be the logic of an argument tendered at our bar—that the President having, on his own responsibility, sent American troops abroad derives from that act "affirmative power" to seize the means of producing a supply of steel for them. . . .

I cannot foresee all that it might entail if the Court should indorse this argument. Nothing in our Constitution is plainer than that declaration of a war is entrusted only to Congress. Of course, a state of war may in fact exist without a formal declaration. But no doctrine that the Court could promulgate would seem to me more sinister and alarming than that a President whose conduct of foreign affairs is so largely uncontrolled, and often even is unknown, can vastly enlarge his mastery over the internal affairs of the country by his own commitment of the Nation's armed forces to some foreign venture. . . .

The Solicitor General lastly grounds support of the seizure upon nebulous, inherent powers never expressly granted but said to have accrued to the office from the customs and claims of preceding administrations. The plea is for a resulting power to deal with a crisis or an emergency according to the necessities of the case, the unarticulated assumption being that necessity knows no law. . . .

The appeal, however, that we declare the existence of inherent powers ex necessitate to meet an emergency asks us to do what many think would be wise, although it is something the forefathers omitted. They knew what emergencies were, knew the pressures they engender for authoritative action, knew, too, how they afford a ready pretext for usurpation. We may also suspect that they suspected that emergency powers would tend to kindle emergencies. . . .

In the practical working of our Government we already have evolved a technique within the framework of the Constitution by which normal executive powers may be considerably expanded to meet an emergency. Congress may and has granted extraordinary authorities which lie dormant in normal times but may be called into play by the Executive in war or upon proclamation of a national emergency. In 1939, upon congressional request, the Attorney General listed ninety-nine such separate statutory grants by Congress of emergency or wartime executive powers. They were invoked from time to time as need appeared. Under this procedure we retain Government by law—special, temporary law, perhaps, but law nonetheless. The public may know the extent and limitations of the powers that can be asserted, and persons affected may be informed from the statute of their rights and duties.

In view of the ease, expedition and safety with which Congress can grant and has granted large emergency powers, certainly ample to embrace this crisis, I am quite unimpressed with the argument that we should affirm possession of them without statute. Such power either has no beginning or it has no end. If it exists, it need submit to no legal restraint. I am not alarmed that it would plunge us straightway into dictatorship, but it is at least a step in that wrong direction. . . .

But I have no illusion that any decision by this Court can keep power in the hands of Congress if it is not wise and timely in meeting its problems. A crisis that challenges the President equally, or perhaps primarily, challenges Congress. If not good law, there was worldly wisdom in the maxim attributed to Napoleon that "The tools belong to the man who can use them." We may say that power to legislate for emergencies belongs in the hands of Congress, but only Congress itself can prevent power from slipping through its fingers.

The essence of our free Government is "leave to live by no man's leave, underneath the law"—to be governed by those impersonal forces which we call law. Our Government is fashioned to fulfill this concept so far as humanly possible. The Executive, except for recommendation and veto, has no legislative power. The executive action we have here originates in the individual will of the President and represents an exercise of authority without law. No one, perhaps not even the President, knows the limits of the power he may seek to exert in this instance and the parties affected cannot learn the limit of their rights. We do not know today what powers over labor or property would be claimed to flow from Government possession if we should legalize it, what rights to compensation would be claimed or recognized, or on what contingency it would end. With all its defects, delays and inconveniences, men have discovered no technique for long preserving free government except that the Executive be under the law, and that the law be made by parliamentary deliberations.

Such institutions may be destined to pass away. But it is the duty of the Court to be last, not first, to give them up.

Mr. Justice **Burton,** concurring in the opinion and judgment of the Court, said in part:

. . . In the case before us, Congress authorized a procedure which the President declined to follow. Instead, he followed another procedure which he hoped might eliminate the need for the first. Upon its failure, he issued an executive order to seize the steel properties in the face of the reserved right of Congress to adopt or reject that course as a matter of legislative policy.

This brings us to a further crucial question. Does the President, in such a situation, have inherent constitutional power to seize private property which makes congressional action in relation thereto unnecessary? We find no such power available to him under the present circumstances. The present situation is not comparable to that of an imminent invasion or threatened attack. We do not face the issue of what might be the President's constitutional power to meet such catastrophic situations. Nor is it claimed that the current seizure is in the nature of a military command addressed by the President, as Commander-in-Chief, to a mobilized nation waging, or imminently threatened with, total war.

The controlling fact here is that Congress, within its constitutionally delegated power, has prescribed for the President specific procedures, exclusive of seizure, for his use in meeting the present type of emergency. Congress has reserved to itself the right to determine where and when to authorize the seizure of property in meeting such an emergency. Under these circumstances, the President's order of April 8 invaded the jurisdiction of Congress. It violated the essence of the principle of the separation of governmental powers. Accordingly, the injunction against its effectiveness should be sustained.

Mr. Justice **Clark,** concurring in the judgment of the Court, said in part:

. . . In my view . . . the Constitution does grant to the President extensive authority in times of grave and imperative national emergency. In fact, to my thinking, such a grant may well be necessary to the very existence of the Constitution itself. As Lincoln aptly said, "[is] it possible to lose the nation and yet preserve the Constitution?" In describing this authority I care not whether one calls it "residual," "inherent," "moral," "implied," "aggregate," "emergency," or otherwise. . . .

I conclude that where Congress has laid down specific procedures to deal with the type of crisis confronting the President, he must follow those procedures in meeting the crisis; but that in the absence of such action by Congress, the President's independent power to act depends upon the gravity of the situation confronting the nation. I cannot sustain the seizure in question because here . . . Congress had prescribed methods to be followed by the President in meeting the emergency at hand. . . .

. . . The Government made no effort to comply with the procedures established by the Selective Service Act of 1948, a statute which expressly authorizes seizures when producers fail to supply necessary defense matèriel. . . .

Mr. Chief Justice Vinson, with whom Justices **Reed** and **Minton** joined, dissented, saying in part:

Focusing now on the situation confronting the President on the night of April 8, 1952, we cannot but conclude that the President was performing his duty under the Constitution ''to take Care that the Laws be faithfully executed''—a duty described by President Benjamin Harrison as ''the central idea of the office.''

The President reported to Congress the morning after the seizure that he acted because a work stoppage in steel production would immediately imperil the safety of the Nation by preventing execution of the legislative programs for procurement of military equipment. And, while a shutdown could be averted by granting the price concessions requested by plaintiffs, granting such concessions would disrupt the price stabilization program also enacted by Congress. Rather than fail to execute either legislative program, the President acted to execute both.

Much of the argument in this case has been directed at straw men. We do not now have before us the case of a President acting solely on the basis of his own notions of the public welfare. Nor is there any question of unlimited executive power in this case. The President himself closed the door to any such claim when he sent his Message to Congress stating his purpose to abide by any action of Congress, whether approving or disapproving his seizure action. Here, the President immediately made sure that Congress was fully informed of the temporary action he had taken only to preserve the legislative programs from destruction until Congress could act.

The absence of a specific statute authorizing seizure of the steel mills as a mode of executing the laws—both the military procurement program and the anti-inflation program—has not until today been thought to prevent the President from executing the laws. Unlike an administrative commission confined to the enforcement of the statute under which it was created, or the head of a department when administering a particular statute, the President is a constitutional officer charged with taking care that a ''mass of legislation'' be executed. Flexibility as to mode of execution to meet critical situations is a matter of practical necessity. . . .

As the District Judge stated, this is no time for ''timorous'' judicial action. But neither is this a time for timorous executive action. Faced with the duty of executing the defense programs which Congress had enacted and the disastrous effects that any stoppage in steel production would have on those programs, the President acted to preserve those programs by seizing the steel mills. There is no question that the possession was other than temporary in character and subject to congressional direction—either approving, disapproving or regulating the manner in which the mills were to be administered and returned to the owners. The President immediately informed Congress of his action and clearly stated his intention to abide by the legislative will. No basis for claims of arbitrary action, unlimited powers or dictatorial usurpation of congressional power appears from the facts of this case. On the contrary, judicial, legislative and executive precedents throughout our history demonstrate that in this case the President acted in full conformity with his duties under the Constitution. Accordingly, we would reverse the order of the District Court.

UNITED STATES v. NIXON

418 U. S. 683; 94 S. Ct. 3090; 41 L. Ed. 2d 1039
(1974)

In setting up a government based on the separation of powers, the framers deliberately devised a form in which authority was divided and policies would necessarily be made as a result of compromise rather than by a single person or body. Given what they viewed as a choice between ''liberty'' and ''tyranny,'' they opted for liberty, but the decision to sacrifice speed and efficiency for debate and compromise was perhaps easier to make then than it would be now. The image of George III and the teachings of Montesquieu were fresh in their minds, government played a minimal role in people's lives, and the slowness of communications made quick decisions less important than they are today.

Since the turn of the century, and especially in the last forty years, all this has changed dramatically. The role of government has grown until it is the dominant force in people's lives, the world has shrunk until the most distant part is only a few hours away, the specter of George III has been relegated to the pages of history, and effective policy-making power has been steadily shifted to the President. With the new pace of the world and our intimate involvement in the affairs of other countries, the frustration and delays imposed by the separation of powers seem barely tolerable. Although given virtually dictatorial powers, presidents like Lincoln and Franklin Roosevelt had not betrayed the public trust and that kind of presidency seemed essential to the effectiveness of the United States in that area of world politics upon which our national safety depended. Demands for more government and more efficiency were inexorable and few people saw in them a threat to essential democratic values. The choice made by the framers seemed scarcely relevant.

Against this background it is easy to view Water-gate as a turn in destiny—a Gilbert and Sullivan operetta played to awaken us to our danger. For it is hard to imagine a more improbable plot in which to set a crucial test of presidential power. Any competent writer of fiction could do better. On June 17, 1972, seven men were caught breaking into the Democratic National Committee headquarters in the Watergate, a luxury apartment-office complex a few blocks from the White House. (The reasons for the break-in are still obscure.) Instead of immediately admitting White House involvement in the affair with an apology for the enthusiasm of his followers (a course which he could almost certainly have survived politically), the President and his staff undertook the bizarre and dramatically ill-fated "Watergate cover-up." The outcome was the resignation, on August 9, 1974, of the President of the United States.

The burglary itself was the culmination of some three years of White House-directed investigation and harassment of political enemies, sparked in part by leaks to the press of the secret bombing of Cambodia and the "Pentagon Papers," and in part by a growing fear that President Nixon might not be reelected in 1972. A successful entry into the Democratic National Committee headquarters the month before had netted nothing of value, and this entry was apparently for the purpose of placing additional electronic bugging equipment.

Five of the "Watergate Seven" pleaded guilty to the burglary and the other two, both members of the Committee to Reelect the President, were convicted. While the upshot of the trial was to suggest that Watergate was merely the work of a few enthusiastic but misguided underlings whose intense loyalty to the President had led them into illegal activities, something about the trial itself belied this conclusion. At its close the presiding judge, John J. Sirica, stated that in his opinion the entire truth had not come out, and on the day of the sentencing he read in court a letter from James W. McCord, Jr., one of those convicted, stating that others involved in the break-in had not been prosecuted, that there had been perjury during the trial, and that pressure had been brought on him and others to plead guilty and keep silent.

A shocked Senate investigating committee heard McCord's story; then called John W. Dean III, a former counsel to the President. Dean testified for a week, explaining how the White House staff, and ultimately the President, had congratulated him on successfully limiting the case to the few who had been tried and discussed with him the question of executive clemency and hush money for some of them. He said the President had known of the White House involvement almost from the beginning and had been actively involved in permitting the cover-up to continue. Implicated by Dean's testimony were former Attorney General John Mitchell and top presidential aides H. R. Haldeman and John Ehrlichman. White House denials raised the question: Who was telling the truth?

The present constitutional issue appeared with the startling disclosure that presidential conversations for the previous two years had been recorded on tape including, apparently, those crucial conversations with John Dean. Since it seemed the credibility issue could thus be easily resolved, an immediate demand was made for the tapes; but the President, citing the separation of powers and the absolute right of the President to keep his conversations confidential, refused to release them either to the Senate committee or to Archibald Cox, the special prosecutor heading the government's investigation of the matter.

There the issue was joined. Judge Sirica, after hearing argument in August of 1973, ordered the President to turn the tapes over to Cox. (He declined to enforce the Senate committee's subpoena for want of jurisdiction.) He conceded that executive privilege did exist, but denied "that it is the Executive that finally determines whether its privilege is properly invoked. . . . Judicial control over the evidence in a case cannot be abdicated to the caprice of executive officers." Nor was he persuaded by the argument based on the separation of powers. Whatever the merits of Mississippi v. Johnson (1867), it would be unrealistic to argue since Youngstown Sheet and Tube Co. v. Sawyer (1952) that compulsory court process cannot touch the White House. "In all candor," he added, "the court fails to perceive any reason for suspending the power of courts to get evidence and rule on questions of privilege in criminal matters simply because it is the President of the United States who holds the evidence." He ordered the tapes turned over to him for in-camera inspection with the understanding that unprivileged portions would be made available to the grand jury. After an abortive effort to get the two parties to compromise, the court of appeals sustained Judge Sirica's order; Nixon v. Sirica, 487 Fed. 2d 700 (1973).

Despite a widespread assumption that the President would seek from the Supreme Court that "definitive decision" by which he had announced he would abide, he instead decided to avoid a "constitutional crisis" by declining to appeal the decision and ordered Cox, as "an employee of the executive branch," not to pursue the matter further. Declining to follow the court's order, he proposed instead to provide White House "summaries" of the tapes. Cox rejected the offer, and on October 20, in what has become known as the "Saturday Night Massacre," the President accepted the resignation of Attorney General Elliot Richardson when he refused to fire Cox, then fired Deputy Attorney General Ruckelshaus when he refused to fire Cox, and finally persuaded Solicitor General Robert H. Bork to fire Cox and his staff of ninety investigators.

Three days later, bowing to a "fire storm" of public protest and the start of formal impeachment proceedings in the House of Representatives, the President agreed to turn over the tapes themselves. By the end of the week Leon Jaworski, a former head of the American Bar Association, had been chosen as the new special prosecutor and was assured even more independence than Cox had enjoyed. (To assure the independence of prosecutors chosen to investigate malfeasance in the ex-

ecutive branch, Congress in 1978 passed the Ethics in Government Act discussed in the note to Buckley v. Valeo, below.)

Although two of the nine tapes ordered released turned out to be missing, and one had an unexplained eighteen-minute gap in it, enough was produced to clinch the indictments of seven more conspirators, including Mitchell, Haldeman, and Ehrlichman, on charges of conspiring to obstruct justice. On Jaworski's advice that a sitting president could not be indicted, President Nixon was named merely as an "unindicted co-conspirator." On order of Judge Sirica the grand jury evidence, including the tapes Jaworski had received, was turned over to the House Judiciary Committee for use in its impeachment investigation.

But the constitutional confrontation was not over. The House committee subpoenaed forty-two more conversations and Jaworski sixty-four, but the President refused to yield and instead made public some 1200 pages of White House-edited transcripts—among them some which had already been released under court order. The public response to this brutally candid glimpse of the workings of the Nixon presidency was one of horrified shock, and demands for his impeachment became overwhelming. If he would release this kind of material, the argument ran, what was he concealing?

In a last-ditch stand the President not only elected to carry Jaworski's subpoena to the Supreme Court, but to protest his being named an unindicted co-conspirator (a point later dismissed by the Court). Over the objection of the President, the Court agreed to by-pass the court of appeals and hear argument in the closing days of its term. The President, in a series of procedural maneuvers, argued that no case or controversy existed, since the dispute between the President and Jaworski was entirely within the executive branch and the President could decide what evidence he wanted to present in prosecuting a case. The Court, in the case below, rejected this argument on the ground that Jaworski had been given freedom to ask for just such information, that the President had promised him complete freedom to pursue in court any interference by the executive, and this was, in fact, "the kind of controversy courts traditionally resolve."

It is important to note that President Nixon did not claim executive privilege from the tapes on the ground that they contained material involving either military or diplomatic matters. He claimed, rather, that all personal presidential conversations with his aides were privileged because without the assurance of such confidentiality the President could not get the uninhibited advice he needed and the presidency would thus be weakened. It was, in effect, a claim that the sanctity of the presidency was the highest constitutional value, and it was this claim that the Court rejected in the present case.

The President's last constitutional crisis came in the wake of the Court's decision. In 1832, following the Supreme Court's decision in Worcester v. Georgia, President Andrew Jackson is reputed to have said,

"John Marshall has made his decision, now let him enforce it." The realization that the court has no enforcement machinery at its command must make such a response a tempting one, and President Nixon, who alone knew what the tapes contained, reputedly agonized a whole day over the question whether or not to defy the Supreme Court. But wiser counsel prevailed and he agreed to comply with the Court's order.

Within a week of the Court's decision, while arguing whether to wait for the contents of the tapes, the House Judiciary Committee voted three articles of impeachment against the President. And President Nixon, even as he began complying with the Court order to release the tapes, elected to release transcripts of three of them which showed that he had known about the Watergate break-in from the beginning. With his concession that he had from the outset lied not only to his supporters in Congress, but even to his own lawyer, those on the judiciary committee who had argued that the President should not be impeached changed their minds. Next morning three members of the congressional leadership visited the President to tell him he could count on no more than 10 votes in the House against impeachment and no more than 15 votes in the Senate against removal. That night, in a television broadcast to the nation, President Nixon resigned his office, effective the following noon.

Mr. Chief Justice **Burger** delivered the opinion of the Court, saying in part:

IV. The Claim of Privilege

A.

Having determined that the requirements of Rule 17(c) were satisfied, we turn to the claim that the subpoena should be quashed because it demands "confidential conversations between a President and his close advisors that it would be inconsistent with the public interest to produce." The first contention is a broad claim that the separation of powers doctrine precludes judicial review of a President's claim of privilege. The second contention is that if he does not prevail on the claim of absolute privilege, the court should hold as a matter of constitutional law that the privilege prevails over the subpoena duces tecum.

In the performance of assigned constitutional duties each branch of the Government must initially interpret the Constitution, and the interpretation of its powers by any branch is due great respect from the others. The President's counsel, as we have noted, reads the Constitution as providing an absolute privilege of confidentiality for all Presidential communications. Many decisions of this Court, however, have unequivocally reaffirmed the holding of Marbury v. Madison (1803) that "[i]t is emphatically the province and duty of the judicial department to say what the law is."

No holding of the Court has defined the scope of judicial power specifically relating to the enforcement of a subpoena for confidential Presidential communications for use in a criminal prosecution, but other exercises of power by the Executive Branch and the Legislative Branch have been found invalid as in conflict with the Constitution. Powell v. McCormack (1969); Youngstown Sheet & Tube Co. v. Sawyer (1952). In a series of cases, the Court interpreted the explicit immunity conferred by express provisions of the Constitution on Members of the House and Senate by the Speech or Debate Clause, U. S. Const. Art. I, § 6. Doe v. McMillan (1973); Gravel v. United States (1972). . . . Since this Court has consistently exercised the power to construe and delineate claims arising under express powers, it must follow that the Court has authority to interpret claims with respect to powers alleged to derive from enumerated powers.

Our system of government "requires that federal courts on occasion interpret the Constitution in a manner at variance with the construction given the document by another branch." Powell v. McCormack. And in Baker v. Carr [1962], the Court stated: "Deciding whether a matter has in any measure been committed by the Constitution to another branch of government, or whether the action of that branch exceeds whatever authority has been committed, is itself a delicate exercise in constitutional interpretation, and is a responsibility of this Court as ultimate interpreter of the Constitution." Notwithstanding the deference each branch must accord the others, the "judicial Power of the United States" vested in the federal courts by Art. III, § 1, of the Constitution can no more be shared with the Executive Branch than the Chief Executive, for example, can share with the Judiciary the veto power, or the Congress share with the Judiciary the power to override a Presidential veto. Any other conclusion would be contrary to the basic concept of separation of powers and the checks and balances that flow from the scheme of a tripartite government. . . . We therefore reaffirm that it is the province and duty of this Court "to say what the law is" with respect to the claim of privilege presented in this case. Marbury v. Madison.

B.

In support of his claim of absolute privilege, the President's counsel urges two grounds, one of which is common to all governments and one of which is peculiar to our system of separation of powers. The first ground is the valid need for protection of communications between high Government officials and those who advise and assist them in the performance of their manifold duties; the importance of this confidentiality is too plain to require further discussion. Human experience teaches that those who expect public dissemination of their remarks may well temper candor with a concern for appearances and for their own interests to the detriment of the decision-making process.* Whatever the nature of the privilege of confidentiality of Presidential communications in the exercise of Art. II powers the privilege can be said to derive from the supremacy of each branch within its own assigned area of constitutional duties. Certain powers and privileges flow from the nature of enumerated powers;† the protection of the confidentiality of Presidential communications has similar constitutional underpinnings.

The second ground asserted by the President's counsel in support of the claim of absolute privilege rests on the doctrine of separation of powers. Here it is argued that the independence of the Executive Branch within its own sphere, Humphrey's Executor v. United States (1935); Kilbourn v. Thompson (1881), insulates a President from a judicial subpoena in an ongoing criminal prosecution, and thereby protects confidential Presidential communications.

However, neither the doctrine of separation of powers, nor the need for confidentiality of high-level communications, without more, can sustain an absolute, unqualified Presidential privilege of immunity from judicial process under all circumstances. The President's need for complete candor and objectivity from advisers calls for great deference from the courts. However, when the privilege depends solely on the broad, undifferentiated claim of public interest in the confidentiality of such conversations, a confrontation with other values arises. Absent a claim of need to protect military, diplomatic, or sensitive national security secrets, we find it difficult to accept the argument that even the very important interest in confidentiality of Presidential communications is significantly diminished by production of such material for in camera inspection with all the protection that a district court will be obliged to provide.

The impediment that an absolute, unqualified privilege would place in the way of the primary constitutional duty of the Judicial Branch to do justice in criminal prosecutions would plainly conflict with the function of the courts under Art. III. In designing the structure of our Government and dividing and allocating the sovereign power among three co-equal branches, the Framers of the Constitution sought to provide a comprehensive

---

*There is nothing novel about governmental confidentiality. The meetings of the Constitutional Convention in 1787 were conducted in complete privacy. 1 M. Farrand, The Records of the Federal Convention of 1787, pp. xi-xxv (1911). Moreover, all records of those meetings were sealed for more than 30 years after the Convention. Most of the Framers acknowledged that without secrecy no constitution of the kind that was developed could have been written. C. Warren, The Making of the Constitution 134-139 (1937).

†The Special Prosecutor argues that there is no provision in the Constitution for a Presidential privilege as to the President's communications corresponding to the privilege of Members of Congress under the Speech or Debate Clause. But the silence of the Constitution on this score is not dispositive. "The rule of constitutional interpretation announced in McCulloch v. Maryland [1819] that that which was reasonably appropriate and relevant to the exercise of a granted power was to be considered as accompanying the grant, has been so universally applied that it suffices merely to state it." Marshall v. Gordon (1917).

system, but the separate powers were not intended to operate with absolute independence. "While the Constitution diffuses power the better to secure liberty, it also contemplates that practice will integrate the dispersed powers into a workable government. It enjoins upon its branches separateness but interdependence, autonomy but reciprocity." Youngstown Sheet & Tube Co. v. Sawyer. (Jackson, J., concurring). To read the Art. II powers of the President as providing an absolute privilege as against a subpoena essential to enforcement of criminal statutes on no more than a generalized claim of the public interest in confidentiality of nonmilitary and nondiplomatic discussions would upset the constitutional balance of "a workable government" and gravely impair the role of the courts under Art. III.

C.

Since we conclude that the legitimate needs of the judicial process may outweigh Presidential privilege, it is necessary to resolve those competing interests in a manner that preserves the essential functions of each branch. The right and indeed the duty to resolve that question does not free the judiciary from according high respect to the representations made on behalf of the President. United States v. Burr, 25 F. Cas. 187 (No. 14,694) (1807).

The expectation of a President to the confidentiality of his conversations and correspondence, like the claim of confidentiality of judicial deliberations, for example, has all the values to which we accord deference for the privacy of all citizens and added to those values the necessity for protection of the public interest in candid, objective, and even blunt or harsh opinions in Presidential decision making. A President and those who assist him must be free to explore alternatives in the process of shaping policies and making decisions and to do so in a way many would be unwilling to express except privately. These are the considerations justifying a presumptive privilege for Presidential communications. The privilege is fundamental to the operation of government and inextricably rooted in the separation of powers under the Constitution. In Nixon v. Sirica, 487 F. 2d 700 (1973), the Court of Appeals held that such Presidential communications are "presumptively privileged," and this position is accepted by both parties in the present litigation. We agree with Mr. Chief Justice Marshall's observation, therefore, that "[i]n no case of this kind would a court be required to proceed against the President as against an ordinary individual." United States v. Burr.

But this presumptive privilege must be considered in light of our historic commitment to the rule of law. This is nowhere more profoundly manifest than in our view that "the twofold aim [of criminal justice] is that guilt shall not escape or innocence suffer." Berger v. United States [1935]. We have elected to employ an adversary system of criminal justice in which the parties contest all issues before a court of law. The need to develop all relevant facts in the adversary system is both fundamental and comprehensive. The ends of criminal justice would be defeated if judgments were to be founded on a partial or speculative presentation of the facts. The very integrity of the judicial system and public confidence in the system depend on full disclosure of all the facts, within the framework of the rules of evidence. To ensure that justice is done, it is imperative to the function of courts that compulsory process be available for the production of evidence needed either by the prosecution or by the defense. . . .

In this case the President challenges a subpoena served on him as a third party requiring the production of materials for use in a criminal prosecution; he does so on the claim that he has a privilege against disclosure of confidential communications. He does not place his claim of privilege on the ground they are military or diplomatic secrets. As to these areas of Art. II duties the courts have traditionally shown the utmost deference to Presidential responsibilities. In [Chicago] & S. Air Lines v. Waterman S. S. Corp. (1948), dealing with Presidential authority involving foreign policy considerations, the court said: "The President, both as Commander-in-Chief and as the Nation's organ for foreign affairs, has available intelligence services whose reports are not and ought not to be published to the world. It would be intolerable that courts, without the relevant information, should review and perhaps nullify actions of the Executive taken on information properly held secret." In United States v. Reynolds (1953), dealing with a claimant's demand for evidence in a damage case against the Government the Court said: "It may be possible to satisfy the court, from all the circumstances of the case, that there is a reasonable danger that compulsion of the evidence will expose military matters which, in the interest of national security, should not be divulged. When this is the case, the occasion for the privilege is appropriate, and the court should not jeopardize the security which the privilege is meant to protect by insisting upon an examination of the evidence, even by the judge alone, in chambers." No case of the Court, however, has extended this high degree of deference to a President's generalized interest in confidentiality. Nowhere in the Constitution, as we have noted earlier, is there any explicit reference to a privilege of confidentiality, yet to the extent this interest relates to the effective discharge of a President's powers, it is constitutionally based.

The right to the production of all evidence at a criminal trial similarly has constitutional dimensions. The Sixth Amendment explicitly confers upon every defendant in a criminal trial the right "to be confronted with the witnesses against him" and "to have compulsory process for obtaining witnesses in his favor." Moreover, the Fifth Amendment also guarantees that no person shall be deprived of liberty without due process of law. It is the manifest duty of the courts to vindicate those guarantees, and to accomplish that it is essential that all relevant and admissible evidence be produced.

In this case we must weigh the importance of the general privilege of confidentiality of Presidential communications in performance of his responsibilities against the inroads of such a privilege on the fair administration of criminal justice.[3] The interest in preserving confidentiality is weighty indeed and entitled to great respect. However, we cannot conclude that advisers will be moved to temper the candor of their remarks by the infrequent occasions of disclosure because of the possibility that such conversations will be called for in the context of a criminal prosecution.

On the other hand, the allowance of the privilege to withhold evidence that is demonstrably relevant in a criminal trial would cut deeply into the guarantee of due process of law and gravely impair the basic function of the courts. . . . Without access to specific facts a criminal prosecution may be totally frustrated. The President's broad interest in confidentiality of communications will not be vitiated by disclosure of a limited number of conversations preliminarily shown to have some bearing on the pending criminal cases.

We conclude that when the ground for asserting privilege as to subpoenaed materials sought for use in a criminal trial is based only on the generalized interest in confidentiality, it cannot prevail over the fundamental demands of due process of law in the fair administration of criminal justice. The generalized assertion of privilege must yield to the demonstrated, specific need for evidence in a pending criminal trial. . . .

Mr. Justice **Rehnquist** took no part in the consideration or decision of these cases.

NIXON v. FITZGERALD

457 U. S. 731; 102 S. Ct. 2690; 73 L. Ed. 2d 349
(1982)

While the Supreme Court has made clear that it alone is the final arbiter of the powers of the three branches of government, like so many judges who have a stake in the outcome of a case, the Court has not been entirely impartial in the distribution of these powers. Thus, while a person who violates a legislative act will not be punished if the act is found unconstitutional, the violation of a court injunction can be punished even though the court had no right to issue the injunction in the first place. Cf. Walker v. Birmingham (1967) and Shuttlesworth v. Birmingham (1969). The Court has also held that the executive branch cannot use evidence to convict a person which has been gotten unconstitutionally, while such unconstitutional evidence can be used to convict a person of perjury before a court. In United States v. Nixon the

Court upheld the right of the judiciary to evidence it needed in a criminal trial while carefully leaving open whether or not the legislature would have a right to such evidence.

Justice White's dissent in the present case emphasizes the danger to constitutional rights posed by the majority's opinion. He argues that the absolute immunity from civil suits conferred on the President by the majority opinion would extend "even to actions taken with express knowledge that the conduct . . . clearly violated the Constitution." It is interesting to compare White's concern that unconstitutional actions of the President might go unremedied with the holding in Walker v. Birmingham mentioned above which gives judges the right to enforce unconstitutional injunctions, thereby allowing unconstitutional actions by judges to go unremedied.

In Harlow v. Fitzgerald, a companion to the present case, the Court held that Presidential aides only enjoy immunity under certain circumstances and remanded the case to see if those circumstances existed.

In the closing months of the Johnson administration Ernest Fitzgerald, a civilian cost analyst employed by the Air Force, testified before Congress that the cost of the C-5A transport plane could run as much as $2 billion above estimates and that unexpected technical difficulties had arisen in the development of the plane. Defense Department officials, angered and embarrassed by Fitzgerald's testimony, explored a number of ways of removing him from his post and finally decided to reorganize the department and eliminate his position. Upon taking office President Nixon considered moving Fitzgerald to another position in the administration, but apparently decided against it on the judgment of his advisors that Fitzgerald lacked loyalty to the administrative branch. The President announced at a news conference that he had been personally responsible for Fitzgerald's removal, but later retracted the statement.

Considerable publicity attended the removal, sixty members of Congress wrote the President in protest, and Fitzgerald took the matter to the Civil Service Commission. After hearing over 4,000 pages of testimony the CSC examiner found that Fitzgerald had been removed because "he was not on the Air Force team," although he had not been removed in retaliation for his congressional testimony. However, the reorganization was found not to be a bona fide economy measure but a removal for "personal" reasons which violated Civil Service regulations and Fitzgerald was ordered reinstated. Although the Air Force ultimately agreed to comply with the order, effective in 1982, Fitzgerald sued the President for damages. When the court of appeals rejected the President's claim of immunity from suit, he appealed to the Supreme Court.

Justice **Powell** delivered the opinion of the Court, saying in part:

The plaintiff in this law suit seeks relief in civil damages from a former President of the United States.

---

*We are not here concerned with the balance between the President's generalized interest in confidentiality and the need for relevant evidence in civil litigation, nor with that between the confidentiality interest and congressional demands for information, nor with the President's interest in preserving state secrets. We address only the conflict between the President's assertion of a generalized privilege of confidentiality and the constitutional need for relevant evidence in criminal trials.

The claim rests on actions allegedly taken in the former President's official capacity during his tenure in office. The issue before us is the scope of the immunity possessed by the President of the United States. . . .

III. . . .

B.

Our decisions concerning the immunity of government officials from civil damages liability have been guided by the Constitution, federal statutes, and history. Additionally, at least in the absence of explicit constitutional or congressional guidance, our immunity decisions have been informed by the common law. . . . This Court necessarily also has weighed concerns of public policy, especially as illuminated by our history and the structure of our government. . . .

This case now presents the claim that the President of the United States is shielded by absolute immunity from civil damages liability. In the case of the President the inquiries into history and policy, though mandated independently by our cases, tend to converge. Because the Presidency did not exist through most of the development of common law, any historical analysis must draw its evidence primarily from our constitutional heritage and structure. Historical inquiry thus merges almost at its inception with the kind of "public policy" analysis appropriately undertaken by a federal court. This inquiry involves policies and principles that may be considered implicit in the nature of the President's office in a system structured to achieve effective government under a constitutionally mandated separation of powers.

IV.

Here a former President asserts his immunity from civil damages claims of two kinds. He stands named as a defendant in a direct action under the Constitution and in two statutory actions under federal laws of general applicability. In neither case has Congress taken express legislative action to subject the President to civil liability for his official acts.

Applying the principles of our cases to claims of this kind, we hold that petitioner, as a former President of the United States, is entitled to absolute immunity from damages liability predicated on his official acts. We consider this immunity a functionally mandated incident of the President's unique office, rooted in the constitutional tradition of the separation of powers and supported by our history. . . .

A.

The President occupies a unique position in the constitutional scheme. Article II of the Constitution provides that "[t]he executive Power shall be vested in a President of the United States. . . . " This grant of authority establishes the President as the chief constitutional officer of the Executive Branch, entrusted with supervisory and policy responsibilities of utmost discretion and sensitivity. These include the enforcement of federal

law—it is the President who is charged constitutionally to "take care that the laws be faithfully executed"; the conduct of foreign affairs—a realm in which the Court has recognized that "[i]t would be intolerable that courts, without the relevant information, should review and perhaps nullify actions of the Executive taken on information properly held secret"; and management of the Executive Branch—a task for which "imperative reasons requir[e] an unrestricted power [in the President] to remove the most important of his subordinates in their most important duties." . . .

Because of the singular importance of the President's duties, diversion of his energies by concern with private lawsuits would raise unique risks to the effective functioning of government. As is the case with prosecutors and judges—for whom absolute immunity now is established—a President must concern himself with matters likely to "arouse the most intense feelings." . . . Yet, as our decisions have recognized, it is in precisely such cases that there exists the greatest public interest in providing an official "the maximum ability to deal fearlessly and impartially with" the duties of his office. . . . This concern is compelling where the officeholder must make the most sensitive and far-reaching decisions entrusted to any official under our constitutional system. Nor can the sheer prominence of the President's office be ignored. In view of the visibility of his office and the effect of his actions on countless people, the President would be an easily identifiable target for suits for civil damages. Cognizance of this personal vulnerability frequently could distract a President from his public duties, to the detriment not only of the President and his office but also the Nation that the Presidency was designed to serve.

B.

Courts traditionally have recognized the President's constitutional responsibilities and status as factors counselling judicial deference and restraint. For example, while courts generally have looked to the common law to determine the scope of an official's evidentiary privilege, we have recognized that the Presidential privilege is "rooted in the separation of powers under the Constitution." United States v. Nixon (1974). It is settled law that the separation of powers doctrine does not bar every exercise of jurisdiction over the President of the United States. See, e.g., United States v. Nixon. . . . But our cases also have established that a court, before exercising jurisdiction, must balance the constitutional weight of the interest to be served against the dangers of intrusion on the authority and functions of the Executive Branch. . . . When judicial action is needed to serve broad public interests—as when the Court acts, not in derogation of the separation of powers, but to maintain their proper balance, . . . or to vindicate the public interest in an ongoing criminal prosecution, see United States v. Nixon—the exercise of jurisdiction has been held warranted. In the case of this merely private suit for damages based on a President's official acts, we hold it is not.

C.

In defining the scope of an official's absolute privilege, this Court has recognized that the sphere of protected action must be related closely to the immunity's justifying purposes. Frequently our decisions have held that an official's absolute immunity should extend only to acts in performance of particular functions of his office. . . . But the Court also has refused to draw functional lines finer than history and reason would support. . . . In view of the special nature of the President's constitutional office and functions, we think it appropriate to recognize absolute Presidential immunity from damages liability for acts within the "outer perimeter" of his official responsibility.

Under the Constitution and laws of the United States the President has discretionary responsibilities in a broad variety of areas, many of them highly sensitive. In many cases it would be difficult to determine which of the President's innumerable "functions" encompassed a particular action. . . .

. . . It clearly is within the President's constitutional and statutory authority to prescribe the manner in which the Secretary will conduct the business of the Air Force. Because this mandate of office must include the authority to prescribe reorganizations and reductions in force, we conclude that petitioner's alleged wrongful acts lay well within the outer perimeter of his authority.

V.

A rule of absolute immunity for the President will not leave the Nation without sufficient protection against misconduct on the part of the chief executive. There remains the constitutional remedy of impeachment. In addition, there are formal and informal checks on Presidential action that do not apply with equal force to other executive officials. The President is subjected to constant scrutiny by the press. Vigilant oversight by Congress also may serve to deter Presidential abuses of office, as well as to make credible the threat of impeachment. Other incentives to avoid misconduct may include a desire to earn re-election, the need to maintain prestige as an element of Presidential influence, and a President's traditional concern for his historical stature.

The existence of alternative remedies and deterrents establishes that absolute immunity will not place the President "above the law."* For the President, as

---

*The dissenting opinions argue that our decision places the President "above the law." This contention is rhetorically chilling but wholly unjustified. The remedy of impeachment demonstrates that the President remains accountable under law for his misdeeds in office. This case involves only a damages remedy. Although the President is not liable in civil damages for official misbehavior, that does not lift him "above" the law. The dissent does not suggest that a judge is "above" the law when he enters a judgment for which he cannot be held answerable in civil damages; or a prosecutor is above the law when he files an indictment; or a Congressman is above the law when he engages in legislative speech or debate. It is simple error to characterize an official as "above the law" because a particular remedy is not available against him.

for judges and prosecutors, absolute immunity merely precludes a particular private remedy for alleged misconduct in order to advance compelling public ends.

Chief Justice **Burger** wrote a concurring opinion, saying in part:

I fully agree that the constitutional concept of separation of independent co-equal powers dictates that a President be immune from civil damages actions based on acts within the scope of the Executive authority while in office. Far from placing a President above the law, the Court's holding places a President on essentially the same footing with judges and other officials whose absolute immunity we have recognized.

Justice **White**, with whom Justice **Brennan**, Justice **Marshall**, and Justice **Blackmun** join, dissented, saying in part:

The four dissenting members of the Court in Butz v. Economou (1978) argued that all federal officials are entitled to absolute immunity from suit for any action they take in connection with their official duties. That immunity would extend even to actions taken with express knowledge that the conduct was clearly contrary to the controlling statute or clearly violative of the Constitution. Fortunately, the majority of the Court rejected that approach: We held that although public officials perform certain functions that entitle them to absolute immunity, the immunity attaches to particular functions—not to particular offices. Officials performing functions for which immunity is not absolute enjoy qualified immunity; they are liable in damages only if their conduct violated well-established law and if they should have realized that their conduct was illegal.

The Court now applies the dissenting view in Butz to the office of the President: A President acting within the outer boundaries of what Presidents normally do may, without liability, deliberately cause serious injury to any number of citizens even though he knows his conduct violates a statute or tramples on the constitutional rights of those who are injured. Even if the President in this case ordered Fitzgerald fired by means of a trumped-up reduction in force, knowing that such a discharge was contrary to the civil service laws, he would be absolutely immune from suit. By the same token, if a President, without following the statutory procedures which he knows apply to himself as well as to other federal officials, orders his subordinates to wiretap or break into a home for the purpose of installing a listening device, and the officers comply with his request, the President would be absolutely immune from suit. He would be immune regardless of the damage he inflicts, regardless of how violative of the statute and of the Constitution he knew his conduct to be, and regardless of his purpose.

The Court intimates that its decision is grounded in the Constitution. If that is the case, Congress can not provide a remedy against presidential misconduct and the criminal laws of the United States are wholly inapplicable to the President. I find this approach completely unacceptable. I do not agree that if the office of President is to operate effectively, the holder of that office must be permitted, without fear of liability and regardless of the function he is performing, deliberately to inflict injury on others by conduct that he knows violates the law.

We have not taken such a scatter-gun approach in other cases. Butz held that absolute immunity did not attach to the office held by a member of the President's Cabinet but only to those specific functions performed by that officer for which absolute immunity is clearly essential. Members of Congress are absolute immune under the Speech or Debate Clause of the Constitution, but the immunity extends only their legislative acts. We have /ever held that in order for legislative work to be done, it is necessary to immunize all of the tasks that legislators must perform. Constitutional immunity does not extend to those many things that Senators and Representatives regularly and necessarily do that are not legislative acts. . . .

Attaching absolute immunity to the office of the President, rather than to particular activities that the President might perform, places the President above the law. It is a reversion to the old notion that the King can do no wrong. Until now, this concept had survived in this country only in the form of sovereign immunity. That doctrine forecloses suit against the government itself and against government officials, but only when the suit against the the latter actually seeks relief against the sovereign. . . . Suit against an officer, however, may be maintained where it seeks specific relief against him for conduct contrary to his statutory authority or to the Constitution. Now, however, the Court clothes the office of the President with sovereign immunity, placing it beyond the law. . . .

Unfortunately, the Court now abandons basic principles that have been powerful guides to decision. It is particularly unfortunate since the judgment in this case has few, if any, indicia of a judicial decision; it is almost wholly a policy choice, a choice that is without substantial support and that in all events is ambiguous in its reach and import. . . .

. . . The Court casually, but candidly, abandons the functional approach to immunity that has run through all of our decisions. Indeed, the majority turns this rule on its head by declaring that because the functions of the President's office are so varied and diverse and some of them so profoundly important, the office is unique and must be clothed with office-wide, absolute immunity. This is policy, not law, and in my view, very poor policy.

I. . . .

The petitioner and the Solicitor General, as amicus, rely principally on two arguments to support the claim of absolute immunity for the President from civil liability: absolute immunity is an ''incidental power'' of the Presidency, historically recognized as implicit in the Constitution, and absolute immunity is required by the separation of powers doctrine. I will address each of these contentions.

A.

The Speech or Debate Clause, Art. I, § 6, guarantees absolute immunity to members of Congress; nowhere, however, does the Constitution directly address the issue of presidential immunity. . . .

Moreover, the Convention debate did not focus on wrongs the President might commit against individuals, but rather on whether there should be a method of holding him accountable for what might be termed wrongs against the state. Thus, examples of the abuses that concerned delegates were betrayal, oppression, and bribery; the delegates feared that the alternative to an impeachment mechanism would be ''tumults and insurrections'' by the people in response to such abuses. The only conclusions that can be drawn from this debate are that the independence of the Executive was not understood to require a total lack of accountability to the other branches and that there was no general desire to insulate the President from the consequences of his improper acts. . . .

. . . From the history discussed above, however, all that can be concluded is that absolute immunity from civil liability for the President finds no support in constitutional text or history, or in the explanations of the earliest commentators. This is too weak a ground to support a declaration by this Court that the President is absolutely immune from civil liability, regardless of the source of liability or the injury for which redress is sought. This much the majority implicitly concedes since history and text, traditional sources of judicial argument, merit only a footnote in the Court's opinion.

B. . . .

That the President should have the same remedial obligations toward those whom he injures as any other federal officer is not a surprising proposition. The fairness of the remedial principle the Court has so far followed—that the wrongdoer, not the victim, should ordinarily bear the costs of the injury—has been found to be outweighed only in instances where potential liability is ''thought to injure the governmental decisionmaking process.'' . . . The argument for immunity is that the possibility of a damages action will, or at least should, have an effect on the performance of official responsibilities. That effect should be to deter unconstitutional, or otherwise illegal, behavior. This may, however, lead officers to be more careful and ''less vigorous'' in the performance of their duties. Caution, of course, is not always a virtue and undue caution is to be avoided. . . .

The Court's response, until today, to this problem has been to apply the argument to individual functions, not offices, and to evaluate the effect of liability on governmental decisionmaking within that function, in light of the substantive ends that are to be encouraged or discouraged. In this case, therefore, the Court should examine the functions implicated by the causes of action at issue here and the effect of potential liability on the performance of those functions. . . .

III. . . .

Focusing on the actual arguments the majority offers for its holding of absolute immunity for the President, one finds surprisingly little. As I read the relevant section of the Court's opinion, I find just three contentions from which the majority draws this conclusion. Each of them is little more than a makeweight; together they hardly suffice to justify the wholesale disregard of our traditional approach to immunity questions.

First, the majority informs us that the President occupies a "unique position in the constitutional scheme," including responsibilities for the administration of justice, foreign affairs, and management of the Executive Branch. True as this may be, it says nothing about why a "unique" rule of immunity should apply to the President. The President's unique role may indeed encompass functions for which he is entitled to a claim of absolute immunity. It does not follow from that, however, that he is entitled to absolute immunity either in general or in this case in particular. . . .

Second, the majority contends that because the President's "visibility" makes him particularly vulnerable to suits for civil damages, a rule of absolute immunity is required. The force of this argument is surely undercut by the majority's admission that "there is no historical record of numerous suits against the President." . . .

Finally, the Court suggests that potential liability "frequently could distract a President from his public duties." Unless one assumes that the President himself makes the countless high level executive decisions required in the administration of government, this rule will not do much to insulate such decisions from the threat of liability. The logic of the proposition cannot be limited to the President; its extension, however, has been uniformly rejected by this Court. . . . Furthermore, in no instance have we previously held legal accountability in itself to be an unjustifiable cost. The availability of the courts to vindicate constitutional and statutory wrongs has been perceived and protected as one of the virtues of our system of delegated and limited powers. . . .

IV.

The majority may be correct in its conclusions that "a rule of absolute immunity will not leave the Nation without sufficient remedies for misconduct on the part of the chief executive." Such a rule will, however, leave Mr. Fitzgerald without an adequate remedy for the harms that he may have suffered. More importantly, it will leave future plaintiffs without a remedy, regardless of the substantiality of their claims. . . .

Justice **Blackmun,** with whom Justice **Brennan** and Justice **Marshall** join, wrote a dissenting opinion.

UNITED STATES v. BELMONT

301 U. S. 324; 57 S. Ct. 758; 81 L. Ed. 1134
(1937)

Exec. agreements

The conduct of foreign affairs has traditionally been the concern of the executive branch of government, and the Constitution of the United States recognizes this fact. The President appoints our foreign ambassadors, ministers, and consuls. He alone receives ambassadors and other public ministers from abroad and thereby "recognizes" the governments by which such officers are sent. It is he who, usually through his Secretary of State, negotiates treaties. But Congress has some power with respect to foreign affairs. Treaties or other agreements which call for the expenditure of money will be ineffective unless Congress appropriates that money by statute. The Senate must consent to the appointments of our diplomatic representatives, and two-thirds of the Senate must give its approval to a treaty. This latter requirement has tended to limit the use of the treaty power to fairly formal and important international agreements, among which have been military alliances, the making of peace, and adherence to international organizations. A substantial proportion of our international agreements take the form of executive agreements concluded between the President and the executive of a foreign nation. Some of these, particularly in the field of foreign trade, are specifically authorized by Congress. Others are made solely on the authority of the President as chief executive. While the Constitution provides that treaties shall be the law of the land, and executive agreements made with congressional consent would also have the authority of law, there has long been some doubt about the binding nature of an agreement made by the executive alone. The Belmont case is important because the Court assumes that executive agreements have a domestic authority which makes them, like treaties, the law of the land.

In 1918 the Soviet government nationalized the Petrograd Metal Works and confiscated its property and assets, wherever situated. Some of these assets were on deposit in Belmont's bank in New York. In 1933 the President, by receiving the Soviet ambassador, recognized the Soviet government as the legitimate government of Russia. A final settlement of the claims and counter-claims between the two countries was concluded in the Litvinov Assignments, and the claim to all money due the Soviet government from American nationals was assigned to the United States, including the deposits in Belmont's bank. The assignments were made by an exchange of diplomatic correspondence between the Soviet government and the United States and were not submitted to the Senate in the form of a treaty. The district court refused to grant title to the United States. It agreed that the Litvinov Assignments embraced the claims in question but held that the Soviet nationalization had been mere confiscation, and confiscation was against the public policy of both New York and the United States.

Mr. Justice **Sutherland** delivered the opinion of the Court, saying in part:

First. We do not pause to inquire whether in fact there was any policy of the State of New York to be infringed, since we are of opinion that no state policy can prevail against the international compact here involved.

This court has held, Underhill v. Hernandez [1897], that every sovereign state must recognize the independence of every other sovereign state; and that the courts of one will not sit in judgment upon the acts of the government of another, done within its own territory.

. . . This court held that the conduct of foreign relations was committed by the Constitution to the political departments of the government, and the propriety of what may be done in the exercise of this political power was not subject to judicial inquiry or decision; that who is the sovereign of a territory is not a judicial question, but one the determination of which by the political departments conclusively binds the courts; and that recognition by these departments is retroactive and validates all actions and conduct of the government so recognized from the commencement of its existence. . . .

We take judicial notice of the fact that coincident with the assignment set forth in the complaint, the President recognized the Soviet Government, and normal diplomatic relations were established between that government and the Government of the United States, followed by an exchange of ambassadors. The effect of this was to validate, so far as this country is concerned, all acts of the Soviet Government here involved from the commencement of its existence. The recognition, establishment of diplomatic relations, the assignment, and agreements with respect thereto, were all parts of one transaction, resulting in an international compact between the two governments. That the negotiations, acceptance of the assignment and agreements and understandings in respect thereof were within the competence of the President may not be doubted. Governmental power over internal affairs is distributed between the national government and the several states. Governmental power over external affairs is not distributed, but is vested exclusively in the national government. And in respect of what was done here, the Executive had authority to speak as the sole organ of that government. The assignment and the agreements in connection therewith did not, as in the case of treaties, as that term is used in the treaty making clause of the Constitution (Art. II, § 2), require the advice and consent of the Senate.

A treaty signifies "a compact made between two or more independent nations with a view to the public welfare." . . . But an international compact, as this was, is not always a treaty which requires the participation of the Senate. There are many such compacts, of which a protocol, a modus vivendi, a postal convention, and agreements like that now under consideration are illustrations. . . . The distinction was pointed out by this court in the B. Altman & Co. Case 1912, which arose under § 3 of the Tariff Act of 1897, authorizing the President to conclude commercial agreements with foreign countries in certain specified matters. We held that although this might not be a treaty requiring ratification by the Senate, it was a compact negotiated and proclaimed under the authority of the President, and as such was a "treaty" within the meaning of the Circuit Court of Appeals Act, the construction of which might be reviewed upon direct appeal to this court.

Plainly, the external powers of the United States are to be exercised without regard to state laws or policies. The supremacy of a treaty in this respect has been recognized from the beginning. Mr. Madison, in the Virginia Convention, said that if a treaty does not supersede existing state laws, as far as they contravene its operation, the treaty would be ineffective. "To counteract it by the supremacy of the state laws, would bring on the Union the just charge of national perfidy, and involve us in war." . . . And while this rule in respect of treaties is established by the express language of cl. 2, Art. 6, of the Constitution, the same rule would result in the case of all international compacts and agreements from the very fact that complete power over international affairs is in the national government and is not and cannot be subject to any curtailment or interference on the part of the several states. . . . In respect of all international negotiations and compacts, and in respect of our foreign relations generally, state lines disappear. As to such purposes the State of New York does not exist. Within the field of its powers, whatever the United States rightfully undertakes, it necessarily has warrant to consummate. And when judicial authority is invoked in aid of such consummation, state constitutions, state laws, and state policies are irrelevant to the inquiry and decision. It is inconceivable that any of them can be interposed as an obstacle to the effective operation of a federal constitutional power. . . .

Second. The public policy of the United States relied upon as a bar to the action is that declared by the Constitution, namely, that private property shall not be taken without just compensation. But the answer is that our Constitution, laws and policies have no extraterritorial operation, unless in respect of our own citizens. . . . What another country has done in the way of taking over property of its nationals, and especially of its corporations, is not a matter for judicial consideration here. Such nationals must look to their own government for any redress to which they may be entitled. So far as the record shows, only the rights of the Russian corporation have been affected by what has been done; and it will be time enough to consider the rights of our nationals when, if ever, by proper judicial proceeding, it shall be made to appear that they are so affected as to entitle them to judicial relief. The substantive right to the moneys, as now disclosed, became vested in the Soviet Government as the successor to the corporation; and this right that government has passed to the United States. It does not appear that respondents have any interest in the matter beyond that of a custodian. Thus far no question under the Fifth Amendment is involved. . . .

In line with Curtis l.we case?

Judgment reversed.

Justices **Stone, Brandeis,** and **Cardozo** concurred.

POLITICAL CONTROL OVER ADMINISTRATION

② Questn

Power to remove

MYERS v. UNITED STATES

The Pres. power to remove is in his power to apont

272 U. S. 52; 47 S. Ct. 21; 71 L. Ed. 160 (1926)

"Whom the President may remove he may dominate." In this statement Professor E. S. Corwin, in The President: Office and Powers, *points to the keystone of the President's authority to control the administrative branch of government. The Constitution indicates how federal executive officers shall be appointed; it is entirely silent, however, as to their removal save by impeachment—a clumsy process applicable only to cases of grave misconduct which has been successfully invoked only four times out of twelve attempts in our nation's history. May the President remove his subordinates at will? Or may Congress deny or limit his power to do so? These are questions of great practical importance. Congresses and Presidents, from 1789 on, have guessed at the answers, and those guesses have often conflicted. The Supreme Court does not answer constitutional questions, however important, unless they squarely arise in actual litigation; and 137 years elapsed before a case came up which clearly involved a question of the President's power of removal. It arose then only because a Mr. Myers saw fit to sue the government in the United States Court of Claims for his salary. The facts were these: in 1917, President Wilson appointed Myers to a first-class postmastership at Portland, Oregon, for a term of four years. He removed him from office in 1920. A statute of 1876, still in force, provided that "postmasters of the first, second, and third classes shall be appointed and may be removed by the President by and with the advice and consent of the Senate and shall hold their offices for four years unless sooner removed or suspended according to law." The removal of Myers was not referred to the Senate for its consent. The President did not nominate a successor to Myers but made a recess appointment which the Senate never confirmed. This fact is important because such confirmation of Myers' successor would have amounted to senatorial consent to Myers' removal. He protested against his removal; refrained from accepting other remunerative employment; and when the four-year period for which he had been appointed expired, he sued in the United States Court of Claims for the salary for about eighteen months of which his removal had deprived him. This amounted to $8,838.72.*

The case was first argued before the Supreme Court in December, 1924. Recognizing its far-reaching importance, the Court ordered a reargument in the spring of 1925 and invited Senator Pepper of Pennsylvania to file a brief as amicus curiae which would present the interests of the Senate in the controversy. The Court divided six to three in its decision. The majority opinion, written by Chief Justice Taft, occupies seventy-one pages in the official reports, while Justices McReynolds and Brandeis required sixty-one and fifty-six pages respectively to express their disagreement. Justice Holmes' dissent occupies one page. This is the first case in which the government through the Department of Justice ever appeared in the Supreme Court to attack the constitutionality of an act of Congress.

The majority opinion of Chief Justice Taft was undoubtedly based upon his conviction, gained from his experience as President of the United States, that the President cannot effectively administer his office unless he can control his subordinates through an unrestricted power of removal. Obviously the President cannot execute the laws personally; he must rely on subordinates whose offices must be created by Congress, and whose duties and responsibilities are set out in statutes. On occasion there have been disputes between the President and Congress as to the right to direct these officers in the performance of their duties. A notable conflict of this kind came to the Supreme Court in Kendall v. United States ex rel. Stokes (1838). Stokes had presented the government a bill for additional expenses incurred while carrying the mail under government contract. Congress ordered the Postmaster General to pay Stokes an amount to be decided by the Solicitor of the Treasury, but the Postmaster considered the Solicitor's award too high, and acting upon the orders of the President, refused to pay the full amount. The Court ordered the money paid in full. "There are," the Court pointed out, "certain political duties imposed upon many officers in the executive department, the discharge of which is under the direction of the President. But it would be an alarming doctrine that Congress cannot impose upon any executive officer any duty they may think proper, which is not repugnant to any rights secured and protected by the Constitution; and in such cases, the duty and responsibility grow out of and are subject to the control of the law, and not to the direction of the President." Moreover, the Court added, "To contend that the obligation imposed on the President to see the laws faithfully executed implies a power to forbid their execution, is a novel construction of the Constitution, and entirely inadmissible."

Since 1887, Congress has been creating independent regulatory commissions—a policy whose effect has been to remove from direct presidential control whole areas of federal regulation and administration. See Humphrey's Executor v. United States (1935).

← former Pres.

Mr. Chief Justice **Taft** delivered the opinion of the Court, saying in part:

The question where the power of removal of executive officers appointed by the President by and with the advice and consent of the Senate was vested, was presented early in the first session of the First Congress. There is no express provision respecting removals in the

Constitution, except as § 4 of article 2, provides for removal from office by impeachment. The subject was not discussed in the Constitutional Convention. . . .

In the House of Representatives of the First Congress, on Tuesday, May 18, 1789, Mr. Madison moved in the Committee of the Whole that there should be established three executive departments—one of Foreign Affairs, another of the Treasury, and a third of War, at the head of each of which there should be a Secretary to be appointed by the President by and with the advice and consent of the Senate, and to be removable by the President. The committee agreed to the establishment of a Department of Foreign Affairs, but a discussion ensued as to making the Secretary removable by the President. . . .

On June 16, 1789, the House resolved itself into a Committee of the Whole on a bill proposed by Mr. Madison for establishing an executive department to be denominated the Department of Foreign Affairs, in which the first clause, after stating the title of the officer and describing his duties, had these words "to be removable from office by the President of the United States." . . .

On June 22, in the renewal of the discussion, "Mr. Benson moved to amend the bill, by altering the second clause, so as to imply the power of removal to be in the President alone. . . .

"Mr. Benson stated that his objection to the clause 'to be removable by the President' arose from an idea that the power of removal by the President hereafter might appear to be exercised by virtue of a legislative grant only, and consequently be subjected to legislative instability, when he was well satisfied in his own mind that it was fixed by a fair legislative construction of the Constitution." . . .

Mr. Benson's first amendment to alter the second clause by the insertion of the italicized words, made that clause to read as follows:

"That there shall be in the State Department an inferior officer to be appointed by the said principal officer, and to be employed therein as he shall deem proper, to be called the Chief Clerk in the Department of Foreign Affairs, *and who, whenever the principal officer shall be removed from office by the President of the United States,* or in any other case of vacancy, shall, during such vacancy, have charge and custody of all records, books and papers appertaining to said department."

The first amendment was then approved by a vote of thirty to eighteen. . . . Mr. Benson then moved to strike out in the first clause the words "to be removable by the President," in pursuance of the purpose he had already declared, and this second motion of his was carried by a vote of thirty-one to nineteen. . . .

It is very clear from this history that the exact question which the House voted upon was whether it should recognize and declare the power of the President under the Constitution to remove the Secretary of Foreign Affairs without the advice and consent of the Senate. That was what the vote was taken for. Some effort has been made to question whether the decision carries

the result claimed for it, but there is not the slightest doubt, after an examination of the record, that the vote was, and was intended to be, a legislative declaration that the power to remove officers appointed by the President and the Senate vested in the President alone, and until the Johnson impeachment trial in 1868, its meaning was not doubted even by those who questioned its soundness. . . .

The bill was discussed in the House at length and with great ability. . . . James Madison was then a leader in the House, as he had been in the Convention. His arguments in support of the President's constitutional power of removal independently of Congressional provision, and without the consent of the Senate, were masterly, and he carried the House.

It is convenient in the course of our discussion of this case to review the reasons advanced by Mr. Madison and his associates for their conclusion, supplementing them, so far as may be, by additional considerations which lead this Court to concur therein.

First. Mr. Madison insisted that article 2 by vesting the executive power in the President was intended to grant to him the power of appointment and removal of executive officers except as thereafter expressly provided in that article. He pointed out that one of the chief purposes of the Convention was to separate the legislative from the executive functions. He said:

"If there is a principle in our Constitution, indeed in any free Constitution more sacred than another, it is that which separates the legislative, executive and judicial powers. If there is any point in which the separation of the legislative and executive powers ought to be maintained with great caution, it is that which relates to officers and offices." . . .

Mr. Madison and his associates in the discussion in the House dwelt at length upon the necessity there was for construing article 2 to give the President the sole power of removal in his responsibility for the conduct of the executive branch, and enforced this by emphasizing his duty expressly declared in the third section of the Article to "take care that the laws be faithfully executed." . . .

The vesting of the executive power in the President was essentially a grant of the power to execute the laws. But the President alone and unaided could not execute the laws. He must execute them by the assistance of subordinates. . . . As he is charged specifically to take care that they be faithfully executed, the reasonable implication, even in the absence of express words, was that as part of his executive power he should select those who were to act for him under his direction in the execution of the laws. The further implication must be, in the absence of any express limitation respecting removals, that as his selection of administrative officers is essential to the execution of the laws by him, so must be his power of removing those for whom he cannot continue to be responsible. . . . It was urged that the natural meaning of the term "executive power" granted the President included the appointment and removal of executive subordinates. If such appointments and removals were not an exercise of the executive power, what were they? They certainly were not the exercise of legislative or judicial power in government as usually understood. . . .

Second. The view of Mr. Madison and his associates was that not only did the grant of executive power to the President in the first section of article 2 carry with it the power of removal, but the express recognition of the power of appointment in the second section enforced this view on the well approved principle of constitutional and statutory construction that the power of removal of executive officers was incident to the power of appointment. It was agreed by the opponents of the bill, with only one or two exceptions, that as a constitutional principle the power of appointment carried with it the power of removal. . . . This principle as a rule of constitutional and statutory construction, then generally conceded, has been recognized ever since. . . . The reason for the principle is that those in charge of and responsible for administering functions of government who select their executive subordinates need in meeting their responsibility to have the power to remove those whom they appoint.

Under § 2 of article 2, however, the power of appointment by the Executive is restricted in its exercise by the provision that the Senate, a part of the legislative branch of the government, may check the action of the Executive by rejecting the officers he selects. Does this make the Senate part of the removing power? And this, after the whole discussion in the House is read attentively, is the real point which was considered and decided in the negative by the vote already given.

The history of the clause by which the Senate was given a check upon the President's power of appointment makes it clear that it was not prompted by any desire to limit removals. As already pointed out, the important purpose of those who brought about the restriction was to lodge in the Senate, where the small states had equal representation with the larger states, power to prevent the President from making too many appointments from the larger states. . . .

It was pointed out in this great debate that the power of removal, though equally essential to the executive power is different in its nature from that of appointment. . . . A veto by the Senate—a part of the legislative branch of the government—upon removals is a much greater limitation upon the executive branch and a much more serious blending of the legislative with the executive than a rejection of a proposed appointment. It is not to be implied. The rejection of a nominee of the President for a particular office does not greatly embarrass him in the conscientious discharge of his high duties in the selection of those who are to aid him, because the President usually has an ample field from which to select for office, according to his preference, competent and capable men. The Senate has full power to reject newly proposed appointees whenever the President shall remove the incumbents. Such a check enables the Senate to prevent the filling of offices with bad or incompetent men or with those against whom there is tenable objection.

The power to prevent the removal of an officer who has served under the President is different from the authority to consent to or reject his appointment. When a nomination is made, it may be presumed that the Senate is, or may become, as well advised as to the fitness of the nominee as the President, but in the nature of things the defects in ability or intelligence or loyalty in the administration of the laws of one who has served as an officer under the President, are facts as to which the President, or his trusted subordinates, must be better informed than the Senate, and the power to remove him may, therefore, be regarded as confined, for very sound and practical reasons, to the governmental authority which has administrative control. The power of removal is incident to the power of appointment, not to the power of advising and consenting to appointment, and when the grant of the executive power is enforced by the express mandate to take care that the laws be faithfully executed, it emphasizes the necessity for including within the executive power as conferred the exclusive power of removal. . . .

Third. Another argument urged against the constitutional power of the President alone to remove executive officers appointed by him with the consent of the Senate is that, in the absence of an express power of removal granted to the President, power to make provision for removal of all such officers is vested in the Congress by § 8 of article 1. . . .

The constitutional construction that excludes Congress from legislative power to provide for the removal of superior officers finds support in the second section of article 2. . . . This is "but the Congress may by law vest the appointment of such inferior officers, as they think proper, in the President alone, in the courts of law, or in the heads of Departments." These words, it has been held by this court, give to Congress the power to limit and regulate removal of such inferior officers by heads of departments when it exercises its constitutional power to lodge the power of appointment with them. United States v. Perkins [1886]. Here, then, is an express provision introduced in words of exception for the exercise by Congress of legislative power in the matter of appointments and removals in the case of inferior executive officers. The phrase "But Congress may by law vest" is equivalent to "excepting that Congress may by law vest." By the plainest implication it excludes Congressional dealing with appointments or removals of executive officers not falling within the exception and leaves unaffected the executive power of the President to appoint and remove them. . . .

It is reasonable to suppose also that, had it been intended to give to Congress power to regulate or control removals in the manner suggested, it would have been included among the specifically enumerated legislative powers in article 1, or in the specified limitations on the executive power in article 2. The difference between the grant of legislative power under article 1 to Congress which is limited to powers therein enumerated, and the more general grant of the executive power to the President under article 2, is significant. The fact that the executive power is given in general terms strengthened by specific terms where emphasis is appropriate, and limited by direct expressions where limitation is needed and that no express limit is placed on the power of removal by the executive is a convincing indication that none was intended. . . .

Fourth. Mr. Madison and his associates pointed out with great force the unreasonable character of the view that the Convention intended, without express provision, to give to Congress or the Senate, in case of political or other differences, the means of thwarting the Executive in the exercise of his great powers and in the bearing of his great responsibility by fastening upon him, as subordinate executive officers, men who by their inefficient service under him, by their lack of loyalty to the service, or by their different views of policy might make his taking care that the laws be faithfully executed most difficult or impossible. . . .

Made responsible under the Constitution for the effective enforcement of the law, the President needs as an indispensable aid to meet it the disciplinary influence upon those who act under him of a reserve power of removal. . . .

In all such cases, the discretion to be exercised is that of the President in determining the national public interest and in directing the action to be taken by his executive subordinates to protect it. In this field his cabinet officers must do his will. He must place in each member of his official family, and his chief executive subordinates, implicit faith. The moment that he loses confidence in the intelligence, ability, judgment or loyalty of any one of them, he must have the power to remove him without delay. To require him to file charges and submit them to the consideration of the Senate might make impossible that unity and co-ordination in executive administration essential to effective action.

The duties of the heads of departments and bureaus in which the discretion of the President is exercised and which we have described are the most important in the whole field of executive action of the government. There is nothing in the Constitution which permits a distinction between the removal of the head of a department or a bureau, when he discharges a political duty of the President or exercises his discretion, and the removal of executive officers engaged in the discharge of their other normal duties. The imperative reasons requiring an unrestricted power to remove the most important of his subordinates in their most important duties must, therefore, control the interpretation of the Constitution as to all appointed by him.

But this is not to say that there are not strong reasons why the President should have a like power to remove his appointees charged with other duties than those above described. The ordinary duties of officers prescribed by statute come under the general administrative control of the President by virtue of the general grant to him of the executive power, and he may properly supervise and guide their construction of the statutes under which they act in order to secure that unitary and uniform execution of the laws which article 2 of the Constitution evidently contemplated in vesting general executive power in the President alone. Laws are often passed with specific provision for the adoption of regulations by a department or bureau head to make the law workable and effective. The ability and judgment manifested by the official thus empowered, as well as his energy and stimulation of his subordinates, are subjects which the President must consider and supervise in his administrative control. Finding such officers to be negligent and inefficient, the President should have the power to remove them. Of course there may be duties so peculiarly and specifically committed to the discretion of a particular officer as to raise a question whether the President may overrule or revise the officer's interpretation of his statutory duty in a particular instance. Then there may be duties of a quasi-judicial character imposed on executive officers and members of executive tribunals whose decisions after hearing affect interests of individuals, the discharge of which the President can not in a particular case properly influence or control. But even in such a case he may consider the decision after its rendition as a reason for removing the officer, on the ground that the discretion regularly entrusted to that officer by statute has not been on the whole intelligently or wisely exercised. Otherwise he does not discharge his own constitutional duty of seeing that the laws be faithfully executed.

We have devoted much space to this discussion and decision of the question of the Presidential power of removal in the First Congress, not because a congressional conclusion on a constitutional issue is conclusive, but first because of our agreement with the reasons upon which it was avowedly based, second because this was the decision of the First Congress on a question of primary importance in the organization of the government, made within two years after the Constitutional Convention and within a much shorter time after its ratification, and third because that Congress numbered among its leaders those who had been members of the Convention. . . . As we shall see it was soon accepted as a final decision of the question by all branches of the government. . . .

[Here follows an analysis of the views of several statesmen of the early period.]

We come now to consider an argument advanced and strongly pressed on behalf of the complainant, that this case concerns only the removal of a postmaster, that a postmaster is an inferior officer, that such an office was not included within the legislative decision of 1789, which related only to superior officers to be appointed by the President by and with the advice and consent of the Senate. . . .

[The court rejects this distinction.]

It is further pressed on us that even though the legislative decision of 1789 included inferior officers, yet under the legislative power given Congress with respect to such officers it might directly legislate as to the method of their removal without changing their method of appointment by the President with the consent of the Senate. We do not think the language of the Constitution justifies such a contention. . . .

The power to remove inferior executive officers, like that to remove superior executive officers, is an incident of the power to appoint them, and is in its nature an executive power. The authority of Congress given by the excepting clause to vest the appointment of such inferior officers in the heads of departments carries with it authority incidentally to invest the heads of departments with power to remove. It has been the practice of Congress to do so and this court has recognized that power. The court also has recognized in the Perkins Case that Congress in committing the appointment of such inferior officers to the heads of departments may prescribe incidental regulations controlling and restricting the latter in the exercise of the power of removal. But the court never has held, nor reasonably could hold, although it is argued to the contrary on behalf of the appellant, that the excepting clause enables Congress to draw to itself, or to either branch of it, the power to remove or the right to participate in the exercise of that power. To do this would be to go beyond the words and implications of that clause and to infringe the constitutional principle of the separation of governmental powers. . . .

Summing up then the facts as to acquiescence by all branches of the Government in the legislative decision of 1789 as to executive officers whether superior or inferior, we find that from 1789 until 1863, a period of seventy-four years, there was no act of Congress, no executive act, and no decision of this court at variance with the declaration of the First Congress, but there was, as we have seen, clear affirmative recognition of it by each branch of the Government. . . .

We come now to a period in the history of the Government when both Houses of Congress attempted to reverse this constitutional construction and to subject the power of removing executive officers appointed by the President and confirmed by the Senate to the control of the Senate, indeed finally to the assumed power in Congress to place the removal of such officers anywhere in the Government.

This reversal grew out of the serious political difference between the two Houses of Congress and President Johnson. There was a two-thirds majority of the Republican party in control of each House of Congress, which resented what it feared would be Mr. Johnson's obstructive course in the enforcement of the reconstruction measures in respect of the States whose people had lately been at war against the National Government. This led the two Houses to enact legislation to curtail the then acknowledged powers of the President. . . .

But the chief legislation in support of the reconstruction policy of Congress was the Tenure of Office Act of March 2, 1867, providing that all officers appointed by and with the consent of the Senate should hold their offices until their successors should have in like manner been appointed and qualified, that certain heads of departments, including the Secretary of War, should hold their offices during the terms of the President by whom appointed and one month thereafter subject to removal by consent of the Senate. The Tenure of Office Act was vetoed, but it was passed over the veto. The House of Representatives preferred articles of impeachment against President Johnson for refusal to comply

with, and for conspiracy to defeat, the legislation above referred to, but he was acquitted for lack of a two-thirds vote for conviction in the Senate. . . .

. . . The feeling growing out of the controversy with President Johnson retained the act on the statute book until 1887, when it was repealed. During this interval, on June 8, 1872, Congress passed an act reorganizing and consolidating the Postoffice Department and provided that the Postmaster General and his three assistants should be appointed by the President by and with the advice and consent of the Senate and might be removed in the same manner. In 1876 the act here under discussion was passed, making the consent of the Senate necessary both to the appointment and removal of first, second and third class postmasters. . . .

An argument ab inconvenienti has been made against our conclusion in favor of the executive power of removal by the President, without the consent of the Senate that it will open the door to a reintroduction of the spoils system. The evil of the spoils system aimed at in the civil service law and its amendments is in respect of inferior offices. It has never been attempted to extend that law beyond them. Indeed Congress forbids its extension to appointments confirmed by the Senate except with the consent of the Senate. . . . It may still be enlarged by further legislation. The independent power of removal by the President alone under present conditions works no practical interference with the merit system. Political appointments of inferior officers are still maintained in one important class, that of the first, second and third class postmasters, collectors of internal revenue, marshals, collectors of customs and other officers of that kind distributed through the country. They are appointed by the President with the consent of the Senate. It is the intervention of the Senate in their appointment and not in their removal which prevents their classification into the merit system. If such appointments were vested in the heads of departments to which they belong, they could be entirely removed from politics, and that is what a number of Presidents have recommended. . . . The extension of the merit system rests with Congress. . . .

. . . Without animadverting on the character of the measures taken, we are certainly justified in saying that they should not be given the weight affecting proper constitutional construction to be accorded to that reached by the First Congress of the United States during a political calm and acquiesced in by the whole Government for three-quarters of a century, especially when the new construction contended for has never been acquiesced in by either the executive or the judicial departments. While this court has studiously avoided deciding the issue until it was presented in such a way that it could not be avoided, in the references it has made to the history of the question, and in the presumptions it has indulged in favor of a statutory construction not inconsistent with the legislative decision of 1789, it has indicated a trend of view that we should not and can not ignore. When on the merits we find our conclusion strongly favoring the view which prevailed in the First Congress, we have no hesitation in holding that conclusion to be correct; and it therefore follows that the Tenure of Office Act of 1867, in so far as it attempted to prevent the President from removing executive officers who had been appointed by him by and with the advice and consent of the Senate, was invalid and that subsequent legislation of the same effect was equally so.

For the reasons given, we must therefore hold that the provision of the law of 1876 by which the unrestricted power of removal of first class postmasters is denied to the President is in violation of the Constitution and invalid. This leads to an affirmance of the judgment of the Court of Claims. . . .

Judgment affirmed.

Mr. Justice **Holmes,** dissenting, said in part:

The arguments drawn from the executive power of the President and from his duty to appoint officers of the United States (when Congress does not vest the appointment elsewhere), to take care that the laws be faithfully executed, and to commission all officers of the United States, seem to me spiders' webs inadequate to control the dominant facts.

We have to deal with an office that owes its existence to Congress and that Congress may abolish tomorrow. Its duration and the pay attached to it while it lasts depend on Congress alone. Congress alone confers on the President the power to appoint to it and at any time may transfer the power to other hands. With such power over its own creation, I have no more trouble in believing that Congress has power to prescribe a term of life for it free from any interference than I have in accepting the undoubted power of Congress to decree its end. I have equally little trouble in accepting its power to prolong the tenure of an incumbent until Congress or the Senate shall have assented to his removal. The duty of the President to see that the laws be executed is a duty that does not go beyond the laws or require him to achieve more than Congress sees fit to leave within his power.

In a dissenting opinion Mr. Justice **McReynolds** said in part:

The long struggle for civil service reform and the legislation designed to insure some security of official tenure ought not to be forgotten. Again and again Congress has enacted statutes prescribing restrictions on removals and by approving them many Presidents have affirmed its power therein. . . .

Nothing short of language clear beyond serious disputation should be held to clothe the President with authority wholly beyond congressional control arbitrarily to dismiss every officer whom he appoints except a few judges. There are no such words in the Constitution, and the asserted inference conflicts with the heretofore accepted theory that this government is one of carefully enumerated power under an intelligible charter. . . .

If the phrase "executive power" infolds the one now claimed many others heretofore totally unsuspected may lie there awaiting future supposed necessity; and no human intelligence can define the field of the President's permissible activities. "A masked battery of constructive powers would complete the destruction of liberty." . . .

HUMPHREY'S EXECUTOR v. UNITED STATES

295 U.S. 602; 55 S. Ct. 869; 79 L. Ed. 1611
(1935)

The decision in the Myers case was rightly viewed as of great importance, although the immediate point involved, the removal of a postmaster, was of no broad interest. What did arouse much controversy and rather general concern was the sweeping dictum of the Chief Justice that the President's unrestricted removal power extended not merely to his immediate executive subordinates but also to the members of the great independent commissions, such as the Interstate Commerce Commission and the Federal Trade Commission, and presumably, also, to the Comptroller General. These officers are appointed under the provisions of statutes conferring upon them duties with respect to which a high degree of independence and freedom from political control is deemed desirable. Congress has carefully specified the causes for which they may be removed with the intention that they be free from removals of a "political" nature. If, however, the Taft theory were to prevail, their independence from presidential control would be broken down. It was expected, therefore, that sooner or later the question of whether the President's unlimited removal power did actually extend to these independent commissions and officers would be presented to the Court on facts requiring a specific answer. This was done in the Humphrey case. It is interesting to note that in overruling Chief Justice Taft's dictum and holding that the President's removal power extends only to executive officers, the Court invokes the same doctrine of the separation of powers which serves as the basis of the Myers decision. The separation of powers protects the President in the exercise of his power to remove executive officers appointed by him, but it also prevents him from removing officers who are not essentially executive and whose removal has been restricted by Congress.

The decision in the Humphrey case does not transfer the removal power to Congress. While Congress may limit the President's removal power by declaring the causes for which he may exercise it, it is still the President who must remove the officer for any one of those causes. But Congress, in its efforts to control the way in which its policies are executed, has from time to time attempted to remove members of the executive branch in whom it lacked confidence, but without resorting to the impeachment process. Such attempts have not been particularly successful. However, Congress has another ace up its sleeve. Under its authority to create an executive office, Congress has frequently listed qualifications which the officer must possess, and such qualifications limit the President's appointing power since they can be readily enforced through the Senate's power to refuse confirmation.

Occasionally Congress has gone further and has added qualifications to an existing office for the purpose of ousting an incumbent. In 1938, Congress provided by a rider to an appropriation act that no salary should be paid any reclamation commissioner who had not had ten years' experience as an engineer. The rider was aimed at a particular reclamation commissioner on the West Coast who had incurred the displeasure of certain Senators, and whose sole training as a newspaperman barred him from drawing further salary under the new law. The officer, however, continued in office without pay, and the following year Congress repealed the rider and reimbursed him. Eventually, Congress went too far. In 1943 Congress provided that no salary should be paid to three named individuals whom the House Committee on Un-American Activities had charged with subversion until they were reappointed by the President and confirmed by the Senate. Although the Court refused to consider the question of the removal power of Congress, in United States v. Lovett (1946) it held the statute void as a bill of attainder. In 1931 the Senate attempted to withdraw the confirmation it had given to the appointment of a member of the Federal Power Commission, after he had assumed office; in United States v. Smith (1932) the Court, in an unusual decision, avoided any constitutional issue by holding that such a move was forbidden by the rules of the Senate.

Thus the question of whether Congress can exercise a direct removal power of its own has never been judicially decided. The statute creating the office of Comptroller General provides that he shall be appointed by the President with the consent of the Senate, but that he may be removed only by impeachment or by the joint address of both houses of Congress. Neither Congress nor the President has ever attempted to remove a Comptroller General, although President Franklin Roosevelt made an unsuccessful effort to have the office abolished. The statute creating the board of directors of the Tennessee Valley Authority provides that "any member of the board may be removed at any time by a concurrent resolution of the Senate and House of Representatives," while providing removal by the President for any violation of the merit principle in dealing with TVA personnel. In 1938 the President removed Dr. A. E. Morgan, chairman of the board of the TVA, for the purpose of ironing out internal dissension which had grown up in the board. The circuit court of appeals upheld the removal on the ground that the TVA was an executive or administrative agency, and that the TVA statute clearly indicated that Congress expected the President to exercise wide powers of control over it; see Morgan v. Tennessee Valley Authority (1940). The Supreme Court refused to review the decision; see Morgan v. Tennessee Valley Authority (1941).

As Justice Sutherland acutely observes in the last paragraph of the Humphrey opinion, there are a number of problems regarding the President's power of removal which remain unsolved. It seems clear from the Myers and Humphrey cases that Congress cannot validly restrict the President's power to remove purely executive officers, but that it may restrict his removal of those who are not executive officers. Federal officers, however, do not fall into any such dichotomy. There are numerous executive officers, not to mention some of our independent regulatory commissions and other administrative agencies, to whom Congress has given both executive duties and quasi-judicial or quasi-legislative functions. The Secretary of Agriculture, in administering the Packers and Stockyards Act, performs functions which are identical with those of the Federal Trade Commission, and yet the Secretary is clearly removable by the President in his discretion. The Civil Aeronautics Board, on the other hand, whose members, under the statute, are removable by the President only for inefficiency, neglect of duty, or malfeasance in office, exercises a melange of executive and quasi-judicial functions which preclude classifying it under either the Myers or the Humphrey rule.

However vague the concept of the separation of powers may be, the one area in which it has real meaning for the public is in the concept of an independent judiciary. Since the time of the historic battle between Lord Coke and James I of England people in common law countries have agreed that the scales of justice should not be tilted by the heavy thumb of the executive. When a person goes into court to contest the action of the police or a regulatory agency, he or she does not think of the court as "part of the government," but as an impartial arbiter of his or her dispute.

Following World War II Congress created a War Claims Commission to handle legal claims against the government growing out of the damage caused to our allies from the conduct of the war on their soil. The Commission was short-lived and no provision was made for removal of its members. President Eisenhower removed one of the members explaining that "I regard it as in the national interest to complete the administration of the War Claims Act . . . with personnel of my own selection." In Wiener v. United States (1958) the Supreme Court held the removal void. It discussed at length the judicial nature of the commission's work and "inferred that Congress did not wish to have hang over the Commission the Damocles' sword of removal by the President . . . . Judging the matter in all the nakedness in which it is presented, namely, the claim that the President could remove a member of an adjudicatory body like the War Claims Commission merely because he wanted his own appointees on such a Commission, we are compelled to conclude that no such power is given to the President directly by the Constitution, and none is impliedly conferred upon him by statute simply because Congress said nothing about it. The philosophy of Humphrey's Executor, in its explicit language as well as its implications, precludes such a claim."

Mr. Justice **Sutherland** delivered the opinion of the Court, saying in part:

Plaintiff brought suit in the Court of Claims against the United States to recover a sum of money alleged to be due the deceased for salary as a Federal Trade Commissioner from October 8, 1933, when the President undertook to remove him from office, to the time of his death on February 14, 1934. The court below has certified to this court two questions . . . in respect of the power of the President to make the removal. The material facts which give rise to the question are as follows:

William E. Humphrey, the decedent, on December 10, 1931, was nominated by President Hoover to succeed himself as a member of the Federal Trade Commission and was confirmed by the United States Senate. He was duly commissioned for a term of seven years expiring September 25, 1938; and, after taking the required oath of office, entered upon his duties. On July 25, 1933, President Roosevelt addressed a letter to the commissioner asking for his resignation, on the ground "that the aims and purposes of the Administration with respect to the work of the Commission can be carried out most effectively with personnel of my own selection," but disclaiming any reflection upon the commissioner personally or upon his services. The commissioner replied, asking time to consult his friends. After some further correspondence upon the subject, the President, on August 31, 1933, wrote the commissioner expressing the hope that the resignation would be forthcoming and saying:

"You will, I know, realize that I do not feel that your mind and my mind go along together on either the policies or the administering of the Federal Trade Commission, and, frankly, I think it is best for the people of this country that I should have a full confidence."

The commissioner declined to resign, and on October 7, 1933, the President wrote him:

"Effective as of this date, you are hereby removed from the office of Commissioner of the Federal Trade Commission."

Humphrey never acquiesced in this action, but continued thereafter to insist that he was still a member of the commission, entitled to perform its duties and receive the compensation provided by law at the rate of $10,000 per annum. Upon these and other facts set forth in the certificate, which we deem it unnecessary to recite, the following questions are certified:

"1. Do the provisions of § 1 of the Federal Trade Commission Act, stating that 'any commissioner may be removed by the President for inefficiency, neglect of duty, or malfeasance in office,' restrict or limit the power of the President to remove a commissioner except upon one or more of the causes named?

"If the foregoing question is answered in the affirmative, then—

"2. If the power of the President to remove a commissioner is restricted or limited as shown by the foregoing interrogatory and the answer made thereto, is such a restriction or limitation valid under the Constitution of the United States?"

The Federal Trade Commission Act creates a commission of five members to be appointed by the President by and with the advice and consent of the Senate, and § 1 provides:

"Not more than three of the commissioners shall be members of the same political party. The first commissioners appointed shall continue in office for terms of three, four, five, six and seven years, respectively, from the date of the taking effect of this act, the term of each to be designated by the President, but their successors shall be appointed for terms of seven years, except that any person chosen to fill a vacancy shall be appointed only for the unexpired term of the commissioner whom he shall succeed. The commission shall choose a chairman from its own membership. No commissioner shall engage in any other business, vocation, or employment. Any commissioner may be removed by the President for inefficiency, neglect of duty, or malfeasance in office."

Section 5 of the act in part provides:

"Unfair methods of competition in commerce are hereby declared unlawful.

"The commission is hereby empowered and directed to prevent persons, partnerships or corporations, except banks and common carriers subject to the acts to regulate commerce, from using unfair methods of competition in commerce."

In exercising this power the commission must issue a complaint stating its charges and giving notice of hearing upon a day to be fixed. A person, partnership, or corporation proceeded against is given the right to appear at the time and place fixed and show cause why an order to cease and desist should not be issued. There is provision for intervention by others interested. If the commission finds the method of competition is one prohibited by the act, it is directed to make a report in writing stating its findings as to the facts, and to issue and cause to be served a cease and desist order. If the order is disobeyed the commission may apply to the appropriate Circuit Court of Appeals for its enforcement. This party subject to the order may seek and obtain a review in the Circuit Court of Appeals in a manner provided by the act.

Section 6, among other things, gives the commission wide powers of investigation in respect of certain corporations subject to the act, and in respect of other matters, upon which it must report to Congress with recommendations. Many such investigations have been made, and some have served as the basis of congressional legislation.

Section 7 provides:

"That in any suit in equity brought by or under the direction of the Attorney General, as provided in the anti-trust acts, the court may, upon the conclusion of the testimony therein, if it shall be then of opinion that the complainant is entitled to relief, refer said suit to the commission, as a master in chancery, to ascertain and report an appropriate form of decree therein. The commission shall proceed upon such notice to the parties and under such rules of procedure as the court may prescribe and upon the coming in of such report such exceptions may be filed and such proceedings had in relation thereto as upon the report of a master in other equity causes, but the court may adopt or reject such report, in whole or in part, and enter such decree as the nature of the case may in its judgment require.''

First. The question first to be considered is whether, by the provisions of § 1 of the Federal Trade Commission Act already quoted, the President's power is limited to removal for the specific causes enumerated therein. . . .

. . . The statute fixes a term of office in accordance with many precedents. The first commissioners appointed are to continue in office for terms of three, four, five, six and seven years, respectively; and their successors are to be appointed for terms of seven years—any commissioner being subject to removal by the President for inefficiency, neglect of duty, or malfeasance in office. The words of the act are definite and unambiguous.

The government says the phrase "continue in office" is of no legal significance, and, moreover, applies only to the first commissioners. We think it has significance. It may be that, literally, its application is restricted as suggested; but it, nevertheless, lends support to a view contrary to that of the government as to the meaning of the entire requirement in respect of tenure; for it is not easy to suppose that Congress intended to secure the first commissioners against removal except for the causes specified and deny like security to their successors. Putting this phrase aside, however, the fixing of a definite term subject to removal for cause, unless there be some countervailing provision or circumstance indicating the contrary, which here we are unable to find, is enough to establish the legislative intent that the term is not to be curtailed in the absence of such cause. But if the intention of Congress that no removal should be made during the specified term except for one or more of the enumerated causes were not clear upon the face of the statute, as we think it is, it would be made clear by a consideration of the character of the commission and the legislative history which accompanied and preceded the passage of the act.

The commission is to be nonpartisan; and it must, from the very nature of its duties, act with entire impartiality. It is charged with the enforcement of no policy except the policy of the law. Its duties are neither political nor executive, but predominantly quasi-judicial and quasi-legislative. Like the Interstate Commerce Commission, its members are called upon to exercise the trained judgment of a body of experts "appointed by law and informed by experience." . . .

The legislative reports in both houses of Congress clearly reflect the view that a fixed term was necessary to the effective and fair administration of the law. . . .

The debates in both houses demonstrate that the prevailing view was that the commission was not to be "subject to anybody in the government but . . . only to the people of the United States," free from "political domination or control," or the "probability or possibility of such a thing;" to be "separate and apart from any existing department of the government—not subject to the orders of the President." . . .

Thus, the language of the act, the legislative reports and the general purposes of the legislation as reflected by the debates, all combine to demonstrate the Congressional intent to create a body of experts who shall gain experience by length of service—a body which shall be independent of Executive authority, *except in its selection*, and free to exercise its judgment without the leave or hindrance of any other official or any department of the government. To the accomplishment of these purposes it is clear that Congress was of opinion that length and certainty of tenure would vitally contribute. And to hold that, nevertheless, the members of the commission continue in office at the mere will of the President, might be to thwart, in large measure, the very ends which Congress sought to realize by definitely fixing the term of office.

We conclude that the intent of the act is to limit the executive power of removal to the causes enumerated, the existence of none of which is claimed here; and we pass to the second question.

Second. To support its contention that the removal provision of § 1, as we have just construed it, is an unconstitutional interference with the executive power of the President, the government's chief reliance is Myers v. United States [1926]. . . . Nevertheless, the narrow point actually decided was only that the President had power to remove a postmaster of the first class, without the advice and consent of the Senate, as required by act of Congress. In the course of the opinion of the court, expressions occur which tend to sustain the government's contention, but these are beyond the point involved, and therefore, do not come within the rule of stare decisis. In so far as they are out of harmony with the views here set forth, these expressions are disapproved. . . .

The office of a postmaster is so essentially unlike the office now involved that the decision in the Myers case cannot be accepted as controlling our decision here. A postmaster is an executive officer restricted to the performance of executive functions. He is charged with no duty at all related to either the legislative or judicial power. The actual decision in the Myers case finds support in the theory that such an officer is merely one of the units in the executive department and hence inherently subject to the exclusive and illimitable power of removal by the chief executive, whose subordinate and aide he is. Putting aside dicta, which may be followed if sufficiently persuasive but which are not controlling, the necessary reach of the decision goes far enough to include all purely executive officers. It goes no farther—much less does it include an officer who occupies no place in the executive department and who exercises no part of the executive power vested by the Constitution in the President.

The Federal Trade Commission is an administrative body created by Congress to carry into effect legislative policies embodied in the statute, in accordance with the legislative standard therein prescribed, and to perform other specified duties as a legislative or as a judicial aid. Such a body cannot in any proper sense be characterized as an arm or an eye of the executive. Its duties are performed without executive leave and, in the contemplation of the statute, must be free from executive control. In administrating the provisions of the statute in respect of "unfair methods of competition"—that is to say in filling in and administering the details embodied by the general standard—the commission acts in part quasi-legislatively and in part quasi-judicially. In making investigations and reports thereon for the information of Congress under § 6, in aid of the legislative power it acts as a legislative agency. Under § 7, which authorizes the commission to act as a master in chancery under rules prescribed by the court, it acts as an agency of the judiciary. To the extent that it exercises any executive function—as distinguished from executive power in the constitutional sense—it does so in the discharge and effectuation of its quasi-legislative or quasi-judicial powers, or as an agency of the legislative or judicial departments of the government.

If Congress is without authority to prescribe causes for removal of members of the Trade Commission and limit executive power of removal accordingly, that power at once becomes practically all inclusive in respect of civil officers, with the exception of the judiciary provided for by the Constitution. The Solicitor General, at the bar, apparently recognizing this to be true, with commendable candor agreed that his view in respect of the removability of members of the Federal Trade Commission necessitated a like view in respect of the Interstate Commerce Commission and the Court of Claims. We are thus confronted with the serious question whether not only the members of these quasi-legislative and quasi-judicial bodies, but the judges of the legislative Court of Claims, exercising judicial power . . . continue in office only at the pleasure of the President.

We think it plain under the Constitution that illimitable power of removal is not possessed by the President in respect of officers of the character of those just named. The authority of Congress, in creating quasi-legislative or quasi-judicial agencies, to require them to act in discharge of their duties independently of executive control, cannot well be doubted and that authority includes, as an appropriate incident, power to fix the period during which they shall continue, and to forbid their removal except for cause in the meantime. For it is quite evident that one who holds his office only during the pleasure of another cannot be depended upon to maintain an attitude of independence against the latter's will.

The fundamental necessity of maintaining each of the three general departments of government entirely free from the control or coercive influence, direct or indirect, of either of the others, has often been stressed and is hardly open to serious question. So much is implied in the very fact of the separation of the powers of these departments by the Constitution, and in the rule which recognizes their essential co-equality. The sound application of a principle that makes one master in his own house precludes him from imposing his control in the house of another who is master there. . . .

The power of removal here claimed for the President falls within this principle, since its coercive influence threatens the independence of a commission, which is not only wholly disconnected from the executive department, but which, as already fully appears, was created by Congress as a means of carrying into operation legislative and judicial powers, and as an agency of the legislative and judicial department.

In the light of the question now under consideration, we have reexamined the precedents referred to in the Myers case, and find nothing in them to justify a conclusion contrary to that which we have reached. . . .

The result of what we now have said is this: Whether the power of the President to remove an officer shall prevail over the authority of Congress to condition the power by fixing a definite term and precluding a removal except for cause will depend upon the character of the office. The Myers decision, affirming the power of the President alone to make the removal, is confined to purely executive officers. And as to officers of the kind here under consideration, we hold that no removal can be made during the prescribed term for which the officer is appointed, except for one or more of the causes named in the applicable statute.

To the extent that, between the decision in the Myers case, which sustains the unrestrictable power of the President to remove purely executive officers, and our present decision that such power does not extend to an office such as that here involved, there shall remain a field of doubt, we leave such cases as may fall within it for future consideration and determination as they may arise.

In accordance with the foregoing the questions submitted are answered.

Question No. 1, Yes.
Question No. 2, Yes.

BUCKLEY v. VALEO

424 U. S. 1; 96 S. Ct.612; 46 L. Ed. 2d 659
(1976)

The grant of presidential power in Article II to see that the laws are faithfully executed suggests that it is the President's role to carry out the policies of Congress as set out in the statutes, and it is probable that this was the role the framers had in mind when the clause was drafted. While the President must necessarily interpret the law when he enforces it, where the congressional policy embodied in the law is clear, the President is expected to carry that policy out. In Kendall v. United States (1838), discussed in connection with the Myers case, the Court made it clear that the constitutional powers of the President to see the laws faithfully executed did not imply "a power to forbid their execution." Clearly, the President is expected to carry out the laws of Congress.

But can Congress enact its policies into law and assign the job of carrying them out to someone other than the President? In the Humphrey case the Court indicated that it could. There it condoned the creation by

Congress of agencies independent of direct presidential control on the ground that they were "charged with the enforcement of no policy except the policy of the law"; and since they were "created by Congress to carry into effect legislative policies embodied in the statute," they "cannot in any proper sense be characterized as an arm or an eye of the executive." Hence they could be made virtually immune from presidential removal.

If Congress can have its policies carried out by agencies not subject to presidential control by removal, can it also have them carried out by agencies whose members are not subject to presidential appointment but are appointed by Congress itself? Can Congress, in other words, create an executive branch of its own to carry out its policies? In the Federal Election Campaign Act of 1971, Congress enacted an elaborate statute which limited in various ways the amount of money candidates could spend in seeking office, required reporting of what monies were spent and whence they came, and provided for the public financing of presidential control by removal, can it also have them carried out by agencies whose members are subject to presidential nominating conventions, primary election campaigns, and the final general election campaign.

To carry out the provisions of this complex act, Congress created a Federal Election Commission with six voting members, two of whom were to be appointed by the President Pro Tempore of the Senate, two by the Speaker of the House, and two by the President of the United States. All six were to be subject to confirmation by a majority of both houses of Congress. While the Court was divided upon other issues raised by the case, it held unanimously that the Election Commission was invalidly appointed.

In the wake of the Watergate affair Congress passed the Ethics in Government Act of 1978 which provided sharp limits on when, if at all, a former government employee could lobby before Congress and also provided for the appointment of special prosecutors to investigate and prosecute malfeasance in the executive branch. These prosecutors are appointed by a three-judge appellate panel chosen by the Chief Justice and are removable by the Attorney General only for "extraordinary improprieties." Two individuals, Michael Deever, a former advisor to the President, has been indicted for violating the lobbying provisions of the act, and Lt. Col. Oliver North, aide to the President's national security advisor and involved in the arms-to-Iran deal is suspected of obstructing justice. Both have challenged the special prosecutors assigned to their cases under the rationale of Humphrey and Buckley.

Query: Can a court, whose appointing power normally extends to court functionaries such as masters and estate administrators, appoint a prosecutor whose job is normally executive?

Can a prosecutor who is essentially independent of the Attorney General, exercise a normally executive power?

The Court, per curiam, said in part:

IV. THE FEDERAL ELECTION COMMISSION . . .

B. The Merits

Appellants urge that since Congress has given the Commission wide-ranging rule-making and enforcement powers with respect to the substantive provisions of the Act, Congress is precluded under the principle of separation of powers from vesting in itself the authority to appoint those who will exercise such authority. Their argument is based on the language of Art. II, § 2, cl. 2, of the Constitution, which provides in pertinent part as follows: "[The President] shall nominate, and by and with the Advice and Consent of the Senate, shall appoint . . . all other Officers of the United States, whose Appointments are not herein otherwise provided for, and which shall be established by Law: but the Congress may by Law vest the Appointment of such inferior Officers, as they think proper, in the President alone, in the Courts of Law, or in the Heads of Departments."

Appellants' argument is that this provision is the exclusive method by which those charged with executing the laws of the United States may be chosen. Congress, they assert, cannot have it both ways. If the Legislature wishes the Commission to exercise all of the conferred powers, then its members are in fact "Officers of the United States" and must be appointed under the Appointments Clause. But if Congress insists upon retaining the power to appoint, then the members of the Commission may not discharge those many functions of the Commission which can be performed only by "Officers of the United States," as that term must be construed within the doctrine of separation of powers.

Appellee Commission and amici in support of the Commission urge that the Framers of the Constitution, while mindful of the need for checks and balances among the three branches of the National Government, had no intention of denying to the Legislative Branch authority to appoint its own officers. Congress, either under the Appointments Clause or under its grants of substantive legislative authority and the Necessary and Proper Clause in Art. I, is in their view empowered to provide for the appointment to the Commission in the manner which it did because the Commission is performing "appropriate legislative functions." . . .

1. Separation of Powers

. . . Our inquiry of necessity touches upon the fundamental principles of the Government established by the Framers of the Constitution, and all litigants and all of the courts which have addressed themselves to the matter start on common ground in the recognition of the intent of the Framers that the powers of the three great branches of the National Government be largely separate from one another.

James Madison, writing in the Federalist No. 47, defended the work of the Framers against the charge that these three governmental powers were not *entirely* separate from one another in the proposed Constitution. He asserted that while there was some admixture, the Constitution was nonetheless true to Montesquieu's well-known maxim that the legislative, executive, and judicial departments ought to be separate and distinct:

"The reasons on which Montesquieu grounds his maxim are a further demonstration of his meaning. 'When the legislative and executive powers are united in the same person or body,' says he, 'there can be no liberty, because apprehensions may arise lest *the same* monarch or senate should *enact* tyrannical laws to *execute* them in a tyrannical manner.' Again: 'Were the power of judging joined with the legislative, the life and liberty of the subject would be exposed to arbitrary control, for the *judge* would then be the *legislator*. Were it joined to the executive power, the *judge* might behave with all the violence of *an oppressor*.' Some of these reasons are more fully explained in other passages; but briefly stated as they are here, they sufficiently establish the meaning which we have put on this celebrated maxim of this celebrated author."

Yet it is also clear from the provisions of the Constitution itself, and from the Federalist Papers, that the Constitution by no means contemplates total separation of each of these three essential branches of Government. The President is a participant in the lawmaking process by virtue of his authority to veto bills enacted by Congress. The Senate is a participant in the appointive process by virtue of its authority to refuse to confirm persons nominated to office by the President. The men who met in Philadelphia in the summer of 1787 were practical statesmen, experienced in politics, who viewed the principle of separation of powers as a vital check against tyranny. But they likewise saw that a hermetic sealing off of the three branches of Government from one another would preclude the establishment of a Nation capable of governing itself effectively. . . .

The Framers regarded the checks and balances that they had built into the tripartite Federal Government as a self-executing safeguard against the encroachment or aggrandizement of one branch at the expense of the other. As Madison put it in Federalist No. 51:

"This policy of supplying, by opposite and rival interests, the defect of better motives, might be traced through the whole system of human affairs, private as well as public. We see it particularly displayed in all the subordinate distributions of power, where the constant aim is to divide and arrange the several offices in such a manner as that each may be a check on the other—that the private interest of every individual may be a sentinel over the public rights. These inventions of prudence cannot be less requisite in the distribution of the supreme powers of the State." . . .

2. The Appointments Clause

The principle of separation of powers was not simply an abstract generalization in the minds of the Framers: it was woven into the document that they drafted in Philadelphia in the summer of 1787. . . .

[The Court here quotes the relevant provisions of Articles I, II and III providing for the distribution of power among the three branches.]

It is in the context of these cognate provisions of the document that we must examine the language of Art. II, § 2, cl. 2, which appellants contend provides the only authorization for appointment of those to whom substantial executive or administrative authority is given by statute. . . .

The Appointments Clause could, of course, be read as merely dealing with etiquette or protocol in describing "Officers of the United States," but the drafters had a less frivolous purpose in mind. This conclusion is supported by language from United States v. Germaine (1879):

"The Constitution for purposes of appointment very clearly divides all its officers into two classes. The primary class requires a nomination by the President and confirmation by the Senate. But foreseeing that when offices became numerous, and sudden removals necessary, this mode might be inconvenient, it was provided that, in regard to officers inferior to those specially mentioned, Congress might by law vest their appointment in the President alone, in the courts of law, or in the heads of departments. *That all persons who can be said to hold an office under the government about to be established under the Constitution were intended to be included within one or the other of these modes of appointment there can be but little doubt*." (Emphasis supplied.) . . .

If "all persons who can be said to hold an office under the government about to be established under the Constitution were intended to be included within one or the other of these modes of appointment," United States v. Germaine, supra, it is difficult to see how the members of the Commission may escape inclusion. . . .

Although two members of the Commission are initially selected by the President, his nominations are subject to confirmation not merely by the Senate, but by the House of Representatives as well. The remaining four voting members of the Commission are appointed by the President pro tempore of the Senate and by the Speaker of the House. While the second part of the Clause authorizes Congress to vest the appointment of the officers described in that part in "the Courts of Law, or in the Heads of Departments," neither the Speaker of the House nor the President pro tempore of the Senate comes within this language.

The phrase "Heads of Departments," used as it is in conjunction with the phrase "Courts of Law," suggests that the Departments referred to are themselves in the Executive Branch or at least have some connection with that branch. While the Clause expressly authorizes Congress to vest the appointment of certain officers in the "Courts of Law," the absence of similar language to include Congress must mean that neither Congress nor its officers were included within the language "Heads of Departments" in this part of cl. 2.

Thus with respect to four of the six voting members of the Commission, neither the President, the head of any department, nor the Judiciary has any voice in their selection.

The Appointments Clause specifies the method of appointment only for "Officer of the United States" whose appointment is not "otherwise provided for" in the Constitution. But there is no provision of the Constitution remotely providing any alternative means for the selection of the members of the Commission or for anybody like them. Appellee Commission has argued, and the Court of Appeals agreed, that the Appointments Clause of Art. II should not be read to exclude the "inherent power of Congress" to appoint its own officers to perform functions necessary to that body as an institution. But there is no need to read the Appointments Clause contrary to its plain language in order to reach the result sought by the Court of Appeals. Article I, § 3, cl. 5, expressly authorizes the selection of the President pro tempore of the Senate, and § 2, cl. 5, of that Article provides for the selection of the Speaker of the House. Ranking nonmembers, such as the Clerk of the House of Representatives, are elected under the internal rules of each House and are designated by statute as "officers of the Congress." There is no occasion for us to decide whether any of these member officers are "Officers of the United States" whose "appointment" is otherwise provided for within the meaning of the Appointments Clause, since even if they were such officers their appointees would not be. Contrary to the fears expressed by the majority of the Court of Appeals, nothing in our holding with respect to Art. II, § 2, cl. 2, will deny to Congress "all power to appoint its own inferior officers to carry out appropriate legislative functions."

Appellee Commission and amici contend somewhat obliquely that because the Framers had no intention of relegating Congress to a position below that of the co-equal Judicial and Executive Branches of the National Government, the Appointments Clause must somehow be read to include Congress or its officers as among those in whom the appointment power may be vested. But the debates of the Constitutional Convention, and the Federalist Papers, are replete with expressions of fear that the Legislative Branch of the National Government will aggrandize itself at the expense of the other two branches. The debates during the Convention, and the evolution of the draft version of the Constitution, seem to us to lend considerable support to our reading of the language of the Appointments Clause itself.

An interim version of the draft Constitution had vested in the Senate the authority to appoint Ambassadors, public Ministers, and Judges of the Supreme Court, and the language of Art. II as finally adopted is a distinct change in this regard. We believe that it was a deliberate change made by the Framers with the intent to deny Congress any authority itself to appoint those who were "Officers of the United States." The debates on the floor of the Convention reflect at least in part the way the change came about. . . . [The Court here reviews the debates.]

Appellee Commission and amici urge that because of what they conceive to be the extraordinary authority reposed in Congress to regulate elections, this case stands on a different footing than if Congress had exercised its legislative authority in another field. There is, of course, no doubt that Congress has express authority to regulate congressional elections, by virtue of the power conferred in Art. I § 4. . . . We see no reason to believe that the authority of Congress over federal election practices is of such a wholly different nature from the other grants of authority to Congress that it may be employed in such a manner as to offend well-established constitutional restrictions stemming from the separation of powers.

The position that because Congress has been given explicit and plenary authority to regulate a field of activity, it must therefore have the power to appoint those who are to administer the regulatory statute is both novel and contrary to the language of the Appointments Clause. Unless their selection is elsewhere provided for, all officers of the United States are to be appointed in accordance with the Clause. Principal officers are selected by the President with the advice and consent of the Senate. Inferior officers Congress may allow to be appointed by the President alone, by the heads of departments, or by the Judiciary. No class or type of officer is excluded because of its special functions. The President appoints judicial as well as executive officers. Neither has it been disputed—and apparently it is not now disputed—that the Clause controls the appointment of the members of a typical administrative agency even though its functions, as this Court recognized in Humphrey's Executor v. United States (1935), may be "predominantly quasi-judicial and quasi-legislative" rather than executive. The Court in that case carefully emphasized that although the members of such agencies were to be independent of the Executive in their day-to-day operations, the Executive was not excluded from selecting them. . . .

We are also told by appellees and amici that Congress had good reason for not vesting in a Commission composed wholly of Presidential appointees the authority to administer the Act, since the administration of the Act would undoubtedly have a bearing on any incumbent President's campaign for re-election. While one cannot dispute the basis for this sentiment as a practical matter, it would seem that those who sought to challenge incumbent Congressmen might have equally good reason to fear a Commission which was unduly responsive to Members of Congress whom they were seeking to unseat. But such fears, however rational, do not by themselves warrant a distortion of the Framers' work.

Appellee Commission and amici finally contend, and the majority of the Court of Appeals agreed with them, that whatever shortcomings the provisions for the appointment of members of the Commission might have under Art. II, Congress had ample authority under the Necessary and Proper Clause of Art. I to effectuate this result. We do not agree. The proper inquiry when considering the Necessary and Proper Clause is not the authority of Congress to create an office or a commission, which is broad indeed, but rather its authority to provide that its own officers may make appointments to such office or commission.

So framed, the claim that Congress may provide for this manner of appointment under the Necessary and Proper Clause of Art. I stands on no better footing than the claim that it may provide for such manner of appointment because of its substantive authority to regulate federal elections. Congress could not, merely because it concluded that such a measure was "necessary and proper" to the discharge of its substantive legislative authority, pass a bill of attainder or ex post facto law contrary to the prohibitions contained in § 9 of Art. I. No more may it vest in itself, or in its officers, the authority to appoint officers of the United States when the Appointments Clause by clear implication prohibits it from doing so.

The trilogy of cases from this Court dealing with the constitutional authority of Congress to circumscribe the President's power to *remove* officers of the United States is entirely consistent with this conclusion. In Myers v. United States (1926), the Court held that Congress could not by statute divest the President of the power to remove an officer in the Executive Branch whom he was initially authorized to appoint. In explaining its reasoning in that case, the Court said:

"The vesting of the executive power in the President was essentially a grant of the power to execute the laws. But the President alone and unaided could not execute the laws. He must execute them by the assistance of subordinates. . . . As he is charged specifically to take care that they be faithfully executed, the reasonable implication, even in the absence of express words, was that as part of his executive power he should select those who were to act for him under his direction in the execution of the laws. . . .

"Our conclusion on the merits, sustained by the arguments before stated is that Article II grants to the President the executive power of the Government, i. e., the general administrative control of those executing the laws, including the power of appointment and removal of executive officers—a conclusion confirmed by his obligation to take care that the laws be faithfully executed. . . ."

In the later case of Humphrey's Executor, where it was held that Congress could circumscribe the President's power to remove members of independent regulatory agencies, the Court was careful to note that it was dealing with an agency intended to be independent of executive authority "*except in its selection.*" (emphasis in original). Wiener v. United States (1958), which applied the holding in Humphrey's Executor to a member of the War Claims Commission, did not question in any respect that members of independent agencies are not independent of the Executive with respect to their appointments. . . .

3. The Commission's Powers

Thus, on the assumption that all of the powers granted in the statute may be exercised by an agency whose members *have been* appointed in accordance with the Appointments Clause, the ultimate question is which, if any, of those powers may be exercised by the present voting Commissioners, none of whom *was* appointed as provided by that Clause. Our previous description of the statutory provisions disclosed that the Commission's powers fall generally into three categories: functions relating to the flow of necessary information—receipt, dissemination, and investigation; functions with respect to the Commission's task of fleshing out the statute—rulemaking and advisory opinions; and functions necessary to ensure compliance with the statute and rules—informal procedures, administrative determinations and hearings, and civil suits.

Insofar as the powers confided in the Commission are essentially of an investigative and informative nature, falling in the same general category as those powers which Congress might delegate to one of its own committees, there can be no question that the Commission as presently constituted may exercise them. Kilbourn v. Thompson (1881); McGrain v. Daugherty (1927). . . .

But when we go beyond this type of authority to the more substantial powers exercised by the Commission, we reach a different result. The Commission's enforcement power, exemplified by its discretionary power to seek judicial relief, is authority that cannot possibly be regarded as merely in aid of the legislative function of Congress. A lawsuit is the ultimate remedy for a breach of the law, and it is to the President, and not to the Congress, that the Constitution entrusts the responsibility to "take Care that the Laws be faithfully executed." Art. II, § 3. . . .

We hold that these provisions of the Act, vesting in the Commission primary responsibility for conducting civil litigation in the courts of the United States for vindicating public rights, violate Art. II, § 2 cl. 2, of the Constitution. Such functions may be discharged only by persons who are "Officers of the United States" within the language of that section.

All aspects of the Act are brought within the Commission's broad administrative powers: rulemaking, advisory opinions, and determinations of eligibility for funds and even for federal elective office itself. These functions, exercised free from day-to-day supervision of either Congress or the Executive Branch, are more legislative and judicial in nature than are the Commission's enforcement powers, and are of kinds usually performed by independent regulatory agencies or by some department in the Executive Branch under the direction of an Act of Congress. Congress viewed these broad powers as essential to effective and impartial administration of the entire substantive framework of the Act. Yet each of these functions also represents the performance of a significant governmental duty exercised pursuant to a public law. While the President may not insist that such functions be delegated to an appointee of his removable at will, Humphrey's Executor v. United States (1935), none of them operates merely in aid of congressional authority to legislate or is sufficiently removed from the administration and enforcement of public law to allow it to be performed by the present Commission. These administrative functions may therefore be exercised only by persons who are "Officers of the United States."

It is also our view that the Commission's inability to exercise certain powers because of the method by which its members have been selected should not affect the validity of the Commission's administrative actions and determinations to this date, including its administration of those provisions, upheld today, authorizing the public financing of federal elections. The past acts of the Commission are therefore accorded de facto validity. . . . We also draw on the Court's practice in the apportionment and voting rights cases and stay, for a period not to exceed 30 days, the Court's judgment insofar as it affects the authority of the Commission to exercise the duties and powers granted it under the Act. This limited stay will afford Congress an opportunity to reconstitute the Commission by law or to adopt other valid enforcement mechanisms . . . .

Mr. Justice **Stevens** took no part in the consideration or decision of these cases.

IMMIGRATION AND NATURALIZATION SERVICE v. CHADHA

462 U. S. 919; 103 S. Ct. 2764; 77 L. Ed. 2d 317
(1983)

There is no way the framers of the Constitution sitting in Philadelphia could have foreseen the growth in power and size of the national government, and had they or the people even suspected what was in the future, the national government would probably not have come into being. With a civil service of over two million persons dispensing annually billions of dollars, the question of "who's in charge here?" has become the major factor in the structuring of governmental relationships. The Supreme Court has sat on the sidelines as an umpire undertaking, as its wisdom permitted, to permit sound changes and veto dangerous ones.

One response to the growth in the size of government was the recognition that Congress did not have time to deal in detail with all the rules necessary for the operation of the country. The response was the delegation of legislative power, and after struggling with the problem in the 1920s and 1930s the Court finally conceded the right to give rule-making power to the executive as long as it was subject to guiding principles which embodied the carefully conceived policies of Congress. In this way, through their votes and lobbying efforts, the people would have a say in what the policies would be, while their actual effectuation would be placed in the hands of technically trained career civil servants. In theory the Court was to police the delegations, watching to see that Congress had provided guidance clear enough that a court, viewing the administrative rules resulting from the delegation, could see that they were within the legislative policy. In practice Congress' policies have been allowed to get vaguer and vaguer and the policing function has been virtually abandoned.

A second response to the growth in government came as a result of its undertaking the regulation and su-

pervision of large areas of the economy. In answer to this need Congress created a string of so-called "independent regulatory commissions" whose job it was to police various aspects of the economy, setting rates to be charged and insuring the fairness of business practices. These commissions were deliberately created outside the traditional departmental structure, given authority that included both legislative and judicial, and in some cases their members were made exempt from the removal power of the president. Without any very clear explanation of how these agencies fit into the separation-of-powers picture, the Court in Humphrey's Executor v. United States (1935) upheld their creation and independence of the President and they became known as the "headless fourth branch of government." These agencies, while enjoying very real independence, have their protagonists among the committees of Congress and their appointments and operating budgets are subject to presidential control.

While the Court had been tolerant of legislative delegation and the creation of independent commissions, it refused to take the step of permitting Congress to appoint administrative officers. In Buckley v. Valeo (1976) it made clear that the separation of powers limited the appointing power to the President, and congressional efforts to take on this important aspect of administrative control were held unconstitutional. Here Congress had provided by law for the congressional appointment of four of the six members of the Federal Election Commission, an agency whose duties involved regulating the ways in which candidates for office raised and spent their campaign funds.

One of the most complex and persistent problems resulting from the enormous growth of government was that of structural organization. How, with nearly two million people on your staff, do you organize them so they are subject to some kind of control by the policy-making levels of the government? Since the creation of administrative agencies and the assignment of powers to them is a legislative task, Congress was under increasing pressure to undertake a comprehensive reorganization. For years presidents had been pressing for action, but each agency lived in dread of being abolished, people who did business with the agencies feared loss of influence should changes be made, and a general fear of increased presidential power resulting from increased efficiency held the matter at a standstill. Finally President Hoover, with a solid reputation as an administrator, persuaded Congress to delegate to him the authority to restructure the government and Congress agreed, reserving to itself the power to nullify any changes of which it disapproved by a vote of both houses of Congress. The bill was signed in the closing hours of the Hoover administration and it was not until 1939, following the report of the Commission on Administrative Management, that President Franklin Roosevelt got through the first of a series of reorganization acts. While the independent commissions, and some favored agencies like the Comptroller General and the Corp of Army Engineers were not to be touched, five measures finally be-

came law without being blocked by the veto power reserved by Congress. The "legislative veto" was peculiarly adapted to the problems of administrative reorganization with whose complexities and political ramifications Congress was ill-equipped to deal and it reappeared in the Reorganization Act of 1949 under which President Truman put into effect many of the recommendations made by the Hoover Commission for dealing with the potpourri of agencies resulting from the war. The extension of the legislative veto into other areas of legislative policy has become increasingly popular and instead of requiring a veto by both houses, Congress in some cases has required a veto by only one.

The result of the legislative veto is not only to turn the law-making process end for end but to bring the Congress into an active role in administering the laws—a role for which it is ill suited and which the framers pretty clearly did not intend it to play. Under normal circumstance Congress passes a general law and leaves it to the administrative branch, under the direction of the President whose job it is to see the laws faithfully executed, to interpret and apply it to particular individuals. Administrative or judicial hearings, or sometimes both, assure that the law is properly applied. The background of the Chadha case illustrates how the turn-about took place in the field of alien deportation. In 1924 Congress by law required the Secretary of Labor to deport any alien who was in the United States unlawfully. No discretion was given the Secretary and it was clearly the policy of Congress that no illegal alien was to remain in the country. However, an alien with political influence could get a congressman to introduce a "private bill" exempting him or her from the order. A committee of Congress, sitting as a quasi-judicial body, would decide whether the alien was deserving of exemption and if he was the bill was reported for a vote of the house involved. If it passed both houses and was signed by the President the alien could stay.

Thousands of applications for suspension were received each year and the enormous burden of this task finally prompted Congress in 1940 to authorize the Attorney General to exercise his discretion and suspend deportation in deserving cases. But Congress, unwilling to release administrative control completely, provided that the Attorney General's decision to suspend could be set aside by a vote of both houses of Congress. In 1948 this was changed to provide that both houses had to approve the Attorney General's suspension, but this proved as onerous as the private bill technique and in 1952 Congress provided that either house could veto the Attorney General's suspension. Chadha was an East Indian whose student visa had expired and following full hearing before an immigration judge at which he demonstrated "extreme hardship" the Attorney General recommended to Congress that his deportation be suspended. A year and a half later, and one day before the congressional veto power would have expired, the resolution opposing permanent residence was brought to the House floor and voted on, debate apparently consisting of the subcommittee chairman's decision that

of 340 cases, Chadha and five others "did not meet these statutory requirements, particularly as it relates to hardship."

The assertion in Justice White's dissent that nearly 200 statutes would be held invalid by the Chadha decision, even if overstated, far exceeds the total number of statutes heretofore held invalid by the Court and gives some idea of the extent to which Congress has been exchanging with the President the roles prescribed for it by the Constitution. In Alaska Airlines v. Brock (1987) the Court reaffirmed the Chadha decision and held the legislative veto provision severable from the rest of the statute.

Chief Justice **Burger** delivered the opinion of the Court, saying in part:

III.

A.

We turn now to the question whether action of one House of Congress under § 244(c)(2) violates strictures of the Constitution. We begin, of course, with the presumption that the challenged statute is valid. Its wisdom is not the concern of the courts; if a challenged action does not violate the Constitution it must be sustained. . . .

By the same token, the fact that a given law or procedure is efficient, convenient, and useful in facilitating functions of government, standing alone, will not save it if it is contrary to the Constitution. Convenience and efficiency are not the primary objectives—or the hallmarks—of democratic government and our inquiry is sharpened rather than blunted by the fact that Congressional veto provisions are appearing with increasing frequency in statutes which delegate authority to executive and independent agencies: "Since 1932, when the first veto provision was enacted into law, 295 congressional veto-type procedures have been inserted in 196 different statutes as follows: from 1932 to 1939, five statutes were affected; from 1940-49, nineteen statutes; between 1950-59, thirty-four statutes; and from 1960-69, forty-nine. From the year 1970 through 1975, at least one hundred sixty-three such provisions were included in eighty-nine laws." . . .

Justice White undertakes to make a case for the proposition that the one-House veto is useful "political invention," and we need not challenge that assertion. We can even concede this utilitarian argument although the long range political wisdom of this "invention" is arguable. It has been vigorously debated and it is instructive to compare the views of the protagonists. . . . But policy arguments supporting even useful "political inventions" are subject to the demands of the Constitution which defines powers and, with respect to this subject, sets out just how those powers are to be exercised.

Explicit and unambiguous provisions of the Constitution prescribe and define the respective functions of the Congress and of the Executive in the legislative process. Since the precise terms of those familiar provisions are critical to the resolution of this case, we set them out verbatim.

[The Court here prints Article I, § 1, Article I, § 7, cl.2 and Article I, § 7, cl. 3, with selected emphasis.]

These provisions of Art. I are integral parts of the constitutional design for the separation of powers. We have recently noted that "[t]he principle of separation of powers was not simply an abstract generalization in the minds of the Framers: it was woven into the documents that they drafted in Philadelphia in the summer of 1787." Buckley v. Valeo [1976]. Just as we relied on the textual provision of Art. II, § 2, cl. 2, to vindicate the principle of separation of powers in Buckley, we find that the purposes underlying the Presentment Clauses, Art. I, § 7, cls. 2, 3 and the bicameral requirement of Art. I, § 1 and § 7, cl. 2, guide our resolution of the important question presented in this case. The very structure of the articles delegating and separating powers under Arts. I, II, and III exemplify the concept of separation of powers and we now turn to Art. I.

B.

The Presentment Clauses

The records of the Constitutional Convention reveal that the requirement that all legislation be presented to the President before becoming law was uniformly accepted by the Framers. Presentment to the President and the Presidential veto were considered so imperative that the draftsmen took special pains to assure that these requirements could not be circumvented. During the final debate on Art. I, § 7, cl. 2, James Madison expressed concern that it might easily be evaded by the simple expedient of calling a proposed law a "resolution" or "vote" rather than a "bill." . . . As a consequence, Art. I, § 7, cl. 3 was added.

The decision to provide the President with a limited and qualified power to nullify proposed legislation by veto was based on the profound conviction of the Framers that the powers conferred on Congress were the powers to be most carefully circumscribed. It is beyond doubt that lawmaking was a power to be shared by both Houses and the President. In The Federalist No. 73, Hamilton focused on the President's role in making laws: "If even no propensity had ever discovered itself in the legislative body to invade the rights of the Executive, the rules of just reasoning and theoretic propriety would of themselves teach us that the one ought not to be left to the mercy of the other, but ought to possess a constitutional and effectual power of self-defense." . . .

The President's role in the lawmaking process also reflects the Framers' careful efforts to check whatever propensity a particular Congress might have to enact oppressive, improvident, or ill-considered measures. The President's veto role in the legislative process was described later during public debates on ratification: "It es-

tablishes a salutary check upon the legislative body, calculated to guard the community against the effects of faction, precipitancy, or of any impulse unfriendly to the public good which may happen to influence a majority of that body. . . . The primary inducement to conferring the power in question upon the Executive is to enable him to defend himself; the secondary one is to increase the chances in favor of the community against the passing of bad laws through haste, inadvertence, or design." The Federalist No. 73. (Hamilton). . . . The Court also has observed that the Presentment Clauses serve the important purpose of assuring that a "national" perspective is grafted on the legislative process: "The President is a representative of the people just as the members of the Senate and of the House are, and it may be, at some times, on some subjects, that the President elected by all the people is rather more representative of them all than are the members of either body of the Legislature whose constituencies are local and not countrywide. . . ." Myers v. United States.

C.

Bicameralism

The bicameral requirement of Art. I, ... 1,7 was of scarcely less concern to the Framers than was the Presidential veto and indeed the two concepts are interdependent. By providing that no law could take effect without the concurrence of the prescribed majority of the Members of both Houses, the Framers reemphasized their belief, already remarked upon in connection with the Presentment Clauses, that legislation should not be enacted unless it has been carefully and fully considered by the Nation's elected officials. In the Constitutional Convention debates on the need for a bicameral legislature, James Wilson, later to become a Justice of this Court, commented: "Despotism comes on mankind in different shapes. Sometimes in an Executive, sometimes in a military, one. Is there danger of a Legislative despotism? Theory & practice both proclaim it. If the Legislative authority be not restrained, there can be neither liberty nor stability; and it can only be restrained by dividing it within itself, into distinct and independent branches. In a single house there is no check, but the inadequate one, of the virtue & good sense of those who compose it." . . .

Hamilton argued that a Congress comprised of a single House was antithetical to the very purposes of the Constitution. Were the Nation to adopt a Constitution providing for only one legislative organ, he warned: "we shall finally accumulate, in a single body, all the most important prerogatives of sovereignty, and thus entail upon our posterity one of the most execrable forms of government that human infatuation ever contrived. Thus we should create in reality that very tyranny which the adversaries of the New Constitution either are, or affect to be, solicitous to avert." The Federalist No. 22.

This view was rooted in a general skepticism regarding the fallibility of human nature later commented on by Joseph Story: "Public bodies, like private persons, are occasionally under the dominion of strong passions and excitements; impatient, irritable, and impetuous. . . . If [a legislature] feels no check but its own will, it rarely has the firmness to insist upon holding a question long enough under its own view, to see and mark it in all its bearings and relations to society." . . . These observations are consistent with what many of the Framers expressed, none more cogently than Hamilton in pointing up the need to divide and disperse power in order to protect liberty: "In republican government, the legislative authority necessarily predominates. The remedy for this inconveniency is to divide the legislature into different branches; and to render them, by different modes of election and different principles of action, as little connected with each other as the nature of their common functions and their common dependence on the society will admit." The Federalist No. 51. . . .

We see therefore that the Framers were acutely conscious that the bicameral requirement and the Presentment Clauses would serve essential constitutional functions. The President's participation in the legislative process was to protect the Executive Branch from Congress and to protect the whole people from improvident laws. The division of the Congress into two distinctive bodies assures that the legislative power would be exercised only after opportunity for full study and debate in separate settings. The President's unilateral veto power, in turn, was limited by the power of two thirds of both Houses of Congress to overrule a veto thereby precluding final arbitrary action of one person. . . . It emerges clearly that the prescription for legislative action in Art. I, §§ 1, 7 represents the Framers' decision that the legislative power of the Federal government be exercised in accord with a single, finely wrought and exhaustively considered procedure.

IV.

The Constitution sought to divide the delegated powers of the new federal government into three defined categories, legislative, executive and judicial, to assure, as nearly as possible, that each Branch of government would confine itself to its assigned responsibility. The hydraulic pressure inherent within each of the separate Branches to exceed the outer limits of its power, even to accomplish desirable objectives, must be resisted.

Although not "hermetically" sealed from one another, . . . the powers delegated to the three Branches are functionally identifiable. When any Branch acts, it is presumptively exercising the power the Constitution has delegated to it. . . . When the Executive acts, it presumptively acts in an executive or administrative capacity as defined in Art. II. And when, as here, one House of Congress purports to act, it is presumptively acting within its assigned sphere.

Beginning with this presumption, we must nevertheless establish that the challenged action under § 244(c)(2) is of the kind to which the procedural requirements of Art. I, § 7 apply. Not every action taken by either House is subject to the bicameralism and presentment requirements of Art. I. Whether actions taken by either House are, in law and fact, an exercise of legislative power depends not on their form but upon "whether they contain matter which is properly to be regarded as legislative in its character and effect."

Examination of the action taken here by one House pursuant to § 244(c)(2) reveals that it was essentially legislative in purpose and effect. In purporting to exercise power defined in Art. I. § 8, cl. 4 to "establish an uniform Rule of Naturalization, " the House took action that had the purpose and effect of altering the legal rights, duties and relations of persons, including the Attorney General, Executive Branch officials and Chadha, all outside the legislative branch. Section 244(c)(2) purports to authorize one House of Congress to require the Attorney General to deport an individual alien whose deportation otherwise would be cancelled under § 244. The one-House veto operated in this case to overrule the Attorney General and mandate Chadha's deportation; absent the House action, Chadha would remain in the United States. Congress has *acted* and its action has altered Chadha's status.

The legislative character of the one-House veto in this case is confirmed by the character of the Congressional action it supplants. Neither the House of Representatives nor the Senate contends that, absent the veto provision in § 244(c)(2), either of them, or both of them acting together, could effectively require the Attorney General to deport an alien once the Attorney General, in the exercise of legislatively delegated authority,* had determined the alien should remain in the United States. Without the challenged provision in § 244(c)(2), this could have been achieved, if at all, only by legislation requiring deportation. Similarly, a veto by one House of Congress under § 244(c)(2) cannot be justified as an attempt at amending the standards set out in § 244(a)(1), or

---

*Congress protests that affirming the Court of Appeals in this case will sanction "lawmaking by the Attorney General. . . . Why is the Attorney General exempt from submitting his proposed changes in the law to the full bicameral process?" To be sure, some administrative agency action—rule making, for example—may resemble "lawmaking." . . . This Court has referred to agency activity as being "quasi-legislative" in character. Humphrey's Executor v. United States (1935). Clearly, however, "[i]n the framework of our Constitution, the President's power to see that the laws are faithfully executed refutes the idea that he is to be a lawmaker." Youngstown Sheet & Tube Co. v. Sawyer (1952). When the Attorney General performs his duties pursuant to § 244 he does not exercise "legislative" power. . . . It is clear, therefore, that the Attorney General acts in his presumptively Art. II capacity when he administers the Immigration and Nationality Act. Executive action under legislatively delegated authority that might resemble "legislative" action in some respects is not subject to the approval of both Houses of Congress and the President for the reason that the Constitution does not so require. That kind of Executive action is always subject to check by the terms of the legislation that authorized it; and if that authority is exceeded it is open to judicial review as well as the power of Congress to modify or revoke the authority entirely. A one-House veto is clearly legislative in both character and effect and is not so checked; the need for the check provided by Art. I, §§ 1, 7 is therefore clear. Congress' authority to delegate portions of its power to administrative agencies provides no support for the argument that Congress can constitutionally control administration of the laws by way of a Congressional veto.

as a repeal of § 244 as applied to Chadha. Amendment and repeal of statutes, no less than enactment, must conform with Art. I.

The nature of the decision implemented by the one-House veto in this case further manifests its legislative character. After long experience with the clumsy, time consuming private bill procedure, Congress made a deliberate choice to delegate to the Executive Branch, and specifically to the Attorney General, the authority to allow deportable aliens to remain in this country in certain specified circumstances. It is not disputed that this choice to delegate authority is precisely the kind of decision that can be implemented only in accordance with the procedures set out in Art. I. Disagreement with the Attorney General's decision on Chadha's deportation—that is, Congress' decision to deport Chadha—no less than Congress' original choice to delegate to the Attorney General the authority to make that decision, involves determinations of policy that Congress can implement in only one way; bicameral passage followed by presentment to the President. Congress must abide by its delegation of authority until that delegation is legislatively altered or revoked. . . .

. . . The bicameral requirement, the Presentment Clauses, the President's veto, and Congress' power to override a veto were intended to erect enduring checks on each Branch and to protect the people from the improvident exercise of power by mandating certain prescribed steps. To preserve those checks, and maintain the separation of powers, the carefully defined limits on the power of each Branch must not be eroded. To accomplish what has been attempted by one House of Congress in this case requires action in conformity with the express procedures of the Constitution's prescription for legislative actions: passage by a majority of both Houses and presentment to the President.

The veto authorized by § 244(c)(2) doubtless has been in many respects a convenient shortcut; the "sharing" with the Executive by Congress of its authority over aliens in this manner is, on its face, an appealing compromise. In purely practical terms, it is obviously easier for action to be taken by one House without submission to the President; but it is crystal clear from the records of the Convention, contemporaneous writings and debates, that the Framers ranked other values higher than efficiency. The records of the Convention and debates in the States preceding ratification underscore the common desire to define and limit the exercise of the newly created federal powers affecting the states and the people. There is an unmistakable expression of a determination that legislation by the national Congress be a step-by-step, deliberate and deliberative process.

Justice Powell, concurring in the judgment, said in part:

The Court's decision, based on the Presentment Clauses, Art. I, § 7, cl. 2 and 3, apparently will invalidate every use of the legislative veto. The breadth of this holding gives one pause. Congress has included the veto in literally hundreds of statutes, dating back to the 1930s. Congress clearly views this procedure as essential to controlling the delegation of power to administrative agencies.* One reasonably may disagree with Congress' assessment of the veto's utility, but the respect due its judgment as a coordinate branch of Government cautions that our holding should be no more extensive than necessary to decide this case. In my view, the case may be decided on a narrower ground. When Congress finds that a particular person does not satisfy the statutory criteria for permanent residence in this country it has assumed a judicial function in violation of the principle of separation of powers. Accordingly, I concur in the judgment. . . .

I.

A. . . .

One abuse that was prevalent during the Confederation was the exercise of judicial power by the state legislatures. The Framers were well acquainted with the danger of subjecting the determination of the rights of one person to the "tyranny of shifting majorities." Jefferson observed that members of the General Assembly in his native Virginia had not been prevented from assuming judicial power, and " '[t]hey have accordingly *in many* instances *decided rights* which should have been left to *judiciary controversy.*' " . . .

It was to prevent the recurrence of such abuses that the Framers vested the executive, legislative, and judicial powers in separate branches. Their concern that a legislature should not be able unilaterally to impose a substantial deprivation on one person was expressed not only in this general allocation of power, but also in more specific provisions, such as the Bill of Attainder Clause. . . . This Clause, and the separation of powers doctrine generally, reflect the Framer's concern that trial by a legislature lacks the safeguards necessary to prevent the abuse of power. . . .

On its face, the House's action appears clearly adjudicatory. The House did not enact a general rule; rather it made its own determination that six specific persons did not comply with certain statutory criteria. It thus undertook the type of decision that traditionally has been left to other branches. Even if the House did not make a de novo determination, but simply reviewed the Immigration and Naturalization Services's findings, it still assumed a function ordinarily entrusted to the federal courts. . . .

The impropriety of the House's assumption of this function is confirmed by the fact that its action raises the very danger the Framers sought to avoid—the exercise of unchecked power. In deciding whether Chadha deserves to be deported, Congress is not subject to any internal constraints that prevent it from arbitrarily depriving him

---

*As Justice White's dissenting opinion explains, the legislative veto has been included in a wide variety of statutes, ranging from bills for executive reorganization to the War Powers Resolution. Whether the veto complies with the Presentment Clauses may well turn on the particular context in which it is exercised, and I would be hesitant to conclude that every veto is unconstitutional on the basis of the unusual example presented by this litigation.

of the right to remain in this country. Unlike the judiciary or an administrative agency, Congress is not bound by established substantive rules. Nor is it subject to the procedural safeguards, such as the right to counsel and a hearing before an impartial tribunal, that are present when a court or an agency adjudicates individual rights. The only effective constraint on Congress' power is political, but Congress is most accountable politically when it prescribes rules of general applicability. When it decides rights of specific persons, those rights are subject to "the tyranny of a shifting majority."

Justice White, dissenting, said in part:

Today the Court not only invalidates § 244(c)(2) of the Immigration and Nationality Act, but also sounds the death knell for nearly 200 other statutory provisions in which Congress has reserved a "legislative veto." For this reason, the Court's decision is of surpassing importance. And it is for this reason that the Court would have been well-advised to decide the case, if possible, on the narrower grounds of separation of powers, leaving for full consideration the constitutionality of other congressional review statutes operating on such varied matters as war powers and agency rulemaking, some of which concern the independent regulatory agencies.

The prominence of the legislative veto mechanism in our contemporary political system and its importance to Congress can hardly be overstated. It has become a central means by which Congress secures the accountability of executive and independent agencies. Without the legislative veto, Congress is faced with a Hobson's choice: either to refrain from delegating the necessary authority, leaving itself with a hopeless task of writing laws with the requisite specificity to cover endless special circumstance across the entire policy landscape, or in the alternative, to abdicate its lawmaking function to the executive branch and independent agencies. To choose the former leaves major national problems unresolved; to opt for the latter risks unaccountable policymaking by those not elected to fill that role. Accordingly, over the past five decades, the legislative veto has been placed in nearly 200 statutes. The device is known in every field of governmental concern: reorganization, budgets, foreign affairs, war powers, and regulation of trade, safety, energy, the environment and the economy. . . .

II. . . .

If the legislative veto were as plainly unconstitutional as the Court strives to suggest, its broad ruling today would be more comprehensible. But, the constitutionality of the legislative veto is anything but clear cut. The issue divides scholars, courts, attorneys general, and the two other branches of the National Government. If the veto devices so flagrantly disregarded the requirements of Article I as the Court today suggests, I find it incomprehensible that Congress, whose members are bound by oath to uphold the Constitution, would have

placed these mechanisms in nearly 200 separate laws over a period of 50 years. . . .

. . . The power to exercise a legislative veto is not the power to write new law without bicameral approval or presidential consideration. The veto must be authorized by statute and may only negate what an Executive department or independent agency has proposed. On its face, the legislative veto no more allows one House of Congress to make law than does the presidential veto confer such power upon the President. . . .

Justice Rehnquist, with whom Justice **White** joined, wrote a short dissenting opinion.

BOWSHER v. SYNAR

92 L. Ed. 2d 583 (1986)

While the Constitution makes reasonably clear that it is the job of Congress to make the laws (policies) of the country, and it is up to the President to see that they "be faithfully executed" or carried out, in reality it is not that which is written but that which is actually carried out that forms the policies of the country. On the other hand, what is actually carried out is dependent in large measure on what is written, so a struggle exists between Congress and the President, each trying to influence or control as much as possible the way in which the other branch does its job. So successful is the President in exercising political control that he is typically thought of as the country's legislative leader; it is he who promises what the country's policies will be if he is elected President, and it is he who gets the blame if a policy turns out to be a failure. The centralized nature of the President's office gives him a marked edge over the 100 Senators and 435 Representatives in Congress.

Congress has been forced to recognize this edge. As early as the turn of the century the physical job of making "all" the laws of the country had become overwhelming, and Congress began delegating to the President some of its power. The Supreme Court condoned this delegation of legislative power, considering it first simply "fact finding" (see Field v. Clark, 1892); but as the complexity of the rules increased the Court was forced to recognize what came to be known as "quasi-legislative" power. "If Congress shall lay down by legislative action an intelligible principle to which the person or body authorized to [make such rules] is directed to conform, such legislative action is not a forbidden delegation of legislative power"; see J. W. Hampton, Jr., & Co. v. United States (1928). As a practical matter, the executive branch is the original source of most of the legislation emerging from Congress.

The efforts of Congress to gain some control over how these laws were administered have not been particularly successful. In Buckley v. Valeo (1976) the Court forbade Congress a share in the power to appoint the officers who administer the laws, and in INS v. Chadha

(1983) Congress was denied the power to veto decisions made by the executive branch; Congress can reject policies by legislating but it cannot constitutionally vote to veto. Only in its efforts to curb the removal power of the President has it been even partially successful (see Humphrey's Executor v. United States, 1935) and in Myers v. United States (1926) the Court had stressed that it could not "reasonably" hold "that the excepting clause enables Congress to draw to itself, or either branch of it, the power or the right to participate in the exercise of that power."

Under President Reagan, who won election on a platform calling for a balanced budget amendment and who remains a supporter of such an amendment, the nation's budget deficit reached record proportions. While the President's policy of reducing taxes and increasing defense spending increased the budget deficit, skillful management persuaded much of the public that the excessive overrun was the fault of an irresponsible and spendthrift Congress rather than of administration policy. The Gramm-Rudman-Hollings act was touted as the belt-tightening first step to a new, more cost-conscious, responsible Congress. Congress would meet certain spending goals and if it failed, it would be forced into austerity by the Comptroller-General who would institute "automatic, across-the-board cuts" whenever the sum total of congressional appropriations exceeded Congress' goals. Gramm-Rudman-Hollings was Congress tying itself to the mast to avoid the sirens. The President, like Odysseus' crew, assisted by lobbying for the measure and signing it into law. However, when the act was challenged in the present case, the Justice Department, doubtless alerted to the unfavorable effect an across-the-board cut would have on the defense budget, argued against its constitutionality. The result of the Court's holding is that Congress now has to agree on a budget and the President has to sign it into law.

Chief Justice **Burger** delivered the opinion of the Court, saying in part:

The question presented by these appeals is whether the assignment by Congress to the Comptroller General of the United States of certain functions under the Balanced Budget and Emergency Deficit Control Act of 1985 violates the doctrine of separation of powers.

I.

A.

On December 12, 1985, the President signed into law the Balanced Budget and Emergency Deficit Control Act of 1985, popularly known as the "Gramm-Rudman-Hollings Act." The purpose of the Act is to eliminate the federal budget deficit. To that end, the Act sets a "maximum deficit amount" for federal spending for each of fiscal years 1986 through 1991. The size of that maximum deficit amount progressively reduces to zero in fiscal year 1991. If in any fiscal year the federal budget deficit exceeds the maximum deficit amount by more than a specified sum, the Act requires across-the-board cuts in federal spending to reach the targeted deficit level, with half the cuts made to defense programs and the other half made to non-defense programs. The Act exempts certain priority programs from these cuts.

These "automatic" reductions are accomplished through a rather complicated procedure, spelled out in the so-called "reporting provisions" of the Act. Each year, the Directors of the Office of Management and Budget (OMB) and the Congressional Budget Office (CBO) independently estimate the amount of the federal budget deficit for the upcoming fiscal year. If that deficit exceeds the maximum targeted deficit amount for that fiscal year by more than the specified amount, the Directors of OMB and CBO independently calculate, on a program-by-program basis, the budget reductions necessary to ensure that the deficit does not exceed the maximum deficit amount. The Act then requires the Directors to report jointly their deficit estimates and budget reduction calculations to the Comptroller General.

The Comptroller General, after reviewing the Directors' reports, then reports his conclusions to the President. The President in turn must issue a "sequestration" order mandating the spending reductions specified by the Comptroller General. There follows a period during which Congress may by legislation reduce spending to obviate, in whole or in part, the need for the sequestration order. If such reductions are not enacted, the sequestration order becomes effective and the spending reductions included in that order are made.

Anticipating constitutional challenge to these procedures, the Act also contains a "fallback" deficit reduction process to take effect "[i]n the event that any of the reporting procedures described . . . are invalidated." Under these provisions, the report prepared by the Directors of OMB and CBO is submitted directly to a specially-created Temporary Joint Committee on Deficit Reduction, which must report in five days to both Houses a joint resolution setting forth the content of the Directors' report. If the resolution is passed and signed by the President, it then serves as the basis for a Presidential sequestration order.

B.

Within hours of the President's signing of the Act, Congressman Synar, who had voted against the Act, filed a complaint seeking declaratory relief that the Act was unconstitutional. Eleven other Members later joined Congressman Synar's suit. A virtually identical lawsuit was also filed by the National Treasury Employees Union. The Union alleged that its members had been injured as a result of the Act's automatic spending reduction provisions, which have suspended certain cost-of-living benefit increases to the Union's members.

A three-judge District Court . . . invalidated the reporting provision. . . .

Although the District Court concluded that the Act survived a delegation doctrine challenge, it held that the role of the Comptroller General in the deficit reduction process violated the constitutionally imposed separation of powers. The court first explained that the Comptroller General exercises executive functions under the Act. However, the Comptroller General, while appointed by the President with the advice and consent of the Senate, is removable not by the President but only by a joint resolution of Congress or by impeachment. The District Court reasoned that this arrangement could not be sustained under this Court's decisions in Myers v. United States (1926) and Humphrey's Executor v. United States (1935). Under the separation of powers established by the Framers of the Constitution, the court concluded, Congress may not retain the power of removal over an officer performing executive functions. The congressional removal power created a "here-and-now subservience" of the Comptroller General to Congress. . . . We affirm. . . .

[The Court here reviews the Myers and Humphrey cases discussed in the note.]

III. . . .

In light of these precedents, we conclude that Congress cannot reserve for itself the power of removal of an officer charged with the execution of the laws except by impeachment. To permit the execution of the laws to be vested in an officer answerable only to Congress would, in practical terms, reserve in Congress control over the execution of the laws. As the District Court observed, "Once an officer is appointed, it is only the authority that can remove him, and not the authority that appointed him, that he must fear and, in the performance of his functions, obey." The structure of the Constitution does not permit Congress to execute the laws; it follows that Congress cannot grant to an officer under its control what it does not possess.

Our decision in INS v. Chadha (1983) supports this conclusion. In Chadha, we struck down a one house "legislative veto" provision by which each House of Congress retained the power to reverse a decision Congress had expressly authorized the Attorney General to make:

"Disagreement with the Attorney General's decision on Chadha's deportation—that is, Congress' decision to deport Chadha—no less than Congress' original choice to delegate to the Attorney General the authority to make that decision, involves determinations of policy that Congress can implement in only one way; bicameral passage followed by presentment to the President. Congress must abide by its delegation of authority until that delegation is legislatively altered or revoked." To permit an officer controlled by Congress to execute the laws would be, in essence, to permit a congressional veto. Congress could simply remove, or threaten to remove, an officer for executing the laws in any fashion found to be unsatisfactory to Congress. This kind of congressional control over the execution of the laws, Chadha makes clear, is constitutionally impermissible.

The dangers of congressional usurpation of Executive Branch functions have long been recognized. "[T]he debates of the Constitutional Convention, and the Federalist Papers, are replete with expressions of fear that the Legislative Branch of the National Government will aggrandize itself at the expense of the other two branches." Buckley v. Valeo (1976). Indeed, we also have observed only recently that "[t]he hydraulic pressure inherent within each of the separate Branches to exceed the outer limits of its power, even to accomplish desirable objectives, must be resisted." Chadha. With these principles in mind, we turn to consideration of whether the Comptroller General is controlled by Congress.

IV.

Appellants urge that the Comptroller General performs his duties independently and is not subservient to Congress. We agree with the District Court that this contention does not bear close scrutiny.

The critical factor lies in the provisions of the statute defining the Comptroller General's office relating to removability. Although the Comptroller General is nominated by the President from a list of three individuals recommended by the Speaker of the House of Representatives and the President pro tempore of the Senate and confirmed by the Senate, he is removable only at the initiative of Congress. He may be removed not only by impeachment but also by Joint Resolution of Congress "at any time" resting on any one of the following bases:

"(i) permanent disability;

"(ii) inefficiency;

"(iii) neglect of duty;

"(iv) malfeasance; or

"(v) a felony or conduct involving moral turpitude."

This provision was included, as one Congressman explained in urging passage of the Act, because Congress "felt that [the Comptroller General] should be brought under the sole control of Congress, so that Congress at the moment when it found he was inefficient and was not carrying on the duties of his office as he should and as the Congress expected, could remove him without the long, tedious process of a trial by impeachment."

The removal provision was an important part of the legislative scheme, as a number of Congressmen recognized. Representative Hawley commented: "[H]e is our officer, in a measure, getting information for us. . . . If he does not do his work properly, we, as practically his employers, ought to be able to discharge him from office." Representative Sisson observed that the removal provisions would give "[t]he Congress of the United States . . . absolute control over the man's destiny in office." The ultimate design was to "give the legislative branch of the Government control of the audit, not through the power of appointment, but through the power of removal." . . .

Justice White, however, assures us that "[r]ealistic consideration" of the "practical result of the removal provision," reveals that the Comptroller General is unlikely to be removed by Congress. The separated powers of our government cannot be permitted to turn on judicial assessment of whether an officer exercising executive powers is on good terms with Congress. The Framers recognized that, in the long term, structural protections against abuse of power were critical to preserving liberty. In constitutional terms, the removal powers over the Comptroller General's office dictate that he will be subservient to Congress.

This much said, we must also add that the dissent is simply in error to suggest that the political realities reveal that the Comptroller General is free from influence by Congress. The Comptroller General heads the General Accounting Office, "an instrumentality of the United States Government independent of the executive departments" which was created by Congress in 1921 as part of the Budget and Accounting Act of 1921. Congress created the office because it believed that it "needed an officer, responsible to it alone, to check upon the application of public funds in accordance with appropriations." H. Mansfield, The Comptroller General: A Study in the Law and Practice of Financial Administration 65 (1939).

It is clear that Congress has consistently viewed the Comptroller General as an officer of the Legislative Branch. The Reorganization Acts of 1945 and 1949, for example, both stated that the Comptroller General and the GAO are "part of the legislative branch of the Government." Similarly, in the Accounting and Auditing Act of 1950, Congress required the Comptroller General to conduct audits "as an agent of the Congress." . . .

Against this background, we see no escape from the conclusions that, because Congress had retained removal authority over the Comptroller General, he may not be entrusted with executive powers. The remaining question is whether the Comptroller General has been assigned such powers in the Balanced Budget and Emergency Deficit Control Act of 1985.

V.

The primary responsibility of the Comptroller General under the instant Act is the preparation of a "report." This report must contain detailed estimates of projected federal revenues and expenditures. The report must also specify the reductions, if any, necessary to reduce the deficit to the target for the appropriate fiscal year. The reductions must be set forth on a program-by-program basis.

In preparing the report, the Comptroller General is to have "due regard" for the estimates and reductions set forth in a joint report submitted to him by the Director of CBO and the Director of OMB, the President's fiscal and budgetary advisor. However, the Act plainly contemplates that the Comptroller General will exercise his independent judgment and evaluation with respect to those estimates. The Act also provides that the Comptroller General's report "shall explain fully any differences between the contents of such report and the report of the Directors."

Appellants suggest that the duties assigned to the Comptroller General in the Act are essentially ministerial and mechanical so that their performance does not constitute "execution of the law" in a meaningful sense. On the contrary, we view these functions as plainly entailing execution of the law in constitutional terms. Interpreting a law enacted by Congress to implement the legislative mandate is the very essence of "execution" of the law. Under [the Act], the Comptroller General must exercise judgment concerning facts that affect the application of the Act. He must also interpret the provisions of the Act to determine precisely what budgetary calculations are required. Decisions of that kind are typically made by officers charged with executing a statute.

The executive nature of the Comptroller General's functions under the Act is revealed in § 252(b)(3) which gives the Comptroller General the ultimate authority to determine the budget cuts to be made. Indeed, the Comptroller General commands the President himself to carry out, without the slightest variation (with exceptions not relevant to the constitutional issues presented), the directive of the Comptroller General as to the budget reductions: "The [Presidential] order *must provide* or reductions in the manner specified in section 251(a)(3), *must incorporate* the provisions of the [Comptroller General's] report submitted under section 251(b), and *must be consistent with such report in all respects.* The President *may not modify or recalculate any of the estimates. determinations, specifications, bases, amounts, or percentages* set forth in the report. . . ." (emphasis added).

Congress of course initially determined the content of the Balanced Budget and Emergency Deficit Control Act; and undoubtedly the content of the Act determines the nature of the executive duty. However, as Chadha makes clear, once Congress makes its choice in enacting legislation, its participation ends. Congress can thereafter control execution of its enactment only indirectly—by passing new legislation. By placing the responsibility for execution of the Balanced Budget and Emergency Deficit Control Act in the hands of an officer who is subject to removal only by itself, Congress in effect has retained control over the execution of the Act and has intruded into the executive function. The Constitution does not permit such intrusion. . . .

Justice **Stevens,** with whom Justice **Marshall** joined, concurred in the judgment saying in part:

. . . I agree with the Court that the "Gramm-Rudman-Hollings" Act contains a constitutional infirmity so severe that the flawed provision may not stand. I disagree with the Court, however, on the reasons why the Constitution prohibits the Comptroller General from exercising the powers assigned to him by the Act. It is not the dormant, carefully circumscribed congressional removal power that presents the primary constitutional evil. Nor do I agree with the conclusion of both the majority and the dissent that the analysis depends on a labeling of the functions assigned to the Comptroller General as "executive powers." Rather, I am convinced that the Comptroller General must be characterized as an agent of Congress because of his longstanding statutory responsibilities; that the powers assigned to him under the Gramm-Rudman-Hollings Act require him to make policy that will bind the Nation; and that, when Congress, or a component or an agent of Congress, seeks to make policy that will bind the Nation, it must follow the procedures mandated by Article I of the Constitution—through passage by both Houses and presentment to the President. In short, Congress may not exercise its fundamental power to formulate national policy by delegating that power to one of its two Houses, to a legislative committee, or to an individual agent of the Congress such as the Speaker of the House of Representatives, the Sergeant at Arms of the Senate, or the Director of the Congressional Budget Office. INS v. Chadha. That principle, I believe, is applicable to the Comptroller General.

Justice **White,** dissenting, said in part:

I. . . .

It is evident (and nothing in the Court's opinion is to the contrary) that the powers exercised by the Comptroller General under the Gramm-Rudman Act are not such that vesting them in an officer not subject to removal at will by the President would in itself improperly interfere with Presidential powers. Determining the level of spending by the Federal Government is not by nature a function central either to the exercise of the President's enumerated powers or to his general duty to ensure execution of the law; rather, appropriating funds is a peculiarly legislative function, and one expressly committed to Congress by Art. I, § 9 . . . . Delegating the execution of this legislation—that is, the power to apply the Act's criteria and make the required calculations—to an officer independent of the President's will does not deprive the President of any power that he would otherwise have or that is essential to the performance of the duties of his office. . . .

II.

If, as the Court seems to agree, the assignment of "executive" power under Gramm-Rudman to an officer

not removable at will by the President would not in itself represent a violation of the constitutional scheme of separated powers, the question remains whether, as the Court concludes, the fact that the officer to whom Congress has delegated the authority to implement the Act is removable by joint resolution of Congress should require invalidation of the Act. The Court's decision . . . is based on a syllogism: the Act vests the Comptroller General with "executive power"; such power may not be exercised by Congress or its agents; the Comptroller General is an agent of Congress because he is removable by Congress; therefore the Act is invalid. I have no quarrel with the proposition that the powers exercised by the Comptroller General under the Act may be characterized as "executive" in that they involve the interpretation and carrying out of the Act's mandate. I can also accept the general proposition that although Congress has considerable authority in designating the officers who are to execute legislation, the constitutional scheme of separated powers does prevent Congress from reserving an executive role for itself or for its "agents." I cannot accept, however, that the exercise of authority by an officer removable for cause by a joint resolution of Congress is analogous to the impermissible execution of the law by Congress itself, nor would I hold that the congressional role in the removal process renders the Comptroller an "agent" of Congress, incapable of receiving "executive" power. . . .

. . . The substantial role played by the President in the process of removal through joint resolution reduces to utter insignificance the possibility that the threat of removal will induce subservience to the Congress. As I have pointed out above, a joint resolution must be presented to the President and is ineffective if it is vetoed by him, unless the veto is overridden by the constitutionally prescribed two-thirds majority of both Houses of Congress. The requirement of presidential approval obviates the possibility that the Comptroller will perceive himself as so completely at the mercy of Congress that he will function as its tool. . . .

Justice **Blackmun** wrote a dissenting opinion.

4

The Electorate

CITIZENSHIP

DRED SCOTT v. SANDFORD

19 How. 393; 15 L. Ed. 691 (1857)

It is a curious fact that while the Constitution carefully outlined the basic structure of the United States government and spelled out both its powers and limitations, nowhere did it indicate who were to be citizens of the newly formed nation. Clearly the idea of citizenship was not simply overlooked. Article I requires that senators and representatives shall have been citizens for a term of years and Article II provides that "no person except a natural born citizen" shall be President. But the document was silent as to who such citizens were to be. In the absence of such provision it was generally assumed that the English rule of "jus soli," whereby a person born in a country was a citizen, would prevail—in contrast to the rule of "jus sanguinis" of the European continent where citizenship came from one's parents. However, in 1790 Congress by law extended United States citizenship to those born of American parents outside the country.

Even less helpful was the reference to state citizenship. Article IV, in what is known as the "comity clause," provided that "the citizens of each State shall be entitled to all the privileges and immunities of citizens of the several States." But who were these citizens and how was such citizenship acquired? Could a person be a citizen of a state without being a citizen of the United States? Some 20 states have at one time or another permitted aliens (from the federal point of view) to vote provided they had applied for United States citizenship. Were they then citizens of the state? These questions have never been answered by the Supreme Court.

It is against this background that the present case must be viewed. Prior to the adoption of the Fourteenth Amendment the prevailing view probably was that, save in cases of naturalization, persons were automatically citizens of the United States if they were citizens of a state. This had been the view of Calhoun, and also of such constitutional authorities as Story and Rawle. The Court in the present case recognized state citizenship as the source of federal citizenship, but insisted that the state had no further power to confer federal citizenship on persons by making them state citizens.

The Dred Scott decision is probably the most notorious one ever handed down by the Supreme Court, and certainly brought the prestige of that institution to an all-time low. Further, it destroyed the reputation of Chief Justice Taney, until that time widely regarded as an effective and respected jurist. The issue could have been decided without raising the constitutional issue by finding, as the Court had done in previous cases, that whatever Scott's status while in a free state or territory, upon his return to a slave state with his master he had again become a slave. Justice Nelson had written what was to be the Court opinion based on this argument, but when it was learned that Justices McLean and Curtis were raising the constitutional issue in their dissents,

Chief Justice Taney wrote a new Court opinion dealing with the points raised.

The facts of the case were these: Dred Scott had been taken by his master from Missouri into Illinois—a free state—and later into federal territory (now Minnesota) made free by the Missouri Compromise of 1820. When Scott was returned to Missouri his new owner, an abolitionist, arranged to be sued for Scott's freedom in a Missouri court—an early example of a test case—and while Scott won his freedom, he lost it again on appeal. To bring the issue to a federal court, a fictitious sale was arranged to a New Yorker named Sandford. The legal issue before the Court was whether Dred Scott was a citizen of Missouri and thus could sue in the federal courts on the ground of diversity of citizenship.

Mr. Chief Justice **Taney** delivered the opinion of the Court, saying in part:

The question is simply this: can a negro, whose ancestors were imported into this country and sold as slaves, become a member of the political community formed and brought into existence by the Constitution of the United States, and as such become entitled to all the rights, and privileges, and immunities, guarantied by that instrument to the citizen. One of these rights is the privilege of suing in a court of the United States in the cases specified in the Constitution.

It will be observed, that the plea applies to that class of persons only whose ancestors were negroes of the African race, and imported into this country, and sold and held as slaves. The only matter in issue before the court, therefore, is, whether the descendants of such slaves, when they shall be emancipated, or who are born of parents who had become free before their birth, are citizens of a state, in the sense in which the word "citizen" is used in the Constitution of the United States. And this being the only matter in dispute on the pleadings, the court must be understood as speaking in this opinion of that class only; that is, of those persons who are the descendants of Africans who were imported into this country and sold as slaves. . . .

The words "people of the United States" and "citizens" are synonymous terms, and mean the same thing. They both describe the political body, who, according to our republican institutions, form the sovereignty, and who hold the power and conduct the government through their representatives. They are what we familiarly call the "sovereign people," and every citizen is one of this people, and a constituent member of this sovereignty. The question before us is, whether the class of persons described in the plea in abatement compose a portion of this people, and are constituent members of this sovereignty. We think they are not, and that they are not included, and were not intended to be included, under the word "citizens" in the Constitution, and can, therefore, claim none of the rights and privileges which that instrument provides for and secures to citizens of the United States. On the contrary, they were at that time considered as a subordinate and inferior class of beings, who

had been subjugated by the dominant race, and whether emancipated or not, yet remained subject to their authority, and had no rights or privileges but such as those who held the power and the government might choose to grant them. . . .

In discussing this question, we must not confound the rights of citizenship which a state may confer within its own limits, and the rights of citizenship as a member of the Union. It does not by any means follow, because he has all the rights and privileges of a citizen of a State, that he must be a citizen of the United States. He may have all the rights and privileges of the citizen of a State, and yet not be entitled to the rights and privileges of a citizen in any other State. For, previous to the adoption of the Constitution of the United States, every State had the undoubted right to confer on whomsoever it pleased the character of a citizen, and to endow him with all its rights. But this character, of course, was confined to the boundaries of the State, and gave him no rights or privileges in other States beyond those secured to him by the laws of nations and the comity of States. Nor have the several States surrendered the power of conferring these rights and privileges by adopting the Constitution of the United States. Each State may still confer them upon an alien, or any one it thinks proper, or upon any class or description of persons; yet he would not be a citizen in the sense in which that word is used in the Constitution of the United States, nor entitled to sue as such in one of its courts, nor to the privileges and immunities of a citizen in the other States. The rights which he would acquire would be restricted to the State which gave them. The Constitution has conferred on Congress the right to establish an uniform rule of naturalization, and this right is evidently exclusive, and has always been held by this court to be so. Consequently, no State, since the adoption of the Constitution, can, by naturalizing an alien, invest him with the rights and privileges secured to a citizen of a State under the federal government, although, so far as the State alone was concerned, he would undoubtedly be entitled to the rights of a citizen, and clothed with all the rights and immunities which the Constitution and laws of the State attached to that character.

It is very clear, therefore, that no State can, by any Act or law of its own, passed since the adoption of the Constitution, introduce a new member into the political community created by the Constitution of the United States. It cannot make him a member of this community by making him a member of its own. And for the same reason it cannot introduce any person, or description of persons, who were not intended to be embraced in this new political family, which the Constitution brought into existence, but were intended to be excluded from it. . . .

It is true, every person, and every class and description of persons, who were at the time of the adoption of the Constitution recognized as citizens in the several States, became also citizens of this new political body; but none other; it was formed by them, and for them and their posterity, but for no one else. And the personal rights and privileges guarantied to citizens of this new sovereignty were intended to embrace those only who were then members of the several state communities, or who should afterwards, by birthright or otherwise, become members, according to the provisions of the Constitution and the principles on which it was founded. . . .

It becomes necessary, therefore, to determine who were citizens of the several States when the Constitution was adopted. And in order to do this, we must recur to the governments and institutions of the thirteen Colonies, when they separated from Great Britain and formed new sovereignties, and took their places in the family of independent nations. We must inquire who, at that time, were recognized as the people or citizens of a State, whose rights and liberties had been outraged by the English Government; and who declared their independence, and assumed the powers of government to defend their rights by force of arms.

In the opinion of the court, the legislation and histories of the times, and the language used in the Declaration of Independence, show, that neither the class of persons who had been imported as slaves, nor their descendants, whether they had become free or not, were then acknowledged as a part of the people, nor intended to be included in the general words used in that memorable instrument.

It is difficult at this day to realize the state of public opinion in relation to that unfortunate race, which prevailed in the civilized and enlightened portions of the world at the time of the Declaration of Independence, and when the Constitution of the United States was framed and adopted. But the public history of every European nation displays it, in a manner too plain to be mistaken.

They had for more than a century before been regarded as beings of an inferior order; and altogether unfit to associate with the white race, either in social or political relations; and so far inferior, that they had no rights which the white man was bound to respect; and that the negro might justly and lawfully be reduced to slavery for his benefit. He was bought and sold, and treated as an ordinary article of merchandise and traffic, whenever a profit could be made by it. This opinion was at that time fixed and universal in the civilized portion of the white race. It was regarded as an axiom in morals as well as in politics, which no one thought of disputing, or supposed to be open to dispute; and men in every grade and position in society daily and habitually acted upon it in their private pursuits, as well as in matters of public concern, without doubting for a moment the correctness of this opinion.

And in no nation was this opinion more firmly fixed or more uniformly acted upon than by the English government and English people. They not only seized them on the coast of Africa, and sold them or held them in slavery for their own use; but they took them as ordinary articles of merchandise to every country where they could make a profit on them, and were far more extensively engaged in this commerce than any other nation in the world.

The opinion thus entertained and acted upon in En-

gland was naturally impressed upon the colonies they founded on this side of the Atlantic. And, accordingly, a negro of the African race was regarded by them as an article of property, and held, and bought and sold as such, in every one of the thirteen Colonies which united in the Declaration of Independence, and afterwards formed the Constitution of the United States. The slaves were more or less numerous in the different Colonies, as slave labor was found more or less profitable. But no one seems to have doubted the correctness of the prevailing opinion of the time.

The legislation of the different Colonies furnishes positive and indisputable proof of this fact. . . . [The Court here reviews this legislation.]

We refer to these historical facts for the purpose of showing the fixed opinions concerning that race, upon which the statesmen of that day spoke and acted. It is necessary to do this, in order to determine whether the general terms used in the Constitution of the United States, as to the rights of man and the rights of the people, was intended to include them, or to give to them or their posterity the benefit of any of its provisions. . . .

No one, we presume, supposes that any change in public opinion or feeling in relation to this unfortunate race, in the civilized nations of Europe or in this country, should induce the court to give to the words of the Constitution a more liberal construction in their favor than they were intended to bear when the instrument was framed and adopted. Such an argument would be altogether inadmissible in any tribunal called on to interpret it. If any of its provisions are deemed unjust, there is a mode prescribed in the instrument itself by which it may be amended; but while it remains unaltered, it must be construed now as it was understood at the time of its adoption. It is not only the same in words, but the same in meaning, and delegates the same powers to the government, and reserves and secures the same rights and privileges to the citizen; and as long as it continues to exist in its present form, it speaks not only in the same words, but with the same meaning and intent with which it spoke when it came from the hands of its framers, and was voted on and adopted by the people of the United States. Any other rule of construction would abrogate the judicial character of this court, and make it the mere reflex of the popular opinion or passion of the day. This court was not created by the Constitution for such purposes. Higher and graver trusts have been confided to it, and it must not falter in the path of duty. . . .

And upon a full and careful consideration of the subject, the court is of opinion that, upon the facts stated in the plea in abatement, Dred Scott was not a citizen of Missouri within the meaning of the Constitution of the United States, and not entitled as such to sue in its courts; and, consequently, that the Circuit Court had no jurisdiction of the case, and that the judgment on the plea in abatement is erroneous. . . .

It is true that the result either way, by dismissal or by a judgment for the defendant, makes very little, if any difference in a pecuniary or personal point of view to either party. But the fact that the result would be very nearly the same to the parties in either form of judgment, would not justify this court in sanctioning an error in the judgment which is patent on the record, and which, if sanctioned, might be drawn into precedent, and lead to serious mischief and injustice in some future suit.

We proceed, therefore, to inquire whether the facts relied on by the plaintiff entitled him to his freedom. . . .

In considering this part of the controversy, two questions arise: 1st. Was he, together with his family, free in Missouri by reason of the stay in the territory of the United States hereinbefore mentioned? And 2d. If they were not, is Scott himself free by reason of his removal to Rock Island, in the State of Illinois, as stated in the above admissions?

We proceed to examine the first question.

The Act of Congress, upon which the plaintiff relies, declares that slavery and involuntary servitude, except as a punishment for crime, shall be forever prohibited in all that part of that territory ceded by France, under the name of Louisiana, which lies north of thirty-six degrees thirty minutes north latitude, and not included within the limits of Missouri. And the difficulty which meets us at the threshold of this part of the inquiry is, whether Congress was authorized to pass this law under any of the powers granted to it by the Constitution; for if the authority is not given by that instrument, it is the duty of this court to declare it void and inoperative, and incapable of conferring freedom upon one who is held as a slave under the laws of any one of the States.

The counsel for the plaintiff has laid much stress upon that article in the Constitution which confers on Congress the power ''to dispose of and make all needful rules and regulations respecting the territory or other property belonging to the United States;'' but, in the judgment of the court, that provision has no bearing on the present controversy, and the power there given, whatever it may be, is confined, and was intended to be confined, to the territory which at that time belonged to, or was claimed by, the United States, and was within their boundaries as settled by the Treaty with Great Britain, and can have no influence upon a territory afterwards acquired from a foreign government. It was a special provision for a known and particular Territory, and to meet a present emergency, and nothing more.

A brief summary of the history of the times, as well as the careful and measured terms in which the article is framed, will show the correctness of this proposition. . . .

This brings us to examine by what provision of the Constitution the present Federal Government under its delegated and restricted powers, is authorized to acquire territory outside of the original limits of the United States, and what powers it may exercise therein over the person or property of a citizen of the United States, while it remains a territory, and until it shall be admitted as one of the States of the Union.

There is certainly no power given by the Constitution to the Federal Government to establish or maintain Colonies bordering on the United States or at a distance,

to be ruled and governed at its own pleasure; nor to enlarge its territorial limits in any way, except by the admission of new States. . . .

We do not mean, however, to question the power of Congress in this respect. The power to expand the territory of the United States by the admission of new States is plainly given; and in the construction of this power by all the departments of the government, it has been held to authorize the acquisition of territory, not fit for admission at the time, but to be admitted as soon as its population and situation would entitle it to admission. It is acquired to become a State, and not to be held as a colony and governed by Congress with absolute authority. . . .

. . . And when the territory becomes a part of the United States, the Federal Government enters into possession in the character impressed upon it by those who created it. It enters upon it with its powers over the citizen strictly defined, and limited by the Constitution, from which it derives its own existence, and by virtue of which alone it continues to exist and act as a government and sovereignty. It has no power of any kind beyond it; and it cannot, when it enters a territory of the United States, put off its character, and assume discretionary or despotic powers which the Constitution has denied to it. . . .

A reference to a few of the provisions of the Constitution will illustrate this proposition.

For example, no one, we presume, will contend that Congress can make any law in a territory respecting the establishment of religion or the free exercise thereof, or abridging the freedom of speech or of the press, or the right of the people of the territory peaceably to assemble and to petition the government for the redress of grievances.

Nor can Congress deny to the people the right to keep and bear arms, nor the right to trial by jury, nor compel anyone to be a witness against himself in a criminal proceeding.

These powers, and others in relation to rights of person, which it is not necessary here to enumerate, are, in express and positive terms, denied to the general government; and the rights of private property have been guarded with equal care. Thus the rights of property are united with the rights of person, and placed on the same ground by the fifth amendment to the Constitution, which provides that no person shall be deprived of life, liberty and property, without due process of law. And an Act of Congress which deprives a citizen of the United States of his liberty or property, merely because he came himself or brought his property into a particular Territory of the United States, and who had committed no offense against the laws, could hardly be dignified with the name of due process of law. . . .

Now, as we have already said in an earlier part of this opinion, upon a different point, the right of property in a slave is distinctly and expressly affirmed in the Constitution. The right to traffic in it, like an ordinary article of merchandise and property, was guaranteed to the citizens of the United States, in every State that might desire it, for twenty years. And the government in express terms is pledged to protect it in all future time, if the slave escapes from his owner. This is done in plain words—too plain to be misunderstood. And no word can be found in the Constitution which gives Congress a greater power over slave property, or which entitles property of that kind to less protection than property of any other description. The only power conferred is the power coupled with the duty of guarding and protecting the owner in his rights.

Upon these considerations, it is the opinion of the court that the Act of Congress which prohibited a citizen from holding and owning property of this kind in the territory of the United States north of the line therein mentioned, is not warranted by the Constitution, and is therefore void; and that neither Dred Scott himself, nor any of his family, were made free by being carried into this territory; even if they had been carried there by the owner, with the intention of becoming a permanent resident.

But there is another point in the case which depends on state power and state law. And it is contended, on the part of the plaintiff, that he is made free by being taken to Rock Island, in the State of Illinois, independently of his residence in the territory of the United States; and being so made free he was not again reduced to a state of slavery by being brought back to Missouri.

Our notice of this part of the case will be very brief; for the principle on which it depends was decided in this court, upon much consideration, in the case of Strader et al. v. Graham [1850]. In that case, the slaves had been taken from Kentucky to Ohio, with the consent of the owner, and afterwards brought back to Kentucky. And this court held that their status or condition, as free or slave, depended upon the laws of Kentucky, when they were brought back into that State, and not of Ohio; and that this court had no jurisdiction to revise the judgment of a state court upon its own laws. This was the point directly before the court, and the decision that this court had not jurisdiction, turned upon it, as will be seen by the report of the case.

So in this case: as Scott was a slave when taken into the State of Illinois by his owner, and was there held as such, and brought back in that character, his status, as free or slave, depended on the laws of Missouri, and not of Illinois. . . .

Upon the whole, therefore, it is the judgment of this court, that it appears by the record before us that the plaintiff in error is not a citizen of Missouri, in the sense in which that word is used in the Constitution; and that the Circuit Court of the United States, for that reason, had no jurisdiction in the case, and could give no judgment in it.

Its judgment for the defendant must, consequently, be reversed, and a mandate issued directing the suit to be dismissed for want of jurisdiction.

Mr. Justice **Wayne** wrote a concurring opinion.

Mr. Justice **Nelson** wrote a concurring opinion.

Mr. Justice **Grier** concurred with Mr. Justice **Nelson,** and also wrote a concurring opinion.

Mr. Justice **Campbell** wrote a concurring opinion.

Mr. Justice **Catron** wrote a concurring opinion.

Mr. Justice **McLean** wrote a dissenting opinion.

Mr. Justice **Curtis,** dissenting, said in part:

To determine whether any free persons, descended from Africans held in slavery, were citizens of the United States under the Confederation, and consequently at the time of the adoption of the Constitution of the United States, it is only necessary to know whether any such persons were citizens of either of the States under the Confederation at the time of the adoption of the Constitution.

Of this there can be no doubt. At the time of the ratification of the Articles of Confederation, all free native-born inhabitants of the States of New Hampshire, Massachusetts, New York, New Jersey and North Carolina, though descended from African slaves, were not only citizens of those States, but such of them as had the other necessary qualifications possessed the franchise of electors on equal terms with other citizens. . . .

Did the Constitution of the United States deprive them or their descendants of citizenship?

That Constitution was ordained and established by the people of the United States through the action, in each State, of those persons who were qualified by its laws to act thereon, in behalf of themselves and all other citizens of that State. In some of the States, as we have seen, colored persons were among those qualified by law to act on this subject. These colored persons were not only included in the body of ''the people of the United States by whom the Constitution was ordained and established,'' but in at least five of the States they had the power to act, and doubtless did act, by their suffrages, upon the question of its adoption. It would be strange, if we were to find in that instrument anything which deprived of their citizenship any part of the people of the United States who were among those by whom it was established.

I can find nothing in the Constitution which, proprio vigore, deprives of their citizenship any class of persons who were citizens of the United States at the time of its adoption, or who should be native-born citizens of any State after its adoption; nor any power enabling Congress to disfranchise persons born on the soil of any State, and entitled to citizenship of such State by its constitution and laws. And my opinion is, that, under the Constitution of the United States, every free person born on the soil of a State, who is a citizen of that State by force of its Constitution or laws, is also a citizen of the United States. . . .

THE SLAUGHTER-HOUSE CASES

16 Wallace 36; 21 L. Ed. 394 (1873)

At the close of the Civil War it seemed clear that without the intervention of the federal government the Southern states would by legislative restrictions strip the newly freed black of most of the ordinary rights and immunities of free citizens. To place the civil rights of the black upon a firm basis Congress proposed the Fourteenth Amendment, authorizing the national government to step in and protect the black against actions by his own state government. The states were forbidden to take life, liberty, or property without due process of law, or to deny anyone the equal protection of the laws. The amendment defined United States citizenship in terms which included the black, and the states were forbidden to make laws abridging the privileges and immunities of that citizenship.

Exactly what the framers of the amendment intended to include in the phrase "privileges and immunities of citizens of the United States" is not altogether clear, and there is evidence to indicate that it was not clear even to the framers. Some apparently believed that the clause would include within its protection those basic rights enjoyed by all persons—such as the right to marry, to own property, to do business, and to move about freely. Others thought that it would include all or part of the protections listed in the federal Bill of Rights. In the Slaughter-House Cases the Court held that the privileges and immunities clause not only protected none of these rights, but by inference protected no rights that were not already amply protected elsewhere in the Constitution. With the exception of one case, mentioned below and later overruled, the Court has never held the clause to be violated. It is ironic that while the privileges and immunities clause was the one which occupied the attention of Congress at the time of its passage, it was the due process and equal protection clauses, added virtually without debate, which became the basis for the Court's later civil rights decisions.

The Slaughter-House Cases were the first cases brought under the Fourteenth Amendment, and they had nothing whatever to do with the rights of freedmen. The case arose on the following facts: the Reconstruction or "carpetbag" government in Louisiana, unquestionably under corrupt influence, had granted a monopoly of the slaughterhouse business to a single concern, thus preventing over one thousand other persons and firms from continuing in that business. The validity of the law was attacked under the Fourteenth Amendment. The case was argued before the Supreme Court twice and was decided by a majority of five to four.

The importance of the case can hardly be overestimated. By distinguishing between state citizenship and national citizenship, and by emphasizing that the rights and privileges of federal citizenship do not include the protection of ordinary civil liberties such as freedom of speech and press, religion, etc., but only the privileges which one enjoys by virtue of his federal citizenship, the Court averted, for the time being at least, the revolution in our constitutional system apparently intended by the framers of the amendment and reserved to the states the responsibility for protecting civil rights generally. Nor has the Court been willing to expand the scope of the privileges and immunities clause beyond this early, limited interpretation. Five years before the Slaughter-House Cases the Supreme Court had held void, in Crandall v. Nevada (1868), a state tax on transporting persons out of the state, on the ground that such a tax would obstruct the citizen in his inherent federal right to come to the seat of his government. Two members of the Court, while concurring in the judgment, held the tax to be a violation of the commerce clause. In his opinion in the Slaughter-House Cases, Justice Miller cites this freedom of movement as an example of the privileges and immunities of United States citizens, and in 1941 in Edwards v. California, four members of the Court strongly urged that the California "anti-Okie" law should be held invalid on this ground. The majority had rested their decision, as had the minority in the Crandall case, upon the commerce power.

The Slaughter-House Cases held that the privileges and immunities of United States citizenship did not include the right to engage in a business of one's choice since such a privilege did not owe its existence to the national Constitution or laws. But did they include the rights listed in the Bill of Rights—rights which were certainly extended by the Constitution to United States citizens? The Court in Maxwell v. Dow (1900) held that they did not, reasoning that such privileges were those enjoyed exclusively by citizens, and since all persons enjoyed the protection of the Bill of Rights, its guarantees could not be considered privileges and immunities of that citizenship.

It looked for a time (1935–1940) as though the Court might broaden the scope and applicability of the privileges and immunities clause of the Fourteenth Amendment. In Colgate v. Harvey (1935) the Court held void a provision of a Vermont income tax law which taxed income from money loaned outside the state at a higher rate than that loaned inside the state. Besides denying the equal protection of the laws, this act was held to abridge the privileges and immunities of citizens of the United States. The right to carry on business freely across state lines was declared to be a privilege or immunity of federal citizenship, a doctrine sharply differing from the rule of the Slaughter-House Cases. In 1939, in Hague v. CIO, involving the validity under the Fourteenth Amendment of various repressions of free speech, assembly, etc., in Jersey City, two justices of the Supreme Court from the majority held that the right of citizens to assemble and discuss their rights under the National Labor Relations Act was a privilege or immunity of citizens of the United States within the meaning of the Fourteenth Amendment. There was also speculation as to whether protection against unreasonable searches and seizures was also a privilege and immunity of federal citizenship, but no decision was made on that point.

There was sharp dissent in both cases against this tendency to enlarge the scope of the privileges and immunities clause; and in Madden v. Kentucky (1940), in a case similar to Colgate v. Harvey, the Court specifically overruled that case and returned to the timeworn narrow construction of the privileges and immunities clause embodied in the Slaughter-House Cases.

The result of the Court's interpretation of the privileges and immunities clause is to equate those privileges to those of a member of an exclusive private club. Clearly membership in such a club does not entitle one to free speech or to own property, but it does entitle one to vote in the club elections and to the extent the club can and does extend exclusive privileges to its members, such as the right to hold parties in its clubhouse, these could be considered privileges and immunities of membership. As a matter of policy the United States has not generally limited its largesse to citizens, and many persons live their lives out as resident aliens barely conscious of any difference between themselves and their citizen neighbors. Even state attempts to discriminate against them must be justified by some ''compelling state interest.'' (See the chapter on Equal Protection of the Laws.) They cannot vote (a privilege not exercised by some 60 percent of those who can) and they cannot homestead on federal land, but if these were to be viewed as the measure of the value of United States citizenship its importance to the thousands who seek it every year would be hard to understand. The single overriding value that such citizenship offers is not in anything tangible, but in the right to reside permanently in one of the richest, freest countries in the world.

Query: It seems altogether probable that the framers of the privileges and immunities clause intended it to protect at least fundamental rights from infringement by the states. Can you draft an opinion for the Court which will produce this result, dealing adequately with the Court's interpretation of the language of the Amendment?

Mr. Justice **Miller** delivered the opinion of the Court, saying in part:

The plaintiffs in error accepting this issue, allege that the statute is a violation of the Constitution of the United States in these several particulars:

That it creates an involuntary servitude forbidden by the 13th article of amendment;

That it abridges the privileges and immunities of citizens of the United States;

That it denies to the plaintiffs the equal protection of the laws; and,

That it deprives them of their property without due process of law; contrary to the provisions of the first section of the 14th article of amendment.

This court is thus called upon for the first time to give construction to these articles. . . .

Twelve articles of amendment were added to the Federal Constitution soon after the original organization of the government under it in 1789. Of these all but the last were adopted so soon afterwards as to justify the statement that they were practically contemporaneous with the adoption of the original; and the twelfth, adopted in eighteen hundred and three, was so nearly so as to have become, like the others, historical and of another age. But within the last eight years three other articles of amendment of vast importance have been added, by the voice of the people, to that now venerable instrument.

The most cursory glance at these articles discloses a unity of purpose, when taken in connection with the history of the times, which cannot fail to have an important bearing on any question of doubt concerning their true meaning. . . . Fortunately that history is fresh within the memory of us all, and its leading features, as they bear upon the matter before us, free from doubt. . . . [Here follows a discussion of the Thirteenth and Fifteenth Amendments.]

The 1st section of the 14th article, to which our attention is more specially invited, opens with a definition of citizenship—not only citizenship of the United States, but citizenship of the states. No such definition was previously found in the Constitution, nor had any attempt been made to define it by act of Congress. It had been the occasion of much discussion in the courts, by the executive departments and in the public journals. It had been said by eminent judges that no man was a citizen of the United States except as he was a citizen of one of the states composing the Union. Those, therefore, who had been born and resided always in the District of Columbia or in the territories, though within the United States, were not citizens. Whether this proposition was sound or not had never been judicially decided. But it had been held by this court, in the celebrated Dred Scott Case [1857], only a few years before the outbreak of the Civil War, that a man of African descent, whether a slave or not, was not and could not be a citizen of a state or of the United States. This decision, while it met the condemnation of some of the ablest statesmen and constitutional lawyers of the country, had never been overruled; and, if it was to be accepted as a constitutional limitation of the right of citizenship, then all the negro race who had recently been made freemen were still, not only not citizens, but were incapable of becoming so by anything short of an amendment to the Constitution.

To remove this difficulty primarily, and to establish a clear and comprehensive definition of citizenship which should declare what should constitute citizenship of the United States and also citizenship of a state, the 1st clause of the 1st section was framed:

''All persons born or naturalized in the United States and subject to the jurisdiction thereof are citizens of the United States and of the state wherein they reside.''

The first observation we have to make on this clause is that it puts at rest both the questions which we stated to have been the subject of differences of opinion. It declares that persons may be citizens of the United States without regard to their citizenship of a particular state, and it overturns the Dred Scott decision by making all persons born within the United States and subject to its jurisdiction citizens of the United States. That its main purpose was to establish the citizenship of the negro can admit of no doubt. The phrase ''subject to its jurisdiction'' was intended to exclude from its operation children of ministers, consuls and citizens or subjects of foreign states born within the United States.

The next observation is more important in view of the arguments of counsel in the present case. It is that the distinction between citizenship of the United States and citizenship of a state is clearly recognized and established. Not only may a man be a citizen of the United States without being a citizen of a state, but an important element is necessary to convert the former into the latter. He must reside within the state to make him a citizen of it, but it is only necessary that he should be born or naturalized in the United States to be a citizen of the Union.

It is quite clear, then, that there is a citizenship of the United States and a citizenship of a state, which are distinct from each other and which depend upon different characteristics or circumstances in the individual.

We think this distinction and its explicit recognition in this Amendment of great weight in this argument, because the next paragraph of this same section, which is the one mainly relied on by the plaintiffs in error, speaks only of privileges and immunities of citizens of the United States, and does not speak of those of citizens of the several states. The argument, however, in favor of the plaintiffs, rests wholly on the assumption that the citizenship is the same and the privileges and immunities guaranteed by the clause are the same.

The language is: ''No state shall make or enforce any law which shall abridge the privileges or immunities of citizens of the United States.'' It is a little remarkable, if this clause was intended as a protection to the citizen of a state against the legislative power of his own state, that the words ''citizen of the state'' should be left out when it is so carefully used, and used in contradistinction to ''citizens of the United States'' in the very sentence which precedes it. It is too clear for argument that the change in phraseology was adopted understandingly and with a purpose.

Of the privileges and immunities of the citizens of the United States, and of the privileges and immunities of the citizen of the state, and what they respectively are, we will presently consider; but we wish to state here that it is only the former which are placed by this clause under the protection of the Federal Constitution, and that the latter, whatever they may be, are not intended to have any additional protection by this paragraph of the Amendment.

If, then, there is a difference between the privileges and immunities belonging to a citizen of the United States as such, and those belonging to the citizen of the state as such, the latter must rest for their security and protection where they have heretofore rested; for they are not embraced by this paragraph of the Amendment.

The first occurrence of the words ''privileges and immunities'' in our constitutional history is to be found in the fourth of the Articles of the old Confederation.

It declares ''That, the better to secure and perpetuate mutual friendship and intercourse among the people of the different states in this Union, the free inhabitants of each of these states, paupers, vagabonds, and fugitives from justice excepted, shall be entitled to all the privileges and immunities of free citizens in the several states; and the people of each state shall have free ingress and regress to and from any other state, and shall enjoy therein all the privileges of trade and commerce, subject to the same duties, impositions, and restrictions as the inhabitants thereof respectively.''

In the Constitution of the United States, which superseded the Articles of Confederation, the corresponding provision is found in section two of the 4th article, in the following words: The citizens of each state shall be entitled to all the privileges and immunities of citizens of the several states.

There can be but little question that the purpose of both these provisions is the same, and that the privileges and immunities intended are the same in each. In the Articles of the Confederation we have some of these specifically mentioned, and enough perhaps to give some general idea of the class of civil rights meant by the phrase.

Fortunately we are not without judicial construction of this clause of the Constitution. The first and the leading case on the subject is that of Corfield v. Coryell, decided by Mr. Justice Washington in the circuit court for the district of Pennsylvania in 1823.

''The inquiry,'' he says, ''is, what are the privileges and immunities of citizens of the several states? We feel no hesitation in confining these expressions to those privileges and immunities which are fundamental; which belong of right to the citizens of all free governments, and which have at all times been enjoyed by citizens of the several states which compose this Union, from the time of their becoming free, independent, and sovereign. What these fundamental principles are, it would be more tedious than difficult to enumerate.'' ''They may all, however, be comprehended under the following general heads: protection by the government, with the right to acquire and possess property of every kind, and to pursue and obtain happiness and safety, subject, nevertheless, to such restraints as the government may prescribe for the general good of the whole.''

This definition of the privileges and immunities of citizens of the states is adopted in the main by this court in the recent case of Ward v. Maryland [1871], while it declines to undertake an authoritative definition beyond what was necessary to that decision. The description, when taken to include others not named, but which are of the same general character, embraces nearly every civil right for the establishment and protection of which organized government is instituted. They are, in the language of Judge Washington, those rights which are fundamental. Throughout his opinion, they are spoken of as rights belonging to the individual as a citizen of a state. They are so spoken of in the constitutional provision which he was construing. And they have always been held to be the class of rights which the state governments were created to establish and secure. . . .

The constitutional provision there alluded to did not create those rights, which it called privileges and immunities of citizens of the states. It threw around them in that clause no security for the citizen of the state in which they were claimed or exercised. Nor did it profess to control the power of the state governments over the rights of its own citizens.

Its sole purpose was to declare to the several states, that whatever those rights, as you grant or establish them to your own citizens, or as you limit or qualify, or impose restrictions on their exercise, the same, neither more nor less, shall be the measure of the rights of citizens of other states within your jurisdiction.

It would be the vainest show of learning to attempt to prove by citations of authority, that up to the adoption of the recent Amendments, no claim or pretense was set up that those rights depended on the Federal government for their existence or protection, beyond the very few express limitations which the Federal Constitution imposed upon the states—such, for instance, as the prohibition against ex post facto laws, bills of attainder, and laws impairing the obligation of contracts. But with the exception of these and a few other restrictions, the entire domain of the privileges and immunities of citizens of the states, as above defined, lay within the constitutional and legislative power of the states, and without that of the Federal government. Was it the purpose of the 14th Amendment, by the simple declaration that no state should make or enforce any law which shall abridge the privileges and immunities of citizens of the United States, to transfer the security and protection of all the civil rights which we have mentioned, from the states to the Federal government? And where it is declared that Congress shall have the power to enforce that article, was it intended to bring within the power of Congress the entire domain of civil rights heretofore belonging exclusively to the states?

All this and more must follow, if the proposition of the plaintiffs in error be sound. For not only are these rights subject to the control of Congress whenever in its discretion any of them are supposed to be abridged by state legislation, but that body may also pass laws in advance, limiting and restricting the exercise of legislative power by the states, in their most ordinary and usual functions, as in its judgment it may think proper on all such subjects. And still further, such a construction followed by the reversal of the judgments of the supreme court of Louisiana in these cases would constitute this court a perpetual censor upon all legislation of the states, on the civil rights of their own citizens, with authority to nullify such as it did not approve as consistent with those rights, as they existed at the time of the adoption of this Amendment. The argument, we admit, is not always the most conclusive which is drawn from the consequences urged against the adoption of a particular construction of

an instrument. But when, as in the case before us, these consequences are so serious, so far reaching and pervading, so great a departure from the structure and spirit of our institutions; when the effect is to fetter and degrade the state governments by subjecting them to the control of Congress, in the exercise of powers heretofore universally conceded to them of the most ordinary and fundamental character; when in fact it radically changes the whole theory of the relations of the state and Federal governments to each other and of both these governments to the people; the argument has a force that is irresistible, in the absence of language which expresses such a purpose too clearly to admit of doubt.

We are convinced that no such results were intended by the Congress which proposed these amendments, nor by the legislatures of the states, which ratified them.

Having shown that the privileges and immunities relied on in the argument are those which belong to citizens of the states as such, and that they are left to the state governments for security and protection, and not by this article placed under the special care of the Federal government, we may hold ourselves excused from defining the privileges and immunities of citizens of the United States which no state can abridge, until some case involving those privileges may make it necessary to do so.

But lest it should be said that no such privileges and immunities are to be found if those we have been considering are excluded, we venture to suggest some which owe their existence to the Federal government, its national character, its Constitution, or its laws.

One of these is well described in the case of Crandall v. Nevada [1868]. It is said to be the right of the citizen of this great country, protected by implied guaranties of its Constitution, ''to come to the seat of government to assert any claim he may have upon that government, to transact any business he may have with it, to seek its protection, to share its offices, to engage in administering its functions. He has the right of free access to its seaports, through which all operations of foreign commerce are conducted, to the sub-treasuries, land-offices, and courts of justice in the several states.'' . . .

Another privilege of a citizen of the United States is to demand the care and protection of the Federal government over his life, liberty, and property when on the high seas or within the jurisdiction of a foreign government. Of this there can be no doubt, nor that the right depends upon his character as a citizen of the United States. The right to peaceably assemble and petition for redress of grievances, the privilege of the writ of habeas corpus, are rights of the citizen guaranteed by the Federal Constitution. The right to use the navigable waters of the United States, however they may penetrate the territory of the several states, and all rights secured to our citizens by treaties with foreign nations, are dependent upon citizenship of the United States, and not citizenship of a state. One of these privileges is conferred by the very article under consideration. It is that a citizen of the United

States can, of his own volition, become a citizen of any state of the Union by a bona fide residence therein, with the same rights as other citizens of that state. To these may be added the rights secured by the 13th and 15th articles of Amendment, and by the other clause of the Fourteenth, next to be considered.

But it is useless to pursue this branch of the inquiry, since we are of opinion that the rights claimed by these plaintiffs in error, if they have any existence, are not privileges and immunities of citizens of the United States within the meaning of the clause of the 14th Amendment under consideration.

"All persons born or naturalized in the United States, and subject to the jurisdiction thereof, are citizens of the United States and of the state, wherein they reside. No state shall make or enforce any law which shall abridge the privileges or immunities of citizens of the United States; nor shall any state deprive any person of life, liberty or property without due process of law, nor deny to any person within its jurisdiction the equal protection of its laws."

The argument has not been much pressed in these cases that the defendant's charter deprives the plaintiffs of their property without due process of law, or that it denies to them the equal protection of the law. The first of these paragraphs has been in the Constitution since the adoption of the 5th Amendment, as a restraint upon the Federal power. It is also to be found in some form of expression in the constitutions of nearly all the states, as a restraint upon the power of the states. This law, then, has practically been the same as it now is during the existence of the government, except so far as the present Amendment may place the restraining power over the states in this matter in the hands of the Federal government.

We are not without judicial interpretation, therefore, both state and national, of the meaning of this clause. And it is sufficient to say that under no construction of that provision that we have ever seen, or any that we deem admissible, can the restraint imposed by the state of Louisiana upon the exercise of their trade by the butchers of New Orleans be held to be a deprivation of property within the meaning of that provision.

"Nor shall any state deny to any person within its jurisdiction the equal protection of the laws."

In the light of the history of these amendments, and the pervading purpose of them, which we have already discussed, it is not difficult to give a meaning to this clause. The existence of laws in the states where the newly emancipated negroes resided, which discriminated with gross injustice and hardship against them as a class, was the evil to be remedied by this clause, and by it such laws are forbidden.

If, however, the states did not conform their laws to its requirements, then by the 5th section of the article of amendment Congress was authorized to enforce it by suitable legislation. We doubt very much whether any action of a state not directed by way of discrimination against the negroes as a class, or on account of their race, will ever be held to come within the purview of this pro-

vision. It is so clearly a provision for that race and that emergency, that a strong case would be necessary for its application to any other. But as it is a state that is to be dealt with, and not alone the validity of its laws, we may safely leave that matter until Congress shall have exercised its power, or some case of state oppression, by denial of equal justice in its courts, shall have claimed a decision at our hands. We find no such case in the one before us, and do not deem it necessary to go over the argument again, as it may have relation to this particular clause of the Amendment. . . .

The judgments of the Supreme Court of Louisiana in these cases are affirmed.

Mr. Justice **Field,** with whom Mr. Chief Justice **Chase,** Mr. Justice **Swayne,** and Mr. Justice **Bradley** concurred, dissented, saying in part:

The Amendment does not attempt to confer any new privileges or immunities upon citizens or to enumerate or define those already existing. It assumes that there are such privileges and immunities which belong of right to citizens as such, and ordains that they shall not be abridged by state legislation. If this inhibition has no reference to privileges and immunities of this character, but only refers, as held by the majority of the court in their opinion, to such privileges and immunities as were before its adoption specially designated in the Constitution or necessarily implied as belonging to citizens of the United States, it was a vain and idle enactment, which accomplished nothing, and most unnecessarily excited Congress and the people on its passage. With privileges and immunities thus designated no state could ever have interfered by its laws, and no new constitutional provision was required to inhibit such interference. The supremacy of the Constitution and the laws of the United States always controlled any state legislation of that character. But if the Amendment refers to the natural and inalienable rights which belong to all citizens, the inhibition has a profound significance and consequence. . . .

Mr. Justice **Swayne** and Mr. Justice **Bradley** filed separate dissenting opinions.

KENNEDY v. MENDOZA-MARTINEZ

372 U. S. 144; 83 S. Ct. 544; 9 L. Ed. 2d 644
(1963)

In 1857 the Supreme Court had established an important exception to the rule that birth in the country conferred citizenship, by holding in the infamous Dred Scott case that a native-born black was not and could not become an American citizen. The Fourteenth Amendment "recalled" the Dred Scott decision on this point and definitely defined United States citizenship in terms of birth in the country and subjection to its jurisdiction, thus enacting the English or "jus soli" doctrine into the

Constitution. The exact purport of the phrase "subject to its jurisdiction" was for some time the subject of dispute and uncertainty. In the Slaughter-House Cases (1873) the Court had gone out of its way to express the opinion that a child born in the United States to parents who were subjects of a foreign state was not born subject to the jurisdiction of the United States and would not, therefore, acquire citizenship by birth.

This view, however, was rejected by the Court in the case of United States v. Wong Kim Ark (1898). Wong had been born in San Francisco in 1873 of Chinese parents who were subjects of the emperor of China but were permanently domiciled in the United States. He went to China in 1894 and upon his return was refused admission on the ground that he was a Chinese laborer, not a citizen, whose admission was forbidden by the Chinese Exclusion Acts then in force. He sued out a writ of habeas corpus, claiming American citizenship on the ground of birth, and the Court sustained him on the ground that he had been born "subject to the jurisdiction" of the United States. The Nationality Act of 1952 repealed the exclusion acts and made all persons eligible for naturalization regardless of race or color.

An important case relating to the acquisition of United States citizenship is that of Perkins v. Elg (1939). Miss Elg was born in the United States of Swedish parents in 1907. The Supreme Court upheld her claim to citizenship on the ground that she had become a citizen of the United States by being born in New York. She might, it is true, have chosen Swedish citizenship on coming of age, since her parents had meanwhile returned to Swedish citizenship. But her relinquishment of her right to enjoy the status of American citizenship upon coming of age had to be her own voluntary act. That right was not destroyed by a change in the citizenship status of her parents while she was still a minor.

While the Constitution provides that persons may become citizens by naturalization, a naturalized citizen is not quite as secure in that status as though he were a Fourteenth Amendment citizen. A naturalized citizen may have his or her citizenship revoked if he or she procured it by fraud; as, for example, by making a false statement about the length of his or her residence in the country. See Johannessen v. United States (1912). The courts have also held that a naturalized citizen who later engages in disloyal conduct may have his or her citizenship cancelled on the ground of fraud, since the person's later behavior indicates that he or she took the oath of allegiance to this country either dishonestly or with mental reservations which made it fraudulent. Many naturalized citizens have been "denaturalized" on such grounds. In Schneiderman v. United States (1943), however, the Supreme Court held that the government in such cases must show beyond a reasonable doubt that the oath of allegiance was fraudulently taken, and it set aside the denaturalization of Schneiderman, a Communist, because this burden of proof was not fully met.

During the "cold war" era following World War II Congress undertook to "denaturalize" persons whom if felt posed a threat to the country's security. In the Sub-

versive Activities Control Act of 1950, Congress provided that membership in a subversive organization was itself grounds for denying citizenship; hence subsequent proof of such membership is sufficient to effect denaturalization. Since 1952 a refusal to testify before a congressional committee concerning subversive activities is ground for denaturalization; an irrebuttable presumption is created that a "material fact" was concealed at the time the naturalization was granted. Joining a "subversive" organization within five years is made prima facie evidence that the oath was taken with mental reservations.

Despite the Constitution's apparent clarity to the contrary, not even a Fourteenth Amendment citizen is entirely immune from loss of citizenship. Although the Fourteenth Amendment explained how United States citizenship could be acquired, it did not indicate how, if at all, it could be lost, or the extent to which Congress had any control over the matter. At the time of the adoption of the Fourteenth Amendment (1868) Congress recognized the right of a person to expatriate himself if he wished; and from this approach, two kinds of federal legislation have flowed. One kind provided that certain acts of allegiance to a foreign country—such as taking an oath of allegiance, holding its public office, or voting in its elections—amounted to a voluntary renunciation of United States citizenship, whether or not it had the effect of making the person a citizen of the other country. In the case of Perez v. Brownell (1958) the Court held valid the law that a person forfeited his or her citizenship by voting in a foreign election, since this was a legitimate exercise of the power over foreign affairs. Termination of citizenship, it was held, enables the government to avoid the international embarrassment that might result if our nationals participated in foreign elections. The Court held that while the act of voting itself had to be voluntary, there need be present no desire to renounce citizenship. Left unanswered by that case was the extent to which Congress could, if it chose, provide for the expatriation of anyone, who, by statements or conduct, embarrassed the United States in its conduct of foreign affairs.

The second kind of legislation made the commission of certain crimes conclusive evidence of the renunciation of citizenship. The earliest of these was a Civil War measure (which, of course, antedated the Fourteenth Amendment) providing that deserters from the armed services and persons leaving the country to avoid the draft "shall be deemed and taken to have voluntarily relinquished and forfeited their rights of citizenship." In the years that followed, Congress added to this list the crimes of treason and conspiring to overthrow the government by force and violence.

In Trop v. Dulles (1958), decided the same day as Perez, a divided Court found that expatriation could not be used as a punishment for the crime of desertion from the armed forces. Four members of the Court in that case argued that American citizenship was conferred by the Fourteenth Amendment upon persons born here, and "is not subject to the general powers of the National

Government and therefore cannot be divested in the exercise of those powers.'' (Justice Whittaker declined to concur in such a statement in the Perez case, but did so in Trop.) Justice Brennan, while conceding the right of Congress to expatriate, voted with the majority on the ground that expatriation of a deserter was not a reasonable exercise of the power of Congress to wage war. The dissenting justices argued that expatriation was not punishment and was within the war power of Congress. In 1967 in Afroyim v. Rusk the Court overruled Perez v. Brownell, rejecting the idea that ''Congress has any general power, express or implied, to take away an American citizen's citizenship without his assent.''

Three important differences have always existed between a native-born citizen and one who became a citizen by naturalization. Only native-born citizens can become President of the United States (Article II, Sec. 1, Cl. 4); naturalized citizens can have their citizenship cancelled if it is obtained by fraud or willful misrepresentation; and up until 1964 their citizenship could be revoked if they left the country to live in their former homeland for two years, or any other country for five years.

In 1964, in Schneider v. Rusk, this last basis of distinction was abolished. The Court held that naturalized citizens were not second-class citizens, and rejected the ''impermissible assumption,'' implicit in the law, that ''naturalized citizens as a class are less reliable and bear less allegiance to this country than do the native born.''

While those who obtain their citizenship either by birth or naturalization may not be deprived of it without their consent, the same is not true of those who derive their citizenship from their parents. Aldo Mario Bellei was born in Italy of an Italian father and native-born citizen mother who had lived in the United States for the ten years required by law to give citizenship to her son. Bellei had never lived in the United States and on the several occasions when he visited here, traveling on a United States passport, he was warned that he would lose his citizenship if he did not reside in this country for at least five years between the ages of fourteen and twenty-eight. He lost his citizenship at the age of twenty-eight and sued to get it back.

With Justice Blackmun speaking for the five-man majority, the Court in Rogers v. Bellei (1970) rejected his claim, noting that Congress was under no constitutional obligation to confer citizenship by descent and had never done so without requiring that the child live some time in this country. It was apparent that if Congress wished, it could require the child to spend the five years in the country before granting citizenship and the Court felt ''that it does not make good constitutional sense, or comport with logic, to say, on the one hand, that Congress may impose a condition precedent, with no constitutional complication and yet be powerless to impose precisely the same condition subsequent.'' Bellei ''was not born in the United States. He was not naturalized in the United States. And he has not been subject to the jurisdiction of the United States. All this being so . . . the first sentence of the Fourteenth Amendment has no application to [him]. He simply is not a Fourteenth-Amendment-first-sentence citizen.''

It is, of course, still possible to denaturalize a person who obtains his or her citizenship by fraud. Thus the Court upheld the denaturalization of Frank Costello on the ground that in 1925, when he applied for citizenship, he swore his occupation was ''real-estate'' when it was really ''bootlegging.'' See Costello v. United States (1961). Efforts to deport Costello, then a man in his seventies, were thwarted by the Court in 1963 in Costello v. Immigration and Naturalization Service. The provision of the statute stating that those who have had their naturalization cancelled never were citizens was not, the Court said, intended to apply to deportation questions. Hence Costello was a citizen from 1925 to 1959. Furthermore, the ''two crimes involving moral turpitude'' which justify deporting an alien had taken place while he was still a citizen and so could not be made the basis of his deportation.

Among the rights enjoyed by an American citizen is the right to travel abroad. While such travel could be, and often was in peacetime, done without a passport, some method of proving United States citizenship was almost vital and the State Department had long issued passports on request. In 1952, however, Congress made it illegal during a national emergency for a citizen to enter or leave the country without a passport. The State Department had always issued passports freely unless the person was not a citizen or did not owe allegiance, or was clearly going to use it for some unlawful purpose. But in 1952 the Secretary of State began requiring statements regarding Communist Party affiliation, and in 1958 a passport was denied to the artist Rockwell Kent because he would not file the required statement. The Supreme Court held only that Congress had not authorized the Secretary of State to withhold passports from persons because they held Communist views, but in its discussion it indicated that it considered the right to travel a ''part of the 'liberty' of which the citizen cannot be deprived without due process of law under the Fifth Amendment.'' See Kent v. Dulles (1958).

In 1981 in Haig v. Agee the Court limited the freedom suggested by the Kent case. Agee, a former Central Intelligence Agency agent, had mounted a campaign to ''fight the CIA wherever it is operating'' and to ''expose CIA officers and agents and to take the measures necessary to drive them out of the countries where they are operating.'' The success of his campaign prompted the State Department to revoke his passport and the Supreme Court upheld the revocation. It found the statute did authorize passport revocation to prevent the kind of damage that Agee was doing to the national security and disposed of his First Amendment argument on the ground that it was his ''actions'' that were being limited and not his ''views.'' It noted that since a passport was in effect a letter of introduction to a foreign sovereign and a request for his aid ''the freedom to travel outside *the United States must be distinguished from the* right *to travel within the United States,'' and that the former can be regulated within the bounds of due process.*

The present case involves two native-born citizens who had been stripped of their citizenship. Mendoza-Martinez, who also possessed Mexican citizenship, fled to Mexico in 1942 to avoid the draft. He voluntarily returned and in 1947 pleaded guilty to draft evasion and served a prison sentence. Five years after his release he was arrested for deportation on the ground that his flight to Mexico had cost him his American citizenship. Cort, the second defendant, had gone to England in 1951 to do medical research. His request for draft deferment was denied, but he refused to return, on the grounds that he was not physically fit for military service and that the draft board was harassing him because of his membership in the Communist party. When England refused to extend his residence permit, he went to Czechoslovakia, where he lived for five years doing medical research. In 1959 he tried to get a passport to return and do his military service, but was turned down by the embassy in Prague on the ground that he had forfeited his United States citizenship.

Mr. Justice **Goldberg** delivered the opinion of the Court, saying in part:

We are called upon in these two cases to decide the grave and fundamental problem, common to both, of the constitutionality of Acts of Congress which divest an American of his citizenship for ''[d]eparting from or remaining outside of the jurisdiction of the United States in time of war or . . . national emergency for the purpose of evading or avoiding training and service'' in the Nation's armed forces. . . .

VI. The Constitutional Issues

A. Basic Principles

Since the validity of an Act of Congress is involved, we begin our analysis mindful that the function we are now discharging is ''the gravest and most delicate duty that this Court is called upon to perform.'' Blodgett v. Holden [1928] (separate opinion of Holmes, J.). This responsibility we here fulfill with all respect for the powers of Congress, but with recognition of the transcendent status of our Constitution.

We deal with the contending constitutional arguments in the context of certain basic and sometimes conflicting principles. Citizenship is a most precious right. It is expressly guaranteed by the Fourteenth Amendment to the Constitution, which speaks in the most positive terms. The Constitution is silent about the permissibility of involuntary forfeiture of citizenship rights. While it confirms citizenship rights, plainly there are imperative obligations of citizenship, performance of

which Congress in the exercise of its powers may constitutionally exact. One of the most important of these is to serve the country in time of war and national emergency. The powers of Congress to require military service for the common defense are broad and far-reaching, for while the Constitution protects against invasions of individual rights, it is not a suicide pact. Similarly, Congress has broad power under the Necessary and Proper Clause to enact legislation for the regulation of foreign affairs. Latitude in this area is necessary to ensure effectuation of this indispensable function of government.

These principles, stemming on the one hand from the precious nature of the constitutionally guaranteed rights of citizenship, and on the other from the powers of Congress and the related obligations of individual citizens, are urged upon us by the parties here. The Government argues that §§ 401 (j) and 349 (a) (10) are valid as an exercise of Congress' power over foreign affairs, of its war power, and of the inherent sovereignty of the Government. Appellees urge the provisions' invalidity as not within any of the powers asserted, and as imposing a cruel and unusual punishment.

We recognize at the outset that we are confronted here with an issue of the utmost import. Deprivation of citizenship—particularly American citizenship, which is ''one of the most valuable rights in the world today,'' Report of the President's Commission on Immigration and Naturalization (1953), 235—has grave practical consequences. An expatriate who, like Cort, had no other nationality becomes a stateless person—a person who not only has no rights as an American citizen, but no membership in any national entity whatsoever. ''Such individuals as do not possess any nationality enjoy, in general, no protection whatever, and if they are aggrieved by a State they have no means of redress, since there is no State which is competent to take up their case. As far as the Law of Nations is concerned, there is, apart from restraints of morality or obligations expressly laid down by treaty . . . no restriction whatever to cause a State to abstain from maltreating to any extent such stateless individuals.'' . . . The calamity is ''[n]ot the loss of specific rights, then, but the loss of a community willing and able to guarantee any rights whatsoever. . . .'' The stateless person may end up shunted from nation to nation, there being no one obligated or willing to receive him, or, as in Cort's case, may receive the dubious sanctuary of a Communist regime lacking the essential liberties precious to American citizenship.

B. The Perez and Trop Cases

The basic principles here involved, the gravity of the issue, and the arguments bearing upon Congress' power to forfeit citizenship were considered by the Court in relation to different provisions of the Nationality Act of 1940 in two cases decided on the same day less than five years ago: Perez v. Brownell [1958] and Trop v.

Dulles [1958]. . . . [The Court here reviews the decisions in these two cases.]

C. Sections 401 (j) and 349 (a) (10) as Punishment

The present cases present for decision the constitutionality of a section not passed upon in either Perez or Trop—§ 401 (j), added in 1944, and its successor and present counterpart, § 349 (a) (10) of the Immigration and Nationality Act of 1952. We have come to the conclusion that there is a basic question in the present cases, the answer to which obviates a choice here between the powers of Congress and the constitutional guarantee of citizenship. That issue is whether the statutes here, which automatically—without prior court or administrative proceedings—impose forfeiture of citizenship, are essentially penal in character, and consequently have deprived the appellees of their citizenship without due process of law and without according them the rights guaranteed by the Fifth and Sixth Amendments, including notice, confrontation, compulsory process for obtaining witnesses, trial by jury, and assistance of counsel. This issue was not relevant in Trop because, in contrast to §§ 401 (j) and 349 (a) (10), [the statute there involved] required conviction by court-martial for desertion before forfeiture of citizenship could be inflicted. . . .

It is fundamental that the great powers of Congress to conduct war and to regulate the Nation's foreign relations are subject to the constitutional requirements of due process. The imperative necessity for safeguarding these rights to procedural due process under the gravest of emergencies has existed throughout our constitutional history, for it is then, under the pressing exigencies of crisis, that there is the greatest temptation to dispense with fundamental constitutional guarantees which, it is feared, will inhibit governmental action. "The Constitution of the United States is a law for rulers and people, equally in war and in peace, and covers with the shield of its protection all classes of men, at all times, and under all circumstances." Ex parte Milligan [1866]. The rights guaranteed by the Fifth and Sixth Amendments are "preserved to every one accused of crime who is not attached to the army, or navy, or militia in actual service." "[I]f society is disturbed by civil commotion—if the passions of men are aroused and the restraints of law weakened, if not disregarded—these safeguards need, and should receive, the watchful care of those intrusted with guardianship of the Constitution and laws. In no other way can we transmit to posterity unimpaired the blessings of liberty, consecrated by the sacrifices of the Revolution."

We hold §§ 401 (j) and 349 (a) (10) invalid because in them Congress has plainly employed the sanction of deprivation of nationality as a punishment—for the offense of leaving or remaining outside the country to evade military service—without affording the procedural safeguards guaranteed by the Fifth and Sixth Amendments. Our forefathers "intended to safeguard the people of this country from punishment without trial by duly constituted courts. . . . And even the courts to which this important function was entrusted were commanded to stay their hands until and unless certain tested safeguards were observed. An accused in court must be tried by an impartial jury, has a right to be represented by counsel, [and] must be clearly informed of the charge against him. . . ." United States v. Lovett [1946]. . . .

As the Government concedes, §§ 401 (j) and 349 (a) (10) automatically strip an American of his citizenship, with concomitant deprivation "of all that makes life worth living," Ng Fung Ho v. White [1922], whenever a citizen departs from or remains outside the jurisdiction of this country for the purpose of evading his military obligations. Conviction for draft evasion, as Cort's Case illustrates, is not prerequisite to the operation of this sanction. Independently of prosecution, forfeiture of citizenship attaches when the statutory set of facts develops. It is argued that the availability after the fact of administrative and judicial proceedings . . . to contest the validity of the sanction meets the measure of due process. But the legislative history and judicial expression with respect to every congressional enactment relating to the provisions in question dating back to 1865 establish that forfeiture of citizenship is a penalty for the act of leaving or staying outside the country to avoid the draft. This being so, the Fifth and Sixth Amendments mandate that this punishment cannot be imposed without a prior criminal trial and all its incidents, including indictment, notice, confrontation, jury trial, assistance of counsel, and compulsory process for obtaining witnesses. If the sanction these sections impose is punishment, and it plainly is, the procedural safeguards required as incidents of a criminal prosecution are lacking. We need go no further.

The punitive nature of the sanction here is evident under the tests traditionally applied to determine whether an Act of Congress is penal or regulatory in character, even though in other cases this problem has been extremely difficult and elusive of solution. Whether the sanction involves an affirmative disability or restraint, whether it has historically been regarded as a punishment, whether it comes into play only on a finding of scienter, whether its operation will promote the traditional aims of punishment—retribution and deterrence, whether the behavior to which it applies is already a crime, whether an alternative purpose to which it may rationally be connected is assignable for it, and whether it appears excessive in relation to the alternative purpose assigned are all relevant to the inquiry, and may often point in differing directions. Absent conclusive evidence of congressional intent as to the penal nature of the statute, these factors must be considered in relation to the statute on its face. Here, although we are convinced that application of these criteria to the face of the statutes supports the conclusion that they are punitive, a detailed examination along such lines is unnecessary, because the objective manifestations of congressional purpose indicate conclusively that the provisions in question can only be interpreted as punitive. A study of the history of the predecessor of § 401 (j), which "is worth a volume of logic," New York Trust Co. v. Eisner [1921], coupled with a reading of Congress' reasons for enacting § 401 (j), compels a conclusion that the statute's primary function is to serve as an additional penalty for a special category of draft evader. Compare Trop v. Dulles (Brennan, J., concurring). . . .

[The Court here reviews the legislative and judicial history of similar legislation enacted during the Civil War, the legislative history of the sections here involved, and concludes that "Congress was concerned solely with inflicting effective retribution upon this class of draft evaders."]

V. Conclusion

It is argued that our holding today will have the unfortunate result of immunizing the draft evader who has left the United States from having to suffer any sanction against his conduct, since he must return to this country before he can be apprehended and tried for his crime. The compelling answer to this is that the Bill of Rights which we guard so jealously and the procedures it guarantees are not to be abrogated merely because a guilty man may escape prosecution or for any other expedient reason. Moreover, the truth is that even without being expatriated, the evader living abroad is not in a position to assert the vast majority of his component rights as an American citizen. If he wishes to assert those rights in any real sense he must return to this country, and by doing that he will subject himself to prosecution. In fact, while he is outside the country evading prosecution, the United States may, by proper refusal to exercise its largely discretionary power to afford him diplomatic protection, decline to invoke its sovereign power on his behalf. Since the substantial benefits of American citizenship only come into play upon return to face prosecution, the draft evader who wishes to exercise his citizenship rights will inevitably come home and pay his debt, which within constitutional limits Congress has the power to define. This is what Mendoza-Martinez did, what Cort says he is willing to do, and what others have done. Thus our holding today does not frustrate the effective handling of the problem of draft evaders who leave the United States.

We conclude, for the reasons stated, that §§ 401 (j) and 349 (a) (10) are punitive and as such cannot constitutionally stand, lacking as they do the procedural safeguards which the Constitution commands. We recognize that draft evasion, particularly in time of war, is a heinous offense, and should and can be properly punished. Dating back to Magna Carta, however, it has been an abiding principle governing the lives of civilized men that "no freeman shall be taken or imprisoned or disseised or outlawed or exiled . . . without the judgment of his peers or by the law of the land. . . ." What we hold is only that, in keeping with this cherished tradition, punishment cannot be imposed "without due process of law." Any lesser holding would ignore the constitutional mandate upon which our essential liberties depend.

Therefore the judgments of the District Courts in these cases are
Affirmed.

Mr. Justice **Douglas** and Mr. Justice **Black,** while joining the opinion of the Court, adhere to the views expressed in the dissent of Mr. Justice **Douglas,** in which Mr. Justice **Black** joined, in Perez v. Brownell, that Congress has no power to deprive a person of the citizenship granted the native-born by § 1, cl. 1, of the Fourteenth Amendment.

Mr. Justice **Brennan** wrote a concurring opinion.

Mr. Justice **Stewart,** with whom Mr. Justice **White** joins, dissenting, said in part:

The Court's opinion is lengthy, but its thesis is simple: (1) The withdrawal of citizenship which these statutes provide is "punishment." (2) Punishment cannot constitutionally be imposed except after a criminal trial and conviction. (3) The statutes are therefore unconstitutional. As with all syllogisms, the conclusion is inescapable if the premises are correct. But I cannot agree with the Court's major premise—that the divestiture of citizenship which these statutes prescribe is punishment in the constitutional sense of that term. . . .

[Mr. Justice Stewart's opinion reviews the legislative history of the act and concludes that it was *not* punishment but a legitimate way of boosting soldier morale, and as such, a valid exercise of the war power of Congress.]

THE RIGHT TO VOTE

EX PARTE YARBROUGH

110 U. S. 651; 4 S. Ct. 152; 28 L. Ed. 274 (1884)

It has long been established that there is no necessary connection between citizenship and suffrage. While it is usual to require that voters be citizens, there are some twenty states which at one time or other have allowed aliens to vote before their naturalization was complete. On the other hand the right to vote has been withheld from substantial classes of citizens, for instance, minors, women (before the adoption of woman suffrage), and those who have no permanent residence in any state.

It should also be kept in mind that the determination of the actual qualifications for suffrage is left by the United States Constitution to the various states. When the federal Constitution was framed, any attempt to establish uniformity among the widely varying state qualifications for suffrage would have been difficult, if not impossible, and would have been so resented by the various states as to imperil the ratification of the Constitution. Consequently it was provided that congressional suffrage should be given to those qualified under state law to vote for members of the most numerous branch of the state legislature, while the method of choosing presidential electors was left to the discretion of the state legislatures. It should be noted that the Fifteenth and Nineteenth Amendments do not guarantee anyone the right to vote in a positive way; they merely stipulate that persons shall not be denied the right to vote because of race, or color, or sex.

In Minor v. Happersett (1875) the Supreme Court held that the right to vote was not one of the privileges and immunities of citizens of the United States which the states were forbidden by the recently adopted Fourteenth Amendment to abridge; that amendment did not deprive the states of their right to establish qualifications for the suffrage, nor did it operate to enfranchise any classes of citizens who had previously been denied the right to vote. The case of Ex parte Yarbrough, on the other hand, established the doctrine that there is a certain sense in which the right to vote for federal officers may be regarded as a right of United States citizenship which will be accorded federal protection.

Yarbrough and others were members of one of the Ku Klux Klan organizations prevalent in the South at the close of the Civil War. They were indicted in the federal district court in Georgia of the crime of conspiring together to intimidate a black, named Berry Saunders, in the exercise of his right to vote for a member of the Congress of the United States. It was shown that the conspirators used physical violence and that they went in disguise upon the public highways. They were convicted and sentenced to prison. The federal crime they committed was defined by a section of the Enforcement Act of 1870 (later invoked in United States v. Classic, 1941) forbidding under heavy penalties two or more persons to "conspire to injure, oppress, threaten, or intimidate any citizen in the free exercise or enjoyment of any right or privilege secured to him by the Constitution or laws of the United States . . ." or to "go in disguise on the highway, or on the premises of another, with intent to prevent or hinder [such citizen in] his free exercise or enjoyment" of any such right; or to "conspire to prevent by force, intimidation, or threat, any citizen who is lawfully entitled to vote" from voting for presidential electors or members of Congress. Yarbrough contended that Congress had no delegated authority to protect the right to vote in federal elections. The Supreme Court, in a powerful opinion by Justice Miller, sustained Yarbrough's conviction and held the federal statute valid. It made clear that the right to vote for representatives in Congress is a right which one gets from the federal Constitution, even though the precise measure of this right is fixed by the suffrage qualifications of the several states. In other words, the right to vote for representatives is a privilege of United States citizenship, provided one has the qualifications which the state requires of those who vote for the most numerous branch of the state legislature. Congress has full authority under the doctrine of implied powers to protect this privilege of federal citizenship against individual or state aggression.

Mr. Justice **Miller** delivered the opinion of the Court, saying in part:

That a government whose essential character is republican, whose executive head and legislative body are both elective, whose most numerous and powerful branch of the Legislature is elected by the people directly, has no power by appropriate laws to secure this election from the influence of violence, of corruption, and of fraud, is a proposition so startling as to arrest attention and demand the gravest consideration.

If this government is anything more than a mere aggregation of delegated agents of other States and governments, each of which is superior to the General Government, it must have the power to protect the elections on which its existence depends from violence and corruption.

If it has not this power, it is left helpless before the two great natural and historical enemies of all republics, open violence and insidious corruption.

The proposition that it has no such power is supported by the old argument often heard, often repeated and in this court never assented to, that when a question of the power of Congress arises the advocate of the power must be able to place his finger on words which expressly grant it. The brief of counsel before us, though directed to the authority of that body to pass criminal laws, uses the same language. Because there is no *express* power to provide for preventing violence exercised on the voter as a means of controlling his vote, no such law can be enacted. It destroys at one blow, in construing the Constitution of the United States, the doctrine universally applied to all instruments of writing, that what is implied is as much a part of the instrument as what is expressed. This principle, in its application to the Constitution of the United States, more than to almost any other writing, is a necessity, by reason of the inherent inability to put into words all derivative powers: a difficulty which the instrument itself recognizes by conferring on Congress the authority to pass all laws necessary and proper to carry into execution the powers expressly granted and all other powers vested in the government or any branch of it by the Constitution. Art. I, sec. 8, clause 18.

We know of no express authority to pass laws to punish theft or burglary of the Treasury of the United States. Is there, therefore, no power in Congress to protect the Treasury by punishing such theft and burglary?

Are the mails of the United States and the money carried in them to be left to the mercy of robbers and of thieves who may handle the mail because the Constitution contains no express words of power in Congress to enact laws for the punishment of those offenses? The principle, if sound, would abolish the entire criminal jurisdiction of the courts of the United States and the laws which confer that jurisdiction.

It is said that the States can pass the necessary law on this subject, and no necessity exists for such action by Congress. But the existence of state laws punishing the counterfeiting of the coin of the United States has never been held to supersede the Acts of Congress passed for that purpose, or to justify the United States in failing to enforce its own laws to protect the circulation of the coin which it issues. . . .

So, also, has the Congress been slow to exercise the powers expressly conferred upon it in relation to elections by the 4th section of the 1st article of the Constitution.

This section declares that: "The times, places and manner of holding elections for Senators and Representatives shall be prescribed in each State by the Legislature thereof; but the Congress may at any time make or alter such regulations, except as to the place of choosing Senators."

It was not until 1842 that Congress took any action under the power here conferred, when, conceiving that the system of electing all the members of the House of Representatives from a State by general ticket, as it was called, that is, every elector voting for as many names as the State was entitled to representatives in that house, worked injustice to other States which did not adopt that system, and gave an undue preponderance of power to the political party which had a majority of votes in the State, however small, enacted that each member should be elected by a separate district, composed of contiguous territory.

And to remedy more than one evil arising from the election of members of Congress occurring at different times in the different States, Congress, by the Act of February 2, 1872, thirty years later, required all the elections for such members to be held on the Tuesday after the first Monday in November in 1876, and on the same day of every second year thereafter.

The frequent failures of the Legislatures of the States to elect Senators at the proper time, by one branch of the Legislature voting for one person and the other branch for another person, and refusing in any manner to reconcile their differences, led Congress to pass an Act which compelled the two bodies to meet in joint convention, and fixing the day when this should be done, and requiring them so to meet on every day thereafter and vote for a Senator until one was elected.

In like manner Congress has fixed a day, which is to be the same in all the States, when the electors for President and Vice-President shall be appointed.

Now the day fixed for electing members of Congress has been established by Congress without regard to the time set for election of state officers in each State, and but for the fact that the State Legislatures have, for their own accommodation, required state elections to be held at the same time, these elections would be held for Congressmen alone at the time fixed by the Act of Congress.

Will it be denied that it is in the power of that body to provide laws for the proper conduct of those elections? To provide, if necessary, the officers who shall conduct them and make return of the result? And especially to provide, in an election held under its own authority, for security of life and limb to the voter while in the exercise of this function? Can it be doubted that Congress can by law protect the act of voting, the place where it is done and the man who votes, from personal violence or intimidation and the election itself from corruption or fraud?

If this be so, and it is not doubted, are such powers annulled because an election for state officers is held at the same time and place? Is it any less important that the election of members of Congress should be the free choice of all the electors because state officers are to be elected at the same time? . . .

These questions answer themselves; and it is only because the Congress of the United States, through long habit and long years of forbearance, has, in deference and respect to the States, refrained from the exercise of these powers, that they are now doubted.

But when, in the pursuance of a new demand for action, that body, as it did in the cases just enumerated, finds it necessary to make additional laws for the free, the pure and the safe exercise of this right of voting, they stand upon the same ground and are to be upheld for the same reasons.

It is said that the parties assaulted in these cases are not officers of the United States, and their protection in exercising the right to vote by Congress does not stand on the same ground.

But the distinction is not well taken. The power in either case arises out of the circumstance that the function in which the party is engaged or the right which he is about to exercise is dependent on the laws of the United States.

In both cases it is the duty of that government to see that he may exercise this right freely and to protect him from violence while so doing or on account of so doing. This duty does not arise solely from the interest of the party concerned, but from the necessity of the government itself, that its service shall be free from the adverse influence of force and fraud practiced on its agents, and that the votes by which its members of Congress and its President are elected shall be the *free* votes of the electors, and the officers thus chosen the free and uncorrupted choice of those who have the right to take part in that choice.

This proposition answers, also, another objection to the constitutionality of the laws under consideration, namely: that the right to vote for a member of Congress is not dependent upon the Constitution or laws of the United States, but is governed by the law of each State respectively.

If this were conceded, the importance to the General Government of having the actual election, the voting for those members, free from force and fraud is not diminished by the circumstance that the qualification of the voter is determined by the law of the State where he votes. It equally affects the government; it is as indispensable to the proper discharge of the great function of legislating for that government, that those who are to control this legislation shall not owe their election to bribery or violence, whether the class of persons who shall vote is determined by the law of the State, or by the law of the United States, or by their united result.

But it is not correct to say that the right to vote for

a member of Congress does not depend on the Constitution of the United States.

The office, if it be properly called an office, is created by that Constitution and by that alone. It also declares how it shall be filled, namely: by election.

Its language is: "The House of Representatives shall be composed of members chosen every second year by the people of the several States, and the electors in each State shall have the same qualifications requisite for electors of the most numerous branch of the State Legislature." Article I, section 2. The States in prescribing the qualifications of voters for the most numerous branch of their own Legislatures, do not do this with reference to the election for members of Congress. Nor can they prescribe the qualification for voters for those eo nomine. They define who are to vote for the popular branch of their own Legislature, and the Constitution of the United States says the same persons shall vote for members of Congress in that State. It adopts the qualification thus furnished as the qualification of its own electors for members of Congress.

It is not true, therefore, that electors for members of Congress owe their right to vote to the state law in any sense which makes the exercise of the right to depend exclusively on the law of the State.

Counsel for petitioners, seizing upon the expression found in the opinion of the court in the case of Minor v. Happersett [1875] that "the Constitution of the United States does not confer the right of suffrage upon any one," without reference to the connection in which it is used, insists that the voters in this case do not owe their right to vote in any sense to that instrument.

But the court was combating the argument that this right was conferred on all citizens, and therefore upon women as well as men.

In opposition to that idea, it was said the Constitution adopts as the qualification for voters of members of Congress that which prevails in the State where the voting is to be done; therefore, said the opinion, the right is not definitely conferred on any person or class of persons by the Constitution alone, because you have to look to the law of the State for the description of the class. But the court did not intend to say that when the class or the person is thus ascertained, his right to vote for a member of Congress was not fundamentally based upon the Constitution, which created the office of member of Congress, and declared it should be elective, and pointed to the means of ascertaining who should be electors. . . .

It is as essential to the successful working of this government that the great organisms of its executive and legislative branches should be the free choice of the people, as that the original form of it should be so. In absolute governments, where the monarch is the source of all power, it is still held to be important that the exercise of that power shall be free from the influence of extraneous violence and internal corruption.

In a republican government, like ours, where political power is reposed in representatives of the entire body of the people, chosen at short intervals by popular elections, the temptations to control these elections by violence and by corruption is a constant source of danger.

Such has been the history of all republics and, though ours has been comparatively free from both these evils in the past, no lover of his country can shut his eyes to the fear of future danger from both sources.

If the recurrence of such acts as these prisoners stand convicted of are too common in one quarter of the country, and give omen of danger from lawless violence, the free use of money in elections, arising from the vast growth of recent wealth in other quarters, presents equal cause for anxiety.

If the Government of the United States has within its constitutional domain no authority to provide against these evils, if the very sources of power may be poisoned by corruption or controlled by violence and outrage, without legal restraint, then, indeed, is the country in danger and its best powers, its highest purposes, the hopes which it inspires and the love which enshrines it, are at the mercy of the combinations of those who respect no right but brute force, on the one hand, and unprincipled corruptionists on the other.

The rule to show cause in this case is discharged and the writ of habeas corpus denied.

UNITED STATES v. CLASSIC

313 U. S. 299; 61 S. Ct. 1031; 85 L. Ed. 1368
(1941)

While the states fix the qualifications for voting for federal officers, Congress is not without power to control by law the conduct of federal elections. Article I, sec. 4, of the Constitution provides that: "The times, places and manner of holding elections for Senators and Representatives, shall be prescribed in each State by the legislature thereof; but the Congress may at any time by law make or alter such regulations, except as to the places of choosing Senators." Congress has found it more satisfactory to use the election laws and election machinery of the states for the choice of congressional senators and representatives than to replace these by its own separate laws and machinery. In 1871 Congress made it a federal crime for any officer of an election at which members of Congress were voted for to violate any duty imposed upon him in regard to such election by any state or federal law. In Ex parte Siebold (1880) the Court upheld the conviction in a federal court of Siebold and others who, being state election officers, stuffed the ballot box at a congressional election in Maryland in violation of a Maryland statute. Congress could validly adopt in this manner the election laws of the states, and could add its own penalties to the violation of these laws. Such cooperative action by state and nation is constitutional.

A somewhat different constitutional problem is presented by congressional efforts to regulate presidential elections. The Constitution provides merely that "each state shall appoint" its presidential electors "in such a manner as the legislature thereof may direct," and it was after the Civil War before the last state provided that they be "appointed" by popular vote rather than by the state legislature itself. Congress may, and has, provided for the time of choosing electors, but it has no power to regulate the manner and places of holding their elections. As a practical matter this limitation on Congress is of little importance. Presidential electors are in practice chosen at the same election as are representatives to Congress, and Congress can control the manner and places of choosing the latter. The distinction did, however, become important during the World War II debates over efforts of the government to provide a "federal ballot" by which soldiers away from home could cast an absentee vote for federal officers.

Despite this ostensible lack of power over presidential elections, the Supreme Court has taken a practical stand in recognizing the national interest in such elections. In Burroughs v. United States (1934) the Court held valid a federal statute of 1925 which requires the public disclosure of presidential campaign contributions, the names of contributors, and other details. The Court said, "To say that Congress is without power to pass appropriate legislation to safeguard such an election from the improper use of money to influence the result is to deny to the nation in a vital particular the power of self protection."

Another practical recognition of the actualities of the electoral system is seen in the case of Ray v. Blair (1952), in which the Court held that Alabama could validly require of those nominated to be presidential electors a pledge to support the choice of the Democratic National Convention. The Court recognized that the framers had intended electors to be free agents, but consistent usage had been the other way; now some twenty states do not even print the names of electors on the ballot. Such a pledge, the Court held, was not forbidden by anything in the Twelfth Amendment, although it deliberately left open the question of whether the pledge could be enforced if anyone chose to violate it.

In January 1964, the long fight to outlaw the poll tax in federal elections resulted in the adoption of the Twenty-fourth Amendment. Five states still had poll taxes whose payment was a prerequisite to voting, and two of them, Virginia and Texas, made plans prior to the adoption of the amendment to separate those eligible to vote only in federal elections from those who, by paying the poll tax, were eligible to vote in both state and federal elections. The Virginia law required federal voters to register annually and to provide a notarized certificate of residence at least six months before the election, while state voters who paid the poll tax were permanently registered and could vote for both state and federal officers. In Harman v. Forssenius (1965) the Court held the Virginia act void under the Twenty-fourth Amendment, since it imposed a "material requirement solely upon those who refuse to surrender their constitutional right to vote in federal elections without paying a poll tax." Whatever plans the remaining four states might have devised became academic in 1966 when the Court, in Harper v. Virginia Board of Elections, held void poll taxes in state elections as a denial of equal protection of the laws.

In Newberry v. United States (1921) the question arose whether the power of Congress to make regulations affecting congressional elections extends to primary elections in which representatives are nominated, or only to the elections in which they are finally chosen. A federal corrupt practices act of 1910 limited by criminal penalties the sums which might be spent in congressional election campaigns. In 1918 Senator Newberry from Michigan spent a great deal more than the statutory amount in winning from Henry Ford the Republican nomination for the Senate, and he was convicted of violating the federal statute. The Supreme Court in a five-to-four decision (explained in the opinion in the Classic case given below) set the conviction aside. Only eight justices, however, passed on the constitutional question of whether Congress could regulate congressional primaries, and they divided four to four. In spite of this the Newberry case was popularly regarded as holding congressional primary elections immune from any federal control, although this supposed result was bitterly criticized.

In 1939 Attorney General Murphy created in the Criminal Division of the Department of Justice the Civil Liberties Unit (now itself a Division of the Department) and ordered it to "direct, supervise and conduct prosecutions of violations of the provisions of the Constitution or Acts of Congress guaranteeing civil rights to individuals." As part of a varied and aggressive program for the protection of civil liberties, the Unit won a signal victory in its successful prosecution of the case of United States v. Classic. Classic, a crooked New Orleans politician, guilty of the crudest kind of election frauds, must have felt that the arm of the law was indeed long to bring about his conviction in a federal court for having violated two sections of the old Enforcement Act of 1870 which forbade obstruction or interference with the rights guaranteed to citizens by the Constitution or statutes of the United States. This result was possible only because the Court was willing to ignore the supposed ruling of the Newberry case and to hold that the right of the citizen to vote in a congressional primary election, and to have his ballot honestly counted, is a right which Congress has validly protected in its laws relating generally to congressional elections. In short, a primary election is an election within the meaning of the Constitution and statutes. The three justices who dissented in this case did so not because they doubted the constitutional power of Congress to regulate congressional primaries, but because they did not agree that Congress, in a statute passed seventy years before, had exercised this power.

Mr. Justice **Stone** delivered the opinion of the Court, saying in part:

Two counts of an indictment found in a federal district court charged that appellees [Classic and others], Commissioners of Elections, conducting a primary election under Louisiana law, to nominate a candidate of the Democratic Party for representative in Congress, willfully altered and falsely counted and certified the ballots of voters cast in the primary election. The questions for decision are whether the right of qualified voters to vote in the Louisiana primary and to have their ballots counted is a right "secured by the Constitution" within the meaning of §§ 19 and 20 of the Criminal Code, and whether the acts of appellees charged in the indictment violate those sections. . . .

Section 19 of the Criminal Code condemns as a criminal offense any conspiracy to injure a citizen in the exercise "of any right or privilege secured to him by the Constitution or laws of the United States." Section 20 makes it a penal offense for anyone who, "acting under color of any law" "willfully subjects, or causes to be subjected, any inhabitant of any State . . . to the deprivation of any rights, privileges and immunities secured and protected by the Constitution and laws of the United States." The government argues that the right of a qualified voter in a Louisiana congressional primary election to have his vote counted as cast is a right secured by Article 1, §§ 2 and 4 of the Constitution, and that a conspiracy to deprive the citizen of that right is a violation of § 19, and also that the willful action of appellees as state officials, in falsely counting the ballots at the primary election and in falsely certifying the count, deprived qualified voters of that right and of the equal protection of the laws guaranteed by the Fourteenth Amendment, all in violation of § 20 of the Criminal Code.

Article 1, § 2 of the Constitution, commands that "The House of Representatives shall be composed of Members chosen every second Year by the People of the several States, and the Electors in each State shall have the Qualifications requisite for Electors of the most numerous Branch of the State Legislature." By § 4 of the same article "The Times, Places and Manner of holding Elections for Senators and Representatives, shall be prescribed in each State by the Legislature thereof; but the Congress may at any time by Law make or alter such Regulations, except as to the Places of chusing Senators." Such right as is secured by the Constitution to qualified voters to choose members of the House of Representatives is thus to be exercised in conformity to the requirements of state law subject to the restrictions prescribed by § 2 and to the authority conferred on Congress by § 4, to regulate the times, places and manner of holding elections for representatives.

We look then to the statutes of Louisiana here involved to ascertain the nature of the right which under the constitutional mandate they define and confer on the voter and the effect upon its exercise of the acts with which appellees are charged, all with the view to determining, first, whether the right or privilege is one secured by the Constitution of the United States, second, whether the effect under the state statute of appellee's alleged acts is such that they operate to injure or oppress citizens in the exercise of that right within the meaning of § 19 and to deprive inhabitants of the state of that right

within the meaning of § 20, and finally, whether §§ 19 and 20 respectively are in other respects applicable to the alleged acts of appellees.

[Under the Constitution] the states are given, and in fact exercise a wide discretion in the formulation of a system for the choice by the people of representatives in Congress. In common with many other states Louisiana has exercised that discretion by setting up machinery for the effective choice of party candidates for representative in Congress by primary elections and by its laws it eliminates or seriously restricts the candidacy at the general election of all those who are defeated at the primary. . . .

The right to vote for a representative in Congress at the general election is, as a matter of law, thus restricted to the successful party candidate at the primary, to those not candidates at the primary who file nomination papers, and those whose names may be lawfully written into the ballot by the electors. . . . In fact, as alleged in the indictment, the practical operation of the primary in Louisiana, is and has been since the primary election was established in 1900 to secure the election of the Democratic primary nominee for the Second Congressional District of Louisiana.

Interference with the right to vote in the congressional primary in the Second Congressional District for the choice of Democratic candidate for Congress is thus as a matter of law and in fact an interference with the effective choice of the voters at the only stage of the election procedure when their choice is of significance, since it is at the only stage when such interference could have any practical effect on the ultimate result, the choice of the Congressman to represent the district. The primary in Louisiana is an integral part of the procedure for the popular choice of Congressman. The right of qualified voters to vote at the congressional primary in Louisiana and to have their ballots counted is thus the right to participate in that choice.

We come then to the question whether that right is one secured by the Constitution. Section 2 of Article 1 commands that Congressmen shall be chosen by the people of the several states by electors, the qualifications of which it prescribes. The right of the people to choose . . . is a right established and guaranteed by the Constitution and hence is one secured by it to those citizens and inhabitants of the state entitled to exercise the right. Ex parte Yarbrough [1884]. . . .

Obviously included within the right to choose, secured by the Constitution, is the right of qualified voters within a state to cast their ballots and have them counted at congressional elections. This Court has consistently held that this is a right secured by the Constitution. . . . And since the constitutional command is without restriction or limitation, the right, unlike those guaranteed by the Fourteenth and Fifteenth Amendments, is secured against the action of individuals as well as of states. Ex parte Yarbrough. . . .

But we are now concerned with the question whether the right to choose at a primary election, a candidate for election as representative, is embraced in the right to choose representatives secured by Article 1, § 2. We may assume that the framers of the Constitution in adopting that section, did not have specifically in mind the selection and elimination of candidates for Congress by the direct primary any more than they contemplated the application of the commerce clause to interstate telephone, telegraph and wireless communication which are concededly within it. But in determining whether a provision of the Constitution applies to a new subject matter, it is of little significance that it is one with which the framers were not familiar. For in setting up an enduring framework of government they undertook to carry out for the indefinite future and in all the vicissitudes of the changing affairs of men, those fundamental purposes which the instrument itself discloses. Hence we read its words, not as we read legislative codes which are subject to continuous revision with the changing course of events, but as the revelation of the great purposes which were intended to be achieved by the Constitution as a continuing instrument of government. . . . If we remember that "it is a Constitution we are expounding," we cannot rightly prefer, of the possible meanings of its words, that which will defeat rather than effectuate the constitutional purpose.

That the free choice by the people of representatives in Congress, subject only to the restrictions to be found in . . . the Constitution, was one of the great purposes of our constitutional scheme of government cannot be doubted. We cannot regard it as any the less the constitutional purpose or its words as any the less guaranteeing the integrity of that choice when a state, exercising its privilege in the absence of congressional action, changes the mode of choice from a single step, a general election, to two, of which the first is the choice at a primary of those candidates from whom, as a second step, the representative in Congress is to be chosen at the election.

Nor can we say that that choice which the Constitution protects is restricted to the second step because § 4 of Article 1, as a means of securing a free choice of representatives by the people, has authorized Congress to regulate the manner of elections, without making any mention of primary elections. For we think that the authority of Congress, given by § 4, includes the authority to regulate primary elections when, as in this case, they are a step in the exercise by the people of their choice of representatives in Congress. . . .

Long before the adoption of the Constitution the form and mode of that expression had changed from time to time. There is no historical warrant for supposing that the framers were under the illusion that the method of effecting the choice of the electors would never change or that if it did, the change was for that reason to be permitted to defeat the right of the people to choose representatives for Congress which the Constitution had guaranteed. The right to participate in the choice of representatives for Congress includes, as we have said, the right to cast a ballot and to have it counted at the general election whether for the successful candidate or not.

Where the state law has made the primary an integral part of the procedure of choice, or where in fact the primary effectively controls the choice, the right of the elector to have his ballot counted at the primary, is likewise included in the right protected by Article 1, § 2. And this right of participation is protected just as is the right to vote at the election, where the primary is by law made an integral part of the election machinery, whether the voter exercises his right in a party primary which invariably, sometimes or never determines the ultimate choice of the representative. Here, even apart from the circumstance that the Louisiana primary is made by law an integral part of the procedure of choice, the right to choose a representative is in fact controlled by the primary because, as is alleged in the indictment, the choice of candidates at the Democratic primary determines the choice of the elected representative.

. . . Words, especially those of a constitution, are not to be read with such stultifying narrowness. The words of §§ 2 and 4 of Article 1, read in the sense which is plainly permissible and in the light of the constitutional purpose, require us to hold that a primary election which involves a necessary step in the choice of candidates for election as representatives in Congress, and which in the circumstances of this case controls that choice, is an election within the meaning of the constitutional provision and is subject to congressional regulation as to the manner of holding it. . . .

There remains the question whether §§ 19 and 20 are an exercise of the congressional authority applicable to the acts with which appellees are charged in the indictment. Section 19 makes it a crime to conspire to "injure" or "oppress" any citizen "in the free exercise of any right or privilege secured to him by the Constitution." In Ex parte Yarbrough, . . . it was held that the right to vote in a congressional election is a right secured by the Constitution, and that a conspiracy to prevent the citizen from voting or to prevent the official count of his ballot when cast, is a conspiracy to injure and oppress the citizen in the free exercise of a right secured by the Constitution within the meaning of § 19. In reaching this conclusion the Court found no uncertainty or ambiguity in the statutory language, obviously devised to protect the citizen "in the free exercise or enjoyment of any right or privilege secured to him by the Constitution," and concerned itself with the question whether the right to participate in choosing a representative is so secured. Such is our function here. Conspiracy to prevent the official count of a citizen's ballot, held in United States v. Mosley [1915] to be a violation of § 19 in the case of a congressional election, is equally a conspiracy to injure and oppress the citizen when the ballots are cast in a primary election prerequisite to the choice of party candidates for a congressional election. In both cases the right infringed is one secured by the Constitution. The injury suffered by the citizen in the exercise of the right is an injury which the statute describes and to which it applies in the one case as in the other. . . .

If a right secured by the Constitution may be infringed by the corrupt failure to include the vote at a primary in the official count, it is not significant that the primary, like the voting machine, was unknown when § 19 was adopted. Abuse of either may infringe the right and therefore violate § 19. . . .

The right of the voters at the primary to have their votes counted is, as we have stated, a right or privilege secured by the Constitution, and to this § 20 also gives protection. The alleged acts of appellees were committed in the course of their performance of duties under the Louisiana statute requiring them to count the ballots, to record the result of the count, and to certify the result of the election. Misuse of power, possessed by virtue of state law and made possible only because the wrongdoer is clothed with the authority of state law, is action taken "under color of" state law. . . . Here the acts of appellees infringed the constitutional right and deprived the voters of the benefit of it within the meaning of § 20. . . .

Reversed

Mr. Chief Justice **Hughes** took no part in the consideration or decision of this case.

Mr. Justice **Douglas** wrote a dissenting opinion in which Justices **Black** and **Murphy** joined.

SMITH v. ALLWRIGHT

321 U.S. 649; 64 S. Ct. 757; 88 L. Ed. 987 (1944)

The act of Congress of March 2, 1867, imposed black voting rights on the ten Southern states as a part of the congressional policy of Reconstruction, and three years later the Fifteenth Amendment undertook to establish, upon a permanent constitutional basis, the right of blacks to vote. It was only natural that such a policy should meet with bitter hostility from Southern whites, and for upwards of two decades the blacks were pretty effectively disfranchised throughout the South by intimidation, violence, and other irregular practices. Such methods, however, provided no permanent solution of the problem; and gradually means were perfected by which it was thought blacks could be disfranchised in a technically constitutional way. Mississippi proved a pioneer in this direction by requiring of the voter the payment of a poll tax and the display of the receipt therefor, and the ability to read the state constitution and to understand and interpret it reasonably when read to him. Fortressed behind clauses such as these the white election officials did not find it difficult to exclude the blacks without disturbing the voting rights of whites. The Supreme Court of the United States held, in Williams v. Mississippi (1898), that such provisions do not violate the Fifteenth Amendment since they do not deny to anyone the right to vote because of race or color. In Lassiter v. Northampton County Board of Elections (1959) the Court held unanimously that a North Carolina statute of

1957 was not unconstitutional "on its face" in requiring that "Every person presenting himself for registration shall be able to read and write any section of the Constitution of North Carolina in the English language." The case involved no direct racial discrimination, since Lassiter had refused to submit to this literacy test.

An even more effective device for disfranchising black voters, however, was the "grandfather clause." The essential features of this plan were two: first, the establishment of a rigorous educational qualification (in some states a property qualification) drastic enough to permit the disfranchisement of most blacks; second, a provision that the qualification need not be met by those who were legal voters in 1866, or in 1867 (prior to the adoption of the act of March 2), or who were lineal descendants of such legal voters. In the case of Guinn v. United States (1915) the Court held that the Oklahoma grandfather clause was a violation of the Fifteenth Amendment. The clause read as follows: "No person shall be registered as an elector of this state or be allowed to vote in any election held herein, unless he be able to read and write any section of the constitution of the State of Oklahoma; but no person who was, on January 1, 1866, or at any time prior thereto, entitled to vote under any form of government, or who at that time resided in some foreign nation, and no lineal descendant of such person, shall be denied the right to register and vote because of his inability to so read and write sections of such constitution." The Court emphasized that while the Fifteenth Amendment does not guarantee to any citizen the right to vote, since voting qualifications are fixed by state law, it does protect him against being denied the right to vote because of race or color. It held that while the grandfather clause did not mention race or color, it was entirely clear that it set up a racial discrimination in the matter of voting since the only possible reason for picking out the date January 1, 1866, as a basis for classifying citizens was that before that date blacks were not allowed to vote.

Perhaps the most ingenious attempt to disfranchise the Southern black was the "white primary" invented by the state of Texas. Relying on the facts that the South was solidly Democratic and whoever won the primary election was certain to be elected, Texas passed a law forbidding blacks to vote in the Democratic primaries. In Nixon v. Herndon (1927) the Court struck the law down not because the primary was an "election" but because the law was blatantly discriminatory. Texas replied with a law authorizing the Democratic State Committee to exclude blacks and when this was held void (Nixon v. Condon, 1932) it simply repealed the law and left it to the Committee to decide who should vote. Since no state action was now involved in the Committee decision the Court held it valid in Grovey v. Townsend (1935).

Following the present case a last valiant effort to convert the Democratic party into a private club was undertaken by South Carolina. The legislature repealed some 150 statutory provisions in which primaries were authorized, regulated, or just mentioned and the constitution was amended to delete all mention of primaries.

The Democratic party then proceeded to bar blacks from its primaries. While a wholly extra-legal election system presents problems and dangers quite unrelated to race, these were never given a chance to develop. The United States district court, finding that for all its informality the primary did produce candidates for the final election, held that it was part of the election machinery and blacks could not be barred from voting in it. The Supreme Court declined to review the decision; see Rice v. Elmore (1948).

When the Court decided United States v. Classic (1941), it did not mention Grovey v. Townsend. It was perfectly obvious that the two cases rested on conflicting principles. If, according to the Classic doctrine, a primary election is a vital part of the election machinery of the state, then clearly it is not the nongovernmental and unofficial activity of a private voluntary association which Grovey v. Townsend held it to be. Accordingly, steps were at once taken to bring before the Court for reexamination the question of the constitutionality of the Texas "white primary." In due course, Smith v. Allwright reached the Supreme Court, and Grovey v. Townsend was overruled.

With the adoption of the Civil Rights Acts of 1957, 1960, and 1964, and the Voting Rights Act of 1965, attention turned to the meaning of these statutes and their effectiveness in halting voting discrimination. See South Carolina v. Katzenbach (1966). After the Twenty-fourth Amendment outlawed poll taxes in federal elections and the Civil Rights Act of 1965 waived them in certain state elections, the Court in 1966 held that state poll taxes violated the equal protection clause of the Fourteenth Amendment; see Harper v. Virginia Bd. of Elections.

While sex and race have long been outlawed as bases for denying the right to vote, a number of other limitations on the franchise were accepted almost without question and only since the mid-1960's have they been subject to serious challenge under the equal protection clause of the Fourteenth Amendment. One of these was the rule limiting the vote on special questions to those who seemed to have a special interest in the outcome. Without actually holding that such a limitation could never be valid, the Supreme Court made clear in Kramer v. Union Free School District (1969) that it had, at the very least, to be precisely limited to those who actually were "primarily interested." In Kramer, parents and real property taxpayers were found to be not sufficiently more interested in school affairs than others in the community to justify letting them alone elect the school board. And in Cipriano v. Houma (1969), decided the same day as Kramer, the Court held that a vote on the issuance of bonds to finance the state's public utilities could not be limited to property taxpayers, since everyone had an interest in utility operation and the bonds were not to be paid from property tax revenue. In both cases, the Court held, the state had failed to meet the "exacting standard of precision required of statutes which selectively distribute the franchise." In 1970 these decisions were reaffirmed in Evans v. Cornman when the Court held that residents of a federal enclave located in Maryland had sufficient interest to vote in Maryland elections since they were subject to that state's criminal, tax, and automobile licensing laws and their children went to Maryland schools.

A widespread limitation on those wishing to run for public office is the requirement that a prospective candidate for statewide office get petitions signed by voters scattered around the state to show that he is not the candidate merely of a single interest or area. In 1948, the Court, relying on Colegrove v. Green (1946), had decided in MacDougal v. Green that Illinois could validly require a prospective candidate to get 200 signatures from each of 50 of the state's 102 counties in order to get on the ballot—a task that Henry Wallace's Progressive party was unable to accomplish. The state, the Court observed, has "the power to assure a proper diffusion of political initiative as between its thinly populated counties and those having concentrated masses, in view of the fact that the latter have practical opportunities for exerting their political weight at the polls not available to the former." In Moore v. Ogilvie (1969), the Court, noting that Illinois' smallest fifty-three counties now contained less than 7 percent of the population, overruled MacDougal v. Green on the basis of the one man-one vote rule. Assuming without discussion that voting rights included the right to nominate candidates, the Court found that while voters in the fifty-three least populous counties could get persons on the ballot, those in the forty-nine most populous ones, with 93 percent of the people, could not. "This law thus discriminates against the residents of the populous counties of the State in favor of rural sections. It, therefore, lacks the equality to which the exercise of political rights is entitled under the Fourteenth Amendment."

The Court did, however, make clear that reasonable registration requirements would be sustained. In Jenness v. Fortson (1971) it upheld a Georgia requirement that a person who has not entered and won a party primary must get petitions signed by 5 percent of the voters in order to get his name on the ballot. The Court pointed out that there was no limit on the write-in votes, no requirement that a new party hold a primary or meet an unreasonably early filing deadline, no limit on anyone's right to run as a new-party candidate, and any eligible voter—even an unregistered one—could sign a petition. Nor was the 5 percent signature requirement a more difficult hazard to meet than winning a party primary so there was no discrimination in favor of regular party candidates over independents. "In a word, Georgia in no way freezes the status quo, but implicitly recognizes the potential fluidity of American political life."

The qualifications needed to vote for public office have always been established by state law. Even the qualifications for voting in federal elections are those "requisite for electors of the most numerous branch of the state legislature." In setting these qualifications all states have required a period of residence both within the state and within the voting district. As early as 1904, in Pope v. Williams, the Supreme Court held valid a one-year residence requirement for voting in a Maryland election with the observation that "a state, so far as the Federal Constitution is concerned, might provide by its own constitution and laws that none but native-born citizens should be able to vote." In that case a newcomer to the state not only had to reside in the state a year but had to declare his intention to become a citizen-voter one year before he could register to vote.

The first move to impose a constitutional limit on a state's control over voter registration came in 1965 in the case of Carrington v. Rash. Texas had a law which forbade a person in the armed forces to acquire a voting residence in Texas while still in uniform. The state conceded that Carrington had acquired a bona fide residence in Texas, but defended its policy on the ground that most service personnel were transient because the service could move them at will and that for administrative purposes the state was entitled to make irrebuttable the presumption that they were always transient. Moreover, since most military bases were located near small towns, the state was entitled to "prevent the danger of a 'takeover' of the civilian community resulting from concentrated voting by large numbers of military personnel."

The Supreme Court found the law denied equal protection. Other persons, such as college students and civilian government employees were no more likely to be permanent than military personnel but they were given a chance to prove they were bona fide residents. Even military personnel seeking to establish residence for the purpose of getting a divorce in the state courts were given such an opportunity. "The right . . . to choose," United States v. Classic (1941), "that this Court has been so zealous to protect, means, at the least, that States may not casually deprive a class of individuals of the vote because of some remote administrative benefit to the State." As for protecting small communities from the military, " 'fencing out' from the franchise a sector of the population because of the way they may vote is constitutionally impermissible."

In Dunn v. Blumstein (1972) the Court struck down a requirement, present in nearly every state, that a person be a resident of the state for a year, and of an election district for a lesser time, before he could vote. These restrictions applied even to bona fide residents—persons who had made their permanent home within the state or district. After considering the importance both of the right to vote and the right to travel interstate, the Court concluded that a durational residence requirement had to be justified by some compelling state interest. It examined and rejected the state's two arguments—that it prevented multiple voting and thus preserved the purity of the ballot box, and that it ensured knowledgeable voters.

The identification of a bona fide resident qualified to vote in the district, as distinguished from a transient able to vote in several districts, was established by a system of registration. Since the state uniformly accepted the voter's oath that he or she was a qualified resident nothing further was gained in the prevention of fraud by a durational residence requirement. As for "knowledge-ability," the Court reiterated its stand in Carrington v. Rash that a community could not fence out voters with different points of view and quite clearly long-time residence in a district was no assurance that a voter was more knowledgeable about local issues and candidates than a relative newcomer.

Congressional passage of the Voting Rights Act Amendments of 1970 eased still further state limitations on the right to vote. The Act reduced the voting age to eighteen, abolished literacy tests for five years and durational residence requirements for voting for president and vice-president. While the Court was unable to agree on an opinion, in Oregon v. Mitchell (1970) it held that Congress could validly reduce the voting age for federal but not state elections, could abolish literacy tests for both state and federal elections, and could abolish durational residency requirements for persons voting for president and vice-president. Following the decision, the states ratified the Twenty-sixth Amendment, establishing the minimum voting age at eighteen years.

Mr. Justice **Reed** delivered the opinion of the Court, saying in part:

The State of Texas by its Constitution and statutes provides that every person, if certain other requirements are met which are not here in issue, qualified by residence in the district or county "shall be deemed a qualified elector." . . . Primary elections for United States Senators, Congressmen and state officers are provided for by Chapters Twelve and Thirteen of the statutes. Under these chapters, the Democratic Party was required to hold the primary which was the occasion of the alleged wrong to petitioner. . . . These nominations are to be made by the qualified voters of the party. . . .

The Democratic party on May 24, 1932, in a State Convention adopted the following resolution, which has not since been "amended, abrogated, annulled or avoided":

"Be it resolved that all white citizens of the State of Texas who are qualified to vote under the Constitution and laws of the State shall be eligible to membership in the Democratic party and, as such, entitled to participate in its deliberations." It was by virtue of this resolution that the respondents refused to permit the petitioner to vote.

Texas is free to conduct her elections and limit her electorate as she may deem wise, save only as her action may be affected by the prohibitions of the United States Constitution or in conflict with powers delegated to and exercised by the National Government. The Fourteenth Amendment forbids a state from making or enforcing any law which abridges the privileges or immunities of citizens of the United States and the Fifteenth Amendment specifically interdicts any denial or abridgement by a state of the right of citizens to vote on account of color. Respondents appeared in the District Court and the Circuit Court of Appeals and defended on the ground that the Democratic party of Texas is a voluntary organization with members banded together for the purpose of selecting individuals of the group representing the common political beliefs as candidates in the general election. As such a voluntary organization, it was claimed, the Democratic party is free to select its own membership and limit to whites participation in the party primary. Such action, the answer asserted, does not violate the Fourteenth, Fifteenth or Seventeenth Amendment as officers of government cannot be chosen at primaries and the Amendments are applicable only to general elections where governmental officers are actually elected. Primaries, it is said, are political party affairs, handled by party not governmental officers. . . .

The right of a Negro to vote in the Texas primary has been considered heretofore by this Court. . . . [Here follows a summary of the decisions in Nixon v. Herndon (1927), and Nixon v. Condon (1932), which are commented upon in the introductory note.]

In Grovey v. Townsend [1935] this Court had before it another suit for damages for the refusal in a primary of a county clerk, a Texas officer with only public functions to perform, to furnish petitioner, a Negro, an absentee ballot. The refusal was solely on the ground of race. This case differed from Nixon v. Condon, in that a state convention of the Democratic party had passed the resolution of May 24, 1932, hereinbefore quoted. It was decided that the determination by the state convention of the membership of the Democratic party made a significant change from a determination by the Executive Committee. The former was party action, voluntary in character. The latter, as had been held in the Condon Case, was action by authority of the State. The managers of the primary election were therefore declared not to be state officials in such sense that their action was state action. A state convention of a party was said not to be an organ of the state. This Court went on to announce that to deny a vote in a primary was a mere refusal of party membership with which ''the state need have no concern,'' while for a state to deny a vote in a general election on the ground of race or color violated the Constitution. Consequently, there was found no ground for holding that the county clerk's refusal of a ballot because of racial ineligibility for party membership denied the petitioner any right under the Fourteenth or Fifteenth Amendment.

Since Grovey v. Townsend and prior to the present suit, no case from Texas involving primary elections has been before this Court. We did decide, however, United States v. Classic [1941]. We there held that § 4 of Article 1 of the Constitution authorized Congress to regulate primary as well as general elections, ''where the primary is by law made an integral part of the election machinery.'' Consequently, in the Classic Case, we upheld the applicability to frauds in a Louisiana primary of §§ 19 and 20 of the Criminal Code. Thereby corrupt acts of election officers were subjected to Congressional sanctions because that body had power to protect rights of Federal suffrage secured by the Constitution in primary as in general elections. This decision depended, too, on the determination that under the Louisiana statutes the primary was a part of the procedure for choice of Federal officials. By this decision the doubt as to whether or not such primaries were a part of ''elections'' subject to Federal control, which had remained unanswered since Newberry v. United States [1921] was erased. The Nixon Cases were decided under the equal protection clause of the Fourteenth Amendment without a determination of the status of the primary as a part of the electoral process. The exclusion of Negroes from the primaries by action of the State was held invalid under that Amendment. The fusing by the Classic Case of the primary and general elections into a single instrumentality for choice of officers has a definite bearing on the permissibility under the Constitution of excluding Negroes from primaries. . . . Classic bears upon Grovey v. Townsend not because exclusion of Negroes from primaries is any more or less state action by reason of the unitary character of the electoral process but because the recognition of the place of the primary in the electoral scheme makes clear that state delegation to a party of the power to fix the qualifications of primary elections is delegation of a state function that may make the party's action the action of the state. When Grovey v. Townsend was written, the Court looked upon the denial of a vote in a primary, as a mere refusal by a party of party membership. As the Louisiana statutes for holding primaries are similar to those of Texas, our ruling in Classic as to the unitary character of the electoral process calls for a reexamination as to whether or not the exclusion of Negroes from a Texas party primary was state action. . . .

It may now be taken as a postulate that the right to vote in such a primary for the nomination of candidates without discrimination by the State, like the right to vote in a general election, is a right secured by the Constitution. . . . By the terms of the Fifteenth Amendment that right may not be abridged by any state on account of race. Under our Constitution the great privilege of the ballot may not be denied a man by the State because of his color.

We are thus brought to an examination of the qualifications for Democratic primary electors in Texas, to determine whether state action or private action has excluded Negroes from participation. . . . [Here follows a summary of the various ways in which Texas primaries are regulated by state statutes.]

We think that this statutory system for the selection of party nominees for inclusion on the general election ballot makes the party which is required to follow these legislative directions an agency of the state in so far as it determines the participants in a primary election. The party takes its character as a state agency from the duties imposed upon it by state statutes; the duties do not become matters of private law because they are performed by a political party. The plan of the Texas primary follows substantially that of Louisiana, with the exception that in Louisiana the state pays the cost of the primary while Texas assesses the cost against candidates. In numerous instances, the Texas statutes fix or limit the fees to be charged. Whether paid directly by the state or through state requirements, it is state action which compels. When primaries become a part of the machinery for choosing officials, state and national, as they have here, the same tests to determine the character of discrimination or abridgement should be applied to the primary as are applied to the general election. If the state requires a certain electoral procedure, prescribes a general election ballot made up of party nominees so chosen and limits the choice of the electorate in general elections for state offices, practically speaking, to those whose names appear on such a ballot, it endorses, adopts and enforces the discrimination against Negroes, practiced by a party entrusted by Texas law with the determination of the qualifications of participants in the primary. This is state action within the meaning of the Fifteenth Amendment. . . .

The United States is a constitutional democracy. Its organic law grants to all citizens a right to participate in the choice of elected officials without restriction by any state because of race. This grant to the people of the opportunity for choice is not to be nullified by a state through casting its electoral process in a form which permits a private organization to practice racial discrimination in the election. Constitutional rights would be of little value if they could be thus indirectly denied. . . .

The privilege of membership in a party may be, as this Court said in Grovey v. Townsend, no concern of a state. But when, as here, that privilege is also the essential qualification for voting in a primary to select nominees for a general election, the state makes the action of the party the action of the state. In reaching this conclusion we are not unmindful of the desirability of continuity of decision in constitutional questions. However, when convinced of former error, this Court has never felt constrained to follow precedent. In constitutional questions, where correction depends upon amendment and not upon legislative action this Court throughout its history has freely exercised its power to reexamine the basis of its constitutional decisions. This has long been accepted practice, and this practice has continued to this day. This is particularly true when the decision believed erroneous is the application of a constitutional principle rather than an interpretation of the Constitution to extract the principle itself. Here we are applying, contrary to the recent decision in Grovey v. Townsend, the well established principle of the Fifteenth Amendment, forbidding the abridgement by a state of a citizen's right to vote. Grovey v. Townsend is overruled.

Judgment reversed.

Mr. Justice **Frankfurter** concurred in the result.

Mr. Justice **Roberts** wrote a dissenting opinion.

RIGHT TO EQUAL REPRESENTATION

REYNOLDS v. SIMS

377 U. S. 533; 84 S. Ct. 1362; 12 L. Ed. 2d 506
(1964)

The decision of the Court in Baker v. Carr (1962) that the fairness of legislative apportionment was a justiciable issue brought immediate and far-reaching results. In two-thirds of the states suits were started in either state or federal courts challenging the apportionment of state legislatures; and by the time of the 1962 elections, nearly twenty states had either reapportioned or put reapportionment plans before the voters in the election. Outstanding among these were Georgia and Alabama. In Georgia, reapportionment resulted in the election of a black state legislator for the first time since Reconstruction; in Alabama, reapportionment was done by a three-judge federal court after the state legislature, which had failed to reapportion for sixty-one years, was unable to come up with a satisfactory plan.

Baker v. Carr did not set any guides for apportionment beyond the requirement that it be "fair." In Gray v. Sanders (1963), however, the Court did hold that "Once the geographical unit for which a representative is to be chosen is designated, all who participate in the election are to have an equal vote—whatever their race, whatever their sex, whatever their occupation, whatever their income, and wherever their home may be in that geographical unit. This is required by the Equal Protection Clause of the Fourteenth Amendment." The case involved the County Unit System in Georgia which, though revised, still permitted a majority of voters in counties having only a third of the population to decide statewide elections. The Court rejected the district court's test that a weighting system was valid if it "showed no greater disparity against a county than exists against any State in the conduct of national elections." The electoral college, the Court pointed out, was the product of historical concerns having nothing to do with statewide elections within a state.

Significant as it was, the Gray decision left unanswered the questions of states which did not use Georgia's unique County Unit System for electing state officers. Did fairness require that all legislative districts within the state be equal in population; and if so, how much deviation from absolute equality was permissible? Could a state, if it wished, apportion one of its two houses on some basis other than population, as is the case with the United States Senate? If so, what bases were permissible? In the event a state failed to provide a fair apportionment scheme, could the United States district court draw the district lines; or was the judicial function limited to forbidding the use of such districts for election purposes?

The first of these questions was answered for congressional districts in Wesberry v. Sanders (1964), a case involving the fairness of congressional districts in the state of Georgia. Speaking for six members of the Court, Justice Black concluded from historical evidence that "the command of Article I, § 2, that Representatives be chosen 'by the People of the several States' means that as nearly as is practicable one man's vote in a congressional election is to be worth as much as another's." It would, he said, "defeat the principle solemnly embodied in the Great Compromise—equal representation in the House for equal numbers of people—for us to hold that, within the States, legislatures may draw the lines of congressional districts in such a way as to give some voters a greater voice in choosing a Congressman than others. The House of Representatives, the Convention agreed, was to represent the people as individuals, and on a basis of complete equality for each voter." Inasmuch as the Georgia apportionment "grossly discriminates against voters in the Fifth Congressional District," the apportionment statute is void.

In a long and impassioned dissent, Justice Harlan, joined by Justice Stewart, took issue with the majority's contention that the framers had intended one citizen's vote to be worth as much as another's. First, in speaking of allocating representatives according to "the number of the state's inhabitants" the Constitution clearly referred to apportionment of representatives among the states, rather than within the states. "In all of the discussion surrounding the basis of representation of the House and all the discussion whether Representatives should be elected by the legislatures or the people of the States, there is nothing which suggests even remotely that the delegates had in mind the problem of districting within a State." Second, both the three-fifths compromise regarding representation for slaves and the provision that each state, no matter how small, have one representative, showed the framers intended "weighted" votes to some extent. He emphasized that this last provision "is not a mere exception to the principle framed by the majority; it shows that no such principle is to be found." Third, the Court, in deciding the issue at all, was derogating the authority of both the states and Congress, clearly given in the provision of Article I, Sec. 4, that "the Times, Places and Manner of holding elections for Senators and Representatives shall be prescribed in each state by the legislature thereof; but the Congress may at any time by Law make or alter such Regulations. . . ."

In four cases decided the same day as Reynolds the Court held void state apportionment schemes because too small a percentage of the population could elect a majority of the legislature. But in a fifth case, Lucas v. Colorado General Assembly (1964), the Court faced the situation that not only did the majority have the power to remedy malapportionment, but as recently as 1962 the people had rejected by a two-to-one vote a system that could have provided equal popular representation in both houses, adopting instead one which took into account "other factors" in apportioning the senate. As a result the senate was malapportioned. The Court rejected the contention that the plan was made valid by the fact that it was the choice of the people, who could change it if they didn't like it. The result was to debase some persons' votes and "a citizen's constitutional rights can hardly be infringed simply because a majority of the people choose to do so."

When the Supreme Court handed down its one-man-one vote rule in Reynolds v. Sims (1964), it required legislative single-member districts to be equal in population without indicating clearly how precise such equality had to be. "The Equal Protection Clause," the Court said, "requires that a State make an honest and good faith effort to construct districts, in both houses of its legislature, as nearly of equal population as is practicable." In most cases the exact dimensions of this holding were unimportant, because the discrepancies between districts were so great as to be indefensible however it was interpreted. In the cases decided the same day as Reynolds, the Court relied to some extent on the percentage of the population which could elect a majority of a legislative body, and in Avery v. Midland County in 1968, in which the Court applied the rule to local governments, it noted merely that the four districts involved in the case had, respectively, populations of 67,906; 852; 414; and 828.

In Kirkpatrick v. Preisler (1969), however, the Court, citing the Reynolds case, made it clear that neither percentages nor population figures were the test to be used for congressional districts but rather the good-faith efforts of the legislature to make the differences as small as possible. Missouri's 1967 reapportionment had produced districts in which the largest and smallest varied only about 3 percent from the ideal, but the state conceded it could have come closer if it had chosen to do so, and the Court insisted it do so.

While the Court in the case below noted in passing the contrast between those cases involving congressional apportionment arising under Article I, Sec. 2 of the Constitution, and those involving the apportionment of state legislatures arising under the equal protection clause, in the ensuing years the Court largely ignored this difference and in dealing with congressional districts in the Kirkpatrick case the Court appeared to assume that the same rules applied to both. No scheme was excused if the deviations between large and small districts could be made smaller, and no justification for not adhering to the one-man-one vote rule passed constitutional muster.

Then, in 1973 in Mahan v. Howell, the Court resurrected the distinction made in Reynolds between federal and state districts and upheld an apportionment scheme adopted by the Virginia legislature that resulted in a 16.4 percent difference between the largest and smallest districts. Rejecting the argument that the state should make "every good-faith effort" to provide the smallest possible difference between the districts, the Court held instead that the state could provide "representation to subdivisions qua subdivisions" and minimize the crossing of local area lines. Since the state legislature had power to legislate for local areas, such a policy was not irrational.

In Gaffney v. Cummings (1973) the Court further widened the gap by holding that where state legislative districts were concerned "it is now time to recognize . . . that minor deviations from mathematical equality among state legislative districts are insufficient to make out a prima facie case of invidious discrimination under the Fourteenth Amendment so as to require justification by the state." It stressed that "there are fundamental differences between congressional districting under Article I and . . . state legislative reapportionment governed by the Fourteenth Amendment. . . ." Here the maximum deviation between Connecticut's legislative districts was 7.83 percent. The Court did emphasize that any districting scheme could be held bad if it fenced out racial groups or was used to cancel the voting strength of racial or political elements in the community, but found this rule was not violated by the drawing of district lines so as to achieve within each district "a rough approximation of the statewide political strength of the Democratic and Republican Parties. . . ." In *White v. Weiser*, decided the same day, it held Texas to the stricter standard in the drawing of congressional district lines.

The Court has made clear that the one-man-one vote rule does not limit all legislative bodies to single member districts. In *Whitcomb v. Chavis (1971)* the Court upheld an Indiana legislative plan in which several of the districts were represented by two or more legislators running at large. It conceded that "voters in multi-member districts vote for and are represented by more legislators than voters in single member districts" and that such legislators might increase their strength by block voting. However, no invidious discrimination against single-member districts had been shown, and the Court was unwilling to "agree that multi-member districts, wherever they exist overrepresent their voters as compared with voters in single-member districts." Nor was there any suggestion that the multi-member districts were "conceived or operated as purposeful devices to further racial or economic discrimination." Where a federal district court rather than a state legislature is doing the reapportioning, however, "unless there are persuasive justifications [it] must avoid use of multimember districts;" see *Chapman v. Meier (1975)*.

In the present case the United States district court had held void the sixty-year-old apportionment of the state of Alabama under which the thirty-five counties, ranging in size from 635,000 to 15,000, each elected one senator. This population-variance ratio of about forty-one to one was matched by a ratio of about sixteen to one in the house. Representatives of about 25 percent of the people constituted a majority in both houses. The Alabama legislature had met in special session and provided two alternative apportionment schemes. The first, known as the "sixty-seven-Senator Amendment," provided for sixty-seven counties and would have put control into the hands of senators representing 19.4 percent of the people, and house members representing about 43 percent. While the population-variance ratio was increased to fifty-nine to one in the senate, it was reduced to four and seventh tenths to one in the house. The second scheme was the Crawford-Webb Act, a legislative stop-gap to be used if the amendment failed to pass or to satisfy the courts. The plan, using the existing counties, permitted control of the house by representatives of 37 percent of the population, and of the senate by representatives of 27.6 percent. Population-variance ratios were about five to one in the house and twenty to one in the senate.

The district court found that neither of these schemes in its entirety met the constitutional test, so it ordered the 1962 elections to be held under the provisions of the "sixty-seven-Senator Amendment" for the house and the Crawford-Webb Act for the senate. This temporary arrangement, it hoped, would break the stranglehold of the small counties and permit the legislature to produce a fair apportionment scheme of its own, but it retained jurisdiction of the case against the chance that this might not be accomplished. The legislature elected under the plan did nothing in 1963. Meanwhile an appeal from the district court's decision reached the Supreme Court of the United States.

Chief Justice **Warren** delivered the opinion of the Court, saying in part:

II.

Undeniably the Constitution of the United States protects the right of all qualified citizens to vote, in state as well as in federal elections. A consistent line of decisions by this Court in cases involving attempts to deny or restrict the right of suffrage has made this indelibly clear. . . . And the right of suffrage can be denied by a debasement or dilution of the weight of a citizen's vote just as effectively as by wholly prohibiting the free exercise of the franchise.

In Baker v. Carr [1962] we held that a claim asserted under the Equal Protection Clause challenging the constitutionality of a State's apportionment of seats in its legislature, on the ground that the right to vote of certain citizens was effectively impaired since debased and diluted, in effect presented a justiciable controversy subject to adjudication by federal courts. . . . We intimated no view as to the proper constitutional standards for evaluating the validity of a state legislative apportionment scheme. Nor did we give any consideration to the question of appropriate remedies. . . .

We indicated in Baker, however, that the Equal Protection Clause provides discoverable and manageable standards for use by lower courts in determining the constitutionality of a state legislative apportionment scheme. . . .

[The Court here reviews briefly its holding in Gray v. Sanders (1963) and Wesberry v. Sanders (1964), discussed in the note above.]

Gray and Wesberry are of course not dispositive of or directly controlling on our decision in these cases involving state legislative apportionment controversies. Admittedly, those decisions, in which we held that, in statewide and in congressional elections, one person's vote must be counted equally with those of all other voters in a State, were based on different constitutional considerations and were addressed to rather distinct problems. But neither are they wholly inapposite. Gray, though not determinative here since involving the weighting of votes in statewide elections, established the basic principle of equality among voters within a State, and held that voters cannot be classified, constitutionally, on the basis of where they live, at least with respect to voting in statewide elections. And our decision in Wesberry was of course grounded on that language of the Constitution which prescribes that members of the Federal House of Representatives are to be chosen "by the People," while attacks on state legislative apportionment schemes, such as that involved in the instant cases, are principally based on the Equal Protection Clause of the Fourteenth Amendment. Nevertheless, Wesberry clearly established that the fundamental principle of representative government in this country is one of equal representation for equal numbers of people, without regard to race, sex, economic status, or place of residence within a State. Our problem, then, is to ascertain, in the instant cases, whether there are any constitutionally cognizable principles which would justify departures from the basic standard of equality among voters in the apportionment of seats in state legislatures.

III.

A predominant consideration in determining whether a State's legislative apportionment scheme constitutes an invidious discrimination violative of rights asserted under the Equal Protection Clause is that the rights allegedly impaired are individual and personal in nature. . . .

Legislators represent people, not trees or acres. Legislators are elected by voters, not farms or cities or economic interests. As long as ours is a representative form of government, and our legislatures are those instruments of government elected directly by and directly representative of the people, the right to elect legislators in a free and unimpaired fashion is a bedrock of our political system. It could hardly be gainsaid that a constitutional claim had been asserted by an allegation that certain otherwise qualified voters had been entirely prohibited from voting for members of their state legislature. And, if a State should provide that the votes of citizens in one part of the State should be given two times, or five times, or ten times the weight of votes of citizens in another part of the State, it could hardly be contended that the right to vote of those residing in the disfavored areas had not been effectively diluted. . . . Of course, the effect of state legislative districting schemes which give the same number of representatives to unequal numbers of constituents is identical. Overweighting and overvaluation of the votes of those living here has the certain effect of dilution and undervaluation of the votes of those living there. The resulting discrimination against those individual voters living in disfavored areas is easily demonstrable mathematically. Their right to vote is simply not the same right to vote as that of those living in a favored part of the State. . . .

State legislatures are, historically, the fountainhead of representative government in this country. A number of them have their roots in colonial times, and substantially antedate the creation of our Nation and our Federal Government. In fact, the first formal stirrings of American political independence are to be found, in large part, in the views and actions of several of the colonial legislative bodies. With the birth of our National Government, and the adoption and ratification of the Federal Constitution, state legislatures retained a most important place in our Nation's governmental structure.

But representative government is in essence self-government through the medium of elected representatives of the people, and each and every citizen has an inalienable right to full and effective participation in the political processes of his State's legislative bodies. Most citizens can achieve this participation only as qualified voters through the election of legislators to represent them. Full and effective participation by all citizens in state government requires, therefore, that each citizen have an equally effective voice in the election of members of his state legislature. Modern and viable state government needs, and the Constitution demands, no less.

Logically, in a society ostensibly grounded on representative government, it would seem reasonable that a majority of the people of a State could elect a majority of that State's legislators. To conclude differently, and to sanction minority control of state legislative bodies, would appear to deny majority rights in a way that far surpasses any possible denial of minority rights that might otherwise be thought to result. Since legislatures are responsible for enacting laws by which all citizens are to be governed, they should be bodies which are collectively responsive to the popular will. . . . Our constitutional system amply provides for the protection of minorities by means other than giving them majority control of state legislatures. And the democratic ideals of equality and majority rule, which have served this Nation so well in the past, are hardly of any less significance for the present and the future. . . .

To the extent that a citizen's right to vote is debased, he is that much less a citizen. The fact that an individual lives here or there is not a legitimate reason for overweighting or diluting the efficacy of his vote. The complexions of societies and civilizations change, often with amazing rapidity. A nation once primarily rural in character becomes predominantly urban. Representation schemes once fair and equitable become archaic and outdated. But the basic principle of representative government remains, and must remain, unchanged—the weight of a citizen's vote cannot be made to depend on where he lives. Population is, of necessity, the starting point for consideration and the controlling criterion for judgment in legislative apportionment controversies. A citizen, a qualified voter, is no more nor no less so because he lives in the city or on the farm. This is the clear and strong command of our Constitution's Equal Protection Clause. This is an essential part of the concept of a government of laws and not men. This is at the heart of Lincoln's vision of "government of the people, by the people, [and] for the people." The Equal Protection Clause demands no less than substantially equal state legislative representation for all citizens, of all places as well as of all races.

IV.

We hold that, as a basic constitutional standard, the Equal Protection Clause requires that the seats in both houses of a bicameral state legislature must be apportioned on a population basis. Simply stated, an individual's right to vote for state legislators is unconstitutionally impaired when its weight is in a substantial fashion diluted when compared with votes of citizens living in other parts of the State. Since, under neither the existing apportionment provisions nor either of the proposed plans was either of the houses of the Alabama Legislature apportioned on a population basis, the District Court correctly held that all three of these schemes were constitutionally invalid. Furthermore, the existing apportionment, and also to a lesser extent the apportionment under the Crawford-Webb Act, presented little more than crazy quilts, completely lacking in rationality, and could be found invalid on that basis alone. . . .

[The Court here details the inequalities present in the various schemes.] And none of the other apportionments of seats in either of the bodies of the Alabama Legislature, under the three plans considered by the District Court, came nearly as close to approaching the required constitutional standard as did that of the House of Representatives under the 67-Senator Amendment. . . .

V.

Since neither of the houses of the Alabama Legislature, under any of the three plans considered by the District Court, was apportioned on a population basis, we would be justified in proceeding no further. However, one of the proposed plans, that contained in the so-called 67-Senator Amendment, at least superficially resembles the scheme of legislative representation followed in the Federal Congress. Under this plan, each of Alabama's 67 counties is allotted one senator, and no counties are given more than one Senate seat. Arguably, this is analogous to the allocation of two Senate seats, in the Federal Congress, to each of the 50 States, regardless of population. Seats in the Alabama House, under the proposed constitutional amendment, are distributed by giving each of the 67 counties at least one, with the remaining 39 seats being allotted among the more populous counties on a population basis. This scheme, at least at first glance, appears to resemble that prescribed for the Federal House of Representatives, where the 435 seats are distributed among the States on a population basis, although each State, regardless of its population, is given at least one Congressman. Thus, although there are substantial differences in underlying rationale and result, the 67-Senator Amendment, as proposed by the Alabama Legislature, at least arguably presents for consideration a scheme analogous to that used for apportioning seats in Congress.

Much has been written since our decision in Baker v. Carr about the applicability of the so-called federal analogy to state legislative apportionment arrangements. After considering the matter, the court below concluded that no conceivable analogy could be drawn between the federal scheme and the apportionment of seats in the Alabama Legislature under the proposed constitutional amendment. We agree with the District Court, and find the federal analogy inapposite and irrelevant to state legislative districting schemes. Attempted reliance on the

federal analogy appears often to be little more than an after-the-fact rationalization offered in defense of maladjusted state apportionment arrangements. The original constitutions of 36 of our States provided that representation in both houses of the state legislatures would be based completely, or predominantly, on population. And the Founding Fathers clearly had no intention of establishing a pattern or model for the apportionment of seats in state legislatures when the system of representation in the Federal Congress was adopted. Demonstrative of this is the fact that the Northwest Ordinance, adopted in the same year, 1787, as the Federal Constitution, provided for the apportionment of seats in territorial legislatures solely on the basis of population.

The system of representation in the two Houses of the Federal Congress is one ingrained in our Constitution, as part of the law of the land. It is one conceived out of compromise and concession indispensable to the establishment of our federal republic. Arising from unique historical circumstances, it is based on the consideration that in establishing our type of federalism a group of formerly independent States bound themselves together under one national government. Admittedly, the original 13 States surrendered some of their sovereignty in agreeing to join together ''to form a more perfect Union.'' But at the heart of our constitutional system remains the concept of separate and distinct governmental entities which have delegated some, but not all, of their formerly held powers to the single national government. The fact that almost three-fourths of our present States were never in fact independently sovereign does not detract from our view that the so-called federal analogy is inapplicable as a sustaining precedent for state legislative apportionments. The developing history and growth of our republic cannot cloud the fact that, at the time of the inception of the system of representation in the Federal Congress, a compromise between the larger and smaller States on this matter averted a deadlock in the Constitutional Convention which had threatened to abort the birth of our Nation. . . .

Political subdivisions of States—counties, cities, or whatever—never were and never have been considered as sovereign entities. Rather, they have been traditionally regarded as subordinate governmental instrumentalities created by the State to assist in the carrying out of state governmental functions. As stated by the Court in Hunter v. City of Pittsburgh [1907], these governmental units are ''created as convenient agencies for exercising such of the governmental powers of the State as may be entrusted to them,'' and the ''number, nature and duration of the powers conferred upon [them] . . . and the territory over which they shall be exercised rests in the absolute discretion of the State.'' The relationship of the States to the Federal Government could hardly be less analogous.

Thus, we conclude that the plan contained in the 67-Senator Amendment for apportioning seats in the Alabama Legislature cannot be sustained by recourse to the so-called federal analogy. Nor can any other inequitable state legislative apportionment scheme be justified on such an asserted basis. This does not necessarily mean that such a plan is irrational or involves something other than a "republican form of government." We conclude simply that such a plan is impermissible for the States under the Equal Protection Clause, since perforce resulting, in virtually every case, in submergence of the equal-population principle in at least one house of a state legislature.

Since we find the so-called federal analogy inapposite to a consideration of the constitutional validity of state legislative apportionment schemes, we necessarily hold that the Equal Protection Clause requires both houses of a state legislature to be apportioned on a population basis. The right of a citizen to equal representation and to have his vote weighted equally with those of all other citizens in the election of members of one house of a bicameral state legislature would amount to little if States could effectively submerge the equal-population principle in the apportionment of seats in the other house. If such a scheme were permissible, an individual citizen's ability to exercise an effective voice in the only instrument of state government directly representative of the people might be almost as effectively thwarted as if neither house were apportioned on a population basis. . . .

We do not believe that the concept of bicameralism is rendered anachronistic and meaningless when the predominant basis of representation in the two state legislative bodies is required to be the same—population. A prime reason for bicameralism, modernly considered, is to insure mature and deliberate consideration of, and to prevent precipitate action on, proposed legislative measures. Simply because the controlling criterion for apportioning representation is required to be the same in both houses does not mean that there will be no differences in the composition and complexion of the two bodies. . . .

VI.

By holding that as a federal constitutional requisite both houses of a state legislature must be apportioned on a population basis, we mean that the Equal Protection Clause requires that a State make an honest and good faith effort to construct districts, in both houses of its legislature, as nearly of equal population as is practicable. We realize that it is a practical impossibility to arrange legislative districts so that each one has an identical number of residents, or citizens, or voters. Mathematical exactness or precision is hardly a workable constitutional requirement.

In Wesberry v. Sanders the Court stated that congressional representation must be based on population as nearly as is practicable. In implementing the basic constitutional principle of representative government as enunciated by the Court in Wesberry—equality of population among districts—some distinctions may well be made between congressional and state legislative representation. Since, almost invariably, there is a significantly larger number of seats in state legislative bodies to be distributed within a State than congressional seats, it

may be feasible to use political subdivision lines to a greater extent in establishing state legislative districts than in congressional districting while still affording adequate representation to all parts of the State. To do so would be constitutionally valid, so long as the resulting apportionment was one based substantially on population and the equal-population principle was not diluted in any significant way. Somewhat more flexibility may therefore be constitutionally permissible with respect to state legislative apportionment than in congressional districting. . . .

A consideration that appears to be of more substance in justifying some deviations from population-based representation in state legislatures is that of insuring some voice to political subdivisions, as political subdivisions. . . . In many States much of the legislature's activity involves the enactment of so-called local legislation, directed only to the concerns of particular political subdivisions. And a State may legitimately desire to construct districts along political subdivision lines to deter the possibilities of gerrymandering. However, permitting deviations from population-based representation does not mean that each local governmental unit or political subdivision can be given separate representation, regardless of population. . . . But if, even as a result of a clearly rational state policy of according some legislative representation to political subdivisions, population is submerged as the controlling consideration in the apportionment of seats in the particular legislative body, then the right of all of the State's citizens to cast an effective and adequately weighted vote would be unconstitutionally impaired.

VII.

One of the arguments frequently offered as a basis for upholding a State's legislative apportionment arrangement, despite substantial disparities from a population basis in either or both houses, is grounded on congressional approval, incident to admitting States into the Union, of state apportionment plans containing deviations from the equal-population principle. Proponents of this argument contend that congressional approval of such schemes, despite their disparities from population-based representation, indicates that such arrangements are plainly sufficient as establishing a "republican form of government." As we stated in Baker v. Carr, some questions raised under the Guaranty Clause are nonjusticiable, where "political" in nature and where there is a clear absence of judicially manageable standards. Nevertheless, it is not inconsistent with this view to hold that, despite congressional approval of state legislative apportionment plans at the time of admission into the Union, even though deviating from the equal-population principle here enunciated, the Equal Protection Clause can and does require more. And an apportionment scheme in which both houses are based on population can hardly be considered as failing to satisfy the Guaranty Clause requirement. Congress presumably does not assume, in admitting States into the Union, to pass on all constitutional questions relating to the character of state governmental organization. In any event, congressional approval, however well-considered, could hardly validate an unconstitutional state legislative apportionment. Congress simply lacks the constitutional power to insulate States from attack with respect to alleged deprivations of individual constitutional rights. . . .

X.

We do not consider here the difficult question of the proper remedial devices which federal courts should utilize in state legislative apportionment cases. Remedial techniques in this new and developing area of the law will probably often differ with the circumstances of the challenged apportionment and a variety of local conditions. . . .

We feel that the District Court in this case acted in a most proper and commendable manner. . . .

. . . In retaining jurisdiction while deferring a hearing on the issuance of a final injunction in order to give the provisionally reapportioned legislature an opportunity to act effectively, the court below proceeded in a proper fashion. Since the District Court evinced its realization that its ordered reapportionment could not be sustained as the basis for conducting the 1966 election of Alabama legislators, and avowedly intends to take some further action should the reapportioned Alabama Legislature fail to enact a constitutionally valid, permanent apportionment scheme in the interim, we affirm the judgment below and remand the cases for further proceedings consistent with the views stated in this opinion.

It is so ordered.

Mr. Justice **Clark,** concurring in the affirmance, said in part:

It seems to me that all the Court need say in this case is that each plan considered by the trial court is "a crazy quilt," clearly revealing invidious discrimination in each house of the Legislature and therefore violative of the Equal Protection Clause. . . .

Mr. Justice **Stewart,** concurring, said in part:

I would affirm the judgment of the District Court holding that this apportionment violated the Equal Protection Clause. . . .

Mr. Justice **Harlan** dissented, saying in part:

Preliminary Statement

Today's holding is that the Equal Protection Clause of the Fourteenth Amendment requires every State to structure its legislature so that all the members of each house represent substantially the same number of people; other factors may be given play only to the extent that they do not significantly encroach on this basic "population" principle. Whatever may be thought of this holding as a piece of political ideology—and even on that score the political history and practices of this country from its earliest beginning leave wide room for debate (see the dissenting opinion of Frankfurter, J., in Baker v. Carr)—I think it demonstrable that the Fourteenth Amendment does not impose this political tenet on the States or authorize this Court to do so.

. . . Stripped of aphorisms, the Court's argument boils down to the assertion that appellees' right to vote has been invidiously "debased" or "diluted" by systems of apportionment which entitle them to vote for fewer legislators than other voters, an assertion which is tied to the Equal Protection Clause only by the constitutionally frail tautology that "equal" means "equal."

Had the Court paused to probe more deeply into the matter, it would have found that the Equal Protection Clause was never intended to inhibit the States in choosing any democratic method they pleased for the apportionment of their legislatures. This is shown by the language of the Fourteenth Amendment taken as a whole, by the understanding of those who proposed and ratified it, and by the political practices of the States at the time the Amendment was adopted. It is confirmed by numerous state and congressional actions since the adoption of the Fourteenth Amendment, and by the common understanding of the Amendment as evidenced by subsequent constitutional amendments and decisions of this Court before Baker v. Carr made an abrupt break with the past in 1962.

The failure of the Court to consider any of these matters cannot be excused or explained by any concept of "developing" constitutionalism. It is meaningless to speak of constitutional "development" when both the language and history of the controlling provisions of the Constitution are wholly ignored. Since it can, I think, be shown beyond doubt that state legislative apportionments, as such, are wholly free of constitutional limitations, save such as may be imposed by the Republican Form of Government Clause (Const., Art. IV, § 4), the Court's action now bringing them within the purview of the Fourteenth Amendment amounts to nothing less than an exercise of the amending power by this Court.

5

Division of Power Between Nation and States

NATURE OF NATIONAL POWER

McCULLOCH v. MARYLAND

4 Wheaton 316; 4 L. Ed. 579 (1819)

Perhaps the most difficult problem faced by the government of a large nation is the reconciliation of local and national interests. To be strong, a country must have a strong central government. To be strong it must also have the support of its people, and this support will come only if the people are allowed to solve at the local level those problems which they regard as local in nature. The American Revolution stemmed from the failure of George III to allow his American colonies sufficient local autonomy, and the framers of the new Constitution knew that they must find a wiser adjustment of these competing interests and loyalties if the country was to endure as a political unit. The solution they worked out was to delegate in Article I, Sec. 8, certain enumerated powers to the national government. The Tenth Amendment declared that those powers not so delegated were left to the states, or to the people, to be later assigned by constitutional amendments.

One of the axioms of American constitutional law is that Congress has only powers that are delegated to it by the Constitution, or are reasonably implied from those so delegated. The origin and history of this theory of national power is as follows: when Randolph proposed the Virginia Plan in the Constitutional Convention of 1787, it contained the only sound principle by which

the powers of nation and state could be divided. It stated: "... the national legislature ought to be empowered ... to legislate in all cases to which the separate states are incompetent, or in which the harmony of the United States may be interrupted by the exercise of individual legislation." This stated a principle rather than a method of allocating powers, and as a principle it was received with approval by the Convention. After two months of debate the Convention created a committee of detail to formulate the text of a constitution and gave it various instructions. The instruction with regard to national powers was that: "The national legislature ought to possess the legislative rights vested in Congress by the Confederation; and, moreover, to legislate in all cases for the general interests of the Union, and also in those to which the states are separately incompetent, or in which the harmony of the United States may be interrupted by individual legislation." Acting upon this instruction the committee of detail reported back to the Convention the specific enumeration of the powers of Congress found in Article I, Sec. 8. The committee, adhering, as did the entire Convention, to the principle of delegated powers, thus gave to the new Congress all of the powers then believed to be described in the article of instruction; and by providing for amendments in Article V, it created the means by which those powers could be increased or altered when it seemed desirable to do so.

When Congress in 1791 chartered the First Bank of the United States, it was only after a most full and bitter argument as to whether it had the power to do so. Hamilton, who had proposed the creation of the bank, had written an elaborate opinion defending it as an exer-

cise of a power reasonably implied from those expressly delegated to Congress. Jefferson and his friends had stoutly maintained that congressional powers must be strictly construed and that the granting of the charter was an act of unwarrantable usurpation. Nevertheless the charter of the First Bank was never attacked in the courts as being unconstitutional, and the institution continued to exist until its charter expired in 1811.

The financial conditions ensuing after the War of 1812 made the reestablishment of the bank desirable, and the Second Bank of the United States was accordingly chartered in 1816. Almost immediately it incurred the bitter odium of large sections of the country, especially of the West and South. The bank was largely under the control of the Federalists, who were accused of using it as a political machine and of wielding its great influence for political purposes; its stock was largely held by British capitalists and other foreign investors; and it was accused of being responsible for a period of financial depression which brought ruin to thousands. It is true that the bank had begun operations under corrupt and inefficient management and had encouraged a high degree of inflation of credits. This had resulted in heavy losses to investors; in the state of Maryland the Baltimore branch collapsed with a loss to Maryland investors alone of a sum variously estimated from $1,700,000 to $3,000,000. Wiser counsel prevailed shortly, however, and the bank faced about and embarked upon a financial course as conservative as it had hitherto been headlong. It refused to accept the bank notes of the imprudent state banks and insisted upon the liquidation of its credits. One after another these overinflated state banks failed, and hundreds of speculators were ruined. Money was almost unobtainable.

While most of this financial disaster was the inevitable result of the orgies of inflation and speculation in which the frontier communities in particular had been indulging, the Bank of the United States was popularly regarded as the cause of the disaster, as the ruthless "money trust" which was ruining the prosperity of the country. A popular demand for legislative control of the bank was set up, and eight states passed either laws or constitutional amendments restricting the activities of the bank or imposing heavy burdens upon it. The law involved in this case, passed by the legislature of Maryland, which was particularly hostile to the bank because of its earlier debacle, is typical of this legislative onslaught.

The Maryland statute forbade all banks not chartered by the state itself to issue bank notes save upon special stamped paper obtainable upon the payment of a very heavy tax. This requirement could be commuted by the payment of an annual tax to the state of $15,000. A penalty of $500 forfeiture was inflicted for each offense, an amount which in the case of the now large and prosperous Baltimore branch of the Bank of the United States would have come possibly to millions of dollars. McCulloch, the cashier of the branch in Baltimore, issued notes without complying with the state law, and this action was brought on behalf of the state of Maryland to recover the penalties.

The case was argued for nine days before the Supreme Court by the greatest lawyers of the day; William Pinkney, Daniel Webster, and William Wirt defended the bank, while Luther Martin, Joseph Hopkinson, and Walter Jones represented the state of Maryland. The opinion of Marshall in the case is commonly regarded as his greatest state paper.

The announcement of the decision was the signal for a veritable storm of abuse directed against the Supreme Court. Judge Roane of the Virginia court of appeals published a series of newspaper attacks upon the decision so bitter that Marshall was led to write a reply in his defense. The Virginia legislature passed a resolution urging that the Supreme Court be shorn of its power to pass upon cases to which states were parties. Ohio, which had previously passed a law taxing each branch of the Bank of the United States within its limits $50,000 a year, defied the Supreme Court and proceeded to collect the tax in spite of its decision, a position from which it was later obliged to withdraw; see Osborn v. The Bank of the United States (1824). The attack upon the Court in this case was directed in large part against the failure of that tribunal to invalidate an act of Congress (incorporating the bank) and not against the exercise of the judicial veto. The decision was particularly odious to the strict constructionists because it not only sustained the doctrine of the implied powers of Congress but also recognized the binding effect of an implied limitation upon the states preventing them from interfering with the functioning of federal agencies.

The doctrine of implied powers in Congress was not new in this case. Not only had it been ably expounded by Hamilton, as mentioned above, but in the case of United States v. Fisher (1805), which had been decided fourteen years before, Marshall himself had given expression to the doctrine; but as that case did not relate to any such important political issue as did the bank case, the decision at that time had evoked no comment.

Later cases make it clear that the implied powers of Congress may be derived not only from a single delegated power but also from a combination of such powers taken together. Thus the power to condemn by eminent domain the land for the national cemetery at Gettysburg was sustained upon the theory that it could thus be implied from a group of federal powers combined. This has sometimes been called the theory of "resulting powers." See United States v. Gettysburg Electric Ry. Co. (1896).

While it is clear not only that the national government has implied powers beyond those explicitly delegated and that those powers are supreme over those of the states, there is another source of national power not so easily traceable to the Constitution. In many decisions the Supreme Court has held that in conducting its relations with foreign nations the United States is a sovereign nation which possesses all the powers that other sovereign nations enjoy, and these powers are not limited by the Tenth Amendment. In 1856 Congress passed an act authorizing the annexation of any unoccupied guano islands which might be discovered by an American citizen. Such an island was discovered in the Caribbean Sea in 1859, was annexed by proclamation, and criminal jurisdiction was extended over it by federal statute. In Jones v. United States (1890), Jones, who had been convicted of murder committed on the island, contended that the statute authorizing the acquisition of the island was invalid and that the court therefore had no jurisdiction to try him. The Supreme Court upheld the statute on the ground that under the law of nations recognized by all civilized states new territory may be acquired by discovery and occupation. This fact fully justified the legislation under which the island was annexed.

It was on the strength of this inherent sovereign power that the Court in Fong Yue Ting v. United States (1893) upheld the authority of Congress to exclude or deport aliens. Fong was born in China and came to the United States prior to 1879, during a period when the United States and China had a treaty according the rights of domicile in this country to Chinese. In 1892 Congress passed a statute prohibiting further Chinese immigration and requiring the registration of those who were permitted to remain. Fong's failure to comply with the statute resulted in deportation proceedings against him, and in resisting such action he set up the unconstitutionality of the statute. The Court characterized the "right to exclude or expel aliens" as an "inherent and inalienable right of every sovereign and independent nation" and pointed out that the United States "are a sovereign and independent nation." The theory forms the constitutional basis of all our immigration legislation not resting upon treaty provisions.

In Afroyim v. Rusk (1967) the Supreme Court overturned a century of practice and held that the inherent power over foreign affairs did not include the power to deprive a person of United States citizenship.

The Court made clear, however, that the sovereign power relied upon in Fong Yue Ting did not encompass a general power on the part of Congress to deal with domestic problems simply because they were beyond the power of the individual states to handle. In Kansas v. Colorado (1907) a dispute arose between the two states as to how the right to use the waters of the Arkansas River was to be divided between them. President Theodore Roosevelt, who believed the national government should have power to deal with any truly national problem, urged his Attorney General to intervene in the suit on the ground that the United States had a right to control the waters in question for the purpose of the reclamation of arid lands. The Court rejected the contention, noting that in domestic affairs Congress was limited by the Tenth Amendment to the powers delegated to it, and if the people did not like the assignment made in the original Constitution they had power to change it by amendment.

Mr. Chief Justice **Marshall** delivered the opinion of the Court, saying in part:

In the case now to be determined, the defendant, a sovereign State, denies the obligation of a law enacted by the legislature of the Union; and the plaintiff, on his part, contests the validity of an Act which has been passed by the legislature of that State. The Constitution of our country, in its most interesting and vital parts, is to be considered; the conflicting powers of the government of the Union and of its members, as marked in that Constitution, are to be discussed; and an opinion given, which may essentially influence the great operations of the government. No tribunal can approach such a question without a deep sense of its importance, and of the awful responsibility involved in its decision. But it must be decided peacefully, or remain a source of hostile legislation, perhaps of hostility of a still more serious nature; and if it is to be so decided, by this tribunal alone can the decision be made. On the Supreme Court of the United States has the Constitution of our country devolved this important duty.

The first question made in the cause is, has Congress power to incorporate a bank? . . .

In discussing this question, the counsel for the State of Maryland have deemed it of some importance, in the construction of the Constitution, to consider that instrument not as emanating from the people, but as the act of sovereign and independent states. The powers of the general government, it has been said, are delegated by the states, who alone are truly sovereign; and must be exercised in subordination to the states, who alone possess supreme dominion.

It would be difficult to sustain this proposition. The convention which framed the Constitution was, indeed, elected by the state legislatures. But the instrument, when it came from their hands, was a mere proposal, without obligation, or pretensions to it. It was reported to the then existing Congress of the United States, with a request that it might "be submitted to a convention of delegates, chosen in each state, by the people thereof, under the recommendation of its legislature, for their assent and ratification." This mode of proceeding was adopted; and by the convention, by Congress, and by the state legislatures, the instrument was submitted to the people. They acted upon it, in the only manner in which they can act safely, effectively, and wisely, on such a subject, by assembling in convention. It is true, they assembled in their several states; and where else should they have assembled? No political dreamer was ever wild enough to think of breaking down the lines which separate the states, and of compounding the American people into one common mass. Of consequence, when they act, they act in their states. But the measures they adopt do not, on that account, cease to be the measures of the people themselves, or become the measures of the state governments.

From these conventions the Constitution derives its whole authority. The government proceeds directly from the people; is "ordained and established" in the name of the people; and is declared to be ordained, "in order to form a more perfect union, establish justice, insure domestic tranquility, and secure the blessings of liberty to themselves and to their posterity." The assent of the states, in their sovereign capacity, is implied in calling a convention, and thus submitting that instrument to the people. But the people were at perfect liberty to accept or reject it; and their act was final. It required not the affirmance, and could not be negatived, by the state governments. The Constitution, when thus adopted, was of complete obligation, and bound the state sovereignties.

It has been said, that the people had already surrendered all their powers to the state sovereignties, and had nothing more to give. But, surely, the question whether they may resume and modify the powers granted to government, does not remain to be settled in this country. Much more might the legitimacy of the general government be doubted, had it been created by the states. The powers delegated to the state sovereignties were to be exercised by themselves, not by a distinct and independent sovereignty, created by themselves. To the formation of a league, such as was the Confederation, the state sovereignties were certainly competent. But when, "in order to form a more perfect union," it was deemed necessary to change this alliance into an effective government, possessing great and sovereign powers, and acting directly on the people, the necessity of referring it to the people, and of deriving its powers directly from them, was felt and acknowledged by all.

The government of the Union, then (whatever may be the influence of this fact on the case), is emphatically and truly a government of the people. In form and in substance it emanates from them, its powers are granted by them, and are to be exercised directly on them, and for their benefit.

This government is acknowledged by all to be one of enumerated powers. The principle, that it can exercise only the powers granted to it, would seem too apparent to have required to be enforced by all those arguments which its enlightened friends, while it was depending before the people, found it necessary to urge. That principle is now universally admitted. But the question respecting the extent of the powers actually granted, is perpetually arising, and will probably continue to arise, as long as our system shall exist.

In discussing these questions, the conflicting powers of the general and State governments must be brought into view, and the supremacy of their respective laws, when they are in opposition, must be settled.

If any one proposition could command the universal assent of mankind, we might expect it would be this: that the government of the Union, though limited in its powers, is supreme within its sphere of action. This would seem to result necessarily from its nature. It is the government of all; its powers are delegated by all; it represents all, and acts for all. Though any one State may be willing to control its operations, no State is willing to allow others to control them. The nation, on those subjects on which it can act, must necessarily bind its component parts. But this question is not left to mere reason: the people have, in express terms, decided it, by saying, "this Constitution, and the laws of the United States, which shall be made in pursuance thereof," "shall be the supreme law of the land," and by requiring that the members of the State legislatures, and the officers of the executive and judicial departments of the States, shall take the oath of fidelity to it.

The government of the United States, then, though limited in its powers, is supreme; and its laws, when made in pursuance of the Constitution, form the supreme law of the land, "anything in the Constitution or laws of any State to the contrary notwithstanding."

Among the enumerated powers, we do not find that of establishing a bank or creating a corporation. But there is no phrase in the instrument which, like the Articles of Confederation, excludes incidental or implied powers; and which requires that everything granted shall be expressly and minutely described. Even the Tenth Amendment, which was framed for the purpose of quieting the excessive jealousies which had been excited, omits the word "expressly," and declares only that the powers "not delegated to the United States, nor prohibited to the States, are reserved to the States or to the people"; thus leaving the question, whether the particular power which may become the subject of contest, has been delegated to the one government, or prohibited to the other, to depend on a fair construction of the whole instrument. The men who drew and adopted this amendment, had experienced the embarrassments resulting from the insertion of this word in the Articles of Confederation, and probably omitted it to avoid those embarrassments. A constitution, to contain an accurate detail of all the subdivisions of which its great powers will admit, and of all the means by which they may be carried into execution, would partake of the prolixity of a legal code, and could scarcely be embraced by the human mind. It would probably never be understood by the public. Its nature, therefore, requires, that only its great outlines should be marked, its important objects designated, and the minor ingredients which compose those objects be deduced from the nature of the objects themselves. That this idea was entertained by the framers of the American Constitution, is not only to be inferred from the nature of the instrument, but from the language. Why else were some of the limitations, found in the ninth section of the first article, introduced? It is also, in some degree, warranted by their having omitted to use any restrictive term which might prevent its receiving a fair and just interpretation. In considering this question, then, we must never forget, that it is a constitution we are expounding.

Although, among the enumerated powers of government, we do not find the word "bank," or "incorporation," we find the great powers to lay and collect taxes; to borrow money; to regulate commerce; to declare and conduct a war; and to raise and support armies and navies. The sword and the purse, all the external relations, and no inconsiderable portion of the industry of the nation, are entrusted to its government. It can never be pretended that these vast powers draw after them others of inferior importance, merely because they are inferior. Such an idea can never be advanced. But it may, with great reason, be contended, that a government, entrusted with such ample powers, on the due execution of which the happiness and prosperity of the nation so vitally depends, must also be entrusted with ample means for their execution. The power being given, it is the interest of the nation to facilitate its execution. It can never be their interest, and cannot be presumed to have been their intention, to clog and embarrass its execution by withholding the most appropriate means. Throughout this vast republic, from the St. Croix to the Gulf of Mexico, from the Atlantic to the Pacific, revenue is to be collected and expended, armies are to marched and supported. The exigencies of the nation may require, that the treasure raised in the North should be transported to the South, that raised in the East conveyed to the West, or that this order should be reversed. Is that construction of the Constitution to be preferred which would render these operations difficult, hazardous, and expensive? Can we adopt that construction (unless the words imperiously require it) which would impute to the framers of that instrument, when granting these powers for the public good, the intention of impeding their exercise by withholding a choice of means? If, indeed, such be the mandate of the Constitution, we have only to obey; but that instrument does not profess to enumerate the means by which the powers it confers may be executed; nor does it prohibit the creation of a corporation, if the existence of such a being be essential to the beneficial exercise of those powers. It is, then, the subject of fair inquiry, how far such means may be employed. It is not denied, that the powers given to the government imply the ordinary means of execution. That, for example, of raising revenue, and applying it to national purposes, is admitted to imply the power of conveying money from place to place, as the exigencies of the nation may require, and of employing the usual means of conveyance. But it is denied that the government has its choice of means; or, that it may employ the most convenient means, if, to employ them, it be necessary to erect a corporation.

. . . The power of creating a corporation, though appertaining to sovereignty, is not, like the power of making war, or levying taxes, or of regulating commerce, a great substantive and independent power, which cannot be implied as incidental to other powers, or used as a means of executing them. It is never the end for which other powers are exercised, but a means by which other objects are accomplished. No contributions are made to charity for the sake of an incorporation, but a corporation is created to administer the charity; no seminary of learning is instituted in order to be incorporated, but the corporate character is conferred to subserve the purposes of education. No city was ever built with the sole object of being incorporated, but is incorporated as affording the best means of being well governed. The power of creating a corporation is never used for its own sake, but for the purpose of effecting something else. No sufficient reason is, therefore, perceived, why it may not pass as incidental to those powers which are expressly given, if it be a direct mode of executing them.

But the Constitution of the United States has not left the right of Congress to employ the necessary means, for the execution of the powers conferred on the government, to general reasoning. To its enumeration of powers is added that of making "all laws which shall be necessary and proper, for carrying into execution the foregoing powers, and all other powers vested by this Constitution, in the government of the United States, or in any department thereof.''

The counsel for the State of Maryland have urged various arguments, to prove that this clause, though in terms a grant of power, is not so in effect; but is really restrictive of the general right, which might otherwise be implied, of selecting means for executing the enumerated powers.

In support of this proposition, they have found it necessary to contend, that this clause was inserted for the purpose of conferring on Congress the power of making laws. That, without it, doubts might be entertained, whether Congress could exercise its powers in the form of legislation.

But could this be the object for which it was inserted? . . . That a legislature, endowed with legislative powers, can legislate, is a proposition too self-evident to have been questioned.

But the argument on which most reliance is placed, is drawn from the peculiar language of this clause. Congress is not empowered by it to make all laws, which may have relation to the powers conferred on the government, but such only as may be "necessary and proper" for carrying them into execution. The word "necessary" is considered as controlling the whole sentence, and as limiting the right to pass laws for the execution of the granted powers, to such as are indispensable, and without which the power would be nugatory. That it excludes the choice of means, and leaves to Congress, in each case, that only which is most direct and simple.

Is it true, that this is the sense in which the word "necessary" is always used? Does it always import an absolute physical necessity, so strong, that one thing, to which another may be termed necessary, cannot exist without that other? We think it does not. If reference be had to its use, in the common affairs of the world, or in approved authors, we find that it frequently imports no more than that one thing is convenient, or useful, or essential to another. To employ the means necessary to an end, is generally understood as employing any means calculated to produce the end, and not as being confined to those single means, without which the end would be entirely unattainable. Such is the character of human language that no word conveys to the mind, in all situations, one single definite idea; and nothing is more common than to use words in a figurative sense. Almost all compositions contain words, which, taken in their rigorous sense, would convey a meaning different from that which is obviously intended. It is essential to just construction, that many words which import something excessive, should be understood in a more mitigated sense—in that sense which common usage justifies. The word "necessary" is of this description. It has not a fixed character peculiar to itself. It admits of all degrees of comparison; and is often connected with other words, which increase or diminish the impression the mind receives of the urgency it imports. A thing may be necessary, very necessary, absolutely or indispensably necessary. To no mind would the same idea be conveyed, by these several phrases. . . . This word, then, like others, is used in various senses; and, in its construction, the subject, the context, the intention of the person using them, are all to be taken into view.

Let this be done in the case under consideration. The subject is the execution of those great powers on which the welfare of a nation essentially depends. It must have been the intention of those who gave these powers, to insure, as far as human prudence could insure, their beneficial execution. This could not be done by confiding the choice of means to such narrow limits as not to leave it in the power of Congress to adopt any which might be appropriate, and which were conducive to the end. This provision is made in a constitution intended to endure for ages to come, and, consequently, to be adapted to the various crises of human affairs. To have prescribed the means by which government should, in all future time, execute its powers, would have been to change, entirely, the character of the instrument, and give it the properties of a legal code. It would have been an unwise attempt to provide, by immutable rules, for exigencies which, if foreseen at all, must have been seen dimly, and which can be best provided for as they occur. To have declared that the best means shall not be used, but those alone without which the power given would be nugatory, would have been to deprive the legislature of the capacity to avail itself of experience, to exercise its reason, and to accommodate its legislation to circumstances. . . .

But the argument which most conclusively demonstrates the error of the construction contended for by the counsel for the State of Maryland, is founded on the intention of the convention, as manifested in the whole clause. To waste time and argument in proving that, without it, Congress might carry its powers into execution, would be not much less idle than to hold a lighted taper to the sun. As little can it be required to prove, that in the absence of this clause, Congress would have some choice of means. That it might employ those which, in its judgment, would most advantageously effect the object to be accomplished. That any means adapted to the end, any means which tended directly to the execution of the constitutional powers of the government, were in themselves constitutional. This clause, as construed by the State of Maryland, would abridge and almost annihilate this useful and necessary right of the legislature to select its means. That this could not be intended, is, we should think, had it not been already controverted, too apparent for controversy. We think so for the following reasons:

1st. The clause is placed among the powers of Congress, not among the limitations on those powers.

2d. Its terms purport to enlarge, not to diminish the powers vested in the government. It purports to be an additional power, not a restriction on those already granted. No reason has been or can be assigned, for thus concealing an intention to narrow the discretion of the national legislature, under words which purport to enlarge it. The framers of the Constitution wished its adoption, and well knew that it would be endangered by its strength, not by its weakness. Had they been capable of using language which would convey to the eye one idea, and after deep reflection, impress on the mind another, they would rather have disguised the grant of power, than its limitation. If then, their intention had been, by this clause, to restrain the free use of means which might otherwise have been implied, that intention would have been inserted in another place, and would have been expressed in terms resembling these: ''In carrying into execution the foregoing powers, and all others,'' etc., ''no laws shall be passed but such as are necessary and proper.'' Had the intention been to make this clause restrictive, it would unquestionably have been so in form as well as in effect.

The result of the most careful and attentive consideration bestowed upon this clause is, that if it does not enlarge, it cannot be construed to restrain the powers of Congress, or to impair the right of the legislature to exercise its best judgment in the selection of measures, to carry into execution the constitutional powers of the government. If no other motive for its insertion can be suggested, a sufficient one is found in the desire to remove all doubts respecting the right to legislate on that vast mass of incidental powers which must be involved in the Constitution, if that instrument be not a splendid bauble.

We admit, as all must admit, that the powers of the government are limited, and that its limits are not to be transcended. But we think the sound construction of the Constitution must allow to the national legislature that discretion, with respect to the means by which the powers it confers are to be carried into execution, which will enable that body to perform the high duties assigned to it, in the manner most beneficial to the people. Let the end be legitimate, let it be within the scope of the Constitution, and all means which are appropriate, which are plainly adapted to that end, which are not prohibited, but consist with the letter and spirit of the Constitution, are constitutional. . . .

If a corporation may be employed indiscriminately with other means to carry into execution the powers of the government, no particular reason can be assigned for excluding the use of a bank, if required for its fiscal operations. To use one, must be within the discretion of Congress, if it be an appropriate mode of executing the powers of government. That it is a convenient, a useful, and essential instrument in the prosecution of its fiscal operations, is not now a subject of controversy. All those who have been concerned in the administration of our finances, have concurred in representing its importance and necessity; and so strongly have they been felt, that statesmen of the first class, whose previous opinions against it had been confirmed by every circumstance which can fix the human judgment, have yielded those opinions to the exigencies of the nation. . . .

But, were its necessity less apparent, none can deny its being an appropriate measure; and if it is, the degree of its necessity, as has been very justly observed, is to be discussed in another place. Should Congress, in the execution of its powers, adopt measures which are prohibited by the constitution; or should Congress, under the pretext of executing its powers, pass laws for the accomplishment of objects not entrusted to the government, it would become the painful duty of this tribunal, should a case requiring such a decision come before it, to say that such an act was not the law of the land. But where the law is not prohibited, and is really calculated to effect any of the objects entrusted to the government, to undertake here to inquire into the degree of its necessity, would be to pass the line which circumscribes the judicial department, and to tread on legislative ground. This court disclaims all pretensions to such a power. . . .

After the most deliberate consideration, it is the unanimous and decided opinion of this court, that the Act to incorporate the Bank of the United States is a law made in pursuance of the Constitution, and is a part of the supreme law of the land. . . .

It being the opinion of the court that the act incorporating the bank is constitutional; and that the power of establishing a branch in the State of Maryland might be properly exercised by the bank itself, we proceed to inquire: —

2. Whether the State of Maryland may, without violating the Constitution, tax that branch?

That the power of taxation is one of vital importance; that it is retained by the States; that it is not abridged by the grant of a similar power to the government of the Union; that it is to be concurrently exercised by the two governments: are truths which have never been denied. But, such is the paramount character of the Constitution, that its capacity to withdraw any subject from the action of even this power, is admitted. The States are expressly forbidden to lay any duties on imports or exports, except what may be absolutely necessary for executing their inspection laws. If the obligation of this prohibition must be conceded—if it may restrain a State from the exercise of its taxing power on imports and exports; the same paramount character would seem to restrain, as it certainly may restrain, a State from such other exercise of this power, as is in its nature incompatible with, and repugnant to, the constitutional laws of the Union. A law, absolutely repugnant to another, as entirely repeals that other as if express terms of repeal were used.

On this ground the counsel for the bank place its claim to be exempted from the power of a State to tax its operations. There is no express provision for the case, but the claim has been sustained on a principle which so entirely pervades the Constitution, is so intermixed with the materials which compose it, so interwoven with its web, so blended with its texture, as to be incapable of being separated from it, without rending it into shreds.

This great principle is, that the Constitution and the laws made in pursuance thereof are supreme; that they control the Constitution and laws of the respective States, and cannot be controlled by them. From this, which may be almost termed an axiom, other propositions are deduced as corollaries, on the truth or error of which, and on their application to this case, the cause has been supposed to depend. These are, 1st. That a power to create implies a power to preserve. 2d. That a power to destroy, if wielded by a different hand, is hostile to, and incompatible with, these powers to create and pre-

serve. 3d. That where this repugnancy exists, that authority which is supreme must control, not yield to that over which it is supreme . . .

The power of Congress to create, and of course to continue, the bank, was the subject of the preceding part of this opinion; and is no longer to be considered as questionable.

That the power of taxing it by the States may be exercised so as to destroy it, is too obvious to be denied. But taxation is said to be an absolute power, which acknowledges no other limits than those expressly prescribed in the Constitution, and like sovereign power of every other description, is trusted to the discretion of those who use it. . . .

The argument on the part of the State of Maryland, is, not that the States may directly resist a law of Congress, but that they may exercise their acknowledged powers upon it, and that the Constitution leaves them this right in the confidence that they will not abuse it. . . .

That the power to tax involves the power to destroy; that the power to destroy may defeat and render useless the power to create; that there is a plain repugnance, in conferring on one government a power to control the constitutional measures of another, which other, with respect to those very measures, is declared to be supreme over that which exerts the control, are propositions not to be denied. But all inconsistencies are to be reconciled by the magic of the word "confidence." Taxation, it is said, does not necessarily and unavoidably destroy. To carry it to the excess of destruction would be an abuse, to presume which, would banish that confidence which is essential to all government.

But is this a case of confidence? Would the people of any one State trust those of another with a power to control the most insignificant operations of their State government? We know they would not. Why, then, should we suppose that the people of any one State should be willing to trust those of another with a power to control the operations of a government to which they have confided their most important and most valuable interests? In the legislature of the Union alone, are all represented. The legislature of the Union alone, therefore, can be trusted by the people with the power of controlling measures which concern all, in the confidence that it will not be abused. This, then, is not a case of confidence, and we must consider it as it really is.

If we apply the principle for which the State of Maryland contends, to the Constitution generally, we shall find it capable of changing totally the character of that instrument. We shall find it capable of arresting all the measures of the government, and of prostrating it at the foot of the States. The American people have declared their Constitution, and the laws made in pursuance thereof, to be supreme; but this principle would transfer the supremacy, in fact, to the States.

If the States may tax one instrument, employed by the government in the execution of its powers, they may tax any and every other instrument. They may tax the mail; they may tax the mint; they may tax patent rights;

they may tax the papers of the custom-house; they may tax judicial process; they may tax all the means employed by the government, to an excess which would defeat all the ends of government. This was not intended by the American people. They did not design to make their government dependent on the States. . . .

It has also been insisted, that, as the power of taxation in the general and State governments is acknowledged to be concurrent, every argument which would sustain the right of the general government to tax banks chartered by the States, will equally sustain the right of the States to tax banks chartered by the general government.

But the two cases are not on the same reason. The people of all the States have created the general government, and have conferred upon it the general power of taxation. The people of all the States, and the States themselves, are represented in Congress, and, by their representatives, exercise this power. When they tax the chartered institutions of the States, they tax their constituents; and these taxes must be uniform. But when a State taxes the operations of the government of the United States, it acts upon institutions created, not by their own constituents, but by people over whom they claim no control. It acts upon the measures of a government created by others as well as themselves, for the benefit of others in common with themselves. The difference is that which always exists, and always must exist, between the action of the whole on a part, and the action of a part on the whole—between the laws of a government declared to be supreme, and those of a government which, when in opposition to those laws, is not supreme.

But if the full application of this argument could be admitted, it might bring into question the right of Congress to tax the State banks, and could not prove the right of the States to tax the Bank of the United States.

The court has bestowed on this subject its most deliberate consideration. The result is a conviction that the States have no power, by taxation or otherwise, to retard, impede, burden or in any manner control, the operations of the constitutional laws enacted by Congress to carry into execution the powers vested in the general government. This is, we think, the unavoidable consequence of that supremacy which the Constitution has declared.

We are unanimously of opinion, that the law passed by the legislature of Maryland, imposing a tax on the Bank of the United States, is unconstitutional and void.

This opinion does not deprive the States of any resources which they originally possessed. It does not extend to a tax paid by the real property of the bank, in common with the other real property within the State, nor to a tax imposed on the interest which the citizens of Maryland may hold in this institution, in common with other property of the same description throughout the State. But this is a tax on the operations of the bank, and is, consequently, a tax on the operation of an instrument employed by the government of the Union to carry its powers into execution. Such a tax must be unconstitutional. . . .

MARTIN v. HUNTER's LESSEE

1 Wheaton 304; 4 L. Ed. 97 (1816)

McCulloch v. Maryland (1819) invoked the doctrine of the supremacy of national law to prevent the state of Maryland from attempting to destroy an agency of the national government. The case presented one example of state interference with, or burden upon, the federal government and its activities. Over the years many other instances of state interference with federal authority have come before the Court. In Johnson v. Maryland (1920) the driver of a mail truck was arrested for driving without a Maryland driver's license. The Supreme Court held the license requirement to be an unconstitutional burden on the government: if the license required of the mail truck driver is a means of revenue to the state, it is a tax on the federal postal system; if it is a means whereby the state determines the competence of mail truck drivers, it is equally an interference with the management of the postal system. This case does not answer the question whether the state could punish the driver for traffic violations, but it is probable that it could. In an old case in the United States circuit court in 1817, United States v. Hart, a constable in Philadelphia was held not to have obstructed the mails when he acted to prevent reckless driving; he stopped a stage "going very rapidly through Market Street; some of the witnesses supposed it to be at a rate of eight or nine miles an hour."

Clashes between federal and state authority take various forms. Thus in 1936 the Supreme Court held in United States v. California that a railroad owned and operated by the state and engaging in interstate commerce was bound to obey the Federal Safety Appliance Acts or be liable to the payment of a civil penalty. In 1946 in Case v. Bowles the Court held that the sale of state-owned timber cut from state school lands was subject to OPA price regulations, while in Motor Coach Employees v. Missouri (1963) the federally guaranteed right to conduct peaceful strikes was held applicable to a transit company, and state efforts to outlaw the strike by seizing the company were void under the supremacy clause.

The present case, which preceded McCulloch v. Maryland by three years, raised the question of the power of the Supreme Court to review decisions of the state courts on questions of federal law. Lord Fairfax, a citizen and resident of Virginia, died in 1781 and willed to Denny Martin, his nephew and a British subject, his vast land holdings in northern Virginia. Virginia, whose common law forbade an enemy alien to inherit anyway, passed a special law after the death of Fairfax confiscating the property and in 1789 sold part of the land to David Hunter. Litigation started in 1791, and finally in 1810 the Virginia court of appeals sustained Hunter's title to the land. Three years later the Supreme Court took the case on a writ of error and reversed the Virginia court, holding that the Treaty of 1794 with England protected British property (including Martin's) from confiscation. Although the Supreme Court had been issuing writs of error to state courts for years without arousing protest, in this important case the Virginia court determined to stem what it considered to be the unconstitutional extension of federal power over the states. In open defiance it declared unconstitutional the grant of this jurisdiction to the Supreme Court in the Judiciary Act of 1789 and refused to obey the Court's mandate. This refusal brought the present case to the Supreme Court.

Five years later came the case of Cohens v. Virginia (1821). Congress had authorized a municipal lottery in the District of Columbia, and the Cohens had proceeded to sell tickets in Virginia. They were convicted under a Virginia law which forbade the sale of lottery tickets, and sued out a writ of error in the Supreme Court of the United States. The possibility that the Supreme Court would take jurisdiction in the case brought to a virtual frenzy the bitterness engendered by the McCulloch and Fairfax decisions. The Virginia legislature passed a resolution protesting the jurisdiction of the Supreme Court and instructing the state's counsel not to argue the case on the merits if he lost the jurisdictional fight. The Court did take jurisdiction, and with Daniel Webster arguing Virginia's side "in consequence of his being counsel for the State of New York in a similar case," the Court decided that Congress had not intended to protect the sale of lottery tickets in Virginia and affirmed the conviction of the Cohens. With this victory on the merits (and for Virginia) the storm abated and the power of the Supreme Court to review federal questions arising in state courts was clearly established.

On occasion states have attempted to interfere by court action with the administration of federal law. The dramatic case of Ableman v. Booth (1859) arose out of the fact that the supreme court of Wisconsin had sustained the release by the state on a writ of habeas corpus of an abolitionist editor who was being held in federal custody for violating the Fugitive Slave Law. In a decision which aroused the fury of the abolitionists, who believed the Fugitive Slave Law to be unconstitutional, the Supreme Court of the United States denied the power of the state court to interfere with federal law enforcement and reversed the state court. In his opinion Chief Justice Taney said: "This right to inquire by process of habeas corpus, and the duty of the officer to make a return, grow, necessarily, out of the complex character of our government, and the existence of two distinct and separate sovereignties within the same territorial space, each of them restricted in its powers, and each within its sphere of action, prescribed by the Constitution of the United States, independent of the other. But, after the return is made, and the state judge or court judicially apprized that the party is in custody under the authority of the United States, they can proceed no further. They then know that the prisoner is within the dominion and jurisdiction of another government, and that neither the writ of habeas corpus, nor any other process issued under state authority, can pass over the line of division between the two sovereignties. He is then within the dominion and exclusive jurisdiction of the United States."

To prevent United States officers acting under federal revenue laws from being held accountable to state authorities, Congress at an early date provided by statute that in case any civil or criminal action be brought against a revenue officer in the state courts arising out of the performance of his official duties, such a case could be removed into a federal court for trial. In Tennessee v. Davis (1880) a federal revenue officer was indicted for murder in a state court for having killed a man, in self-defense as he claimed, in the discharge of his duty. The Supreme Court sustained the validity of the act and allowed the case to be removed for jury trial to the federal district court.

Two cases involving the supremacy of national law arose out of attempts to thwart integration of the public schools in Arkansas and Louisiana. In Cooper v. Aaron (1958) the Court refused to postpone desegregation in Little Rock because of violence incited by the action of state officials attempting to prevent integration. And in 1960 the Court held void a series of statutes designed to "interpose" the power of the state between the federal government and its citizens and thus prevent integration. In United States v. Louisiana (1960) the Supreme Court agreed with the statement by the federal district court that "interposition is not a constitutional doctrine. If taken seriously, it is an illegal defiance of constitutional authority."

Mr. Justice **Story** delivered the opinion of the Court, saying in part:

This is a writ of error from the Court of Appeals of Virginia, founded upon the refusal of that court to obey the mandate of this court, requiring the judgment rendered in this very cause, at February Term, 1813, to be carried into due execution. The following is the judgment of the Court of Appeals rendered on the mandate: "The court is unanimously of opinion, that the appellate power of the Supreme Court of the United States does not extend to this court, under a sound construction of the Constitution of the United States; that so much of the 25th section of the Act of Congress to establish the Judicial Courts of the United States, as extends the appellate jurisdiction of the Supreme Court to this court, is not in pursuance of the Constitution of the United States; that the writ of error in this cause was improvidently allowed under the authority of that Act; that the proceedings thereon in the Supreme Court were coram non judice, in relation to this court, and that obedience to its mandate be declined by the court."

The questions involved in this judgment are of great importance and delicacy. Perhaps it is not too much to affirm that, upon their right decision, rest some of the most solid principles which have hitherto been supposed to sustain and protect the Constitution itself. . . .

Before proceeding to the principal questions, it may not be unfit to dispose of some preliminary considerations which have grown out of the arguments at the Bar.

The Constitution of the United States was ordained and established, not by the States in their sovereign capacities, but emphatically, as the preamble of the Constitution declares, by "the people of the United States." There can be no doubt that it was competent to the people to invest the general government with all the powers which they might deem proper and necessary; to extend or restrain these powers according to their own good pleasure, and to give them a paramount and supreme authority. As little doubt can there be, that the people had a right to prohibit to the States the exercise of any powers which were, in their judgment, incompatible with the objects of the general compact; to make the powers of the State governments, in given cases, subordinate to those of the nation, or to reserve to themselves those sovereign authorities which they might not choose to delegate to either. The Constitution was not, therefore, necessarily carved out of existing State sovereignties, nor a surrender of powers already existing in State institutions, for the powers of the States depend upon their own constitutions; and the people of every State had the right to modify and restrain them, according to their own views of policy or principle. On the other hand, it is perfectly clear that the sovereign powers vested in the State governments, by their respective constitutions, remained unaltered and unimpaired except so far as they were granted to the government of the United States.

These deductions do not rest upon general reasoning, plain and obvious as they seem to be. They have been positively recognized by one of the articles in amendment of the Constitution, which declares, that "the powers not delegated to the United States by the Constitution, nor prohibited by it to the States, are reserved to the States respectively, or to the people."

The government, then, of the United States, can claim no powers which are not granted to it by the Constitution, and the powers actually granted must be such as are expressly given, or given by necessary implication. On the other hand, this instrument, like every other grant, is to have a reasonable construction, according to the import of its terms; and where a power is expressly given in general terms, it is not to be restrained to particular cases, unless that construction grows out of the context expressly, or by necessary implication. The words are to be taken in their natural and obvious sense, and not in a sense unreasonably restricted or enlarged.

The Constitution, unavoidably, deals in general language. It did not suit the purposes of the people, in framing this great charter of our liberties, to provide for minute specifications of its powers, or to declare the means by which those powers should be carried into execution. It was foreseen that this would be a perilous and difficult, if not an impracticable, task. The instrument was not intended to provide merely for the exigencies of a few years, but was to endure through a long lapse of ages, the events of which were locked up in the inscrutable purposes of Providence. It could not be foreseen what new changes and modifications of power might be indispensable to effectuate the general objects of the charter; and restrictions and specifications, which at the present might seem salutary, might, in the end, prove the overthrow of the system itself. Hence its powers are expressed in general terms, leaving to the legislature, from time to time, to adopt its own means to effectuate legitimate objects, and to mould and model the exercise of its powers, as its own wisdom and the public interest should require.

With these principles in view, principles in respect to which no difference of opinion ought to be indulged, let us now proceed to the interpretation of the Constitution, so far as regards the great points in controversy. The third article of the Constitution is that which must principally attract our attention. . . .

This leads us to the consideration of the great question as to the nature and extent of the appellate jurisdiction of the United States. We have already seen that appellate jurisdiction is given by the Constitution to the Supreme Court in all cases where it has not original jurisdiction, subject, however, to such exceptions and regulations as Congress may prescribe. It is, therefore, capable of embracing every case enumerated in the Constitution, which is not exclusively to be decided by way of original jurisdiction. But the exercise of appellate jurisdiction is far from being limited by the terms of the Constitution, to the Supreme Court. There can be no doubt that Congress may create a succession of inferior tribunals, in each of which it may vest appellate as well as original jurisdiction. . . .

As, then, by the terms of the Constitution, the appellate jurisdiction is not limited as to the Supreme Court, and as to this court it may be exercised in all other cases than those of which it has original cognizance, what is there to restrain its exercise over State tribunals in the enumerated cases? The appellate power is not limited by the terms of the third article to any particular courts. The words are, "the judicial power (which includes appellate power) shall extend to all cases," &c., and "in all other cases before mentioned the Supreme Court shall have appellate jurisdiction." It is the case, then, and not the court, that gives the jurisdiction. If the judicial power extends to the case, it will be in vain to search in the letter of the Constitution for any qualification as to the tribunal where it depends. It is incumbent, then, upon those who assert such a qualification to show its existence by necessary implication. If the text be clear and distinct, no restriction upon its plain and obvious import ought to be admitted, unless the inference be irresistible. . . .

But it is plain that the framers of the Constitution did contemplate that cases within the judicial cognizance of the United States not only might but would arise in the State courts, in the exercise of their ordinary jurisdiction. With this view the sixth article declares, that "this Constitution, and the laws of the United States which shall be made in pursuance thereof, and all treaties made, or which shall be made, under the authority of the United States, shall be the supreme law of the land, and the judges in every State shall be bound thereby, anything in the Constitution, or laws of any State to the contrary notwithstanding." It is obvious, that this obligation is imperative upon the State judges in their official, and not merely in their private, capacities. From the very nature of their judicial duties they would be called upon to pronounce the law applicable to the case in judgment. They were not to decide merely according to the laws or Constitution of the State, but according to the Constitution, laws, and treaties of the United States, "the supreme law of the land." . . .

It must, therefore, be conceded that the Constitution not only contemplated, but meant to provide for cases within the scope of the judicial power of the United States, which might yet depend before State tribunals. It was foreseen that in the exercise of their ordinary jurisdiction, State courts would incidentally take cognizance of cases arising under the Constitution, the laws and treaties of the United States. Yet to all these cases the judicial power, by the very terms of the Constitution, is to extend. It cannot extend by original jurisdiction if that was already rightfully and exclusively attached in the State courts, which (as has been already shown) may occur; it must therefore extend by appellate jurisdiction, or not at all. It would seem to follow that the appellate power of the United States must, in such cases, extend to State tribunals; and if in such cases, there is no reason why it should not equally attach upon all others within the purview of the Constitution.

It has been argued that such an appellate jurisdiction over State courts is inconsistent with the genius of our governments, and the spirit of the Constitution. That the latter was never designed to act upon State sovereignties, but only upon the people, and that, if the power exists, it will materially impair the sovereignty of the States, and the independence of their courts. We cannot yield to the force of this reasoning; it assumes principles which we cannot admit, and draws conclusions to which we do not yield our assent.

It is a mistake that the Constitution was not designed to operate upon States, in their corporate capacities. It is crowded with provisions which restrain or annul the sovereignty of the States in some of the highest branches of their prerogatives. The tenth section of the first article contains a long list of disabilities and prohibitions imposed upon the States. Surely, when such essential portions of State sovereignty are taken away, or prohibited to be exercised, it cannot be correctly asserted that the Constitution does not act upon the States. The language of the Constitution is also imperative upon the States, as to the performance of many duties. It is imperative upon the State legislatures to make laws prescribing the time, places, and manner of holding elections for Senators and Representatives, and for electors of President and Vice-President. And in these, as well as in some other cases, Congress have a right to revise, amend, or supersede the laws which may be passed by State legislatures. When, therefore, the States are stripped of some of the highest attributes of sovereignty, and the same are given to the United States; when the legislatures of the States are, in some respects, under the control of Congress, and in every case are, under the Constitution, bound by the paramount authority of the United States; it is certainly difficult to support the argument that the appellate power over the decisions of State courts is contrary to the genius of our institutions. The

courts of the United States can, without question, revise the proceedings of the executive and legislative authorities of the States, and if they are found to be contrary to the Constitution, may declare them to be of no legal validity. Surely, the exercise of the same right over judicial tribunals is not a higher or more dangerous act of sovereign power.

Nor can such a right be deemed to impair the independence of State judges. It is assuming the very ground in controversy to assert that they possess an absolute independence of the United States. In respect to the powers granted to the United States, they are not independent; they are expressly bound to obedience by the letter of the Constitution; and if they should unintentionally transcend their authority, or misconstrue the Constitution, there is no more reason for giving their judgments an absolute and irresistible force, than for giving it to the acts of the other coordinate departments of State sovereignty.

The argument urged from the possibility of the abuse of the revising power, is equally unsatisfactory. It is always a doubtful course, to argue against the use or existence of a power, from the possibility of its abuse. It is still more difficult, by such an argument, to engraft upon a general power, a restriction which is not to be found in the terms in which it is given. From the very nature of things, the absolute right of decision, in the last resort, must rest somewhere—wherever it may be vested it is susceptible of abuse. In all questions of jurisdiction the inferior, or appellate court must pronounce the final judgment; and common-sense, as well as legal reasoning, has conferred it upon the latter. . . .

This is not all. A motive of another kind, perfectly compatible with the most sincere respect for State tribunals, might induce the grant of appellate power over their decisions. That motive is the importance, and even necessity of uniformity of decisions throughout the whole United States, upon all subjects within the purview of the Constitution. Judges of equal learning and integrity, in different States, might differently interpret a statute, or a treaty of the United States, or even the Constitution itself. If there were no revising authority to control these jarring and discordant judgments, and harmonize them into uniformity, the laws, the treaties, and the Constitution of the United States would be different in different States, and might perhaps never have precisely the same construction, obligation, or efficacy, in any two States. The public mischiefs that would attend such a state of things would be truly deplorable; and it cannot be believed that they could have escaped the enlightened convention which formed the Constitution. What, indeed, might then have been only prophecy has now become fact; and the appellate jurisdiction must continue to be the only adequate remedy for such evils. . . .

It is the opinion of the whole court, that the judgment of the Court of Appeals of Virginia, rendered on the mandate in this cause, be reversed, and the judgment of the District Court, held at Winchester, be, and the same is hereby affirmed.

Mr. Justice **Johnson** delivered a concurring opinion.

THE NATURE OF STATE POWER

COYLE v. SMITH

221 U. S. 559; 31 S. Ct. 688; 55 L. Ed. 853
(1911)

The power which Congress possesses to admit new states into the Union is a purely discretionary power. No territory has any right to claim statehood, but must wait until it seems wise to Congress to confer that status. It is not surprising, therefore, that it should be assumed that Congress in the exercise of an unquestioned power to grant or withhold such a privilege might make the enjoyment of the right contingent upon the meeting of such conditions by the incoming state as might seem to the congressional mind desirable. This seems to have been the theory upon which Congress proceeded with reference to the admission of states; and as early as 1802 we find Ohio compelled, as the price of admission into the Union, to enter into an agreement, irrevocable without the consent of Congress, not to tax for a period of five years lands within the state which were sold by the United States government. The imposing of conditions of various kinds upon the incoming states became a settled policy of Congress, and the stipulations agreed to covered a considerable range of topics. They related to the disposition of public lands, many of them being much more detailed than the Ohio provision; to the use of navigable waters; to the protection of the rights of citizens of the United States; to slavery; to civil and religious liberty; to the right to vote. When Utah came into the Union in 1894 it was obliged to make an irrevocable agreement that there should be perfect religious toleration maintained in the state, that the public schools should be kept free from sectarian control, and that polygamous marriages should be forever prohibited.

In 1910 Arizona was authorized by a congressional enabling act to draw up a state constitution preparatory to entering the Union. The constitution framed contained provisions for the popular recall of judges. While Congress somewhat reluctantly passed a resolution admitting Arizona into the Union, President Taft, being bitterly opposed to the recall of judges, vetoed the resolution. A new resolution was then passed providing that Arizona be admitted on condition that the objectionable provision be stricken out of the constitution. This was done and Arizona became a member of the Union. The state thereupon promptly restored the recall of judges by amending the new state constitution, and has retained the provision ever since.

But if Congress can thus impose conditions upon the new states as they assume statehood, the question arises: are the states equal? Do we actually have states in the Union which do not have the power enjoyed by other states, as, for instance, to decide how judges shall be removed from office, or what shall constitute a lawful marriage? It is a rather curious fact that the question of the binding nature of these restrictions was not brought before the Supreme Court until 1911 in the case of Coyle v. Smith. This case grew out of a congressional restriction imposed upon Oklahoma in the enabling act passed in 1906 which provided (1) that the new state should locate its capital at Guthrie, (2) that it should irrevocably agree not to move it from that place before the year 1913, and (3) that it should not appropriate any unnecessary money for public buildings. This agreement was ratified by the voters of the state at the time that the new constitution was adopted; and, thus bound, Oklahoma entered the Union. In 1910, a bill initiated by the people providing that the state capital should forthwith be moved to Oklahoma City and appropriating $600,000 for public buildings was approved by the voters of Oklahoma. This was, of course, in plain violation of the "irrevocable" agreement which the state had made, and a proceeding was instituted to test the validity of the law. In sustaining the right of the state to move its capital at its discretion regardless of its agreement, the Supreme Court enunciated the important doctrine of the political equality of the states.

A distinction, however, should be noted between those conditions imposed upon incoming states which relate to political or governmental authority and which would therefore place the state upon an unequal footing in the Union, and those conditions in the nature of business agreements or contracts which relate to property. Thus, for example, the agreement of a new state to conditions in its Enabling Act that lands given to it by the United States in trust for certain purposes has been held enforceable like any other trust agreement. See Ervien v. United States (1919) in which New Mexico, which was given lands for school purposes, was held properly enjoined from using them for advertising the resources of the state.

It may be said that the vital question of whether one of the states of the Union may constitutionally secede was effectively and permanently answered upon the battlefields of the Civil War. Four years after the war had ended, however, the Supreme Court found itself under the necessity of deciding, in the case of Texas v. White (1869), whether the Southern states had at any time during the period of attempted secession been actually out of the Union. Was secession, in point of law, constitutionally possible? The facts in this case were as follows:

In 1850 the United States gave the state of Texas $10 million in 5 percent bonds in settlement of certain boundary claims. Half were held in Washington; half were delivered to the state, and made payable to the state or bearer and redeemable after December 31, 1864. A Texas law was passed providing that the bonds should not be available in the hands of any holder until after their endorsement by the governor. Texas joined the Confederacy at the outbreak of the war, and in 1862 the state legislature repealed the act requiring the endorsement of the bonds by the governor and created a military board to provide for the expenses of the war, empowering the board to use any bonds in the state treasury for this purpose up to $1 million. In 1865 this board made a contract with White and others for the transfer of some of the bonds for military supplies. None of the bonds was endorsed by the governor of the state. Immediately upon the close of the war, but while the state was still "unreconstructed" or unrestored to its former normal status as a member of the Union, suit was brought by the governor of the state to get the bonds back and to enjoin White and the other defendants from receiving payment for them from the federal government. *The suit was brought by Texas in the Supreme Court of the United States as an original action,* and at the very threshold of the case arose the question whether *Texas, after her efforts at secession, was still a "state"* within the meaning of *Article III,* of the Constitution extending the *original jurisdiction* of the Supreme Court to those cases "*in which a State shall be party.*" Texas at this time was still unrepresented in Congress and the radical Republicans like Stevens claimed that she was out of the Union.

The Court held that secession was constitutionally impossible and that Texas had never ceased to be a state in the Union. Chief Justice Chase said *the Articles of Confederation created* what was solemnly declared to be a "*perpetual Union*"; that the Constitution *was ordained "to form a more perfect Union*"; and he concluded that: "*The Constitution, in all of its provisions, looks to an indestructible union, composed of indestructible states.*" The fact that Texas, by her own efforts at secession, had temporarily given up the rights and privileges of membership in the Union did not alter the fact that she could not sever the constitutional ties which bound her to that Union. *The Court accordingly took jurisdiction in the case and decided that Texas was entitled to recover the bonds.*

In cases of spectacular importance the Supreme Court faced the issue of who holds title to the land beneath the sea within the so-called "three-mile" limit. The discovery of oil off the coasts of California, Louisiana, and Texas gave this underwater land tremendous value; and the three states, assuming the land was theirs, leased to various oil companies the right to drill for offshore oil. The United States, asserting that it was "the owner in fee simple, or possessed of paramount rights in and powers over" this land, brought suit to enjoin the states from trespassing upon it. The Supreme Court, in United States v. California (1947), invoked the "equal footing" rule to sustain the United States, at least in its claim to "paramount rights." The original 13 states, the Court found, had not "separately acquired ownership to the three-mile belt or the soil under it" so as to require the extension of similar rights to California.

A similar question had reached the Court in 1845 in Pollard v. Hagan. Alabama had been admitted to the Union on an equal footing with the other states, but in the act of admission it had been stipulated that Alabama disclaimed title to waste and unappropriated lands within the state, and that its navigable waters should remain public highways and free to the citizens of the state and of the United States. On the strength of this the United States claimed title to the submerged lands under the navigable waters within the state of Alabama. The

Court found that all the other states had had common-law title to these submerged lands when they came into the Union. "Alabama is therefore entitled to the sovereignty and jurisdiction over all the territory within her limits, . . . to the same extent that Georgia possessed it before she ceded it to the United States. To maintain any other doctrine, is to deny that Alabama has been admitted into the Union on an equal footing with the original states. . . .''

The Court decided the claims of Louisiana (United States v. Louisiana, 1950) on the basis of the California decision. But United States v. Texas (1950) presented a slightly different problem. Texas had been an independent nation prior to its admission to the Union and had had undoubted title to its offshore lands. The Court applied the Pollard argument in reverse: "The 'equal footing' clause, we hold, works the same way in the converse situation presented by this case. It negatives any implied, special limitation of any of the paramount powers of the United States in favor of a State. . . . When Texas came into the Union, she ceased to be an independent nation. She then became a sister State on an 'equal footing' with all the other States. That act concededly entailed a relinquishment of some of her sovereignty. . . . We hold that as an incident to the transfer of that sovereignty any claim that Texas may have had to the marginal sea was relinquished to the United States."

The tidelands' oil question became an issue in the 1952 presidential campaign, and the victorious Republican Congress redeemed its campaign pledge to cede to the three states the lands which they claimed. Since the acts ceded title to the land extending to the original boundaries of the states, the Gulf states claimed three leagues (nine nautical miles) of marginal sea. Congress' right to make this cession was upheld in Alabama v. Texas in 1954, but in 1960 the Court held that only Texas and Florida were entitled to three leagues. The fact that this apparently leaves these states sticking out some six miles beyond the boundaries of the United States raises potential problems in international law which the Court declined to answer. "It is sufficient for present purposes to note that there is no question of Congress' power to fix state land and water boundaries as a domestic matter. Such a boundary, fully effective as between Nation and State, undoubtedly circumscribes the extent of navigable inland waters and underlying lands owned by the State under the Pollard rule." See United States v. Louisiana (1960).

In the years since 1937, the substance of the power reserved to the states has diminished steadily as Congress, under the pressure of public opinion, has extended its authority under the taxing and commerce powers to areas once under state control. So clear was this trend, and so unwavering the approval of the Supreme Court, that the future seemed bleak for the "residuum of sovereignty" to which the Court alluded in the case below. In 1976, however, in National League of Cities of Usery, the Court suddenly appeared to reverse this trend and resurrect the Tenth Amendment, then reversed itself again in Garcia v. San Antonio Metro. (1985); see the cases printed below.

Mr. Justice **Lurton** delivered the opinion of the Court, saying in part:

. . . The only question for review by us is whether the provision of the enabling act was a valid limitation upon the power of the State after its admission, which overrides any subsequent state legislation repugnant thereto.

The power to locate its own seat of government, and to determine when and how it shall be changed from one place to another, and to appropriate its own public funds for that purpose, are essentially and peculiarly state powers. That one of the original thirteen States could now be shorn of such powers by an act of Congress would not be for a moment entertained. The question, then, comes to this: Can a State be placed upon a plane of inequality with its sister States in the Union if the Congress chooses to impose conditions which so operate, at the time of its admission? The argument is, that while Congress may not deprive a State of any power which it possesses, it may, as a condition to the admission of a new State, constitutionally restrict its authority, to the extent, at least, of suspending its powers for a definite time in respect to the location of its seat of government. This contention is predicated upon the constitutional power of admitting new States to this Union, and the constitutional duty of guaranteeing to "every State in this Union a republican form of government." The position of counsel for the appellants is substantially this: That the power of Congress to admit new States, and to determine whether or not its fundamental law is republican in form, are political powers, and as such, uncontrollable by the courts. That Congress may, in the exercise of such power, impose terms and conditions upon the admission of the proposed new State, which, if accepted, will be obligatory, although they operate to deprive the State of powers which it would otherwise possess, and, therefore, not admitted upon "an equal footing with the original States."

The power of Congress in respect to the admission of new States is found in the 3rd section of the 4th article of the Constitution. That provision is that, "new states may be admitted by the Congress into this Union." The only expressed restriction upon this power is that no new State shall be formed within the jurisdiction of any other State, nor by the junction of two or more States, or parts of States, without the consent of such States, as well as of the Congress.

But what is this power? It is not to admit political organizations which are less or greater, or different in dignity or power, from those political entities which constitute the Union. It is, as strongly put by counsel, a "power to admit States."

The definition of "a state" is found in the powers possessed by the original states which adopted the Constitution,—a definition emphasized by the term employed in all subsequent acts of Congress admitting new States into the Union. The first two States admitted into the Union were the States of Vermont and Kentucky, one as of March 4, 1791, and the other as of June 1, 1792. No terms or conditions were exacted from either. Each act declares that the State is admitted "as a new and *entire member* of the United States of America." . . . Emphatic and significant as is the phrase admitted as "an entire member," even stronger was the declaration upon the admission in 1796 of Tennessee as the third new State, it being declared to be "one of the United States of America," "on an equal footing with the original States in all respects whatsoever,"—phraseology which has ever since been substantially followed in admission acts, concluding with the Oklahoma act, which declares that Oklahoma shall be admitted "on an equal footing with the original states."

The power is to admit "new States into *this* Union."

"This Union" was and is a union of States, equal in power, dignity, and authority, each competent to exert that residuum of sovereignty not delegated to the United States by the Constitution itself. To maintain otherwise would be to say that the Union, through the power of Congress to admit new States, might come to be a union of States unequal in power, as including States whose powers were restricted only by the Constitution, with others whose powers had been further restricted by an act of Congress accepted as a condition of admission. Thus it would result, first, that the powers of Congress would not be defined by the Constitution alone, but in respect to new States, enlarged or restricted by the conditions imposed upon new States by its own legislation admitting them into the Union; and, second, that such new States might not exercise all of the powers which had not been delegated by the Constitution, but only such as had not been further bargained away as conditions of admission.

The argument that Congress derives from the duty of "guaranteeing to each State in this Union a republican form of government," power to impose restrictions upon a new State which deprive it of equality with other members of the Union, has no merit. It may imply the duty of such new State to provide itself with such state government, and impose upon Congress the duty of seeing that such form is not changed to one anti-republican, . . . but it obviously does not confer power to admit a new State which shall be any less a State than those which compose the Union.

We come now to the question as to whether there is anything in the decisions of this court which sanctions the claim that Congress may, by the imposition of conditions in an enabling act, deprive a new State of any of those attributes essential to its equality in dignity and power with other States. In considering the decisions of this court bearing upon the question, we must distinguish, first, between provisions which are fulfilled by the admission of the State; second, between compacts or affirmative legislation intended to operate in futuro, which are within the scope of the conceded powers of Congress over the subject; and third, compacts or affirmative legislation which operates to restrict the powers of such new States in respect of matters which would otherwise be exclusively within the sphere of state power.

As to requirements in such enabling acts as relate

only to the contents of the constitution for the proposed new State, little needs to be said. The constitutional provision concerning the admission of new States is not a mandate, but a power to be exercised with discretion. From this alone it would follow that Congress may require, under penalty of denying admission, that the organic laws of a new State at the time of admission shall be such as to meet its approval. A constitution thus supervised by Congress, would, after all, be a constitution of a State, and as such subject to alteration and amendment by the State after admission. Its force would be that of a state constitution, and not that of an act of Congress. . . .

So far as this court has found occasion to advert to the effect of enabling acts as affirmative legislation affecting the power of new states after admission, there is to be found no sanction for the contention that any state may be deprived of any of the power constitutionally possessed by other states, as states, by reason of the terms in which the acts admitting them to the Union have been framed. . . .

[Here follows discussion of a case involving the construction of the act under which Alabama was admitted to the Union.]

The plain deduction from this case is that when a new state is admitted into the Union, it is so admitted with all of the powers of sovereignty and jurisdiction which pertain to the original states, and that such powers may not be constitutionally diminished, impaired, or shorn away by any conditions, compacts, or stipulations embraced in the act under which the new state came into the Union, which would not be valid and effectual if the subject of congressional legislation after admission. . . .

It may well happen that Congress should embrace in an enactment introducing a new state into the Union legislation intended as a regulation of commerce among the states, or with Indian tribes situated within the limits of such new state, or regulations touching the sole care and disposition of the public lands or reservations therein which might be upheld as legislation within the sphere of the plain power of Congress. But in every such case such legislation would derive its force not from any agreement or compact with the proposed new state, nor by reason of its acceptance of such enactment as a term of admission, but solely because the power of Congress extended to the subject, and therefore would not operate to restrict the state's legislative power in respect of any matter which was not plainly within the regulative power of Congress. . . .

No such question is presented here. The legislation in the Oklahoma enabling act relating to the location of the capital of the state, if construed as forbidding a removal by the state after its admission as a state, is referable to no power granted to Congress over the subject, and if it is to be upheld at all, it must be implied from the power to admit new states. If power to impose such a restriction upon the general and undelegated power of a state be conceded as implied from the power to admit a new state, where is the line to be drawn against restrictions imposed upon new states? . . .

If anything was needed to complete the argument

against the assertion that Oklahoma has not been admitted to the Union upon an equality of power, dignity, and sovereignty with Massachusetts or Virginia, it is afforded by the express provision of the act of admission, by which it is declared that when the people of the proposed new state have complied with the terms of the act, that it shall be the duty of the President to issue his proclamation, and that "thereupon the proposed state of Oklahoma shall be deemed admitted by Congress into the Union under and by virtue of this act, *on an equal footing with the original states.*" The proclamation has been issued and the Senators and Representatives from the state admitted to their seats in the Congress.

Has Oklahoma been admitted upon an equal footing with the original states? If she has, she, by virtue of her jurisdictional sovereignty as such a state, may determine for her own people the proper location of the local seat of government. She is not equal in power to them if she cannot. . . .

To this we may add that the constitutional equality of the states is essential to the harmonious operation of the scheme upon which the Republic was organized. When that equality disappears we may remain a free people, but the Union will not be the Union of the Constitution.

Judgment affirmed.

Mr. Justice **McKenna** and Mr. Justice **Holmes** dissent.

UNITED STATES v. BUTLER

297 U. S. 1; 56 S. Ct. 312; 80 L. Ed. 477 (1936)

While it is clear from Coyle v. Smith (1911) that a state has a "residuum" of state sovereignty that cannot be taken away from it, and from Kansas v. Colorado (1907) and McCulloch v. Maryland (1819) that Congress has only delegated powers or those reasonably implied from such delegation, are there limits to the way in which Congress can exercise those powers that are clearly delegated? From time to time the Court has held that there are. In Collector v. Day (1871) the taxing power of Congress was held limited by the sovereign right of the states to an unimpaired existence, and in Ashton v. Cameron County Water Dist. (1936) Congress was held unable to extend the bankruptcy power to a state agency, since to do so would be to "pass laws inconsistent with the idea of sovereignty."

In Hammer v. Dagenhart (1918) the Court held for the first time that the powers reserved to the states by the Tenth Amendment acted as a limit on the use of congressional power. There the Court struck down the use of the commerce power to control child labor. The philosophy underlying this decision is that the powers of Congress cannot be used to achieve ends which have not been delegated to Congress, and hence, according to the Tenth Amendment, are reserved to the states.

Perhaps the most lucid explanation of this doctrine, dubbed "dual federalism" by Professor E. S.

Corwin, is that made by Justice Roberts in the Butler case below. One of the crucial problems of the Great Depression of the 1930s was the presence of agricultural surpluses so great that the market price often failed to cover the cost of production. So, as a major part of the New Deal recovery program, Congress passed the Agricultural Adjustment Act of 1933. The AAA undertook to solve the problem of low farm prices and agricultural surpluses by paying farmers to limit the growing of certain commodities. The necessary money was raised by a processing tax on the industries which prepared farm products for market, and over a billion dollars was collected before the Court held the act void. The Court does not contend that such a processing tax, taken alone, would be void; but when coupled with a clear attempt to regulate agriculture, it was an unconstitutional use of a delegated power.

The doctrine of dual federalism, in the form that appears here, was destined to be short-lived. In the Social Security Act Cases in 1937 the Court sustained an almost identical use of the tax power, and in United States v. Darby in 1941 the Court consciously abandoned it, noting that the Tenth Amendment "states but a truism that all is retained which has not been surrendered." The conservative resurgence of the 1970s and 1980s once again made state sovereignty a political issue—see the Usery and Garcia cases printed below—and revives questions about the meaning of the Tenth Amendment.

Mr. Justice **Roberts** delivered the opinion of the Court, saying in part:

Second. The Government asserts that even if the respondents may question the propriety of the appropriation embodied in the statute their attack must fail because Article I, § 8 of the Constitution authorizes the contemplated expenditure of the funds raised by the tax. This contention presents the great and the controlling question in the case. We approach its decision with a sense of our grave responsibility to render judgment in accordance with the principles established for the governance of all three branches of the Government.

There should be no misunderstanding as to the function of this court in such a case. It is sometimes said that the court assumes a power to overrule or control the action of the people's representatives. This is a misconception. The Constitution is the supreme law of the land ordained and established by the people. All legislation must conform to the principles it lays down. When an act of Congress is appropriately challenged in the courts as not conforming to the constitutional mandate the judicial branch of the Government has only one duty,—to lay the article of the Constitution which is invoked beside the statute which is challenged and to decide whether the latter squares with the former. All the court does, or can do, is to announce its considered judgment upon the question. The only power it has, if such it may be called, is the power of judgment. This court neither approves nor condemns any legislative policy. Its delicate and

difficult office is to ascertain and declare whether the legislation is in accordance with, or in contravention of, the provisions of the Constitution; and, having done that, its duty ends.

The question is not what power the federal Government ought to have but what powers in fact have been given by the people. It hardly seems necessary to reiterate that ours is a dual form of government; that in every state there are two governments,—the state and the United States. Each State has all governmental powers save such as the people, by their Constitution, have conferred upon the United States, denied to the States, or reserved to themselves. The federal union is a government of delegated powers. It has only such as are expressly conferred upon it and such as are reasonably to be implied from those granted. In this respect we differ radically from nations where all legislative power, without restriction or limitation, is vested in a parliament or other legislative body subject to no restrictions except the discretion of its members.

Article I, § 8, of the Constitution vests sundry powers in the Congress. But two of its clauses have any bearing upon the validity of the statute under review.

The third clause endows the Congress with power "to regulate Commerce . . . among the several States." Despite a reference in its first section to a burden upon, and an obstruction of the normal currents of commerce, the act under review does not purport to regulate transactions in interstate or foreign commerce. Its stated purpose is the control of agricultural production, a purely local activity, in an effort to raise the prices paid the farmer. Indeed, the Government does not attempt to uphold the validity of the act on the basis of the commerce clause, which, for the purpose of the present case, may be put aside as irrelevant.

The clause thought to authorize the legislation,—the first,—confers upon the Congress power "to lay and collect Taxes, Duties, Imposts and Excises, to pay the Debts and provide for the common Defence and general Welfare of the United States. . . ." It is not contended that this provision grants power to regulate agricultural production upon the theory that such legislation would promote the general welfare. The Government concedes that the phrase "to provide for the general welfare" qualifies the power "to lay and collect taxes." The view that the clause grants power to provide for the general welfare, independently of the taxing power, has never been authoritatively accepted. Mr. Justice Story points out that if it were adopted "it is obvious that under color of the generality of the words, to 'provide for the common defence and general welfare,' the government of the United States is, in reality, a government of general and unlimited powers, notwithstanding the subsequent enumeration of specific powers." The true construction undoubtedly is that the only thing granted is the power to tax for the purpose of providing funds for payment of the nation's debts and making provision for the general welfare.

Nevertheless the Government asserts that warrant is found in this clause for the adoption of the Agricultural Adjustment Act. The argument is that Congress may appropriate and authorize the spending of moneys for the "general welfare;" that the phrase should be liberally construed to cover anything conducive to national welfare; that decision as to what will promote such welfare rests with Congress alone, and the courts may not review its determination; and finally that the appropriation under attack was in fact for the general welfare of the United States.

The Congress is expressly empowered to lay taxes to provide for the general welfare. Funds in the Treasury as a result of taxation may be expended only through appropriation. (Art. I, § 9, cl. 7.) They can never accomplish the objects for which they were collected unless the power to appropriate is as broad as the power to tax. The necessary implication from the terms of the grant is that the public funds may be appropriated "to provide for the general welfare of the United States." These words cannot be meaningless, else they would not have been used. The conclusion must be that they were intended to limit and define the granted power to raise and to expend money. How shall they be construed to effectuate the intent of the instrument?

Since the foundation of the nation sharp differences of opinion have persisted as to the true interpretation of the phrase. Madison asserted it amounted to no more than a reference to the other powers enumerated in the subsequent clauses of the same section; that, as the United States is a government of limited and enumerated powers, the grant of power to tax and spend for the general national welfare must be confined to the enumerated legislative fields committed to the Congress. In this view the phrase is mere tautology, for taxation and appropriation are or may be necessary incidents of the exercise of any of the enumerated legislative powers. Hamilton, on the other hand, maintained the clause confers a power separate and distinct from those later enumerated, is not restricted in meaning by the grant of them, and Congress consequently has a substantive power to tax and to appropriate, limited only by the requirement that it shall be exercised to provide for the general welfare of the United States. Each contention has had the support of those whose views are entitled to weight. This court has noticed the question, but has never found it necessary to decide which is the true construction. Mr. Justice Story, in his Commentaries, espouses the Hamiltonian position. We shall not review the writings of public men and commentators or discuss the legislative practice. Study of all these leads us to conclude that the reading advocated by Mr. Justice Story is the correct one. While, therefore, the power to tax is not unlimited, its confines are set in the clause which confers it, and not in those of § 8 which bestow and define the legislative powers of the Congress. It results that the power of Congress to authorize expenditure of public moneys for public purposes is not limited by the direct grants of legislative power found in the Constitution. . . .

We are not now required to ascertain the scope of the phrase "general welfare of the United States" or to determine whether an appropriation in aid of agriculture falls within it. Wholly apart from that question, another principle embedded in our Constitution prohibits the enforcement of the Agricultural Adjustment Act. The act invades the reserved rights of the states. It is a statutory plan to regulate and control agricultural production, a matter beyond the powers delegated to the federal government. The tax, the appropriation of the funds raised, and the direction for their disbursement, are but parts of the plan. They are but means to an unconstitutional end.

From the accepted doctrine that the United States is a government of delegated powers, it follows that those not expressly granted, or reasonably to be implied from such as are conferred, are reserved to the states or to the people. To forestall any suggestion to the contrary, the Tenth Amendment was adopted. The same proposition, otherwise stated, is that powers not granted are prohibited. None to regulate agricultural production is given, and therefore legislation by Congress for that purpose is forbidden.

It is an established principle that the attainment of a prohibited end may not be accomplished under the pretext of the exertion of powers which are granted.

"Should Congress, in the execution of its powers, adopt measures which are prohibited by the constitution; or should Congress, under the pretext of executing its powers, pass laws for the accomplishment of objects not intrusted to the government; it would become the painful duty of this tribunal, should a case requiring such a decision come before it, to say that such an act was not the law of the land." M'Culloch v. Maryland [1819].

"Congress cannot, under the pretext of executing delegated power, pass laws for the accomplishment of objects not intrusted to the Federal Government. And we accept as established doctrine that any provision of an act of Congress ostensibly enacted under power granted by the Constitution, not naturally and reasonably adapted to the effective exercise of such power but solely to the achievement of something plainly within power reserved to the States, is invalid and cannot be enforced." Linder v. United States [1925].

These principles are as applicable to the power to lay taxes as to any other federal power. Said the court, in M'Culloch v. Maryland:

"Let the end be legitimate, let it be within the scope of the constitution, and all means which are appropriate, which are plainly adapted to that end, which are not prohibited, but consist with the letter and spirit of the constitution, are constitutional."

The power of taxation, which is expressly granted, may, of course, be adopted as a means to carry into operation another power also expressly granted. But resort to the taxing power to effectuate an end which is not legitimate, not within the scope of the Constitution, is obviously inadmissible. . . .

COLLECTOR v. DAY

11 Wallace 113; 20 L. Ed. 122 (1871)

The doctrine of "dual federalism" had its roots in the theory that the Tenth Amendment reserved to the states the "police power"—a term used to describe the power of a state to promote by its laws the public health, safety and welfare—and that Congress not only did not have any such power but could not use its delegated powers in a way that suggested that it did. But there was another area in which the states asserted their independence from the national government and that was in the area of intergovernmental tax immunity. What was at stake here was not the state's power to control public policy, but rather its right to continued existence, unimpeded by the "power to destroy" implicit in the federal tax power.

Marshall's decision in McCulloch v. Maryland (1819) that Maryland could not constitutionally tax the Bank of the United States rested on three propositions: first, "the power to tax involves the power to destroy" since, if the power exists at all, the rate of the tax is merely a question of legislative policy; second, the supremacy clause denies the state's power to destroy instrumentalities of the federal government; and third, the Bank is such an instrumentality.

It is worth noting that in McCulloch, Marshall plainly rejected the converse of his rule, i.e., that the states are constitutionally free from federal taxation. He said: "The difference is that which always exists, and always must exist, between the action of the whole on a part, and the action of a part on the whole—between the laws of a government declared to be supreme, and those of a government which, when in opposition to those laws, is not supreme." The Maryland tax in this case was both discriminatory and destructive. The state plainly intended to destroy the branch of the Bank of the United States in Baltimore. But later, in Weston v. Charleston (1829), Marshall made it clear that the immunity of the federal government from state taxes was not limited to taxes which were actually destructive, but included all state taxes. The states could not tax the United States at all. In this case a nondiscriminatory state property tax had hit, among other things, stock (bonds) issued by the United States. This, Marshall explained, was a tax on the borrowing power of the United States—an important instrumentality of fiscal policy. Two justices dissented from this extension of the doctrine on the ground that the tax was nondiscriminatory and the burden on the United States was only indirect: "It is said the states cannot tax the mint," Justice Thompson said, "but this does not imply that they may not tax the money coined at the mint, when held and owned by individuals."

In Dobbins v. Commissioners of Erie County (1842) the Court had extended this doctrine to hold that the salaries of federal officials were immune from state taxation. Erie County had levied an income tax on persons holding offices and posts of profit and sought to collect the tax from Dobbins, the captain of a federal revenue cutter. The Court held the tax on Dobbin's salary invalid on the ground that the captain of a vessel is as much a means of carrying out government policy as the vessel itself, and the compensation paid the officer was the means used by the government to obtain his services; therefore the tax was an "interference with the constitutional means which have been legislated by the government of the United States to carry into effect its powers."

. . ." The Court relied on this theory in Collector v. Day when it held the salaries of state officers immune from federal taxation.

From the time of Collector v. Day down to the 1920's the Supreme Court steadily broadened the scope of intergovernmental tax immunity and, with a reservation or two, was inclined to hold the two governments, federal and state, equally immune from taxation by the other. Various instrumentalities of government were held to be covered by the tax-immunity rule. In 1888 the Court held in California v. Central Pacific Railroad Co. that the state could not tax the franchise given by Congress to the Central Pacific to build a railroad, and in Ambrosini v. United States (1902) the federal government was forbidden to place a federal stamp tax on a state bond required as a condition of getting a state liquor license. When the federal government leases property, such leases are instrumentalities of government; therefore in Indian Territory Illuminating Oil Co. v. Oklahoma (1916) the Court held void a state tax on the leases of Indian land to private companies. In Gillespie v. Oklahoma (1922) the immunity was extended to the income earned from such leased land. "A tax upon such profits," said the Court, "is a direct hamper upon the effort of the United States to make the best terms that it can for its wards." Burnet v. Coronado Oil & Gas Co. (1932) extended immunity from federal taxes to the income from lands leased from the state. In 1928 the states were denied the right to tax income in the form of royalties earned under a patent (or copyright), on the theory that a patent is the federal government's instrumentality for promoting science and the arts, and such instrumentalities are immune from state taxation; see Long v. Rockwood.

The sale of goods to a government was also held to enjoy tax immunity, on the theory that purchases are government transactions and exercises of sovereign power which cannot be burdened. In Panhandle Oil Co. v. Mississippi (1928) the Court held void a state gasoline tax as applied to the sale of gasoline to the United States Coast Guard, while in Indian Motocycle Co. v. United States (1931) the federal government was forbidden to collect a sales tax on motorcycles sold to a municipal police department.

In one area the Court refused to extend immunity. When a state engaged in what was commonly thought of as a private business, as South Carolina did when it went into the liquor business, it had to pay federal taxes on the business like everyone else. The state could not deprive the federal government of its sources of revenue by taking over businesses on which that revenue depended. See South Carolina v. United States (1905). Nor did the Court extend immunity from taxation to those who were not government employees, but who merely had contractual relations with the government. Thus in Metcalf & Eddy v. Mitchell (1926) the Court found that a firm of private contractors was not the kind of agency "through which either government immediately and directly exercises its sovereign power," and after assuring itself that the tax was nondiscriminatory and would not impair the ability of the contractors to do their job, held the tax valid.

The Court eventually came to the realization that the true beneficiaries of all this immunity were not the governments involved but a select group of favored individuals, and in the 1930's began retracting the doctrine. The climax came with the Court's decision in Graves v. New York ex rel. O'Keefe (1939) in which it held that individuals working for a federal agency were no longer to be considered "instrumentalities" enjoying a form of sovereign immunity, but, like the contractors in Metcalf & Eddy, were merely persons whose salaries were being taxed by the state. The Court stated that "the theory . . . that a tax on income is legally or economically a tax on its source, is no longer tenable," and added that to the extent such taxes raised the cost of labor so as to be a burden on either government this was "but the normal incident of the organization within the same territory of two governments, each possessing the taxing power. The burden, so far as it can be said to exist or to affect the government in any indirect or incidental way, is one which the Constitution presupposes. . . ." To the extent that it had immunized officers or employees, Collector v. Day was overruled.

Despite the drastic contraction of the scope of tax immunity, the doctrine itself has not been abolished. Things which are instrumentalities of government are still immune, and in Mayo v. United States (1943) the Court held void a Florida attempt to collect from the Department of Agriculture an inspection fee on fertilizer it brought into the state under its soil conservation program. Still intact, too, is the immunity from taxation of the bonds issued by the state and federal governments, although it is arguable whether a nondiscriminatory tax on the income earned by the bonds would now be held a threat to the borrowing power of the governments. Statutory exemption of such bonds from taxation has precluded a constitutional test of the issue, but in 1985 Congress moved to tax them in an indirect way. Persons receiving social security benefits were taxed on those benefits if their total income was above a certain level—and that income included the earnings from tax-exempt bonds. And in 1987 Congress levied a tax on the income from municipal bonds issued for "nonessential" purposes, while those for "essential" purposes remained exempt.

Mr. Justice **Nelson** delivered the opinion of the Court, saying in part:

Day, the plaintiff in the court below and defendant in error, brought a suit against Buffington, collector of the internal revenue, to recover back $61.51 and interest, assessed upon his salary in the years 1866 and 1867, as judge of the court of probate and insolvency for the county of Barnstable, state of Massachusetts, paid under protest. The salary is fixed by law, and payable out of the treasury of the state. The case was submitted to the court below on an agreed statement of facts, and upon which judgment was rendered for the plaintiff. It is now here for reexamination. It presents the question whether or not it is competent for Congress, under the Constitution of the United States, to impose a tax upon the salary of a judicial officer of a state. . . .

The general government, and the states, although both exist within the same territorial limits, are separable and distinct sovereignties, acting separately and independently of each other, within their respective spheres. The former, in its appropriate sphere, is supreme; but the states within the limits of their powers not granted; or, in the language of the 10th Amendment, "reserved," are as independent of the general government as that government within its sphere is independent of the states.

The relations existing between the two governments are well stated by the present Chief Justice in the case of Lane County v. Oregon [1869]. "Both the states and the United States," he observed, "existed before the Constitution. The people, through that instrument, established a more perfect union, by substituting a national government, acting with ample powers directly upon the citizens, instead of the confederate government, which acted with powers, greatly restricted, only upon the states. But, in many of the articles of the Constitution, the necessary existence of the states, and within their proper spheres, the independent authority of the states are distinctly recognized. To them nearly the whole charge of interior regulation is committed or left; to them, and to the people, all powers, not expressly delegated to the national government, are reserved." Upon looking into the Constitution it will be found that but a few of the articles in that instrument could be carried into practical effect without the existence of the states.

Two of the great departments of the government, the executive and legislative, depend upon the exercise of the powers, or upon the people of the states. The Constitution guarantees to the states a republican form of government, and protects each against invasion or domestic violence. Such being the separate and independent condition of the states in our complex system, as recognized by the Constitution, and the existence of which is so indispensable, that, without them, the general government itself would disappear from the family of nations, it would seem to follow, as a reasonable, if not a necessary consequence, that the means and instrumentalities employed for carrying on the operations of their governments for preserving their existence, and fulfilling the high and responsible duties assigned to them in the Constitution, should be left free and unimpaired; should not be liable to be crippled, much less defeated by the taxing power of another government, which power acknowledges no limits but the will of the legislative body imposing the tax. And, more especially, those means and instrumentalities which are the creation of their sovereign and reserved rights, one of which is the establishment of the judicial department, and the appointment of officers to administer their laws. Without this power, and the exercise of it, we risk nothing in saying that no one of the states, under the form of government guaranteed by the Constitution, could long preserve its existence. A despotic government might. We have said that one of the reserved powers was that to establish a judicial department, it would have been more accurate, and in accordance with the existing state of things at the time, to have said the power to maintain a judicial department. All of the thirteen states were in the possession of this power, and had exercised it at the adoption of the Constitution; and it is not pretended that any grant of it to the general government is found in that instrument. It is, therefore, one of the sovereign powers vested in the states by their constitutions which remained unaltered and unimpaired, and in respect to which the state is as independent of the general government as that government is independent of the states.

The supremacy of the general government, therefore, so much relied on in the argument of the counsel for the plaintiff in error, in respect to the question before us, cannot be maintained. The two governments are upon an equality, and the question is whether the power "to lay and collect taxes" enables the general government to tax the salary of a judicial officer of the state, which officer is a means or instrumentality employed to carry into execution one of its most important functions, the administration of the laws, and which concerns the exercise of a right reserved to the states.

We do not say the mere circumstance of the establishment of the judicial department, and the appointment of officers to administer the laws, being among the reserved powers of the state, disables the general government from levying the tax, as that depends upon the express power "to lay and collect taxes," but it shows that it is an original inherent power never parted with, and in respect to which, the supremacy of that government does not exist, and is of no importance in determining the question; and further, that being an original and reserved power, and the judicial officers appointed under it being a means or instrumentality employed to carry it into effect, the right and necessity of its unimpaired exercise, and the exemption of the officer from taxation by the general government, stand upon as solid a ground, and are maintained by principles and reasons as cogent as those which led to the exemption of the Federal officer in Dobbins v. Erie Co. [1842] from taxation by the state; for, in this respect, that is, in respect to the reserved powers, the state is as sovereign and independent as the general government. And if the means and instrumentalities employed by that government to carry into operation the powers granted to it are necessarily, and, for the sake of self-preservation, exempt from taxation by the states, why are not those of the states depending upon their reserved powers, for like reasons, equally exempt from Federal taxation? Their unimpaired existence in the one case is as essential as in the other. It is admitted that there is no express provision in the Constitution that prohibits the general government from taxing the means and instrumentalities of the states, nor is there any prohibiting the states from taxing the means and instrumentalities of that government. In both cases the exemption rests upon necessary implication, and is upheld by the great law of self-preservation; as any government, whose means employed in conducting its operations, if subject to the control of another and distinct government, can exist only at the mercy of that government. Of what avail are these means if another power may tax them at discretion? . . .

The judgment of the court below is affirmed.

Mr. Justice **Bradley** dissenting:

I dissent from the opinion of the court in this case, because it seems to me that the general government has the same power of taxing the income of officers of the state governments as it has of taxing that of its own officers. It is the common government of all alike; and every citizen is presumed to trust his own government in the matter of taxation. No man ceases to be a citizen of the United States by being an officer under the state government. I cannot accede to the doctrine that the general government is to be regarded as in any sense foreign or antagonistic to the state governments, their officers, or people; nor can I agree that a presumption can be admitted that the general government will act in a manner hostile to the existence or functions of the state governments, which are constituent parts of the system or body politic forming the basis on which the general government is founded. The taxation by the state governments of the instruments employed by the general government in the exercise of its powers is a very different thing. Such taxation involves an interference with the powers of a government in which other states and their citizens are equally interested with the state which imposes the taxation. In my judgment, the limitation of the power of taxation in the general government, which the present decision establishes, will be found very difficult of control. Where are we to stop in enumerating the functions of the state governments which will be interfered with by Federal taxation? If a state incorporates a railroad to carry out its purposes of internal improvement, or a bank to aid its financial arrangements, reserving, perhaps, a percentage on the stock or profits, for the supply of its own treasury, will the bonds or stock of such an institution be free from Federal taxation? How can we now tell what the effect of this decision will be? I cannot but regard it as founded on a fallacy, and that it will lead to mischievous consequences. I am as much opposed as any one can be to any interference by the general government with the just powers of the state governments. But no concession of any of the just powers of the general government can easily be recalled. I, therefore, consider it my duty to at least record my dissent when such concession appears to be made. An extended discussion of the subject would answer no useful purpose.

UNIVERSITY OF ILLINOIS v. UNITED STATES

289 U. S. 48; 53 S. Ct. 509; 77 L. Ed. 1025
(1933)

There could never be any doubt as to the propriety of using the taxing power as a means of raising revenue, since that is the obvious and primary reason for establishing the power. But no tax is without economic effect upon the thing taxed and almost immediately after the organization of the national government Congress, over the protest of the strict constructionist school, passed a protective tariff; and during most of our subsequent history we have had similar legislation on our statute books. Recent competition from Asia, especially in the automotive and hi-tech fields, has spurred calls for even more protection. Some tariff schedules have been so high as to prevent entirely the importation of certain commodities, and in such cases it would seem that Congress had used its power of taxation for the purpose of destroying the thing taxed.

A still more striking instance of a prohibitive tax is to be found in the federal tax on state bank notes levied by Congress in 1866. This imposed a tax of 10 percent upon all bank notes issued by state banks and had the desired result of preventing the further issue of such notes.

The validity of this tax came before the Court in the case of Veazie Bank v. Fenno (1869). After holding that the tax in question was not a tax on a state instrumentality, and also that a tax may not be held invalid simply because it is thought to be too high, the Court pointed out that it need not be considered a tax at all. The power being exercised was the power to control the currency: "Having thus, in the exercise of undisputed constitutional powers, undertaken to provide a currency for the whole country, it cannot be questioned that Congress may, constitutionally, secure the benefit of it to the people by appropriate legislation. To this end, Congress has denied the quality of legal tender to foreign coins, and has provided by law against the imposition of counterfeit and base coin on the community. To the same end, Congress may restrain, by suitable enactments, the circulation as money of any notes not issued under its own authority. Without this power, indeed, its attempts to secure a sound and uniform currency for the country must be futile."

A similar result was reached with respect to the commerce power in the Head Money Cases (1884), in which the Court sustained a tax of 50 cents on every alien passenger brought into the United States by ship: "But the true answer to all these objections is, that the power exercised in this instance is not the taxing power. The burden imposed on the ship owner by this statute is the mere incident of the regulation of commerce, of that branch of foreign commerce which is involved in immigration. The title of the Act, 'An Act to Regulate Immigration,' is well chosen. It describes, as well as any short sentence can describe it, the real purpose and effect of the statute. . . .

"If this is an expedient regulation of commerce by Congress, and the end to be attained is one falling within that power, the Act is not void because, within a loose and more extended sense than was used in the Constitution, it is called a tax."

Mr. Chief Justice **Hughes** delivered the opinion of the Court, saying in part:

The University of Illinois imported scientific apparatus for use in one of its educational departments. Customs duties were exacted at the rates prescribed by the Tariff Act of 1922. The University paid under protest, insisting that as an instrumentality of the State of Illinois, and discharging a governmental function, it was entitled to import the articles duty free. At the hearing on the protest, the Customs Court decided in favor of the Government and the Court of Customs and Patent Appeals affirmed the decision. This Court granted certiorari. . . .

The Tariff Act of 1922 is entitled—"An Act to provide revenue, to regulate commerce with foreign countries, to encourage the industries of the United States, and for other purposes." The Congress thus asserted that it was exercising its constitutional authority "to regulate commerce with foreign nations." Art. 1, § 8, cl. 3. The words of the Constitution "Comprehend every species of commercial intercourse between the United States and foreign nations. No sort of trade can be carried on between this country and any other, to which this power does not extend." Gibbons v. Ogden [1824]. It is an essential attribute of the power that it is exclusive and plenary. As an exclusive power, its exercise may not be limited, qualified or impeded to any extent by state action. . . . The power is buttressed by the express provision of the Constitution denying to the States authority to lay imposts or duties on imports or exports without the consent of the Congress. Art. 1, § 10, cl. 2.

The Congress may determine what articles may be imported into this country and the terms upon which importation is permitted. No one can be said to have a vested right to carry on foreign commerce with the United States. . . . If the Congress saw fit to lay an embargo or to prohibit altogether the importation of specified articles, as the Congress may . . . , no State by virtue of any interest of its own would be entitled to override the restriction. The principle of duality in our system of government does not touch the authority of the Congress in the regulation of foreign commerce.

Appellant argues that the Tariff Act is a revenue measure; that it is not the less so because it is framed with a view, as its title states, of encouraging the industries of the United States . . . , that the duty is a tax, that the Act is not one for the regulation of commerce but is an exertion of the taxing power, and that, as such, it is subject to the constitutional limitation that the Congress, may not lay a tax so as to impose a direct burden upon an instrumentality of a State used in the performance of a governmental function.

It is true that the taxing power is a distinct power; that it is distinct from the power to regulate commerce. . . . It is also true that the taxing power embraces the power to lay duties. Art. 1, § 8, cl.1. But because the taxing power is a distinct power and embraces the power to lay duties, it does not follow that duties may not be imposed in the exercise of the power to regulate commerce. The contrary is well established. . . . The laying of duties is "a common means of executing the power." . . . And the Congress may, and undoubtedly does, in its tariff legislation consider the conditions of foreign trade in all its aspects and effects. Its requirements are not the less regulatory because they are not prohibitory or retaliatory. They embody the congressional conception of the extent to which regulation should go. But if the Congress may thus exercise the power, and asserts, as it has asserted here, that it is exercising it, the judicial department may not attempt in its own conception of policy to distribute the duties thus fixed by allocating some of them to the exercise of the admitted power to regulate commerce and others to an independent exercise of the taxing power. The purpose to regulate foreign commerce permeates the entire congressional plan. The revenue resulting from the duties "is an incident to such an exercise of the power. It flows from, but does not create the power."

The principle invoked by the petitioner, of the immunity of state instrumentalities from Federal taxation, has its inherent limitations. . . . It is a principle implied from the necessity of maintaining our dual system of government. . . . Springing from that necessity it does not extend beyond it. Protecting the functions of government in its proper province, the implication ceases when the boundary of that province is reached. The fact that the State in the performance of state functions may use imported articles does not mean that the importation is a function of the state government independent of federal power. The control of importation does not rest with the State but with the Congress. In international relations and with respect to foreign intercourse and trade the people of the United States act through a single government with unified and adequate national power. There is thus no violation of the principle which petitioner invokes, for there is no encroachment on the power of the State as none exists with respect to the subject over which the Federal power has been exerted. To permit the States and their instrumentalities to import commodities for their own use, regardless of the requirements imposed by the Congress, would undermine, if not destroy, the single control which it was one of the dominant purposes of the Constitution to create. It is for the Congress to decide to what extent, if at all, the States and their instrumentalities shall be relieved of the payment of duties on imported articles.

The contention of the petitioner finds no support in the history of tariff acts or in departmental practice. It is not necessary to review this practical construction. It is sufficient to say that only in recent years has any question been raised by state officials as to the authority of Congress to impose duties upon their imports.

In view of these conclusions we find it unnecessary to consider the questions raised with respect to the particular functions of the petitioner and its right to invoke the principle for which it contends.

Judgment affirmed.

UNITED STATES v. CALIFORNIA

297 U. S. 175; 56 S. Ct. 421; 80 L. Ed 567 (1936)

When is a tax not a tax? Curiously enough only the tax power had ever been held limited by the sovereign power of the states and in a series of cases, including the University of Illinois case, the power underwent a radical transformation. The Court did not deny that a tax was a tax but it did deny that it was levied under the power of Congress to lay and collect taxes. And since it was not an exercise of the tax power it could not be a tax on an instrumentality of a state and hence did not fall afoul of the doctrine of intergovernmental tax immunity (discussed more fully under The Tax Power). Moreover, since it was an exercise of the commerce power, a power clearly delegated to Congress, the supremacy clause settled any question of the claims of state sovereignty. The case below raised again the question of a state's sovereign immunity from federal interference with its essential state functions and Justice Stone's opinion deals with the contrast between the taxing and commerce powers.

The State Belt Railroad paralleled the waterfront of San Francisco harbor and served both as a terminal railroad for industries located along its right of way and as a link for through traffic passing over its trackage to other railroads. It was thus engaged in interstate commerce and was subject to the provisions of the federal Safety Appliance Act. It was wholly owned by the state of California and the United States brought suit against the state to collect a $100 penalty for hauling a car with a defective coupler in violation of the act.

Mr. Justice **Stone** delivered the opinion of the Court, saying in part:

2. The state urges that it is not subject to the federal Safety Appliance Act. It is not denied that the omission charged would be a violation if by a privately-owned rail carrier in interstate commerce. But it is said that as the state is operating the railroad without profit, for the purpose of facilitating the commerce of the port, and is using the net proceeds of operation for harbor improvement . . . it is engaged in performing a public function in its sovereign capacity and for that reason cannot constitutionally be subjected to the provisions of the federal Act. In any case it is argued that the statute is not to be construed as applying to the state acting in that capacity.

Despite reliance upon the point both by the government and the state, we think it unimportant to say whether the state conducts its railroad in its "sovereign" or in its "private" capacity. That in operating its railroad it is acting within a power reserved to the states cannot be doubted. . . . The only question we need consider is whether the exercise of that power, in whatever capacity, must be in subordination to the power to regulate interstate commerce, which has been granted specifically to the national government. The sovereign power of the states is necessarily diminished to the extent of the grants of power to the federal government in the Constitution. The power of a state to fix intrastate railroad rates must yield to the power of the national government when their regulation is appropriate to the regulation of interstate commerce. . . . Shreveport Rate Cases [1914]. A contract between a state and a rail carrier fixing intrastate rates is subject to regulation and control by Congress, acting within the commerce clause, New York v. United States [1922], as are state agencies created to effect a public purpose, see . . . University of Illinois v. United States [1933]. . . . In each case the power of the state is subordinate to the constitutional exercise of the granted federal power.

The analogy of the constitutional immunity of state instrumentalities from federal taxation, on which respondent relies, is not illuminating. That immunity is implied from the nature of our federal system and the relationship within it of state and national governments, and is equally a restriction on taxation by either of the instrumentalities of the other. Its nature requires that it be so construed as to allow to each government reasonable scope for its taxing power, see Metcalf v. Mitchell [1926], which would be unduly curtailed if either by extending its activities could withdraw from the taxing power of the other subjects of taxation traditionally within it. . . . Hence we look to the activities in which the states have traditionally engaged as marking the boundary of the restriction upon the federal taxing power. But there is no such limitation upon the plenary power to regulate commerce. The state can no more deny the power if its exercise has been authorized by Congress than can an individual.

California, by engaging in interstate commerce by rail, has subjected itself to the commerce power and is liable for a violation of the Safety Appliance Act, as are other carriers. . . .

NATIONAL LEAGUE OF CITIES v. USERY

426 U. S. 833; 96 S. Ct. 2465; 49 L. Ed. 2d 245
(1976)

In the forty year period between United States v. California and the case below dramatic changes had taken place in the power relationship between the states and the nation. The California case was decided only one month after the Court had struck down the AAA in United States v. Butler (1936), and three years before it finally abandoned the essentials of intergovernmental tax immunity in Graves v. New York ex rel. O'Keefe (1939). In a dramatic reversal of attitude, probably aided by an increased sensitivity to public opinion and a threat by President Roosevelt to "pack" the Court (see the note to West Coast Hotel Co. v. Parrish), the Court abandoned its highly restrictive interpretation of the commerce clause. During the next four decades the power of Congress to regulate the nation's economy and provide for the general welfare of its citizens grew to be a truly national "police power." The chief vehicle for this constitutional growth was the commerce power and virtually no facet of American life was left untouched.

By and large, the regulatory provisions provided by Congress for the country generally specifically exempted the state governments, although these were among the nation's largest users of goods moving in interstate commerce. But in 1961 Congress amended the Fair Labor Standards Act of 1938 to make applicable the minimum wage and maximum hour provisions of the law to all schools and hospitals, even those run by the states themselves. The Supreme Court held the law valid. In

Maryland v. Wirtz (1968) the Court reassured the state that "the Court has ample power to prevent what the appellants purport to fear, 'the utter destruction of the State as a sovereign political entity,' " but added that "while the commerce power has limits, valid general regulations of commerce do not cease to be regulations of commerce because a State is involved. . . . This was settled by the unanimous decision in United States v. California [1936]." In 1975 in Fry v. United States the Court upheld on the same ground the application of the federal wage freeze to state employees under the Economic Stabilization Act of 1970.

Mr. Justice **Rehnquist** delivered the opinion of the Court, saying in part:

II.

It is established beyond peradventure that the Commerce Clause of Art. I of the Constitution is a grant of plenary authority to Congress. That authority is, in the words of Mr. Chief Justice Marshall in Gibbons v. Ogden (1824), "the power to regulate; that is, to prescribe the rule by which commerce is to be governed."

When considering the validity of asserted applications of this power to wholly private activity, the Court has made it clear that "[e]ven activity that is purely intrastate in character may be regulated by Congress, where the activity, combined with like conduct by others similarly situated, affects commerce among the States or with foreign nations." Fry v. United States (1975). . . .

Appellants in no way challenge these decisions establishing the breadth of authority granted Congress under the commerce power. Their contention, on the contrary, is that when Congress seeks to regulate directly the activities of States as public employers, it transgresses an affirmative limitation on the exercise of its power akin to other commerce power affirmative limitations contained in the Constitution. Congressional enactments which may be fully within the grant of legislative authority contained in the Commerce Clause may nonetheless be invalid because found to offend against the right to trial by jury. . . .

This Court has never doubted that there are limits upon the power of Congress to override state sovereignty, even when exercising its otherwise plenary powers to tax or to regulate commerce which are conferred by Art. I of the Constitution. In [Maryland v. Wirtz (1968)], for example, the Court took care to assure the appellants that it had "ample power to prevent . . . 'the utter destruction of the State as a sovereign political entity,' " which they feared. . . . In Fry, the Court recognized that an express declaration of this limitation is found in the Tenth Amendment: "While the Tenth Amendment has been characterized as a 'truism,' stating merely that 'all is retained which has not been surrendered,' United States v. Darby (1941), it is not without significance. The Amendment expressly declares the constitutional policy that Congress may not exercise power in a fashion that impairs the States' integrity or

their ability to function effectively in a federal system.''
. . .

In Metcalf & Eddy v. Mitchell (1926), the Court likewise observed that ''neither government may destroy the other nor curtail in any substantial manner the exercise of its powers.''

Appellee Secretary argues that the cases in which this Court has upheld sweeping exercises of authority by Congress, even though those exercises pre-empted state regulation of the private sector, have already curtailed the sovereignty of the States quite as much as the 1974 amendments to the Fair Labor Standards Act. We do not agree. It is one thing to recognize the authority of Congress to enact laws regulating individual business necessarily subject to the dual sovereignty of the government of the Nation and of the State in which they reside. It is quite another to uphold a similar exercise of congressional authority directed, not to private citizens, but to the States as States. We have repeatedly recognized that there are attributes of sovereignty attaching to every state government which may not be impaired by Congress, not because Congress may lack an affirmative grant of legislative authority to reach the matter, but because the Constitution prohibits it from exercising the authority in that manner. In Coyle v. Oklahoma [Smith] (1911), the Court gave this example of such an attribute:

''The power to locate its own seat of government and to determine when and how it shall be changed from one place to another, and to appropriate its own public funds for that purpose, are essentially and peculiarly state powers. That one of the original thirteen States could now be shorn of such powers by an act of Congress would not be for a moment entertained.''

One undoubted attribute of state sovereignty is the States' power to determine the wages which shall be paid to those whom they employ in order to carry out their governmental functions, what hours those persons will work, and what compensation will be provided where these employees may be called upon to work overtime. The question we must resolve here, then, is whether these determinations are '' 'functions essential to separate and independent existence,' '' so that Congress may not abrogate the States' otherwise plenary authority to make them.

In their complaint appellants advanced estimates of substantial costs which will be imposed upon them by the 1974 amendments. . . .

Judged solely in terms of increased costs in dollars, these allegations show a significant impact on the functioning of the governmental bodies involved. The Metropolitan Government of Nashville and Davidson County, Tenn., for example, asserted that the Act will increase its costs of providing essential police and fire protection, without any increase in service or in current salary levels, by $938,000 per year. . . .

Increased costs are not, of course, the only adverse effects which compliance with the Act will visit upon state and local governments, and in turn upon the citizens who depend upon those governments. In its complaint in intervention, for example, California asserted

that it could not comply with the overtime costs (approximately $750,000 per year) which the Act required to be paid to California Highway Patrol cadets during their academy training program. California reported that it had thus been forced to reduce its academy training program from 2,080 hours to only 960 hours, a compromise undoubtedly of substantial importance to those whose safety and welfare may depend upon the preparedness of the California Highway Patrol. . . .

Quite apart from the substantial costs imposed upon the States and their political subdivisions, the Act displaces state policies regarding the manner in which they will structure delivery of those governmental services which their citizens require. The Act, speaking directly to the States qua States, requires that they shall pay all but an extremely limited minority of their employees the minimum wage rates currently chosen by Congress. It may well be that as a matter of economic policy it would be desirable that States, just as private employers, comply with these minimum wage requirements. But it cannot be gainsaid that the federal requirement directly supplants the considered policy choices of the States' elected officials and administrators as to how they wish to structure pay scales in state employment. The State might wish to employ persons with little or no training, or those who wish to work on a casual basis, or those who for some other reason do not possess minimum employment requirements, and pay them less than the federally prescribed minimum wage. It may wish to offer part-time or summer employment to teenagers at a figure less than the minimum wage, and if unable to do so may decline to offer such employment at all. But the Act would forbid such choices by the States. . . .

. . . If Congress may withdraw from the States the authority to make those fundamental employment decisions upon which their systems for performance of these functions must rest, we think there would be little left of the States' '' 'separate and independent existence.' '' Coyle. Thus, even if appellants may have overestimated the effect which the Act will have upon their current levels and patterns of governmental activity, the dispositive factor is that Congress has attempted to exercise its Commerce Clause authority to prescribe minimum wages and maximum hours to be paid by the States in their capacities as sovereign governments. In so doing, Congress has sought to wield its power in a fashion that would impair the States' ''ability to function effectively in a federal system.'' Fry. This exercise of congressional authority does not comport with the federal system of government embodied in the Constitution. We hold that insofar as the challenged amendments operate to directly displace the States' freedom to structure integral operations in areas of traditional governmental functions, they are not within the authority granted Congress by Art. I, § 8, cl. 3.

III.

One final matter requires our attention. Appellee has vigorously urged that we cannot, consistently with the Court's decisions in Maryland v. Wirtz (1968), and

Fry, rule against him here. It is important to examine this contention so that it will be clear what we hold today, and what we do not. . . .

We think our holding today quite consistent with Fry. The enactment at issue there was occasioned by an extremely serious problem which endangered the well-being of all the component parts of our federal system and which only collective action by the National Government might forestall. The means selected were carefully drafted so as not to interfere with States' freedom beyond a very limited, specific period of time. . . . The limits imposed upon the commerce power when Congress seeks to apply it to the States are not so inflexible as to preclude temporary enactments tailored to combat a national emergency. . . .

With respect to the Court's decision in Wirtz, we reach a different conclusion. . . . There are undoubtedly factual distinctions between the two situations, but in view of the conclusions expressed earlier in this opinion we do not believe the reasoning in Wirtz may any longer be regarded as authoritative.

Wirtz relied heavily on the Court's decision in United States v. California (1936). The opinion quotes the following language from that case: " '[We] look to the activities in which the states have traditionally engaged as marking the boundary of the restriction upon the federal taxing power. But there is no such limitation upon the plenary power to regulate commerce. The state can no more deny the power if its exercise has been authorized by Congress than can an individual.' "

But we have reaffirmed today that the States as States stand on a quite different footing from an individual or a corporation when challenging the exercise of Congress' power to regulate commerce. We think the dicta* from United States v. California, simply wrong.† Congress may not exercise that power so as to force directly upon the States its choices as to how essential decisions regarding the conduct of integral governmental functions are to be made. . . .

While there are obvious differences between the schools and hospitals involved in Wirtz, and the fire and police departments affected here, each provides an integral portion of those governmental services which the States and their political subdivisions have traditionally afforded their citizens. We are therefore persuaded that Wirtz must be overruled. . . .

---

*The holding of United States v. California, as opposed to the language quoted in the texts, is quite consistent with our holding today. There California's activity to which the congressional command was directed was not in an area that the States have regarded as integral parts of their governmental activities. It was, on the contrary, the operation of a railroad engaged in "common carriage by rail in interstate commerce. . . ."

†Mr. Justice Brennan's dissent leaves no doubt from its discussion that in its view Congress may under its commerce power deal with the States as States just as they might deal with private individuals. We venture to say that it is this conclusion, rather than the one we reach, which is in the words of the dissent a "startling restructuring of our federal system. . . ."

Mr. Justice **Blackmun,** concurring, said in part:

I may misinterpret the Court's opinion, but it seems to me that it adopts a balancing approach, and does not outlaw federal power in areas such as environmental protection, where the federal interest is demonstrably greater and where state facility compliance with imposed federal standards would be essential. With this understanding on my part of the Court's opinion, I join it.

Mr. Justice **Brennan,** with whom Mr. Justice **White** and Mr. Justice **Marshall** join, dissenting, said in part:

My Brethren do not successfully obscure today's patent usurpation of the role reserved for the political process by their purported discovery in the Constitution of a restraint derived from sovereignty of the States on Congress' exercise of the commerce power. Mr. Chief Justice Marshall recognized that limitations "prescribed in the constitution," Gibbons v. Ogden [1824], restrain Congress' exercise of the power. . . . Thus laws within the commerce power may not infringe individual liberties protected by the First Amendment . . . or the Sixth Amendment. . . . But there is no restraint based on state sovereignty requiring or permitting judicial enforcement anywhere expressed in the Constitution; our decisions over the last century and a half have explicitly rejected the existence of any such restraint on the commerce power.

We said in United States v. California (1936), for example: "The sovereign power of the states is necessarily diminished to the extent of the grants of power to the federal government in the Constitution. . . . [T]he power of the state is subordinate to the constitutional exercise of the granted federal power." . . . "[It] is not a controversy between equals" when the Federal government "is asserting its sovereign power to regulate commerce. . . . [T]he interests of the nation are more important than those of any State." Sanitary District v. United States (1925). . . .

My Brethren thus have today manufactured an abstraction without substance, founded neither in the words of the Constitution nor on precedent. An abstraction having such profoundly pernicious consequences is not made less so by characterizing the 1974 amendments as legislation directed against the "States qua States." Of course, regulations that this Court can say are not regulations of "commerce" cannot stand, . . . and in this sense "[t]he Court has ample power to prevent . . . 'the utter destruction of the State as a sovereign political entity.' " Maryland v. Wirtz (1968). But my Brethren make no claim that the 1974 amendments are not regulations of "commerce"; rather they overrule Wirtz in disagreement with historic principles that United States v. California reaffirmed: "[W]hile the commerce power has limits, valid general regulations of commerce do not cease to be regulations of commerce because a State is involved. If a state is engaging in economic activities that are validly regulated by the Federal Government when engaged in by private persons, the State too may be forced to conform its activities to federal regulation.'' Wirtz. . . .

The reliance of my Brethren upon the Tenth Amendment as ''an express declaration of [a state sovereignty] limitation,'' not only suggests that they overrule governing decisions of this Court that address this question but must astound scholars of the Constitution. For not only early decisions, Gibbons v. Ogden, McCulloch v. Maryland, and Martin v. Hunter's Lessee, (1816), hold that nothing in the Tenth Amendment constitutes a limitation on congressional exercise of powers delegated by the Constitution to Congress. . . . Rather, as the Tenth Amendment's significance was more recently summarized:

''The amendment states but a truism that all is retained which has not been surrendered. *There is nothing in the history of its adoption to suggest that it was more than declaratory of the relationship between the national and state governments as it had been established by the Constitution before the amendment* or that its purpose was other than to allay fears that the new national government might seek to exercise powers not granted, and that the states might not be able to exercise fully their reserved powers. . . .'' . . . United States v. Darby (emphasis added). . . .

[The Court here discusses the rejection in Case v. Bowles (1946) of the idea that the war power was limited by state sovereignty. Among the cases relied on there was United States v. California.]

Even more significant for our purposes is the Court's citation of United States v. California, a case concerned with Congress' power to regulate commerce, as supporting the rejection of the State's contention that state sovereignty is a limitation on Congress' war power. California directly presented the question whether any state sovereignty restraint precluded application of the Federal Safety Appliance Act to a state-owned and -operated railroad. The State argued ''that as the state is operating the railroad without profit, for the purpose of facilitating the commerce of the port, and is using the net proceeds of operation for harbor improvement, . . . it is engaged in performing a public function in its sovereign capacity and for that reason cannot constitutionally be subjected to the provisions of the federal Act.'' Mr. Justice Stone rejected the contention in an opinion for a unanimous Court. His rationale is a complete refutation of today's holding: ''That in operating its railroad [the State] is acting within a power reserved to the states cannot be doubted. . . . The only question we need consider is whether the exercise of that power, in whatever capacity, must be in subordination to the power to regulate interstate commerce, which has been granted specifically to the national government. The sovereign power of the states is necessarily diminished to the extent of the grants of power to the federal government in the Constitution. . . .

''The analogy of the constitutional immunity of state instrumentalities from federal taxation, on which [California] relies, is not illuminating. That immunity is implied from the nature of our federal system and the re-lationship within it of state and national governments, and is equally a restriction on taxation by either of the instrumentalities of the other. Its nature requires that it be so construed as to allow to each government reasonable scope for its taxing power . . . which would be unduly curtailed if either by extending its activities could withdraw from the taxing power of the other subjects of taxation traditionally within it. . . . Hence, we look to the activities in which the states have traditionally engaged as marking the boundary of the restriction upon the federal taxing power. *But there is no such limitation upon the plenary power to regulate commerce. The state can no more deny the power if its exercise has been authorized by Congress than can an individual.*'' (emphasis added).

Today's repudiation of this unbroken line of precedents that firmly reject my Brethren's ill-conceived abstraction can only be regarded as a transparent cover for invalidating a congressional judgment with which they disagree. The only analysis even remotely resembling that adopted today is found in a line of opinions dealing with the Commerce Clause and the Tenth Amendment that ultimately provoked a constitutional crisis for the Court in the 1930's. E.g. Carter v. Carter Coal Co. (1936); United States v. Butler (1936); Hammer v. Dagenhart (1918). . . . It may have been the eventual abandonment of the overly restrictive construction of the commerce power that spelled defeat for the Court-packing plan, and preserved the integrity of this institution, see, e.g., United States v. Darby (1941); Mulford v. Smith (1939); NLRB v. Jones & Laughlin Steel Corp. (1937), but my Brethren today are transparently trying to cut back on that recognition of the scope of the commerce power. My Brethren's approach to this case is not far different from the dissenting opinions in the cases that averted the crisis. . . .

. . . I cannot recall another instance in the Court's history when the reasoning of so many decisions covering so long a span of time has been discarded in such a roughshod manner. That this is done without any justification not already often advanced and consistently rejected, clearly renders today's decision an ipse dixit reflecting nothing but displeasure with a congressional judgment.

My Brethren's treatment of Fry v. United States (1975), further illustrates the paucity of legal reasoning or principle justifying today's result. Although the Economic Stabilization Act ''displace[d] the States' freedom''—the reason given for invalidating the 1974 amendments—the result in Fry is not disturbed since the interference was temporary and only a national program enforced by the Federal Government could have alleviated the country's economic crisis. Thus, although my Brethren by fiat strike down the 1974 amendments without analysis of countervailing national considerations, Fry by contrary logic remains undisturbed because, on balance, countervailing national considerations override the interference with the State's freedom. Moreover, it is sophistry to say the Economic Stabilization Act ''displaced no state choices,'' but that the 1974 amendments do. Obviously the Stabilization Act—no less than every exercise of a national power delegated to Congress by the Constitution—displaced the State's freedom. It is absurd to suggest that there is a constitutionally significant distinction between curbs against increasing wages and curbs against paying wages lower than the federal minimum. . . .

A sense of the enormous impact of States' political power is gained by brief reference to the federal budget. The largest estimate by any of the appellants of the cost impact of the 1974 amendments—$1 billion—pales in comparison with the financial assistance the States receive from the Federal Government. In fiscal 1977 the President's proposed budget recommends $60.5 billion in federal assistance to the States, exclusive of loans. . . . Appellants complain of the impact of the amended FLSA on police and fire departments, but the 1977 budget contemplates outlays for law enforcement assistance of $716 million. Concern is also expressed about the diminished ability to hire students in the summer if States must pay them a minimum wage, but the Federal Government's "summer youth program" provides $400 million for 670,000 jobs. Given this demonstrated ability to obtain funds from the Federal Government for needed state services, there is little doubt that the States' influence in the political process is adequate to safeguard their sovereignty.

Mr. Justice **Stevens,** dissenting, said in part:

I agree that it is unwise for the federal Government to exercise its power in the ways described in the Court's opinion. For the proposition that regulation of the minimum price of a commodity—even labor—will increase the quantity consumed is not one that I can readily understand. That concern, however, applies with even greater force to the private sector of the economy where the exclusion of the marginally employable does the greatest harm and, in all events, merely reflects my views on a policy issue which has been firmly resolved by the branches of government having power to decide such questions.

GARCIA v. SAN ANTONIO METRO

469 U. S. 528; 105 S. Ct. 1005; 83 L. Ed. 2d
1016 (1985)

After Usery, a number of cases raising challenges under the Tenth Amendment came before the Court. In those cases the Court found unanimously that Congress was exercising its commerce power properly. But it was not until Equal Employment Opportunity Commission v. Wyoming (1983) that the Court again faced a problem that raised the issues of the Usery case. In 1974 Congress had amended the Age Discrimination in Employment Act to apply to the states and the EEOC brought suit under the act to protest the enforced retirement of a supervisor in the state's Fish and Game Department.

In a five-to-four decision the act was held validly applicable to the state. The Court reviewed the three-prong test of the Usery case that the law be directed at the state as a state, that it impinge on matters indisputably attributes of state sovereignty, and that state compliance with the law would impair its ability to structure "integral operations in areas of traditional functions." It conceded that the first part of the test was met, declined to resolve on the grounds of vagueness whether an undoubted attribute of state sovereignty was involved, but found that in view of the slight financial effect of the act and the flexibility still allowed the states in their retirement policies the act "does not 'directly impair' the State's ability to 'structure integral operations in areas of traditional governmental functions.' " In a sharp dissent Justices Burger, Powell, Rehnquist and O'Connor argued that the right to ensure the physical preparedness of game wardens was certainly an attribute of state sovereignty and that, in fact, the statute would cost the state money and prevent its hiring those physically best able to do the job.

Justice **Blackmun** delivered the opinion of the Court, saying in part:

We revisit in these cases an issue raised in National League of Cities v. Usery (1976). In that litigation, this Court, by a sharply divided vote, ruled that the Commerce Clause does not empower Congress to enforce the minimum-wage and overtime provisions of the Fair Labor Standards Act (FLSA) against the States "in areas of traditional governmental functions." Although National League of Cities supplied some examples of "traditional governmental functions," it did not offer a general explanation of how a "traditional" function is to be distinguished from a "nontraditional" one. Since then, federal and state courts have struggled with the task, thus imposed, of identifying a traditional function for purposes of state immunity under the Commerce Clause.

In the present cases, a Federal District Court concluded that municipal ownership and operation of a mass-transit system is a traditional governmental function and thus, under National League of Cities, is exempt from the obligations imposed by the FLSA. Faced with the identical question, three Federal Courts of Appeals and one state appellate court have reached the opposite conclusion.

Our examination of this "function" standard applied in these and other cases over the last eight years now persuades us that the attempt to draw the boundaries of state regulatory immunity in terms of "traditional governmental function" is not only unworkable but is inconsistent with established principles of federalism and, indeed, with those very federalism principles on which National League of Cities purported to rest. That case, accordingly, is overruled.

II.

Appellees have not argued that SAMTA [San Antonio Metropolitan Transit Authority] is immune from regulations under the FLSA on the ground that it is a local transit system engaged in intrastate commercial activity. In a practical sense, SAMTA's operation might well be characterized as "local." Nonetheless, it long has been settled that Congress' authority under the Commerce clause extends to intrastate economic activities that affect interstate commerce. . . . Heart of Atlanta Motel, Inc. v. United States (1964); . . . United States v. Darby (1941). . . . Were SAMTA a privately owned and operated enterprise, it could not credibly argue that Congress exceeded the bounds of its Commerce Clause powers in prescribing minimum wages and overtime rates for SAMTA's employees. Any constitutional exemption from the requirements of the FLSA therefore must rest on SAMTA's status as a governmental entity rather than on the "local" nature of its operations.

The prerequisites for governmental immunity under National League of Cities were summarized by this Court in Hodel [v. Virginia Surface Mining & Recl. Assn. (1981)]. Under that summary, four conditions must be satisfied before a state activity may be deemed immune from a particular federal regulation under the Commerce Clause. First, it is said that the federal statute at issue must regulate "the 'States as States.' " Second, the statute must "address matters that are indisputably "attribute[s] of state sovereignty.' " Third, state compliance with the federal obligation must "directly impair [the States'] ability 'to structure integral operations in areas of traditional governmental functions. 4 Finally, the relation of state and federal interests must not be such that "the nature of the federal interest . . . justifies state submission."

The controversy in the present cases has focused on the third Hodel requirement—that the challenged federal statute trench on "traditional governmental functions." The District Court voiced a common concern: "Despite the abundance of adjectives, identifying which particular state functions are immune remains difficult." Just how troublesome the task has been is revealed by the results reached in other federal cases. Thus, [lower federal] courts have held that regulating ambulance services . . . ; licensing automobile drivers . . . ; operating a municipal airport . . . ; performing solid waste disposal . . . ; and operating a highway authority . . . , are functions protected under National League of Cities. At the same time, court have held that issuance of industrial development bonds . . . ; regulation of intrastate natural gas sales . . . ; regulation of traffic on public roads . . . ; regulation of air transportation . . . ; operation of a telephone system . . . ; leasing and sale of natural gas . . . ; operation of a mental health facility . . . ; and provision of in-house domestic services for the aged and handicapped . . . , are not entitled to immunity. We find it difficult, if not impossible, to identify an organizing principle that places each of the cases in the first group on one side of a line and each of the cases in the second group on the other side. The constitutional distinction between licensing drivers and regulating traffic, for example, or between operating a highway authority and operating a mental health facility, is elusive at best.

Thus far, this Court itself has made little headway in defining the scope of the governmental functions deemed protected under National League of Cities. In that case the Court set forth examples of protected and unprotected functions, but provided no explanation of how those examples were identified. The only other case in which the Court has had occasion to address the problem is [Transportation Union v.] Long Island [1982]. We there observed: "The determination of whether a federal law impairs a state's authority with respect to 'areas of traditional [state] functions' may at times be a difficult one." The accuracy of that statement is demonstrated by this Court's own difficulties in Long Island in developing a workable standard for "traditional governmental function." We relied in large part there on "the historical reality that the operation of railroads is not among the functions traditionally performed by state and local governments," but we simultaneously disavowed "a static historical view of state functions generally immune from federal regulation." We held that the inquiry into a particular function's "traditional" nature was merely a means of determining whether the federal statute at issue unduly handicaps "basic state prerogatives," but we did not offer an explanation of what makes one state function a "basic prerogative" and another function not basic. Finally, having disclaimed a rigid reliance on the historical pedigree of state involvement in a particular area, we nonetheless found it appropriate to emphasize the extended historical record of federal involvement in the field of rail transportation.

Many constitutional standards involve "undoubte[d] . . . gray areas," and, despite the difficulties that this Court and other courts have encountered so far, it normally might be fair to venture the assumption that case-by-case development would lead to a workable standard for determining whether a particular governmental function should be immune from federal regulation under the Commerce Clause. A further cautionary note is sounded, however, by the Court's experience in the related field of state immunity from federal taxation. In South Carolina v. United States (1905), the Court held for the first time that the state tax immunity recognized in Collector v. Day, extended only to the "ordinary" and "strictly governmental" instrumentalities of state governments and not to instrumentalities "used by the State in the carrying on of an ordinary private business." While the Court applied the distinction outlined in South Carolina for the following 40 years, at no time during that period did the Court develop a consistent formulation of the kinds of governmental functions that were entitled to immunity. . . .

If these tax immunity cases had any common thread, it was in the attempt to distinguish between "governmental" and "proprietary" functions. To say that the distinction between "governmental" and "proprietary" proved to be stable, however, would be something of an overstatement. . . .

Even during the heyday of the governmental/proprietary distinction in intergovernmental tax immunity-doctrine the Court never explained the constitutional basis for that distinction. . . .

The distinction the Court discarded as unworkable in the field of tax immunity has proved no more fruitful in the field of regulatory immunity under the Commerce Clause. Neither do any of the alternative standards that might be employed to distinguish between protected and unprotected governmental functions appear manageable. We rejected the possibility of making immunity turn on a purely historical standard of "tradition" in Long Island, and properly so. The most obvious defect of a historical approach to state immunity is that it prevents a court from accommodating changes in the historical functions of States, changes that have resulted in a number of once-private functions like education being assumed by the States and their subdivisions. At the same time, the only apparent virtue of a rigorous historical standard, namely, its promise of a reasonably objective measure for state immunity, is illusory. Reliance on history as an organizing principle results in linedrawing of the most arbitrary sort; the genesis of state governmental functions stretches over a historical continuum from before the Revolution to the present, and courts would have to decide by fiat precisely how longstanding a pattern of state involvement had to be for federal regulatory authority to be defeated.* A nonhistorical standard for selecting immune governmental functions is likely to be just as unworkable as is a historical standard. The goal of identifying "uniquely" governmental functions, for example, has been rejected by the Court in the field of government tort liability in part because the notion of a "uniquely" governmental function is unmanageable. . . . Another possibility would be to confine immunity to "necessary" governmental services, that is, services that would be provided inadequately or not at all unless the government provided them. The set of services that fits into this category, however, may well be negligible. . . .

We believe, however, that there is a more fundamental problem at work here, a problem that explains why the Court was never able to provide a basis for the governmental/proprietary distinction in the intergovernmental tax immunity cases and why an attempt to draw similar distinctions with respect to federal regulatory authority under National League of Cities is unlikely to succeed regardless of how the distinctions are phrased. The problem is that neither the governmental/proprietary distinction nor any other that purports to separate out important governmental functions can be faithful to the role of federalism in a democratic society. The essence of our federal system is that within the realm of authority left open to them under the Constitution, the States must be equally free to engage in any activity that their citizens choose for the common weal, no matter how unorthodox or unnecessary anyone else—including the judiciary—deems state involvement to be. Any rule of state immunity that looks to the "traditional," "integral," or "necessary" nature of governmental functions inevitably invites an unelected federal judiciary to make decisions about which state policies it favors and which ones it dislikes. "The science of government . . . is the science of

---

*For much the same reasons, the existence vel non of a tradition of federal involvement in a particular area does not provide an adequate standard for state immunity. Most of the Federal Government's current regulatory activity originated less than 50 years ago with the New Deal, and a good portion of it has developed within the past two decades. The recent vintage of this regulatory activity does not diminish the strength of the federal interest in applying regulatory standards to state activities, nor does it affect the strength of the States' interest in being free from federal supervision. . . .

experiment," Anderson v. Dunn (1821), and the States cannot serve as laboratories for social and economic experiment . . . if they must pay an added price when they meet the changing needs of their citizenry by taking up functions that an earlier day and a different society left in private hands. . . .

We therefore now reject, as unsound in principle and unworkable in practice, a rule of state immunity from federal regulation that turns on a judicial appraisal of whether a particular governmental function is "integral" or "traditional." Any such rule leads to inconsistent results at the same time that it disserves principles of democratic self-governance, and it breeds inconsistency precisely because it is divorced from those principles. If there are to be limits on the Federal Government's power to interfere with state functions—as undoubtedly there are—we must look elsewhere to find them. We accordingly return to the underlying issue that confronted the Court in National League of Cities—the manner in which the Constitution insulates States from the reach of Congress' power under the Commerce Clause.

III.

The central theme of National League of Cities was that the States occupy a special position in our constitutional system and that the scope of Congress' authority under the Commerce Clause must reflect that position. Of course, the Commerce Clause by its specific language does not provide any special limitation on Congress' actions with respect to the States. . . . It is equally true, however, that the text of the Constitution provides the beginning rather than the final answer to every inquiry into questions of federalism, for "[b]ehind the words of the constitutional provisions are postulates which limit and control." . . . National League of Cities reflected the general conviction that the Constitution precludes, "the National Government [from] devouring the essentials of state sovereignty." Maryland v. Wirtz (dissenting opinion) [1968]. In order to be faithful to the underlying federal premises of the Constitution, courts must look for the "postulates which limit and control."

What has proved problematic is not the perception that the constitution's federal structure imposes limitations on the Commerce Clause, but rather the nature and content of those limitations. One approach . . . is to identify certain underlying elements of political sovereignty that are deemed essential to the States' "separate and independent existence." . . . This approach obviously underlay the Court's use of the "traditional governmental function" concept in National League of Cities. . . . In [that case], the Court concluded that decisions by a State concerning the wages and hours of its employees are an "undoubted attribute of state sovereignty." The opinion did not explain what aspects of such decision made them such an "undoubted attribute," and the Court since then has remarked on the uncertain scope of the concept. See EEOC v. Wyoming (1983). The point of the inquiry, however, has remained to single out, particular features of a State's internal governance that are deemed to be intrinsic parts of state sovereignty.

We doubt that courts ultimately can identify principled constitutional limitations on the scope of Congress' Commerce Clause powers over the States merely by relying on a priori definitions of state sovereignty. In part, this is because of the elusiveness of objective criteria for "fundamental" elements of state sovereignty, a problem we have witnessed in the search for "traditional governmental functions." There is, however, a more fundamental reason: the sovereignty of the States is limited by the Constitution itself. A variety of sovereign powers . . . are withdrawn from the States. . . .

The States unquestionably do "retai[n] a significant measure of sovereign authority." EEOC v. Wyoming (Powell, J., dissenting). They do so, however, only to the extent that the Constitution has not divested them of their original powers and transferred those powers to the Federal Government. . . .

As a result, to say that the Constitution assumes the continued role of the States is to say little about the nature of that role. Only recently, this Court recognized that the purpose of the constitutional immunity recognized in National League of Cities is not to preserve "a sacred province of state autonomy." EEOC v. Wyoming. . . .

When we look for the States' "residuary and inviolable sovereignty," The Federalist No. 39 (J. Madison), in the shape of the constitutional scheme rather than in predetermined notions of sovereign power, a different measure of state sovereignty emerges. Apart from the limitation on federal authority inherent in the delegated nature of Congress' Article I powers, the principal means chosen by the Framers to ensure the role of the States in the federal system lies in the structure of the Federal Government itself. It is no novelty to observe that the composition of the Federal Government was designed in large part to protect the States from overreaching by Congress. The Framers thus gave the States a role in the selection both of the Executive and the Legislative Branches of the Federal Government. The States were vested with indirect influence over the House of Representatives and the Presidency by their control of electoral qualifications and their role in presidential election. U. S. Const. Art. I, § 2, and Art. II, § 1. They were given more direct influence in the Senate, where each State received equal representation and each Senator was to be selected by the legislature of his State. Art. I, § 3. The significance attached to the States' equal representation in the Senate is underscored by the prohibition of any constitutional amendment divesting a State of equal representation without the State's consent. Art. V.

The extent to which the structure of the Federal Government itself was relied on to insulate the interests of the States is evident in the views of the Framers. . . . The Framers chose to rely on a federal system in which special restraints on federal power over the States inhered principally in the workings of the National Government itself, rather than in discrete limitations on the objects of federal authority. State sovereign interests, then, are more properly protected by procedural safeguards inherent in the structure of the federal system than by judicially created limitations on federal power.

The effectiveness of the federal political process in preserving the States' interests is apparent even today in the course of federal legislation. . . . At the same time that the States have exercised their influence to obtain federal support, they have been able to exempt themselves from a wide variety of obligations imposed by congress under the Commerce Clause. For example, the Federal Power Act, the National Labor Relations Act, the Labor-Management Reporting and Disclosure Act, the Occupational Safety and Health Act, the Employee Retirement Insurance Act, and the Sherman Act all contain express or implied exemptions for States and their subdivisions. The fact that some federal statutes such as FLSA extend general obligations to the States cannot obscure the extent to which the political position of the States in the federal system has served to minimize the burdens that the States bear under the Commerce Clause.

We realize that changes in the structure of the Federal Government have taken place since 1789, not the least of which has been the substitution of popular election of Senators by the adoption of the Seventeenth Amendment in 1913, and that these changes may work to alter the influence of the States in the federal political process. Nonetheless, against this background, we are convinced that the fundamental limitation that the constitutional scheme imposes on the Commerce Clause to protect the "States as States" is one of process rather than one of result. Any substantive restraint on the exercise of Commerce Clause powers must find its justification in the procedural nature of this basic limitation, and it must be tailored to compensate for possible failings in the political process rather than to dictate a "sacred province of state autonomy." EEOC v. Wyoming.

In so far as the present cases are concerned, then, we need go no further than to state that we perceive nothing in the overtime and minimum-wage requirements of the FLSA, as applied to SAMTA, that is destructive of state sovereignty or violative of any constitutional provision. SAMTA faces nothing more than the same minimum-wage and overtime obligations that hundreds of thousands of other employers, public as well as private, have to meet. . . .

IV.

This analysis makes clear that Congress' action in affording SAMTA employees the protections of the wage and hour provisions of FLSA contravened no affirmative limit on Congress' power under the Commerce Clause. The judgment of the District Court therefore must be reversed.

Of course, we continue to recognize that the States occupy a special and specific position in our constitutional system and that the scope of Congress' authority under the Commerce Clause must reflect that position. But the principal and basic limit on the federal commerce power is that inherent in all congressional action—the built-in restraints that our system provides through state participation in federal governmental action. The political process ensures that laws that unduly burden the States will not be promulgated. In the factual setting of these cases the internal safeguards of the political process have performed as intended.

These cases do not require us to identify or define

what affirmative limits the constitutional structure might impose on federal action affecting the States under the Commerce Clause. . . .

Though the separate concurrence providing the fifth vote in National League of Cities was "not untroubled by certain possible implications" of the decision, the Court in that case attempted to articulate affirmative limits on the Commerce Clause power in terms of core governmental functions and fundamental attributes of state sovereignty. But the model of democratic decisionmaking the Court there identified underestimated, in our view, the solicitude of the national political process for the continued vitality of the States. Attempts by other courts since then to draw guidance from this model have proved it both impracticable and doctrinally barren. In sum, in National League of Cities the Court tried to repair what did not need repair.

We do not lightly overrule recent precedent. . . . Due respect for the reach of congressional power within the federal system mandates that we do so now. National League of Cities v. Usery (1976) is overruled. The judgment of the District Court is reversed. . . .

Justice **Powell,** with whom the **Chief Justice,** Justice **Rehnquist,** and Justice **O'Connor** join, dissenting, said in part:

The Court today, in its 5–4 decision, overrules National League of Cities v. Usery, a case in which we held that Congress lacked authority to impose the requirements of the Fair Labor Standards Act on state and local governments. Because I believe this decision substantially alters the federal system embodied in the Constitution, I dissent.

I.

There are, of course, numerous examples over the history of this Court in which prior decisions have been reconsidered and overruled. There have been few cases, however, in which the principle of stare decisis and the rationale of recent decisions were ignored as abruptly as we now witness. . . .

Although the doctrine is not rigidly applied to constitutional questions, "any departure from the doctrine of stare decisis demands special justification." . . . In the present case, the five Justices who compose the majority today participated in National League of Cities and the cases reaffirming it. The stability of judicial decision, and with it respect for the authority of this Court, are not served by the precipitous overruling of multiple precedents that we witness in this case.

Whatever effect the Court's decision may have in weakening the application of stare decisis, it is likely to be less important than what the Court has done to the Constitution itself. A unique feature of the United States is the *federal* system of government guaranteed by the Constitution and implicit in the very name of our country. Despite some genuflecting in the Court's opinion to the concept of federalism, today's decision effectively reduces the Tenth Amendment to meaningless

rhetoric when Congress acts pursuant to the Commerce Clause. . . .

II. . . .

B.

Today's opinion does not explain how the States' role in the electoral process guarantees that particular exercises of the Commerce Clause power will not infringe on residual State sovereignty.* Members of Congress are elected from the various States, but once in office they are members of the federal government. Although the States participate in the Electoral College, this is hardly a reason to view the President as a representative of the States' interest against federal encroachment. . . .

. . . At least since Marbury v. Madison [1803] it has been the settled province of the federal judiciary "to say what the law is" with respect to the constitutionality of acts of Congress. In reflecting the role of the judiciary in protecting the States from federal overreaching, the Court's opinion offers no explanation for ignoring the teaching of the most famous case in our history. . . .

III. . . .

D.

. . . The Court today propounds a view of federalism that pays only lip service to the role of the States. . . . Indeed, the Court barely acknowledges that the Tenth Amendment exists.† That Amendment states explicitly that "[t]he powers not delegated to the United States . . . are reserved to the States." U. S. Const. Amend. 10. The Court recasts this language to say that the States retain their sovereign powers "only to the extent that the Constitution has not divested them of their original powers and transferred those powers to the Federal Government." This rephrasing is not a distinction without a difference; rather, it reflects the Court's unprecedented view that Congress is free under the Commerce Clause to assume a State's traditional sovereign power, and to do so without judicial review of its action. Indeed, the Court's view of federalism appears to relegate the States to precisely the trivial role that opponents of the Constitution feared they would occupy.

Justice **Rehnquist** wrote a dissenting opinion.

Justice **O'Connor** wrote a dissenting opinion with which Justice **Powell** and Justice **Rehnquist** joined.

---

*Late in its opinion, the Court suggests that after all there may be some "affirmative limits the constitutional structure might impose on federal action affecting the States under the Commerce Clause." . . . The Court's failure to specify the "affirmative limits" on federal power, or when and how these limits are to be determined, may well be explained by the transparent fact that any such attempt would be subject to precisely the same objections on which it relies to overrule National League of Cities.

†The Court's opinion mentions the Tenth Amendment only once, when it restates the question put to the parties for reargument in these cases.

6

Basis and Growth of a National Police Power

THE TAX POWER

HYLTON v. UNITED STATES

3 Dallas 171; 1 L. Ed. 556 (1796)

So accustomed are we to the Internal Revenue Service knocking on our door every April 15th that we forget that there was a time when there was no income tax. The economic requirements of the government were small and what was needed was raised by excise taxes on items like liquor and tobacco, and on duties on goods imported from abroad. The Convention of 1787 disagreed upon many things, but they were virtually unanimous that the Congress of the new national government should have the power to lay and collect taxes. That heads the list of delegated powers. But the power to tax is a potent economic weapon, and the framers sought to make sure that it could not be used to the advantage of some states at the expense of others. To accomplish this they provided that direct taxes (as well as representatives) should be apportioned among the states on the basis of population. Concretely this means that Congress in levying a direct tax must decide in advance how much money it wishes to raise. The sum is then assessed against the states on the basis of the ratio which each state's population bears to the population of the nation. Since the number of a state's seats in the House of Representatives (with certain exceptions) is computed in this way, a state's share

of a direct tax would be approximately the same share that its delegation bears to the total size of the House.

The carriage tax challenged in the present case had been bitterly opposed by the Anti-Federalists in Virginia who owned ten carriages to the New Englander's one. It was exactly the kind of tax the apportionment rule was designed to discourage, since the New Englander with his one carriage, living in a more densely populated state, would pay a much greater share of the tax and a very much higher tax per carriage than would his fellow Virginian. It was this very inequity that had been counted on to prevent the passage of such taxes, but it had been passed on the assumption it was an indirect tax and if the courts agreed the burden of the tax would fall most heavily on the Virginians.

The case is remarkable in a number of ways. First, it confronted the Court for the first time with the duty of deciding whether a law passed by Congress was constitutional or not; the Court upheld the law rather than invalidate it as it did in Marbury v. Madison (1803). Second, the case was so obviously trumped up that no modern court would consider taking it. Hylton owned one carriage on which he owed a tax of $16. Hamilton, as Secretary of the Treasury, was anxious to have the validity of the carriage tax established, but the $16 was far short of the $2000 necessary to give the circuit court jurisdiction. Accordingly Hylton and the Treasury Department entered into a stipulation that Hylton owned the astounding number of "125 chariots . . . kept exclusively for the defendant's own private use, and not to let out to

*hire, or for the conveyance of personal [sic] for hire.
. . ." This brought the amount of the tax to $2000,
which the Treasury promised could be discharged by the
payment of $16. Third, when the circuit court divided
evenly in its decision, Hylton's enthusiasm waned; and
the Treasury, in order to bring the issue before the Supreme Court, agreed to pay all the costs of the appeal.
Fourth, the case was decided by only three of the six justices on the Court; and Alexander Hamilton, who had
just retired as Secretary of the Treasury, argued the case
as special counsel for the government.*

*Only five times has Congress resorted to the com-
plicated plan of apportioning direct taxes, the last being
in 1861 during the Civil War. This tax, levied on real
property and household furnishings, was apportioned to
include the seceded states on the theory that they were
still in the Union; and the attempts to collect it were so
unsuccessful that in 1891 Congress reimbursed those
states who had paid.*

*While the Court now receives over 5000 requests
for review a year, in the first few years of its existence
the Court had almost no business—one year the term
lasted only three days. With no precedents to guide it, it
developed its procedures as it went along. In the "pre-
Marshall" period of the Supreme Court's history, each
justice of the Court wrote a separate opinion announcing
his decision in the case and his reasons for it. These
were called "seriatim" opinions. In the Hylton case, the
earliest case included in this book, they were as follows:*

Chase, Justice, said in part:

The Constitution evidently contemplated no taxes
as direct taxes, but only such as Congress could lay in
proportion to the census. The rule of apportionment is
only to be adopted in such cases where it can reasonably
apply; and the subject taxed must ever determine the application of the rule.

If it is proposed to tax any specific article by the
rule of apportionment and it would evidently create great
inequality and injustice, it is unreasonable to say that the
Constitution intended such tax should be laid by that
rule.

It appears to me that a tax on carriages cannot be
laid by the rule of apportionment, without very great inequality and injustice. For example, suppose two States
equal in census, to pay 80,000 dollars [$80,000] each,
by a tax of 8 dollars on every carriage, and in one State
there are 100 carriages, and in the other 1,000. The owners of carriages in one State would pay ten times the tax
of owners in the other. A, in one State, would pay for his
carriage 8 dollars; but B, in the other State, would pay
for his carriage; 80 dollars. . . .

I think an annual tax on carriages for the conveyance of persons, may be considered as within the power
granted to Congress to lay duties. The term duty is the
most comprehensive next to the generical term tax; and
practically in Great Britain, whence we take our general
ideas of taxes, duties, imposts, excises, customs, etc.,
embraces taxes on stamps, tolls for passage, etc., etc.,
and is not confined to taxes on importation only.

It seems to me that a tax on expense is an indirect
tax; and I think an annual tax on a carriage for the conveyance of persons, is of that kind; because a carriage is
a consumable commodity, and such annual tax on it is on
the expense of the owner.

I am inclined to think, but of this I do not give a
judicial opinion, that the direct taxes contemplated by
the Constitution, are only two, to wit, a capitation or poll
tax, simply without regard to property, profession, or
any other circumstance; and a tax on land,—I doubt
whether a tax, by a general assessment of personal property, within the United States, is included within the
term direct tax.

As I do not think the tax on carriages is a direct
tax, it is unnecessary at this time for me to determine
whether this court constitutionally possesses the power
to declare an Act of Congress void, on the ground of its
being made contrary to, and in violation of the Constitution; but if the court have such power, I am free to declare, that I will never exercise it but in a very clear case.
. . .

Paterson, Justice, said in part:

. . . What are direct taxes within the meaning of
the Constitution? The Constitution declares that a capitation tax is a direct tax; and both in theory and practice, a
tax on land is deemed to be a direct tax. In this way, the
terms direct taxes, and capitation and other direct tax,
are satisfied. It is not necessary to determine, whether a
tax on the product of land be a direct or indirect tax. Perhaps the immediate product of land, in its original and
crude state, ought to be considered as the land itself; it
makes part of it; or else the provision made against
taxing exports would be easily eluded. Land, independently of its produce, is of no value. When the produce is
converted into a manufacture it assumes a new shape; its
nature is altered; its original state is changed, it becomes
quite another subject, and will be differently considered.
Whether direct taxes, in the sense of the Constitution,
comprehend any other tax than a capitation tax, and tax
on land, is a questionable point. If Congress, for instance, should tax, in the aggregate or mass, things that
generally pervade all the states in the Union, then perhaps the rule of apportionment would be the most
proper, especially if an assessment was to intervene.
This appears, by the practice of some of the states, to
have been considered as a direct tax. Whether it be so
under the Constitution of the United States is a matter of
some difficulty; but as it is not before the court, it would
be improper to give any decisive opinion upon it. I never
entertained a doubt that the principal, I will not say the
only objects, that the framers of the Constitution contemplated as falling within the rule of apportionment, were a
capitation tax and a tax on land. Local considerations,
and the particular circumstances and relative situation of
the States, naturally lead to this view of the subject. The
provision was made in favor of the southern states. They
possessed a large number of slaves; they had extensive
tracts of territory, thinly settled and not very productive.

A majority of the States had but few slaves, and several of them a limited territory, well settled, and in a high state of cultivation. The southern states, if no provision had been introduced in the Constitution, would have been wholly at the mercy of the other states. Congress in such case might tax slaves, at discretion or arbitrarily, and land in every part of the Union after the same rate or measure; so much a head in the first instance, and so much an acre in the second. To guard them against imposition, in these particulars, was the reason of introducing the clause in the Constitution which directs that representatives and direct taxes shall be apportioned among the states according to their respective numbers. . . .

All taxes on expenses or consumption are indirect taxes; a tax on carriages is of this kind, and of course, is not a direct tax. Indirect taxes are circuitous modes of reaching the revenue of individuals, who generally live according to their income. In many cases of this nature the individual may be said to tax himself. . . .

I am, therefore, of opinion that the judgment rendered in the Circuit Court of Virginia ought to be affirmed.

Iredell, Justice, said in part:

I agree in opinion with my brothers, who have already expressed theirs, that the tax in the question is agreeable to the Constitution; and the reasons which have satisfied me can be delivered in a very few words, since I think the Constitution itself affords a clear guide to decide the controversy.

The Congress possess the power of taxing all taxable objects, without limitation, with the particular exception of a duty on exports.

There are two restrictions only on the exercise of this authority.

1. All direct taxes must be apportioned.
2. All duties, imposts, and excises must be uniform.

If the carriage tax be a direct tax, within the meaning of the Constitution, it must be apportioned. If it be a duty, impost, or excise, within the meaning of the Constitution, it must be uniform.

If it can be considered as a tax, neither direct within the meaning of the Constitution, nor comprehended within the term duty, impost, or excise; there is no provision in the constitution, one way or another, and then it must be left to such an operation of the power, as if the authority to lay taxes had been given generally in all instances, without saying whether they should be apportioned or uniform; and in that case, I should presume, the tax ought to be uniform; because the present constitution was particularly intended to affect individuals, and not states, except in particular cases specified; and this is the leading distinction between the articles of confederation and the present constitution.

As all direct taxes must be apportioned, it is evident that the constitution contemplated none as direct but such as could be apportioned.

If this cannot be apportioned, it is, therefore, not a direct tax in the sense of the constitution.

That this tax cannot be apportioned is evident. Suppose 10 dollars contemplated as a tax on each chariot, or post chaise, in the United States, and the number of both in all the United States be computed at 105, the number of representatives in Congress.

This would produce in the whole..........................		1050.00
The share of Virginia being 19/105 parts, would be................. Dollars	190.00	
The share of Connecticut being 7/105 parts, would be	70.00	
Then suppose Virginia had 50 carriages, Connecticut 2,		
The share of Virginia being 190 dollars, this must of course be collected from the owners of carriages, and there would therefore be collected from each carriage		3.80
The share of Connecticut being 70 dollars, each carriage would pay..............................		35.00

If any state had no carriages, there could be no apportionment at all. This mode is too manifestly absurd to be supported, and has not even been attempted in debate. . . .

There is no necessity or propriety in determining what is, or is not a direct or indirect tax in all cases.

Some difficulties may occur which we do not at present foresee. Perhaps a direct tax, in the sense of the constitution, can mean nothing but a tax on something inseparably annexed to the soil, something capable of apportionment under all such circumstances.

A land or a poll tax may be considered of this description.

The latter is to be considered so particularly under the present constitution, on account of the slaves in the southern states, who give a ratio in the representation in the proportion of three to five.

Either of these is capable of apportionment. In regard to other articles there may possibly be considerable doubt.

It is sufficient, on the present occasion, for the court to be satisfied that this is not a direct tax contemplated by the constitution, in order to affirm the present judgment; since, if it cannot be apportioned, it must necessarily be uniform.

I am clearly of opinion this is not a direct tax in the sense of the constitution, and, therefore, that the judgment ought to be affirmed. . . .

By the Court: Let the judgment of the circuit court be affirmed.

Wilson, Justice, who had sat in the court below and therefore did not sit in the case: . . . My sentiments, in favor of the constitutionality of the tax in question, have not been changed.

Mr. Chief Justice **Ellsworth** and Mr. Justice **Cushing** did not participate in the decision.

POLLOCK v. FARMERS' LOAN & TRUST COMPANY

158 U.S. 601; 15 S. Ct. 912; 39 L. Ed. 1108
(1895)

The decision in the Hylton case (1796) that a carriage tax was an excise was of no lasting practical significance, but the dictum of the justices that direct taxes comprised only taxes on land and capitation taxes was of far-reaching importance. During the Civil War, Congress, badly in need of money, enacted the first national income tax law. Was this tax, levied on income, gains, and profits, a direct tax? Springer, a lawyer upon whom the tax had been levied, argued that it was. Relying on generally accepted theories of political economy, Springer argued that a tax which hit an individual directly and could not be passed on was a direct tax, in contrast to an indirect tax on manufacture or sales which could be passed on to the ultimate consumer in the form of higher prices. In Springer v. United States (1881) the Supreme Court rejected this economic definition of a direct tax in favor of the judicial-historical definition, and quoting at length from Hylton v. United States, held the income tax to be an excise: "Our conclusions are, that direct taxes, within the meaning of the Constitution, are only capitation taxes, as expressed in that instrument, and taxes on real estate; and that the tax of which the plaintiff in error complains is within the category of an excise or duty." Congress repealed the act five years after the war.

More than twenty years passed before Congress again enacted an income tax law, the legality of which was decided in the present case. In 1894, fulfilling promises made in the campaign of 1892, a Democratic Congress passed a law that levied an income tax graduated to the extent that it exempted incomes under $4000 and taxed those above at 2 percent. Subject to the tax were incomes from (1) real estate, (2) stocks, bonds, and other securities, (3) state and municipal bonds, and (4) wages, salaries, and professional earnings. Adopted and defended as a measure to relieve the victims of the panic of 1893 and to shift most of the tax burden to the wealthy, the act was bitterly denounced as socialistic; and capital industry girded its loins for a last-ditch fight in the Supreme Court. Ignoring a well-established principle that taxes can be contested only after they have been paid, the Supreme Court agreed to hear on appeal a suit in which a stockholder sought to enjoin a bank from paying the new tax. The best legal talent of the country was brought into the case, and the Court heard argument twice, one justice being ill during the first argument. In a five-to-four decision, one unidentified justice having switched over on the second argument, the Court held the income tax law invalid. The provision taxing income derived from wages, salaries, and professional earnings was declared valid as an excise, but under the rule governing the partial unconstitutionality of statutes, the entire act was held void.

The adoption of the Sixteenth Amendment in 1912 gave Congress power to tax incomes from whatever source derived, but the wording of the amendment raised certain difficulties. The decision in the Pollock case, which was generally construed to mean that income taxes were direct taxes and must therefore be apportioned, seemed to infer that they were not excise taxes which had to be uniform, since obviously they could not be both at once. But with the removal by the Sixteenth Amendment of the requirement of apportionment, the income tax was not required to be either uniform or apportioned. The Court extracted itself from this apparent dilemma in Brushaber v. Union Pacific R. Co. (1916). Chief Justice White, in one of his famous nonstop sentences, solved the problem to the satisfaction of everyone. He said: "Moreover, in addition, the conclusion reached in the Pollock Case did not in any degree involve holding that income taxes generically and necessarily came within the class of direct taxes on property, but, on the contrary, recognized the fact that taxation on income was in its nature an excise entitled to be enforced as such unless and until it was concluded that to enforce it would amount to accomplishing the result which the requirement as to apportionment of direct taxation was adopted to prevent, in which case the duty would arise to disregard form and consider substance alone, and hence subject the tax to the regulation as to apportionment which otherwise as an excise would not apply to it." What this means is that income taxes are now returned to the status of excise taxes, which must be "uniform throughout the United States."

The language of the Sixteenth Amendment, authorizing Congress to tax incomes "from whatever source derived," raised other issues. Could Congress subject federal judges to income taxation on their salaries, in the face of the clause in Article III forbidding diminution of such judicial salaries? In Evans v. Gore (1920) the Court held it could not, although Justice Holmes urged in dissent that such salaries were "income from whatever source derived." It was also responsibly urged that this phrase in the amendment destroyed the immunity from federal taxation of income from state and municipal bonds, an immunity established in the Pollock case. Again it was plausibly argued that the income from these bonds fell within the meaning of the phrase "income from whatever source derived." The Court's language in Evans v. Gore has been accepted as the answer to these problems. The words "from whatever source derived" are not to be construed literally, but rather in the context of the purpose of Congress in drafting the Sixteenth Amendment. The Court said: ". . . The genesis and words of the Amendment unite in showing that it does not extend the taxing power to new or excepted subjects, but merely removes all occasion otherwise existing for an apportionment among the states of taxes laid on income, whether derived from one source or another." While there has been no judicial utterance on the precise point, income from state and municipal bonds remains immune from federal taxation, and Congress has acquiesced in this result.

While the Constitution requires that direct taxes shall be apportioned, it also says that "duties, imposts, and excises shall be uniform throughout the United States." In 1882 Congress had passed "An Act to Regulate Immigration" which levied a tax of 50 cents on ev-

ery alien immigrant passenger arriving by steam or sail vessel, the tax to be collected from the master of the vessel involved. In the Head Money Cases (1884), a number of steamship companies challenged the uniformity of the tax because it was not exacted from those bringing in alien passengers by rail, carriage, horse, or rowboat. Although the Court held that the levy in question was a regulation of commerce rather than a tax, in a famous dictum it pointed out that uniformity means geographical uniformity: "The tax is uniform when it operates with the same force and effect in every place where the subject of it is found. The tax in this case, which, as far as it can be called a tax, is an excise duty on the business of bringing passengers from foreign countries into this by ocean navigation, is uniform and operates precisely alike in every port of the United States where such passengers can be landed."

The decision of the Court in Knowlton v. Moore (1900) reaffirmed this statement. A congressional inheritance tax which varied with the amount of the inheritance and the closeness of the relationship of the heir was held to be uniform, since "what the Constitution commands is the imposition of a tax by the rule of geographical uniformity, not that in order to levy such a tax objects must be selected which exist uniformly in the several states." The argument that the statute violated the "uniformity" requirement of the Constitution was grounded on the theory that "uniformity" means "intrinsic" uniformity. This theory would require that all persons to whom the tax applied would be subject to identical rates, exemptions, etc., and the modern principle of "progressive rates of taxation," embodied in virtually all modern tax statutes, would be completely outlawed.

Mr. Chief Justice **Fuller** delivered the opinion of the Court, saying in part:

As heretofore stated, the Constitution divided federal taxation into two great classes, the class of direct taxes and the class of duties, imposts, and excises and prescribed two rules which qualified the grant of power as to each class.

The power to lay direct taxes, apportioned among the several States in proportion to their representation in the popular branch of Congress, a representation based on population as ascertained by the census, was plenary and absolute, but to lay direct taxes without apportionment was forbidden. The power to lay duties, imposts, and excises was subject to the qualification that the imposition must be uniform throughout the United States.

Our previous decision was confined to the consideration of the validity of the tax on the income from real estate and on the income from municipal bonds. The question thus limited, was whether such taxation was direct or not, in the meaning of the Constitution, and the court went no further as to the tax on the incomes from real estate than to hold that it fell within the same class as the source whence the income was derived, that is, that a tax upon the realty and a tax upon the receipts therefrom were alike direct; while as to the income from municipal bonds, that could not be taxed, because of want of power

to tax the source, and no reference was made to the nature of the tax being direct or indirect.

We are now permitted to broaden the field of inquiry and determine to which of the two great classes a tax upon a person's entire income, whether derived from rents or products or otherwise, of real estate, or from bonds, stocks or other forms of personal property, belongs; and we are unable to conclude that the enforced subtraction from the yield of all the owner's real or personal property, in the manner prescribed, is so different from a tax upon the property itself that it is not a direct but an indirect tax in the meaning of the Constitution. . . .

We know of no reason for holding otherwise than that the words "direct taxes" on the one hand, and "duties, imposts, and excises" on the other, were used in the Constitution in their natural and obvious sense, nor, in arriving at what those terms embrace, do we perceive any ground for enlarging them beyond, or narrowing them within, their natural and obvious import at the time the Constitution was framed and ratified. . . .

Whatever the speculative views of political economists or revenue reformers may be, can it be properly held that the Constitution, taken in its plain and obvious sense, and with due regard to the circumstances attending the formation of the government, authorizes a general unapportioned tax on the products of the farm and the rents of real estate, although imposed merely because of ownership and with no possible means of escape from payment, as belonging to a totally different class from that which includes the property from whence the income proceeds?

There can be only one answer, unless the constitutional restriction is to be treated as utterly illusory and futile, and the object of its framers defeated. We find it impossible to hold that a fundamental requisition, deemed so important as to be enforced by two provisions, one affirmative and one negative, can be refined away by forced distinctions between that which gives value to property and the property itself.

Nor can we conceive any ground why the same reasoning does not apply to capital in personalty held for the purpose of income or ordinarily yielding income, and to the income therefrom. All the real estate of the country, and all its invested personal property, are open to the direct operation of the taxing power if an apportionment be made according to the Constitution. . . .

The stress of the argument is thrown, however, on the assertion that an income tax is not a property tax at all; that it is not a real estate tax, nor a crop tax, nor a bond tax; that it is an assessment upon the taxpayer on account of his money-spending power as shown by his revenue for the year preceding the assessment; that rents received, crops harvested, interest collected, have lost all connection with their origin, and although once not taxable have become transmuted in their new form into taxable subject-matter; in other words, that income is taxable irrespective of the source whence it is derived. . . .

We have unanimously held in this case that, so far as this law operates on the receipts from municipal bonds, it cannot be sustained because it is a tax on the power of the States, and on their instrumentalities to borrow money, and consequently repugnant to the Constitution. But if, as contended, the interest when received has become merely money in the recipient's pocket, and taxable as such without reference to the source from which it came, the question is immaterial whether it should have been originally taxed at all or not. This was admitted by the Attorney General with characteristic candor; and it follows that, if the revenue derived from municipal bonds cannot be taxed because the source cannot be, the same rule applies to revenue from any other source not subject to the tax; and the lack of power to levy any but an apportioned tax on real estate and personal property equally exists as to the revenue therefrom.

Admitting that this Act taxes the income of property irrespective of its source, still we cannot doubt that such a tax is necessarily a direct tax in the meaning of the Constitution. . . .

Our conclusions may, therefore, be summed up as follows:

First. We adhere to the opinion already announced, that, taxes on real estate being indisputably direct taxes, taxes on the rents or incomes of real estate are equally direct taxes.

Second. We are of opinion that taxes on personal property, or on the income of personal property, are likewise direct taxes.

Third. The tax imposed by sections twenty-seven to thirty-seven, inclusive, of the act of 1894, so far as it falls on the income of real estate and of personal property, being a direct tax within the meaning of the Constitution, and, therefore, unconstitutional and void because not apportioned according to representation, all those sections, constituting one entire scheme of taxation, are necessarily invalid.

The decrees hereinbefore entered in this court will be vacated; the decrees below will be reversed, and the case remanded, with instructions to grant the relief prayed.

Mr. Justice **Harlan,** Mr. Justice **Brown,** Mr. Justice **Jackson,** and Mr. Justice **White** delivered dissenting opinions.

BAILEY v. DREXEL FURNITURE COMPANY

259 U. S. 20; 42 S. Ct. 449; 66 L. Ed. 817(1922)

In its holding in the McCray case (1904) the Court expressed neither approval nor disapproval of the use by Congress of its taxing power to regulate or destroy things lying outside its delegated powers, though we know that Justice White strongly disapproved. The Court merely refused to examine the motives of Congress in order to determine whether they were lawful motives or not. Inevitably, Congress was encouraged to feel that it now had in the taxing power a device for controlling or prohibiting a number of interests and activities which it could validly reach in no other way.

Therefore, following the disappointment of the Su-preme Court's decision in the case of Hammer v. Dagenhart (1918), it was natural for the opponents of child labor who sought a constitutional basis for the enactment of a new child labor law to turn their attention to the taxing clause. Here they felt they would be on safer ground. Accordingly there emerged after some debate the child labor tax provision of the general Revenue Act of February 24, 1919. This imposed a 10 percent excise tax upon the annual net income of mines, quarries, factories, and other establishments which during any portion of the taxable year employed children contrary to the regulations established. These regulations as to age, hours, and days of labor, etc. were identical with those in the first Child Labor Act. The Drexel Furniture Company permitted a boy under the age of fourteen years to work in its factory during the taxable year 1919. It received notice from Bailey, who was United States collector of internal revenue for the district, that the firm would be assessed 10 percent of its net income for the year, or $6,312.79, under the provisions of the child labor tax act. It paid the tax under protest and brought suit to recover the amount of the tax upon the ground that the law imposing it was unconstitutional. The Supreme Court in the present case held that it was, establishing the doctrine that when Congress levies taxes which the Court can clearly see are penalties rather than taxes, they can be held void. Thus the Bailey case established an important check upon the exercise by Congress of its taxing power for police purposes.

Can the McCray case and the Bailey case be distinguished on rational grounds? Superficially they may seem to be in conflict, and yet neither has been overruled. The Court has insisted that there is a real difference between them, and that difference could be stated as follows: there was nothing in the language of the statute taxing colored oleomargarine 10 cents a pound to disclose to the Court that Congress was really trying to cripple or destroy the oleomargarine business. Ten cents per pound on oleomargarine ''looks'' just like the tax of 18 cents per pound on smoking tobacco found in the same statute. On what basis could the Court declare one tax good and the other bad? In the child labor tax, however, the regulatory purpose of Congress was explicitly written into the language of the statute. A major portion of the act was nothing but a child labor law, setting out specifically the conditions under which children either could or could not be employed; then to this was added a section which imposed a crippling tax (10 percent of net profits) on any employer who violated the ban on child labor as set forth in the first part of the statute. The Court needed no clairvoyance to learn exactly what Congress was trying to do. The regulatory and destructive purpose was all written out; it could be seen with the naked eye.

This doctrine of a ''penalty'' tax was held applicable to the grain futures tax held void in Hill v. Wallace (1922). Here a destructive tax of 20 cents per bushel was imposed upon those who sold grain on future contracts on grain exchanges which had not submitted themselves to elaborate regulations set out in detail in the statute and administered by the Secretary of Agriculture. On *this ground the Court held void the special federal excise tax of $1000 imposed annually upon those who carry on the liquor business in violation of state law; see United States v. Constantine (1935).*

On the other hand, if Congress can make a regulatory or destructive tax look like a revenue statute, the Court, following the McCray case, will uphold it. Thus in Sonzinsky v. United States (1937) the Court upheld the National Firearms Act of 1934, which not only imposed a $200 annual license tax on dealers in firearms but also laid a tax of $200 on each transfer of a machine gun, sawed-off shotgun, or silencer. "On its face," said the Court, "it is only a taxing measure."

Query: *Can Congress constitutionally levy a tax of 100 percent on the profits on stocks sold within one year of the date of purchase?*

Mr. Chief Justice **Taft** delivered the opinion of the Court, saying in part:

The law is attacked on the ground that it is a regulation of the employment of child labor in the states,—an exclusively state function under the Federal Constitution and within the reservations of the 10th Amendment. It is defended on the ground that it is a mere excise tax, levied by the Congress of the United States under its broad power of taxation conferred by § 8, article I, of the Federal Constitution. We must construe the law and interpret the intent and meaning of Congress from the language of the act. The words are to be given their ordinary meaning unless the context shows that they are differently used. Does this law impose a tax with only that incidental restraint and regulation which a tax must inevitably involve? Or does it regulate by the use of a so-called tax as a penalty? If a tax, it is clearly an excise. If it were an excise on a commodity or other thing of value we might not be permitted, under previous decisions of this court, to infer solely from its heavy burden, that the act intends a prohibition instead of a tax. But this act is more. It provides a heavy exaction for a departure from a detailed and specified course of conduct in business. That course of business is that employers shall employ in mines and quarries, children of an age greater than sixteen years; in mills and factories, children of an age greater than fourteen years; and shall prevent children of less than sixteen years in mills and factories from working more than eight hours a day or six days in the week. If an employer departs from this prescribed course of business, he is to pay to the government one tenth of his entire net income in the business for a full year. The amount is not to be proportioned in any degree to the extent or frequency of the departures, but is to be paid by the employer in full measure whether he employs five hundred children for a year, or employs only one for a day. Moreover, if he does not know the child is within the named age limit, he is not to pay; that is to say, it is only where he knowingly departs from the prescribed course that payment is to be exacted. Scienters are associated with penalties, not with taxes. The employer's factory is to be subject to inspection at any time not only

by the taxing officers of the Treasury, the Department normally charged with the collection of taxes, but also by the Secretary of Labor and his subordinates, whose normal function is the advancement and protection of the welfare of the workers. In the light of these features of the act, a court must be blind not to see that the so-called tax is imposed to stop the employment of children within the age limits prescribed. Its prohibitory and regulatory effect and purpose are palpable. All others can see and understand this. How can we properly shut our minds to it?

It is the high duty and function of this court in cases regularly brought to its bar to decline to recognize or enforce seeming laws of Congress, dealing with subjects not intrusted to Congress, but left or committed by the supreme law of the land to the control of the states. We cannot avoid the duty even though it require us to refuse to give effect to legislation designed to promote the highest good. The good sought in unconstitutional legislation is an insidious feature because it leads citizens and legislators of good purpose to promote it without thought of the serious breach it will make in the ark of our covenant, or the harm which will come from breaking down recognized standards. In the maintenance of self-government, on the one hand, and the national power, on the other, our country has been able to endure and prosper for near a century and a half.

Out of a proper respect for the acts of a co-ordinate branch of the government, this Court has gone far to sustain taxing acts as such, even though there has been ground for suspecting, from the weight of the tax, it was intended to destroy its subject. But in the act before us, the presumption of validity cannot prevail, because the proof of the contrary is found on the very face of its provisions. Grant the validity of this law, and all that Congress would need to do hereafter, in seeking to take over to its control any one of the great number of subjects of public interest, jurisdiction of which the states have never parted with, and which are reserved to them by the 10th Amendment, would be to enact a detailed measure of complete regulation of the subject and enforce it by a so-called tax upon departures from it. To give such magic to the word "tax" would be to break down all constitutional limitation of the powers of Congress and completely wipe out the sovereignty of the states.

The difference between a tax and a penalty is sometimes difficult to define, and yet the consequences of the distinction in the required method of their collection often are important. Where the sovereign enacting the law has power to impose both tax and penalty, the difference between revenue production and mere regulation may be immaterial; but not so when one sovereign can impose a tax only, and the power of regulation rests in another. Taxes are occasionally imposed in the discretion of the legislature on proper subjects with the primary motive of obtaining revenue from them, and with the incidental motive of discouraging them by making their continuance onerous. They do not lose their character as taxes because of the incidental motive. But there comes a time in the extension of the penalizing features of the so-called tax when it loses its character as such and becomes a mere penalty, with the characteristics of regulation and punishment. Such is the case in the law before us. Although Congress does not invalidate the contract of employment, or expressly declare that the employment within the mentioned ages is illegal, it does exhibit its intent practically to achieve the latter result by adopting the criteria of wrongdoing, and imposing its principal consequence on those who transgress its standard.

The case before us cannot be distinguished from that of Hammer v. Dagenhart [1918]. . . .

In the case at the bar, Congress, in the name of a tax which, on the face of the act, is a penalty, seeks to do the same thing, and the effort must be equally futile.

The analogy of the Dagenhart case is clear. The congressional power over interstate commerce is, within its proper scope, just as complete and unlimited as the congressional power to tax; and the legislative motive in its exercises is just as free from judicial suspicion and inquiry. Yet when Congress threatened to stop interstate commerce in ordinary and necessary commodities, unobjectionable as subjects of transportation, and to deny the same to the people of a state, in order to coerce them into compliance with Congress's regulation of state concerns, the court said this was not in fact regulation of interstate commerce, but rather that of state concerns, and was invalid. So here the so-called tax is a penalty to coerce people of a state to act as Congress wishes them to act in respect of a matter completely the business of the state government under the Federal Constitution. This case requires, as did the Dagenhart case, the application of the principle announced by Chief Justice Marshall in M'Culloch v. Maryland [1819], in a much-quoted passage:

"Should Congress, in the execution of its powers, adopt measures which are prohibited by the Constitution, or should Congress, under the pretext of executing its powers, pass laws for the accomplishment of objects not intrusted to the government, it would become the painful duty of this tribunal, should a case requiring such a decision come before it, to say that such an act was not the law of the land." . . .

For the reasons given, we must hold the Child Labor Tax Law invalid, and the judgment of the District Court is affirmed.

Mr. Justice **Clarke** dissented.

SOUTH DAKOTA v. DOLE

97 L. Ed. 2d 171 (1987)

While it is clear that the framers intended the tax power as a way to raise revenue, the fact that any tax has an economic effect of some kind has led it to be viewed, even from earliest times, as a potential mechanism for control. As the cases discussed above show, the tax power has been used as a regulatory measure in two somewhat different ways.

The first way has been to place an economic bur- *den on certain kinds of conduct that Congress had power to control directly by criminal sanctions had it so chosen. Examples are the tariff acts discouraging the importation of certain items and the prohibition on the sale of state bank notes in Veazie Bank v. Fenno (1869); see note to University of Illinois v. United States (1933).*

The second technique—an off-shoot of the first—was the levying of taxes to discourage conduct which Congress had no delegated authority to control; see McCray v. United States (1904). The restriction upon Congress in this area was that the tax had to look like a tax, and if it looked like a penalty it was void; see Bailey v. Drexel Furniture Co. (1922). The resulting sophistication of Congress in drafting tax statutes coupled with the change in the attitude of the Court toward governmental control of the economy has resulted in all taxes since the Child Labor tax being held valid.

A third, and somewhat more subtle method of control, involved the granting of funds by Congress to the states to be used for specific purposes. Typical was the Morrill Act of 1862 providing federal aid to so-called "land grant" colleges—state schools which agreed to offer courses in the science of agriculture and in military science and tactics.

The restrictions accompanying these grants were few and it was not used as a systematic method of controlling policy until the Great Depression of the 1930s when Congress began a wide-ranging effort to revive the economy and restore purchasing power. The first attempt at such control to come before the Supreme Court was the Agricultural Adjustment Act of 1933 in which Congress undertook to reduce surpluses and raise prices of certain agricultural products by paying farmers to reduce their production. The Court held the act void in United States v. Butler (1936). While it appeared to concede that aid to farmers was within the concept of "general welfare" for which federal money could be spent, since Congress had no authority to regulate farm production the whole scheme was illegal.

Two other major efforts by Congress which involved grants-in-aid involved a nationwide retirement system and protection for workers who lost their jobs. It became clear, as the Depression continued, that the acute problems of unemployment and old age relief could be adequately met, not by casual or emergency measures, but only a permanent, constructive, and self-respecting policy grounded on the principles of insurance. Furthermore, national action was imperative. Not only was it beyond the financial capacity of some of the states to extend needed relief to their own citizens, but those able to do so put themselves at a serious competitive disadvantage by assuming the heavy burdens involved. The whole problem received careful study. Early in 1935 the President's Committee on Economic Security filed its report and recommendations; extensive Senate and House hearings were held; and in August 1935 the Social Security Act was passed. The act was an elaborate and complex assembly of policies, including unemployment compensation and aid to the blind, but except for the old-age and survivors insurance which was federally administered, the program was administered by the states under plans approved by the Social Security Board and largely financed from the United States treasury.

In Charles C. Steward Machine Co. v. Davis (1937) the Court upheld the unemployment insurance aspects of the act, noting that with between ten and sixteen million unemployed in the country "it is too late today for the argument to be heard with tolerance that in a crisis so extreme the use of the moneys of the nation to relieve the unemployed and their dependents is a use for any purpose narrower than the promotion of the general welfare." It rejected the assumptions of the Butler case that an offer of financial help amounted to coercion and found that most of the conditions with which the Court had found fault in Butler were not present here. Relying heavily on Steward Machine, the Court in Helvering v. Davis (1937) upheld the old-age benefits provisions of the Act.

Chief Justice **Rehnquist** delivered the opinion of the Court, saying in part:

Petitioner South Dakota permits persons 19 years of age or older to purchase beer containing up to 3.2% alcohol. In 1984 Congress enacted 23 U. S. C. § 158 ("§ 158"), which directs the Secretary of Transportation to withhold a percentage of federal highway funds otherwise allocable from States "in which the purchase or public possession of any alcoholic beverage by a person who is less than twenty-one years of age is lawful." The State sued in United States District Court seeking a declaratory judgment that § 158 violates the constitutional limitations on congressional exercise of the spending power and violates the Twenty-first Amendment to the United States Constitution. The District Court rejected the State's claims, and the Court of Appeals for the Eighth Circuit affirmed.

In this Court, the parties direct most of their efforts to defining the proper scope of the Twenty-first Amendment. . . .

. . . Despite the extended treatment of the question by the parties, however, we need not decide in this case whether that Amendment would prohibit an attempt by Congress to legislate directly a national minimum drinking age. Here, Congress has acted indirectly under its spending power to encourage uniformity in the States' drinking ages. As we explain below, we find this legislative effort within constitutional bounds even if Congress may not regulate drinking ages directly.

The Constitution empowers Congress to "lay and collect Taxes, Duties, Imposts, and Excises, to pay the Debts and provide for the common Defence and general Welfare of the United States. "Art. I, § 8, cl. 1. Incident to this power, Congress may attach conditions on the receipt of federal funds, and has repeatedly employed the power "to further broad policy objectives by conditioning receipt of federal moneys upon compliance by the recipient with federal statutory and administrative directives." . . . The breadth of this power was made clear in United States v. Butler (1936) where the Court, resolving a long standing debate over the scope of the Spending Clause, determined that "the power of Con-

gress to authorize expenditure of public moneys for public purposes is not limited by the direct grants of legislative power found in the Constitution." Thus, objectives not thought to be within Article I's "enumerated legislative fields," may nevertheless be attained through the use of the spending power and the conditional grant of federal funds.

The spending power is of course not unlimited . . . , but is instead subject to several general restrictions articulated in our cases. The first of these limitations is derived from the language of the Constitution itself: the exercise of the spending power must be in pursuit of "the general welfare." . . . In considering whether a particular expenditure is intended to serve general public purposes, courts should defer substantially to the judgment of Congress. . . . Second, we have required that if Congress desires to condition the States' receipt of federal funds, it "must do so unambiguously . . . , enabl[ing] the States to exercise their choice knowingly, cognizant of the consequences of their participation." . . . Third, our cases have suggested (without significant elaboration) that conditions on federal grants might be illegitimate if they are unrelated "to the federal interest in particular national projects or programs." . . .

South Dakota does not seriously claim that § 158 is inconsistent with any of the . . . three restrictions mentioned above. We can readily conclude that the provision is designed to serve the general welfare, especially in light of the fact that "the concept of welfare or the opposite is shaped by Congress. . . ." . . . Congress found that the differing drinking ages in the States created particular incentives for young persons to combine their desire to drink with their ability to drive, and that this interstate problem required a national solution. The means it chose to address this dangerous situation were reasonably calculated to advance the general welfare. The conditions upon which States received the funds, moreover, could not be more clearly stated by Congress. And the State itself, rather than challenging the germaneness of the condition to federal purposes, admits that it "has never contended that the congressional action was . . . unrelated to a national concern in the absence of the Twenty-first Amendment." Indeed, the condition imposed by Congress is directly related to one of the main purposes for which highway funds are expended—safe interstate travel. This goal of the interstate highway system had been frustrated by varying drinking ages among the States. A presidential commission appointed to study alcohol-related accidents and fatalities on the Nation's highways concluded that the lack of uniformity in the States' drinking ages created "an incentive to drink and drive" because "young persons commut[e] to border States where the drinking age is lower." . . . By enacting § 158, Congress conditioned the receipt of federal funds in a way reasonably calculated to address this particular impediment to a purpose for which the funds are expended.

The remaining question about the validity of § 158—and the basic point of disagreement between the parties—is whether the Twenty-first Amendment constitutes an "independent constitutional bar" to the conditional grant of federal funds. . . . But our cases show that this "independent constitutional bar" limitation on the spending power is not of the kind petitioner suggests. United States v. Butler [1936], for example, established that the constitutional limitations on Congress when exercising its spending power are less exacting than those on its authority to regulate directly.

We have also held that a perceived Tenth Amendment limitation on congressional regulation of state affairs did not concomitantly limit the range of conditions legitimately placed on federal grants. In Oklahoma v. Civil Service Comm'n (1947), the Court considered the validity of the Hatch Act insofar as it was applied to political activities of state officials whose employment was financed in whole or in part with federal funds. The State contended that an order under this provision to withhold certain federal funds unless a state official was removed invaded its sovereignty in violation of the Tenth Amendment. Though finding that "the United States is not concerned with, and has no power to regulate, local political activities as such, of state officials," the Court nevertheless held that the Federal Government "does have power to fix the terms upon which its money allotments to states shall be disbursed." The Court found no violation of the State's sovereignty because the State could, and did, adopt "the 'simple expedient' of not yielding to what she urges is federal coercion. The offer of benefits to a state by the United States dependent upon cooperation by the state with federal plans, assumedly for the general welfare, is not unusual." . . .

These cases establish that the "independent constitutional bar" limitation on the spending power is not, as petitioner suggests, a prohibition on the indirect achievement of objectives which Congress is not empowered to achieve directly. Instead, we think that the language in our earlier opinions stands for the unexceptionable proposition that the power may not be used to induce the States to engage in activities that would themselves be unconstitutional. Thus, for example, a grant of federal funds conditioned on invidiously discriminatory state action or the infliction of cruel and unusual punishment would be an illegitimate exercise of the Congress' broad spending power. But no such claim can be or is made here. Were South Dakota to succumb to the blandishments offered by Congress and raise its drinking age to 21, the State's action in so doing would not violate the constitutional rights of anyone.

Our decisions have recognized that in some circumstances the financial inducement offered by Congress might be so coercive as to pass the point at which "pressure turns into compulsion." Steward Machine Co. v. Davis [1937]. Here, however, Congress has directed only that a State desiring to establish a minimum drinking age lower than 21 lose a relatively small percentage of certain federal highway funds. Petitioner contends that the coercive nature of this program is evident from the degree of success it has achieved. We cannot conclude, however, that a conditional grant of federal money of this sort is unconstitutional simply by reason of its success in achieving the congressional objective.

When we consider, for a moment, that all South Dakota would lose if she adheres to her chosen course as to a suitable minimum drinking age is 5% of the funds otherwise obtainable under specified highway grant programs, the argument as to coercion is shown to be more rhetoric than fact. As we said half a century ago in Steward Machine Co. v. Davis: "[E]very rebate from a tax when conditioned upon conduct is in some measure a temptation. But to hold that motive or temptation is equivalent to coercion is to plunge the law in endless difficulties. The outcome of such a doctrine is the acceptance of a philosophical determinism by which choice becomes impossible. Till now the law has been guided by a robust common sense which assumes the freedom of the will as a working hypothesis in the solution of its problems."

Here Congress has offered relatively mild encouragement to the States to enact higher minimum drinking ages than they would otherwise choose. But the enactment of such laws remains the prerogative of the States not merely in theory but in fact. Even if Congress might lack the power to impose a national minimum drinking age directly, we concluded that encouragement to state action found in § 158 is a valid use of the spending power. Accordingly, the judgment of the Court of Appeals is

Affirmed.

Justice **Brennan,** dissenting, said in part:

I agree with Justice O'Connor that regulation of the minimum age of purchasers of liquor falls squarely within the ambit of those powers reserved to the States by the Twenty-first Amendment. . . .

Justice **O'Connor,** dissenting, said in part:

. . . § 158 is not a condition on spending reasonably related to the expenditure of federal funds and cannot be justified on that ground. Rather, it is an attempt to regulate the sale of liquor, an attempt that lies outside Congress' power to regulate commerce because it falls within the ambit of § 2 of the Twenty-first Amendment.

THE COMMERCE POWER

GIBBONS v. OGDEN

9 Wheaton 1; 6 L. Ed. 23 (1824)

In 1798 Robert R. Livingston secured from the New York legislature an exclusive twenty-year grant to navigate by steam the rivers and other waters of the state, provided that within two years he should build a boat which would make four miles an hour against the current of the Hudson River. The grant was made amidst the ribald jeers of the legislators, who had no faith whatever in the project. The terms of the grant were not met, however, and it was renewed in 1803—this time to Livingston together with his partner, Robert Fulton—and again for two years in 1807. In August, 1807, Fulton's steamboat made its first successful trip from New York to Albany, and steamboat navigation became a reality. The following year the legislature, now fully aware of the practical significance of Fulton's achievement, passed a law providing that for each new boat placed on New York waters by Fulton and Livingston they should be entitled to a five-year extension of their monopoly, which should, however, not exceed thirty years. The monopoly was made effective by further providing that no one should be allowed to navigate New York waters by steam without a license from Fulton and Livingston, and any unlicensed vessel should be forfeited to them. The business of steamboat navigation developed rapidly. Boats were put in operation between New York and Albany and intervening points, and steam ferries ran between Fulton Street, New York City, and points in New Jersey. In 1811 the partners obtained from the Territory of Orleans (later Louisiana) a monopoly of steam navigation on the waters of Louisiana similar to that granted by New York, thus assuring them a pivotal position in the two greatest ports of the land. Naturally the monopolistic nature of the Fulton-Livingston rights worked hardship on their would-be competitors, and neighboring states began to pass retaliatory laws directed against the New York partners. The New Jersey legislature in 1811 authorized the owner of any boat seized under the forfeiture clause of the Fulton-Livingston charter to capture and hold in retaliation any boat belonging to any New York citizen. Connecticut in 1822 forbade any vessel licensed by Fulton and Livingston to enter the waters of that state, and Ohio passed a somewhat similar law in the same year. Granting such exclusive franchises was a game at which more than one state could play; and such grants were made by Georgia, Massachusetts, Pennsylvania, Tennessee, New Hampshire, and Vermont. With the inevitable increase of feeling created by such policies, retaliatory acts became common. In short, an achievement of science which had seemed destined to enlarge the means of communication and develop the commerce of the nation appeared rather to be embroiling the states in bitter antagonisms and commercial warfare such as prevailed during the dismal period of the Confederation. It is against the background of this intensely acute economic situation that the case of Gibbons v. Ogden must be read.

Ogden had secured a license for steam navigation from Fulton and Livingston. Gibbons had originally been his partner but was now his rival and was operating steamboats between two points in New York under the authority of a coasting license obtained from the United States government. Upon Ogden's petition the New York court had enjoined Gibbons from continuing in business. The great jurist Chancellor James Kent wrote the opinion in this case claiming the whole Hudson River belonged to New York, upholding the validity of the New York statute establishing the monopoly and repudiating

the idea that there was any conflict involved between federal and state authority. An appeal was taken by Gibbons to the Supreme Court of the United States, thus presenting to that tribunal its first case under the commerce clause of the Constitution.

So accustomed are we to the free flow of commerce among the states that it is hard to conceive how the nation might have developed had the arguments in favor of the monopoly prevailed, for it was urged that the powers of state and nation to regulate interstate commerce were concurrent; that in the absence of a conflicting congressional statute the state was free to exercise this concurrent power as it pleased; and the "commerce" which Congress may regulate was "the transportation and sale of commodities." Had that argument prevailed, the federal coasting license under which Gibbons operated would have given him no protection, since he was carrying passengers, not goods. But the most crucial argument of all was that the New York monopoly law was not a regulation of interstate commerce but was merely a regulation of commerce within the boundaries of the state of New York. "It [the law] does not deny the right of entry into its waters to any vessel navigated by steam; it only forbids such vessel, when within its waters and jurisdiction, to be moved by steam; but that vessel may still navigate by all other means; and it leaves the people of other states, or of New York, in full possession of the right of navigation, by all the means known or used at the time of the passage of the law. [Most early steam boats were also sailboats.] It is, therefore, strictly a regulation of internal trade and navigation, which belongs to the state. This may, indeed, indirectly affect the right of commercial intercourse between the states. But so do all other laws regulating internal trade." . . .

Webster's argument against the validity of the steamboat monopoly was perhaps his greatest effort before the Supreme Court, and some writers believe that Marshall's opinion invalidating the New York law is his greatest state paper; others would place it second only to the opinion in McCulloch v. Maryland (1819). It was perhaps the only genuinely popular decision which Marshall ever handed down. It was received with widespread expressions of approval, for it was, as one writer has put it, "the first great anti-trust decision." The economic consequences of it in freeing a developing commerce from the shackles of state monopoly can hardly be overestimated; and it established for all time the supremacy of the national government in all matters affecting interstate and foreign commerce.

Mr. Chief Justice **Marshall** delivered the opinion of the Court, saying in part:

The appellant contends that this decree is erroneous, because the laws which purport to give the exclusive privilege it sustains are repugnant to the constitution and laws of the United States.

They are said to be repugnant:

1st. To that clause in the constitution which authorizes Congress to regulate commerce.

2d. To that which authorizes Congress to promote the progress of science and useful arts. . . .

As preliminary to the very able discussions of the constitution which we have heard from the bar, and as having some influence on its construction, reference has been made to the political situation of these states, anterior to its formation. It has been said that they were sovereign, were completely independent, and were connected with each other only by a league. This is true. But when these allied sovereigns converted their league into a government, when they converted their congress of ambassadors, deputed to deliberate on their common concerns, and to recommend measures of general utility, into a legislature, empowered to enact laws on the most interesting subjects, the whole character in which the states appear, underwent a change, the extent of which must be determined by a fair consideration of the instrument by which that change was effected.

This instrument contains an enumeration of powers expressly granted by the people to their government. It has been said that these powers ought to be construed strictly. But why ought they to be so construed? Is there one sentence in the constitution which gives countenance to this rule? In the last of the enumerated powers, that which grants, expressly, the means for carrying all others into execution, Congress is authorized ''to make all laws which shall be necessary and proper'' for the purpose. But this limitation on the means which may be used, is not extended to the powers which are conferred; nor is there one sentence in the constitution, which has been pointed out by the gentlemen of the bar or which we have been able to discern, that prescribes this rule. We do not, therefore, think ourselves justified in adopting it. What do gentlemen mean by a strict construction? If they contend only against that enlarged construction which would extend words beyond their natural and obvious import, we might question the application of the term, but should not controvert the principle. If they contend for that narrow construction which, in support of some theory not to be found in the constitution, would deny to the government those powers which the words of the grant, as usually understood, import, and which are consistent with the general views and objects of the instrument; for the narrow construction, which would cripple the government and render it unequal to the objects for which it is declared to be instituted, and to which the powers given, as fairly understood, render it competent; then we cannot perceive the propriety of this strict construction, nor adopt it as the rule by which the constitution is to be expounded. As men, whose intentions require no concealment, generally employ the words which most directly and aptly express the ideas they intend to convey, the enlightened patriots who framed our constitution, and the people who adopted it, must be understood to have employed words in their natural sense, and to have intended what they have said. If, from the imperfection of human language, there should be serious doubts respecting the extent of any given power, it is a well-settled rule that the objects for which it was given, especially when those objects are expressed in the instrument itself, should have great influence in the construction. We know of no reason for excluding this rule from the present case. The grant does not convey power which might be beneficial to the grantor, if retained by himself, or which can enure solely to the benefit of the grantee; but is an investment of power for the general advantage, in the hands of agents selected for that purpose; which power can never be exercised by the people themselves, but must be placed in the hands of agents or lie dormant. We know of no rule for construing the extent of such powers, other than is given by the language of the instrument which confers them, taken in connection with the purposes for which they were conferred.

The words are: ''Congress shall have power to regulate commerce with foreign nations, and among the several states, and with the Indian tribes.''

The subject to be regulated is commerce; and our constitution being, as was aptly said at the bar, one of enumeration, and not of definition, to ascertain the extent of the power it becomes necessary to settle the meaning of the word. Counsel for the appellee would limit it to traffic, to buying and selling, or the interchange of commodities, and do not admit that it comprehends navigation. This would restrict a general term, applicable to many objects, to one of its significations. Commerce, undoubtedly, is traffic, but it is something more; it is intercourse. It describes the commercial intercourse between nations, and parts of nations, in all its branches, and regulated by prescribing rules for carrying on that intercourse. The mind can scarcely conceive a system for regulating commerce between nations, which shall exclude all laws concerning navigation, which shall be silent on the admission of the vessels of the one nation into the ports of the other, and be confined to prescribing rules for the conduct of individuals, in the actual employment of buying and selling, or of barter.

If commerce does not include navigation, the government of the Union has no direct power over that subject, and can make no law prescribing what shall constitute American vessels, or requiring that they shall be navigated by American seamen. Yet this power has been exercised from the commencement of the government, has been exercised with the consent of all, and has been understood by all to be a commercial regulation. All America understands, and has uniformly understood, the word ''commerce'' to comprehend navigation. It was so understood, and must have been so understood, when the constitution was framed. The power over commerce, including navigation, was one of the primary objects for which the people of America adopted their government, and must have been contemplated in forming it. The convention must have used the word in that sense, because all have understood it in that sense, and the attempt to restrict it comes too late. . . .

The word used in the constitution, then, comprehends, and has been always understood to comprehend, navigation within its meaning; and a power to regulate navigation is as expressly granted as if that term had been added to the word ''commerce.''

To what commerce does this power extend? The

constitution informs us, to commerce "with foreign nations, and among the several states, and with the Indian tribes."

It has, we believe, been universally admitted that these words comprehend every species of commercial intercourse between the United States and foreign nations. No sort of trade can be carried on between this country and any other to which this power does not extend. It has been truly said that commerce, as the word is used in the constitution, is a unit, every part of which is indicated by the term.

If this be the admitted meaning of the word, in its application to foreign nations, it must carry the same meaning throughout the sentence, and remain a unit, unless there be some plain intelligible cause which alters it.

The subject to which the power is next applied, is to commerce "among the several states." The word "among" means intermingled with. A thing which is among others is intermingled with them. Commerce among the states cannot stop at the external boundary line of each state, but may be introduced into the interior.

It is not intended to say that these words comprehend that commerce which is completely internal, which is carried on between man and man in a state, or between different parts of the same state, and which does not extend to or affect other states. Such a power would be inconvenient, and is certainly unnecessary.

Comprehensive as the word "among" is, it may very properly be restricted to that commerce which concerns more states than one. . . . The completely internal commerce of a state, then, may be considered as reserved for the state itself.

But, in regulating commerce with foreign nations, the power of Congress does not stop at the jurisdictional lines of the several states. It would be a very useless power if it could not pass those lines. The commerce of the United States with foreign nations, is that of the whole United States. Every district has a right to participate in it. The deep streams which penetrate our country in every direction, pass through the interior of almost every state in the Union, and furnish the means of exercising this right. If Congress has the power to regulate it, that power must be exercised whenever the subject exists. If it exists within the states, if a foreign voyage may commence or terminate at a port within a state, then the power of Congress may be exercised within a state.

This principle is, if possible, still more clear when applied to commerce "among the several states." They either join each other, in which case they are separated by a mathematical line, or they are remote from each other, in which case other states lie between them. What is commerce "among" them; and how is it to be conducted? Can a trading expedition between two adjoining states commence and terminate outside of each? And if the trading intercourse be between two states remote from each other, must it not commence in one, terminate in the other, and probably pass through a third? Commerce among the states must, of necessity, be commerce with the states. In the regulation of trade with the Indian

tribes, the action of the law, especially when the constitution was made, was chiefly within a state. The power of Congress, then, whatever it may be, must be exercised within the territorial jurisdiction of the several states. . . .

We are now arrived at the inquiry, What is this power?

It is the power to regulate; that is, to prescribe the rule by which commerce is to be governed. This power, like all others vested in Congress, is complete in itself, may be exercised to its utmost extent, and acknowledges no limitations other than are prescribed in the constitution. These are expressed in plain terms, and do not affect the questions which arise in this case, or which have been discussed at the bar. . . .

The power of Congress, then, comprehends navigation within the limits of every state in the Union, so far as that navigation may be, in any manner, connected with "commerce with foreign nations, or among the several states, or with the Indian tribes." It may, of consequence, pass the jurisdictional line of New York, and act upon the very waters to which the prohibition now under consideration applies.

But it has been urged with great earnestness, that although the power of Congress to regulate commerce with foreign nations, and among the several states, be co-extensive with the subject itself, and have no other limits than are prescribed in the constitution, yet the states may severally exercise the same power within their respective jurisdictions. In support of this argument, it is said that they possessed it as an inseparable attribute of sovereignty before the formation of the Constitution, and still retain it, except so far as they have surrendered it by that instrument; that this principle results from the nature of the government, and is secured by the tenth amendment; that an affirmative grant of power is not exclusive, unless in its own nature it be such that the continued exercise of it by the former possessor is inconsistent with the grant, and that this is not of that description.

The appellant, conceding these postulates, except the last, contends that full power to regulate a particular subject implies the whole power, and leaves no residuum; that a grant of the whole is incompatible with the existence of a right in another to any part of it. . . .

In discussing the question, whether this power is still in the states, in the case under consideration, we may dismiss from it the inquiry, whether it is surrendered by the mere grant to Congress, or is retained until Congress shall exercise the power. We may dismiss that inquiry, because it has been exercised, and the regulations which Congress deemed it proper to make, are now in full operation. The sole question is, can a state regulate commerce with foreign nations and among the states, while Congress is regulating it? . . .

The act passed in 1803, prohibiting the importation of slaves into any state which shall itself prohibit their importation, implies, it is said, an admission that the states possessed the power to exclude or admit them; from which it is inferred that they possess the same power with respect to other articles.

If this inference were correct; if this power was exercised, not under any particular clause in the constitution, but in virtue of a general right over the subject of commerce, to exist as long as the constitution itself, it might now be exercised. Any state might now import African slaves into its own territory. But it is obvious that the power of the states over this subject, previous to the year 1808, constitutes an exception to the power of Congress to regulate commerce, and the exception is expressed in such words as to manifest clearly the intention to continue the pre-existing right of the states to admit or exclude for a limited period. The words are: "The migration or importation of such persons as any of the states, now existing, shall think proper to admit, shall not be prohibited by the Congress prior to the year 1808." The whole object of the exception is to preserve the power to those states which might be disposed to exercise it; and its language seems to the court to convey this idea unequivocally. The possession of this particular power, then, during the time limited in the constitution, cannot be admitted to prove the possession of any other similar power.

It has been said that the act of August 7th, 1789, acknowledges a concurrent power in the states to regulate the conduct of pilots, and hence is inferred an admission of their concurrent right with Congress to regulate commerce with foreign nations and amongst the states. But this inference is not, we think, justified by the fact.

Although Congress cannot enable a state to legislate, Congress may adopt the provisions of a state on any subject. When the government of the Union was brought into existence, it found a system for the regulation of its pilots in full force in every state. The act which has been mentioned adopts this system, and gives it the same validity as if its provisions had been specially made by Congress. But the act, it may be said, is prospective also, and the adoption of laws to be made in future presupposes the right in the maker to legislate on the subject.

The act unquestionably manifests an intention to leave this subject entirely to the states, until Congress should think proper to interpose; but the very enactment of such a law indicates an opinion that it was necessary; that the existing system would not be applicable to the new state of things, unless expressly applied to it by Congress. . . .

These acts were cited at the bar for the purpose of showing an opinion in Congress that the states possess, concurrently with the legislature of the Union, the power to regulate commerce with foreign nations and among the states. Upon reviewing them, we think they do not establish the proposition they were intended to prove. They show the opinion that the states retain powers enabling them to pass the laws to which allusion has been made, not that those laws proceed from the particular power which has been delegated to Congress.

It has been contended by the counsel for the appellant, that, as the word "to regulate" implies in its nature full power over the thing to be regulated, it excludes, necessarily, the action of all others that would perform the same operation on the same thing. That regulation is

designed for the entire result, applying to those parts which remain as they were, as well as to those which are altered. It produces a uniform whole, which is as much disturbed and deranged by changing what the regulating power designs to leave untouched, as that on which it has operated.

There is great force in this argument, and the court is not satisfied that it has been refuted.

Since, however, in exercising the power of regulating their own purely internal affairs, whether of trading or police, the states may sometimes enact laws, the validity of which depends on their interfering with, and being contrary to, an act of Congress passed in pursuance of the constitution, the court will enter upon the inquiry, whether the laws of New York, as expounded by the highest tribunal of that state, have, in their application to this case, come into collision with an act of Congress, and deprived a citizen of a right to which that act entitles him. Should this collision exist, it will be immaterial whether those laws were passed in virtue of a concurrent power "to regulate commerce with foreign nations and among the several states," or in virtue of a power to regulate their domestic trade and police. In one case and the other, the acts of New York must yield to the law of Congress; and the decision sustaining the privilege they confer, against a right given by a law of the Union, must be erroneous. . . .

The questions, then, whether the conveyance of passengers be a part of the coasting trade, and whether a vessel can be protected in that occupation by a coasting license, are not, and cannot be, raised in this case. The real and sole question seems to be, whether a steam machine, in actual use, deprives a vessel of the privileges conferred by a license.

In considering this question, the first idea which presents itself, is that the laws of Congress for the regulation of commerce, do not look to the principle by which vessels are moved. That subject is left entirely to individual discretion; and, in that vast and complex system of legislative enactment concerning it, which embraces everything that the legislature thought it necessary to notice, there is not, we believe, one word respecting the peculiar principle by which vessels are propelled through the water, except what may be found in a single act, granting a particular privilege to steamboats. With this exception, every act, either prescribing duties, or granting privileges, applies to every vessel, whether navigated by the instrumentality of wind or fire, of sails or machinery. The whole weight of proof, then, is thrown upon him who would introduce a distinction to which the words of the law give no countenance.

If a real difference could be admitted to exist between vessels carrying passengers and others, it has already been observed that there is no fact in this case which can bring up that question. And, if the occupation of steamboats be a matter of such general notoriety that the court may be presumed to know it, although not specially informed by the record, then we deny that the transportation of passengers is their exclusive occupation. It is a matter of general history, that, on our western waters, their principal employment is the transportation of merchandise; and all know, that in the waters of the Atlantic they are frequently so employed.

But all inquiry into this subject seems to the court to be put completely at rest by the act already mentioned, entitled, "An act for the enrolling and licensing of steamboats."

This act authorizes a steamboat employed, or intended to be employed, only in a river or bay of the United States, owned wholly or in part by an alien, resident within the United States, to be enrolled and licensed as if the same belonged to a citizen of the United States.

This act demonstrates the opinion of Congress, that steamboats may be enrolled and licensed, in common with vessels using sails. They are, of course, entitled to the same privileges, and can no more be restrained from navigating waters, and entering ports which are free to such vessels, than if they were wafted on their voyage by the winds, instead of being propelled by the agency of fire. The one element may be as legitimately used as the other, for every commercial purpose authorized by the laws of the Union; and the act of a state inhibiting the use of either to any vessel having a license under the act of Congress, comes, we think, in direct collision with that act.

As this decides the cause, it is unnecessary to enter in an examination of that part of the constitution which empowers Congress to promote the progress of science and the useful arts. . . .

COOLEY v. THE BOARD OF WARDENS OF THE PORT OF PHILADELPHIA

12 Howard 299; 13 L. Ed. 996 (1852)

In the early judicial construction of the commerce clause of the Constitution, one important and difficult question remained long unanswered: namely, whether the power of Congress to regulate foreign and interstate commerce was absolutely exclusive, or could be shared in part by the states. Gibbons v. Ogden (1824) had held that state action affecting commerce which is in conflict with congressional regulation is invalid, but it had left unsettled the question whether a state may lawfully legislate regarding subjects pertaining to interstate commerce in the absence of conflicting federal regulation. It was this issue which came before the Court in the case of Cooley v. The Board of Wardens.

The legislature of Pennsylvania in 1803 had passed a statute establishing an elaborate system of regulations affecting pilotage in the port of Philadelphia and imposing certain penalties of money in case of the failure of a master, owner, or consignee to comply with these rules. Cooley had rendered himself liable to the enforcement of these penalties against him, but alleged in appealing his case to the Supreme Court that the state statute was unconstitutional as an invasion of the exclusive authority of Congress over foreign and interstate commerce. In holding the state statute valid because Congress had not legislated independently with respect to pilotage and in view of the local nature of the prob-

lems of pilotage, the Court laid down a rule for determining the exclusive or nonexclusive character of federal commercial regulations which has been of utmost importance and value. It is interesting to note that two justices dissented vigorously on the ground that the power of Congress over commerce should be held absolutely exclusive.

The doctrine of the Cooley case, while simple enough to state, is by no means so simple to apply. Involving as it does the determination by the Court of the question of whether a particular subject of commercial regulation admits of and requires uniform and national control or whether it is sufficiently local in character to make state regulation permissible, it imposes upon the Court the solution of many complicated and difficult questions. The doctrine has been criticized on the ground that the determination of such a question properly belongs to Congress rather than to the courts; but aside from that the rule has generally been regarded as a wise one, sufficiently protecting federal commercial interests on the one hand while permitting the local control of local commercial problems on the other.

The importance of the rule in operation can perhaps best be judged in terms of the railroad problem. During the first 100 years of our national history following the ratification of the Constitution there was no significant congressional regulation of interstate commerce. The Supreme Court, following the rules of Gibbons v. Ogden and the Cooley case, policed the boundaries of interstate commerce to prevent state interference with that commerce. In the absence of federal regulation, the line between interstate commerce and intrastate commerce separated those businesses which were subject to state regulation from those which were not. The Supreme Court, recognizing the need for regulation in the post-Civil War era, had leaned in the direction of upholding the power of the states. In 1877, in Peik v. Chicago & N. W. R. Co., one of the Granger Cases, state regulation of railroad rates had been held valid as "to state commerce, or such interstate commerce as directly affects the people of Wisconsin." But state regulation of railroads fell far short of meeting the problems posed by the coast-to-coast railroad empires of men like James J. Hill and Jay Gould. For more than ten years Congress had been considering federal regulation, but the railroad interests had successfully thwarted all proposals. Then in October of 1886 the Supreme Court decided the famous Wabash case (Wabash, St. L. & P. Ry. Co. v. Illinois), which held void all state control over the rates charged by interstate railroads. Such rates, the Court held, require nationally uniform regulation and therefore, under the doctrine of the Cooley case, cannot be controlled by the individual states. Four months after the Wabash decision Congress passed the Interstate Commerce Act authorizing the regulation of railroad rates and practices and establishing the Interstate Commerce Commission. This was followed two years later by the Sherman Antitrust Act, and the 100 years of national inactivity were at an end.

The aspects of interstate commerce which may still be regulated by the states on the ground that "uniform national control'' is unnecessary include such things as the rates or tolls charged on ferries, bridges, and tunnels which span the boundaries between states.

Although the states under the Cooley rule are permitted to regulate certain aspects of interstate commerce which do not require uniform treatment, the Court has made clear that such regulation must be local in nature and must not burden the commerce. A state can neither extend its regulations beyond its borders nor make the regulations so onerous as to interfere with the interstate movement of persons and goods.

In 1950, before the Court held segregation unconstitutional, it held in an unusual case that questions of segregation in transportation could be local in impact and thus be subject to state control under the Cooley rule. Bois Blanc (Bob-Lo) Island lies in the Detroit River about fifteen miles from Detroit, but it lies beyond the international boundary in Canada. It is almost wholly owned by a Michigan corporation which operates it as an amusement park, bringing patrons to it in excursion boats and returning them to Detroit the same day. Although the patrons pass through Canadian customs and immigration inspection when they land on the island, there is no way for Canadians to get to the island except on the excursion boats from Detroit. In Bob-Lo Excursion Co. v. Michigan (1948) the Supreme Court held the Michigan civil rights act forbidding racial discrimination validly applicable to the excursion steamers, which were clearly plying in foreign commerce. The Cooley case itself, the Court pointed out, dealt with foreign as well as interstate commerce. The Court distinguished two earlier cases, Hall v. De Cuir (1878) and Morgan v. Virginia (1946) which had held that segregation in transportation was a matter of interstate commerce, since neither ''involved so completely and locally insulated a segment of foreign or interstate commerce. In none was the business affected merely an adjunct of a single locality or community as in the business here so largely.'' In a rather caustic dissent, Justice Jackson observed, ''The Court admits that the commerce involved in this case is foreign commerce, but subjects it to the state police power on the ground that it is not very foreign.''

A similar result was reached in 1963, when the Court held valid Colorado's antidiscrimination law as applied to the hiring of airline pilots by an interstate carrier. The Court acknowledged that the changed rules regarding segregation had made obsolete the Hall and Morgan cases. ''Were there a possibility that a pilot hired in Colorado could be barred solely because of his color from serving a carrier in another State, then this case might well be controlled by our prior holdings.'' But, since Brown v. Board of Education (1954), ''the kind of burden that was thought possible in the Hall and Morgan Cases . . . simply cannot exist here.'' See Colorado Commission v. Continental Air Lines.

Mr. Justice **Curtis** delivered the opinion of the Court, saying in part:

That the power to regulate commerce includes the regulation of navigation, we consider settled. And when we look to the nature of the service performed by pilots, to the relations which that service and its compensations bear to navigation between the several States, and between the ports of the United States, and foreign countries, we are brought to the conclusion, that the regulation of the qualifications of pilots, of the modes and times of offering and rendering their services, of the responsibilities which shall rest upon them, of the powers they shall possess, of the compensation they may demand, and of the penalties by which their rights and duties may be enforced do constitute regulations of navigation, and consequently of commerce, within the just meaning of this clause of the Constitution.

The power to regulate navigation is the power to prescribe rules in conformity with which navigation must be carried on. It extends to the persons who conduct it, as well as to the instruments used. Accordingly, the first Congress assembled under the Constitution passed laws, requiring the masters of ships and vessels of the United States to be citizens of the United States, and established many rules for the government and regulation of officers and seamen. These have been from time to time added to and changed, and we are not aware that their validity has been questioned.

Now, a pilot, so far as respects the navigation of the vessel in that part of the voyage which is his pilotage ground, is the temporary master charged with the safety of the vessel and cargo, and of the lives of those on board, and intrusted with the command of the crew. He is not only one of the persons engaged in navigation, but he occupies a most important and responsible place among those thus engaged. And if Congress has power to regulate the seamen who assist the pilot in the management of the vessel, a power never denied, we can perceive no valid reason why the pilot should be beyond the reach of the same power. It is true that, according to the usages of modern commerce on the ocean, the pilot is on board only during a part of the voyage between ports of different states, or between ports of the United States and foreign countries; but if he is on board for such a purpose and during so much of the voyage as to be engaged in navigation, the power to regulate navigation extends to him while thus engaged, as clearly as it would if he were to remain on board throughout the whole passage, from port to port. For it is a power which extends to every part of the voyage, and may regulate those who conduct or assist in conducting navigation in one part of a voyage as much as in another part, or during the whole voyage.

Nor should it be lost sight of, that this subject of the regulation of pilots and pilotage has an intimate connection with, and an important relation to, the general subject of commerce with foreign nations and among the several States, over which it was one main object of the Constitution to create a national control. . . .

. . . And a majority of the court are of opinion that a regulation of pilots is a regulation of commerce, within the grant to Congress of the commercial power, contained in the third clause of the eighth section of the first article of the Constitution.

It becomes necessary, therefore, to consider

whether this law of Pennsylvania, being a regulation of commerce, is valid.

The Act of Congress of the 7th of August, 1789, sec. 4, is as follows:

"That all pilots in the bays, inlets, rivers, harbors, and ports of the United States shall continue to be regulated in conformity with the existing laws of the States, respectively, wherein such pilots may be, or with such laws as the States may respectively hereafter enact for the purpose, until further legislative provision shall be made by Congress." . . .

. . . We are brought directly and unavoidably to the consideration of the question, whether the grant of the commercial power to Congress, did per se deprive the States of all power to regulate pilots. This question has never been decided by this court, nor, in our judgment, has any case depending upon all the considerations which must govern this one, come before this court. The grant of commercial power to Congress does not contain any terms which exclude the States from exercising an authority over its subject matter. If they are excluded it must be because the nature of the power, thus granted to Congress, requires that a similar authority should not exist in the States. If it were conceded on the one side that the nature of this power, like that to legislate for the District of Columbia, is absolutely and totally repugnant to the existence of similar power in the States, probably no one would deny that the grant of the power to Congress, as effectually and perfectly excludes the States from all future legislation on the subject, as if express words had been used to exclude them. And on the other hand, if it were admitted that the existence of this power in Congress, like the power of taxation, is compatible with the existence of a similar power in the States, then it would be in conformity with the contemporary exposition of the Constitution (Federalist, No. 32), and with the judicial construction given from time to time by this court, after the most deliberate consideration, to hold that the mere grant of such a power to Congress, did not imply a prohibition on the States to exercise the same power; that it is not the mere existence of such a power, but its exercise by Congress, which may be incompatible with the exercise of the same power by the States, and that the States may legislate in the absence of congressional regulations. . . .

The diversities of opinion, therefore, which have existed on this subject, have arisen from the different views taken of the nature of this power. But when the nature of a power like this is spoken of, when it is said that the nature of the power requires that it should be exercised exclusively by Congress, it must be intended to refer to the subjects of that power, and to say they are of such a nature as to require exclusive legislation by Congress. Now, the power to regulate commerce, embraces a vast field, containing not only many, but exceedingly various subjects, quite unlike in their nature; some imperatively demanding a single uniform rule, operating equally on the commerce of the United States in every port; and some, like the subject now in question, as imperatively demanding that diversity, which alone can meet the local necessities of navigation.

Either absolutely to affirm, or deny, that the nature of this power requires exclusive legislation by Congress, is to lose sight of the nature of the subjects of this power, and to assert concerning all of them, what is really applicable but to a part. Whatever subjects of this power are in their nature national, or admit only of one uniform system, or plan of regulation, may justly be said to be of such a nature as to require exclusive legislation by Congress. That this cannot be affirmed of laws for the regulation of pilots and pilotage is plain. The Act of 1789 contains a clear and authoritative declaration by the first Congress, that the nature of this subject is such, that until Congress should find it necessary to exert its power, it should be left to the legislation of the States; that it is local and not national; that it is likely to be the best provided for, not by one system, or plan of regulations, but by as many as the legislative discretion of the several States should deem applicable to the local peculiarities of the ports within their limits. . . .

It is the opinion of a majority of the court that the mere grant to Congress of the power to regulate commerce, did not deprive the States of power to regulate pilots, and that although Congress has legislated on this subject, its legislation manifests an intention, with a single exception, not to regulate this subject, but to leave its regulation to the several States. To these precise questions, which are all we are called on to decide, this opinion must be understood to be confined. It does not extend to the question what other subjects, under the commercial power, are within the exclusive control of Congress, or may be regulated by the States in the absence of all congressional legislation; nor to the general question how far any regulation of a subject by Congress may be deemed to operate as an exclusion of all legislation by the States upon the same subject. We decide the precise questions before us, upon what we deem sound principles, applicable to this particular subject in the state in which the legislation of Congress has left it. We go no farther. . . .

Mr. Justice **McLean,** with Mr. Justice **Wayne** concurring, rendered a dissenting opinion.

Mr. Justice **Daniel** rendered an opinion which differed in reasoning but concurred in the judgment of the Court.

EDWARDS v. CALIFORNIA

314 U.S. 160; 62 S. Ct. 164; 86 L. Ed. 119 (1941)

Many states have set up quarantine regulations and applied them to persons or goods entering the state. These are valid if they do not cut off legitimate interstate commerce or compete with existing federal controls. In an early case, Hannibal & St. J. R. Co. v. Husen (1878), a Missouri statute, in order to keep out of the state any cattle which might be infected with Texas fever, forbade the bringing into the state of any "Texas, Mexican or Indian cattle between March 1 and November 1 of each year."

This was held void since it imposed a complete embargo upon all interstate shipments of cattle from the areas specified instead of confining itself to barring diseased animals. However, in Mintz v. Baldwin (1933) the state of New York was upheld in forbidding the bringing into the state for dairy or breeding purposes any cattle unless such cattle, and the herds from which they came, were certified by the chief sanitary officer of the state of origin to be free from Bang's disease. This requirement was held not to be an invalid burden upon interstate commerce. In Minnesota v. Barber (1890) the Supreme Court held invalid a state requirement that fresh meat could not be sold in the state unless inspected by a state inspector not more than twenty-four hours before it was slaughtered. The practical effect of the statute, the Court found, was to exclude from Minnesota markets all meat slaughtered outside the state. In 1951 a similar fate befell a Madison, Wisconsin, ordinance which forbade the sale within the city of milk that had not been pasteurized within five miles of the center of the city and produced in establishments inspected by city health officials, which officials were not required to travel more than twenty-five miles from Madison; see Dean Milk Co. v. Madison (1951). In both cases the Court noted that there were reasonable alternatives by which the public health could be safeguarded.

The statute of California at issue in Edwards v. California, printed below, was known popularly as the "anti-Okie" law. Along with similar statutes passed by more than twenty other states it penalized the bringing into the state of indigent persons. The importance and sweep of the social problem involved in this legislation lifted the Edwards case out of the usual category of conflicts between state police power and interstate commerce, and, in fact, led four members of the Court to conclude that the invalidity of the statute ought not to rest on the commerce clause but on the more basic ground that the act abridged the privileges and immunities of citizens of the United States in violation of the Fourteenth Amendment. To make this minority position amply clear, the concurring opinion of Justice Jackson is printed below. It is interesting to recall that in Crandall v. Nevada (1868) the Court had held invalid a state statute which imposed on common carriers a charge of $1.00 for each passenger transported out of the state. This was held to abridge the privilege of national citizenship to move freely about the country. Two justices concurred in the result, but stated that the act should have been held void as unconstitutional obstruction of interstate commerce. In the Edwards case the majority of the Court preferred to invalidate the California statute as an obstruction of commerce, leaving the concurring justices to defend the position taken by the majority in the Crandall case.

Mr. Justice **Byrnes** delivered the opinion of the Court, saying in part:

The facts of this case are simple and are not disputed. Appellant is a citizen of the United States and a resident of California. In December, 1939, he left his home in Marysville, California, for Spur, Texas, with the intention of bringing back to Marysville his wife's brother, Frank Duncan, a citizen of the United States and a resident of Texas. When he arrived in Texas, appellant learned that Duncan had last been employed by the Works Progress Administration. Appellant thus became aware of the fact that Duncan was an indigent person and he continued to be aware of it throughout the period involved in this case. The two men agreed that appellant should transport Duncan from Texas to Marysville in appellant's automobile. Accordingly, they left Spur on January 1, 1940, entered California by way of Arizona on January 3, and reached Marysville on January 5. When he left Texas, Duncan had about $20. It had all been spent by the time he reached Marysville. He lived with appellant for about ten days until he obtained financial assistance from the Farm Security Administration. During the ten-day interval, he had no employment.

In Justice Court a complaint was filed against appellant under § 2615 of the Welfare and Institutions Code of California, which provides: Every person, firm or corporation, or officer or agent thereof that brings or assists in bringing into the State any indigent person who is not a resident of the State, knowing him to be an indigent person, is guilty of a misdemeanor." . . . [The] appellant was convicted and sentenced to six months imprisonment in the county jail, and sentence was suspended. . . .

Article 1, § 8 of the Constitution delegates to the Congress the authority to regulate interstate commerce. And it is settled beyond question that the transportation of persons is "commerce," within the meaning of that provision. It is nevertheless true that the States are not wholly precluded from exercising their police power in matters of local concern even though they may thereby affect interstate commerce. . . . The issue presented in this case, therefore, is whether the prohibition embodied in § 2615 against the "bringing" or transportation of indigent persons into California is within the police power of that State. We think that it is not, and hold that it is an unconstitutional barrier to interstate commerce.

The grave and perplexing social and economic dislocation which this statute reflects is a matter of common knowledge and concern. We are not unmindful of it. We appreciate that the spectacle of large segments of our population constantly on the move has given rise to urgent demands upon the ingenuity of government. Both the brief of the Attorney General of California and that of the Chairman of the Select Committee of the House of Representatives of the United States, as amicus curiae, have sharpened this appreciation. The State asserts that the huge influx of migrants into California in recent years has resulted in problems of health, morals, and especially finance, the proportions of which are staggering. It is not for us to say that this is not true. We have repeatedly and recently affirmed, and we now reaffirm, that we do not conceive it our function to pass upon "the wisdom, need, or appropriateness" of the legislative efforts of the States to solve such difficulties. . . .

But this does not mean that there are no boundaries to the permissible area of State legislative activity. There are. And none is more certain than the prohibition against attempts on the part of any single State to isolate itself from difficulties common to all of them by restraining the transportation of persons and property across its borders. It is frequently the case that a State might gain a momentary respite from the pressure of events by the simple expedient of shutting its gates to the outside world. But, in the words of Mr. Justice Cardozo: "The Constitution was framed under the dominion of a political philosophy less parochial in range. It was framed upon the theory that the peoples of the several States must sink or swim together, and that in the long run prosperity and salvation are in union and not division." Baldwin v. Seelig [1935].

It is difficult to conceive of a statute more squarely in conflict with this theory than the section challenged here. Its express purpose and inevitable effect is to prohibit the transportation of indigent persons across the California border. The burden upon interstate commerce is intended and immediate; it is the plain and sole function of the statute. Moreover, the indigent nonresidents who are the real victims of the statute are deprived of the opportunity to exert political pressure upon the California legislature in order to obtain a change in policy. . . . We think this statute must fail under any known test of the validity of State interference with interstate commerce.

It is urged, however, that the concept which underlies § 2615 enjoys a firm basis in English and American history. This is the notion that each community should care for its own indigent, that relief is solely the responsibility of local government. Of this it must first be said that we are not now called upon to determine anything other than the propriety of an attempt by a State to prohibit the transportation of indigent nonresidents into its territory. The nature and extent of its obligation to afford relief to newcomers is not here involved. We do, however, suggest that the theory of the Elizabethan poor laws no longer fits the facts. Recent years, and particularly the past decade, have been marked by a growing recognition that in an industrial society the task of providing assistance to the needy has ceased to be local in character. The duty to share the burden, if not wholly to assume it, has been recognized not only by State governments, but by the Federal government as well. The changed attitude is reflected in the Social Security laws under which the Federal and State governments cooperate for the care of the aged, the blind and dependent children. It is reflected in the works programs under which work is furnished the unemployed, with the States supplying approximately 25% and the Federal government approximately 75% of the cost. . . . It is further reflected in the Farm Security laws, under which the entire cost of the relief provisions is borne by the Federal government.

Indeed the record in this very case illustrates the inadequate basis in fact for the theory that relief is presently a local matter. Before leaving Texas, Duncan had received assistance from the Works Progress Administration. After arriving in California he was aided by the Farm Security Administration, which, as we have said, is wholly financed by the Federal government. This is not to say that our judgment would be different if Duncan had received relief from local agencies in Texas and California. Nor is it to suggest that the financial burden of assistance to indigent persons does not continue to fall heavily upon local and State governments. It is only to illustrate that in not inconsiderable measure the relief of the needy has become the common responsibility and concern of the whole nation.

What has been said with respect to financing relief is not without its bearing upon the regulation of the transportation of indigent persons. For the social phenomenon of large-scale interstate migration is as certainly a matter of national concern as the provision of assistance to those who have found a permanent or temporary abode. Moreover, and unlike the relief problem, this phenomenon does not admit of diverse treatment by the several States. The prohibition against transporting indigent nonresidents into one State is an open invitation to retaliatory measures, and the burdens upon the transportation of such persons become cumulative. Moreover, it would be a virtual impossibility for migrants and those who transport them to acquaint themselves with the peculiar rules of admission of many States. "This Court has repeatedly declared that the grant [the commerce clause] established the immunity of interstate commerce from the control of the States respecting all those subjects embraced within the grant which are of such a nature as to demand that, if regulated at all, their regulation must be prescribed by a single authority." Milk Control Board v. Eisenberg Farm Products [1939]. We are of the opinion that the transportation of indigent persons from State to State clearly falls within this class of subjects. The scope of congressional power to deal with this problem we are not now called upon to decide.

There remains to be noticed only the contention that the limitation upon State power to interfere with the interstate transportation of persons is subject to an exception in the case of "paupers." It is true that support for this contention may be found in early decisions of this Court. In New York v. Miln [1837], it was said that it is "as competent and as necessary for a State to provide precautionary measures against the moral pestilence of paupers, vagabonds, and possibly convicts, as it is to guard against the physical pestilence which may arise from unsound and infectious articles imported. . . ." This language has been casually repeated in numerous later cases up to the turn of the century. . . . In none of these cases, however, was the power of a State to exclude "paupers" actually involved.

Whether an able-bodied but unemployed person like Duncan is a "pauper" within the historical meaning of the term is open to considerable doubt. . . . But assuming that the term is applicable to him and to persons similarly situated, we do not consider ourselves bound by the language referred to. New York v. Miln was decided in 1837. Whatever may have been the notion then prevailing, we do not think that it will now be seriously contended that because a person is without employment and without funds he constitutes a "moral pestilence." Poverty and immorality are not synonymous.

We are of the opinion that § 2615 is not a valid

exercise of the police power of California, that it imposes an unconstitutional burden upon interstate commerce, and that the conviction under it cannot be sustained. In the view we have taken it is unnecessary to decide whether the section is repugnant to other provisions of the Constitution.

Reversed.

Mr. Justice **Douglas** wrote a concurring opinion, in which Justices **Black** and **Murphy** joined. He contended that the statute was void because "The right to move freely from State to State is an incident of *national* citizenship protected by the privileges and immunities clause of the Fourteenth Amendment against State interference."

Mr. Justice **Jackson,** concurring, said:

I concur in the result reached by the Court, and I agree that the grounds of its decision are permissible ones under applicable authorities. But the migrations of a human being, of whom it is charged that he possesses nothing that can be sold and has no wherewithal to buy, do not fit easily into my notions as to what is commerce. To hold that the measure of his rights is the commerce clause is likely to result eventually either in distorting the commercial law or in denaturing human rights. I turn, therefore, away from principles by which commerce is regulated to that clause of the Constitution by virtue of which Duncan is a citizen of the United States and which forbids any state to abridge his privileges or immunities as such.

This clause was adopted to make United States citizenship the dominant and paramount allegiance among us. The return which the law had long associated with allegiance was protection. The power of citizenship as a shield against oppression was widely known from the example of Paul's Roman citizenship, which sent the centurion scurrying to his higher-ups with the message: "Take heed what thou doest: for this man is a Roman." I suppose none of us doubts that the hope of imparting to American citizenship some of this vitality was the purpose of declaring in the Fourteenth Amendment: "All persons born or naturalized in the United States, and subject to the jurisdiction thereof, are citizens of the United States and of the State wherein they reside. No State shall make or enforce any law which shall abridge the privileges or immunities of citizens of the United States. . . ."

But the hope proclaimed in such generality soon shriveled in the process of judicial interpretation. For nearly three-quarters of a century this Court rejected every plea to the privileges and immunities clause. The judicial history of this clause and the very real difficulties in the way of its practical application to specific cases have been too well and recently reviewed to warrant repetition.

While instances of valid "privileges or immunities" must be but few, I am convinced that this is one. I do not ignore or belittle the difficulties of what has been characterized by this Court as an "almost forgotten" clause. But the difficulty of the task does not excuse us from giving these general and abstract words whatever of specific content and concreteness they will bear as we mark out their application, case by case. That is the method of the common law, and it has been the method of this Court with other no less general statements in our fundamental law. This Court has not been timorous about giving concrete meaning to such obscure and vagrant phrases as "due process," "general welfare," "equal protection," or even "commerce among the several States." But it has always hesitated to give any real meaning to the privileges and immunities clause lest it improvidently give too much.

This Court should, however, hold squarely that it is a privilege of citizenship of the United States, protected from state abridgment, to enter any state of the Union, either for temporary sojourn or for the establishment of permanent residence therein and for gaining resultant citizenship thereof. If national citizenship means less than this, it means nothing.

The language of the Fourteenth Amendment declaring two kinds of citizenship is discriminating. It is: "All persons born or naturalized in the United States, and subject to the jurisdiction thereof, are citizens of the United States and of the State wherein they reside." While it thus establishes national citizenship from the mere circumstance of birth within the territory and jurisdiction of the United States, birth within a state does not establish citizenship thereof. State citizenship is ephemeral. It results only from residence and is gained or lost therewith. That choice of residence was subject to local approval is contrary to the inescapable implications of the westward movement of our civilization.

Even as to an alien who had "been admitted to the United States under the Federal law," this Court, through Mr. Justice Hughes, declared that "He was thus admitted with the privilege of entering and abiding in the United States, and hence of entering and abiding in any State in the Union." Truax v. Raich [1915]. Why we should hesitate to hold that federal citizenship implies rights to enter and abide in any state of the Union at least equal to those possessed by aliens passes my understanding. The world is even more upside down than I had supposed it to be, if California must accept aliens in deference to their federal privileges but is free to turn back citizens of the United States unless we treat them as subjects of commerce.

The right of the citizen to migrate from state to state which, I agree with Mr. Justice Douglas, is shown by our precedents to be one of national citizenship, is not, however, an unlimited one. In addition to being subject to all constitutional limitations imposed by the federal government, such citizen is subject to some control by state governments. He may not, if a fugitive from justice, claim freedom to migrate unmolested, nor may he endanger others by carrying contagion about. These causes, and perhaps others that do not occur to me now, warrant any public authority in stopping a man where it finds him and arresting his progress across a state line quite as much as from place to place within the state.

It is here that we meet the real crux of this case. Does "indigence" as defined by the application of the California statute constitute a basis for restricting the freedom of a citizen, as crime or contagion warrants its restriction? We should say now, and in no uncertain terms, that a man's mere property status, without more, cannot be used by a state to test, qualify, or limit his rights as a citizen of the United States. "Indigence" in itself is neither a source of rights nor a basis for denying them. The mere state of being without funds is a neutral fact—constitutionally an irrelevance, like race, creed, or color. I agree with what I understand to be the holding of the Court that cases which may indicate the contrary are overruled.

Any measure which would divide our citizenry on the basis of property into one class free to move from state to state and another class that is poverty-bound to the place where it has suffered misfortune is not only at war with the habit and custom by which our country has expanded, but is also a short-sighted blow at the security of property itself. Property can have no more dangerous, even if unwitting, enemy than one who would make its possession a pretext for unequal or exclusive civil rights. Where those rights are derived from national citizenship no state may impose such a test, and whether the Congress could do so we are not called upon to inquire.

I think California had no right to make the condition of Duncan's purse, with no evidence of violation by him of any law or social policy which caused it, the basis of excluding him or of punishing one who extended him aid.

If I doubted whether his federal citizenship alone were enough to open the gates of California to Duncan, my doubt would disappear on consideration of the obligations of such citizenship. Duncan owes a duty to render military service, and this Court has said that this duty is the result of his citizenship. Mr. Chief Justice White declared in the Selective Draft Law Cases [1918]: "It may not be doubted that the very conception of a just government and its duty to the citizen includes the reciprocal obligation of the citizen to render military service in case of need and the right to compel it." A contention that a citizen's duty to render military service is suspended by "indigence" would meet with little favor. Rich or penniless, Duncan's citizenship under the Constitution pledges his strength to the defense of California as a part of the United States, and his right to migrate to any part of the land he must defend is something she must respect under the same instrument. Unless this Court is willing to say that citizenship of the United States means at least this much to the citizen, then our heritage of constitutional privileges and immunities is only a promise to the ear to be broken to the hope, a teasing illusion like a munificent bequest in a pauper's will.

UNITED STATES v. E. C. KNIGHT CO.

156 U. S. 1; 15 S. Ct. 249; 39 L. Ed. 325 (1895)

For one hundred years prior to 1887 the Supreme Court had struggled with the question: what constitutes interstate commerce and when is a business engaged in it? The question was important because the answer deter- mined the power of the states to tax and regulate commercial enterprises within their borders. Since the only regulation there was was state regulation, if a business could show that it was engaged in interstate commerce it could escape regulation entirely. In 1888 a liquor distiller argued that he could not be forbidden by an Iowa prohibition law to manufacture liquor within the state, since all his product went into interstate commerce and putting him out of business would burden that commerce. In Kidd v. Pearson the Supreme Court rejected the contention and held that manufacturing was not interstate commerce but a separate process antecedent thereto, and that his plan to ship the liquor out of the state did not alter this situation.

Following the passage in 1887 of the Interstate Commerce Act and in 1890 of the Sherman Antitrust Act, activities which had previously argued they were interstate in order to avoid state regulation now argued they were local to avoid the new federal laws. The Court, which was largely antagonistic to regulation of any kind, continued to draw the lines of definition where they had been before but their effect now was to determine what things Congress could and could not regulate under its commerce power. The doctrine of the Kidd case was applied in the case below and in Oliver Iron Mining Co. v. Lord (1923) the Court extended it to hold that mining, like manufacturing, was not interstate commerce.

In Federal Baseball Club v. National League (1922) the Court held that major league baseball games were local activities and not subject to the Antitrust Act, despite the fact that the players traveled interstate to play games which had been arranged through interstate transactions. As Justice Holmes expressed it, "The business is giving exhibitions of baseball, which are purely state affairs." In 1953 the Federal Baseball Club holding was reaffirmed by the Court in Toolson v. New York Yankees, Inc. to the extent that it "determines that Congress had no intention of including the business of baseball within the scope of the federal antitrust laws" (a determination not apparent in the Federal Baseball case itself). However, in United States v. International Boxing Club of New York (1955) and United States v. Shubert (1955) the Court departed from Toolson and refused to hold either prize fighting or theatrical productions exempt from the antitrust controls of Congress. When, in 1957, in Radovich v. National Football League the Court refused to apply an exemption to football, it became clear that the Toolson case would have no progeny. The Court distinguished baseball from boxing, football, and the theater on the basis of the relative volume of interstate business involved in the four fields of activity. "If this ruling is unrealistic, inconsistent, or illogical, it is sufficient to answer . . . that were we considering the question of baseball for the first time upon a clean slate we would have no doubts. But Federal Baseball held the business of baseball outside the scope of the Act. No other business claiming the coverage of those cases has such an adjudication."

The decisions of Federal Baseball and Toolson were reaffirmed in Flood v. Kuhn (1972). There the Court noted that baseball was a business engaged in interstate commerce but pointed out that over fifty bills had been introduced in Congress dealing with the applicability of the antitrust laws to baseball and the only ones to pass either house would have extended the exemption to other sports rather than remove it from baseball. Conceding that it was an aberration, the Court made clear that "it is an aberration that has been with us now for half a century" and if any changes were going to come in it they would have to come from Congress.

The Supreme Court, as a general rule, has had little difficulty in keeping the commerce clause up to date. As new techniques have been devised or as local activities have spread across state lines, the Court has spread the clause to cover them. Thus in the field of communications the Court held in Pensacola Teleg. Co. v. Western Union Teleg. Co. (1878) that telegraphic communication is interstate commerce and in Federal Radio Comm. v. Nelson Bros. Bond and Mortgage Co. (1933) a similar result was reached with respect to radio transmission. When television made its appearance, it became interstate commerce without the question ever being raised. Transportation of persons and things received similar treatment; and as they appeared, the commerce clause was extended to steamships, railroads, automobiles, and aircraft. In United States v. Ohio Oil Co. (Pipe Line Cases) (1914) the transmission of one's own oil by pipe line was held to be interstate commerce.

Nor is it necessary that the interstate transaction be a business transaction undertaken for profit. In Covington & Cincinnati Bridge Co. v. Kentucky (1894) persons crossing an interstate bridge were said to be in interstate commerce and in United States v. Simpson (1920) a person carrying his own liquor across a state line in his own car was held to be engaged in such commerce. In Caminetti v. United States (1917) the Mann "White Slave" Act was held applicable to those who transport women across state lines for immoral, although noncommercial, purposes and in Cleveland v. United States (1946) to a Mormon who was taking one of his wives across a state line.

It is apparent that Congress must have the power to control the avenues along which interstate commerce moves, since only in that way can such movement be protected from real or threatened obstruction. From the first, Congress has required the licensing of those using vessels on the navigable waters of the United States. As early as 1852 in The Genesee Chief the Court rejected the English common-law rule which defined as navigable only those waters in which the tide ebbed and flowed, and in The Daniel Ball (1871) it held that "those rivers must be regarded as public navigable rivers in law which are navigable in fact." There the Court upheld the licensing of a steamer which never left the state but which plied waters flowing into Lake Michigan carrying goods some of which moved out of state.

In United States v. Appalachian Electric Power Co. (1940) control over navigable streams was extended to those which could be made navigable "after reasonable improvements which might be made." In upholding the need for a Federal Power Commission license to build a power dam across the New River in Tennessee, the Court made clear that "In our view, it cannot properly be said that the constitutional power of the United States over its waters is limited to control for navigation. . . . Navigability, . . . is but a part of [the] whole. Flood protection, watershed development, recovery of the cost of improvements through utilization of power are likewise parts of commerce control." And in Cappaert v. United States (1976), the Court held that the commerce and property power gave the federal government power to assure the water level in Devil's Hole, a deep limestone cavern in Nevada, in order to protect a unique species of desert fish. Devil's Hole had been made a national monument and Cappaert, by pumping water from wells on his ranch two and a half miles away, was lowering the water level in the cave.

Mr. Chief Justice **Fuller** delivered the opinion of the Court, saying in part:

By the purchase of the stock of . . . four Philadelphia refineries, with shares of its own stock, the American Sugar Refining Company acquired nearly complete control of the manufacture of refined sugar within the United States. The bill charged that the contracts under which these purchases were made constituted combinations in restraint of trade, and that in entering into them the defendants combined and conspired to restrain the trade and commerce in refined sugar among the several states and with foreign nations, contrary to the Act of Congress of July 2, 1890.

. . . The monopoly and restraining denounced by the Act are the monopoly and restraining of interstate and international trade or commerce, while the conclusion to be assumed on this record is that the result of the transaction complained of was the creation of a monopoly in the manufacture of a necessary of life. . . .

The fundamental question is whether conceding that the existence of a monopoly in manufacture is established by the evidence, that monopoly can be directly suppressed under the Act of Congress in the mode attempted by this bill.

It cannot be denied that the power of a state to protect the lives, health, and property of its citizens, and to preserve good order and the public morals, "the power to govern men and things within the limits of its dominion," is power originally and always belonging to the states, not surrendered by them to the general government, nor directly restrained by the Constitution of the United States, and essentially exclusive. The relief of the citizens of each state from the burden of monopoly and the evils resulting from the restraint of trade among such citizens was left with the states to deal with. . . .

The argument is that the power to control the manufacture of refined sugar is a monopoly over a necessary of life, to the enjoyment of which by a large population of the United States interstate commerce is indispensable, and that, therefore, the general government in the exercise of the power to regulate commerce may repress such monopoly directly and set aside the instruments which have created it. But this argument cannot be confined to the necessaries of life merely, and must include all articles of general consumption. Doubtless the power to control the manufacture of a given thing involves in a certain sense the control of its disposition, but this is a secondary and not the primary sense; and although the exercise of that power may result in bringing the operation of commerce into play, it does not control it, and affects it only incidentally and indirectly. Commerce succeeds to manufacture, and is not a part of it. The power to regulate commerce is the power to prescribe the rule by which commerce shall be governed, and is a power independent of the power to suppress monopoly. But it may operate in repression of monopoly whenever that comes within the rules by which commerce is governed or whenever the transaction is itself a monopoly of commerce.

It is vital that the independence of the commercial power and of the police power, and the delimitation between them, however sometimes perplexing, should always be recognized and observed, for while the one furnishes the strongest bond of union, the other is essential to the preservation of the autonomy of the states as required by our dual form of government; and acknowledged evils, however grave and urgent they may appear to be, had better be borne, than the risk be run, in the effort to suppress them, of more serious consequences by resort to expedients of even doubtful constitutionality. . . .

. . . In Kidd v. Pearson [1888], where the question was discussed whether the right of a state to enact a statute prohibiting within its limits the manufacture of intoxicating liquors, except for certain purposes, could be overthrown by the fact that the manufacturer intended to export the liquors when made, it was held that the intent of the manufacturer did not determine the time when the article or product passed from the control of the state and belonged to commerce. . . . And Mr. Justice Lamar remarked: ". . . If it be held that the term includes the regulation of all such manufactures as are intended to be the subject of commercial transactions in the future, it is impossible to deny that it would also include all productive industries that contemplate the same thing. The result would be that Congress would be invested, to the exclusion of the states, with the power to regulate, not only manufactures, but also agriculture, horticulture, stock raising, domestic fisheries, mining—in short, every branch of human industry. For is there one of them that does not contemplate, more or less clearly, an interstate market? Does not the wheat grower of the northwest, and the cotton planter of the south, plant, cultivate, and harvest his crop with an eye on the prices at Liverpool, New York and Chicago? The power being vested in Congress and denied to the states, it would follow as an inevitable result that the duty would devolve on Congress to regulate all of these delicate multiform, and vital interests—interests which in their nature are and must be local in all the details of their successful management. . . . The demands of such supervisions would require, not uniform legislation generally applicable throughout the United States, but a swarm of statutes only locally applicable and utterly inconsistent. . . . Any movement toward the local, detailed, and incongruous legislation required by such interpretation would be about the widest possible

departure from the declared object of the clause in question. . . ."

Contracts, combinations, or conspiracies to control domestic enterprise in manufacture, agriculture, mining, production in all its forms, or to raise or lower prices or wages, might unquestionably tend to restrain external as well as domestic trade, but the restraint would be an indirect result, however inevitable and whatever its extent, and such result would not necessarily determine the object of the contract, combination, or conspiracy. . . .

. . . The contracts and acts of the defendants related exclusively to the acquisition of the Philadelphia refineries and the business of sugar refining in Pennsylvania, and bore no direct relation to commerce between the states or with foreign nations. The object was manifestly private gain in the manufacture of the commodity, but not through the control of interstate or foreign commerce. It is true that the bill alleged that the products of these refineries were sold and distributed among the several states, and that all the companies were engaged in trade or commerce with the several states and with foreign nations; but this was no more than to say that trade and commerce served manufacture to fulfill its function. . . . There was nothing in the proofs to indicate any intention to put a restraint upon trade or commerce, and the fact, as we have seen, that trade or commerce might be indirectly affected was not enough to entitle complainants to a decree. . . .

Mr. Justice **Harlan** dissented.

THE SHREVEPORT CASE.
HOUSTON, EAST & WEST TEXAS RY. CO.
v. UNITED STATES

234 U. S. 342; 34 S. Ct. 833; 58 L. Ed. 1341
(1914)

The language of the commerce clause, together with that of the Tenth Amendment, seemed to indicate that the internal commerce of a state—that which is not commerce "among the several States"—is reserved exclusively for state control. That a class of commerce existed which was beyond the reach of Congress was generally accepted, and in Covington & Cincinnati Bridge Co. v. Kentucky (1894) the Court had noted that it included the power to construct railways "and regulate the tolls for the use of the same." The Court, in effect, drew a clear-cut and somewhat mechanical line between interstate commerce and local commerce and this line divided the power of Congress from that of the states. Hence the E. C. Knight case (1895), in which manufacturing was held to be a local activity and therefore beyond the reach of federal control.

In the Shreveport Case printed below, the Court abandoned this outmoded concept of two mutually exclusive areas of intrastate and interstate commerce, each clearly and safely under the control of state or federal government. *In its place, as a rule for measuring federal authority in the field of commerce, it adopted the realistic test of whether commercial or business activities— even though they be local—so impinge upon or affect interstate commerce as to bring them reasonably within the range of federal control. The Court recognized a functional relationship between local and interstate commerce. In the Transportation Act of 1920 Congress made explicit the power of the ICC to deal with local rates which unduly discriminate against interstate rates, and the validity of this was sustained in Railroad Commission v. Chicago, B. & Q. R. Co. (1922).*

In 1922 the doctrine of the Shreveport Case was extended to cover local businesses other than common carriers. In 1921 Congress had passed the Packers and Stockyards Act in an effort to break up discriminatory practices resulting from control of the stockyards by the "Big Five" meat packers: Swift, Armour, Cudahy, Wilson, and Morris. Livestock was shipped into Chicago from producers throughout the West and was received by brokers called "commission men," who unloaded the stock into pens in the stockyard, watered and cared for them, and then sold them on a commission basis, largely to the big meat packers. Most of the meat, either before or after packing, was shipped to eastern markets. The control of the stockyards by the packers and their resultant influence over the commission men resulted in discrimination against the western shipper as well as against other buyers. The act provided an elaborate scheme of regulation, including approval by the Secretary of Agriculture of all rates and charges for services and facilities in the stockyards.

In Stafford v. Wallace (1922) the Supreme Court sustained this regulation, rejecting the argument that Congress had no authority to control purely local sales of cattle after they had come to rest in the stockyards. "The stockyards," the Court said, "are not a place of rest or final destination. Thousands of head of live stock arrive daily by carloads and trainload lots, and must be promptly sold and disposed of and moved out to give place to the constantly flowing traffic that presses behind. The stockyards are but a throat through which the current flows, and the transactions which occur therein are only incident to this current from the West to the East, and from one State to another. Such transactions cannot be separated from the movement to which they contribute, and necessarily take on its character. . . . The sales are not, in this aspect, merely local transactions. They create a local change of title, it is true, but they do not stop the flow; they merely change the private interests in the subject of the current, not interfering with, but, on the contrary, being indispensable to, its continuity." The essentially local nature of the sales which were being regulated was emphasized in Minnesota v. Blasius (1933), in which the Court upheld a state property tax upon cattle which had come to rest in the stockyards awaiting sale. "But because there is a flow of interstate commerce which is subject to the regulating power of the Congress, it does not necessarily follow that . . . a State may not lay a non-discriminatory tax

upon property which, although connected with that flow as a general course of business, has come to rest and has acquired a situs within the State."

Mr. Justice **Hughes** delivered the opinion of the Court, saying in part:

These suits were brought in the commerce court by the Houston, East & West Texas Railway Company and the Houston & Shreveport Railroad Company, and by the Texas & Pacific Railway Company, respectively, to set aside an order of the Interstate Commerce Commission, dated March 11, 1912, upon the ground that it exceeded the Commission's authority. . . .

The order of the Interstate Commerce Commission was made in a proceeding initiated in March, 1911, by the Railroad Commission of Louisiana. The complaint was that the appellants, and other interstate carriers, maintained unreasonable rates from Shreveport, Louisiana, to various points in Texas, and further, that these carriers, in the adjustment of rates over their respective lines, unjustly discriminated in favor of traffic within the state of Texas, and against similar traffic between Louisiana and Texas. The carriers filed answers; numerous pleas of intervention by shippers and commercial bodies were allowed; testimony was taken and arguments were heard.

The gravamen of the complaint, said the Interstate Commerce Commission, was that the carriers made rates out of Dallas and other Texas points into eastern Texas which were much lower than those which they extended into Texas from Shreveport. The situation may be briefly described: Shreveport, Louisiana, is about 40 miles from the Texas state line, and 231 miles from Houston, Texas, on the line of the Houston, East & West Texas and Houston & Shreveport Companies (which are affiliated in interest); it is 189 miles from Dallas, Texas, on the line of the Texas & Pacific. Shreveport competes with both cities for the trade of the intervening territory. The rates on these lines from Dallas and Houston, respectively, eastward to intermediate points in Texas, were much less, according to distance, than from Shreveport westward to the same points. It is undisputed that the difference was substantial, and injuriously affected the commerce of Shreveport. It appeared, for example, that a rate of 60 cents carried first-class traffic a distance of 160 miles to the eastward from Dallas, while the same rate would carry the same class of traffic only 55 miles into Texas from Shreveport. . . . The rate on wagons from Dallas to Marshall, Texas, 147.7 miles, was 36.8 cents, and from Shreveport to Marshall, 42 miles, 56 cents. . . . These instances of differences in rates are merely illustrative; they serve to indicate the character of the rate adjustment.

. . . The Interstate Commerce Commission . . . found that the carriers maintained "higher rates from Shreveport to points in Texas" than were in force "from cities in Texas to such points under substantially similar conditions and circumstances," and that thereby "an unlawful and undue preference and advantage" was given to the Texas cities, and a "discrimination" that was "undue and unlawful" was effected against Shreveport. In order to correct this discrimination, the carriers were directed to desist from charging higher rates for the transportation of any commodity from Shreveport to Dallas and Houston, respectively, and intermediate points, than were contemporaneously charged for the carriage of such commodity from Dallas and Houston toward Shreveport for equal distances, as the Commission found that relation of rates to be reasonable. . . .

. . . There are, it appears, commodity rates fixed by the Railroad Commission of Texas for intrastate hauls, which are substantially less than the class, or standard, rates prescribed by that Commission; and thus the commodity rates charged by the carriers from Dallas and Houston eastward to Texas points are less than the rates which they demand for the transportation of the same articles for like distances from Shreveport into Texas. The present controversy relates to these commodity rates.

The point of the objection to the order is that, as the discrimination found by the Commission to be unjust arises out of the relation of intrastate rates, maintained under state authority, to interstate rates that have been upheld as reasonable, its correction was beyond the Commission's power. Manifestly the order might be complied with, and the discrimination avoided, either by reducing the interstate rate from Shreveport to the level of the competing intrastate rates, or by raising these intrastate rates to the level of the interstate rates, or by such reduction in the one case and increase in the other as would result in equality. But it is urged that, so far as the interstate rates were sustained by the Commission as reasonable, the Commission was without authority to compel their reduction in order to equalize them with the lower intrastate rates. The holding of the commerce court was that the order relieved the appellants from further obligation to observe the intrastate rates, 'and that they were at liberty to comply with the Commission's requirements by increasing these rates sufficiently to remove the forbidden discrimination. The invalidity of the order in this aspect is challenged upon two grounds:

(1) That Congress is impotent to control the intrastate charges of an interstate carrier even to the extent necessary to prevent injurious discrimination against interstate traffic; and

(2) That, if it be assumed that Congress has this power, still it has not been exercised, and hence the action of the Commission exceeded the limits of the authority which has been conferred upon it.

First. It is necessary to repeat what has frequently been said by this court with respect to the complete and paramount character of the power confided to Congress to regulate commerce among the several states. It is of the essence of this power that, where it exists, it dominates. Interstate trade was not left to be destroyed or impeded by the rivalries of local government. The purpose was to make impossible the recurrence of the evils which had overwhelmed the Confederation, and to provide the necessary basis of national unity by insuring "uniformity of regulation against conflicting and discriminating state legislation." By virtue of the comprehensive terms of the grant, the authority of Congress is at all times adequate to meet the varying exigencies that arise, and to protect the national interest by securing the freedom of interstate commercial intercourse from local control. . . .

Congress is empowered to regulate,—that is, to provide the law for the government of interstate commerce; to enact "all appropriate legislation" for its "protection and advancement" . . . ; to adopt measures "to promote its growth and insure its safety." Its authority, extending to these interstate carriers as instruments of interstate commerce, necessarily embraces the right to control their operations in all matters having such a close and substantial relation to interstate traffic that the control is essential or appropriate to the security of that traffic, to the efficiency of the interstate service, and to the maintenance of conditions under which interstate commerce may be conducted upon fair terms and without molestation or hindrance. As it is competent for Congress to legislate to these ends, unquestionably it may seek their attainment by requiring that the agencies of interstate commerce shall not be used in such manner as to cripple, retard, or destroy it. The fact that carriers are instruments of intrastate commerce, as well as of interstate commerce, does not derogate from the complete and paramount authority of Congress over the latter, or preclude the Federal power from being exerted to prevent the intrastate operations of such carriers from being made a means of injury to that which has been confided to Federal care. Wherever the interstate and intrastate transactions of carriers are so related that the government of the one involves the control of the other, it is Congress, and not the state, that is entitled to prescribe the final and dominant rule, for otherwise Congress would be denied the exercise of its constitutional authority, and the state, and not the nation, would be supreme within the national field. . . .

. . . This is not to say that Congress possesses the authority to regulate the internal commerce of a state, as such, but that it does possess the power to foster and protect interstate commerce, and to take all measures necessary or appropriate to that end, although intrastate transactions of interstate carriers may thereby be controlled.

This principle is applicable here. We find no reason to doubt that Congress is entitled to keep the highways of interstate communication open to interstate traffic upon fair and equal terms. That an unjust discrimination in the rates of a common carrier, by which one person or locality is unduly favored as against another under substantially similar conditions of traffic, constitutes an evil, is undeniable; and where this evil consists in the action of an interstate carrier in unreasonably discriminating against interstate traffic over its line, the authority of Congress to prevent it is equally clear. It is immaterial, so far as the protecting power of Congress is concerned, that the discrimination arises from intrastate rates as compared with interstate rates. The use of the instrument of interstate commerce in a discriminatory manner so as to inflict injury upon that commerce, or some part thereof, furnishes abundant ground for Federal intervention. Nor can the attempted exercise of state authority alter the matter, where Congress has acted, for a state may not authorize the carrier to do that which Congress is entitled to forbid and has forbidden. . . .

In conclusion: Reading the order in the light of the report of the Commission, it does not appear that the Commission attempted to require the carriers to reduce their interstate rates out of Shreveport below what was found to be a reasonable charge for that service. So far as these interstate rates conformed to what was found to be reasonable by the Commission, the carriers are entitled to maintain them, and they are free to comply with the order by so adjusting the other rates, to which the order relates, as to remove the forbidden discrimination. But this result they are required to accomplish.

The decree of the Commerce Court is affirmed in each case.

Affirmed.

Mr. Justice **Lurton** and Mr. Justice **Pitney** dissent.

HAMMER v. DAGENHART

247 U.S. 251; 38 S. Ct. 529; 62 L. Ed. 1101
(1918)

In the cases discussed above, the Supreme Court permitted federal control over local affairs on the ground that they affected interstate commerce, and only by controlling them could the national government ensure that the free flow of commerce among the states would not be impeded or adversely affected. A quite different use of the commerce power is involved when Congress closes the channels of interstate commerce to things of which it disapproves. By preventing the free flow of commerce for certain purposes or commodities, Congress in effect localizes those things and permits each state to have its own police regulations within its borders without fear of competition or interference from across state lines.

In 1895 Congress forbade the sending of lottery tickets through interstate commerce or the mails. The Court held the act valid in the Lottery Case (Champion v. Ames, 1903) against the charge that the power to regulate commerce did not include the power to prohibit that commerce. Noting that lotteries were a "widespread pestilence" "confessedly injurious to the public morals," and that lottery tickets were articles of commerce, the Court found that Congress' plenary power over commerce enabled it to "provide that such commerce shall not be polluted by the carrying of lottery tickets from one state to another."

Congress was not slow to exercise the kind of power sustained in the Lottery Case. It excluded from interstate commerce impure or misbranded food and drugs, meat not properly inspected, obscene literature, prize fight films (later modified in part), and other injurious or fraudulent commodities. Under a somewhat similar sort of law, if fabrics shipped in interstate commerce are marked "all wool," they must in fact be all wool. It

may be noted in passing that the power of Congress over the postal system has enabled it to exercise a wide police power by excluding objectionable articles from the mails and by forbidding the use of the mails for purposes of fraud.

The Court found no difference in principle between barring objectionable articles from interstate commerce and forbidding the use of the facilities of interstate commerce to aid immoral or criminal activities. In Hoke v. United States (1913) it held valid the Mann Act of 1910 which makes it a crime to transport women across a state line for immoral purposes. The act was not aimed at localized prostitution, but at the organized gangs of white slavers who carried on the interstate traffic in girls and women upon which commercialized vice depends. In 1925 Congress made it a crime knowingly to drive a stolen automobile across a state line, and this was upheld in Brooks v. United States (1925). Under the "anti-fence" laws, the same ban was put upon the interstate shipment of stolen goods in general. The so-called Lindbergh Act makes kidnapping a federal crime if the kidnapped person is carried across a state line (held valid in Gooch v. United States, 1936); and it is also a federal crime to use the mails, telephone, telegraph, or any system of interstate communication for purposes of extortion or blackmail. The Fleeing Felon Act of 1934 makes it a crime to travel in interstate commerce in order to escape from the criminal jurisdiction of a state, and in 1967 Congress forbade persons to travel in interstate commerce for the purpose of inciting a riot. The theory in all these cases is clear and convincing. Congress, which is responsible for interstate commerce and for the uses to which it is put, may punish those who use the facilities of that commerce for immoral or criminal purposes.

It was not unnatural, therefore, that Congress should turn to this power in an effort to solve an increasingly difficult and divisive economic and social problem—the competition in states which had outlawed child labor from the products of those states which had not, with the resultant encouragement of such labor in the latter states. The movement for the enactment of such legislation developed in strength, and in 1916 the Keating-Owen Act was passed. This law forbade the transportation in interstate commerce of the product of any mine or quarry in which within thirty days prior to its removal therefrom children under the age of sixteen had been allowed to work, or the product of any mill, cannery, workshop, factory, or manufacturing establishment in which within thirty days prior to the shipment of the product children under fourteen were allowed to work, or children under sixteen were allowed to work more than eight hours per day or more than six days per week or between the hours of seven in the evening and six in the morning. The prohibition extended to all the products of establishments employing children, not merely to the products made by children themselves. And if a manufacturer employed but one child for but a fraction of a day, the ban would fall upon the entire product of his plant for the thirty-day period subsequent to which such employment occurred.

Almost immediately after the law became operative

Dagenhart, the father of two children, one under four-teen and one between fourteen and sixteen, who were employed in a cotton mill in Charlotte, North Carolina, brought action to enjoin Hammer, the United States district attorney for that district, from enforcing the law against the employment of the two children. The federal district judge granted the injunction on the ground that the Keating-Owen Act was unconstitutional, and Hammer took an appeal to the Supreme Court.

Mr. Justice **Day** delivered the opinion of the Court, saying in part:

The attack upon the act rests upon three propositions: First. It is not a regulation of interstate and foreign commerce. Second. It contravenes the 10th Amendment to the Constitution. Third. It conflicts with the 5th amendment to the Constitution.

The controlling question for decision is: Is it within the authority of Congress in regulating commerce among the states to prohibit the transportation in interstate commerce of manufactured goods, the product of a factory in which, within thirty days prior to their removal therefrom, children under the age of fourteen have been employed or permitted to work, or children between the ages of fourteen and sixteen years have been employed or permitted to work more than eight hours in any day, or more than six days in any week, or after the hour of 7 o'clock p.m. or before the hour of 6 o'clock a.m.?

The power essential to the passage of this act, the government contends, is found in the commerce clause of the Constitution which authorizes Congress to regulate commerce with foreign nations and among the states.

In Gibbons v. Ogden [1824], Chief Justice Marshall, speaking for this court, and defining the extent and nature of the commerce power, said: "It is the power to regulate,—that is, to prescribe the rule by which commerce is to be governed." In other words, the power is one to control the means by which commerce is carried on, which is directly the contrary of the assumed right to forbid commerce from moving and thus destroy it as to particular commodities. But it is insisted that adjudged cases in this court establish the doctrine that the power to regulate given to Congress incidentally includes the authority to prohibit the movement of ordinary commodities, and therefore the subject is not open for discussion. The cases demonstrate the contrary. They rest upon the character of the particular subjects dealt with and the fact that the scope of governmental authority, state or national, possessed over them, is such that the authority to prohibit is, as to them, but the exertion of the power to regulate. [The Court here discusses the several cases mentioned in the note introducing this case.]

In each of these instances the use of interstate transportation was necessary to the accomplishment of harmful results. In other words, although the power over interstate transportation was to regulate, that could only be accomplished by prohibiting the use of the facilities of interstate commerce to effect the evil intended.

This element is wanting in the present case. The thing intended to be accomplished by this statute is the denial of the facilities of interstate commerce to those manufacturers in the states who employ children within the prohibited ages. The act in its effect does not regulate transportation among the states, but aims to standardize the ages at which children may be employed in mining and manufacturing within the states. The goods shipped are of themselves harmless. The act permits them to be freely shipped after thirty days from the time of their removal from the factory. When offered for shipment, and before transportation begins, the labor of their production is over, and the mere fact that they were intended for interstate commerce transportation does not make their production subject to Federal control under the commerce power.

Commerce "consists of intercourse and traffic . . . and includes the transportation of persons and property, as well as the purchase, sale and exchange of commodities." The making of goods and the mining of coal are not commerce, nor does the fact that these things are to be afterwards shipped, or used in interstate commerce, make their production a part thereof. . . .

Over interstate transportation, or its incidents, the regulatory power of Congress is ample, but the production of articles intended for interstate commerce is a matter of local regulation. "When the commerce begins is determined not by the character of the commodity, nor by the intention of the owner to transfer it to another state for sale, nor by his preparation of it for transportation, but by its actual delivery to a common carrier for transportation, or the actual commencement of its transfer to another state." . . . This principle has been recognized often in this court. . . . If it were otherwise, all manufacture intended for interstate shipment would be brought under federal control to the practical exclusion of the authority of the states,—a result certainly not contemplated by the framers of the Constitution when they vested in Congress the authority to regulate commerce among the states. . . .

It is further contended that the authority of Congress may be exerted to control interstate commerce in the shipment of child-made goods because of the effect of the circulation of such goods in other states where the evil of this class of labor has been recognized by local legislation, and the right to thus employ child labor has been more rigorously restrained than in the state of production. In other words, that the unfair competition thus engendered may be controlled by closing the channels of interstate commerce to manufacturers in those states where the local laws do not meet what Congress deems to be the more just standard of other states.

There is no power vested in Congress to require the states to exercise their police power so as to prevent possible unfair competition. Many causes may cooperate to give one state, by reason of local laws or conditions, an economic advantage over others. The commerce clause was not intended to give to Congress a general authority to equalize such conditions. In some of the states laws have been passed fixing minimum wages for women, in others the local law regulates the hours of labor of women in various employments. Business done in such states may be at an economic disadvantage when compared with states which have no such regulation; surely, this fact does not give Congress the power to deny transportation in interstate commerce to those who carry on business where the hours of labor and the rate of compensation for women have not been fixed by a standard in use in other states and approved by Congress.

The grant of power to Congress over the subject of interstate commerce was to enable it to regulate such commerce, and not to give it authority to control the states in their exercise of the police power over local trade and manufacture.

The grant of authority over a purely Federal matter was not intended to destroy the local power always existing and carefully reserved to the states in the 10th Amendment of the Constitution.

Police regulations relating to the internal trade and affairs of the states have been uniformly recognized as within such control. "This," said this court in United States v. Dewitt [1870], "has been so frequently declared by this court, results so obviously from the terms of the Constitution, and has been so fully explained and supported on former occasions, that we think it unnecessary to enter again upon the discussion." . . .

That there should be limitations upon the right to employ children in mines and factories in the interest of their own and the public welfare, all will admit. That such employment is generally deemed to require regulation is shown by the fact that the brief of counsel states that every state in the Union has a law upon the subject, limiting the right to thus employ children. In North Carolina, the state wherein is located the factory in which the employment was had in the present case, no child under twelve years of age is permitted to work.

It may be desirable that such laws be uniform, but our Federal government is one of enumerated powers. . . .

In interpreting the Constitution it must never be forgotten that the nation is made up of states, to which are intrusted the powers of local government. And to them and to the people the powers not expressly delegated to the national government are reserved. . . . The power of the states to regulate their purely internal affairs by such laws as seem wise to the local authority is inherent, and has never been surrendered to the general government. . . . To sustain this statute would not be, in our judgment, a recognition of the lawful exertion of congressional authority over interstate commerce, but would sanction an invasion by the federal power of the control of a matter purely local in its character, and over which no authority has been delegated to Congress in conferring the power to regulate commerce among the states.

We have neither authority nor disposition to question the motives of Congress in enacting this legislation. The purposes intended must be attained consistently with constitutional limitations, and not by an invasion of the powers of the states. This court has no more important function than that which devolves upon it the obligation to preserve inviolate the constitutional limitations upon the exercise of authority, federal and state, to the end that each may continue to discharge, harmoniously with the other, the duties intrusted to it by the Constitution.

In our view the necessary effect of this act is, by means of a prohibition against the movement in interstate commerce of ordinary commercial commodities, to regulate the hours of labor of children in factories and mines within the states, a purely state authority. Thus the act in a twofold sense is repugnant to the Constitution. It not only transcends the authority delegated to Congress over commerce, but also exerts a power as to a purely local matter to which the Federal authority does not extend. The far-reaching result of upholding the act cannot be more plainly indicated than by pointing out that if Congress can thus regulate matters intrusted to local authority by prohibition of the movement of commodities in interstate commerce, all freedom of commerce will be at an end, and the power of the states over local matters may be eliminated, and thus our system of government be practically destroyed.

For these reasons we hold that this law exceeds the constitutional authority of Congress. It follows that the decree of the District Court must be affirmed.

Mr. Justice **Holmes,** dissenting, said in part:

The single question in this case is whether Congress has power to prohibit the shipment in interstate or foreign commerce of any product of cotton mill [etc.]. . . . The objection urged against the power is that the states have exclusive control over their methods of production and that Congress cannot meddle with them, and taking the proposition in the sense of direct intermeddling I agree to it and suppose that no one denies it. But if an act is within the powers specifically conferred upon Congress, it seems to me that it is not made any less constitutional because of the indirect effects that it may have, however obvious it may be that it will have those effects; and that we are not at liberty upon such grounds to hold it void.

The first step in my argument is to make plain what no one is likely to dispute,—that the statute in question is within the power expressly given to Congress if considered only as to its immediate effects, and that if invalid it is so only upon some collateral ground. The statute confines itself to prohibiting the carriage of certain goods in interstate or foreign commerce. Congress is given power to regulate such commerce in unqualified terms. It would not be argued to-day that the power to regulate does not include the power to prohibit. Regulation means the prohibition of something, and when interstate commerce is the matter to be regulated I cannot doubt that the regulations may prohibit any part of such commerce that Congress sees fit to forbid. At all events it is established by the Lottery Case and others that have followed it that a law is not beyond the regulative power of Congress merely because it prohibits certain transportation out and out. Champion v. Ames [1903]. So I repeat that this statute in its immediate operation is clearly within the Congress's constitutional power.

The question, then, is narrowed to whether the exercise of its otherwise constitutional power by Congress can be pronounced unconstitutional because of its possible reaction upon the conduct of the states in a matter upon which I have admitted that they are free from direct control. I should have thought that that matter had been disposed of so fully as to leave no room for doubt. I should have thought that the most conspicuous decisions of this court had made it clear that the power to regulate commerce and other constitutional powers could not be cut down or qualified by the fact that it might interfere with carrying out of the domestic policy of any state.

The manufacture of oleomargarine is as much a matter of state regulation as the manufacture of cotton cloth. Congress levied a tax upon the compound when colored so as to resemble butter that was so great as obviously to prohibit the manufacture and sale. In a very elaborate discussion the present Chief Justice excluded any inquiry into the purpose of an act which, apart from that purpose, was within the power of Congress. McCray v. United States [1904]. . . . Fifty years ago a tax on state banks, the obvious purpose and actual effect of which was to drive them, or at least their circulation, out of existence, was sustained, although the result was one that Congress had no constitutional power to require. The court made short work of the argument as to the purpose of the act. "The judicial cannot prescribe to the legislative departments of the government limitations upon the exercise of its acknowledged powers." Veazie Bank v. Fenno [1869]. . . . And to come to cases upon interstate commerce, notwithstanding United States v. E. C. Knight Co. [1895], the Sherman Act has been made an instrument for the breaking up of combinations in restraint of trade and monopolies, using the power to regulate commerce as a foothold, but not proceeding because that commerce was the end actually in mind. The objection that the control of the states over production was interfered with was urged again and again, but always in vain. Standard Oil Co. v. United States [1911]. . . .

The Pure Food and Drug Act was sustained in Hipolite Egg Co. v. United States [1911], with the intimation that "no trade can be carried on between the states to which it [the power of Congress to regulate commerce] does not extend," applies not merely to articles that the changing opinions of the time condemn as intrinsically harmful, but to others innocent in themselves, simply on the ground that the order for them was induced by a preliminary fraud. . . . It does not matter whether the supposed evil precedes or follows the transportation. It is enough that, in the opinion of Congress, the transportation encourages the evil. . . .

The notion that prohibition is any less prohibition when applied to things now thought evil I do not understand. But if there is any matter upon which civilized countries have agreed,—far more unanimously than they have with regard to intoxicants and some other matters over which this country is now emotionally aroused,—it is the evil of premature and excessive child labor. I should have thought that if we were to introduce our own moral conceptions where, in my opinion, they do not belong, this was pre-eminently a case for upholding the exercise of all its powers by the United States.

But I had thought that the propriety of the exercise of a power admitted to exist in some cases was for the consideration of Congress alone, and that this court always had disavowed the right to intrude its judgment upon questions of policy or morals. It is not for this court

to pronounce when prohibition is necessary to regulation if it ever may be necessary,—to say that it is permissible as against strong drink, but not as against the product of ruined lives.

The act does not meddle with anything belonging to the states. They may regulate their internal affairs and their domestic commerce as they like. But when they seek to send their products across the state line they are no longer within their rights. If there were no Constitution and no Congress their power to cross the line would depend upon their neighbors. Under the Constitution such commerce belongs not to the states, but to Congress to regulate. It may carry out its views of public policy whatever indirect effect they may have upon the activities of the states. Instead of being encountered by a prohibitive tariff at her boundaries, the state encounters the public policy of the United States which it is for Congress to express. The public policy of the United States is shaped with a view to the benefit of the nation as a whole. If, as has been the case within the memory of men still living, a state should take a different view of the propriety of sustaining a lottery from that which generally prevails, I cannot believe that the fact would require a different decision from that reached in Champion v. Ames. Yet in that case it would be said with quite as much force as in this that Congress was attempting to intermeddle with the state's domestic affairs. The national welfare as understood by Congress may require a different attitude within its sphere from that of some self-seeking state. It seems to me entirely constitutional for Congress to enforce its understanding by all the means at its command.

Mr. Justice **McKenna,** Mr. Justice **Brandeis,** and Mr. Justice **Clarke** concur in this opinion.

SCHECHTER POULTRY CORPORATION v. UNITED STATES

295 U. S. 495; 55 S. Ct. 837; 79 L. Ed. 1570
(1935)(Continued from p. 55)

While the decision in Hammer v. Dagenhart was limited to Congressional efforts to keep products out of interstate commerce, it is apparent in retrospect that it was probably more an expression of the Court's hostility to federal regulation of traditional business affairs than a reasoned argument regarding the commerce clause. This is suggested by its comments in Bailey v. Drexel Furniture Co. (1922), the Child Labor Tax Case, to the effect that it "knew what Congress was up to," while at the same time it was holding valid a virtually indistinguishable prohibition on the interstate shipment of stolen automobiles; see Brooks v. United States (1925).

One question, however, had never been answered by the Court and that was when interstate commerce came to an end and state power took over. As was the case with the distinction between manufacturing and commerce, what theories there were had developed in the era prior to federal regulation. As early as 1827 in

Brown v. Maryland the Court had devised the "original package" doctrine to tell when imported goods ceased to enjoy the constitutional protection against state taxation conferred by Article 1, Sec. 10: when the original package was broken and the goods sold or mixed with other merchandise they lost their protection from state control and taxation.

In the State Freight Tax Case (1873) a state tax upon freight in transit was held void as applied to freight moving in interstate commerce, so it is important to know at what point goods moving in interstate commerce acquire whatever immunity from the state they may possess. Customarily goods enter interstate commerce when they are committed to a common carrier for transportation out of the state or have started on their ultimate passage out of the state, and they remain in interstate commerce until they come to rest in the state of their destination and are in the possession of those to whom they were consigned. Thus in Coe v. Errol (1886), logs piled on the bank of the Androscoggin River in New Hampshire were subject to a New Hampshire property tax until the river had actually risen and started them on their journey to the state of Maine, while logs which were launched further upstream in Maine did not become subject to the New Hampshire tax merely because they accidentally washed ashore in that state on their way to the mills at Lewiston, Maine. On the other hand, a taxi service provided by a railroad to bring interstate passengers to and from the depot was held to be local commerce preliminary or subsequent to the interstate journey rather than part of the interstate journey itself; see New York ex rel. Pennsylvania R. Co. v. Knight (1904).

But when do items moving in interstate commerce cease to enjoy federal protection? The original package doctrine had proved unsuitable once domestic shippers tried to subvert it (a freight car containing cigarettes loose in packets of ten was held not to be an "original package") and the Court has since relegated it to the area of importation from which it started; see Department of Revenue v. Beam Distilling Co. (1964). While the case below was decided just before the "switch" in the Court (discussed in detail in the note to West Coast Hotel v. Parrish) it reflects the attitude of the Court that federal control does end and, despite its bitter division in many cases of the period, its decision in this case was unanimous.

Mr. Chief Justice **Hughes**, continuing, said in part:

Third. *The question of the application of the provisions of the Live Poultry Code to intrastate transactions.* Although the validity of the codes (apart from the question of delegation) rests upon the commerce clause of the Constitution, § 3 (a) is not in terms limited to interstate and foreign commerce. From the generality of terms, and from the argument of the Government at the bar it would appear that § 3 (a) was designed to authorize codes without that limitation. But under § 3 (f) penalties are confined to violations of a code provision "in any transaction in or affecting interstate or foreign com-

merce." This aspect of the case presents the question whether the particular provisions of the Live Poultry Code, which the defendants were convicted for violating and for having conspired to violate, were within the regulating power of Congress.

These provisions relate to the hours and wages of those employed by defendants in their slaughterhouses in Brooklyn and to the sales there made to retail dealers and butchers.

(1) Were these transactions "*in*" interstate commerce? Much is made of the fact that almost all the poultry coming to New York is sent there from other States. But the code provisions, as here applied, do not concern the transportation of the poultry from other States to New York, or the transactions of the commission men or others to whom it is consigned, or the sales made by such consignees to defendants. When defendants had made their purchases, whether at the West Washington Market in New York City or at the railroad terminals serving the city, or elsewhere, the poultry was trucked to their slaughterhouses in Brooklyn for local disposition. The interstate transactions in relation to that poultry then ended. Defendants held the poultry at their slaughterhouse markets for slaughter and local sale to retail dealers and butchers, who in turn sold directly to consumers. Neither the slaughtering nor the sales by defendants were transactions in interstate commerce. . . .

The undisputed facts thus afford no warrant for the argument that the poultry handled by defendants at their slaughterhouse markets was in a "*current*" or "*flow*" of interstate commerce and was thus subject to congressional regulation. The mere fact that there may be a constant flow of commodities into a State does not mean that the flow continues after the property has arrived and has become commingled with the mass of property within the State and is there held solely for local disposition and use. So far as the poultry herein questioned is concerned, the flow in interstate commerce has ceased. The poultry had come to a permanent rest within the State. It was not held, used or sold by defendants in relation to any further transactions in interstate commerce and was not destined for transportation to other States. Hence, decisions which deal with a stream of interstate commerce—where goods come to rest within a State temporarily and are later to go forward in interstate commerce—and with the regulations of transactions involved in that practical continuity of movement, are not applicable here. . . .

(2) Did the defendants' transactions directly "affect" interstate commerce so as to be subject to Federal regulation? The power of Congress extends not only to the regulation of transactions which are part of interstate commerce, but to the protection of that commerce from injury. It matters not that the injury may be due to the conduct of those engaged in intrastate operations. Thus, Congress may protect the safety of those employed in interstate transportation "no matter what may be the source of the dangers which threaten it." . . . We said in Second Employers' Liability Cases [1912], that it is the "effect upon interstate commerce," not "the source of the injury," which is "the criterion of congressional power." We have held that, in dealing with common

carriers engaged in both interstate and intrastate commerce, the dominant authority of Congress necessarily embraces the right to control their intrastate operations in all matters having such a close and substantial relation to interstate traffic that the control is essential or appropriate to secure the freedom of that traffic from interference or unjust discrimination and to promote the efficiency of the interstate service. The Shreveport Case [1914]. . . . And combinations and conspiracies to restrain interstate commerce, or to monopolize any part of it, are none the less within the reach of the Anti-Trust Act, because the conspirators seek to attain their end by means of intrastate activities. . . .

. . . This is not a prosecution for a conspiracy to restrain or monopolize interstate commerce in violation of the Anti-Trust Act. Defendants have been convicted, not upon direct charges of injury to interstate commerce or of interference with persons engaged in that commerce, but of violations of certain provisions of the Live Poultry Code and of conspiracy to commit these violations. Interstate commerce is brought in only upon the charge that violations of these provisions—as to hours and wages of employes and local sales—"affected" interstate commerce.

In determining how far the Federal Government may go in controlling intrastate transactions upon the ground that they "affect" interstate commerce, there is a necessary and well-established distinction between direct and indirect effects. The precise line can be drawn only as individual cases arise, but the distinction is clear in principle. Direct effects are illustrated by the railroad cases we have cited, as, e.g., the effect of failure to use prescribed safety appliances on railroads which are the highways of both interstate and intrastate commerce, injury to an employe engaged in interstate transportation by the negligence of an employe engaged in an intrastate movement, the fixing of rates for intrastate transportation which unjustly discriminate against interstate commerce. But where the effect of intrastate transactions upon interstate commerce is merely indirect, such transactions remain within the domain of State power. If the commerce clause were construed to reach all enterprises and transactions which could be said to have an indirect effect upon interstate commerce, the Federal authority would embrace practically all the activities of the people and the authority of the State over its domestic concerns would exist only by sufferance of the Federal Government. Indeed, on such a theory, even the development of the State's commercial facilities would be subject to Federal control. . . .

The question of chief importance relates to the provisions of the Code as to the hours and wages of those employed in defendants' slaughterhouse markets. It is plain that these requirements are imposed in order to govern the details of defendants' management of their local business. The persons employed in slaughtering and selling in local trade are not employed in interstate commerce. Their hours and wages have no direct relation to interstate commerce. The question of how many hours these employes should work and what they should be paid differs in no essential respect from similar questions

in other local businesses which handle commodities brought into a State and there dealt in as a part of its internal commerce. This appears from an examination of the considerations urged by the Government with respect to conditions in the poultry trade. Thus, the Government argues that hours and wages affect prices; that slaughterhouse men sell at a small margin above operating costs; that labor represents 50 to 60 per cent of these costs; that a slaughterhouse operator paying lower wages or reducing his cost by exacting long hours of work translates his saving into lower prices; that this results in demands for a cheaper grade of goods, and that the cutting of prices brings about a demoralization of the price structure. Similar conditions may be adduced in relation to other businesses. The argument of the Government proves too much. If the Federal Government may determine the wages and hours of employes in the internal commerce of a State, because of their relation to cost and prices and their indirect effect upon interstate commerce, it would seem that a similar control might be exerted over other elements of cost, also affecting prices, such as the number of employes, rents, advertising, methods of doing business, etc. All the processes of production and distribution that enter into cost could likewise be controlled. If the cost of doing an intrastate business is in itself the permitted object of Federal control, the extent of the regulation of cost would be a question of discretion and not of power.

The Government also makes the point that efforts to enact State legislation establishing high labor standards have been impeded by the belief that unless similar action is taken generally, commerce will be diverted from the States adopting such standards, and that this fear of diversion has led to demands for Federal legislation on the subject of wages and hours. The apparent implication is that the Federal authority under the commerce clause should be deemed to extend to the establishment of rules to govern wages and hours in intrastate trade and industry generally throughout the country, thus overriding the authority of the States to deal with domestic problems arising from labor conditions in their internal commerce.

It is not the province of the Court to consider the economic advantages or disadvantages of such a centralized system. It is sufficient to say that the Federal Constitution does not provide for it. Our growth and development have called for wide use of the commerce power of the Federal Government in its control over the expanded activities of interstate commerce and in protecting that commerce from burdens, interferences and conspiracies to restrain and monopolize it. But the authority of the Federal Government may not be pushed to such an extreme as to destroy the distinction, which the commerce clause itself establishes, between commerce "among the several States" and the internal concerns of a State. The same answer must be made to the contention that is based upon the serious economic situation which led to the passage of the Recovery Act—the fall in prices, the decline in wages and employment, and the curtailment of the market for commodities. Stress is laid upon the great importance of maintaining wage distributions which would provide the necessary stimulus in starting "the cumulative forces making for expanding commercial activity." Without in any way disparaging this motive, it is enough to say that the recuperative efforts of the Federal Government must be made in a manner consistent with the authority granted by the Constitution.

We are of the opinion that the attempt through the provisions of the Code to fix the hours and wages of employes of defendants in their intrastate business was not a valid exercise of Federal power.

On both the grounds we have discussed, the attempted delegation of legislative power and the attempted regulation of intrastate transactions which affect interstate commerce only indirectly, we hold the code provisions here in question to be invalid and that the judgment of conviction must be reversed.

Mr. Justice **Cardozo** concurred.

NLRB v. JONES & LAUGHLIN STEEL CORPORATION

301 U. S. 1; 57 S. Ct. 615; 81 L. Ed. 893 (1937)

It is, by and large, the nature of courts to be conservative institutions and when the burgeoning labor movement which accompanied the industrial revolution began to raise legal claims the Supreme Court stood firmly by the laissez-faire economic doctrine of the time under which a businessman was the absolute ruler of his business and it was the role of government to support him. The same year that E. C. Knight was decided saw the Court strike down the income tax in Pollock v. Farmers' Loan and Trust Co. (1895) and confirm the jailing of Eugene V. Debs for his role in the Pullman strike; In re Debs (1895).

Even before the turn of the century the grievances of labor had produced both state and federal legislation designed to curb some of the worst abuses. Such state legislation was struck down under the due process clause guarantee of "liberty of contract," (see Lochner v. New York, 1905) while the federal legislation was held an invalid use of the commerce clause, even though it was applied to interstate carriers. In 1898 Congress passed a statute outlawing so-called "yellow-dog contracts" (by which workmen were forced to agree not to join labor unions) and punishing railroads for discriminating against an employee because of union membership. In Adair v. United States (1908) the Court held the act void not only as a denial of due process of law under the Fifth Amendment but on the ground that there is no "possible legal or logical connection . . . between an employee's membership in a labor organization and the carrying on of interstate commerce. . . ." A week later the Court in Loewe v. Lawlor, the "Danbury Hatters Case,", held the Sherman Act applicable to labor union activities.

*After nearly twenty years of legislative experimentation in the railway labor field, Congress passed the Railway Labor Act of 1926, which was strengthened in 1934 to outlaw again the yellow-dog contract and pro-*vide *employees the widest possible freedom to organize into labor unions. All forms of interference upon the part of the railroads with the labor organizations of their men were forbidden together with company formation or financial support of unions. The Court, in a unanimous opinion, held this act valid in the case of Virginian Ry. Co. v. System Federation No. 40 (1937), decided on March 29, the same day as West Coast Hotel v. Parrish.*

Less than two months after the NIRA had been held void in the Schechter case, Congress passed the National Labor Relations Act (known as the Wagner Act, or NLRA), the first thoroughgoing and genuinely regulatory federal act to deal with the relations between labor and capital. The act was unique both in scope and in method. Its scope included all labor disputes which burdened or obstructed interstate commerce. Such burden or obstruction might take the form (1) of impairing the efficiency or safety of the instrumentalities of commerce, (2) of restraining the flow of raw materials or manufactured goods through interstate commerce, or controlling the prices thereof, (3) of reducing employment and wages sufficiently to reduce substantially the market for goods moving in interstate commerce, or (4) of obstructing directly the actual current of commerce. The method employed by the act was that of defining carefully seven or eight "unfair labor practices" which were forbidden, and of creating a new National Labor Relations Board with power upon investigation to issue "cease and desist orders," enforceable in the courts, against those guilty of these practices.

The NLRA clearly rested upon precarious footing, since its provisions extended to labor relations in the processes of manufacturing goods which were to be moved in interstate commerce. Ever since the E. C. Knight case (1895) the Court had insisted that manufacturing was antecedent to and clearly separate from the interstate commerce in which the manufactured goods later move, and while the Shreveport Case (1914) and Stafford v. Wallace (1922) indicated that the Court's attitude toward this distinction was becoming less rigid, the emphasis in the Schechter case upon "direct" and "indirect" effects which local activities produce on interstate commerce did not give supporters of the NLRA much encouragement. Moreover, in Carter v. Carter Coal Co. (1936), which held the Guffey Coal Act void, the Court said that the relations between employers and workmen in the coal industry did not directly affect interstate commerce in coal and could not therefore be regulated by Congress. The Court might very consistently have held the NLRA void in its application to labor relations in the field of manufacturing. But this it did not do.

In discussing the "judicial revolution of 1937" there will always be speculation as to the part played by public pressure and by President Franklin Roosevelt's threat to "pack" the Court, discussed more fully in the note to the Parrish case. But whether the Court responded to such pressure or whether its change of attitude was a spontaneous response to a new perception of social needs, its reversal in attitude was complete and permanent. While it is instructive to study the way in which the Court handled the change, and important to understand the reasoning upon which the post-1937 cases rest, today it is only with the greatest caution that one cites as authority cases from the earlier period. The Court had, in the economic sphere at least, turned over to the legislatures of the states and the nation the power to govern.

Perhaps even more striking than the extension of federal control in the field of labor relations has been the development of such control in the field of agriculture. The Agricultural Adjustment Act of 1933, which was held void in United States v. Butler (1936), had relied for its constitutional underpinnings upon the delegated powers of Congress to tax and to spend money. The Agricultural Adjustment Act of 1938, which aimed at similar objectives, was based on the commerce power. The act declared that its policy (in part) was: "to regulate interstate and foreign commerce in cotton, wheat, corn, tobacco and rice to the extent necessary to provide an orderly, adequate, and balanced flow of such commodities in interstate and foreign commerce through storage of reserve supplies, loans, marketing quotas, assisting farmers to obtain, in so far as practicable, parity prices for such commodities and parity of income, and assisting consumers to obtain an adequate and steady supply of such commodities at fair prices."

The attack upon the validity of the statute arose under the sections providing for the establishment of marketing quotas for flue-cured tobacco. There were similar sections dealing with cotton, wheat, corn, and rice. The act authorized the Secretary of Agriculture, when he found that the supply of tobacco had increased beyond a certain point, to put into effect a national marketing quota, provided that not more than one-third of the previous year's tobacco growers were opposed. The quotas were allocated in such a way that each grower was given a quota which he must not exceed. If tobacco in excess of the quota for a particular farm was marketed through a warehouse man, the latter paid to the Secretary a penalty equal to 50 percent of the market price of the excess, and might deduct this amount from the prices paid to the producer. In Mulford v. Smith (1939) the Supreme Court held the act valid. It was not, the Court said, a regulation of production but only a regulation of the interstate commerce in tobacco at the "throat where tobacco enters the stream of commerce,—the marketing warehouse." The fact that not all the tobacco was sold interstate was considered immaterial since the "regulation, to be effective, must, and therefore may constitutionally, apply to all sales."

A more extreme application of the 1938 statute was upheld in Wickard v. Filburn (1942). Quotas were established for the production of wheat, in order to prevent surpluses and maintain prices. Filburn raised twenty-three acres of wheat, none of which was intended for interstate commerce, and all of which he consumed or fed to his stock. The quota allotted to him, however, was 11.1 acres; and the Court held him validly liable to the statutory penalties on the wheat produced in excess of this quota. His production of this wheat affected interstate commerce "directly" just as much as though he had farmed 23,000 acres instead of 23.

In the present case the NLRB found that the Jones & Laughlin Steel Corporation had discharged some of its men because of their labor union activities. The board ordered the company to reinstate them and to cease such discrimination. The company was the fourth largest producer of steel in the country. It had nineteen subsidiaries which comprised an integrated system. It owned mines, ships, railroads, furnaces, and mills. The board found that the plants in which the labor troubles occurred "might be likened to the heart of a self-contained, highly integrated body. They draw in the raw materials from Michigan, Minnesota, West Virginia, Pennsylvania in part through arteries and by means controlled by the company; they transform the materials and then pump them out to all parts of the nation through the vast mechanism which the respondent has elaborated."

Mr. Chief Justice **Hughes** delivered the opinion of the Court, saying in part:

First. The scope of the Act.—The Act is challenged in its entirety as an attempt to regulate all industry, thus invading the reserved powers of the States over their local concerns. It is asserted that the references in the Act to interstate and foreign commerce are colorable at best; that the Act is not a true regulation of such commerce or of matters which directly affect it but on the contrary has the fundamental object of placing under the compulsory supervision of the Federal government all industrial labor relations within the nation. The argument seeks support in the broad words of the preamble (section one) and in the sweep of the provisions of the Act, and it is further insisted that its legislative history shows an essential universal purpose in the light of which its scope cannot be limited by either construction or by the application of the separability clause.

If this conception of terms, intent and consequent inseparability were sound, the Act would necessarily fall by reason of the limitation upon the Federal power which inheres in the constitutional grant, as well as because of the explicit reservation of the Tenth Amendment. . . . The authority of the Federal government may not be pushed to such an extreme as to destroy the distinction, which the commerce clause itself establishes, between commerce "among the several States" and the internal concerns of a State. That distinction between what is national and what is local in the activities of commerce is vital to the maintenance of our federal system. . . .

We think it clear that the National Labor Relations Act may be construed so as to operate within the sphere of constitutional authority. The jurisdiction conferred upon the Board, and invoked in this instance, is found in § 10 (a), which provides:

"Sec. 10 (a). The Board is empowered, as hereinafter provided, to prevent any person from engaging in any unfair labor practice (listed in § 8) affecting commerce."

The critical words of this provision, prescribing the limits of the Board's authority in dealing with the labor practices, are "affecting commerce." The Act specifically defines the "commerce" to which it refers (§ 2 (6)):

"The term 'commerce' means trade, traffic, commerce, transportation, or communication among the several States, or between the District of Columbia or any Territory of the United States and any State or other Territory, or between any foreign country and any State, Territory, or the District of Columbia, or within the District of Columbia or any Territory, or between points in the same State but through any other State or any Territory or the District of Columbia or any foreign country."

There can be no question that the commerce thus contemplated by the Act (aside from that within a Territory or the District of Columbia) is interstate and foreign commerce in the constitutional sense. The Act also defines the term "affecting commerce" (§ 2 (7)):

"The term 'affecting commerce' means in commerce, or burdening or obstructing commerce or the free flow of commerce, or having led or tending to lead to a labor dispute burdening or obstructing commerce or the free flow of commerce."

This definition is one of exclusion as well as inclusion. The grant of authority to the Board does not purport to extend to the relationship between all industrial employees and employers. Its terms do not impose collective bargaining upon all industry regardless of effects upon interstate or foreign commerce. It purports to reach only what may be deemed to burden or obstruct that commerce and, thus qualified, it must be construed as contemplating the exercise of control within constitutional bounds. It is a familiar principle that acts which directly burden or obstruct interstate or foreign commerce, or its free flow, are within the reach of the congressional power. Acts having that effect are not rendered immune because they grow out of labor disputes. . . . It is the effect upon commerce, not the source of the injury, which is the criterion. . . . Whether or not particular action does affect commerce in such a close and intimate fashion as to be subject to Federal control, and hence to lie within the authority conferred upon the Board, is left by the statute to be determined as individual cases arise. We are thus to inquire whether in the instant case the constitutional boundary has been passed.

Second. The unfair labor practices in question.
. . .

[The Court finds that Congress may forbid employers to interfere with the right of employees, guaranteed by the act, to organize labor unions and to bargain collectively.]

*Third. The application of the Act to employees engaged in production.—The principle involved.—*Respondent says that whatever may be said of employees engaged in interstate commerce, the industrial relations and activities in the manufacturing department of respondent's enterprise are not subject to Federal regulation. The argument rests upon the proposition that manufacturing in itself is not commerce. Kidd v. Pearson [1888]; . . . A. L. A. Schechter Poultry Corp. v. United States [1935]; Carter v. Carter Coal Co. [1936].

The Government distinguishes these cases. The various parts of respondent's enterprise are described as interdependent and as thus involving "a great movement of iron ore, coal and limestone along well-defined paths to the steel mills, thence through them, and thence in the form of steel products into the consuming centers of the country—a definite and well-understood course of business." It is urged that these activities constitute a "stream" or "flow" of commerce, of which the Aliquippa manufacturing plant is the focal point, and that industrial strife at that point would cripple the entire movement. Reference is made to our decision sustaining the Packers and Stockyards Act. Stafford v. Wallace [1922]. The Court found that the stockyards were but a "throat" through which the current of commerce flowed and the transactions which there occurred could not be separated from that movement. Hence the sales at the stockyards were not regarded as merely local transactions, for while they created "a local change of title" they did not "stop the flow," but merely changed the private interests in the subject of the current. . . . Applying the doctrine of Stafford v. Wallace, the Court sustained the Grain Futures Act of [September 11] 1922 with respect to transactions on the Chicago Board of Trade, although these transactions were "not in and of themselves interstate commerce." Congress had found that they had become "a constantly recurring burden and obstruction to that commerce." Board of Trade v. Olsen [1923]. . . .

Respondent contends that the instant case presents material distinctions. Respondent says that the Aliquippa plant is extensive in size and represents a large investment in buildings, machinery and equipment. The raw materials which are brought to the plant are delayed for long periods and, after being subjected to manufacturing processes "are changed substantially as to character, utility and value." The finished products which emerge "are to a large extent manufactured without reference to pre-existing orders and contracts and are entirely different from the raw materials which enter at the other end." Hence respondent argues that "If importation and exportation in interstate commerce do not singly transfer purely local activities into the field of congressional regulation, it should follow that their combination would not alter the local situation." . . .

We do not find it necessary to determine whether these features of defendant's business dispose of the asserted analogy to the "stream of commerce" cases. The instances in which that metaphor has been used are but particular, and not exclusive, illustrations of the protective power which the Government invokes in support of the present Act. The congressional authority to protect interstate commerce from burdens and obstructions is not limited to transactions which can be deemed to be an essential part of a "flow" of interstate or foreign commerce. Burdens and obstructions may be due to injurious action springing from other sources. The fundamental principle is that the power to regulate commerce is the power to enact "all appropriate legislation" for "its protection and advancement" . . . ; to adopt measures "to promote its growth and insure its safety" . . . ; "to foster, protect, control and restrain." . . . That power is plenary and may be exerted to protect interstate commerce "no matter what the source of the dangers which threaten it." . . . Although activities may be intrastate in character when separately considered, if they have such a close and substantial relation to interstate commerce that their control is essential or appropriate to protect that commerce from burdens and obstructions, Congress cannot be denied the power to exercise that control. . . . Undoubtedly the scope of this power must be considered in the light of our dual system of government and may not be extended so as to embrace effects upon interstate commerce so indirect and remote that to embrace them, in view of our complex society, would effectually obliterate the distinction between what is national and what is local and create a completely centralized government. The question is necessarily one of degree. . . .

That intrastate activities, by reason of close and intimate relation to interstate commerce, may fall within Federal control is demonstrated in the case of carriers who are engaged in both interstate and intrastate transportation. There Federal control has been found essential to secure the freedom of interstate traffic from interference or unjust discrimination and to promote the efficiency of the interstate service. Shreveport Case [1914]; . . . It is manifest that intrastate rates deal *primarily* with a local activity. But in rate-making they bear such a close relation to interstate rates that effective control of the one must embrace some control over the other. Under the Transportation Act [February 28] 1920, Congress went so far as to authorize the Interstate Commerce Commission to establish a state-wide level of intrastate rates in order to prevent an unjust discrimination against interstate commerce. . . .

The close and intimate effect which brings the subject within the reach of Federal power may be due to activities in relation to productive industry although the industry when separately viewed is local. This has been abundantly illustrated in the application of the Federal Anti-Trust Act. In the Standard Oil Co. Case [1911], and American Tobacco Co. Case [1911], that statute was applied to combinations of employers engaged in productive industry.

Upon the same principle, the Anti-Trust Act has been applied to the conduct of employees engaged in production. Loewe v. Lawlor [1908]. . . .

It is thus apparent that the fact that the employees here concerned were engaged in production is not determinative. The question remains as to the effect upon interstate commerce of the labor practice involved. In the A. L. A. Schechter Poultry Corp. Case we found that the effect there was so remote as to be beyond the Federal power. To find "immediacy or directness" there was to find it "almost everywhere," a result inconsistent with the maintenance of our federal system. In the Carter Case the Court was of the opinion that the provisions of the statute relating to production were invalid upon several grounds,—that there was improper delegation of legislative power, and that the requirements not only went beyond sustainable measure of protection of interstate commerce but were also inconsistent with due process. These cases are not controlling here.

Fourth. Effects of the unfair labor practice in respondent's enterprise.—Giving full weight to respondent's contention with respect to a break in the complete continuity of the "stream of commerce" by reason of respondent's manufacturing operations, the fact remains that the stoppage of those operations by industrial strife would have a most serious effect upon interstate commerce. In view of respondent's far-flung activities, it is idle to say that the effect would be indirect or remote. It is obvious that it would be immediate and might be catastrophic. We are asked to shut our eyes to the plainest facts of our national life and to deal with the question of direct and indirect effects in an intellectual vacuum. Because there may be but indirect and remote effects upon interstate commerce in connection with a host of local enterprises throughout the country, it does not follow that other industrial activities do not have such a close and intimate relation to interstate commerce as to make the presence of industrial strife a matter of the most urgent national concern. When industries organize themselves on a national scale, making their relation to interstate commerce the dominant factor in their activities, how can it be maintained that their industrial labor relations constitute a forbidden field into which Congress may not enter when it is necessary to protect interstate commerce from the paralyzing consequences of industrial war? We have often said that interstate commerce itself is a practical conception. It is equally true that interferences with that commerce must be appraised by a judgment that does not ignore actual experience.

Experience has abundantly demonstrated that the recognition of the right of employees to self-organization and to have representatives of their own choosing for the purpose of collective bargaining is often an essential condition of industrial peace. Refusal to confer and negotiate has been one of the most prolific causes of strife. This is such an outstanding fact in the history of labor disturbances that it is a proper subject of judicial notice and requires no citation of instances. The opinion in the case of Virginian Railway Co. v. System Federation No. 40 [1937], points out that, in the case of carriers, experience has shown that before the amendment, of 1934, of the Railway Labor Act "when there was no dispute as to the organizations authorized to represent the employees, and when there was a willingness of the employer to meet such representative for a discussion of their grievances, amicable adjustment of differences had generally followed and strikes had been avoided." That, on the other hand, "a prolific source of dispute had been the maintenance by the railroads of company unions and the denial by railway management of the authority of representatives chosen by their employees." The opinion in that case also points to the large measure of success of the labor policy embodied in the Railway Labor Act. But with respect to the appropriateness of the recognition of self-organization and representation in the promotion of peace, the question is not essentially different in the case of employees in industries of such a character that interstate commerce is put in jeopardy from the case of employees of transportation companies. And of what avail is it to protect the facility of transportation, if interstate commerce is throttled with respect to the commodities to be transported!

These questions have frequently engaged the attention of Congress and have been the subject of many inquiries. The steel industry is one of the great basic industries of the United States, with ramifying activities affecting interstate commerce at every point. The Government aptly refers to the steel strike of 1919–1920 with its far-reaching consequences. The fact that there appears to have been no major disturbance in that industry in the more recent period did not dispose of the possibilities of future and like dangers to interstate commerce which Congress was entitled to foresee and to exercise its protective power to forestall. It is not necessary again to detail the facts as to respondent's enterprise. Instead of being beyond the pale, we think that it presents in a most striking way the close and intimate relation which a manufacturing industry may have to interstate commerce and we have no doubt that Congress had constitutional authority to safeguard the right of respondent's employees to self-organization and freedom in the choice of representatives for collective bargaining.

Fifth. The means which the Act employs.—Questions under the due process clause and other constitutional restrictions.—Respondent asserts its right to conduct its business in an orderly manner without being subjected to arbitrary restraints. What we have said points to the fallacy in the argument. Employees have their correlative right to organize for the purpose of securing the redress of grievances and to promote agreements with employers relating to rate of pay and conditions of work. . . . Restraint for the purpose of preventing an unjust interference with that right cannot be considered arbitrary or capricious. . . .

The Act does not compel agreements between employers and employees. It does not compel any agreement whatever. It does not prevent the employer "from refusing to make a collective contract and hiring individuals on whatever terms" the employer "may by unilateral action determine." The Act expressly provides in § 9 (a) that any individual employee or a group of employees shall have the right at any time to present grievances to their employer. The theory of the Act is that free opportunity for negotiation with accredited representatives of employees is likely to promote industrial peace and may bring about the adjustments and agreements which the Act in itself does not attempt to compel. . . . The Act does not interfere with the normal exercise of the right of the employer to select its employees or to discharge them. The employer may not, under cover of that right, intimidate or coerce its employees with respect to their self-organization and representation, and, on the other hand, the Board is not entitled to make its authority a pretext for interference with the right of discharge when that right is exercised for other reasons than such intimidation and coercion. The true purpose is the subject of investigation with full opportunity to show the facts. It would seem that when employers freely recognize the right of their employees to their own organizations and their unrestricted right of representation there will be much less occasion for controversy in respect to the free and appropriate exercise of the right of selection and discharge.

The Act has been criticized as one-sided in its application; that it subjects the employer to supervision and restraint and leaves untouched the abuses for which employees may be responsible; that it fails to provide a more comprehensive plan,—with better assurances of fairness to both sides and with increased chances of success in bringing about, if not compelling, equitable solutions of industrial disputes affecting interstate commerce. But we are dealing with the power of Congress, not with a particular policy, or with the extent to which policy should go. We have frequently said that the legislative authority, exerted within its proper field, need not embrace all the evils within its reach. The Constitution does not forbid "cautious advance, step by step," in dealing with the evils which are exhibited in activities within the range of legislative power. . . . The question in such cases is whether the legislature, in what it does prescribe, has gone beyond constitutional limits. . . .

Our conclusion is that the order of the Board was within its competency and that the Act is valid as here applied. . . .

Reversed.

Mr. Justice **McReynolds** delivered the following dissenting opinion, saying in part:

Mr. Justice **Van Devanter**, Mr. Justice **Sutherland**, Mr. Justice **Butler** and I are unable to agree with the decisions just announced. . . .

The Court as we think departs from well-established principles followed in . . . Schechter Poultry Corp. v. United States and Carter v. Carter Coal Co. Upon the authority of those decisions . . . the power of Congress under the commerce clause does not extend to relations between employers and their employees engaged in manufacture, and therefore the Act conferred upon the National Labor Relations Board no authority in respect of matters covered by the questioned orders. . . . No decision or judicial opinion to the contrary has been cited, and we find none. Every consideration brought forward to uphold the Act before us was applicable to support the Acts held unconstitutional in causes decided within two years. And the lower courts rightly deemed them controlling. . . .

Any effect on interstate commerce by the discharge of employees shown here, would be indirect and remote in the highest degree, as consideration of the facts will show. In No. 419 [The Jones & Laughlin case] ten men out of ten thousand were discharged; in the other cases only a few. The immediate effect in the factory may be to create discontent among all those employed and a strike may follow, which, in turn, may result in reducing production, which ultimately may reduce the volume of goods moving in interstate commerce. By this chain of indirect and progressively remote events we finally reach the evil with which it is said the legislation under consideration undertakes to deal. A more remote and indirect interference with interstate commerce or a more definite invasion of the powers reserved to the states is difficult, if not impossible, to imagine.

The Constitution still recognizes the existence of States with indestructible powers; the Tenth Amendment was supposed to put them beyond controversy. . . .

HEART OF ATLANTA MOTEL v. UNITED STATES

379 U. S. 241; 85 S. Ct. 348; 13 L. Ed. 2d 258 (1964)

It used to be said that the federal government has no police power. In a narrow sense this is true, for the police power is defined as the general power to pass regulatory laws for the protection of the health, morals, safety, good order, and general welfare of the community. The Constitution grants no such broad power to Congress, and so, by the operation of the Tenth Amendment, it is reserved to the states. Since the turn of the century, however, what may fairly be called a federal police power has come into existence through the use by Congress of certain of its delegated powers to achieve some of the same social objectives which the states achieve through the police power. Thus Congress has no delegated power to regulate local labor conditions, but if they can be shown to affect interstate commerce, then Congress can regulate them under the commerce power. It cannot punish ordinary business swindles, but it may make it a crime to use the mails for purposes of fraud. Another major exercise of the federal police power through the commerce clause is in the regulation of the sale of securities on the country's stock exchanges. In this way Congress has been able to implement policies for the national welfare which it has no direct authority to adopt by hanging these policies on the "constitutional pegs" found in its powers to regulate interstate commerce, to operate the postal service, and to tax. By this somewhat indirect method Congress has come to exercise control over an ever-increasing number of social and economic problems. By far the largest part of this growing federal police power is based upon the commerce clause.

From the start this penetration of federal power into new areas aroused plenty of protest on constitutional grounds, and in the early years the Supreme Court moved cautiously in dealing with the new forms of federal social legislation. It found little difficulty, however, in sustaining the validity of the federal safety appliance acts, laws regulating the transportation of explosives, restrictions upon the hours of labor of trainmen and telegraphers, the federal employers' liability statute applicable to railroads, the federal antitrust laws, the licensing of radio, television and telephone communications, and many similar statutes. While Congress in passing these acts was often seeking to control social and economic problems, the Court held the statutes valid on the rather narrow ground that they all tended to keep interstate commerce safe, efficient, and unobstructed. If the power to regulate commerce means anything, it means the power to protect that commerce and promote its effi-

ciency. See, e.g., Baltimore & O. R. Co. v. Interstate Commerce Commission (1911), sustaining the Hours of Service Act, and Second Employers' Liability Cases (1912), upholding the Federal Employers' Liability Act of 1908. While the revolution in the Court's thinking of 1937 eased the burden upon Congress, it did not exempt it from the necessity of justifying its social legislation in terms of specific delegated powers.

To a person unfamiliar with our institutions and constitutional history, it must seem strange that the national government, in its efforts to abolish race discrimination, should be forced to act under a grant of power to regulate interstate commerce. Of course, if a state government does the discriminating, either through its laws or its officials, the courts can interfere under the equal protection clause of the Fourteenth Amendment. But as early as 1883 in the Civil Rights Cases the Court made clear that private discrimination was not forbidden by the Fourteenth Amendment, and Congress had no "police power" under which it could outlaw it generally.

The passage of the Civil Rights Act of 1964, Title II of which was sustained in the present cases, brought to an all-time high congressional efforts to abolish race discrimination in the United States. The act itself was remarkable for a number of reasons. First, for the first time since the ill-fated Civil Rights Act of 1875, Congress made a sweeping attack on race discrimination. Second, the act commanded overwhelming bipartisan support. After five months of committee hearings, 2800 pages of testimony, and seven months of debates, the measure passed the House 289 to 126. In an unusual move, the Senate did not even send it to committee, but worked out a bill with informal bipartisan conferences. The House adopted the Senate bill without change. Third, for the first time in history the Senate, with the all-out support of both majority and minority leaders, invoked cloture to stop a Southern filibuster on a civil rights measure.

In the 1960s the Supreme Court suggested subtly that the "back-stairs legislation" approach to civil rights may no longer be needed, and that an overt reliance on the enforcement power granted in the three amendments would be received more sympathetically than it had been before. In upholding the Voting Rights Act of 1965, the Court permitted Congress to substitute federal for state voting machinery where necessary to prevent discrimination, and to outlaw voting qualifications which might not, of themselves, violate the Fourteenth Amendment. These provisions were upheld in South Carolina v. Katzenbach (1966) and Katzenbach v. Morgan (1966). In United States v. Guest (1966), six justices indicated that Congress could protect an individual right to use state facilities, and in the Civil Rights Act of 1968 Congress acted on this suggestion and outlawed interference with "any person because of his race . . . and because he is or has been . . . participating in or enjoying any benefit, service, privilege, program, facility or activity provided or administered by any State or subdivision thereof. . . .

Finally, in a dramatic reversal of an eighty-five-

year-old policy, the Court made the "back-stairs" approach to civil rights legislation obsolete. In the closing days of the Reconstruction, with the white race rapidly resuming control of Southern state governments, Congress had passed the Civil Rights Act of 1875 to insure continued federal power to prevent racial discrimination in the South. This act made it both a crime and a civil wrong for any person to deny to any other person "the full and equal enjoyment of any of the accommodations, advantages, facilities and privileges of inns, public conveyances on land or water, theaters and other places of public amusement; subject only to the conditions and limitations established by law, and applicable alike to citizens of every race and color. . . ." In the Civil Rights Cases (1883) the Supreme Court held the act unconstitutional. It pointed out that the Fourteenth Amendment was a limit only upon state power, not individual actions, and while the Thirteenth Amendment did apply to individuals, to consider discrimination against blacks to be a "badge of slavery or servitude" "would be running the slavery argument into the ground."

Finally in 1968, in Jones v. Alfred H. Mayer Co., the Court overruled the Civil Rights Cases. It rejected the idea "that only conduct which actually enslaves someone" is slavery and held that "Congress has the power under the Thirteenth Amendment rationally to determine what are the badges and the incidents of slavery, and the authority to translate that determination into effective legislation." Certainly such badges "included restraints upon 'those fundamental rights which are the essence of civil freedom, namely, the same right . . . to inherit, purchase, lease, sell and convey property, as is enjoyed by white citizens.' "

Following the above decision the Court held that a cause of action existed under the old Ku Klux Act of 1871 where a black mistakenly thought to be a civil rights worker was stopped on the highway and beaten up by two armed white men. The law forbids private individuals to deprive other private individuals of the "equal protection of the laws." The Court conceded that "a century of Fourteenth Amendment adjudication has . . . made it understandably difficult to conceive of what might constitute a deprivation of the equal protection of the laws by private persons. Yet there is nothing inherent in the phrase that requires the action working the deprivation to come from the State. . . . Indeed, the failure to mention any such requisite can be viewed as an important indication of congressional intent to speak in [the act] of all deprivation of 'equal protection of the laws' and 'equal privileges and immunities under the laws,' whatever their source." Nor is the power to control individual conduct limited to the kinds of things traditionally thought of as privileges and immunities of citizenship and hence subject to federal power. Citing Jones v. Alfred H. Mayer Co., the Court found that "Congress was wholly within its powers under § 2 of the Thirteenth Amendment in creating a statutory cause of action for Negro citizens who have been the victims of conspiratorial, racially discriminatory private action aimed at de-priving them of the basic rights that the law secures to all free men." See Griffin v. Breckenridge (1971).

Mr. Justice **Clark** delivered the opinion of the Court, saying in part:

This is a declaratory judgment action attacking the constitutionality of Title II of the Civil Rights Act of 1964. . . . Appellees counterclaimed for enforcement under § 206 (a) of the Act and asked for a three-judge district court under § 206 (b). A three-judge court . . . sustained the validity of the Act and issued a permanent injunction on appellees' counterclaim restraining appellant from continuing to violate the Act. . . . We affirm the judgment.

1. The Factual Background and Contentions of the Parties

The case comes here on admissions and stipulated facts. Appellant owns and operates the Heart of Atlanta Motel which has 216 rooms available to transient guests. The motel is located on Courtland Street, two blocks from downtown Peachtree Street. It is readily accessible to interstate highways 75 and 85 and state highways 23 and 41. Appellant solicits patronage from outside the State of Georgia through various national advertising media, including magazines of national circulation; it maintains over 50 billboards and highway signs within the State, soliciting patronage for the motel; it accepts convention trade from outside Georgia and approximately 75% of its registered guests are from out of State. Prior to passage of the Act the motel had followed a practice of refusing to rent rooms to Negroes, and it alleged that it intended to continue to do so. In an effort to perpetuate that policy this suit was filed.

The appellant contends that Congress in passing this Act exceeded its power to regulate commerce under Art. I, § 8, cl. 3, of the Constitution of the United States; that the Act violates the Fifth Amendment because appellant is deprived of the right to choose its customers and operate its business as it wishes, resulting in a taking of its liberty and property without due process of law and a taking of its property without just compensation; and, finally, that by requiring appellant to rent available rooms to Negroes against its will, Congress is subjecting it to involuntary servitude in contravention of the Thirteenth Amendment. . . .

2. The History of the Act

[The Court notes the passage by Congress of earlier civil rights acts, and reviews briefly the struggle to enact the present statute.]

The Act as finally adopted was most comprehensive, undertaking to prevent through peaceful and voluntary settlement discrimination in voting, as well as in places of accommodation and public facilities, federally secured programs and in employment. Since Title II is the only portion under attack here, we confine our consideration to those public accommodation provisions.

3. Title II of the Act

This Title is divided into seven sections beginning with § 201 (a) which provides that:

"All persons shall be entitled to the full and equal enjoyment of the goods, services, facilities, privileges, advantages, and accommodations of any place of public accommodation, as defined in this section, without discrimination or segregation on the ground of race, color, religion, or national origin."

There are listed in § 201 (b) four classes of business establishments, each of which "serves the public" and "is a place of public accommodation" within the meaning of § 201 (a) "if its operations affect commerce, or if discrimination or segregation by it is supported by State action." The covered establishments are:

"(1) any inn, hotel, motel, or other establishment which provides lodging to transient guests, other than an establishment located within a building which contains not more than five rooms for rent or hire and which is actually occupied by the proprietor of such establishment as his residence; (2) any restaurant, cafeteria . . . [not here involved]; (3) any motion picture house . . . [not here involved]; (4) any establishment . . . which is physically located within the premises of any establishment otherwise covered by this subsection, or . . . within the premises of which is physically located any such covered establishment . . . [not here involved]."

Section 201 (c) defines the phrase "affect commerce" as applied to the above establishments. It first declares that "any inn, hotel, motel, or other establishment which provides lodging to transient guests" affects commerce per se. . . .

Finally, § 203 prohibits the withholding or denial, etc., of any right or privilege secured by § 201 . . . or the intimidation, threatening or coercion of any person with the purpose of interfering with any such right or the punishing, etc., of any person for exercising or attempting to exercise any such right.

The remaining sections of the Title are remedial ones for violations of any of the previous sections. Remedies are limited to civil actions for preventive relief. The Attorney General may bring suit where he has "reasonable cause to believe that any person or group of persons is engaged in a pattern or practice of resistance to the full enjoyment of any of the rights secured by this title, and that the pattern or practice is of such a nature and is intended to deny the full exercise of the rights herein described. . . ."

4. Application of Title II to Heart of Atlanta Motel

It is admitted that the operation of the motel brings it within the provisions of § 201 (a) of the Act and that appellant refused to provide lodging for transient Negroes because of their race or color and that it intends to continue that policy unless restrained.

The sole question posed is, therefore, the constitutionality of the Civil Rights Act of 1964 as applied to these facts. The legislative history of the Act indicates that Congress based the Act on § 5 and the Equal Protection Clause of the Fourteenth Amendment as well as its power to regulate interstate commerce under Art. I, § 8, cl. 3 of the Constitution.

The Senate Commerce Committee made it quite clear that the fundamental object of Title II was to vindicate "the deprivation of personal dignity that surely accompanies denials of equal access to public establishments." At the same time, however, it noted that such an objective has been and could be readily achieved "by congressional action based on the commerce power of the Constitution." . . . Our study of the legislative record, made in the light of prior cases, has brought us to the conclusion that Congress possessed ample power in this regard, and we have therefore not considered the other grounds relied upon. This is not to say that the remaining authority upon which it acted was not adequate, a question upon which we do not pass, but merely that since the commerce power is sufficient for our decision here we have considered it alone. . . .

5. The Civil Rights Cases (1883) and their Application

In light of our ground for decision, it might be well at the outset to discuss the Civil Rights Cases, which declared provisions of the Civil Rights Act of 1875 unconstitutional. We think that decision inapposite, and without precedential value in determining the constitutionality of the present Act. Unlike Title II of the present legislation, the 1875 Act broadly proscribed discrimination in "inns, public conveyances on land or water, theaters, and other public places of amusement," without limiting the categories of affected businesses to those impinging upon interstate commerce. In contrast, the applicability of Title II is carefully limited to enterprises having a direct and substantial relation to the interstate flow of goods and people, except where state action is involved. Further, the fact that certain kinds of businesses may not in 1875 have been sufficiently involved in interstate commerce to warrant bringing them within the ambit of the commerce power is not necessarily dispositive of the same question today. Our populace had not reached its present mobility, nor were facilities, goods and services circulating as readily in interstate commerce as they are today. Although the principles which we apply today are those first formulated by Chief Justice Marshall in Gibbons v. Ogden [1824], the conditions of transportation and commerce have changed dramatically, and we must apply those principles to the present state of commerce. The sheer increase in volume of interstate traffic alone would give discriminatory practices which inhibit travel a far larger impact upon the Nation's commerce than such practices had on the economy of another day. . . .

6. The Basis of Congressional Action

While the Act as adopted carried no congressional findings the record of its passage through each house is replete with evidence of the burdens that discrimination by race or color places upon interstate commerce. . . . This testimony included the fact that our people have become increasingly mobile with millions of people of all races traveling from State to State; that Negroes in particular have been the subject of discrimination in transient accommodations, having to travel great distances to secure the same; that often they have been unable to obtain accommodations and have had to call upon friends to put them up overnight . . . ; and that these conditions have become so acute as to require the listing of available lodging for Negroes in a special guidebook which was itself "dramatic testimony to the difficulties" Negroes encounter in travel. . . . These exclusionary practices were found to be nationwide, the Under Secretary of Commerce testifying that there is "no question that this discrimination in the North still exists to a large degree" and in the West and Midwest as well. . . . This testimony indicated a qualitative as well as quantitative effect on interstate travel by Negroes. The former was the obvious impairment of the Negro traveler's pleasure and convenience that resulted when he continually was uncertain of finding lodging. As for the latter, there was evidence that this uncertainty stemming from racial discrimination had the effect of discouraging travel on the part of a substantial portion of the Negro community. . . . This was the conclusion not only of the Under Secretary of Commerce but also of the Administrator of the Federal Aviation Agency who wrote the Chairman of the Senate Commerce Committee that it was his "belief that air commerce is adversely affected by the denial to a substantial segment of the traveling public of adequate and desegregated public accommodations." . . . We shall not burden this opinion with further details since the voluminous testimony presents overwhelming evidence that discrimination by hotels and motels impedes interstate travel.

7. The Power of Congress Over Interstate Travel

The power of Congress to deal with these obstructions depends on the meaning of the Commerce Clause. Its meaning was first enunciated 140 years ago by the great Chief Justice John Marshall in Gibbons v. Ogden, in these words:

[The Court here quotes at length from the opinion concerning the nature of interstate commerce and congressional power over it.]

In short, the determinative test of the exercise of power by the Congress under the Commerce Clause is simply whether the activity sought to be regulated is "commerce which concerns more States than one" and has a real and substantial relation to the national interest. Let us now turn to this facet of the problem.

That the "intercourse" of which the Chief Justice spoke included the movement of persons through more States than one was settled as early as 1849, in the Passenger Cases where Mr. Justice McLean stated: "That the transportation of passengers is a part of commerce is not now an open question." Again in 1913 Mr. Justice McKenna, speaking for the Court, said: "Commerce among the States, we have said, consists of intercourse and traffic between their citizens, and includes the transportation of persons and property." Hoke v. United States. And only four years later in 1917 in Caminetti v. United States, Mr. Justice Day held for the Court:

"The transportation of passengers in interstate commerce, it has long been settled, is within the regulatory power of Congress, under the commerce clause of the Constitution, and the authority of Congress to keep the channels of interstate commerce free from immoral and injurious uses has been frequently sustained, and is no longer open to question."

Nor does it make any difference whether the transportation is commercial in character. In Morgan v. Virginia (1946), Mr. Justice Reed observed as to the modern movement of persons among the States:

"The recent changes in transportation brought about by the coming of automobiles [do] not seem of great significance in the problem. People of all races travel today more extensively than in 1878 when this Court first passed upon state regulation of racial segregation in commerce. [It but] emphasizes the soundness of this Court's early conclusion in Hall v. De Cuir."

The same interest in protecting interstate commerce which led Congress to deal with segregation in interstate carriers and the white slave traffic has prompted it to extend the exercise of its power to gambling . . . ; to criminal enterprises . . . ; to deceptive practices in the sale of products . . . ; to fraudulent security transactions . . . ; to misbranding of drugs . . . ; to wages and hours . . . ; to members of labor unions . . . ; to crop control . . . ; to discrimination against shippers . . . ; to the protection of small business from injurious price cutting . . . ; to discriminate against shippers . . . ; to the protection of small business from injurious price cutting . . . ; to resale price maintenance . . . ; to professional football . . . ; and to racial discrimination by owners and managers of terminal restaurants. . . .

That Congress was legislating against moral wrongs in many of these areas rendered its enactments no less valid. In framing Title II of this Act Congress was also dealing with what it considered a moral problem. But that fact does not detract from the overwhelming evidence of the disruptive effect that racial discrimination has had on commercial intercourse. It was this burden which empowered Congress to enact appropriate legislation, and, given this basis for the exercise of its power, Congress was not restricted by the fact that the particular obstruction to interstate commerce with which it was dealing was also deemed a moral and social wrong.

It is said that the operation of the motel here is of a purely local character. But, assuming this to be true, "[i]f it is interstate commerce that feels the pinch, it does not matter how local the operation which applies the squeeze." . . . As Chief Justice Stone put it in United States v. Darby [1941]:

"The power of Congress over interstate commerce is not confined to the regulation of commerce among the states. It extends to those activities interstate which so affect interstate commerce or the exercise of the power of Congress over it as to make regulation of them appropriate means to the attainment of a legitimate end, the exercise of the granted power of Congress to regulate interstate commerce. . . ."

Thus the power of Congress to promote interstate commerce also includes the power to regulate the local incidents thereof, including local activities in both the States of origin and destination, which might have a substantial and harmful effect upon that commerce. One need only examine the evidence which we have discussed above to see that Congress may—as it has—prohibit racial discrimination by motels serving travelers, however "local" their operations may appear.

Nor does the Act deprive appellant of liberty or property under the Fifth Amendment. The commerce power invoked here by the Congress is a specific and plenary one authorized by the Constitution itself. The only questions are: (1) whether Congress had a rational basis for finding that racial discrimination by motels affected commerce, and (2) if it had such a basis, whether the means it selected to eliminate that evil are reasonable and appropriate. If they are, appellant has no "right" to select its guests as it sees fit, free from governmental regulation.

There is nothing novel about such legislation. Thirty-two States now have it on their books either by statute or executive order and many cities provide such regulation. Some of these Acts go back fourscore years. It has been repeatedly held by this Court that such laws do not violate the Due Process Clause of the Fourteenth Amendment. . . .

. . . As a result the constitutionality of such state statutes stands unquestioned. "The authority of the Federal Government over interstate commerce does not differ . . . in extent or character from that retained by the states over intrastate commerce." . . .

It is doubtful if in the long run appellant will suffer economic loss as a result of the Act. Experience is to the contrary where discrimination is completely obliterated as to all public accommodations. But whether this be true or not is of no consequence since this Court has specifically held that the fact that a "member of the class which is regulated may suffer economic losses not shared by others . . . has never been a barrier" to such legislation. . . . Likewise in a long line of cases this Court has rejected the claim that the prohibition of racial discrimination in public accommodations interferes with personal liberty. . . .

We find no merit in the remainder of appellant's contentions, including that of "involuntary servitude." . . .

We, therefore, conclude that the action of the Congress in the adoption of the Act as applied here to a motel which concededly serves interstate travelers is within the power granted it by the Commerce Clause of the Constitution, as interpreted by this Court for 140 years. It may be argued that Congress could have pursued other methods to eliminate the obstructions it found in interstate commerce caused by racial discrimination. But this is a matter of policy that rests entirely with the Congress not with the courts. How obstructions in commerce may be removed—what means are to be employed—is within the sound and exclusive discretion of the Congress. It is subject only to one caveat—that the means chosen by it must be reasonably adapted to the end permitted by the Constitution. We cannot say that its choice here was not so adapted. The Constitution requires no more.

Affirmed.

Mr. Justice **Black,** concurring, said in part:

Long ago this Court, again speaking through Mr. Chief Justice Marshall, said:

"Let the end be legitimate, let it be within the scope of the constitution, and all means which are appropriate, which are plainly adapted to that end, which are not prohibited, but consist with the letter and spirit of the constitution, are constitutional." McCulloch v. Maryland [1819].

By this standard Congress acted within its power here. In view of the Commerce Clause it is not possible to deny that the aim of protecting interstate commerce from undue burdens is a legitimate end. In view of the Thirteenth, Fourteenth and Fifteenth Amendments, it is not possible to deny that the aim of protecting Negroes from discrimination is also a legitimate end. The means adopted to achieve these ends are also appropriate, plainly adopted to achieve them and not prohibited by the Constitution but consistent with both its letters and spirit. . . .

Mr. Justice **Douglas,** concurring, said in part:

1

Though I join the Court's opinion, I am somewhat reluctant here, as I was in Edwards v. California [1941], to rest solely on the Commerce Clause. My reluctance is not due to any conviction that Congress lacks power to regulate commerce in the interests of human rights. It is rather my belief that the right of people to be free of state action that discriminates against them because of race, like the "right of persons to move freely from State to State" . . . "occupies a more protected position in our constitutional system than does the movement of cattle, fruit, steel and coal across state lines." Moreover, when we come to the problem of abatement in Hamm v. Rock Hill [1964], the result reached by the Court is for me much more obvious as a protective measure under the Fourteenth Amendment than under the Commerce Clause. For the former deals with the constitutional status of the individual not with the impact on commerce of local activities or vice versa.

Hence I would prefer to rest on the assertion of legislative power contained in § 5 of the Fourteenth Amendment which states: "The Congress shall have power to enforce, by appropriate legislation, the provisions of this article"—a power which the Court concedes was exercised at least in part in this Act.

A decision based on the Fourteenth Amendment would have a more settling effect, making unnecessary litigation over whether a particular restaurant or inn is within the commerce definitions of the Act or whether a particular customer is an interstate traveler. Under my construction, the Act would apply to all customers in all the enumerated places of public accommodation. And that construction would put an end to all obstructionist strategies and finally close one door on a bitter chapter in American history. . . .

Mr. Justice **Goldberg**, concurring, said in part:

I join in the opinions and judgments of the Court, since I agree "that the action of the Congress in the adoption of the Act as applied here . . . is within the power granted it by the Commerce Clause of the Constitution, as interpreted by this Court for 140 years." . . .

In my concurring opinion in Bell v. Maryland [1964], . . . I expressed my conviction that § 1 of the Fourteenth Amendment guarantees to all Americans the constitutional right "to be treated as equal members of the community with respect to public accommodations," and that "Congress [has] authority under § 5 of the Fourteenth Amendment, or under the Commerce Clause, Art. I, § 8, to implement the rights protected by § 1 of the Fourteenth Amendment. In the give-and-take of the legislative process, Congress can fashion a law drawing the guidelines necessary and appropriate to facilitate practical administration and to distinguish between genuinely public and private accommodations." The challenged Act is just such a law and, in my view, Congress clearly had authority under both § 5 of the Fourteenth Amendment and the Commerce Clause to enact the Civil Rights Act of 1964.

KATZENBACH v. McCLUNG

379 U. S. 294; 85 S. Ct. 377; 13 L. Ed. 2d 290
(1964)

Mr. Justice **Clark** delivered the opinion of the Court, saying in part:

This case was argued with Heart of Atlanta Motel v. United States in which we upheld the constitutional validity of Title II of the Civil Rights Act of 1964 against an attack by hotels, motels, and like establishments. This complaint for injunctive relief against appellants attacks the constitutionality of the Act as applied to a restaurant. . . .

2. The Facts

Ollie's Barbecue is a family-owned restaurant in Birmingham, Alabama, specializing in barbecued meats and homemade pies, with a seating capacity of 220 cus-

tomers. It is located on a state highway 11 blocks from an interstate one and a somewhat greater distance from railroad and bus stations. The restaurant caters to a family and white-collar trade with a take-out service for Negroes. It employs 36 persons, two-thirds of whom are Negroes.

In the 12 months preceding the passage of the Act, the restaurant purchased locally approximately $150,000 worth of food, $69,683 or 46% of which was meat that it bought from a local supplier who had procured it from outside the State. The District Court expressly found that a substantial portion of the food served in the restaurant had moved in interstate commerce. The restaurant has refused to serve Negroes in its dining accommodations since its original opening in 1927, and since July 2, 1964, it has been operating in violation of the Act. The court below concluded that if it were required to serve Negroes it would lose a substantial amount of business.

On the merits, the District Court held that the Act could not be applied under the Fourteenth Amendment because it was conceded that the State of Alabama was not involved in the refusal of the restaurant to serve Negroes. . . . As to the Commerce Clause, the court found . . . that the clause was . . . a grant of power "to regulate intrastate activities, but only to the extent that action on its part is necessary or appropriate to the effective execution of its expressly granted power to regulate interstate commerce." There must be, it said, a close and substantial relation between local activities and interstate commerce which requires control of the former in the protection of the latter. The court concluded, however, that the Congress, rather than finding facts sufficient to meet this rule, had legislated a conclusive presumption that a restaurant affects interstate commerce if it serves or offers to serve interstate travelers or if a substantial portion of the food which it serves has moved in commerce. This, the court held, it could not do because there was no demonstrable connection between food purchased in interstate commerce and sold in a restaurant and the conclusion of Congress that discrimination in the restaurant would affect that commerce. . . .

3. The Act As Applied

Section 201 (a) of Title II commands that all persons shall be entitled to the full and equal enjoyment of the goods and services of any place of public accommodation without discrimination or segregation on the ground of race, color, religion, or national origin; and § 201 (b) defines establishments as places of public accommodation if their operations affect commerce or segregation by them as supported by state action. Sections 201 (b) (2) and (c) place any "restaurant . . . principally engaged in selling food for consumption on the premises" under the Act "if . . . it serves or offers to serve interstate travelers or a substantial portion of the food which it serves . . . has moved in commerce."

Ollie's Barbecue admits that it is covered by these provisions of the Act. The Government makes no contention that the discrimination at the restaurant was supported by the State of Alabama. There is no claim that interstate travelers frequented the restaurant. The sole question, therefore, narrows down to whether Title II, as applied to a restaurant annually receiving about $70,000 worth of food which has moved in commerce, is a valid exercise of the power of Congress. The Government has contended that Congress had ample basis upon which to find that racial discrimination at restaurants which receive from out of state a substantial portion of the food served does, in fact, impose commercial burdens of national magnitude upon interstate commerce. The appellees' major argument is directed to this premise. They urge that no such basis existed. It is to that question that we now turn.

4. The Congressional Hearings

As we noted in Heart of Atlanta Motel both houses of Congress conducted prolonged hearings on the Act. And, as we said there, while no formal findings were made, which of course are not necessary, it is well that we make mention of the testimony at these hearings the better to understand the problem before Congress and determine whether the Act is a reasonable and appropriate means toward its solution. The record is replete with testimony of the burdens placed on interstate commerce by racial discrimination in restaurants. A comparison of per capita spending by Negroes in restaurants, theaters, and like establishments indicated less spending, after discounting income differences, in areas where discrimination is widely practiced. This condition, which was especially aggravated in the South, was attributed in the testimony of the Under Secretary of Commerce to racial segregation. . . . This diminutive spending springing from a refusal to serve Negroes and their total loss as customers has, regardless of the absence of direct evidence, a close connection to interstate commerce. The fewer customers a restaurant enjoys the less food it sells and consequently the less it buys. . . . In addition, the Attorney General testified that this type of discrimination imposed "an artificial restriction on the market" and interfered with the flow of merchandise. . . . In addition, there were many references to discriminatory situations causing wide unrest and having a depressant effect on general business conditions in the respective communities. . . .

Moreover there was an impressive array of testimony that discrimination in restaurants had a direct and highly restrictive effect upon interstate travel by Negroes. This resulted, it was said, because discriminatory practices prevent Negroes from buying prepared food served on the premises while on a trip, except in isolated and unkempt restaurants and under most unsatisfactory and often unpleasant conditions. This obviously discourages travel and obstructs interstate commerce for one can hardly travel without eating. Likewise, it was said, that discrimination deterred professional, as well as skilled, people from moving into areas where such practices occurred and thereby caused industry to be reluctant to establish there. . . .

We believe that this testimony afforded ample basis for the conclusion that established restaurants in such areas sold less interstate goods because of the discrimination, that interstate travel was obstructed directly by it, that business in general suffered and that many new businesses refrained from establishing there as a result of it. Hence the District Court was in error in concluding that there was no connection between discrimination and the movement of interstate commerce. The court's conclusion that such a connection is outside "common experience" flies in the face of stubborn fact.

It goes without saying that, viewed in isolation, the volume of food purchased by Ollie's Barbecue from sources supplied from out of state was insignificant when compared with the total foodstuffs moving in commerce. But, as our late Brother Jackson said for the Court in Wickard v. Filburn (1942):

"That appellee's own contribution to the demand for wheat may be trivial by itself is not enough to remove him from the scope of federal regulation where, as here, his contribution, taken together with that of many others similarly situated, is far from trivial."

We noted in Heart of Atlanta Motel that a number of witnesses attested the fact that racial discrimination was not merely a state or regional problem but was one of nationwide scope. Against this background, we must conclude that while the focus of the legislation was on the individual restaurant's relation to interstate commerce, Congress appropriately considered the importance of that connection with the knowledge that the discrimination was but "representative of many others throughout the country, the total incidence of which if left unchecked may well become far-reaching in its harm to commerce." . . .

With this situation spreading as the record shows, Congress was not required to await the total dislocation of commerce. . . .

5. The Power of Congress to Regulate Local Activities

Article I, § 8, cl. 3, confers upon Congress the power "[t]o regulate Commerce . . . among the several States" and Clause 18 of the same Article grants it the power "[t]o make all Laws which shall be necessary and proper for carrying into Execution the foregoing Powers. . . ." This grant, as we have pointed out in Heart of Atlanta Motel "extends to those activities intrastate which so affect interstate commerce, or the exertion of the power of Congress over it, as to make regulation of them appropriate means to the attainment of a legitimate end, the effective execution of the granted power to regulate interstate commerce." . . . Much is said about a restaurant business being local but "even if appellee's activity be local and though it may not be regarded as commerce, it may still, whatever its nature, be reached by Congress if it exerts a substantial economic effect on interstate commerce. . . ." . . . The activities that are beyond the reach of Congress are "those which are completely within a particular State, which do not affect other States, and with which it is not necessary to interfere, for the purpose of executing some of the general powers of the government." . . . This rule is as good today as it was when Chief Justice Marshall laid it down almost a century and a half ago. . . .

Nor are the cases holding that interstate commerce ends when goods come to rest in the State of destination apposite here. That line of cases has been applied with reference to state taxation or regulation but not in the field of federal regulation.

The appellees contend that Congress has arbitrarily created a conclusive presumption that all restaurants meeting the criteria set out in the Act "affect commerce." Stated another way, they object to the omission of a provision for a case-by-case determination—judicial or administrative—that racial discrimination in a particular restaurant affects commerce.

But Congress' action in framing this Act was not unprecedented. In United States v. Darby, this Court held constitutional the Fair Labor Standards Act of 1938. There Congress determined that the payment of substandard wages to employees engaged in the production of goods for commerce, while not itself commerce, so inhibited it as to be subject to federal regulation. The appellees in that case argued, as do the appellees here, that the Act was invalid because it included no provision for an independent inquiry regarding the effect on commerce of substandard wages in a particular business. . . . But the Court rejected the argument, observing that:

"Sometimes Congress itself has said that a particular activity affects the commerce, as it did in the present Act, the Safety Appliance Act and the Railway Labor Act. In passing on the validity of legislation of the class last mentioned the only function of courts is to determine whether the particular activity regulated or prohibited is within the reach of the federal power."

Here, as there, Congress has determined for itself that refusals of service to Negroes have imposed burdens both upon the interstate flow of food and upon the movement of products generally. Of course, the mere fact that Congress has said when particular activity shall be deemed to affect commerce does not preclude further examination by this Court. But where we find that the legislators, in light of the facts and testimony before them, have a rational basis for finding a chosen regulatory scheme necessary to the protection of commerce, our investigation is at an end. The only remaining question—one answered in the affirmative by the court below—is whether the particular restaurant either serves or offers to serve interstate travelers or serves food a substantial portion of which has moved in interstate commerce. . . .

Confronted as we are with the facts laid before Congress, we must conclude that it had a rational basis for finding that racial discrimination in restaurants had a direct and adverse effect on the free flow of interstate commerce. Insofar as the sections of the Act here relevant are concerned, §§ 201 (b) (2) and (c), Congress prohibited discrimination only in those establishments having a close tie to interstate commerce, i.e., those, like the McClungs', serving food that has come from out of the State. We think in so doing that Congress acted well within its power to protect and foster commerce in extending the coverage of Title II only to those restaurants offering to serve interstate travelers or serving food, a substantial portion of which has moved in interstate commerce.

The absence of direct evidence connecting discriminatory restaurant service with the flow of interstate food, a factor on which the appellees place much reliance, is not, given the evidence as to the effect of such practices on other aspects of commerce, a crucial matter.

The power of Congress in this field is broad and sweeping; where it keeps within its sphere and violates no express constitutional limitation it has been the rule of this Court, going back almost to the founding days of the Republic, not to interfere. The Civil Rights Act of 1964, as here applied, we find to be plainly appropriate in the resolution of what the Congress found to be a national commercial problem of the first magnitude. We find it in no violation of any express limitations of the Constitution and we therefore declare it valid.

The judgment is therefore
Reversed.

Justices **Black, Douglas,** and **Goldberg** wrote concurring opinions.

UNITED STATES v. DARBY

312 U. S. 100; 61 S. Ct. 451; 85 L. Ed. 609
(1941)

The final remnant of the pre-1937 Court's attitude toward the commerce power still standing was Hammer v. Dagenhart (1918), the case in which the Court had found that keeping child-labor-made goods out of interstate commerce was really a regulation of local manufacturing rather than of interstate commerce. With the assurance gained from the judicial acceptance of the National Labor Relations Act Congress boldly set forth to deal not only with child labor but with labor conditions in general.

In 1938 Congress enacted the Fair Labor Standards (Wages and Hours) Act, which provided the first comprehensive regulation of the working standards of persons engaged in interstate commerce or producing goods for that commerce. The act provided (the first year) for a minimum wage of 25 cents an hour and a maximum forty-four-hour week without overtime pay, and required employers subject to the act to keep records of the hours and pay of their workers. Prohibited, also, was the employment of children under sixteen in manufacturing and mining, and under eighteen in hazardous occupations. The act not only made it a crime to ship in interstate commerce goods manufactured in violation of these standards but, in addition, made it a crime to employ persons in the manufacture of goods for commerce under conditions which did not meet the prescribed standards. Darby, the president of a lumber company, was indicted for violating the wages, hours, and record-keeping provisions of the act.

2 Questions

Mr. Justice **Stone** delivered the opinion of the Court, saying in part:

The two principal questions raised by the record in this case are, *first*, whether Congress has constitutional power to prohibit the shipment in interstate commerce of lumber manufactured by employees whose wages are less than a prescribed minimum or whose weekly hours of labor at that wage are greater than a prescribed maximum, and, *second*, whether it has power to prohibit the employment of workmen in the production of goods "for interstate commerce" at other than prescribed wages and hours. A subsidiary question is whether in connection with such prohibitions Congress can require the employer subject to them to keep records showing the hours worked each day and week by each of his employees including those engaged "in the production and manufacture of goods to wit, lumber, for 'interstate commerce.' " . . .

The Fair Labor Standards Act set up a comprehensive legislative scheme for preventing the shipment in interstate commerce of certain products and commodities produced in the United States under labor conditions as respects wages and hours which fail to conform to standards set up by the Act. Its purpose, as we judicially know from the declaration of policy in § 2(a) of the Act, and the reports of Congressional committees proposing the legislation, . . . is to exclude from interstate commerce goods produced for the commerce and to prevent their production for interstate commerce, under conditions detrimental to the maintenance of the minimum standards of living necessary for health and general well-being; and to prevent the use of interstate commerce as the means of competition in the distribution of goods so produced, and as the means of spreading and perpetuating such substandard labor conditions among the workers of the several states. The Act also sets up an administrative procedure whereby those standards may from time to time be modified generally as to industries subject to the Act or within an industry in accordance with specified standards, by an administrator acting in collaboration with "Industry Committees" appointed by him. . . .

The indictment charges that appellee is engaged, in the state of Georgia, in the business of acquiring raw materials, which he manufactures into finished lumber with the intent, when manufactured, to ship it in interstate commerce to customers outside the state, and that he does in fact so ship a large part of the lumber so produced. There are numerous counts charging appellee with the shipment in interstate commerce from Georgia to points outside the state of lumber in the production of which, for interstate commerce, appellee has employed workmen at less than the prescribed minimum wage or more than the prescribed maximum hours without payment to them of any wage for overtime. Other counts charge the employment by appellee of workmen in the production of lumber for interstate commerce at wages [of] less than 25 cents an hour or for more than the maximum hours per week without payment to them of the

prescribed overtime wage. Still another count charges appellee with failure to keep records showing the hours worked each day a week by each of his employees as required by § 11(c) and the regulation of the administrator, . . . and also that appellee unlawfully failed to keep such records of employees engaged "in the production and manufacture of goods, to-wit lumber, for interstate commerce." . . .

The case comes here on assignments by the Government that the district court erred in so far as it held that Congress was without constitutional power to penalize the acts set forth in the indictment, and appellee seeks to sustain the decision below on the grounds that the prohibition by Congress of those Acts is unauthorized by the commerce clause and is prohibited by the Fifth Amendment. . . . Hence we . . . confine our decision to the validity and construction of the statute.

The prohibition of shipment of the proscribed goods in interstate commerce. Section 15(a) (1) prohibits, and the indictment charges, the shipment in the interstate commerce, of goods produced for interstate commerce by employees whose wages and hours of employment do not conform to the requirements of the Act. Since this section is not violated unless the commodity shipped has been produced under labor conditions prohibited by § 6 and § 7, the only question arising under the commerce clause with respect to such shipments is whether Congress has the constitutional power to prohibit them.

While manufacture is not of itself interstate commerce the shipment of manufactured goods interstate is such commerce and the prohibition of such shipment by Congress is indubitably a regulation of the commerce. The power to regulate commerce is the power "to prescribe the rule by which commerce is governed." Gibbons v. Ogden [1824]. It extends not only to those regulations which aid, foster and protect the commerce, but embraces those which prohibit it. . . . It is conceded that the power of Congress to prohibit transportation in interstate commerce includes noxious articles, Lottery Case (Champion v. Ames) [1903] . . . ; stolen articles, Brooks v. United States [1925]; kidnapped persons, Gooch v. United States [1936] . . . and articles such as intoxicating liquor or convict made goods, traffic in which is forbidden or restricted by the laws of the state of destination. Kentucky Whip & Collar Co. v. Illinois C. R. Co. [1937].

But it is said that the present prohibition falls within the scope of none of these categories; that while the prohibition is nominally a regulation of the commerce its motive or purpose is regulation of wages and hours of persons engaged in manufacture, the control of which has been reserved to the states and upon which Georgia and some of the states of destination have placed no restriction; that the effect of the present statute is not to exclude the prescribed articles from interstate commerce in aid of state regulation as in Kentucky Whip & Collar Co. v. Illinois C. R. Co., but instead, under the guise of a regulation of interstate commerce, it undertakes to regulate wages and hours within the state con-

Congress has power

trary to the policy of the state which has elected to leave them unregulated.

The power of Congress over interstate commerce "is complete in itself, may be exercised to its utmost extent, and acknowledges no limitations other than are prescribed in the Constitution." Gibbons v. Ogden. That power can neither be enlarged nor diminished by the exercise or nonexercise of state power. . . . Congress, following its own conception of public policy concerning the restrictions which may appropriately be imposed on interstate commerce, is free to exclude from the commerce articles whose use in the states for which they are destined it may conceive to be injurious to the public health, morals or welfare, even though the state has not sought to regulate their use. . . .

Such regulation is not a forbidden invasion of state power merely because either its motive or its consequence is to restrict the use of articles of commerce within the states of destination and is not prohibited unless by other constitutional provisions. It is no objection to the assertion of the power to regulate interstate commerce that its exercise is attended by the same incidents which attend the exercise of the police power of the states. . . .

The motive and purpose of the present regulation are plainly to make effective the Congressional conception of public policy that interstate commerce should not be made the instrument of competition in the distribution of goods produced under substandard labor conditions, which competition is injurious to the commerce and to the states from and to which the commerce flows. The motive and purpose of a regulation of interstate commerce are matters for the legislative judgment upon the exercise of which the Constitution places no restriction and over which the courts are given no control. . . . "The judicial cannot prescribe to the legislative department of the government limitations upon the exercise of its acknowledged power." Veazie Bank v. Fenno [1869]. Whatever their motive and purpose, regulations of commerce which do not infringe some constitutional prohibition are within the plenary power conferred on Congress by the Commerce Clause. Subject only to that limitation, presently to be considered, we conclude that the prohibition of the shipment interstate of goods produced under the forbidden substandard labor conditions is within the constitutional authority of Congress.

In the more than a century which has elapsed since the decision of Gibbons v. Ogden, these principles of constitutional interpretation have been so long and repeatedly recognized by this Court as applicable to the Commerce Clause, that there would be little occasion for repeating them now were it not for the decision of this Court twenty-two years ago in Hammer v. Dagenhart [1918]. In that case it was held by a bare majority of the Court over the powerful and now classic dissent of Mr. Justice Holmes setting forth the fundamental issues involved, that Congress was without power to exclude the products of child labor from interstate commerce. The reasoning and conclusion of the Court's opinion there cannot be reconciled with the conclusion which we have reached, that the power of Congress under the Com-

merce Clause is plenary to exclude any article from interstate commerce subject only to the specific prohibitions of the Constitution.

Hammer v. Dagenhart has not been followed. The distinction on which the decision was rested that congressional power to prohibit interstate commerce is limited to articles which in themselves have some harmful or deleterious property—a distinction which was novel when made and unsupported by any provision of the Constitution—has long since been abandoned. Brooks v. United States; Kentucky Whip & Collar Co. v. Illinois C. R. Co.; . . . Mulford v. Smith [1939]. The thesis of the opinion that the motive of the prohibition or its effect to control in some measure the use or production within the states of the article thus excluded from the commerce can operate to deprive the regulation of its constitutional authority has long since ceased to have force. . . . And finally we have declared "The authority of the federal government over interstate commerce does not differ in extent or character from that retained by the states over intrastate commerce." United States v. Rock Royal Cooperative [1939].

The conclusion is inescapable that Hammer v. Dagenhart was a departure from the principles which have prevailed in the interpretation of the commerce clause both before and since the decision and that such vitality, as a precedent, as it then had has long since been exhausted. It should be and now is overruled.

Validity of the wage and hour requirements. Section 15(a) (2) and §§ 6 and 7 require employers to conform to the wage and hour provisions with respect to all employees engaged in the production of goods for interstate commerce. As appellee's employees are not alleged to be "engaged in interstate commerce" the validity of the prohibition turns on the question whether the employment, under other than the prescribed labor standards, of employees engaged in the production of goods for interstate commerce is so related to the commerce and so affects it as to be within the reach of the power of Congress to regulate it. . . .

. . . The power of Congress over interstate commerce is not confined to the regulation of commerce among the states. It extends to those activities intrastate which so affect interstate commerce or the exercise of the power of Congress over it as to make regulation of them appropriate means to the attainment of a legitimate end, the exercise of the granted power of Congress to regulate interstate commerce. . . .

. . . A recent example is the National Labor Relations Act for the regulation of employer and employee relations in industries in which strikes, induced by unfair labor practices named in the Act, tend to disturb or obstruct interstate commerce. See National Labor Relations Bd. v. Jones & L. Steel Corp. [1937]. . . . But long before the adoption of the National Labor Relations Act this Court had many times held that the power of Congress to regulate interstate commerce extends to the regulation through legislative action of activities intrastate which have a substantial effect on the commerce or the exercise of the Congressional power over it.

In such legislation Congress has sometimes left it

to the courts to determine whether the intrastate activities have the prohibited effect on the commerce, as in the Sherman Act. It has sometimes left it to an administrative board or agency to determine whether the activities sought to be regulated or prohibited have such effect, as in the case of the Interstate Commerce Act, and the National Labor Relations Act or whether they come within the statutory definition of the prohibited Act as in the Federal Trade Commission Act. And sometimes Congress itself has said that a particular activity affects the commerce as it did in the present act, the Safety Appliance Act and the Railway Labor Act. In passing on the validity of legislation of the class last mentioned the only function of courts is to determine whether the particular activity regulated or prohibited is within the reach of the federal power. . . .

Congress having by the present Act adopted the policy of excluding from interstate commerce all goods produced for the commerce which do not conform to the specified labor standards, it may choose the means reasonably adapted to the attainment of the permitted end, even though they involve control of intrastate activities. . . . A familiar like exercise of power is the regulation of intrastate transactions which are so commingled with or related to interstate commerce that all must be regulated if the interstate commerce is to be effectively controlled. Shreveport Case [1914]. . . . Similarly Congress may require inspection and preventive treatment of all cattle in a disease infected area in order to prevent shipment in interstate commerce of some of the cattle without the treatment. . . . It may prohibit the removal, at destination, of labels required by the Pure Food & Drugs Act to be affixed to articles transported in interstate commerce. . . . And we have recently held that Congress in the exercise of its power to require inspection and grading of tobacco shipped in interstate commerce may compel such inspection and grading of all tobacco sold at local auction rooms from which a substantial part but not all of the tobacco sold is shipped in interstate commerce. . . .

We think also that § 15(a) (2) now under consideration, is sustainable independently of § 15(a) (1), which prohibits shipment or transportation of the proscribed goods. As we have said the evils aimed at by the Act are the spread of substandard labor conditions through the use of the facilities of interstate commerce for competition by the goods so produced with those produced under the prescribed or better labor conditions; and the consequent dislocation of the commerce itself caused by the impairment or destruction of local businesses by competition made effective through interstate commerce. The Act is thus directed at the suppression of a method or kind of competition in interstate commerce which it has in effect condemned as "unfair," as the Clayton Act has condemned other "unfair methods of competition" made effective through interstate commerce. . . .

The Sherman Act and the National Labor Relations Act are familiar examples of the exertion of the commerce power to prohibit or control activities wholly intrastate because of their effect on interstate commerce. . . .

The means adopted by § 15(a) (2) for the protec-

tion of interstate commerce by the suppression of the production of the condemned goods for interstate commerce is so related to the commerce and so affects it as to be within the reach of the commerce power. . . . Congress, to attain its objective in the suppression of nationwide competition in interstate commerce by goods produced under substandard labor conditions, has made no distinction as to the volume or amount of shipments in the commerce or of production for commerce by any particular shipper or producer. It recognized that in present day industry, competition by a small part may affect the whole and that the total effect of the competition of many small producers may be great. . . . The legislation aimed at a whole embraces all its parts.

So far as Carter v. Carter Coal Co. [1936] is inconsistent with this conclusion, its doctrine is limited in principle by the decisions under the Sherman Act and the National Labor Relations Act, which we have cited and which we follow. . . .

Our conclusion is unaffected by the Tenth Amendment which provides: "The powers not delegated to the United States by the Constitution nor prohibited by it to the states are reserved to the states respectively or to the people." The amendment states but a truism that all is retained which has not been surrendered. There is nothing in the history of its adoption to suggest that it was more than declaratory of the relationship between the national and state governments as it had been established by the Constitution before the amendment or that its purpose was other than to allay fears that the new national government might seek to exercise powers not granted, and that the states might not be able to exercise fully their reserved powers. . . .

From the beginning and for many years the amendment has been construed as not depriving the national government of authority to resort to all means for the exercise of a granted power which are appropriate and plainly adapted to the permitted end. . . . Whatever doubts may have arisen of the soundness of that conclusion they have been put at rest by the decisions under the Sherman Act and the National Labor Relations Act which we have cited. . . .

Reversed.

SOVEREIGN POWER

WOODS v. MILLER

333 U. S. 138; 68 S. Ct. 421; 92 L. Ed. 596(1948)

While nearly all the regulatory measures enacted by Congress are exercises of one of the powers delegated to it in Article I, Sec. 8—usually tax or commerce—there are two sources of power that do not owe their existence to such delegation. These are the "war power" and the "treaty" power, and they are in a sense truly "federal" powers, owing their ultimate effectiveness to cooperation between Congress and the President.

The Constitution gives Congress the power to de-

clare war and to raise and support armies but the war power which has developed from these simple grants staggers the imagination by its scope and variety. This is because, as Chief Justice Hughes put it in Home Building & Loan Ass'n. v. Blaisdell (1934), "the war power of the Federal Government . . . is a power to wage war successfully." In short, what is necessary to win the war Congress may do, and the Supreme Court has shown no inclination to hold void new and drastic war measures. In World War II the war power was invoked to fix price ceilings, to ration food and fuel, to commandeer factories, and to direct the production, distribution, and consumption of commodities. Our entire economy was mobilized for the war effort. A number of specific war powers exercised by Congress have been challenged in the courts, but in every case unsuccessfully.

Another question is whether Congress has to declare war in order for the country to fight one. Both the Korean War, euphemistically called a "police action," and the Vietnam War were undeclared wars, although Congress appropriated money to fight them. Attempts to have the Vietnam War declared unconstitutional were thwarted, over Justice Douglas's lone dissent, by the Court's refusal to grant certiorari.

The power of Congress to draft men into the armed services was attacked during World War I, although the draft had been resorted to sporadically and inefficiently during the Civil War. In 1917 Congress passed the Selective Draft Act, which made all male citizens between the ages of 21 and 30 subject to national military service. Public officers, ministers of religion, and theological students were exempt from the draft, while conscientious objectors who were affiliated with a "well recognized" pacifist religious sect were permitted to engage in noncombatant duty. In Selective Draft Law Cases (Arver v. United States, 1918) the Supreme Court unanimously held the act valid. The power to compel men to serve in the armed forces is reasonably implied from the power to raise and support armies, for a grant of power with no compulsion behind it is no power at all. The exemption of ministers and theological students is not an "establishment of religion" forbidden by the First Amendment; nor does compulsory military service constitute "involuntary servitude" forbidden by the Thirteenth Amendment. The First Amendment holding was reaffirmed in Gillette v. United States (1971) when the Court rejected a claim that it discriminated among religions by permitting conscientious objection to all wars but not just to one war. The government's need to provide a fair and administratively manageable conscription system constituted a "neutral and secular" basis for limiting the exemption to objectors to all wars and hence did not violate the establishment clause.

In the Selective Training and Service Act of 1940, Congress changed the exemption rule, making it unnecessary to belong to a pacifist sect if a person's conscientious objection were based on "religious training and belief." The meaning of this phrase was spelled out in more detail in the Selective Service Act of 1948 (renamed in 1951 the Universal Military Training and Service Act): "Religious training and belief," according to the

act, was to be defined as "an individual's belief in a relation to a Supreme Being involving duties superior to those arising from any human relation, but [not including] essentially political, sociological, or philosophical views or a merely personal moral code." In United States V. Seeger (1965), the Supreme Court held that this belief in a Supreme Being was not confined to a belief in God, in the traditional sense, but included any "sincere and meaningful belief which occupies in the life of its possessor a place parallel to that filled by the God of those admittedly qualifying for the exemption. . . ."

In 1967, following continued bitter and sometimes violent demonstrations against the draft, General Lewis B. Hershey, then head of the Selective Service System, recommended to the country's draft boards that persons engaged in illegal demonstrations be reclassified if necessary and inducted promptly into the armed service. In 1968 over 500 students who returned their draft cards as a protest against the Vietnam War had their student deferment cancelled and were inducted into the army. The Supreme Court, in Gutknecht v. United States (1970), held that the Selective Service System was not authorized by law to use "immediate induction as a disciplinary or vindictive measure."

Congress, following the Seeger decision, amended the draft act to make explicit that only religiously motivated CO's could be exempted from service, and in United States v. Sisson (297 Fed. Supp. 902, 1969), district judge Charles E. Wyzanski, Jr., of Boston upset the conviction of a nonreligious objector to the Vietnam War both on the ground that the act amounted to an establishment of religion, and that the government's interest in fighting in Vietnam was insufficient to outweigh Sisson's individual rights. The Supreme Court held that Sisson had in effect been ordered acquitted and refused to review the case.

Among the techniques devised for protesting both the war and the draft was the public burning of a person's draft card, and following a wave of such draft-card burning episodes an outraged Congress had in 1965 made it a crime to "knowingly destroy" a draft card. The following year a Boston University philosophy student publicly burned his draft card as part of a "demonstration against the [Vietnam] war and against the draft." In United States v. O'Brien (1968) the Supreme Court denied that the First Amendment had been violated and sustained his conviction under the act. ". . . We think it clear that a government regulation is sufficiently justified if it is within the constitutional power of the government; if it furthers an important or substantial governmental interest; if the governmental interest is unrelated to the suppression of free expression; and if the incidental restriction on alleged First Amendment freedom is no greater than is essential to the furtherance of that interest." Judged by these standards, "the many functions performed by the Selective Service certificates establish beyond doubt that Congress has a legitimate and substantial interest in preventing their wanton and unrestrained destruction."

In 1973 Congress amended the Military Selective Service Act to forbid actual conscription but authorized the President in his discretion to register those eligible for compulsory military service. President Carter, in 1980, ordered all male persons between the ages of 18 and 26 to register for the draft. Failure to so register was a criminal offense. In *Rostker v. Goldberg (1981)* this was challenged on the ground that only men had to register, but was held valid. While roughly 8.4 of the 9 million eligibles registered, an estimated 674,000 refused to do so and the government, faced with the impossibility of prosecuting that many violators, resorted to two techniques. One of these, a purely administrative action, involved instigating prosecution (after pleading with them to register) against those who publicly announced that they were not registered or were not going to register, or whose identity as nonregistrants was reported by others to the Department of Justice. In *Wayte v. United States* the Supreme Court, while conceding that the thirteen chosen for prosecution had all been ''vocal'' nonregistrants, rejected the charge that their First Amendment rights of protest has been infringed. Relying on *O'Brien*, it noted that ''when, as here, ' ''speech'' and ''nonspeech'' elements are combined in the same course of conduct, a sufficiently important governmental interest in regulating the nonspeech element can justify incidental limitations on First Amendment freedoms.' '' Moreover, ''the passive enforcement policy also meets the final requirement of the *O'Brien* test, for it placed no more limitation on speech than was necessary to ensure registration for the national defense.'' The Court also rejected the view that a person could gain immunity from prosecution under the statute simply by reporting his refusal to abide by it.

A second technique devised for obtaining compliance with the draft law was a congressional statute of 1983 withholding financial aid to college students who were not registered for the draft. In *Selective Service v. Minnesota Pub. Int. Res. Gp. (1984)* the Court found that the statute was not a bill of attainder since it did not inflict punishment. Any eligible student could obtain the financial aid simply by registering. Nor was there a problem of compulsory self-incrimination as a result of having to date a late registration, since none of those involved in the suit had sought to register and hence had had no occasion either to assert a Fifth Amendment privilege or to press a claim of immunity.

During World War I Congress passed a limited type of rent control act applicable to the District of Columbia. It forbade a landlord to evict a tenant at the expiration of his lease if the latter wished to remain and continued to pay the former rent and observed the other conditions of the lease. In *Block v. Hirsh (1921)* the Supreme Court held that the housing emergency growing out of the war justified the exercise of this power. In World War II Congress resorted to rent and price controls in earnest. The Emergency Price Control Act of 1942 gave the Administrator of the Office of Price Administration (OPA) broad authority to fix maximum prices on most commodities and on residential rents. The act created a special Emergency Court of Appeals, manned by federal judges designated by the Chief Justice of the United States, to pass upon the validity of OPA regulations. In *Yakus v. United States (1944)* the Court held valid the price-fixing provisions of the statute, while in *Bowles v. Willingham (1944)* it upheld the rent-control sections of the act. In pithy language it rejected Mrs. Willingham's claim that, while the rents fixed might be generally fair, the rents she was allowed to charge were so low as to be a taking of her property without due process of law. ''Of course, price control, the same as other forms of regulation, may reduce the value of the property regulated. But . . . that does not mean that the regulation is unconstitutional. . . . A nation which can demand the lives of its men and women in the waging of . . . war is under no constitutional necessity of providing a system of price control on the domestic front which will assure each landlord a 'fair return' on his property.''

It is interesting to note that in these two cases there was no frontal attack upon the power of Congress to control rents and prices under its war power. The act was challenged upon the ground that it invalidly delegated legislative power to the OPA Administrator, and that it did not provide fair procedure for the review of the rights of those subject to the act. In *Steuart & Bros. Inc. v. Bowles (1944)* the Court held that the Second War Powers Act of 1942, which authorized the rationing of materials and commodities, empowered the President through the OPA to withhold rationed goods from those who acquired or distributed them in violation of ration regulations. Here, again, the power of Congress to authorize rationing was taken for granted.

In *Woods v. Miller*, below, the issue is not whether the war power of Congress validly supports rent control, but whether it can keep on supporting it after hostilities have ended. The question was not new to the Court. The World War I rent-control act which had been held valid in *Block v. Hirsh* had been extended by Congress until 1924. In *Chastleton Corp. v. Sinclair (1924)* the Court agreed that ''a law depending upon the existence of an emergency or other certain state of facts to uphold it may cease to operate if the emergency ceases or the facts change, even though valid when passed.'' The Court then sent the case back to the lower court for a determination of the facts, noting only that ''if about all that remains of war conditions is the increased cost of living, that is not, in itself, a justification of the act.'' On December 31, 1946, President Truman issued a proclamation declaring the termination of hostilities. Congress itself, however, had passed no act or resolution declaring the war to be ended. On June 30, 1947, Congress enacted the Housing and Rent Act, effective on July 1, 1947, continuing in force the rent-control provisions of the Emergency Price Control Act of 1942.

Query: Does the war power continue after the fighting is over? Does it continue, as the Court intimates, as long as the problems generated by the war still face us?

Mr. Justice **Douglas** delivered the opinion of the Court, saying in part:

The case is here on a direct appeal . . . from a

judgment of the District Court holding unconstitutional Title II of the Housing and Rent Act of 1947.

The act became effective on July 1, 1947, and the following day the appellee demanded of its tenants increases of 40% and 60% for rental accommodations in the Cleveland Defense-Rental Area, an admitted violation of the act and regulations adopted pursuant thereto. . . .

The District Court was of the view that the authority of Congress to regulate rents by virtue of the war power . . . ended with the Presidential Proclamation terminating hostilities on December 31, 1946, since that proclamation inaugurated "peace-in-fact" though it did not mark termination of the war. It also concluded that, even if the war power continues, Congress did not act under it because it did not say so, and only if Congress says so, or enacts provisions so implying, can it be held that Congress intended to exercise such power. That Congress did not so intend, said the District Court, follows from the provision that the Housing Expediter can end controls in any area without regard to the official termination of the war, and from the fact that the preceding federal rent control laws (which were concededly exercises of the war power) were neither amended nor extended. The District Court expressed the further view that rent control is not within the war power because "the emergency created by housing shortage came into existence long before the war." . . .

We conclude, in the first place, that the war power sustains this legislation. The Court said in Hamilton v. Kentucky Distilleries Co. [1919] that the war power includes the power "to remedy the evils which have arisen from its rise and progress" and continues for the duration of that emergency. Whatever may be the consequences when war is officially terminated, the war power does not necessarily end with the cessation of hostilities. We recently held that it is adequate to support the preservation of rights created by wartime legislation. Fleming v. Mohawk Wrecking & Lumber Co. [1947]. But it has a broader sweep. In Hamilton v. Kentucky Distilleries Co., and Ruppert v. Caffey [1920], prohibition laws which were enacted after the Armistice in World War I were sustained as exercises of the war power because they conserved manpower and increased efficiency of production in the critical days during the period of demobilization, and helped to husband the supply of grains and cereals depleted by the war effort. . . .

The constitutional validity of the present legislation follows a fortiori from those cases. The legislative history of the present Act makes abundantly clear that there has not yet been eliminated the deficit in housing which in considerable measure was caused by the heavy demobilization of veterans and by the cessation or reduction in residential construction during the period of hostilities due to the allocation of building materials to military projects. Since the war effort contributed heavily to that deficit, Congress has the power even after the cessation of hostilities to act to control the forces that a short supply of the needed article created. If that were not true, the Necessary and Proper Clause, Art. I, § 8, cl. 18, would be drastically limited in its application to the several war powers. The Court has declined to follow that course in the past. . . . We decline to take it today. The result would be paralyzing. It would render Congress powerless to remedy conditions the creation of which necessarily followed from the mobilization of men and materials for successful prosecution of the war. So to read the Constitution would be to make it self-defeating.

We recognize the force of the argument that the effects of the war under modern conditions may be felt in the economy for years and years, and that if the war power can be used in days of peace to treat all the wounds which war inflicts on our society, it may not only swallow up all other powers of Congress but largely obliterate the Ninth and the Tenth Amendments as well. There are no such implications in today's decision. We deal here with the consequences of a housing deficit greatly intensified during the period of hostilities by the war effort. Any power, of course, can be abused. But we cannot assume that Congress is not alert to its constitutional responsibilities. And the question whether the war power has been properly employed in cases such as this is open to judicial inquiry. . . .

The question of the constitutionality of action taken by Congress does not depend on recitals of the power which it undertakes to exercise. Here it is plain from the legislative history that Congress was invoking its war power to cope with a current condition of which the war was a direct and immediate cause. Its judgment on that score is entitled to the respect granted like legislation enacted pursuant to the police power. . . .

Reversed.

Mr. Justice **Jackson,** concurring, said:

I agree with the result in this case, but the arguments that have been addressed to us lead me to utter more explicit misgivings about war powers than the Court has done. The Government asserts no constitutional basis for this legislation other than this vague, undefined and undefinable "war power."

No one will question that this power is the most dangerous one to free government in the whole catalogue of powers. It usually is invoked in haste and excitement when calm legislative consideration of constitutional limitation is difficult. It is executed in a time of patriotic fervor that makes moderation unpopular. And, worst of all, it is interpreted by the Judges under the influence of the same passions and pressures. Always, as in this case, the Government urges hasty decision to forestall some emergency or serve some purpose and pleads that paralysis will result if its claims to power are denied or their confirmation delayed.

Particularly when the war power is invoked to do things to the liberties of people, or to their property or economy that only indirectly affect conduct of the war and do not relate to the management of the war itself, the constitutional basis should be scrutinized with care.

I think we can hardly deny that the war power is as valid a ground for federal rent control now as it has been at any time. We still are technically in a state of war. I would not be willing to hold that war powers may be indefinitely prolonged merely by keeping legally alive a state of war that had in fact ended. I cannot accept the argument that war powers last as long as the effects and consequences of war for if so they are permanent—as permanent as the war debts. But I find no reason to conclude that we could find fairly that the present state of war is merely technical. We have armies abroad exercising our war power and have made no peace terms with our allies not to mention our principal enemies. I think the conclusion that the war power has been applicable during the lifetime of this legislation is unavoidable.

MISSOURI v. HOLLAND

252 U. S. 416; 40 S. Ct. 382; 64 L. Ed. 641 (1920)

The "treaty power," like the war power, is a mixture of congressional and presidential authority, resting on the power of the President to "make" treaties with the consent of the Senate and the power of Congress to pass laws to carry them out. While the laws of Congress on domestic matters owe their validity to the Constitution, treaties, on the other hand, are valid if made "under the authority of the United States." Thus Congress may derive legislative authority from the power to carry out the provisions of a treaty when it could not derive it from any of the specific grants of legislative power enumerated in Article I. The traditional reluctance of the nation to commit itself to international agreements in any way limiting its own sovereign powers has meant that the scope of the power, unlike the war power, has never been really tested.

That such treaties are, as the Constitution says, "the supreme law of the land" was made clear as early as 1796 in Ware v. Hylton, reaffirmed in Hauenstein v. Lynham (1880), both cases in which the Court held invalid a Virginia statute denying an alien rights which the federal government had guaranteed him by a treaty with his native land. These points are clearly emphasized by the judicial history of the two migratory-birds acts passed by Congress. In 1913 Congress passed an act forbidding, save under strict regulations, the killing of migratory birds. The control of bird life is not one of the powers which the Constitution grants to Congress, and two lower federal courts held the law unconstitutional: United States v. Shauver (1914) and United States v. McCullagh (1915). These cases have been generally regarded as correct.

In 1916 we entered into a treaty with Great Britain by the terms of which the United States and Canada agreed to protect migratory birds and to propose legislation for that purpose. In 1918 Congress passed such a law, much more elaborate than the act of 1913, forbidding the killing, capturing, or selling of the birds included within the provisions of the treaty, except in accordance with regulations set by the Secretary of Agriculture. The Secretary of Agriculture promulgated suitable regulations; and the state of Missouri, on the ground that her reserved powers were invaded by the act, brought action to enjoin a game warden of the United States from enforcing the provisions of the act and the rules established by the Secretary of Agriculture. The decision of the Court makes it clear that Congress may regulate bird life as a means of carrying into effect the provisions of a treaty when it could not regulate it as an independent exercise of legislative power.

This broad doctrine has been sharply attacked. In 1954 the Senate by only a narrow margin defeated the so-called Bricker Amendment, one section of which provided that "A treaty shall become effective as internal law in the United States only through legislation which would be valid in the absence of a treaty." This would have reversed Missouri v. Holland, and was so intended.

Certain questions arise in connection with the treaty power. First, is a treaty "self-executing," or is a statute of Congress necessary before it goes into effect? Marshall answered this question in Foster v. Neilson (1829), where he said: "Our Constitution declares a treaty to be the law of the land. It is, consequently, to be regarded in courts of justice as equivalent to an Act of the Legislature, whenever it operates of itself, without the aid of any legislative provision. But when the terms of the stipulation import a contract—when either of the parties engages to perform a particular act—the treaty addresses itself to the political, not the judicial department; and the Legislature must execute the contract before it can become a rule for the Court." Whether or not a treaty is self-executing is, of course, a question for the Court to decide. Public attention was focused on this question when a California court held that the state's Alien Land Law had been nullified by our adherence to the United Nations Charter, an interpretation which was rejected by the state's supreme court; see Sei Fujii v. California, 38 Cal. 2d 718 (1952).

A second problem arises when a treaty and a congressional statute conflict with each other. Since they are of equal weight, both being the law of the land, the more recent is deemed to express the policy of the government. On a number of occasions the Supreme Court has held that a later act of Congress abrogates a prior treaty. In Chae Chan Ping v. United States (1889) a treaty with China guaranteeing certain Chinese laborers the right to leave and reenter the United States was held to be superseded by a statute forbidding such reentry. The abrogation of treaties in this way does not, of course, relieve the government of the international obligations it may have incurred, but these are not problems with which the courts are concerned; the offended nation must appeal for redress to the political branches of the government.

There are few cases in which a treaty has been held to nullify a prior act of Congress. This did occur, however, in the case of Cook v. United States (1933). The Tariff Act of 1922 had been superseded in 1924 by a treaty with Britain substituting for a flat congressional twelve-mile limit the "distance which can be traversed in one hour by the suspected vessel" as the offshore distance within which we could stop vessels in order to enforce our prohibition laws against rumrunners. In the Tariff Act of 1930, however, Congress reenacted the *provision for a twelve-mile limit in the identical language of the 1922 act. The Court held that there was no evidence that Congress had intended to modify the provision of the 1924 treaty, and therefore the one-hour distance provisions of the treaty remained in force.*

An important problem raised by Missouri v. Holland was the extent to which, if at all, Congress was free to make treaties which limited the rights of citizens guaranteed them by the Constitution. If Congress was freed from the restrictions of the Tenth Amendment, as the Court in the present case held, was it also freed from the limitations of the Bill of Rights? Despite Justice Holmes's reassuring statement that the migratory-birds treaty "does not contravene any prohibitory words to be found in the Constitution," there was no firm decision on this important point. Speaking for four members of the Court in Reid v. Covert (1957), Justice Black emphasized that the "obvious and decisive answer to this, of course, is that no agreement with a foreign nation can confer power on the Congress, or on any other branch of government, which is free from the restraints of the Constitution."

Public attention was focused on this problem in the spring of 1957 when Girard, an American soldier, was turned over to the Japanese authorities for trial on charges of having killed a Japanese woman. A United States district court ordered the military authorities not to turn Girard over to the Japanese, and the Supreme Court, in a per curiam opinion, reversed this order. The Court pointed out that "a sovereign nation has exclusive jurisdiction to punish offenses against its laws committed within its borders," and nothing in the Constitution or subsequent legislation was found to nullify the provision in our security treaty with Japan (a Status of Forces Agreement) under which we would give "sympathetic consideration" to a request that we relinquish our jurisdiction in such cases. See Wilson v. Girard (1957).

Mr. Justice **Holmes** delivered the opinion of the Court, saying in part:

. . . As we have said, the question raised is the general one whether the treaty and statute are void as an interference with the rights reserved to the states.

To answer this question it is not enough to refer to the 10th Amendment, reserving the powers not delegated to the United States, because by article 2, § 2, the power to make treaties is delegated expressly, and by article 6, treaties made under the authority of the United States, along with the Constitution and laws of the United States, made in pursuance thereof, are declared the supreme law of the land. If the treaty is valid, there can be no dispute about the validity of the statute under article 1, § 8, as a necessary and proper means to execute the powers of the government. The language of the Constitution as to the supremacy of treaties being general, the question before us is narrowed to an inquiry into the ground upon which the present supposed exception is placed.

It is said that a treaty cannot be valid if in infringes

the Constitution; that there are limits, therefore, to the treaty-making power; and that one such limit is that what an act of Congress could not do unaided, in derogation of the powers reserved to the states, a treaty cannot do. An earlier act of Congress that attempted by itself, and not in pursuance of a treaty, to regulate the killing of migratory birds within the states, had been held bad in the district court. United States v. Shauver [1914]; United States v. McCullagh [1915]. Those decisions were supported by arguments that migratory birds were owned by the states in their sovereign capacity, for the benefit of their people, and that under cases like Geer v. Connecticut [1896], this control was one that Congress had no power to displace. The same argument is supposed to apply now with equal force.

Whether the two cases cited were decided rightly or not, they cannot be accepted as a test of the treaty power. Acts of Congress are the supreme law of the land only when made in pursuance of the Constitution, while treaties are declared to be so when made under the authority of the United States. It is open to question whether the authority of the United States means more than the formal acts prescribed to make the convention. We do not mean to imply that there are no qualifications to the treaty-making power; but they must be ascertained in a different way. It is obvious that there may be matters of the sharpest exigency for the national well-being that an act of Congress could not deal with, but that a treaty followed by such an act could, and it is not lightly to be assumed that, in matters requiring national action, "a power which must belong to and somewhere reside in every civilized government" is not to be found. . . . We are not yet discussing the particular case before us, but only are considering the validity of the test proposed. With regard to that, we may add that when we are dealing with words that also are a constituent act, like the Constitution of the United States, we must realize that they have called into life a being the development of which could not have been foreseen completely by the most gifted of its begetters. It was enough for them to realize or to hope that they had created an organism; it has taken a century and has cost their successors much sweat and blood to prove that they created a nation. The case before us must be considered in the light of our whole experience, and not merely in that of what was said a hundred years ago. The treaty in question does not contravene any prohibitory words to be found in the Constitution. The only question is whether it is forbidden by some invisible radiation from the general terms of the 10th Amendment. We must consider what this country has become in deciding what that amendment has reserved.

The state, as we have intimated, founds its claim of exclusive authority upon an assertion of title to migratory birds,—an assertion that is embodied in statute. No doubt it is true that, as between a state and its inhabitants, the state may regulate the killing and sale of such birds, but it does not follow that its authority is exclusive of paramount powers. To put the claim of the state upon title is to lean upon a slender reed. Wild birds are not in the possession of anyone; and possession is the beginning of ownership. The whole foundation of the state's rights is the presence within their jurisdiction of birds that yesterday had not arrived, tomorrow may be in another state, and in a week a thousand miles away. If we are to be accurate, we cannot put the case of the state upon higher ground than that the treaty deals with creatures that for the moment are within the state borders, that it must be carried out by officers of the United States within the same territory, and that, but for the treaty, the state would be free to regulate this subject itself.

As most of the laws of the United States are carried out within the states, and as many of them deal with matters which, in the silence of such laws, the state might regulate, such general grounds are not enough to support Missouri's claim. Valid treaties, of course, "are as binding within the territorial limits of the states as they are effective throughout the dominion of the United States." . . . No doubt the great body of private relations usually falls within the control of the state, but a treaty may override its power. . . .

Here a national interest of very nearly the first magnitude is involved. It can be protected only by national action in concert with that of another power. The subject-matter is only transitorily within the state, and has no permanent habitat therein. But for the treaty and the statute, there soon might be no birds for any powers to deal with. We see nothing in the Constitution that compels the government to sit by while a food supply is cut off and the protectors of our forests and our crops are destroyed. It is not sufficient to rely upon the states. The reliance is vain, and were it otherwise, the question is whether the United States is forbidden to act. We are of opinion that the treaty and statute must be upheld. . . .

Decree affirmed.

Mr. Justice **Van Devanter** and Mr. Justice **Pitney** dissent.

7

Rights in the Early Constitution

EX POST FACTO LAWS

CALDER v. BULL

3 Dallas 386; 1 L. Ed. 648 (1798)

While the original Constitution contained no comprehensive Bill of Rights, it did include a number of provisions designed to protect individuals against governmental action. One of these, the contract clause, was a guarantee against state action only; some, like the guarantee of habeas corpus, were applied to the national government only. Two of them, the clauses forbidding bills of attainder and ex post facto laws, applied to both state and national governments.

There is some historical evidence (not wholly conclusive) that the framers intended the ex post facto clauses to apply to civil as well as criminal retroactive laws, thus protecting property interests from retroactive legislative attack. Any such result was defeated by the Court in Calder v. Bull. In an opinion, most of which is still good law, Justice Chase pointed out that ex post facto laws were only retrospective criminal statutes which operated to the disadvantage of accused persons.

This definition raises difficult problems. What is criminal law? Obviously any law which declares an action to be a crime and provides for its punishment meets the test. But what about statutes that impose so-called civil penalties or disabilities? In the Test Oath Cases, discussed below in connection with bills of attainder, the Court held that to bar a person from a profession was punishment despite the argument that the laws in question were not punitive but merely defined necessary professional qualifications. The grounds for disqualification, the Court found, were irrelevant to the fitness of the individuals to carry on their profession. And since it provided for punishment, the law was considered to be "criminal" within the meaning of the ex post facto and bill of attainder clauses.

In Hawker v. New York (1898) the Court backed away from its stand in the Test Oath Cases. Hawker was a physician who in 1878 had been sent to prison for the crime of performing an abortion. In 1893 New York made it a misdemeanor for anyone who had ever been convicted of a felony to practice medicine. Hawker was convicted under the statute for continuing to practice and appealed to the Supreme Court on the ground that the statute increased the penalty for the original crime and was ex post facto. The Court held, however, that the state was merely setting qualifications for the practice of medicine. Under its police power the state could require good moral character of physicians and could validly make the previous violation of law conclusive evidence of bad moral character. It was unnecessary to look back of the general rule to see if Hawker actually was unfit to practice. The Court followed this doctrine in holding that former Communists could be barred from public employment (Garner v. Los Angeles Board of Public Works, 1951) and that ex-convicts could not hold union offices on New York's waterfront (De Veau v. Braisted, 1960).

The denaturalization of naturalized citizens and

231

the deportation of aliens are considered civil rather than criminal proceedings. Congress in 1906 provided for the cancellation of naturalization on grounds of fraud, and this was held validly applicable to a person who had been fraudulently naturalized in 1892. See Johannessen v. United States (1912). In the Internal Security Act of 1950, Congress made even "innocent" membership in the Communist party grounds for deportation. In Galvan v. Press (1954) the Court held that this could validly be applied retroactively, although with obvious misgivings about the justice of the decision. ". . . Were we writing on a clean slate," said the Court, ". . . since the intrinsic consequences of deportation are so close to punishment for crime, it might fairly be said also that the ex post facto clause, even though applicable only to punitive legislation, should be applied to deportation. But the slate is not clean." In 1957, in Rowoldt v. Perfetto, the Court overruled the effect of Galvan v. Press by construing the Internal Security Act as requiring proof of "meaningful association" with the Communist party, and in Gastelum-Quinones v. Kennedy (1963) the Court emphasized that such association was not to be inferred from the mere fact that a person paid dues and attended a few meetings.

A state generally has a right to alter its trial procedure and rules of evidence and to make such changes retroactive to crimes already committed. Such changes are not ex post facto unless they "dispense with any of those substantial protections with which the existing law surrounds the person accused of crime." Thus in Thompson v. Utah (1898) the retroactive reduction in the size of the jury from twelve to eight persons was held ex post facto because it is easier to get eight jurors to agree to convict than it is twelve. On the other hand, in Thompson v. Missouri (1898), where the rules of evidence were altered by law so that letters to Thompson's wife which had previously been excluded became admissible, the Court held that the "substantial rights of the accused" had not been affected. Under the new rule, which was designed merely to give the jury all the light it could get on the disputed facts, both the accused and the state had equal rights to introduce evidence.

In Dobbert v. Florida (1977) the Court held valid as a mere procedural change the enactment of a new death penalty statute (following the commission of the crime) to replace one that had been held unconstitutional following the Court's decision in Furman v. Georgia (1972). What changes there were in the act served to benefit the accused, and since he was on notice that the state could seek the death penalty for murder he was not without warning, despite the invalidity of the statute at the time the murder was actually committed. On the other hand, a statute which reduced retroactively the amount of time to be deducted from a prisoner's sentence for good behavior was held to be a substantive disadvantage to the prisoner and ex post facto; see Weaver v. Graham (1981).

In 1793, as a result of a suit over a contested will, one Calder acquired title to certain property. Two years later the Connecticut legislature passed a law setting aside this decree of the probate court and ordered a new

hearing to be held. As a result of the new hearing the property went to Bull. Calder contended that the Connecticut law was ex post facto.

Mr. Justice **Chase** delivered the opinion of the Court, saying in part:

The effect of the resolution or law of Connecticut, above stated, is to revise a decision of one of its inferior courts, called the court of probate for Hartford, and to direct a new hearing of the case by the same court of probate, that passed the decree against the will of Normand Morrison. By the existing law of Connecticut a right to recover certain property had vested in Calder and wife (the appellants) in consequence of a decision of a court of justice, but, in virtue of a subsequent resolution or law, and the new hearing thereof, and the decision in consequence, this right to recover certain property was divested, and the right to the property declared to be in Bull and wife, the appellees. The sole enquiry is, whether this resolution or law of Connecticut, having such operation, is an ex post facto law, within the prohibition of the federal constitution? . . .

All the restrictions contained in the constitution of the United States on the power of the state Legislatures, were provided in favor of the authority of the federal government. The prohibition against their making any ex post facto laws was introduced for greater caution, and very probably arose from the knowledge, that the Parliament of Great Britain claimed and exercised a power to pass such laws, under the denomination of bills of attainder, or bills of pains and penalties; the first inflicting capital, and the other less, punishment. These acts were legislative judgments; and an exercise of judicial power. . . . The ground for the exercise of such legislative power was this, that the safety of the kingdom depended on the death, or other punishment, of the offender; as if traitors, when discovered, could be so formidable, or the government so insecure! With very few exceptions, the advocates of such laws were stimulated by ambition, or personal resentment, and vindictive malice. To prevent such, and similar, acts of violence and injustice, I believe, the Federal and State Legislatures, were prohibited from passing any bill of attainder; or any ex post facto law. . . .

I shall endeavor to show what law is to be considered an ex post facto law, within the words and meaning of the prohibition in the Federal constitution. The prohibition, "that no state shall pass any ex post facto law," necessarily requires some explanation; for naked, and without explanation, it is unintelligible, and means nothing. Literally, it is only that a law shall not be passed concerning, and after the fact, or thing done, or action committed. I would ask, what fact; of what nature, or kind; and by whom done? That Charles 1st king of England, was beheaded; that Oliver Cromwell was Protector of England, that Louis 16th, late king of France, was guillotined, are all facts, that have happened; but it would be nonsense to suppose, that the states were prohibited from making any law after either of these events, and with reference thereto. The prohibition, in the letter, is not to pass any law concerning and after the fact; but the plain and obvious meaning and intention of the prohibition is this; that the Legislatures of the several states shall not pass laws, after a fact done by a subject or citizen, which shall have relation to such fact, and shall punish him for having done it. The prohibition considered in this light, is an additional bulwark in favor of the personal security of the subject, to protect his person from punishment by legislative acts, having a retrospective operation. I do not think it was inserted to secure the citizen in his private rights, of either property, or contracts. The prohibition not to make anything but gold and silver coin a tender in payment of debts, and not to pass any law impairing the obligations of contracts, were inserted to secure private rights; but the restriction not to pass any ex post facto law, was to secure the person of the subject from injury, or punishment, in consequence of such law. If the prohibition against making ex post facto laws was intended to secure personal rights from being affected, or injured, by such laws, and the prohibition is sufficiently extensive for that object, the other restraints I have enumerated, were unnecessary, and therefore improper; for both of them are retrospective.

I will state what laws I consider ex post facto laws, within the words and the intent of the prohibition. 1st. Every law that makes an action done before the passing of the law; and which was innocent when done, criminal; and punishes such action. 2d. Every law that aggravates a crime, or makes it greater than it was, when committed. 3d. Every law that changes the punishment, and inflicts a greater punishment, than the law annexed to the crime, when committed. 4th. Every law that alters the legal rules of evidence, and receives less, or different, testimony, than the law required at the time of the commission of the offense, in order to convict the offender. All these, and similar laws, are manifestly unjust and oppressive. In my opinion, the true distinction is between ex post facto laws, and retrospective laws. Every ex post facto law must necessarily be retrospective; but every retrospective law is not an ex post facto law: The former, only, are prohibited. Every law that takes away, or impairs, rights vested, agreeably to existing laws, is retrospective, and is generally unjust; and may be oppressive; and it is a good general rule, that a law should have no retrospect: but there are cases in which laws may justly, and for the benefit of the community, and also of individuals, relate to a time antecedent to their commencement; as statutes of oblivion, or of pardon. They are certainly retrospective, and literally both concerning, and after, the facts committed. But I do not consider any law ex post facto, within the prohibition, that mollifies the rigor of the criminal law; but only those that create, or aggravate, the crime; or increase the punishment, or change the rules of evidence, for the purpose of conviction. Every law that is to have an operation before the making thereof, as to commence at an antecedent time; or to save time from the statute of limitations; or to excuse acts which were unlawful, and before committed, and the like; is retrospective. But such laws may be proper or necessary, as the case may be. There is a great and apparent difference between making an unlawful act lawful; and the making an innocent action criminal, and punishing it as a crime. The expressions "ex post facto laws" are technical, they had been in use long before the Revolution, and had acquired an appropriate meaning, by legislators, lawyers, and authors. The celebrated and judicious Sir William Blackstone in his commentaries, considers an ex post facto law precisely in the same light I have done. His opinion is confirmed by his successor, Mr. Wooddeson; and by the author of the Federalist, whom I esteem superior to both, for his extensive and accurate knowledge of the true principles of government.

I also rely greatly on the definition, or explanation of ex post facto laws, as given by the conventions of Massachusetts, Maryland, and North Carolina; in their several constitutions, or forms of government. . . .

I am of the opinion that the decree of the Supreme Court of Errors of Connecticut be affirmed, with costs.

Judgment affirmed.

Mr. Justice **Paterson,** Mr. Justice **Iredell,** and Mr. Justice **Cushing** each delivered concurring opinions.

BILLS OF ATTAINDER

UNITED STATES v. BROWN

381 U.S. 437; 85 S. Ct. 1707; 14 L. Ed. 2d 484
(1965)

A bill of attainder is a statute which inflicts punishment upon a person without a judicial trial. Where the punishment is for a newly defined offense, which is frequently the case, the law is also ex post facto. This was the situation in the two Test Oath Cases arising out of the Civil War. The Missouri constitution was amended by the Reconstruction government to require all persons wishing to pursue a variety of callings, including teaching, the ministry, and the law, to take an oath that they had among other things never '' 'by act or word' manifested . . . adherence to the cause of the enemies of the United States . . . or . . . sympathy with those engaged in rebellion. . . .'' Cummings, a Catholic priest, was convicted of preaching without taking the oath and fined $500. See Cummings v. Missouri (1867). Ex parte Garland (1867) involved a statute of Congress that forbade anyone to practice law in the courts of the United States unless he took an oath that he had never supported the Confederacy. Garland, who later became Attorney General of the United States, was seeking readmission to practice before the Supreme Court and was unable to take the oath. The Court found in both cases that the deprivation of the right to practice their professions was punishment, and that it was being imposed by legislative act since it in effect declared the guilt of these persons and adjudged their punishment. The acts were therefore bills of attainder. Since some of the acts punished were not already crimes, the statutes were also held to be ex post facto.

The case of United States v. Lovett (1946) involved three federal employees who had been on a list of thirty-

nine alleged subversives compiled by the House Committee on Un-American Activities. Congressman Dies, as chairman of the committee, asked that all these men be removed at once from the federal payroll, but the House decided instead to set up a special committee to pass on the charges. This committee heard charges against nine out of the thirty-nine and found that Messrs. Lovett, Watson, and Dodd were subversive and unfit for government service. Whereupon the House passed a rider (§ 304) to an appropriation act which forbade the payment of salaries to these three men, mentioned by name, unless they were renominated by the President and confirmed by the Senate. The three continued to work for a few months and then brought suit for the amount of salary thus earned and not received. The Court found § 304 to be a bill of attainder. The proceedings in the House were analogous to a trial of three named individuals on charges of subversion—in fact, members had spoken of giving each man "his day in court"—and the attempt "permanently to bar them from government service" constituted punishment within the meaning of a bill of attainder. The Court reaffirmed the two Test Oath Cases, noting that "they stand for the proposition that legislative acts, no matter what their form, that apply either to named individuals or to easily ascertainable members of a group in such a way as to inflict punishment on them without a judicial trial are bills of attainder prohibited by the Constitution."

In the light of the Lovett case it was argued that those persons removed for disloyalty under the President's Loyalty Program of 1947 were being punished, and hence should be able to confront their accusers in accordance with due process of law. In Bailey v. Richardson (1950) the court of appeals for the District of Columbia agreed that barring a person from federal service (in this case for three years) was punishment invalidly imposed, but held that dismissal on grounds of loyalty was not. The Supreme Court, dividing four to four, affirmed the decision without opinion.

The present case represents something of a departure from the Court's recent attitude toward the bill of attainder clause. In American Communications Assn. v. Douds (1950), discussed in the case below, the Court had upheld the noncommunist oath provision (§ 9h) of the Taft Hartley Act against the charge that it was a bill of attainder. Then in De Veau v. Braisted, in 1960, it had held that a state statute barring ex-convicts from holding office in the longshoreman's union was not a bill of attainder, since the intent of the New York legislature was not to punish such persons, but to reform the waterfront. It noted the finding of a Senate subcommittee that criminals "whose long records belie any suggestion that they can be reformed have been monopolizing controlling positions in the International Longshoremen's Association and in local unions. Under their regimes gambling, the narcotics traffic, loansharking, shortganging, payroll 'phantoms', the 'shakedown' in all its forms—and the brutal ultimate of murder—have flourished, often virtually unchecked." It concluded that "duly mindful as we are of the promising record of rehabilitation by ex-felons, and of the emphasis on rehabilitation by mod-

ern penological efforts, it is not for this Court to substitute its judgment for that of Congress and the Legislatures of New York and New Jersey regarding the social surgery required by a situation as gangrenous as exposure of the New York waterfront had revealed."

Nor was it considered punishment (and hence a bill of attainder) to deprive deported aliens of their social security benefits; see Flemming v. Nestor (1960). Nestor was a sixty-nine-year-old alien who had resided in the United States for forty-three years, had paid into the social security system for nineteen years, and had been a member of the Communist party from 1933 to 1939. In 1956 he was deported for having been a Communist; and under a statute denying social security benefits to persons deported for this reason, his social security payments were stopped. The Court held that he had no contractual right to social security payments, despite having contributed toward them, and the act was not a bill of attainder since "the presumption of constitutionality with which this enactment, like any other, comes to us" forbade it to read the legislative history of the act as manifesting an intent on the part of Congress to inflict punishment.

Mr. Chief Justice **Warren** delivered the opinion of the Court, saying in part:

In this case we review for the first time a conviction under § 504 of the Labor-Management Reporting and Disclosure Act of 1959, which makes it a crime for a member of the Communist Party to serve as an officer or (except in clerical or custodial positions) as an employee of a labor union. Section 504, the purpose of which is to protect the national economy by minimizing the danger of political strikes, was enacted to replace § 9(h) of the National Labor Relations [Act], as amended by the Taft-Hartley Act, which conditioned a union's access to the National Labor Relations Board upon the filing of affidavits by all of the union's officers attesting that they were not members of or affiliated with the Communist Party.

Respondent has been a working longshoreman on the San Francisco docks, and an open and avowed Communist, for more than a quarter of a century. He was elected to the Executive Board of Local 10 of the International Longshoremen's and Warehousemen's Union for consecutive one-year terms in 1959, 1960, and 1961. On May 24, 1961, respondent was charged in a one-count indictment returned in the Northern District of California with "knowingly and wilfully serv[ing] as a member of an executive board of a labor organization . . . while a member of the Communist Party, in wilful violation of Section 504." It was neither charged nor proven that respondent at any time advocated or suggested illegal activity by the union, or proposed a political strike. The jury found respondent guilty and he was sentenced to six months' imprisonment. The Court of Appeals for the Ninth Circuit, sitting en banc, reversed and remanded with instructions to set aside the conviction and dismiss the indictment, holding that § 504 violates the First and Fifth Amendments to the Constitution. . . .

Respondent urges—in addition to the grounds relied on by the court below—that the statute under which he was convicted is a bill of attainder, and therefore violates Art. I, § 9, of the Constitution. We agree that § 504 is void as a bill of attainder and affirm the decision of the Court of Appeals on that basis. We therefore find it unnecessary to consider the First and Fifth Amendment arguments.

I.

The provisions outlawing bills of attainder were adopted by the Constitutional Convention unanimously, and without debate.

"No Bill of Attainder or ex post facto Law shall be passed [by the Congress]." Art. 1, § 9, cl. 3.

"No State shall . . . pass any Bill of Attainder, ex post facto Law, or Law impairing the Obligation of Contracts. . . ." Art. I, § 10.

A logical starting place for an inquiry into the meaning of the prohibition is its historical background. The bill of attainder, a parliamentary act sentencing to death one or more specific persons, was a device often resorted to in sixteenth, seventeenth and eighteenth century England for dealing with persons who had attempted, or threatened to attempt, to overthrow the government. In addition to the death sentence, attainder generally carried with it a "corruption of blood," which meant that the attainted party's heirs could not inherit his property. The "bill of pains and penalties" was identical to the bill of attainder, except that it prescribed a penalty short of death, e.g., banishment, deprivation of the right to vote, or exclusion of the designated party's sons from Parliament. Most bills of attainder and bills of pains and penalties named the parties to whom they were to apply; a few, however, simply described them. While some left the designated parties a way of escaping the penalty, others did not. The use of bills of attainder and bills of pains and penalties was not limited to England. During the American Revolution, the legislatures of all thirteen States passed statutes directed against the Tories; among these statutes were a large number of bills of attainder and bills of pains and penalties.

While history thus provides some guidelines, the wide variation in form, purpose and effect of ante-Constitution bills of attainder indicates that the proper scope of the Bill of Attainder Clause, and its relevance to contemporary problems, must ultimately be sought by attempting to discern the reasons for its inclusion in the Constitution, and the evils it was designed to eliminate. The best available evidence, the writings of the architects of our constitutional system, indicates that the Bill of Attainder Clause was intended not as a narrow, technical (and therefore soon to be outmoded) prohibition, but rather as an implementation of the separation of powers, a general safeguard against legislative exercise of the judicial function, or more simply—trial by legislature. . . .

[The Court here reviews the theory of the separation of powers and concludes that the bill of attainder

provision was intended to keep the legislature from doing judicial work.]

Thus the Bill of Attainder Clause not only was intended as one implementation of the general principle of fractionalized power, but also reflected the Framers' belief that the Legislative Branch is not so well suited as politically independent judges and juries to the task of ruling upon the blameworthiness of, and levying appropriate punishment upon, specific persons.

"Every one must concede that a legislative body, from its numbers and organization, and from the very intimate dependence of its members upon the people which renders them liable to be peculiarly susceptible to popular clamor, is not properly constituted to try with coolness, caution, and impartiality a criminal charge, especially in those cases in which the popular feeling is strongly excited,—the very class of cases most likely to be prosecuted by this mode."

By banning bills of attainder, the Framers of the Constitution sought to guard against such dangers by limiting legislatures to the task of rulemaking. "It is the peculiar province of the legislature to prescribe general rules for the government of society; the application of those rules to individuals in society would seem to be the duty of other departments." Fletcher v. Peck [1810].

II.

It is in this spirit that the Bill of Attainder Clause was consistently interpreted by this Court—until the decision in American Communications Assn. v. Douds [1950], which we shall consider hereafter. In 1810, Chief Justice Marshall, speaking for the Court in Fletcher v. Peck stated that "[a] bill of attainder may affect the life of an individual, or may confiscate his property, or may do both." This means, of course, that what were known at common law as bills of pains and penalties are outlawed by the Bill of Attainder Clause. The Court's pronouncement therefore served notice that the Bill of Attainder Clause was not to be given a narrow historical reading (which would exclude bills of pains and penalties), but was instead to be read in light of the evil the Framers had sought to bar: legislative punishment, of any form or severity, of specifically designated persons or groups. . . .

The approach which Chief Justice Marshall had suggested was followed in the twin post-Civil War cases of Cummings v. Missouri [1867] and Ex parte Garland [1867]. Cummings involved the constitutionality of amendments to the Missouri Constitution of 1865 which provided that no one could engage in a number of specified professions (Cummings was a priest) unless he first swore that he had taken no part in the rebellion against the Union. At issue in Garland was a federal statute which required attorneys to take a similar oath before they could practice in federal courts. This Court struck down both provisions as bills of attainder on the ground that they were legislative acts inflicting punishment on a specific group: clergymen and lawyers who had taken part in the rebellion and therefore could not truthfully take the oath. In reaching its result, the Court emphatically rejected the argument that the constitutional prohibition outlawed only a certain class of legislatively imposed penalties:

"The deprivation of any rights, civil or political, previously enjoyed, may be punishment, the circumstances attending and the causes of the deprivation determining this fact. Disqualification from office may be punishment, as in cases of conviction upon impeachment. Disqualification from the pursuits of a lawful avocation, or from positions of trust, or from the privilege of appearing in the courts, or acting as an executor, administrator, or guardian, may also, and often has been, imposed as punishment."

The next extended discussion of the Bill of Attainder Clause came in 1946, in United States v. Lovett where the Court invalidated § 304 of the Urgent Deficiency Appropriation Act, 1943, which prohibited payment of further salary to three named federal employees, as a bill of attainder.

"[L]egislative acts, no matter what their form, that apply either to named individuals or to easily ascertainable members of a group in such a way as to inflict punishment on them without a judicial trial are bills of attainder prohibited by the Constitution. . . . This permanent proscription from any opportunity to serve the Government is punishment, and of a most severe type. . . . No one would think that Congress could have passed a valid law, stating that after investigation it had found Lovett, Dodd, and Watson 'guilty' of the crime of engaging in 'subversive activities,' defined that term for the first time, and sentenced them to perpetual exclusion from any government employment. Section 304, while it does not use that language, accomplishes that result."

III.

Under the line of cases just outlined, § 504 of the Labor Management Reporting and Disclosure Act plainly constitutes a bill of attainder. Congress undoubtedly possesses power under the Commerce Clause to enact legislation designed to keep from positions affecting interstate commerce persons who may use such positions to bring about political strikes. In § 504, however, Congress has exceeded the authority granted it by the Constitution. The statute does not set forth a generally applicable rule decreeing that any person who commits certain acts or possesses certain characteristics (acts and characteristics which, in Congress' view, make them likely to initiate political strikes) shall not hold union office, and leave to courts and juries the job of deciding what persons have committed the specified acts or possessed the specified characteristics. Instead, it designates in no uncertain terms the persons who possess the feared characteristics and therefore cannot hold union office without incurring criminal liability—members of the Communist Party.

Communist Party v. Subversive Activities Control Board [1961] lends support to our conclusion. That case involved an appeal from an order by the Control Board ordering the Communist Party to register as a "Communist-action organization," under the Subversive Activities Control Act of 1950. The definition of "Communist-action organization" which the Board is to apply is set forth in § 3 of the Act:

"[A]ny organization in the United States . . . which (i) is substantially directed, dominated, or controlled by the foreign government or foreign organization controlling the world Communist movement referred to in section 2 of this title, and (ii) operates primarily to advance the objectives of such world Communist movement. . . ."

A majority of the Court rejected the argument that the Act was a bill of attainder, reasoning that § 3 does not specify the persons or groups upon which the deprivations set forth in the Act are to be imposed, but instead sets forth a general definition. Although the Board had determined in 1953 that the Communist Party was a "Communist-action organization," the Court found the statutory definition not to be so narrow as to insure that the Party would always come within it:

"In this proceeding the Board has found, and the Court of Appeals has sustained its conclusion, that the Communist Party, by virtue of the activities in which it now engages, comes within the terms of the Act. If the Party should at any time choose to abandon these activities, after it is once registered pursuant to § 7, the Act provides adequate means of relief."

The entire Court did not share the view of the majority that § 3's definition constituted rule-making rather than specification. . . . However, language incorporated in the majority opinion indicates that there was agreement on one point: by focusing upon "the crucial constitutional significance of what Congress did when it rejected the approach of outlawing the Party by name and accepted instead a statutory program regulating not enumerated organizations but designated activities," the majority clearly implied that if the Act had applied to the Communist Party by name, it would have been a bill of attainder:

"The Act is not a bill of attainder. It attaches not to specified organizations but to described activities in which an organization may or may not engage. . . . The Subversive Activities Control Act . . . requires the registration only of organizations which, after the date of the Act, are found to be under the direction, domination, or control of certain foreign powers and to operate primarily to advance certain objectives. This finding must be made after full administrative hearing, subject to judicial review which opens the record for the reviewing court's determination whether the administrative findings as to fact are supported by the preponderance of the evidence."

In this case no disagreement over whether the statute in question designates a particular organization can arise for § 504 in terms inflicts its disqualification upon members of the Communist Party. The moment § 504 was enacted, respondent was given the choice of declining a leadership position in his union or incurring criminal liability.

The Solicitor General points out that in Board of Governors v. Agnew [1947], this Court applied § 32 of the Banking Act of 1933, which provides:

"No officer, director, or employee of any corporation or unincorporated association, no partner or employee of any partnership, and no individual, primarily engaged in the issue, flotation, underwriting, public sale, or distribution, at wholesale or retail, or through syndicate participation, of stocks, bonds, or other similar securities, shall serve the same time as an officer, director, or employee of any member bank except in limited classes of cases in which the Board of Governors of the Federal Reserve System may allow such service by general regulations when in the judgment of the said Board it would not unduly influence the investment policies of such member bank or the advice it gives its customers regarding investments."

He suggests that for purposes of the Bill of Attainder Clause, such conflict-of-interest laws are not meaningfully distinguishable from the statute before us. We find this argument without merit. First, we note that § 504, unlike § 32 of the Banking Act, inflicts its deprivation upon the members of a political group thought to present a threat to the national security. As we noted above, such groups were the targets of the overwhelming majority of English and early American bills of attainder. Second, § 32 incorporates no judgment censuring or condemning any man or group of men. In enacting it, Congress relied upon its general knowledge of human psychology, and concluded that the concurrent holding of the two designated positions would present a temptation to *any* man—not just certain men or members of a certain political party. Thus insofar as § 32 incorporates a condemnation, it condemns all men. Third, we cannot accept the suggestion that § 32 constitutes an exercise in specification rather than rule-making. It seems to us clear that § 32 establishes an objective standard of conduct. Congress determined that a person who both (a) held a position in a bank which could be used to influence the investment policies of the bank or its customers, and (b) was in a position to benefit financially from investment in the securities handled by a particular underwriting house, might well be tempted to "use his influence in the bank to involve it or its customers in securities which his underwriting house has in its portfolio or has committed itself to take." In designating bank officers, directors, and employees as those persons in position (a), and officers, directors, partners and employees of underwriting houses as those persons in position (b), Congress merely expressed the characteristics it was trying to reach in an alternative, shorthand way. That Congress was legislating with respect to general characteristics rather than with respect to a specific group of men is well demonstrated by the fact that § 32 provides that the prescribed disqualification should not obtain whenever the Board of Governors determined that "it would not unduly influence the investment policies of such member bank or the advice it gives its customers regarding investments." We do not suggest that such an escape clause is essential to the constitutionality of § 32, but

point to it only further to underscore the infirmity of the suggestion that § 32, like § 504, incorporates an empirical judgment of, and inflicts its deprivation upon, a particular group of men.

It is argued, however, that in § 504 Congress did no more than it did in enacting § 32: it promulgated a general rule to the effect that persons possessing characteristics which make them likely to incite political strikes should not hold union office, and simply inserted in place of a list of those characteristics an alternative, shorthand criterion—membership in the Communist Party. Again, we cannot agree. The designation of Communists as those persons likely to cause political strikes is not the substitution of a semantically equivalent phrase; on the contrary, it rests, as the Court in Douds explicitly recognized, upon an empirical investigation by Congress of the acts, characteristics and propensities of Communist Party members. . . . Even assuming that Congress had reason to conclude that some Communists would use union positions to bring about political strikes, "it cannot automatically be inferred that all members shar[e] their evil purposes or participat[e] in their illegal conduct." . . . In utilizing the term "members of the Communist Party" to designate those persons who are likely to incite political strikes, it plainly is not the case that Congress has merely substituted a convenient shorthand term for a list of the characteristics it was trying to reach.

IV.

The Solicitor General argues that § 504 is not a bill of attainder because the prohibition it imposes does not constitute "punishment." In support of this conclusion, he urges that the statute was enacted for preventive rather than retributive reasons—that its aim is not to punish Communists for what they have done in the past, but rather to keep them from positions where they will in the future be able to bring about undesirable events. He relies on American Communications Assn. v. Douds which upheld § 9(h) of the National Labor Relations Act, the predecessor of the statute presently before us. In Douds the Court distinguished Cummings, Garland and Lovett on the ground that in those cases "the individuals involved were in fact being punished for *past* actions; whereas in this case they are subject to possible loss of position only because there is substantial ground for the congressional judgment that their beliefs and loyalties will be transformed into *future* conduct."

This case is not necessarily controlled by Douds. For to prove its assertion that § 9(h) was preventive rather than retributive in purpose, the Court in Douds focused on the fact that members of the Communist Party could escape from the class of persons specified by Congress simply by resigning from the Party:

"Here the intention is to forestall future dangerous acts; there is no one who may not, by a voluntary alteration of the loyalties which impel him to action, become eligible to sign the affidavit. We cannot conclude that this section is a bill of attainder."

Section 504, unlike § 9(h), disqualifies from the holding of union office not only present members of the Communist Party, but also anyone who has within the past five years been a member of the Party. However, even if we make the assumption that the five-year provision was inserted not out of desire to visit retribution but purely out of a belief that failure to include it would lead to pro forma resignations from the Party which would not decrease the threat of political strikes, it still clearly appears that § 504 inflicts "punishment" within the meaning of the Bill of Attainder Clause. It would be archaic to limit the definition of "punishment" to "retribution." Punishment serves several purposes: retributive, rehabilitative, deterrent—and preventive. One of the reasons society imprisons those convicted of crimes is to keep them from inflicting future harm, but that does not make imprisonment any the less punishment.

Historical considerations by no means compel restriction of the bill of attainder ban to instances of retribution. A number of English bills of attainder were enacted for preventive purposes—that is, the legislature made a judgment, undoubtedly based largely on past acts and associations (as § 504 is) that a given person or group was likely to cause trouble (usually, overthrow the government) and therefore inflicted deprivations upon that person or group in order to keep it from bringing about the feared event. It is also clear that many of the early American bills attainting the Tories were passed in order to impede their effectively resisting the Revolution. . . .

We think that the Court in Douds misread United States v. Lovett when it suggested that that case could be distinguished on the ground that the sanction there imposed was levied for purely retributive reasons. In Lovett the Court, after reviewing the legislative history of § 304 of the Urgent Deficiency Appropriation Act, concluded that the statute was the product of a congressional drive to oust from government persons whose (congressionally determined) "subversive" tendencies made their continued employment dangerous to the national welfare: "the purpose of all who sponsored § 304 . . . clearly was to 'purge' the then existing and all future lists of government employees of those whom Congress deemed guilty of 'subversive activities' and therefore 'unfit' to hold a federal job." Similarly, the purpose of the statute before us is to purge the governing boards of labor unions of those whom Congress regards as guilty of subversive acts and associations and therefore unfit to fill positions which might affect interstate commerce.

The Solicitor General urges us to distinguish Lovett on the ground that the statute struck down there "singled out three identified individuals." It is of course true that § 504 does not contain the words "Archie Brown," and that it inflicts its deprivation upon more than three people. However, the decisions of this Court, as well as the historical background of the Bill of Attainder Clause, make it crystal clear that these are distinctions without a difference. It was not uncommon for English acts of attainder to inflict their deprivations upon relatively large groups of people, sometimes by description rather than name. Moreover, the statutes voided in

Cummings and Garland were of this nature. We cannot agree that the fact that § 504 inflicts its deprivation upon the membership of the Communist Party rather than upon a list of named individuals takes it out of the category of bills of attainder.

We do not hold today that Congress cannot weed dangerous persons out of the labor movement, any more than the Court held in Lovett that subversives must be permitted to hold sensitive government positions. Rather, we make again the point made in Lovett: that Congress must accomplish such results by rules of general applicability. It cannot specify the people upon whom the sanction it prescribes is to be levied. Under our Constitution, Congress possesses full legislative authority, but the task of adjudication must be left to other tribunals.

This Court is always reluctant to declare that an Act of Congress violates the Constitution, but in this case we have no alternative. . . .

The judgment of the Court of Appeals is Affirmed.

Mr. Justice **White,** with whom Mr. Justice **Clark,** Mr. Justice **Harlan,** and Mr. Justice **Stewart** join, dissenting, said in part:

. . . When an enactment is challenged as an attainder, the central inquiry must be whether the disability imposed by the act is "punishment" (i.e., is directed at an individual or a group of individuals) or is "regulation" (i.e., is directed at controlling future conduct). . . . Whether a punitive purpose would be inferred has depended in past cases on a number of circumstances, including the nature of the disability, whether it was traditionally regarded as punishment, whether it is rationally connected to a permissible legislative objective, as well as the specificity of the legislature's designation of the persons to be affected. . . .

I.

It is not difficult to find some of the cases and statutes which the necessary implications of the Court's approach which will overrule or invalidate.

American Communications Assn. v. Douds which upheld the predecessor statute to § 504 is obviously overruled. In that case the Court accepted the congressional findings about the Communist Party and about the propensity of Party members "to subordinate legitimate trade union objectives to obstructive strikes when dictated by Party leaders, often in support of the policies of a foreign government." Moreover, Congress was permitted to infer from a person's "political affiliations and beliefs" that such a person would be likely to instigate political strikes. Like § 504, the statute there under consideration did not cover all persons who might be likely to call political strikes. Nevertheless, legislative findings that *some* Communists would engage in illegal activities were sufficient to sustain the exercise of legislative power. The Bill of Attainder Clause now forbids Congress to do precisely what was validated in Douds.

Similarly invalidated are statutes denying positions of public importance to groups of persons identified by their business affiliations, commonly known as conflict-of-interest statutes. . . .

In term of the Court's analysis of the Bill of Attainder Clause, no meaningful distinction may be drawn between § 32 of the Banking Act and § 504. Both sections disqualify a specifically described group, officers and employees of underwriting firms in the one one case and members of the Communist Party in the other. Both sections may be said to be underinclusive: others besides underwriters may have business interests conflicting with the duties of a bank director and others than Communists may call political strikes. Equally, both sections may be deemed overinclusive: neither section finds that all members of the group affected would violate their obligations to the office from which they are disqualified; some members would and perhaps others would not. Both sections are based on a probability or likelihood that this would occur. Both sections leave to the courts the task of determining whether particular persons are members of the designated groups and occupy the specified positions.

In attempting to distinguish the two sections, the Court states that in enacting § 32 of the Banking Act Congress made no judgment or condemnation of any specific group of persons. Instead, the Court reasons, "Congress relied upon its general knowledge of human psychology, and concluded that the concurrent holding of the two designated positions would present a temptation to *any* man—not just certain men or members of a certain political party." But § 32 disqualifies only partners and employees of underwriting firms, not other businessmen with conflicting interests. And § 504 applies to *any* man who occupies the two positions of labor union leader and member of the Communist Party. If based upon "its general knowledge of human psychology" Congress may make findings about a group including members and employees of underwriting firms which disqualify such persons from a certain office, why may not Congress on a similar basis make such a finding about members of the Communist Party? "Because of their business connections, carrying as they do certain loyalties, interests and disciplines," § 32 disqualifies members and employees of underwriting firms as posing "a continuing threat of participation in the harmful activities. . . ." Douds. The same might be said about § 504, as was said about its predecessor: "Political affiliations of the kind here involved, no less than business affiliations, provide rational ground for the legislative judgment that those persons proscribed by § 9(h) would be subject to 'tempting opportunities' to commit acts deemed harmful to the national economy. In this respect, § 9(h) is not unlike a host of other statutes which prohibit specified groups of persons from holding positions of power and public interest because, in the legislative judgment, they threaten to abuse the trust that is a necessary concomitant of the power of office."

Conflict-of-interest statutes are an accepted type of legislation. Indeed, our Constitution contains a conflict-of-interest provisions in Art. I, § 6, cl. 2, which prohib-

its any Congressman from simultaneously holding office under the United States. If the Court would save the conflict-of-interest statutes, which apparently it would, it is difficult to understand why § 504 is stricken down as a bill of attainder.

Other legislative enactments relevant here are those statutes disqualifying felons from occupying certain positions. The leading case is Hawker v New York [1898], which upheld a provision prohibiting convicted felons from practicing medicine against a claim that, as applied to one convicted before its enactment, it was an ex post facto law. The Court noted that a legislature may establish qualifications for the practice of medicine, and character may be such a qualification. Conviction of a felony, the Court reasoned, may be evidence of character:

"It is not open to doubt that the commission of crime . . . has some relation to the question of character. It is not, as a rule, the good people who commit crime. When the legislature declares that whoever has violated the criminal laws of the State shall be deemed lacking in good moral character it is not laying down an arbitrary or fanciful rule—one having no relation to the subject-matter, but is only appealing to a well recognized fact of human experience. . . .

"It is no answer to say that this test of character is not in all cases absolutely certain, and that sometimes it works harshly. Doubtless, one who has violated the criminal law may thereafter reform and become in fact possessed of a good moral character. But the legislature has power in cases of this kind to make a rule of universal application, and no inquiry is permissible back of the rule to ascertain whether the fact of which the rule is made the absolute test does or does not exist." . . .

The Court apparently agrees that the Subversive Activities Control Act was not a bill of attainder with regard to the Communist Party because, as the Court pointed out in Communist Party v. Subversive Activities Control Board, the finding that the Party was a Communist-action organization was not made by the legislature but was made administratively, after a trial-type hearing and subject to judicial review. But this apparently does not settle whether the statute is a bill of attainder with respect to Party members; for under today's approach, a finding about the Party and about some of its members does not cure the vice of overinclusiveness. The Subversive Activities Control Act attaches certain disqualifications to each Party member following the administrative-judicial finding that the Party is a Communist-action organization. Among other things, each Party member is disqualified from holding union office, almost the same disqualification as is involved here. I do not see how this and the other consequences attached to Party membership in that Act could survive examination under the principles announced today.

On the other hand, if the statutes involved in Hawker and Agnew are not bills of attainder, how can the Subversive Activities Control Act be an attainder with respect to members of the Communist Party? In the Communist Party case, the Board found that the "[Party's] principal leaders and a substantial number of its members are subject to and recognize the disciplinary power of the Soviet Union and its representatives. This evidences domination and control over [the Party] by the Soviet Union, and a purpose to advance the objectives of the world Communist movement.'' . . . That finding was expressly sustained by this Court. Certainly, if Hawker and Agnew are to be followed at all, these nonlegislative findings establish a sufficient probability or likelihood with regard to Party members—a sufficient temptation to Party members who are also union officers—to permit the legislature to disqualify Party members from union office as it did in the Subversive Activities Control Act. . . .

But how does one prove that a person would be disloyal? The Communist Party's illegal purpose and its domination by a foreign power have already been adjudicated, both administratively and judicially. If this does not in itself provide a sufficient probability with respect to the individual who persists in remaining a member of the Party, or if a probability is in any event insufficient, what evidence with regard to the individual will be sufficient to disqualify him? If he must be apprehended in the act of calling one political strike or in one act of disloyalty before steps can be taken to exclude him from office, there is little or nothing left of the preventive or prophylactic function of § 504 or of the statutes such as the Court had before it in Hawker and Agnew. . . .

THE CONTRACT CLAUSE

THE DARTMOUTH COLLEGE CASE: THE TRUSTEES OF DARTMOUTH COLLEGE v. WOODWARD

4 Wheaton 518; 4 L. Ed. 629 (1819)

When the framers of the Constitution forbade the states to pass laws impairing the obligation of contracts, they had in mind the ordinary executory contracts between individuals, which during the ''critical period'' had so frequently been interfered with by the enactment of ''stay laws,'' legal tender laws, and other legislation for the benefit of insolvent debtors. The first interpretation of the contract clause by the Supreme Court was given in the case of Fletcher v. Peck (1810), which did not relate to this variety of contract at all, but which involved the question of whether an executed contract in the form of a legislative grant of land made by the state itself through its legislature could be later rescinded by the state. The Court held here that the grant of land, even though made under circumstances of the most scandalous corruption, is a contract within the meaning of the constitutional provision and cannot be rescinded by the state after the land in question has passed into the hands of innocent purchasers.

Of far greater significance was the Dartmouth College Case, in which the contract clause was given an even wider application. In 1769 Dartmouth College was chartered by the English Crown. The charter created a college to be governed by a board of trustees but in 1816 the New Hampshire legislature passed a law reorganizing the college as a state university. The trustees of the old college refused to be governed by the law and, undaunted, gathered about them their sympathizers among the professors, hired rooms nearby, and continued to operate as the ''college,'' most of the students remaining loyal to the old regime. The trustees then brought an action to regain control of the college, thus raising the general question of the constitutionality of the reorganizing statute.

The case was argued before the supreme court of New Hampshire in 1817. Little reference was made to the contract clause. The state court decided against the college on the ground that the institution had become public in character and as such was subject to state control. The case was argued before the Supreme Court in 1818. Daniel Webster, a Dartmouth graduate not yet at the height of his fame, represented the college and made an argument which included the now famous quote: ''It is a small college and yet there are those who love it.'' He laid much more emphasis on the necessity of protecting vested rights than upon the contract clause. Rumor has it that the Court was divided in its opinion on the case at the close of the argument and that Marshall, who favored the college, postponed the decision until the next term and in the meantime won over his colleagues to his own position. At the opening of the next term of court the decision was handed down in favor of the college.

The doctrine of this case, that a corporate charter is a contract which may not be impaired by legislative enactment, was criticized because it made it possible for corrupt and ignorant legislatures, in granting charters, irrevocably to grant away privileges and rights contrary to the public interest and welfare. In an economic sense the decision was of great importance in giving to those who invested money in corporate enterprises assurance that the corporations would be free from legislative interference, and it thus encouraged the expansion of business enterprise in the fields of railroad construction, insurance, commerce, and industry.

About ten days after its decision in the Dartmouth College Case, the Court decided another contract clause case with which the business world was deeply concerned. This was the case of Sturges v. Crowninshield (1819), in which the question was raised of whether the New York bankruptcy act impaired the obligation of contracts. There was at this time no federal bankruptcy law. The Court held that the New York statute impaired the obligation of contracts of debt entered into before the act was passed. But in speaking for the Court, Marshall went beyond this and declared his view that the state law was also invalid as applied to contracts made after its passage, a point not before the Court for decision. This dictum, which caused widespread uncertainty and concern, was rejected in Ogden v. Saunders (1827), the first case in which Marshall dissented on a constitutional law question. The Court held that a state bankruptcy law when applied to future debt contracts did not impair the obligation of those contracts. Marshall argued that the obligation of a contract was to be found in the terms of the agreement between the parties and nowhere else; under no circumstances could that agreement be modified by state law. The majority opinion in Ogden was of far-reaching importance. The validity of the so-called "reservation clauses," by which the states retain certain powers to modify or repeal corporate charters or franchises, rests upon it.

With the replacement of Marshall by Chief Justice Taney, the direction of the Court away from the rigid Dartmouth College rule was made clearer. In Charles River Bridge v. Warren Bridge (1837) the Court laid down the important rule that the terms of a charter contract must be strictly construed, and that no rights or privileges can be held to be granted away by the public by mere implication. The Charles River Bridge Company was privately owned, and under a state franchise operated a toll bridge for profit. During the life of this franchise the state incorporated the Warren Bridge Company, which was authorized to build and operate a toll bridge within a few rods of the Charles River Bridge, but with the stipulation that within a short time it should become a free bridge and part of the public highway. The charter of the Charles River Bridge Company said nothing about its grant being exclusive, but since its business would be ruined by the opening of a free bridge close by, the company plausibly contended that its charter contract, reasonably construed, implied the grant of a monopoly; and the obligation of the contract was therefore impaired by the chartering of the new bridge. The Court rejected this contention. No grant of monopoly can be "read into" a charter, the words of which make no such grant.

In the years that followed, the scope and power of the contract clause dwindled under the pressure of the rising doctrine of "paramount power." This doctrine holds that certain powers possessed by the state are so vital and indispensable to its existence and its power to govern that they cannot be contracted away. If one legislature does contract them away, a subsequent legislature may rescind the agreement and recover the power. This does not violate the contract clause because the state had no authority to contract away this power permanently in the first place.

This doctrine is evident in West River Bridge Co. v. Dix (1848) which held that a state cannot contract away its power of eminent domain. The Supreme Court held that the state could validly condemn the 100-year franchise of a toll bridge company and convert the bridge into a free public highway. This point was even more sharply made in Pennsylvania Hospital v. Philadelphia (1917). In 1845 the hospital secured an agreement with the state that no streets or alleys should ever be opened through its grounds, and in return the hospital granted some land and paid some money to the state. In 1913 the city, under authority from the state, sought to condemn a street through the hospital grounds in plain violation of the 1845 contract. The Court held that the power of eminent domain overrode the contract and the condemnation was valid.

Nor can the state contract away its police power. A lottery corporation had been chartered by the state of Mississippi in 1867 and in 1869 the state's new constitution forbade lotteries. The state sued to close up the lottery, and in Stone v. Mississippi (1880) the Supreme Court held that the constitutional provision did not violate the contract clause. There was, in fact, no real contract, because the state had no power to "bargain away the police power." "Anyone, therefore, who accepts a lottery charter, does so with the implied understanding that the People, in their sovereign capacity . . . may resume it at any time. . . ." It need hardly be emphasized that if the police power of the state may be exercised to override contracts which the state itself has made, it certainly may limit or destroy contracts between private individuals which come within its reach.

The most devastating blow to the contract clause came in 1934 in Home Building and Loan Assn. v. Blaisdell, in which the Court upheld the Minnesota Mortgage Moratorium Law. In an effort to alleviate one of the most pressing problems of the Great Depression, the state had provided a two-year moratorium on the foreclosure of real-estate mortgages, thus making it impossible for banks to dispossess homeowners and small businessmen.

In upholding the Act, the Court emphasized that the prohibition of the contract clause "is not an absolute one and is not to be read with literal exactness like a mathematical formula. . . . Not only is the constitutional provision qualified by the measure of control which the State retains over remedial processes, but the State also continues to possess authority to safeguard the vital interests of its people. It does not matter that legislation appropriate to that end 'has the result of modifying or abrogating contracts already in effect.' . . . Not only are existing laws read into contracts in order to fix obligations as between the parties, but the reservation of essential attributes of sovereign power is also read into contracts as a postulate of the legal order. The policy of protecting contracts against impairment presupposes the maintenance of a government by virtue of which contractual relations are worthwhile,—a government which retains adequate authority to secure the peace and good order of society. This principle of harmonizing the constitutional prohibition with the necessary residuum of state power has had progressive recognition in the decisions of this Court."

Mr. Chief Justice **Marshall**, in delivering the opinion of the Court, said in part:

This court can be insensible neither to the magnitude nor delicacy of this question. The validity of a legislative act is to be examined; and the opinion of the highest law tribunal of a state is to be revised: an opinion which carries with it intrinsic evidence of the diligence, of the ability, and the integrity, with which it was formed. On more than one occasion this court has expressed the cautious circumspection with which it approaches the consideration of such questions; and has declared that, in no doubtful case would it pronounce a legislative act to be contrary to the constitution. But the American people have said, in the constitution of the United States, that "no state shall pass any bill of attainder, ex post facto law, or law impairing the obligation of contracts." In the same instrument they have also said, "that the judicial power shall extend to all cases in law and equity arising under the constitution." On the judges of this court, then, is imposed the high and solemn duty of protecting, from even legislative violation, those contracts which the constitution of our country has placed beyond legislative control; and however irksome the task may be, this is a duty from which we dare not shrink.

. . .

It can require no argument to prove that the circumstances of this case constitute a contract. An application is made to the crown for a charter to incorporate a religious and literary institution. In the application, it is stated that large contributions have been made for the object, which will be conferred on the corporation as soon as it shall be created. The charter is granted, and on its faith the property is conveyed. Surely in this transaction every ingredient of a complete and legitimate contract is to be found.

The points for consideration are: 1. Is this contract protected by the constitution of the United States? 2. Is it impaired by the acts under which the defendant holds?

1. On the first point it has been argued that the word "contract," in its broadest sense, would comprehend the political relations between the government and its citizens, would extend to offices held within a state for state purposes, and to many of those laws concerning civil institutions, which must change with circumstances, and be modified by ordinary legislation; which deeply concern the public, and which, to preserve good government, the public judgment must control. That even marriage is a contract, and its obligations are affected by the laws respecting divorces. That the clause in the constitution, if construed in its greatest latitude, would prohibit these laws. Taken in its broad unlimited sense, the clause would be an unprofitable and vexatious interference with the internal concerns of a state, would unnecessarily and unwisely embarrass its legislation, and render immutable those civil institutions which are established for purposes of internal government, and which, to subserve those purposes, ought to vary with varying circumstances. That as the framers of the constitution could never have intended to insert in that instrument a provision so unnecessary, so mischievous, and so repugnant to its general spirit, the term "contract" must be understood in a more limited sense. That it must be understood as intended to guard against a power of at least doubtful utility, the abuse of which had been extensively felt; and to restrain the legislature in future from violating the right to property. That anterior to the formation of the constitution, a course of legislation had prevailed in many, if not in all, of the states, which weakened the confidence of man in man, and embarrassed all transactions between individuals, by dispensing with a faithful performance of engagements. To correct this mischief, by restraining the power which produced it, the state legislatures were forbidden "to pass any law impairing the obligation of contracts," that is, of contracts respecting property, under which some individual could claim a right to something beneficial to himself; and that since the clause in the constitution must in construction receive some limitation, it may be confined, and ought to be confined, to cases of this description; to cases within the mischief it was intended to remedy.

The general correctness of these observations cannot be controverted. That the framers of the constitution did not intend to restrain the states in the regulation of their civil institutions, adopted for internal government, and that the instrument they have given us is not to be so construed, may be admitted. The provision of the constitution never has been understood to embrace other contracts than those which respect property or some object of value, and confer rights which may be asserted in a court of justice. It never has been understood to restrict the general right of the legislature to legislate on the subject of divorces. Those acts enable some tribunal, not to impair a marriage contract, but to liberate one of the parties because it has been broken by the other. When any state legislature shall pass an act annulling all marriage contracts, or allowing either party to annul it without the consent of the other, it will be time enough to inquire whether such an act be constitutional.

The parties in this case differ less on general principles, less on the true construction of the constitution in the abstract, than on the application of those principles to this case, and on the true construction of the charter of 1769. This is the point on which the cause essentially depends. If the act of incorporation be a grant of political power, if it create a civil institution to be employed in the administration of the government, or if the funds of the college be public property, or if the state of New Hampshire, as a government, be alone interested in its transactions, the subject is one in which the legislature of the state may act according to its own judgment, unrestrained by any limitation of its power imposed by the constitution of the United States.

But if this be a private eleemosynary institution, endowed with a capacity to take property for objects unconnected with government, whose funds are bestowed by individuals on the faith of the charter; if the donors have stipulated for the future disposition and management of those funds in the manner prescribed by themselves, there may be more difficulty in the case, although neither the persons who have made these stipulations nor those for whose benefit they are made, should be parties to the cause. Those who are no longer interested in the property, may yet retain such an interest in the preservation of their own arrangements as to have a right [to] insist that those arrangements shall be held sacred. Or, if they have themselves disappeared, it becomes a subject of serious and anxious inquiry, whether those whom they have legally empowered to represent them forever may not assert all the rights which they possessed, while in being; whether, if they be without personal representatives who may feel injured by a violation of the compact, the trustees be not so completely their representatives, in the eye of the law, as to stand in their place, not only as respects the government of the college, but also as respects the maintenance of the college charter.

It becomes, then, the duty of the court most seriously to examine this charter, and to ascertain its true character. . . .

[In the course of his comment upon the charitable objects of the donors of Dartmouth College occurs Marshall's classic description of a corporation.]

A corporation is an artificial being, invisible, intangible, and existing only in contemplation of law. Being the mere creature of law, it possesses only those properties which the charter of its creation confers upon it, either expressly or as incidental to its very existence. These are such as are supposed best calculated to effect the object for which it was created. Among the most important are immortality, and, if the expression may be allowed, individuality; properties by which a perpetual succession of many persons are considered as the same, and may act as a single individual. They enable a corporation to manage its own affairs, and to hold property without the perplexing intricacies, the hazardous and endless necessity, of perpetual conveyances for the purpose of transmitting it from hand to hand. It is chiefly for the purpose of clothing bodies of men, in succession, with these qualities and capacities that corporations were invented and are in use. By these means, a perpetual succession of individuals are capable of acting for the promotion of the particular object, like one immortal being. . . .

From this review of the charter, it appears that Dartmouth College is an eleemosynary institution, incorporated for the purpose of perpetuating the application of the bounty of the donors, to the specified objects of that bounty; that its trustees or governors were originally named by the founder, and invested with the power of perpetuating themselves; that they are not public officers, nor is it a civil institution, participating in the administration of government; but a charity school, or a seminary of education, incorporated for the preservation of its property, and the perpetual application of that property to the objects of its creation. . . .

According to the theory of the British constitution, their parliament is omnipotent. To annul corporate rights might give a shock to public opinion, which that government has chosen to avoid; but its power is not questioned. Had parliament, immediately after the emanation of this charter and the execution of those conveyances which followed it, annulled the instrument, so that the living donors would have witnessed the disappointment of their hopes, the perfidy of the transaction would have been universally acknowledged. Yet then, as now, the donors would have had no interest in the property; then, as now, those who might be students would have had no rights to be violated; then, as now, it might be said, that the trustees, in whom the rights of all were combined, possessed no private, individual, beneficial interest in the property confided to their protection. Yet the contract would at that time have been deemed sacred by all. What has since occurred to strip it of its inviolability? Circumstances have not changed it. In reason, in justice, and in law, it is now what it was in 1769.

This is plainly a contract to which the donors, the trustees, and the crown (to whose rights and obligations New Hampshire succeeds), were the original parties. It is a contract made on a valuable consideration. It is a contract for the security and disposition of property. It is a contract, on the faith of which real and personal estate has been conveyed to the corporation. It is then a contract within the letter of the constitution, and within its spirit also, unless the fact that the property is invested by the donors in trustees for the promotion of religion and education, for the benefit of persons who are perpetually changing, though the objects remain the same, shall create a particular exception, taking this case out of the prohibition contained in the constitution.

It is more than possible that the preservation of rights of this description was not particularly in the view of the framers of the constitution when the clause under consideration was introduced into that instrument. It is probable that interferences of more frequent recurrence, to which the temptation was stronger and of which the mischief was more extensive, constituted the great motive for imposing this restriction on the state legislatures. But although a particular and a rare case may not in itself be of sufficient magnitude to induce a rule, yet it must be governed by the rule, when established unless some plain and strong reason for excluding it can be given. It is not enough to say that this particular case was not in the mind of the convention when the article was framed, nor of the American people when it was adopted. It is necessary to go farther, and to say that, had this particular case been suggested, the language would have been so varied as to exclude it, or it would have been made a special exception. The case being within the words of the rule, must be within its operation likewise, unless there be something in the literal construction so obviously absurd, or mischievous, or repugnant to the general spirit of the instrument, as to justify those who expound the constitution in making it an exception.

On what safe and intelligible ground can this exception stand[?] There is no expression in the constitution, no sentiment delivered by its contemporaneous expounders, which would justify us in making it. In the absence of all authority of this kind, is there, in the nature and reason of the case itself, that which would sustain a construction of the constitution, not warranted by its words? Are contracts of this description of a character to excite so little interest that we must exclude them from the provisions of the constitution, as being unworthy of the attention of those who framed the instrument? Or does public policy so imperiously demand their remaining exposed to legislative alteration, as to compel us, or rather permit us to say that these words, which were introduced to give stability to contracts, and which in their plain import comprehend this contract, must yet be so construed as to exclude it?

Almost all eleemosynary corporations, those which are created for the promotion of religion, of charity, or of education, are of the same character. The law of this case is the law of all. . . .

The opinion of the court, after mature deliberation, is, that this is a contract, the obligation of which cannot be impaired without violating the constitution of the United States. This opinion appears to us to be equally supported by reason, and by the former decisions of this court.

2. We next proceed to the inquiry whether its obligation has been impaired by those acts of the legislature of New Hampshire to which the special verdict refers.

From the review of this charter, which has been taken, it appears that the whole power of governing the college, of appointing and removing tutors, of fixing their salaries, of directing the course of study to be pursued by the students, and of filling up vacancies created in their own body, was vested in the trustees. On the part of the crown it was expressly stipulated that this corporation, thus constituted, should continue forever; and that the number of trustees should forever consist of twelve, and no more. By this contract the crown was bound, and could have made no violent alteration in its essential terms without impairing its obligation.

By the revolution, the duties, as well as the powers, of government devolved on the people of New Hampshire. It is admitted, that among the latter was comprehended the transcendent power of parliament, as well as that of the executive department. It is too clear to require the support of argument that all contracts, and rights, respecting property, remained unchanged by the revolution. The obligations, then, which were created by the charter to Dartmouth College, were the same in the new that they had been in the old government. The power of the government was also the same. A repeal of this charter at any time prior to the adoption of the present constitution of the United States, would have been an extraordinary and unprecedented act of power, but one which could have been contested only by the restrictions upon the legislature, to be found in the constitution of the state. But the constitution of the United States has imposed this additional limitation, that the legislature of a state shall pass no act "impairing the obligation of contracts."

It has been already stated that the act "to amend the charter, and enlarge and improve the corporation of Dartmouth College," increases the number of trustees to twenty-one, gives the appointment of the additional members to the executive of the state, and creates a board of overseers, to consist of twenty-five persons, of whom twenty-one are also appointed by the executive of New Hampshire, who have power to inspect and control the most important acts of the trustees.

On the effect of this law two opinions cannot be entertained. Between acting directly, and acting through the agency of trustees and overseers, no essential difference is perceived. The whole power of governing the college is transformed from trustees appointed according to the will of the founder, expressed in the charter, to the executive of New Hampshire. The management and application of the funds of this eleemosynary institution, which are placed by the donors in the hands of trustees named in the charter, and empowered to perpetuate themselves, are placed by this act under the control of the government of the state. The will of the state is substituted for the will of the donors in every essential operation of the college. This is not an immaterial change. The founders of the college contracted, not merely for the perpetual application of the funds which they gave, to the objects for which those funds were given; they contracted also to secure that application by the constitution of the corporation. They contracted for a system which should, as far as human foresight can provide, retain forever the government of the literary institution they had formed, in the hands of persons approved by themselves. This system is totally changed. The charter of 1769 exists no longer. It is reorganized; and reorganized in such a manner as to convert a literary institution, molded according to the will of its founders, and placed under the control of private literary men, into a machine entirely subservient to the will of government. This may be for the advantage of this college in particular, and may be for the advantage of literature in general, but it is not according to the will of the donors, and is subversive of that contract, on the faith of which their property was given.

In the view which has been taken of this interesting case, the court has confined itself to the right possessed by the trustees, as the assignees and representatives of the donors and founders, for the benefit of religion and literature. Yet it is not clear that the trustees ought to be considered as destitute of such beneficial interest in themselves as the law may respect. In addition to their being the legal owners of the property, and to their having a freehold right in the powers confided to them, the charter itself countenances the idea that trustees may also be tutors with salaries. The first president was one of the original trustees; and the charter provides, that in case of vacancy in that office, "the senior professor or tutor, being one of the trustees, shall exercise the office of president, until the trustees shall make choice of, and appoint a president." According to the tenor of the charter, then, the trustees might, without impropriety, appoint a president and other professors from their own body. This is a power not entirely unconnected with an interest. Even if the proposition of the counsel for the defendant were sustained; if it were admitted that those contracts only are protected by the constitution, a beneficial interest in which is vested in the party, who appears in court to assert that interest; yet it is by no means clear that the trustees of Dartmouth College have no beneficial interest in themselves.

But the court has deemed it unnecessary to investigate this particular point, being of opinion, on general principles, that in these private eleemosynary institutions, the body corporate, as possessing the whole legal and equitable interest, and completely representing the donors, for the purpose of executing the trust, has rights which are protected by the constitution.

It results from this opinion, that the acts of the legislature of New Hampshire, which are stated in the special verdict found in this cause, are repugnant to the constitution of the United States; and that the judgment on this special verdict ought to have been for the plaintiffs. The judgment of the State Court must therefore be reversed.

Mr. Justice **Washington** and Mr. Justice **Story** rendered separate concurring opinions.

Mr. Justice **Duvall** dissented.

8

The Nationalization of the Bill of Rights

EARLY EFFORTS TO EXTEND THE BILL OF RIGHTS TO THE STATES

BARRON v. BALTIMORE

7 Peters 243; 8 L. Ed. 672 (1833)

One of the bitter criticisms of our federal Constitution as it came from the hands of the Convention was that it contained no bill of rights. It was feared that without specific guarantees the civil rights and liberties of the people and the states would be at the mercy of the proposed national government. Ratification was secured, but with a tacit understanding that a bill of rights should promptly be added which should restrict the national government in behalf of individual liberty. That the early statesmen thought of a federal bill of rights only in terms of restrictions on national power is emphasized by Hamilton's ingenious argument in The Federalist *(No. 84) that since the proposed central government was one which possessed only the powers delegated to it, it would be not only unnecessary but unwise to prohibit it from doing things which were clearly outside the scope of its delegated authority.*

When the First Congress convened, the House of Representatives proposed seventeen amendments in the nature of a bill of rights. One of these, the fourteenth, provided that ''no state should infringe the right of trial by jury in criminal cases, nor the rights of conscience, nor the freedom of speech or of the press.'' (Emphasis added). This amendment, which was the only one re- *stricting the powers of the states, was rejected by the Senate. The substance of the others was consolidated into twelve amendments, ten of which were finally ratified by the states.*

The First Amendment indicates by its own language that it is directed only against the federal government, for it begins, ''Congress shall make no law. . . .'' The other amendments are couched in terms of general prohibition; and in spite of the perfectly clear historical evidence as to the intention of those who framed them, it came to be argued that these guarantees of civil liberty ought to be construed as restrictions upon state and federal governments alike. Whether this view is correct is the issue involved in Barron v. Baltimore, the last constitutional decision in which Chief Justice Marshall participated.

While paving its streets, the city of Baltimore had diverted from their natural courses certain streams, with the result that sand and gravel were deposited near Barron's wharf. The wharf, which had previously enjoyed the deepest water in the harbor, was rendered practically useless, for the deposits prevented the approach of vessels. A verdict of $4500 for Barron had been reversed by the state court of appeals, and a writ of error was taken to the Supreme Court of the United States. It was alleged by Barron that this action upon the part of the city constituted a violation of that clause of the Fifth Amendment which forbids taking private property for public use without just compensation. He insisted that this amendment, being a guarantee in behalf of individual liberty, ought to be construed to restrain the states as well as the national government.

The decision in Barron v. Baltimore has left an indelible impression on the development of civil rights in this country. While today Barron would have brought his case under the due process clause of the Fourteenth Amendment (which does restrict the states), the process of change by which parts of the Bill of Rights have come to be applicable to the states has been slow, uncertain, and confusing. Most rights in the Bill of Rights now do apply to the states, but they do so only because they are essential to due process of law. The ruling in the present case that the Bill of Rights does not apply directly to the states has never been overruled.

Mr. Chief Justice **Marshall** delivered the opinion of the court:

The judgment brought up by this writ of error having been rendered by the court of a State, this tribunal can exercise no jurisdiction over it unless it be shown to come within the provisions of the twenty-fifth section of the Judicial Act.

The plaintiff in error contends that it comes within that clause in the fifth amendment to the Constitution which inhibits the taking of private property for public use without just compensation. He insists that this amendment, being in favor of the liberty of the citizen, ought to be so construed as to restrain the legislative power of a State, as well as that of the United States. If this proposition be untrue, the court can take no jurisdiction of the cause.

The question thus presented is, we think, of great importance, but not of much difficulty.

The Constitution was ordained and established by the people of the United States for themselves, for their own government, and not for the government of the individual States. Each State established a constitution for itself, and in that constitution provided such limitations and restrictions on the powers of its particular government as its judgment dictated. The people of the United States framed such a government for the United States as they supposed best adapted to their situation, and best calculated to promote their interests. The powers they conferred on this government were to be exercised by itself; and the limitations on power, if expressed in general terms, are naturally, and, we think, necessarily applicable to the government created by the instrument. They are limitations of power granted in the instrument itself; not of distinct governments, framed by different persons and for different purposes.

If these propositions be correct, the fifth amendment must be understood as restraining the power of the general government, not as applicable to the States. In their several constitutions they have imposed such restrictions on their respective governments as their own wisdom suggested; such as they deemed most proper for themselves. It is a subject on which they judge exclusively, and with which others interfere no farther than they are supposed to have a common interest.

The counsel for the plaintiff in error insists that the Constitution was intended to secure the people of the several States against the undue exercise of power by their respective State governments; as well as against that which might be attempted by their general government. In support of this argument he relies on the inhibitions contained in the tenth section of the first article.

We think that section affords a strong if not a conclusive argument in support of the opinion already indicated by the court.

The preceding section contains restrictions which are obviously intended for the exclusive purpose of restraining the exercise of power by the departments of the general government. Some of them use language applicable only to Congress; others are expressed in general terms. The third clause, for example, declares that "no bill of attainder or ex post facto law shall be passed." No language can be more general; yet the demonstration is complete that it applies solely to the government of the United States. In addition to the general arguments furnished by the instrument itself, some of which have been already suggested, the succeeding section, the avowed purpose of which is to restrain State legislation, contains in terms the very prohibition. It declares that "no State shall pass any bill of attainder or ex post facto law." This provision, then, of the ninth section, however comprehensive its language, contains no restriction on State legislation.

The ninth section having enumerated, in the nature of a bill of rights, the limitations intended to be imposed on the powers of the general government, the tenth proceeds to enumerate those which were to operate on the State legislatures. These restrictions are brought together in the same section, and are by express words applied to the States. "No State shall enter into any treaty," etc. Perceiving that in a constitution framed by the people of the United States for the government of all, no limitation of the action of government on the people would apply to the State government, unless expressed in terms; the restrictions contained in the tenth section are in direct words so applied to the States.

It is worthy of remark, too, that these inhibitions generally restrain State legislation on subjects intrusted to the general government, or in which the people of all the States feel an interest.

A State is forbidden to enter into any treaty, alliance or confederation. If these compacts are with foreign nations, they interfere with the treaty-making power which is conferred entirely on the general government; if with each other, for political purposes, they can scarcely fail to interfere with the general purpose and intent of the Constitution. To grant letters of marque and reprisal would lead directly to war, the power of declaring which is expressly given to Congress. To coin money is also the exercise of a power conferred on Congress. It would be tedious to recapitulate the several limitations on the powers of the States which are contained in this section. They will be found, generally, to restrain State legislation on subjects intrusted to the government of the Union, in which the citizens of all the States are interested. In these alone were the whole people concerned. The question of their application to States is not left to construction. It is averred in positive words.

If the original Constitution, in the ninth and tenth sections of the first article, draws this plain and marked line of discrimination between the limitations it imposes on the powers of the general government and on those of the States; if in every inhibition intended to act on State power, words are employed which directly express that intent, some strong reason must be assigned for departing from this safe and judicious course in framing the amendments, before that departure can be assumed.

We search in vain for that reason.

Had the people of the several States, or any of them, required changes in their constitutions; had they required additional safeguards to liberty from the apprehended encroachments of their particular governments, the remedy was in their own hands, and would have been applied by themselves. A convention would have been assembled by the discontented State, and the required improvements would have been made by itself. The unwieldy and cumbrous machinery of procuring a recommendation from two-thirds of Congress, and the assent of three-fourths of their sister States, could never have occurred to any human being as a mode of doing that which might be effected by the State itself. Had the framers of these amendments intended them to be limitations on the powers of the State governments they would have imitated the framers of the original Constitution, and have expressed that intention. Had Congress engaged in the extraordinary occupation of improving the constitutions of the several States by affording the people additional protection from the exercise of power by their own governments in matters which concerned themselves alone, they would have declared this purpose in plain and intelligible language.

But it is universally understood, it is a part of the history of the day, that the great revolution which established the Constitution of the United States was not effected without immense opposition. Serious fears were extensively entertained that those powers which the patriot statesmen who then watched over the interests of our country, deemed essential to union, and to the attainment of those invaluable objects for which union was sought, might be exercised in a manner dangerous to liberty. In almost every convention by which the Constitution was adopted, amendments to guard against the abuse of power were recommended. These amendments demanded security against the apprehended encroachments of the general government—not against those of the local governments.

In compliance with a sentiment thus generally expressed, to quiet fears thus extensively entertained, amendments were proposed by the required majority in Congress, and adopted by the States. These amendments contain no expression indicating an intention to apply them to the State governments. This court cannot so apply them.

We are of opinion that the provision in the fifth amendment to the Constitution, declaring that private property shall not be taken for public use without just compensation, is intended solely as a limitation on the exercise of power by the government of the United States, and is not applicable to the legislation of the States. We are therefore of opinion that there is no repugnancy between the several acts of the General Assembly of Maryland, given in evidence by the defendants at the trial of this cause in the court of that State, and the Constitution of the United States.

This court, therefore, has no jurisdiction of the cause, and [it] is dismissed.

SUBSTANTIVE DUE PROCESS AND THE POLICE POWER

MUNN v. ILLINOIS

94 U. S. 133; 24 L. Ed. 77 (1877)

At the time the Fourteenth Amendment was adopted the due process clause of the Fifth Amendment had been in effect against the federal government for three-quarters of a century. During that entire period the Supreme Court had decided only four or five cases interpreting the clause, but from Coke and Blackstone the ancient lineage and narrow meaning of the clause were abundantly clear. The clause traces its beginning to the guarantee embodied in Magna Charta that "no freeman shall be taken or imprisoned or deprived of his freehold or his liberties or free customs, or outlawed or exiled, or in any manner destroyed, nor shall we come upon him or send against him, except by a legal judgment of his peers or by the law of the land." With the reaffirmation of these guarantees in the Statute of Westminster (1354) Ed. III, "per legem terrae" became "due process of the law," although at the time of the adoption of the Bill of Rights the eight state constitutions providing such protection used the term "law of the land." Whichever words were used, the guarantee involved was the same: the government was forbidden to limit in any way the individual's personal or property rights unless it did so through proper procedures. In short, it was a check not on what the government could do, but on the process it had to follow in order to do it.

This "procedural" due process was the only kind of due process there was until after the middle of the nineteenth century, when pressure from important property interests for a "substantive" content to the due process clause began to make itself felt. Among the leading purposes for which the United States Constitution had been framed was the protection of private property from the attacks of the "too-popular" state governments. Hence those with vested property rights looked from the beginning to the judicially enforceable Constitution to protect them from legislation, particularly state legislation. They turned first to the protection against bills of attainder and ex post facto laws, but in Calder v. Bull

(1798) the Supreme Court held that the ex post facto clause applied only to criminal legislation. Better luck was had with the contract clause, and in such cases as *Fletcher v. Peck* (1810) and the *Dartmouth College Case* (1819) the Court held that a vested right implied a contract not to divest it or interfere with its exercise. But with the passing of Chief Justice Marshall the strength of even this doctrine began to wane. In *Charles River Bridge v. Warren Bridge* (1837) the Court under Taney made clear that henceforth contracts would be strictly construed in favor of the people and against the vested interests; and much later, in *Stone v. Mississippi* (1880), the Court held that the police power to legislate in the public interest could not be limited by the contract clause.

So it was natural that pressure should mount to persuade the courts that the guarantee of due process of law should provide constitutional protection to the vested interests. In 1856 in *Wynhammer v. New York* a state court finally struck down a provision of a state prohibition statute as a denial of due process of law because the law provided for the confiscation of stocks of liquor in possession when the law took effect. The court's basic premise was that liquor was property which could not be transformed into a nuisance merely by the whim of the legislature; hence a statute providing for its confiscation was void, even though the procedures by which the confiscation took place followed "the forms which belong to due process of law." The court said, "The act . . . itself pronounces the sentence of condemnation, and the judicial machinery, such as it is, which it provides are agencies merely to insure the execution of the sentence."

This theory that the substance of a law itself could be held void for want of due process made its way slowly into the Supreme Court. In 1857, Chief Justice Taney in the *Dred Scott* case, after holding the Missouri Compromise Act void on a number of grounds, added that "an act of Congress which deprives a citizen of the United States of his liberty or property merely because he came himself or brought his property into a particular territory of the United States and who had committed no offense against the laws could hardly be dignified with the name of due process of law." But the Court was not yet ready to receive the doctrine. Justice Miller rejected it in the *Slaughter-House Cases* (1873); and in 1875 in *Loan Association v. Topeka,* the Court, instead of relying on the due process clause, held bad the expenditure of public money for a private purpose on the ground that this was a violation of those limits on governmental power "which grow out of the essential nature of all free governments; implied reservations of individual rights, without which the social compact could not exist. . . ." Again in 1878 in *Davidson v. New Orleans,* the Court made clear its attitude toward due process, going so far as to scold the bar for pressing upon them this new concept of due process. "There is here abundant evidence that there exists some strange misconception of the scope of this provision as found in the Fourteenth Amendment. In fact, it would seem, from the character of many of the cases before us, and the arguments made in them, that the clause under consideration is looked upon as a means of bringing to the test of the decision of this court the abstract opinions of every unsuccessful litigant in a State court of the justice of the decision against him, and of the merits of the legislation on which such a decision may be founded."

The present case was the first of a famous group of cases known as the "Granger Cases," which brought to the Supreme Court for the first time the important question of the right of a state legislature to regulate private business. The close of the Civil War ushered in a period of rapid railroad expansion. In the East, where industrial development tended to keep pace with the multiplication of transportation facilities, railroad building proved satisfactorily profitable. In the West, however, where new country was being opened up and population was sparse, the railroads had difficulty in paying dividends and frequently yielded to the temptation to indulge in stock-watering, questionable manipulation of credits, and doubtful practices in respect to grants of lands; to rebating and discrimination; and to other objectionable practices. Pitted against the desperate efforts of the railroads to make profits was the Western farmer, who wished to enjoy adequate railroad facilities at reasonable rates in order to facilitate the movement of crops in sparsely settled communities and who resented the unfair or dishonest methods of which some of the roads were known to be guilty. Out of this conflict of interests grew the Granger Movement, an organized effort on the part of the Western farmers which finally culminated in state legislation designed to cure the worst abuses. Starting in Illinois in 1871, the movement spread to other states; and soon railroads and warehousemen in Minnesota, Iowa, and Wisconsin found themselves subject to severe regulation with respect to rates and services. It was these laws which were challenged in the Granger Cases.

The present case involved an Illinois statute requiring the licensing of grain elevators and fixing the prices they could charge for the storage of grain. Munn was one of a group of elevator owners in Chicago who annually got together and fixed the prices to be charged by the elevators in the city during the coming year. The prices set by the law were lower than those set by the owners, and Munn refused to take out a license or submit to the regulation.

Mr. Chief Justice **Waite** delivered the opinion of the Court, saying in part:

Every statute is presumed to be constitutional. The courts ought not to declare one to be unconstitutional, unless it is clearly so. If there is doubt, the expressed will of the Legislature should be sustained.

The Constitution contains no definition of the word "deprive," as used in the 14th Amendment. To determine its signification, therefore, it is necessary to ascertain the effect which usage has given it, when employed in the same or a like connection.

While this provision of the Amendment is new in the Constitution of the United States as a limitation upon the powers of the States, it is old as a principle of civilized government. It is found in Magna Charta, and, in substance if not in form, in nearly or quite all the constitutions that have been from time to time adopted by the several States of the Union. By the 5th Amendment, it was introduced into the Constitution of the United States as a limitation upon the powers of the National Government, and by the 14th, as a guaranty against any encroachment upon an acknowledged right of citizenship by the Legislatures of the States. . . .

When one becomes a member of society, he necessarily parts with some rights or privileges which, as an individual not affected by his relations to others, he might retain. "A body politic," as aptly defined in the preamble of the Constitution of Massachusetts, "is a social compact by which the whole people covenants with each citizen, and each citizen with the whole people, that all shall be governed by certain laws for the common good." This does not confer power upon the whole people to control rights which are purely and exclusively private . . . , but it does authorize the establishment of laws requiring each citizen to so conduct himself, and so use his own property as not unnecessarily to injure another. This is the very essence of government, and has found expression in the maxim, Sic utere tuo ut alienum non laedas. From this source come the police powers, which . . . [a]re nothing more or less than the powers of government inherent in every sovereignty, . . . that is to say, . . . the power to govern men and things." Under these powers the government regulates the conduct of its citizens one towards another, and the manner in which each shall use his own property, when such regulation becomes necessary for the public good. In their exercise it has been customary in England from time immemorial, and in this country from its first colonization, to regulate ferries, common carriers, hackmen, bakers, millers, wharfingers, innkeepers, etc., and in so doing to fix a maximum of charge to be made for services rendered, accommodations furnished, and articles sold. To this day, statutes are to be found in many of the states upon some or all these subjects; and we think it has never yet been successfully contended that such legislation came within any of the constitutional prohibitions against interference with private property. . . .

From this it is apparent that, down to the time of the adoption of the 14th Amendment, it was not supposed that statutes regulating the use, or even the price of the use, of private property necessarily deprived an owner of his property without due process of law. Under some circumstances they may, but not under all. The Amendment does not change the law in this particular; it simply prevents the states from doing that which will operate as such a deprivation.

This brings us to inquire as to the principles upon which this power of regulation rests, in order that we may determine what is within and what without its operative effect. Looking, then, to the common law, from whence came the right which the Constitution protects, we find that when private property is "affected with a public interest, it ceases to be juris privati only." This was said by Lord Chief Justice Hale more than two hundred years ago. . . . Property does become clothed with a public interest when used in a manner to make it of public consequence, and affect the community at large. When, therefore, one devotes his property to a use in which the public has an interest, he, in effect, grants to the public an interest in that use, and must submit to be controlled by the public for the common good, to the extent of the interest he has thus created. He may withdraw his grant by discontinuing the use; but, so long as he maintains the use, he must submit to the control. . . .

And the same has been held as to warehouses and warehousemen. . . .

From the same source comes the power to regulate the charges of common carriers, which was done in England as long ago as the third year of the reign of William and Mary, and continued until within a comparatively recent period. . . .

Common carriers exercise a sort of public office, and have duties to perform in which the public is interested. . . .

Their business is, therefore, "affected with a public interest," within the meaning of the doctrine which Lord Hale has so forcibly stated.

But we need not go further. Enough has already been said to show that, when private property is devoted to a public use, it is subject to public regulation. It remains only to ascertain whether the warehouses of these plaintiffs in error, and the business which is carried on there, come within the operation of this principle.

For this purpose we accept as true the statements of fact contained in the elaborate brief of one of the counsel of the plaintiffs in error. From these it appears that ". . . The quantity (of grain) received in Chicago has made it the greatest grain market in the world. This business has created a demand for means by which the immense quantity of grain can be handled or stored, and these have been found in grain warehouses. . . . In this way the largest traffic between the citizens of the country north and west of Chicago, and the citizens of the country lying on the Atlantic coast north of Washington is in grain which passes through the elevators of Chicago. In this way the trade in grain is carried on by the inhabitants of seven or eight of the great States of the West with four or five of the States lying on the seashore, and forms the largest part of interstate commerce in these States. The grain warehouses or elevators in Chicago are immense structures, holding from 300,000 to 1,000,000 bushels at one time, according to size. . . . It has been found impossible to preserve each owner's grain separate, and this has given rise to a system of inspection and grading, by which the grain of different owners is mixed, and receipts issued for the number of bushels which are negotiable, and redeemable in like kind, upon demand. This mode of conducting the business was inaugurated more than twenty years ago, and has grown to immense proportions. The railways have found it impracticable to own such elevators, and public policy forbids the transaction of such business by the carrier; the ownership has, therefore, been by private individuals, who have embarked their capital and devoted their industry to such business as a private pursuit."

In this connection it must also be borne in mind that, although in 1874 there were in Chicago fourteen warehouses adapted to this particular business, and owned by about thirty persons, nine business firms controlled them, and that the prices charged and received for storage were such "as have been from year to year agreed upon and established by the different elevators or warehouses in the city of Chicago, and which rates have been annually published in one or more newspapers printed in said city, in the month of January in each year, as the established rates for the year then next ensuing such publication." Thus it is apparent that all the elevating facilities through which these vast productions "of seven or eight great States of the West" must pass on the way "to four or five of the States on the seaboard" may be a "virtual" monopoly.

Under such circumstances it is difficult to see why, if the common carrier, or the miller, or the ferryman, or the innkeeper, or the wharfinger, or the baker, or the cartman, or the hackney-coachman, pursues a public employment and exercises "a sort of public office," these plaintiffs in error do not. They stand, to use again the language of their counsel, in the very "gateway of commerce," and take toll from all who pass. Their business most certainly "tends to a common charge, and is become a thing of public interest and use." . . . Certainly, if any business can be clothed "with a public interest, and cease to be juris privati only," this has been. It may not be made so by the operation of the Constitution of Illinois or this statute, but it is by the facts.

We also are not permitted to overlook the fact that, for some reason, the people of Illinois, when they revised their Constitution in 1870, saw fit to make it the duty of the general assembly to pass laws "for the protection of producers, shippers and receivers of grain and produce," Art. XIII., sec. 7; and by sec. 5 of the same article, to require all railroad companies receiving and transporting grain in bulk or otherwise to deliver the same at any elevator to which it might be consigned, that could be reached by any track that was or could be used by such company, and that all railroad companies should permit connections to be made with their tracks, so that any public warehouse, etc., might be reached by the cars on their railroads. This indicates very clearly that during the twenty years in which this peculiar business had been assuming its present "immense proportions," something had occurred which led the whole body of the people to suppose that remedies such as are usually employed to prevent abuses by virtual monopolies might not be inappropriate here. For our purposes we must assume that, if a state of facts could exist that would justify such legislation, it actually did exist when the statute now under consideration was passed. For us the question is one of power, not of expediency. If no state of circumstances could exist to justify such a statute, then we may declare this one void, because in excess of the legislative power of the State. But if it could, we must presume it did. Of the propriety of legislative interference within the scope of legislative power, the Legislature is the exclusive judge.

Neither is it a matter of any moment that no precedent can be found for a statute precisely like this. It is conceded that the business is one of recent origin, that its growth has been rapid, and that it is already of great importance. And it must also be conceded that it is a business in which the whole public has a direct and positive interest. It presents, therefore, a case for the application of a long known and well established principle in social science, and this statute simply extends the law so as to meet this new development of commercial progress. There is no attempt to compel these owners to grant the public an interest in their property, but to declare their obligations, if they use it in this particular manner.

It matters not in this case that these plaintiffs in error had built their warehouses and established their business before the regulations complained of were adopted. What they did was, from the beginning, subject to the power of the body politic to require them to conform to such regulations as might be established by the proper authorities for the common good. They entered upon their business and provided themselves with the means to carry it on subject to this condition. If they did not wish to submit themselves to such interference, they should not have clothed the public with an interest in their concerns. . . .

It is insisted, however, that the owner of property is entitled to a reasonable compensation for its use, even though it be clothed with a public interest, and that what is reasonable is a judicial and not a legislative question.

As has already been shown, the practice has been otherwise. In countries where the common law prevails, it has been customary from time immemorial for the Legislature to declare what shall be a reasonable compensation under such circumstances, or, perhaps more properly speaking, to fix a maximum beyond which any charge made would be unreasonable. Undoubtedly, in mere private contracts, relating to matters in which the public has no interest, what is reasonable must be ascertained judicially. But this is because the Legislature has no control over such a contract. So, too, in matters which do affect the public interest, and as to which legislative control may be exercised, if there are no statutory regulations upon the subject, the courts must determine what is reasonable. The controlling fact is the power to regulate at all. If that exists, the right to establish the maximum of charge, as one of the means of regulation, is implied. In fact, the common law rule, which requires the charge to be reasonable, is itself a regulation as to price. Without it the owner could make his rates at will, and compel the public to yield to his terms, or forego the use.

But a mere common law regulation of trade or business may be changed by statute. A person has no property, no vested interest, in any rule of the common law. That is only one of the forms of municipal law, and is no more sacred than any other. Rights of property which have been created by the common law cannot be taken away without due process; but the law itself, as a rule of conduct, may be changed at the will, or even at the whim, of the Legislature, unless prevented by constitutional limitations. Indeed, the great office of statutes is to remedy defects in the common law as they are developed, and to adapt it to the changes of time and circumstances. To limit the rate of charge for services rendered in a public employment, or for the use of property in which the public has an interest, is only changing a regulation which existed before. It establishes no new principle in the law, but only gives a new effect to an old one.

We know that this is a power which may be abused; but that is no argument against its existence. For protection against abuses by Legislatures the people must resort to the polls, not to the courts. . . .

We conclude, therefore, that the statute in question is not repugnant to the Constitution of the United States, and that there is no error in the judgment. . . . Judgment affirmed.

Mr. Justice **Field,** with Mr. Justice **Strong** concurring, dissenting, said in part:

I am compelled to dissent from the decision of the court in this case, and from the reasons upon which that decision is founded. The principle upon which the opinion of the majority proceeds is, in my judgment, subversive of the rights of private property, heretofore believed to be protected by constitutional guaranties against legislative interference, and is in conflict with the authorities cited in its support. . . .

The declaration of the Constitution of 1870, that private buildings used for private purposes shall be deemed public institutions, does not make them so. The receipt and storage of grain in a building erected by private means for that purpose does not constitute the building a public warehouse. There is no magic in the language, though used by a constitutional convention, which can change a private business into a public one, or alter the character of the building in which the business is transacted. . . . One might as well attempt to change the nature of colors, by giving them a new designation. . . .

If this be sound law, if there be no protection, either in the principles upon which our republican government is founded, or in the prohibitions of the Constitution against such invasion of private rights, all property and all business in the State are held at the mercy of a majority of its Legislature. The public has no greater interest in the use of buildings for the storage of grain than it has in the use of buildings for the residences of families, nor, indeed, anything like so great an interest; and, according to the doctrine announced, the Legislature may fix the rent of all tenements used for residences, without reference to the cost of their erection. If the owner does not like the rates prescribed, he may cease renting his houses. . . .

By the term ''liberty,'' as used in the provisions, something more is meant than mere freedom from physical restraint or the bounds of a prison. It means freedom to go where one may choose, and to act in such manner, not inconsistent with the equal rights of others, as his judgment may dictate for the promotion of his happiness; that is, to pursue such callings and avocations as may be most suitable to develop his capacities, and to give them their highest enjoyment.

The same liberal construction which is required for the protection of life and liberty, in all particulars in which life and liberty are of any value, should be applied to the protection of private property. If the Legislature of a State, under pretense of providing for the public good, or for any other reason, can determine, against the consent of the owner, the uses to which private property shall be devoted, or the prices which the owner shall receive for its uses, it can deprive him of the property as completely as by a special Act for its confiscation or destruction. . . .

There is nothing in the character of the business of the defendants as warehousemen which called for the interference complained of in this case. Their buildings are not nuisances; their occupation of receiving and storing grain infringes upon no rights of others, disturbs no neighborhood, infects not the air, and in no respect prevents others from using and enjoying their property as to them may seem best. The legislation in question is nothing less than a bold assertion of absolute power by the State to control, at its discretion, the property and business of the citizen, and fix the compensation he shall receive. The will of the Legislature is made the condition upon which the owner shall receive the fruits of his property and the just reward of his labor, industry and enterprise. ''That government,'' says Story, ''can scarcely be deemed to be free where the rights of property are left solely dependent upon the will of a legislative body without any restraint. The fundamental maxims of a free government seem to require that the rights of personal liberty and private property should be held sacred.'' Wilkinson v. Leland [1829]. The decision of the court in this case gives unrestrained license to legislative will.

NEBBIA v. NEW YORK

291 U. S. 502; 54 S. Ct. 505; 78 L. Ed. 940
(1934)

The acceptance by the Supreme Court of ''substantive'' due process, in addition to the earlier exclusively ''procedural'' due process, took place gradually over a period of nearly twenty years as cases involving the validity of state laws came before it. The change came first in the area of rate controls. Within a decade after the Munn case (1877) the Court started to backtrack from Chief Justice Waite's dictum in that case—that the only appeal from an unjust rate was to elect a new legislature to enact a just one. In the Railroad Commission Cases (Stone v. Farmers' Loan & Trust Co., 1886) the Court, while confirming the legislature's power to regulate rates, added that ''this power to regulate is not a power to destroy, and limitation is not the equivalent of confiscation. Under pretense of regulating fares and freights, the State cannot require a railroad corporation to carry persons or property without reward; neither can it do that which in law amounts to taking of private property for public use without just compensation, or without due process of law.'' Thus the legislature is apparently forbidden by due process to enact a regulatory measure which in substance is unreasonable. For over fifty years following Stone the courts had the last word as to what rates set for regulated industries were fair. Finally, in *Federal Power Commission v. Hope Natural Gas Co.*, it abandoned its earlier policy of scrutinizing the precise formula by which rates were fixed. Noting that the value of a company depends on the rates it is allowed to charge, the Court indicated that henceforth it would judge the rate in terms of its general effect on the business, and leave to the proper agency the method by which the rate was to be set.

In *Munn v. Illinois* and the cases which followed it, the Court established the doctrine that the government could regulate prices and control terms of service (within limits) only of businesses which were "affected with a public interest." To impose these regulations upon a business not affected with a public interest was to deprive it of its liberty and property without due process of law. This doctrine seemed fair on its face and comported with the tradition of American individualism. But what is a business "affected with a public interest"? The Court found it difficult to answer this question because as cases involving it arose, it became obvious that there was no single characteristic by which a business so affected with a public interest could invariably be identified. In *Wolff Packing Co. v. Industrial Court* (1923), holding that a meat-packing establishment is not a business affected with public interest, Chief Justice Taft went on to say that such businesses fall into three categories. These are as follows: "(1) Those which are carried on under the authority of a public grant of privileges which either expressly or impliedly imposes the affirmative duty of rendering a public service demanded by any member of the public. Such are the railroads, other common carriers and public utilities. (2) Certain occupations, regarded as exceptional, the public interest attaching to which, recognized from earliest times, has survived the period of arbitrary laws by Parliament or colonial legislatures for regulating all trades and callings. Such are those of the keepers of inns, cabs, and gristmills. . . . (3) Businesses which, though not public at their inception, may be fairly said to have risen to be such, and have become subject in consequence to some government regulation. They have come to hold such a peculiar relation to the public that this is superimposed upon them. In the language of the cases, the owner by devoting his business to the public use, in effect grants the public an interest in that use, and subjects himself to public regulation to the extent of that interest, although the property continues to belong to its private owner, and to be entitled to protection accordingly." None of this seemed very helpful as a guide for the decision of future cases.

The continued application of so vague a judicial test did not fail to produce criticism, and some of the sharpest of this came from the members of the Court itself. In a powerful dissenting opinion in *Ribnik v. McBride* (1928), Justice Stone declared: "[Price] . . .

regulation is within the state's power whenever any combination of circumstances seriously curtails the regulative force of competition, so that buyers or sellers are placed at such a disadvantage in the bargaining struggle that a legislature might reasonably anticipate serious consequences to the community as a whole." And in his dissenting opinion in *New State Ice Co. v. Liebmann* (1932), Justice Brandeis struck out boldly with the assertion: "The notion of a distinct category of business 'affected with a public interest' employing property 'devoted to a public use' rests upon historical error. . . . In my opinion, the true principle is that the State's power extends to every regulation of any business reasonably required and appropriate for the public protection. I find in the due process clause no other limitation upon the character or the scope of regulation permissible."

These minority views finally prevailed in the area of rate-making. The *Nebbia* case printed below abandons entirely the concept of a business affected with a public interest as the constitutional test of price control. The milk business admittedly is not affected with a public interest in the traditional sense. Price control is merely a phase of the police power of the state subject only to the limitations of due process of law upon arbitrary interference with liberty and property.

Mr. Justice **Roberts** delivered the opinion of the Court, saying in part:

The Legislature of New York established a Milk Control Board with power, among other things, to "fix minimum and maximum . . . retail prices to be charged by . . . stores to consumers for consumption off the premises where sold." The Board fixed nine cents as the price to be charged by a store for a quart of milk. Nebbia, the proprietor of a grocery store in Rochester, sold two quarts and a five cent loaf of bread for eighteen cents; and was convicted for violating the Board's order. At his trial he asserted the statute and order contravene the equal protection clause and the due process clause. . . .

The question for decision is whether the Federal Constitution prohibits a state from so fixing the selling price of milk. We first inquire as to the occasion for the legislation and its history.

During 1932 the prices received by farmers for milk were much below the cost of production. The decline in prices during 1931 and 1932 was much greater than that of prices generally. The situation of the families of dairy producers had become desperate and called for state aid similar to that afforded the unemployed, if conditions should not improve.

On March 10, 1932, the senate and assembly resolved "That a joint legislative committee is hereby created . . . to investigate the causes of the decline of the price of milk to producers and the resultant effect of the low prices upon the dairy industry. . . ."

In part those conclusions [of the committee] are:

Milk is an essential item of diet. It cannot long be stored. It is an excellent medium for growth of bacteria.

These facts necessitate safeguards in its production and handling for human consumption which greatly increase the cost of the business. Failure of producers to receive a reasonable return for their labor and investment over an extended period threatens a relaxation of vigilance against contamination.

The production and distribution of milk is a paramount industry of the state, and largely affects the health and prosperity of its people. Dairying yields fully one-half of the total income from all farm products. Dairy farm investment amounts to approximately $1,000,000. Curtailment or destruction of the dairy industry would cause a serious economic loss to the people of the state.

In addition to the general price decline, other causes for the low price of milk include a periodic increase in the number of cows and in milk production, the prevalence of unfair and destructive trade practices in the distribution of milk, leading to a demoralization of prices in the metropolitan area and other markets, and the failure of transportation and distribution charges to be reduced in proportion to the reduction in retail prices for milk and cream.

The fluid milk industry is affected by factors of instability peculiar to itself which call for special methods of control. . . . [The Court here analyzes these factors in detail.]

The legislature adopted Chapter 158 [creating a Milk Control Board with power to fix prices] as a method of correcting the evils, which the report of the committee showed could not be expected to right themselves through the ordinary play of the forces of supply and demand, owing to the peculiar and uncontrollable factors affecting the industry. . . .

First. The appellant urges that the order of the Milk Control Board denies him the equal protection of the laws. It is shown that the order requires him, if he purchases his supply from a dealer, to pay eight cents per quart and five cents per pint, and to resell at not less than nine and six, whereas the same dealer may buy his supply from a farmer at lower prices and deliver milk to consumers at ten cents the quart and six cents the pint. We think the contention that the discrimination deprives the appellant of equal protection is not well founded. For aught that appears, the appellant purchased his supply of milk from a farmer as do distributors, or could have procured it from a farmer if he so desired. There is therefore no showing that the order placed him at a disadvantage, or in fact affected him adversely, and this alone is fatal to the claim of denial of equal protection. But if it were shown that the appellant is compelled to buy from a distributor, the difference in the retail price he is required to charge his customers from that prescribed for sales by distributors is not on its face arbitrary or unreasonable, for there are obvious distinctions between the two sorts of merchants which may well justify a difference of treatment, if the legislature possesses the power to control the prices to be charged for fluid milk. . . .

Second. The more serious question is whether in the light of the conditions disclosed, . . . [the price-regulation] denied the appellant the due process secured to him by the Fourteenth amendment. . . .

Under our form of government the use of property and the making of contracts are normally matters of private and not of public concern. The general rule is that both shall be free of governmental interference. But neither property rights nor contract rights are absolute; for government cannot exist if the citizen may at will use his property to the detriment of his fellows, or exercise his freedom of contract to work them harm. Equally fundamental with the private right is that of the public to regulate it in the common interest. . . .

The milk industry in New York has been the subject of long-standing and drastic regulation in the public interest. The legislative investigation of 1932 was persuasive of the fact that for this and other reasons unrestricted competition aggravated existing evils and the normal law of supply and demand was insufficient to correct maladjustments detrimental to the community. The inquiry disclosed destructive and demoralizing competitive conditions and unfair trade practices which resulted in retail price cutting and reduced the income of the farmer below the cost of production. We do not understand the appellant to deny that in these circumstances the legislature might reasonably consider further regulation and control desirable for protection of the industry and the consuming public. That body believed conditions could be improved by preventing destructive price-cutting by stores which, due to the flood of surplus milk, were able to buy at much lower prices than the larger distributors and to sell without incurring the delivery costs of the latter. In the order of which complaint is made the Milk Control Board fixed a price of ten cents per quart for sales by a distributor to a consumer, and nine cents by a store to a consumer, thus recognizing the lower costs of the store, and endeavoring to establish a differential which would be just to both. In the light of the facts the order appears not to be unreasonable or arbitrary, or without relation to the purpose to prevent ruthless competition from destroying the wholesale price structure on which the farmer depends for his livelihood, and the community for an assured supply of milk.

But we are told that because the law essays to control prices it denies due process. Notwithstanding the admitted power to correct existing economic ills by appropriate regulation of business, even though an indirect result may be a restriction of the freedom of contract or a modification of charges for services or the price of commodities, the appellant urges that direct fixation of prices is a type of regulation absolutely forbidden. His position is that the Fourteenth Amendment requires us to hold the challenged statute void for this reason alone. The argument runs that the public control of rates or prices is per se unreasonable and unconstitutional, save as applied to businesses affected with a public interest; that a business so affected is one in which property is devoted to an enterprise of a sort which the public itself might appropriately undertake, or one whose owner relies on a public grant or franchise for the right to conduct the business, or in which he is bound to serve all who apply; in short, such as is commonly called a public utility; or a business in its nature a monopoly. The milk industry, it is said, possesses none of these characteristics, and, therefore, not being affected with a public interest, its charges may not be controlled by the state. Upon the soundness of this contention the appellant's case against the statute depends.

We may as well say at once that the dairy industry is not, in the accepted sense of the phrase, a public utility. We think the appellant is also right in asserting that there is in this case no suggestion of any monopoly or monopolistic practice. It goes without saying that those engaged in the business are in no way dependent upon public grants or franchises for the privilege of conducting their activities. But if, as must be conceded, the industry is subject to regulation in the public interest, what constitutional principle bars the state from correcting existing maladjustments by legislation touching prices? We think there is no such principle. The due process clause makes no mention of sales or of prices any more than it speaks of business or contracts or buildings or other incidents of property. The thought seems nevertheless to have persisted that there is something peculiarly sacrosanct about the price one may charge for what he makes or sells, and that, however able to regulate other elements of manufacture or trade, with incidental effect upon price, the state is incapable of directly controlling the price itself. This view was negatived many years ago. Munn v. Illinois [1877]. . . . [Here follows an analysis of the Munn case in which it is pointed out that the Court therein regarded the term "affected with a public interest" as the equivalent of "subject to the exercise of the police power."]

It is clear that there is no closed class or category of businesses affected with a public interest, and the function of courts in the application of the Fifth and Fourteenth Amendments is to determine in each case whether circumstances vindicate the challenged regulation as a reasonable exertion of governmental authority or condemn it as arbitrary or discriminatory. . . . The phrase "affected with a public interest" can, in the nature of things, mean no more than that an industry, for adequate reason, is subject to control for the public good. In several of the decisions of this court wherein the expressions "affected with a public interest," and "clothed with a public use," have been brought forward as the criteria of the validity of price control, it has been admitted that they are not susceptible of definition and form an unsatisfactory test of the constitutionality of legislation directed at business practices or prices. These decisions must rest, finally, upon the basis that the requirements of due process were not met because the laws were found arbitrary in their operation and effect. But there can be no doubt that upon proper occasion and by appropriate measures the state may regulate a business in any of its aspects, including the prices to be charged for the products or commodities it sells.

So far as the requirement of due process is concerned, and in the absence of other constitutional restriction, a state is free to adopt whatever economic policy may reasonably be deemed to promote public welfare, and to enforce that policy by legislation adapted to its purpose. The courts are without authority either to declare such policy, or, when it is declared by the legislature, to override it. . . .

. . . The constitution does not secure to any one liberty to conduct his business in such fashion as to inflict injury upon the public at large, or upon any substantial group of the people. Price control, like any other form of regulation, is unconstitutional only if arbitrary, discriminatory, or demonstrably irrelevant to the policy the legislature is free to adopt, and hence an unnecessary and unwarranted interference with individual liberty.

Tested by these considerations we find no basis in the due process clause of the Fourteenth Amendment for condemning the provisions of the Agriculture and Markets Law here drawn into question.

The judgment is affirmed.

Mr. Justice **McReynolds** dissented in an opinion concurred in by Justices **Van Devanter, Sutherland** and **Butler,** saying in part:

Regulation to prevent recognized evils in business has long been upheld as permissible legislative action. But fixation of the price at which "A," engaged in an ordinary business, may sell, in order to enable "B," a producer, to improve his condition, has not been regarded as within legislative power. This is not regulation, but management, control, dictation—it amounts to the deprivation of the fundamental right which one has to conduct his own affairs honestly and along customary lines. . . .

The statement by the court below that—"Doubtless the statute before us would be condemned by an earlier generation as a temerarious interference with the rights of property and contract . . . ; with the natural law of supply and demand," is obviously correct. But another, that "statutes . . . aiming to stimulate the production of a vital food product by fixing living standards of prices for the producer, are to be interpreted with that degree of liberality which is essential to the attainment of the end in view," conflicts with views of constitutional rights accepted since the beginning. An end although apparently desirable cannot justify inhibited means. Moreover the challenged act was not designed to stimulate production—there was too much milk for the demand and no prospect of less for several years; also "standards of prices" at which the producer might sell were not prescribed. The Legislature cannot lawfully destroy guaranteed rights of one man with the prime purpose of enriching another, even if for the moment, this may seem advantageous to the public. And the adoption of any "concept of jurisprudence" which permits facile disregard of the Constitution as long interpreted and respected will inevitably lead to its destruction. Then, all rights will be subject to the caprice of the hour; government by stable laws will pass.

LOCHNER v. NEW YORK

198 U. S. 45; 25 S. Ct. 539; 49 L. Ed. 937 (1905)

At the same time that the states were trying to regulate rates, they were also trying to alleviate some of the more abusive labor conditions that had arisen with the industrial revolution. The Court's hostility to these efforts was similar to that shown to rate control in the post-Munn era. What persuaded the Supreme Court to assert a supervisory power over the substance of state legislation which it had so carefully rejected in the Slaughter-House Cases (1873) is not difficult to surmise. During the two decades involved, the entire personnel of the Court, with the exception of Justice Field, had changed; and Field, who had dissented in the Slaughter-House Cases, had always been an apostle of the new faith. The new members coming onto the Court tended to reflect the social and economic pressures of the post-Civil War period: the tremendous expansion of the railroads and industry, the brawling struggle between management and labor with the growth of the trade union movement, and the increasing use of political power by the workingman to secure the enactment of protective labor legislation. Naturally, organized industry looked upon legislative efforts to ameliorate factory conditions and hours of labor as intolerable interferences with the employer's private affairs and a deprivation of his liberty and property. A generation of judges steeped in the individualism of the common law tended to share this view. Due process of law came to seem the completely appropriate and adequate constitutional weapon with which to combat the onward march of the new social control—the new police power.

This individualistic interpretation by the courts of due process of law found finally a definite basis in the development in the state courts during the 1880s of the doctrine of "liberty of contract," which was first introduced into the Supreme Court by Justice Peckham in Allgeyer v. Louisiana (1897), a case involving the right to buy insurance. There he interpreted due process as including "the right of the citizen . . . to live and work where he will; to earn his livelihood by any lawful calling; to pursue any livelihood or avocation, and for that purpose to enter into all contracts which may be proper, necessary, and essential to his carrying out to a successful conclusion the purposes above mentioned."

The concept of "liberty of contract" was both plausible and alluring. It asserted in substance that when two parties, neither of whom was under any legal disability, came together to make a contract which was not contrary to public policy, the legislature had no right to interfere and dictate the terms of the agreement. The application of this doctrine to the problem of protective labor legislation produced, however, some very startling results, due in large measure to the naïve assumption by the courts that the individual employee of a great industrial corporation possessed full liberty of contract and could dicker with an employer upon equal terms. Naturally, as time went on the courts found frequently that this vaunted liberty of contract was infringed by the laws regulating hours of labor, method and time of wage payment, employer's liability, factory conditions, and similar matters.

Sir Henry Maine's statement that "the movement of the progressive societies has hitherto been a movement from status to contract" marked this as a liberal doctrine which emancipated the individual, especially the laborer, from governmental controls and allowed the person to bargain freely about his or her affairs. Hence it was only natural that it should receive a preferred place in the constitutional scheme. The normal presumption that a state statute is constitutional gradually gave way, and the burden of proof was placed upon those who would sustain a law alleged to limit such liberty of contract. The Court's insistence in Mugler v. Kansas (1887) that a state statute purporting to protect the public health, safety, and morals must bear a "real or substantial relation to those objects" meant that the Court had to be shown that such was the case before the act could be upheld.

The difficulty came in persuading the Court that such a relationship did in fact exist. In the Mugler case the Court had taken judicial notice of the evils of drink and had upheld the validity of a state prohibition statute; but the judges themselves had no knowledge of the social and economic conditions which led to the passage of laws regulating the hours of labor and working conditions, and to the extent they had such knowledge their inclination was to protect the right of entrepreneurs to conduct their affairs under the old common-law rules to which they were accustomed—rules which gave them virtually uncontrolled discretion over marketing policies, labor relations and working conditions. Nor was the bar, if it had such knowledge, in a position to transmit such knowledge to the bench, since the traditional method of arguing cases was to cite case precedents and attempt to show by rational analysis how the case at bar was similar. Thus the protagonists of protective labor laws found themselves with a strong presumption against the validity of the laws and no effective way to rebut the presumption.

Most of the court decisions now regarded as more or less reactionary were rendered by the state courts. They had been invalidating state social legislation for nearly twenty years before the Supreme Court followed suit. The case of Lochner v. New York is interesting for two reasons: first, because it is the earliest and one of the most important cases in which the Supreme Court invalidated a state law under the liberty of contract phrase of the due process clause; and second, because it contains Justice Holmes's dissenting opinion upholding the validity of such reform laws. Lochner was convicted of violating a New York statute called the Labor Law, which provided that no employee should be "required or permitted to work in a biscuit, bread or cake bakery or confectionery establishment more than sixty hours in any one week, or more than ten hours in any one day unless for the purpose of making a shorter day on the last day of the week." The legislature had proceeded upon the assumption that the conditions in the baking industry were such as to demand the intervention of the state in behalf of the employees. The majority of the Supreme Court did not agree that such protection was reasonably necessary and accordingly held that there was no adequate justification for this infringement of the private rights of the employer. Four justices dissented on the ground that there was sufficient support for the view of the legislature to make it a debatable question whether the law was arbitrary or not and that when such was the case, the *courts should not override the legislative judgment. The dissenting opinion of Justice Holmes has become almost a classic as a statement of the more liberal judicial attitude toward the question of the validity of social and economic legislation under the Fourteenth Amendment. It is interesting to note that in the 1980s, under the rubric of "law and economics," the assumption that individuals and corporations are equal bargaining agents—a basic assumption of Lochner—is undergoing a revival.*

Mr. Justice **Peckham** delivered the opinion of the Court, saying in part:

The statute necessarily interferes with the right of contract between the employer and employees, concerning the number of hours in which the latter may labor in the bakery of the employer. The general right to make a contract in relation to his business is part of the liberty of the individual protected by the 14th Amendment of the Federal Constitution. . . . Under that provision no state can deprive any person of life, liberty, or property without due process of law. The right to purchase or to sell labor is part of the liberty protected by this amendment, unless there are circumstances which exclude the right. There are, however, certain powers, existing in the sovereignty of each state in the Union, somewhat vaguely termed police powers, the exact description and limitation of which have not been attempted by the courts. Those powers, broadly stated, and without, at present, any attempt at a more specific limitation, relate to the safety, health, morals, and general welfare of the public. Both property and liberty are held on such reasonable conditions as may be imposed by the governing power of the state in the exercise of those powers, and with such conditions the 14th Amendment was not designed to interfere. . . .

The state, therefore, has power to prevent the individual from making certain kinds of contracts, and in regard to them the Federal Constitution offers no protection. If the contract be one which the state, in the legitimate exercise of its police power, has the right to prohibit, it is not prevented from prohibiting it by the 14th Amendment. Contracts in violation of a statute, either of the Federal or state government, or a contract to let one's property for immoral purposes, or to do any other unlawful act, could obtain no protection from the Federal Constitution, as coming under the liberty of person or of free contract. Therefore, when the state, by its legislature, in the assumed exercise of its police powers, has passed an act which seriously limits the right to labor or the right of contract in regard to their means of livelihood between persons who are sui juris (both employer and employee), it becomes of great importance to determine which shall prevail,—the right of the individual to labor for such time as he may choose, or the right of the state to prevent the individual from laboring, or from entering into any contract to labor, beyond a certain time prescribed by the state. . . .

It must, of course, be conceded that there is a limit to the valid exercise of the police power by the state.

There is no dispute concerning this general proposition. Otherwise the 14th Amendment would have no efficacy and the legislatures of the states would have unbounded power, and it would be enough to say that any piece of legislation was enacted to conserve the morals, the health, or the safety of the people; such legislation would be valid, no matter how absolutely without foundation the claim might be. The claim of the police power would be a mere pretext,—become another and delusive name for the supreme sovereignty of the state to be exercised free from constitutional restraint. This is not contended for. In every case that comes before this court, therefore, where legislation of this character is concerned, and where the protection of the Federal Constitution is sought, the question necessarily arises: Is this a fair, reasonable, and appropriate exercise of the police power of the state, or is it an unreasonable, unnecessary, and arbitrary interference with the right of the individual to his personal liberty, or to enter into those contracts in relation to labor which may seem to him appropriate or necessary for the support of himself and his family? Of course the liberty of contract relating to labor includes both parties to it. The one has as much right to purchase as the other to sell labor.

This is not a question of substituting the judgment of the court for that of the legislature. If the act be within the power of the state it is valid, although the judgment of the court might be totally opposed to the enactment of such a law. But the question would still remain: Is it within the police power of the state? and that question must be answered by the court.

The question whether this act is valid as a labor law, pure and simple, may be dismissed in a few words. There is no reasonable ground for interfering with the liberty of person or the right of free contract, by determining the hours of labor, in the occupation of a baker. There is no contention that bakers as a class are not equal in intelligence and capacity to men in other trades or manual occupations, or that they are not able to assert their rights and care for themselves without the protecting arm of the state, interfering with their independence of judgment and of action. They are in no sense wards of the state. Viewed in the light of a purely labor law, with no reference whatever to the question of health, we think that a law like the one before us involves neither the safety, the morals, nor the welfare, of the public, and that the interest of the public is not in the slightest degree affected by such an act. The law must be upheld, if at all, as a law pertaining to the health of the individual engaged in the occupation of a baker. It does not affect any other portion of the public than those who are engaged in that occupation. Clean and wholesome bread does not depend upon whether the baker works but ten hours per day or only sixty hours a week. The limitation of the hours of labor does not come within the police power on that ground.

It is a question of which of two powers or rights shall prevail,—the power of the state to legislate or the right of the individual to liberty of person and freedom of contract. The mere assertion that the subject relates, though but in a remote degree, to the public health, does not necessarily render the enactment valid. The act must have a more direct relation, as a means to an end, and the end itself must be appropriate and legitimate, before an act can be held to be valid which interferes with the general right of an individual to be free in his person and in his power to contract in relation to his own labor. . . .

We think the limit of the police power has been reached and passed in this case. There is, in our judgment, no reasonable foundation for holding this to be necessary or appropriate as a health law to safeguard the public health, or the health of the individuals who are following the trade of a baker. If this statute be valid, and if, therefore, a proper case is made out in which to deny the right of an individual, sui juris, as employer or employee, to make contracts for the labor of the latter under the protection of the provisions of the Federal Constitution, there would seem to be no length to which legislation of this nature might not go. . . .

We think that there can be no fair doubt that the trade of a baker, in and of itself, is not an unhealthy one to that degree which would authorize the legislature to interfere with the right to labor, and with the right of free contract on the part of the individual, either as employer or employee. In looking through statistics regarding all trades and occupations, it may be true that the trade of a baker does not appear to be as healthy as some other trades, and is also vastly more healthy than still others. To the common understanding the trade of a baker has never been regarded as an unhealthy one. Very likely physicians would not recommend the exercise of that or of any other trade as a remedy for ill health. Some occupations are more healthy than others, but we think there are none which might not come under the power of the legislature to supervise and control the hours of working therein, if the mere fact that the occupation is not absolutely and perfectly healthy is to confer that right upon the legislative department of the government. It might be safely affirmed that almost all occupations more or less affect the health. There must be more than the mere fact of the possible existence of some small amount of unhealthiness to warrant legislative interference with liberty. It is unfortunately true that labor, even in any department, may possibly carry with it the seeds of unhealthiness. But are we all, on that account, at the mercy of legislative majorities? A printer, a tinsmith, a locksmith, a carpenter, a cabinetmaker, a dry goods clerk, a bank's, a lawyer's, or a physician's clerk, or a clerk in almost any kind of business, would all come under the power of the legislature, on this assumption. No trade, no occupation, no mode of earning one's living, could escape this all-pervading power, and the acts of the legislature in limiting the hours of labor in all employments would be valid, although such limitation might seriously cripple the ability of the laborer to support himself and his family. In our large cities there are many buildings into which the sun penetrates for but a short time in each day, and these buildings are occupied by people carrying on the business of bankers, brokers, lawyers, real estate, and many other kinds of business, aided by many clerks, messengers, and other employees. Upon the assumption of the validity of this act under review, it

is not possible to say that an act, prohibiting lawyers' or bank clerks, or others, from contracting to labor for their employers more than eight hours a day would be invalid. It might be said that it is unhealthy to work more than that number of hours in an apartment lighted by artificial light during the working hours of the day; that the occupation of the bank clerk, the lawyer's clerk, the real-estate clerk, or the broker's clerk, in such offices is therefore unhealthy, and the legislature, in its paternal wisdom, must, therefore, have the right to legislate on the subject of and to limit, the hours for such labor; and, if it exercises that power, and its validity be questioned, it is sufficient to say, it has reference to the public health; it has reference to the health of the employees condemned to labor day after day in buildings where the sun never shines; it is a health law, and therefore it is valid, and cannot be questioned by the courts.

It is also urged, pursuing the same line of argument, that it is to the interest of the state that its population should be strong and robust, and therefore any legislation which may be said to tend to make people healthy must be valid as health laws, enacted under the police power. If this be a valid argument and a justification for this kind of legislation, it follows that the protection of the Federal Constitution from undue interference with liberty of person and freedom of contract is visionary, wherever the law is sought to be justified as a valid exercise of the police power. Scarcely any law but might find shelter under such assumptions, and conduct, properly so called, as well as contract, would come under the restrictive sway of the legislature. Not only the hours of employees, but the hours of employers, could be regulated, and doctors, lawyers, scientists, all professional men, as well as athletes and artisans, could be forbidden to fatigue their brains and bodies by prolonged hours of exercise, lest the fighting strength of the state be impaired. We mention these extreme cases because the contention is extreme. We do not believe in the soundness of the views which uphold this law. On the contrary, we think that such a law as this, although passed in the assumed exercise of the police power, and as relating to the public health, or the health of the employees named, is not within that power, and is invalid. The act is not, within any fair meaning of the term, a health law, but is an illegal interference with the rights of individuals, both employers and employees, to make contracts regarding labor upon such terms as they may think best, or which they may agree upon with the other parties to such contracts. Statutes of the nature of that under review, limiting the hours in which grown and intelligent men may labor to earn their living, are mere meddlesome interferences with the rights of the individual, and they are not saved from condemnation by the claim that they are passed in the exercise of the police power and upon the subject of the health of the individual whose rights are interfered with, unless there be some fair ground, reasonable in and of itself, to say that there is material danger to the public health, or to the health of the employees, if the hours of labor are not curtailed. . . .

It was further urged on the argument that restricting the hours of labor in the case of bakers was valid because it tended to cleanliness on the part of the workers, as a man was more apt to be cleanly when not overworked, and if cleanly then his "output" was also more likely to be so. . . . The connection, if any exist, is too shadowy and thin to build any argument for the interference of the legislature. If the man works ten hours a day it is all right, but if ten and a half or eleven his health is in danger and his bread may be unhealthy, and, therefore, he shall not be permitted to do it. This, we think, is unreasonable and entirely arbitrary. . . .

. . . It seems to us that the real object and purpose were simply to regulate the hours of labor between the master and his employees (all being men, sui juris), in a private business, not dangerous in any degree to morals, or in any real and substantial degree to the health of the employees. Under such circumstances the freedom of master and employee to contract with each other in relation to their employment, and in defining the same, cannot be prohibited or interfered with, without violating the Federal Constitution.

The judgment . . . must be reversed. . . .

Mr. Justice **Harlan,** with whom Mr. Justice **White** and Mr. Justice **Day** concurred in dissenting, said in part:

. . . I find it impossible, in view of common experience, to say that there is here no real or substantial relation between the means employed by the state and the end sought to be accomplished by its legislation. . . .

We judicially know that the question of the number of hours during which a workman should continuously labor has been, for a long period, and is yet, a subject of serious consideration among civilized peoples, and by those having special knowledge of the laws of health. Suppose the statute prohibited labor in bakery and confectionery establishments in excess of eighteen hours each day. No one, I take it, could dispute the power of the state to enact such a statute. But the statute before us does not embrace extreme or exceptional cases. It may be said to occupy a middle ground in respect of the hours of labor. What is the true ground for the state to take between legitimate protection, by legislation, of the public health and liberty of contract is not a question easily solved, nor one in respect of which there is or can be absolute certainty. There are very few, if any, questions in political economy about which entire certainty may be predicated. . . .

I do not stop to consider whether any particular view of this economic question presents the sounder theory. What the precise facts are it may be difficult to say. It is enough for the determination of this case, and it is enough for this court to know, that the question is one about which there is room for debate and for an honest difference of opinion. There are many reasons of a weighty, substantial character, based upon the experience of mankind, in support of the theory that, all things considered, more than ten hours steady work each day, from week to week, in a bakery or confectionery establishment, may endanger the health and shorten the lives of the workmen, thereby diminishing their physical and mental capacity to serve the state and to provide for those dependent upon them.

If such reasons exist that ought to be the end of this case, for the state is not amenable to the judiciary, in respect of its legislative enactments, unless such enactments are plainly, palpably, beyond all question, inconsistent with the Constitution of the United States. . . .

Mr. Justice **Holmes** dissenting:

I regret sincerely that I am unable to agree with the judgment in this case, and I think it my duty to express my dissent.

This case is decided upon an economic theory which a large part of the country does not entertain. If it were a question whether I agreed with that theory, I should desire to study it further and long before making up my mind. But I do not conceive that to be my duty, because I strongly believe that my agreement or disagreement has nothing to do with the right of a majority to embody their opinions in law. It is settled by various decisions of this court that state constitutions and state laws may regulate life in many ways which we as legislators might think as injudicious, or if you like as tyrannical, as this, and which equally with this, interfere with the liberty to contract. Sunday laws and usury laws are ancient examples. A more modern one is the prohibition of lotteries. The liberty of the citizen to do as he likes so long as he does not interfere with the liberty of others to do the same, which has been a shibboleth for some well-known writers, is interfered with by school laws, by the Postoffice, by every state or municipal institution which takes his money for purposes thought desirable, whether he likes it or not. The 14th Amendment does not enact Mr. Herbert Spencer's Social Statics. The other day we sustained the Massachusetts vaccination law. Jacobson v. Massachusetts [1905]. United States and state statutes and decisions cutting down the liberty to contract by way of combination are familiar to this court. Northern Securities Co. v. United States [1904]. Two years ago we upheld the prohibition of sales of stock on margins, or for future delivery, in the Constitution of California. . . . The decision sustaining an eight-hour law for miners is still recent. Holden v. Hardy [1898]. Some of these laws embody convictions or prejudices which judges are likely to share. Some may not. But a constitution is not intended to embody a particular economic theory, whether of paternalism and the organic relation of the citizen to the state or of laissez faire. It is made for people of fundamentally differing views, and the accident of our finding certain opinions natural and familiar, or novel, and even shocking, ought not to conclude our judgment upon the question whether statutes embodying them conflict with the Constitution of the United States.

General propositions do not decide concrete cases. The decision will depend on a judgment or intuition more subtle than any articulate major premise. But I think that the proposition just stated, if it is accepted, will carry us far toward the end. Every opinion tends to become a law. I think that the word "liberty," in the

14th Amendment, is perverted when it is held to prevent the natural outcome of a dominant opinion, unless it can be said that a rational and fair man necessarily would admit that the statute proposed would infringe fundamental principles as they have been understood by the traditions of our people and our law. It does not need research to show that no such sweeping condemnation can be passed upon the statute before us. A reasonable man might think it a proper measure on the score of health. Men whom I certainly could not pronounce unreasonable would uphold it as a first instalment of a general regulation of the hours of work. Whether in the latter aspect it would be open to the charge of inequality I think it unnecessary to discuss.

WEST COAST HOTEL CO. v. PARRISH

300 U. S. 379; 57 S. Ct. 578; 81 L. Ed. 703
(1937)

The first break in the doctrine of the Lochner case came three years later in Muller v. Oregon (1908). The case involved the validity of the Oregon ten-hour day for women, which had been challenged on the ground that it bore no reasonable relation to the public health, safety, and morals and therefore denied due process. Louis D. Brandeis, who had been invited to participate by the state of Oregon, undertook to persuade the justices that the law was a valid exercise of the state's police power. He filed with the Court the first of the famous "Brandeis briefs." It contained two pages of legal argument and over 100 pages of sociological facts and statistics showing the evil effect of long working hours upon women. The Court was obviously impressed and paid one of its rare personal tributes to counsel: "It may not be amiss, in the present case, before examining the constitutional question, to notice the course of legislation, as well as expressions of opinion from other than judicial sources. In the brief filed by Mr. Louis D. Brandeis for the defendant in error is a very copious collection of all these matters, an epitome of which is found in the margin." More important, Brandeis had succeeded in getting his information across to the Court. "The legislation and opinions referred to in the margin may not be, technically speaking, authorities, and in them is little or no discussion of the constitutional questions presented to us for determination, yet they are significant of a widespread belief that woman's physical structure, and the functions she performs in consequence thereof, justify special legislation restricting or qualifying the conditions under which she should be permitted to toil. Constitutional questions, it is true, are not settled by even a consensus of present public opinion. . . . At the same time, when a question of fact is debated and debatable, and the extent to which a special constitutional limitation goes is affected by the truth in respect to that fact, a widespread and long continued belief concerning it is worthy of consideration. We take judicial cognizance of all matters of general knowledge." The Court unanimously sustained the act.

A second break in the doctrine of the Lochner case came in 1917 in the case of Bunting v. Oregon, a case involving an Oregon statute providing a ten-hour day for all industrial workers. In a five-to-three decision the Court sustained the act and in doing so made it plain that the burden of proof had shifted to those who attacked its validity. "But we need not cast about for reasons for the legislative judgment. We are not required to be sure of the precise reasons for its exercise, or be convinced of the wisdom of its exercise. . . . It is enough for our decision if the legislation under review was passed in the exercise of an admitted power of government. . . . There is a contention made that the law . . . is not either necessary or useful 'for preservation of the health of employees. . . .' The record contains no facts to support the contention, and against it is the judgment of the legislature and the supreme court. . . ." The same day the Court divided four to four to sustain the Oregon minimum wage law in Stettler v. O'Hara (1917). Justice Brandeis took no part in the decision of either of these cases. He had been counsel in the cases in the beginning, and with his appointment to the Supreme Court his place on the briefs had been taken by Felix Frankfurter, a professor in the Harvard Law School.

While the Court decided the Bunting case without any mention of the Lochner decision, it was widely assumed that the Lochner doctrine had been permanently abandoned. But in 1922 George Sutherland and Pierce Butler were appointed to the Court, and the following year the minimum wage statute of the District of Columbia was held void as a denial of due process of law. This was the case of Adkins v. Children's Hospital (1923). The Court divided five to three. Again Justice Brandeis did not sit, this time because his daughter was a member of the minimum wage commission. The majority opinion of Justice Sutherland reads like the opinion of the Court in the Lochner case, from which it quotes at length with approval. It held that there is no connection between the wages women receive and their health, morals, or welfare that can be justified by destroying by law the freedom of contract of employers and the women who work for them. Furthermore, the Court said, the act does not guarantee that the minimum wage fixed shall not exceed the fair value of the service for which it is paid. Thus the Court returned to the old presumption of the invalidity of the statute and announced that while the materials in Professor Frankfurter's brief were useful enough to the legislature in passing the law, "they reflect no legitimate light upon the question of its validity." Chief Justice Taft and Justice Holmes wrote dissenting opinions. Justice Sanford concurred with the Chief Justice. In 1925 and in 1927 the Court without opinion ruled that the Adkins case rendered invalid the state minimum wage laws of Arizona and Arkansas respectively.

In 1933 New York passed a minimum wage law for women and children. Its framers sought to escape the ban of the Adkins decision by providing that the wages fixed should be based on the fair value of the labor paid for. The attempt failed. In Morehead v. New York ex rel. Tipaldo (1936) the Supreme Court in a five-to-four decision held the New York statute invalid. In the majority opinion Justice Butler stated that the statute was like the one held void in the Adkins case, but further said in substance that any minimum wage law, regardless of its provisions, would be invalid as a denial of due process of law. In a dissenting opinion Justice Stone observed: "It is difficult to imagine any grounds, other than our own personal economic predilections, for saying that the contract of employment is any the less an appropriate subject of legislation than are scores of others, in dealing with which this court has held that legislatures may curtail individual freedom in the public interest."

Public disenchantment with the Tipaldo decision was almost universal. Even the Republican Party repudiated it as it organized for the 1936 presidential campaign, and President Roosevelt, following his overwhelming reelection that November, immediately began laying plans for an attack on a Supreme Court he was convinced would ultimately strike down his entire New Deal program. On February 5, with his national prestige at an all-time high, he sent to Congress his ill-fated court-packing plan calling for the addition of a new justice to the Court for every justice over the age of seventy (of which there were six). While it presented no technical constitutional problems, since Congress sets the size of the Supreme Court, it aroused almost as much public antagonism as had the Tipaldo decision before it. A public which badly wanted New Deal legislation declared constitutional was clearly unprepared to sacrifice the independence of the Supreme Court to get it.

During all this time Washington's minimum wage law of 1913 had been in force and the case below attacking its validity had been argued in December, shortly after FDR's reelection. In March, with the court-packing battle in full swing, the Court handed down its decision. Two months later the judiciary committee reported the court-packing plan unfavorably and it ultimately failed to pass the Senate.

Mr. Chief Justice **Hughes** delivered the opinion of the Court, saying in part:

This case presents the question of the constitutional validity of the minimum wage law of the State of Washington. [Passed in 1913.]

. . . It provides:

"Section 1. The welfare of the State of Washington demands that women and minors be protected from conditions of labor which have a pernicious effect on their health and morals. The State of Washington, therefore, exercising herein its police and sovereign power declares that inadequate wages and unsanitary conditions of labor exert such pernicious effect.

"Sec. 2. It shall be unlawful to employ women or minors in any industry or occupation within the State of Washington under conditions of labor detrimental to their health or morals; and it shall be unlawful to employ women workers in any industry within the State of Washington at wages which are not adequate for their maintenance.

"Sec. 3. There is hereby created a commission to be known as the 'Industrial Welfare Commission' for the State of Washington, to establish such standards of wages and conditions of labor for women and minors employed within the State of Washington, as shall be held hereunder to be reasonable and not detrimental to health and morals, and which shall be sufficient for the decent maintenance of women." . . .

[Further provisions outlined the procedure to be followed by the commission in fixing minimum wages in various occupations.]

The appellant conducts a hotel. The appellee Elsie Parrish was employed as a chambermaid and (with her husband) brought this suit to recover the difference between the wages paid her and the minimum wage fixed pursuant to the state law. The minimum wage was $14.50 per week of 48 hours. The appellant challenged the act as repugnant to the due process clause of the Fourteenth Amendment of the Constitution of the United States. The Supreme Court of the State, reversing the trial court, sustained the statute and directed judgment for the plaintiffs. . . .

The appellant relies upon the decision of this Court in Adkins v. Children's Hospital [1923] which held invalid the District of Columbia Minimum Wage Act which was attacked under the due process clause of the Fifth Amendment. . . . [Here follows comment upon Morehead v. New York ex rel. Tipaldo (1936), discussed above, and a review of the judicial history of minimum wage legislation.]

The principle which must control our decision is not in doubt. The constitutional provision invoked is the due process clause of the Fourteenth Amendment governing the States, as the due process clause invoked in the Adkins Case governed Congress. In each case the violation alleged by those attacking minimum wage regulation for women is deprivation of freedom of contract. What is this freedom? The Constitution does not speak of freedom of contract. It speaks of liberty and prohibits the deprivation of liberty without due process of law. In prohibiting that deprivation the Constitution does not recognize an absolute and uncontrollable liberty. Liberty in each of its phases has its history and connotation. But the liberty safeguarded is liberty in a social organization which requires the protection of law against the evils which menace the health, safety, morals and welfare of the people. Liberty under the Constitution is thus necessarily subject to the restraints of due process, and regulation which is reasonable in relation to its subject and is adopted in the interests of the community is due process.

This essential limitation of liberty in general governs freedom of contract in particular. More than twenty-five years ago we set forth the applicable principle in these words, after referring to the cases where the liberty guaranteed by the Fourteenth Amendment had been broadly described:

"But it was recognized in the cases cited, as in many others, that freedom of contract is a qualified and not an absolute right. There is no absolute freedom to do as one wills or to contract as one chooses. The guaranty of liberty does not withdraw from legislative supervision that wide department of activity which consists of the making of contracts, or deny to government the power to provide restrictive safeguards. Liberty implies the absence of arbitrary restraint, not immunity from reasonable regulations and prohibitions imposed in the interests of the community." Chicago, B. & Q. R. Co. v. McGuire [1911].

This power under the Constitution to restrict freedom of contract has had many illustrations. That it may be exercised in the public interest with respect to contracts between employer and employee is undeniable. . . . [The Court lists here numerous cases holding valid under the Fourteenth Amendment various types of protective labor legislation.]

The point that has been strongly stressed that adult employees should be deemed competent to make their own contracts was decisively met nearly forty years ago in Holden v. Hardy [1898], where we pointed out the inequality in the footing of the parties. We said:

"The legislature has also recognized the fact, which the experience of legislators in many States has corroborated, that the proprietors of these establishments and their operatives do not stand upon an equality, and that their interests are, to a certain extent, conflicting. The former naturally desire to obtain as much labor as possible from their employees, while the latter are often induced by the fear of discharge to conform to regulations which their judgment, fairly exercised, would pronounce to be detrimental to their health or strength. In other words, the proprietors lay down the rules and the laborers are practically constrained to obey them. In such cases self-interest is often an unsafe guide, and the legislature may properly interpose its authority."

And we added that the fact "that both parties are of full age and competent to contract does not necessarily deprive the State of the power to interfere where the parties do not stand upon an equality, or where the public health demands that one party to the contract shall be protected against himself." . . .

It is manifest that this established principle is peculiarly applicable in relation to the employment of women in whose protection the State has a special interest. That phase of the subject received elaborate consideration in Muller v. Oregon (1908), where the constitutional authority of the State to limit the working hours of women was sustained. We emphasized the consideration that "woman's physical structure and the performance of maternal functions place her at a disadvantage in the struggle for subsistence" and that her physical well-being "becomes an object of public interest and care in order to preserve the strength and vigor of the race." We emphasized the need of protecting women against oppression despite her possession of contractual rights. We said that "though limitations upon personal and contractual rights may be removed by legislation, there is that in her disposition and habits of life which will operate against a full assertion of those rights. She will still be where some legislation to protect her seems necessary to secure a real equality or right." Hence she was "prop-

erly placed in a class by herself, and legislation designed for her protection may be sustained even when like legislation is not necessary for men and could not be sustained." We concluded that the limitations which the statute there in question "placed upon her contractual powers, upon her right to agree with her employer as to the time she shall labor" were "not imposed solely for her benefit, but also largely for the benefit of all." . . .

This array of precedents and the principles they applied were thought by the dissenting justices in the Adkins Case to demand that the minimum wage statute be sustained. The validity of the distinction made by the Court between a minimum wage and a maximum of hours in limiting liberty of contract was especially challenged. That challenge persists and is without any satisfactory answer. As Chief Justice Taft observed: "In absolute freedom of contract the one term is as important as the other, for both enter equally into the consideration given and received; a restriction as to one is not any greater in essence than the other, and is of the same kind. One is the multiplier and the other the multiplicand." And Mr. Justice Holmes, while recognizing that "the distinctions of the law are distinctions of degree," could "perceive no difference in the kind or degree of interference with liberty, the only matter with which we have any concern, between the one case and the other. The bargain is equally affected whichever half you regulate." . . .

The minimum wage to be paid under the Washington statute is fixed after full consideration by representatives of employers, employees and the public. It may be assumed that the minimum wage is fixed in consideration of the services that are performed in the particular occupations under normal conditions. Provision is made for special licenses at less wages in the case of women who are incapable of full service. The statement of Mr. Justice Holmes in the Adkins Case is pertinent: "This statute does not compel anybody to pay anything. It simply forbids employment at rates below those fixed as the minimum requirement of health and right living. It is safe to assume that women will not be employed at even the lowest wages allowed unless they earn them, or unless the employer's business can sustain the burden. In short the law in its character and operation is like hundreds of so-called police laws that have been upheld." And Chief Justice Taft forcibly pointed out the consideration which is basic in a statute of this character: "Legislatures which adopt a requirement of maximum hours or minimum wages may be presumed to believe that when sweating employers are prevented from paying unduly low wages by positive law they will continue their business, abating that part of their profits, which were wrung from the necessities of their employees, and will concede the better terms required by the law; and that while in individual cases hardship may result, the restriction will enure to the benefit of the general class of employees in whose interest the law is passed and so to that of the community at large."

We think that the views thus expressed are sound and that the decision in the Adkins Case was a departure from the true application of the principles governing the regulation by the State of the relation of employer and employed. . . .

With full recognition of the earnestness and vigor which characterize the prevailing opinion of the Adkins Case, we find it impossible to reconcile that ruling with these well-considered declarations. What can be closer to the public interest than the health of women and their protection from unscrupulous and overreaching employers? And if the protection of women is a legitimate end of the exercise of state power, how can it be said that the requirement of the payment of a minimum wage fairly fixed in order to meet the very necessities of the existence is not an admissible means to that end? The legislature of the State was clearly entitled to consider the situation of women in employment, the fact that they are in the class receiving the least pay, that their bargaining power is relatively weak, and that they are the ready victims of those who would take advantage of their necessitous circumstances. The legislature was entitled to adopt measures to reduce the evils of the "sweating system," the exploiting of workers at wages so low as to be insufficient to meet the bare cost of living, thus making their very helplessness the occasion of a most injurious competition. The legislature had the right to consider that its minimum wage requirements would be an important aid in carrying out its policy of protection. The adoption of similar requirements by many States evidences a deep-seated conviction both as to the presence of the evil and as to the means adapted to check it. Legislative response to that conviction cannot be regarded as arbitrary or capricious and that is all we have to decide. Even if the wisdom of the policy be regarded as debatable and its effects uncertain, still the legislature is entitled to its judgment.

There is an additional and compelling consideration which recent economic experience has brought into a strong light. The exploitation of a class of workers who are in an unequal position with respect to bargaining power and are thus relatively defenseless against the denial of a living wage is not only detrimental to their health and well being but casts a direct burden for their support upon the community. What these workers lose in wages the taxpayers are called upon to pay. The bare cost of living must be met. We may take judicial notice of the unparalleled demands for relief which arose during the recent period of depression and still continue to an alarming extent despite the degree of economic recovery which has been achieved. It is unnecessary to cite official statistics to establish what is of common knowledge through the length and breadth of the land. While in the instant case no factual brief has been presented, there is no reason to doubt that the State of Washington has encountered the same social problem that is present elsewhere. The community is not bound to provide what is in effect a subsidy for unconscionable employers. The community may direct its law-making power to correct the abuse which springs from their selfish disregard of the public interest. The argument that the legislation in question constitutes an arbitrary discrimination, because it does not extend to men, is unavailing. This Court has frequently held that the legislative authority, acting

within its proper field, is not bound to extend its regulation to all cases which it might possibly reach. The legislature "is free to recognize degrees of harm and it may confine its restrictions to those classes of cases where the need is deemed to be clearest." If "the law presumably hits the evil where it is most felt, it is not to be overthrown because there are other instances to which it might have been applied." There is no "doctrinaire requirement" that the legislation should be couched in all embracing terms. . . .

Our conclusion is that the case of Adkin's v. Children's Hospital should be, and it is, overruled. The judgment of the Supreme Court of the State of Washington is affirmed.

Mr. Justice **Sutherland** dissented in an opinion in which Justices **Van Devanter, McReynolds,** and **Butler** concurred.

CRIMINAL PROCEDURE AND THE BILL OF RIGHTS

HURTADO v. CALIFORNIA

110 U. S. 516; 4 S. Ct. 111; 28 L. Ed. 232 (1884)

While the due process clauses of the Fifth and Fourteenth Amendments came to be restrictions by which the validity of the substance of legislation was tested in the courts, it should not be forgotten that originally due process was construed only as a limitation on governmental procedure. Whatever the government did, it had to do in accordance with the "process" which was "due" under the law of the land. But what, concretely, did such process include? To nonprofessionals, thinking in terms of criminal procedure, it undoubtedly included the common-law procedures with which they were familiar— procedures spelled out in detail in the Bill of Rights. The Supreme Court, however, rejected the idea that due process required adherence to a fixed list of prescribed procedures, and in Davidson v. New Orleans (1878) it explained that the meaning of the clause would be determined "by the gradual process of judicial inclusion and exclusion, as the cases presented for decision shall require, with the reasoning on which such decisions may be founded."

The Court had already decided, in the case of Murray's Lessee v. Hoboken Land and Improvement Co. (1856), that "due" process did not always mean "judicial" process; and an administrative agency could employ procedures which had the sanction of long-established custom. In this case an administrative warrant authorizing the seizure of a man's property to satisfy a debt to the government was found to be a well-established procedure and hence due process of law.

But if old established procedures were due process of law, then surely those common-law procedures listed in the Bill of Rights were due process of law. And if this were the case, why were they not guaranteed by the Fourteenth Amendment in state criminal cases? This was the argument of Hurtado in the present case. He had been convicted of murder by the state of California and sentenced to be hanged. He claimed a denial of due process because instead of a grand jury indictment, to which he would have been entitled under the common law, he had been charged by an information prepared by the prosecuting attorney—a form of charge authorized by the state of California, but limited at common law to misdemeanors.

Mr. Justice **Matthews** delivered the opinion of the Court, saying in part:

. . . The proposition of law we are asked to affirm is, that an indictment or presentment by a grand jury, as known to the common law of England, is essential to that "due process of law," when applied to prosecutions for felonies, which is secured and guaranteed by this provision of the Constitution of the United States, and which accordingly it is forbidden to the States respectively to dispense with in the administration of criminal law.

. . . It is maintained on behalf of the plaintiff in error that the phrase "due process of law" is equivalent to "law of the land," as found in the [thirty-]ninth chapter of Magna Charta; that, by immemorial usage, it has acquired a fixed, definite and technical meaning; that it refers to and includes, not only the general principles of public liberty and private right, which lie at the foundation of all free government, but the very institutions which, venerable by time and custom, have been tried by experience and found fit and necessary for the preservation of those principles, and which, having been the birthright and inheritance of every English subject, crossed the Atlantic with the colonists and were transplanted and established in the fundamental laws of the State; that, having been originally introduced into the Constitution of the United States as a limitation upon the powers of the government, brought into being by that instrument, it has now been added as an additional security to the individual against oppression by the States themselves; that one of these institutions is that of the grand jury, an indictment or presentment by which against the accused in cases of alleged felonies is an essential part of due process of law, in order that he may not be harassed or destroyed by prosecutions founded only upon private malice or popular fury. . . .

It is urged upon us, however, in argument, that the claim made in behalf of the plaintiff in error is supported by the decision of this court in Murray's Lessee v. Hoboken Land & Improvement Company [1856]. There, Mr. Justice Curtis delivering the opinion of the court, after showing that due process of law must mean something more than the actual existing law of the land, for otherwise it would be no restraint upon legislative power, proceeds as follows: "To what principle, then, are we to resort to ascertain whether this process, enacted by Congress, is due process? To this the answer must be twofold. We must examine the Constitution itself to see whether this process be in conflict with any of its provisions. If not found to be so, we must look to those settled usages and modes of proceeding existing in the common and statute law of England before the emigration of our ancestors, and which are shown not to have been unsuited to their civil and political condition by having been acted on by them after the settlement of this country."

This, it is argued, furnishes an indispensable test of what constitutes "due process of law"; that any proceeding otherwise authorized by law, which is not thus sanctioned by usage, or which supersedes and displaces one that is, cannot be regarded as due process of law.

But this inference is unwarranted. The real syllabus of the passage quoted is, that a process of law, which is not otherwise forbidden, must be taken to be due process of law, if it can show the sanction of settled usage both in England and in this country; but it by no means follows, that nothing else can be due process of law. The point in the case cited arose in reference to a summary proceeding, questioned on that account, as not due process of law. The answer was: however exceptional it may be, as tested by definitions and principles of ordinary procedure, nevertheless, this, in substance, has been immemorially the actual law of the land, and, therefore, is due process of law. But to hold that such a characteristic is essential to due process of law, would be to deny every quality of the law but its age, and to render it incapable of progress or improvement. It would be to stamp upon our jurisprudence the unchangeableness attributed to the laws of the Medes and Persians.

This would be all the more singular and surprising, in this quick and active age, when we consider that, owing to the progressive development of legal ideas and institutions in England, the words of Magna Charta stood for very different things at the time of the separation of the American Colonies from what they represented originally. . . .

The Constitution of the United States was ordained, it is true, by descendants of Englishmen, who inherited the traditions of English law and history; but it was made for an undefined and expanding future, and for a people gathered and to be gathered from many Nations and of many tongues. And while we take just pride in the principles and institutions of the common law, we are not to forget that in lands where other systems of jurisprudence prevail, the ideas and processes of civil justice are also not unknown. Due process of law, in spite of the absolutism of continental governments, is not alien to that Code which survived the Roman Empire as the foundation of modern civilization in Europe, and which has given us that fundamental maxim of distributive justice, *suum cuique tribuere.* There is nothing in Magna Charta, rightly construed as a broad charter of public right and law, which ought to exclude the best ideas of all systems and of every age; and as it was the characteristic principle of the common law to draw its inspiration from every fountain of justice, we are not to assume that the sources of its supply have been exhausted. On the contrary, we should expect that the new and various experiences of our own situation and system will mold and shape it into new and not less useful forms. . . .

We are to construe this phrase in the 14th Amendment by the *usus loquendi* of the Constitution itself. The same words are contained in the 5th Amendment. That article makes specific and express provision for perpetuating the institution of the grand jury, so far as relates to prosecutions, for the more aggravated crimes under the laws of the United States. It declares that "No person shall be held to answer for a capital or otherwise infamous crime, unless on a presentment or indictment of a grand jury, except in cases arising in the land or naval forces, or in the militia when in actual service in time of war or public danger; nor shall any person be subject for the same offense to be twice put in jeopardy of life or limb; nor shall he be compelled in any criminal case to be a witness against himself." It then immediately adds: "nor be deprived of life, liberty or property, without due process of law." According to a recognized canon interpretation, especially applicable to formal and solemn instruments of constitutional law, we are forbidden to assume, without clear reason to the contrary, that any part of this most important Amendment is superfluous. The natural and obvious inference is, that in the sense of the Constitution, "due process of law" was not meant or intended to include, *ex vi termini*, the institution and procedure of a grand jury in any case. The conclusion is equally irresistible, that when the same phrase was employed in the 14th Amendment to restrain the action of the States, it was used in the same sense and with no greater extent; and that if in the adoption of that Amendment it had been part of its purpose to perpetuate the institution of the grand jury in all the States, it would have embodied, as did the 5th Amendment, express declarations to that effect. Due process of law in the latter refers to that law of the land, which derives its authority from the legislative powers conferred upon Congress by the Constitution of the United States, exercised within the limits therein prescribed, and interpreted according to the principles of the common law. In the 14th Amendment, by parity of reason, it refers to that law of the land in each State, which derives its authority from the inherent and reserved powers of the State, exerted within the limits of those fundamental principles of liberty and justice which lie at the base of all our civil and political institutions, and the greatest security for which resides in the right of the people to make their own laws, and alter them at their pleasure. "The 14th Amendment," as was said by Mr. Justice Bradley in Mo. v. Lewis [1880], "does not profess to secure to all persons in the United States the benefit of the same laws and the same remedies. Great diversities in these respects may exist in two States separated only by an imaginary line. On one side of this line there may be a right of trial by jury, and on the other side no such right. Each State prescribes its own modes of judicial proceeding."

But it is not to be supposed that these legislative powers are absolute and despotic, and that the Amendment prescribing due process of law is too vague and indefinite to operate as a practical restraint. It is not every Act, legislative in form, that is law. Law is something more than mere will exerted as an act of power. . . . Arbitrary power, enforcing its edicts to the injury of the persons and property of its subjects, is not law, whether manifested as the decree of a personal monarch or of an impersonal multitude. And the limitations imposed by our constitutional law upon the action of the governments, both state and national, are essential to the preservation of public and private rights, notwithstanding the representative character of our political institutions. . . .

It follows that any legal proceeding enforced by public authority, whether sanctioned by age and custom, or newly devised in the discretion of the legislative power, in furtherance of the general public good, which regards and preserves these principles of liberty and justice, must be held to be due process of law. . . .

Tried by these principles, we are unable to say that the substitution for a presentment or indictment by a grand jury of the proceeding by information, after examination and commitment by a magistrate, certifying to the probable guilt of the defendant, with the right on his part to the aid of counsel, and to the cross-examination of the witnesses produced for the prosecution, is not due process of law. It is, as we have seen, an ancient proceeding at common law, which might include every case of an offense of less grade than a felony, except misprision of treason; and in every circumstance of its administration, as authorized by the Statute of California, it carefully considers and guards the substantial interest of the prisoner. It is merely a preliminary proceeding, and can result in no final judgment, except as the consequence of a regular judicial trial, conducted precisely as in cases of indictments. . . .

For these reasons, finding no error therein, the judgment of the Supreme Court of California is affirmed.

Mr. Justice **Harlan,** dissenting, said in part:

. . . I cannot agree that the State may, consistently with due process of law, require a person to answer for a capital offense, except upon the presentment or indictment of a grand jury. . . .

. . . To what principles are we to resort to ascertain whether this process . . . is due process? To this the answer must be twofold. We must examine the Constitution itself to see whether this process be in conflict with any of its provisions. If not found to be so, we must look *"to those settled usages and modes of proceeding existing in the common and statute law of England before the emigration of our ancestors, and which are shown not to have been unsuited to their civil and political condition by having been acted on by them after the settlement of this country."* . . .

. . . Let us inquire (and no other inquiry is at all pertinent) whether according to the settled usages and modes of proceeding to which, this court has said, reference must be had, an information for a capital offense was, prior to the adoption of our Constitution, regarded as due process of law. . . . [Justice Harlan here reviews the authorities and finds it was not.]

My brethren concede that there are principles of liberty and justice, lying at the foundation of our civil and political institutions, which no State can violate consistently with that due process of law required by the 14th Amendment in proceedings involving life, liberty or property. Some of these principles are enumerated in the opinion of the court. But, for reasons which do not impress my mind as satisfactory, they exclude from that enumeration the exemption from prosecution, by information, for a public offense involving life. By what authority is that exclusion made? Is it justified by the settled usages and modes of procedure, existing under the common and statute law of England at the emigration of our ancestors or at the foundation of our government? Does not the fact that the people of the original States required an amendment of the National Constitution, securing exemption from prosecution, for a capital offense, except upon the indictment or presentment of a grand jury, prove that, in their judgment, such an exemption was essential to protection against accusation and unfounded prosecution and, therefore, was a fundamental principle in liberty and justice? . . .

But it is said that the framers of the Constitution did not suppose that due process of law necessarily required for a capital offense the institution and procedure of a grand jury, else they would not in the same amendment prohibiting the deprivation of life, liberty or property without due process of law, have made specific and express provision for a grand jury where the crime is capital or otherwise infamous; therefore, it is argued, the requirement by the 14th Amendment, of due process of law in all proceedings involving life, liberty and property, without specific reference to grand juries in any case whatever, was not intended as a restriction upon the power which it is claimed that the States previously had, so far as the express restrictions of the National Constitution are concerned, to dispense altogether with grand juries.

The line of argument, it seems to me, would lead to results which are inconsistent with the vital principles of republican government. If the presence in the 5th Amendment of a specific provision for grand juries in capital cases, alongside the provision for due process of law in proceedings involving life, liberty or property, is held to prove that due process of law did not, in the judgment of the framers of the Constitution, necessarily require a grand jury in capital cases, inexorable logic would require it to be, likewise, held that the right not to be put twice in jeopardy of life and limb for the same offense, nor compelled in a criminal case to testify against one's self (rights and immunities also specifically recognized in the 5th Amendment) were not protected by that due process of law required by the settled usages and proceedings existing under the common and statute law of England at the settlement of this country. More than that, other Amendments of the Constitution proposed at the same time, expressly recognize the right of persons to just compensation for private property taken for public use; their right, when accused of crime, to be informed of the nature and cause of the accusation against them, and to a speedy and public trial, by an impartial jury of the State and district wherein the crime was committed; to be confronted by the witnesses against them; and to have compulsory process for obtaining witnesses in their

favor. Will it be claimed that these rights were not secured by the "law of the land" or by "due process of law," as declared and established at the foundation of our government? Are they to be excluded from the enumeration of the fundamental principles of liberty and justice and, therefore, not embraced by "due process of law?" . . .

It seems to me that too much stress is put upon the fact that the framers of the Constitution made express provision for the security of those rights which at common law were protected by the requirement of due process of law and, in addition, declared, generally, that no person shall "be deprived of life, liberty or property without due process of law." The rights, for the security of which these express provisions were made, were of a character so essential to the safety of the people that it was deemed wise to avoid the possibility that Congress, in regulating the processes of law, would impair or destroy them. Hence their specific enumeration in the earlier Amendments of the Constitution. . . .

POWELL v. ALABAMA

287 U. S. 45; 53 S. Ct. 55; 77 L. Ed. 158 (1932)

The Court in the Hurtado case (1884) not only rejected the idea that the protections listed in the Bill of Rights are included in due process, but the reasoning on which the decision was based made logically impossible their inclusion in the future. In 1897, however, following the advent of the concept of substantive due process in Munn v. Illinois (1877), the Court held that due process forbade a state to seize private property without just compensation; see Chicago, B. & Q. R. Co. v. Chicago. Justice Harlan, who had dissented in Hurtado, wrote the opinion of the Court without alluding to that case or calling attention to the fact that the right was one listed in the Bill of Rights. He held, simply, that the right to compensation was a right "founded in natural equity" and "laid down as a principle of universal law. Indeed, in a free government almost all other rights would become worthless if the government possessed an uncontrollable power over the private fortune of every citizen." He emphasized that "in determining what is due process of law regard must be had to substance, not to form," and pointed out that while "the legislature may prescribe a form of procedure to be observed in the taking of private property for public use, . . . it is not due process of law if provision be not made for compensation."

The C. B. & Q. decision had not overruled Hurtado, but since the two cases were in some ways incompatible, it seemed plausible to suppose that some of the Bill of Rights guarantees for persons accused of crime might also be found essential to due process. In Twining v. New Jersey (1908), however, the Court rejected the notion. The right to just compensation, it noted, was part of due process because of its fundamental nature, not because it was listed in the Bill of Rights. Not only was the guarantee against self-incrimination not of this funda-

mental nature, as Twining claimed, but added that the Court had never held void any state criminal procedure for want of due process of law. "Salutary as the principle [self-incrimination] may seem to the great majority, it cannot be ranked with the right to hearing before condemnation, the immunity from arbitrary power not acting by general laws, and the inviolability of private property." Clearly, the rights protected by due process were property rights—not rights involving criminal procedure. It was not until 1964, in Malloy v. Hogan, that the Court overruled Twining and held the protection against self-incrimination essential to due process.

With the rise of the doctrine of substantive due process it was increasingly urged on the Court that the "liberty" protected by the due process clause of the Fourteenth Amendment should include, at the very least, the freedom of speech and press mentioned in the First Amendment. The pressure was not only from members of the bar, but from the Court itself. In 1907 Justice Harlan, in a dissenting opinion in Patterson v. Colorado, declared, "I go further and hold that the privileges of free speech and a free press, belonging to every citizen of the United States, constitute essential parts of every man's liberty, and are protected against violation by that clause of the Fourteenth Amendment forbidding a state to deprive any person of his liberty without due process of law." Essentially the same view was expressed by Justice Brandeis in his dissenting opinion in Gilbert v. Minnesota (1920), a case in which the Court assumed for the sake of argument that freedom of speech was "a natural and inherent" right but held that it had not been violated. Although in Prudential Insurance Co. v. Cheek (1922) the Court insisted that "neither the Fourteenth Amendment nor any other provision of the Constitution of the United States imposes upon the states any restrictions about 'freedom of speech,' " the following year it began to show signs of conversion to a broader conception of the term "liberty." In Meyer v. Nebraska (1923) Justice McReynolds, in an opinion holding invalid a Nebraska statute forbidding the teaching of any subject in any language but English in any private, parochial, or public school, defined the "liberty" protected by the due process clause as follows: "Without doubt, it denotes not merely freedom from bodily restraint, but also the right of the individual to contract, to engage in any of the common occupations of life, to acquire useful knowledge, to marry, establish a home and bring up children, to worship God according to the dictates of his own conscience, and, generally, to enjoy those privileges long recognized at common law as essential to the orderly pursuit of happiness by free men."

Two years later, in what was in fact a constitutional revolution, the Court, in Gitlow v. New York (1925), reversed its stand. Gitlow had challenged a state statute as violating his freedom of speech and thereby denying him due process; the Supreme Court took jurisdiction under the due process clause, declaring that "For present purposes we may and do assume that freedom of speech and of the press—which are protected by the First Amendment from abridgment by Congress—are among the fundamental personal rights and 'liberties'

protected by the due process clause of the Fourteenth Amendment from impairment by the states." In Gitlow's case the Court held the state statute valid and upheld Gitlow's conviction; but in 1931, in Near v. Minnesota, the Court held a state statute void on the ground that it denied due process by unreasonably restricting freedom of speech and press. With these two cases these important liberties became effectively "nationalized," and the states came under federal judicial scrutiny and discipline in dealing with freedom of speech and press.

The other liberties mentioned in the First Amendment followed in due course. In Hamilton v. Board of Regents of the University of California (1934) freedom of religion was held to be protected by the Fourteenth Amendment, although the Court held that Hamilton's religious liberty was not abridged by making him take military drill as a condition of attending the state university. In De Jonge v. Oregon (1937) freedom of assembly was added to the list. The assimilation of the First Amendment into the Fourteenth was completed in Everson v. Board of Education (1947). The preceding cases were decided on the theory that the due process clause protects "liberty" and that "liberty" includes freedom of speech, press, religion, and assembly. The Everson case, however, which involved state aid to parochial school pupils, raised no question of "freedom" of religion but the question of whether the state action amounted to an "establishment" of religion. It could be argued that a state-supported religion does not abridge freedom of religion and hence is not an abridgment of "liberty" protected by due process of law, but the Supreme Court in the Everson case did not argue the point; it simply declared that "the First Amendment, as made applicable to the states by the Fourteenth . . . commands that a state 'shall make no law respecting an establishment of religion. . . .' "

With the incorporation of First Amendment rights into the due process clause of the Fourteenth, pressure was brought on the Court to reconsider its stand in Hurtado (1884) and Twining (1908) to find other rights in the Bill of Rights to be "essential to due process" and hence applicable to the states. The present case, one of the famous Scottsboro Cases, raises the question of whether the right to counsel, guaranteed against federal infringement by the Sixth Amendment, is applicable to the states through the Fourteenth.

Mr. Justice **Sutherland** delivered the opinion of the Court, saying in part:

The petitioners, hereinafter referred to as defendants, are negroes charged with the crime of rape, committed upon the persons of two white girls. The crime is said to have been committed on March 25, 1931. The indictment was returned in a state court of first instance on March 31, and the record recites that on the same day the defendants were arraigned and entered pleas of not guilty. There is a further recital to the effect that upon the arraignment they were represented by counsel. But no counsel had been employed, and aside from a statement made by the trial judge several days later during a colloquy immediately preceding the trial, the record does not disclose when, or under what circumstances, an appointment of counsel was made, or who was appointed. During the colloquy referred to, the trial judge, in response to a question, said that he had appointed all the members of the bar for the purpose of arraigning the defendants and then of course anticipated that the members of the bar would continue to help the defendants if no counsel appeared. Upon the argument here both sides accepted that as a correct statement of the facts concerning the matter.

There was a severance upon the request of the state, and the defendants were tried in three several groups, as indicated above. As each of the three cases was called for trial, each defendant was arraigned, and, having the indictment read to him, entered a plea of not guilty. Whether the original arraignment and pleas were regarded as ineffective is not shown. Each of the three trials was completed within a single day. Under the Alabama statute the punishment for rape is to be fixed by jury, and in its discretion may be from ten years' imprisonment to death. The juries found defendants guilty and imposed the death penalty upon all. The trial court overruled motions for new trials and sentenced the defendants in accordance with the verdicts. The judgments were affirmed by the state supreme court. Chief Justice Anderson thought the defendants had not been accorded a fair trial and strongly dissented.

In this court the judgments are assailed upon the grounds that the defendants, and each of them, were denied due process of law and the equal protection of the laws, in contravention of the Fourteenth Amendment, specifically as follows: (1) They were not given a fair, impartial and deliberate trial; (2) they were denied the right of counsel, with the accustomed incidents of consultation and opportunity of preparation for trial; and (3) they were tried before juries from which qualified members of their own race were systematically excluded. These questions were properly raised and saved in the courts below.

The only one of the assignments which we shall consider is the second, in respect of the denial of counsel; and it becomes unnecessary to discuss the facts of the case or the circumstances surrounding the prosecution except in so far as they reflect light upon that question.

The record shows that on the day when the offense is said to have been committed, these defendants, together with a number of other negroes, were upon a freight train on its way through Alabama. On the same train were seven white boys and two white girls. A fight took place between the negroes and the white boys, in the course of which the white boys, with the exception of one named Gilley, were thrown off the train. A message was sent ahead, reporting the fight and asking that every negro be gotten off the train. The participants in the fight, and the two girls, were in an open gondola car. The two girls testified that each of them was assaulted by six different negroes in turn, and they identified the seven defendants as having been among the number.

None of the white boys was called to testify, with the exception of Gilley, who was called in rebuttal.

Before the train reached Scottsboro, Alabama, a sheriff's posse seized the defendants and two other negroes. Both girls and the negroes then were taken to Scottsboro, the county seat. Word of their coming and of the alleged assault had preceded them, and they were met at Scottsboro by a large crowd. It does not sufficiently appear that the defendants were seriously threatened with, or that they were actually in danger of, mob violence; but it does appear that the attitude of the community was one of great hostility. The sheriff thought it necessary to call for the militia to assist in safeguarding the prisoners. Chief Justice Anderson pointed out in his opinion that every step taken from the arrest and arraignment to the sentence was accompanied by the military. Soldiers took the defendants to Gadsden for safekeeping, brought them back to Scottsboro for arraignment, returned them to Gadsden for safekeeping while awaiting trial, escorted them to Scottsboro for trial a few days later, and guarded the courthouse and grounds at every stage of the proceedings. It is perfectly apparent that the proceedings, from beginning to end, took place in an atmosphere of tense, hostile and excited public sentiment. During the entire time, the defendants were closely confined or were under military guard. The record does not disclose their ages, except that one of them was nineteen; but the record clearly indicates that most, if not all, of them were youthful, and they are constantly referred to as "the boys." They were ignorant and illiterate. All of them were residents of other states, where alone members of their families or friends resided.

However guilty defendants, upon due inquiry might prove to have been, they were, until convicted, presumed to be innocent. It was the duty of the court having their cases in charge to see that they were denied no necessary incident of a fair trial. With any error of the state court involving alleged contravention of the state statutes or constitution we, of course, have nothing to do. The sole inquiry which we are permitted to make is whether the federal Constitution was contravened . . . and as to that, we confine ourselves, as already suggested, to the inquiry whether the defendants were in substance denied the right of counsel, and if so, whether such denial infringes the due process clause of the Fourteenth Amendment.

First. The record shows that immediately upon the return of the indictment defendants were arraigned and pleaded not guilty. Apparently they were not asked whether they had, or were able to employ counsel, or wished to have counsel appointed; or whether they had friends or relatives who might assist in that regard if communicated with. That it would not have been an idle ceremony to have given the defendants reasonable opportunity to communicate with their families and endeavor to obtain counsel is demonstrated by the fact that very soon after conviction able counsel appeared in their behalf. . . .

It is hardly necessary to say that the right to counsel being conceded, a defendant should be afforded a fair opportunity to secure counsel of his own choice. Not only was that not done here, but such designation of counsel as was attempted was either so indefinite or so close upon the trial as to amount to a denial of effective and substantial aid in that regard. This will be amply demonstrated by a brief review of the record.

April 6, six days after indictment, the trials began. When the first case was called, the court inquired whether the parties were ready for trial. The state's attorney replied that he was ready to proceed. No one answered for the defendants or appeared to represent or defend them. Mr. Roddy, a Tennessee lawyer not a member of the local bar, addressed the court, saying that he had not been employed, but that people who were interested had spoken to him about the case. He was asked by the court whether he intended to appear for the defendants, and answered that he would like to appear along with counsel that the court might appoint. . . .

It thus will be seen that until the very morning of the trial no lawyer had been named or definitely designated to represent the defendants. Prior to that time, the trial judge had "appointed all the members of the bar" for the limited "purpose of arraigning the defendants." Whether they would represent the defendants thereafter if no counsel appeared in their behalf, was a matter of speculation only, or, as the judge indicated, of mere anticipation on the part of the court. Such a designation, even if made for all purposes, would, in our opinion, have fallen far short of meeting, in any proper sense, a requirement for the appointment of counsel. How many lawyers were members of the bar does not appear; but, in the very nature of things, whether many or few, they would not, thus collectively named, have been given that clear appreciation of responsibility or impressed with that individual sense of duty which should and naturally would accompany the appointment of a selected member of the bar, specifically named and assigned. . . .

. . . In any event, the circumstance lends emphasis to the conclusion that during perhaps the most critical period of the proceedings against these defendants, that is to say, from the time of their arraignment until the beginning of their trial, when consultation, thorough-going investigation and preparation were vitally important, the defendants did not have the aid of counsel in any real sense, although they were as much entitled to such aid during that period as at the trial itself. . . .

Second. The Constitution of Alabama provides that in all criminal prosecutions the accused shall enjoy the right to have the assistance of counsel; and a state statute requires the court in a capital case, where the defendant is unable to employ counsel, to appoint counsel for him. The state supreme court held that these provisions had not been infringed, and with that holding we are powerless to interfere. The question, however, which it is our duty, and within our power, to decide, is whether the denial of the assistance of counsel contravenes the due process clause of the Fourteenth Amendment to the federal Constitution. . . .

One test which has been applied to determine whether due process of law has been accorded in given instances is to ascertain what were the settled usages and modes of proceeding under the common and statute law of England before the Declaration of Independence, subject, however, to the qualification that they be shown not to have been unsuited to the civil and political conditions of our ancestors by having been followed in this country after it became a nation. . . . Plainly, as appears from the foregoing, this test, as thus qualified, has not been met in the present case.

We do not overlook the case of Hurtado v. California [1884], where this court determined that due process of law does not require an indictment by a grand jury as a prerequisite to prosecution by a state for murder. In support of that conclusion the court referred to the fact that the Fifth Amendment, in addition to containing the due process of law clause, provides in explicit terms that "No person shall be held to answer for a capital, or otherwise infamous crime, unless on a presentment or indictment of a grand jury," and said that since no part of this important amendment could be regarded as superfluous, the obvious inference is that in the sense of the Constitution due process of law was not intended to include, ex vi termini, the institution and procedure of a grand jury in any case; and that the same phrase, employed in the Fourteenth Amendment to restrain the action of the states, was to be interpreted as having been used in the same sense and with no greater extent; and that if it had been the purpose of that Amendment to perpetuate the institution of the grand jury in the states, it would have embodied, as did the Fifth Amendment, an express declaration to that effect.

The Sixth Amendment, in terms, provides that in all criminal prosecutions the accused shall enjoy the right "to have the assistance of counsel for his defense." In the face of the reasoning of the Hurtado Case, if it stood alone, it would be difficult to justify the conclusion that the right to counsel, being thus specifically granted by the Sixth Amendment, was also within the intendment of the due process of law clause. But the Hurtado Case does not stand alone. In the later case of Chicago, B. & Q. R. Co. v. Chicago [1897], this court held that a judgment of a state court, even though authorized by statute, by which private property was taken for public use without just compensation, was in violation of the due process of law required by the Fourteenth Amendment, notwithstanding that the Fifth Amendment explicitly declares that private property shall not be taken for public use without just compensation. . . .

Likewise, this court has considered that freedom of speech and of the press are rights protected by the due process clause of the Fourteenth Amendment, although in the First Amendment, Congress is prohibited in specific terms from abridging the right. Gitlow v. New York [1925]. . . .

These later cases establish that notwithstanding the sweeping character of the language in the Hurtado Case, the rule laid down is not without exceptions. The rule is an aid to construction, and in some instances may be conclusive; but it must yield to more compelling considerations whenever such considerations exist. The fact that the right involved is of such a character that it cannot be denied without violating those "fundamental principles of liberty and justice which lie at the base of all our civil and political institutions" (Hebert v. Louisiana [1926]), is obviously one of those compelling considerations which must prevail in determining whether it is embraced within the due process clause of the Fourteenth Amendment, although it be specifically dealt with in another part of the federal Constitution. Evidently this court, in the later cases enumerated, regarded the rights there under consideration as of this fundamental character. That some such distinction must be observed is foreshadowed in Twining v. New Jersey [1908], where Mr. Justice Moody, speaking for the court, said that ". . . it is possible that some of the personal rights safeguarded by the first eight Amendments against national action may also be safeguarded against state action, because a denial of them would be a denial of due process of law. Chicago, B. & Q. R. Co. v. Chicago [1897]. If this is so, it is not because those rights are enumerated in the first eight Amendments, but because they are of such a nature that they are included in the conception of due process of law." While the question has never been categorically determined by this court, a consideration of the nature of the right and a review of the expressions of this and other courts, make it clear that the right to the aid of counsel is of this fundamental character.

It never has been doubted by this court, or any other so far as we know, that notice and hearing are preliminary steps essential to the passing of an enforceable judgment, and that they, together with a legally competent tribunal having jurisdiction of the case, constitute basic elements of the constitutional requirement of due process of law. . . .

What, then, does a hearing include? Historically and in practice, in our own country at least, it has always included the right to the aid of counsel when desired and provided by the party asserting the right. The right to be heard would be, in many cases, of little avail if it did not comprehend the right to be heard by counsel. Even the intelligent and educated layman has small and sometimes no skill in the science of law. If charged with crime, he is incapable, generally, of determining for himself whether the indictment is good or bad. He is unfamiliar with the rules of evidence. Left without the aid of counsel he may be put on trial without a proper charge, and convicted upon incompetent evidence, or evidence irrelevant to the issue or otherwise inadmissible. He lacks both the skill and knowledge adequately to prepare his defense, even though he have a perfect one. He requires the guiding hand of counsel at every step in the proceedings against him. Without it, though he be not guilty, he faces the danger of conviction because he does not know how to establish his innocence. If that be true of men of intelligence, how much more true is it of the ignorant and illiterate, or those of feeble intellect. If in any case, civil or criminal, a state or federal court were arbitrarily to refuse to hear a party by counsel, employed by and appearing for him, it reasonably may not be doubted that such a refusal would be a denial of a hearing, and, therefore, of due process in the constitutional sense.

The decisions all point to that conclusion. . . . In Ex parte Chin Loy You (D. C.) 223 Fed. 833 [1915], also a deportation case, the district judge held that under the particular circumstances of the case the prisoner, having reasonably made demand, was entitled to confer with and have the aid of counsel. Pointing to the fact that the right to counsel as secured by the Sixth Amendment relates only to criminal prosecutions, the judge said, "But it is equally true that the provision was inserted in the Constitution because the assistance of counsel was recognized as essential to any fair trial of a case against a prisoner." . . .

In the light of the facts outlined in the forepart of this opinion—the ignorance and illiteracy of the defendants, their youth, the circumstances of public hostility, the imprisonment and the close surveillance of the defendants by the military forces, the fact that their friends and families were all in other states and communication with them necessarily difficult, and above all that they stood in deadly peril of their lives—we think the failure of the trial court to give them reasonable time and opportunity to secure counsel was a clear denial of due process.

But passing that, and assuming their inability, even if opportunity had been given, to employ counsel, as the trial court evidently did assume, we are of opinion that, under the circumstances just stated, the necessity of counsel was so vital and imperative that the failure of the trial court to make an effective appointment of counsel was likewise a denial of due process within the meaning of the Fourteenth Amendment. Whether this would be so in other criminal prosecutions, or under other circumstances, we need not determine. All that it is necessary now to decide, as we do decide, is that in a capital case, where the defendant is unable to employ counsel, and is incapable adequately of making his own defense because of ignorance, feeblemindedness, illiteracy, or the like, it is the duty of the court, whether requested or not, to assign counsel for him as a necessary requisite of due process of law; and that duty is not discharged by an assignment at such a time or under such circumstances as to preclude the giving of effective aid in the preparation and trial of the case. To hold otherwise would be to ignore the fundamental postulate, already adverted to, "that there are certain immutable principles of justice which inhere in the very idea of free government which no member of the Union may disregard." . . . In a case such as this, whatever may be the rule in other cases, the right to have counsel appointed, when necessary, is a logical corollary from the constitutional right to be heard by counsel. . . .

The United States by statute and every state in the Union by express provision of law, or by the determination of its courts, make it the duty of the trial judge, where the accused is unable to employ counsel, to appoint counsel for him. In most states the rule applies broadly to all criminal prosecutions, in others it is limited to the more serious crimes, and in a very limited number, to capital cases. A rule adopted with such unanimous accord reflects, if it does not establish, the inherent right to have counsel appointed at least in cases like the present, and lends convincing support to the conclusion we have reached as to the fundamental nature of that right.

The judgments must be reversed and the causes remanded for further proceedings not inconsistent with this opinion.

Judgments reversed.

Mr. Justice **Butler** wrote a dissenting opinion in which Mr. Justice **McReynolds** concurred.

PALKO v. CONNECTICUT

302 U. S. 319; 58 S. Ct. 149; 82 L. Ed. 288
(1937)

With the decision in Powell v. Alabama (1932) it appeared that the long struggle to nationalize the Bill of Rights might at last be bearing fruit. The Court had acknowledged that it no longer felt bound by the Hurtado reasoning; the application to the states of the Fifth Amendment right to just compensation and the First Amendment rights of free speech, press, religion, and assembly showed that some of the Bill of Rights guarantees could be applied to the states through due process of law. And now, in Powell, the Court for the first time had found one of the rights of persons accused of crime to be essential to due process.

The Palko case, printed below, made clear that the Court was not prepared to abandon earlier decisions such as Hurtado and Twining. Instead, it undertook to explain why some rights, such as the rights to counsel and free speech, are absorbed into due process; and why others, like jury trial and grand jury indictment, are not. It should be emphasized that the cases "absorbing" rights into the Fourteenth Amendment do not overrule Barron v. Baltimore (1833). The provisions of the federal Bill of Rights still limit directly only the federal government; it is the Fourteenth Amendment which limits the states. What the Court has done is to reverse the practical effect of the rule in Barron v. Baltimore with respect to part, but not all, of the Bill of Rights. Some of these rights are still not considered by the Court to be so fundamental as to be required by due process of law. The Court in case after case has been classifying the provisions of the Bill of Rights into those which are essential to due process of law and thus bind the states through the operation of the Fourteenth Amendment, and those which are not essential to due process and by which the states are not bound. In effect, the Court has established an "honor roll" of superior rights which bind both state and national governments. The opinion in the present case is important since it gives an official summary of this classification up to 1937 and states clearly the principles upon which the classification rests.

One question which the Palko case failed to answer satisfactorily was what was meant by "absorption" or "incorporation" of a Bill of Rights guarantee into due process. Did it mean that the right, as listed in the Bill of Rights and interpreted by the Supreme Court in federal cases, was made applicable to the states? Or was the right as applied to the states a more general right, less clearly defined and permitting more leeway and discretion on the part of the states? Clearly, incorporation of the First Amendment has meant its application to the states exactly as it is applied to the national government. Justices Brandeis and Holmes, in their dissent in the Gitlow case, suggested that the free speech applicable to the states perhaps "may be accepted with a somewhat larger latitude of interpretation than is allowed to Congress by the sweeping language that governs or ought to govern the laws of the United States." The Court, however, with the exception of whether jury verdicts must be unanimous (see Apodaca v. Oregon, 1972), has never acknowledged such a distinction, and the same rules for deciding such cases are applied to the states and the nation alike.

With the gradual extension of due process to include other rights, an important controversy developed as to how these rights would apply to the states. This problem is discussed in connection with the specific rights in the chapter below.

Mr. Justice **Cardozo** delivered the opinion of the Court, saying in part:

. . . Appellant was indicted . . . for the crime of murder in the first degree. A jury found him guilty of murder in the second degree, and he was sentenced to confinement in the state prison for life. Thereafter the state of Connecticut, with the permission of the judge presiding at the trial, gave notice of appeal to the Supreme Court of Errors. This it did pursuant to an act adopted in 1886 which is printed in the margin.* . . . Upon such appeal, the Supreme Court of Errors reversed the judgment and ordered a new trial. . . . It found that there had been error of law to the prejudice of the state. . . .

. . . [The] defendant was brought to trial again. Before a jury was impaneled and also at later stages of the case he made the objection that the effect of the new trial was to place him twice in jeopardy for the same offense, and in so doing to violate the Fourteenth Amendment of the Constitution of the United States. Upon the overruling of the objection the trial proceeded. The jury returned a verdict of murder in the first degree, and the court sentenced the defendant to the punishment of death. . . . The case is here upon appeal.

1. The execution of the sentence will not deprive appellant of his life without the process of law assured to him by the Fourteenth Amendment of the Federal Constitution.

---

*"Sec. 6494. *Appeals by the state in criminal cases.* Appeals from the rulings and decisions of the superior court or of any criminal court of common pleas, upon all questions of law arising on the trial of criminal cases, may be taken by the state, with the permission of the presiding judge, to the supreme court of errors, in the same manner and to the same effect as if made by the accused. . . ."

The argument for appellant is that whatever is forbidden by the Fifth Amendment is forbidden by the Fourteenth also. The Fifth Amendment, which is not directed to the states, but solely to the federal government, creates immunity from double jeopardy. No person shall be "subject for the same offense to be twice put in jeopardy of life or limb." The Fourteenth Amendment ordains, "nor shall any state deprive any person of life, liberty, or property, without due process of law." To retry a defendant, though under one indictment and only one, subjects him, it is said, to double jeopardy in violation of the Fifth Amendment, if the prosecution is one on behalf of the United States. From this the consequence is said to follow that there is a denial of life or liberty without due process of law, if the prosecution is one on behalf of the People of a State. . . .

We have said that in appellant's view the Fourteenth Amendment is to be taken as embodying the prohibitions of the Fifth. His thesis is even broader. Whatever would be a violation of the original bill of rights (Amendments 1 to 8) if done by the federal government is now equally unlawful by force of the Fourteenth Amendment if done by a state. There is no such general rule.

The Fifth Amendment provides, among other things, that no person shall be held to answer for a capital or otherwise infamous crime unless on presentment or indictment of a grand jury. This court has held that, in prosecutions by a state, presentment or indictment by a grand jury may give way to informations at the instance of a public officer. Hurtado v. California [1884]. . . . The Fifth Amendment provides also that no person shall be compelled in any criminal case to be a witness against himself. This court has said that, in prosecutions by a state, the exemption will fail if the state elects to end it. Twining v. New Jersey [1908]. . . . The Sixth Amendment calls for a jury trial in criminal cases and the Seventh for a jury trial in civil cases at common law where the value in controversy shall exceed twenty dollars. This court has ruled that consistently with those amendments trial by jury may be modified by a state or abolished altogether. Walker v. Sauvinet [1876]; Maxwell v. Dow [1900]. . . . As to the Fourth Amendment, one should refer to Weeks v. United States [1914] and as to other provisions of the Sixth, to West v. Louisiana [1904].

On the other hand, the due process clause of the Fourteenth Amendment may make it unlawful for a state to abridge by its statutes the freedom of speech which the First Amendment safeguards against encroachment by the Congress (De Jonge v. Oregon [1937]) or the like freedom of the press (Near v. Minnesota [1931]), or the free exercise of religion (Hamilton v. University of California [1934]; . . .), or the right of peaceable assembly, without which speech would be unduly trammeled (De Jonge v. Oregon), or the right of one accused of crime to the benefit of counsel (Powell v. Alabama [1932]). In these and other situations immunities that are valid as against the federal government by force of the specific pledges of particular amendments have been found to be implicit in the concept of ordered liberty, and thus, through the Fourteenth Amendment, become valid as against the states.

The line of division may seem to be wavering and broken if there is a hasty catalogue of the cases on the one side and the other. Reflection and analysis will induce a different view. There emerges the perception of a rationalizing principle which gives to discrete instances a proper order and coherence. The right to trial by jury and the immunity from prosecution except as the result of an indictment may have value and importance. Even so, they are not of the very essence of a scheme of ordered liberty. To abolish them is not to violate a "principle of justice so rooted in the traditions and conscience of our people as to be ranked as fundamental." . . . Few would be so narrow or provincial as to maintain that a fair and enlightened system of justice would be impossible without them. What is true of jury trials and indictments is true also, as the cases show, of the immunity from compulsory self-incrimination. Twining v. New Jersey. This too might be lost, and justice still be done. Indeed, today as in the past there are students of our penal system who look upon the immunity as a mischief rather than a benefit, and who would limit its scope or destroy it altogether. . . . The exclusion of these immunities and privileges from the privileges and immunities protected against the action of the states has not been arbitrary or casual. It has been dictated by a study and appreciation of the meaning, the essential implications, of liberty itself.

We reach a different plane of social and moral values when we pass to the privileges and immunities that have been taken over from the earlier articles of the federal bill of rights and brought within the Fourteenth Amendment by a process of absorption. These in their origin were effective against the federal government alone. If the Fourteenth Amendment has absorbed them, the process of absorption has had its source in the belief that neither liberty nor justice would exist if they were sacrificed. Twining v. New Jersey. This is true, for illustration, of freedom of thought and speech. Of that freedom one may say that it is the matrix, the indispensable condition, of nearly every other form of freedom. With rare aberrations a pervasive recognition of that truth can be traced in our history, political and legal. So it has come about that the domain of liberty, withdrawn by the Fourteenth Amendment from encroachment by the states, has been enlarged by latter-day judgments to include liberty of the mind as well as liberty of action. . . . Fundamental too in the concept of due process, and so in that of liberty, is the thought that condemnation shall be rendered only after trial. . . . The hearing, moreover, must be a real one, not a sham or a pretense. Moore v. Dempsey [1923]. . . . For that reason, ignorant defendants in a capital case were held to have been condemned unlawfully when in truth, though not in form, they were refused the aid of counsel. Powell v. Alabama. The decision did not turn upon the fact that the benefit of counsel would have been guaranteed to the defendants by the provisions of the Sixth Amendment if they had been prosecuted in a federal court. The decision turned upon the fact that in the particular situation laid before us in the evidence the benefit of counsel was essential to the substance of a hearing.

Our survey of the cases serves, we think, to justify the statement that the dividing line between them, if not unfaltering throughout its course, has been true for the most part to a unifying principle. On which side of the line the case made out by the appellant has appropriate location must be the next inquiry and the final one. Is that kind of double jeopardy to which the statute has subjected him a hardship so acute and shocking that our polity will not endure it? Does it violate those ''fundamental principles of liberty and justice which lie at the base of all our civil and political institutions?'' . . . The answer surely must be ''no.'' What the answer would have to be if the state were permitted after a trial free from error to try the accused over again or to bring another case against him, we have no occasion to consider. We deal with the statute before us and no other. The state is not attempting to wear the accused out by a multitude of cases with accumulated trials. It asks no more than this, that the case against him shall go on until there shall be a trial free from the corrosion of substantial legal error. . . . This is not cruelty at all, nor even vexation in any immoderate degree. If the trial had been infected with error adverse to the accused, there might have been review at his instance, and as often as necessary to purge the vicious taint. A reciprocal privilege, subject at all times to the discretion of the presiding judge . . . , has now been granted to the state. There is here no seismic innovation. The edifice of justice stands, in its symmetry, to many, greater than before.

2. The conviction of appellant is not in derogation of any privileges or immunities that belong to him as a citizen of the United States. . . .

Maxwell v. Dow [1900], gives all the answer that is necessary.

The judgment is affirmed.

Mr. Justice **Butler** dissents.

DUE PROCESS AS FUNDAMENTAL FAIRNESS

BETTS v. BRADY

316 U. S. 455; 62 S. Ct. 1252; 86 L. Ed. 1595 (1942)

The procedural side of due process developed slowly. As late as 1908 the Court in Twining v. New Jersey conceded that no state procedure had ever been held void for want of due process, and in both Hurtado and Twining the Court made clear that due process did not make the procedures of the Bill of Rights applicable to the states. State procedures, as long as they conformed to state law and did not violate the ''fundamental principles of liberty and justice which lie at the base of all our civil and political institutions,'' were due process.

Nor was the Court willing to use the Fifth Amendment's due process clause in the field of criminal procedure. Since the two clauses meant the same thing, the Fifth Amendment protection could not be applied to federal criminal trials without at the same time applying the Fourteenth Amendment to state criminal trials—a step the Court was not prepared to take. So where the Court wished to enforce against the federal government standards of fairness more exacting than those spelled out in the Bill of Rights, it did not invoke the due process clause of the Fifth Amendment; instead it relied on what may be called ''quasi-due process'' based on its general supervisory power over the administration of justice in the United States courts.

This doctrine was enunciated first in 1943 in McNabb v. United States: ''Judicial supervision of the administration of criminal justice in the Federal courts implies the duty of establishing and maintaining civilized standards of procedure and evidence. Such standards are not satisfied merely by observance of those minimal historic safeguards for securing trial by reason which are summarized as 'due process of law' and below which we reach what is really trial by force.'' In this case the Court held inadmissible in a federal court admissions secured from a prisoner who was held by the police without being taken immediately before a committing magistrate as required by statute. It was upon this ground, also, that evidence which federal officers obtain illegally was first held inadmissible in federal courts (see Nardone v. United States, 1937) and stricter standards are maintained in the selection of federal juries.

Despite its obvious reluctance to incorporate the specific guarantees of the Bill of Rights, the Court did take increasing interest in state procedures and machinery, and grew more watchful lest they not meet the requirements of fundamental fairness. Such insistence on fundamental fairness, especially for persons accused of crime, was bound to bring before the Court the widest variety of state activities. In 1927, for instance, the Court in Tumey v. Ohio reversed the conviction of a bootlegger who had been tried before the mayor of a small town. An ordinance provided that the mayor should retain the court costs as payment for his judicial work, but no costs were paid if the defendant were acquitted. Tumey had been fined one hundred dollars, and the costs involved were twelve dollars. The Supreme Court held it to be a denial of due process to ''subject his liberty or property to the judgment of a court, the judge of which has a direct, personal, substantial pecuniary interest in reaching a conclusion against him in his case. . . . There are doubtless mayors,'' the Court conceded, ''who would not allow such a consideration as twelve dollar costs in each case to affect their judgment in it, but the requirement of due process of law in judicial procedure is not satisfied by the argument that men of the highest honor and the greatest self-sacrifice could carry it on without danger of injustice. Every procedure which would offer a possible temptation to the average man as a judge to forget the burden of proof required to convict the defendant, or which might lead him not to hold the balance nice, clear and true between the state and the accused denies the latter due process of law." The doctrine of Tumey was reaffirmed as recently as 1977 when the Court in Connally v. Georgia held void a search warrant issued by a justice of the peace. The justice received five dollars if he issued the warrant but nothing if he didn't.

Nor are jury members expected to be persons of unrestrained self-sacrifice, and a trial conducted in an atmosphere of mob violence is inherently unfair. In Moore v. Dempsey (1923) five blacks were convicted in an Arkansas court of the murder of a white man and sentenced to death. The Court described the trial in these words: "The court and the neighborhood were thronged with an adverse crowd that threatened the most dangerous consequences to any one interfering with the desired result. The counsel did not venture to demand delay or a change of venue, to challenge a juryman, or to ask for separate trials. He had had no preliminary consultation with the accused, called no witnesses for the defense, although they could have been produced, and did not put the defendants on the stand. The trial lasted about three quarters of an hour, and in less than five minutes the jury brought in a verdict of murder in the first degree. According to the allegations and affidavits there never was a chance for the petitioners to be acquitted; no juryman could have voted for an acquittal and continued to live in Phillips County, and if any prisoner, by any chance, had been acquitted by a jury, he could not have escaped the mob." Under these conditions no trial in the true sense was possible and the defendants were denied due process of law.

The Supreme Court has made it clear that due process is denied by an attempt to punish a person for a crime which is not clearly defined. In 1934 New Jersey passed an act punishing by $10,000 or twenty years or both the crime of being "a gangster." A gangster was defined as "any person not engaged in any lawful occupation, known to be a member of any gang consisting of two or more persons, who has been convicted at least three times of being a disorderly person, or who has been convicted of any crime. . . ." In Lanzetta v. New Jersey (1939) the Court held the statute void, noting that "no one may be required at peril of his life, liberty or property to speculate as to the meaning of penal statues. All are entitled to be informed as to what the State commands or forbids."

In 1972 the Supreme Court struck down a Jacksonville vagrancy ordinance which, in the archaic language of the Elizabethan Poor Law, defines as vagrants (among others) "rogues and vagabonds, or dissolute persons who go about begging, . . . common night walkers, . . . common railers and brawlers, persons wandering or strolling around from place to place without any lawful purpose or object, habitual loafers, [and] . . . persons able to work but habitually living upon the earnings of their wives or minor children. . . ." Two white girls and their black dates were arrested on the main thoroughfare in Jacksonville and convicted of "prowling by auto." In Papachristou v. Jacksonville (1972) a unanimous Court found the ordinance void for vagueness both in the sense that it "fails to give a person of ordinary intelligence fair notice that his contemplated conduct is forbidden by the statute, ". . . and because it encourages arbitrary arrests and convictions." Not only does it "make criminal activities which by modern standards are normally innocent," but it puts "unfettered discretion in the hands of the Jacksonville police." "Those generally implicated by the imprecise terms of the ordinance—poor people, nonconformists, dissenters, idlers—may be required to comport themselves according to the life-style deemed appropriate by the Jacksonville police and the courts. Where, as here, there are no standards governing the exercise of the discretion granted by the ordinance, the scheme permits and encourages an arbitrary and discriminatory enforcement of the law . . . It results in a regime in which the poor and unpopular are permitted to 'stand on a public sidewalk . . . only at the whim of any police officer.' Shuttlesworth v. Birmingham [1969]." In 1983 the case was reaffirmed in Kolender v. Lawson where the Court struck down a California statute making it a crime to be unable to produce "credible and reliable" identification when asked to do so by a police officer. The statute was violated unless "the officer [is] satisfied that the identification is reliable."

The fairness which due process requires in civil and criminal procedures alike demands that when the law creates a presumption of guilt or misconduct or incapacity, this presumption may not be made irrebuttable. The person who is the subject of the presumption must be given the chance to rebut it if he can. This principle governed the Court's decision in Slochower v. Board of Education (1956). The New York City charter provides that if any city employee pleads self-incrimination to avoid answering questions relating to his or her official conduct, he or she shall be automatically removed from office and ineligible for reappointment. Slochower was an associate professor at Brooklyn College, maintained by the City of New York. In 1953 he refused on grounds of self-incrimination to testify before a subcommittee of the United States Senate concerning alleged Communist activities. He was dismissed from his post. The Board of Education contended that one of two possible inferences flowed from his plea of self-incrimination: "(1) that the answering of the question would tend to prove him guilty of a crime in some way connected with his official conduct; or (2) that in order to avoid answering the question he falsely invoked the privilege by stating that the answer would tend to incriminate him, and thus committed perjury. Either inference, it insists, is sufficient to justify the termination of his employment."

The Supreme Court held that Slochower's dismissal denied him due process of law, since he had been given no opportunity to rebut the presumption of guilt or unfitness based on his plea of self-incrimination. The New York charter made that presumption conclusive. The Court condemned the "practice of imputing a sinister meaning to the exercise of a person's constitutional right under the Fifth Amendment," and emphasized that "the privilege against self-incrimination would be reduced to a hollow mockery if its exercise could be taken as equivalent either to a confession of guilt or a conclusive presumption of perjury." In 1958, however, the Court held that a Philadelphia schoolteacher could validly be dismissed on grounds of incompetence for the lack of candor shown by refusal to answer questions concerning possible subversive associations at a fairly conducted hearing; see Beilan v. Board of Education. The same result was reached in Lerner v. Casey (1958), in which a New York subway guard who refused to testify was dismissed on grounds of "unreliability."

Among the things a state cannot do is knowingly to permit a conviction to rest upon perjured testimony. In Mooney v. Holohan (1935) the Court held that "depriving a defendant of liberty through a deliberate deception of court and jury by the presentation of testimony known to be perjured . . . is as inconsistent with the rudimentary demands of justice as is the obtaining of a like result by intimidation." The state must also provide "corrective judicial process by which a conviction obtained may be set aside."

Nor can a state through its criminal procedure favor the wealthy over the poor. In order to carry an appeal to the supreme court of Illinois in a criminal case it is necessary to have a stenographic transcript of the trial proceedings. Only an indigent defendant who had been sentenced to death was provided with a free transcript; all other defendants had to buy it. As a result, a poor person convicted of a noncapital crime and therefore not entitled to a free transcript would be deprived of the right to appeal because of poverty—a right easily available to the well-to-do convict. In Griffin v. Illinois, (1956) the Supreme Court held this to be a violation of due process and equal protection of the laws. "In criminal trials," the Court said, "a State can no more discriminate on account of poverty than on account of religion, race, or color. Plainly the ability to pay costs in advance bears no rational relationship to a defendant's guilt or innocence and could not be used as an excuse to deprive a defendant of a fair trial. . . . There is no meaningful distinction between a rule which would deny the poor the right to defend themselves in a trial court and one which effectively denies the poor an adequate appellate review accorded to all who have money enough to pay the costs in advance." In Mayer v. Chicago (1972) the Court extended the rule to include persons charged with a misdemeanor and liable only to a fine. "Griffin," it emphasized, ". . . is a flat protection against pricing indigent defendants out of as effective an appeal as would be available to others able to pay their own way."

It is clear that rights which are not mentioned in the Bill of Rights must be protected, if at all, through that aspect of due process of law that guarantees a person "fundamental fairness" of treatment at the hands of the state. Thus in the Palko case the Court not only declined to "incorporate" the right against double jeopardy into due process, but it found that the state had not, on the facts of his particular case, denied him essentially fair treatment. To use Justice Frankfurter's phrase, while it had not accorded him "civilized" treatment, neither had it dropped to the level of "trial by force."

The language used by the Court to describe these two aspects of due process is often confusing. While it will describe a right listed in the Bill of Rights as sufficiently "fundamental" to be incorporated into due process, it also uses "fundamental" to describe the level of fairness demanded of the states in its exercise of those procedures not so incorporated.

The decision in Powell v. Alabama (1932) was widely regarded as incorporating the Sixth Amendment right to counsel into due process in the sense that a state would have had to supply counsel in all cases where the Sixth Amendment would have required it. This assumption was bolstered by its inclusion in Palko in the list of rights "that have been taken over from the earlier articles of the federal Bill of Rights and brought within the Fourteenth Amendment by a process of absorption." In a number of other cases, mentioned in the opinion below, the Court appeared to assume that the right to counsel was "fundamental" (in the former sense) and had thus been incorporated into due process. But the Court, in deciding the present case, rejected this interpretation. The right to counsel, like the right against double jeopardy involved in the Palko case, is not in its very nature "fundamental" so as to be required in all cases, i. e., incorporated. It is the right to a fair trial, i.e., fair treatment by the state, and not any specific ingredient thereof, that is fundamental and hence guaranteed by due process.

It was not until two decades later, in Gideon v. Wainwright (1963), that Betts v. Brady was overruled and the right to counsel duly "incorporated."

Mr. Justice **Roberts** delivered the opinion of the Court, saying in part:

The petitioner was indicted for robbery in the Circuit Court of Carroll County, Maryland. Due to lack of funds, he was unable to employ counsel, and so informed the judge at his arraignment. He requested that counsel be appointed for him. The judge advised him that this would not be done as it was not the practice in Carroll County to appoint counsel for indigent defendants save in prosecutions for murder and rape.

Without waiving his asserted right to counsel the petitioner pleaded not guilty and elected to be tried without a jury. At his request witnesses were summoned in his behalf. He cross-examined the State's witnesses and examined his own. The latter gave testimony tending to establish an alibi. Although afforded the opportunity, he did not take the witness stand. The judge found him guilty and imposed a sentence of eight years. . . .

3. Was the petitioner's conviction and sentence a deprivation of his liberty without due process of law, in violation of the Fourteenth Amendment, because of the court's refusal to appoint counsel at his request?

The Sixth Amendment of the national Constitution applies only to trials in federal courts. The due process clause of the Fourteenth Amendment does not incorporate, as such, the specific guarantees found in the Sixth Amendment although a denial by a state of rights or privileges specifically embodied in that and others of the first eight amendments may, in certain circumstances, or in connection with other elements, operate, in a given case, to deprive a litigant of due process of law in violation of the Fourteenth. Due process of law is secured against invasion by the federal Government by the Fifth Amendment and is safeguarded against state action in identical words by the Fourteenth. The phrase formulates a concept less rigid and more fluid than those envisaged in other specific and particular provisions of the Bill of rights. Its application is less a matter of rule. Asserted denial is to be tested by an appraisal of the totality of facts in a given case. That which may, in one setting, constitute a denial of fundamental fairness, shocking to the universal sense of justice, may, in other circumstances, and in the light of other considerations, fall short of such denial. In the application of such a concept there is always the danger of falling into the habit of formulating the guarantee into a set of hard and fast rules the application of which in a given case may be to ignore the qualifying factors therein disclosed.

The petitioner, in this instance, asks us, in effect, to apply a rule in the enforcement of the due process clause. He says the rule to be deduced from our former decisions is that, in every case, whatever the circumstances, one charged with crime, who is unable to obtain counsel, must be furnished counsel by the state. Expressions in the opinions of this court lend color to the argument,* but, as the petitioner admits, none of our decisions squarely adjudicates the questions now presented.

In Powell v. Alabama [1932] ignorant and friendless negro youths, strangers in the community, without friends or means to obtain counsel, were hurried to trial for a capital offense without effective appointment of counsel on whom the burden of preparation and trial would rest, and without adequate opportunity to consult even the counsel casually appointed to represent them. This occurred in a State whose statute law required the appointment of counsel for indigent defendants prosecuted for the offense charged. Thus the trial was conducted in disregard of every principle of fairness and in disregard of that which was declared by the law of the State a requisite of a fair trial. This court held the resulting convictions were without due process of law. It said that, in the light of all the facts, the failure of the trial court to afford the defendants reasonable time and opportunity to secure counsel was a clear denial of due process. The court stated further that "under the circumstances, the necessity of counsel was so vital and imperative that the failure of the trial court to make an effective appointment of counsel was likewise a denial of due process," but added: "whether this would be so in other criminal prosecutions, or under other circumstances, we need not determine. All that it is necessary now to decide, as we do decide, is that, in a capital case, where the defendant is unable to employ counsel, and is incapable adequately of making his own defense because of igno-

rance, feeble-mindedness, illiteracy, or the like, it is the duty of the court, whether requested or not, to assign counsel for him as a necessary requisite of due process of law." . . .

Those cases, which are the petitioner's chief reliance, do not rule this. The question we are now to decide is whether due process of law demands that in every criminal case, whatever the circumstances, a state must furnish counsel to an indigent defendant. Is the furnishing of counsel in cases whatever dictated by natural, inherent, and fundamental principles of fairness? The answer to the question may be found in the common understanding of those who have lived under the Anglo-American system of law. By the Sixth Amendment the people ordained that, in all criminal prosecutions, the accused should "enjoy the right . . . to have the assistance of counsel for his defense." We have construed the provision to require appointment of counsel in all cases where a defendant is unable to procure the services of an attorney, and where the right has not been intentionally and competently waived. Though, as we have noted, the amendment lays down no rule for the conduct of the states, the question recurs whether the constraint laid by the amendment upon the national courts expresses a rule so fundamental and essential to a fair trial, and so, to due process of law, that it is made obligatory upon the states by the Fourteenth Amendment. Relevant data on the subject are afforded by constitutional and statutory provisions subsisting in the colonies and the states prior to the inclusion of the Bill of Rights in the national Constitution, and in the constitutional, legislative, and judicial history of the states to the present date. These constitute the most authoritative sources for ascertaining the considered judgment of the citizens of the states upon the question. . . .

In the light of this common law practice, it is evident that the constitutional provisions to the effect that a defendant should be "allowed" counsel or should have a right "to be heard by himself and his counsel," or that he might be heard by "either or both," at his election, were intended to do away with the rules which denied representation, in whole or in part, by counsel in criminal prosecutions, but were not aimed to compel the state to provide counsel for a defendant. At the least, such a construction by state courts and legislators can not be said to lack reasonable basis.

The statutes in force in the thirteen original states at the time of the adoption of the Bill of Rights are also illuminating. It is of interest that the matter of appointment of counsel for defendants, if dealt with at all, was dealt with by statute rather than by constitutional provision. The contemporary legislation exhibits great diversity of policy. . . .

This material demonstrates that, in the great majority of the states, it has been the considered judgment of the people, their representatives and their courts that appointment of counsel is not a fundamental right, essential to a fair trial. On the contrary, the matter has generally been deemed one of legislative policy. In the light of this evidence we are unable to say that the concept of due process incorporated in the Fourteenth Amendment obli-

---

*Powell v. Alabama [1932]; Grosjean v. American Press Co. [1936]; Johnson v. Zerbst [1938]; Avery v. Alabama [1940].

gates the states, whatever may be their own views, to furnish counsel in every such case. Every court has power, if it deems proper, to appoint counsel where that course seems to be required in the interest of fairness.

The practice of the courts of Maryland gives point to the principle that the states should not be strait-jacketed in this respect, by a construction of the Fourteenth Amendment. Judge Bond's opinion states, and counsel at the bar confirmed the fact, that in Maryland the usual practice is for the defendant to waive a trial by jury. This the petitioner did in the present case. Such trials, as Judge Bond remarks, are much more informal than jury trials and it is obvious that the judge can much better control the course of the trial and is in a better position to see impartial justice done than when the formalities of a jury trial are involved.

In this case there was no question of the commission of a robbery. The State's case consisted of evidence identifying the petitioner as the perpetrator. The defense was an alibi. Petitioner called and examined witnesses to prove that he was at another place at the time of the commission of the offense. The simple issue was the veracity of the testimony for the State and that for the defendant. As Judge Bond says, the accused was not helpless, but was a man forty-three years old, of ordinary intelligence and ability to take care of his own interests on the trial of that narrow issue. He had once before been in a criminal court, pleaded guilty to larceny and served a sentence and was not wholly unfamiliar with criminal procedure. It is quite clear that in Maryland, if the situation had been otherwise and it had appeared that the petitioner was, for any reason, at a serious disadvantage by reason of the lack of counsel, a refusal to appoint would have resulted in the reversal of a judgment of conviction. Only recently the Court of Appeals has reversed a conviction because it was convinced on the whole record that an accused tried without counsel had been handicapped by the lack of representation.

To deduce from the due process clause a rule binding upon the states in this matter would be to impose upon them, as Judge Bond points out, a requirement without distinction between criminal charges of different magnitude or in respect of courts of varying jurisdiction. As he says: "Charges of small crimes tried before justices of the peace and capital charges tried in the higher courts would equally require the appointment of counsel. Presumably it would be argued that trials in the Traffic Court would require it." And indeed it was said by petitioner's counsel both below and in this court, that as the Fourteenth Amendment extends the protection of due process to property as well as to life and liberty, if we hold with the petitioner logic would require the furnishing of counsel in civil cases involving property.

As we have said, the Fourteenth Amendment prohibits the conviction and incarceration of one whose trial is offensive to the common and fundamental ideas of fairness and right, and while want of counsel in a particular case may result in a conviction lacking in such fundamental fairness, we cannot say that the amendment embodies an inexorable command that no trial for any offense, or in any court, can be fairly conducted and justice accorded a defendant who is not represented by counsel.

The judgment is affirmed.

Mr. Justice **Black,** dissenting, with whom Mr. Justice **Douglas** and Mr. Justice **Murphy** concur, said in part:

If this case had come to us from a federal court, it is clear we should have to reverse it, because the Sixth Amendment makes the right to counsel in criminal cases inviolable by the federal government. I believe that the Fourteenth Amendment made the Sixth applicable to the states. But this view, although often urged in dissents, has never been accepted by a majority of this Court and is not accepted today. A statement of the grounds supporting it is, therefore, unnecessary at this time. I believe, however, that under the prevailing view of due process, as reflected in the opinion just announced, a view which gives this Court such vast supervisory powers that I am not prepared to accept it without grave doubts, the judgment below should be reversed.

This Court has just declared that due process of law is denied if a trial is conducted in such manner that it is "shocking to the universal sense of justice" or "offensive to the common and fundamental ideas of fairness and right." On other occasion this Court has recognized that whatever is "implicit in the concept of ordered liberty" and "essential to the substance of a hearing" is within the procedural protection afforded by the constitutional guaranty of due process. Palko v. Connecticut [1937].

The right to counsel in a criminal proceeding is "fundamental." Powell v. Alabama. . . .

A practice cannot be reconciled with "common and fundamental ideas of fairness and right," which subjects innocent men to increased dangers of conviction merely because of their poverty. Whether a man is innocent cannot be determined from a trial in which, as here, denial of counsel has made it impossible to conclude, with any satisfactory degree of certainty, that the defendant's case was adequately presented. . . .

ROCHIN v. CALIFORNIA

342 U.S. 165; 72 S. Ct. 205; 96 L. Ed. 183 (1952)

The Supreme Court had held in the case of Wolf v. Colorado (1949) that the right of privacy protected by the search and seizure provision of the Fourth Amendment was essential to due process, but at the same time had refused to hold that evidence gotten by such seizures was inadmissible in court. Thus a state could get evidence against a person in an unconstitutional way and use it against him in court. The Supreme Court, however, took a very different attitude with respect to evidence got by coercion. In Brown v. Mississippi (1936) the conviction of three blacks for murder solely upon the basis of confessions obtained by brutality and physical torture was held to deny them due process of law. The Court explained that merely "because a State may dispense with a jury trial, it does not follow that it may substitute trial by ordeal. The rack and torture chamber may not be substituted for the witness stand. . . . It would be difficult to conceive of methods more revolting to the sense of justice than those taken to procure the confessions of these petitioners, and the use of the confessions thus obtained as the basis for conviction and sentence was a clear denial of due process."

The problem of what constitutes coercion has been a difficult one for the Court. While physical violence clearly amounts to coercion, it is apparent that certain types of psychological pressure may do so, too. In *Chambers v. Florida* (1940) the Court held a denial of due process the "sunrise confessions" of four blacks which followed five days of interrogation in the absence of "friends, advisors or counselors, and under circumstances calculated to break the strongest nerves and the stoutest resistance." The same result was reached in *Ashcraft v. Tennessee* (1944), where the prisoner confessed to a murder after thirty-six hours of continuous questioning under powerful electric lights, though he was not subjected to any physical abuse.

In *Lisenba v. California* (1941), however, the Court upheld the use of a confession despite the fact that the defendant had been subject to two sleepless days and nights of almost continuous questioning by relays of police officers. The confession took place ten days after this questioning, and the Court concluded that he had not "so lost his freedom of action that the statements made were not his but were the result of the deprivation of his free choice to admit, to deny, or to refuse to answer." A similar result was reached in *Stein v. New York* (1953), the Reader's Digest *murder case. Here the judge had left to the jury the question of admissibility, and since the jury had delivered a general verdict of guilty the Court faced two problems: (1) could the jury have constitutionally found the confessions voluntary and used them as the basis of the conviction, and (2) if the jury found the confessions inadmissible, could it convict on the basis of other evidence or did the use of the confessions vitiate the entire trial? The Court held the confessions were " 'voluntary,' in the only sense in which confessions to the police by one under arrest and suspicion ever are" and hence were admissible. After prolonged questioning, one defendant had confessed after receiving assurances that his father and brother would not be molested by the police; the second had confessed when confronted with the confession of the first. "Of course, these confessions were not voluntary in the sense that petitioners wanted to make them or that they were completely spontaneous, like a confession to a priest, a lawyer, or a psychiatrist. But in this sense no criminal confession is voluntary." The Court made it clear that "the limits in any case depend upon a weighing of the circumstances of pressure against the power of resistance of the person confessing." Neither man, the Court noted, was "young, soft, ignorant or timid." Their will to resist had not been broken by psychological coercion. The Court also found that the jury could convict on other

evidence even if it found the confessions to have been coerced.

It is interesting to note that the Court is not entirely consistent in its reasons for excluding evidence obtained by coercion. The common law rule against the admission of forced confessions was not based on any theory of fairness, but was a practical one designed to prevent the admission in court of untrustworthy evidence. A confession was rejected if sufficient force was applied in getting it to cast doubt upon its reliability. In *Lisenba v. California*, however, the Court made clear what was implied in previous cases, that "the aim of the requirement of due process is not to exclude presumptively false evidence, but to prevent fundamental unfairness in the use of evidence whether true or false. . . . Such unfairness exists when a coerced confession is used as a means of obtaining a verdict of guilt." Without mentioning either the Lisenba or Rochin cases, the Court in the Stein case suggested a return to the common law rationale, noting that forced confessions constitute "illusory and deceptive evidence," while stolen or wiretap evidence "often is of the utmost verity." In *Spano v. New York* (1959) it was made clear that only where the Court has not found a confession to be involuntary may a jury convict on the basis of other evidence; a forced confession always voids the conviction. And in *Rogers v. Richmond* (1961) the Court reaffirmed the rule that the truth or falsity of a confession does not determine its admissibility.

Somewhat different problems are presented when the state undertakes to obtain from a suspect evidence other than oral testimony. This occurs when a person is asked to submit to fingerprinting, blood typing, trying on items of clothing, and the like. In *Breithaupt v. Abram* (1957) the Court held valid the taking of a blood sample from the unconscious victim of an automobile accident to see if he was intoxicated. It distinguished the Rochin case on the ground that "there is nothing 'brutal' or 'offensive' in the taking of a sample of blood when done, as in this case, under the protective eye of a physician. . . . Certainly the test as administered here would not be considered offensive by even the most delicate." The holding in Breithaupt was reaffirmed in 1966 in *Schmerber v. California* on a set of facts similar except that the defendant was awake and protested, on the advice of counsel, the taking of the blood sample. In addition, the Court found that the activity violated neither the guarantee against unreasonable searches and seizures nor compulsory self-incrimination—both made applicable to the states since the Breithaupt decision. In 1983 in *South Dakota v. Neville* the Court extended the Schmerber doctrine to permit the admission as trial evidence the fact a drunken motorist had refused to take a blood test at the time of his arrest on the ground that he was "too drunk to pass it." He was warned that his refusal might cost him his license, but not that it could be used in court against him.

In *United States v. Wade* (1967) the Court held that a robbery suspect could be forced to take part in a police line up, wear strips of adhesive tapes on his face as the robber allegedly did, and repeat the words "put

the money in the bag" allegedly spoken by the robber.
Gilbert v. California (1967) held that a suspect could be
forced to furnish a sample of his handwriting.

Mr. Justice **Frankfurter** delivered the opinion of the Court, saying in part:

Having "some information that [the petitioner here] was selling narcotics," three deputy sheriffs of the County of Los Angeles, on the morning of July 1, 1949, made for the two-story dwelling house in which Rochin lived with his mother, common-law wife, brothers and sisters. Finding the outside door open, they entered and then forced open the door to Rochin's room on the second floor. Inside they found petitioner sitting partly dressed on the side of the bed, upon which his wife was lying. On a "night stand" beside the bed the deputies spied two capsules. When asked "Whose stuff is this?" Rochin seized the capsules and put them in his mouth. A struggle ensued, in the course of which the three officers "jumped upon him" and attempted to extract the capsules. The force they applied proved unavailing against Rochin's resistance. He was handcuffed and taken to a hospital. At the direction of one of the officers a doctor forced an emetic solution through a tube into Rochin's stomach against his will. This "stomach pumping" produced vomiting. In the vomited matter were found two capsules which proved to contain morphine.

Rochin was brought to trial before a California Superior Court, sitting without a jury, on the charge of possessing "a preparation of morphine" in violation of the California Health and Safety Code. Rochin was convicted and sentenced to sixty days' imprisonment. The chief evidence against him was the two capsules. They were admitted over petitioner's objection, although the means of obtaining them was frankly set forth in the testimony by one of the deputies, substantially as here narrated. . . .

. . . Regard for the requirements of the Due Process Clause "inescapably imposes upon this Court an exercise of judgment upon the whole course of the proceedings [resulting in a conviction] in order to ascertain whether they offend those canons of decency and fairness which express the notions of justice of English-speaking peoples even toward those charged with the most heinous offenses." Malinski v. New York [1945]. These standards of justice are not authoritatively formulated anywhere as though they were specifics. Due process of law is a summarized constitutional guarantee of respect for those personal immunities which, as Mr. Justice Cardozo twice wrote for the Court, are "so rooted in the traditions and conscience of our people as to be ranked as fundamental," Snyder v. Massachusetts [1934], or are "implicit in the concept of ordered liberty." Palko v. Connecticut [1937].

The Court's function in the observance of this settled conception of the Due Process Clause does not leave us without adequate guides in subjecting State criminal procedures to constitutional judgment. In dealing not with the machinery of government but with human rights, the absence of formal exactitude, or want of fixity of meaning, is not an unusual or even regrettable attribute of constitutional provisions. Words being symbols do not speak without a gloss. On the one hand the gloss may be the deposit of history, whereby a term gains technical content. Thus the requirements of the Sixth and Seventh Amendments for trial by jury in the Federal courts have a rigid meaning. No changes or chances can alter the content of the verbal symbol of "jury"—a body of twelve men who must reach a unanimous conclusion if the verdict is to go against the defendant. On the other hand, the gloss of some of the verbal symbols of the Constitution does not give them a fixed technical content. It exacts a continuing process of application.

When the gloss has thus not been fixed but is a function of the process of judgment, the judgment is bound to fall differently at different times and differently at the same time through different judges. Even more specific provisions, such as the guaranty of freedom of speech and the detailed protection against unreasonable searches and seizures, have inevitably evoked as sharp divisions in this Court as the least specific and most comprehensive protection of liberties, the Due Process Clause.

The vague contours of the Due Process Clause do not leave judges at large. We may not draw on our merely personal and private notions and disregard the limits that bind judges in their judicial function. Even though the concept of due process of law is not final and fixed, these limits are derived from considerations that are fused in the whole nature of our judicial process. See Cardozo, The Nature of the Judicial Process; The Growth of the Law; The Paradoxes of Legal Science. These are considerations deeply rooted in reason and in the compelling traditions of the legal profession. The Due Process Clause places upon this Court the duty of exercising a judgment, within the narrow confines of judicial power in reviewing State convictions, upon interests of society pushing in opposite directions.

Due process of law thus conceived is not to be derided as resort to a revival of "natural law." To believe that this judicial exercise of judgment could be avoided by freezing "due process of law" at some fixed stage of time or thought is to suggest that the most important aspect of constitutional adjudication is a function for inanimate machines and not for judges, for whom the independence safeguarded by Article 3 of the Constitution was designed and who are presumably guided by established standards of judicial behavior. Even cybernetics has not yet made that haughty claim. To practice the requisite detachment and to achieve sufficient objectivity no doubt demands of judges the habit of self-discipline and self-criticism, incertitude that one's own views are incontestable and alert tolerance toward views not shared. But these are precisely the presuppositions of our judicial process. They are precisely the qualities society has a right to expect from those entrusted with ultimate judicial power.

Restraints on our jurisdiction are self-imposed only

in the sense that there is from our decisions no immediate appeal short of impeachment or constitutional amendment. But that does not make due process of law a matter of judicial caprice. The faculties of the Due Process Clause may be indefinite and vague, but the mode of their ascertainment is not self-willed. In each case "due process of law" requires an evaluation based on a disinterested inquiry pursued in the spirit of science, on a balanced order of facts exactly and fairly stated, on the detached consideration of conflicting claims, . . . on a judgment not ad hoc and episodic but duly mindful of reconciling the needs both of continuity and of change in a progressive society.

Applying these general considerations to the circumstances of the present case, we are compelled to conclude that the proceedings by which this conviction was obtained do more than offend some fastidious squeamishness or private sentimentalism about combatting crime too energetically. This is conduct that shocks the conscience. Illegally breaking into the privacy of the petitioner, the struggle to open his mouth and remove what was there, the forcible extraction of his stomach's contents—this course of proceeding by agents of government to obtain evidence is bound to offend even hardened sensibilities. They are methods too close to the rack and the screw to permit of constitutional differentiation.

It has long since ceased to be true that due process of law is heedless of the means by which otherwise relevant and credible evidence is obtained. This was not true even before the series of recent cases enforced the constitutional principle that the States may not base convictions upon confessions, however much verified, obtained by coercion. These decisions are not arbitrary exceptions to the comprehensive right of States to fashion their own rules of evidence for criminal trials. They are not sports in our constitutional law but applications of a general principle. They are only instances of the general requirement that States in their prosecutions respect certain decencies of civilized conduct. Due process of law, as a historic and generative principle, precludes defining, and thereby confining, these standards of conduct more precisely than to say that convictions cannot be brought about by methods that offend "a sense of justice." See Mr. Chief Justice Hughes, speaking for a unanimous Court in Brown v. Mississippi [1936]. It would be a stultification of the responsibility which the course of constitutional history has cast upon this Court to hold that in order to convict a man the police cannot extract by force what is in his mind but can extract what is in his stomach.

To attempt in this case to distinguish what lawyers call "real evidence" from verbal evidence is to ignore the reasons for excluding coerced confessions. Use of involuntary verbal confessions in State criminal trials is constitutionally obnoxious not only because of their unreliability. They are inadmissible under the Due Process Clause even though statements contained in them may be independently established as true. Coerced confessions offend the community's sense of fair play and decency. So here, to sanction the brutal conduct which naturally enough was condemned by the court whose judgment is before us, would be to afford brutality the cloak of law. Nothing would be more calculated to discredit law and thereby to brutalize the temper of a society. . . .

On the facts of this case the conviction of the petitioner has been obtained by methods that offend the Due Process Clause. The judgment below must be
Reversed.

Mr. Justice **Minton** took no part in the consideration or decision of this case.

Mr. Justice **Black,** concurring, said in part:

Adamson v. California [1947] sets out reasons for my belief that state as well as federal courts and law enforcement officers must obey the Fifth Amendment's command that "No person . . . shall be compelled in any criminal case to be a witness against himself." I think a person is compelled to be a witness against himself not only when he is compelled to testify, but also when as here, incriminating evidence is forcibly taken from him by a contrivance of modern science. . . .

Mr. Justice **Douglas** wrote a concurring opinion.

IRVINE v. CALIFORNIA

347 U. S. 128; 74 S. Ct. 381; 98 L. Ed. 561
(1954)

Certain theoretical and practical difficulties accompany the attempts to enforce the essential fairness doctrine—or the "shock-the-conscience" doctrine, as it came to be known after the Rochin case. What is essentially fair, or shocking, tends to be a matter of individual judgment reflecting the background and personality of the judge. Moreover, the lack of clear guidelines as to what is fair and what is not makes it difficult for police and prosecutors, however well intentioned, to know what conduct on their part is prohibited. While Justice Frankfurter's opinion in the Rochin case is a masterful analysis and defense of the doctrine in its purest form, it does not provide completely satisfactory answers on these two points.

In the present case the California police had broken into the home of a suspected bookmaker and placed microphones in several rooms of the house, including the bedroom. For over a month police officers eavesdropped in this way, and on the basis of information thus obtained Irvine was tried and convicted. Justice Jackson, speaking for four members of the Court, conceded that "few police measures have come to our attention that more flagrantly, deliberately, and persistently violated the fundamental principle declared by the Fourth Amendment," but the Court refused to declare the evidence inadmissible although two members of the majority urged the Attorney General of the United States to de-

termine whether the state officials might not be prosecuted under § 242 of the Criminal Code for violating rights guaranteed by the Constitution.

Mr. Justice **Jackson** announced the judgment of the Court and an opinion in which The Chief Justice [**Warren**], Mr. Justice **Reed**, and Mr. Justice **Minton** join, saying in part:

. . . The decision in Wolf v. Colorado [1949], for the first time established that "[t]he security of one's privacy against arbitrary intrusion by the police" is embodied in the concept of due process found in the Fourteenth Amendment.

But Wolf, for reasons set forth therein, declined to make the subsidiary procedural and evidentiary doctrines developed by the federal courts limitations on the states. On the contrary, it declared, "We hold, therefore, that in a prosecution in a State court for a State crime the Fourteenth Amendment does not forbid the admission of evidence obtained by an unreasonable search and seizure." . . . That holding would seem to control here.

An effort is made, however, to bring this case under the sway of Rochin v. California [1952]. That case involved, among other things, an illegal search of the defendant's person. But it also presented an element totally lacking here—coercion . . . applied by a physical assault upon his person to compel submission to the use of a stomach pump. This was the feature which led to a result in Rochin contrary to that in Wolf. Although Rochin raised the search-and-seizure question, this Court studiously avoided it and never once mentioned the Wolf Case. Obviously, it thought that illegal search and seizure alone did not call for reversal. However obnoxious are the facts in the case before us, they do not involve coercion, violence or brutality to the person, but rather a trespass to property, plus eavesdropping.

It is suggested, however, that although we affirmed the conviction in Wolf, we should reverse here because this invasion of privacy is more shocking, more offensive, than the one involved there. The opinions in Wolf were written entirely in the abstract and did not disclose the details of the constitutional violation. Actually, the search was offensive to the law in the same respect, if not the same degree, as here. A deputy sheriff and others went to a doctor's office without a warrant and seized his appointment book, searched through it to learn the names of all his patients, looked up and interrogated certain of them, and filed an information against the doctor on the information that the District Attorney had obtained from the books. The books also were introduced in evidence against the doctor at his trial.

We are urged to make inroads upon Wolf by holding that it applies only to searches and seizures which produce on our minds a mild shock, while if the shock is more serious, the states must exclude the evidence or we will reverse the conviction. We think that the Wolf decision should not be overruled, for the reasons so persuasively stated therein. We think, too, that a distinction of the kind urged would leave the rule so indefinite that no state court could know what it should rule in order to keep its processes on solid constitutional ground. . . .

Judgment affirmed.

Mr. Justice **Clark,** concurring.

Had I been here in 1949 when Wolf was decided, I would have applied the doctrine of Weeks v. United States [1914] to the states. But the Court refused to do so then, and it still refuses today. Thus Wolf remains the law and, as such, is entitled to the respect of this Court's membership.

Of course, we could sterilize the rule announced in Wolf by adopting a case-by-case approach to due process in which inchoate notions of propriety concerning local police conduct guide our decisions. But this makes for such uncertainty and unpredictability that it would be impossible to foretell—other than by guesswork—just how brazen the invasion of the intimate privacies of one's home must be in order to shock itself into the protective arms of the Constitution. In truth, the practical result of this ad hoc approach is simply that when five Justices are sufficiently revolted by local police action, a conviction is overturned and a guilty man may go free. Rochin bears witness to this. We may thus vindicate the abstract principle of due process, but we do not shape the conduct of local police one whit; unpredictable reversals on dissimilar fact situations are not likely to curb the zeal of those police and prosecutors who may be intent on racking up a high percentage of successful prosecutions. I do not believe that the extension of such a vacillating course beyond the clear cases of physical coercion and brutality, such as Rochin, would serve a useful purpose.

In light of the "incredible" activity of the police here, it is with great reluctance that I follow Wolf. Perhaps strict adherence to the tenor of that decision may produce needed converts for its extinction. Thus I merely concur in the judgment of affirmance.

Mr. Justice **Black,** with whom Mr. Justice **Douglas** concurs, wrote a dissenting opinion.

Mr. Justice **Frankfurter,** whom Mr. Justice **Burton** joins, dissenting, said in part:

In the Wolf Case, the Court rejected one absolute. In Rochin, it rejected another. . . .

Rochin decided that the Due Process Clause of the Fourteenth Amendment does not leave States free in their prosecutions for crime. The Clause puts limits on the wide discretion of a State in the process of enforcing its criminal law. The holding of the case is that a State cannot resort to methods that offend civilized standards of decency and fairness. The conviction in the Rochin Case was found to offend due process not because evidence had been obtained through an unauthorized search and seizure or was the fruit of compulsory self-incrimination. Neither of these concepts, relevant to federal prosecutions, was invoked by the Court in Rochin, so of course the Wolf Case was not mentioned. While there is in the case before us, as there was in Rochin, an element of unreasonable search and seizure, what is decisive here, as in Rochin, is additional aggravating conduct which the Court find repulsive. . . .

There was lacking here physical violence, even to the restricted extent employed in Rochin. We have here, however, a more powerful and offensive control over the Irvine's life than a single, limited physical trespass. Certainly the conduct of the police here went far beyond a bare search and seizure. The police devised means to hear every word that was said in the Irvine household for more than a month. Those affirming the conviction find that this conduct, in its entirety, is "almost incredible if it were not admitted." Surely the Court does not propose to announce a new absolute, namely, that even the most reprehensible means for securing a conviction will not taint a verdict so long as the body of the accused was not touched by State officials. . . .

Since due process is not a mechanical yardstick, it does not afford mechanical answers. In applying the Due Process Clause judicial judgment is involved in an empiric process in the sense that results are not predetermined or mechanically ascertainable. But that is a very different thing from conceiving the results as ad hoc decisions in the opprobrious sense of ad hoc. Empiricism implies judgment upon variant situations by the wisdom of experience. Ad hocness in adjudication means treating a particular case by itself and not in relation to the meaning of a course of decisions and the guides they serve for the future. There is all the difference in the world between disposing of a case as though it were a discreet instance and recognizing it as part of the process of judgment, taking its place in relation to what went before and further cutting a channel for what is to come.

The effort to imprison due process within tidy categories misconceives its nature and is a futile endeavor to save the judicial function from the pains of judicial judgment. It is pertinent to recall how the Court dealt with this craving for unattainable certainty in the Rochin Case:

"The vague contours of the Due Process Clause do not leave judges at large. We may not draw on our merely personal and private notions and disregard the limits that bind judges in their judicial function. Even though the concept of due process of law is not final and fixed, these limits are derived from considerations that are fused in the whole nature of our judicial process. See Cardozo, The Nature of the Judicial Process; The Growth of the Law; The Paradoxes of Legal Science. These are considerations deeply rooted in reason and in the compelling traditions of the legal profession. The Due Process Clause places upon this Court the duty of exercising a judgment, within the narrow confines of judicial power in reviewing State convictions, upon interests of society pushing in opposite directions." . . .

McKEIVER v. PENNSYLVANIA

403 U. S. 528; 91 S. Ct. 1976; 29 L. Ed. 2d 647
(1971)

Since the birth of the common law, society has struggled to provide ways of humanizing it, of increasing its flexibility, and of getting around its insistence on procedure.

From time to time, systems of executive justice are instituted to provide needed reforms; supported by the enthusiasm of the reformers, they work well and produce the desired results. But with the passage of time the interest of the reformers wanes, and among the highly competent idealists who made the system work appear others to whom a job is simply a job. Freedom and discretion, exercised wisely and with a broad social conscience by the idealists, become, in the hands of the latter, tools by which to achieve less lofty goals. Incompetent, selfish, and occasionally venal, these people bring criticism on a system that for the most part does not deserve it. The result is a demand for instituting the very procedural protections that were abandoned when the system was set up. Procedures that might not be necessary if demigods were in control or when an alert and conscientious public is watching seem to be the only way to ensure fairness when public interest flags and mere human beings take over. The reversion, of course, is never complete; and the result is usually a modified version of what went before, with the best of the reform ideas being retained. But the unfettered freedom to be a "philosopher king," to act and decide "in the public interest," ends up hedged about with procedures that centuries of experience have shown are necessary if the rights of individuals are not to be overlooked.

In greater or lesser degree this life-span characterizes the history of that branch of the law known as equity, accounts in part for the writing of our own Constitution, and in recent times colors the development of administrative agencies. It is against this background of what Dean Roscoe Pound calls the "vitality and tenacity" of the common-law tradition that the history of the juvenile court system should be read. The system was born at the turn of the century from the feelings of reformers that it was unconscionable to try children by regular criminal proceedings and sentence them to long terms in the same prisons with hardened adult criminals. If the child was to be saved from a life of crime, the state had to see where that child had gone wrong and what could be done to set him or her back on the right track. The result was that the practice of informal proceedings, presided over by juvenile court judges, was adopted throughout the country. The judges, acting as parental figures, determined whether the child was delinquent and, if so, what should be done. The constitutional problem raised by the denial of procedural rights was gotten around by insisting that the state was proceeding "in loco parentis," that the proceedings were civil rather than criminal, and that the child was being rehabilitated rather than punished.

However ideally the system might have worked in its heyday, it was in a sad state of deterioration when its processes were finally challenged in the Supreme Court in In re Gault (1967). Gerald Gault, fifteen, was charged with making obscene phone calls, an offense carrying a maximum sentence of two months if committed by an adult. He was given a hearing for which his parents had no adequate notice of charges against him, at which the complaining witness failed to appear, at which he was not represented by counsel or warned of his right to silence, and from which there was no right of appeal. He was sentenced to six years in the State Industrial School. While acknowledging that much desirable informality could be retained, eight members of the Supreme Court agreed that these procedures failed to provide due process of law. Five justices held that as a matter of fundamental fairness he was entitled at least to adequate notice, the right to counsel, the right to confront his accusers, and a warning that he need not incriminate himself.

The hopes of those pushing for more procedural protection for juveniles were raised by the Supreme Court's decision in In re Winship (1970) that a delinquent child could not be imprisoned unless guilt was established beyond a reasonable doubt. Samuel Winship had been committed to a state training school for theft after a hearing at which his guilt was based "on a preponderance of the evidence." Emphasizing that "the reasonable-doubt standard plays a vital role in the American scheme of criminal procedure" since "it is a prime instrument for reducing the risk of convictions resting on factual error," the Court made clear that such a standard was essential to due process of law.

Moreover, "the same considerations that demand extreme caution in factfinding to protect the innocence of adults apply as well to the innocent child." The Court rejected, as it had in Gault, the state's reliance on the "civil label-of-convenience" as a basis for holding the due process clause inapplicable to juvenile proceedings, and its justification that such proceedings were designed "not to punish, but to save the child." "We made clear in [Gault] that civil labels and good intentions do not themselves obviate the need for criminal due process safeguards in juvenile courts, for '[a] proceeding where the issue is whether the child will be found to be "delinquent" and subject to the loss of his liberty for years is comparable in seriousness to a felony prosecution.'"

The present case involved sixteen-year-old Joseph McKeiver, who was charged with robbery, larceny, and receiving stolen goods (felonies under Pennsylvania law), and Barbara Burrus, who, with some forty-five other black children, was arrested with a group of adults for obstructing traffic in connection with a protest in North Carolina against school segregation policies.

Mr. Justice **Blackmun** announced the judgment of the Court and an opinion in which The Chief Justice **[Burger]**, Mr. Justice **Stewart**, and Mr. Justice **White** join, saying in part:

These cases present the narrow but precise issue whether the Due Process Clause of the Fourteenth Amendment assures the right to trial by jury in the adjudicative phase of a state juvenile court delinquency proceeding. . . .

IV.

The right to an impartial jury "[i]n all criminal prosecutions" under federal law is guaranteed by the Sixth Amendment. Through the Fourteenth Amendment that requirement has now been imposed upon the States "in all criminal cases which—were they to be tried in a federal court—would come within the Sixth Amendment's guarantee." This is because the Court has said it believes "that trial by jury in criminal cases is fundamental to the American scheme of justice." Duncan v. Louisiana [1968]. . . .

This, of course, does not automatically provide the answer to the present jury trial issue, if for no other reason than that the juvenile court proceeding has not yet been held to be a "criminal prosecution," within the meaning and reach of the Sixth Amendment, and also has not yet been regarded as devoid of criminal aspects merely because it usually has been given the civil label. . . .

V.

The Pennsylvania juveniles' basic argument is that they were tried in proceedings "substantially similar to a criminal trial." They say that a delinquency proceeding in their State is initiated by a petition charging a penal code violation in the conclusory language of an indictment; that a juvenile detained prior to trial is held in a building substantially similar to an adult prison; that in Philadelphia juveniles over 16 are, in fact, held in the cells of a prison; that counsel and the prosecution engage in plea bargaining; that motions to suppress are routinely heard and decided; that the usual rules of evidence are applied; that the customary common law defenses are available; that the press is generally admitted in the Philadelphia juvenile courtrooms; that members of the public enter the room; that arrest and prior record may be reported by the press (from police sources, however, rather than from the juvenile court records); that, once adjudged delinquent, a juvenile may be confined until his majority in what amounts to a prison (see In re Bethea, 215 Pa. Super. 75 (1969), describing the state correctional institution at Camp Hill as a "maximum security prison for adjudged delinquents and youthful criminal offenders"); and that the stigma attached upon delinquency adjudication approximates that resulting from conviction in an adult criminal proceeding.

The North Carolina juveniles particularly urge that the requirement of a jury trial would not operate to deny the supposed benefits of the juvenile court system; that the system's primary benefits are its discretionary intake procedure permitting disposition short of adjudication, and its flexible sentencing permitting emphasis on rehabilitation; that realization of these benefits does not depend upon dispensing with the jury; that adjudication of factual issues on the one hand and disposition of the case on the other are very different matters with very different purposes; that the purpose of the former is indistinguishable from that of the criminal trial; that the jury trial provides an independent protective factor; that experience has shown that jury trials in juvenile courts are manageable; that no reason exists why protection traditionally accorded in criminal proceedings should be denied young people subject to involuntary incarceration for lengthy periods; and that the juvenile courts deserve healthy public scrutiny.

VI.

All the litigants here agree that the applicable due process standard in juvenile proceedings, as developed by Gault [1967] and Winship [1970], is fundamental fairness. As that standard was applied in those two cases, we have an emphasis on factfinding procedures. The requirements of notice, counsel, confrontation, cross-examination, and standard of proof naturally flowed from this emphasis. But one cannot say that in our legal system the jury is a necessary component of accurate factfinding. There is much to be said for it, to be sure, but we have been content to pursue other ways for determining facts. Juries are not required, and have not been, for example, in equity cases, in workmen's compensation, in probate, or in deportation cases. Neither have they been generally used in military trials. In Duncan the Court stated, "We would not assert, however, that every criminal trial—or any particular trial—held before a judge alone is unfair or that a defendant may never be as fairly treated by a judge as he would be by a jury." In DeStefano [v. Woods, 1968] for this reason and others, the Court refrained from retrospective application of Duncan, an action it surely would have not taken had it felt that the integrity of the result was seriously at issue. And in Williams v. Florida (1970), the Court saw no particular magic in a 12-man jury for a criminal case, thus revealing that even jury concepts themselves are not inflexible.

We must recognize, as the Court has recognized before, that the fond and idealistic hopes of the juvenile court proponents and early reformers of three generations ago have not been realized. The devastating commentary upon the system's failure as a whole, contained in the Task Force Report: Juvenile Delinquency and Youth Crime (President's Commission on Law Enforcement and the Administration of Justice (1967), pp. 7-9), reveals the depth of disappointment in what has been accomplished. Too often the juvenile court judge falls far short of that stalwart, protective and communicating figure the system envisaged.* The community's unwillingness to provide people and facilities and to be concerned, the insufficiency of time devoted, the scarcity of professional help, the inadequacy of dispositional alternatives, and our general lack of knowledge all contribute to dissatisfaction with the experiment.†

The Task Force Report, however, also said, page 7, "To say that juvenile courts have failed to achieve their goals is to say no more than what is true of criminal courts in the United States. But failure is most striking when hopes are highest."

Despite all these disappointments, all these failures, and all these shortcomings, we conclude that trial by jury in the juvenile court's adjudicative stage is not a constitutional requirement. We so conclude for a number of reasons:

1. The Court has refrained, in the cases heretofore decided, from taking the easy way with a flat holding that all rights constitutionally assured for the adult accused are to be imposed upon the state juvenile proceeding. . . .

2. There is a possibility, at least, that the jury trial, if required as a matter of constitutional precept, will remake the juvenile proceeding into a fully adversary process and will put an effective end to what has been the idealistic prospect of an intimate, informal protective proceeding.

3. The Task Force Report, although concededly pre-Gault, is notable for its not making any recommendation that the jury trial be imposed upon the juvenile court system. . . .

5. The imposition of the jury trial on the juvenile court system would not strengthen greatly, if at all, the factfinding function, and would, contrarily, provide an attrition of the juvenile court's assumed ability to function in a unique manner. It would not remedy the defects of the system. Meager as has been the hoped-for advance in the juvenile field, the alternative would be regressive, would lose what has been gained, and would tend once again to place the juvenile squarely in the routine of the criminal process.

6. The juvenile concept held high promise. We are reluctant to say that, despite disappointments of grave dimensions, it still does not hold promise, and we are particularly reluctant to say, as do the Pennsylvania petitioners here, that the system cannot accomplish its rehabilitative goals. So much depends on the availability of resources, on the interest and commitment of the public, on willingness to learn, and on understanding as to cause and effect and cure. In this field, as in so many others, one perhaps learns best by doing. We are reluctant to disallow the States further to experiment and to seek in new and different ways the elusive answers to the problems of the young, and we feel that we would be impeding that experimentation by imposing the jury trial. The States, indeed, must go forward. If, in its wisdom, any State feels the jury trial is desirable in all cases, or in

---

*"A recent study of juvenile court judges . . . revealed that half had not received undergraduate degrees; a fifth had received no college education at all; a fifth were not members of the bar." Task Force Report, p. 7.

†What emerges, then, is this: In theory the juvenile court was to be helpful and rehabilitative rather than punitive. In fact the distinction often disappears, not only because of the absence of facilities and personnel but also because of the limits of knowledge and technique. In theory the court's action was to affix no stigmatizing label. In fact a delinquent is generally viewed by employers, schools, the armed services—by society generally—as a criminal. In theory the court was to treat children guilty of criminal acts in noncriminal ways. In fact it labels truants and runaways as junior criminals.

"In theory the court's operations could justifiably be informal, its findings and decisions made without observing ordinary procedural safeguards, because it would act only in the best interest of the child.

"In fact it frequently does nothing more nor less than deprive a child of liberty without due process of law—knowing not what else to do and needing, whether admittedly or not, to act in the community's interest even more imperatively than the child's. In theory it was to exercise its protective powers to bring an errant child back into the fold. In fact there is increasing reason to believe that its intervention reinforces the juvenile's unlawful impulses. In theory it was to concentrate on each case the best of current social science learning. In fact it has often become a vested interest in its turn, loathe to cooperate with innovative programs or avail itself of forward-looking methods." Task Force Report, p. 9.

certain kinds, there appears to be no impediment to its installing a system embracing that feature. That, however, is the State's privilege and not its obligation. . . .

10. Since Gault and since Duncan the great majority of States, in addition to Pennsylvania and North Carolina, that have faced the issue have concluded that the considerations that led to the result in those two cases do not compel trial by jury in the juvenile court. . . .

11. Stopping short of proposing the jury trial for juvenile proceedings are the Uniform Juvenile Court Act, § 24(a), approved in July 1968 by the National Conference of Commissioners on Uniform State Laws; the Standard Juvenile Court Act, Article V, § 19, proposed by the National Council on Crime and Delinquency (see W. Sheridan, Standards for Juvenile and Family Courts 73 (1968)); and the Legislative Guide for Drafting Family and Juvenile Court Acts § 29(a) (1969) (issued by the Children's Bureau, Social and Rehabilitation Service, United States Department of H. E. W.).

12. If the jury trial were to be injected into the juvenile court system as a matter of right, it would bring with it into that system the traditional delay, the formality and the clamor of the adversary system and, possibly, the public trial. . . .

13. Finally, the arguments advanced by the juveniles here are, of course, the identical arguments that underlie the demand for the jury trial for criminal proceedings. The arguments necessarily equate the juvenile proceeding—or at least the adjudicative phase of it— with the criminal trial. Whether they should be so equated is our issue. Concern about the inapplicability of exclusionary and other rules of evidence, about the juvenile court judge's possible awareness of the juvenile's prior record and of the contents of the social file; about repeated appearances of the same familiar witnesses in the persons of juvenile and probation officers and social workers—all to the effect that this will create the likelihood of prejudgment—chooses to ignore, it seems to us, every aspect of fairness, of concern, of sympathy, and of paternal attention that the juvenile court system contemplates.

If the formalities of the criminal adjudicative process are to be superimposed upon the juvenile court system, there is little need for its separate existence. Perhaps that ultimate disillusionment will come one day, but for the moment we are disinclined to give impetus to it.

Affirmed.

Mr. Justice **White,** concurring, said in part:

The criminal law proceeds on the theory that defendants have a will and are responsible for their actions. A finding of guilt establishes that they have chosen to engage in conduct so reprehensible and injurious to others that they must be punished to deter them and others from crime. Guilty defendants are considered blameworthy; they are branded and treated as such, however much the State also pursues rehabilitative ends in the criminal justice system.

For the most part, the juvenile justice system rests on more deterministic assumptions. Reprehensible acts by juveniles are not deemed the consequence of mature and malevolent choice but of environmental pressures (or lack of them) or of other forces beyond their control. Hence the state legislative judgment not to stigmatize the juvenile delinquent by branding him a criminal; his conduct is not deemed so blameworthy that punishment is required to deter him or others. Coercive measures, where employed, are considered neither retribution nor punishment. Supervision or confinement is aimed at rehabilitation, not at convincing the juvenile of his error simply by imposing pains and penalties. Nor is the purpose to make the juvenile delinquent an object lesson for others, whatever his own merits or demerits may be. A typical disposition in the juvenile court where delinquency is established may authorize confinement until age 21, but it will last no longer and within that period will last only so long as his behavior demonstrates that he remains an unacceptable risk if returned to his family. Nor is authorization for custody until 21 any measure of the seriousness of the particular act which the juvenile has performed.

Against this background and in light of the distinctive purpose of requiring juries in criminal cases, I am satisfied with the Court's holding. To the extent that the jury is a buffer to the corrupt or overzealous prosecutor in the criminal law system, the distinctive intake policies and procedures of the juvenile court system to a great extent obviate this important function of the jury. As for the necessity to guard against judicial bias, a system eschewing blameworthiness and punishment for evil choice is itself an operative force against prejudice and short-tempered justice. Nor where juveniles are involved is there the same opportunity for corruption to the juvenile's detriment or the same temptation to use the courts for political ends.

Mr. Justice **Brennan,** concurring in No. 322 [Pennsylvania] and dissenting in No. 128 [North Carolina], said in part:

I agree with the plurality opinion's conclusion that the proceedings below in these cases were not "criminal prosecutions" within the meaning of the Sixth Amendment. For me, therefore, the question in these cases is whether jury trial is among the "essentials of due process and fair treatment," . . . required during the adjudication of a charge of delinquency based upon acts which would constitute a crime if engaged in by an adult. . . . This does not, however, mean that the interests protected by the Sixth Amendment's guarantee of jury trial in all "criminal prosecutions" are of no importance in the context of these cases. The Sixth Amendment, where applicable, commands that these interests be protected by a particular procedure, that is, trial by jury. The Due Process Clause commands not a particular procedure, but only a result: in my Brother Blackmun's words, "fundamental fairness . . . in factfinding." In the context of these and similar juvenile delinquency proceedings, what this means is that the States are not bound to provide jury trials on demand so long as some other aspect of the process adequately protects the interests that Sixth Amendment jury trials are intended to serve.

In my view, therefore, the due process question cannot be decided upon the basis of general characteristics of juvenile proceedings, but only in terms of the adequacy of a particular state procedure to "protect the [juvenile] from oppression by the Government," . . . and to protect him against "the compliant, biased, or eccentric judge." . . .

Examined in this light, I find no defect in the Pennsylvania cases before us. The availability of trial by jury allows an accused to protect himself against possible oppression by what is in essence an appeal to the community conscience, as embodied in the jury that hears his case. To some extent, however, a similar protection may be obtained when an accused may in essence appeal to the community at large, by focusing public attention upon the facts of his trial, exposing improper judicial behavior to public view, and obtaining if necessary executive redress through the medium of public indignation. . . .

. . . In the Pennsylvania cases before us, there appears to be no statutory ban upon admission of the public to juvenile trials. Appellants themselves, without contradiction, assert that "the press is generally admitted" to juvenile delinquency proceedings in Philadelphia. Most important, the record in these cases is bare of any indication that any person whom appellants sought to have admitted to the courtroom was excluded. In these circumstances, I agree that the judgment in No. 322 must be affirmed.

The North Carolina cases, however, present a different situation. North Carolina law either permits or requires exclusion of the general public from juvenile trials. In the cases before us, the trial judge "ordered the general public excluded from the hearing room and stated that only officers of the court, the juveniles, their parents or guardians, their attorney and witnesses would be present for the hearing," . . . notwithstanding petitioners' repeated demand for a public hearing. The cases themselves, which arise out of a series of demonstrations by black adults and juveniles who believed that the Hyde County, North Carolina, school system unlawfully discriminated against black schoolchildren, present a paradigm of the circumstances in which there may be a substantial "temptation to use the courts for political ends." Opinion of Mr. Justice White, ante, . . .

Mr. Justice **Harlan,** concurring in the judgments, said in part:

If I felt myself constrained to follow Duncan v. Louisiana (1968), which extended the Sixth Amendment right of jury trial to the States, I would have great difficulty, upon the premise seemingly accepted in my Brother Blackmun's opinion, in holding that the jury trial right does not extend to state juvenile proceedings. That premise is that juvenile delinquency proceedings have in practice actually become in many, if not all, respects criminal trials. . . . If that premise be correct, then I do not see why, given Duncan, juveniles as well

as adults would not be constitutionally entitled to jury trials, so long as juvenile delinquency systems are not restructured to fit their original purpose. When that time comes I would have no difficulty in agreeing with my Brother Blackmun, and indeed with my Brother White, the author of Duncan, that juvenile delinquency proceedings are beyond the pale of Duncan.

I concur in the judgments in these cases however, on the ground that criminal jury trials are not constitutionally required of the States, either as a matter of Sixth Amendment law or due process. See my dissenting opinion in Duncan and my concurring opinion in Williams v. Florida (1970).

Mr. Justice **Douglas,** with whom Mr. Justice **Black** and Mr. Justice **Marshall** concur, dissenting, said in part:

These cases from Pennsylvania and North Carolina present the issue of the right to a jury trial for offenders charged in juvenile court and facing a possible incarceration until they reach their majority. I believe the guarantees of the Bill of Rights, made applicable to the States by the Fourteenth Amendment, require a jury trial. . . . We had held in In re Gault that "neither the Fourteenth Amendment nor the Bill of Rights is for adults alone." As we noted in that case, the Juvenile Court movement was designed to avoid procedures to ascertain whether the child was "guilty" or "innocent" but to bring to bear on these problems a "clinical" approach. It is of course not our task to determine as a matter of policy whether a "clinical" or "punitive" approach to these problems should be taken by the States. But where a State uses its juvenile court proceedings to prosecute a juvenile for a criminal act and to order "confinement" until the child reaches 21 years of age or where the child at the threshold of the proceedings faces that prospect, then he is entitled to the same procedural protection as an adult. As Mr. Justice Black said in In re Gault (concurring):

"Where a person, infant or adult, can be seized by the State, charged, and convicted for violating a state criminal law, and then ordered by the State to be confined for six years, I think the Constitution requires that he be tried in accordance with the guarantees of all the provisions of the Bill of Rights made applicable to the States by the Fourteenth Amendment. Undoubtedly this would be true of an adult defendant, and it would be a plain denial of equal protection of the laws—an invidious discrimination—to hold that others subject to heavier punishments could, because they are children, be denied these same constitutional safeguards."

Just as courts have sometimes confused delinquency with crime, so have law enforcement officials treated juveniles not as delinquents but as criminals. . . .

In the present cases imprisonment or confinement up to 10 years was possible for one child and each faced at least a possible five-year incarceration. No adult could be denied a jury trial in those circumstances. Duncan v. Louisiana. The Fourteenth Amendment which makes trial by jury provided in the Sixth Amendment applicable to States speaks of denial of rights to "any person," not denial of rights to "any adult person"; and we have held indeed that where a juvenile is charged with an act that would constitute a crime if committed by an adult, he is entitled to trial by jury with proof beyond a reasonable doubt. . . .

SUBSTANTIVE DUE PROCESS REVISITED

GRISWOLD v. CONNECTICUT

381 U. S. 479; 85 S. Ct. 1678; 14 L. Ed. 2d 510
(1965)

While the Constitution prescribes certain limits on governmental power, these limits are in a continual state of change. As the Court engages in the endless process of interpreting the constitutional guarantees, certain protections are withdrawn and others are added. Ordinarily this process occurs so slowly and subtly that only a careful observer can detect that a real change is actually taking place. While apparently applying the same principles to a new set of facts, the Court is in reality altering the principle by an almost indistinguishable increment. Now and again the Court will find this process incapable of producing the results that it wants; a former interpretation or principle no longer fills what the Court sees as the needs of society, so that principle must be rejected and another put in its place. On such occasions the Court will overrule its previous interpretation of the Constitution and substitute another interpretation—usually one which has been long clamoring for acceptance. This is what the Court did when, starting in the early 1960s, under the leadership of Chief Justice Warren, it began in a serious way to incorporate Bill of Rights guarantees into the due process clause of the Fourteenth Amendment.

On very rare occasions, when what seems to the Court to be an important right cannot be brought comfortably under any existing constitutional guarantee, the Court is forced to draw upon what it conceives to be the general or fundamental principles of the Constitution to supply the necessary protection. In the early days little effort was made to tie such protection to specific parts of the document: in Loan Association v. Topeka (1875), for example, the Court forbade spending tax money for private purposes on the ground that it violated limits on governmental power that "grow out of the essential nature of all free governments." With the evolution of the due process clause, this right and the celebrated "liberty of contract" became elements of due process of law. See the note to Lochner v. New York (1905).

In raising the "right of privacy" to the status of an independent right, the Court in the present case draws on a "penumbra" cast by a number of specific constitutional rights, without resting the right squarely on any one of them. Three justices, in addition to endorsing the "penumbra" theory, also invoked the Ninth Amendment and Fourteenth Amendment due process. It is interesting to note that Justice Black, a staunch proponent of incorporating the entire Bill of Rights into due process, here dissents on the ground that due process should be limited to what is in the Bill of Rights, as well as extended to it. He rejects the idea that it should include what he views as a "natural justice" component of either fairness or reasonableness.

A test of the validity of Connecticut's birth-control statute first came to the Supreme Court in Tileston v. Ullman (1943). Tileston, a physician, asked a declaratory judgment that the statute was void because it forbade him recommending contraceptives to three patients whose lives would be endangered by childbearing. The Court dismissed the case on the ground that no threatened injury to Tileston was shown. In 1961 a second challenge to the statute was dismissed for lack of justiciable controversy, the Court finding that despite the notorious and common sale of contraceptives in Connecticut, no one had ever been tried for violating the statute; see Poe v. Ullman. The present case was brought after Connecticut abandoned, following the opening of birth-control clinics, its long-standing policy of nonenforcement. In Eisenstadt v. Baird (1972) the Court held that equal protection required that unmarried women, too, be allowed birth control information and articles.

Mr. Justice **Douglas** delivered the opinion of the Court, saying in part:

Appellant Griswold is Executive Director of the Planned Parenthood League of Connecticut. Appellant Buxton is a licensed physician and a professor at the Yale Medical School who served as Medical Director for the League at its Center in New Haven—a center open and operating from November 1 to November 10, 1961, when appellants were arrested.

They gave information, instruction, and medical advice to *married persons* as to the means of preventing conception. They examined the wife and prescribed the best contraceptive device or material for her use. Fees were usually charged, although some couples were serviced free.

The statutes whose constitutionality is involved in this appeal are §§ 53-32 and 54-196 of the General Statutes of Connecticut (1958 rev.). The former provides:

"Any person who uses any drug, medicinal article or instrument for the purpose of preventing conception shall be fined not less than fifty dollars or imprisoned not less than sixty days nor more than one year or be both fined and imprisoned."

Section 54-196 provides:

"Any person who assists, abets, counsels, causes, hires or commands another to commit any offense may be prosecuted and punished as if he were the principal offender."

The appellants were found guilty as accessories and fined $100 each, against the claim that the accessory statute as so applied violated the Fourteenth Amendment. . . .

We think that appellants have standing to raise the constitutional rights of the married people with whom they had a professional relationship. Tileston v. Ullman [1943] is different, for there the plaintiff seeking to represent others asked for a declaratory judgment. In that situation we thought that the requirements of standing should be strict, lest the standards of "case or controversy" in Article III of the Constitution become blurred. Here those doubts are removed by reason of a criminal conviction for serving married couples in violation of an aiding-and-abetting statute. Certainly the accessory should have standing to assert that the offense which he is charged with assisting is not, or cannot constitutionally be, a crime. . . .

Coming to the merits, we are met with a wide range of questions that implicate the Due Process Clause of the Fourteenth Amendment. Overtones of some arguments suggest that Lochner v. New York [1905] should be our guide. But we decline that invitation as we did in West Coast Hotel Co. v. Parrish [1937]. . . . We do not sit as a super-legislature to determine the wisdom, need, and propriety of laws that touch economic problems, business affairs, or social conditions. This law, however, operates directly on an intimate relation of husband and wife and their physician's role in one aspect of that relation.

The association of people is not mentioned in the Constitution nor in the Bill of Rights. The right to educate a child in a school of the parents' choice—whether public or private or parochial—is also not mentioned. Nor is the right to study any particular subject or any foreign language. Yet the First Amendment has been construed to include certain of those rights.

By Pierce v. Society of Sisters [1925] the right to educate one's children as one chooses is made applicable to the States by the force of the First and Fourteenth Amendments. By Meyer v. Nebraska [1923] the same dignity is given the right to study the German language in a private school. In other words, the State may not, consistently with the spirit of the First Amendment, contract the spectrum of available knowledge. The right of freedom of speech and press includes not only the right to utter or to print, but the right to distribute, the right to receive, the right to read . . . and freedom of inquiry, freedom of thought, and freedom to teach . . . —indeed the freedom of the entire university community. . . . Without those peripheral rights the specific rights would be less secure. And so we reaffirm the principle of the Pierce and the Meyer cases.

In NAACP v. Alabama [1958] we protected the "freedom to associate and privacy in one's association," noting that freedom of association was a peripheral First Amendment right. Disclosure of membership lists of a constitutionally valid association, we held, was invalid "as entailing the likelihood of a substantial restraint upon the exercise by petitioner's members of their right to freedom of association." In other words, the First Amendment has a penumbra where privacy is protected from governmental intrusion. In like context, we have protected forms of "association" that are not political in the customary sense but pertain to the social, legal, and economic benefit of the members. NAACP v. Button [1963]. In Schware v. Board of Bar Examiners [1957] we held it not permissible to bar a lawyer from practice, because he had once been a member of the Communist Party. The man's "association with that Party" was not shown to be "anything more than a political faith in a political party" and was not action of a kind proving bad moral character.

Those cases involved more than the "right of assembly"—a right that extends to all irrespective of their race or ideology. . . . The right of "association" like the right of belief . . . is more than the right to attend a meeting; it includes the right to express one's attitudes or philosophies by membership in a group or by affiliation with it or by other lawful means. Association in that context is a form of expression of opinion; and while it is not expressly included in the First Amendment its existence is necessary in making the express guarantees fully meaningful.

The foregoing cases suggest that specific guarantees in the Bill of Rights have penumbras, formed by emanations from those guarantees that help give them life and substance. . . . Various guarantees create zones of privacy. The right of association contained in the penumbra of the First Amendment is one, as we have seen. The Third Amendment in its prohibition against the quartering of soldiers "in any house" in time of peace without the consent of the owner is another facet of that privacy. The Fourth Amendment explicitly affirms the "right of the people to be secure in their persons, houses, papers, and effects, against unreasonable searches and seizures." The Fifth Amendment in its Self-Incrimination Clause enables the citizen to create a zone of privacy which government may not force him to surrender to his detriment. The Ninth Amendment provides: "The enumeration in the Constitution, of certain rights, shall not be construed to deny or disparage others retained by the people." . . .

The present case, then, concerns a relationship lying within the zone of privacy created by several fundamental constitutional guarantees. And it concerns a law which, in forbidding the *use* of contraceptives rather than regulating their manufacture or sale, seeks to achieve its goals by means having a maximum destructive impact upon that relationship. Such a law cannot stand in light of the familiar principle, so often applied by this Court, that a "governmental purpose to control or prevent activities constitutionally subject to state regulation may not be achieved by means which sweep unnecessarily broadly and thereby invade the area of protected freedoms." NAACP v. Alabama [1964]. Would we allow the police to search the sacred precincts of marital bedrooms for telltale signs of the use of contraceptives? The very idea is repulsive to the notions of privacy surrounding the marriage relationship.

We deal with a right of privacy older than the Bill of Rights—older than our political parties, older than our school system. Marriage is a coming together for better or for worse, hopefully enduring, and intimate to the degree of being sacred. It is an association that promotes a way of life, not causes; a harmony in living, not political faiths; a bilateral loyalty, not commercial or social projects. Yet it is an association for as noble a purpose as any involved in our prior decisions.

Reversed.

Mr. Justice **Goldberg,** whom the Chief Justice **[Warren]** and Mr. Justice **Brennan** join, concurring, said in part:

While this Court has had little occasion to interpret the Ninth Amendment, "[i]t cannot be presumed that any clause in the constitution is intended to be without effect." Marbury v. Madison [1803]. . . . To hold that a right so basic and fundamental and so deep-rooted in our society as the right of privacy in marriage may be infringed because that right is not guaranteed in so many words by the first eight amendments to the Constitution is to ignore the Ninth Amendment and to give it no effect whatsoever. Moreover, a judicial construction that this fundamental right is not protected by the Constitution because it is not mentioned in explicit terms by one of the first eight amendments or elsewhere in the Constitution would violate the Ninth Amendment, which specifically states that "[t]he enumeration in the Constitution, of certain rights, shall not be *construed* to deny or disparage others retained by the people." (Emphasis added.)

. . . I do not take the position of my Brother Black . . . that the entire Bill of Rights is incorporated in the Fourteenth Amendment, and I do not mean to imply that the Ninth Amendment is applied against the States by the Fourteenth. Nor do I mean to state that the Ninth Amendment constitutes an independent source of rights protected from infringement by either the States or the Federal Government. Rather, the Ninth Amendment shows a belief of the Constitution's authors that fundamental rights exist that are not expressly enumerated in the first eight amendments and an intent that the list of rights included there not be deemed exhaustive. . . .

. . . In sum, the Ninth Amendment simply lends strong support to the view that the "liberty" protected by the Fifth and Fourteenth Amendments from infringement by the Federal Government or the States is not restricted to rights specifically mentioned in the first eight amendments. . . .

Mr. Justice **Harlan,** concurring in the judgment, said in part:

. . . What I find implicit in the Court's opinion is that the "incorporation" doctrine may be used to *restrict* the reach of Fourteenth Amendment Due Process. For me this is just as unacceptable constitutional doctrine as is the use of the "incorporation" approach to *impose* upon the States all the requirements of the Bill of Rights as found in the provisions of the first eight amendments and in the decisions of this Court interpreting them. . . .

In my view, the proper constitutional inquiry in this case is whether this Connecticut statute infringes the Due Process Clause of the Fourteenth Amendment because the enactment violates basic values "implicit in the concept of ordered liberty," Palko v. Connecticut [1937]. . . .

Mr. Justice **White** concurred in the judgment.

Mr. Justice **Black,** with whom Mr. Justice **Stewart** joins, dissented, saying in part:

The Court talks about a constitutional "right of privacy" as though there is some constitutional provision or provisions forbidding any law ever to be passed which might abridge the "privacy" of individuals. But there is not. There are, of course, guarantees in certain specific constitutional provisions which are designed in part to protect privacy at certain times and places with respect to certain activities. Such, for example, is the Fourth Amendment's guarantee against "unreasonable searches and seizures." But I think it belittles that Amendment to talk about it as though it protects nothing but "privacy." To treat it that way is to give it a niggardly interpretation, not the kind of liberal reading I think any Bill of Rights provision should be given. The average man would very likely not have his feelings soothed any more by having his property seized openly than by having it seized privately and by stealth. He simply wants his property left alone. And a person can be just as much, if not more, irritated, annoyed and injured by an unceremonious public arrest by a policeman as he is by a seizure in the privacy of his office or home.

One of the most effective ways of diluting or expanding a constitutionally guaranteed right is to substitute for the crucial word or words of a constitutional guarantee another word or words more or less flexible and more or less restricted in meaning. This fact is well illustrated by the use of the term "right of privacy" as a comprehensive substitute for the Fourth Amendment's guarantee against "unreasonable searches and seizures." "Privacy" is a broad, abstract and ambiguous concept which can easily be shrunken in meaning but which can also, on the other hand, easily be interpreted as a constitutional ban against many things other than searches and seizures. I have expressed the view many times that First Amendment freedoms, for example, have suffered from a failure of the courts to stick to the simple language of the First Amendment in construing it, instead of invoking multitudes of words substituted for those the Framers used. . . .

I realize that many good and able men have eloquently spoken and written, sometimes in rhapsodical strains, about the duty of this Court to keep the Constitution in tune with the times. The idea is that the Constitution must be changed from time to time and that this Court is charged with a duty to make those changes. For myself, I must with all deference reject that philosophy. The Constitution makers knew the need for change and provided for it. Amendments suggested by the people's elected representatives can be submitted to the people or their selected agents for ratification. That method of change was good for our Fathers, and being somewhat old-fashioned I must add it is good enough for me. And so, I cannot rely on the Due Process Clause or the Ninth Amendment or any mysterious and uncertain natural law concept as a reason for striking down this state law. The Due Process Clause with an "arbitrary and capricious" or "shocking to the conscience" formula was liberally used by this Court to strike down economic legislation in the early decades of this century, threatening, many people thought, the tranquility and stability of the Nation. See, e.g., Lochner v. New York [1905]. That formula, based on subjective considerations of "natural justice," is no less dangerous when used to enforce this Court's views about personal rights than those about economic rights. I had thought that we had laid that formula, as a means for striking down state legislation, to rest once and for all in cases like West Coast Hotel Co. v. Parrish [1937].

Mr. Justice **Stewart** wrote a dissenting opinion in which Mr. Justice **Black** joined.

ROE v. WADE

410 U. S. 113; 93 S. Ct. 705; 35 L. Ed. 2d 147
(1973)

"The Court today does not *pick out particular human activities, characterize them as 'fundamental,' and give them added protection. . . . To the contrary, the Court simply recognizes, as it must, an established constitutional right, and gives to that right no less protection than the Constitution itself demands."*

Although this quotation from Justice Stewart by the Court in San Antonio v. Rodriguez (1973) states the orthodox view of the Court's role, few scholars today would subscribe to it. While in theory all rights in the Constitution are of equal value (the Constitution nowhere suggests that some rights are more important than others), over the years the Court has always cherished certain rights which it considered more important than other rights and hence entitled to greater constitutional protection. The rights so honored have changed from time to time as the Court perceived changes in basic social values. In the early days private property was given special consideration, and later this came to include the rights of businessmen and "liberty of contract." Then in the 1930s and 1940s, while the economic rights fell from grace, the rights listed in the First Amendment rose to favor. In recent years the rights of privacy and the right to vote have joined the ranks of the elite.

Since the ranking of these rights is a matter of value judgment, it has been condemned by those who disapproved the particular ranking as "judicial legislation," "substituting judicial values for those of the community," a "violation of the democratic process," and a "lack of proper judicial restraint." While such attacks seem to challenge the role of the Court in this area, in fact few justices have rejected philosophically the idea that some rights are better than others. The classic example is Justice Holmes, who condemned the judicial fa-

voritism shown to economic rights (see Lochner v. New York, 1905) while insisting that speech could be curtailed only if it presented a "clear and present danger," (see his dissent in Gitlow v. New York, 1925).

Perhaps the easiest method of giving added protection to a right, once it is identified, is to clothe it in language that nullifies the normal presumption in favor of legislative acts and forces the government to show that its laws are reasonable and necessary. Such language abounds in the areas of the First Amendment: the "clear and present danger" test, the statement that First Amendment rights are in a "preferred position" (see Murdock v. Pennsylvania, 1943) and the rule (since modified) that publications cannot be condemned as obscene unless they are utterly without redeeming social value—all serve to tip the scales in favor of the right and against the government wishing to suppress or regulate it.

In 1960 in Bates v. Little Rock a new phrase made its appearance. The Court held bad the demand of the city of Little Rock for the publication of the membership lists of the NAACP on the ground that it would destroy the group's organizational privacy and impair its operations. "Where there is a significant encroachment upon personal liberty, the State may prevail only upon showing a subordinating interest which is compelling." This "compelling state interest" phrase appeared again in several cases in 1963 (see Gibson v. Florida Investigating Committee), where its impact was to make the state produce evidence that it had a compelling interest which could be met only by infringing a claimed right of association. In none of the cases was sufficient interest shown.

In 1969 the "compelling state interest" doctrine was applied to the equal protection clause. The Court in this area had long granted favored status to certain bases of classification, such as race and religion, holding that legislative distinctions based on them were, if not "invidious," at least "inherently suspect." But with Shapiro v. Thompson and Kramer v. U.S.F.D. the Court looked not at the bases of classification alone, but at the aims sought to be achieved by these bases. In striking down the requirement of a year's residence to receive welfare and the requirement of taxpayer (or parental) status to vote in school board elections, the Court found that where a classification limits the right to move freely across state lines or the right to vote, it could only be justified by a compelling state interest.

In the case below, the phrase is moved again—this time into the area of privacy protected by the Constitution. Here the Court not only upholds the right of a mother to decide, in consultation with her doctor, whether or not to have an abortion, but spells out the "compelling points" at which the state's "compelling interest" permits it to undertake regulation of abortions.

While the case below in effect holds invalid the statutes of some thirty states which forbid abortions except to save the life of the mother, in Doe v. Bolton, decided the same day, the Court dealt with a Georgia statute patterned after the American Law Institute's Penal Code and followed in about a dozen states. The Georgia statute permitted abortion if it was necessary to the pres-

ervation of the health of the mother, if the fetus was likely to be born with a serious defect, or if the pregnancy resulted from rape. Although the Court held that the validity of these provisions was not properly before it, the questions they raise are clearly answered in the Texas case below. In addition, the Georgia law required a number of procedural conditions, such as that the woman's doctor and two other doctors put in writing the judgment that an abortion was needed, that the abortion be performed in a hospital accredited by the nongovernmental Joint Committee on Accreditation of Hospitals, and that the abortion be approved in advance by three members of the hospital's abortion committee. All these requirements were held invalid since they were not required in any surgical procedure other than abortion. Two years later the Court made clear that this language did not forbid a state to apply its anti-abortion statute to punish the performance of an abortion by a non-physician with no medical training; see *Connecticut v. Menillo* (1975).

Following the decisions of the Court in Roe and Doe, Missouri enacted an elaborate statute for the regulation of abortions. In *Planned Parenthood of Missouri v. Danforth* (1976) the Court upheld some of these provisions and struck down others. It could find no quarrel with the definition of viability as "that state of fetal development when the life of the unborn child may be continued indefinitely outside the womb by natural or artificial life support systems." This, the Court found, merely endorsed the flexibility called for in Roe, since "the determination of whether a particular fetus is viable is, and must be, a matter for the judgment of the responsible attending physician." Nor did it find fault with the requirement that the woman give her informed consent to the abortion freely, and in writing, and that the physician keep certain records which the state argued would "advance the sum of medical knowledge." The Court found no constitutional reason why the state could not require written consent for any surgery, and it upheld the record-keeping on the assumption that it would not be allowed to become a burden on the abortion procedure.

In addition to the consent of the pregnant woman, the statute also required the consent of her spouse, and, in the case of an unmarried woman under eighteen, the consent of a parent or guardian. Since the state has no power itself to forbid the termination of the pregnancy, it "does not have the constitutional authority to give a third party an absolute, and possibly arbitrary veto over the decision of the physician and his patient to terminate the patient's pregnancy, regardless of the reason for withholding consent." It was unpersuaded that marital harmony would be promoted by the requirement, and since only the wishes of one could prevail, the interests of the woman bearing the child took precedence. Nor could the Court see how giving parents an absolute veto would "strengthen the family unit" or "enhance parental authority or control where the minor and the nonconsenting parent are so fundamentally in conflict and the very existence of the pregnancy already has fractured the family structure. Any independent interest the parent may have in the termination of the minor daughter's

pregnancy is no more weighty than the right of privacy of the competent minor mature enough to have become pregnant."

The Court's decision that a state could not forbid abortions triggered a highly emotional nationwide political battle. With the political and financial support of "anti-abortion" and "right to life" groups, efforts were made to overturn or undo the effects of the case by constitutional amendment, by Congressional statutes defining a fetus as a "person" entitled to due process of law, and by various procedural statutes designed to prevent federal courts from enforcing its ruling. While these failed to pass, a substantial victory was achieved when the Court held valid state laws giving financial aid to normal child birth while withholding it from abortions, since most abortions are sought by those requiring financial aid from the state; see *Maher v. Roe* (1977). It was hoped that this victory was an indication that the Court was weakening in its enthusiasm for Roe, and should the opportunity arise, it would respond to the efforts in Congress and the intense publicity by overruling it.

In a series of three cases decided in June 1983 the Court not only did not overrule Roe v. Wade but reaffirmed in unmistakable terms the right of a woman to have an abortion. Justice Powell, speaking for six members of the Court in *Akron v. Akron Center for Reproductive Health*, noted that "the doctrine of stare decisis . . . demands respect in a society governed by the rule of law," and in a footnote added: "There are especially compelling reasons for adhering to stare decisis in applying the principles of Roe v. Wade. That case was considered with special care. it was first argued during the 1971 Term, and reargued—with extensive briefing—the following term. The decision was joined by the Chief Justice and six other Justices. Since Roe was decided in February 1973, the Court repeatedly and consistently has accepted and applied the basic principle that a woman has a fundamental right to make the highly personal choice whether or not to terminate her pregnancy. . . ."

Over the dissents of Justices O'Connor, Rehnquist and White, the Court struck down a number of requirements imposed by the City of Akron. These included a requirement that all second trimester abortions be performed in a full-service hospital (most of which do not perform such abortions) rather than a clinic; that a minor under the age of fifteen must have either parental consent or a court order before an abortion can be performed (regardless of the maturity of the minor); that a woman must be given detailed information regarding the abortion—much of which, the Court noted, "is designed not to inform the woman's consent but rather to persuade her to withhold it altogether"; and that the physician, under threat of criminal penalties, dispose of the fetus in a "humane and sanitary" manner (which the Court found void for vagueness.) The Court made clear that while the mental health of the woman was a legitimate concern of the state, there were limits beyond which it could not reasonably go.

In *Planned Parenthood v. Ashcroft* the Court conceded that the compelling interest of the state entitled it *to ban abortions entirely once the fetus became viable, and Missouri had done so except to preserve the life or health of the mother. Hence it was not unreasonable to require the presence of a second physician to care for the fetus, since the attending physician would be occupied with the care of the mother. Moreover, the statute requiring parental or judicial consent for a minor to have an abortion required the court to deny such request only for "good cause," which sufficiently protected both the interest of the pregnant minor herself and the state's legitimate interest in protecting immature minors generally. And in Simopoulos v. Virginia it held that a state could require a license of out-patient clinics performing second trimester abortions as a way of protecting the mother's health and upheld the conviction of an operator of an unlicensed clinic. The dissenting justices, while not directly urging the overruling of Roe, argued that the requirement that state regulations not be "unduly burdensome" should be applied throughout the term of the pregnancy, and if it was not unduly burdensome its validity should be judged by whether it "rationally relates to a legitimate state purpose." None of the requirements involved in these cases were found unduly burdensome and all met the rational basis test.*

Mr. Justice **Blackmun** delivered the opinion of the Court, saying in part:

V.

The principal thrust of appellant's attack on the Texas statutes is that they improperly invade a right, said to be possessed by the pregnant woman, to choose to terminate her pregnancy. Appellant would discover this right in the concept of personal "liberty" embodied in the Fourteenth Amendment's Due Process Clause; or in personal, marital, familial, and sexual privacy said to be protected by the Bill of Rights or its penumbras, see Griswold v. Connecticut (1965); Eisenstadt v. Baird (1972); (White, J., concurring); or among those rights reserved to the people by the Ninth Amendment, Griswold v. Connecticut (Goldberg, J., concurring). Before addressing this claim, we feel it desirable briefly to survey, in several aspects, the history of abortion, for such insight as that history may afford us, and then to examine the state purposes and interests behind the criminal abortion laws.

VI.

It perhaps is not generally appreciated that the restrictive criminal abortion laws in effect in a majority of States today are of relatively recent vintage. Those laws, generally proscribing abortion or its attempt at any time during pregnancy except when necessary to preserve the pregnant woman's life, are not of ancient or even of common law origin. Instead, they derive from statutory changes effected, for the most part, in the latter half of the 19th century. . . .

[The Court here reviews the history of attitudes toward abortion and abortion laws since ancient times.]

VII.

Three reasons have been advanced to explain historically the enactment of criminal abortion laws in the 19th century and to justify their continued existence.

It has been argued occasionally that these laws were the product of a Victorian social concern to discourage illicit sexual conduct. Texas, however, does not advance this justification in the present case, and it appears that no court or commentator has taken the argument seriously. The appellants and amici contend, moreover, that this is not a proper state purpose at all and suggest that, if it were, the Texas statutes are overbroad in protecting it since the law fails to distinguish between married and unwed mothers.

A second reason is concerned with abortion as a medical procedure. When most criminal abortion laws were first enacted, the procedure was a hazardous one for the woman. This was particularly true prior to the development of antisepsis. Antiseptic techniques, of course, were based on discoveries by Lister, Pasteur, and others first announced in 1867, but were not generally accepted and employed until about the turn of the century. Abortion mortality was high. Even after 1900, and perhaps until as late as the development of antibiotics in the 1940's, standard modern techniques such as dilation and curettage were not nearly so safe as they are today. Thus it has been argued that a State's real concern in enacting a criminal abortion law was to protect the pregnant woman, that is, to restrain her from submitting to a procedure that placed her life in serious jeopardy.

Modern medical techniques have altered this situation. Appellants and various amici refer to medical data indicating that abortion in early pregnancy, that is, prior to the end of first trimester, although not without its risk, is now relatively safe. Mortality rates for women undergoing early abortions, where the procedure is legal, appear to be as low as or lower than the rates for normal childbirth. Consequently, any interest of the State in protecting the woman from an inherently hazardous procedure, except when it would be equally dangerous for her to forego it, has largely disappeared. Of course, important state interests in the area of health and medical standards do remain. The State has a legitimate interest in seeing to it that abortion, like any other medical procedure, is performed under circumstances that insure maximum safety for the patient. This interest obviously extends at least to the performing physician and his staff, to the facilities involved, to the availability of after-care, and to adequate provision for any complication or emergency that might arise. The prevalence of high mortality rates at illegal "abortion mills" strengthens, rather than weakens, the State's interest in regulating the conditions under which abortions are performed. Moreover, the risk to the woman increases as her pregnancy continues. Thus the State retains a definite interest in protecting the woman's own health and safety when an abortion is proposed at a late stage of pregnancy.

The third reason is the State's interest—some phrase it in terms of duty—in protecting prenatal life. Some of the argument for this justification rests on the theory that a new human life is present from the moment of conception. The State's interest and general obligation to protect life then extends, it is argued, to prenatal life. Only when the life of the pregnant mother herself is at stake, balanced against the life she carries within her, should the interest of the embryo or fetus not prevail. Logically, of course, a legitimate State interest in this area need not stand or fall on acceptance of the belief that life begins at conception or at some other point prior to live birth. In assessing the State's interest, recognition may be given to the less rigid claim that as long as at least *potential* life is involved, the State may assert interests beyond the protection of the pregnant woman alone.

Parties challenging state abortion laws have sharply disputed in some courts the contention that a purpose of these laws, when enacted, was to protect prenatal life. . . .

It is with these interests, and the weight to be attached to them, that this case is concerned.

VIII.

The Constitution does not explicitly mention any right of privacy. In a line of decisions, however, going back perhaps as far as Union Pacific R. Co. v. Botsford (1891), the Court has recognized that a right of personal privacy, or a guarantee of certain areas or zones of privacy, does exist under the Constitution. In varying contexts the Court or individual Justices have indeed found at least the roots of that right in the First Amendment, Stanley v. Georgia (1969); in the Fourth and Fifth Amendments, Terry v. Ohio (1968), Katz v. United States (1967) . . . ; in the penumbras of the Bill of Rights, Griswold v. Connecticut (1965); in the Ninth Amendment; or in the concept of liberty guaranteed by the first section of the Fourteenth Amendment, see Meyer v. Nebraska (1923). These decisions make it clear that only personal rights that can be deemed "fundamental" or "implicit in the concept of ordered liberty," Palko v. Connecticut (1937), are included in this guarantee of personal privacy. They also make it clear that the right has some extension to activities relating to marriage, Loving v. Virginia (1967), procreation, Skinner v. Oklahoma (1942), contraception, Eisenstadt v. Baird (1972). . . .

This right of privacy, whether it be founded in the Fourteenth Amendment's concept of personal liberty and restrictions upon state action, as we feel it is, or, as the District Court determined, in the Ninth Amendment's reservation of rights to the people, is broad enough to encompass a woman's decision whether or not to terminate her pregnancy. The detriment that the State would impose upon the pregnant woman by denying this choice altogether is apparent. Specific and direct harm medically diagnosable even in early pregnancy may be involved. Maternity, or additional offspring, may force upon the woman a distressful life and future. Psychological harm may be imminent. Mental and physical health may be taxed by child care. There is also the distress, for all concerned, associated with the unwanted child, and

there is the problem of bringing a child into a family already unable, psychologically and otherwise, to care for it. In other cases, as in this one, the additional difficulties and continuing stigma of unwed motherhood may be involved. All these are factors the woman and her responsible physician necessarily will consider in consultation.

On the basis of elements such as these, appellants and some amici argue that the woman's right is absolute and that she is entitled to terminate her pregnancy at whatever time, in whatever way, and for whatever reason she alone chooses. With this we do not agree. Appellants' arguments that Texas either has no valid interest at all in regulating the abortion decision, or no interest strong enough to support any limitation upon the woman's sole determination, is unpersuasive. The Court's decisions recognizing a right of privacy also acknowledge that some state regulation in areas protected by that right is appropriate. As noted above, a State may properly assert important interests in safeguarding health, in maintaining medical standards, and in protecting potential life. At some point in pregnancy, these respective interests become sufficiently compelling to sustain regulation of the factors that govern the abortion decision. The privacy right involved, therefore, cannot be said to be absolute. In fact, it is not clear to us that the claim asserted by some amici that one has an unlimited right to do with one's body as one pleases bears a close relationship to the right of privacy previously articulated in the Court's decisions. The Court has refused to recognize an unlimited right of this kind in the past. Jacobson v. Massachusetts (1905) (vaccination); Buck v. Bell (1927) (sterilization).

We therefore conclude that the right of personal privacy includes the abortion decision, but that this right is not unqualified and must be considered against state interests in regulation.

Where certain "fundamental rights" are involved, the Court has held that regulation limiting these rights may be justified only by a "compelling state interest," Kramer v. Union Free School District (1969), Shapiro v. Thompson (1969), . . . and that legislative enactments must be narrowly drawn to express only the legitimate state interests at stake. Griswold v. Connecticut (1965). . . .

IX.

The District Court held that the appellee failed to meet his burden of demonstrating that the Texas statute's infringement upon Roe's rights was necessary to support a compelling state interest. . . . Appellee argues that the State's determination to recognize and protect prenatal life from and after conception constitutes a compelling state interest. As noted above, we do not agree fully with either formulation.

A. The appellee and certain amici argue that the fetus is a "person" within the language and meaning of the Fourteenth Amendment. In support of this they outline at length and in detail the well-known facts of fetal development. If this suggestion of personhood is established, the appellant's case, of course, collapses, for the fetus' right to life is then guaranteed specifically by the Amendment. The appellant conceded as much on reargument. On the other hand, the appellee conceded on reargument that no case could be cited that holds that a fetus is a person within the meaning of the Fourteenth Amendment.

The Constitution does not define "person" in so many words. Section 1 of the Fourteenth Amendment contains three references to "person." The first, in defining "citizens," speaks of "persons born or naturalized in the United States." The word also appears both in the Due Process Clause and in the Equal Protection Clause. "Person" is used in other places in the Constitution. . . . But in nearly all these instances, the use of the word is such that it has application only postnatally. None indicates, with any assurance, that it has any possible pre-natal application.* All this, together with our observation, that throughout the major portion of the 19th century prevailing legal abortion practices were far freer than they are today, persuades us that the word "person," as used in the Fourteenth Amendment, does not include the unborn. . . .

B. The pregnant woman cannot be isolated in her privacy. She carries an embryo and, later, a fetus, if one accepts the medical definitions of the developing young in the human uterus. . . . The situation therefore is inherently different from marital intimacy, or bedroom possession of obscene material, or marriage, or procreation, or education, with which Eisenstadt, Griswold, Stanley, Loving, Skinner, Pierce, and Meyer were respectively concerned. As we have intimated above, it is reasonable and appropriate for a State to decide that at some point in time another interest, that of health of the mother or that of potential human life, becomes significantly involved. The woman's privacy is no longer sole and any right of privacy she possesses must be measured accordingly.

Texas urges that, apart from the Fourteenth Amendment, life begins at conception and is present throughout pregnancy, and that, therefore, the State has a compelling interest in protecting that life from and after conception. We need not resolve the difficult question of when life begins. When those trained in the respective disciplines of medicine, philosophy, and theology are unable to arrive at any consensus, the judiciary, at this point in the development of man's knowledge, is not in a position to speculate as to the answer.

It should be sufficient to note briefly the wide divergence of thinking on this most sensitive and difficult question. . . .

X.

In view of all this, we do not agree that, by adopting one theory of life, Texas may override the rights of the pregnant woman that are at stake. We repeat, however, that the State does have an important and legitimate interest in preserving and protecting the health of the pregnant woman, whether she be a resident of the State or a nonresident who seeks medical consultation and treatment there, and that it has still *another* important and legitimate interest in protecting the potentiality of human life. These interests are separate and distinct. Each grows in substantiality as the woman approaches term and, at a point during pregnancy, each becomes "compelling."

With respect to the State's important and legitimate interest in the health of the mother, the "compelling" point, in the light of present medical knowledge, is at approximately the end of the first trimester. This is so because of the now established medical fact, referred to above . . . that until the end of the first trimester mortality in abortion is less than mortality in normal childbirth. It follows that, from and after this point, a State may regulate the abortion procedure to the extent that the regulation reasonably relates to the preservation and protection of maternal health. Examples of permissible state regulation in this area are requirements as to the qualifications of the person who is to perform the abortion; as to the licensure of that person; as to the facility in which the procedure is to be performed, that is, whether it must be a hospital or may be a clinic or some other place of less-than-hospital status; as to the licensing of the facility; and the like.

This means, on the other hand, that, for the period of pregnancy prior to this "compelling" point, the attending physician, in consultation with his patient, is free to determine, without regulation by the State, that in his medical judgment the patient's pregnancy should be terminated. If that decision is reached, the judgment may be effectuated by an abortion free of interference by the State.

With respect to the State's important and legitimate interest in potential life, the "compelling" point is at viability. This is so because the fetus then presumably has the capability of meaningful life outside the mother's womb. State regulation protective of fetal life after viability thus has both logical and biological justifications. If the State is interested in protecting fetal life after viability, it may go so far as to proscribe abortion during that period except when it is necessary to preserve the life or health of the mother.

Measured against these standards, the Texas Penal Code, in restricting legal abortions to those "procured or attempted by medical advice for the purpose of saving the life of the mother," sweeps too broadly. The statute makes no distinction between abortions performed early in pregnancy and those performed later, and it limits to a

---

*When Texas urges that a fetus is entitled to Fourteenth Amendment protection as a person, it faces a dilemma. Neither in Texas nor in any other State are all abortions prohibited. Despite broad proscription, an exception always exists. The exception contained in Art. 1196, for an abortion procured or attempted by medical advice for the purpose of saving the life of the mother, is typical. But if the fetus is a person who is not to be deprived of life without due process of law, and if the mother's condition is the sole determinant, does not the Texas exception appear to be out of line with the Amendment's command? . . .

single reason, ''saving'' the mother's life, the legal justification for the procedure. The statute, therefore, cannot survive the constitutional attack made upon it here. . . .

XI.

To summarize and to repeat:

1. A state criminal abortion statute of the current Texas type, that excepts from criminality only a *life saving* procedure on behalf of the mother, without regard to pregnancy stage and without recognition of the other interests involved, is violative of the Due Process Clause of the Fourteenth Amendment.

(a) For the stage prior to approximately the end of the first trimester, the abortion decision and its effectuation must be left to the medical judgment of the pregnant woman's attending physician.

(b) For the stage subsequent to approximately the end of the first trimester, the State, in promoting its interest in the health of the mother, may, if it chooses, regulate the abortion procedure in ways that are reasonably related to maternal health.

(c) For the stage subsequent to viability the State, in promoting its interest in the potentiality of human life, may, if it chooses, regulate, and even proscribe, abortion except where it is necessary, in appropriate medical judgment, for the preservation of the life or health of the mother.

2. The State may define the term ''physician,'' as it has been employed in the preceding numbered paragraphs of this Part XI of this opinion, to mean only a physician currently licensed by the State, and may proscribe any abortion by a person who is not a physician as so defined.

In Doe v. Bolton procedural requirements contained in one of the modern abortion statutes are considered. That opinion and this one, of course, are to be read together. . . .

Mr. Chief Justice **Burger** concurred.

Mr. Justice **Douglas** concurred.

Mr. Justice **Stewart,** concurring said in part:

In 1963, this Court, in Ferguson v. Skrupa, purported to sound the death knell for the doctrine of substantive due process, a doctrine under which many state laws had in the past been held to violate the Fourteenth Amendment. As Mr. Justice Black's opinion for the Court in Skrupa put it: ''We have returned to the original constitutional proposition that courts do not substitute their social and economic beliefs for the judgment of legislative bodies, who are elected to pass laws.''

Barely two years later, in Griswold v. Connecticut, the Court held a Connecticut birth control law unconstitutional. In view of what had been so recently said in Skrupa, the Court's opinion in Griswold understandably did its best to avoid reliance on the Due Process Clause of the Fourteenth Amendment as the ground for decision. Yet, the Connecticut law did not violate any provision of the Bill of Rights, nor any other specific provision of the Constitution. So it was clear to me then, and it is equally clear to me now, that the Griswold decision can be rationally understood only as a holding that the Connecticut statute substantively invaded the ''liberty'' that is protected by the Due Process Clause of the Fourteenth Amendment. As so understood, Griswold stands as one in a long line of pre-Skrupa cases decided under the doctrine of substantive due process, and I now accept it as such.

''In a Constitution for a free people, there can be no doubt that the meaning of 'liberty' must be broad indeed.'' . . . The Constitution nowhere mentions a specific right of personal choice in matters of marriage and family life, but the ''liberty'' protected by the Due Process Clause of the Fourteenth Amendment covers more than those freedoms explicitly named in the Bill of Rights. . . .

Several decisions of this Court make clear that freedom of personal choice in matters of marriage and family life is one of the liberties protected by the Due Process Clause of the Fourteenth Amendment. Loving v. Virginia, Griswold v. Connecticut . . . . That right necessarily includes the right of a woman to decide whether or not to terminate her pregnancy. ''Certainly the interests of a woman in giving of her physical and emotional self during pregnancy and the interests that will be affected throughout her life by the birth and raising of a child are of a far greater degree of significance and personal intimacy than the right to send a child to private school protected in Pierce v. Society of Sisters (1925), or the right to teach a foreign language protected in Meyer v. Nebraska (1923).'' . . .

Mr. Justice **Rehnquist,** dissenting, said in part:

. . . I have difficulty in concluding, as the Court does, that the right of ''privacy'' is involved in this case. Texas by the statute here challenged bars the performance of a medical abortion by a licensed physician on a plaintiff such as Roe. A transaction resulting in an operation such as this is not ''private'' in the ordinary usage of that word. . . .

If the Court means by the term ''privacy'' no more than that the claim of a person to be free from unwanted state regulation of consensual transactions may be a form of ''liberty'' protected by the Fourteenth Amendment, there is no doubt that similar claims have been upheld in our earlier decisions on the basis of that liberty. I agree with the statement of Mr. Justice Stewart in his concurring opinion that the ''liberty,'' against deprivation of which without due process the Fourteenth Amendment protects, embraces more than the rights found in the Bill of Rights. But that liberty is not guaranteed absolutely against deprivation, but only against deprivation without due process of law. The test traditionally applied in the area of social and economic legislation is whether or not a law such as that challenged has a rational relation to a valid state objective. . . . But the Court's sweeping invalidation of any restrictions on abortion during the first trimester is impossible to justify under that standard, and the conscious weighing of competing factors which the Court's opinion apparently substitutes for the established test is far more appropriate to a legislative judgment than to a judicial one.

The Court eschews the history of the Fourteenth Amendment in its reliance on the "compelling state interest" test. . . . But the Court adds a new wrinkle to this test by transposing it from the legal considerations associated with the Equal Protection Clause of the Fourteenth Amendment to this case arising under the Due Process Clause of the Fourteenth Amendment. Unless I misapprehend the consequences of this transplanting of the "compelling state interest test," the Court's opinion will accomplish the seemingly impossible feat of leaving this area of the law more confused than it found it.

While the Court's opinion quotes from the dissent of Mr. Justice Holmes in Lochner v. New York (1905), the result it reaches is more closely attuned to the majority opinion of Mr. Justice Peckham in that case. As in Lochner and similar cases applying substantive due process standards to economic and social welfare legislation, the adoption of the compelling state interest standard will inevitably require this Court to examine the legislative policies and pass on the wisdom of these policies in the very process of deciding whether a particular state interest put forward may or may not be "compelling." . . .

The fact that a majority of the States, reflecting after all the majority sentiment in those States, have had restrictions on abortions for at least a century is a strong indication, it seems to me, that the asserted right to an abortion is not "so rooted in the traditions and conscience of our people as to be ranked as fundamental," Snyder v. Massachusetts (1934). . . .

Mr. Justice **White,** with whom Mr. Justice **Rehnquist** joins, dissented.

9

Rights of Persons Accused of Crime

THE EXCLUSION OF UNCONSTITUTIONAL EVIDENCE

WEEKS v. UNITED STATES

232 U. S. 383; 34 S. Ct. 341; 58 L. Ed. 652
(1914)

At common law the admission of evidence in court had nothing to do with any illegal action by the police in securing the evidence. A lawyer could argue that certain evidence was incompetent, irrelevant, and immaterial; but if the court found it wasn't, it was admissible. The court was not concerned with the legality of the methods used to obtain it. If it had been stolen, either by a private person or by a police officer, the common law provided for prosecution of the thief or a civil action for trespass and the return of the property.

With the growth of professional police forces and the burgeoning of personal rights against searches and seizures and compulsory self-incrimination, it became clear that these approaches were not effective restraints on enthusiastic police investigation. Not only were juries, who as individuals depended on these same police for the protection of themselves and their homes, reluctant to convict an officer who had turned up evidence of crime or induced a confession, but such financial awards as were made were normally not large enough to serve as a serious deterrent. It was long argued, therefore, that evidence illegally obtained should not be admitted in court, because refusal to admit it provided the only effec-

tive deterrent to the illegal conduct. This argument was slow to find favor, and for years most of the states continued to follow the common-law rule. The Supreme Court itself apparently adhered to it until the decision in the present case. See Adams v. New York (1904).

In Silverthorne Lumber Co. v. United States (1920) the Court made it clear that the "Weeks" rule requiring the exclusion of illegal evidence was not merely the formal requirement that things stolen from an accused must be returned. Here the government had seized all the company's books without warrant and made photographic copies of them. The trial court ordered the return of the originals but impounded the photographs and issued a subpoena for the production of the originals. Justice Holmes, speaking for the Court, rejected the claim that "the protection of the Constitution covers the physical possession, but not any advantages that the government can gain over the object of its pursuit by doing the forbidden act. Weeks v. United States . . . is taken to mean only that two steps are required instead of one. In our opinion such is not the law. It reduces the Fourth Amendment to a form of words. The essence of a provision forbidding the acquisition of evidence in a certain way is that not merely evidence so acquired shall not be used before the court, but that it shall not be used at all."

Despite the undisputed acceptance of the Weeks "exclusion of evidence" doctrine in the federal system, two problems have plagued the Supreme Court: (1) how, as a rational matter, can the rule be justified, and (2) is it really a Constitutional requirement or is it just a convenient rule of evidence promulgated by the Court. One justification for the rule, characterized as the "imperative of judicial integrity," was expressed in two classic dissents in *Olmstead v. United States* (1928). In the words of Justice Holmes, "We have to choose, and for my part I think it a less evil that some criminals should escape than that the government should play an ignoble part." Or, as Justice Brandeis put it, "Decency, security, and liberty alike demand that government officials shall be subjected to the same rules of conduct that are commands to the citizen. In a government of laws, existence of the government will be imperiled if it fails to observe the law scrupulously. Our government is the potent, the omnipresent, teacher. For good or for ill, it teaches the whole people by its example. Crime is contagious. If the government becomes a law-breaker, it breeds contempt for the law; it invites every man to become a law unto himself; it invites anarchy. To declare that in the administration of the criminal law the end justifies the means—to declare that the government may commit crimes in order to secure the conviction of a private criminal—would bring terrible retribution. Against that pernicious doctrine this court should resolutely set its face." The underlying assumption that makes these two classic statements relevant here is that a court which makes use of illegally or unconstitutionally gotten evidence, like a fence who receives stolen goods, shares in the criminality of the original theft.

The "deterrent effect" argument is the one on which the Court has clearly placed its reliance. Since it is apparent that the traditional common-law actions against a police officer by the victim of an unreasonable search are totally ineffective in preventing such searches, the Court has concluded that only by making it unrewarding to search illegally will the practice be abandoned. Although persuasive in theory, the technique has not proven as effective as it might be in practice. In the first place many investigative goals, such as the location and identification of witnesses, conspirators, and investigative leads, are furthered by illegal searches even though the results cannot be used in court. In the second place, the Court has not set the kind of comprehensive ban on the use of unconstitutional searches that would produce a really deterrent effect. Clearly it has not been designed to deter stealing evidence in general, as shown both by the fact the Court admits evidence stolen by private individuals and by the *Weeks* case itself, in which evidence stolen by the state police was held admissible. This "silver platter" doctrine was later abandoned as to evidence stolen by state officials; see *Benanti v. United States* (1957) and *Elkins v. United States* (1960).

Nor has the Court held inadmissible evidence gotten unconstitutionally, even by federal officers, where it was not used directly against the victim of the search. In *Goldstein v. United States* (1942) the telephones of Goldstein's accomplices had been illegally tapped, and, when they were confronted with the transcript of their conversation, they agreed to testify against Goldstein. The Court upheld the use of the testimony on the ground that the protection against unconstitutional search and seizure, like that against self-incrimination, was a purely personal right.

There are, in addition, purposes for which illegally gotten evidence may be used even against the victim himself. Thus, in *Walder v. United States* (1954) the Court held that narcotics which had been unreasonably seized from the defendant could be used to impeach his credibility at a later (and unrelated) trial at which he had testified broadly that he had never possessed narcotics before. The Court distinguished between using the evidence to convict him and using it to make him out a liar. In 1971 in *Harris v. New York*, the Court reaffirmed the *Walder* doctrine and permitted statements taken from the accused without the warnings required by *Miranda v. Arizona* (1966) to be used to impeach his credibility. In both cases the accused had taken the stand in his own defense, but unlike Walder, the statements introduced in Harris contradicted his protestations of innocence. The jury had been instructed to use the statement only to assess the defendant's credibility and not as evidence of guilt, and there was no denial that the statements made were voluntary. "The shield provided by Miranda," said Chief Justice Burger, "cannot be perverted into a license to use perjury by way of a defense, free from the risk of confrontation with prior inconsistent utterances."

In the case which follows, Weeks was arrested by a city police officer at his place of business and indicted in a federal court on a charge of sending lottery tickets through the mails. The police also searched his house and turned over to a United States marshal papers and articles found there. Thereupon the marshal himself, accompanied by police officers, searched Week's room and carried away other documents and letters. No warrants had been obtained either for the arrest or for the search by the police or marshal. Before the trial Weeks petitioned the federal district court to return all the papers and articles seized by the various officers. The district court, however, allowed the papers to be used against Weeks at the trial.

Mr. Justice **Day** delivered the opinion of the Court, saying in part:

The defendant assigns error, among other things, in the court's refusal to grant his petition for the return of his property, and in permitting the papers to be used at the trial. . . .

. . . The tendency of those who execute the criminal laws of the country to obtain conviction by means of unlawful seizures and enforced confessions, the latter often obtained after subjecting accused persons to unwarranted practices destructive of rights secured by the federal Constitution, should find no sanction in the judgments of the courts, which are charged at all times with the support of the Constitution, and to which people of all conditions have a right to appeal for the maintenance of such fundamental rights. . . .

. . . If letters and private documents can thus be seized and held and used in evidence against a citizen accused of an offense, the protection of the 4th Amendment, declaring his right to be secure against such searches and seizures, is of no value, and, so far as those thus placed are concerned, might as well be stricken from the Constitution. The efforts of the courts and their officials to bring the guilty to punishment, praiseworthy as they are, are not to be aided by the sacrifice of those great principles established by years of endeavor and suffering which have resulted in their embodiment in the fundamental law of the land. . . .

. . . While there is no opinion in the case, the court in this proceeding doubtless relied upon what is now contended by the government to be the correct rule of law under such circumstances, that the letters having come into the control of the court, it would not inquire into the manner in which they were obtained, but, if competent, would keep them and permit their use in evidence. . . .

The right of the court to deal with papers and documents in the possession of the district attorney and other officers of the court, and subject to its authority, was recognized in Wise v. Henkel [1911]. That papers wrongfully seized should be turned over to the accused has been frequently recognized in the early as well as later decisions of the courts.

We therefore reach the conclusion that the letters in question were taken from the house of the accused by an official of the United States, acting under color of his office in direct violation of the constitutional rights of the defendant; that having made a seasonable application for their return, which was heard and passed upon by the court, there was involved in the order refusing the application a denial of the constitutional rights of the accused, and that the court should have restored these letters to the accused. In holding them and permitting their use upon the trial, we think prejudicial error was committed. As to the papers and property seized by the policemen, it does not appear that they acted under any claim of federal authority such as would make the amendment applicable to such unauthorized seizures. The record shows that what they did by way of arrest and search and seizure was done before the finding of the indictment in the Federal court; under what supposed right or authority does not appear. What remedies the defendant may have against them we need not inquire, as the 4th Amendment is not directed to individual misconduct of such officials. Its limitations reach the Federal government and its agencies. . . .

Reversed.

WOLF v. COLORADO

338 U. S. 25; 69 S. Ct. 1359; 93 L. Ed. 1782
(1949)

The question whether the "exclusionary rule" was required by the Fourth Amendment or was merely a rule of evidence did not reach the Court as a problem until the present case, and it did so here as an aspect of the "incorporation" doctrine. Justice Frankfurter's reference to the "security of one's privacy against arbitrary intrusion by the police—which is at the core of the Fourth Amendment . . ." appeared to incorporate the search and seizure provision of the Fourth Amendment; the four dissenting justices clearly assumed this, dissenting only from the Court's failure to exclude the evidence. The Court in Elkins v. United States (1960) assumed that incorporation had taken place in Wolf, while Justice Frankfurter, in his dissent in Mapp v. Ohio (1961), denied that this was so.

For twelve years following the Wolf decision the Court continued to hold the Weeks rule regarding the exclusion of evidence not applicable to state search and seizure cases, regardless of how offensive to the sense of fairness the search had been. In Stefanelli v. Minard (1951) the Supreme Court refused to exercise its equity jurisdiction to suppress unconstitutionally gotten evidence, although in Rea v. United States (1956) the Court did forbid a federal officer to turn over evidence which he had illegally gotten to a state for use as evidence, and in Monroe v. Pape (1961) it held that the victim of an unreasonable search (in which no evidence had been turned up) could sue the Chicago police under the Civil Rights Act.

In the present case a deputy sheriff went to a doctor's office and, without a warrant, seized his appointment book, obtaining from it the names of patients who were then interrogated; and on evidence contained in the book the district attorney filed an information. The books were introduced against Wolf at his trial.

Mr. Justice **Frankfurter** delivered the opinion of the Court, saying in part:

The precise question for consideration is this: Does a conviction by a State court for a State offense deny the "due process of law" required by the Fourteenth Amendment, solely because evidence that was admitted at the trial was obtained under circumstances which would have rendered it inadmissible in a prosecution for violation of a federal law in a court of the United States because there deemed to be an infraction of the Fourth Amendment as applied in Weeks v. United States [1914]? . . .

Unlike the specific requirements and restrictions placed by the Bill of Rights (Amendments I to VIII) upon the administration of criminal justice by federal authority, the Fourteenth Amendment did not subject criminal justice in the States to specific limitations. The notion that the "due process of law" guaranteed by the Fourteenth Amendment is shorthand for the first eight amendments of the Constitution and thereby incorporates them has been rejected by this Court again and again, after impressive consideration. . . . Only the other day the Court reaffirmed this rejection after thorough reexamination of the scope and function of the Due Process Clause of the Fourteenth Amendment. Adamson v. California [1947]. The issue is closed.

For purposes of ascertaining the restriction which the Due Process Clause imposed upon the States in the enforcement of their criminal law, we adhere to the views expressed in Palko v. Connecticut [1937]. That decision speaks to us with the great weight of the authority, particularly in matters of civil liberty, of a court that included Mr. Chief Justice Hughes, Mr. Justice Brandeis, Mr. Justice Stone and Mr. Justice Cardozo, to name only the dead. In rejecting the suggestion that the Due Process Clause incorporated the original Bill of Rights, Mr. Justice Cardozo reaffirmed on behalf of that Court a different but deeper and more pervasive conception of the due process clause. This Clause exacts from the States for the lowliest and most outcast all that is "implicit in the concept of ordered liberty."

Due process of law thus conveys neither formal nor fixed nor narrow requirements. It is the compendious expression for all those rights which the courts must enforce because they are basic to our free society. But basic rights do not become petrified as of any one time, even though, as a matter of human experience, some may not too rhetorically be called eternal verities. It is of the very nature of a free society to advance in its standards of what is deemed reasonable and right. Representing as it does a living principle, due process is not confined within a permanent catalogue of what may at a given time be deemed the limits or the essentials of fundamental rights.

To rely on a tidy formula for the easy determination of what is a fundamental right for purposes of legal enforcement may satisfy a longing for certainty but ignores the movements of a free society. It belittles the scale of the conception of due process. The real clue to the problem confronting the judiciary in the application of the Due Process Clause is not to ask where the line is once and for all to be drawn but to recognize that it is for the Court to draw it by the gradual and empiric process of "inclusion and exclusion." . . .

The security of one's privacy against arbitrary intrusion by the police—which is at the core of the Fourth Amendment—is basic to a free society. It is therefore implicit in "the concept of ordered liberty" and as such enforceable against the States through the Due Process Clause. The knock at the door, whether by day or by night, as a prelude to a search, without authority of law but solely on the authority of the police, did not need the commentary of recent history to be condemned as inconsistent with the conception of human rights enshrined in the history and the basic constitutional documents of English-speaking peoples.

Accordingly, we have no hesitation in saying that were a State affirmatively to sanction such police incursion into privacy it would run counter to the guaranty of the Fourteenth Amendment. But the ways of enforcing such a basic right raise questions of a different order. How such arbitrary conduct should be checked, what remedies against it should be afforded, the means by which the right should be made effective, are all questions that are not to be so dogmatically answered as to preclude the varying solutions which spring from an allowable range of judgment on issues not susceptible of quantitative solution.

In Weeks v. United States, this Court held that in a federal prosecution the Fourth Amendment barred the use of evidence secured through an illegal search and sei-

zure. This ruling was made for the first time in 1914. It was not derived from the explicit requirements of the Fourth Amendment; it was not based on legislation expressing Congressional policy in the enforcement of the Constitution. The decision was a matter of judicial implication. Since then it has been frequently applied and we stoutly adhere to it. But the immediate question is whether the basic right to protection against arbitrary intrusion by the police demands the exclusion of logically relevant evidence obtained by an unreasonable search and seizure because, in a federal prosecution for a federal crime, it would be excluded. As a matter of inherent reason, one would suppose this to be an issue as to which men with complete devotion to the protection of the right of privacy might give different answers. When we find that in fact most of the English-speaking world does not regard as vital to such protection the exclusion of evidence thus obtained, we must hesitate to treat this remedy as an essential ingredient of the right. The contrariety of views of the States is particularly impressive in view of the careful reconsideration which they have given the problem in the light of the Weeks decision.

I. Before the Weeks decision 27 States had passed on the admissibility of evidence obtained by unlawful search and seizure.
   A. Of these, 26 States opposed the Weeks doctrine.
   B. Of these, 1 State anticipated the Weeks doctrine.
II. Since the Weeks decision 47 States all told have passed on the Weeks doctrine.
   A. Of these, 20 passed on it for the first time.
      1. Of the foregoing States, 6 followed the Weeks doctrine.
      2. Of the foregoing States, 14 rejected the Weeks doctrine.
   B. Of these, 26 States reviewed prior decisions contrary to the Weeks doctrine.
      1. Of these, 10 States have followed Weeks, overruling or distinguishing their prior decisions.
      2. Of these, 16 States adhered to their prior decisions against Weeks.
   C. Of these, 1 State adhered to its prior formulation of the Weeks doctrine.
III. As of today 30 States reject the Weeks doctrine, 17 States are in agreement with it.
IV. Of 10 jurisdictions with the United Kingdom and the British Commonwealth of Nations which have passed on the question, none has held evidence obtained by illegal search and seizure inadmissible.

[An appendix to the opinion lists the states and countries which comprise the categories just listed.]

The jurisdictions which have rejected the Weeks doctrine have not left the right to privacy without other means of protection. Indeed, the exclusion of evidence is a remedy which directly serves only to protect those upon whose person or premises something incriminating has been found. We cannot, therefore, regard it as a departure from basic standards to remand such persons, together with those who emerge scatheless from a search, to the remedies of private action and such protection as the internal discipline of the police, under the eyes of an alert public opinion, may afford. Granting that in practice the exclusion of evidence may be an effective way of deterring unreasonable searches, it is not for this Court to condemn as falling below the minimal standards assured by the Due Process Clause a State's reliance upon other methods which, if consistently enforced, would be equally effective. Weighty testimony against such an insistence on our own view is furnished by the opinion of Mr. Justice (then Judge) Cardozo in People v. Defore, 242 N. Y. 13 [1926]. We cannot brush aside the experience of States which deem the incidence of such conduct by the police too slight to call for a deterrent remedy not by way of disciplinary measures but by overriding the relevant rules of evidence. There are, moreover, reasons for excluding evidence unreasonably obtained by the federal police which are less compelling in the case of police under State or local authority. The public opinion of a community can far more effectively be exerted against oppressive conduct on the part of police directly responsible to the community itself than can local opinion, sporadically aroused, be brought to bear upon remote authority pervasively exerted throughout the country.

We hold, therefore, that in a prosecution in a State court for a State crime the Fourteenth Amendment does not forbid the admission of evidence obtained by an unreasonable search and seizure. And though we have interpreted the Fourth Amendment to forbid the admission of such evidence, a different question would be presented if Congress under its legislative powers were to pass a statute purporting to negate the Weeks doctrine. We would then be faced with the problem of the respect to be accorded the legislative judgment on an issue as to which, in default of that judgment, we have been forced to depend upon our own. Problems of a converse character, also not before us, would be presented should Congress under § 5 of the Fourteenth Amendment undertake to enforce the rights there guaranteed by attempting to make the Weeks doctrine binding upon the States.

Affirmed.

Mr. Justice **Black** concurred.

Justices **Douglas, Murphy,** and **Rutledge** dissented.

MAPP v. OHIO

367 U. S. 643; 81 S. Ct. 1684; 6 L. Ed. 2d 1081 (1961)

The Supreme Court was very slow to add to the list of Bill of Rights guarantees which had been assimilated, or incorporated, into the due process clause of the Fourteenth Amendment. There was no serious doubt that the First Amendment rights had been incorporated, but Betts v. Brady (1942) made it clear that the right to counsel, at least as the Sixth Amendment applied it to the federal government, had not been. A lack of agreement as to what incorporation really meant made it difficult to determine whether or not it had taken place in a given case. An example is the early attempt to incorporate the Eighth Amendment protection against cruel and unusual punishments. In 1946 one Willie Francis was to be electrocuted for murder and through some failure of the equipment did not receive enough electric current to kill him. Before the state could make a second attempt he obtained a writ of habeas corpus on the ground that such an attempt would subject him to cruel and unusual punishment in violation of the due process clause of the Fourteenth Amendment. The Supreme Court rejected his contentions in Louisiana ex rel. Francis v. Resweber (1947). Four members of the majority declared that "the Fourteenth [Amendment] would prohibit by its due process clause execution by a state in a cruel manner," but they did not say whether or not they considered this an "incorporation" of the provisions of the Eighth Amendment into the Fourteenth. Justice Frankfurter concurred in a separate opinion in order to state that in his view "the penological policy of a State is not to be tested by the scope of the Eighth Amendment. . . ." In 1962, however, the Court held that a California law providing a jail sentence for being addicted to narcotics amounted to a cruel and unusual punishment "in violation of the Eighth and Fourteenth Amendments," and cited Resweber as the case in which the right had been incorporated. See Robinson v. California (1962). And in Ker v. California (1963) eight justices made clear the effect of the Mapp decision by holding that state officers were subject to federal standards in searches and seizures.

Query: What is the significance of Justice Black's separate concurring opinion in the present case in view of the fact the Court had not yet incorporated the Fifth Amendment into the due process clause? Does the case incorporate the exclusionary rule?

Mr. Justice **Clark** delivered the opinion of the Court [sic], saying in part:

Appellant stands convicted of knowingly having had in her possession and under her control certain lewd and lascivious books, pictures, and photographs in violation of § 2905.34 of Ohio's Revised Code. . . . The Supreme Court of Ohio found that her conviction was valid though "based primarily upon the introduction in evidence of lewd and lascivious books and pictures unlawfully seized during an unlawful search of defendant's home. . . ."

On May 23, 1957, three Cleveland police officers arrived at appellant's residence in that city pursuant to information that "a person [was] hiding out in the home, who was wanted for questioning in connection with a recent bombing, and that there was a large amount of policy paraphernalia being hidden in the home." . . . Upon their arrival at that house, the officers knocked on the door and demanded entrance but appellant, after telephoning her attorney, refused to admit them without a search warrant. They advised their headquarters of the situation and undertook a surveillance of the house.

The officers again sought entrance some three hours later when four or more additional officers arrived on the scene. When Miss Mapp did not come to the door immediately, at least one of the several doors to the house was forcibly opened and the policemen gained admittance. Meanwhile Miss Mapp's attorney arrived, but the officers, having secured their own entry, and continuing in their defiance of the law, would permit him neither to see Miss Mapp nor to enter the house. It appears that Miss Mapp was halfway down the stairs from the upper floor to the front door when the officers, in this highhanded manner, broke into the hall. She demanded to see the search warrant. A paper, claimed to be a warrant, was held up by one of the officers. She grabbed the "warrant" and placed it in her bosom. A struggle ensued in which the officers recovered the piece of paper and as a result of which they handcuffed appellant because she had been "belligerent" in resisting their official rescue of the "warrant" from her person. Running roughshod over appellant, a policeman "grabbed" her, "twisted [her] hand," and she "yelled [and] pleaded with him" because "it was hurting." Appellant, in handcuffs, was then forcibly taken upstairs to her bedroom where the officers searched a dresser, a chest of drawers, a closet and some suitcases. They also looked into a photo album and through personal papers belonging to the appellant. The search spread to the rest of the second floor including . . . the living room, the kitchen and a dinette. The basement of the building and a trunk found therein were also searched. The obscene materials for possession of which she was ultimately convicted were discovered in the course of that widespread search.

At the trial no search warrant was produced by the prosecution, nor was the failure to produce one explained or accounted for. At best, "There is, in the record, considerable doubt as to whether there ever was any warrant for the search of defendant's home." . . .

The State says that even if the search were made without authority, or otherwise unreasonably, it is not prevented from using the unconstitutionally seized evidence at trial, citing Wolf v. Colorado [1949], in which this Court did indeed hold "that in a prosecution in a State court for a State crime the Fourteenth Amendment does not forbid the admission of evidence obtained by an unreasonable search and seizure." On this appeal . . . it is urged once again that we review that holding. . . .

[The Court here discusses the appearance of the exclusion doctrine in Boyd v. United States (1886) and Weeks v. United States (1914).]

There are in the cases of this Court some passing references to the Weeks rule as being one of evidence. But the plain and unequivocal language of Weeks—and its later paraphrase in Wolf—to the effect that the Weeks rule is of constitutional origin, remains entirely undisturbed. . . . The Court, in Olmstead v. United States [1928] in unmistakable language restated the Weeks rule:

"The striking outcome of the Weeks case and those which followed it was the sweeping declaration that the Fourth Amendment, although not referring to or limiting the use of evidence in courts, really forbade its introduction if obtained by government officers through a violation of the Amendment." . . .

In 1949, 35 years after Weeks was announced, this Court, in Wolf v. Colorado, again for the first time, discussed the effect of the Fourth Amendment upon the States through the operation of the Due Process Clause of the Fourteenth amendment. . . .

Nevertheless, after declaring that the "security of one's privacy against arbitrary intrusion by the police" is "implicit in 'the concept of ordered liberty' and as such enforceable against the States through the Due Process Clause," . . . the Court decided that the Weeks exclusionary rule would not then be imposed upon the States as "an essential ingredient of the right." The Court's reasons . . . were bottomed on factual considerations. . . .

[The Court here notes that at the time Wolf was decided almost two-thirds of the states rejected the Weeks doctrine, but that this situation has changed. Moreover, the futility of other means of protection and remedies to prevent police lawlessness has become apparent since Wolf.]

It, therefore, plainly appears that the factual considerations supporting the failure of the Wolf Court to include the Weeks exclusionary rule when it recognized the enforceability of the right to privacy against the States in 1949, while not basically relevant to the constitutional consideration, could not, in any analysis, now be deemed controlling. . . .

. . . Today we once again examine Wolf's constitutional documentation of the right to privacy free from unreasonable state intrusion, and, after its dozen years on our books, are led by it to close the only courtroom door remaining open to evidence secured by official lawlessness in flagrant abuse of that basic right, reserved to all persons as a specific guarantee against that very same unlawful conduct. We hold that all evidence obtained by searches and seizures in violation of the Constitution is, by that same authority, inadmissible in a state court.

Since the Fourth Amendment's right of privacy has been declared enforceable against the States through the Due Process Clause of the Fourteenth, it is enforceable against them by the same sanction of exclusion as is used against the Federal Government. Were it otherwise, then just as without the Weeks rule the assurance against unreasonable federal searches and seizures would be "a form of words," valueless and undeserving of mention in a perpetual charter of inestimable human liberties, so too, without that rule the freedom from state invasions of privacy would be so ephemeral and so neatly severed from its conceptual nexus with the freedom from all brutish means of coercing evidence as not to merit this Court's high regard as a freedom "implicit in the concept of ordered liberty." At the time that the Court held in Wolf that the Amendment was applicable to the States through the Due Process Clause, the cases of this Court, as we have seen, had steadfastly held that as to federal officers the Fourth Amendment included the exclusion of the evidence seized in violation of its provisions. Even

Wolf "stoutly adhered" to that proposition. The right to privacy, when conceded operatively enforceable against the States, was not susceptible of destruction by avulsion of the sanction upon which its protection and enjoyment had always been deemed dependent under the Boyd, Weeks and Silverthorne cases. Therefore, in extending the substantive protections of due process to all constitutionally unreasonable searches—state or federal—it was logically and constitutionally necessary that the exclusion doctrine—an essential part of the right to privacy—be also insisted upon as an essential ingredient of the right newly recognized by the Wolf Case. In short, the admission of the new constitutional right by Wolf could not consistently tolerate denial of its most important constitutional privilege, namely, the exclusion of the evidence which an accused had been forced to give by reason of the unlawful seizure. To hold otherwise is to grant the right but in reality to withhold its privilege and enjoyment. Only last year the Court itself recognized that the purpose of the exclusionary rule "is to deter—to compel respect for the constitutional guaranty in the only effectively available way—by removing the incentive to disregard it." Elkins v. United States [1960].

Indeed, we are aware of no restraint, similar to that rejected today, conditioning the enforcement of any other basic constitutional right. The right to privacy, no less important than any other right carefully and particularly reserved to the people, would stand in marked contrast to all other rights declared as "basic to a free society." Wolf v. Colorado. This Court has not hesitated to enforce as strictly against the States as it does against the Federal Government the rights of free speech and of a free press, the rights to notice and to a fair, public trial, including, as it does, the right not to be convicted by use of a coerced confession, however logically relevant it be, and without regard to its reliability. . . . And nothing could be more certain than that when a coerced confession is involved, "the relevant rules of evidence" are overridden without regard to "the incidence of such conduct by the police," slight or frequent. Why should not the same rule apply to what is tantamount to coerced testimony by way of unconstitutional seizure of goods, papers, effects, documents, etc.? We find that, as to the Federal Government, the Fourth and Fifth Amendments and, as to the States, the freedom from unconscionable invasions of privacy and the freedom from convictions based upon coerced confessions do enjoy an "intimate relation" in their perpetuation of "principles of humanity and civil liberty [secured] . . . only after years of struggle," Bram v. United States (1897). . . .

Moreover, our holding that the exclusionary rule is an essential part of both the Fourth and Fourteenth Amendments is not only the logical dictate of prior cases, but it also makes very good sense. There is no war between the Constitution and common sense. Presently, a federal prosecutor may make no use of evidence illegally seized, but a State's attorney across the street may, although he supposedly is operating under the enforceable prohibitions of the same Amendment. Thus the State, by admitting evidence unlawfully seized, serves to encourage disobedience to the Federal Constitution which it is bound to uphold. Moreover, as was said in Elkins, "[t]he very essence of a healthy federalism depends upon the avoidance of needless conflict between state and federal courts." . . . Yet the double standard recognized until today hardly put such a thesis into practice. In nonexclusionary States, federal officers, being human, were by it invited to and did, as our cases indicate, step across the street to the State's attorney with their unconstitutionally seized evidence. Prosecution on the basis of that evidence was then had in a state court in utter disregard of the enforceable Fourth Amendment. If the fruits of an unconstitutional search had been inadmissible in both state and federal courts, this inducement to evasion would have been sooner eliminated. . . .

Federal-state cooperation in the solution of crime under constitutional standards will be promoted, if only by recognition of their now mutual obligation to respect the same fundamental criteria in their approaches. "However much in a particular case insistence upon such rules may appear as a technicality that inures to the benefit of a guilty person, the history of the criminal law proves that tolerance of shortcut methods in law enforcement impairs its enduring effectiveness." . . . Denying shortcuts to only one of two cooperating law enforcement agencies tends naturally to breed legitimate suspicion of "working arrangements" whose results are equally tainted. . . .

There are those who say, as did Justice (then Judge) Cardozo, that under our constitutional exclusionary doctrine "[t]he criminal is to go free because the constable has blundered." People v. Defore, 242 N. Y., at page 21 [1926]. In some cases this will undoubtedly be the result. But, as was said in Elkins, "there is another consideration—the imperative of judicial integrity." The criminal goes free, if he must, but it is the law that sets him free. Nothing can destroy a government more quickly than its failure to observe its own laws, or worse, its disregard of the charter of its own existence. . . .

The ignoble shortcut to conviction left open to the State tends to destroy the entire system of constitutional restraints on which the liberties of the people rest. Having once recognized that the right to privacy embodied in the Fourth Amendment is enforceable against the States, and that the right to be secure against rude invasions of privacy by state officers is, therefore, constitutional in origin, we can no longer permit that right to remain an empty promise. Because it is enforceable in the same manner and to like effect as other basic rights secured by the Due Process Clause, we can no longer permit it to be revocable at the whim of any police officer who, in the name of law enforcement itself, chooses to suspend its enjoyment. Our decision, founded on reason and truth, gives to the individual no more than that which the Constitution guarantees him, to the police officer no less than that to which honest law enforcement is entitled, and, to the courts, that judicial integrity so necessary in the true administration of justice.

The judgment of the Supreme Court of Ohio is reversed and the cause remanded for further proceedings not inconsistent with this opinion.

Reversed and remanded.

Mr. Justice **Black,** concurring, said in part:

I am still not persuaded that the Fourth Amendment, standing alone, would be enough to bar the introduction into evidence against an accused of papers and effects seized from him in violation of its commands. For the Fourth Amendment does not itself contain any provision expressly precluding the use of such evidence, and I am extremely doubtful that such a provision could properly be inferred from nothing more than the basic command against unreasonable searches and seizures. Reflection on the problem, however, in the light of cases coming before the Court since Wolf, has led me to conclude that when the Fourth Amendment's ban against unreasonable searches and seizures is considered together with the Fifth Amendment's ban against compelled self-incrimination, a constitutional basis emerges which not only justifies but actually requires the exclusionary rule.

The close interrelationship between the Fourth and Fifth Amendments, as they apply to this problem, has long been recognized and, indeed, was expressly made the ground for this Court's holding in Boyd v. United States. There the Court fully discussed this relationship and declared itself "unable to perceive that the seizure of a man's private books and papers to be used in evidence against him is substantially different from compelling him to be a witness against himself." . . . And, although I rejected the argument at that time, its force has, for me at least, become compelling with the more thorough understanding of the problem brought on by recent cases. In the final analysis, it seems to me that the Boyd doctrine, though perhaps not required by the express language of the Constitution strictly construed, is amply justified from an historical standpoint, soundly based in reason, and entirely consistent with what I regard to be the proper approach to interpretation of our Bill of Rights. . . . [After discussing cases involving the "shock the conscience" standard, Mr. Justice Black goes on to say:]

. . . As I understand the Court's opinion in this case, we again reject the confusing "shock-the-conscience" standard of the Wolf and Rochin cases and, instead, set aside this state conviction in reliance upon the precise, intelligible and more predictable constitutional doctrine enunciated in the Boyd Case. . . . The Court's opinion, in my judgment, dissipates the doubt and uncertainty in this field of constitutional law and I am persuaded, for this and other reasons stated, to depart from my prior views, to accept the Boyd doctrine as controlling in this state case and to join the Court's judgment and opinion which are in accordance with that constitutional doctrine.

Mr. Justice **Douglas,** concurring, said in part:

Though I have joined the opinion of the Court, I add a few words. This criminal proceeding started with a lawless search and seizure. The police entered a home forcefully, and seized documents that were later used to convict the occupant of a crime. . . .

We held in Wolf v. Colorado that the Fourth Amendment was applicable to the States by reason of the Due Process Clause of the Fourteenth Amendment. But a majority held that the exclusionary rule of the Weeks Case was not required of the States, that they could apply such sanctions as they chose. That position had the necessary votes to carry the day. But with all respect it was not the voice of reason or principle.

As stated in the Weeks Case, if evidence seized in violation of the Fourth Amendment can be used against an accused, "his right to be secure against such searches and seizures is of no value, and . . . might as well be stricken from the Constitution."

When we allowed States to give constitutional sanction to the "shabby business" of unlawful entry into a home (to use an expression of Mr. Justice Murphy, Wolf v. Colorado), we did indeed rob the Fourth Amendment of much meaningful force. . . .

Wolf v. Colorado was decided in 1949. The immediate result was a storm of constitutional controversy which only today finds its end. I believe that this is an appropriate case in which to put an end to the asymmetry which Wolf imported into the law. . . .

Mr. Justice **Harlan,** with whom Mr. Justice **Frankfurter** and Mr. Justice **Whittaker** join, dissenting, said in part:

In overruling the Wolf Case the Court, in my opinion, has forgotten the sense of judicial restraint which, with due regard for stare decisis, is one element that should enter into deciding whether a past decision of this Court should be overruled. Apart from that I also believe that the Wolf rule represents sounder Constitutional doctrine than the new rule which now replaces it.

I.

From the Court's statement of the case one would gather that the central, if not controlling, issue on this appeal is whether illegally state seized evidence is Constitutionally admissible in a state prosecution, an issue which would of course face us with the need for reexamining Wolf. However, such is not the situation. For, although that question was indeed raised here and below among appellant's subordinate points, the new and pivotal issue brought to the Court by this appeal is whether § 2905.34 of the Ohio Revised Code making criminal the *mere* knowing possession or control of obscene material, and under which appellant has been convicted, is consistent with rights of free thought and expression assured against state action by the Fourteenth Amendment. That was the principal issue which was decided by the Ohio Supreme Court, . . . and which was briefed and argued in this Court.

In this posture of things, I think it fair to say that five members of this Court have simply "reached out" to overrule Wolf. With all respect for the views of the majority, and recognizing that stare decisis carries different weight in Constitutional adjudication than it does in nonconstitutional decision, I can perceive no justification for regarding this case as an appropriate occasion for reexamining Wolf. . . .

II.

Essential to the majority's argument against Wolf is the proposition that the rule of Weeks v. United States excluding in federal criminal trials the use of evidence obtained in violation of the Fourth Amendment, derives not from the "supervisory power" of this Court over the federal judicial system, but from Constitutional requirement. This is so because no one, I suppose, would suggest that this Court possesses any general supervisory power over the state courts. Although I entertain considerable doubt as to the soundness of this foundational proposition of the majority, . . . I shall assume, for present purposes, that the Weeks rule "is of constitutional origin."

At the heart of the majority's opinion in this case is the following syllogism: (1) the rule excluding in federal criminal trials evidence which is the product of an illegal search and seizure is "part and parcel" of the Fourth Amendment; (2) Wolf held that the "privacy" assured against federal action by the Fourth Amendment is also protected against state action by the Fourteenth Amendment; and (3) it is therefore "logically and constitutionally necessary" that the Weeks exclusionary rule should also be enforced against the States.

This reasoning ultimately rests on the unsound premise that because Wolf carried into the States, as part of "the concept of ordered liberty" embodied in the Fourteenth Amendment, the principle of "privacy" underlying the Fourth Amendment, it must follow that whatever configurations of the Fourth Amendment have been developed in the particularizing federal precedents are likewise to be deemed a part of "ordered liberty," and as such are enforceable against the States. For me, this does not follow at all.

It cannot be too much emphasized that what was recognized in Wolf was not that the Fourth Amendment *as such* is enforceable against the States as a facet of due process, a view of the Fourteenth Amendment which, as Wolf itself pointed out, has long since been discredited, but the principle of privacy "which is at the core of the Fourth Amendment." . . .

. . . Here we are reviewing not a determination that what the state police did was Constitutionally permissible (since the state court quite evidently assumed that it was not), but a determination that appellant was properly found guilty of conduct which, for present purposes, it is to be assumed the State could Constitutionally punish. Since there is not the slightest suggestion that Ohio's policy is "affirmatively to sanction . . . police incursion into privacy," . . . what the Court is now doing is to impose upon the States not only federal substantive standards of "search and seizure" but also the basic federal remedy for violation of those standards. For

I think it entirely clear that the Weeks exclusionary rule is but a remedy which, by penalizing past official misconduct, is aimed at deterring such conduct in the future.

I would not impose upon the States this federal exclusionary remedy. The reasons given by the majority for now suddenly turning its back on Wolf seem to me notably unconvincing.

First, it is said that "the factual grounds upon which Wolf was based" have since changed, in that more States now follow the Weeks exclusionary rule than was so at the time Wolf was decided. While that is true, a recent survey indicates that at present one-half of the States still adhere to the common-law non-exclusionary rule, and one, Maryland, retains the rule as to felonies. . . . But in any case surely all this is beside the point, as the majority itself indeed seems to recognize. . . .

Further, we are told that imposition of the Weeks rule on the States makes "very good sense," in that it will promote recognition by state and federal officials of their "mutual obligation to respect the same fundamental criteria" in their approach to law enforcement, and will avoid "needless conflict between state and federal courts." . . .

An approach which regards the issue as one of achieving procedural symmetry or of serving administrative convenience surely disfigures the boundaries of this Court's functions in relation to the state and federal courts. . . . I do not believe that the Fourteenth Amendment empowers this Court to mould state remedies effectuating the right to freedom from "arbitrary intrusion by the police" to suit its own notions of how things should be done . . . .

. . . I do not see how it can be said that a trial becomes unfair simply because a State determines that evidence may be considered by the trier of fact, regardless of how it was obtained, if it is relevant to the one issue with which the trial is concerned, the guilt or innocence of the accused. Of course, a court may use its procedures as an incidental means of pursuing other ends than the correct resolution of the controversies before it. Such indeed is the Weeks rule, but if a State does not choose to use its courts in this way, I do not believe that this Court is empowered to impose this much-debated procedure on local courts, however efficacious we may consider the Weeks rule to be as a means of securing Constitutional rights.

Finally, it is said that the overruling of Wolf is supported by the established doctrine that the admission in evidence of an involuntary confession renders a state conviction Constitutionally invalid. Since such a confession may often be entirely reliable, and therefore of the greatest relevance to the issue of the trial, the argument continues, this doctrine is ample warrant in precedent that the way evidence was obtained, and not just its relevance, is Constitutionally significant to the fairness of a trial. I believe this analogy is not a true one. The "coerced confession" rule is certainly not a rule that any illegally obtained statements may not be used in evidence. . . .

The point, then, must be that in requiring exclusion of an involuntary statement of an accused, we are concerned not with an appropriate remedy for what the police have done, but with something which is regarded as going to the heart of our concepts of fairness in judicial procedure. . . . The pressures brought to bear against an accused leading to a confession, unlike an unconstitutional violation of privacy, do not, apart from the use of the confession at trial, necessarily involve independent Constitutional violations. What is crucial is that the trial defense to which an accused is entitled should not be rendered an empty formality by reason of statements wrung from him, for then "a prisoner . . . [has been] made the deluded instrument of his own conviction." . . . That this is a *procedural right*, and that its violation occurs at the time his improperly obtained statement is admitted at trial, is manifest. For without this right all the careful safeguards erected around the giving of testimony, whether by an accused or any other witness, would become empty formalities in a procedure where the most compelling possible evidence of guilt, a confession, would have already been obtained at the unsupervised pleasure of the police.

This, and not the disciplining of the police, as with illegally seized evidence, is surely the true basis for excluding a statement of the accused which was unconstitutionally obtained. In sum, I think the coerced confession analogy works strongly *against* what the Court does today. . . .

Memorandum of Mr. Justice **Stewart**.

Agreeing fully with Part I of Mr. Justice Harlan's dissenting opinion, I express no view as to the merits of the constitutional issue which the Court today decides. I would, however, reverse the judgment in this case, because I am persuaded that the provision of § 2905.34 of the Ohio Revised Code, upon which the petitioner's conviction was based, is, in the words of Mr. Justice Harlan, not "consistent with the rights of free thought and expression assured against state action by the Fourteenth Amendment."

EXCLUSION IN ACTION: SELF-INCRIMINATION

MIRANDA v. ARIZONA

384 U. S. 436; 86 S. Ct. 1602; 16 L. Ed. 2d 694 (1966)

The privilege against compulsory self-incrimination grew up in England as a revolt against procedures, especially those in the ecclesiastical courts and the Court of Star Chamber, whereby persons were questioned by the judges in order both to get evidence on which to accuse them and to secure a confession from them after they were accused. Immunity from such questioning gradually became established in the common law, and it was this immunity that was written into the Fifth Amendment of the Constitution. Over the years it has been one of the most controversial guarantees in the Bill of Rights. At the time the first colonists came to America it was still not universally accepted in England, and important deviations occurred during the colonial period, notably in the Salem "witch trials." Throughout much of its history the desirability of the protection has been questioned by various bodies of opinion on two grounds: First, it is considered no longer a necessary protection; modern courts would prevent any attempt to get evidence from an accused by means of torture or intimidation. The second ground is that the protection is a shield only to the guilty, since only guilty persons can legitimately refuse to give evidence on the ground that their testimony would tend to incriminate them. This position is bolstered by the historical fact that prominent among those who brought about the adoption of the protection in England were the early Puritans, who were obviously guilty of heresy but who objected to being forced to provide the only testimony upon which they could be convicted in the ecclesiastical courts and the Court of Star Chamber.

Despite these attacks, the protection against compulsory self-incrimination continues to command strong support. There is a strong moral sense which regards it as uncivilized to put a person, whether innocent or guilty, through the degrading process of having to give the evidence upon which he may be convicted of crime. The protection is also felt to promote sound police methods by preventing the lazy prosecutor from relying upon evidence he can secure by the relatively easy method of torturing his suspects. Sir James Fitzjames Stephens illustrates this point by quoting an Indian policeman who said, "It is far pleasanter to sit comfortably in the shade rubbing red pepper into a poor devil's eyes than to go about in the sun hunting up evidence." Wigmore, the great authority on evidence, while criticizing many aspects of the guarantee, supported it on the ground that it protected innocent and guilty alike from the overzealousness of prosecuting officials who are forced by public opinion to maintain a high conviction record if they are to continue to hold their offices.

Unlike the protection against unreasonable searches and seizures, the protection against self-incrimination contains what amounts to a built-in exclusionary rule. Evidence that is coerced cannot be used in court to convict a person. Thus, although the Court in Mapp v. Ohio held that the exclusionary rule of the Weeks case (1914) was incorporated into the Fourteenth Amendment, the five-man majority could not agree on which constitutional clause actually embodied the rule. Four members held it to be an aspect of the Fourth Amendment, while Justice Black held it was required by the self-incrimination provision of the Fifth Amendment. At the time Mapp was decided, self-incrimination had not been incorporated and when the Court finally did incorporate the doctrine in Malloy v. Hogan (1964), Justice Clark, who had joined the majority in Mapp, agreed with the dissenting opinion of Justice Harlan that in neither Mapp nor Gideon did "incorporation," as such, take place. So, while the results of Mapp were to make the exclusionary rule applicable to the states, it is not possible to point to a constitutional clause that dictates this result, let alone be sure that such clause was "incorporated," since only four members of the Court appeared to agree with either of these propositions.

The Hogan case made the question academic and with both searches and seizures and self-incrimination made applicable to the states, which clause actually does the work ceases to be of crucial importance. With the decision in Ker v. California (1963) that federal standards applied in state search and seizure cases, even Justice Harlan conceded that incorporation of this clause had taken place.

The Court had always made clear that the right not to be a witness against one's self was not limited to being excused from taking the witness stand at one's criminal trial. Any statement coerced from a person by the government, wherever the coercion took place, constituted self-incrimination and in addition any information gotten by the government as a result of such coerced statements were excluded from court as "fruit of the poisoned tree." Since statements could be gotten from a person under an almost unlimited range of circumstances, the Court was continually faced with the question whether they were voluntary or coerced. As a result of the slow convergence of two very different doctrines the Court finally arrived at what it hoped would be a solution to its problem. Have a lawyer on hand when the person makes a statement!

In 1963, in the celebrated case of Gideon v. Wainwright, the Supreme Court held applicable to trials in state courts the Sixth Amendment right to counsel and in the years following it decided a series of cases, some of them highly controversial, extending that right to points both earlier and later in the criminal process. In Hamilton v. Alabama (1961) it held that an accused was entitled to counsel (at state expense, if necessary) at the time of his arraignment, since certain defenses such as insanity had to be plead at that time or completely forfeited. In White v. Maryland (1963) it was pushed back to the preliminary hearing stage, because a guilty plea made at that stage became a permanent part of the record; and in Douglas v. California (1963) it was moved forward to cover the first appeal from a criminal conviction which is normally given by the state as a matter of right. The rationale behind all these cases was that these were "critical stages" in the criminal process. It was at these points that a person might do or fail to do, or say or fail to say, something that could irrevocably prejudice his chances of acquittal. It was at these points that the "guiding hand of counsel" was vital if his rights were to receive full protection. In United States v. Wade (1967) and Gilbert v. California (1967) the Court extended the right of counsel to include that point where an accused is identified as a wanted suspect by being picked out of a police line-up by an eyewitness, although it did hold in Gilbert that taking a handwriting sample from a man before he saw his lawyer did not violate his rights. Here, too, the suspect's right to an unprejudiced identification may easily be jeopardized by an excess of police enthusiasm.

While these changes were going on the Court was also struggling with the somewhat unrelated problem of coerced confessions; see the note to Rochin v. California. Although it had held in Brown v. Mississippi (1936) that a confession based on coercion—in this case physical torture—was void, it was continually plagued by the problem of what constituted coercion. It conceded that coercion could be psychological as well as physical, but it was haunted by the fact so clearly stated in Stein v. New York (1953), that "no criminal confession is voluntary" in the "sense that petitioners wanted to make them." A definition of "voluntary" that meant some pressure could be used, but not too much, raised endless difficulties for the Court. Since most confessions are secured before a person is formally charged with crime, the Court had managed to solve much of the problem in the federal courts by requiring that an accused be taken immediately before a committing magistrate. But this ruling rested on the supervisory authority of the Court over the administration of federal justice and so could not be extended to the states. Consequently the Court had to trace a guideline for the states as cases came before it, and as the Court noted in Spano v. New York (1959), as "the methods used to extract confessions become more sophisticated, our duty . . . only becomes more difficult because of the more delicate judgments to be made." In the Spano case the defendant was persuaded to confess by fatigue and the false sympathy aroused by a boyhood friend on the police force, while in subsequent cases the techniques used included threatening to bring the defendant's wife in for questioning (Rogers v. Richmond, 1961), threatening to take her infant children from her and give them to strangers (Lynumn v. Illinois, 1963), injecting "truth serum" into his veins (Townsend v. Sain, 1963), and refusing to let him call his wife or lawyer until he had confessed (Haynes v. Washington, 1963). While in some of these cases the police disputed the defendant's version, in all of them the defendants were denied access to counsel who might have given them moral support and perhaps furnished a dispassionate version of the proceedings. Claims that the right to counsel was being denied were noted by the Court but not reached because the confessions were held to be coerced. Clearly the amount of "pressure" a state could use to invoke a confession was getting less and less.

Then in 1964 the Court moved sharply to merge these two lines of development, extending the right to counsel, but in such a way that would serve also as a protection against forced confessions. In Massiah v. United States (1964) the government was forbidden to question an accused, who was under indictment, in the absence of his lawyer, and in Escobedo v. Illinois (1964) it held that where "the investigation is no longer a general inquiry into an unsolved crime but has begun to focus on a particular suspect, the suspect has been taken into police custody, the police carry out a process of interrogations that lends itself to eliciting incriminating statements, the suspect has requested and been denied an opportunity to consult with his lawyer, and the police have not effectively warned him of his absolute constitutional right to remain silent, the accused has been denied 'the Assistance of Counsel' in violation of the Sixth Amendment to the Constitution as 'made obligatory upon the States by the Fourteenth Amendment.' "

The two years following the Escobedo decision (1964) witnessed a nationwide debate on the implications and wisdom of what the Court had done. The case itself had involved only the denial of Danny Escobedo's request to see his attorney and reaffirmed his absolute right to remain silent. But did it imply, in effect, an adoption of the English "Judge's Rule" that a suspect must be warned of his right to silence and cautioned that anything he said could be used against him? Did it require that he be told of his right to counsel? That he be furnished counsel at state expense? Did it, perhaps, outlaw all confessions? All police interrogation?

The Court itself was bitterly attacked for what was considered a gratuitous hamstringing of the police in their efforts to protect society against criminals. It was asserted that between 75 and 80 percent of the convictions in major crimes were dependent upon confessions; and police officers and prosecutors across the country, together with some courts, echoed the conviction of New York City's police commissioner, Michael J. Murphy, that "if suspects are told of their rights they will not confess." Certainly a competent lawyer would tell them not to confess, and then this effective method of solving crimes would come to an end.

Meanwhile, public confidence in the reliability of confessions as a substitute for investigatory evidence was badly shaken in early 1965 when George Whitmore, Jr., was conceded to be innocent of the sensational murder of career girls Janice Wylie and Emily Hoffert in their New York apartment. Whitmore had been arrested a year and a half after the murders and during twenty-eight hours of questioning had given a sixty-one-page confession filled with details "which only he, as the killer, could have known." Although Whitmore repudiated his confession to this and two other major crimes, the police contended it had been freely given, and his indictment was not dismissed until eight months later when incontrovertible evidence of his innocence was presented—evidence which the police could have obtained at once had they checked into the truth of his alibi.

Not until 1971 in Harris v. New York did the Court move to reduce the impact of Miranda by permitting the use in court of evidence gotten in violation of the rule. Harris, on trial for a narcotics violation, took the stand and testified that a bag of powder he had sold to an undercover agent was baking powder rather than heroin. He was asked on cross-examination if this did not contradict statements made to the police at the time of his arrest and without the Miranda warnings and the statements were then read to him. The jury was instructed that they could not be used to determine his guilt, but only his credibility. In a five-to-four decision the Court held this use of the statements valid. Conceding that "some comments in the Miranda opinion can indeed be read as indicating a bar to use of any uncounseled statement for any purpose," they were only dicta and "it does not follow from Miranda that evidence inadmissible against an accused in the prosecution's case in chief is barred for all purposes, provided of course that the trustworthiness of the evidence satisfies legal standards." The Court reaffirmed Walder v. United States (1954) in which a similar decision had been reached with regard to illegally seized evidence (see the note to Weeks v. United States, 1914) and added, "the shield provided by Miranda cannot be perverted into a license to use perjury by way of a defense, free from the risk of confrontation with prior inconsistent utterances."

In Oregon v. Hass (1975) the Court not only reaffirmed Harris but extended it to a defendant who had been given the Miranda warnings and had his request for an attorney ignored. "One might concede that when proper Miranda warnings have been given, and the officer then continues his interrogation after the suspect asks for an attorney, the officer may be said to have little to lose and perhaps something to gain by way of possibly uncovering impeachment material. . . . In any event, the balance was struck in Harris, and we are not disposed to change it now." Where the testimony is used to convict, however, the Court has adhered firmly to Miranda. In Edwards v. Arizona (1981) Edwards' request for a lawyer was ignored and a resumption of questioning produced a confession. The Court held he had not waived his right to counsel.

While the Miranda case seems to rest on the ground that the right to "Miranda warnings" stems from the right against self-incrimination, the Court in New Jersey v. Portash (1979) drew a distinction between statements obtained in violation of the Miranda rule and those obtained from direct compulsion. Here the defendant was faced with having his testimony in a criminal trial impeached by the use of testimony he had given before the grand jury under a grant of immunity from prosecution. "Testimony given in response to a grant of legislative immunity is the essence of coerced testimony. In such cases there is no question whether physical or psychological pressures overrode the defendant's will; the witness is told to talk or face the government's coercive sanctions, notably a conviction for contempt. . . . Balancing of interests was thought to be necessary in Harris and Hass when the attempt to deter unlawful police conduct collided with the need to prevent perjury. Here, by contrast, we deal with the constitutional privilege against compulsory self-incrimination in its most pristine form. Balancing, therefore, is not simply unnecessary, it is impermissible."

The purpose of the Miranda warnings is to inform suspects that they need not aid the police in making a case against them and that they are entitled to legal counsel as to what they should say and not say. But suppose a person is arrested without probable cause, given the Miranda warnings, and voluntarily confesses. Does the invalidity of the arrest make the confession inadmissible even though it was voluntarily made? In Brown v.

Illinois (1975) Justice Blackmun, speaking for six members of a unanimous court, held that it did. Here Brown had been illegally seized by the police (a Fourth Amendment violation) and voluntarily confessed after Miranda warnings which assured there was no Fifth Amendment violation. The Court pointed out that despite the intimate relationship between the two amendments the exclusionary rule did not serve the same purpose with regard to each. When used with the Fourth Amendment it excluded all statements or evidence—not just those which were self-incriminating. Not only do the Miranda warnings not inform the suspect about the right not to be illegally detained, but they do nothing to deter other Fourth Amendment violations. "If Miranda warnings, by themselves, were held to attenuate the taint of an unconstitutional arrest, regardless of how wanton and purposeful the Fourth Amendment violation, the effect of the exclusionary rule would be substantially diluted. . . . Arrests made without warrant or without probable cause, for questioning or 'investigation,' would be encouraged by the knowledge that evidence derived therefrom hopefully could well be made admissible at trial by the simple expedient of giving Miranda warnings. Any incentive to avoid the Fourth Amendment violations would be eviscerated by making the warnings, in effect, a 'cure-all' and the constitutional guarantee against unlawful searches and seizures could be said to be reduced to a 'form of words.' " Of course it is possible for a person to confess voluntarily even though subjected to an unreasonable search and seizure, but the Court made clear that in passing on the validity of such confessions "the temporal proximity of the arrest and the confession, the presence of intervening circumstances, . . . and, particularly, the purpose and flagrancy of the official misconduct are all relevant." The decision was reaffirmed in Taylor v. Alabama (1982)

The case below is a combination of four cases, all raising questions of the admissibility of confessions. Miranda was convicted of kidnapping and rape on the basis of a confession obtained after two hours of questioning in which he was not told of his right to counsel or silence.

Mr. Chief Justice **Warren** delivered the opinion of the Court, saying in part:

The cases before us raise questions which go to the roots of our concepts of American criminal jurisprudence: the restraints society must observe consistent with the Federal Constitution in prosecuting individuals for crime. More specifically, we deal with the admissibility of statements obtained from an individual who is subjected to custodial police interrogation and the necessity for procedures which assure that the individual is accorded his privilege under the Fifth Amendment to the Constitution not to be compelled to incriminate himself. . . .

Our holding will be spelled out with some specificity in the pages which follow but briefly stated it is this: the prosecution may not use statements, whether excul-patory or inculpatory, stemming from custodial interrogation of the defendant unless it demonstrates the use of procedural safeguards effective to secure the privilege against self-incrimination. By custodial interrogation, we mean questioning initiated by law enforcement officers after a person has been taken into custody or otherwise deprived of his freedom of action in any significant way. As for the procedural safeguards to be employed, unless other fully effective means are devised to inform accused persons of their right of silence and to assure a continuous opportunity to exercise it, the following measures are required. Prior to any questioning, the person must be warned that he has a right to remain silent, that any statement he does make may be used as evidence against him, and that he has a right to the presence of an attorney, either retained or appointed. The defendant may waive effectuation of these rights, provided the waiver is made voluntarily, knowingly and intelligently. If, however, he indicates in any manner and at any stage of the process that he wishes to consult with an attorney before speaking there can be no questioning. Likewise, if the individual is alone and indicates in any manner that he does not wish to be interrogated, the police may not question him. The mere fact that he may have answered some questions or volunteered some statements on his own does not deprive him of the right to refrain from answering any further inquiries until he has consulted with an attorney and thereafter consents to be questioned.

I.

The constitutional issue we decide in each of these cases is the admissibility of statements obtained from a defendant questioned while in custody or otherwise deprived of his freedom of action in any significant way. In each, the defendant was questioned by police officers, detectives, or a prosecuting attorney in a room in which he was cut off from the outside world. In none of these cases was the defendant given a full and effective warning of his rights at the outset of the interrogation process. In all the cases, the questioning elicited oral admissions, and in three of them, signed statements as well which were admitted at their trials. They all thus share salient features—incommunicado interrogation of individuals in a police-dominated atmosphere, resulting in self-incriminating statements without full warnings of constitutional rights.

. . . The use of physical brutality and violence is not, unfortunately, relegated to the past. . . .

. . . Unless a proper limitation upon custodial interrogation is achieved—such as these decisions will advance—there can be no assurance that practices of this nature will be eradicated in the foreseeable future. . . .

Again we stress that the modern practice of in-custody interrogation is psychologically rather than physically oriented. As we have stated before, "Since Chambers v. Florida [1940] this Court has recognized that coercion can be mental as well as physical, and that the blood of the accused is not the only hallmark of an unconstitutional inquisition." Blackburn v. Alabama (1960). Interrogation still takes place in privacy. Privacy results in secrecy and this in turn results in a gap in our knowledge as to what in fact goes on in the interrogation rooms. A valuable source of information about present police practices, however, may be found in various police manuals and texts which document procedures employed with success in the past, and which recommend various other effective tactics. These texts are used by law enforcement agencies themselves as guides. It should be noted that these texts professedly present the most enlightened and effective means presently used to obtain statements through custodial interrogation. By considering these texts and other data, it is possible to describe procedures observed and noted around the country. . . . [The Court here quotes at length from a number of books on criminal investigation.]

From these representative samples of interrogation techniques, the setting prescribed by the manuals and observed in practice becomes clear. In essence, it is this: To be alone with the subject is essential to prevent distraction and to deprive him of any outside support. The aura of confidence in his guilt undermines his will to resist. He merely confirms the preconceived story the police seek to have him describe. Patience and persistence, at times relentless questioning are employed. To obtain a confession, the interrogator must "patiently maneuver himself or his quarry into a position from which the desired objective may be obtained." When normal procedures fail to produce the needed result, the police may resort to deceptive stratagems such as giving false legal advice. It is important to keep the subject off balance, for example, by trading on his insecurity about himself or his surroundings. The police then persuade, trick, or cajole him out of exercising his constitutional rights.

Even without employing brutality, the "third degree" or the specific stratagems described above, the very fact of custodial interrogation exacts a heavy toll on individual liberty and trades on the weakness of individuals. This fact may be illustrated simply by referring to three confession cases decided by this Court in the Term immediately preceding our Escobedo decision. In Townsend v. Sain (1963), the defendant was a 19 year-old heroin addict, described as a "near mental defective." The defendant in Lynumn v. Illinois (1963), was a woman who confessed to the arresting officer after being importuned to "cooperate" in order to prevent her children from being taken by relief authorities. This Court as in those cases reversed the conviction of a defendant in Haynes v. Washington (1963), whose persistent request during his interrogation was to phone his wife or attorney. In other settings, these individuals might have exercised their constitutional rights. In the incommunicado police-dominated atmosphere, they succumbed.

[The Court here discusses the facts of the cases before it, noting that in each the questioning in an "incommunicado police-dominated atmosphere" had resulted in a confession.]

In these cases, we might not find the defendant's statements to have been involuntary in traditional terms. Our concern for adequate safeguards to protect precious Fifth Amendment rights is, of course, not lessened in the slightest. In each of the cases, the defendant was thrust into an unfamiliar atmosphere and run through menacing police interrogation procedures. The potentiality for compulsion is forcefully apparent, for example, in Miranda, where the indigent Mexican defendant was a seriously disturbed individual with pronounced sexual fantasies, and in Stewart, in which the defendant was an indigent Los Angeles Negro who had dropped out of school in the sixth grade. To be sure, the records do not evince overt physical coercion or patent psychological ploys. The fact remains that in none of these cases did the officers undertake to afford appropriate safeguards at the outset of the interrogation to insure that the statements were truly the product of free choice.

It is obvious that such an interrogation environment is created for no purpose other than to subjugate the individual to the will of his examiner. This atmosphere carries its own badge of intimidation. To be sure, this is not physical intimidation, but it is equally destructive of human dignity. The current practice of incommunicado interrogation is at odds with one of our Nation's most cherished principles—that the individual may not be compelled to incriminate himself. Unless adequate protective devices are employed to dispel the compulsion inherent in custodial surroundings, no statement obtained from the defendant can truly be the product of his free choice.

From the foregoing, we can readily perceive an intimate connection between the privilege against self-incrimination and police custodial questioning. . . .

II.

. . . We have recently noted that the privilege against self-incrimination—the essential mainstay of our adversary system—is founded on a complex of values. . . . All these policies point to one overriding thought: the constitutional foundation underlying the privilege is the respect a government—state or federal—must accord to the dignity and integrity of its citizens. To maintain a "fair state-individual balance," to require the government "to shoulder the entire load," . . . to respect the inviolability of the human personality, our accusatory system of criminal justice demands that the government seeking to punish an individual produce the evidence against him by its own independent labors, rather than by the cruel, simple expedient of compelling it from his own mouth. . . . In sum, the privilege is fulfilled only when the person is guaranteed the right "to remain silent unless he chooses to speak in the unfettered exercise of his will." . . .

The question in these cases is whether the privilege is fully applicable during a period of custodial interrogation. . . . We are satisfied that all the principles embodied in the privilege apply to informal compulsion exerted by law-enforcement officials during in-custody questioning. An individual swept from familiar surroundings into police custody, surrounded by antagonistic forces, and subjected to the techniques of persuasion described above cannot be otherwise than under compulsion to speak. As a practical matter, the compulsion to speak in the isolated setting of the police station may well be greater than in courts or other official investigations, where there are often impartial observers to guard against intimidation or trickery.

This question, in fact, could have been taken as settled in federal courts almost 70 years go, when, in Bram v. United States (1897), this Court held:

"In criminal trials, in the courts of the United States, wherever a question arises whether a confession is incompetent because not voluntary, the issue is controlled by that portion of the Fifth Amendment . . . commanding that no person 'shall be compelled in any criminal case to be a witness against himself.' " . . .

III. . . .

It is impossible for us to foresee the potential alternatives for protecting the privilege which might be devised by Congress or the States in the exercise of their creative rule-making capacities. Therefore we cannot say that the Constitution necessarily requires adherence to any particular solution for the inherent compulsions of the interrogation process as it is presently conducted. Our decision in no way creates a constitutional straitjacket which will handicap sound efforts at reform, nor is it intended to have this effect. We encourage Congress and the States to continue their laudable search for increasingly effective ways of protecting the rights of the individual while promoting efficient enforcement of our criminal laws. However, unless we are shown other procedures which are at least as effective in apprising accused persons of their right of silence and in assuring a continuous opportunity to exercise it, the following safeguards must be observed. . . .

[The Court here elaborates on and justifies the requirements summarized at the beginning of the opinion.]

If the interrogation continues without the presence of an attorney and a statement is taken, a heavy burden rests on the government to demonstrate that the defendant knowingly and intelligently waived his privilege against self-incrimination and his right to retained or appointed counsel. . . . This Court has always set high standards of proof for the waiver of constitutional rights, Johnson v. Zerbst (1938), and we reassert these standards as applied to in-custody interrogation. Since the State is responsible for establishing the isolated circumstances under which the interrogation takes place and has the only means of making available corroborated evidence of warnings given during incommunicado interrogation, the burden is rightly on its shoulders. . . .

The warnings required and the waiver necessary in accordance with our opinion today are, in the absence of a fully effective equivalent, pre-requisites to the admissibility of any statement made by a defendant. No distinction can be drawn between statements which are direct confessions and statements which amount to "admissions" of part or all of an offense. The privilege against self-incrimination protects the individual from being compelled to incriminate himself in any manner; it does not distinguish degrees of incrimination. Similarly for precisely the same reason, no distinction may be drawn between inculpatory statements and statements alleged to be merely "exculpatory." If a statement made were in fact truly exculpatory it would, of course, never be used by the prosecution. In fact, statements merely intended to be exculpatory by the defendant are often used to impeach his testimony at trial or to demonstrate untruths in the statement given under interrogation and thus to prove guilt by implication. These statements are incriminating in any meaningful sense of the word and may not be used without the full warnings and effective waiver required for any other statements. In Escobedo itself, the defendant fully intended his accusation of another as the slayer to be exculpatory as to himself.

The principles announced today deal with the protection which must be given to the privilege against self-incrimination when the individual is first subjected to police interrogation while in custody at the station or otherwise deprived of his freedom of action in any significant way. It is at this point that our adversary system of criminal proceedings commences, distinguishing itself at the outset from the inquisitorial system recognized in some countries. Under the system of warnings we delineate today or under any other system which may be devised and found effective, the safeguards to be erected about the privilege must come into play at this point. . . .

In dealing with statements obtained through interrogation, we do not purport to find all confessions inadmissible. Confessions remain a proper element in law enforcement. Any statement given freely and voluntarily without any compelling influences is, of course, admissible in evidence. The fundamental import of the privilege while an individual is in custody is not whether he is allowed to talk to the police without the benefit of warnings and counsel, but whether he can be interrogated. There is no requirement that police stop a person who enters a police station and states that he wishes to confess to a crime, or a person who calls the police to offer a confession or any other statement he desires to make. Volunteered statements of any kind are not barred by the Fifth Amendment and their admissibility is not affected by our holding today. . . .

IV.

A recurrent argument made in these cases is that society's need for interrogation outweighs the privilege. This argument is not unfamiliar to this Court. . . . The whole thrust of our foregoing discussion demonstrates that the Constitution has prescribed the rights of the individual when confronted with the power of government when it provided in the Fifth Amendment that an individual cannot be compelled to be a witness against himself. That right cannot be abridged. As Mr. Justice Brandeis once observed:

"Decency, security and liberty alike demand that government officials shall be subjected to the same rules of conduct that are commands to the citizen. In a government of laws, existence of the government will be imperilled if it fails to observe the law scrupulously. Our Government is the potent, the omnipresent teacher. For good or for ill, it teaches the whole people by its example.

Crime is contagious. If the Government becomes a law-breaker, it breeds contempt for law; it invites every man to become a law unto himself; it invites anarchy. To declare that in the administration of the criminal law the end justifies the means . . . would bring terrible retribution. Against that pernicious doctrine this Court should resolutely set its face." Olmstead v. United States [1928] (dissenting opinion). . . .

V.

Because of the nature of the problem and because of its recurrent significance in numerous cases, we have to this point discussed the relationship of the Fifth Amendment privilege to police interrogation without specific concentration on the facts of the cases before us. We turn now to these facts to consider the application to these cases of the constitutional principles discussed above. In each instance, we have concluded that statements were obtained from the defendant under circumstances that did not meet constitutional standards for protection of the privilege.

[The Court here reviews in detail the facts of the four cases and concludes either that the defendant did not waive his right to silence, or was not informed that he had a right to silence or to counsel.]

Mr. Justice **Clark** dissented in part.

Mr. Justice **Harlan,** whom Mr. Justice **Stewart** and Mr. Justice **White** joined, dissented, saying in part:

I believe the decision of the Court represents poor constitutional law and entails harmful consequences for the country at large. How serious these consequences may prove to be only time can tell. But the basic flaws in the Court's justification seem to me readily apparent now once all sides of the problem are considered. . . .

While the fine points of this scheme are far less clear than the Court admits, the tenor is quite apparent. The new rules are not designed to guard against police brutality or other unmistakably banned forms of coercion. Those who use third-degree tactics and deny them in court are equally able and destined to lie as skillfully about warnings and waivers. Rather, the thrust of the new rules is to negate all pressures, to reinforce the nervous or ignorant suspect, and ultimately to discourage any confession at all. The aim in short is toward "voluntariness" in a utopian sense, or to view it from a different angle, voluntariness with a vengeance. . . .

What the Court largely ignores is that its rules impair, if they will not eventually serve wholly to frustrate, an instrument of law enforcement that has long and quite reasonably been thought worth the price paid for it. There can be little doubt that the Court's new code would markedly decrease the number of confessions. To warn the suspect that he may remain silent and remind him that his confession may be used in court are minor obstructions. To require also an express waiver by the suspect and an end to questioning whenever he demurs must heavily handicap questioning. And to suggest or provide counsel for the suspect simply invites the end of the interrogation.

How much harm this decision will inflict on law enforcement cannot fairly be predicted with accuracy. Evidence on the role of confessions is notoriously incomplete, . . . and little is added by the Court's reference to the FBI experience and the resources believed wasted in interrogation. . . . We do know that some crimes cannot be solved without confessions, that ample expert testimony attests to their importance in crime control, and that the Court is taking a real risk with society's welfare in imposing its new regime on the country. The social costs of crime are too great to call the new rules anything but a hazardous experimentation.

While passing over the costs and risks of its experiment, the Court portrays the evils of normal police questioning in terms which I think are exaggerated. Albeit stringently confined by the due process standards interrogation is no doubt often inconvenient and unpleasant for the suspect. However, it is not less so for a man to be arrested and jailed, to have his house searched, or to stand trial in court, yet all this may properly happen to the most innocent given probable cause, a warrant, or an indictment. Society has always paid a stiff price for law and order, and peaceful interrogation is not one of the dark moments of the law. . . .

Mr. Justice **White,** with whom Mr. Justice **Harlan** and Mr. Justice **Stewart** joined, dissented, saying in part:

The proposition that the privilege against self-incrimination forbids in-custody interrogation without the warnings specified in the majority opinion and without a clear waiver of counsel has no significant support in the history of the privilege or in the language of the Fifth Amendment. As for the English authorities and the common-law history, the privilege, firmly established in the second half of the seventeenth century, was never applied except to prohibit compelled judicial interrogations. The rule excluding coerced confessions matured about 100 years later, "[b]ut there is nothing in the reports to suggest that the theory has its roots in the privilege against self-incrimination. And so far as the cases reveal, the privilege, as such, seems to have been given effect only in judicial proceedings, including the preliminary examinations by authorized magistrates." . . .

EXCLUSION IN ACTION: SEARCHES AND SEIZURES

TERRY v. OHIO

392 U. S. 1; 88 S. Ct. 1868; 20 L. Ed. 2d 889 (1968)

One of the areas in which the Supreme Court has had the most difficulty agreeing on a consistent philosophy is that of unreasonable searches and seizures. In part this is merely a reflection of the conflicting values in the country as a whole, but it is also the result of the methods by which the guarantee is enforced. Individual rights can be divided into two types. Those like free speech and religion have intrinsic value to the individual and are thought of as "substantive" rights, while those like the right to counsel and a jury trial are termed "procedural" because their purpose is to ensure that one will only be convicted of crime on the basis of true evidence fairly presented and impartially appraised. Appellate courts will normally enforce the substantive rights by ordering the government either to stop interfering with their exercise or to grant those which are being withheld. The procedural rights, on the other hand, are usually policed by ordering a new, untainted trial to take the place of the unfair one.

The guarantee against unreasonable searches and seizures, like the protection against compulsory self-incrimination, is in the anomalous position of being a substantive right, of value to the individual for its own sake, but enforceable by the courts only through the procedural technique of ordering excluded at a new trial the evidence gotten by its violation. The result in those cases where the tainted evidence was essential to conviction is the release of a person who has been found guilty on the basis of probative evidence fairly appraised, not because the person might be innocent, but because the police have violated his or her rights. In Justice Cardozo's famous phrase, "the criminal is to go free because the constable has blundered." People v. Defore, 242 N. Y. 13 (1926). While Supreme Court justices are not supposed to be influenced in constitutional judgments by the apparent guilt or innocence of a particular defendant, it is hard to escape the conclusion that a more consistent concern for the rights of the accused might emerge if the price were not the freeing of so many obviously guilty defendants.

The flexibility needed by the Court to provide reasoned arguments to go with its ever-changing views on searches and seizures has been provided by what has become known as the "talismanic" approach. Essentially this involves taking a constitutional theory, giving it a shorthand name, then using that name until it comes to have an entity of its own quite unrelated to the theory from which it sprang. When using the talisman the Court does not look back to the original theory, but interprets the talisman as though it were the true statement of the rule. This has the advantage of freeing it from the restraints of the rule without apparently abandoning the rule itself.

For example, the basic constitutional theory underlying the Fourth Amendment is that a magistrate, not a police officer, should decide when a person's privacy should yield to a search, and a search without a magistrate's warrant is "unreasonable" unless it can be justified by some "exigent circumstance" that makes getting a warrant impractical. Two such exceptions discussed in the cases below are the warrantless search of an automobile before it can escape and the warrantless search of a person by an arresting officer to protect both the officer and the evidence of the crime. However, since probable cause is necessary to get a search warrant, there must be probable cause to search without a warrant; and the arresting officer must be prepared to satisfy the court that the probable cause existed before the search was made.

The talismans that have evolved from these two exceptions to the warrant requirement are the "Carroll" and the "search incident" doctrines. Carroll v. United States (1925) involved stopping and searching without a warrant a bootlegger's car. The Supreme Court upheld the search, but emphasized that "where the securing of a warrant is reasonably practicable it must be used. . . . In cases where seizure is impossible except without a warrant, the seizing officer acts unlawfully and at his peril unless he can show the court probable cause." In its talismanic form these last requirements are dropped and the Carroll doctrine becomes the right to search a car without a warrant.

The common law authorized a police officer to conduct a limited search, or "frisk," at the time of a lawful arrest. The obvious justification was that an arrested person might then be carrying either a weapon with which the person could effect an escape, or evidence which he or she might find an opportunity to destroy. On this theory the extent of a search, both in time and space, is limited to what is necessary to protect the arresting officer or the evidence. But "search incident," once it had been given a name, took on a life of its own and in its talismanic form became an automatic right to search any arrested person. While the original theory had built-in limits stemming from the need that gave rise to it, the talismanic form knew no limits at all.

In the past half-century the Supreme Court has wandered back and forth between the theory and the talisman like a restless ghost. In Agnello v. United States (1925) it said that a search incident could extend "to the place where the arrest is made," but held it could not extend to another house several blocks away, and in Harris v. United States (1947) it upheld the search of Harris' four-room apartment because it was "under his immediate control." A year later, in Trupiano v. United States (1948), the talismanic approach was abandoned. Revenue agents had watched an illegal still being constructed and put into operation for a period of several weeks, during which they could have obtained both search and arrest warrants. When they finally closed in, one man was engaged in running the still and the Court sustained his arrest. But returning to the basic theory, it held that the "fortuitous circumstance" that he was in the building rather than out in the yard did not justify seizing the still without a warrant as incident to lawful arrest, since there had been plenty of time to get one. In McDonald v. United States (1948), after a two-month surveillance of McDonald in connection with a numbers racket investigation, the police broke into McDonald's room, arrested him, and seized an adding machine and other lottery paraphernalia. Without discussing the question of lawful arrest, the Court held the search unreasonable. "Where, as here, officers are not responding to an emergency, there must be compelling reasons to justify the absence of a search warrant. A search without a warrant demands exceptional circumstances. . . ."

Two years later in United States v. Rabinowitz (1950) the Court abruptly overruled Trupiano and held valid a widespread search of the defendant's property on the strength of his lawful arrest alone. Noting that the Constitution required only that a search be reasonable, not that it be made with a warrant if practicable, the Court found that, considering all the circumstances, this search was reasonable. The impact of this holding was to make possible a much broader search in conjunction with lawful arrest than could be made under a search warrant—as long as the arrest took place on the premises to be searched—since there were no limits as in the case of search warrants, as to "places to be searched" or "things to be seized." This was so much easier that in some communities the traditional search warrant became virtually extinct.

After nearly twenty years of this approach the Supreme Court overruled Harris and Rabinowitz and returned to the restrictive doctrines of Trupiano. Although in Chimel v. California (1969), the police had, as incident to arrest, searched an entire house including a garage and workshop, the Court declined to draw distinguishing lines between this search and that of the single room involved in Rabinowitz or the four rooms in Harris. "The only reasoned distinction is one between a search of the person arrested and the area within his reach on the one hand, and more extensive searches on the other." Furthermore, the theory justifying the search incident to arrest, the Court explained, itself marks its proper extent. "When an arrest is made, it is reasonable for the arresting officer to search the person arrested in order to remove any weapons that the latter might seek to use in order to resist arrest or effect his escape. Otherwise, the officer's safety might well be endangered, and the arrest itself frustrated. In addition, it is entirely reasonable for the arresting officer to search and seize any evidence on the arrestee's person in order to prevent its concealment or destruction. And the area into which an arrestee might reach in order to grab a weapon or evidentiary items must, of course, be governed by a like rule. A gun on a table or in a drawer in front of one who is arrested can be as dangerous to the arresting officer as one concealed in the clothing of the person arrested. There is ample justification, therefore, for a search of the arrestee's person and the area "within his immediate control"—construing that phrase to mean the area from within which he might gain possession of a weapon or destructible evidence.

"There is no comparable justification, however, for routinely searching rooms other than that in which an arrest occurs—or, for that matter, for searching through all the desk drawers or other closed or concealed areas in that room itself. Such searches, in the absence of well-recognized exceptions, may be made only under the authority of a search warrant. The 'adherence to judicial processes' mandated by the Fourth Amendment requires no less."

Any idea that the Court had abandoned the talismanic approach to the search incident doctrine was destined to be short-lived. While it had been rejected in 1971 in Coolidge v. New Hampshire, by 1974 it was back in full force in United States v. Edwards. There the defendant had been arrested for burglarizing a United States post office by jimmying a window—an operation which had chipped the paint on the window sill. The next day the police came to his cell, gave him new clothes, and without a warrant took his clothes and searched them for evidence of paint chips (which they found). In upholding the validity of the search, the Court, dividing five to four, argued that the mere fact of a full "custodial" arrest justified a complete warrantless search of his clothing, and since they could have searched him that night, it was not unreasonable to wait until the next morning when substitute clothes could be made available. Referring with approval to a case decided two years prior to Chimel, the Court noted that "it was no answer [in that case] to say that the police could have obtained a search warrant, for the Court held the test to be not whether it was reasonable to procure a search warrant, but whether the search itself was reasonable, which it was." Four dissenting justices pointed out that this language had been expressly rejected in Chimel and that, in view of the time-lapse, "the considerations that typically justify a warrantless search incident to a lawful arrest were wholly absent here . . . The police had ample time to seek a warrant, and no exigent circumstances were present to excuse their failure to do so."

The persistent attractiveness of the talismanic approach is exemplified by New York v. Belton (1981). There four men were stopped for speeding and when the police smelled burned marijuana in the car they ordered them out of the car, arrested them for possession and separated them from one another along the Thruway. They then searched the car and found heroin in the pocket of a jacket left on the back seat. The Court converted the Chimel doctrine into a "workable rule" by holding that "when a policeman has made a lawful custodial arrest of the occupant of an automobile, he may, as a contemporaneous incident of that arrest, search the passenger compartment of that automobile." He may, "also examine the contents of any containers found within the passenger compartment, for if the passenger compartment is within reach of the arrestee, so also will containers in it be within his reach."

The right of the police to arrest a person, like any other "seizure," has to be made on probable cause. If the arrest is to be made by warrant the magistrate who is to issue it must be told the facts so he can decide if there is probable cause. This does not necessarily mean sufficient evidence to obtain a conviction. It is enough that it reflect the "practical considerations of everyday life on which reasonable and prudent men, not legal technicians, act"; see Brinegar v. United States (1949). Where a police officer actually sees a felony being committed, or where the officer knows a felony has been committed and has probable cause to believe the suspect committed it, the officer may arrest the person without a *warrant. These situations, however, involve the actual commission of a felony and it is this that is involved when the search incident doctrine speaks of a search incident to a "valid arrest." The policeman in the case below was not witnessing the commission of a crime, nor even overt preparations for the commission of a crime. There was nothing he could have taken to a magistrate to obtain either a search or arrest warrant based upon probable cause.*

The Court, in holding valid the "frisk" in this case, opened up an entirely new dimension to the law of search and seizure. Never before had there been a valid way in which an officer could stop persons against their will and conduct a quick, superficial check to see if they passed some elementary test. Thus in United States v. Brignoni-Ponce (1975) the Court applied Terry in upholding the brief stop of a car near the Mexican border to check the citizenship of its occupants, while in United States v. Place (1983) it made clear that a ninety-minute detention at an airport while a suspect's luggage was subjected to a "sniff" test by narcotic-hunting dogs was well beyond the limits in both time and personal inconvenience permitted by Terry.

Nor was the Terry-type search to be used as a substitute for more traditional searches where these were in order. In United States v. Robinson (1973) the police stopped Robinson with probable cause to believe he was driving a car after the revocation of his license. He was placed under arrest and given a full-scale search which turned up a crumpled cigarette package containing capsules of heroin, for whose possession he was later convicted. The Court rejected the claim that since Robinson was being stopped for a license violation, and no search, however thorough, would turn up further evidence on that score, that the police should be limited to a Terry-type search which would determine whether or not Robinson was armed. The search incident to arrest could be a full-scale search, whatever the charge.

Mr. Chief Justice **Warren** delivered the opinion of the Court, saying in part:

This case presents serious questions concerning the role of the Fourth Amendment in the confrontation on the street between the citizen and the policeman investigating suspicious circumstances.

Petitioner Terry was convicted of carrying a concealed weapon and sentenced to the statutorily prescribed term of one to three years in the penitentiary. Following the denial of a pretrial motion to suppress, the prosecution introduced in evidence two revolvers and a number of bullets seized from Terry and a codefendant, Richard Chilton, by Cleveland Police Detective Martin McFadden. At the hearing on the motion to suppress this evidence, Officer McFadden testified that while he was patrolling in plain clothes in downtown Cleveland at approximately 2:30 in the afternoon of October 31, 1963, his attention was attracted by two men, Chilton and Terry, standing on the corner of Huron Road and Euclid

Avenue. He had never seen the two men before, and he was unable to say precisely what first drew his eye to them. However, he testified that he had been a policeman for 39 years and a detective for 35 and that he had been assigned to patrol this vicinity of downtown Cleveland for shoplifters and pickpockets for 30 years. He explained that he had developed routine habits of observation over the years and that he would "stand and watch people or walk and watch people at many intervals of the day." He added: "Now, in this case when I looked over they didn't look right to me at the time."

His interest aroused, Officer McFadden took up a post of observation in the entrance to a store 300 to 400 feet away from the two men. "I got more purpose to watch them when I seen their movements," he testified. He saw one of the men leave the other one and walk southwest on Huron Road, past some stores. The man paused for a moment and looked in a store window, then walked on a short distance, turned around and walked back toward the corner, pausing once again to look in the same store window. He rejoined his companion at the corner, and the two conferred briefly. Then the second man went through the same series of motions, strolling down Huron Road, looking in the same window, walking on a short distance, turning back, peering in the store window again, and returning to confer with the first man at the corner. The two men repeated this ritual alternately between five and six times apiece—in all, roughly a dozen trips. At one point, while the two were standing together on the corner, a third man approached them and engaged them briefly in conversation. This man then left the two others and walked west on Euclid Avenue. Chilton and Terry resumed their measured pacing, peering, and conferring. After this had gone on for 10 to 12 minutes, the two men walked off together, heading west on Euclid Avenue, following the path taken earlier by the third man.

By this time Officer McFadden had become thoroughly suspicious. He testified that after observing their elaborately casual and oft-repeated reconnaissance of the store window on Huron Road, he suspected the two men of "casing a job, a stick-up," and that he considered it his duty as a police officer to investigate further. He added that he feared "they may have a gun." Thus, Officer McFadden followed Chilton and Terry and saw them stop in front of Zucker's store to talk to the same man who had conferred with them earlier on the street corner. Deciding that the situation was ripe for direct action, Officer McFadden approached the three men, identified himself as a police officer and asked for their names. At this point his knowledge was confined to what he had observed. He was not acquainted with any of the three men by name or by sight, and he had received no information concerning them from any other source. When the men "mumbled something" in response to his inquiries, Officer McFadden grabbed petitioner Terry, spun him around so that they were facing the other two, with Terry between McFadden and the others, and patted down the outside of his clothing. In the left breast pocket of Terry's overcoat Officer McFadden felt a pistol. He reached inside the overcoat pocket, but was unable to remove the gun. At this point, keeping Terry between himself and the others, the officer ordered all three men to enter Zucker's store. As they went in, he removed Terry's overcoat completely, retrieved a .38 caliber revolver from the pocket and ordered all three men to face the wall with their hands raised. Officer McFadden proceeded to pat down the outer clothing of Chilton and the third man, Katz. He discovered another revolver in the outer pocket of Chilton's overcoat, but no weapons were found on Katz. The officer testified that he only patted the men down to see whether they had weapons, and that he did not put his hands beneath the outer garments of either Terry or Chilton until he felt their guns. So far as appears from the record, he never placed his hands beneath Katz's outer garments. Officer McFadden seized Chilton's gun, asked the proprietor of the store to call a police wagon, and took all three men to the station, where Chilton and Terry were formally charged with carrying concealed weapons.

On the motion to suppress the guns the prosecution took the position that they had been seized following a search incident to a lawful arrest. The trial court rejected this theory, stating that it "would be stretching the facts beyond reasonable comprehension" to find that Officer McFadden had had probable cause to arrest the men before he patted them down for weapons. However, the court denied the defendant's motion on the ground that Officer McFadden, on the basis of his experience, "had reasonable cause to believe . . . that the defendants were conducting themselves suspiciously, and some interrogation should be made of their action." Purely for his own protection, the court held, the officer had the right to pat down the outer clothing of these men, whom he had reasonable cause to believe might be armed. The court distinguished between an investigatory "stop" and an arrest, and between a "frisk" of the outer clothing for weapons and a full-blown search for evidence of crime. The frisk, it held, was essential to the proper performance of the officer's investigatory duties, for without it "the answer to the police officer may be a bullet, and a loaded pistol discovered during the frisk is admissible."

After the court denied their motion to suppress, Chilton and Terry waived jury trial and pleaded not guilty. The court adjudged them guilty. . . . We granted certiorari (1967) to determine whether the admission of the revolvers in evidence violated petitioner's rights under the Fourth Amendment, made applicable to the States by the Fourteenth. Mapp v. Ohio (1961). We affirm the conviction. . . .

II.

Our first task is to establish at what point in this encounter the Fourth Amendment becomes relevant. That is, we must decide whether and when Officer McFadden "seized" Terry and whether and when he conducted a "search." There is some suggestion in the use of such terms as "stop" and "frisk" that such police conduct is outside the purview of the Fourth Amendment because neither action rises to the level of a "search" or "seizure" within the meaning of the Constitution. We emphatically reject this notion. It is quite plain that the Fourth Amendment governs "seizures" of the person which do not eventuate in a trip to the station house and prosecution for crime—"arrests" in traditional terminology. It must be recognized that whenever a police officer accosts an individual and restrains his freedom to walk away, he has "seized" that person. And it is nothing less than sheer torture of the English language to suggest that a careful exploration of the outer surfaces of a person's clothing all over his or her body in an attempt to find weapons is not a "search." Moreover, it is simply fantastic to urge that such a procedure performed in public by a policeman while the citizen stands helpless, perhaps facing a wall with his hands raised, is a "petty indignity." It is a serious intrusion upon the sanctity of the person, which may inflict great indignity and arouse strong resentment, and it is not to be undertaken lightly.

The danger in the logic which proceeds upon distinctions between a "stop" and an "arrest," or "seizure" of the person, and between a "frisk" and a "search" is twofold. It seeks to isolate from constitutional scrutiny the initial stages of the contact between the policeman and the citizen. And by suggesting a rigid all-or-nothing model of justification and regulation under the Amendment, it obscures the utility of limitations upon the scope, as well as the initiation, of police action as a means of constitutional regulation. This Court has held in the past that a search which is reasonable at its inception may violate the Fourth Amendment by virtue of its intolerable intensity and scope. . . . The scope of the search must be "strictly tied to and justified by" the circumstances which rendered its initiation permissible. Warden v. Hayden (1967) (Mr. Justice Fortas, concurring). . . .

The distinctions of classical "stop-and-frisk" theory thus serve to divert attention from the central inquiry under the Fourth Amendment—the reasonableness in all the circumstances of the particular governmental invasion of a citizen's personal security. "Search" and "seizure" are not talismans. We therefore reject the notions that the Fourth Amendment does not come into play at all as a limitation upon police conduct if the officers stop short of something called "technical arrest" or a "full-blown search."

In this case there can be no question, then, that Officer McFadden "seized" petitioner and subjected him to a "search" when he took hold of him and patted down the outer surfaces of his clothing. We must decide whether at that point it was reasonable for Officer McFadden to have interfered with petitioner's personal security as he did.* And in determining whether the sei-

---

*We thus decide nothing today concerning the constitutional propriety of an investigative "seizure" upon less than probable cause for purposes of "detention" and/or interrogation. Obviously, not all personal intercourse between policemen and citizens involves "seizures" of persons. Only when the officer, by means of physical force or show of authority, has in some way restrained the liberty of a citizen may we conclude that a "seizure" has occurred. We cannot tell with any certainty upon this record whether any such "seizure" took place here prior to Officer McFadden's initiation of physical contact for purposes of searching Terry for weapons, and we thus may assume that up to that point no intrusion upon constitutionally protected rights had occurred.

zure and search were "unreasonable" our inquiry is a dual one—whether the officer's action was justified at its inception, and whether it was reasonably related in scope to the circumstances which justified the interference in the first place.

III.

If this case involved police conduct subject to the Warrant Clause of the Fourth Amendment, we would have to ascertain whether "probable cause" existed to justify the search and seizure which took place. However, that is not the case. We do not retreat from our holdings that the police must, whenever practicable, obtain advance judicial approval of searches and seizures through the warrant procedure, see, e. g., Katz v. United States (1967); Beck v. Ohio (1964); Chapman v. United States (1961), or that in most instances failure to comply with the warrant requirement can only be excused by exigent circumstances, see, e. g., Warden v. Hayden (1967) (hot pursuit); cf. Preston v. United States (1964). But we deal here with an entire rubric of police conduct—necessarily swift action predicated upon the on-the-spot observations of the officer on the beat—which historically has not been, and as a practical matter could not be, subjected to the warrant procedure. Instead, the conduct involved in this case must be tested by the Fourth Amendment's general proscription against unreasonable searches and seizures.

Nonetheless, the notions which underlie both the warrant procedure and the requirement of probable cause remain fully relevant in this context. In order to assess the reasonableness of Officer McFadden's conduct as a general proposition, it is necessary "first to focus upon the governmental interest which allegedly justifies official intrusion upon the constitutionally protected interests of the private citizen," for there is "no ready test for determining reasonableness other than by balancing the need to search [or seize] against the invasion which the search [or seizure] entails." Camara v. Municipal Court (1967). And in justifying the particular intrusion the police officer must be able to point to specific and articulate facts which, taken together with rational inferences from those facts reasonably warrant that intrusion. . . .

Applying these principles to this case, we consider first the nature and extent of the governmental interests involved. One general interest is of course that of effective crime prevention and detection; it is this interest which underlies the recognition that a police officer may in appropriate circumstances and in an appropriate manner approach a person for purposes of investigating possibly criminal behavior even though there is no probable cause to make an arrest. It was this legitimate investigative function Officer McFadden was discharging when he decided to approach petitioner and his companions. He had observed Terry, Chilton, and Katz go through a series of acts, each of them perhaps innocent in itself, but which taken together warranted further investigation . . .

The crux of this case, however, is not the propriety of Officer McFadden's taking steps to investigate petitioner's suspicious behavior, but rather, whether there was justification for McFadden's invasion of Terry's personal security by searching him for weapons in the course of that investigation. . . .

Petitioner does not argue that a police officer should refrain from making any investigation of suspicious circumstances until such time as he has probable cause to make an arrest; nor does he deny that police officers in properly discharging their investigative function may find themselves confronting persons who might well be armed and dangerous. Moreover, he does not say that an officer is always unjustified in searching a suspect to discover weapons. Rather, he says it is unreasonable for the policeman to take that step until such time as the situation evolves to a point where there is probable cause to make an arrest. When that point has been reached, petitioner would concede the officer's right to conduct a search of the suspect for weapons, fruits or instrumentalities of the crime, or "mere" evidence, incident to the arrest.

There are two weaknesses in this line of reasoning, however. First, it fails to take account of traditional limitations upon the scope of searches, and thus recognizes no distinction in purpose, character, and extent between a search incident to an arrest and a limited search for weapons. The former, although justified in part by the acknowledged necessity to protect the arresting officer from assault with a concealed weapon . . . , is also justified on other grounds and can therefore involve a relatively extensive exploration of the person. A search for weapons in the absence of probable cause to arrest, however, must, like any other search, be strictly circumscribed by the exigencies which justify its initiation. . . . Thus it must be limited to that which is necessary for the discovery of weapons which might be used to harm the officer or others nearby, and may realistically be characterized as something less than a "full" search, even though it remains a serious intrusion.

A second, and related, objection to petitioner's argument is that it assumes that the law of arrest has already worked out the balance between the particular interests involved here—the neutralization of danger to the policeman in the investigative circumstance and the sanctity of the individual. But this is not so. An arrest is a wholly different kind of intrusion upon individual freedom from a limited search for weapons, and the interests each is designed to serve are likewise quite different. An arrest is the initial stage of a criminal prosecution. It is intended to vindicate society's interest in having its laws obeyed, and it is inevitably accompanied by future interference with the individual's freedom of movement, whether or not trial or conviction ultimately follows. The protective search for weapons, on the other hand, constitutes a brief, though far from inconsiderable, intrusion upon the sanctity of the person. It does not follow that because an officer may lawfully arrest a person only when he is apprised of facts sufficient to warrant a belief that the person has committed or is committing a crime, the officer is equally unjustified, absent that kind of evidence, in making any intrusions short of an arrest. Moreover, a perfectly reasonable apprehension of danger may arise long before the officer is possessed of adequate information to justify taking a person into custody for the purpose of prosecuting him for a crime. Petitioner's reliance on cases which have worked out standards of reasonableness with regard to ''seizures'' constituting arrests and searches incident thereto is thus misplaced. It assumes that the interests sought to be vindicated and the invasions of personal security may be equated in the two cases, and thereby ignores a vital aspect of the analysis of the reasonableness of particular types of conduct under the Fourth Amendment. . . .

Our evaluation of the proper balance that has to be struck in this type of case leads us to conclude that there must be a narrowly drawn authority to permit a reasonable search for weapons for the protection of the police officer, where he has reason to believe that he is dealing with an armed and dangerous individual, regardless of whether he has probable cause to arrest the individual for a crime. The officer need not be absolutely certain that the individual is armed; the issue is whether a reasonably prudent man in the circumstances would be warranted in the belief that his safety or that of others was in danger. . . . And in determining whether the officer acted reasonably in such circumstances, due weight must be given, not to his inchoate and unparticularized suspicion or ''hunch,'' but to the specific reasonable inferences which he is entitled to draw from the facts in light of his experience. . . .

IV.

We must now examine the conduct of Officer McFadden in this case to determine whether his search and seizure of petitioner were reasonable, both at their inception and as conducted. He had observed Terry, together with Chilton and another man, acting in a manner he took to be preface to a ''stick-up.'' We think on the facts and circumstances Officer McFadden detailed before the trial judge a reasonably prudent man would have been warranted in believing petitioner was armed and thus presented a threat to the officer's safety while he was investigating his suspicious behavior. . . .

The scope of the search in this case presents no serious problem in light of these standards. Officer McFadden patted down the outer clothing of petitioner and his two companions. He did not place his hands in their pockets or under the outer surface of their garments until he had felt weapons, and then he merely reached for and removed the guns. He never did invade Katz's person beyond the outer surfaces of his clothes, since he discovered nothing in his pat down which might have been a weapon. Officer McFadden confined his search strictly to what was minimally necessary to learn whether the men were armed and to disarm them once he discovered the weapons. He did not conduct a general exploratory search for whatever evidence of criminal activity he might find.

V.

We conclude that the revolver seized from Terry was properly admitted in evidence against him. At the time he seized petitioner and searched him for weapons, Officer McFadden had reasonable grounds to believe that petitioner was armed and dangerous, and it was necessary for the protection of himself and others to take swift measures to discover the true facts and neutralize the threat of harm if it materialized. The policeman carefully restricted his search to what was appropriate to the discovery of the particular items which he sought. Each case of this sort will, of course, have to be decided on its own facts. We merely hold today that where a police officer observes unusual conduct which leads him reasonably to conclude in light of his experience that criminal activity may be afoot and that the persons with whom he is dealing may be armed and presently dangerous; where in the course of investigating this behavior he identifies himself as a policeman and makes reasonable inquiries; and where nothing in the initial stages of the encounter serves to dispel his reasonable fear for his own or others' safety, he is entitled for the protection of himself and others in the area to conduct a carefully limited search of the outer clothing of such persons in an attempt to discover weapons which might be used to assault him. Such a search is reasonable search under the Fourth Amendment, and any weapons seized may properly be introduced in evidence against the person from whom they were taken.

Affirmed.

Mr. Justice **Black** concurs in the judgment and the opinion except where the opinion quotes from and relies upon this Court's opinion in Katz v. United States and the concurring opinion in Warden v. Hayden.

Justices **Harlan** and **White** wrote concurring opinions.

Mr. Justice **Douglas,** dissenting, said in part:

I agree that petitioner was ''seized'' within the meaning of the Fourth Amendment. I also agree that frisking petitioner and his companions for guns was a ''search.'' But it is a mystery how that ''search'' and that ''seizure'' can be constitutional by Fourth Amendment standards, unless there was ''probable cause'' to believe that (1) a crime had been committed or (2) a crime was in the process of being committed or (3) a crime was about to be committed.

The opinion of the Court disclaims the existence of ''probable cause.'' If loitering were an issue and that was the offense charged, there would be ''probable cause'' shown. But the crime here is carrying concealed weapons; and there is no basis for concluding that the officer had ''probable cause'' for believing that crime was being committed. Had a warrant been sought, a magistrate would, therefore, have been unauthorized to issue one, for he can act only if there is a showing of ''probable cause.'' We hold today that the police have greater authority to make a ''seizure'' and conduct a ''search'' than a judge has to authorize such action. We have said precisely the opposite over and over again.

KATZ v. UNITED STATES

389 U. S. 347; 88 S. Ct. 507, 19 L. Ed. 2d 576
(1967)

The common law set narrow limits to the things that could be seized under a search warrant. A warrant would issue only to seize smuggled goods, the fruits and instruments of crime, and contraband articles. The Court in the Boyd v. United States (1886) stressed this rule, explaining that only "stolen or forfeited goods or goods liable to duties and concealed to avoid the payment thereof" were subject to seizure because only there did the government have a property interest. "In the case of stolen goods, the owner . . . is entitled to their possession; and in the case of excisable or dutiable articles, the Government has an interest in them for the payment of duties thereon, and until such duties are paid has a right to keep them under observation, or to pursue and drag them from concealment. . . ."

This decision was reaffirmed in 1921 in Gouled v. United States. There an officer, "pretending to make a friendly call upon the defendant, gained admission to his office, and, in his absence, without warrant of any character, seized and carried away several documents . . . [one of which was] 'of evidential value only.'" . . . Later, certain papers and documents tending to show mail fraud were seized under a search warrant. The Court not only found that the fraudulent entrance violated the Fourth Amendment, but held that none of the seized documents could be admitted as evidence. "Although search warrants have . . . been used in many cases ever since the adoption of the Constitution, and although their use has been extended from time to time to meet new cases within the old rules, nevertheless it is clear that, at common law and as the result of the Boyd and Weeks [Weeks v. United States, 1914] Cases, they may not be used as a means of gaining access to a person's house or office and papers solely for the purpose of making search to secure evidence to be used against him in a criminal or penal proceeding, but that they may be resorted to only when a primary right to such search and seizure may be found in the interest which the public or the complainant may have in the property to be seized, or in the right to the possession of it, or when a valid exercise of the police power renders possession of the property by the accused unlawful, and provides that it may be taken. . . ."

In the years following the Gouled decision the Court paid lip-service to its holding in several dicta, but no further evidence was actually held inadmissible on the ground that it was "mere evidence." Federal statutes authorized search warrants for those limited kinds of evidence only, and in the lower courts there was a tendency to find nearly all things remotely connected with a crime to be "instruments," since the crime could not have been committed without them.

Finally, in Warden v. Hayden (1967), the pretense was abandoned and the Gouled case overruled. The Court pointed out that over the years it had "recognized that the principal object of the Fourth Amendment is the protection of privacy rather than property, and [had] increasingly discarded fictional and procedural barriers rest[ing] on property concepts." That being the case, the "mere evidence" rule served no useful purpose, since "the requirements of the Fourth Amendment can secure the same protection of privacy whether the search is for 'mere evidence' or for fruits, instrumentalities or contraband. There must, of course, be a nexus—automatically provided in the case of fruits, instrumentalities or contraband—between the item to be seized and criminal behavior. Thus in the case of 'mere evidence,' probable cause must be examined in terms of cause to believe that the evidence sought will aid in a particular apprehension or conviction. In so doing, consideration of police purposes will be required. . . . But no such problem is presented in this case. The clothes found in the washing machine matched the description of those worn by the robber and the police therefore could reasonably believe that the items would aid in the identification of the culprit."

While the protection against unreasonable searches and seizures has come to protect individual privacy, it was originally, as its wording suggests, a protection only against the physical invasion of persons or their houses and the seizure of tangible things belonging to them. What could be heard by the eavesdropper under the window or seen by peeping at the keyhole was not being seized, and the search of a defendant's open field which resulted in the finding of a whiskey bottle was held to be neither a search nor a seizure. See Hester v. United States (1924).

The protection of the Fourth Amendment had been extended in Ex parte Jackson (1878) to sealed letters in the United States mails, and the Court in Olmstead v. United States (1928) faced for the first time the question whether such protection should be extended to other forms of communication, in this case the telephone. Olmstead was the ringleader of a gigantic conspiracy of rum-runners and bootleggers operating mainly from Seattle, involving two seagoing vessels and several coastwise craft, underground storage caches, and elaborate offices. The yearly income from the business was over two million dollars. Federal prohibition officers tapped the telephone wires in the basement of Olmstead's office building and the transcribed record was introduced in court to prove the conspiracy. The question was whether either the Fourth or Fifth Amendment forbade wiretapping.

The decision of the Court that neither amendment was violated rested first on the proposition that since Olmstead had not been compelled to talk, there was no room for a claim that he had been forced to incriminate himself unless he had been the victim of an unreasonable search or seizure in violation of the Fourth. That he had not been was evident from a number of facts. In the first place, the wire tap had not taken place on Olmstead's property—there had been no trespass. "The language of the Amendment can not be extended and expanded to in-

clude telephone wires reaching to the whole world from the defendant's house or office. The intervening wires are not part of his house or office, any more than are the highways along which they are stretched. . . ."

In the second place, Olmstead had not intended to limit his conversations to those in the room with him. "The reasonable view is that one who installs in his house a telephone instrument with connecting wires intends to project his voice to those quite outside, and that the wires beyond his house and messages while passing over them are not within the protection of the fourth Amendment." And third, since the Fourth Amendment speaks only of "things" to be seized, it clearly was not intended to cover merely verbal material. "The Amendment does not forbid what was done here. There was no searching. There was no seizure. The evidence was secured by the use of the sense of hearing and that only."

In deciding that wiretapping did not violate the Fourth Amendment, the Court rejected the warning of four justices that electronic inventions would ultimately make physical search and seizure unnecessary and completely destroy privacy. Time has not blunted the argument of Justice Brandeis that the Fourth Amendment should keep pace with discoveries and inventions which have "made it possible for the Government by means far more effective than stretching upon the rack, to obtain disclosure in court of what is whispered in the closet."

After the decision in the Olmstead case several bills were introduced in Congress to forbid wiretapping by federal officers. None of these passed, but in the Federal Communications Act of 1934 Congress provided that "no person not being authorized by the sender shall intercept any communication and divulge or publish the existence, contents, substance . . . of such intercepted communication to any person." This act, applying to individuals and government agents alike, remained law until 1968 when Congress passed the Omnibus Crime Control and Safe Streets Act which set up rules by which state and federal law enforcement officials could tap telephone wires under court order and use the results in the prosecution of a wide variety of crimes.

When the Supreme Court decided in Olmstead v. United States (1928) that wire tapping did not constitute an unreasonable search and seizure in violation of the Fourth Amendment, it did so on three grounds. First, there was no physical trespass. Second, Olmstead had intended "to project his voice to those quite outside." And third, what had been seized from Olmstead was his spoken word. Nothing tangible had been taken that would make applicable the constitutional injunction requiring a warrant describing "things to be seized."

The last of these grounds was the first to go. In Goldman v. United States (1942) the Court held that eavesdropping by means of a detectophone, a sensitive device which could pick up conversations in an adjoining room, was not an unreasonable search and seizure; and in 1952 the rule was reaffirmed in On Lee v. United States, in which an undercover narcotics agent with a hidden pocket transmitter engaged a shopkeeper in conversation and transmitted damaging admissions to an agent in a car outside. In both these cases the Court relied on the absence of trespass to sustain the use of the evidence rather than upon the fact that nothing tangible was being seized. Finally, in Silverman v. United States (1961) the Court held void a search for intangibles where there was trespass. A "spike-mike" had been driven into a hot-air duct in a building wall so that police could overhear conversations within the building. While probably not amounting to trespass under local law, it was considered by the Court to be a "physical intrusion into a constitutionally protected area." The Court emphasized that physical trespass distinguished the case from Olmstead, but simply ignored Olmstead's limitation of the amendment to "things" that were tangible.

While breaking into a home or office, or an obvious physical intrusion however slight (like a spike-mike), could clearly be viewed as trespass, what was the status of the traditional undercover agent who posed as a member of the "gang" in order to gain evidence of crime? In 1921 the Court in Gouled v. United States had held unanimously that "whether entrance to the home or office of a person suspected of crime be obtained by a representative of . . . the government . . . by stealth or through social acquaintance, or in the guise of a business call, and whether the owner be present or not when he enters, any search and seizure subsequently and secretly made in his absence falls within the scope of the Fourth Amendment." Does this mean that planting an informer in a criminal conspiracy violates the Fourth Amendment right of the conspirators? In Hoffa v. United States (1966), the Court held that it did not. Partin, a local teamster official, acted as a paid informer to bring federal officials reports on Hoffa's efforts to bribe the jury in a federal trial in which Hoffa was involved. The Court conceded that a hotel room can be an area protected by the Fourth Amendment, that the amendment can be violated by guile as well as by forceful entry, and that its protection is not limited to tangibles. But Hoffa had no protection in this instance because "what the Fourth Amendment protects is the security a man relies upon when he places himself or his property within a constitutionally protected area." In this case Hoffa "was not relying on the security of the hotel room; he was relying upon his misplaced confidence that Partin would not reveal his wrongdoing." A similar result was reached in Lewis v. United States (1966) where a narcotics pusher had invited a federal agent to his home and sold him narcotics, not knowing what he was. By converting his home into a "commercial center to which outsiders are invited for purposes of transacting unlawful business" the pusher forfeited its sanctity under the Fourth Amendment.

Mr. Justice **Stewart** delivered the opinion of the Court, saying in part:

The petitioner was convicted in the District Court for the Southern District of California under an eight-count indictment charging him with transmitting wagering information by telephone from Los Angeles to Miami and Boston, in violation of a federal statute. At the trial the Government was permitted, over the petitioner's objection, to introduce evidence of the petitioner's end of telephone conversations, overheard by FBI agents who had attached an electronic listening and recording device to the outside of the public telephone booth from which he had placed his calls. In affirming his conviction, the Court of Appeals rejected the contention that the recordings had been obtained in violation of the Fourth Amendment, because "[t]here was no physical entrance into the area occupied by [the petitioner]." We granted certiorari in order to consider the constitutional questions thus presented.

The petitioner has phrased those questions as follows:

"A. Whether a public telephone booth is a constitutionally protected area so that evidence obtained by attaching an electronic listening recording device to the top of such a booth is obtained in violation of the right to privacy of the user of the booth.

"B. Whether physical penetration of a constitutionally protected area is necessary before a search and seizure can be said to be violative of the Fourth Amendment to the United States Constitution."

We decline to adopt this formulation of the issues. In the first place, the correct solution of Fourth Amendment problems is not necessarily promoted by incantation of the phrase "constitutionally protected area." Secondly, the Fourth Amendment cannot be translated into a general constitutional "right to privacy." That Amendment protects individual privacy against certain kinds of governmental intrusion, but its protections go further, and often have nothing to do with privacy at all. Other provisions of the Constitution protect personal privacy from other forms of governmental invasion. But the protection of a person's *general* right to privacy—his right to be let alone by other people—is, like the protection of his property and of his life, left largely to the law of the individual states.

Because of the misleading way the issues have been formulated, the parties have attached great significance to the characterization of the telephone booth from which the petitioner placed his calls. The petitioner has strenuously argued that the booth was a "constitutionally protected area." The Government has maintained with equal vigor that it was not. But this effort to decide whether or not a given "area," viewed in the abstract, is "constitutionally protected" deflects attention from the problem presented by this case.* For the Fourth Amendment protects people, not places. What a person knowingly exposes to the public, even in his own home or office, is not a subject of Fourth Amendment protection. . . . But what he seeks to preserve as private, even in an area accessible to the public, may be constitutionally protected. See . . . Ex parte Jackson [1878].

---

*It is true that this Court has occasionally described its conclusions in terms of "constitutionally protected areas," see, e.g., Silverman v. United States [1961]; Lopez v. United States [1963]; Berger v. New York [1967], but we have never suggested that this concept can serve as a talismanic solution to every Fourth Amendment problem.

The Government stresses the fact that the telephone booth from which the petitioner made his calls was constructed partly of glass, so that he was as visible after he entered it as he would have been if he had remained outside. But what he sought to exclude when he entered the booth was not the intruding eye—it was the uninvited ear. He did not shed his right to do so simply because he made his calls from a place where he might be seen. No less than an individual in a business office, in a friend's apartment, or in a taxicab, a person in a telephone booth may rely upon the protection of the Fourth Amendment. One who occupies it, shuts the door behind him, and pays the toll that permits him to place a call, is surely entitled to assume that the words he utters into the mouthpiece will not be broadcast to the world. To read the Constitution more narrowly is to ignore the vital role that the public telephone has come to play in private communication.

The Government contends, however, that the activities of its agents in this case should not be tested by Fourth Amendment requirements, for the surveillance technique they employed involved no physical penetration of the telephone booth from which the petitioner placed his calls. It is true that the absence of such penetration was at one time thought to foreclose further Fourth Amendment inquiry, Olmstead v. United States [1928]; Goldman v. United States [1942], for that Amendment was thought to limit only searches and seizures of tangible property. But "[t]he premise that property interests control the right of the Government to search and seize has been discredited." Warden v. Hayden [1967]. Thus, although a closely divided Court supposed in Olmstead that surveillance without any trespass and without the seizure of any material object fell outside the ambit of the Constitution, we have since departed from the narrow view on which that decision rested. Indeed, we have expressly held that the Fourth Amendment governs not only the seizure of tangible items, but extends as well to the recording of oral statements, overheard without any "technical trespass under . . . local property law." Silverman v. United States [1961]. Once this much is acknowledged, and once it is recognized that the Fourth Amendment protects people—and not simply "areas"—against unreasonable searches and seizures, it becomes clear that the reach of that Amendment cannot turn upon the presence or absence of a physical intrusion into any given enclosure. We conclude that the underpinnings of Olmstead and Goldman have been so eroded by our subsequent decisions that the "trespass" doctrine there enunciated can no longer be regarded as controlling. The Government's activities in electronically listening to and recording the petitioner's words violated the privacy upon which he justifiably relied while using the telephone booth and thus constituted a "search and seizure" within the meaning of the Fourth Amendment. The fact that the electronic device employed to achieve that end did not happen to penetrate the wall of the booth can have no constitutional significance.

The question remaining for decision, then, is whether the search and seizure conducted in this case complied with constitutional standards. In that regard, the Government's position is that its agents acted in an entirely defensible manner: They did not begin their electronic surveillance until investigation of the petitioner's activities had established a strong probability that he was using the telephone in question to transmit gambling information to persons in other States, in violation of federal law. Moreover, the surveillance was limited, both in scope and in duration, to the specific purpose of establishing the contents of the petitioner's unlawful telephonic communications. The agents confined their surveillance to the brief periods during which he used the telephone booth, and they took great care to overhear only the conversations of the petitioner himself.

Accepting this account of the Government's actions as accurate, it is clear that this surveillance was so narrowly circumscribed that a duly authorized magistrate, properly notified of the need for such investigation, specifically informed of the basis on which it was to proceed, and clearly apprised of the precise intrusion it would entail, could constitutionally have authorized, with appropriate safeguards, the very limited search and seizure that the Government asserts in fact took place. . . .

The Government urges that, because its agents relied upon the decisions in Olmstead and Goldman, and because they did no more here than they might properly have done with prior judicial sanction, we should retroactively validate their conduct. That we cannot do. It is apparent that the agents in this case acted with restraint. Yet the inescapable fact is that this restraint was imposed by the agents themselves, not by a judicial officer. They were not required, before commencing the search, to present their estimate of probable cause for detached scrutiny by a neutral magistrate. They were not compelled, during the conduct of the search itself, to observe precise limits established in advance by a specific court order. Nor were they directed, after the search had been completed, to notify the authorizing magistrate in detail of all that had been seized. In the absence of such safeguards, this Court has never sustained a search upon the sole ground that officers reasonably expected to find evidence of a particular crime and voluntarily confined their activities to the least intrusive means consistent with that end. Searches conducted without warrants have been held unlawful "notwithstanding facts unquestionably showing probable cause," Agnello v. United States [1925], for the Constitution requires "that the deliberate, impartial judgment of a judicial officer . . . be interposed between the citizen and the police. . . ." Wong Sun v. United States [1963] . . . —subject only to a few specifically established and well-delineated exceptions.

It is difficult to imagine how many of those exceptions could ever apply to the sort of search and seizure involved in this case. Even electronic surveillance substantially contemporaneous with an individual's arrest could hardly be deemed an "incident" of that arrest. Nor could the use of electronic surveillance without prior authorization be justified on grounds of "hot pursuit." And, of course, the very nature of electronic surveillance precludes its use pursuant to the suspect's consent.

The Government does not question these basic principles. Rather, it urges the creation of a new exception to cover this case.* It argues that surveillance of a telephone booth should be exempted from the usual requirement of advance authorization by a magistrate upon a showing of probable cause. We cannot agree. Omission of such authorization "bypasses the safeguards provided by an objective predetermination of probable cause, and substitutes instead the far less reliable procedure of an after-the-event justification for the . . . search, too likely to be subtly influenced by the familiar shortcomings of hindsight judgment." . . .

And bypassing a neutral predetermination of the *scope* of a search leaves individuals secure from Fourth Amendment violations "only in the discretion of the police." . . .

These considerations do not vanish when the search in question is transferred from the setting of a home, an office, or a hotel room, to that of a telephone booth. Wherever a man may be, he is entitled to know that he will remain free from unreasonable searches and seizures. The government agents here ignore "the procedure of antecedent justification . . . that is central to the Fourth Amendment, a procedure that we hold to be a constitutional precondition of the kind of electronic surveillance involved in this case. Because the surveillance here failed to meet that condition, and because it led to the petitioner's conviction, the judgment must be reversed.

It is so ordered.

Mr. Justice **Marshall** took no part in the consideration or decision of this case.

Mr. Justice **Douglas,** with whom Mr. Justice **Brennan** joins, concurring, said in part:

While I join the opinion of the Court, I feel compelled to reply to the separate concurring opinion of my Brother White, which I view as a wholly unwarranted green light for the Executive Branch to resort to electronic eavesdropping without a warrant in cases which the Executive Branch itself labels "national security" matters.

Neither the President nor the Attorney General is a magistrate. In matters where they believe national security may be involved they are not detached, disinterested, and neutral as a court or magistrate must be. . . . They may even be the intended victims of subversive action. Since spies and saboteurs are as entitled to the protection of the Fourth Amendment as suspected gamblers like petitioner, I cannot agree that where spies and saboteurs are involved adequate protection of Fourth Amendment rights is assured when the President and Attorney General assume both the position of adversary-and-prosecutor and disinterested, neutral magistrate.

Mr. Justice **Harlan,** concurring, said in part:

I join the opinion of the Court, which I read to hold only (a) that an enclosed telephone booth is an area

---

*Whether safeguards other than prior authorization by a magistrate would satisfy the Fourth Amendment in a situation involving the national security is a question not presented by this case.

where, like a home, Weeks v. United States [1914], and unlike a field, Hester v. United States [1924], a person has a constitutionally protected reasonable expectation of privacy; (b) that electronic as well as physical intrusion into a place that is in this sense private may constitute a violation of the Fourth Amendment; and (c) that the invasion of a constitutionally protected area by federal authorities is, as the Court has long held, presumptively unreasonable in the absence of a warrant.

As the Court's opinion states, "The Fourth Amendment protects people, not places." The question, however, is what protection it affords to those people. Generally, as here, the answer to that question requires reference to a "place." . . . Thus a man's home is, for most purposes, a place where he expects privacy, but objects, activities, or statements that he exposes to the "plain view" of outsiders are not "protected" because no intention to keep them to himself has been exhibited. On the other hand, conversations in the open would not be protected against being overheard, for the expectation of privacy under the circumstances would be unreasonable. Hester v. United States. . . .

Mr. Justice **White,** concurring, said in part:

In joining the Court's opinion, I note the Court's acknowledgment that there are circumstances in which it is reasonable to search without a warrant. In this connection the Court points out that today's decision does not reach national security cases. Wiretapping to protect the security of the Nation has been authorized by successive Presidents. The present Administration would apparently save national security cases from restrictions against wiretapping. . . . We should not require the warrant procedure and the magistrate's judgment if the President of the United States or his chief legal officer, the Attorney General, has considered the requirements of national security and authorized electronic surveillance as reasonable.

Mr. Justice **Black,** dissenting, said in part:

If I could agree with the Court that eavesdropping carried on by electronic means (equivalent to wiretapping) constitutes a "search" or "seizure," I would be happy to join the Court's opinion. . . .

My basic objection is twofold: (1) I do not believe that the words of the Amendment will bear the meaning given them by today's decision, and (2) I do not believe that it is the proper role of this Court to rewrite the Amendment in order "to bring it into harmony with the times" and thus reach a result that many people believe to be desirable.

UNITED STATES v. ROSS

456 U. S. 798; 102 S. Ct. 2157; 72 L. Ed. 2d 572 (1982)

While the "search incident" exception to the warrant requirement is of ancient origin, the "Carroll" doctrine exempting automobiles from the requirement stems from the Court's decision in Carroll v. United States decided in 1925. Carroll, a known bootlegger, was recognized and stopped by federal prohibition agents without a warrant and his car searched. The agents had ample cause to believe Carroll would be carrying contraband and since there was no time in which to get a warrant the Supreme Court held the search valid. In reaching its decision it made clear that "where the securing of a warrant is reasonably practicable it must be used. . . . In cases where seizure is impossible except without a warrant, the seizing officer acts unlawfully and at his peril unless he can show the court probable cause."

Like the search incident doctrine, the Carroll doctrine has become a talisman or shorthand for the right to search an automobile without a warrant, and a number of justices have argued that it should be independent of whether or not there was time to get a warrant. The Court in Coolidge v. New Hampshire (1971) rejected the argument of the state that "the police may make a warrantless search of an automobile whenever they have probable cause to do so" and also Justice White's suggestion that "for Fourth Amendment purposes the difference between a moving and movable vehicle is tenuous at best." "The word 'automobile' ," said the Court, "is not a talisman in whose presence the Fourth Amendment fades away and disappears."

The Carroll case left unanswered two problems that have since come before the Court. The first of these, the question of timing, was answered in Chambers v. Maroney (1970) in which the Court extended the Carroll doctrine to justify a search later in time than the arrest. There the police had been given a description of a car, its occupants, and the clothing they wore, seen near the scene of a nighttime holdup. Within an hour a car answering the description, and containing the described occupants and clothing was stopped. The occupants were arrested and the car driven to the police station where it was searched and incriminating evidence discovered.

The Court agreed unanimously that the evidence was properly admitted. Speaking for seven members of the Court, Justice White conceded that the "search incident" doctrine could not apply because the search was not made at the time and place of arrest. But while the right to search incident to lawful arrest expired when the car was moved, the right to search under the Carroll doctrine did not. In view of the facts, the police had probable cause to search the car for guns and loot before it escaped their jurisdiction. Since it was impractical to follow it around, either they had to search it on the spot without a warrant, or they had to seize it without a warrant and detain it until a search warrant could be obtained. Conceding that arguably the search was the greater infringement and should only be made with a warrant, the Court held that where there was probable cause to search, either course was reasonable under the Fourth Amendment.

Cardwell v. Lewis (1974) involved the warrantless seizure of the defendant's car from a public parking lot after he was in police custody. The car was impounded by the police and tire imprints and paint scrapings were taken to compare with information found at the scene of a murder. Justice Blackmun, writing for himself and Justices Burger, White and Rehnquist, argued that a search of the outside of the car was not really a breach of privacy and that in any event, cars were not entitled to as "stringent warrant requirements" as other places. Not only were they mobile, but "one has a lesser expectation of privacy in a motor vehicle because its function is transportation and it seldom serves as one's residence or as the repository of personal effects. A car has little capacity for escaping public scrutiny. It travels public thoroughfares where both its occupants and its contents are in plain view." Repeating the Court's statement in *Katz v. United States* (1976) that "what a person knowingly exposes to the public, even in his own home or office, is not a subject of Fourth Amendment protection," he added, "this is not to say that no part of the interior of an automobile has Fourth Amendment protection; the exercise of a desire to be mobile does not, of course, waive one's right to be free of unreasonable government intrusion. But insofar as Fourth Amendment protection extends to a motor vehicle, it is the right to privacy that is the touchstone of our inquiry." Justice Powell concurred on the ground that such questions, if fairly litigated in the state courts, should not be subject to federal court review. Justices Steward, Douglas, Brennan and Marshall dissented, pointing out that the Carroll doctrine did not apply since the car was immobilized, and while "the plurality opinion suggests that other 'exigent circumstances' might have excused the failure of the police to procure a warrant, . . . the opinion nowhere states what these mystical exigencies might have been, and counsel for the petitioner has not been so inventive as to suggest any."

The second question left unanswered by Carroll was the status of a sealed container found within an automobile which was itself subject to search without warrant. Since the very existence of such a container suggests the owner's desire for privacy and since the container can be immobilized until a search warrant can be obtained, what is the exigency that permits opening it without such a warrant? Encouraged by the language of the Cardwell case, the government in *United States v. Chadwick* (1977) argued that "the Fourth Amendment warrant clause protects only interests traditionally identified with the home." It had been tipped off that a suspicious-looking footlocker was arriving in Boston by rail, and a number of agents were on hand to witness its arrival. They watched while the owners claimed it and a specially trained police dog signaled secretly that it contained drugs. After it was loaded into the trunk of their car and before the engine was started, the agents arrested the defendants and took them and the footlocker to the federal building where, over an hour later, they opened and searched it without a warrant. It contained some 200 pounds of marijuana.

In a seven-to-two decision the Court held the search unconstitutional. It rejected the government's interpretation, noting that "a fundamental purpose of the Fourth Amendment is to safeguard individuals from unreasonable government invasions of legitimate privacy interests, and not simply those interests found inside the four walls of the home. . . . By placing personal effects inside a double-locked footlocker, respondents manifested an expectation that the contents would remain free from public examination. No less than one who locks the doors of his home against intruders, one who safeguards his personal possessions in this manner is due the protection of the Fourth Amendment Warrant Clause."

Nor was "luggage analogous to motor vehicles for Fourth Amendment purposes," as the government argued. While the Court reaffirmed the language in Cardwell that there was a diminished expectation of privacy surrounding an automobile, it pointed out that the same factors did not apply here. "Unlike an automobile, whose primary function is transportation, luggage is intended as a repository of personal effects. In sum, a person's expectations of privacy in personal luggage are substantially greater than in an automobile.

"Nor does the footlocker's mobility justify dispensing with the added protections of the Warrant Clause. Once the federal agents had seized it at the railroad station and had safely transferred it to the Boston federal building under their exclusive control, there was not the slightest danger that the footlocker or its contents could have been removed before a valid search warrant could be obtained."

But if Chadwick had settled the status of formal luggage, what of things like paper bags, cigarette packages, plastic baggies, and the like that might contain drugs? In the years that followed the police and lower courts disagreed on the immunity of such items from search and it was with the express hope of settling the law in this area that the Court took the present case. Following a tip by a reliable informant that Ross was selling narcotics out of the trunk of his car, Ross was identified by the District of Columbia police, ordered to pull his car over to the curb and get out. The police searched the car and found a bullet on the seat, a gun in the glove compartment, and a closed paper bag in the trunk which contained a number of glassine bags containing white powder. The car was driven to police headquarters where a further search turned up a zippered leather pouch containing $3,200 in cash. The powder in the bags turned out to be heroin. The district court denied a motion to suppress the evidence and Ross was convicted of possession with intent to distribute.

Justice **Stevens** delivered the opinion of the Court, saying in part:

In Carroll v. United States (1925), the Court held that a warrantless search of an automobile stopped by police officers who had probable cause to believe the vehicle contained contraband was not unreasonable within the meaning of the Fourth Amendment. The Court in Carroll did not explicitly address the scope of the search that is permissible. In this case, we consider the extent to which police officers—who have legitimately stopped an automobile and who have probable cause to believe that contraband is concealed somewhere within it—may conduct a probing search of compartments and containers within the vehicle whose contents are not in plain view. We hold that they may conduct a search of the vehicle that is as thorough as a magistrate could authorize in a warrant ''particularly describing the place to be searched.''

I. . . .

There is . . . no dispute among judges about the importance of striving for clarification in this area of the law. For countless vehicles are stopped on highways on public streets every day and our cases demonstrate that it is not uncommon for police officers to have probable cause to believe that contraband may be found in a stopped vehicle. In every such case a conflict is presented between the individual's constitutionally protected interest in privacy and the public interest in effective law enforcement. No single rule of law can resolve every conflict, but our conviction that clarification is feasible led us to grant the Government's petition for certiorari in this case and to invite the parties to address the question whether the decision in Robbins should be reconsidered. . . .

III.

The rationale justifying a warrantless search of an automobile that is believed to be transporting contraband arguably applies with equal force to any movable container that is believed to be carrying an illicit substance. This argument, however, was squarely rejected in United States v. Chadwick [1977]. . . .

The Court in Chadwick specifically rejected the argument that the warrantless search was ''reasonable'' because a footlocker has some of the mobile characteristics that support warrantless searches of automobiles. The Court recognized that ''a person's expectations of privacy in personal luggage are substantially greater than in an automobile,'' and noted that the practical problems associated with the temporary detention of a piece of luggage during the period of time necessary to obtain a warrant are significantly less than those associated with the detention of an automobile. In ruling that the warrantless search of the footlocker was unjustified, the Court reaffirmed the general principle that closed packages and containers may not be searched without a warrant. Cf. Ex parte Jackson [1878]. . . . In sum, the Court in Chadwick declined to extend the rationale of the ''automobile exception'' to permit a warrantless search of any movable container found in a public place.

The facts in Arkansas v. Sanders, [1979], were similar to those in Chadwick. In Sanders, a Little Rock police officer received information from a reliable informant that Sanders would arrive at the local airport on a specified flight that afternoon carrying a green suitcase containing marijuana. The officer went to the airport. Sanders arrived on schedule and retrieved a green suitcase from the airline baggage service. Sanders gave the suitcase to a waiting companion who placed it in the trunk of a taxi. Sanders and his companion drove off in

the cab; police officers followed and stopped the taxi several blocks from the airport. The officers opened the trunk, seized the suitcase, and searched it on the scene without a warrant. As predicted, the suitcase contained marijuana.

The Arkansas Supreme Court ruled that the warrantless search of the suitcase was impermissible under the Fourth Amendment, and this Court affirmed. As in Chadwick, the mere fact that the suitcase had been placed in the trunk of the vehicle did not render the automobile exception of Carroll applicable; the police had probable cause to seize the suitcase before it was placed in the trunk of the cab and did not have probable cause to search the taxi itself. Since the suitcase had been placed in the trunk, no danger existed that its contents could have been secreted elsewhere in the vehicle. As The Chief Justice noted in his opinion concurring in the judgment:

''Because the police officers had probable cause to believe that respondent's green suitcase contained marijuana before it was placed in the trunk of the taxicab, their duty to obtain a search warrant before opening it is clear under United States v. Chadwick (1977). . . .

''Here, as in Chadwick, it was the luggage being transported by respondent at the time of the arrest, not the automobile in which it was being carried, that was the suspected locus of the contraband. The relationship between the automobile and the contraband was purely coincidental, as in Chadwick. The fact that the suitcase was resting in the trunk of the automobile at the time of respondent's arrest does not turn this into an 'automobile' exception case. The Court need say no more.'' . . .

Robbins v. California [1981], however, was a case in which suspicion was not directed at a specific container. In that case the Court for the first time was forced to consider whether police officers who are entitled to conduct a warrantless search of an automobile stopped on a public roadway may open a container found within the vehicle. In the early morning of January 5, 1975, police officers stopped Robbins' station wagon because he was driving erratically. Robbins got out of the car, but later returned to obtain the vehicle's registration papers. When he opened the car door, the officers smelled marijuana smoke. One of the officers searched Robbins and discovered a vial of liquid; in a search of the interior of the car the officer found marijuana. The police officers then opened the tailgate of the station wagon and raised the cover of a recessed luggage compartment. In the compartment they found two packages wrapped in green opaque plastic. The police unwrapped the packages and discovered a large amount of marijuana in each. . . .

. . . Writing for a plurality, Justice Stewart rejected the argument that the outward appearance of the packages precluded Robbins from having a reasonable expectation of privacy in their contents. He also squarely rejected the argument that there is a constitutional distinction between searches of luggage and searches of ''less worthy'' containers. Justice Stewart reasoned that all containers are equally protected by the Fourth Amendment, unless their contents are in plain view. The plurality concluded that the warrantless search was impermissible because Chadwick and Sanders had established that "a closed piece of luggage found in a lawfully searched car is constitutionally protected to the same extent as are closed pieces of luggage found anywhere else." . . .

. . . Unlike Chadwick and Sanders, in this case police officers had probable cause to search respondent's entire vehicle. Unlike Robbins, in this case the parties have squarely addressed the question whether, in the course of a legitimate warrantless search of an automobile, police are entitled to open containers found within the vehicle. We now address that question. Its answer is determined by the scope of the search that is authorized by the exception to the warrant requirement set forth in Carroll.

IV.

In Carroll itself, the whiskey that the prohibition agents seized was not in plain view. It was discovered only after an officer opened the rumble seat and tore open the upholstery of the lazyback. The Court did not find the scope of the search unreasonable. Having stopped Carroll and Kiro on a public road and subjected them to the indignity of a vehicle search—which the Court found to be a reasonable intrusion on their privacy because it was based on probable cause that their vehicle was transporting contraband—prohibition agents were entitled to tear open a portion of the roadster itself. The scope of the search was no greater than a magistrate could have authorized by issuing a warrant based on the probable cause that justified the search. Since such a warrant could have authorized to open the rear portion of the roadster and to rip the upholstery in their search for concealed whiskey, the search was constitutionally permissible.

In Chambers v. Maroney [1975] the police found weapons and stolen property "concealed in a compartment under the dashboard." No suggestion was made that the scope of the search was impermissible. It would be illogical to assume that the outcome of Chambers—or the outcome of Carroll itself—would have been different if the police had found the secreted contraband enclosed within a secondary container and had opened that container without a warrant. If it was reasonable for prohibition agents to rip open the upholstery in Carroll, it certainly would have been reasonable for them to look into a burlap sack stashed inside; if it was reasonable to open the concealed compartment in Chambers, it would have been equally reasonable to open a paper bag crumpled within it. A contrary rule could produce absurd results inconsistent with the decision in Carroll itself. . . .

As we have stated, the decision in Carroll was based on the Court's appraisal of practical considerations viewed in the perspective of history. It is therefore significant that the practical consequences of the Carroll decision would be largely nullified if the permissible scope of a warrantless search of an automobile did not include containers and packages found inside the vehicle. Contraband goods rarely are strewn across the trunk or floor

of a car; since by their very nature such goods must be withheld from public view, they rarely can be placed in an automobile unless they are enclosed within some form of container. The Court in Carroll held that "contraband goods *concealed* and illegally transported in an automobile or other vehicle may be searched for without a warrant." (emphasis added). As we noted in Henry v. United States [1959], the decision in Carroll "merely relaxed the requirements for a warrant on grounds of impracticability." It neither broadened nor limited the scope of a lawful search based on probable cause. . . .

As Justice Stewart stated in Robbins, the Fourth Amendment provides protection to the owner of every container that conceals its contents from plain view. But the protection afforded by the Amendment varies in different settings. The luggage carried by a traveler entering the country may be searched at random by a customs officer; the luggage may be searched no matter how great the traveler's desire to conceal the contents may be. A container carried at the time of arrest often may be searched without a warrant and even without any specific suspicion concerning its contents. A container that may conceal the object of a search authorized by a warrant may be opened immediately; the individual's interest in privacy must give way to the magistrate's official determination of probable cause.

In the same manner, an individual's expectation of privacy in a vehicle and its contents may not survive if probable cause is given to believe that the vehicle is transporting contraband. Certainly the privacy interests in a car's trunk or glove compartment may be no less than those in a movable container. An individual undoubtedly has a significant interest that the upholstery of his automobile will not be ripped or a hidden compartment within it opened. These interests must yield to the authority of a search, however, which—in light of Carroll—does not itself require the prior approval of a magistrate. The scope of a warrantless search based on probable cause is no narrower—and no broader—than the scope of a search authorized by a warrant supported by probable cause. Only the prior approval of the magistrate is waived; the search otherwise is as the magistrate could authorize.

The scope of a warrantless search of an automobile thus is not defined by the nature of the container in which the contraband is secreted. Rather, it is defined by the object of the search and the places in which there is probable cause to believe that it may be found. Just as probable cause to believe that a stolen lawnmower may be found in a garage will not support a warrant to search an upstairs bedroom, probable cause to believe that undocumented aliens are being transported in a van will not justify a warrantless search of a suitcase. Probable cause to believe that a container placed in the trunk of a taxi contains contraband or evidence does not justify a search of the entire cab. . . .

Justice **Blackmun**, concurring, said in part:

My dissents in prior cases have indicated my continuing dissatisfaction and discomfort with the Court's vacillation in what is rightly described as "this troubled area." . . .

. . . It is important, however, not only for the court as an institution, but also for law enforcement officials and defendants, that the applicable legal rules be clearly established. Justice Stevens' opinion for the Court now accomplishes much in this respect, and it should clarify a good bit of the confusion that has existed. In order to have an authoritative ruling, I join the Court's opinion and judgment.

Justice **Powell**, concurring, said in part:

. . . It became evident last Term, however, from the five opinions written in Robbins—in none of which The Chief Justice joined—that it is essential to have a Court opinion in *automobile* search cases that provides "specific guidance to police and courts in this reoccurring situation." Robbins v. California (1981) (Powell, J., concurring). The Court's opinion today, written by Justice Stevens and now joined by four other Justices, will afford this needed guidance. It is fair also to say that, given Carroll v. United States (1925) and Chambers v. Maroney (1970), the Court's decision does not depart substantially from Fourth Amendment doctrine in enunciating a readily understood and applied rule. Today's decision is consistent with the similar step taken last Term in New York v. Belton (1981).

Justice **Marshall**, with whom Justice **Brennan** joins, dissenting, said in part:

The majority today not only repeals all realistic limits on warrantless automobile searches, it repeals the Fourth Amendment warrant requirement itself. By equating a police officer's estimation of probable cause with a magistrate's, the Court utterly disregards the value of a neutral and detached magistrate. . . .

A police officer on the beat hardly satisfies these standards. In adopting today's new rule, the majority opinion shows contempt for these Fourth Amendment values, ignores this Court's precedents, is internally inconsistent, and produces anomalous and unjust consequences. I therefore dissent.

I.

According to the majority, whenever police have probable cause to believe that contraband may be found within an automobile that they have stopped on the highway, they may search not only the automobile but also any container found inside it, without obtaining a warrant. The scope of the search, we are told, is as broad as a magistrate could authorize in a warrant to search the automobile. The majority makes little attempt to justify this rule in terms of recognized Fourth Amendment values. The Court simply ignores the critical function that a magistrate serves. And although the Court purports to rely on the mobility of an automobile and the impracticability of obtaining a warrant, it never explains why these concerns permit the warrantless search of a con-

tainer, which can easily be seized and immobilized while police are obtaining a warrant.

The new rule adopted by the Court today is completely incompatible with established Fourth Amendment principles, and takes a first step toward an unprecedented "probable cause" exception to the warrant requirement. In my view, under accepted standards, the warrantless search of the container in this case clearly violates the Fourth Amendment.

UNITED STATES v. LEON

468 U. S. 897; 104 S. Ct. 3424; 82 L. Ed. 2d 677 (1984)

[Over the years in a wide variety of decisions the Court had manifested a basic discontent with the exclusionary rule of Weeks v. United States. The Court seemed to agree that blatant violations of the right of personal privacy could only be discouraged by the use of the doctrine, yet it balked at having to exclude from court unimpeachable evidence of a person's guilt simply because of some legal flaw in the way it was obtained. It had vacillated in its application of the Carroll and "search incident" doctrines and in Terry v. Ohio it had eased dramatically the restrictions on warrantless searches. But it had still failed to find a doctrine that would let it ban illegal evidence gotten in ways it found objectionable, while admitting equally illegal evidence whose admission seemed to promote the cause of justice.

Curiously enough, it was in the context of the retroactivity question that the Court finally devised a theory that it hoped would provide this flexibility. The abrupt reversal of many long-standing constitutional rules in the years of the Warren Court brought to the fore a new kind of problem: To what extent were the new interpretations of the Constitution to be made retroactive so as to free prisoners held under the old interpretations. The traditional rule had always been to apply any new interpretation retroactively, but faced with the specter of thousands of retrials, the Court reexamined this doctrine and in Linkletter v. Walker (1965) set a precedent for limiting the retroactivity of certain rights. Whether a holding is to be applied retroactively depends on the nature of the right and the purposes it is designed to serve. In its decision in United States v. Calandra (1974) the Court had leaned heavily on the "deterrent effect" of the exclusionary rule and concluded that if, in fact, excluding the evidence would not have deterred the police conduct, there was no point in excluding the evidence through a retroactive application of the rule.

A year later in United States v. Peltier (1975) the Court refined the doctrine into what has become known as the "good faith" exception to the exclusion rule. Bluntly stated, if the purpose of the exclusion of evidence is to deter the police from making illegal searches, there is no point in excluding the evidence if the police did not know the search was illegal. Why punish a police offi-

cer? If the police are acting "in good faith," then the evidence should be admissible.

The Peltier case arose out of the enforcement of legislation regulating our border patrols and again involved the questions of the retroactivity of a newly announced interpretation of the law. The Court found that the guards along the Mexican border were relying on what they believed to be valid rules regarding the stopping and searching of vehicles near the border and there was no point in "punishing" them by refusing to admit their evidence simply because the rules had been changed.

Four years later, in Michigan v. DeFillippo (1979), the Court extended the "good faith" doctrine of Peltier beyond the confines of the retroactivity question to hold admissible evidence gotten by a search incident to an unconstitutional arrest. DeFillippo was stopped by the police in a Detroit alley under suspicious circumstances and asked to identify himself. When he refused he was arrested under a city ordinance that made it a crime to refuse such identification, was searched incident to the arrest, and marijuana was found in his pocket. He was charged with possession but the Michigan court, holding the identification ordinance void for vagueness and hence the arrest invalid, held the evidence inadmissible as the product of an invalid search.

The Supreme Court reversed. A police officer, it held, has a duty to enforce a law until it is held void unless it is "so grossly and flagrantly unconstitutional that any person of reasonable prudence would be bound to see its flaws." Such was not the case here, and since the refusal to give his name was a crime being committed in the presence of the officer, the arrest and incident search were valid. The unconstitutionality of the ordinance under which DeFillippo had been arrested was stressed in a companion case holding void on its face an El Paso ordinance making it a crime for a person to refuse to identify himself to a police officer; see Brown v. Texas (1979).

Originally limited to evidence gotten by an unreasonable search and seizure, the "good faith" doctrine moved within a year into the area of evidence obtained by questioning suspects. After giving a murder suspect Miranda warnings, three police officers were taking him to the police station for questioning. During the ride, two of them discussed the danger posed to the community by the fact that the murder gun was still missing. A school for handicapped children was nearby "and God forbid one of them might find a weapon with shells and might hurt themselves." The suspect interrupted and asked the officers to return to the scene of the crime. There he produced the hidden weapon because " 'he wanted to get the gun out of the way because of the kids in the area in the school.' " The Court upheld the admission of the gun and the defendant's statements pointing out that the officers, acting in good faith, had not intended their conversation as interrogation and they could not have known of the defendant's sensitivity where handicapped children were concerned. See Rhode Island v. Innis (1980).

In the present case a confidential informant of unproven reliability tipped off the police of Burbank, Calif., that Leon and others were selling cocaine and methaqualone from their home and other places. The police watched the comings and goings of the five or six persons involved, some of whom were known to have been involved in the drug traffic, and concluded that they were engaged in a drug smuggling operation. Several district attorneys reviewed the evidence collected by the police, and at their request a state judge issued a warrant to search a number of residences and vehicles. The defendants were indicted on drug charges. They filed a motion to suppress the evidence seized under the warrant and the district court granted the motion on the ground that the reliability and credibility of the informant had not been established. "I just cannot find this warrant sufficient for a showing of probable cause" for the issuance of a search warrant.

Justice **White** delivered the opinion of the Court, saying in part:

This case presents the question whether the Fourth Amendment exclusionary rule should be modified so as not to bar the use in the prosecutions's case-in-chief of evidence obtained by officers acting in reasonable reliance on a search warrant issued by a detached and neutral magistrate but ultimately found to be unsupported by probable cause. To resolve this question, we must consider once again the tension between the sometimes competing goals of, on the one hand, deterring official misconduct and removing inducements to unreasonable invasions of privacy and, on the other, establishing procedures under which criminal defendants are "acquitted or convicted on the basis of all the evidence which exposes the truth." . . .

I. . . .

We have concluded that, in the Fourth Amendment context, the exclusionary rule can be modified somewhat without jeopardizing its ability to perform its intended functions. . . .

II. . . .

A.

The Fourth Amendment contains no provision expressly precluding the use of evidence obtained in violation of its commands, and an examination of its origin and purposes makes clear that the use of fruits of a past unlawful search or seizure "work[s] no new Fourth Amendment wrong." United States v. Calandra (1974). The wrong condemned by the Amendment is "fully accomplished" by the unlawful search or seizure itself, and the exclusionary rule is neither intended nor able to "cure the invasion of the defendant's rights which he has already suffered." . . . The rule thus operates as "a judicially created remedy designed to safeguard Fourth

Amendment rights generally through its deterrent effect, rather than a personal constitutional right of the person aggrieved.'' . . .

Whether the exclusionary sanction is appropriately imposed in a particular case, our decisions make clear, is ''an issue separate from the question whether the Fourth Amendment rights of the party seeking to invoke the rule were violated by police conduct.'' Illinois v. Gates [1983]. Only the former question is currently before us, and it must be resolved by weighing the costs and benefits of preventing the use in the prosecution's case-in-chief of inherently trustworthy tangible evidence obtained in reliance on a search warrant issued by a detached and neutral magistrate that ultimately is found to be defective.

The substantial social costs exacted by the exclusionary rule for the vindication of Fourth Amendment rights have long been a source of concern. ''Our cases have consistently recognized that unbending application of the exclusionary sanction to enforce ideals of government rectitude would impede unacceptably the truth-finding functions of judge and jury.'' . . . An objectionable collateral consequence of this interference with the criminal justice system's truth-finding function is that some guilty defendants may go free or receive reduced sentences as a result of favorable plea bargains. Particularly when law enforcement officers have acted in objective good faith or their transgressions have been minor, the magnitude of the benefit conferred on such guilty defendants offends basic concepts of the criminal justice system. . . . Indiscriminate application of the exclusionary rule, therefore, may well ''generat[e] disrespect for the law and the administration of justice.'' . . .

B.

. . . The Court has, to be sure, not seriously questioned, ''in the absence of a more efficacious sanction, the continued application of the rule to suppress evidence from the [prosecution's] case where a Fourth Amendment violation has been substantial and deliberate. . . .'' Nevertheless, the balancing approach that has evolved in various contexts—including criminal trials—''forcefully suggest[s] that the exclusionary rule be more generally modified to permit the introduction of evidence obtained in the reasonable good-faith belief that a search or seizure was in accord with the Fourth Amendment.'' . . .

[The Court here reviews the past cases and the exceptions to the exclusionary rule.]

As yet, we have not recognized any form of good-faith exception to the Fourth Amendment exclusionary rule. But the balancing approach that has evolved during the years of experience with the rule provides strong support for the modification currently urged upon us. As we discuss below, our evaluation of the costs and benefits of suppressing reliable physical evidence seized by officers reasonably relying on a warrant issued by a detached and neutral magistrate leads to the conclusion that such evidence should be admissible in the prosecution's case-in-chief.

III.

A.

Because a search warrant ''provides the detached scrutiny of a neutral magistrate, which is a more reliable safeguard against improper searches than the hurried judgment of a law enforcement officer 'engaged in the often competitive enterprise of ferreting out crime,' '' . . . we have expressed a strong preference for warrants and declared that ''in a doubtful or marginal case a search under a warrant may be sustainable where without one it would fail'' . . . Reasonable minds frequently may differ on the question whether a particular affidavit establishes probable cause, and we have thus concluded that the preference for warrants is most appropriately effectuated by according ''great deference'' to a magistrate's determination. . . .

Deference to the magistrate, however, is not boundless. It is clear, first, that the deference accorded to a magistrate's finding of probable cause does not preclude inquiry into the knowing or reckless falsity of the affidavit on which that determination was based. . . . Second, the courts must also insist that the magistrate purport to ''perform his 'neutral and detached' function and not serve merely as a rubber stamp for the police.'' . . . A magistrate failing to ''manifest that neutrality and detachment demanded of a judicial officer when presented with a warrant application'' and who acts instead as ''an adjunct law enforcement officer'' cannot provide valid authorization for an otherwise unconstitutional search. . . .

Third, reviewing courts will not defer to a warrant based on an affidavit that does not ''provide the magistrate with a substantial basis for determining the existence of probable cause.'' Illinois v. Gates. ''Sufficient information must be presented to the magistrate to allow that official to determine probable cause; his action cannot be a mere ratification of the bare conclusions of others.'' . . . Even if the warrant application was supported by more than a ''bare bones'' affidavit, a reviewing court may properly conclude that, notwithstanding the deference that magistrates deserve, the warrant was invalid because the magistrate's probable-cause determination reflected an improper analysis of the totality of the circumstances . . . or because the form of the warrant was improper in some respect.

Only in the first of these three situations, however, has the Court set forth a rationale for suppressing evidence obtained pursuant to a search warrant; in the other areas, it has simply excluded such evidence without considering whether Fourth Amendment interests will be advanced. To the extent that proponents of exclusion rely on its behavioral effects on judges and magistrates in these areas, their reliance is misplaced. First, the exclusionary rule is designed to deter police misconduct rather than to punish the errors of judges and magistrates. Second, there exists no evidence suggesting that judges and magistrates are inclined to ignore or subvert the Fourth

Amendment or that lawlessness among these actors requires application of the extreme sanction of exclusion.

Third, and most important, we discern no basis, and are offered none, for believing that exclusion of evidence seized pursuant to a warrant will have a significant deterrent effect on the issuing judge or magistrate. Many of the factors that indicate that the exclusionary rule cannot provide an effective "special" or "general" deterrent for individual offending law enforcement officers apply as well to judges or magistrates⟩ And, to the extent that the rule is thought to operate as a "systemic" deterrent on a wider audience, it clearly can have no such effect on individuals empowered to issue search warrants. Judges and magistrates are not adjuncts to the law enforcement team; as neutral judicial officers, they have no stake in the outcome of particular criminal prosecutions. the threat of exclusion thus cannot be expected significantly to deter them. Imposition of the exclusionary sanction is not necessary meaningfully to inform judicial officers of their errors, and we cannot conclude that admitting evidence obtained pursuant to a warrant while at the same time declaring that the warrant was somehow defective will in any way reduce judicial officers' professional incentives to comply with the Fourth Amendment, encourage them to repeat their mistakes, or lead to the granting of all colorable warrant requests.

B.

If exclusion of evidence obtained pursuant to a subsequently invalidated warrant is to have any deterrent effect, therefore, it must alter the behavior of individual law enforcement officers or the policies of their departments. One could argue that applying the exclusionary rule in cases where the police failed to demonstrate probable cause in the warrant application deters future inadequate presentations or "magistrate shopping" and thus promotes the ends of the Fourth Amendment. Suppressing evidence obtained pursuant to a technically defective warrant supported by probable cause also might encourage officers to scrutinize more closely the form of the warrant and to point out suspected judicial errors. We find such arguments speculative and conclude that suppression of evidence obtained pursuant to a warrant should be ordered only on a case-by-case basis and only in those unusual cases in which exclusion will further the purposes of the exclusionary rule.

⟨We have frequently questioned whether the exclusionary rule can have any deterrent effect when the offending officers acted in the objectively reasonable belief that their conduct did not violate the Fourth Amendment. "No empirical researcher, proponent or opponent of the rule, has yet been able to establish with any assurance whether the rule has a deterrent effect. . . ." . . . But even assuming that the rule effectively deters some police misconduct and provides incentives for the law enforcement profession as a whole to conduct itself in accord with the Fourth Amendment, it cannot be expected, and should not be applied, to deter objectively reasonable law enforcement activity. . . .

This is particularly true, we believe, when an officer acting with objective good faith has obtained a search warrant from a judge or magistrate and acted within its scope. In most such cases, there is no police illegality and thus nothing to deter. It is the magistrate's responsibility to determine whether the officer's allegations establish probable cause and, if so, to issue a warrant comporting in form with the requirements of the Fourth Amendment. In the ordinary case, an officer cannot be expected to question the magistrate's probable-cause determination or his judgment that the form of the warrant is technically sufficient. . . . Penalizing the officer for the magistrate's error, rather than his own, cannot logically contribute to the deterrence of Fourth Amendment violations.

C.

We conclude that the marginal or nonexistent benefits produced by suppressing evidence obtained in objectively reasonable reliance on a subsequently invalidated search warrant cannot justify the substantial costs of exclusion. We do not suggest, however, that exclusion is always inappropriate in cases where an officer has obtained a warrant and abided by its terms. . . .

Suppression . . . remains an appropriate remedy if the magistrate or judge in issuing a warrant was misled by information in an affidavit that the affiant knew was false or would have known was false except for his reckless disregard of the truth. . . . The exception we recognize today will also not apply in cases where the issuing magistrate wholly abandoned his judicial role . . . ; in such circumstances, no reasonably well-trained officer should rely on the warrant. Nor would an officer manifest objective good faith in relying on a warrant based on an affidavit "so lacking in indicia of probable cause as to render official belief in its existence entirely unreasonable.⟩ . . . Finally, depending on the circumstances of the particular case, a warrant may be so facially deficient—i.e., in failing to particularize the place to be searched or the things to be seized—that the executing officers cannot reasonably presume it to be valid. . . .

Justice **Blackmun,** concurring, said in part:

. . . I write separately . . . to underscore what I regard as the unavoidably provisional nature of today's decisions. . . .

What must be stressed . . . is that any empirical judgment about the effect of the exclusionary rule in a particular class of cases necessarily is a provisional one. By their very nature, the assumptions on which we proceed today cannot be cast in stone. To the contrary, they now will be tested in the real world of state and federal law enforcement, and this Court will attend to the results. If it should emerge from experience that, contrary to our expectations, the good faith exception to the exclusionary rule results in a material change in police compliance with the Fourth Amendment, we shall have to reconsider what we have undertaken here. The logic of a decision that rests on untested predictions about police conduct demands no less.

Justice **Brennan**, with whom Justice **Marshall** joins, dissenting said in part:

I. . . .

A.

. . . Because seizures are executed principally to secure evidence, and because such evidence generally has utility in our legal system only in the context of a trial supervised by a judge, it is apparent that the admission of illegally obtained evidence implicates the same constitutional concerns as the initial seizure of that evidence. Indeed, by admitting unlawfully seized evidence, the judiciary becomes a part of what is in fact a single governmental action prohibited by the terms of the Amendment. . . .

It is difficult to give any meaning at all to the limitations imposed by the Amendment if they are read to proscribe only certain conduct by the police but to allow other agents of the same government to take advantage of evidence secured by the police in violation of its requirements. The Amendment therefore must be read to condemn not only the initial unconstitutional invasion of privacy—which is done, after all, for the purpose of securing evidence—but also the subsequent use of any evidence so obtained.

The Court evades this principle by drawing an artificial line between the constitutional rights and responsibilities that are engaged by actions of the police and those that are engaged when a defendant appears before the courts. According to the Court, the substantive protections of the Fourth Amendment are wholly exhausted at the moment when police unlawfully invade an individual's privacy and thus no substantive force remains to those protections at the time of trial when the government seeks to use evidence obtained by the police.

I submit that such a crabbed reading of the Fourth Amendment casts aside the teaching of those Justices who first formulated the exclusionary rule, and rests ultimately on an impoverished understanding of judicial responsibility in our constitutional scheme. For my part, "[t]he right of the people to be secure in their persons, houses, papers and effects, against unreasonable searches and seizures" comprises a personal right to exclude all evidence secured by means of unreasonable searches and seizures. The right to be free from the initial invasion of privacy and the right of exclusion are coordinate components of the central embracing right to be free from unreasonable searches and seizures. . . .

B.

. . . The Court since Calandra has gradually pressed the deterrence rationale for the rule back to center stage. . . . The various arguments advanced by the Court in this campaign have only strengthened my conviction that the deterrence theory is both misguided and unworkable. First, the Court has frequently bewailed the "cost" of excluding reliable evidence. In large part, this criticism rests upon a refusal to acknowledge the function of the Fourth Amendment itself. If nothing else, the Amendment plainly operates to disable the government from gathering information and securing evidence in certain ways. In practical terms, of course, this restriction of official power means that some incriminating evidence inevitably will go undetected if the government obeys these constitutional restraints. It is the loss of that evidence that is the "price" our society pays for enjoying the freedom and privacy safeguarded by the Fourth Amendment. Thus, some criminals will go free *not*, in Justice (then Judge) Cardozo's misleading epigram, "because the constable has blundered," People v. Defore, 242 N. Y. 13 (1926), but rather because official compliance with Fourth Amendment requirements makes it more difficult to catch criminals. Understood in this way, the Amendment directly contemplates that some reliable and incriminating evidence will be lost to the government; therefore, it is not the exclusionary rule, but the Amendment itself that has imposed this cost.

In addition, the Court's decisions over the past decade have made plain that the entire enterprise of attempting to assess the benefits and costs of the exclusionary rule in various contexts is a virtually impossible task for the judiciary to perform honestly or accurately. Although the Court's language in those cases suggests that some specific empirical basis may support its analyses, the reality is that the Court's opinions represent inherently unstable compounds of intuition, hunches, and occasional pieces of partial and often inconclusive data. In Calandra, for example, the Court, in considering whether the exclusionary rule should apply in grand jury proceedings, had before it no concrete evidence whatever concerning the impact that application of the rule in such proceedings would have either in terms of the long-term costs or the expected benefits. To the extent empirical data is available regarding the general costs and benefits of the exclusionary rule, it has shown, on the one hand, as the Court acknowledges today, that the costs are not as substantial as critics have asserted in the past, and, on the other hand, that while the exclusionary rule may well have certain deterrent effects, it is extremely difficult to determine with any degree of precision whether the incidence of unlawful conduct by police is now lower than it was prior to Mapp. . . . The Court has sought to turn this uncertainty to its advantage by casting the burden of proof upon proponents of the rule. . . . "Obviously," however, "the assignment of the burden of proof on an issue where evidence does not exist and cannot be obtained is outcome determinative. [The] assignment of the burden is merely a way of announcing a predetermined conclusion."* By remaining within its

---

*Dworkin, Fact Style Adjudication and the Fourth Amendment: The Limits of Lawyering, 48 Ind. L. J. 329, 332-333 (1973). . . .

redoubt of empiricism and by basing the rule solely on the deterrence rationale, the Court has robbed the rule of legitimacy. A doctrine that is explained as if it were an empirical proposition but for which there is only limited empirical support is both inherently unstable and an easy mark for critics. The extent of this Court's fidelity to Fourth Amendment requirements, however, should not turn on such statistical uncertainties. . . .

III.

Even if I were to accept the Court's general approach to the exclusionary rule, I could not agree with today's result. There is no question that in the hands of the present Court the deterrence rationale has proved to be a powerful tool for confining the scope of the rule. In Calandra, for example, the Court concluded that the "speculative and undoubtedly minimal advance in the deterrence of police misconduct," was insufficient to outweigh the "expense of substantially impeding the grand jury." In Stone v. Powell [1976], the Court found that "the additional contribution, if any, of the consideration of search-and-seizure claims of state prisoners on collateral review is small in relation to the costs." In United States v. Janis (1976), the Court concluded that "exclusion from federal civil proceedings of evidence unlawfully seized by a state criminal enforcement officer has not been shown to have a sufficient likelihood of deterring the conduct of the state police so that it outweighs the societal costs imposed by the exclusion." And in an opinion handed down today, the Court finds that the "balance between costs and benefits comes out against applying the exclusionary rule in civil deportation hearings held by the Immigration and Naturalization Service." INS v. Lopez-Mendoza [1984]. . . .

At the outset, the Court suggests that society has been asked to pay a high price—in terms either of setting guilty persons free or of impeding the proper functioning of trials—as a result of excluding relevant physical evidence in cases where the police, in conducting searches and seizing evidence, have made only an "objectively reasonable" mistake concerning the constitutionality of their actions. But what evidence is there to support such a claim?

Significantly, the Court points to none, and, indeed, as the Court acknowledges, recent studies have demonstrated that the "costs" of the exclusionary rule—calculated in terms of dropped prosecutions and lost convictions—are quite low. Contrary to the claims of the rule's critics that exclusion leads to "the release of countless guilty criminals," . . . these studies have demonstrated that federal and state prosecutors very rarely drop cases because of potential search and seizure problems. For example, a 1979 study prepared at the request of Congress by the General Accounting Office reported that only 0.4% of all cases actually declined for prosecution by federal prosecutors were declined primarily because of illegal search problems. . . .

What then supports the Court's insistence that this evidence be admitted? Apparently, the Court's only answer is that even though the costs of exclusion are not very substantial, the potential deterrent effect in these circumstances is so marginal that exclusion cannot be justified. . . .

. . . But what the Court overlooks is that the deterrence rationale for the rule is not designed to be, nor should it be thought of as, a form of "punishment" of individual police officers for their failures to obey the restraints imposed by the Fourth Amendment. . . . Instead, the chief deterrent function of the rule is its tendency to promote institutional compliance with Fourth Amendment requirements on the part of law enforcement agencies generally. Thus, as the Court has previously recognized, "over the long term, [the] demonstration [provided by the exclusionary rule] that our society attaches serious consequences to violations of constitutional rights is thought to encourage those who formulate law enforcement policies, and the officers who implement them, to incorporate Fourth Amendment ideals into their value system." . . . It is only through such an institution-wide mechanism that information concerning the Fourth Amendment standards can be effectively communicated to rank and file officers. . . .

After today's decision, however, that institutional incentive will be lost. Indeed, the Court's "reasonable mistake" exception to the exclusionary rule will tend to put a premium on police ignorance of the law. . . .

. . . A chief consequence of today's decision will be to convey a clear and unambiguous message to magistrates that their decisions to issue warrants are now insulated from subsequent judicial review. Creation of this new exception for good faith reliance upon a warrant implicitly tells magistrates that they need not take much care in reviewing warrant applications, since their mistakes will from now on have virtually no consequences: If their decision to issue a warrant was correct, the evidence will be admitted; if their decision was incorrect but the police relied in good faith on the warrant, the evidence will also be admitted. Inevitably, the care and attention devoted to such an inconsequential chore will dwindle.

THE RIGHT OF COUNSEL

GIDEON v. WAINWRIGHT

372 U.S. 335; 83 S. Ct. 792; 9 L. Ed. 2d 799
(1963)

The right of a person being tried for a crime to be represented by counsel trained in the law has been recognized in this country since earliest times. It rests on an appreciation of the fact that trial procedure is complex and confusing, that its rules are highly technical, and that a nonprofessional's ignorance of them may cause a mistrial, may cause the loss of valuable procedural rights, and may hopelessly frustrate efforts to get the accused's story into the record. There is much truth in the apho-

rism that one who defends oneself has a fool for a lawyer.

The Sixth Amendment expressly guarantees that in "all criminal prosecutions the accused shall . . . have the assistance of counsel for his defense." Designed originally to ensure to the accused the presence of his or her own counsel, it has long since come to include the right to court-appointed counsel if one cannot afford an attorney. The importance attached by the Supreme Court to the right to counsel in a federal court is shown by two rules which the Court has laid down. One is that if the right to counsel is not accorded to a defendant in a federal court, the court loses its jurisdiction to proceed with the case. The other rule is that while the right to counsel, like some other constitutional rights, may be waived by an accused person, such waiver must be both clear and intelligently made. The right is not waived merely by failure to claim it, nor is the waiver valid unless the accused understands adequately the consequences of waiving the right.

Both of the rules were set out clearly in the landmark case of Johnson v. Zerbst (1938). Here a young marine on leave had been arraigned, tried for forgery, convicted, and sentenced to four years in prison, all in one afternoon. He informed the district court on arraignment that he had no counsel, but was ready for trial. He conducted his own defense, and failed, through ignorance of the law, to make timely application for an appeal. The Supreme Court held that he had not "intelligently" waived his right to counsel, and it also stated that "if this requirement of the Sixth Amendment is not complied with, the court no longer has jurisdiction to proceed." The Court emphasized that "the Sixth Amendment withholds from Federal Courts, in all criminal proceedings, the power and authority to deprive an accused of his life or liberty unless he has or waives the assistance of Counsel . . . [and the] 'courts indulge every reasonable presumption against waiver'. . . ." Moreover, "the constitutional right of an accused to be represented by Counsel invokes, of itself, the protection of a trial court, in which the accused—whose life or liberty is at stake—is without Counsel. This protecting duty imposes the serious and weighty responsibility upon the trial judge of determining whether there is an intelligent and competent waiver by the accused. While an accused may waive the right to Counsel, whether there is a proper waiver should be clearly determined by the trial court; and it would be fitting and appropriate for that determination to appear upon the record."

This doctrine was reaffirmed in Von Moltke v. Gillies (1948), where the signing of a formal waiver of the right to counsel even by an "intelligent, mentally acute woman" was not, in the circumstances, the kind of "intelligent" waiver which could deprive her of her Sixth Amendment right. The Court said: "To be valid such waiver must be made with an apprehension of the nature of the charges, the statutory offenses included within them, the range of allowable punishments thereunder, possible defenses to the charges and circumstances in mitigation thereof, and all other facts essential to a broad understanding of the whole matter. A judge can make certain that an accused's professed waiver of counsel is understandingly and wisely made only from a penetrating and comprehensive examination of all the circumstances under which such a plea is tendered." Mrs. Von Moltke had pleaded guilty without the aid of counsel to espionage charges under which she could have been sentenced to death or thirty years in prison.

The right to counsel includes the right to consult a lawyer without the conversation being monitored by the government, as in wiretapping, or relayed to the government through a government informer planted in the same cell block where the defendant was awaiting trial in the hope that the defendant would volunteer incriminating statements in the absence of counsel. Here the informer, also an inmate, was paid on a contingency fee basis and testified against the defendant at trial. United States v. Henry (1980).

By the language of the Sixth Amendment the right to counsel is guaranteed "in all criminal prosecutions." It is not guaranteed in noncriminal proceedings. Thus a congressional investigating committee, which conducts a civil—not criminal—proceeding, may do as it pleases about allowing witnesses called before it to be represented by counsel. In recent years committees have usually allowed witnesses this privilege, though the role played by the attorney is very narrowly limited.

In the years following Betts v. Brady (1942) the Supreme Court continued to deal with state right-to-counsel cases under the due process rule requiring essential fairness, the cases turning on the question whether the defendant was capable of conducting his or her own defense. The Court clearly assumed, however, that the right to counsel in a capital case was absolute, and since 1950, even in noncapital cases, no one had been found capable enough to be tried without counsel. In 1954 in Chandler v. Fretag the defendant had been denied a chance to obtain counsel at his own expense, and the Supreme Court held that he had been denied due process. "Regardless of whether petitioner would have been entitled to the appointment of counsel, his right to be heard through his own counsel was unqualified. See Palko v. Connecticut [1937] . . . Powell v. Alabama [1932]. . . ."

Following the reversal of his conviction in the present case, Gideon was retried by the state of Florida in the same courtroom, before the same judge, with the same witnesses, but with a lawyer appointed by the court at Gideon's request. This time he was acquitted.

Mr. Justice **Black** delivered the opinion of the Court, saying in part:

Petitioner was charged in a Florida state court with having broken and entered a poolroom with intent to commit a misdemeanor. This offense is a felony under Florida law. Appearing in court without funds and without a lawyer, petitioner asked the court to appoint counsel for him, whereupon the following colloquy took place:

"The Court: Mr. Gideon, I am sorry, but I cannot appoint Counsel to represent you in this case. Under the laws of the State of Florida, the only time the Court can appoint Counsel to represent a Defendant is when that person is charged with a capital offense. I am sorry, but I will have to deny your request to appoint Counsel to defend you in this case.

"The Defendant: The United States Supreme Court says I am entitled to be represented by Counsel."

Put to trial before a jury, Gideon conducted his defense about as well as could be expected from a layman. He made an opening statement to the jury, cross-examined the State's witnesses, presented witnesses in his own defense, declined to testify himself, and made a short argument "emphasizing his innocence to the charge contained in the Information filed in this case." The jury returned a verdict of guilty, and petitioner was sentenced to serve five years in the state prison. . . . Since 1942, when Betts v. Brady was decided by a divided Court, the problem of a defendant's federal constitutional right to counsel in a state court has been a continuing source of controversy and litigation in both state and federal courts. To give this problem another review here, we granted certiorari. Since Gideon was proceeding in forma pauperis, we appointed counsel to represent him and requested both sides to discuss in their briefs and oral arguments the following: "Should this Court's holding in Betts v. Brady be reconsidered?"

I.

The facts upon which Betts claimed that he had been unconstitutionally denied the right to have counsel appointed to assist him are strikingly like the facts upon which Gideon here bases his federal constitutional claim. Betts was indicted for robbery in a Maryland state court. On arraignment, he told the trial judge of his lack of funds to hire a lawyer and asked the court to appoint one for him. Betts was advised that it was not the practice in that county to appoint counsel for indigent defendants except in murder and rape cases. He then pleaded not guilty, had witnesses summoned, cross-examined the State's witnesses, examined his own, and chose not to testify himself. He was found guilty by the judge, sitting without a jury, and sentenced to eight years in prison. Like Gideon, Betts sought release by habeas corpus, alleging that he had been denied the right to assistance of counsel in violation of the Fourteenth Amendment. Betts was denied any relief, and on review this Court affirmed. It was held that a refusal to appoint counsel for an indigent defendant charged with a felony did not necessarily violate the Due Process Clause of the Fourteenth Amendment, which for reasons given the Court deemed to be the only applicable federal constitutional provision. The Court said:

"Asserted denial [of due process] is to be tested by an appraisal of the totality of facts in a given case. That which may, in one setting, constitute a denial of fundamental fairness, shocking to the universal sense of justice, may, in other circumstances, and in the light of other considerations, fall short of such denial."

Treating due process as "a concept less rigid and more fluid than those envisaged in other specific and particular provisions of the Bill of Rights," the Court held that refusal to appoint counsel under the particular facts and circumstances in the Betts Case was not so "offensive to the common and fundamental ideas of fairness" as to amount to a denial of due process. Since the facts and circumstances of the two cases are so nearly indistinguishable, we think the Betts v. Brady holding if left standing would require us to reject Gideon's claim that the Constitution guarantees him the assistance of counsel. Upon full reconsideration we conclude that Betts v. Brady should be overruled.

II.

The Sixth Amendment provides, "In all criminal prosecutions, the accused shall enjoy the right . . . to have the Assistance of Counsel for his defence." We have construed this to mean that in federal courts counsel must be provided for defendants unable to employ counsel unless the right is competently and intelligently waived. Betts argued that this right is extended to indigent defendants in state courts by the Fourteenth Amendment. In response the Court stated that, while the Sixth Amendment laid down "no rule for the conduct of the States, the question recurs whether the constraint laid by the Amendment upon the national courts expresses a rule so fundamental and essential to a fair trial, and so, to due process of law, that it is made obligatory upon the States by the Fourteenth Amendment." In order to decide whether the Sixth Amendment's guarantee of counsel is of this fundamental nature, the Court in Betts set out and considered "[r]elevant data on the subject . . . afforded by constitutional and statutory provisions subsisting in the colonies and the States prior to the inclusion of the Bill of Rights in the national Constitution, and in the constitutional, legislative, and judicial history of the States to the present date." On the basis of this historical data the Court concluded that "appointment of counsel is not a fundamental right, essential to a fair trial." It was for this reason the Betts Court refused to accept the contention that the Sixth Amendment's guarantee of counsel for indigent federal defendants was extended to or, in the words of that Court, "made obligatory upon the States by the Fourteenth Amendment." Plainly, had the Court concluded that appointment of counsel for indigent criminal defendant was "a fundamental right, essential to a fair trial," it would have held that the Fourteenth Amendment requires appointment of counsel in a state court, just as the Sixth Amendment requires in a federal court.

We think the Court in Betts had ample precedent for acknowledging that those guarantees of the Bill of Rights which are fundamental safeguards of liberty immune from federal abridgment are equally protected against state invasion by the Due Process Clause of the Fourteenth Amendment. This same principle was recognized, explained and applied in Powell v. Alabama (1932), a case upholding the right of counsel, where the

Court held that despite sweeping language to the contrary in Hurtado v. California (1884), the Fourteenth Amendment "embraced" those "fundamental principles of liberty and justice which lie at the base of all our civil and political institutions," even though they had been "specifically dealt with in another part of the federal Constitution." In many cases other than Powell and Betts, this Court has looked to the fundamental nature of original Bill of Rights guarantees to decide whether the Fourteenth Amendment makes them obligatory on the States. Explicitly recognized to be of this "fundamental nature" and therefore made immune from state invasion by the Fourteenth, or some part of it, are the First Amendment's freedoms of speech, press, religion, assembly, association, and petition for redress of grievances. For the same reason, though not always in precisely the same terminology, the Court has made obligatory on the States the Fifth Amendment's command that private property shall not be taken for public use without just compensation, the Fourth Amendment's prohibition of unreasonable searches and seizures, and the Eighth's ban on cruel and unusual punishment. On the other hand, this Court in Palko v. Connecticut (1937), refused to hold that the Fourteenth Amendment made the double jeopardy provision of the Fifth Amendment obligatory on the States. In so refusing, however, the Court, speaking through Mr. Justice Cardozo, was careful to emphasize that "immunities that are valid as against the federal government by force of the specific pledges of particular amendments have been found to be implicit in the concept of ordered liberty, and thus, through the Fourteenth Amendment, become valid as against the states" and that guarantees "in their origin . . . effective against the federal government alone" had by prior cases "been taken over from the earlier articles of the federal bill of rights and brought within the Fourteenth Amendment by a process of absorption."

We accept Betts v. Brady's assumption, based as it was on our prior cases, that a provision of the Bill of Rights which is "fundamental and essential to a fair trial" is made obligatory upon the States by the Fourteenth Amendment. We think the Court in Betts was wrong, however, in concluding that the Sixth Amendment's guarantee of counsel is not one of these fundamental rights. Ten years before Betts v. Brady, this Court, after full consideration of all the historical data examined in Betts, had unequivocally declared that "the right to the aid of counsel is of this fundamental character." . . . While the Court at the close of its Powell opinion did by its language, as this Court frequently does, limit its holding to the particular facts and circumstances of that case, its conclusions about the fundamental nature of the right to counsel are unmistakable. Several years later, in 1936, the Court reemphasized what it had said about the fundamental nature of the right to counsel in this language:

"We concluded that certain fundamental rights, safeguarded by the first eight amendments against federal action, were also safeguarded against state action by the due process of law clause of the Fourteenth Amendment, and among them the fundamental right of the ac-

cused to the aid of counsel in a criminal prosecution." Grosjean v. American Press Co. (1936).

And again in 1938 this Court said:

"[The assistance of counsel] is one of the safeguards of the Sixth Amendment deemed necessary to insure fundamental human rights of life and liberty. . . . The Sixth Amendment stands as a constant admonition that if the constitutional safeguards it provides be lost, justice will not 'still be done,' " Johnson v. Zerbst (1938). . . .

In light of these many other prior decisions of this Court, it is not surprising that the Betts Court, when faced with the contention that "one charged with crime, who is unable to obtain counsel, must be furnished counsel by the State," conceded that "[e]xpressions in the opinions of this court lend color to the argument. . . ." The fact is that in deciding as it did—that "appointment of counsel is not a fundamental right, essential to a fair trial"—the Court in Betts v. Brady made an abrupt break with its own well-considered precedents. In returning to these old precedents, sounder we believe than the new, we but restore constitutional principles established to achieve a fair system of justice. Not only these precedents but also reason and reflection require us to recognize that in our adversary system of criminal justice, any person haled into court, who is too poor to hire a lawyer, cannot be assured a fair trial unless counsel is provided for him. This seems to us to be an obvious truth. Governments, both state and federal, quite properly spend vast sums of money to establish machinery to try defendants accused of crime. Lawyers to prosecute are everywhere deemed essential to protect the public's interest in an orderly society. Similarly, there are few defendants charged with crime, few indeed, who fail to hire the best lawyers they can get to prepare and present their defenses. That government hires lawyers to prosecute and defendants who have the money hire lawyers to defend are the strongest indications of the widespread belief that lawyers in criminal courts are necessities, not luxuries. The right of one charged with crime to counsel may not be deemed fundamental and essential for fair trials in some countries, but it is in ours. From the very beginning, our state and national constitutions and laws have laid great emphasis on procedural and substantive safeguards designed to assure fair trials before impartial tribunals in which every defendant stands equal before the law. This noble ideal cannot be realized if the poor man charged with crime has to face his accusers without a lawyer to assist him. A defendant's need for a lawyer is nowhere better stated than in the moving words of Mr. Justice Sutherland in Powell v. Alabama:

"The right to be heard would be, in many cases, of little avail if it did not comprehend the right to be heard by counsel. Even the intelligent and educated layman has small and sometimes no skill in the science of law. If charged with crime, he is incapable, generally, of determining for himself whether the indictment is good or bad. He is unfamiliar with the rules of evidence. Left without the aid of counsel he may be put on trial without a proper charge, and convicted upon incompetent evidence, or evidence irrelevant to the issue or otherwise inadmissible. He lacks both the skill and knowledge adequately to prepare his defense, even though he have a perfect one. He requires the guiding hand of counsel at every step in the proceedings against him. Without it, though he be not guilty, he faces the danger of conviction because he does not know how to establish his innocence.''

The Court in Betts v. Brady departed from the sound wisdom upon which the Court's holding in Powell v. Alabama rested. Florida, supported by two other States, has asked that Betts v. Brady be left intact. Twenty-two States, as friends of the Court, argue that Betts was ''an anachronism when handed down'' and that it should now be overruled. We agree.

The judgment is reversed and the cause is remanded to the Supreme Court of Florida for further action not inconsistent with this opinion.

Reversed.

Mr. Justice **Douglas,** while joining the opinion of the Court, wrote a separate opinion, saying in part:

My Brother Harlan is of the view that a guarantee of the Bill of Rights that is made applicable to the States by reason of the Fourteenth Amendment is a lesser version of that same guarantee as applied to the Federal Government. Mr. Justice Jackson shared the view. But that view has not prevailed and rights protected against state invasion by the Due Process Clause of the Fourteenth Amendment are not watered-down versions of what the Bill of Rights guarantees.

Mr. Justice **Clark,** concurring in the result, wrote a separate opinion.

Mr. Justice **Harlan,** concurring, said in part:

I agree that Betts v. Brady should be overruled, but consider it entitled to a more respectful burial than has been accorded, at least on the part of those of us who were not on the Court when that case was decided.

I cannot subscribe to the view that Betts v. Brady represented ''an abrupt break with its own well-considered precedents.'' In 1932, in Powell v. Alabama, a capital case, this Court declared that under the particular facts there presented—''the ignorance and illiteracy of the defendants, their youth, the circumstances of public hostility . . . and above all that they stood in deadly peril of their lives''—the state court had a duty to assign counsel for the trial as a necessary requisite of due process of law. It is evident that these limiting facts were not added to the opinion as an afterthought; they were repeatedly emphasized, and were clearly regarded as important to the result.

Thus when this Court, a decade later, decided Betts v. Brady, it did no more than to admit of the possible existence of special circumstances in noncapital as well as capital trials, while at the same time insisting that such circumstances be shown in order to establish a denial of due process. The right to appointed counsel had been recognized as being considerably broader in federal prosecutions, see Johnson v. Zerbst, but to have imposed these requirements on the States would indeed have been ''an abrupt break'' with the almost immediate past. The declaration that the right to appointed counsel in state prosecutions, as established in Powell v. Alabama, was not limited to capital cases was in truth not a departure from, but an extension of, existing precedent. . . .

[Mr. Justice Harlan here notes the ''troubled journey'' of the Powell and Betts doctrines and concedes that since 1950 no ''special circumstances'' have been found to justify the absence of counsel.]

. . . The Court has come to recognize, in other words, that the mere existence of a serious criminal charge constituted in itself special circumstances requiring the services of counsel at trial. In truth the Betts v. Brady rule is no longer a reality.

This evaluation, however, appears not to have been fully recognized by many state courts, in this instance charged with the front-line responsibility for the enforcement of constitutional rights. To continue a rule which is honored by this Court only with lip service is not a healthy thing and in the long run will do disservice to the federal system. . . .

In agreeing with the Court that the right to counsel in a case such as this should now be expressly recognized as a fundamental right embraced in the Fourteenth Amendment, I wish to make a further observation. When we hold a right or immunity, valid against the Federal Government, to be ''implicit in the concept of ordered liberty'' and thus valid against the States, I do not read our past decisions to suggest that by so holding, we automatically carry over an entire body of federal law and apply it in full sweep to the States. Any such concept would disregard the frequently wide disparity between the legitimate interests of the States and of the Federal Government, the divergent problems that they face, and the significantly different consequences of their actions. . . . In what is done today I do not understand the Court to depart from the principles laid down in Palko v. Connecticut, or to embrace the concept that the Fourteenth Amendment ''incorporates'' the Sixth Amendment as such.

On these premises I join in the judgment of the Court.

CRUEL AND UNUSUAL PUNISHMENTS

GREGG v. GEORGIA

428 U. S. 153; 96 St. Ct. 2909; 49 L. Ed. 2d 859
(1976)

The Eighth Amendment prohibits the infliction of cruel and unusual punishment, but makes no effort to define such punishment. In early England most felonies were punished by hanging, and for certain serious crimes, such as treason, a person could be drawn and quartered. In colonial America the pillory and stocks were a feature of nearly every town square, and flogging was common for many offenses. At the time the Constitution was adopted both branding and piercing the nostrils were accepted punishments in some jurisdictions. Many, if not all, of these forms of punishment would be considered uncivilized today, and have long since been abolished. In 1963 the supreme court of Delaware, the last state to permit flogging (except for infraction of prison rules), upheld the sentence of twenty lashes for breaking parole in a car theft case; but the state pardons board freed the man and the sentence was not carried out. In *Louisiana ex rel. Francis v. Resweber* (1947) the Supreme Court, assuming capital punishment to be valid, rejected the contention that the state's failure to electrocute the defendant on the first try made subsequent tries cruel and unusual. In *Wilkerson v. Utah* (1879) the Court had held shooting was not cruel and unusual, but suggested the ban would include both drawing and quartering and burning alive.

The idea that punishment could be cruel and unusual not in the abstract, but because it did not "fit the crime" to which it was attached, was argued as early as 1892 by Justice Field in his dissent in *O'Neil v. Vermont*, a case in which a New Yorker selling liquor illegally in Vermont stood to serve 19,914 days in jail for 307 separate illegal sales. The Court found that since the Eighth Amendment did not limit the states, no federal question was involved. In reviewing a case arising under the Philippine constitution, whose cruel and unusual punishment clause was identical to the Eighth Amendment's, the Court struck down as cruel and unusual a twelve-year sentence at hard labor in irons for knowingly making a false statement in a public document; see *Weems v. United States* (1910). The Court, however, appeared to reject this approach in the 1980s. It upheld a sentence of life imprisonment for violating Texas' recidivist statute despite the fact that none of the three felonies involved the theft of more than a $120.75; see *Rummel v. Estelle* (1980). And in *Hutto v. Davis* (1982) it held that a person with nine ounces of marijuana could be sentenced to two consecutive twenty-year terms in prison and a $20,000 fine for the two crimes of possession and possession with intent to distribute.

Then in 1983, with Justice Blackmun switching over, it again held that the punishment should fit the crime. In *Solem v. Davis*, it held void as disproportionately cruel a life sentence for a series of crimes virtually indistinguishable from those of *Rummel*. It did not overrule *Rummel*, but noted that while Rummel would become eligible for parole in twelve years, Solem would spend his life in prison unless his sentence were commuted by the governor.

It is also cruel to punish a person for being sick or having some affliction over which he has no control. In *Robinson v. California* (1962) the Court struck down a state statute making it a misdemeanor "to be addicted to the use of narcotics." While the state was free to punish the use of narcotics or prescribe a mandatory program of treatment for addicts, such addiction was an "illness which may be contracted innocently or involuntarily. We hold that a state law which imprisons a person thus afflicted as a criminal, even though he has never touched any narcotic drug within the State or been guilty of any irregular behavior there, inflicts cruel and unusual punishment in violation of the Fourteenth Amendment. To be sure, imprisonment for ninety days is not, in the abstract, a punishment which is either cruel or unusual. But the question cannot be considered in the abstract. Even one day in prison would be a cruel and unusual punishment for the 'crime' of having a common cold."

Following the *Robinson* case, a sixty-year-old bootblack with over one hundred convictions for public drunkenness argued that alcoholism, like drug addiction, was a disease and could not be punished. Five members of the Court agreed that his conviction for public drunkenness was not a cruel and unusual punishment. While they were unable to agree on an opinion regarding alcoholism, they did agree that Powell was not being punished for alcoholism, but for being in public while drunk. Four members of the Court dissented on the ground that his affliction was such that he could not resist being drunk in public. See *Powell v. Texas* (1968).

Unlike most constitutional developments, which take place gradually with the Court hinting broadly at the path it plans to follow, the inclusion of the death penalty in the Eighth Amendment came with startling suddenness. In nearly every case involving cruel and unusual punishment, the Court had discussed the death penalty, and while none of these cases had raised the Eighth Amendment question directly, in each of them the Court had left no doubt that the penalty, as such, was valid. As late as 1958, four members of the majority (Justice Brennan concurred on other grounds) said in *Trop v. Dulles* that while expatriation was a cruel and unusual punishment, the death penalty "cannot be said to violate the constitutional concept of cruelty."

Then in the 1960s an all-out legal attack was launched against the penalty, underwritten largely by the American Civil Liberties Union and the NAACP Legal Defense Fund, which had evidence that most of those executed since 1930 were black. The penalty was challenged on a variety of grounds, and on June 3, 1967, the execution of more than 500 condemned prisoners throughout the country came to a halt while courts and governors waited to see what the Supreme Court would do.

The first of these challenges reached the Supreme Court in *Witherspoon v. Illinois* (1968), and for the first time the Court gave an indication that the death penalty was in trouble. Illinois permitted a verdict of guilty and a sentence of death to be handed down by a jury from which the state had deliberately excluded all persons with scruples against capital punishment. The Court declined to reverse the verdict of guilty, since the jury would not be necessarily prone to convict, but it held that no jury so constituted could hand down a sentence of death since such a jury "fell woefully short of that impartiality to which the petitioner was entitled under the Sixth and Fourteenth Amendments." "A jury that must choose between life imprisonment and capital punishment can do little more—and must do nothing less—than express the conscience of the community on the ultimate question of life or death. Yet, in a nation less than half of whose people believe in the death penalty, a jury composed exclusively of such people cannot speak for the community. Culled of all who harbor doubts about the wisdom of capital punishment—of all who would be reluctant to pronounce the extreme penalty—such a jury can speak only for a distinct and dwindling minority." Justice Black, dissenting with Justices Harlan and White, pointed up the majority's underlying motives. "If this Court is to hold capital punishment unconstitutional, I think it should do so forthrightly, not by making it impossible for States to get juries that will enforce the death penalty."

The hopes of opponents of the death penalty that it had been abolished by the Witherspoon case proved unduly optimistic, but the moratorium on executions remained in effect while other challenges were readied for Supreme Court review. One such challenge involved the question of whether a jury could constitutionally impose the death penalty without any governing standards, and in McGautha v. California (1971) the Court held that it could. Justice Harlan, writing for a six-man majority, traced the efforts of the states to reduce the rigors of mandatory death sentences, first by introducing "degrees" of murder, and, when juries still took the law into their own hands, finally giving way to reality and providing for complete jury discretion to hang or not to hang.

On the basis of this history the Court concluded that "to identify before the fact those characteristics of criminal homicides and their perpetrators which call for the death penalty, and to express these characteristics in language which can be fairly understood and applied by the sentencing authority, appear to be tasks which are beyond present human ability." It cited the efforts of a British Royal Commission to solve the same problem and its conclusion that "no simple formula can take account of the innumerable degrees of culpability, and no formula which fails to do so can claim to satisfy public opinion." The list of "aggravating and mitigating circumstances" provided in the Model Penal Code for jury consideration, the Court said, "bear witness to the intractable nature of the problem of 'standards'. . . . [and] caution against this Court's undertaking to establish such standards itself." . . .

The Court concluded that "in the light of history, experience, and the present limitations of human knowledge, we find it quite impossible to say that committing to the untrammeled discretion of the jury the power to pronounce life or death in capital cases is offensive to anything in the Constitution." At the same time it held that the Ohio system of having the jury decide both guilt and punishment together did not deny due process merely because a defendant who wanted to argue for clemency could hardly do so without incriminating himself. "The criminal process, like the rest of the legal system, is replete with situations requiring 'the making of difficult judgments' as to which course to follow."

In a long and carefully reasoned dissent Justice Brennan, joined by Justices Douglas and Marshall, attacked the discretion of the sentencing jury to kill or not to kill as it wished as amounting to "nothing more than

government by whim"—a form totally at odds with the "government of laws" protected by the due process clause. "We are not presented with the slightest attempt to bring the power of reason to bear on the considerations relevant to capital sentencing. We are faced with nothing more than stark legislative abdication. Not once in the history of this Court, until today, have we sustained against a due process challenge such an unguided, unbridled, unreviewable exercise of naked power. Almost a century ago, we found an almost identical California procedure constitutionally inadequate to license a laundry. Yick Wo v. Hopkins (1886). Today we hold it adequate to license life."

The decision in McGautha was widely viewed as the Supreme Court's final word on the death penalty. No more cases involving it were pending before the Court, and with the right of juries to act arbitrarily firmly guaranteed, there seemed little likelihood that an Eighth Amendment argument would prevail. As states made preparations to start executing the now almost 700 prisoners on death row, the Court announced it would hear a group of cases involving the Eighth Amendment. In June 1972, in Furman v. Georgia, it held the death penalty void.

None of the five members of the majority could agree on an opinion. Justices Marshall and Brennan agreed that all capital punishment was cruel and unusual, with the latter reasoning that "a punishment may not be so severe as to be degrading to the dignity of human beings," and no punishment met this test which was inflicted arbitrarily, which was unacceptable to contemporary society, and which was excessive in view of the purpose to be achieved. In view of its waning popularity and erratic application, the death penalty failed on all counts. Justice Douglas argued that since it was applied disproportionately to the underprivileged, it was therefore "not compatible with the idea of equal protection of the laws that is implicit in the ban on 'cruel and unusual' punishments." Justice Marshall agreed about the discrimination, but stressed that it was ineffective as a deterrent of the crimes for which it was inflicted and would be rejected by a public that was truly "informed" about its operation and impact. Justices Stewart and White, without arguing that the death penalty was cruel per se, noted that the cruelty of the provisions currently in use lay in the results they produced—that the infliction of the penalty was so infrequent and unpredictable that it served neither the goal of deterrence nor of retribution.

The dissenting justices argued that since the Fifth Amendment alluded to capital offenses, it was clear that the framers of the Eighth did not consider death cruel and unusual; that the Court had said uniformly over the years and as recently as Trop v. Dulles in 1958 that it was not cruel; and that the evidence did not show "that capital punishment offends the conscience of society to such a degree that our traditional deference to legislative judgment must be abandoned."

The effect of Furman was to invalidate every death penalty statute in the country, and legislatures studied the case in the hope of discerning from the multitude of opinions what sort of statute might pass constitutional muster. *Since the fault of previous statutes seemed to lie in the erratic use of the penalty, two answers suggested themselves. Either the discretion of the sentencing authority could be carefully guided to produce more consistent results, or it could be taken away altogether in an effort to have the penalty inflicted in all cases.*

The first of these approaches came to the Court in the case below while the validity of mandatory death penalties came the same day in the cases of Stanislaus Roberts v. Louisiana and Woodson v. North Carolina. Here, Justices Stewart, Powell and Stevens joined Justices Brennan and Marshall to hold the statutes void. Insistence that the death penalty always be applied, the Court found, would merely perpetuate the pre-Furman pattern in which juries would simply refuse to convict if they felt the death penalty inappropriate for a particular case. A similar result was reached in Sumner v. Shuman (1987) where a mandatory death penalty for murder for a life-sentence prison inmate was held void as not allowing for mitigating circumstances.

A year after the decision in the present case, the Court in Coker v. Georgia (1977) held the same statute invalid as applied to the crime of rape of an adult woman. Here the Court, with only Justices Burger and Rehnquist dissenting, found that in the absence of gross brutality in the act itself, death "is a disproportionate punishment for rape." Not only was Georgia the only state to punish the rape of an adult woman by death, but in 90 percent of the rape convictions under the new law the jury had not imposed the death sentence. In Lockett v. Ohio (1978) the Court held, for a variety of reasons, that the death penalty could not be imposed on the driver of a get-away car where the victim of an attempted robbery had been shot. A similar result was reached in Ennmund v. Florida (1982), but not in Tison v. Arizona (1987) where the non-shooter played a major role in the felony leading to the murder and showed reckless indifference regarding human life. In Godfrey v. Georgia (1980) the Court held the limiting aggravating circumstance provided in the statute that the murder be "outrageously and wantonly vile" was unconstitutionally vague and without force as a standard where it was clear a jury could find every murder outrageously and wantonly vile. Here the defendant had simply shot his wife and mother-in-law instantly to death.

McCleskey v. Kemp (1987) presented a new challenge to the death penalty. McCleskey, a black, had killed a white police officer in the course of committing a robbery. One of the aggravating circumstances called for by Georgia law was present and after his conviction for murder the sentencing jury imposed the death penalty. Statistics accepted by the Court showed that a someone killing a white person was 4.3 times as apt to draw the death penalty as though the victim were black, and black defendants were 1.1 times as likely to receive a death sentence as other defendants. Justice Powell, writing for five members of the Court, upheld the conviction. They rejected McCleskey's equal protection argument on the ground that there had been no showing of "purposeful discrimination" against him and they rejected the claim that Georgia's capital punishment

scheme was "arbitrary and capricious in application," noting that "even Professor Baldus [author of the statistical analysis] does not contend that his statistics prove that race enters into any capital sentencing decisions or that race was a factor in McCleskey's particular case." "Individual jurors bring to their deliberations 'qualities of human nature and varieties of human experience, the range of which is unknown and perhaps unknowable.' . . . The capital sentencing decision requires the individual jurors to focus their collective judgment on the unique characteristics of a particular criminal defendant. It is not surprising that such collective judgments often are difficult to explain. But the inherent lack of predictability of jury decisions does not justify their condemnation."

Justice Brennan, speaking for Justices Marshall, Blackmun and Stevens, condemned a system in which "defendants killing white victims . . . are 4.3 times as likely to be sentenced to death as defendants charged with killing blacks" and "six of every eleven defendants convicted of killing a white person would not have received the death penalty if their victims had been black. . . . The Court's evaluation of the significance of petitioner's evidence is fundamentally at odds with our consistent concern for rationality in capital sentencing." The dissenters pointed out that "since Furman v. Georgia (1972), the Court has been concerned with the risk of the imposition of an arbitrary sentence, rather than the proven fact of one." "Once we can identify a pattern of arbitrary sentencing outcomes, we can say that a defendant runs a risk of being sentenced arbitrarily." "Defendants challenging their death sentences thus never have had to prove that impermissible considerations have actually infected sentencing decisions. We have required instead that they establish that the system under which they were sentenced posed a significant risk of such an occurrence. McCleskey's claim does differ, however, in one respect from earlier cases: it is the first to base a challenge not on speculation about how a system might operate, but on empirical documentation of how it does operate." It is clear that "the statistical evidence in this case . . . relentlessly documents the risk that McCleskey's sentence was influenced by racial considerations. This evidence shows that there is a better than even chance in Georgia that race will influence the decision to impose the death penalty. . . ."

Mr. Justice **Stewart**, Mr. Justice **Powell**, and Mr. Justice **Stevens** announced the judgment of the Court and filed an opinion delivered by Mr. Justice **Stewart**, saying in part:

The issue in this case is whether the imposition of the sentence of death for the crime of murder under the law of Georgia violates the Eight and Fourteenth Amendments.

I.

The petitioner, Troy Gregg, was charged with committing armed robbery and murder. In accordance with Georgia procedure in capital cases, the trial was in two stages, a guilt stage and a sentencing stage. The evidence at the guilt trial established that on November 21, 1973, the petitioner and a traveling companion, Floyd Allen, while hitchhiking north in Florida were picked up by Fred Simmons and Bob Moore. Their car broke down, but they continued north after Simmons purchased another vehicle with some of the cash he was carrying. While still in Florida, they picked up another hitchhiker, Denis Weaver, who rode with them to Atlanta, where he was let out about 11 p.m. A short time later the four men interrupted their journey for a rest stop along the highway. The next morning the bodies of Simmons and Moore were discovered in a ditch nearby.

On November 23, after reading about the shootings in an Atlanta newspaper, Weaver communicated with the Gwinnett County police and related information concerning the journey with the victims, including a description of the car. The next afternoon, the petitioner and Allen, while in Simmons' car, were arrested in Asheville, N. C. In the search incident to the arrest a .25-caliber pistol, later shown to be that used to kill Simmons and Moore, was found in the petitioner's pocket. After receiving the warnings required by Miranda v. Arizona (1966), and signing a written waiver of his rights, the petitioner signed a statement in which he admitted shooting, then robbing Simmons and Moore. He justified the slayings on grounds of self-defense. The next day, while being transferred to Lawrenceville, Ga., the petitioner and Allen were taken to the scene of the shootings. Upon arriving there, Allen recounted the events leading to the slayings. His version of these events was as follows: After Simmons and Moore left the car, the petitioner stated that he intended to rob them. The petitioner then took his pistol in hand and positioned himself on the car to improve his aim. As Simmons and Moore came up an embankment toward the car, the petitioner fired three shots and the two men fell near a ditch. The petitioner, at close range, then fired a shot into the head of each. He robbed them of valuables and drove away with Allen. . . .

The trial judge submitted the murder charges to the jury on both felony-murder and nonfelony-murder theories. He also instructed on the issue of self-defense but declined to instruct on manslaughter. He submitted the robbery case to the jury on both an armed-robbery theory and on the lesser included offense of robbery by intimidation. The jury found the petitioner guilty of two counts of armed robbery and two counts of murder.

At the penalty stage, which took place before the same jury, neither the prosecutor nor the petitioner's lawyer offered any additional evidence. Both counsel, however, made lengthy arguments dealing generally with the propriety of capital punishment under the circumstances and with the weight of the evidence of guilt. The trial judge instructed the jury that it could recommend either a death sentence or a life prison sentence on each count. The judge further charged the jury that in determining what sentence was appropriate the jury was free to consider the facts and circumstances, if any, presented by the parties in mitigation or aggravation.

Finally, the judge instructed the jury that it

"would not be authorized to consider [imposing] the penalty of death" unless it first found beyond a reasonable doubt one of these aggravating circumstances:

"One—That the offense of murder was committed while the offender was engaged in the commission of two other capital felonies, to-wit the armed robbery of [Simmons and Moore].

"Two—That the offender committed the offense of murder for the purpose of receiving money and the automobile described in the indictment.

"Three—The offense of murder was outrageously and wantonly vile, horrible and inhuman, in that they [sic] involved the depravity of [the] mind of the defendant."

Finding the first and second of these circumstances, the jury returned verdicts of death on each count.

The Supreme court of Georgia affirmed the convictions and the imposition of the death sentences for murder. After reviewing the trial transcript and the record, including the evidence, and comparing the evidence and sentence in similar cases in accordance with the requirements of Georgia law, the court concluded that, considering the nature of the crime and the defendant, the sentences of death had not resulted from prejudices or any other arbitrary factor and were not excessive or disproportionate to the penalty applied in similar cases. The death sentences imposed for armed robbery, however, were vacated on the grounds that the death penalty had rarely been imposed in Georgia for that offense and that the jury improperly considered the murders as aggravating circumstances for the robberies after having considered the armed robberies as aggravating circumstances for the murders. . . .

II.

Before considering the issues presented it is necessary to understand the Georgia statutory scheme for the imposition of the death penalty. The Georgia statute, as amended after our decision in Furman v. Georgia (1972), retains the death penalty for six categories of crime: murder, kidnapping for ransom or where the victim is harmed, armed robbery, rape, treason, and aircraft hijacking. The capital defendant's guilt or innocence is determined in the traditional manner, either by a trial judge or a jury, in the first stage of a bifurcated trial.

If trial is by jury, the trial judge is required to charge lesser included offenses when they are supported by any view of the evidence. . . . After a verdict, finding, or plea of guilty to a capital crime, a presentence hearing is conducted before whoever made the determination of guilt. the sentencing procedures are essentially the same in both bench and jury trials. At the hearing: "[T]he judge [or jury] shall hear additional evidence in extenuation, mitigation, and aggravation of punishment, including the record of any prior criminal convictions and pleas of guilty or pleas of nolo contendere of the defendant, or the absence of any prior conviction and pleas: Provided, however, that only such evidence in aggravation as the State has made known to the defendant prior to his trial shall be admissible. The judge [or jury] shall also hear argument by the defendant or his counsel and the prosecuting attorney . . . regarding the punishment to be imposed." . . .

III. . . .

[The Court here review previous cases dealing with the death penalty.]

It is clear from the foregoing precedents that the Eighth Amendment has not been regarded as a static concept. As Mr. Chief Justice Warren said, in an oft-quoted phrase, "[t]he Amendment must draw its meaning from the evolving standards of decency that mark the progress of a maturing society." Trop v. Dulles [1958]. . . . Thus, an assessment of contemporary values concerning the infliction of a challenged sanction is relevant to the application of the Eighth Amendment. As we develop below more fully, this assessment does not call for a subjective judgment. It requires, rather, that we look to objective indicia that reflect the public attitude toward a given sanction.

But our cases also make clear that public perceptions of standards of decency with respect to criminal sanctions are not conclusive. A penalty also must accord with "the dignity of man," which is the "basic concept underlying the Eighth Amendment." Trop v. Dulles. This means, at least, that the punishment not be "excessive." When a form of punishment in the abstract (in this case, whether capital punishment may ever be imposed as a sanction for murder) rather than in the particular (the propriety of death as a penalty to be applied to a specific defendant for a specific crime) is under consideration, the inquiry into "excessiveness" has two aspects. First, the punishment must not involve the unnecessary and wanton infliction of pain. Furman v. Georgia (Burger, C.J., dissenting). . . . Second, the punishment must not be grossly out of proportion to the severity of the crime. Trop v. Dulles. . . .

C.

. . . We now consider specifically whether the sentence of death for the crime of murder is a per se violation of the Eighth and Fourteenth Amendments to the Constitution. We note first that history and precedent strongly support a negative answer to this question.

The imposition of the death penalty for the crime of murder has a long history of acceptance both in the United States and in England. The common-law rule imposed a mandatory death sentence on all convicted murderers. McGautha v. California (1971). . . .

It is apparent from the text of the Constitution itself that the existence of capital punishment was accepted by the Framers. At the time the Eighth Amendment was ratified, capital punishment was a common sanction in every State. Indeed, the First Congress of the United States enacted legislation providing death as the penalty for specified crimes. The Fifth Amendment, adopted at the same time as the Eighth, contemplated the continued existence of the capital sanction by imposing certain limits on the prosecution of capital cases. . . . And the Fourteenth Amendment, adopted over three-quarters of a century later, similarly contemplates the existence of the capital sanction in providing that no State shall deprive any person of "life, liberty, or property" without due process of law.

For nearly two centuries, this Court, repeatedly and often expressly, has recognized that capital punishment is not invalid per se. . . .

Four years ago, the petitioners in Furman and its companion cases predicated their argument primarily upon the asserted proposition that standards of decency had evolved to the point where capital punishment no longer could be tolerated. The petitioners in those cases said, in effect, that the evolutionary process had come to an end, and that standards of decency required that the Eighth Amendment be construed finally as prohibiting capital punishment for any crime regardless of its depravity and impact on society. This view was accepted by two Justices. Three other justices were unwilling to go so far; focusing on the procedures by which convicted defendants were selected for the death penalty rather than on the actual punishment inflicted, they joined in the conclusion that the statutes before the Court were constitutionally invalid.

The petitioners in the capital cases before the Court today renew the "standards of decency" argument, but developments during the four years since Furman have undercut substantially the assumptions upon which their argument rested. Despite the continuing debate, dating back to the 19th century, over the morality and utility of capital punishment, it is now evident that a large proportion of American society continues to regard it as an appropriate and necessary criminal sanction.

The most marked indication of society's endorsement of the death penalty of murder is the legislative response to Furman. The legislatures of at least 35 States have enacted new statutes that provide for the death penalty for at least some crimes that result in the death of another person. And the Congress of the United States, in 1974, enacted a statute providing the death penalty for aircraft conspiracy that results in death. These recently adopted statutes have attempted to address the concerns expressed by the Court in Furman primarily (i) by specifying the factors to be weighed and the procedures to be followed in deciding when to impose a capital sentence, or (ii) by making the death penalty mandatory for specified crimes. But all of the post-Furman statutes make clear that capital punishment itself has not been rejected by the elected representatives of the people.

In the only statewide referendum occurring since Furman and brought to our attention, the people of California adopted a constitutional amendment that authorized capital punishment, in effect negating a prior ruling by the Supreme Court of California . . . that the death penalty violated the California Constitution. . . .

As we have seen, however, the Eighth Amendments demands more than that a challenged punishment be acceptable to contemporary society. The Court also must ask whether it comports with the basic concept of human dignity at the core of the Amendment. . . .

The death penalty is said to serve two principal social purposes: retribution and deterrence of capital crimes by prospective offenders.

In part, capital punishment is an expression of society's moral outrage at particularly offensive conduct. This function may be unappealing to many, but it is essential in an ordered society that asks its citizens to rely on legal processes rather than self-help to vindicate their wrongs. "The instinct for retribution is part of the nature of man, and channeling that instinct in the administration of criminal justice serves an important purpose in promoting the stability of a society governed by law. When people begin to believe that organized society is unwilling or unable to impose upon criminal offenders the punishment they 'deserve,' then there are sown the seeds of anarchy—of self-help, vigilante justice, and lynch law." Furman v. Georgia (Stewart, J., concurring). . . .

Statistical attempts to evaluate the worth of the death penalty as a deterrent to crimes by potential offenders have occasioned a great deal of debate. The results simply have been inconclusive. As one opponent of capital punishment has said: "[A]fter all possible inquiry, including the probing of all possible methods of inquiry, we do not know, and for systematic and easily visible reasons cannot know, what the truth about this 'deterrent' effect may be . . . ." . . .

In sum, we cannot say that the judgment of the Georgia legislature that capital punishment may be necessary in some cases is clearly wrong. Considerations of federalism, as well as respect for the ability of a legislature to evaluate, in terms of its particular state the moral consensus concerning the death penalty and its social utility as a sanction, require us to conclude, in the absence of more convincing evidence, that the infliction of death as a punishment for murder is not without justification and thus is not unconstitutionally severe.

Finally, we must consider whether the punishment of death is disproportionate in relation to the crime for which it is imposed. There is no question that death as a punishment is unique in its severity and irrevocability. Furman v. Georgia, (Stewart, J., concurring). When a defendant's life is at stake, the Court has been particularly sensitive to insure that every safeguard is observed. . . . But we are concerned here only with the imposition of capital punishment for the crime of murder, and when a life has been taken deliberately by the offender, we cannot say that the punishment is invariably disproportionate to the crime. It is an extreme sanction, suitable to the most extreme of crimes.

We hold that the death penalty is not a form of punishment that may never be imposed, regardless of the circumstances of the offense, regardless of the character of the offender, and regardless of the procedure followed in reaching the decision to impose it.

IV.

We now consider whether Georgia may impose the death penalty on the petitioner in this case.

A. . . .

Furman mandates that where discretion is afforded a sentencing body on a matter so grave as the determination of whether a human life should be taken or spared, that discretion must be suitably directed and limited so as to minimize the risk of wholly arbitrary and capricious action.

It is certainly not a novel proposition that discretion in the area of sentencing be exercised in an informed manner. We have long recognized that "[f]or the determination of sentences, justice generally requires . . . that there be taken into account the circumstances of the offense together with the character and propensities of the offender." . . .

Jury sentencing has been considered desirable in capital cases in order "to maintain a link between contemporary community values and the penal system--a link without which the determination of punishment could hardly reflect 'the evolving standards of decency that mark the progress of a maturing society.' But it creates special problems. Much of the information that is relevant to the sentencing decision may have no relevance to the question of guilt, or may even be extremely prejudicial to a fair determination of that question. This problem, however, is scarcely insurmountable. Those who have studied the question suggest that a bifurcated procedure—one in which the question of sentence is not considered until the determination of guilt has been made—is the best answer. . . .

. . . When a human life is at stake and when the jury must have information prejudicial to the question of guilt but relevant to the question of penalty in order to impose a rational sentence, a bifurcated system is more likely to ensure elimination of the constitutional deficiencies identified in Furman. . . .

The idea that a jury should be given guidance in its decision making is also hardly a novel proposition. Juries are invariably given careful instruction on the law and how to apply it before they are authorized to decide the merits of a lawsuit. It would be virtually unthinkable to follow any other course in a legal system that has traditionally operated by following prior precedents and fixed rules of law. . . .

While some have suggested that standards to guide a capital jury's sentencing deliberations are impossible to formulate, the fact is that such standards have been developed. When the drafters of the Model Penal Code faced this problem, they concluded "that it is within the realm of possibility to point to the main circumstances of aggravation and of mitigation that should be weighted, *and weighed against each other*, when they are presented in a concrete case." . . .

B.

We now turn to consideration of the constitutionality of Georgia's capital-sentencing procedures. In the wake of Furman, Georgia amended its capital punishment statute, but chose not to narrow the scope of its murder provisions. Thus, now as before Furman, in Georgia "[a] person commits murder when he unlawfully and with malice aforethought, either express or implied, causes the death of another human being." All persons convicted of murder "shall be punished by death or by imprisonment for life."

Georgia did act, however, to narrow the class of

murderers subject to capital punishment by specifying 10 statutory aggravating circumstances, one of which must be found by the jury to exist beyond a reasonable doubt before a death sentence can ever be imposed. In addition, the jury is authorized to consider any other appropriate aggravating or mitigating circumstances. The jury is not required to find any mitigating circumstance in order to make a recommendation of mercy that is binding on the trial court, but it must find a *statutory* aggravating circumstance before recommending a sentence of death.

These procedures require the jury to consider the circumstances of the crime and the criminal before it recommends sentence. No longer can a Georgia jury do as Furman's jury did: reach a finding of the defendant's guilt, and then, without guidance or direction, decide whether he should live or die. Instead, the jury's attention is directed to the specific circumstances of the crime: Was it committed in the course of another capital felony? Was it committed for money? Was it committed upon a peace officer or judicial officer? Was it committed in a particularly heinous way or in a manner that endangered the lives of many persons? In addition, the jury's attention is focused on the characteristics of the person who committed the crime: Does he have a record of prior convictions for capital offenses? Are there any special acts about this defendant that mitigate against imposing capital punishment (e.g., his youth, the extent of his cooperation with the police, his emotional state at the time of the crime). As a result, while some jury discretion still exists, "the discretion to be exercised is controlled by clear and objective standards so as to produce nondiscriminatory application." . . .

3.

Finally, the Georgia statute has an additional provision designed to assure that the death penalty will not be imposed on a capriciously selected group of convicted defendants. The new sentencing procedures require that the state supreme court review every death sentence to determine whether it was imposed under the influence of passion, prejudice, or any other arbitrary factor, whether the evidence supports the findings of a statutory aggravating circumstance, and "[w]hether the sentence of death is excessive or disproportionate to the penalty imposed in similar cases, considering both the crime and the defendant." In performing its sentence-review function, the Georgia court has held that "if the death penalty is only rarely imposed for an act or it is substantially out of line with sentences imposed for other acts it will be set aside as excessive." . . . The court on another occasion stated that "we view it to be our duty under the similarity standard to assure that no death sentence is affirmed unless in similar cases throughout the state the death penalty has been imposed generally. . . ." . . .

It is apparent that the Supreme Court of Georgia has taken its review responsibilities seriously. . . . Although armed robbery is a capital offense under Georgia law, the Georgia court concluded that the death sentences imposed in this case for that crime were "unusual in that they are rarely imposed for [armed robbery]. Thus, under the test provided by statute, . . . they must be considered to be excessive or disproportionate to the penalties imposed in similar cases." The Court therefore vacated Gregg's death sentences for armed robbery and has followed a similar course in every other armed robbery death penalty case to come before it. . . .

The provision for appellate review in the Georgia capital-sentencing system serves as a check against the random or arbitrary imposition of the death penalty. In particular, the proportionality review substantially eliminates the possibility that a person will be sentenced to die by the action of an aberrant jury. If a time comes when juries generally do not impose the death sentence in a certain kind of murder case, the appellate review procedures assures that no defendant convicted under such circumstances will suffer a sentence of death.

V. . . .

. . . For the reasons expressed in this opinion, we hold that the statutory system under which Gregg was sentenced to death does not violate the Constitution. Accordingly, the judgment of the Georgia Supreme Court is affirmed.

It is so ordered.

Mr. Justice **White,** with whom **The Chief Justice** and Mr. Justice **Rehnquist** join, concurring in the judgment, said in part:

III. . . .

. . . The Georgia Legislature has made an effort to identify those aggravating factors which it considers necessary and relevant to the question whether a defendant convicted of capital murder should be sentenced to death. The jury which imposes sentences is instructed on all statutory aggravating factors which are supported by the evidence, and is told that it may not impose the death penalty unless it unanimously finds at least one of those factors to have been established beyond a reasonable doubt. The Georgia Legislature has plainly made an effort to guide the jury in the exercise of its discretion, while at the same time permitting the jury to dispense mercy on the basis of factors too intangible to write into a statute, and I cannot except the naked assertion that the effort is bound to fail. As the types of murders of which the death penalty may be imposed become more narrowly defined and are limited to those which are particularly serious or for which the death penalty is peculiarly appropriate as they are in Georgia by reason of the aggravating-circumstance requirement, it becomes reasonable to expect that juries—even given discretion not to impose the death penalty—will impose the death penalty in a substantial portion of the cases so defined. If they do, it can no longer be said that the penalty is being imposed wantonly and freakishly or so infrequently that it loses its usefulness as a sentencing device. There is, therefore, reason to expect that Georgia's current system would escape the infirmities which invalidated its previous system under Furman. However, the Georgia Legislature was not satisfied with a system which might, but also might not turn out in practice to result in death sentences being imposed with reasonable consistence for certain serious murders. Instead, it gave the Georgia Supreme Court the power and the obligation to perform precisely the task which three Justices of this Court, whose opinions were necessary to the result, performed in Furman: namely, the task of deciding whether *in fact* the death penalty was being administered for any given class of crime in a discriminatory, standardless, or rare fashion. . . .

Statement of The Chief Justice and Mr. Justice Rehnquist:

We concur in the judgment and join the opinion of Mr. Justice White, agreeing with its analysis that Georgia's system of capital punishment comports with the Court's holding in Furman v. Georgia.

Mr. Justice Blackmun, concurring in the judgment.

I concur in the judgment. See Furman v. Georgia, (1972) (Blackmun, J., dissenting).

Mr. Justice Brennan, dissenting, said in part:

The Cruel and Unusual Punishments Clause "must draw its meaning from the evolving standards of decency that mark the progress of a maturing society." The opinions of Mr. Justice Stewart, Mr. Justice Powell, and Mr. Justice Stevens today hold that "evolving standards of decency" require focus not on the essence of the death penalty itself but primarily upon the procedures employed by the State to single out persons to suffer the penalty of death. Those opinions hold further that, so viewed, the Clause invalidates the mandatory infliction of the death penalty but not its infliction under sentencing procedures that Mr. Justice Stewart, Mr. Justice Powell, and Mr. Justice Stevens conclude adequately safeguard against the risk that the death penalty was imposed in an arbitrary and capricious manner.

In Furman v. Georgia (1972), I read "evolving standards of decency" as requiring focus upon the essence of the death penalty itself and not primarily or solely upon the procedures under which the determination to inflict the penalty upon a particular person was made. . . .

This Court inescapably has the duty, as the ultimate arbiter of the meaning of our Constitution, to say whether, when individuals condemned to death stand before our Bar, "moral concepts" require us to hold that the law has progressed to the point where we should declare that the punishment of death, like punishments on the rack, the screw, and the wheel, is no longer morally tolerable in our civilized society. My opinion in Furman v. Georgia concluded that our civilization and the law had progressed to this point and that therefore the punishment of death, for whatever crime and under all circumstances, is "cruel and unusual" in violation of the Eighth and Fourteenth Amendments of the Constitution. . . .

The fatal constitutional infirmity in the punishment of death is that it treats "members of the human race as nonhumans, as objects to be toyed with and discarded. [It is] thus inconsistent with the fundamental premise of the Clause, that even the vilest criminal remains a human being possessed of common human dignity." As such it is a penalty that "subjects the individual to a fate forbidden by the principle of civilized treatment guaranteed by the [Clause]." I therefore would hold, on that ground alone, that death is today a cruel and unusual punishment prohibited by the Clause. "Justice of this kind is obviously no less shocking than the crime itself, and the new 'official' murder, far from offering redress for the offense committed against society, adds instead a second defilement to the first."

Mr. Justice Marshall, dissenting, said in part:

In Furman I concluded that the death penalty is constitutionally invalid for two reasons. First, the death penalty is excessive. And second, the American people, fully informed as to the purposes of the death penalty and its liabilities, would in my view reject it as morally unacceptable.

Since the decision in Furman, the legislatures of 35 States have enacted new statutes authorizing the imposition of the death sentence for certain crimes, and Congress has enacted a law providing the death penalty for air piracy resulting in death. I would be less than candid if I did not acknowledge that these developments have a significant bearing on a realistic assessment of the moral acceptability of the death penalty to the American people. But if the constitutionality of the death penalty turns, as I have urged, on the opinion of an *informed* citizenry, then even the enactment of new death statutes cannot be viewed as conclusive. In Furman, I observed that the American people are largely unaware of the information critical to a judgment on the morality of the death penalty, and concluded that if they were better informed they would consider it shocking, unjust, and unacceptable. A recent study, conducted after the enactment of the post-Furman statutes, has confirmed that the American people know little about the death penalty, and that the opinions of an informed public unaware of the consequences and efforts of the death penalty.

TRIAL BY JURY

DUNCAN v. LOUISIANA

391 U. S. 145; 88 S. Ct. 1444; 20 L. Ed. 2d 491
(1968)

The present century has seen the increasing erosion of one of the most venerable procedures of the common law—the jury trial. In England, its birthplace, it has been virtually abandoned in civil cases and in all but the most important criminal cases. Increasingly in the United States it is waived by the contending parties, and some states have moved to streamline their jury systems by reducing the number of jurors or providing for less than a unanimous verdict. Such changes were held in *Maxwell v. Dow* (1900) not to deny the accused due process of law. But the framers of the Constitution clearly intended that the right of jury trial be maintained; both in Article III of the original document and in the Sixth Amendment the right of jury trial in criminal cases is ensured, and the Seventh Amendment guarantees it in all civil cases involving over $20.

In *Patton v. United States* (1930) the Court made clear that this meant the traditional common-law jury trial—a presiding judge and twelve jurors rendering a unanimous verdict. The agreement of the defendant in that case to go on with eleven jurors after one got sick was as much a waiver of a jury as if he had elected to be tried by the judge alone. Such waiver requires the consent of both the government and the trial court, and the defendant has no constitutional right to be tried by a judge alone in the absence of such consent; see *Singer v. United States* (1965). To reduce the likelihood of a mistrial because of a sick juror, especially in long trials, the federal rules of procedure now provide for the selection of alternate jurors who meet all the qualifications and hear all the evidence, but who do not retire with the jury to consider the verdict unless a regular juror has had to be replaced.

In the guarantee of jury trial in the Sixth it is stated that the jury shall be "impartial," a requirement normally met through a system of challenges. Each prospective juror is examined under oath (voir dire) and may be áhallenged by either party for "cause." If found by the presiding judge to be prejudiced or to have an interest in the case, the potential juror is disqualified for service in that trial. Each side is also allowed a certain number of "peremptory challenges," which may be exercised without any assignment of cause. In cases involving sensational crimes which have received widespread local publicity it is sometimes impossible to impanel an impartial jury. Lurid or inflammatory crime reporting by press, radio, or television may create a climate of opinion in which a fair trial is impossible, and in which to conduct a trial denies the defendant due process of law. There is no easy solution to this conflict between the two major civil liberties, freedom of the press and the right to a fair trial. In such cases the defendant, even though only charged with a misdemeanor, may request a change of venue so the trial may be held in another community; see *Groppi v. Wisconsin* (1971).

In 1962 a national scandal broke involving Texas millionaire Billie Sol Estes, accused of influence and fraud in grain-storage and cotton-acreage dealings. Against a backdrop of a dead Department of Agriculture official, two congressional inquiries, and four fraud indictments, Estes was convicted before a national TV audience of swindling a farmer. In *Estes v. Texas* (1965) the Court reversed for lack of due process. Noting that "we start with the proposition that it is a 'public trial' that the Sixth Amendment guarantees to the 'accused,' " it concluded that a day in court is not a day in a "stadium . . . or nationwide arena."

In *Walker v. Sauvinet* (1876) and *Maxwell v. Dow* (1900) the Supreme Court held that trial by jury was not required of the states by either the privileges and immunities or the due process clauses of the Fourteenth Amendment, but as the Court said in *Brown v. Mississippi* (1936), "because a State may dispense with a jury trial, it does not follow that it may substitute trial by ordeal." The trial must meet the test of essential fairness, and the Court incorporated some of the specifics of the Sixth Amendment designed to ensure such fairness. In *Pointer v. Texas* (1965) the right of the accused "to be confronted with the witnesses against him" was held applicable to the states; in *Parker v. Gladden* (1966) the right to a trial "by an impartial jury" was added, apparently to cover such jury trials as the state actually provided; and in *Klopfer v. North Carolina* (1967) the Court incorporated the "right to a speedy . . . trial." In *Washington v. Texas* (1967) the Court held applicable to the states the right of an accused "to have compulsory process for obtaining witnesses in his favor."

There are well-established exceptions to the general rule requiring trial by jury in criminal cases. Even at common law, petty offenses were tried without a jury, and punishment for contempt of court has always been imposed summarily by the presiding judge. One of the most tangible distinctions between "law" and "equity" is the absence of a jury in equity cases, although these normally do not involve criminal matters.

A jury trial problem of recent origin involved the right of Congress to subject civilian citizens to the jurisdiction of a military court. Article I of the Constitution authorizes Congress "to make rules for the government and regulation of the land and naval forces," and under this authority the first Congress adopted from the British the Articles of War to be administered by a system of courts-martial. This body of military law not only includes the common-law crimes but in addition covers purely military offenses the punishment of which is necessary to the discipline of the armed forces. Courts-martial are an essential part of this system of discipline, and differ in many ways from civilian courts of justice.

They are specifically exempt by the Fifth Amendment from the requirement of grand jury indictment, and by implication they are also exempt from the jury trial provisions of the Sixth. While the federal courts can review court-martial convictions on habeas corpus, their review is largely limited to ensuring the jurisdiction of the military court. Legal errors are subject to review only within the executive branch of the government, and in *Hiatt v. Brown* (1950) a United States district court was held in error "in extending its review, for the purpose of determining compliance with the due process clause, to such matters as the propositions of law set forth . . . , the sufficiency of the evidence . . . , the adequacy of the pretrial investigation, and the competence of the law member and defense counsel."

In 1950 Congress adopted the Uniform Code of Military Justice, which provided for all the armed forces a system of military justice more in harmony with the concept of due process of law as it has developed in civilian courts. In two controversial sections the new code undertook to extend court-martial jurisdiction to civilians. One of these (Art. 3a) provided that a person who had been discharged from the armed forces could thereafter still be tried by court-martial for certain offenses committed while in the service. In *United States ex rel. Toth v. Quarles* (1955) the Supreme Court held this section of the act void. Toth had been discharged from the Air Force and returned to his civilian job. Five months later he was arrested by the military police and returned to Korea to stand trial for murder. Relying on *Ex parte Milligan* (1866), the Court rejected the theory that the "commander-in-chief" clause provided such power; nor could it, except by "an extremely broad construction," be brought under the power of Congress to make rules for governing the armed forces, whose natural meaning clearly limited it to persons actually in military service. "There is a compelling reason for construing the clause this way; any expansion of court-martial jurisdiction like that in the 1950 Act necessarily encroaches on the jurisdiction of federal courts set up under Article III of the Constitution where persons on trial are surrounded with more constitutional safeguards than in military tribunals. . . . We find nothing in the history or constitutional treatment of military tribunals which entitles them to rank along with Article III courts as adjudicators of the guilt or innocence of people charged with offenses for which they can be deprived of their life, liberty or property."

The post-World War II policy of the United States has resulted, for the first time in our history, in the stationing abroad of American military personnel on a more or less permanent basis. Such troops normally serve a three-year tour of duty overseas, and Congress has wisely made it possible for them to be accompanied by their families. These troops are, in a sense, the guests of the country in which they are stationed, and would normally be subject to the penal laws of that country in the same way as would a civilian tourist. But, by the Status of Forces Agreements concluded with the NATO countries and Japan, the United States has jurisdiction to try criminal cases involving its military personnel by its own courts-martial, provided the host country agrees to waive its jurisdiction. The host country normally does waive its jurisdiction, and there is no question of the right of the United States to subject military personnel to trial by court-martial. An awkward question arises, however, in cases involving the civilian dependents of these troops. On the rare occasions when they commit crimes, can they be tried, as those actually in the armed forces would be, by an army court-martial?

After the Status of Forces Agreements went into effect Mrs. Dorothy Krueger Smith and Mrs. Clarice B. Covert were accused of murdering their soldier-husbands on foreign military bases. The countries where the crimes were committed waived jurisdiction, and they were tried and convicted by Army courts-martial under the provision of the Status of Forces Agreements.

Although the Supreme Court at first upheld their convictions, the decision was apparently hastily reached and at the opening of the following term of Court the case was reheard and the decision reversed. Although there was no majority opinion, four members of the

Court relied on the *Toth* case, and the Court clearly agreed that, at least in capital cases, civilians could not be denied their right to a jury trial by an agreement to try them by court-martial. See *Reid v. Covert* (1957).

In 1960 three cases came to the Court involving the scope of the *Reid* holding. In *Kinsella v. United States ex rel. Singleton* (civilian dependent in a noncapital case); *Grisham v. Hagan* (American civilian employee in a capital case); and *McElroy v. United States ex rel. Guagliardo* (American civilian employee in a noncapital case) the Court held void trial by court-martial. To the criticism that in these cases persons accused of serious crimes escaped trial, the Court replied that Congress has power to establish civilian courts in which the constitutional rights of such persons, including jury trial, will be guaranteed.

In 1969, in *O'Callahan v. Parker*, the Supreme Court again reaffirmed its faith in the common-law judicial process by ruling that the armed forces could not court-martial a soldier for a non-service-connected crime—in this case an attempted rape that took place while the soldier was away on leave. Quoting at length from *United States ex rel. Toth v. Quarles* (1955), the Court emphasized the command influence in military trials and the resultant shortcomings from the standpoint of judicial impartiality. The Court found that the Fifth Amendment's guarantee of grand jury indictment "except in cases arising in the land or naval forces, or in the militia, when in actual service in time of war or public danger," did not entitle Congress to authorize the trial by court-martial of soldiers for purely civilian crimes. The absence of especially persuasive logical or historical reasoning to back its decision, together with a failure to tell the military what crimes they could and could not try, prompted a strong dissent from Justices Harlan, Stewart, and White. "Absolutely nothing," they concluded, "in the language, history, or logic of the Constitution justifies this uneasy state of affairs which the Court has today created." In *Relford v. Commandant* (1971) the situation was eased somewhat when the Court agreed unanimously that the rape by a serviceman, on a military base, of members of another serviceman's family was a "service connected crime" within the meaning of *O'Callahan*.

While recent years have seen most of the rights of criminal defendants listed in the Bill of Rights incorporated into due process, jury trial and grand jury indictment remained conspicuously absent from the list. Both rights have been subject to a good deal of professional criticism that raised serious questions as to whether or not they should be considered fundamental and hence required of the states. Many states have substituted the "information," a charge signed by the prosecutor alone, for the grand jury indictment, and the argument is made that it is a fairer, more efficient procedure. The grand jury, it is contended, is usually under the thumb of the prosecutor anyway, yet lets the prosecutor escape the onus of bringing to trial someone who is later found to be innocent.

Serious question was raised, too, about the competence of trial juries, especially in complex civil cases, to understand the facts of a case and apply the law to it *properly. Public concern for the concept of jury secrecy has made the gathering of information on the subject extremely difficult, so the charges have gone largely unrefuted.*

Mr. Justice **White** delivered the opinion of the Court, saying in part:

Appellant, Gary Duncan, was convicted of simple battery in the Twenty-fifth Judicial District Court of Louisiana. Under Louisiana law simple battery is a misdemeanor, punishable by two years' imprisonment and a $300 fine. Appellant sought trial by jury, but because the Louisiana Constitution grants jury trials only in cases in which capital punishment or imprisonment at hard labor may be imposed, the trial judge denied the request. Appellant was convicted and sentenced to serve 60 days in the parish prison and pay a fine of $150. Appellant sought review in the Supreme Court of Louisiana, asserting that the denial of jury trial violated rights guaranteed to him by the United States Constitution. The Supreme Court, finding "no error of law in the ruling complained of," denied appellant a writ of certiorari. . . . Appellant sought review in this Court, alleging that the Sixth and Fourteenth Amendments to the United States Constitution secure the right to jury trial in state criminal prosecutions where a sentence as long as two years may be imposed. . . .

I.

The Fourteenth Amendment denies the States the power to "deprive any person of life, liberty, or property, without due process of law." In resolving conflicting claims concerning the meaning of this spacious language, the Court has looked increasingly to the Bill of Rights for guidance; many of the rights guaranteed by the first eight Amendments to the Constitution have been held to be protected against state action by the Due Process Clause of the Fourteenth Amendment. That clause now protects the right to compensation for property taken by the State, the rights of speech, press, and religion covered by the First Amendment; the Fourth Amendment rights to be free from unreasonable searches and seizures and to have excluded from criminal trials any evidence illegally seized, the right guaranteed by the Fifth Amendment to be free of compelled self-incrimination; and the Sixth Amendment rights to counsel, to a speedy and public trial, to confrontation of opposing witnesses, and to compulsory process for obtaining witnesses.

The test for determining whether a right extended by the Fifth and Sixth Amendments with respect to federal criminal proceedings is also protected against state action by the Fourteenth Amendment has been phrased in a variety of ways in the opinions of this Court. The question has been asked whether a right is among those " 'fundamental principles of liberty and justice which lie at the base of all our civil and political institutions,' " Powell v. Alabama, (1932); whether it is "basic in our system of jurisprudence," In re Oliver (1948); and

whether it is "a fundamental right, essential to a fair trial," Gideon v. Wainwright (1963). . . . The claim before us is that the right to trial by jury guaranteed by the Sixth Amendment meets these tests. The position of Louisiana, on the other hand, is that the Constitution imposes upon the States no duty to give a jury trial in any criminal case, regardless of the seriousness of the crime or the size of the punishment which may be imposed. Because we believe that trial by jury in criminal cases is fundamental to the American scheme of justice, we hold that the Fourteenth Amendment guarantees a right of jury trial in all criminal cases which—were they to be tried in a federal court—would come within the Sixth Amendment's guarantee.* Since we consider the appeal before us to be such a case, we hold that the Constitution was violated when appellant's demand for jury trial was refused.

The history of trial by jury in criminal cases has been frequently told. It is sufficient for present purposes to say that by the time our Constitution was written, jury trial in criminal cases had been in existence in England for several centuries and carried impressive credentials traced by many to Magna Carta. Its preservation and proper operation as a protection against arbitrary rule

---

*In one sense recent cases applying provisions of the first eight amendments to the States represent a new approach to the "incorporation" debate. Earlier the Court can be seen as having asked, when inquiring into whether some particular procedural safeguard was required of a State, if a civilized system could be imagined that would not accord the particular protection. For example, Palko v. Connecticut (1937) stated: "The right to trial by jury and the immunity from prosecution except as the result of an indictment may have value and importance. Even so, they are not of the very essence of a scheme of ordered liberty. . . . Few would be so narrow or provincial as to maintain that a fair and enlightened system of justice would be impossible without them." The recent cases, on the other hand, have proceeded upon the valid assumption that state criminal processes are not imaginary and theoretical schemes but actual systems bearing virtually every characteristic of the common-law system that has been developing contemporaneously in England and in this country. The question thus is whether given this kind of system a particular procedure is fundamental—whether, that is, a procedure is necessary to an Anglo-American regime of ordered liberty. . . . Of immediate relevance for this case are the Court's holdings that the States must comply with certain provisions of the Sixth Amendment, specifically that the States may not refuse a speedy trial, confrontation of witnesses, and the assistance, at state expense if necessary, of counsel. Of each of these determinations that a constitutional provision originally written to bind the Federal Government should bind the States as well it might be said that the limitation in question is not necessarily fundamental to fairness in every criminal system that might be imagined but is fundamental in the context of the criminal process maintained by the American States.

When the inquiry is approached in this way the question whether the States can impose criminal punishment without granting a jury trial appears quite different from the way it appeared in the older cases opining that States might abolish jury trial. See, e. g., Maxwell v. Dow (1900). A criminal process which was fair and equitable but used no juries is easy to imagine. It would make use of alternative guarantees and protections which would serve the purposes that the jury serves in the English and American systems. Yet no American State has undertaken to construct such a system. Instead, every American State, including Louisiana, uses the jury extensively, and imposes very serious punishments only after a trial at which the defendant has a right to a jury's verdict. In every State, including Louisiana, the structure and style of the criminal process—the supporting framework and the subsidiary procedures—are of the sort that naturally complement jury trial, and have developed in connection with and in reliance upon jury trial.

were among the major objectives of the revolutionary settlement which was expressed in the Declaration and Bill of Rights of 1689. In the 18th century Blackstone could write:

"Our law has therefore wisely placed this strong and two-fold barrier, of a presentment and a trial by jury, between the liberties of the people and the prerogative of the crown. It was necessary, for preserving the admirable balance of our constitution, to vest the executive power of the laws in the prince: and yet this power might be dangerous and destructive to that very constitution, if exerted without check or control, by justices of oyer and terminer occasionally named by the crown; who might then, as in France or Turkey, imprison, dispatch, or exile any man that was obnoxious to the government, by an instant declaration that such is their will and pleasure. But the founders of the English law have, with excellent forecast, contrived that . . . the truth of every accusation, whether preferred in the shape of indictment, information, or appeal, should afterwards be confirmed by the unanimous suffrage of twelve of his equals and neighbors, indifferently chosen and superior to all suspicion."

Jury trial came to America with English colonists, and received strong support from them. Royal interference with the jury trial was deeply resented. Among the resolutions adopted by the First Congress of the American Colonies (the Stamp Act Congress) on October 19, 1765—resolutions deemed by their authors to state "the most essential rights and liberties of the colonists"—was the declaration: "That trial by jury is the inherent and invaluable right of every British subject in these colonies." . . . The Declaration of Independence stated solemn objections to the King making "judges dependent on his will alone, for the tenure of their offices, and the amount and payment of their salaries," to his "depriving us, in many cases, of the benefits of trial by jury," and to his "transporting us beyond the seas to be tried for pretended offenses." The Constitution itself, in Art. III, § 2, commanded:

"The Trial of all Crimes, except in cases of Impeachment, shall be by Jury; and such Trial shall be held in the State where the said Crimes shall have been committed."

Objections to the Constitution because of the absence of a bill of rights were met by the immediate submission and adoption of the Bill of Rights. Included was the Sixth Amendment which, among other things, provided:

"In all criminal prosecutions, the accused shall enjoy the right to a speedy and public trial, by an impartial jury of the State and district wherein the crime shall have been committed."

The constitutions adopted by the original States guaranteed jury trial. Also, the constitution of every State entering the Union thereafter in one form or another protected the right to jury trial in criminal cases.

Even such skeletal history is impressive support for considering the right to jury trial in criminal cases to be fundamental to our system of justice, an importance frequently recognized in the opinions of this Court. . . .

Jury trial continues to receive strong support. The laws of every State guarantee a right to jury trial in serious criminal cases; no State has dispensed with it; nor are there significant movements underway to do so. Indeed, the three most recent state constitutional revisions, in Maryland, Michigan, and New York, carefully preserved the right of the accused to have the judgment of a jury when tried for a serious crime.

We are aware of prior cases in this Court in which the prevailing opinion contains statements contrary to our holding today that the right to jury trial in serious criminal cases is a fundamental right and hence must be recognized by the States as part of their obligation to extend due process of law to all persons within their jurisdiction. Louisiana relies especially on Maxwell v. Dow (1900); Palko v. Connecticut (1937); and Snyder v. Massachusetts (1934). None of these cases, however, dealt with a State which had purported to dispense entirely with a jury trial in serious criminal cases. Maxwell held that no provision of the Bill of Rights applied to the States—a position long since repudiated—and that the Due Process Clause of the Fourteenth Amendment did not prevent a State from trying a defendant for a noncapital offense with fewer than 12 men on the jury. It did not deal with a case in which no jury at all had been provided. In neither Palko nor Snyder was jury trial actually at issue, although both cases contain important dicta asserting that the right to jury trial is not essential to ordered liberty and may be dispensed with by the States regardless of the Sixth and Fourteenth Amendments. These observations, though weighty and respectable, are nevertheless dicta, unsupported by holdings in this Court that a State may refuse a defendant's demand for a jury trial when he is charged with a serious crime. . . .

The guarantees of jury trial in the Federal and State Constitutions reflect a profound judgment about the way in which law should be enforced and justice administered. A right to jury trial is granted to criminal defendants in order to prevent oppression by the Government. Those who wrote our constitutions knew from history and experience that it was necessary to protect against unfounded criminal charges brought to eliminate enemies and against judges too responsive to the voice of higher authority. The framers of the constitutions strove to create an independent judiciary but insisted upon further protection against arbitrary action. Providing an accused with the right to be tried by a jury of his peers gave him an inestimable safeguard against the corrupt or overzealous prosecutor and against the compliant, biased, or eccentric judge. If the defendant preferred the common-sense judgment of a jury to the more tutored but perhaps less sympathetic reaction of the single judge, he was to have it. Beyond this, the jury trial provisions in the Federal and State Constitutions reflect a fundamental decision about the exercise of official power—a reluctance to entrust plenary powers over the life and liberty of the citizen to one judge or to a group of judges. Fear of unchecked power, so typical of our State and Federal Governments in other respects, found expression in the criminal law in this insistence upon community participation in the determination of guilt or innocence. The deep commitment of the Nation to the right of jury trial in serious criminal cases as a defense against arbitrary law enforcement qualifies for protection under the Due Process Clause of the Fourteenth Amendment, and must therefore be respected by the States.

Of course jury trial has "its weaknesses and the potential for misuse." . . . We are aware of the long debate, especially in this century, among those who write about the administration of justice, as to the wisdom of permitting untrained laymen to determine the facts in civil and criminal proceedings. Although the debate has been intense, with powerful voices on either side, most of the controversy has centered on the jury in civil cases. Indeed, some of the severest critics of civil juries acknowledge that the arguments for criminal juries are much stronger. In addition, at the heart of the dispute have been express or implicit assertions that juries are incapable of adequately understanding evidence or determining issues of fact, and that they are unpredictable, quixotic, and little better than a roll of dice. Yet, the most recent and exhaustive study of the jury in criminal cases concluded that juries do understand the evidence and come to sound conclusions in most of the cases presented to them and that when juries differ with the result at which the judge would have arrived, it is usually because they are serving some of the very purposes for which they were created and for which they are now employed.

The State of Louisiana urges that holding that the Fourteenth Amendment assures a right to jury trial will cast doubt on the integrity of every trial conducted without a jury. . . . We would not assert, however, that every criminal trial—or any particular trial—held before a judge alone is unfair or that a defendant may never be as fairly treated by a judge as he would be by a jury. Thus we hold no constitutional doubts about the practices, common in both federal and state courts, of accepting waivers of jury trial and prosecuting petty crimes without extending a right to jury trial. However, the fact is that in most places more trials for serious crimes are to juries than to a court alone; a great many defendants prefer the judgment of a jury to that of a court. Even where defendants are satisfied with bench trials, the right to a jury trial very likely serves its intended purpose of making judicial or prosecutorial unfairness less likely.*

---

*. . . Louisiana objects to application of the decisions of this Court interpreting the Sixth Amendment as guaranteeing a 12-man jury in serious criminal cases, Thompson v. Utah (1898); as requiring a unanimous verdict before guilt can be found, Maxwell v. Dow (1900); and as barring procedures by which crimes subject to the Sixth Amendment jury trial provision are tried in the first instance without a jury but at the first appellate stage by de novo trial with a jury, Callan v. Wilson (1888). It seems very unlikely to us that our decision today will require widespread changes in state criminal processes. First, our decisions interpreting the Sixth Amendment are always subject to reconsideration, a fact amply demonstrated by the instant decision. In addition, most of the States have provisions for jury trials equal in breadth to the Sixth Amendment, if that amendment is construed, as it has been, to permit

II.

Louisiana's final contention is that even if it must grant jury trials in serious criminal cases, the conviction before us is valid and constitutional because here the petitioner was tried for simple battery and was sentenced to only 60 days in the parish prison. We are not persuaded. It is doubtless true that there is a category of petty crimes or offenses which is not subject to the Sixth Amendment jury trial provision and should not be subject to the Fourteenth Amendment jury trial requirement here applied to the States. Crimes carrying possible penalties up to six months do not require a jury trial if they otherwise qualify as petty offenses, Cheff v. Schnackenberg (1966). But the penalty authorized for a particular crime is of major relevance in determining whether it is serious or not and may in itself, if severe enough, subject the trial to the mandates of the Sixth Amendment. . . . In the case before us the Legislature of Louisiana has made simple battery a criminal offense punishable by imprisonment for two years and a fine. The question, then, is whether a crime carrying such a penalty is an offense which Louisiana may insist on trying without a jury.

We think not. So-called petty offenses were tried without juries both in England and in the Colonies and have always been held to be exempt from the otherwise comprehensive language of the Sixth Amendment's jury trial provisions. . . . Of course the boundaries of the petty offense category have always been ill defined, if not ambulatory. In the absence of an explicit constitutional provision, the definitional task necessarily falls on the courts, which must either pass upon the validity of legislative attempts to identify those petty offenses which are exempt from jury trial or, where the legislature has not addressed itself to the problem, themselves face the question in the first instance. In either case it is necessary to draw a line in the spectrum of crime, separating petty from serious infractions. This process, although essential, cannot be wholly satisfactory, for it requires attaching different consequences to events which, when they lie near the line, actually differ very little. . . .

. . . We need not, however, settle in this case the exact location of the line between petty offenses and serious crimes. It is sufficient for our purposes to hold that a crime punishable by two years in prison is, based on past and contemporary standards in this country, a serious crime and not a petty offense. Consequently, appellant was entitled to a jury trial and it was error to deny it.

The judgment below is reversed and the case is remanded for proceedings not inconsistent with this opinion.

---

the trial of petty crimes and offenses without a jury. Indeed, there appear to be only four States in which juries of fewer than 12 can be used without the defendant's consent for offenses carrying a maximum penalty of greater than one year. Only in Oregon and Louisiana can a less-than-unanimous jury convict for an offense with a maximum penalty greater than one year. However 10 States authorize first-stage trials without juries for crimes carrying lengthy penalties; these States give a convicted defendant the right to a de novo trial before a jury in a different court. . . .

Mr. Justice **Fortas** joined the judgment and opinion of the Court in a concurring opinion.

Mr. Justice **Black,** with whom Mr. Justice **Douglas** concurred, wrote a concurring opinion.

Mr. Justice **Harlan,** with whom Mr. Justice **Stewart** joined, wrote a dissenting opinion.

WILLIAMS v. FLORIDA

399 U. S. 78; 90 S. Ct. 1893; 26 L. Ed. 2d 446
(1970)

Two important questions were raised by the Court's decision in Duncan v. Louisiana (1968). First, would it mean that all states now had to go back to the old common-law jury of 12 persons, since the Sixth Amendment had consistently been held to require that kind of jury in the federal courts? Second, to what kind of cases would the jury requirement apply? Traditionally, petty offenses were tried before a judge rather than a jury, and in the Duncan case the Court held that the rule applied to the states as well as to the federal government—the severity of the crime to be determined not by the sentence actually imposed, but by the maximum sentence provided by law. In Baldwin v. New York (1970), decided the same day as Williams v. Florida, the Court struck down a conviction for "jostling" handed down by the New York City Criminal Court, which by law operated without a jury. The misdemeanor of jostling carried a maximum sentence of one year in jail, and Justices White, Brennan, and Marshall agreed that "no offense can be deemed 'petty' for purposes of the right to trial by jury where imprisonment for more than six months is authorized." In this case the defendant had been given the maximum sentence of one year in jail. Justices Black and Douglas concurred on the ground that all crimes should be tried by jury regardless of seriousness.

In McKeiver v. Pennsylvania (1971) the Court, without agreeing upon an opinion, held that a state was not required to provide a jury trial in juvenile court adjudications. Four members of the Court stressed there that "if the jury trial were to be injected into the juvenile court system as a matter of right, it would bring with it into that system the traditional delay, the formality and the clamor of the adversary system and, possibly, the public trial."

In a number of cases, the most notable being the conspiracy trial of the "Chicago Seven" before district Judge Julius J. Hoffman, a systematic attempt had been made to disrupt the orderly trial process as a way either of showing contempt for that process or of preventing the trial proceeding to a conviction. In two important cases the Court has laid down rules regarding the power of judges to deal with such disruption. In Illinois v. Allen (1970) the defendant, an accused robber whose mental stability was dubious, had so disrupted his trial that the judge had removed him from the courtroom. The Supreme Court held that while it was within the authority of

the judge to bind and gag him or fine him for contempt, the Sixth Amendment guarantee of confrontation did forbid removing him from the courtroom if he refused to behave. Following this decision, New York state made plans to resume, with the aid of closed circuit TV so the defendants could follow the trial, the disrupted trial of thirteen Black Panthers accused of plotting to bomb public places. Although there were further disruptions, the plans were never put into effect.

While the court clearly has what power it needs to prevent disruption of a trial, it cannot tolerate the disruptive conduct and then, at the end of the trial, accumulate the contempts into one summary contempt sentence. In Mayberry v. Pennsylvania (1971) a prisoner on trial for jail break insulted and provoked the judge on eleven occasions. Before the judge pronounced sentence on his conviction, he pronounced him guilty of contempt and sentenced him to one to two years for each contempt. The Supreme Court, while sympathizing with the judge and praising his patience, held that "no one so cruelly slandered is likely to maintain that calm detachment necessary for fair adjudication," and that the question of contempt should be returned for trial before another judge.

In the present case the defendant was tried for robbery before a six-man jury provided by Florida law in all but capital cases. His request for a twelve-man jury was denied and he was sentenced to life imprisonment.

Mr. Justice **White** delivered the opinion of the Court, saying in part:

III

In Duncan v. Louisiana (1968), we held that the Fourteenth Amendment guarantees a right to trial by jury in all criminal cases which—were they to be tried in a federal court—would come within the Sixth Amendment's guarantee. . . .

The question in this case then is whether the constitutional guarantee of a trial by "jury" necessarily requires trial by exactly 12 persons, rather than some lesser number—in this case six. We hold that the 12-man panel is not a necessary ingredient of "trial by jury," and that respondent's refusal to impanel more than the six members provided for by Florida law did not violate petitioner's Sixth Amendment rights as applied to the States through the Fourteenth.

We had occasion in Duncan v. Louisiana to review briefly the oft-told history of the development of trial by jury in criminal cases. That history revealed a long tradition attaching great importance to the concept of relying on a body of one's peers to determine guilt or innocence as a safeguard against arbitrary law enforcement. That same history, however, affords little insight into the considerations which gradually led the size of that body to be generally fixed at 12. Some have suggested that the number 12 was fixed upon simply because that was the number of the presentment jury from the hundred, from which the petty jury developed. Other, less circular but more fanciful reasons for the number 12 have been given, "but they were all brought forward after the number was fixed," and rest on little more than mystical or superstitious insights into the significance of "12." Lord Coke's explanation that the "number of twelve is much respected in holy writ, as 12 apostles, 12 stones, 12 tribes, etc." is typical. In short, while sometime in the 14th century the size of the jury at common law came to be fixed generally at 12, that particular feature of the jury system appears to have been an historical accident, unrelated to the great purposes which gave rise to the jury in the first place. The question before us is whether this accidental feature of the jury has been immutably codified into our Constitution.

. This Court's earlier decisions have assumed an affirmative answer to this question. The leading case so construing the Sixth Amendment if Thompson v. Utah (1898). There the defendant had been tried and convicted by a 12-man jury for a crime committed in the Territory of Utah. A new trial was granted, but by that time Utah had been admitted as a State. The defendant's new trial proceeded under Utah's Constitution, providing for a jury of only eight members. This Court reversed the resulting conviction, holding that Utah's constitutional provision was an ex post facto law as applied to the defendant. In reaching its conclusion, the Court announced that the Sixth Amendment was applicable to the defendant's trial when Utah was a territory, and that the jury referred to in the Amendment was a jury "constituted, as it was at common law, of twelve persons, neither more nor less." Arguably unnecessary for the result,* this announcement was supported simply by referring to the Magna Carta, and by quoting passages from treatises which noted—what has already been seen—that at common law the jury did indeed consist of 12. Noticeably absent was any discussion of the essential step in the argument: namely, that every feature of the jury as it existed at common law—whether incidental or essential to that institution—was necessarily included in the Constitution wherever that document referred to a "jury." Subsequent decisions have reaffirmed the announcement in Thompson, often in dictum† and usually by relying—where there was any discussion of the issue at all—solely on the fact that the common law jury consisted of 12. See Patton v. United States (1930);‡ Rassmussen v. United States (1905); Maxwell v. Dow (1900).

---

*At the time of the crime and at the first trial the statutes of the Territory of Utah—wholly apart from the Sixth Amendment—ensured Thompson a 12-man jury. The court found the ex post facto question easy to solve, once it was assumed that Utah's subsequent constitutional provision deprived Thompson of a right previously guaranteed him by the United States Constitution; the possibility that the same result might have been reached solely on the basis of the rights formerly accorded Thompson under the territorial statute was hinted at, but was not explicitly considered.

†A ruling that the Sixth Amendment refers to a common law jury was essential to the holding in Rassmussen v. United States (1905), where the Court held invalid a conviction by a six-man jury in Alaska. The ruling was accepted at the Government's concession without discussion or citation. . . .

‡The Patton opinion furnishes an interesting illustration of the Court's willingness to re-examine earlier assertions about the nature of "jury trial" in almost every respect except the 12-man jury requirement. Patton reaffirmed the 12-man requirement with a simple citation to

While "the intent of the Framers" is often an elusive quarry, the relevant constitutional history casts considerable doubt on the easy assumption in our past decisions that if a given feature existed in a jury at common law in 1789, then it was necessarily preserved in the Constitution. Provisions for jury trial were first placed in the Constitution in Article III's provision that "[t]he Trial of all Crimes . . . shall be by jury; and such Trial shall be held in the State where the said Crimes shall have been committed." The "very scanty history [on this provision] in the records of the Constitutional Convention" sheds little light either way on the intended correlation between Article III's "jury" and the features of the jury at common law. . . .

[The Court here reviews in detail the unsuccessful efforts to write a Sixth Amendment explicitly calling for the "accustomed requisites" of the common law and concludes that Congress at the very least showed no interest in being specific about the matter.]

We do not pretend to be able to divine precisely what the word "jury" imported to the Framers, the First Congress, or the States in 1789. It may well be that the usual expectation was that the jury would consist of 12, and that hence, the most likely conclusion to be drawn is simply that little thought was actually given to the specific question we face today. But there is absolutely no indication in "the intent of the Framers" of an explicit decision to equate the constitutional and common law characteristics of the jury. Nothing in this history suggests, then, that we do violence to the letter of the Constitution by turning to other than purely historical considerations to determine which features of the jury system, as it existed at common law, were preserved in the Constitution. The relevant inquiry, as we see it, must be the function which the particular feature performs and its relation to the purposes of the jury trial. Measured by this standard, the 12-man requirement cannot be regarded as an indispensable component of the Sixth Amendment.

The purpose of the jury trial, as we noted in Duncan, is to prevent oppression by the Government. "Providing an accused with the right to be tried by a jury of his peers gave him an inestimable safeguard against the corrupt or overzealous prosecutor and against the compliant, biased, or eccentric judge." Duncan v. Louisiana. Given this purpose, the essential feature of a jury obviously lies in the interposition between the accused and his accuser of the common-sense judgment of a group of laymen, and in the community participation and shared responsibility which results from that group's determination of guilt or innocence. The performance of this role is not a function of the particular number of the body which makes up the jury. To be sure, the number should probably be large enough to promote group deliberation, free from outside attempts at intimidation, and to provide a fair possibility for obtaining a representative cross section of the community. But we find little reason to think that these goals are in any meaningful sense less

---

Thompson v. Utah, while at the same time discarding as "dictum" the equally dogmatic assertion in Thompson that the requirement could not be waived.

likely to be achieved when the jury numbers six, than when it numbers 12—particularly if the requirement of unanimity is retained.* And, certainly the reliability of the jury as a factfinder hardly seems likely to be a function of its size.

It might be suggested that the 12-man jury gives a defendant a greater advantage since he has more "chances" of finding a juror who will insist on acquittal and thus prevent conviction. But the advantage might just as easily belong to the State, which also needs only one juror out of twelve insisting on guilt to prevent acquittal. What few experiments have occurred—usually in the civil area—indicate that there is no discernible difference between the results reached by the two different-sized juries. In short, neither currently available evidence nor theory suggests that the 12-man jury is necessarily more advantageous to the defendant than a jury composed of fewer members.

Similarly, while in theory the number of viewpoints represented on a randomly selected jury ought to increase as the size of the jury increases, in practice the difference between the 12-man and the six-man jury in terms of the cross section of the community represented seems likely to be negligible. Even the 12-man jury cannot insure representation of every distinct voice in the community, particularly given the use of the peremptory challenge. As long as arbitrary exclusions of a particular class from the jury rolls are forbidden, . . . the concern that the cross section will be significantly diminished if the jury is decreased in size from 12 to six seems an unrealistic one.

We conclude, in short, as we began: the fact that the jury at common law was composed of precisely 12 is an historical accident, unnecessary to effect the purposes of the jury system and wholly without significance "except to mystics." . . . To read the Sixth Amendment as forever codifying a feature so incidental to the real purpose of the Amendment is to ascribe a blind formalism to the Framers which would require considerably more evidence than we have been able to discover in the history and language of the Constitution or in the reasoning of our past decisions. . . . We conclude that petitioner's Sixth Amendment rights, as applied to the States through the Fourteenth Amendment, were not violated by Florida's decision to provide a six-man rather than a 12-man jury. The judgment of the Florida District Court of Appeal is

Affirmed.

Mr. Justice **Blackmun** took no part in the consideration or decision of this case.

Mr. Chief Justice **Burger** joined the opinion of the Court and wrote a brief concurring opinion dealing with Part I.

---

*We intimate no view whether or not the requirement of unanimity is an indispensable element of the Sixth Amendment jury trial. While much of the above historical discussion applies as well to the unanimity as to the 12-man requirement, the former, unlike the latter, may well serve an important role in the jury function, for example, as a device for insuring that the Government bear the heavier burden of proof.

Mr. Justice **Harlan,** dissenting in [Baldwin v. New York], and concurring in [Williams v. Florida] said in part:

In Duncan v. Louisiana (1968), the Court held, over my dissent and that of Mr. Justice Stewart, that a state criminal defendant is entitled to a jury trial in any case which, if brought in a federal court, would require a jury under the Sixth Amendment. Today the Court holds, in Baldwin v. New York, that New York cannot constitutionally provide that misdemeanors carrying sentences up to one year shall be tried in New York City without a jury. At the same time the Court holds in Williams v. Florida that Florida's six-member jury statute satisfies the Sixth Amendment as carried to the States by the Duncan holding. The necessary consequence of this decision is that 12-member juries are not *constitutionally* required in *federal* criminal trials either.

The historical argument by which the Court undertakes to justify its view that the Sixth Amendment does not require 12-member juries is, in my opinion, much too thin to mask the true thrust of this decision. The decision evinces, I think, a recognition that the "incorporationist" view of the Due Process Clause of the Fourteenth Amendment, which underlay Duncan and is now carried forward into Baldwin, must be tempered to allow the States more elbow room in ordering their own criminal systems. With that much I agree. But to accomplish this by diluting constitutional protections within the federal system itself is something to which I cannot possibly subscribe. Tempering the rigor of Duncan should be done forthrightly, by facing up to the fact that at least in this area the "incorporation" doctrine does not fit well with our federal structure, and by the same token that Duncan was wrongly decided. . . .

Mr. Justice **Stewart,** dissenting in [Baldwin v. New York], and concurring in [Williams v. Florida], said in part:

I substantially agree with the separate opinion Mr. Justice Harlan has filed in these cases—an opinion that fully demonstrates some of the basic errors in a mechanistic "incorporation" approach to the Fourteenth Amendment. I cannot subscribe to his opinion in its entirety, however, if only for the reason that it relies in part upon certain dissenting and concurring opinions in previous cases in which I did not join. . . .

Mr. Justice **Black,** with whom Mr. Justice **Douglas** joins, concurring in part and dissenting in part, said in part:

The Court today holds that a State can, consistently with the Sixth Amendment to the United States Constitution, try a defendant in a criminal case with a jury of six members. I agree with that decision for substantially the same reasons given by the Court. . . .

Mr. Justice **Marshall,** dissenting in part, said in part:

. . . Since I believe that the Fourteenth Amendment guaranteed Williams a jury of 12 to pass upon the question of his guilt or innocence before he could be sent to prison for the rest of his life, I dissent from the affirmance of his conviction. . . .

APODACA v. OREGON

406 U. S. 404; 92 S. Ct. 1628; 32 L. Ed. 2d 184 (1972)

If, as the Court held in Williams v. Florida (1970), the old common-law jury is not the measure of the jury required by the Constitution, what kind of jury is required? Two cases decided in 1972 added a new and unexpected dimension to this problem. Both cases raised the question of non-unanimous jury verdicts, but because one was started before Duncan v. Louisiana (1968) and the other after it, the first raised only a fundamental fairness question under the due process clause while the second involved the applicability to the states of the Sixth Amendment.

In Johnson v. Louisiana (1972) the Court upheld the conviction of a man who was tried for robbery before a twelve-member jury and convicted by a nine-to-three verdict, in accordance with Louisiana law. Two years before in In re Winship (1970), a case involving the rights of juveniles to a fair trial, the Court had held explicitly "that the Due Process Clause protects the accused against conviction except upon proof beyond a reasonable doubt . . ." and the question was whether a less-than-unanimous verdict met such a standard. Justice White, joined by the recent appointees to the Court, stressed that "want of jury unanimity is not to be equated with the existence of a reasonable doubt. . . ." If this were not the case, the failure of the common-law jury required by the federal law to reach a unanimous verdict in any case would call for a directed verdict of acquittal rather than a mistrial and there would be no such thing as a hung jury. "Of course, the State's proof could perhaps be regarded as more certain if it had convinced all twelve jurors instead of only nine; it would have been more compelling if it had been required to convince and had, in fact, convinced twenty-four or thirty-six jurors. But the fact remains that nine jurors—a substantial majority of the jury—were convinced by the evidence. . . . That rational men disagree is not in itself equivalent to a failure of proof by the state, nor does it indicate infidelity to the reasonable doubt standard." Justice Blackmun joined the Court's opinion but noted that use of a seven-to-five standard rather than nine-to-three minimum would afford him "great difficulty."

Justice Stewart, joined by Justices Brennan and Marshall, pointed out in dissent that the effect of the decision was to undermine the principle that a jury had to be an indiscriminate cross-section of the community. "The clear purpose of these decisions has been to ensure universal participation of the citizenry in the administration of criminal justice. Yet today's judgment approves the elimination of the one rule that can ensure that such participation will be meaningful. . . . Under today's judgment, nine jurors can simply ignore the views of their fellow panel members of a different race or class."

When the Court decided Williams v. Florida, it expressly left unanswered the question of whether the ruling applied to federal trials under the Seventh Amendment which provides that "in suits at common law . . . the right of trial by jury shall be preserved," and the agreement of five justices in the case below that the Sixth Amendment requires a unanimous verdict in federal trials suggested that it might not. In Colegrove v. Battin (1973), with Justice Brennan switching sides and writing the opinion, the Court held on the basis of an historical argument that seems to answer the unanimity question as well, that a six-member jury met the Seventh Amendment requirement. "We can only conclude, therefore, that by referring to the 'common law,' the Framers of the Seventh Amendment were concerned with preserving the right of trial by jury in civil cases where it existed at common law, rather than the various incidents of trial by jury. In short, what was said in Williams with respect to the criminal jury is equally applicable here: constitutional history reveals no intention on the part of the Framers 'to equate the constitutional and common-law characteristics of the Jury.' " Two of the four dissenters did not reach the constitutional question, arguing only that Congress had not intended to permit federal courts to use a six-member jury.

Mr. Justice **White** announced the judgment of the Court and an opinion in which The Chief Justice [**Burger**], Mr. Justice **Blackmun,** and Mr. Justice **Rehnquist** joined, and said in part:

Robert Apodaca, Henry Morgan Cooper, Jr., and James Arnold Madden were convicted respectively of assault with a deadly weapon, burglary in a dwelling, and grand larceny before separate Oregon juries, all of which returned less than unanimous verdicts. The vote in the cases of Apodaca and Madden was 10–2, while the vote in the case of Cooper was ten to two, the minimum requisite vote under Oregon law for sustaining a conviction. After their convictions had been affirmed by the Oregon Court of Appeals and review had been denied by the Supreme Court of Oregon, all three sought review in this Court upon a claim that conviction of crime by a less than unanimous jury violates the right to trial by jury in criminal cases specified by the Sixth Amendment and made applicable to the States by the Fourteenth. See Duncan v. Louisiana (1968). We granted certiorari to consider this claim, which we now find to be without merit.

In Williams v. Florida (1970), we had occasion to consider a related issue: whether the Sixth Amendment's right to trial by jury requires that all juries consist of 12 men. After considering the history of the 12-man requirement and the functions it performs in contemporary society, we concluded that it was not of constitutional stature. We reach the same conclusion today with regard to the requirement of unanimity.

I.

Like the requirement that juries consist of 12 men, the requirement of unanimity arose during the middle ages and had become an accepted feature of the common-law jury by the 18th century. But, as we observed in Williams, "the relevant constitutional history casts considerable doubt on the easy assumption . . . that if a given feature existed in a jury at common law in 1789, then it was necessarily preserved in the Constitution." . . .

As in Williams, we must accordingly consider what is meant by the concept "jury" and determine whether a feature commonly associated with it is constitutionally required. And, as in Williams, our inability to divine "the intent of the Framers" when they eliminated references to the "accustomed requisites" requires that in determining what is meant by a jury we must turn to other than purely historical considerations.

II.

Our inquiry must focus upon the function served by the jury in contemporary society. . . . As we said in Duncan the purpose of trial by jury is to prevent oppression by the Government by providing a "safeguard against the corrupt or overzealous prosecutor and against the compliant, biased, or eccentric judge." . . . "Given this purpose, the essential feature of a jury obviously lies in the interposition between the accused and his accuser of the commonsense judgment of a group of laymen. . . ." Williams v. Florida. A requirement of unanimity, however, does not materially contribute to the exercise of this commonsense judgment. As we said in Williams, a jury will come to such a judgment as long as it consists of a group of laymen representative of a cross section of the community who have the duty and the opportunity to deliberate, free from outside attempts at intimidation, on the question of a defendant's guilt. In terms of this function we perceive no difference between juries required to act unanimously and those permitted to convict or acquit by votes of 10 to two or 11 to one. Requiring unanimity would obviously produce hung juries in some situations where nonunanimous juries will convict or acquit. But in either case, the interest of the defendant in having the judgment of his peers interposed between himself and the officers of the State who prosecute and judge him is equally well served.

III.

Petitioners nevertheless argue that unanimity serves other purposes constitutionally essential to the continued operation of the jury system. Their principal contention is that a Sixth Amendment "jury trial" made mandatory on the States by virtue of the Due Process Clause of the Fourteenth Amendment . . . should be held to require a unanimous jury verdict in order to give substance to the reasonable doubt standard otherwise mandated by the Due Process Clause. See In re Winship (1970).

We are quite sure, however, that the Sixth Amendment itself has never been held to require proof beyond a reasonable doubt in criminal cases. The reasonable doubt standard developed separately from both the jury trial and the unanimous verdict. As the Court noted in the Winship case, the rule requiring proof of crime beyond a reasonable doubt did not crystallize in this country until after the Constitution was adopted. And in that case, which held such a burden of proof to be constitutionally required, the Court purported to draw no support from the Sixth Amendment.

Petitioners' argument that the Sixth Amendment requires jury unanimity in order to give effect to the reasonable doubt standard thus founders on the fact that the Sixth Amendment does not require proof beyond a reasonable doubt at all. The reasonable doubt argument is rooted, in effect, in due process and has been rejected in Johnson v. Louisiana [1972].

IV.

Petitioners also cite quite accurately a long line of decisions of this Court upholding the principle that the Fourteenth Amendment requires jury panels to reflect a cross section of the community. . . . They then contend that unanimity is a necessary precondition for effective application of the cross section requirement, because a rule permitting less than unanimous verdicts will make it possible for convictions to occur without the acquiescence of minority elements within the community.

There are two flaws in this argument. One is petitioners' assumption that every distinct voice in the community has a right to be represented on every jury and a right to prevent conviction of a defendant in any case. All that the Constitution forbids, however, is systematic exclusion of identifiable segments of the community from jury panels and from the juries ultimately drawn from those panels; a defendant may not, for example, challenge the makeup of a jury merely because no members of his race are on the jury, but must prove that his race has been systematically excluded. . . . No group, in short, has the right to block convictions; it has only the right to participate in the overall legal processes by which criminal guilt and innocence are determined.

We also cannot accept petitioners' second assumption—that minority groups, even when they are represented on a jury, will not adequately represent the viewpoint of those groups simply because they may be outvoted in the final result. They will be present during all deliberations, and their views will be heard. We cannot assume that the majority of the jury will refuse to weigh the evidence and reach a decision upon rational grounds, just as it must now do in order to obtain unanimous verdicts, or that a majority will deprive a man of his liberty on the basis of prejudice when a minority is presenting a reasonable argument in favor of acquittal. We simply find no proof for the notion that a majority will disregard its instructions and cast its votes for guilt or innocence based on prejudice rather than the evidence.

We accordingly affirm the judgment of the Court of Appeals of Oregon.

It is so ordered.

Mr. Justice **Blackmun**, concurring, said in part:

I do not hesitate to say that a system employing a 7–5 standard, rather than a 9–3 or 75% minimum, would afford me great difficulty. As Mr. Justice White points out [in Johnson], "a substantial majority of the jury" are to be convinced. That is all that is before us in each of these cases.

Mr. Justice **Powell** concurring in the judgment said in part:

II.

. . . I concur in the plurality opinion in this case insofar as it concludes that a defendant in a state court may constitutionally be convicted by less than a unanimous verdict, but I am not in accord with a major premise upon which that judgment is based. Its premise is that the concept of jury trial, as applicable to the States under the Fourteenth Amendment, must be identical in every detail to the concept required in federal courts by the Sixth Amendment. I do not think that all of the elements of jury trial within the meaning of the Sixth Amendment are necessarily embodied in or incorporated into the Due Process Clause of the Fourteenth Amendment. As Mr. Justice Fortas, concurring in Duncan v. Louisiana said: "Neither logic nor history nor the intent of the draftsmen of the Fourteenth Amendment can possibly be said to require that the Sixth Amendment or its jury trial provision be applied to the States together with the total gloss that the Court's decisions have supplied."

In an unbroken line of cases reaching back into the late 1800's, the Justices of this Court have recognized, virtually without dissent, that unanimity is one of the indispensable features of *federal* jury trial. Andres v. United States (1948); Patton v. United States (1930); Hawaii v. Mankichi, (1903) (see also Mr. Justice Harlan's dissenting opinion); Maxwell v. Dow, (1900) (see also Mr. Justice Harlan's dissenting opinion); Thompson v. Utah, (1898). In these cases, the Court has presumed that unanimous verdicts are essential in federal jury trials, not because unanimity is necessarily fundamental to the function performed by the jury, but because that result is mandated by history.* The reasoning which revision runs throughout this Court's Sixth Amendment precedents is that, in amending the Constitution to guarantee the right to jury trial, the Framers desired to preserve the jury safeguard as it was known to them at common law. At the time the Bill of Rights was adopted, unanimity had long been established as one of the attributes of a jury conviction at common law. It therefore seems to me, in accord both with history and precedent, that the Sixth Amendment requires a unanimous jury verdict to convict in a federal criminal trial.

But it is the Fourteenth Amendment, rather than the Sixth, which imposes upon the States the requirement that they provide jury trials to those accused of serious crimes. This Court has said, in cases decided when the intendment of that Amendment was not as clouded by the passage of time, that due process does not require that the States apply the federal jury trial right with all its

gloss. In Maxwell v. Dow, Mr. Justice Peckham, speaking for eight of the nine members of the Court, so stated: "[W]hen providing in their constitution and legislation for the manner in which civil or criminal actions shall be tried, it is in entire conformity with the character of the Federal Government that [the States] should have the right to decide for themselves what shall be the form and character of the procedure in such trials, . . . whether there shall be a jury of twelve or a lesser number, and whether the verdict must be unanimous or not. . . ." Again, in Jordan v. Massachusetts (1912), the Court concluded that "[i]n criminal cases due process of law is not denied by a state law which dispenses with . . . the necessity of a jury of twelve, or unanimity in the verdict." . . .

The question, therefore, which should be addressed in this case is whether unanimity is in fact so fundamental to the essentials of jury trial that this particular requirement of the Sixth Amendment is necessarily binding on the States under the Due Process Clause of the Fourteenth Amendment. An affirmative answer, ignoring the strong views previously expressed to the contrary by this Court in Maxwell and Jordan, would give unwarranted and unwise scope to the incorporation doctrine as it applies to the due process right of state criminal defendants to trial by jury. . . .

Viewing the unanimity controversy as one requiring a fresh look at the question of what is fundamental in jury trial, I see no constitutional infirmity in the provision adopted by the people of Oregon. It is the product of a constitutional amendment, approved by a vote of the people in the State, and appears to be patterned on a provision of the American Law Institute's Code of Criminal Procedure. A similar decision has been echoed more recently in England where the unanimity requirement was abandoned by statutory enactment. Less than unanimous verdict provisions also have been viewed with approval by the American Bar Association's Criminal Justice Project. Those who have studied the jury mechanism and recommended deviation from the historic rule of unanimity have found a number of considerations to be significant. Removal of the unanimity requirement could well minimize the potential for hung juries occasioned either by bribery or juror irrationality. Furthermore, the rule that juries must speak with a single voice often leads, not to full agreement among the 12 but to agreement by none and compromise by all, despite the frequent absence of a rational basis for such compromise. Quite apart from whether Justices sitting on this Court would have deemed advisable the adoption of any particular less than unanimous jury provision, I think that considerations of this kind reflect a legitimate basis for experimentation and deviation from the federal blueprint.

Mr. Justice **Douglas**, with whom Mr. Justice **Brennan** and Mr. Justice **Marshall** concur, dissenting, said in part:

II.

The plurality approves a procedure which diminishes the reliability of jury. First, it eliminates the cir-

---

*. . . No reason, other than the conference committee's revision of the House draft of the Sixth Amendment, has been offered to justify departure from this Court's prior precedents. The admitted ambiguity of that piece of legislative history is not sufficient, in my view, to override the unambiguous history of the common law right. Williams v. Florida.

cumstances in which a minority of jurors (a) could have rationally persuaded the entire jury to acquit, or (b) while unable to persuade the majority to acquit, nonetheless could have convinced them to convict only on a lesser-included offense. Second, it permits prosecutors in Oregon and Louisiana to enjoy a conviction-acquittal ratio substantially greater than that ordinarily returned by unanimous juries.

The diminution of verdict reliability flows from the fact that nonunanimous juries need not debate and deliberate as fully as must unanimous juries. As soon as the requisite majority is attained, further consideration is not required either by Oregon or by Louisiana even though the dissident jurors might, if given the chance, be able to convince the majority. Such persuasion does in fact occasionally occur in States where the unanimous requirement applies: "In roughly one case in ten, the minority eventually succeeds in reversing an initial majority, and these may be cases of special importance."* One explanation for this phenomenon is that because jurors are often not permitted to take notes and because they have imperfect memories, the forensic process of forcing jurors to defend their conflicting recollections and conclusions flushes out many nuances which otherwise would go overlooked. This collective effort to piece together the puzzle of historical truth, however, is cut short as soon as the requisite majority is reached in Oregon and Louisiana. Indeed, if a necessary majority is immediately obtained, then no deliberation at all is required in these States. (There is a suggestion that this may have happened in the 10–2 verdict rendered in only 41 minutes in Apodaca's case.) To be sure, in jurisdictions other than these two States, initial majorities normally prevail in the end, but about a tenth of the time the rough and tumble of the juryroom operates to reverse completely their preliminary perception of guilt or innocence. The Court now extracts from the juryroom this automatic check against hasty fact-finding by relieving jurors of the duty to hear out fully the dissenters.

It is said that there is no evidence that majority jurors will refuse to listen to dissenters whose votes are unneeded for conviction. Yet human experience teaches that polite and academic conversation is no substitute for the earnest and robust argument necessary to reach unanimity. As mentioned earlier, in Apodaca's case, whatever courtesy dialogue transpired could not have lasted more than 41 minutes. I fail to understand why the Court should lift from the States the burden of justifying so radical a departure from an accepted and applauded tradition and instead demand that these defendants document with empirical evidence what has always been thought to be too obvious for further study.

To be sure in Williams v. Florida, we held that a State could provide a jury less than 12 in number in criminal trial. We said "What few experiments have occurred—usually in the civil area—indicate that there is no discernible difference between the results reached by the two different-sized juries. In short, neither currently available evidence nor theory suggests that the 12-man

---

*Kalven & Zeisel, The American Jury 490(1966). . . .

jury is necessarily more advantageous to the defendant than a jury composed of fewer members."

That rationale of Williams can have no application here. Williams requires that the change be neither more nor less advantageous to either the State or the defendant. It is said that such a showing is satisfied here since a 3:9 (Louisiana) or 2:10 (Oregon) verdict will result in acquittal. Yet experience shows that the less than unanimous jury overwhelmingly favors the States.

Moreover, even where an initial majority wins the dissent over to its side, the ultimate result in unanimous jury States may nonetheless reflect the reservations of uncertain jurors. I refer to many compromise verdicts on lesser-included offenses and lesser sentences. Thus, even though a minority may not be forceful enough to carry the day, their doubts may nonetheless cause a majority to exercise caution. Obviously, however, in Oregon and Louisiana, dissident jurors will not have the opportunity through full deliberation to temper the opposing faction's degree of certainty of guilt.

The new rule also has an impact on cases in which a unanimous jury would have neither voted to acquit nor to convict, but would have deadlocked. In unanimous jury States, this occurs about 5.6 percent of the time. Of these deadlocked juries, Kalven and Zeisel say that 56% contain either one, two, or three dissenters. In These latter cases, the majorities favor the prosecution 44% (of the 56%) but the defendant only 12% (of the 56%). Thus, by eliminating these deadlocks, Louisiana wins 44 cases for every 12 that it loses, obtaining in this band of outcomes a substantially more favorable conviction ratio (3.67) than the unanimous jury ratio of slightly less than two guilty verdicts for every acquittal. . . . By eliminating the one and two dissenting juror cases, Oregon does even better, gaining 4.25 convictions for every acquittal. While the statutes on their face deceptively appear to be neutral, the use of the nonunanimous jury stacks the truth-determining process against the accused. Thus, we take one step more away from the accusatorial system that has been our proud boast.

Mr. Justice **Brennan,** with whom Mr. Justice **Marshall** joins, dissenting, said in part:

. . . When verdicts must be unanimous, no member of the jury may be ignored by the others. When less than unanimity is sufficient, consideration of minority views may become nothing more than a matter of majority grace. In my opinion, the right of all groups in this Nation to participate in the criminal process means the right to have their voices heard. A unanimous verdict vindicates that right. Majority verdicts could destroy it.

Mr. Justice **Stewart,** with whom Mr. Justice **Brennan** and Mr. Justice **Marshall** join, dissenting, said in part:

In Duncan v. Louisiana, the court squarely held that the Sixth Amendment right to trial by jury in a federal criminal case is made wholly applicable to state criminal trials by the Fourteenth Amendment. Unless Duncan is to be overruled, therefore, the only relevant question here is whether the Sixth Amendment's guarantee of trial by jury embraces a guarantee that the verdict of the jury must be unanimous. The answer to that question is clearly "yes," as my Brother Powell has cogently demonstrated in that part of his concurring opinion that reviews almost a century of Sixth Amendment adjudication.

Until today, it has been universally understood that a unanimous verdict is an essential element of a Sixth Amendment jury trial. . . .

I would follow these settled Sixth Amendment precedents and reverse the judgment before us.

Mr. Justice **Marshall,** with whom Mr. Justice **Brennan** joins, dissenting, said in part:

Today the Court cuts the heart out of two of the most important and inseparable safeguards the Bill of Rights offers a criminal defendant: the right to submit his case to a jury, and the right to proof beyond a reasonable doubt. Together, these safeguards occupy a fundamental place in our constitutional scheme, protecting the individual defendant from the awesome power of the State. After today, the skeleton of these safeguards remains, but the Court strips them of life and of meaning. I cannot refrain from adding my protest to that of my Brothers Douglas, Brennan, and Stewart, whom I join.

In Apodaca v. Oregon, the question is too frighteningly simple to bear much discussion. We are asked to decide what is the nature of the "jury" that is guaranteed by the Sixth Amendment. I would have thought that history provided the appropriate guide, and as Mr. Justice Powell has demonstrated so convincingly, history compels the decision that unanimity is an essential feature of that jury. But the majority has embarked on a "functional" analysis of the jury that allows it to strip away, one by one, virtually all the characteristic features of the jury as we know it. Two years ago, over my dissent, the Court discarded as an essential feature the traditional size of the jury. Williams v. Florida (1970). Today the Court discards, at least in state trials, the traditional requirement of unanimity. It seems utterly and ominously clear that so long as the tribunal bears the label "jury," it will meet Sixth Amendment requirements as they are presently viewed by this Court. The Court seems to require only that jurors be laymen, drawn from the community without systematic exclusion of any group, who exercise common sense judgment.

More distressing still than the Court's treatment of the right to jury trial is the cavalier treatment the Court gives to proof beyond a reasonable doubt. The Court asserts that when a jury votes nine to three for conviction, the doubts of the three do not impeach the verdict of the nine. The argument seems to be that since, under Williams, nine jurors are enough to convict, the three dissenters are mere surplusage. But there is all the difference in the world between three jurors who aren't there, and three jurors who entertain doubts after hearing all the evidence. In the first case we can never know, and it is senseless to ask, whether the prosecutor might have persuaded additional jurors had they been present. But in the second case we know what has happened: the prosecutor has tried and failed to persuade those jurors of the

defendant's guilt. In such circumstances, it does violence to language and to logic to say that the government has proved the defendant's guilt beyond a reasonable doubt.

It is said that this argument is fallacious because a deadlocked jury does not, under our law, bring about an acquittal or bar a retrial. The argument seems to be that if the doubt of a dissenting juror were the "reasonable doubt" that constitutionally bars conviction, then it would necessarily result in an acquittal and bar retrial. But that argument rests on a complete non sequitur. The reasonable doubt rule, properly viewed, simply establishes that, as a prerequisite to obtaining a valid conviction, the prosecutor must overcome all of the jury's reasonable doubts; it does not, of itself, determine what shall happen if he fails to do so. That is a question to be answered with reference to a wholly different constitutional provision, the Fifth Amendment ban on double jeopardy, made applicable to the States through the Due Process Clause of the Fourteenth Amendment in Benton v. Maryland (1969).

Under prevailing notions of double jeopardy, if a jury has tried and failed to reach a unanimous verdict, a new trial may be held. United States v. Perez (1824). The State is free, consistent with the ban on double jeopardy, to treat the verdict of a nonunanimous jury as a nullity rather than as an acquittal. On retrial, the prosecutor may be given the opportunity to make a stronger case if he can: new evidence may be available, old evidence may have disappeared, and even the same evidence may appear in a different light if, for example, the demeanor of witnesses is different. Because the second trial may vary substantially from the first, the doubts of the dissenting jurors at the first trial do not necessarily impeach the verdict of a new jury on retrial. But that conclusion is wholly consistent with the view that the doubts of dissenting jurors create a constitutional bar to conviction at the trial which produced those doubts. Until today, I had thought that was the law.

THE BARGAINING AWAY OF CONSTITUTIONAL RIGHTS

WYMAN v. JAMES

400 U. S. 309; 91 S. Ct. 381; 27 L. Ed. 2d 408 (1971)

When Justice Holmes was still serving on the Supreme Judicial Court of Massachusetts he said, in the course of upholding the dismissal of a policeman for political activities, he "may have a constitutional right to talk politics, but he has no constitutional right to be a policeman"; McAuliffe v. Mayor of New Bedford, 155 Mass. 216 (1892). While the matter would not be handled in this offhand manner today, the problem is symbolic of a relationship between the public and the government that because of its nature bears careful and constant scrutiny. On the one hand stands an individual with certain guaranteed rights against the powers of government; on the other stands that government with almost unlimited resources with which to buy those rights from the individual. What is to prevent a state offering to educate its children free and feed them a free lunch on condition that the child's parents, should they be accused under the criminal law, agree to waive their right to a court trial and accept the decision of the prosecuting attorney as to guilt and appropriate punishment? The parents are free to reject the offer if they are prepared to pay the expenses of educating their children. They are not coerced out of their rights, they are merely tempted out of them. Given the enormous variety of rights and benefits involved, it is scarcely surprising that the courts have not come up with a single rule for all cases.

In an earlier period the courts eased the problem somewhat by drawing a distinction between "rights" and "privileges." Privileges, since they were a gift of the state, could be withdrawn at will, while rights could only be withdrawn for cause and after a full hearing to see that such cause existed. Historically, a license to operate a pool hall or a saloon was granted as a privilege and could be revoked summarily, while the license to practice law or medicine was a right which could only be revoked for cause and after notice and hearing. The courts, over time, have blunted this distinction and now nearly any advantage offered by statute is held by those eligible as a matter of right.

Although, as W. S. Gilbert put it, there are times when a "policeman's lot is not a happy one" he or she does not have to forfeit political rights, including the right to express the hope the President may be assassinated, in order to hold his or her his job; see Rankin v. McPherson (1987). On the other hand, an assistant district attorney is not free to circulate a critical questionnaire within the office raising questions of office procedure which are not matters of public concern; see Connick v. Myers (1983).

The Supreme Court early recognized the dangers latent in the exaction of "unconstitutional conditions" and in Terral v. Burke Construction Co. (1922) held void a state law that required any out-of-state corporation, as a condition of doing business in the state, to waive its right to sue in the federal courts. And in Frost v. Railroad Commission (1926) it struck down as unconstitutional a stipulation that all truckers, as a condition of using the highways of the state, convert themselves into common carriers for hire. In both cases the conditions were being used to favor one economic group over another.

The area in which the Court has been the most unyielding in this matter is where the person applying for state benefits is asked to forfeit some First Amendment right. In Speiser v. Randall (1958) and First Unitarian Church v. Los Angeles (1958) the Court struck down California laws denying tax exemption to anyone who refused to take a loyalty oath so structured as to place on them the burden of proving their innocence, and in Sherbert v. Verner (1936) it held bad a rule whereby unemployment compensation was withheld from a woman who would not accept "suitable employment" involving Saturday work in violation of her religious beliefs.

As the quotation from Justice Holmes would suggest, the group most vulnerable to the temptation to accept unconstitutional conditions is that of public servants, especially security forces, and it is from this group that the legislature is most apt to exact such conditions as the price of employment. During the Cold War era of the 1950s states and municipalities began demanding loyalty oaths of their employees, especially teachers. The Court struggled with the problem in a substantial group of cases, but the general result was that the employee's right to protest was protected while the right to try to overthrow the government by force and violence was forbidden. See Cole v. Richardson (1972). Nor has the Court permitted the state to require of a police officer as a condition of employment a waiver of the right against self-incrimination; see Garrity v. New Jersey (1967) and Gardner v. Broderick (1968). The Court did say in the latter case, however, that while the officer could not be deprived of immunity from prosecution, if the testimony he or she gave justified dismissal the officer could be dismissed.

The present case involves another group that is peculiarly susceptible to the temptation to waive their right, and that is the group that receives public assistance in one form or another. It is an enormous group, ranging from cotton farmers and airlines to all recipients of Social Security benefits. With the exception of the situation below, the government has refrained from demanding as a price of these benefits the waiver of constitutional rights.

Mr. Justice **Blackmun** delivered the opinion of the Court, saying in part:

III

When a case involves a home and some type of official intrusion into that home, as this case appears to do, an immediate and natural reaction is one of concern about Fourth Amendment rights and the protection which that Amendment is intended to afford. Its emphasis indeed is upon one of the most precious aspects of personal security in the home. "The right of the people to be secure in their persons, houses, papers, and effects. . . ." This Court has characterized that right as "basic to our free society." Wolf v. Colorado (1949); Camara v. Municipal Court (1967). And over the years the Court consistently has been most protective of the privacy of the dwelling. See, for example, Boyd v. United States (1886); Mapp v. Ohio (1961). . . . In Camara Mr. Justice White, after noting that the "translation of the abstract prohibition against 'unreasonable searches and seizures' into workable guidelines for the decision of particular cases is a difficult task," went on to observe, "Nevertheless, one governing principle, justified by history and by current experience, has consistently been followed: except in certain carefully defined classes of cases, a search of private property without proper consent is 'unreasonable' unless it has been authorized by a valid search warrant." He pointed out, too, that one's

Fourth Amendment protection subsists apart from his being suspected of criminal behavior.

IV.

This natural and quite proper protective attitude, however, is not a factor in this case, for the seemingly obvious and simple reason that we are not concerned here with any search by the New York social service agency in the Fourth Amendment meaning of that term. It is true that the governing statute and regulations appear to make mandatory the initial home visit and the subsequent periodic "contacts" (which may include home visits) for the inception and continuance of aid. It is also true that the caseworker's posture in the home visit is perhaps, in a sense, both rehabilitative and investigative. But this latter aspect, we think, is given too broad a character and far more emphasis than it deserves if it is equated with a search in the traditional criminal law context. We note, too, that the visitation in itself is not forced or compelled, and that the beneficiary's denial of permission is not a criminal act. If consent to the visitation is withheld, no visitation takes place. The aid then never begins or merely ceases, as the case may be. There is no entry of the home and there is no search.

V.

If however, we were to assume that a caseworker's home visit, before or subsequent to the beneficiary's initial qualification for benefits, somehow (perhaps because the average beneficiary might feel she is in no position to refuse consent to the visit), and despite its interview nature, does possess some of the characteristics of a search in the traditional sense, we nevertheless conclude that the visit not fall within the Fourth Amendment's proscription. This is because it does not descend to the level of unreasonableness. It is unreasonableness which is the Fourth Amendment's standard. Terry v. Ohio (1968). . . .

There are a number of factors which compel us to conclude that the home visit proposed for Mrs. James is not unreasonable:

1. The public's interest in this particular segment of the area of assistance to the unfortunate is protection and aid for the dependent child whose family requires such aid for that child. The focus is on the *child* and, further, it is on the child who is *dependent*. There is no more worthy object of the public's concern. The dependent child's needs are paramount, and only with hesitancy would we relegate those needs, in the scale of comparative values, to a position secondary to what the mother claims as her rights.

2. The agency, with tax funds provided from federal as well as from state sources, is fulfilling a public trust. The State, working through its qualified welfare agency, has appropriate and paramount interest and concern in seeing and assuring that the intended and proper objects of that tax-produced assistance are the ones who benefit from the aid it dispenses. Surely it is not unreasonable, in the Fourth Amendment sense or in any other

sense of that term, that the State have at its command a gentle means, of limited extent and of practical and considerate application, of achieving that assurance.

3. One who dispenses purely private charity naturally has an interest in and expects to know how his charitable funds are utilized and put to work. The public, when it is the provider, rightly expects the same. It might well expect more, because of the trust aspect of public funds, and the recipient, as well as the caseworker, has not only an interest but an obligation.

4. The emphasis of the New York statutes and regulations is upon the home, upon "close (contact)" with the beneficiary, upon restoring the aid recipient "to a condition of self-support," and upon the relief of his distress. The federal emphasis is no different. . . . And it is concerned about any possible exploitation of the child. . . .

7. Mrs. James, in fact, on this record presents no specific complaint of any unreasonable intrusion of her home and nothing which supports an inference that the desired home visit had as its purpose the obtaining of information as to criminal activity. She complains of no proposed visitation at an awkward or retirement hour. She suggests no forcible entry. She refers to no snooping. She describes no impolite or reprehensible conduct of any kind. She alleges only, in general and nonspecific terms, that on previous visits and, on information and belief, on visitation at the home of other aid recipients, "questions concerning personal relationships, beliefs and behavior are raised and pressed which are unnecessary for a determination of continuing eligibility." Paradoxically, this same complaint could be made of a conference held elsewhere than in the home, and yet this is what is sought by Mrs. James. The same complaint could be made of the census taker's questions. . . . What Mrs. James appears to want from the agency which provides her and her infant son with the necessities for life is the right to receive those necessities upon her own informational terms, to utilize the Fourth Amendment as a wedge for imposing those terms and to avoid questions of any kind.*

8. We are not persuaded, as Mrs. James would have us be, that all information pertinent to the issue of eligibility can be obtained by the agency through an interview at a place other than the home, or, as the District Court majority suggested, by examining a lease or a birth certificate, or by periodic medical examinations, or by interviews with school personnel. Although these secondary sources might be helpful, they would not always assure verification of actual residence or of actual physi-

---

*We have examined Mrs. James' case record with the New York City Department of Social Services, which, as an exhibit, accompanied defendant Wyman's answer. It discloses numerous interviews from the time of the initial one on April 27, 1967, until the attempted closing in June 1969. The record is revealing as to Mrs. James' failure ever really to satisfy the requirements for eligibility; as to constant and repeated demands; as to attitude toward the caseworker; as to reluctance to cooperate; as to evasiveness; and as to occasional belligerency. There are indications that all was not always well with the infant Maurice (skull fracture, a dent in the head, a possible rat bite). The picture is a sad and unhappy one.

cal presence in the home, which are requisites for AFDC benefits, or of impending medical needs. And, of course, little children, such as Maurice James, are not yet registered in school.

9. The visit is not one by police or uniformed authority. It is made by a caseworker of some training* whose primary objective is, or should be, the welfare, not the prosecution, of the aid recipient for whom the worker has profound responsibility. As has already been stressed, the program concerns dependent children and the needy families of those children. It does not deal with crime or with the actual or suspected perpetrators of crime. The caseworker is not a sleuth but rather, we trust, is a friend in need.

10. The home visit is not a criminal investigation, does not equate with a criminal investigation, and despite the announced fears of Mrs. James and those who would join her, is not in aid of any criminal proceeding. If the visitation serves to discourage misrepresentation or fraud, such a byproduct of that visit does not impress upon the visit itself a dominant criminal investigative aspect. And if the visit should, by chance, lead to the discovery of fraud and a criminal prosecution should follow, then, even assuming that the evidence discovered upon the home visitation is admissible, an issue upon which we express no opinion, that is a routine and expected fact of life and a consequence no greater than that which necessarily ensues upon any other discovery by a citizen of criminal conduct. . . .

It seems to us that the situation is akin to that where an Internal Revenue Service agent, in making a routine civil audit of a taxpayer's income tax return, asks that the taxpayer produce for the agent's review some proof of a deduction the taxpayer has asserted to his benefit in the computation of his tax. If the taxpayer refuses, there is, absent fraud, only a disallowance of the claimed deduction and a consequent additional tax. The taxpayer is fully within his "rights" in refusing to produce the proof, but in maintaining and asserting those rights a tax detriment results and it is a detriment of the taxpayer's own making. So here Mrs. James has the "right" to refuse the home visit, but a consequence in the form of cessation of aid, similar to the taxpayer's resultant additional tax, flows from that refusal. The choice is entirely hers, and nothing of constitutional magnitude is involved.

VI.

Camara v. Municipal Court (1967) and its companion case, See v. City of Seattle (1967), both by a di-

---

*The amicus brief submitted on behalf of the Social Services Employees Union Local 371, AFSCME, AFL–CIO, the bargaining representative for the social service staff employed in the New York City Department of Social Services, recites that "caseworkers are either badly trained or untrained" and that "[g]enerally, a caseworker is not only poorly trained, but also young and inexperienced. . . ." Despite this astonishing description by the union of the lack of qualification of its own members for the work they are employed to do, we must assume that the caseworker possesses at least some qualifications and some dedication to duty.

vided Court, are not inconsistent with our result here. Those cases concerned, respectively, a refusal of entry to city housing inspectors checking for a violation of a building's occupancy permit, and a refusal of entry to a fire department representative interested in compliance with a city's fire code. In each case a majority of this Court held that the Fourth Amendment barred prosecution for refusal to permit the desired warrantless inspection. Frank v. Maryland (1959), a case which reached an opposing result and which concerned a request by a health officer for entry in order to check the source of a rat infestation, was pro tanto overruled. Both Frank and Camara involved dwelling quarters. See had to do with a commercial warehouse.

But the facts of the three cases are significantly different from those before us. Each concerned a true search for violations. Frank was a criminal prosecution for the owner's refusal to permit entry. So, too, was See. Camara had to do with a writ of prohibition sought to prevent an already pending criminal prosecution. The community welfare aspects, of course, were highly important, but each case arose in a criminal context where a genuine search was denied and prosecution followed.

In contrast, Mrs. James is not being prosecuted for her refusal to permit the home visit and is not about to be so prosecuted. Her wishes in that respect are fully honored. We have not been told, and have not found, that her refusal is made a criminal act by any applicable New York or federal statute. The only consequence of her refusal is that the payment of benefits ceases. Important and serious as this is, the situation is no different than if she had exercised a similar negative choice initially and refrained from applying for AFDC benefits. If a statute made her refusal a criminal offense, and if this case were one concerning her prosecution under that statute, Camara and See would have conceivable pertinency. . . .

Mr. Justice **White** concurs in the judgment and joins the opinion of the Court with the exception of Part IV thereof.

Mr. Justice **Douglas,** dissenting, said in part:

In 1969 roughly 126 billion dollars were spent by the federal, state, and local governments on "social welfare." To farmers alone, over four billion dollars was paid, in part for not growing certain crops. Almost 129,000 farmers received $5,000 or more, their total benefit exceeding $1,450,000,000. Those payments were in some instances very large, a few running a million or more a year. But the majority were payments under $5,000 each.

Yet almost every beneficiary whether rich or poor, rural or urban, has a "house"—one of the places protected by the Fourth Amendment against "unreasonable searches and seizures." The question in this case is whether receipt of largesse from the government makes the *home* of the beneficiary subject to access by an inspector of the agency of oversight, even though the beneficiary objects to the intrusion and even though the

Fourth Amendment's procedure for access to one's *house* or *home* is not followed. The penalty here is not, of course, invasion of the privacy of Barbara James, only her loss of federal or state largesse. That, however, is merely rephrasing the problem. Whatever the semantics, the central question is whether the government by force of its largesse has the power to "buy up" rights guaranteed by the Constitution. But for the assertion of her constitution right, Barbara James in this case would have received the welfare benefit.

[Justice Douglas here discusses Speiser v. Randall (1958), Hannegan v. Esquire (1946) and Sherbert v. Verner (1963), in which state benefits were conditioned on the forfeiture of First Amendment rights.]

These cases are in the tradition of United States v. Chicago M. St. P. & PR Co. [1931], where Mr. Justice Sutherland, writing for the Court said: " . . . the rule is that the right to continue the exercise of a privilege granted by the state cannot be made to depend upon the grantee's submission to a condition prescribed by the state which is hostile to the provisions of the federal Constitution."

What we said in those cases is as applicable to Fourth Amendment rights as to those of the First. The Fourth, of course, speaks of "unreasonable" searches and seizures, while the First is written in absolute terms. But the right of privacy which the Fourth protects is perhaps as vivid in our lives as the right of expression sponsored by the First. Griswold v. Connecticut [1965]. If the regime under which Barbara James lives were enterprise capitalism as, for example, if she ran a small factory geared into the Pentagon's procurement program, she certainly would have a right to deny inspectors access to her *home* unless they came with a warrant. . . .

. . . It is a strange jurisprudence indeed which safeguards the businessman at his place of work from warrantless searches but will not do the same for a mother in her *home*.

Is a search of her home without a warrant made "reasonable" merely because she is dependent on government largesse? . . .

If the welfare recipient was not Barbara James but a prominent, affluent cotton or wheat farmer receiving benefit payments for not growing crops, would not the approach be different? Welfare in aid of dependent children, like social security and unemployment benefits, has an aura of suspicion. There doubtless are frauds in every sector of public welfare whether the recipient be a Barbara James or someone who is prominent or influential. But constitutional rights—here the privacy of the *home*—are obviously not dependent on the poverty or on the affluence of the beneficiary. It is the precincts of the *home* that the Fourth Amendment protects; and their privacy is as important to the lowly as to the mighty. . . .

I would place the same restrictions on inspectors entering the *homes* of welfare beneficiaries as are on inspectors entering the *homes* of those on the payroll of government, or the *homes* of those who contract with the government, or the *homes* of those who work for those having government contracts. . . .

Mr. Justice **Marshall,** whom Mr. Justice **Brennan** joins, dissenting, said in part:

Although I substantially agree with its initial statement of the issue in this case, the Court's opinion goes on to imply that the appellee has refused to provide information germane to a determination of her eligibility for AFDC benefits. The record plainly shows, however, that Mrs. James offered to furnish any information that the appellants desired and to be interviewed at any place other than her home. Appellants rejected her offers and terminated her benefits solely on the ground that she refused to permit a home visit. In addition, appellants make no contention that any sort of probable cause exists to suspect appellee of welfare fraud or child abuse.

Simply stated, the issue in this case is whether a state welfare agency can require all recipients of AFDC benefits to submit to warrantless "visitations" of their homes. In answering that question, the majority dodges between constitutional issues to reach a result clearly inconsistent with the decisions of this Court. We are told that there is no search involved in this case; that even if there were a search, it would not be unreasonable; and that even if this were an unreasonable search, a welfare recipient waives her right to object by accepting benefits. I emphatically disagree with all three conclusions. Furthermore, I believe that binding regulations of the Department of Health, Education, and Welfare prohibit appellants from requiring the home visit.

I.

The Court's assertion that this case concerns no search "in the Fourth Amendment meaning of the term" is neither "obvious" nor "simple." I should have thought that the Fourth Amendment governs all intrusions by agents of the public upon personal security, Terry v. Ohio (1968). . . .

Even if the Fourth Amendment does not apply to each and every governmental entry into the home, the welfare visit is not some sort of purely benevolent inspection. No one questions the motives of the dedicated welfare caseworker. Of course, caseworkers seek to be friends, but the point is that they are also required to be sleuths. The majority concedes that the "visitation" is partially investigative, but claims that this investigative aspect has been given "too much emphasis." Emphasis has indeed been given. Time and again, in briefs and at oral argument, appellants emphasized the need to enter AFDC homes to guard against welfare fraud and child abuse, both of which are felonies. The New York statutes provide emphasis by requiring all caseworkers to report any evidence of fraud which a home visit uncovers. . . . And appellants have strenuously emphasized the importance of the visit to provide evidence leading to civil forfeitures including elimination of benefits and loss of child custody.

Actually, the home visit is precisely the type of inspection proscribed by Camara and its companion case, See v. City of Seattle (1967), except that the welfare visit is a more severe intrusion upon privacy and family dignity. . . .

The Court attempts to distinguish See and Camara by telling us that those cases involved "true" and "genuine" searches. The only concrete distinction offered is that See and Camara concerned criminal prosecutions for refusal to permit the search. The Camara opinion did observe that one could be prosecuted for a refusal to allow that search; but, apart from the issue of consent, there is neither logic in, nor precedent for, the view that the ambit of the Fourth Amendment depends not on the character of the governmental intrusion but on the size of the club that the State wields against a resisting citizen. Even if the magnitude of the penalty were relevant, which sanction for resisting the search is more severe? For protecting the privacy of her home, Mrs. James lost the sole means of support for herself and her infant son. For protecting the privacy of his commercial warehouse, Mr. See received a $100 suspended fine.

Conceding for the sake of argument that someone might view the "visitation" as a search, the majority nonetheless concludes that such a search is not unreasonable. However, their mode of reaching that conclusion departs from the entire history of Fourth Amendment case law. Of course, the Fourth Amendment test is reasonableness, but in determining whether a search is reasonable, this Court is not free merely to balance, in a totally ad hoc fashion, any number of subjective factors. An unbroken line of cases holds that, subject to a few narrowly drawn exceptions, any search without a warrant is constitutionally unreasonable. . . . In this case, no suggestion that evidence will disappear, that a criminal will escape, or that an officer will be injured, justifies the failure to obtain a warrant. Instead, the majority asserts what amounts to three state interests which allegedly render this search reasonable. None of these interests is sufficient to carve out a new exception to the warrant requirement.

First, it is argued that the home visit is justified to protect dependent children from "abuse" and "exploitation." These are heinous crimes, but they are not confined to indigent households. Would the majority sanction, in the absence of probable cause, compulsory visits to all American homes for the purpose of discovering child abuse? Or is this Court prepared to hold as a matter of constitutional law that a mother, merely because she is poor, is substantially more likely to injure or exploit her children? Such a categorical approach to an entire class of citizens would be dangerously at odds with the tenets of our democracy.

Second, the Court contends that caseworkers must enter the homes of AFDC beneficiaries to determine eligibility. Interestingly, federal regulations do not require the home visit. In fact, the regulations specify the recipient himself as the primary source of eligibility information thereby rendering an inspection of the home only one of several alternative secondary sources. The majority's implication that a biannual home visit somehow assures the verification of actual residence or actual physical presence in the home strains credulity in the context of urban poverty. Despite the caseworker's responsibility for dependent children, he is not even required to see the children as a part of the home visit. Appellants offer scant explanation for their refusal even to attempt to utilize public records, expenditure receipts, documents such as leases, non-home interviews, personal financial records, sworn declarations, etc.—all sources which governmental agencies regularly accept as adequate to establish eligibility for other public benefits. In this setting, it ill behooves appellants to refuse to utilize informational sources less drastic than an invasion of the privacy of the home.

We are told that the plight of Mrs. James is no different from that of a taxpayer who is required to document his right to a tax deduction, but this analogy is seriously flawed. The record shows that Mrs. James has offered to be interviewed anywhere other than her home, to answer any questions and to provide any documentation which the welfare agency desires. The agency curtly refused all these offers and insisted on its "right" to pry into appellee's home. Tax exemptions are also governmental "bounty." A true analogy would be an Internal Revenue Service requirement that in order to claim a dependency exemption, a taxpayer *must* allow a specially trained IRS agent to invade the home for the purpose of questioning the occupants and looking for evidence that the exemption is being properly utilized for the benefit of the dependent. If such a system were even proposed, the cries of constitutional outrage would be unanimous.

Appellants offer a third state interest which the Court seems to accept as partial justification for this search. We are told that the visit is designed to rehabilitate, to provide aid. This is strange doctrine indeed. A paternalistic notion that a complaining citizen's constitutional rights can be violated so long as the State is somehow helping him is alien to our Nation's philosophy. More than 40 years ago, Mr. Justice Brandeis warned: ". . . experience should teach us to be most on our guard to protect liberty when the government's purposes are beneficent." Olmstead v. United States (1928) (dissenting opinion). . . .

Although the Court does not agree with my conclusion that the home visit is an unreasonable search, its opinion suggests that even if the visit were unreasonable, appellee has somehow waived her right to object. Surely the majority cannot believe that valid Fourth Amendment consent can be given under the threat of the loss of one's sole means of support. Nor has Mrs. James waived her rights. Had the Court squarely faced the question of whether the State can condition welfare payments on the waiver of clear constitutional rights, the answer would be plain. The decisions of this Court do not support the notion that a State can use welfare benefits as a wedge to coerce "waiver" of Fourth Amendment rights. . . . In Sherbert v. Verner this Court did not say, "Aid merely ceases. There is no abridgement of religious freedom." Nor did the Court say in Speiser v. Randall, "The tax is simply increased. No one is compelled to relinquish First Amendment rights." As my Brother Douglas points out, the majority's statement that Mrs. James' "choice (to be searched or to lose her benefits) is entirely hers and nothing of constitutional magnitude is involved" merely restates the issue. To Mr. Justice Douglas' eloquent discussion of the law of unconstitutional conditions, I would add only that this Court last Term reaffirmed Sherbert and Speiser as applicable to the law of public welfare:

"Relevant constitutional restraints apply as much to the withdrawal of public assistance benefits as to the disqualification for unemployment compensation . . . denial of tax exemptions . . . or discharge from public employment." Goldberg v. Kelly (1970).

BORDENKIRCHER v. HAYES

434 U. S. 357; 98 S.Ct. 663; 54 L. Ed.2d 604
(1978)

In a simpler era when communities were less congested and the crime rate lower, it was expected that someone charged with crime would be duly examined before a magistrate, held for a grand jury if the crime were serious enough, and if the grand jury returned an indictment he or she would be tried by a court. Now, with the crime rate soaring and the number of judges dwindling, another technique has developed to take the place of the criminal trial. This is the negotiated guilty plea, or "plea bargain." The exact routine varies, but in essence an accused person is presented by the prosecuting attorney with the evidence against him or her, told what the sentence might be if he or she went to trial and were found guilty, and given the option of pleading guilty to a lesser offense carrying a smaller sentence. While a prosecutor is not authorized by law to guarantee what sentence will result from this guilty plea, in practice criminal judges, recognizing that the system is vital to the efficient operation of their court, accept the prosecutor's recommendation. In 1964, of the criminal convictions recorded in New York and California, 95.5 percent in the first and 74 percent in the second were the result of guilty pleas. It is safe to assume that these percentages have not diminished in the intervening years.

The plea bargain has much to offer both parties. It saves the state enormous sums in trial costs, saves the prosecutor from having to present his case and saves the time involved in empaneling a jury and trying the case. The defendant is given a chance to serve a far lighter sentence than might otherwise be the case and he or she can get about the business of serving the sentence without having to languish in jail for an extended period waiting for the case to come to trial.

The drawbacks to the system are less obvious and their implications less well-understood. However it is viewed, the accused person is clearly bargaining away the right to a court trial. If he or she is really getting a bargain, then the public, which has an interest in having criminals punished according to their deserts, is being cheated. If, on the other hand, the accused is not guilty of any crime, but the crime for which the prosecutor threatens to prosecute him or her carries an intolerable sentence, the person accused dares not take the chance on acquittal and is thus pressured into jail even though innocent. A simple example is a case of mistaken identity where an entirely innocent person is identified as a murderer by several witnesses. The accused is offered a bargain of a maximum of thirty years for a lesser degree of homicide if he or she pleads guilty, or a possible death sentence if he or she goes to trial and is convicted. In some measure the voluntariness of the guilty plea, which is an essential ingredient of the plea, has been cast in doubt. Clearly the system of justice has been fundamentally altered.

In Santabello v. New York (1971) the Supreme Court gave its first official approval to the practice of plea bargaining, at the same time laying down the rule that the prosecution had to live up to its side of the bargain. Here the defendant, with the aid of his attorney, worked out a plea which was accepted by the judge. A date was set for sentencing but when, after a delay of two months, the moment came for sentencing a different judge and different prosecutor were in the courtroom and there was no record of the original bargain. The Court scolded the New York City attorney's office for its inadequate communications and record keeping and remanded the case to the New York court.

Mr. Justice **Stewart** delivered the opinion of the Court, saying in part:

The question in this case is whether the Due Process Clause of the Fourteenth Amendment is violated when a state prosecutor carries out a threat made during plea negotiations to reindict the accused on more serious charges if he does not plead guilty to the offense with which he was originally charged.

I.

. . . Paul Lewis Hayes was indicted by a Fayette County, Ky., grand jury on a charge of uttering a forged instrument in the amount of $88.30, an offense then punishable by a term of 2 to 10 years in prison. After arraignment, Hayes, his retained counsel, and the Commonwealth's Attorney met in the presence of the Clerk of the Court to discuss a possible plea agreement. During these conferences the prosecutor offered to recommend a sentence of five years in prison if Hayes would plead guilty to the indictment. He also said that if Hayes did not plead guilty and "save the court the inconvenience and necessity of a trial," he would return to the grand jury to seek an indictment under the Kentucky Habitual Criminal Act,* which would subject Hayes to a mandatory sentence of life imprisonment by reason of his two

---

*While cross-examining Hayes during the subsequent trial proceedings the prosecutor described the plea offer in the following language: "Isn't it a fact that I told you at that time [the initial bargaining session] if you did not intend to plead guilty to five years for this charge and . . . save the court the inconvenience and necessity of a trial and taking up this time that I intended to return to the grand jury and ask them to indict you based upon these prior felony convictions?"

prior felony convictions. Hayes chose not to plead guilty, and the prosecutor did obtain an indictment charging him under the Habitual Criminal Act. It is not disputed that the recidivist charge was fully justified by the evidence, that the prosecutor was in possession of this evidence at the time of the original indictment, and that Hayes' refusal to plead guilty to the original charge was what led to his indictment under the habitual criminal statute.

A jury found Hayes guilty on the principal charge of uttering a forged instrument, and, in a separate proceeding, further found that he had twice before been convicted of felonies. As required by the habitual offender statute, he was sentenced to a life term in the penitentiary. . . .

II.

It may be helpful to clarify at the outset the nature of the issue in this case. While the prosecutor did not actually obtain the recidivist indictment until after the plea conferences had ended, his intention to do so was clearly expressed at the outset of the plea negotiations. Hayes was thus fully informed of the true terms of the offer when he made his decision to plead not guilty. This is not a situation, therefore, where the prosecutor brought an additional and more serious charge after plea negotiations relating only to the original indictment had ended with the defendant's insistence on pleading not guilty. As a practical matter, in short, this case would be no different if the grand jury had indicted Hayes as a recidivist from the outset, and the prosecutor had offered to drop that charge as part of the plea bargain.

The Court of Appeals nonetheless drew a distinction between "concessions relating to prosecution under an existing indictment," and threats to bring more severe charges not contained in the original indictment—a line it thought necessary in order to establish a prophylactic rule to guard against the evil of prosecutorial vindictiveness.* Quite apart from this chronological distinction, however, the Court of Appeals found that the prosecutor had acted vindictively in the present case since he had conceded that the indictment was influenced by his desire to induce a guilty plea.† The ultimate conclusion of the Court of Appeals thus seems to have been that a prosecutor acts vindictively and in violation of due process of law whenever his charging decision is influenced by what he hopes to gain in the course of plea bargaining negotiations.

---

*"Although a prosecutor may in the course of plea negotiations offer a defendant concessions relating to prosecution under an existing indictment . . . he may not threaten a defendant with the consequence that more severe charges may be brought if he insists on going to trial. When a prosecutor obtains an indictment less severe than the facts known to him at the time might permit, he makes a discretionary determination that the interests of the state are served by not seeking more serious charges. . . . Accordingly, if after plea negotiations fail, he then procures an indictment charging a more serious crime, a strong inference is created that the only reason for the more serious charge is vindictiveness. Under these circumstances, the prosecutor should be required to justify his action."

†"In this case, a vindictive motive need not be inferred. The prosecutor has admitted it."

III.

We have recently had occasion to observe that "[w]hatever might be the situation in an ideal world, the fact is that the guilty plea and the often concomitant plea bargain are important components of this country's criminal justice system. Properly administered, they can benefit all concerned. . . . The open acknowledgement of this previously clandestine practice has led this Court to recognize the importance of counsel during plea negotiations, . . . the need for a public record indicating that a plea was knowingly and voluntarily made, . . . and the requirement that a prosecutor's plea bargaining promise must be kept. . . . The decision of the Court of appeals in the present case, however, did not deal with considerations such as these, but held that the substance of the plea offer itself violated the limitations imposed by the Due Process Cause of the Fourteenth Amendment. For these reasons, we have concluded that the Court of Appeals was mistaken in so ruling.

IV.

This Court held in North Carolina v. Pearce [1969], that the Due Process Clause of the Fourteenth Amendment "requires that vindictiveness against a defendant for having successfully attacked his first conviction must play no part in the sentence he receives after a new trial." The same principle was later applied to prohibit a prosecutor from reindicting a convicted misdemeanant on a felony charge after the defendant had invoked an appellate remedy, since in this situation there was also a "realistic likelihood of 'vindictiveness.' " Blackledge v. Perry [1974].

In those cases, the Court was dealing with the State's unilateral imposition of a penalty upon a defendant who had chosen to exercise a legal right to attack his original conviction—a situation "very different from the give-and-take negotiation common in plea bargaining between the prosecution and defense, which arguably possess relatively equal bargaining power." . . . The Court has emphasized that the due process violation in cases such as Pearce and Perry lay not in the possibility that a defendant might be deterred from the exercise of a legal right . . . but rather in the danger that the State might be retaliating against the accused for lawfully attacking his conviction. . . .

To punish a person because he has done what the law plainly allows him to do is a due process violation of the most basic sort, . . . and for an agent of the State to pursue a course of action whose objective is to penalize a person's reliance on his legal rights is "patently unconstitutional." . . . But in the "give-and-take" of plea bargaining, there is no such element of punishment or retaliation so long as the accused is free to accept or reject the prosecution's offer.

Plea bargaining flows from "the mutuality of advantage" to defendants and prosecutors, each with his own reasons for wanting to avoid trial. . . . Defendants advised by competent counsel and protected by other procedural safeguards are presumptively capable of intelligent choice in response to prosecutorial persuasion, and unlikely to be driven to false self-condemnation. Indeed, acceptance of the basic legitimacy of plea bargaining necessarily implies rejection of any notion that a guilty plea is involuntary in a constitutional sense simply because it is the end result of the bargaining process. By hypothesis, the plea may have been induced by promises of a recommendation of a lenient sentence or a reduction of charges, and thus by fear of the possibility of a greater penalty upon conviction after a trial. . . .

While confronting a defendant with the risk of more severe punishment clearly may have a "discouraging effect on the defendant's assertion of his trial rights, the imposition of these difficult choices [is] an inevitable"—and permissible—"attribute of any legitimate system which tolerates and encourages the negotiation of pleas." . . . It follows that, by tolerating and encouraging the negotiation of pleas, this Court has necessarily accepted as constitutionally legitimate the simple reality that the prosecutor's interest at the bargaining table is to persuade the defendant to forgo his right to plead not guilty.

It is not disputed here that Hayes was properly chargeable under the recidivist statute, since he had in fact been convicted of two previous felonies. In our system, so long as the prosecutor has probable cause to believe that the accused committed an offense defined by statute, the decision whether or not to prosecute, and what charge to file or bring before a grand jury, generally rests entirely in his discretion.* Within the limits set by the legislatures constitutionally valid definition of chargeable offenses, "the conscious exercise of some selectivity in enforcement is not in itself a federal constitutional violation" so long as "the selection was [not] deliberately based upon an unjustifiable standard such as race, religion, or other arbitrary classification." . . . To hold that the prosecutor's desire to induce a guilty plea is an "unjustifiable standard," which, like race or religion, may play no part in his charging decision, would contradict the very premises that underlie the concept of plea bargaining itself. Moreover, a rigid constitutional rule that would prohibit a prosecutor from acting forthrightly in his dealings with the defense could only invite unhealthy subterfuge that would drive the practice of plea bargaining back into the shadows from which it has so recently emerged.

There is no doubt that the breadth of discretion that our country's legal system vests in prosecuting attorneys carries with it the potential for both individual and institutional abuse. And broad though that discretion may be, there are undoubtedly constitutional limits upon its exercise. We hold only that the course of conduct engaged in by the prosecutor in this case, which no more than openly presented the defendant with the unpleasant alternatives of forgoing trial or facing charges on which he was plainly subject to prosecution, did not violate the Due Process Clause of the Fourteenth Amendment.

---

*This case does not involve the constitutional implications of a prosecutor's offer during plea bargaining of adverse or lenient treatment for some person *other* than the accused . . . which might pose a greater danger of inducing a false guilty plea by skewing the assessment of the risks a defendant must consider. . . .

Accordingly, the judgment of the Court of Appeals is reversed.

Mr. Justice **Blackmun,** with whom Mr. Justice **Brennan** and Mr. Justice **Marshall** join, dissenting, said in part:

I feel that the Court, although purporting to rule narrowly (that is, on "the course of conduct engaged in by the prosecutor in this case," is departing from, or at least restricting, the principles established in North Carolina v. Pearce (1969), and in Blackledge v. Perry (1974). If those decisions are sound and if those principles are salutary, as I must assume they are, they require, in my view, an affirmance, not a reversal, of the judgment of the Court of Appeals in the present Case.

In Pearce, as indeed the Court notes, it was held that "vindictiveness against a defendant for having successfully attacked his first conviction must play no part in the sentence he receives after a new trial." Accordingly, if, on the new trial, the sentence the defendant receives from the court is greater than that imposed after the first trial, it must be explained by reasons "based upon objective information concerning identifiable conduct on the part of the defendant occurring after the time of the original sentencing proceeding," other than his having pursued the appeal or collateral remedy. On the other hand, if the sentence is imposed by the jury and not by the court, if the jury is not aware of the original sentence, and if the second sentence is not otherwise shown to be a product of vindictiveness, Pearce has no application.

Then later, in Perry, the Court applied the same principle to prosecutorial conduct where there was a "realistic likelihood of 'vindictiveness.' " It held that the requirement of Fourteenth Amendment due process prevented a prosecutor's reindictment of a convicted misdemeanant on a felony charge after the defendant had exercised his right to appeal the misdemeanor conviction and thus to obtain a trial de novo. It noted the prosecution's "considerable stake" in discouraging the appeal.

The Court now says, however, that this concern with vindictiveness is of no import in the present case, despite the difference between five years in prison and a life sentence, because we are here concerned with plea bargaining where there is give-and-take negotiation, and where, it is said, "there is no such element of punishment or retaliation so long as the accused is free to accept or reject the prosecution's offer." Yet in this case vindictiveness is present to the same extent as it was thought to be in Pearce and in Perry; the prosecutor here admitted that the sole reason for the new indictment was to discourage the respondent from exercising his right to a trial. Even had such an admission not been made, when plea negotiations, conducted in the face of the less serious charge under the first indictment, fail, charging by a second indictment a more serious crime for the same conduct creates "a strong inference" of vindictiveness. As then Judge McCree aptly observed, in writing for a unanimous panel of the Sixth Circuit, the prosecutor initially "makes a discretionary determination that the interests of the state are served by not seeking more serious charges.'' I therefore do not understand why, as in Pearce, due process does not require that the prosecution justify its action on some basis other than discouraging respondent from the exercise of his right to a trial.

Prosecutorial vindictiveness, it seems to me, in the present narrow context, is the fact against which the Due Process Clause ought to protect. I perceive little difference between vindictiveness after what the Court describes as the exercise of a "legal right to attack his original conviction,'' and vindictiveness in the '' 'give-and-take negotiation common in plea bargaining.' '' Prosecutorial vindictiveness in any context is still prosecutorial vindictiveness. The Due Process Clause should protect an accused against it, however it asserts itself. The Court of Appeals so held, and I would affirm the judgment.

It might be argued that it really makes little difference how this case, now that it is here, is decided. The Court's holding gives plea bargaining full sway despite vindictiveness. A contrary result, however, merely would prompt the aggressive prosecutor to bring the greater charge initially in every case, and only thereafter to bargain. The consequences to the accused would still be adverse, for then he would bargain against a greater charge, face the likelihood of increased bail, and run the risk that the court would be less inclined to accept a bargained plea. Nonetheless, it is far preferable to hold the prosecution to the charge it was originally content to bring and to justify it in the eyes of its public.*

Mr. Justice **Powell,** dissenting, said in part:

Although I agree with much of the Court's opinion, I am not satisfied that the result in this case is just or that the conduct of plea bargaining met the requirements of due process. . . .

The prosecutor's initial assessment of respondent's case led him to forgo an indictment under the habitual criminal statute. The circumstances of respondent's prior convictions are relevant to this assessment and to my view of the case. Respondent was 17 years old when he committed his first offense. He was charged with rape but pleaded guilty to the lesser included offense of "detaining a female.'' One of the other participants in the incident was sentenced to life imprisonment. Respondent was sent not to prison but to a reformatory where he served five years. Respondent's second offense was robbery. This time he was found guilty by a jury and was sentenced to five years in prison, but he was placed on probation and served no time. Although respondent's prior convictions brought him within the terms of the Ha-

bitual Criminal Act, the offenses themselves did not result in imprisonment; yet the addition of a conviction on a charge involving $88.30 subjected respondent to a mandatory sentence of imprisonment for life. Persons convicted of rape and murder often are not punished so severely.

No explanation appears in the record for the prosecutor's decision to escalate the charge against respondent other than respondent's refusal to plead guilty. The prosecutor has conceded that his purpose was to discourage respondent's assertion of constitutional rights, and the majority accepts this characterization of events.

It seems to me that the question to be asked under the circumstances is whether the prosecutor reasonably might have charged respondent under the Habitual Criminal Act in the first place. The deference that courts properly accord the exercise of a prosecutor's discretion perhaps would foreclose judicial criticism if the prosecutor originally had sought an indictment under that Act, as unreasonable as it would have seemed.† But here the prosecutor evidently made a reasonable, responsible judgment not to subject an individual to a mandatory life sentence when his only new offense had societal implications as limited as those accompanying the uttering of a single $88 forged check and when the circumstances of his prior convictions confirmed the inappropriateness of applying the habitual criminal statute. I think it may be inferred that the prosecutor himself deemed it unreasonable and not in the public interest to put this defendant in jeopardy of a sentence of life imprisonment.

There may be situations in which a prosecutor would be fully justified in seeking a fresh indictment for a more serious offense. . . .

But this is not such a case. Here, any inquiry into the prosecutor's purpose is made unnecessary by his candid acknowledgement that he threatened to procure and in fact procured the habitual criminal indictment because of respondent's insistence on exercising his constitutional rights. We have stated in unequivocal terms . . . ''. . . if the only objective of a state practice is to discourage the assertion of constitutional rights it is "patently unconstitutional' '' . . .

. . . In this case, the prosecutor's actions denied respondent due process because their admitted purpose was to discourage and then to penalize with unique severity his exercise of constitutional rights. Implementation of a strategy calculated solely to deter the exercise of constitutional rights is not a constitutionally permissible exercise of discretion. . . .

---

*That prosecutors, without saying so, may sometimes bring charges more serious than they think appropriate for the ultimate disposition of a case, in order to gain bargaining leverage with a defendant, does not add support to today's decision, for this Court, in its approval of the advantages to be gained from plea negotiations has never openly sanctioned such deliberate overcharging or taken such a cynical view of the bargaining process. . . . Normally, of course, it is impossible to show that this is what the prosecutor is doing, and the courts necessarily have deferred to the prosecutor's exercise of discretion in initial charging decisions. . . .

†The majority suggests that this case cannot be distinguished from the case where the prosecutor initially obtains an indictment under an enhancement statute and later agrees to drop the enhancement charge in exchange for a guilty plea. I would agree that these two situations would be alike only if it were assumed that the hypothetical prosecutor's decision to charge under the enhancement statute was occasioned not by consideration of the public interest but by a strategy to discourage the defendant from exercising his constitutional rights. In theory, I would condemn both practices. In practice, the hypothetical situation is largely unreviewable. The majority's view confuses the propriety of a particular exercise of prosecutorial discretion with its unreviewability. In the instant case, however, we have no problem of proof.

10

First Amendment Rights

FREE SPEECH AND SECURITY

SCHENCK v. UNITED STATES

249 U. S. 47; 39 S. Ct. 247; 63 L. Ed. 470 (1919)

Freedom of speech and press are not absolute rights and were never intended to be so. They are relative, in the sense that they are limited by the coexisting rights of others (as in the matter of libel) and by the demands of national security and public decency. As Justice Holmes put it (below), ''The most stringent protection of free speech would not protect a man in falsely shouting fire in a theatre and causing a panic.'' Free-speech and free-press cases present to the courts difficult questions of degree: questions involved in drawing the line that separates the speech and publication which government must suppress in order to be safe and decent from that which it must allow and protect in order to be free and democratic.

Perhaps the most conspicuous and interesting instance in our history of interference with freedom of expression never came before the Supreme Court of the United States. The Sedition Act of 1798 provided among other things for the severe punishment of false, scandalous, and malicious writings against the government, either house of Congress, or the President if published with intent to defame any of them, or to excite against them the hatred of the people, or to stir up sedition. It was limited in operation to two years. Ten persons were

convicted under it, and many others were indicted but not tried. Its enactment and enforcement called forth great popular indignation, and President Jefferson upon assuming office pardoned all persons still imprisoned under its provisions. Many years later Congress refunded with interest the fines which had been imposed.

The relative character of the right of free speech and press becomes particularly obvious in time of war. Where is the line to be drawn between legitimate and salutary freedom of discussion and utterances which, by reason of their disloyal or seditious character, must be deemed incompatible with the public safety? This is a delicate and important question. During the Civil War such interferences with freedom of speech and press as occurred were perpetrated by military officers under the sanction of martial law, and no question of the validity of these acts of repression ever came squarely before the Supreme Court. World War I brought forth a large grist of restrictive legislation, both state and federal, and numerous judicial questions arose as to the validity of these acts and their application to specific cases. Most conspicuous of these laws were the Espionage Act of 1917—which penalized any circulation of false statements made with intent to interfere with military success, as well as any attempt to cause disloyalty in the Army or Navy or to obstruct recruiting—and the Sedition Act of 1918—which made it a crime to say or do anything which could obstruct the sale of government bonds, or to utter or publish words intended to bring into contempt or disrepute the form of government of the United States, the Constitution, flag, uniform, etc., or to incite resistance to the government or promote the cause of its ene-

mies. *Nearly a thousand persons were convicted under these two acts. Their validity was sustained in six cases coming to the Supreme Court after the close of the war. Schenck v. United States, printed below, was the first of these cases; and in it Justice Holmes announced the now famous "clear and present danger" test. A week later the Court decided two more cases, Frohwerk v. United States (1919), involving a pro-German newspaper man, and Debs v. United States (1919), involving the famous Socialist leader. Holmes wrote the opinions sustaining the convictions of the two men on the grounds that their writings and speeches met the test of clear and present danger. Nine months later the Supreme Court decided Abrams v. United States (1919), upholding the conviction under the Sedition Act of 1918 of a group of so-called Bolshevists who were urging strikes in ammunition plants to prevent American military interference with the Russian Revolution. Without mentioning the clear and present danger doctrine the Court found that the defendants had intended to "urge, incite, and advocate" curtailment of production necessary to the war. "It will not do," the Court reasoned, "to say, as is now argued, that the only intent of these defendants was to prevent injury to the Russian cause. Men must be held to have intended, and to be accountable for, the effects which their acts were likely to produce." Holmes, with whom Brandeis concurred, dissented: "I do not doubt for a moment that by the same reasoning that would justify punishing persuasion to murder, the United States constitutionally may punish speech that produces or is intended to produce a clear and imminent danger that it will bring about forthwith certain substantive evils that the United States constitutionally may seek to prevent. . . . It is only the present danger of immediate evil or an intent to bring it about that warrants Congress in setting a limit to the expression of opinion where private rights are not concerned." As for there being such danger here, "nobody can suppose that the surreptitious publishing of a silly leaflet by an unknown man, without more, would present any immediate danger that its opinions would hinder the success of the government. . . ." Nor was there the "intent" required to constitute a violation of the statute, since the intent of the defendants had been to protect Russia, not Germany, with whom we were at war.*

In Schaefer v. United States (1920) and Pierce v. United States (1920) the Court sustained convictions under the Espionage Act of 1917 on the ground that the defendants willfully published "false reports and statements with intent to interfere with the operation or success of military or naval forces of the United States or to promote the success of its enemies." The Court applied to the utterances in the Schaefer case what is called the "bad tendency" test of validity (see Gitlow v. New York, 1925): "Their effect on the persons affected could not be shown, nor was it necessary. The tendency of the articles and their efficacy were enough for offense. . . ." It is in Brandeis's dissent in the Schaefer case that he makes his well-known comment about the test of clear and present danger. He said: "This is a rule of reason. Correctly applied, it will preserve the right of free speech both from suppression by tyrannous, well-meaning majorities, and from abuse by irresponsible, fanatical minorities."

Only one case, Hartzel v. United States (1944), came to the Supreme Court under the Espionage Act of 1917 during or after World War II. (In 1921 Congress had repealed the Sedition Act of 1918.) Hartzel was prosecuted for publishing and mailing "scurrilous and vitriolic attacks on the English, the Jews and the President of the United States" to those on a carefully selected mailing list. These facts, similar in their essentials to those in Schenck, the Court found insufficient to constitute a crime under the statute. The Court emphasized that "two major elements are necessary to constitute an offense under these clauses. The first element is a subjective one, consisting of a specific intent . . . to cause insubordination or disloyalty in the armed forces. . . . This . . . springs from the statutory use of the word 'willfully.' . . . The second element is an objective one, consisting of a clear and present danger that the activities in question will bring about the substantive evils which Congress has a right to prevent. . . . Both elements must be proved by the Government beyond a reasonable doubt." The Court failed to find the requisite intent. Four justices dissented, agreeing with Justice Holmes's earlier comment that "of course the document would not have been sent unless it had been intended to have some effect. . . ."

Mr. Justice **Holmes** delivered the opinion of the Court, saying in part:

[Schenck was convicted in a federal district court of violation of the Espionage Act of 1917, by causing and attempting to cause insubordination in the armed forces of the United States when the United States was at war with Germany. Schenck had circulated among men called and accepted for military service a document alleged to be intended to cause insubordination and obstruction of the draft. He claimed that the statute abridged his freedom of speech and press in violation of the First Amendment.]

. . . The document in question upon its first printed side recited the 1st section of the 13th Amendment, said that the idea embodied in it was violated by the Conscription Act, and that a conscript is little better than a convict. In impassioned language it intimated that conscription was despotism in its worst form and a monstrous wrong against humanity, in the interest of Wall Street's chosen few. It said: "Do not submit to intimidation;" but in form at least confined itself to peaceful measures, such as a petition for the repeal of the act. The other and later printed side of the sheet was headed "Assert Your Rights." It stated reasons for alleging that any one violated the Constitution when he refused to recognize "your right to assert your opposition to the draft," and went on: "If you do not assert and support your rights, you are helping to deny or disparage rights which it is the solemn duty of all citizens and residents of the United States to retain." It described the arguments on the other side as coming from cunning politicians and a mercenary capitalist press, and even silent consent to the Conscription Law as helping to support an infamous conspiracy. It denied the power to send our citizens away to foreign shores to shoot up the people of other lands, and added that words could not express the condemnation such cold-blooded ruthlessness deserves, etc., etc., winding up, "You must do your share to maintain, support and uphold the rights of the people of this country." Of course the document would not have been sent unless it had been intended to have some effect, and we do not see what effect it could be expected to have upon persons subject to the draft except to influence them to obstruct the carrying of it out. The defendants do not deny that the jury might find against them on this point.

But it is said, suppose that that was the tendency of this circular, it is protected by the 1st Amendment to the Constitution. Two of the strongest expressions are said to be quoted respectively from well-known public men. It well may be that the prohibition of laws abridging the freedom of speech is not confined to previous restraints, although to prevent them may have been the main purpose, as intimated in Patterson v. Colorado [1907]. We admit that in many places and in ordinary times the defendants, in saying all that was said in the circular, would have been within their constitutional rights. But the character of every act depends upon the circumstances in which it is done. The most stringent protection of free speech would not protect a man in falsely shouting fire in a theatre, and causing a panic. It does not even protect a man from an injunction against uttering words that may have all the effect of force. Gompers v. Buck's Stove & Range Co. [1911]. The question in every case is whether the words used are used in such circumstances and are of such a nature as to create a clear and present danger that they will bring about the substantive evils that Congress has a right to prevent. It is a question of proximity and degree. When a nation is at war many things that might be said in time of peace are such a hindrance to its effort that their utterance will not be endured so long as men fight, and that no court could regard them as protected by any constitutional right. It seems to be admitted that if an actual obstruction of the recruiting service were proved, liability for words that produced that effect might be enforced. The statute of 1917, in § 4, punishes conspiracies to obstruct as well as actual obstruction. If the act (speaking, or circulating a paper), its tendency and the intent with which it is done, are the same, we perceive no ground for saying that success alone warrants making the act a crime. . . .

Judgments affirmed.

GITLOW v. NEW YORK

268 U. S. 652; 45 S. Ct. 625; 69 L. Ed. 1138
(1925)

The Espionage Act of 1917 forbade certain kinds of action, such as causing or attempting to cause insubordination or obstructing the draft. It did not expressly limit freedom of speech; it limited it only when speech amounted to the kind of action forbidden by the statute. In order to determine when a particular speech became "action" and thus punishable under the statute, the Court resorted to two tests, the "bad tendency" test and the "clear and present danger" test.

The "bad tendency" test was designed, as Professor Chafee put it, "to kill the serpent in the egg" by preventing all speech which had a tendency, however remote, to bring about acts in violation of the law. It had its roots in the doctrine of constructive treason, so infamous in English history, under which criticism of the government was construed as an attempt to accomplish the overthrow of that government and was punished as treason. The "clear and present danger" test, devised by Justice Holmes in the Schenck case (1919), held that speech becomes punishable as action only when there is a danger, clear and present, that it will bring the action about. If there is no clear and present danger the speech does not amount to action, and the statute forbidding the action has not been violated. Holmes's doctrine was not intended as a test of the validity of the statute itself, since presumably the "action" which the statute forbids is, like obstructing the draft, something Congress could legitimately prohibit.

The clear and present danger test is not simple to apply. It is, for instance, difficult to apply to a statute which by its language forbids certain kinds of speech. If a person makes the kind of speech thus forbidden, then he has violated the statute; in other words, once the legislature has decided for itself what kind of speech is dangerous and forbidden it, the courts can hold the statute unconstitutional but they cannot say it has not been violated. Holmes and Brandeis apparently felt that statutes of this kind could not constitutionally be applied to cases in which there was no clear and present danger of serious substantive evil. See Whitney v. California (1927).

In the present case Benjamin Gitlow was prosecuted under the New York Criminal Anarchy Act of 1902 for distributing a document similar to the Communist Manifesto of Marx and Engels (1848). This statute, which formed the model for the federal Smith Act, punishes certain kinds of speech and publication regardless of the intent of the speaker or publisher.

Not until 1965 was the New York act again invoked successfully, when William Epton was convicted of criminal anarchy for conspiring to instigate and inflame the Harlem race riots that followed the killing by a policeman of a fifteen-year-old Negro boy.

Mr. Justice **Sanford** delivered the opinion of the Court, saying in part:

Benjamin Gitlow was indicted in the supreme court of New York, with three others, for the statutory crime of criminal anarchy. . . .

The contention here is that the statute, by its terms and as applied in this case, is repugnant to the due process clause of the 14th Amendment. Its material provisions are:

"§ 160. Criminal anarchy defined.—Criminal anarchy is the doctrine that organized government should be overthrown by force or violence, or by assassination of the executive head or of any of the executive officials of government, or by any unlawful means. The advocacy of such doctrine either by word of mouth or writing is a felony.

"§ 161. Advocacy of criminal anarchy.—Any person who:

"1. By word of mouth or writing advocates, advises or teaches the duty, necessity or propriety of overthrowing or overturning organized government by force or violence, or by assassination of the executive head or of any of the executive officials of government, or by any unlawful means; or

"2. Prints, publishes, edits, issues or knowingly circulates, sells, distributes or publicly displays any book, paper, document, or written or printed matter in any form, containing or advocating, advising or teaching the doctrine that organized government should be overthrown by force, violence or any unlawful means . . . ,

"Is guilty of a felony and punishable" by imprisonment or fine, or both.

The indictment was in two counts. The first charged that the defendants had advocated, advised, and taught the duty, necessity, and propriety of overthrowing and overturning organized government by force, violence, and unlawful means, by certain writings therein set forth, entitled, "The Left Wing Manifesto"; the second, that he had printed, published, and knowingly circulated and distributed a certain paper called "The Revolutionary Age," containing the writings set forth in the first count, advocating, advising, and teaching the doctrine that organized government should be overthrown by force, violence, and unlawful means.

. . . It was admitted that the defendant signed a card subscribing to the Manifesto and Program of the Left Wing, which all applicants were required to sign before being admitted to membership; that he went to different parts of the state to speak to branches of the Socialist party about the principles of the Left Wing, and advocated their adoption; and that he was responsible [as business manager] for the Manifesto as it appeared, that "he knew of the publication, in a general way, and he knew of its publication afterwards, and is responsible for its circulation."

There was no evidence of any effect resulting from the publication and circulation of the Manifesto.

No witnesses were offered in behalf of the defendant.

Extracts from the Manifesto are set forth in the margin. Coupled with a review of the rise of Socialism, it condemned the dominant "moderate Socialism" for its recognition of the necessity of the democratic parliamentary state; repudiated its policy of introducing Socialism by legislative measures; and advocated, in plain and unequivocal language, the necessity of accomplishing the "Communist Revolution" by a militant and "revolutionary Socialism," based on "the class struggle" and mobilizing the "power of the proletariat in action," through mass industrial revolts developing into mass political strikes and "revolutionary mass action"

for the purpose of conquering and destroying the parliamentary state and establishing in its place, through a "revolutionary dictatorship of the proletariat," the system of Communist Socialism. The then recent strikes in Seattle and Winnipeg were cited as instances of a development already verging on revolutionary action and suggestive of proletarian dictatorship, in which the strike workers were "trying to usurp the functions of municipal government"; and Revolutionary Socialism, it was urged, must use these mass industrial revolts to broaden the strike, make it general and militant, and develop it into mass political strikes and revolutionary mass action for the annihilation of the parliamentary state.

. . . The sole contention here is, essentially, that, as there was no evidence of any concrete result flowing from the publication of the Manifesto, or of circumstances showing the likelihood of such result, the statute as construed and applied by the trial court penalizes the mere utterance, as such, of "doctrine" having no quality of incitement, without regard either to the circumstances of its utterance or to the likelihood of unlawful sequences; and that, as the exercise of the right of free expression with relation to government is only punishable "in circumstances involving likelihood of substantive evil," the statute contravenes the due process clause of the Fourteenth Amendment. The argument in support of this contention rests primarily upon the following propositions: 1st, that the "liberty" protected by the 14th Amendment includes the liberty of speech and of the press; and 2nd, that while liberty of expression "is not absolute," it may be restrained "only in circumstances where its exercise bears a causal relation with some substantive evil, consummated, attempted, or likely"; and as the statute "takes no account of circumstances," it unduly restrains this liberty, and is therefore unconstitutional.

The precise question presented, and the only question which we can consider under this writ of error, then, is whether the statute, as construed and applied in this case by the state courts, deprived the defendant of his liberty of expression, in violation of the due process clause of the 14th Amendment.

The statute does not penalize the utterance or publication of abstract "doctrine" or academic discussion having no quality of incitement to any concrete action. It is not aimed against mere historical or philosophical essays. It does not restrain the advocacy of changes in the form of government by constitutional and lawful means. What it prohibits is language advocating, advising, or teaching the overthrow of organized government by unlawful means. These words imply urging to action. Advocacy is defined in the Century Dictionary as: "1. The act of pleading for, supporting, or recommending; active espousal." It is not the abstract "doctrine" of overthrowing organized government by unlawful means which is denounced by the statute, but the advocacy of action for the accomplishment of that purpose. . . .

The Manifesto, plainly, is neither the statement of abstract doctrine nor, as suggested by counsel, mere prediction that industrial disturbances and revolutionary mass strikes will result spontaneously in an inevitable process of evolution in the economic system. It advocates and urges in fervent language mass action which shall progressively foment industrial disturbances, and, through political mass strikes and revolutionary mass action, overthrow and destroy organized parliamentary government. It concludes with a call to action in these words: "The proletariat revolution and the Communist reconstruction of society—*the struggle for these*—is now indispensable. . . . The Communist International calls the proletariat of the world to the final struggle!" This is not the expression of philosophical abstraction, the mere prediction of future events: it is the language of direct incitement.

The means advocated for bringing about the destruction of organized parliamentary government, namely, mass industrial revolts usurping the functions of municipal government, political mass strikes directed against the parliamentary state, and revolutionary mass action for its final destruction, necessarily imply the use of force and violence, and in their essential nature are inherently unlawful in a constitutional government of law and order. That the jury were warranted in finding that the Manifesto advocated not merely the abstract doctrine of overwhelming organized government by force, violence, and unlawful means, but action to that end, is clear.

For present purposes we may and do assume that freedom of speech and of the press—which are protected by the 1st Amendment from abridgment by Congress—are among the fundamental personal rights and "liberties" protected by the due process clause of the 14th Amendment from impairment by the states. . . .

It is a fundamental principle, long established, that freedom of speech and of the press which is secured by the Constitution does not confer an absolute right to speak or publish, without responsibility, whatever one may choose, or an unrestricted and unbridled license that gives immunity for every possible use of language, and prevents the punishment of those who abuse this freedom 2 Story, Const. 5th ed. § 1580, p. 634. . . . Reasonably limited, it was said by Story in the passage cited, this freedom is an inestimable privilege in a free government; without such limitation, it might become the scourge of the Republic.

That a state, in the exercise of its police power, may punish those who abuse this freedom by utterances inimical to the public welfare, tending to corrupt public morals, incite to crime, or disturb the public peace, is not open to question. . . . Thus it was held by this court in the Fox Case [Fox v. Washington, 1915], that a state may punish publications advocating and encouraging a breach of its criminal laws; and, in the Gilbert Case [Gilbert v. Minnesota, 1920], that a state may punish utterances teaching or advocating that its citizens should not assist the United States in prosecuting or carrying on war with its public enemies.

And, for yet more imperative reasons, a state may punish utterances endangering the foundations of organized government and threatening its overthrow by unlawful means. These imperil its own existence as a constitutional state. Freedom of speech and press, said Story

(supra), does not protect disturbances of the public peace or the attempt to subvert the government. It does not protect publications or teachings which tend to subvert or imperil the government, or to impede or hinder it in the performance of its governmental duties. . . . It does not protect publications prompting the overthrow of government by force; the punishment of those who publish articles which tend to destroy organized society being essential to the security of freedom and the stability of the state. . . . And a state may penalize utterances which openly advocate the overthrow of the representative and constitutional form of government of the United States and the several states, by violence or other unlawful means. . . . In short, this freedom does not deprive a state of the primary and essential right of self-preservation, which, so long as human governments endure, they cannot be denied. . . .

By enacting the present statute the state has determined, through its legislative body, that utterances advocating the overthrow of organized government by force, violence, and unlawful means, are so inimical to the general welfare, and involve such danger of substantive evil, that they may be penalized in the exercise of its police power. That determination must be given great weight. Every presumption is to be indulged in favor of the validity of the statute. . . . That utterances inciting to the overthrow of organized government by unlawful means present a sufficient danger of substantive evil to bring their punishment within the range of legislative discretion is clear. Such utterances, by their very nature, involve danger to the public peace and to the security of the state. They threaten breaches of the peace and ultimate revolution. And the immediate danger is none the less real and substantial because the effect of a given utterance cannot be accurately foreseen. The state cannot reasonably be required to measure the danger from every such utterance in the nice balance of a jeweler's scale. A single revolutionary spark may kindle a fire that, smoldering for a time, may burst into a sweeping and destructive conflagration. It cannot be said that the state is acting arbitrarily or unreasonably when, in the exercise of its judgment as to the measures necessary to protect the public peace and safety, it seeks to extinguish the spark without waiting until it has enkindled the flame or blazed into the conflagration. It cannot reasonably be required to defer the adoption of measures for its own peace and safety until the revolutionary utterances lead to actual disturbances of the public peace or imminent and immediate danger of its own destruction; but it may, in the exercise of its judgment, suppress the threatened danger in its incipiency. . . .

We cannot hold that the present statute is an arbitrary or unreasonable exercise of the police power of the state, unwarrantably infringing the freedom of speech or press; and we must and do sustain its constitutionality.

This being so it may be applied to every utterance—not too trivial to be beneath the notice of the law—which is of such a character and used with such intent and purpose as to bring it within the prohibition of the statute. . . . In other words, when the legislative body has determined generally, in the constitutional exercise of its discretion, that utterances of a certain kind involve such danger of substantive evil that they may be punished, the question whether any specific utterance coming within the prohibited class is likely, in and of itself, to bring about the substantive evil, is not open to consideration. It is sufficient that the statute itself be constitutional, and that the use of the language comes within its prohibition.

It is clear that the question in such cases is entirely different from that involved in those cases where the statute merely prohibits certain acts involving the danger of substantive evil, without any reference to language itself, and it is sought to apply its provisions to language used by the defendant for the purpose of bringing about prohibited results. There, if it be contended that the statute cannot be applied to the language used by the defendant because of its protection by the freedom of speech or press, it must necessarily be found, as an original question, without any previous determination by the legislative body, whether the specific language used involved such likelihood of bringing about the substantive evil as to deprive it of the constitutional protection. In such cases it has been held that the general provisions of the statute may be constitutionally applied to the specific utterance of the defendant if its natural tendency and probable effect were to bring about the substantive evil which the legislative body might prevent. Schenck v. United States [1919]; Debs v. United States [1919]. And the general statement in the Schenck Case that the "question in every case is whether the words are used in such circumstances and are of such a nature as to create a clear and present danger that they will bring about the substantive evils,"—upon which great reliance is placed in the defendant's argument,—was manifestly intended, as shown by the context, to apply only in cases of this class, and has no application to those like the present, where the legislative body itself has previously determined the danger of substantive evil arising from utterances of a specified character. . . .

And finding, for the reasons stated, that the statute is not in itself unconstitutional, and that it has not been applied in the present case in derogation of any constitutional right, the judgment of the Court of Appeals is affirmed.

Mr. Justice **Holmes** dissented:

Mr. Justice Brandeis and I are of the opinion that this judgment should be reversed. The general principle of free speech, it seems to me, must be taken to be included in the 14th Amendment, in view of the scope that has been given to the word "liberty" as there used, although perhaps it may be accepted with a somewhat larger latitude of interpretation than is allowed to Congress by the sweeping language that governs, or ought to govern, the laws of the United States. If I am right, then I think that the criterion sanctioned by the full court in Schenck v. United States, applies: "The question in every case is whether the words used are used in such circumstances and are of such a nature as to create a clear and present danger that they will bring about the substantive evils that [the state] has a right to prevent." It is true

that in my opinion this criterion was departed from in Abrams v. United States [1919] but the convictions that I expressed in that case are too deep for it to be possible for me as yet to believe that it and Schaefer v. United States [1920] have settled the law. If what I think the correct test is applied, it is manifest that there was no present danger of an attempt to overthrow the government by force on the part of the admittedly small minority who shared the defendant's views. It is said that this Manifesto was more than a theory, that it was an incitement. Every idea is an incitement. It offers itself for belief, and, if believed, it is acted on unless some other belief outweighs it, or some failure of energy stifles the movement at its birth. The only difference between the expression of an opinion and an incitement in the narrower sense is the speaker's enthusiasm for the result. Eloquence may set fire to reason. But whatever may be thought of the redundant discourse before us, it had no chance of starting a present conflagration. If, in the long run, the beliefs expressed in proletarian dictatorship are destined to be accepted by the dominant forces of the community, the only meaning of free speech is that they should be given their chance and have their way.

If the publication of this document had been laid as an attempt to induce an uprising against government at once, and not at some indefinite time in the future, it would have presented a different question. The object would have been one with which the law might deal, subject to the doubt whether there was any danger that the publication could produce any result; or, in other words, whether it was not futile and too remote from possible consequences. But the indictment alleges the publication and nothing more.

DENNIS v. UNITED STATES

341 U. S. 494; 71 S. Ct. 857; 95 L. Ed. 1137
(1951)

The Smith Act of 1940, which in 1948 became § 2385 of Title 18 of the United States Code, directs a five-pronged attack against subversion. First, it punishes anyone who "knowingly or willfully advocates . . . or teaches the duty . . . or propriety of overthrowing . . . the government of the United States . . . by force or violence. . . ." Second, it punishes the dissemination of literature advocating such overthrow "with intent to cause such overthrow." Third, it punishes anyone who "organizes . . . any society, group or assembly of persons to teach, advocate or encourage" such overthrow. Fourth, it punishes anyone who "becomes or is a member of . . . any such society, group or assembly . . . knowing the purposes thereof." Finally, it makes it a separate offense to conspire to do any of the above things.

The validity of the act was considered by the Supreme Court for the first time in the Dennis case below. In 1948, the eleven top leaders of the American Communist party were indicted under the act for willfully and knowingly conspiring to teach and advocate the overthrow of government by force and violence, and to orga-

nize the Communist party for the purpose of so doing. The trial in District Judge Medina's court in New York ran from January 20 to September 23, 1949, and resulted in conviction. Judge Medina's charge to the jury included two important interpretations of the law. First, he ruled out the possibility that "teaching" or "conspiring to teach" alone would violate the statute. "You must be satisfied from the evidence beyond a reasonable doubt that the defendants had an intent to cause the overthrow or destruction of the Government of the United States by force and violence, and that it was with this intent and for the purpose of furthering that objective that they conspired both (1) to organize the Communist Party . . . and (2) to teach and advocate. . . ." Second, should the jury find that the statute as so construed had been violated, it was their duty to find the defendants guilty. "I find as a matter of law that there is sufficient danger of a substantive evil that the Congress has a right to prevent to justify the application of the statute under the First Amendment. . . ."

Both the conviction and this charge to the jury were upheld by the court of appeals in an opinion by Judge Learned Hand. The Supreme Court limited the scope of its review to the constitutional questions raised, chief of which was the First Amendment question of free speech. It did not review the sufficiency of the evidence to support the verdict.

In the five opinions written in the Dennis case, there are four interpretations of the clear and present danger test. Chief Justice Vinson, speaking for four members of the Court, paid allegiance to Holmes's statement and application of the test, but in reality adopted in its place Judge Hand's test of "clear and probable danger." The danger need not be imminent; it is enough that there is a group willing to attempt the overthrow of government if and when possible. The Chief Justice read the time element out of clear and present danger.

Justice Frankfurter had always rejected the idea that a law which on its face invades free speech must be presumed to be unconstitutional, or that the First Amendment occupies any "preferred position." See Thomas v. Collins (1945). He felt that free-speech cases call for the weighing of competing interests, and that the legislative judgment embodied in the Smith Act, that the Communist threat to the security of the country justifies punitive action, is amply supported by evidence.

In an incisive concurring opinion Justice Jackson bluntly declared that the test of clear and present danger has no applicability to a criminal conspiracy such as that carried on by the Communist party. It was never intended to be applied in a case like this, and should be reserved for cases involving restrictions upon speeches and publications.

Justices Black and Douglas, dissenting, felt that the clear and present danger test had been destroyed. Justice Douglas emphasized that the defendants were charged with no overt acts, only with speeches and publications. He also felt that the question of clear and present danger should be decided by the jury and not by the court.

The decision in the Dennis case provided for the first time a legal basis for the idea that the Communist party is a criminal conspiracy dedicated to overthrowing the government of the United States by force and violence. It therefore seemed logical to suppose that any official of the party, and probably any member who was familiar with the aims of the party, could be convicted for taking part in the conspiracy. Acting upon this assumption the government moved against fourteen second-string Communist leaders, and in Yates v. United States (1957) the Supreme Court reversed their convictions, acquitting five of them outright and remanding the other nine for retrial. The District Court, it explained, had failed to charge the jury that in order to convict it must find the defendants guilty of advocating "action" in the "language of incitement." "The essence of the Dennis holding," the Court said, "was that indoctrination of a group in preparation for future violent action, as well as exhortation to immediate action, by advocacy found to be directed to 'action for the accomplishment' of forcible overthrow, to violence 'as a rule or principle of action,' and employing 'language of incitement,' is not constitutionally protected when the group is of sufficient size and cohesiveness, is sufficiently oriented towards action, and other circumstances are such as reasonably to justify apprehension that action will occur. This is quite a different thing from the view of the District Court here that mere doctrinal justification of forcible overthrow, if engaged in with the intent to accomplish overthrow, is punishable per se under the Smith Act. That sort of advocacy, even though uttered with the hope that it may ultimately lead to violent revolution, is too remote from concrete action to be regarded as the kind of indoctrination preparatory to action which was condemned in Dennis."

Although Justice Harlan stresses that he is merely applying the doctrine of the Dennis case, it seems apparent that in insisting in Yates that advocacy amount to incitement to action, he is, without actually using the well-known phrase, moving back toward the clear and present danger rule of Holmes and Brandeis. The Dennis case was widely believed to have modified and weakened that rule.

Four years after Yates, in Scales v. United States (1961), the Supreme Court passed on the validity of the membership section for the first time, and in a five-to-four decision held it valid as applied to Scales. It stated that this was not mere "guilt by association." The guilt was personal and punishable under the act if it was "active membership in an organization [in this case the Communist party] engaged in illegal advocacy by one having guilty knowledge and intent." Scales had been convicted first in 1955, and after a second trial and two full arguments before the Court his case was finally heard and considered in conjunction with Communist Party v. Subversive Activities Control Board (1961). Scales argued that the membership section of the Smith Act had been repealed by the section of the Subversive Activities Control Act of 1950 (requiring registration of Communists), which provides that : "Neither the holding of office nor membership in any Communist organization by any person shall constitute per se a violation of subsection (a) or subsection (c) of this section or any other criminal statute." Justice Harlan's opinion for the *majority held that the section quoted from the act of 1950 clarified, rather than repealed, the membership section of the Smith Act; and he emphasized the difference between punishing someone for membership per se and punishing the person for membership with guilty knowledge and with intent to aid in the violent overthrow of government. In the dissenting opinions it was urged that the act of 1950 had repealed the Smith Act provision and that the membership section violated the First Amendment.*

In Brandenberg v. Ohio (1969), the Supreme Court held void Ohio's criminal syndicalism act—an act passed in the 1920s and patterned after that of California which had been held valid in Whitney v. California (1927). Without actually using the words "clear and present danger," the Court held the act void as forbidding mere advocacy of violence or sabotage, whether or not it would incite the hearers to lawless action. The Court overruled Whitney v. California.

In Meese v. Keene (1987) a member of the California senate wanted to show three films dealing with acid rain and the effects of nuclear war, and when he imported them from Canada the Justice Department designated them political propaganda. The Court refused to find the statute or the designation a violation of free speech. It argued that Keene was not forbidden to show the films, that the term "propaganda" was not pejorative and thus inhibiting to free expression, and that while Keene had to say that the films were listed as propaganda, he was free to say anything else about them he wished by way of explanation.

Mr. Chief Justice **Vinson** announced the judgment of the Court and an opinion in which Mr. Justice **Reed**, Mr. Justice **Burton**, and Mr. Justice **Minton** join, saying in part:

I.

It will be helpful in clarifying the issues to treat next the contention that the trial judge improperly interpreted the statute by charging that the statute required an unlawful intent before the jury could convict. . . .

. . . The structure and purpose of the statute demand the inclusion of intent as an element of the crime. Congress was concerned with those who advocate and organize for the overthrow of the Government. Certainly those who recruit and combine for the purpose of advocating overthrow intend to bring about that overthrow. We hold that the statute required as an essential element of the crime proof of the intent of those who are charged with its violation to overthrow the Government by force and violence. . . .

II.

The obvious purpose of the statute is to protect existing Government, not from change by peaceable, lawful and constitutional means, but from change by violence, revolution and terrorism. That it is within the *power* of the Congress to protect the Government of the United States from armed rebellion is a proposition which requires little discussion. Whatever theoretical merit there may be to the argument that there is a "right" to rebellion against dictatorial governments is without force where the existing structure of the government provides for peaceful and orderly change. We reject any principle of governmental helplessness in the face of preparation for revolution, which principle, carried to its logical conclusion, must lead to anarchy. No one could conceive that it is not within the power of Congress to prohibit acts intended to overthrow the Government by force and violence. The question with which we are concerned here is not whether Congress has such *power*, but whether the *means* which it has employed conflict with the First and Fifth Amendments to the Constitution.

One of the bases for the contention that the means which Congress has employed are invalid takes the form of an attack on the face of the statute on the grounds that by its terms it prohibits academic discussion of the merits of Marxism-Leninism, that it stifles ideas and is contrary to all concepts of a free speech and a free press. Although we do not agree that the language itself has that significance, we must bear in mind that it is the duty of the federal courts to interpret federal legislation in a manner not inconsistent with the demands of the Constitution. . . . This is a federal statute which we must interpret as well as judge. . . .

The very language of the Smith Act negates the interpretation which petitioners would have us impose on the Act. It is directed at advocacy, not discussion. Thus, the trial judge properly charged the jury that they could not convict if they found that petitioners did "no more than pursue peaceful studies and discussions or teaching and advocacy in the realm of ideas." He further charged that it was not unlawful "to conduct in an American college and university a course explaining the philosophical theories set forth in the books which have been placed in evidence." Such a charge is in strict accord with the statutory language, and illustrates the meaning to be placed on those words. Congress did not intend to eradicate the free discussion of political theories, to destroy the traditional rights of Americans to discuss and evaluate ideas without fear of governmental sanction. Rather Congress was concerned with the very kind of activity in which the evidence showed these petitioners engaged.

III.

But although the statute is not directed at the hypothetical cases which petitioners have conjured, its application in this case has resulted in convictions for the teaching and advocacy of the overthrow of the Government by force and violence, which, even though coupled with the intent to accomplish that overthrow, contains an element of speech. For this reason, we must pay special heed to the demands of the First Amendment marking out the boundaries of speech.

We pointed out in [American Communications Ass'n v. Douds, 1950] that the basis of the First Amendment is the hypothesis that speech can rebut speech, propaganda will answer propaganda, free debate of ideas will result in the wisest governmental policies. It is for this reason that this Court has recognized the inherent value of free discourse. An analysis of the leading cases in this Court which have involved direct limitations on speech, however, will demonstrate that both the majority of the Court and the dissenters in particular cases have recognized that this is not an unlimited, unqualified right, but that the societal value of speech must, on occasion, be subordinated to other values and considerations.

No important case involving free speech was decided by this Court prior to Schenck v. United States (1919). . . . Writing for a unanimous Court, Justice Holmes states that the "question in every case is whether the words used are used in such circumstances and are of such a nature as to create a clear and present danger that they will bring about the substantive evils that Congress has a right to prevent." . . . The fact is inescapable, too, that the phrase bore no connotation that the danger was to be any threat to the safety of the Republic. The charge was causing and attempting to cause insubordination in the military forces and obstruct recruiting. The objectionable document denounced conscription and its most inciting sentence was, "You must do your share to maintain, support and uphold the rights of the people of this country." Fifteen thousand copies were printed and some circulated. This insubstantial gesture toward insubordination in 1917 during war was held to be a clear and present danger of bringing about the evil of military insubordination.

In several later cases involving convictions under the Criminal Espionage Act, the nub of the evidence the Court held sufficient to meet the "clear and present danger" test enunciated in Schenck was as follows: [Five cases, 1919–1920, are here discussed.] . . .

The rule we deduce from these cases is that where an offense is specified by a statute in nonspeech or nonpress terms, a conviction relying upon speech or press as evidence of violation may be sustained only when the speech or publication created a "clear and present danger" of attempting or accomplishing the prohibited crime, e. g., interference with enlistment. The dissents, we repeat, in emphasizing the value of speech, were addressed to the argument of the sufficiency of the evidence.

The next important case before the Court in which free speech was the crux of the conflict was Gitlow v. New York [1925]. There New York had made it a crime to "advocate . . . the necessity or propriety of overthrowing . . . the government by force. . . ." The evidence of violation of the statute was that the defendant had published a Manifesto attacking the Government and capitalism. The convictions were sustained, Justices Holmes and Brandeis dissenting. The majority refused to apply the "clear and present danger" test to the specific utterance. Its reasoning was as follows: The "clear and present danger" test was applied to the utterance itself in Schenck because the question was merely one of sufficiency of evidence under an admittedly constitutional statute. Gitlow, however, presented a different question.

There a legislature had found that a certain kind of speech was, itself, harmful and unlawful. The constitutionality of such a state statute had to be adjudged by this Court just as it determined the constitutionality of any state statute, namely, whether the statute was "reasonable." Since it was entirely reasonable for a state to attempt to protect itself from violent overthrow, the statute was perforce reasonable. The only question remaining in the case became whether there was evidence to support the conviction, a question which gave the majority no difficulty. Justices Holmes and Brandeis refused to accept this approach, but insisted that wherever speech was the evidence of the violation, it was necessary to show that the speech created the "clear and present danger" of the substantive evil which the legislature had the right to prevent. Justices Holmes and Brandeis, then, made no distinction between a federal statute which made certain acts unlawful, the evidence to support the conviction being speech, and a statute which made speech itself the crime. This approach was emphasized in Whitney v. California [1927], where the Court was confronted with a conviction under the California Criminal Syndicalist statute. The Court sustained the conviction, Justices Brandeis and Holmes concurring in the result. In their concurrence they repeated that even though the legislature had designated certain speech as criminal, this could not prevent the defendant from showing that there was no danger that the substantive evil would be brought about.

Although no case subsequent to Whitney and Gitlow has expressly overruled the majority opinions in those cases, there is little doubt that subsequent opinions have inclined toward the Holmes-Brandeis rationale. And in American Communications Ass'n v. Douds . . . we pointed out that Congress did not intend to punish belief, but rather intended to regulate the conduct of union affairs. We therefore held that any indirect sanction on speech which might arise from the oath requirement did not present a proper case for the "clear and present danger" test, for the regulation was aimed at conduct rather than speech. In discussing the proper measure of evaluation of this kind of legislation, we suggested that the Holmes-Brandeis philosophy insisted that where there was a direct restriction upon speech, a "clear and present danger" that the substantive evil would be caused was necessary before the statute in question could be constitutionally applied. And we stated, "[The First] Amendment requires that one be permitted to believe what he will. It requires that one be permitted to advocate what he will unless there is a clear and present danger that a substantial public evil will result therefrom." But we further suggested that neither Justice Holmes nor Justice Brandeis ever envisioned that a shorthand phrase should be crystallized into a rigid rule to be applied inflexibly without regard to the circumstances of each case. Speech is not an absolute, above and beyond control by the legislature when its judgment, subject to review here, is that certain kinds of speech are so undesirable as to warrant criminal sanction. Nothing is more certain in modern society than the principle that there are no absolutes, that a name, a phrase, a standard has meaning only when associated with the considerations which gave birth to the no-menclature. . . . To those who would paralyze our Government in the face of impending threat by encasing it in a semantic straitjacket we must reply that all concepts are relative.

In this case we are squarely presented with the application of the "clear and present danger" test, and must decide what that phrase imports. We first note that many of the cases in which this Court has reversed convictions by use of this or similar tests have been based on the fact that the interest which the State was attempting to protect was itself too insubstantial to warrant restriction of speech. . . . Overthrow of the Government by force and violence is certainly a substantial enough interest for the Government to limit speech. Indeed, this is the ultimate value of any society, for if a society cannot protect its very structure from armed internal attack, it must follow that no subordinate value can be protected. If, then, this interest may be protected, the literal problem which is presented is what has been meant by the use of the phrase "clear and present danger" of the utterances bringing about the evil within the power of Congress to punish.

Obviously, the words cannot mean that before the Government may act, it must wait until the *putsch* is about to be executed, the plans have been laid and the signal is awaited. If Government is aware that a group aiming at its overthrow is attempting to indoctrinate its members and to commit them to a course whereby they will strike when the leaders feel the circumstances permit, action by the Government is required. The argument that there is no need for Government to concern itself, for Government is strong, it possesses ample powers to put down a rebellion, it may defeat the revolution with ease needs no answer. For that is not the question. Certainly an attempt to overthrow the Government by force, even though doomed from the outset because of inadequate numbers or power of the revolutionists, is a sufficient evil for Congress to prevent. The damage which such attempts create both physically and politically to a nation makes it impossible to measure the validity in terms of the probability of success, or the immediacy of a successful attempt. In the instant case the trial judge charged the jury that they could not convict unless they found that petitioners intended to overthrow the Government "as speedily as circumstances would permit." This does not mean, and could not properly mean, that they would not strike until there was certainty of success. What was meant was that the revolutionists would strike when they thought the time was ripe. We must therefore reject the contention that success or probability of success is the criterion.

The situation with which Justices Holmes and Brandeis were concerned in Gitlow was a comparatively isolated event, bearing little relation in their minds to any substantial threat to the safety of the community. . . . They were not confronted with any situation comparable to the instant one—the development of an apparatus designed and dedicated to the overthrow of the Government, in the context of world crisis after crisis.

Chief Judge Learned Hand, writing for the majority below, interpreted the phrase as follows: "In each case [courts] must ask whether the gravity of the 'evil,' discounted by its improbability, justifies such invasion of free speech as is necessary to avoid the danger." We adopt this statement of the rule. As articulated by Chief Judge Hand, it is as succinct and inclusive as any other we might devise at this time. It takes into consideration those factors which we deem relevant, and relates their significances. More we cannot expect from words.

Likewise, we are in accord with the court below, which affirmed the trial court's finding that the requisite danger existed. The mere fact that from the period 1945 to 1948 petitioners' activities did not result in an attempt to overthrow the Government by force and violence is of course no answer to the fact that there was a group that was ready to make the attempt. The formation by petitioners of such a highly organized conspiracy, with rigidly disciplined members subject to call when the leaders, these petitioners, felt that the time had come for action, coupled with the inflammable nature of world conditions, similar uprisings in other countries, and the touch-and-go nature of our relations with countries with whom petitioners were in the very least ideologically attuned, convince us that their convictions were justified on this score. And this analysis disposes of the contention that a conspiracy to advocate, as distinguished from the advocacy itself, cannot be constitutionally restrained, because it comprises only the preparation. It is the existence of the conspiracy which creates the danger. . . . If the ingredients of the reaction are present, we cannot bind the Government to wait until the catalyst is added.

IV.

[The Court here considers whether the trial court was correct in not submitting to the jury the question of the existence of clear and present danger.]

. . . The argument that the action of the trial court is erroneous, in declaring as a matter of law that such violation shows sufficient danger to justify the punishment despite the First Amendment, rests on the theory that a jury must decide a question of the application of the First Amendment. We do not agree.

When facts are found that establish the violation of a statute, the protection against conviction afforded by the First Amendment is a matter of law. The doctrine that there must be a clear and present danger of a substantive evil that Congress has a right to prevent is a judicial rule to be applied as a matter of law by the courts. The guilt is established by proof of facts. Whether the First Amendment protects the activity which constitutes the violation of the statute must depend upon a judicial determination of the scope of the First Amendment applied to the circumstances of the case. . . .

V.

There remains to be discussed the question of vagueness—whether the statute as we have interpreted it is too vague, not sufficiently advising those who would speak of the limitations upon their activity. . . .

We hold that §§ 2(a) (1), (2)(a) (3) and 3 of the Smith Act, do not inherently, or as construed or applied in the instant case, violate the First Amendment and other provisions of the Bill of Rights, or the First and Fifth Amendments because of indefiniteness. Petitioners intended to overthrow the Government of the United States as speedily as the circumstances would permit. Their conspiracy to organize the Communist Party and to teach and advocate the overthrow of the Government of the United States by force and violence created a "clear and present danger" of an attempt to overthrow the Government by force and violence. They were properly and constitutionally convicted for violation of the Smith Act. The judgments of conviction are

Affirmed.

Mr. Justice **Clark** took no part in this case.

Mr. Justice **Frankfurter** wrote a concurring opinion.

Mr. Justice **Jackson** wrote a concurring opinion.

Mr. Justice **Black** wrote a dissenting opinion.

Mr. Justice **Douglas** wrote a dissenting opinion.

FREE ASSEMBLY AND PUBLIC ORDER

ADDERLEY v. FLORIDA

385 U. S. 39; 87 S. Ct. 242; 17 L. Ed. 2d 149
(1966)

During the late 1950s and early 1960s Southern blacks, led by such people as Martin Luther King, Jr., undertook to bring an end to segregation by nonviolent means. This was to be done by attracting public attention to segregation policies in the hope that the public conscience would be aroused and demand their abolition.

Against these efforts the Southern communities rolled out a battery of legal field pieces, some of them dating back to the early days of the common law. One of these was a prosecution for criminal trespass. Among the techniques employed to publicize segregation was the "sit-in" demonstration, in which blacks, sometimes accompanied by sympathetic whites, would enter a restaurant or lunch counter with a **WHITE ONLY** *sign in the window and ask to be served. When service was denied, they refused to leave, and the police would be called to arrest them for trespass.*

In five cases decided in 1964 the Supreme Court reversed on nonconstitutional grounds convictions for sit-in demonstrations. Although the Court carefully avoided the issue of whether state enforcement of trespass laws to effect private discrimination made the state a party to the discrimination, six justices in separate opinions indicated their stand on this issue. Justices Black, Harlan, and White argued that in the absence of a statute forbidding such discrimination, the impartial enforcement of trespass statutes does not make the state a party to the discrimination and hence does not deny

equal protection, while Justices Warren, Goldberg, and Douglas argued that the framers of the Fourteenth Amendment had assumed the continued existence of the right of all citizens to enter places of public accommodation, and the refusal of the state to enforce that right as to blacks denies them the equal protection of the law. See Bell v. Maryland, Bouie v. Columbia, Griffin v. Maryland, Robinson v. Florida, and Barr v. Columbia.

The final chapter in the sit-in cases was written in Hamm v. Rock Hill (1964), decided the same day as Heart of Atlanta Motel v. United States. Again the Court failed to reach the constitutional issue but concluded that the Civil Rights Act of 1964, by making sit-ins no longer a crime, had abated sit-in prosecutions then in progress, since the states no longer had a policy to be served by such prosecutions. Federal statutes would decree this result as far as federal crimes were concerned, and the supremacy clause dictated the same result for state crimes. The effect of the decision was to stop the prosecution of some three thousand sit-in demonstrators.

A second technique relied upon by the Southern communities was the well-established right of any organized community to protect itself from a breach of the peace. Such a breach is "a substantive evil which the state can prevent" through the exercise of its police power; therefore a speech which presents a "clear and present danger" of causing a breach of the peace is punishable. Although the use of such statutes against demonstrations and "marches" presented some novel features, the general rules regarding them had been laid down years before. The Supreme Court, in reviewing cases which allege a violation of freedom of speech on this ground must determine (1) that the statute, as interpreted by the state court or by the judge in his charge to the jury, really defines a breach of the peace, and (2) that a clear and present danger of such breach actually exists.

In Chaplinsky v. New Hampshire (1942) a Jehovah's Witness called a police officer "a God damned racketeer" and "a damned Fascist," in violation of state statute whose purpose, the state court said, was to forbid words "such as have a direct tendency to cause acts of violence by the persons to whom, individually, the remark is addressed." The Court agreed that such speech could constitutionally be punished: "There are certain well-defined and narrowly limited classes of speech, the prevention and punishment of which have never been thought to raise any constitutional problem. These include the lewd and obscene, the profane, the libelous, and the insulting or 'fighting' words—those which by their very utterance inflict injury or tend to incite an immediate breach of the peace. . . . 'Resort to epithets or personal abuse is not in any proper sense communication of information or opinion safeguarded by the Constitution. . . .' " There was, moreover, a clear and present danger: ". . . the appellations 'damned racketeer' and 'damned Fascist' are epithets likely to provoke the average person to retaliation, and thereby cause a breach of the peace."

Another case in which the making of a speech was punished by the city as a breach of the peace was Terminiello v. Chicago (1949), a case which remains bitterly controversial. Terminiello (who denied he was a Fascist) was introduced by Gerald L. K. Smith and spoke in an auditorium in Chicago to a crowd of about eight hundred persons, under the sponsorship of the Christian Veterans of America. Outside, a protesting crowd of over a thousand (who denied they were Communist-led) milled about, yelling and throwing stones at the windows. Inside Terminiello spoke despite the tumult, linking Democrats, Jews, and Communists together in a speech filled with race hatred. A cordon of police assigned to the meeting was unable to prevent several outbreaks of violence, including the smashing of doors and windows.

Terminiello was found guilty of inciting a breach of the peace and fined $100. The trial court charged the jury that " 'breach of the peace' consists of any 'misbehavior which violates the public peace and decorum'; and that the 'misbehavior may constitute a breach of the peace if it stirs the public to anger, invites dispute, brings about a condition of unrest, or creates a disturbance. . . .' " The Supreme Court never reached the question whether the speech itself might be punishable, because it found that the statute as interpreted by the trial judge permitted the punishment of speech that was protected by the Constitution: ". . . A function of free speech under our system of government is to invite dispute. It may indeed best serve its high purpose when it induces a condition of unrest, creates dissatisfaction with conditions as they are, or even stirs people to anger. Speech is often provocative and challenging. It may strike at prejudices and preconceptions and have profound unsettling effects as it presses for acceptance of an idea. . . . The ordinance as construed by the trial court seriously invaded this province.' "

In contrast to the Terminiello decision, the Court in Feiner v. New York (1951) upheld the disorderly conduct conviction of a Syracuse University student for a street-corner speech in which he was apparently "endeavoring to arouse the Negro people against the whites, urging that they rise up in arms and fight for equal rights." The two policemen present later testified that the mixed crowd of seventy-five to eighty persons "was restless and there was some pushing, shoving, and milling around." Fearful that they could not control the crowd if violence erupted, they asked Feiner to stop speaking and arrested him when he refused. The Court held the trial court justified in finding a clear and present danger of causing a riot.

In 1963 in Edwards v. South Carolina the Court upheld the right to demonstrate on public property. A group of black students had gathered on the statehouse lawn to protest state segregation policies. The pickets listened to a religious harangue, sang, stamped their feet, and clapped. They refused to disperse when ordered and were arrested for a breach of the peace. The Court held that "the Fourteenth Amendment does not permit a State to make criminal the peaceful expression of unpopular views . . ." and the breach of the peace statute was so vague as to "permit punishment of the fair use of this opportunity." In this case "there was no violence or threat of violence on their part, or on the part of

any member of the crowd watching them. Police protection was ample. . . . And the record is barren of any evidence of 'fighting words.' "

Two years later, in Cox v. Louisiana (1965), a civil rights leader was arrested when a group of some two thousand students assembled across the street from the courthouse, with police permission, to protest the arrest of twenty-three of their fellows for picketing segregated lunch counters. As in the Edwards case they began to sing and clap, and upon their refusal to disperse when ordered were arrested for breach of the peace. The Court found the facts and the statute almost identical to those in Edwards, and void for the same reasons. The Court also rejected the claim that the pickets had been illegally obstructing the sidewalk. It denied that physical demonstrations enjoyed the same freedom as mere speech, but noted that the city police customarily permitted the obstruction of sidewalks for some purposes "in their completely uncontrolled discretion." In a companion case by the same name and involving the same facts, the Court reversed Cox's conviction for picketing near a courthouse. Conceding that a state could legitimately protect its "judicial system from the pressures which picketing near a courthouse might create" the Court held that Cox had police permission to picket where he did and was not arrested until ordered (invalidly) to move on. (In April 1983 the Court, in United States v. Grace, held void on its face a federal statute forbidding picketing or the display of banners or signs on the grounds of the Supreme Court building itself. One sign carried the text of the First Amendment.)

The courageous efforts of the Southern black to achieve racial equality through nonviolent means won widespread admiration and support from the liberal white community and strong encouragement was given the National Association for the Advancement of Colored People (NAACP) in its efforts to win recognition for black rights in the courts. Since the average victim of race discrimination was ill-equipped to fight for legal rights, the NAACP shouldered the financial burden and provided those victimized with legal assistance, with the result that a number of Southern states made serious efforts to oust or cripple the organization. The result was a series of Supreme Court holdings that the organization need not divulge its membership lists either as a condition of doing business in the state (NAACP v. Alabama, 1958), or to a legislative committee investigating Communism in civil rights organizations (Gibson v. Florida Investigation Committee, 1963). Nor was its bringing of test cases punishable as barratry (NAACP v. Button, 1963), and it could not be forbidden to do business in the state (NAACP v. Alabama, 1964). All these decisions rested on a freedom of association held to be protected by the First Amendment and made applicable to the states by the Fourteenth.

With the outbreak of racial violence in Northern cities in the summer of 1965 and with the breach between the conservative, law-oriented NAACP on the one hand and the more militant Congress of Racial Equality (CORE) and Student Nonviolent Coordinating Committee (SNCC) on the other, Northern white support for the *civil rights movement fell off sharply. The 1966 civil rights bill with provisions against anti-civil rights terrorism and an open housing provision failed to pass Congress, and in the fall elections of that year a number of congressional candidates and advocates of referendum measures exploited the fear of "black power" and looked, in some cases successfully, to a "white backlash" for support.*

In the present case the Supreme Court for the first time held valid a state criminal trespass statute against black demonstrators. A group of some two hundred students from Florida A&M had marched to the jail in Tallahassee to protest the arrest of some of their body for trying to integrate public theaters, as well as against segregation policies generally. Over one hundred remained after being ordered to leave, and were arrested for trespass.

Mr. Justice **Black** delivered the opinion of the Court, saying in part:

Petitioners, Harriett Louise Adderley and 31 other persons, were convicted by a jury in a joint trial in the County Judge's Court of Leon County, Florida, on a charge of "trespass with a malicious and mischievous intent" upon the premises of the county jail contrary to § 821.18 of the Florida statutes. . . . Petitioners, apparently all students of the Florida A. & M. University in Tallahassee, had gone from the school to the jail about a mile away, along with many other students, to "demonstrate" at the jail their protests because of arrests of other protesting students the day before, and perhaps to protest more generally against state and local policies and practices of racial segregation, including segregation of the jail. The county sheriff, legal custodian of the jail and jail grounds, tried to persuade the students to leave the jail grounds. When this did not work, he notified them that they must leave, that if they did not leave he would arrest them for trespassing, and that if they resisted he would charge them with that as well. Some of the students left but others, including petitioners, remained and they were arrested. . . .

I.

Petitioners have insisted from the beginning of this case that they are controlled and must be reversed because of our prior cases of Edwards v. South Carolina [1963] and Cox v. Louisiana [1965]. We cannot agree.

The Edwards case, like this one, did come up when a number of persons demonstrated on public property against their State's segregation policies. They also sang hymns and danced, as did the demonstrators in this case. But here the analogies to this case end. In Edwards, the demonstrators went to the South Carolina State Capitol grounds to protest. In this case they went to the jail. Traditionally, state capitol grounds are open to the public. Jails, built for security purposes, are not. The demonstrators at the South Carolina Capitol went in through a public driveway and as they entered they were told by state officials there that they had a right as citizens to go through the State House grounds as long as they were peaceful. Here the demonstrators entered the jail grounds through a driveway used only for jail purposes and without warning to or permission from the sheriff. More importantly, South Carolina sought to prosecute its State Capitol demonstrators by charging them with the common-law crime of breach of the peace. This Court in Edwards took pains to point out at length the indefinite, loose, and broad nature of this charge; indeed, this Court pointed out . . . that the South Carolina Supreme Court had itself declared that the "breach of the peace" charge is "not susceptible of exact definition." South Carolina's power to prosecute, it was emphasized . . . , would have been different had the State proceeded under a "precise and narrowly drawn regulatory statute evincing a legislative judgment that certain specific conduct be limited or proscribed" such as, for example, "limiting the periods during which the State House grounds were open to the public. . . ." The South Carolina breach-of-the-peace statute was thus struck down as being so broad and all-embracing as to jeopardize speech, press, assembly and petition, under the constitutional doctrine enunciated in Cantwell v. Connecticut [1940], and followed in many subsequent cases. And it was on this same ground of vagueness that in Cox v. Louisiana the Louisiana breach-of-the-peace law used to prosecute Cox was invalidated.

The Florida trespass statute under which these petitioners were charged cannot be challenged on this ground. It is aimed at conduct of one limited kind, that is for one person or persons to trespass upon the property of another with a malicious and mischievous intent. There is no lack of notice in this law, nothing to entrap or fool the unwary.

Petitioners seem to argue that the Florida trespass law is void for vagueness because it requires a trespass to be "with a malicious and mischievous intent. . . ." But these words do not broaden the scope of trespass so as to make it cover a multitude of types of conduct as does the common-law breach-of-the-peace charge. On the contrary, these words narrow the scope of the offense. The trial court charged the jury as to their meaning and petitioners have not argued that this definition . . . is not a reasonable and clear definition of the terms. The use of these terms in the statute, instead of contributing to uncertainty and misunderstanding, actually makes its meaning more understandable and clear.

II.

Petitioners in this Court invoke the doctrine of abatement announced by this Court in Hamm v. Rock Hill [1964]. But that holding was that the Civil Rights Act of 1964, which made it unlawful for places of public accommodation to deny service to any person because of race, effected an abatement of prosecutions of persons for seeking such services that arose prior to the passage of the Act. But this case in no way involves prosecution of petitioners for seeking service in establishments covered by the Act. It involves only an alleged trespass on jail grounds—a trespass which can be prosecuted regardless of the fact that it is the means of protesting segregation of establishments covered by the Act.

III.

Petitioners next argue that "petty criminal statues may not be used to violate minorities' constitutional rights." This of course is true but this abstract proposition gets us nowhere in deciding this case.

IV.

Petitioners here contend that "Petitioners' convictions are based on a total lack of relevant evidence." If true, this would be a denial of due process. . . . Petitioners' summary of facts as well as that of the Circuit Court show an abundance of facts to support the jury's verdict of guilty in this case.

In summary both these statements show testimony ample to prove this: Disturbed and upset by the arrest of their schoolmates the day before, a large number of Florida A. & M. students assembled on the school grounds and decided to march down to the county jail. Some apparently wanted to be put in jail too, along with the students already there. A group of around 200 marched from the school and arrived at the jail singing and clapping. They went directly to the jail-door entrance where they were met by a deputy sheriff, evidently surprised by their arrival. He asked them to move back, claiming they were blocking the entrance to the jail and fearing that they might attempt to enter the jail. They moved back part of the way, where they stood or sat, singing, clapping, and dancing, on the jail driveway and on an adjacent grassy area upon the jail premises. This particular jail entrance and driveway were not normally used by the public, but by the sheriff's department for transporting prisoners to and from the courts several blocks away and by commercial concerns for servicing the jail. Even after their partial retreat, the demonstrators continued to block vehicular passage over this driveway up to the entrance of the jail.* Someone called the sheriff who was at the moment apparently conferring with one of the state court judges about incidents connected with prior arrests for demonstrations. When the sheriff returned to the jail, he immediately inquired if all was safe inside the jail and was told it was. He then engaged in a conversation with two of the leaders. He told them they were trespassing upon jail property and that he would give them 10 minutes to leave or he would arrest them. Neither of the leaders did anything to disperse the crowd, and one of them told the sheriff that they wanted to get

---

*Although some of the petitioners testified that they had no intention of interfering with vehicular traffic to and from the jail entrance and that they noticed no vehicle trying to enter or leave the driveway, the deputy sheriff testified that it would have been impossible for automobiles to drive up to the jail entrance and that one serviceman, finished with his business in the jail, waited inside because the demonstrators were sitting around and leaning against his truck parked outside. The sheriff testified that the time the demonstrators were there, between 9:30 and 10 Monday morning, was generally a very busy time for using the jail entrance to transport weekend inmates to the courts and for tradesmen to make service calls at the jail.

arrested. A local minister talked with some of the demonstrators and told them not to enter the jail, because they could not arrest themselves, but just to remain where they were. After about 10 minutes, the sheriff, in a voice loud enough to be heard by all, told the demonstrators that he was the legal custodian of the jail and its premises, that they were trespassing on county property in violation of the law, that they should all leave forthwith or he would arrest them, and that if they attempted to resist arrest, he would charge them with that as a separate offense. Some of the group then left. Others, including all petitioners, did not leave. Some of them sat down. In a few minutes, realizing that the remaining demonstrators had no intention of leaving, the sheriff ordered his deputies to surround those remaining on jail premises and place them, 107 demonstrators, under arrest. The sheriff unequivocally testified that he did not arrest any persons other than those who were on the jail premises. Of the three petitioners testifying, two insisted that they were arrested before they had a chance to leave, had they wanted to, and one testified that she did not intend to leave. The sheriff again explicitly testified that he did not arrest any person who was attempting to leave.

Under the foregoing testimony the jury was authorized to find that the State had proven every essential element of the crime, as it was defined by the state court. That interpretation is, of course, binding on us, leaving only the question of whether conviction of the state offense, thus defined, unconstitutionally deprives petitioners of their rights to freedom of speech, press, assembly or petition. We hold it does not. The sheriff, as jail custodian, had power, as the state courts have here held, to direct that this large crowd of people get off the grounds. There is not a shred of evidence in this record that this power was exercised, or that its exercise was sanctioned by the lower courts, because the sheriff objected to what was being sung or said by the demonstrators or because he disagreed with the objectives of their protest. The record reveals that he objected only to their presence on that part of the jail grounds reserved for jail uses. There is no evidence at all that on any other occasion had similarly large groups of the public been permitted to gather on this portion of the jail grounds for any purpose. Nothing in the Constitution of the United States prevents Florida from even-handed enforcement of its general trespass statute against those refusing to obey the sheriff's order to remove themselves from what amounted to the curtilage of the jailhouse. The State, no less than a private owner of property, has power to preserve the property under its control for the use to which it is lawfully dedicated. For this reason there is no merit to the petitioners' argument that they had a constitutional right to stay on the property, over the jail custodian's objections, because this "area chosen for the peaceful civil rights demonstration was not only 'reasonable' but also particularly appropriate. . . ." Such an argument has as its major unarticulated premise the assumption that people who want to propagandize protests or views have a constitutional right to do so whenever and however and wherever they please. That concept of constitutional law was vigorously and forthrightly rejected in two of the cases petitioners rely on, Cox v. Louisiana, at 554-555 and 563-564. We reject it again. The United States Constitution does not forbid a State to control the use of its own property for its own lawful nondiscriminatory purpose.

These judgments are
Affirmed.

Mr. Justice **Douglas,** with whom the Chief Justice **[Warren],** Mr. Justice **Brennan,** and Mr. Justice **Fortas** concur, dissenting, said in part:

The First Amendment, applicable to the States by reason of the Fourteenth . . . , provides that "Congress shall make no law abridging . . . the right of the people peaceably to assemble, and to petition the Government for a redress of grievances." These rights, along with religion, speech, and press, are preferred rights of the Constitution, made so by reason of that explicit guarantee and what Edmond Cahn in Confronting Injustice (1966) referred to as "The Firstness of the First Amendment." With all respect, therefore, the Court errs in treating the case as if it were an ordinary trespass case or an ordinary picketing case.

The jailhouse, like an executive mansion, a legislative chamber, a courthouse, or the statehouse itself (Edwards v. South Carolina) is one of the seats of government whether it be the Tower of London, the Bastille, or a small county jail. And when it houses political prisoners or those whom many think are unjustly held, it is an obvious center for protest. The right to petition for the redress of grievances has an ancient history and is not limited to writing a letter or sending a telegram to a congressman; it is not confined to appearing before the local city council, or writing letters to the President or Governor or Mayor. . . . Conventional methods of petitioning may be, and often have been, shut off to large groups of our citizens. Legislators may turn deaf ears; formal complaints may be routed endlessly through a bureaucratic maze; courts may let the wheels of justice grind very slowly. Those who do not control television and radio, those who cannot afford to advertise in newspapers or circulate elaborate pamphlets may have only a more limited type of access to public officials. Their methods should not be condemned as tactics of obstruction and harassment as long as the assembly and petition are peaceable, as these were.

There is no question that petitioners had as their purpose a protest against the arrest of Florida A. & M. students for trying to integrate public theatres. The sheriff's testimony indicates that he well understood the purpose of the rally. The petitioners who testified unequivocally stated that the group was protesting the arrests, and state and local policies of segregation, including segregation of the jail. This testimony was not contradicted or even questioned. The fact that no one gave a formal speech, that no elaborate handbills were distributed, and that the group was not laden with signs would seem to be immaterial. Such methods are not the sine qua non of petitioning for the redress grievances. The group did sing "freedom" songs. And history shows that a song can be a powerful tool of protest. . . . There was no violence; no threat of violence; no attempted jail break; no storm-

ing of a prison; no plan or plot to do anything but protest. The evidence is uncontradicted that the petitioners' conduct did not upset the jailhouse routine; things went on as they normally would. None of the group entered the jail. Indeed, they moved back from the entrance as they were instructed. There was no shoving, no pushing, no disorder or threat of riot. It is said that some of the group blocked part of the driveway leading to the jail entrance. The chief jailer, to be sure, testified that vehicles would not have been able to use the driveway. Never did the students locate themselves so as to cause interference with persons or vehicles going to or coming from the jail. Indeed, it is undisputed that the sheriff and deputy sheriff, in separate cars, were able to drive up the driveway to the parking places near the entrance and that no one obstructed their path. Further, it is undisputed that the entrance to the jail was not blocked. And whenever the students were requested to move they did so. If there was congestion, the solution was a further request to move to lawns or parking areas, not complete ejection and arrest. The claim is made that a tradesman waited inside the jail because some of the protestants were sitting around and leaning on his truck. The only evidence supporting such a conclusion is the testimony of a deputy sheriff that the tradesman "came to the door . . . and then did not leave." His remaining is just as consistent with a desire to satisfy his curiosity as it is with a restraint. Finally, the fact that some of the protestants may have felt their cause so just that they were willing to be arrested for making their protest outside the jail seems wholly irrelevant. A petition is nonetheless a petition, though its futility may make martyrdom attractive.

We do violence to the First Amendment when we permit this "petition for redress of grievances" to be turned into a trespass action. It does not help to analogize this problem to the problem of picketing. Picketing is a form of protest usually directed against private interests. I do not see how rules governing picketing in general are relevant to this express constitutional right to assemble and to petition for redress of grievances. In the first place the jailhouse grounds were not marked with "NO TRESPASSING!" signs, nor does respondent claim that the public was generally excluded from the grounds. Only the sheriff's fiat transformed lawful conduct into an unlawful trespass. To say that a private owner could have done the same if the rally had taken place on private property is to speak of a different case, as an assembly and a petition for redress of grievances run to government, not to private proprietors.

. . . When we allow Florida to construe her "malicious trespass" statute to bar a person from going on property knowing it is not his own and to apply that prohibition to public property, we discard Cox and Edwards. Would the case be any different if, as is common, the demonstration took place outside a building which housed both the jail and the legislative body? I think not.

There may be some public places which are so clearly committed to other purposes that their use for the airing of grievances is anomalous. There may be some instances in which assemblies and petitions for redress of grievances are not consistent with other necessary purposes of public property. A noisy meeting may be out of keeping with the serenity of the statehouse or the quiet of the courthouse. No one, for example, would suggest that the Senate gallery is the proper place for a vociferous protest rally. And in other cases it may be necessary to adjust the right to petition for redress of grievances to the other interests inhering in the uses to which the public property is normally put. . . . But this is quite different than saying that all public places are off limits to people with grievances. . . . And it is farther yet from saying that the "custodian" of the public property in his discretion can decide when public places shall be used for the communication of ideas, especially the constitutional right to assemble and petition for redress of grievances. . . . For to place such discretion in any public official, be he the "custodian" of the public property or the local police commissioner . . . is to place those who assert their First Amendment rights at his mercy. It gives him the awesome power to decide whose ideas may be expressed and who shall be denied a place to air their claims and petition their government. Such power is out of step with all our decisions prior to today where we have insisted that before a First Amendment right may be curtailed under the guise of a criminal law, any evil that may be collateral to the exercise of the right, must be isolated and defined in a "narrowly drawn" statute . . . lest the power to control excesses of conduct be used to suppress the constitutional right itself. . . .

That tragic consequence happens today when a trespass law is used to bludgeon those who peacefully exercise a First Amendment right to protest to government against one of the most grievous of all modern oppressions which some of our States are inflicting on our citizens. . . .

Today a trespass law is used to penalize people for exercising a constitutional right. Tomorrow a disorderly conduct statute, a breach-of-the-peace statute, a vagrancy statute will be put to the same end. It is said that the sheriff did not make the arrests because of the views which petitioners espoused. That excuse is usually given, as we know from the many cases involving arrests of minority groups for breaches of the peace, unlawful assemblies, and parading without a permit. The charge against William Penn, who preached a nonconformist doctrine in a street in London, was that he caused "a great concourse and tumult of people" in contempt of the King and "to the great disturbance of his peace." That was in 1670. In modern times also such arrests are usually sought to be justified by some legitimate function of government. Yet by allowing these orderly and civilized protests against injustice to be suppressed, we only increase the forces of frustration which the conditions of second-class citizenship are generating amongst us.

WALKER v. BIRMINGHAM

388 U. S. 307; 87 S. Ct. 1824; 18 L. Ed. 2d 1210
(1967)

The difficulties that confront a state in imposing those "reasonable" limits on free speech which the Constitu-
tion allows are illustrated by cases involving the suppression of public nuisances. The Supreme Court held that a statute which forbade entirely the distribution of literature was unconstitutional. In Jamison v. Texas (1943) an ordinance forbade the distribution of handbills on the streets of Dallas. Mrs. Jamison, a member of Jehovah's Witnesses, was convicted of violating the ordinance and fined five dollars. The Court held that "one who is rightfully on a street which the state has left open to the public carries with him there as elsewhere the constitutional right to express his views in an orderly fashion. . . . The right to distribute handbills concerning religious subjects on the streets may not be prohibited at all times, at all places, and under all circumstances."

The state may, on the other hand, place freedom of speech under reasonable police regulations for the protection of the recognized social interests of the community. In Kovacs v. Cooper (1949) the Court upheld a Trenton, New Jersey, ordinance which forbade the use on the streets of a sound-truck which emitted "loud and raucous noises." The Court found that "loud and raucous" was a sufficiently clear definition of the crime, since it has "through daily use acquired a content that conveys to any interested person a sufficiently accurate concept of what is forbidden." Moreover, the restriction was a reasonable one, since "the unwilling listener is not like the passer-by who may be offered a pamphlet in the street but cannot be made to take it. In his home or on the street he is practically helpless to escape this interference with his privacy by loud speakers except through the protection of the municipality." Here the Court was striking a balance between the right to quiet and privacy and the right to free speech.

What a state may not limit directly by statute, it may not permit a policeman or other officer to limit under a grant of administrative discretion which amounts to censorship. Many municipalities have used the device of requiring a license for all public modes of expression, and making it a crime to violate the license requirement. The Supreme Court has almost uniformly held these ordinances to be unconstitutional limitations on freedom of speech and press. If the licensing officer has authority to pass on the desirability of the intended speech, or has authority broad enough to forbid a speech protected by the First Amendment, the ordinance is void on its face because it establishes previous censorship, condemned by the Court in Near v. Minnesota (1931). Thus in Lovell v. Griffin (1938) the Court held void a municipal ordinance which punished as a nuisance the distribution of any literature on the streets without a license from the city manager. The Court emphasized that "the ordinance is not limited to 'literature' that is obscene or offensive to public morals or that advocates unlawful conduct. . . . There is . . . no restriction in its application with respect to time or place. It is not limited to ways which might be regarded as inconsistent with the maintenance of public order. . . ." In Largent v. Texas (1943) an ordinance was held void which forbade soliciting orders or selling books without a license which the mayor had power to issue if he deemed it "proper or advisable." In Saia v. New York (1948) the Court held void an ordinance which forbade the use of a sound-truck on the streets without the permission of the chief of police: "There are no standards prescribed for the exercise of his discretion. The statute is not narrowly drawn to regulate the hours or places of use of loud-speakers, or the volume of sound. . . ." And in *Kunz v. New York* (1951) the Court reversed the conviction of an itinerant preacher for preaching without a license after his application had been disapproved with no reason given. "It is noteworthy that there is no mention in the ordinance of reasons for which such a permit application can be refused. This interpretation allows the police commissioner, an administrative official, to exercise discretion in denying subsequent permit applications on the basis of his interpretation, at that time, of what is deemed to be conduct condemned by the ordinance. We have here, then, an ordinance which gives an administrative official discretionary power to control in advance the right of citizens to speak on religious matters on the streets of New York. As such, the ordinance is clearly invalid as a prior restraint on the exercise of First Amendment rights." The Court was unimpressed with the fact that Kunz had had a previous license revoked for ridiculing and denouncing other religions.

What the state may do directly by statute it may also do through the device of administrative discretion provided the discretion is so narrow that the administrator may not censor speech or press. In *Cox v. New Hampshire* (1941) the Court sustained an ordinance that required a permit from a license board in order to parade in the streets. A group of Jehovah's Witnesses staged an "information march" without applying for a permit and were convicted of violating the ordinance; the state court held that any other form of expression was open to them, and "the defendants, separately, or collectively in groups not constituting a parade or procession" were "under no contemplation of the Act." Furthermore, the discretion of the license board had to be exercised with "uniformity of method of treatment upon the facts of each application, free from improper or inappropriate considerations and from unfair discrimination." The statutory mandate was held to be a "systematic consistent and just order of treatment, with reference to the convenience of public use of the highways." This, the Supreme Court found, was a valid use of the authority to "control the use of its public streets for parades or processions."

But if a state may not deny a person a license to speak, may it, nevertheless, enjoin a person from speaking and then punish that person when the injunction is lifted? This problem first arose in the case of *Thomas v. Collins* (1945). A Texas statute required every labor union organizer operating in the state to secure from the secretary of state an organizer's card before soliciting any members for a union. In order to get the card organizers had to give their name and union affiliations and show their credentials. The secretary of state had no discretion to refuse to register such organizers if these requirements were met. When registered, they were given cards which they were required to carry with them and show to any person they solicited for membership. R. J. Thomas, president of the United Automobile Workers, went to Texas after the passage of this act for the express purpose of contesting its validity. He announced his intention to address a labor union meeting, and this plan was widely advertised in advance. He did not apply for registration as a labor organizer as required by the statute. He addressed a meeting of union men and he specifically invited any nonunion person present to join the union. Prior to the meeting, a restraining order was served on Thomas, forbidding him to address the meeting in the capacity of an organizer since he had not registered; and he was later cited for contempt for a deliberate and willful violation of the order.

The Court held the statute void on two grounds. First, the statute was so broad as to make possible the punishment of legitimate speech. It forbade soliciting members, and "how," the Court said, "one might 'laud unionism,' as the State and the State Supreme Court conceded Thomas was free to do, yet in these circumstances not imply an invitation, is hard to conceive. . . . The restriction's effect, as applied, in a very practical sense was to prohibit Thomas not only to solicit members and memberships, but also to speak in advocacy of the cause of trade unionism. . . ." In the second place, there was not a clear and present danger of bringing about a sufficiently substantial injury to the public to justify the restriction: "We cannot say that 'solicit' in this setting is such a dangerous word. So far as free speech alone is concerned, there can be no ban or restriction or burden placed on the use of such a word except on showing of exceptional circumstances where the public safety, morality or health is involved or some other substantial interest of the community is at stake. . . . A restriction so destructive of the right of public discussion, without greater or more imminent danger to the public interest than existed in this case, is incompatible with the freedoms secured by the First Amendment. . . . If the exercise of the rights of free speech and free assembly cannot be made a crime, we do not think this can be accomplished by the device of requiring previous registration as a condition for exercising them and making such a condition the foundation for restraining in advance their exercise and for imposing a penalty for violating such a restraining order."

A similar problem was presented in *Poulos v. New Hampshire* (1953), which arose under an ordinance like the one involved in the *Cox* case. Poulos, a Jehovah's Witness, applied for a permit to speak in Goodwin Park in Portsmouth on a particular Sunday and was refused; Poulos spoke without the permit and was arrested. The state court interpreted the statute as it had in the *Cox* case, as requiring uniformity and impartiality of treatment. It found that Poulos had not received such treatment, and that the denial of the license had been arbitrary and unreasonable. It held, however, that Poulos was properly convicted; he had no right to violate the ordinance, but should have brought a civil suit in the courts to compel the issuance of a license.

The Supreme Court sustained the conviction on the ground that the ordinance was valid and the state could validly require that arbitrary administrative action be corrected by orderly court procedure: "It must be admitted that judicial correction of arbitrary refusal by administrators to perform official duties under valid laws is *exulcerating and costly. But to allow applicants to proceed without the required permits to run businesses, erect structures, purchase firearms, transport or store explosives or inflammatory products, hold public meetings without prior safety arrangements or take other unauthorized action is apt to cause breaches of the peace or create public dangers. The valid requirements of license are for the good of the applicants and the public. It would be unreal to say that such official failures to act in accordance with state law, redressable by state judicial procedures, are state acts violative of the Federal Constitution. Delay is unfortunate, but the expense and annoyance of litigation is a price citizens must pay for life in an orderly society where the rights of the First Amendment have a real and abiding meaning. Nor can we say that a state's requirement that redress must be sought through appropriate judicial procedure violates due process." The Court distinguished this case from Thomas v. Collins, holding that there the statute was void on its face. "The statutes were as though they did not exist. Therefore there were no offenses in violation of a valid law. In the present prosecution there was a valid ordinance, an unlawful refusal of a license, with the remedial state procedure for the correction of the error. . . . Our Constitution does not require that we approve the violation of a reasonable requirement for a license to speak in public parks because an official error occurred in refusing a proper application."*

While Thomas v. Collins suggests that a person is free to ignore a judicial restraining order if the statute under which it is issued is void on its face, the case printed below cast serious doubt upon the vitality of this holding. In April of 1963, Martin Luther King, Jr., together with two other ministers, Wyatt T. Walker and Fred L. Shuttlesworth, announced plans for a "march" on Good Friday. They requested, and were denied, a permit for the march under § 1159 of the Birmingham city code which provided that the city commission "shall grant a written permit for such parade, procession or other public demonstration, prescribing the streets or other public ways which may be used therefor, unless in its judgment the public welfare, peace, safety, health, decency, good order, morals or convenience require that it be refused."

Apparently fearing the march would take place without a permit, city officials applied the Wednesday before Good Friday for an injunction against "participating in or encouraging mass street parades or mass processions without a permit." The injunction was served the following day, and that night a meeting was held at which one of the petitioners announced that "injunction or no injunction we are going to march tomorrow." No attempt was made to seek judicial review of the injunction, and the petitioners marched both on Good Friday and again on Easter Sunday, leading a group of fifty to sixty followers each time.

The petitioners were convicted both of disobeying the injunction and of marching without a license, receiving sentences of five days in jail and a $50 fine for the first and ninety days at hard labor (plus forty-eight days at hard labor in default of payment of a $75 fine and $24 costs) for the second.

Because of their different rates of movement through the judicial labyrinth, the two cases reached the Supreme Court almost two years apart. When Shuttlesworth v. Birmingham (1969) reached the Court it found the parade ordinance void on its face. "There can be no doubt that the Birmingham ordinance, as it was written, conferred upon the City Commission virtually unbridled and absolute power to prohibit any "parade," "procession," or "demonstration" on the city's streets or public ways. For in deciding whether or not to withhold a permit, the members of the Commission were to be guided only by their own ideas of "public welfare, peace, safety, health, decency, good order, morals or convenience." When the ordinance finally reached the Alabama supreme court it was given a very restrictive interpretation which the Supreme Court was prepared to assume made it valid. But "it would have taken extraordinary clairvoyance for anyone to perceive that this language meant what the Supreme Court of Alabama was destined to find that it meant more than four years later" and "we would hesitate long before assuming that either the members of the Commission or the petitioner possessed any such clairvoyance at the time of the Good Friday march." The Court also noted that success of Alabama's attempt to validate the ordinance "would depend upon, among other things, the availability of expeditious judicial review of the Commission's refusal of a permit. . . . Freedman v. Maryland [1965]." It is interesting to speculate what the outcomes might have been had Shuttlesworth been decided before Walker, rather than the other way around.

Mr. Justice **Stewart** delivered the opinion of the Court, saying in part:

. . . On Easter Sunday, April 14, a crowd of between 1,500 and 2,000 people congregated in the midafternoon in the vicinity of Seventh Avenue and Eleventh Street North in Birmingham. One of the petitioners was seen organizing members of the crowd in formation. A group of about 50, headed by three other petitioners, started down the sidewalk two abreast. At least one other petitioner was among the marchers. Some 300 or 400 people from among the onlookers followed in a crowd that occupied the entire width of the street and overflowed onto the sidewalks. Violence occurred. Members of the crowd threw rocks that injured a newspaperman and damaged a police motorcycle.

The next day the city officials who had requested the injunction applied to the state circuit court for an order to show cause why the petitioners should not be held in contempt for violating it. At the ensuing hearing the petitioners sought to attack the constitutionality of the injunction on the ground that it was vague and overbroad, and restrained free speech. They also sought to attack the Birmingham parade ordinance upon similar grounds, and upon the further ground that the ordinance had previously been administered in an arbitrary and discriminatory manner.

The circuit judge refused to consider any of these contentions, pointing out that there had been neither a motion to dissolve the injunction, nor an effort to comply with it by applying for a permit from the city commission before engaging in the Good Friday and Easter Sunday parades. Consequently, the court held that the only issues before it were whether it had jurisdiction to issue the temporary injunction, and whether thereafter the petitioners had knowingly violated it. Upon these issues the court found against the petitioners, and imposed upon each of them a sentence of five days in jail and a $50 fine, in accord with an Alabama statute.

The Supreme Court of Alabama affirmed. . . .

Howat v. Kansas [1922] was decided by this Court almost 50 years ago. That was a case in which people had been punished by a Kansas trial court for refusing to obey an anti-strike injunction issued under the state industrial relations act. They had claimed a right to disobey the court's order upon the ground that the state statute and the injunction based upon it were invalid under the Federal Constitution. The Supreme Court of Kansas had affirmed the judgment, holding that the trial court "had general power to issue injunctions in equity and that, even if its exercise of the power was erroneous, the injunction was not void, and the defendants were precluded from attacking it in this collateral proceeding . . . that, if the injunction was erroneous, jurisdiction was not thereby forfeited, that the error was subject to correction only by the ordinary method of appeal, and disobedience to the order constituted contempt."

This Court, in dismissing the writ of error, not only unanimously accepted but fully approved the validity of the rule of state law upon which the judgment of the Kansas court was grounded:

"An injunction duly issuing out of a court of general jurisdiction with equity powers upon pleadings properly invoking its action, and served upon persons made parties therein and within the jurisdiction, must be obeyed by them however erroneous the action of the court may be, even if the error be in the assumption of the validity of a seeming but void law going to the merits of the case. It is for the court of first instance to determine the question of the validity of the law, and until its decision is reversed for error by orderly review, either by itself or by a higher court, its orders based on its decision are to be respected, and disobedience of them is contempt of its lawful authority, to be punished."

The rule of state law accepted and approved in Howat v. Kansas is consistent with the rule of law followed by the federal courts.

In the present case, however, we are asked to hold that this rule of law, upon which the Alabama courts relied, was constitutionally impermissible. We are asked to say that the Constitution compelled Alabama to allow the petitioners to violate this injunction, to organize and engage in these mass street parades and demonstrations, without any previous effort on their part to have the injunction dissolved or modified, or any attempt to secure a parade permit in accordance with its terms. Whatever the limits of Howat v. Kansas, we cannot accept the petitioners' contentions in the circumstances of this case.

Without question the state court that issued the injunction had, as a court of equity, jurisdiction over the petitioners and over the subject matter of the controversy. And this is not a case where the injunction was transparently invalid or had only a frivolous pretense to validity. We have consistently recognized the strong interest of state and local governments in regulating the use of their streets and other public places. Cox v. New Hampshire [1941]; Kovacs v. Cooper [1949]; Poulos v. New Hampshire [1953]; Adderley v. Florida [1966]. When protest takes the form of mass demonstrations, parades, or picketing on public streets and sidewalks, the free passage of traffic and the prevention of public disorder and violence become important objects of legitimate state concern. As the Court stated, in Cox v. Louisiana, "We emphatically reject the notion . . . that the First and Fourteenth Amendments afford the same kind of freedom to those who would communicate ideas by conduct such as patrolling, marching, and picketing on streets and highways, as these amendments afford to those who communicate ideas by pure speech." . . .

. . . The generality of the language contained in the Birmingham parade ordinance upon which the injunction was based would unquestionably raise substantial constitutional issues concerning some of its provisions. . . . The petitioners, however, did not even attempt to apply to the Alabama courts for an authoritative construction of the ordinance. Had they done so, those courts might have given the licensing authority granted in the ordinance a narrow and precise scope, as did the New Hampshire courts in Cox v. New Hampshire and Poulos v. New Hampshire. . . . Here, just as in Cox and Poulos, it could not be assumed that this ordinance was void on its face.

The breadth and vagueness of the injunction itself would also unquestionably be subject to substantial constitutional question. But the way to raise that question was to apply to the Alabama courts to have the injunction modified or dissolved. The injunction in all events clearly prohibited mass parading without a permit, and the evidence shows that the petitioners fully understood that prohibition when they violated it.

. . . The petitioners also claim that they were free to disobey the injunction because the parade ordinance on which it was based had been administered in the past in an arbitrary and discriminatory fashion. In support of this claim they sought to introduce evidence that, a few days before the injunction issued, requests for permits to picket had been made to a member of the city commission. One request had been rudely rebuffed, and this same official had later made clear that he was without power to grant the permit alone, since the issuance of such permits was the responsibility of the entire city commission. Assuming the truth of this proffered evidence, it does not follow that the parade ordinance was void on its face. The petitioners, moreover, did not apply for a permit either to the commission itself or to any commissioner after the injunction issued. Had they done so, and had the permit been refused, it is clear that their claim of arbitrary or discriminatory administration of the ordinance would have been considered by the state circuit court upon a motion to dissolve the injunction.

This case would arise in quite a different constitutional posture if the petitioners, before disobeying the injunction, had challenged it in the Alabama courts, and had been met with delay or frustration of their constitutional claims. But there is no showing that such would have been the fate of a timely motion to modify or dissolve the injunction. There was an interim of two days between the issuance of the injunction and the Good Friday march. The petitioners give absolutely no explanation of why they did not make some application to the state court during that period. The injunction had issued ex parte; if the court had been presented with the petitioners' contentions, it might well have dissolved or at least modified its order in some respects. If it had not done so, Alabama procedure would have provided for an expedited process of appellate review. It cannot be presumed that the Alabama courts would have ignored the petitioners' constitutional claims. Indeed, these contentions were accepted in another case by an Alabama appellate court that struck down on direct review the conviction under this very ordinance of one of these same petitioners. . . .

The rule of law that Alabama followed in this case reflects a belief that in the fair administration of justice no man can be judge in his own case, however exalted his station, however righteous his motives, and irrespective of his race, color, politics, or religion. This Court cannot hold that the petitioners were constitutionally free to ignore all the procedures of the law and carry their battle to the streets. One may sympathize with the petitioners' impatient commitment to their cause. But respect for judicial process is a small price to pay for the civilizing hand of law, which alone can give abiding meaning to constitutional freedom.

Affirmed.

Mr. Chief Justice **Warren**, whom Mr. Justice **Brennan** and Mr. Justice **Fortas** join, dissenting, said in part:

Petitioners in this case contend that they were convicted under an ordinance that is unconstitutional on its face because it submits their First and Fourteenth Amendment rights to free speech and peaceful assembly to the unfettered discretion of local officials. They further contend that the ordinance was unconstitutionally applied to them because the local officials used their discretion to prohibit peaceful demonstrations by a group whose political viewpoint the officials opposed. The Court does not dispute these contentions, but holds that petitioners may nonetheless be convicted and sent to jail because the patently unconstitutional ordinance was copied into an injunction—issued ex parte without prior notice or hearing on the request of the Commissioner of Public Safety—forbidding all persons having notice of the injunction to violate the ordinance without any limitation of time. I dissent because I do not believe that the fundamental protections of the Constitution were meant to be so easily evaded, or that "the civilizing hand of law" would be hampered in the slightest by enforcing the First Amendment in this case. . . .

The salient facts can be stated very briefly. Petitioners are Negro ministers who sought to express their concern about racial discrimination in Birmingham, Alabama, by holding peaceful protest demonstrations in that city on Good Friday and Easter Sunday, 1963. For obvious reasons, it was important for the significance of the demonstrations that they be held on those particular dates. A representative of petitioners' organization went to the City Hall and asked "to see the person or persons in charge to issue permits, permits for parading, picketing, and demonstrating." She was directed to Public Safety Commissioner Connor, who denied her request for a permit in terms that left no doubt that petitioners were not going to be issued a permit under any circumstances. "He said, 'No, you will not get a permit in Birmingham, Alabama to picket. I will picket you over to the City Jail,' and he repeated that twice." A second, telegraphic request was also summarily denied, in a telegram signed by "Eugene 'Bull' Connor," with the added information that permits could be issued only by the full City Commission, a three-man body consisting of Commissioner Connor and two others.* According to petitioners' offer of proof, the truth of which is assumed for purposes of this case, parade permits had uniformly been issued for all other groups by the city clerk on the request of the traffic bureau of the police department, which was under Commissioner Connor's direction. The requirement that the approval of the full Commission be obtained was applied only to this one group.

Understandably convinced that the City of Birmingham was not going to authorize their demonstrations under any circumstances, petitioners proceeded with their plans despite Commissioner Connor's orders. On Wednesday, April 10, at 9 in the evening, the city filed in a state circuit court a bill of complaint seeking an ex parte injunction. . . .

. . . The Circuit Court issued the injunction in the form requested, and in effect ordered petitioners and all other persons having notice of the order to refrain for an unlimited time from carrying on any demonstrations without a permit. A permit, of course, was clearly unobtainable; the city would not have sought this injunction if it had any intention of issuing one.

Petitioners were served with copies of the injunction at various times on Thursday and on Good Friday. Unable to believe that such a blatant and broadly drawn prior restraint on their First Amendment rights could be valid, they announced their intention to defy it and went ahead with the planned peaceful demonstrations on Easter weekend. On the following Monday, when they

---

*. . . The attitude of the city administration in general and of its Public Safety Commissioner in particular are a matter of public record, of course, and are familiar to this Court from previous litigation. See Shuttlesworth v. City of Birmingham (1965); Shuttlesworth v. City of Birmingham (1964); Shuttlesworth v. City of Birmingham (1963); Gober v. City of Birmingham (1963); In Re Shuttlesworth (1962). The United States Commission on Civil Rights found continuing abuse of civil rights protestors by the Birmingham police, including use of dogs, clubs, and firehoses. . . . Commissioner Eugene "Bull" Connor, a self-proclaimed white supremacist, . . . made no secret of his personal attitude toward the rights of Negroes and the decisions of this Court. He vowed that racial integration would never come to Birmingham, and wore a button inscribed "Never" to advertise that vow. Yet the Court indulges in speculation that these civil rights protesters might have obtained a permit from this city and this man had they made enough repeated applications.

promptly filed a motion to dissolve the injunction, the court found them in contempt, holding that they had waived all their First Amendment rights by disobeying the court order.

These facts lend no support to the court's charges that petitioners were presuming to act as judges in their own case, or that they had a disregard for the judicial process. They did not flee the jurisdiction or refuse to appear in the Alabama courts. Having violated the injunction, they promptly submitted themselves to the courts to test the constitutionality of the injunction and the ordinance it parroted. They were in essentially the same position as persons who challenge the constitutionality of a statute by violating it, and then defend the ensuing criminal prosecution on constitutional grounds. It has never been thought that violation of a statute indicated such a disrespect for the legislature that the violator always must be punished even if the statute was unconstitutional. . . .

I do not believe that giving this Court's seal of approval to such a gross misuse of the judicial process is likely to lead to greater respect for the law any more than it is likely to lead to greater protection for First Amendment freedoms. The ex parte temporary injunction has a long and odious history in this country, and its susceptibility to misuse is all too apparent from the facts of the case. As a weapon against strikes, it proved so effective in the hands of judges friendly to employers that Congress was forced to take the drastic step of removing from federal district courts the jurisdiction to issue injunctions in labor disputes. The labor injunction fell into disrepute largely because it was abused in precisely the same way that the injunctive power was abused in this case. Judges who were not sympathetic to the union cause commonly issued, without notice or hearing, broad restraining orders addressed to large numbers of persons and forbidding them to engage in acts that were either legally permissible or, if illegal, that could better have been left to the regular course of criminal prosecution. The injunctions might later be dissolved, but in the meantime strikes would be crippled because the occasion on which concerted activity might have been effective had passed. Such injunctions, so long discredited as weapons against concerted labor activities, have now been given new life by this Court as weapons against the exercise of First Amendment freedoms. Respect for the courts and for judicial process was not increased by the history of the labor injunction. . . .

. . . The majority opinion in this case rests essentially on a single precedent, and that a case the authority of which has clearly been undermined by subsequent decisions. Howat v. Kansas (1922), was decided in the days when the labor injunction was in fashion. . . .

It is not necessary to question the continuing validity of the holding in Howat v. Kansas, however, to demonstrate that neither it nor the Mine Workers [United States v. United Mine Workers (1947)] case supports the holding of the majority in this case. In Howat the subpoena and injunction were issued to enable the Kansas Court of Industrial Relations to determine an underlying labor dispute. In the Mine Workers case, the District Court issued a temporary anti-strike injunction to preserve existing conditions during the time it took to decide whether it had authority to grant the Government relief in a complex and difficult action of enormous importance to the national economy. In both cases the orders were of questionable legality, but in both cases they were reasonably necessary to enable the court or administrative tribunal to decide an underlying controversy of considerable importance before it at the time. This case involves an entirely different situation. The Alabama Circuit Court did not issue this temporary injunction to preserve existing conditions while it proceeded to decide some underlying dispute. There was no underlying dispute before it, and the court in practical effect merely added a judicial signature to a pre-existing criminal ordinance. Just as the court had no need to issue the injunction to preserve its ability to decide some underlying dispute, the city had no need of an injunction to impose a criminal penalty for demonstrating on the streets without a permit. The ordinance already accomplished that. In point of fact, there is only one apparent reason why the city sought this injunction and why the court issued it: to make it possible to punish petitioners for contempt rather than for violating the ordinance, and thus to immunize the unconstitutional statute and its unconstitutional application from any attack. I regret that this strategy has been so successful. . . .

Mr. Justice **Douglas,** with whom **The Chief Justice,** Mr. Justice **Brennan,** and Mr. Justice **Fortas** concur, dissenting, said in part:

The right to defy an unconstitutional statute is basic in our scheme. Even when an ordinance requires a permit to make a speech, to deliver a sermon, to picket, to parade, or to assemble, it need not be honored when it is invalid on its face. Lovell v. Griffin [1938] . . . Thomas v. Collins [1945]. . . .

Mr. Justice **Brennan,** with whom **The Chief Justice,** Mr. Justice **Douglas,** and Mr. Justice **Fortas** joined, wrote a dissenting opinion.

CENSORSHIP AND THE RIGHT TO PUBLISH

NEAR v. MINNESOTA

283 U. S. 697; 51 S. Ct. 625; 75 L. Ed. 1357 (1931)

The struggle to achieve freedom of the press has been long and difficult. Once the invention of the printing press made possible the dissemination of information to the people generally, it became painfully clear to the monarchs of Europe that here lay a serious threat to their absolute powers. Their first reaction was to outlaw and destroy this new engine of seditious propaganda. Failing in this, they resorted to a system of licensing un-

der which all publications, before being released to the public, had to be submitted to the King's Licenser. Serious penalties were meted out to those whose publications did not bear the official "imprimatur." Obviously no criticism of the sovereign or government, whether just or unjust, could be published under such a system; and the long fight against the official licenser was a major part of the fight to establish democratic institutions.

It is against this background that the case of Near v. Minnesota must be read. The law involved had been dubbed the "Minnesota gag law." It provided for the "padlocking," by injunctive process, of a newspaper for printing matter which was scandalous, malicious, defamatory, or obscene. Such a "padlock" injunction, enforceable by the customary process of summary punishment for contempt of court, could be lifted only by convincing the judge who issued it that the publication would, in the future, be unobjectionable. This, in the judgment of the majority of the Court, amounted to previous censorship of publication and a violation of long-established canons of free speech and press.

The present case represents the climax of a striking evolution in our constitutional law whereby freedom of speech and press was at last effectively "nationalized" or confided to the protection of the federal courts against both national and state impairment. The steps in that evolution are traced in the note to Powell v. Alabama (1932). The case of Near v. Minnesota was the first case in which a state law was held unconstitutional as violating that freedom of press protected by the due process clause of the Fourteenth Amendment.

Mr. Chief Justice **Hughes** delivered the opinion of the Court, saying in part:

Chapter 285 of the Session Laws of Minnesota for the year 1925 provides for the abatement, as a public nuisance, of a "malicious, scandalous and defamatory newspaper, magazine or other periodical." Section one of the act is as follows:

"Section 1: Any person who, as an individual, or as a member or employee of a firm, or association or organization, or as an officer, director, member or employee of a corporation, shall be engaged in the business of regularly or customarily producing, publishing or circulating, having in possession, selling or giving away,

(a) an obscene, lewd and lascivious newspaper, magazine, or other periodical, or

(b) a malicious, scandalous and defamatory newspaper, magazine or other periodical, is guilty of a nuisance, and all persons guilty of such nuisance may be enjoined, as hereinafter provided.

"Participation in such business shall constitute a commission of such nuisance and render the participant liable and subject to the proceedings, orders and judgments provided for in this act. Ownership, in whole or in part, directly or indirectly, of any such periodical, or of any stock or interest in any corporation or organization which owns the same in whole or in part, or which publishes the same, shall constitute such participation." . . .

Section two provides that whenever any such nuisance is committed or exists, the county attorney of any county where any such periodical is published or circulated, or, in case of his failure or refusal to proceed upon written request in good faith of a reputable citizen, the attorney general, or upon like failure or refusal of the latter, any citizen of the county, may maintain an action in the district court of the county in the name of the state to enjoin perpetually the persons committing or maintaining any such nuisance from further committing or maintaining it. Upon such evidence as the court shall deem sufficient, a temporary injunction may be granted. The defendants have the right to plead by demurrer or answer, and the plaintiff may demur or reply as in other cases.

The action, by section three, is to be "governed by the practice and procedure applicable to civil actions for injunctions," and after trial the court may enter judgment permanently enjoining the defendants found guilty of violating the act from continuing the violation and, "in and by such judgment, such nuisance may be wholly abated." The court is empowered, as in other cases of contempt, to punish disobedience to a temporary or permanent injunction by fine of not more than $1000 or by imprisonment in the county jail for not more than twelve months.

Under this statute, (section one, clause (b)), the county attorney of Hennepin county brought this action to enjoin the publication of what was described as a "malicious, scandalous and defamatory newspaper, magazine and periodical," known as "The Saturday Press," published by the defendants in the city of Minneapolis. . . .

Without attempting to summarize the contents of the voluminous exhibits attached to the complaint, we deem it sufficient to say that the articles charged in substance that a Jewish gangster was in control of gambling, bootlegging and racketeering in Minneapolis, and that law enforcing officers and agencies were not energetically performing their duties. Most of the charges were directed against the chief of police; he was charged with gross neglect of duty, illicit relations with gangsters, and with participation in graft. The county attorney was charged with knowing the existing conditions and with failure to take adequate measures to remedy them. The mayor was accused of inefficiency and dereliction. One member of the grand jury was stated to be in sympathy with the gangsters. A special grand jury and a special prosecutor were demanded to deal with the situation in general, and, in particular, to investigate an attempt to assassinate one Guilford, one of the original defendants, who, it appears from the articles, was shot by gangsters after the first issue of the periodical had been published. There is no question but that the articles made serious accusations against the public officers named and others in connection with the prevalence of crimes and the failure to expose and punish them. . . .

[Upon complaint the state court ordered Near to show cause why a temporary injunction should not be issued and forbade, meanwhile, further publication of the periodical. Near demurred on constitutional grounds. The district court certified the question of the constitutionality of the statute to the state supreme court, which held it valid. Near then answered the complaint but presented no evidence, and a permanent injunction was issued.]

From the judgment as thus affirmed, the defendant Near appeals to this court.

This statute, for the suppression as a public nuisance of a newspaper or periodical, is unusual, if not unique, and raises questions of grave importance transcending the local interests involved in the particular action. It is no longer open to doubt that the liberty of the press, and of speech, is within the liberty safeguarded by the due process clause of the 14th Amendment from invasion by state action. . . . In maintaining this guaranty, the authority of the State to enact laws to promote the health, safety, morals and general welfare of its people is necessarily admitted. The limits of this sovereign power must always be determined with appropriate regard to the particular subject of its exercise. . . . Liberty of speech and of the press is also not an absolute right, and the state may punish its abuse. . . . Liberty, in each of its phases, has its history and connotation and, in the present instance, the inquiry is as to the historic conception of the liberty of the press and whether the statute under review violates the essential attributes of that liberty. . . .

With respect to these contentions it is enough to say that in passing upon constitutional questions the court has regard to substance and not to mere matters of form, and that, in accordance with familiar principles, the statute must be tested by its operation and effect. . . . That operation and effect we think are clearly shown by the record in this case. We are not concerned with mere errors of the trial court, if there be such, in going beyond the direction of the statute as construed by the supreme court of the state. It is thus important to note precisely the purpose and effect of the statute as the state court has construed it.

First. The statute is not aimed at the redress of individual or private wrongs. Remedies for libel remain available and unaffected. The statute, said the state court, "is not directed at threatened libel but at an existing business which, generally speaking, involves more than libel." It is aimed at the distribution of scandalous matter as "detrimental to public morals and to the general welfare," tending "to disturb the peace of the community" and "to provoke assaults and the commission of crime." In order to obtain an injunction to suppress the future publication of the newspaper or periodical, it is not necessary to prove the falsity of the charges that have been made in the publication condemned. In the present action there was no allegation that the matter published was not true. It is alleged, and the statute requires the allegation, that the publication was "malicious." But, as in prosecutions for libel, there is no requirement of proof by the state of malice in fact as distinguished from malice inferred from the mere publication of the defamatory matter. The judgment in this case proceeded upon the mere proof of publication. The statute permits the defense, not of the truth alone, but only that the truth was published with good motives and

for justifiable ends. It is apparent that under the statute the publication is to be regarded as defamatory if it injures reputation, and that it is scandalous if it circulates charges of reprehensible conduct, whether criminal or otherwise, and the publication is thus deemed to invite public reprobation and to constitute a public scandal. The court sharply defined the purpose of the statute, bringing out the precise point, in these words: "There is no constitutional right to publish a fact merely because it is true. It is a matter of common knowledge that prosecutions under the criminal libel statutes do not result in efficient repression or suppression of the evils of scandal. Men who are the victims of such assaults seldom resort to the courts. This is especially true if their sins are exposed and the only question relates to whether it was done with good motives and for justifiable ends. This law is not for the protection of the person attacked nor to punish the wrongdoer. It is for the protection of the public welfare."

Second. The statute is directed not simply at the circulation of scandalous and defamatory statements with regard to private citizens, but at the continued publication by newspapers and periodicals of charges against public officers of corruption, malfeasance in office, or serious neglect of duty. Such charges by their very nature create a public scandal. They are scandalous and defamatory within the meaning of the statute, which has its normal operation in relation to publications dealing prominently and chiefly with the alleged derelictions of public officers.

Third. The object of the statute is not punishment, in the ordinary sense, but suppression of the offending newspaper or periodical. The reason for the enactment, as the state court has said, is that prosecutions to enforce penal statutes for libel do not result in "efficient repression or suppression of the evils of scandal." Describing the business of publication as a public nuisance, does not obscure the substance of the proceeding which the statute authorizes. It is the continued publication of scandalous and defamatory matter that constitutes the business and the declared nuisance. In the case of public officers, it is the reiteration of charges of official misconduct, and the fact that the newspaper or periodical is principally devoted to that purpose, that exposes it to suppression. In the present instance, the proof was that nine editions of the newspaper or periodical in question were published on successive dates, and that they were chiefly devoted to charges against public officers and in relation to the prevalence and protection of crime. In such a case, these officers are not left to their ordinary remedy in a suit for libel, or the authorities to a prosecution for criminal libel. Under this statute, a publisher of a newspaper or periodical, undertaking to conduct a campaign to expose and to censure official derelictions, and devoting his publication principally to that purpose, must face not simply the possibility of a verdict against him in a suit or prosecution for libel, but a determination that his newspaper or periodical is a public nuisance to be abated, and that this abatement and suppression will follow unless he is prepared with legal evidence to prove the truth of the charges and also to satisfy the court that, in addition to being true, the matter was published with good motives and for justifiable ends.

This suppression is accomplished by enjoining publications and that restraint is the object and effect of the statute.

Fourth. The statute not only operates to suppress the offending newspaper or periodical but to put the publisher under an effective censorship. When a newspaper or periodical is found to be "malicious, scandalous and defamatory," and is suppressed as such, resumption of publication is punishable as a contempt of court by fine or imprisonment. Thus, where a newspaper or periodical has been suppressed because of the circulation of charges against public officers of official misconduct, it would seem to be clear that the renewal of the publication of such charges would constitute a contempt and that the judgment would lay a permanent restraint upon the publisher, to escape which he must satisfy the court as to the character of a new publication. Whether he would be permitted again to publish matter deemed to be derogatory to the same or other public officers would depend upon the court's ruling. In the present instance the judgment restrained the defendants from "publishing, circulating, having in their possession, selling or giving away any publication whatsoever which is a malicious, scandalous or defamatory newspaper, as defined by law." The law gives no definition except that covered by the words "scandalous and defamatory," and publications charging official misconduct are of that class. While the court, answering the objection that the judgment was too broad, saw no reason for construing it as restraining the defendants "from operating a newspaper in harmony with the public welfare to which all must yield," and said that the defendants had not indicated "any desire to conduct their business in the usual and legitimate manner," the manifest inference is that, at least with respect to a new publication directed against official misconduct, the defendant would be held, under penalty of punishment for contempt as provided in the statute, to a manner of publication which the court considered to be "usual and legitimate" and consistent with the public welfare.

If we cut through mere details of procedure, the operation and effect of the statute in substance is that public authorities may bring the owner or publisher of a newspaper or periodical before a judge upon a charge of conducting a business of publishing scandalous and defamatory matter—in particular that the matter consists of charges against public officers of official dereliction—and unless the owner or publisher is able and disposed to bring competent evidence to satisfy the judge that the charges are true and are published with good motives and for justifiable ends, his newspaper or periodical is suppressed and further publication is made punishable as a contempt. This is of the essence of censorship.

The question is whether a statute authorizing such proceedings in restraint of publication is consistent with the conception of the liberty of the press as historically conceived and guaranteed. In determining the extent of the constitutional protection, it has been generally, if not universally, considered that it is the chief purpose of the guaranty to prevent previous restraints upon publication. The struggle in England, directed against the legislative power of the licenser, resulted in renunciation of the censorship of the press. The liberty deemed to be established was thus described by Blackstone: "The liberty of the press is indeed essential to the nature of a free state; but this consists in laying no *previous* restraints upon publications, and not in freedom from censure for criminal matter when published. Every freeman has an undoubted right to lay what sentiments he pleases before the public; to forbid this, is to destroy the freedom of the press; but if he publishes what is improper, mischievous or illegal, he must take the consequence of his own temerity." . . .

The criticism upon Blackstone's statement has not been because immunity from previous restraint upon publication has not been regarded as deserving of special emphasis, but chiefly because that immunity cannot be deemed to exhaust the conception of the liberty guaranteed by state and Federal constitutions. The point of criticism has been "that the mere exemption from previous restraints cannot be all that is secured by the constitutional provisions;" and that "the liberty of the press might be rendered a mockery and a delusion, and the phrase itself a by-word, if, while every man was at liberty to publish what he pleased, the public authorities might nevertheless punish him for harmless publications." . . . But it is recognized that punishment for the abuse of the liberty accorded to the press is essential to the protection of the public, and that the common law rules that subject the libeler to responsibility for the public offense, as well as for the private injury, are not abolished by the protection extended in our constitutions. . . . In the present case, we have no occasion to inquire as to the permissible scope of subsequent punishment: For whatever wrong the appellant has committed or may commit, by his publications, the state appropriately affords both public and private redress by its libel laws. As has been noted, the statute in question does not deal with punishments; it provides for no punishment, except in case of contempt for violation of the court's order, but for suppression and injunction, that is, for restraint upon publication.

The objection has also been made that the principle as to immunity from previous restraint is stated too broadly, if every such restraint is deemed to be prohibited. That is undoubtedly true; the protection even as to previous restraint is not absolutely unlimited. But the limitation has been recognized only in exceptional cases. "When a nation is at war many things that might be said in time of peace are such a hindrance to its effort that their utterance will not be endured so long as men fight and that no court could regard them as protected by any constitutional right." Schenck v. United States [1919]. No one would question but that a government might prevent actual obstruction to its recruiting service or the publication of the sailing dates of transports or the number and location of troops. On similar grounds, the primary requirements of decency may be enforced against obscene publications. The security of the community life may be protected against incitements to acts of violence and the overthrow by force of orderly government. The constitutional guaranty of free speech does not "protect a man from an injunction against uttering words that may have all the effect of force. . . ."

The exceptional nature of its limitations places in a strong light the general conception that liberty of the press, historically considered and taken up by the Federal Constitution, has meant, principally although not exclusively, immunity from previous restraints or censorship. The conception of the liberty of the press in this country had broadened with the exigencies of the colonial period and with the efforts to secure freedom from oppressive administration. That liberty was especially cherished for the immunity it afforded from previous restraint of the publication of censure of public officers and charges of official misconduct. . . .

The importance of this immunity has not lessened. While reckless assaults upon public men, and efforts to bring obloquy upon those who are endeavoring faithfully to discharge official duties, exert a baleful influence and deserve the severest condemnation in public opinion, it cannot be said that this abuse is greater, and it is believed to be less, than that which characterized the period in which our institutions took shape. Meanwhile, the administration of government has become more complex, the opportunities for malfeasance and corruption have multiplied, crime has grown to most serious proportions, and the danger of its protection by unfaithful officials and of the impairment of the fundamental security of life and property by criminal alliances and official neglect, emphasizes the primary need of a vigilant and courageous press, especially in great cities. The fact that the liberty of the press may be abused by miscreant purveyors of scandal does not make any the less necessary the immunity of the press from previous restraint in dealing with official misconduct. Subsequent punishment for such abuses as may exist is the appropriate remedy, consistent with constitutional privilege. . . .

The statute in question cannot be justified by reason of the fact that the publisher is permitted to show, before injunction issues, that the matter published is true and is published with good motives and for justifiable ends. If such a statute, authorizing suppression and injunction on such a basis, is constitutionally valid, it would be equally permissible for the legislature to provide that at any time the publisher of any newspaper could be brought before a court, or even an administrative officer (as the constitutional protection may not be regarded as resting on mere procedural details) and required to produce proof of the truth of his publication, or of what he intended to publish, and of his motives, or stand enjoined. If this can be done, the legislature may provide machinery for determining in the complete exercise of its discretion what are justifiable ends and restrain publication accordingly. And it would be but a step to a complete system of censorship. The recognition of authority to impose previous restraint upon publication in order to protect the community against the circulation of charges of misconduct, and especially of official misconduct, necessarily would carry with it the admission of the authority of the censor against which the constitutional barrier was erected. The preliminary freedom, by virtue of the very reason for its existence, does not depend, as this court has said, on proof of truth. . . .

Equally unavailing is the insistence that the statute is designed to prevent the circulation of scandal which tends to disturb the public peace and to provoke assaults and the commission of crime. Charges of reprehensible conduct, and in particular of official malfeasance, unquestionably create a public scandal, but the theory of the constitutional guaranty is that even a more serious public evil would be caused by authority to prevent publication. . . . There is nothing new in the fact that charges of reprehensible conduct may create resentment and the disposition to resort to violent means of redress, but this well-understood tendency did not alter the determination to protect the press against censorship and restraint upon publication. . . . The danger of violent reactions becomes greater with effective organization of defiant groups resenting exposure, and if this consideration warranted legislative interference with the initial freedom of publication, the constitutional protection would be reduced to a mere form of words.

For these reasons we hold the statute, so far as it authorized the proceedings in this action under clause (b) of section one, to be an infringement of the liberty of the press guaranteed by the 14th Amendment. We should add that this decision rests upon the operation and effect of the statute, without regard to the question of the truth of the charges contained in the particular periodical. The fact that the public officers named in this case, and those associated with the charges of official dereliction, may be deemed to be impeccable, cannot affect the conclusion that the statute imposes an unconstitutional restraint upon publication. *unconstitutional form of censorship*

Judgment reversed.

Mr. Justice **Butler** dissented in an opinion in which Justices **Van Devanter**, **McReynolds**, and **Sutherland** concurred.

KINGSLEY BOOKS v. BROWN

354 U. S. 436; 77 S. Ct. 1325; 1 L. Ed. 2d 1469
(1957)

One aspect of the broad problem of censorship is that presented by the publication of obscene materials. Although a state may not resort to prior censorship of the press, it does have authority to punish the publication of matter offensive to public morals and decency. While it had long been assumed that clearly obscene publications could validly be punished, the question was never squarely decided by the Supreme Court until 1957 in the case of Roth v. United States. There two cases were combined: one involved the prosecution of one Alberts by the state of California for publishing obscene matter; the other, the prosecution of Roth by the federal government for violation of the law forbidding the sending of obscene matter through the mails. On historical grounds the Court decided that the First Amendment was not intended to protect obscenity, and therefore the question of whether an obscene publication presented a clear and present danger of "antisocial conduct" was entirely irrelevant.

The states, however, have experienced great difficulty in drafting legislation under which the publication of such material can validly be punished. In the first place, the problem of finding a sufficiently clear definition of crime in this area has proved to be an extremely challenging one. The state may, of course, properly forbid the publication of "lewd, lascivious, salacious, obscene and filthy" matter. These are words with which the courts are familiar; and despite the diverse results obtained in their interpretations, they constitute valid definitions of crime. But these words are not adequate to handle a problem which has aroused public concern— the problem of "horror comic books." Some of these cheap pulp-paper publications contain stories of crime and bloodshed, lust and depravity, and are believed by many to contribute directly to delinquency. In Winters v. New York (1948) a statute designed to deal with this problem was held void for vagueness.

In the second place, such machinery as the state provides for enforcement must be so designed that publications which are protected by the First Amendment are not suppressed along with those that enjoy no such protection. In Butler v. Michigan (1957) the Supreme Court held unconstitutional a Michigan statute which forbade "any person" to sell or give away anything "containing obscene, immoral, lewd or lascivious language . . . tending to incite minors to violent or depraved or immoral acts, manifestly tending to the corruption of the morals of youth. . . ." The Court set aside the conviction of an adult who sold such a book to another adult, in this case a policeman, on the ground that the state could not, under its police power, quarantine "the general reading public against books not too rugged for grown men and women in order to shield juvenile innocence. . . ." This, the Court decided, was "legislation not reasonably restricted to the evil with which it is said to deal. The incidence of this enactment is to reduce the adult population of Michigan to reading only what is fit for children. It thereby arbitrarily curtails one of those liberties of the individual, now enshrined in the Due Process Clause. . . ." The Court noted that Michigan had a statute which forbade selling or giving such books to children.

In 1961, in Marcus v. Property Search Warrant, the Court held void a warrant which authorized the police to seize any book they thought obscene. Eleven thousand copies of 280 publications were seized with the idea that the Court would later make a final decision. This, said the Court, lacks "the procedural safeguards which due process demands to assure nonobscene material the constitutional protection to which it is entitled." In 1959 the Court held that persons could not be punished for selling an obscene book unless it were proven that they knew it to be obscene; see Smith v. California. In Bantam Books v. Sullivan (1963) a Rhode Island commission notified a book distributor that certain of his offerings were unfit for juvenile reading, and a few days later a policeman called to see "what action he had taken." Wishing to avoid trouble, he had returned the books to the publisher. In upholding an injunction against the commission, the Court noted that these "informal sanctions" were an effective system of censorship which "provides no safeguards whatever against the suppression of non-obscene, and therefore constitutionally protected, matter. It is a form of regulation that creates hazards to protected freedoms markedly greater than those that attend reliance upon the criminal law." And in A Quantity of Books v. Kansas (1964) the Court struck down a scheme where the attorney general, in an ex parte proceeding, persuaded a judge that certain books were obscene and the judge ordered them seized. The adversary hearing on the question of obscenity was not available until after the seizure. This is in sharp contrast to the process provided by New York state and held valid in the present case.

In two cases the Court shed new light on the procedure by which obscene material can be seized without jeopardizing material protected by the First Amendment. In Heller v. New York (1973) the police saw a blue movie called "Blue Movie" and went and got a judge. The judge saw the movie and at the end of it signed a warrant for the arrest of the theater manager, the projectionist, and the ticket taker and the seizure of the film to preserve it as evidence. Since there was no showing that this was the only copy of the film and there was no injunction against its further exhibition pending a final determination of obscenity, the Court found the procedures valid. In contrast, in Roaden v. Kentucky (1973) a sheriff saw a sexually explicit movie in a drive-in and seized the only copy on the spot, interrupting the performance to do so. The Court held that in the absence of a valid warrant the film was arguably entitled to First Amendment protection and the seizure constituted a prior restraint. "The seizure is unreasonable," the Court said, "not simply because it would have been easy to secure a warrant, but rather because prior restraint of the right of expression, whether by books or films, calls for a higher hurdle in the evaluation of reasonableness."

In the present case New York had provided by law that the legal officer in any town who learns that someone is about to sell obscene matter may go to the state supreme court and request an injunction against such sale. The question whether the injunction should be issued must be tried within one day after the defendant has been properly notified and the court must render its decision within two days of the trial. If the materials are found to be obscene the judge is to order the sheriff to seize and destroy them. Books kept for sale by Kingsley Books were found on trial to be "dirt for dirt's sake," their distribution enjoined and they were ordered destroyed. The sale of future issues was not enjoined since this would constitute a prior restraint.

Mr. Justice **Frankfurter** delivered the opinion of the Court, saying in part:

Neither in the New York Court of Appeals, nor here, did appellants assail the legislation insofar as it outlaws obscenity. The claim they make lies within a very narrow compass. Their attack is upon the power of New York to employ the remedial scheme of § 22-a. Authorization of an injunction pendente lite, as part of this scheme, during the period within which the issue of obscenity must be promptly tried and adjudicated in an adversary proceeding for which "[a]dequate notice, judicial hearing, [and] fair determination" are assured, is a safeguard against frustration of the public interest in effectuating judicial condemnation of obscene matter. It is a brake on the temptation to exploit a filthy business offered by the limited hazards of piecemeal prosecutions, sale by sale, of a publication already condemned as obscene. New York enacted this procedure on the basis of study by a joint legislative committee. Resort to this injunctive remedy, it is claimed, is beyond the constitutional power of New York in that it amounts to a prior censorship of literary product and as such is violative of that "freedom of thought, and speech" which has been "withdrawn by the Fourteenth Amendment from encroachment by the states." Palko v. Connecticut [1937]. Reliance is particularly placed upon Near v. Minnesota [1931].

In an unbroken series of cases extending over a long stretch of this Court's history, it has been accepted as a postulate that "the primary requirements of decency may be enforced against obscene publications." And so our starting point is that New York can constitutionally convict appellants of keeping for sale the booklets incontestably found to be obscene. Alberts v. California, decided this day. The immediate problem then is whether New York can adopt as an auxiliary means of dealing with such obscene merchandising the procedure of § 22-a.

We need not linger over the suggestion that something can be drawn out of the Due Process Clause of the Fourteenth Amendment that restricts New York to the criminal process in seeking to protect its people against the dissemination of pornography. It is not for this Court thus to limit the State in resorting to various weapons in the armory of the law. Whether proscribed conduct is to be visited by a criminal prosecution or by a qui tam action or by an injunction or by some or all of these remedies in combination, is a matter within the legislature's range of choice. . . . If New York chooses to subject persons who disseminate obscene "literature" to criminal prosecution and also to deal with such books as deodands of old, or both, with due regard, of course, to appropriate opportunities for the trial of the underlying issue, it is not for us to gainsay its selection of remedies. Just as Near v. Minnesota, one of the landmark opinions in shaping the constitutional protection of freedom of speech and of the press, left no doubts that "Liberty of speech, and of the press, is also not an absolute right," it likewise made clear that "the protection even as to previous restraint is not absolutely unlimited." To be sure, the limitation is the exception; it is to be closely confined so as to preclude what may fairly be deemed licensing or censorship.

The judicial angle of vision in testing the validity of a statute like § 22-a is "the operation and effect of the statute in substance." The phrase "prior restraint" is not a self-wielding sword. Nor can it serve as a talismanic test. The duty of closer analysis and critical judgment in applying the thought behind the phrase has thus been authoritatively put by one who brings weighty learning to his support of constitutionally protected liberties: "What is needed," writes Professor Paul Freund, "is a pragmatic assessment of its operation in the particular circumstances. The generalization that prior restraint is particularly obnoxious in civil liberties cases must yield to more particularistic analysis." . . .

Wherein does § 22-a differ in its effective operation from the type of statute upheld in Alberts? Section 311 of California's Penal Code provides that "Every person who wilfully and lewdly . . . keeps for sale . . . any obscene . . . book . . . is guilty of a misdemeanor. . . ." Section 1141 of New York's Penal Law is similar. One would be bold to assert that the in terrorem effect of such statutes less restrains booksellers in the period before the law strikes than does § 22-a. Instead of requiring the bookseller to dread that the offer for sale of a book may without prior warning subject him to a criminal prosecution with the hazard of imprisonment, the civil procedure assures him that such consequences cannot follow unless he ignores a court order specifically directed to him for a prompt and carefully circumscribed determination of the issue of obscenity. Until then, he may keep the book for sale and sell it on his own judgment rather than "steer nervously among the treacherous shoals." . . .

Criminal enforcement and the proceeding under § 22-a interfere with a book's solicitation of the public precisely at the same stage. In each situation the law moves after publication; the book need not in either case have yet passed into the hands of the public. The Alberts record does not show that the matter there found to be obscene had reached the public at the time that the criminal charge of keeping such matter for sale was lodged, while here as a matter of fact copies of the booklets whose distribution was enjoined had been on sale for several weeks when process was served. In each case the bookseller is put on notice by the complaint that sale of the publication charged with obscenity in the period before trial may subject him to penal consequences. In the one case he may suffer fine and imprisonment for violation of the criminal statute, in the other, for disobedience of the temporary injunction. The bookseller may of course stand his ground and confidently believe that in any judicial proceeding the book could not be condemned as obscene, but both modes of procedure provide an effective deterrent against distribution prior to adjudication of the book's content—the threat of subsequent penalization. . . .

Nor are the consequences of a judicial condemnation for obscenity under § 22-a more restrictive of freedom of expression than the result of conviction for a misdemeanor. In Alberts, the defendant was fined $500, sentenced to sixty days in prison, and put on probation for two years on condition that he not violate the obscenity statute. Not only was he completely separated from society for two months but he was also seriously restrained from trafficking in all obscene publications for a considerable time. Appellants, on the other hand, were enjoined from displaying for sale or distributing only the particular booklets theretofore published and adjudged to be obscene. Thus, the restraint upon appellants as merchants in obscenity was narrower than that imposed on Alberts.

Section 22-a's provision for the seizure and destruction of the instruments of ascertained wrongdoing expresses resort to a legal remedy sanctioned by the long history of Anglo-American law. . . . It is worth noting that although the Alberts record does not reveal whether the publications found to be obscene were destroyed, provision is made for that by §§ 313 and 314 of the California Penal Code. Similarly, § 1144 of New York's Penal Law provides for destruction of obscene matter following conviction for its dissemination.

It only remains to say that the difference between Near v. Minnesota and this case is glaring in fact. The two cases are no less glaringly different when judged by the appropriate criteria of constitutional law. Minnesota empowered its courts to enjoin the dissemination of future issues of a publication because its past issues had been found offensive. In the language of Mr. Chief Justice Hughes, ''This is of the essence of censorship.'' As such, it was found unconstitutional. This was enough to condemn that statute wholly apart from the fact that the proceeding in Near involved not obscenity but matters deemed to be derogatory to a public officer. Unlike Near, § 22-a is concerned solely with obscenity and, as authoritatively construed, it studiously withholds restraint upon matters not already published and not yet found to be offensive.

The judgment is
Affirmed.

Mr. Chief Justice **Warren,** dissenting.

My views on the rights of a State to protect its people against the purveyance of obscenity were expressed in Alberts v. California, also decided today. Here we have an entirely different situation.

This is not a criminal obscenity case. Nor is it a case ordering the destruction of materials disseminated by a person who has been convicted of an offense for doing so, as would be authorized under provisions in the laws of New York and other States. It is a case wherein the New York police, under a different state statute, located books which, in their opinion, were unfit for public use because of obscenity and then obtained a court order for their condemnation and destruction.

The majority opinion sanctions this proceeding. I would not. Unlike the criminal cases decided today, this New York law places the book on trial. There is totally lacking any standard in the statute for judging the book in context. The personal element basic to the criminal laws is entirely absent. In my judgment, the same object may have wholly different impact depending upon the setting in which it is placed. Under this statute, the setting is irrelevant.

It is the manner of use that should determine obscenity. It is the conduct of the individual that should be judged, not the quality of art or literature. To do otherwise is to impose a prior restraint and hence to violate the Constitution. Certainly in the absence of a prior judicial determination of illegal use, books, pictures and other objects of expression should not be destroyed. It savors too much of book burning.

I would reverse.

Mr. Justice **Douglas,** with whom Mr. Justice **Black** concurs, dissenting, said in part:

There are two reasons why I think this restraining order should be dissolved.

First, the provision for an injunction pendente lite gives the State the paralyzing power of a censor. A decree can issue ex parte—without a hearing and without any ruling or finding on the issue of obscenity. This provision is defended on the ground that it is only a little encroachment, that a hearing must be promptly given and finding of obscenity promptly made. But every publisher knows what awful effect a decree issued in secret can have. We tread here on First Amendment grounds. And nothing is more devastating to the rights that it guarantees than the power to restrain publication before even a hearing is held. This is prior restraint and censorship at its worst.

Second, the procedure for restraining by equity decree the distribution of all the condemned literature does violence to the First Amendment. The judge or jury which finds the publisher guilty in New York City acts on evidence that may be quite different from evidence before the judge or jury that finds the publisher not guilty in Rochester. . . . Yet the present statute makes one criminal conviction conclusive and authorizes a statewide decree that subjects the distributor to the contempt power. I think every publication is a separate offense which entitles the accused to a separate trial. . . .

Mr. Justice **Brennan,** dissenting, said in part:

I believe the absence in this New York obscenity statute of a right to jury trial is a fatal defect. . . .

The jury represents a cross-section of the community and has a special aptitude for reflecting the view of the average person. Jury trial of obscenity therefore provides a peculiarly competent application of the standard for judging obscenity which, by its definition, calls for an appraisal of material according to the average person's application of contemporary community standards. A statute which does not afford the defendant, of right, a jury determination of obscenity falls short, in my view, of giving proper effect to the standard fashioned as the necessary safeguard demanded by the freedoms of speech and press for material which is not obscene. . . .

FREEDMAN v. MARYLAND

380 U. S. 51; 85 S. Ct. 734; 13 L. Ed. 2d 649
(1965)

*Although the Court had insisted as early as Near v. Minnesota (1931) that "the protection even as to previous restraint is not absolutely unlimited," no scheme of previous censorship had ever been found valid and the Court had never undertaken to explain just what this dictum meant. It had spoken of "exceptional" circumstances that might justify such censorship, but it had defined them, not in terms of when or how the state could censor, but in terms of the kinds of ideas that could be suppressed. But how, without resorting to a general scheme of censorship and licensing, were these suppressible ideas to be located? How was a state to identify and suppress "utterances creating a hindrance to the . . . war effort," or which offended "the primary requirements of decency," without examining all utterances before they were published? Since it was this very "examining" before publication that the Court had held void in the Near case, the theory underlying the dictum seemed incompatible with the holding of the case.

The Court's greatest challenge came with the censorship of movies. In early years movies were not considered part of the press of the country, and were therefore not eligible for whatever protection was available at that time; see Mutual Film Corp. v. Industrial Commission of Ohio (1915). Then, in an antitrust case in 1948 (United States v. Paramount Pictures, Inc.), the Court observed by way of dictum: "We have no doubt that moving pictures, like newspapers and radio, are included in the press whose freedom is guaranteed by the First Amendment." It was thus only a matter of time before a movie censorship case came to the Court, and the first one involved a highly controversial Italian film The Miracle. The picture was built up around the birth of a child to a poor, simple-minded girl who, while tending goats on a mountainside, is seduced by a bearded stranger. The girl, in her religious ecstasy, believes the man to be her favorite saint. The film was licensed and shown in New York City. Bitter attacks upon it immediately ensued. The Vatican had considered the film profane, and Catholic prelates in this country denounced it as blasphemous and sacrilegious. It had, however, important and respected defenders. The New York Board of Regents, who had the authority to censor motion pictures, reconsidered the film and withdrew its license on the ground that it was "sacrilegious" within the meaning of the New York censorship statute. The New York courts held that the statute was valid and that the Regents had acted within the proper range of their discretion under it.

In Burstyn v. Wilson (1952) the Supreme Court reversed. Without holding void all movie censorship, it pointed out that "in seeking to apply the broad and all-inclusive definition of 'sacrilegious' given by the New York courts, the censor is set adrift upon a boundless sea amid a myriad of conflicting currents of religious views with no charts but those provided by the most vocal and powerful orthodoxies. New York cannot vest such unlimited restraining control over motion pictures in a censor." Moreover, while such censorship raised serious questions of religious freedom, "from the standpoint of freedom of speech and the press, it is enough to point out that the state has no legitimate interest in protecting any or all religions from views distasteful to them which is sufficient to justify prior restraint upon the expression of those views. It is not the business of government in our nation to suppress real or imagined attacks upon a particular religious doctrine, whether they appear in publications, speeches, or motion pictures."

The motion picture censorship cases that came to the Supreme Court following the Burstyn decision (1952) shed very little light on some of the basic questions involved in the problem. "Immorality," and a tendency to "undermine confidence" in government apparently were not satisfactory standards for censorship. But in the absence of opinions there was no way of knowing whether they were simply too vague or whether they were an improper basis of censorship under the First Amendment. Nor did the Court indicate whether any censorship of films was validly possible.

In one case, however, the Court did make clear the basis of its decision. New York had forbidden the showing of the movie Lady Chatterley's Lover "because its subject matter is adultery presented as being right and desirable for certain people under certain circumstances." This was held to violate the state education law, which forbids the licensing of motion pictures "which are immoral in that they portray 'acts of sexual immorality . . . as desirable, acceptable, or proper patterns of behavior.' " In Kingsley Pictures v. Regents of the University of New York (1959) the Court held this was a clear violation of freedom of the press. "What New York has done," said the Court, ". . . is to prevent the exhibition of a motion picture because that picture advocates an idea—that adultery under certain circumstances may be proper behavior. Yet the First Amendment's basic guarantee is of freedom to advocate ideas. The State, quite simply, has thus struck at the very heart of constitutionally protected liberty." Nor could the censorship be defended because the picture makes immorality attractive. "This argument misconceives what it is that the Constitution protects. Its guarantee is not confined to the expression of ideas that are conventional or shared by a majority. It protects advocacy of the opinion that adultery may sometimes be proper, no less than advocacy of socialism or the single tax. And in the realm of ideas it protects expression which is eloquent no less than that which is unconvincing."

While the Court in the post-Burstyn cases had held bad all movie censorship, it had always confined itself to the particular censorship under review and had carefully avoided saying whether all censorship was void per se. The problem of the [right] to censor finally reached the Court in Times Film Corp. v. Chicago (1961). Times Film Corporation undertook to show in Chicago a picture entitled Don Juan based upon Mozart's opera Don Giovanni. It had paid the license fees required by the city, but had refused to submit the picture for censorship. Thus the validity of whatever standards the censors *might have applied were not an issue—the only question was whether the picture could be shown without being submitted to the censors at all. In a five-to-four decision the Court upheld movie censorship. Stressing that "obscenity is not within the area of constitutionally protected speech or press," it conceded Chicago's right to find out if a movie was obscene and suggested that movies might have a "capacity for evil" that was greater than that of other forms of publication.*

In the Freedman case, printed below, the Court acted to bring the business of movie censorship into line with the Kingsley Books doctrine (Kingsley Books v. Brown, 1957), announcing strict standards which a censorship plan must meet in order to be valid. While it did not actually overrule Times Film, all the censorship plans then in use, including that in Chicago, failed to meet the constitutional test. Since the decision a number of jurisdictions, including New York, have taken steps to comply with the procedural requirements.

Mr. Justice **Brennan** delivered the opinion of the Court, saying in part:

Appellant sought to challenge the constitutionality of the Maryland motion picture censorship statute, and exhibited the film "Revenge at Daybreak" at his Baltimore theatre without first submitting the picture to the State Board of Censors as required by § 2 of the statute. The State concedes that the picture does not violate the statutory standards and would have received a license if properly submitted, but the appellant was convicted of a § 2 violation despite his contention that the statute in its entirety unconstitutionally impaired freedom of expression. The Court of Appeals of Maryland affirmed. . . . We reverse.

I.

In Times Film Corp. v. Chicago [1961] we considered and upheld a requirement of submission of motion pictures in advance of exhibition. The Court of Appeals held, on the authority of that decision, that "the Maryland censorship law must be held to be not void on its face as violative of the freedoms protected against State action by the First and Fourteenth Amendments." This reliance on Times Film was misplaced. The only question tendered for decision in that case was "whether a prior restraint was necessarily unconstitutional *under all circumstances*." . . . The exhibitor's argument that the requirement of submission without more amounted to a constitutionally prohibited prior restraint was interpreted by the Court in Times Film as a contention that the "constitutional protection includes complete and absolute freedom to exhibit, at least once, any and every kind of motion picture . . . even if this film contains the basest type of pornography, or incitement to riot, or forceful overthrow of orderly government. . . ." The Court held that on this "narrow" question, the argument stated the principle against prior restraints too broadly; citing a number of our decisions, the Court quoted the statement from Near v. Minnesota [1931] that "the protection even

as to previous restraint is not absolutely unlimited." In rejecting the proffered proposition in Times Film the Court emphasized, however, that "[i]t is that question alone which we decide," and it would therefore be inaccurate to say that Times Film upheld the specific features of the Chicago censorship ordinance.

Unlike the petitioner in Times Film, appellant does not argue that § 2 is unconstitutional simply because it may prevent even the first showing of a film whose exhibition may legitimately be the subject of an obscenity prosecution. He presents a question quite distinct from that passed on in Times Film; accepting the rule in Times Film, he argues that § 2 constitutes an invalid prior restraint because, in the context of the remainder of the statute, it presents a danger of unduly suppressing protected expression. He focuses particularly on the procedure for an initial decision by the censorship board, which, without any judicial participation, effectively bars exhibition of any disapproved film, unless and until the exhibitor undertakes a time-consuming appeal to the Maryland courts and succeeds in having the Board's decision reversed. Under the statute, the exhibitor is required to submit the film to the Board for examination, but no time limit is imposed for completion of Board action § 17. If the film is disapproved, or any elimination ordered, § 19 provides that "the person submitting such film or view for examination will receive immediate notice of such elimination or disapproval, and if appealed from, such film or view will be promptly reexamined, in the presence of such person, by two or more members of the Board, and the same finally approved or disapproved promptly after such re-examination, with the right of appeal from the decision of the Board to the Baltimore City Court of Baltimore City. There shall be a further right of appeal from the decision of the Baltimore City Court to the Court of Appeals of Maryland, subject generally to the time and manner provided for taking appeal to the Court of Appeals."

Thus there is no statutory provision for judicial participation in the procedure which bars a film, nor even assurance of prompt judicial review. Risk of delay is built into the Maryland procedure, as is borne out by experience; in the only reported case indicating the length of time required to complete an appeal, the initial judicial determination has taken four months and final vindication of the film on appellate review, six months. . .

In the area of freedom of expression it is well established that one has standing to challenge a statute on the ground that it delegates overly broad licensing discretion to an administrative office, whether or not his conduct could be proscribed by a properly drawn statute, and whether or not he applied for a license. "One who might have had a license for the asking may . . . call into question the whole scheme of licensing when he is prosecuted for failure to procure it." Thornhill v. Alabama [1940]. . . . Standing is recognized in such cases because of the ". . . danger of tolerating, in the area of First Amendment freedoms, the existence of a penal statute susceptible of sweeping and improper application." NAACP v. Button [1963]. . . . Although we have no occasion to decide whether the vice of overbroadness infects the Maryland statute, we think that appellant's assertion of a similar danger in the Maryland apparatus of censorship—one always fraught with danger and viewed with suspicion—gives him standing to make that challenge. In substance his argument is that, because the apparatus operates in a statutory context in which judicial review may be too little and too late, the Maryland statute lacks sufficient safeguards for confining the censor's action to judicially determined constitutional limits, and therefore contains the same vice as a statute delegating excessive administration discretion.

II.

Although the Court has said that motion pictures are not "necessarily subject to the precise rules governing any other particular method of expression," Joseph Burstyn, Inc. v. Wilson [1952], it is as true here as of other forms of expression that "[a]ny system of prior restraints of expression comes to this Court bearing a heavy presumption against its constitutional validity." Bantam Books, Inc. v. Sullivan [1963] ". . . [U]nder the Fourteenth Amendment, a State is not free to adopt whatever procedures it pleases for dealing with obscenity . . . without regard to the possible consequences for constitutionally protected speech." Marcus v. Search Warrant [1961]. The administration of a censorship system for motion pictures presents peculiar dangers to constitutionally protected speech. Unlike a prosecution for obscenity, a censorship proceeding puts the initial burden on the exhibitor or distributor. Because the censor's business is to censor, there inheres the danger that he may well be less responsive than a court—part of an independent branch of government—to the constitutionally protected interests in free expression. And if it is made unduly onerous, by reason of delay or otherwise, to seek judicial review, the censor's determination may in practice be final.

Applying the settled rule of our cases, we hold that a noncriminal process which requires the prior submission of a film to a censor avoids constitutional infirmity only if it takes place under procedural safeguards designed to obviate the dangers of a censorship system. First, the burden of proving that the film is unprotected expression must rest on the censor. As we said in Speiser v. Randall [1958], "Where the transcendent value of speech is involved, due process certainly requires . . . that the State bear the burden of persuasion to show that the appellants engaged in criminal speech." Second, while the State may require advance submission of all films, in order to proceed effectively to bar all showings of unprotected films, the requirement cannot be administered in a manner which would lend an effect of finality to the censor's determination whether a film constitutes protected expression. The teaching of our cases is that, because only a judicial determination in an adversary proceeding ensures the necessary sensitivity to freedom of expression, only a procedure requiring a judicial determination suffices to impose a valid final restraint. . . . To this end, the exhibitor must be assured, by statute or authoritative judicial construction, that the censor will,

within a specified brief period, either issue a license or go to court to restrain showing the film. Any restraint imposed in advance of a final judicial determination on the merits must similarly be limited to preservation of the status quo for the shortest fixed period compatible with sound judicial resolution. Moreover, we are well aware that, even after expiration of a temporary restraint, an administrative refusal to license, signifying the censor's view that the film is unprotected, may have a discouraging effect on the exhibitor. . . . Therefore, the procedure must also assure a prompt final judicial decision, to minimize the deterrent effect of an interim and possibly erroneous denial of a license.

Without these safeguards, it may prove too burdensome to seek review or the censor's determination. Particularly in the case of motion pictures, it may take very little to deter exhibition in a given locality. The exhibitor's stake in any one picture may be insufficient to warrant a protracted and onerous course of litigation. The distributor, on the other hand, may be equally unwilling to accept the burdens and delays of litigation in a particular area when, without such difficulties, he can freely exhibit his film in most of the rest of the country; for we are told that only four States and a handful of municipalities have active censorship laws.

It is readily apparent that the Maryland procedural scheme does not satisfy these criteria. First, once the censor disapproves the film, the exhibitor must assume the burden of instituting judicial proceedings and of persuading the courts that the film is protected expression. Second, once the Board has acted against a film, exhibition is prohibited pending judicial review, however protracted. Under the statute, appellant could have been convicted if he had shown the film after unsuccessfully seeking a license, even though no court had ever ruled on the obscenity of the film. Third, it is abundantly clear that the Maryland statute provides no assurance of prompt judicial determination. We hold, therefore, that appellant's conviction must be reversed. The Maryland scheme fails to provide adequate safeguards against undue inhibition of protected expression, and this renders the § 2 requirement of prior submission of films to the Board an invalid previous restraint.

III.

How or whether Maryland is to incorporate the required procedural safeguards in the statutory scheme is, of course, for the State to decide. But a model is not lacking: In Kingsley Books, Inc. v. Brown [1957] we upheld a New York injunctive procedure designed to prevent the sale of obscene books. That procedure postpones any restraint against sale until a judicial determination of obscenity following notice and an adversary hearing. The statute provides for a hearing one day after joinder of issue; the judge must hand down his decision within two days after termination of the hearing. The New York procedure operates without prior submission to a censor, but the chilling effect of a censorship order, even one which requires judicial action for its enforcement, suggests all the more reason for expeditious determination of the question whether a particular film is constitutionally protected.

The requirement of prior submission to a censor sustained in Times Film is consistent with our recognition that films differ from other forms of expression. Similarly, we think that the nature of the motion picture industry may suggest different time limits for a judicial determination. It is common knowledge that films are scheduled well before actual exhibition, and the requirement of advance submission in § 2 recognizes this. One possible scheme would be to allow the exhibitor or distributor to submit his film early enough to ensure an orderly final disposition of the case before the scheduled exhibition date—far enough in advance so that the exhibitor could safely advertise the opening on a normal basis. Failing such a scheme or sufficiently early submission under such a scheme, the statute would have to require adjudication considerably more prompt than has been the case under the Maryland statute. Otherwise, litigation might be unduly expensive and protracted, or the victorious exhibitor might find the most propitious opportunity for exhibition past. We do not mean to lay down rigid time limits or procedures, but to suggest considerations in drafting legislation to accord with local exhibition practices, and in doing so to avoid the potentially chilling effect of the Maryland statute on protected expression.

Reversed.

Mr. Justice **Douglas,** whom Mr. Justice **Black** joined, concurred.

MILLER v. CALIFORNIA

413 U. S. 15; 93 S. Ct. 2067; 37 L. Ed. 2d 419
(1973)

Justice Holmes's wise rule that only those utterances should be suppressed that present a clear and present danger of bringing about some substantive evil probably expresses the ideal of free speech in a democracy. It is, in essence, a reflection of the doctrine that that government is best which governs least. But few people live easily with such a rule when it involves expressions of which they disapprove. There is as natural tendency in most of us to feel that the First Amendment should protect the right to say those things we want to say or hear, while permitting the government to suppress those expressions which we find offensive. Thus, those who find attacks on their religious beliefs offensive see no merit in having "that sort of thing" protected by the First Amendment; at the same time they feel their own beliefs and practices should be immune from governmental interference. Those who find what they consider disloyal or subversive utterances a threat to their way of life see no reason why they should not be suppressed—as long as their own right to complain about the government and agitate for change is not restricted.

The two cases printed below illustrate the kind of judgment the Supreme Court has to make when it abandons the clear and present danger philosophy and substitutes a judgment on the merits of certain kinds of speech. Is there any constitutional reason why those who enjoy the "titillation" of erotic literature shouldn't be allowed to obtain it? But then why shouldn't those who find such material offensive be allowed to raise the moral tone of the community by suppressing it? Probably nothing vital is lost whichever way a particular matter is decided—so few expressions are in themselves really valuable or important—but in the long run the spirit of freedom in a society may well depend on whether the question ceases to be "Why shouldn't one speak?" and becomes instead "Why shouldn't one be suppressed?" It is with this in mind that the role of the Court in deciding most First Amendment cases, but especially obscenity cases, should be judged.

In Roth v. United States (1947), the five members of the Court agreed that obscene material was that "which deals with sex in a manner appealing to prurient interest." In applying this definition, the Court rejected the so-called Hicklin rule, which judged isolated excerpts of writings by their likely effect on the most susceptible persons, and affirmed, instead, the test "whether to the average person, applying contemporary community standards, the dominant theme of the material taken as a whole appeals to prurient interest." Such material, it was emphasized, does not enjoy constitutional protection because it is "utterly without social importance." The Court in Roth found that the jury had been properly instructed on the standard, so the conviction was valid.

In Jacobellis v. Ohio (1964) the Court again applied the Roth rule and reversed the Ohio court finding that the movie The Lovers *was obscene. The Court divided badly on the reasoning for its decision, no more than two justices agreeing on the test to be applied. Justices Brennan and Goldberg reaffirmed the Roth test, but added that "community standards" meant national, not local, standards; and the question whether something was obscene could not be left solely to a jury, but must ultimately be decided by the Supreme Court itself. They also relied on the "redeeming social importance" of any publication, however erotic its contents, to justify First Amendment protection. Justices Black and Douglas joined in the judgment on the ground that punishing any publication was unconstitutional, and Justice Stewart held that the First Amendment forbids only hard-core pornography."I shall not today attempt further to define the kinds of material I understand to be embraced within that shorthand description; and perhaps I could never succeed in intelligibly doing so. But I know it when I see it, and the motion picture involved in this case is not that." Justices Warren and Clark, on the other hand, supported the Roth rule, but dissented on the ground that "community standards" meant local standards, such as those applied by the jury in this case; and obscenity, moreover, was as much a question of the conduct of the purveyors and the purposes to which the material was put, as of the character of the material itself. Justice*

Harlan dissented on the ground that the First and Fourteenth Amendments apply differently, and the state should be allowed to outlaw obscenity as it sees fit.

A Book on Trial

In Memoirs v. Massachusetts (1966) six members of the Court joined in overruling a Massachusetts court decision that Fanny Hill was obscene—still without agreeing on a definition of obscenity. Justices Brennan, Warren, and Fortas reiterated the Roth rule that "(a) the dominant theme of the material taken as a whole appeals to a purient interest in sex; (b) the material is patently offensive because it affronts contemporary community standards relating to the description or representation of sexual matters; and (c) the material is utterly without redeeming social value." They held the Massachusetts court had misapplied this test when they weighed the obscenity of Fanny Hill against its limited social value. "A book can not be proscribed unless it is found to be utterly without redeeming social value. This is so even though the book is found to possess the requisite prurient appeal and to be patently offensive." Justices Black, Douglas, and Stewart concurred; and Justice Harlan dissented for the reasons given in Jacobellis, while Justice White dissented because he felt a lack of redeeming social value was a characteristic of all patently offensive material and should not be used as an independent test.

In the still controversial case of Ginzburg v. United States (1966), decided the same day as Memoirs, the Court upheld the conviction of Ralph Ginzburg for sending through the mails copies of Eros, an American Heritage-style magazine of erotica, and The Housewife's Handbook of Selective Promiscuity. Abandoning the approach of its previous cases, the Court conceded that the publications were not in themselves obscene, but that they took their obscenity from the fact that Ginzburg was in "the sordid business of pandering—'the business of purveying textual or graphic matter openly advertised to appeal to the erotic interest of their customers.'" Moreover, the "leer of the sensualist" permeated his advertising. "The deliberate representation of petitioners' publications as erotically arousing, for example, stimulated the reader to accept them as prurient; he looks for titillation, not for saving intellectual content." Three of the four dissenting justices attacked the Court's jailing of Ginzburg for "pandering" and "titillating," things which Congress had not made illegal and which the Court had not previously declared to be a crime.

Following the Ginzburg decision Congress amended the postal statutes to permit a person receiving "pandering" advertisements through the mail to force the sender to remove his or her name from its mailing lists. The statute was attacked as a denial of the First Amendment right of the mailers to disseminate information, but in Rowan v. United States Post Office (1970) the Supreme Court held it valid. Taking judicial notice of the amount of junk mail inundating the householder, the Court interpreted the statute as allowing "the addressee complete and unfettered discretion in electing whether or not he desired to receive further material from a particular sender." He may, it explained, "prohibit the mailing

of a dry goods catalog because he objects to the contents—or indeed the text of the language touting the merchandise." But broad as it was, it did not abridge the First Amendment. "Weighing the highly important right to communicate, but without trying to determine where it fits into constitutional imperatives, against the very basic right to be free from sights, sounds, and tangible matter we do not want, it seems to us that a mailer's right to communicate must stop at the mailbox of an unreceptive addressee."

While the right to sell obscene material enjoys no protection under the First Amendment, the freedom of thought implicitly guaranteed by that provision ensures one's right to enjoy such material in the privacy of one's own home. Relying on the Court's statement in Roth that "obscenity is not within the area of constitutionally protected speech or press," the state of Georgia forbade the mere possession of obscene material. In Stanley v. Georgia (1969), the Court held the statute void. It conceded the wording of Roth, but pointed out that it and other obscenity cases all involved the sale and distribution of obscene materials to others, and should be read in that context. "This right to receive information and ideas, regardless of their social worth, . . . is fundamental to our free society," and "also fundamental is the right to be free, except in very limited circumstances, from unwanted governmental intrusions into one's privacy." The Court rejected outright the idea that Georgia had a right to "control the moral content of a person's thoughts." "Whatever may be the justification for other statutes regulating obscenity, we do not think they reach into the privacy of one's own home. If the First Amendment means anything, it means that a State has no business telling a man, sitting alone in his own house, what books he may read or what films he may watch. Our whole constitutional heritage rebels at the thought of giving government the power to control men's minds." Nor could Georgia justify its statute on the ground that the possession of pornography led to antisocial conduct. "Given the present state of knowledge, the State may no more prohibit mere possession of obscenity on the ground that it may lead to antisocial conduct than it may prohibit possession of chemistry books on the ground that they may lead to the manufacture of home-made spirits."

The right to enjoy obscene matter in one's home does not, however, ensure one the right to get it there. Emphasizing that Roth had not been overruled, the Court in United States v. Reidel (1971) upheld a conviction for sending obscene matter through the mails, and in United States v. Orito (1973) it upheld the power of Congress under the commerce clause to forbid the private transportation for personal use of obscene matter in interstate commerce. In United States v. Twelve 200-Foot Reels (1973) it added that a person could not import obscene material even for his own personal use.

Although Justice Brennan had written the opinions in both Roth and Ginzburg, in his dissent in the Paris Adult Theater case (1973) he abandoned his approach in Roth of describing how offensive matter must be in order *to be banned, and argued that the right to publish should be protected where no one is injured by such publication. Meanwhile, a majority of the Court, agreeing for the first time since Roth on language to describe obscenity, suggests in the Miller case that it is prepared to let obscenity decisions be made by local juries on the basis of local standards of good taste—although apparently only as long as they ban only ''hard core'' pornography.*

In Paris Theater I, the Court rejected Justice Brennan's contention that ''consenting adults'' should be able to see ''dirty movies'' if they wish. Here the city of Atlanta, Georgia, had moved, under procedures that met the test of Freedman v. Maryland (1965), to suppress two ''adult'' movies shown only to adults in a theater devoid of offensive advertising. The trial court agreed the movies were obscene but refused to enjoin their exhibition. The Georgia Supreme Court reversed.

In Jenkins v. Georgia (1974) a unanimous Court made clear that despite Miller, the last word on questions of obscenity still rested with it. There a theater operator had shown ''Carnal Knowledge,'' a movie dealing with sex, although not in an explicit way. A jury, properly charged to apply local community standards, had found him guilty of showing an obscene film. ''Even though questions of appeal to the 'prurient interest' or of patent offensiveness are 'essentially questions of fact,' it would be a serious misreading of Miller to conclude that juries have unbridled discretion in determining what is 'patently offensive.' . . . Our own view of the film satisfies us that 'Carnal Knowledge' could not be found under the Miller standard to depict sexual conduct in a patently offensive way.''

Mr. Chief Justice **Burger** delivered the opinion of the Court, saying in part:

This is one of a group of ''obscenity-pornography'' cases being reviewed by the Court in a re-examination of standards enunciated in earlier cases involving what Mr. Justice Harlan called ''the intractable obscenity problem.''

Appellant conducted a mass mailing campaign to advertise the sale of illustrated books, euphemistically called ''adult'' material. After a jury trial, he was convicted of violating California Penal Code § 311.2(a), a misdemeanor, by knowingly distributing obscene matter. . . . Appellant's conviction was specifically based on his conduct in causing five unsolicited advertising brochures to be sent through the mail in an envelope addressed to a restaurant in Newport Beach, California. The envelope was opened by the manager of the restaurant and his mother. They had not requested the brochures; they complained to the police.

The brochures advertise four books entitled ''Intercourse,'' ''Man-Woman,'' ''Sex Orgies Illustrated,'' and ''An Illustrated History of Pornography,'' and a film entitled ''Marital Intercourse.'' While the brochures contain some descriptive printed material, primarily they consist of pictures and drawings very explicitly depicting men and women in groups of two or more engaging in a variety of sexual activities, with genitals often prominently displayed.

I.

This case involves the application of a state's criminal obscenity statute to a situation in which sexually explicit materials have been thrust by aggressive sales action upon unwilling recipients who had in no way indicated any desire to receive such materials. This Court has recognized that the States have a legitimate interest in prohibiting dissemination or exhibition of obscene material when the mode of dissemination carries with it a significant danger of offending the sensibilities of unwilling recipients or of exposure to juveniles. Stanley v. Georgia (1969). Ginsberg v. New York (1968). Interstate Circuit, Inc. v. Dallas (1968). Redrup v. New York (1967). Jacobellis v. Ohio (1964). . . . It is in this context that we are called on to define the standards which must be used to identify obscene material that a State may regulate without infringing the First Amendment as applicable to the States through the Fourteenth Amendment.

The dissent of Mr. Justice Brennan reviews the background of the obscenity problem, but since the Court now undertakes to formulate standards more concrete than those in the past, it is useful for us to focus on two of the landmark cases in the somewhat tortured history of the Court's obscenity decisions. In Roth v. United States (1957), the Court sustained a conviction under a federal statute punishing the mailing of ''obscene, lewd, lascivious or filthy . . .'' materials. The key to that holding was the Court's rejection of the claim that obscene materials were protected by the First Amendment. Five Justices joined in the opinion stating:

''All ideas having even the slightest redeeming social importance—unorthodox ideas, controversial ideas, even ideas hateful to the prevailing climate of opinion— have full protection of the [First Amendment] guaranties, unless excludable because they encroach upon the limited area of more important interests. But implicit in the history of the First Amendment is the rejection of obscenity as utterly without redeeming social importance. . . . This is the same judgment expressed by this Court in Chaplinsky v. New Hampshire [1942].

'' '. . . There are certain well-defined and narrowly limited classes of speech, the prevention and punishment of which have never been thought to raise any Constitutional problem. *These include the lewd and obscene . . . . It has been well observed that such utterances are no essential part of any exposition of ideas, and are of such slight social value as a step to truth that any benefit that may be derived from them is clearly outweighed by the social interest in order and morality. . . .*' '' [Emphasis by Court in Roth opinion.]

We hold that obscenity is not within the area of constitutionally protected speech or press.''

Nine years later in Memoirs v. Massachusetts (1966), the Court veered sharply away from the Roth concept and, with only three Justices in the plurality opinion, articulated a new test of obscenity. The plurality held that under the Roth definition: ''. . . as elaborated in subsequent cases, three elements must coalesce: it must be established that (a) the dominant theme of the material taken as a whole appeals to a prurient interest in sex; (b) the material is patently offensive because it affronts contemporary community standards relating to the description or representation of sexual matters; and (c) the material is utterly without redeeming social value.'' The sharpness of the break with Roth, represented by the third element of the Memoirs test and emphasized by Mr. Justice White's dissent, was further underscored when the Memoirs plurality went on to state: ''The Supreme Judicial Court erred in holding that a book need not be 'unqualifiedly worthless before it can be deemed obscene.' A book cannot be proscribed unless it is found to be *utterly* without redeeming social value.'' (Emphasis in original.)

While Roth presumed ''obscenity'' to be ''utterly without redeeming social value,'' Memoirs required that to prove obscenity it must be affirmatively established that the material is ''*utterly* without redeeming social value.'' Thus, even as they repeated the words of Roth, the Memoirs plurality produced a drastically altered test that called on the prosecution to prove a negative, i.e., that the material was ''*utterly* without redeeming social value''—a burden virtually impossible to discharge under our criminal standards of proof. Such considerations caused Mr. Justice Harlan to wonder if the *utterly* without redeeming social value'' test had any meaning at all. . . .

Apart from the initial formulation in the Roth case, no majority of the Court has at any given time been able to agree on a standard to determine what constitutes obscene, pornographic material subject to regulation under the States' police power. . . . We have seen ''a variety of views among the members of the Court unmatched in any other course of constitutional adjudication [footnote omitted].'' Interstate Circuit, Inc. v. Dallas (Harlan, J., concurring and dissenting). This is not remarkable, for in the area of freedom of speech and press the courts must always remain sensitive to any infringement on genuinely serious literary, artistic, political, or scientific expression. This is an area in which there are few eternal verities.

The case we now review was tried on the theory that the California Penal Code § 311 approximately incorporates the three-stage Memoirs test. But now the Memoirs test has been abandoned as unworkable by its author and no member of the Court today supports the Memoirs formulation.

II.

This much has been categorically settled by the Court, that obscene material is unprotected by the First Amendment. . . . We acknowledge, however, the inherent dangers of undertaking to regulate any form of expression. State statutes designed to regulate obscene materials must be carefully limited. . . . As a result, we now confine the permissible scope of such regulation to works which depict or describe sexual conduct. That conduct must be specifically defined by the applicable state law, as written or authoritatively construed. A state offense must also be limited to works which, taken as a whole, appeal to the prurient interest in sex, which portray sexual conduct in a patently offensive way, and which, taken as a whole, do not have serious literary, artistic, political, or scientific value.

The basic guidelines for the trier of fact must be: (a) whether ''the average person, applying contemporary community standards'' would find that the work, taken as a whole, appeals to the prurient interest. . . . (b) whether the work depicts or describes, in a patently offensive way, sexual conduct specifically defined by the applicable state law, and (c) whether the work, taken as a whole, lacks serious literary, artistic, political, or scientific value. We do not adopt as a constitutional standard the ''*utterly* without redeeming social value'' test of Memoirs v. Massachusetts; that concept has never commanded the adherence of more than three Justices at one time. If a state law that regulates obscene material is thus limited, as written or construed, the First Amendment values applicable to the States through the Fourteenth Amendment are adequately protected by the ultimate power of appellate courts to conduct an independent review of constitutional claims when necessary. . . .

We emphasize that it is not our function to propose regulatory schemes for the States. That must await their concrete legislative efforts. It is possible, however, to give a few plain examples of what a state statute could define for regulation under the second part (b) of the standard announced in this opinion, supra:

(a) Patently offensive representations or descriptions of ultimate sexual acts, normal or perverted, actual or simulated.

(b) Patently offensive representations or descriptions of masturbation, excretory functions, and lewd exhibition of the genitals.

Sex and nudity may not be exploited without limit by films or pictures exhibited or sold in places of public accommodation any more than live sex and nudity can be exhibited or sold without limit in such public places. At a minimum, prurient, patently offensive depiction or description of sexual conduct must have serious literary, artistic, political, or scientific value to merit First Amendment protection. . . . For example, medical books for the education of physicians and related personnel necessarily use graphic illustrations and descriptions of human anatomy. In resolving the inevitably sensitive questions of fact and law, we must continue to rely on the jury system, accompanied by the safeguards that judges, rules of evidence, presumption of innocence, and other protective features provide, as we do with rape, murder, and a host of other offenses against society and its individual members.*

Mr. Justice Brennan, author of the opinions of the Court, or the plurality opinions, in Roth v. United States, Jacobellis v. Ohio, Ginzburg v. United States (1966), Mishkin v. New York (1966), and Memoirs v. Massachusetts, has abandoned his former positions and now maintains that no formulation of this Court, the Congress, or the States can adequately distinguish ob-

---

*The mere fact juries may reach different conclusions as to the same material does not mean that constitutional rights are abridged. As this Court observed in Roth v. United States, ''It is common experience that different juries may reach different results under any criminal statute. That is one of the consequences we accept under our jury system.''

scene material unprotected by the First Amendment from protected expression, Paris Adult Theatre v. Slaton (1973) (Brennan, J., dissenting). Paradoxically, Mr Justice Brennan indicates that suppression of unprotected obscene material is permissible to avoid exposure to unconsenting adults, as in this case, and to juveniles, although he gives no indication of how the division between protected and nonprotected materials may be drawn with greater precision for these purposes than for regulation of commercial exposure to consenting adults only. Nor does he indicate where in the Constitution he finds the authority to distinguish between a willing "adult" one month past the state law age of majority and a willing "juvenile" one month younger.

Under the holdings announced today, no one will be subject to prosecution for the sale or exposure of obscene materials unless these materials depict or describe patently offensive "hard core" sexual conduct specifically defined by the regulating state law, as written or construed. We are satisfied that these specific prerequisites will provide fair notice to a dealer in such materials that his public and commercial activities may bring prosecution. . . . If the inability to define regulated materials with ultimate, godlike precision altogether removes the power of the States or the Congress to regulate, then "hard core" pornography may be exposed without limit to the juvenile, the passerby, and the consenting adult alike, as, indeed, Mr. Justice Douglas contends. . . . In this belief, however, Mr. Justice Douglas now stands alone.

Mr. Justice Brennan also emphasizes "institutional stress" in justification of his change of view. Noting that "the number of obscenity cases on our docket gives ample testimony to the burden that has been placed upon this Court," he quite rightly remarks that the examination of contested materials "is hardly a source of edification to members of this Court." Paris Adult Theatre v. Slaton (Brennan, J., dissenting). He also notes, and we agree, that "uncertainty of the standards creates a continuing source of tension between state and federal courts. . . ." "The problem is . . . that one cannot say with certainty that material is obscene until at least five members of this Court, applying inevitably obscure standards, have pronounced it so."

It is certainly true that the absence, since Roth, of a single majority view of this Court as to proper standards for testing obscenity has placed a strain on both state and federal courts. But today, for the first time since Roth was decided in 1957, a majority of this Court has agreed on concrete guidelines to isolate "hard core" pornography from expression protected by the First Amendment. Now we may abandon the casual practice of Redrup v. New York and attempt to provide positive guidance to the federal and state courts alike.

This may not be an easy road, free from difficulty. But no amount of "fatigue" should lead us to adopt a convenient "institutional" rationale—an absolutist, "anything goes" view of the First Amendment—because it will lighten our burdens. "Such an abnegation of judicial supervision in this field would be inconsistent with our duty to uphold the constitutional guarantees."

. . . Nor should we remedy "tension between state and federal courts" by arbitrarily depriving the States of a power reserved to them under the Constitution, a power which they have enjoyed and exercised continuously from before the adoption of the First Amendment to this day. . . . "Our duty admits of no 'substitute for facing up to the tough individual problems of constitutional judgment involved in every obscenity case.' . . ."

III.

Under a national Constitution, fundamental First Amendment limitations on the powers of the States do not vary from community to community, but this does not mean that there are, or should or can be, fixed, uniform national standards of precisely what appeals to the "prurient interest" or is "patently offensive." These are essentially questions of fact, and our nation is simply too big and too diverse for this Court to reasonably expect that such standards could be articulated for all 50 States in a single formulation, even assuming the prerequisite consensus exists. When triers of fact are asked to decide whether "the average person, applying contemporary community standards" would consider certain materials "prurient," it would be unrealistic to require that the answer be based on some abstract formulation. The adversary system, with lay jurors as the usual ultimate fact-finders in criminal prosecutions, has historically permitted triers-of-fact to draw on the standards of their community, guided always by limiting instructions on the law. To require a State to structure obscenity proceedings around evidence of a *national* "community standard" would be an exercise in futility. . . .

It is neither realistic nor constitutionally sound to read the First Amendment as requiring that the people of Maine or Mississippi accept public depiction of conduct found tolerable in Las Vegas, or New York City. . . . People in different States vary in their tastes and attitudes, and this diversity is not to be strangled by the absolutism of imposed uniformity. As the Court made clear in Mishkin v. New York (1966), the primary concern with requiring a jury to apply the standard of "the average person, applying contemporary community standards" is to be certain that, so far as material is not aimed at a deviant group, it will be judged by its impact on an average person, rather than a particularly susceptible or sensitive person—or indeed a totally insensitive one. . . . We hold the requirement that the jury evaluate the materials with reference to "contemporary standards of the State of California" serves this protective purpose and is constitutionally adequate.

IV.

The dissenting justices sound the alarm of repression. But, in our view, to equate the free and robust exchange of ideas and political debate with commercial exploitation of obscene material demeans the grand conception of the First Amendment and its high purposes in the historic struggle for freedom. It is a "misuse of the great guarantees of free speech and free press. . . ." . . .

The First Amendment protects works which, taken as a whole, have serious literary, artistic, political, or scientific value, regardless of whether the government or a majority of the people approve of the ideas these works represent. "The protection given speech and press was fashioned to assure unfettered interchange of *ideas* for the bringing about of political and social changes desired by the people." . . . But the public portrayal of hard core sexual conduct for its own sake, and for the ensuing commercial gain, is a different matter.*

There is no evidence, empirical or historical, that the stern nineteenth century American censorship of public distribution and display of material relating to sex, . . . in any way limited or affected expression of serious literary, artistic, political, or scientific ideas. On the contrary, it is beyond any question that the era following Thomas Jefferson to Theodore Roosevelt was an "extraordinarily vigorous period" not just in economics and politics, but in *belles lettres* and in "the outlying fields of social and political philosophies."† We do not see the harsh hand of censorship of ideas—good or bad, sound or unsound—and "repression" of political liberty lurking in every state regulation of commercial exploitation of human interest in sex.

Mr. Justice Brennan finds "it is hard to see how state ordered regimentation of our minds can ever be forestalled." Paris Adult Theatre I v. Slaton. These doleful anticipations assume that courts cannot distinguish commerce in ideas, protected by the First Amendment, from commercial exploitation of obscene material. Moreover, state regulation of hard core pornography so as to make it unavailable to nonadults, a regulation which Mr. Justice Brennan finds constitutionally permissible, has all the elements of "censorship" for adults; indeed even more rigid enforcement techniques may be called for with such dichotomy of regulation. . . . One can concede that the "sexual revolution" of recent years may have had useful byproducts in striking layers of prudery from a subject long irrationally kept from needed ventilation. But it does not follow that no regulation of patently offensive "hard core" materials is needed or permissible; civilized people do not allow unregulated access to heroin because it is a derivative of medicinal morphine.

In sum we (a) reaffirm the Roth holding that obscene material is not protected by the First Amendment, (b) hold that such material can be regulated by the States, subject to the specific safeguards enunciated above, without a showing that the materials is "*utterly without redeeming social value,*" and (c) hold that obscenity is to be determined by applying "contemporary community standards," . . . not "national standards." . . .

PARIS ADULT THEATER I v. SLATON

413 U. S. 49; 93 S. Ct. 2628; 37 L. Ed. 2d 446 (1973)

Mr. Chief Justice **Burger** delivered the opinion of the Court, saying in part:

II.

We categorically disapprove the theory, apparently adopted by the trial judge, that obscene, pornographic films acquire constitutional immunity from state regulation simply because they are exhibited for consenting adults only. This holding was properly rejected by the Georgia Supreme Court. Although we have often pointedly recognized the high importance of the state interest in regulating the exposure of obscene materials to juveniles and unconsenting adults, see Miller v. California (1973); Stanley v. Georgia (1969); Redrup v. New York (1967), this Court has never declared these to be the only legitimate state interests permitting regulation of obscene material. The states have a long-recognized legitimate interest in regulating the use of obscene material in local commerce and in all places of public accommodation, as long as these regulations do not run afoul of specific constitutional prohibitions. . . .

In particular, we hold that there are legitimate state interests at stake in stemming the tide of commercialized obscenity, even assuming it is feasible to enforce effective safeguards against exposure to juveniles and to the passerby.‡ Rights and interests "other than those of the advocates are involved." . . . These include the interest of the public in the quality of life and the total community environment, the tone of commerce in the great city centers, and, possibly, the public safety itself. The Hill-Link Minority Report of the Commission on Obscenity and Pornography indicates that there is at least an arguable correlation between obscene material and crime. Quite apart from sex crimes, however, there remains one problem of large proportions aptly described by Professor Bickel:

"It concerns the tone of the society, the mode, or to use terms that have perhaps greater currency, the style and quality of life, now and in the future. A man may be

---

*In the apt words of Mr. Chief Justice Warren, the petitioner in this case was "plainly engaged in the commercial exploitation of the morbid and shameful craving for materials with prurient effect. I believe that the State and Federal Governments can constitutionally punish such conduct. That is all that these cases present to us, and that is all that we need to decide." Roth v. United States (1957) (concurring opinion).

†See Parrington, *Main Currents in American Thought*, Vol. 2.

‡It is conceivable that an "adult" theatre can—if it really insists—prevent the exposure of its obscene wares to juveniles. An "adult" bookstore, dealing in obscene books, magazines, and pictures, cannot realistically make this claim. The Hill-Link Minority Report of the Commission on Obscenity and Pornography emphasizes evidence (the Abelson National Survey of Youth and Adults) that, although most pornography may be bought by elders, "the heavy users and most highly exposed people to pornography are adolescent females (among women) and adolescent and young males (among men)." *The Report of the Commission on Obscenity* (1970 ed.), 401. The legitimate interest in preventing exposure of juveniles to obscene materials cannot be fully served by simply barring juveniles from the immediate physical premises of "adult" bookstores, when there is a flourishing "outside business" in these materials.

entitled to read an obscene book in his room, or expose himself indecently there. . . . We should protect his privacy. But if he demands a right to obtain the books and pictures he wants in the market, and to foregather in public places—discreet, if you will, but accessible to all—with others who share his tastes, *then to grant him his right is to affect the world about the rest of us, and to impinge on other privacies.* Even supposing that each of us can, if he wishes, effectively avert the eye and stop the ear (which, in truth, we cannot), what is commonly read and seen and heard and done intrudes upon us all, want it or not." 22 The Public Interest 25, 25-26 (Winter, 1971). (Emphasis supplied.) As Mr. Chief Justice Warren stated there is a "right of the nation and of the states to maintain a decent society. . . ." Jacobellis v. Ohio (1964) (Warren, C. J., dissenting). . . .

But, it is argued, there is no scientific data which conclusively demonstrates that exposure to obscene materials adversely affects men and women or their society. It is urged on behalf of the petitioner that, absent such a demonstration, any kind of state regulation is "impermissible." We reject this argument. It is not for us to resolve empirical uncertainties underlying state legislation, save in the exceptional case where that legislation plainly impinges upon rights protected by the Constitution itself. . . . Although there is no conclusive proof of a connection between antisocial behavior and obscene material, the legislature of Georgia could quite reasonably determine that such a connection does or might exist. In deciding Roth, this Court implicitly accepted that a legislature could legitimately act on such a conclusion to protect "*the social interest in order and morality.*" Roth v. United States quoting Chaplinsky v. New Hampshire (1942) (emphasis added in Roth).

From the beginning of civilized societies, legislators and judges have acted on various unprovable assumptions. Such assumptions underlie much lawful state regulation of commercial and business affairs. . . . On the basis of these assumptions both Congress and state legislatures have, for example, drastically restricted associational rights by adopting antitrust laws, and have strictly regulated public expression by issuers of and dealers in securities, profit sharing "coupons," and "trading stamps," commanding what they must and may not publish and announce. . . . Understandably those who entertain an absolutist view of the First Amendment find it uncomfortable to explain why rights of association, speech, and press should be severely restrained in the marketplace of goods and money, but not in the marketplace of pornography. . . .

If we accept the unprovable assumption that a complete education requires certain books, see Bd. of Education v. Allen (1968), . . . and the well nigh universal belief that good books, plays, and art lift the spirit, improve the mind, enrich the human personality and develop character, can we then say that a state legislature may not act on the corollary assumption that commerce in obscene books, or public exhibitions focused on obscene conduct, have a tendency to exert a corrupting and debasing impact leading to antisocial behavior? . . .

It is argued that individual "free will" must govern, even in activities beyond the protection of the First Amendment and other constitutional guarantees of privacy, and that government cannot legitimately impede an individual's desire to see or acquire obscene plays, movies, and books. We do indeed base our society on certain assumptions that people have the capacity for free choice. Most exercises of individual free choice—those in politics, religion, and expression of ideas—are explicitly protected by the Constitution. Totally unlimited play for free will, however, is not allowed in ours or any other society. We have just noted, for example, that neither the First Amendment nor "free will" precludes States from having "blue sky" laws to regulate what sellers of securities may write or publish about their wares. Such laws are to protect the weak, the uninformed, the unsuspecting, and the gullible from the exercise of their own volition. Nor do modern societies leave disposal of garbage and sewage up to the individual "free will," but impose regulation to protect both public health and the appearance of public places. . . .

. . . This Court, has, on numerous occasions, refused to hold that commercial ventures such as a motion-picture house are "private" for the purpose of civil rights litigation and civil rights statutes. . . .

Our prior decisions recognizing a right to privacy guaranteed by the Fourteenth Amendment included "only those personal rights that can be deemed 'fundamental' or 'implicit in the concept of ordered liberty.' Palko v. Connecticut." Roe v. Wade (1973). This privacy right encompasses and protects the personal intimacies of the home, the family, marriage, motherhood, procreation, and child rearing. . . . Nothing, however, in this Court's decisions intimates that there is any "fundamental" privacy right "implicit in the concept of ordered liberty" to watch obscene movies in places of public accommodation. . . .

. . . The idea of a "privacy" right and a place of public accommodation are, in the context, mutually exclusive. Conduct or depictions of conduct that the state police power can prohibit on a public street does not become automatically protected by the Constitution merely because the conduct is moved to a bar or a "live" theatre stage, any more than a "live" performance of a man and woman locked in a sexual embrace at high noon in Times Square is protected by the Constitution because they simultaneously engage in a valid political dialogue.

It is also argued that the State has no legitimate interest in "control [of] the moral content of a person's thoughts," Stanley v. Georgia (1969), and we need not quarrel with this. But we reject the claim that the state of Georgia is here attempting to control the minds or thoughts of those who patronize theatres. Preventing unlimited display or distribution of obscene material, which by definition lacks any serious literary, artistic, political, or scientific value as communication. . . . The fantasies of a drug addict are his own and beyond the reach of government, but government regulation of drug sales is not prohibited by the Constitution. . . .

Finally, petitioners argue that conduct which directly involves "consenting adults" only has, for that sole reason, a special claim to constitutional protection. Our Constitution establishes a broad range of conditions on the exercise of power by the states, but for us to say that our Constitution incorporates the proposition that conduct involving consenting adults only is always beyond state regulation, that is a step we are unable to take. Commercial exploitation of depictions, descriptions, or exhibitions of obscene conduct on commercial premises open to the adult public falls within a State's broad power to regulate commerce and protect the public environment. The issue in this context goes beyond whether someone, or even the majority, considers the conduct depicted as "wrong" or "sinful." The States have the power to make a morally neutral judgment that public exhibition of obscene material, or commerce in such material, has a tendency to injure the community as a whole, to endanger the public safety, or to jeopardize, in Mr. Chief Justice Warren's words, the States' "right . . . to maintain a decent society." Jacobellis v. Ohio (1964) (dissenting opinion). . . .

Vacated and remanded for further proceedings.

Mr. Justice **Douglas** wrote a dissenting opinion.

Mr. Justice **Brennan,** with whom Mr. Justice **Stewart** and Mr. Justice **Marshall** joined, dissenting, said in part:

III.

Our experience with the Roth approach has certainly taught us that the outright suppression of obscenity cannot be reconciled with the fundamental principles of the First and Fourteenth Amendments. For we have failed to formulate a standard that sharply distinguishes protected from unprotected speech, and out of necessity, we have resorted to the Redrup approach, which resolves cases as between the parties, but offers only the most obscure guidance to legislation, adjudication by other courts, and primary conduct. By disposing of cases through summary reversal or denial certiorari we have deliberately and effectively obscured the rationale underlying the decision. It comes as no surprise that judicial attempts to follow our lead conscientiously have often ended in hopeless confusion.

Of course, the vagueness problem would be largely of our own creation if it stemmed primarily from our failure to reach a consensus on any one standard. But after 15 years of experimentation and debate I am reluctantly forced to the conclusion that none of the available formulas, including the one announced today, can reduce the vagueness to a tolerable level while at the same time striking an acceptable balance between the protections of the First and Fourteenth Amendments, on the one hand, and on the other the asserted state interest in regulating the dissemination of certain sexually oriented materials. Any effort to draw a constitutionally acceptable boundary on state power must resort to such indefinite concepts as "prurient interest," "patent offensiveness," "serious literary value," and the like. The meaning of these concepts necessarily varies with the experience, outlook, and even idiosyncracies of the person defining them. Although we have assumed that obscenity does exist and that we "know it when [we] see it," Jacobellis v. Ohio (1964) (Stewart, J., concurring), we are manifestly unable to describe it in advance except by reference to concepts so elusive that they fail to distinguish clearly between protected and unprotected speech. . . .

In addition to problems that arise when any criminal statute fails to afford fair notice of what it forbids, a vague statute in the areas of speech and press creates a second level of difficulty. We have indicated that "stricter standards of permissible statutory vagueness may be applied to a statute having a potentially inhibiting effect on speech; a man may the less be required to act at his peril here, because the free dissemination of ideas may be the loser." Smith v. California (1959). That proposition draws its strength from our recognition that "[t]he fundamental freedoms of speech and press have contributed greatly to the development and well-being of our free society and are indispensable to its continued growth. Ceaseless vigilance is the watchword to prevent their erosion by Congress or by the states. The door barring federal and state intrusion into this area cannot be left ajar. . . ." Roth [v. United States].

The problems of fair notice and chilling protected speech are very grave standing alone. But it does not detract from their importance to recognize that a vague statute in this area creates a third, although admittedly more subtle, set of problems. These problems concern the institutional stress that inevitably results where the line separating protected from unprotected speech is excessively vague. In Roth we conceded that "there may be marginal cases in which it is difficult to determine the side of the line on which a particular fact situation falls. . . ." Our subsequent experience demonstrates that almost every case is "marginal." And since the "margin" marks the point of separation between protected and unprotected speech, we are left with a system in which almost every obscenity case presents a constitutional question of exceptional difficulty. "The suppression of a particular writing or other tangible form of expression is . . . an *individual* matter, and in the nature of things every such suppression raises an individual constitutional problem, in which a reviewing court must determine for *itself* whether the attacked expression is suppressible within constitutional standards." Roth (separate opinion of Harlan, J.). . . .

. . . The problem is, rather, that one cannot say with certainty that material is obscene until at least five members of this Court, applying inevitably obscure standards, have pronounced it so. The number of obscenity cases on our docket gives ample testimony to the burden that has been placed upon this Court.

But the sheer *number* of the cases does not define the full extent of the institutional problem. For quite apart from the number of cases involved and the need to make a fresh constitutional determination in each case, we are tied to the "absurd business of perusing and viewing the miserable stuff that pours into the Court. . . ." . . . While the material may have varying degrees of social importance, it is hardly a source of edification to the members of this Court who are compelled to view it before passing on its obscenity. . . .

. . . In addition, the uncertainty of the standards creates a continuing source of tension between the state and federal courts, since the need for an independent determination by this Court seems to render superfluous even the most conscientious analysis by state tribunals. And our inability to justify our decisions with a persuasive rationale—or indeed, any rationale at all—necessarily created the impression that we are merely second-guessing state court judges.

The severe problems arising from the lack of fair notice, from the chill on protected expression, and from the stress imposed on the state and federal judicial machinery persuade me that a significant change in direction is urgently required. I turn, therefore, to the alternatives that are now open.

IV.

1. The approach requiring the smallest deviation from our present course would be to draw a new line between protected and unprotected speech, still permitting the States to suppress all material on the unprotected side of the line. In my view, clarity cannot be obtained pursuant to this approach except by drawing a line that resolves all doubts in favor of state power and against the guarantees of the First Amendment. We could hold, for example, that any depiction or description of human sexual organs, irrespective of the manner or purpose of the portrayal, is outside the protection of the First Amendment and therefore open to suppression by the States. . . .

2. The alternative adopted by the Court today recognizes that a prohibition against any depiction or description of human sexual organs could not be reconciled with the guarantees of the First Amendment. But the Court does retain the view that certain sexually oriented material can be considered obscene and therefore unprotected by the First and Fourteenth Amendments. To describe that unprotected class of expression, the Court adopts a restatement of the Roth-Memoirs definition of obscenity. . . .

The differences between this formulation and the three-pronged Memoirs test are, for the most part, academic.* . . .

Although the Court's restatement substantially tracks the three-part test announced in Memoirs v. Mas-

---

*While the Court's modification of the Memoirs test is small, it should still prove sufficient to invalidate virtually every state law relating to the suppression of obscenity. For under the Court's restatement, a statute must specifically enumerate certain forms of sexual conduct, the depiction of which is to be prohibited. It seems highly doubtful to me that state courts will be able to construe state statutes so as to incorporate a carefully itemized list of various forms of sexual conduct, and thus to bring them into conformity with the Court's requirements. . . . The statutes of at least one State should, however, escape the wholesale invalidation. Oregon has recently revised its statute to prohibit only the distribution of obscene materials to juveniles or unconsenting adults. The enactment of this principle is, of course, a choice constitutionally open to every State even under the Court's decision.

sachusetts, it does purport to modify the ''social value'' component of the test. Instead of requiring, as did Roth and Memoirs, that state suppression be limited to materials utterly lacking in social value, the Court today permits suppression if the government can prove that the materials lack ''*serious* literary, artistic, political or scientific value.'' But the definition of ''obscenity'' as expression utterly lacking social importance is the key to the conceptual basis of Roth and our subsequent opinions. In Roth we held that certain expression is obscene, and thus outside the protection of the First Amendment, precisely *because* it lacks even the slightest redeeming social value. . . . The Court's approach necessarily assumes that some works will be deemed obscene—even though they clearly have *some* social value—because the State was able to prove that the value, measured by some unspecified standard, was not sufficiently ''serious'' to warrant constitutional protection. That result is not merely inconsistent with our holding in Roth; it is nothing less than a rejection of the fundamental First Amendment premises and rationale of the Roth opinion and an invitation to widespread suppression of sexually oriented speech. Before today, the protections of the First Amendment have never been thought limited to expression of *serious* literary or political value. See . . . Cohen v. California (1971); Terminiello v. City of Chicago (1949).

Although the Court concedes that ''Roth presumed 'obscenity' to be 'utterly without redeeming social value,' '' it argues that Memoirs produced ''a drastically altered test that called on the prosecution to prove a negative, i. e., that the material was 'utterly without redeeming social value'—a burden virtually impossible to discharge under our criminal standards of proof.'' One should hardly need to point out that under the third component of the Court's test the prosecution is still required to ''prove a negative''—i. e., that the material lacks serious literary, artistic, political, or scientific value. Whether it will be easier to prove that material lacks ''serious'' value than to prove that it lacks any value at all remains, of course, to be seen.

In any case, even if the Court's approach left undamaged the conceptual framework of Roth, and even if it clearly barred the suppression of works with at least some social value, I would nevertheless be compelled to reject it. For it is beyond dispute that the approach can have no ameliorative impact on the cluster of problems that grow out of the vagueness of our current standards. . . .

V.

Our experience since Roth requires us not only to abandon the effort to pick out obscene materials on a case-by-case basis, but also to reconsider a fundamental postulate of Roth: that there exists a definable class of sexually oriented expression that may be totally suppressed by the Federal and State governments. Assuming that such a class of expression does in fact exist, I am forced to conclude that the concept of ''obscenity'' cannot be defined with sufficient specificity and clarity to provide fair notice to persons who create and distribute sexually oriented materials, to prevent substantial erosions of protected speech as a by-product of the attempt to suppress unprotected speech, and to avoid very costly institutional harms. Given these inevitable side-effects of state efforts to suppress what is assumed to be *unprotected* speech, we must scrutinize with care the state interest that is asserted to justify the suppression. For in the absence of some very substantial interest in suppressing such speech, we can hardly condone the ill-effects that seem to flow inevitably from the effort. . . .

Because we assumed—incorrectly, as experience has proven—that obscenity could be separated from other sexually oriented expression without significant costs either to the First Amendment or to the judicial machinery charged with the task of safeguarding First Amendment freedoms, we had no occasion in Roth to probe the asserted state interest in curtailing unprotected, sexually oriented speech. Yet as we have increasingly come to appreciate the vagueness of the concept of obscenity, we have begun to recognize and articulate the state interests at stake. Significantly, in Redrup v. New York where we set aside findings of obscenity with regard to three sets of material, we pointed out that "[i]n none of the cases was there a claim that the statute in question reflected a specific and limited state concern for juveniles. See Prince v. Massachusetts [1944]; cf. Butler v. Michigan [1957]. In none was there any suggestion of an assault upon individual privacy by publication in a manner so obtrusive as to make it impossible for an unwilling individual to avoid exposure to it. . . . And in none was there evidence of the sort of 'pandering' which the Court found significant in Ginzburg v. United States [1966]. . . .

The opinions in Redrup and Stanley v. Georgia reflected our emerging view that the state interest in protecting children and in protecting unconsenting adults may stand on a different footing from the other asserted state interests. It may well be, as one commentator has argued, that "exposure to [erotic material] is for some persons an intense emotional experience. A communication of this nature, imposed upon a person contrary to his wishes, has all the characteristics of a physical assault. . . . [And it] constitutes an invasion of his privacy. . . ." But cf. Cohen v. California (1971). Similarly, if children are "not possessed of that full capacity for individual choice which is the presupposition of the First Amendment guarantees," Ginsberg v. New York (1968) (Stewart, J., concurring), then the State may have a substantial interest in precluding the flow of obscene materials even to consenting juveniles. . . .

But whatever the strength of the state interests in protecting juveniles and unconsenting adults from exposure to sexually oriented materials, those interests cannot be asserted in defense of the holding of the Georgia Supreme Court in this case. That court assumed for the purposes of its decision that the films in issue were exhibited only to persons over the age of 21 who viewed them willingly and with prior knowledge of the nature of their contents. And on that assumption the state court held that the films could still be suppressed. The justification for

the suppression must be found, therefore, in some independent interest in regulating the reading and viewing habits of consenting adults.

At the outset it should be noted that virtually all of the interests that might be asserted in defense of suppression, laying aside the special interests associated with distribution to juveniles and unconsenting adults, were also posited in Stanley v. Georgia, where we held that the State could not make the "mere private possession of obscene material a crime." That decision presages the conclusions I reach here today.

In Stanley we pointed out that "[t]here appears to be little empirical basis for" the assertion that "exposure to obscene materials may lead to deviant sexual behavior or crimes of sexual violence."* In any event, we added that "if the State is only concerned about printed or filmed materials inducing antisocial conduct, we believe that in the context of private consumption of ideas and information we should adhere to the view that 'among free men, the deterrents ordinarily to be applied to prevent crime are education and punishment for violations of the law. . . .' . . ."

Moreover, in Stanley we rejected as "wholly inconsistent with the philosophy of the First Amendment" the notion that there is a legitimate state concern in the "control [of] the moral content of a person's thoughts." . . . That is not to say, of course, that a State must remain utterly indifferent to—and take no action bearing on—the morality of the community. . . . But the State's interest in regulating morality by suppressing obscenity, while often asserted, remains essentially unfocused and ill-defined. And, since the attempt to curtail unprotected speech necessarily spills over into the area of protected speech, the effort to serve this speculative interest through the suppression of obscene material must tread heavily on rights protected by the First Amendment.

In Roe v. Wade (1973), we held constitutionally invalid a state abortion law, even though we were aware of "the sensitive and emotional nature of the abortion controversy, of the vigorous opposing views, even among physicians, and of the deep and seemingly absolute convictions that the subject inspires. One's philosophy, one's experiences, one's exposure to the raw edges of human existence, one's religious training, one's attitudes toward life and family and their values, and the moral standards one establishes and seeks to observe, are all likely to influence and to color one's thinking and conclusions about abortion." Like the proscription of

---

*Indeed, since Stanley was decided, the President's Commission on Obscenity and Pornography has concluded: "In sum, empirical research designed to clarify the question has found no evidence to date that exposure to explicit sexual materials plays a significant role in the causation of delinquent or criminal behavior among youth or adults. The Commission cannot conclude that exposure to erotic materials is a factor in the causation of sex crime or sex delinquency." Report of the Commission on Obscenity and Pornography 27 (1970) (footnote omitted).

To the contrary, the Commission found that "on the positive side, explicit sexual materials are sought as a source of entertainment and information by substantial numbers of American adults. At times, these materials also appear to serve to increase and facilitate constructive communication about sexual matters within marriage."

abortions, the effort to suppress obscenity is predicated on unprovable, although strongly held, assumptions about human behavior, morality, sex, and religion. The existence of these assumptions cannot validate a statute that substantially undermines the guarantees of the First Amendment, any more than the existence of similar assumptions on the issue of abortion can validate a statute that infringes the constitutionally protected privacy interests of a pregnant woman.

If, as the Court today assumes, "a state legislature may . . . act on the . . . assumption that. . . . commerce in obscene books, or public exhibitions focused on obscene conduct, have a tendency to exert a corrupting and debasing impact leading to antisocial behavior," Paris Adult Theatre v. Slaton, then it is hard to see how state-ordered regimentation of our minds can ever be forestalled. For if a State may, in an effort to maintain or create a particular moral tone, prescribe what its citizens cannot read or cannot see, then it would seem to follow that in pursuit of that same objective a State could decree that its citizens must read certain books or must view certain films. . . . However laudable its goal—and that is obviously a question on which reasonable minds may differ—the State cannot proceed by means that violate the Constitution. . . .

. . . Even a legitimate, sharply focused state concern for the morality of the community cannot, in other words, justify an assault on the protections of the First Amendment. . . . Where the state interest in regulation of morality is vague and ill-defined, interference with the guarantees of the First Amendment is even more difficult to justify.

. . . I would hold, therefore, that at least in the absence of distribution to juveniles or obtrusive exposure to unconsenting adults, the First and Fourteenth Amendments prohibit the state and federal governments from attempting wholly to suppress sexually oriented materials on the basis of their allegedly "obscene" contents. Nothing in this approach precludes those governments from taking action to serve what may be strong and legitimate interests through regulation of the manner of distribution of sexually oriented material. . . .

NEW YORK TIMES CO. v. UNITED STATES

403 U. S. 713; 91 S. Ct. 2140; 29 L. Ed. 2d 820
(1971)

On Sunday Morning, June 13, 1971, The New York Times ran on its front page a modest headline spanning columns five, six, and seven:

Vietnam Archive: Pentagon Study Traces
3 Decades of Growing U. S. Involvement

A small box underneath said, "Three pages of documentary material from the Pentagon study begin on page 35."

In this unobtrusive way, the reading public was introduced to what was to become one of the most dramatic and sensational cases ever to reach the Supreme Court. The study, tracing the deliberate involvement of the United States in Vietnam during the administrations of four presidents, was based on a 7000-page top secret study made by the Pentagon and was turned over to the Times by Daniel Ellsberg, a Pentagon employee, as an act of conscience.

The following Monday night, just as the third in the series was about to appear, the Justice Department called the Times and asked them to desist from further publication on the ground that publication violated the Espionage Act. The Times refused, and Tuesday afternoon the Attorney General filed a motion for an injunction in the district court in New York. That afternoon District Judge Gurfein, who just that day had started work as a federal judge, issued the first federal injunction against a newspaper publication in the history of the nation.

Three days later the district court in Washington refused to enjoin the publication of the "Pentagon Papers" by the Washington Post, and the following day Judge Gurfein abolished his restraining order. Both orders freeing the newspapers were set aside by courts of appeal within hours and on Wednesday of the following week the Boston Globe was added to the list.

Following the decision in the present case, Ellsberg, and his assistant, Anthony Russo, were indicted by a federal grand jury for stealing and releasing the papers. The trial jury had been no more than sworn in the case when Justice Douglas, sitting as a circuit justice, stayed the trial pending a determination of whether the defendants were entitled to hear the tapes of unwarranted government eavesdropping involving one of the defense attorneys. The case ultimately resumed, only to be plagued by the disclosures that the FBI had tapped Ellsberg's telephone in 1969 and 1970 (before the Pentagon Papers were published), that investigators under the direction of White House staff members broke into the office of Ellsberg's psychiatrist, and that the presiding judge, W. Matthew Byrne, Jr., had twice been offered the directorship of the FBI by presidential aide John Ehrlichman while the trial was in progress. In mid-May 1973, clearly angered by the government's over-zealous behavior, Judge Byrne dismissed all charges against Ellsberg and Russo and ordered that they not be brought to trial again.

While it is perhaps true, as Justice Holmes said, that great cases make bad law, the importance of the Supreme Court's decision in the present case would be hard to overstate. Over the past forty years, the growing complexity and pervasiveness of government have resulted in a steady increase in presidential power at the expense of congressional power. Nowhere is this more apparent than in the areas of foreign affairs and national defense, in which the President has special constitutional authority, and it is widely assumed that constitutional limitations on presidential prerogatives in these areas should bow to presidential determinations of what the national security requires. The Supreme Court has apparently agreed, and not since Ex parte Milligan (1866), except for the Steel Seizure Case in 1952, has the Supreme Court said "no" to the President on matters of this kind. It thus came as a shock to those who approve such presidential authority that the Court should refuse to prevent the publication of material which the government deemed harmful to the national interest despite the refusal of Congress to provide such a remedy.

While Justice Black was probably right in saying that the First Amendment was drafted to prevent just such assumptions of governmental power over the press, his contention that the Amendment should be applied absolutely literally was so at odds with its judicial development that it attracted few adherents. Far more impressive were the votes of Justices Stewart and White, who felt that the publication was certainly wrong and might even be a crime, but refused to enjoin it because the "heavy burden" borne by the government under the First Amendment had not been met.

In a far less spectacular case decided some six weeks before the Pentagon Papers case the Court also held void an injunction against publication—in this case the distribution of pamphlets in the home neighborhood of an Illinois realtor accused of "block-busting." The leaflets were designed to let "his neighbors know what he was doing to us" in the hope he would agree to stop such tactics. Rejecting the argument that the purpose of the leaflets was to "force" rather than "inform" and that the injunction was a valid protection for the realtor's right of privacy, the Court held it void as a previous restraint on speech and publication. "The claim that the expressions were intended to exercise a coercive impact on respondent does not remove them from the reach of the First Amendment. Petitioners plainly intended to influence respondent's conduct by their activities; this is not fundamentally different from the function of a newspaper. . . . But so long as the means are peaceful, the communication need not meet standards of acceptability." See Organization for a Better Austin v. Keefe (1971).

On similar grounds the Court reviewed the conviction of a young man wearing a jacket bearing the words FUCK THE DRAFT. "The only 'conduct' which the State sought to punish," said the Court, "is the fact of communication. Thus, we deal here with a conviction resting solely upon 'speech'. . . ." Since these were not "fighting words" in the sense of Chaplinsky v. New Hampshire (1942) and were not obscene in the sense of being erotic, they could not be banned merely because some persons objected to them." The ability of government, consonant with the Constitution, to shut off discourse solely to protect others from hearing it is, in other words, dependent upon a showing that substantial privacy interests are being invaded in an essentially intolerable manner. Any broader view of this authority would effectively empower a majority to silence dissidents simply as a matter of personal predilections." See Cohen v. California (1971). And in Schacht v. United States (1970) the Court held void a statute forbidding an actor to wear a United States military uniform unless the actor's portrayal was favorable to the service. While the law could have banned all civilian use of uniforms, forbidding an actor wearing a uniform to say things critical of the service denied him freedom of speech.

In Branzburg v. Hayes (1972) the Supreme Court refused to create a constitutional privilege under the First Amendment for newsmen to withhold confidential sources of information from a grand jury investigating crime. The case involved newspaper reporters who had won the confidence of drug users and of the Black Panther Party and had written behind-the-scenes stories about them. Grand juries investigating these matters subpoenaed the reporters to testify and they refused on the ground that to do so would dry up their news sources and obstruct the free flow of news protected by the First Amendment. A five-man majority rejected their claim, holding that "the First Amendment does not guarantee the press a constitutional right of special access to information not available to the public generally." Nor was there any evidence that there would be "a significant constriction of the flow of news to the public" if reporters had to testify like anyone else, and it was clear that the state's interest in "extirpating the traffic in illegal drugs, in forestalling assassination attempts on the President, and in preventing the community from being disrupted" were "compelling" enough to justify this indirect burden on the press. Justice Stewart, speaking for three of the four dissenters, argues that the Court has now shifted the burden to those trying to defend their First Amendment rights, and notes that the victory of the grand jury is a Pyrrhic one at best. "The sad paradox of the Court's position is that when a grand jury may exercise an unbridled subpoena power, and sources involved in sensitive matters become fearful of disclosing information, the newsman will not only cease to be a useful grand jury witness; he will cease to investigate and publish information about issues of public import."

Per Curiam.

We granted certiorari in these cases in which the United States seeks to enjoin the New York Times and the Washington Post from publishing the contents of a classified study entitled "History of U. S. Decision-Making Process on Viet Nam Policy."

"Any system of prior restraints of expression comes to this Court bearing a heavy presumption against its constitutional validity." Bantam Books, Inc. v. Sullivan (1963); see also Near v. Minnesota (1931). The Government "thus carries a heavy burden of showing justification for the imposition of such a restraint." Organization for a Better Austin v. Keefe (1971). The District Court for the Southern District of New York in the New York Times case and the District Court for the District of Columbia and the Court of Appeals for the District of Columbia Circuit in the Washington Post case held that the Government had not met that burden. We agree.

The judgment of the Court of Appeals for the District of Columbia Circuit is therefore affirmed. The order of the Court of Appeals for the Second Circuit is reversed and the case is remanded with directions to enter a judgment affirming the judgment of the District Court for the Southern District of New York. The stays entered June 25, 1971, by the Court are vacated. The judgments shall issue forthwith.

So ordered.

Mr. Justice **Black,** with whom Mr. Justice **Douglas** joins, concurring, said in part:

. . . I agree completely that we must affirm the judgment of the Court of Appeals for the District of Columbia and reverse the judgment of the Court of Appeals for the Second Circuit for the reasons stated by my Brothers Douglas and Brennan. In my view it is unfortunate that some of my Brethren are apparently willing to hold that the publication of news may sometimes be enjoined. Such a holding would make a shambles of the First Amendment. . . .

In seeking injunctions against these newspapers and its presentation to the Court, the Executive Branch seems to have forgotten the essential purpose and history of the First Amendment. When the Constitution was adopted, many people strongly opposed it because the document contained no Bill of Rights to safeguard certain basic freedoms. They especially feared that the new powers granted to a central government might be interpreted to permit the government to curtail freedom of religion, press, assembly, and speech. In response to an overwhelming public clamor, James Madison offered a series of amendments to satisfy citizens that these great liberties would remain safe and beyond the power of government to abridge. . . . The amendments were offered to *curtail* and *restrict* the general powers granted to the Executive, Legislative, and Judicial Branches two years before in the original Constitution. The Bill of Rights changed the original Constitution into a new charter under which no branch of government could abridge the people's freedoms of press, speech, religion, and assembly. Yet the Solicitor General argues and some members of the Court appear to agree that the general powers of the Government adopted in the original Constitution should be interpreted to limit and restrict the specific and emphatic guarantees of the Bill of Rights adopted later. I can imagine no greater perversion of history. Madison and the other Framers of the First Amendment, able men that they were, wrote in language they earnestly believed could never be misunderstood: "Congress shall make no law . . . abridging the freedom of the press. . . ." Both the history and language of the First Amendment support the view that the press must be left free to publish news, whatever the source, without censorship, injunctions, or prior restraints.

In the First Amendment the Founding Fathers gave the free press the protection it must have to fulfill its essential role in our democracy. The press was to serve the governed, not the governors. The Government's power to censor the press was abolished so that the press would remain forever free to censure the Government. The press was protected so that it could bare the secrets of government and inform the people. Only a free and unrestrained press can effectively expose deception in government. And paramount among the responsibilities of a free press is the duty to prevent any part of the government from deceiving the people and sending them off to distant lands to die of foreign fevers and foreign shot and shell. In my view, far from deserving condemnation for their courageous reporting, the New York Times, the Washington Post, and other newspapers should be commended for serving the purpose that the Founding Fathers saw so clearly. In revealing the workings of government that led to the Viet Nam war, the newspapers nobly did precisely that which the Founders hoped and trusted they would do.

The Government's case here is based on premises entirely different from those that guided the Framers of the First Amendment. . . . And the Government argues in its brief that in spite of the First Amendment, "[t]he authority of the Executive Department to protect the nation against publication of information whose disclosure would endanger the national security stems from two interrelated sources: the constitutional power of the President over the conduct of foreign affairs and his authority as Commander-in-Chief."

. . . To find that the President has "inherent power" to halt the publication of news by resort to the courts would wipe out the First Amendment and destroy the fundamental liberty and security of the very people the Government hopes to make "secure." No one can read the history of the adoption of the First Amendment without being convinced beyond any doubt that it was injunctions like those sought here that Madison and his collaborators intended to outlaw in this Nation for all time.

The word "security" is a broad, vague generality whose contours should not be invoked to abrogate the fundamental law embodied in the First Amendment. The guarding of military and diplomatic secrets at the expense of informed representative government provides no real security for our Republic. The Framers of the First Amendment, fully aware of both the need to defend a new nation and the abuses of the English and Colonial governments, sought to give this new society strength and security by providing that freedom of speech, press, religion, and assembly should not be abridged. This thought was eloquently expressed in 1937 by Mr. Chief Justice Hughes—great man and great Chief Justice that he was—when the Court held a man could not be punished for attending a meeting run by Communists.

"The greater the importance of safeguarding the community from incitements to the overthrow of our institutions by force and violence, the more imperative is the need to preserve inviolate the constitutional rights of free speech, free press and free assembly in order to maintain the opportunity for free political discussion, to the end that government may be responsive to the will of the people and that changes, if desired, may be obtained by peaceful means. Therein lies the security of the Republic, the very foundation of constitutional government" [De Jonge v. Oregon, 1937].

Mr. Justice **Douglas,** with whom Mr. Justice **Black** joins, concurring, said in part:

While I join the opinion of the Court I believe it necessary to express my views more fully.

It should be noted at the outset that the First Amendment provides that "Congress shall make no law . . . abridging the freedom of speech or of the press." That leaves, in my view, no room for governmental restraint on the press.

There is, moreover, no statute barring the publication by the press of the material which the Times and Post seek to use. . . .

[Justice Douglas reviewed the wording of the Espionage Act and argued that Congress, in prohibiting "communication" of defense information, deliberately rejected a prohibition on "publication."]

Judge Gurfein's holding in the Times case that this Act does not apply to this case was therefore pre-eminently sound. Moreover, the Act of September 23, 1950, in amending 18 USC § 793 states in § 1 (b) that: "Nothing in this Act shall be construed to authorize, require, or establish military or civilian censorship or in any way to limit or infringe upon freedom of the press or of speech as guaranteed by the Constitution of the United States and no regulation shall be promulgated hereunder having that effect." Thus Congress had been faithful to the command of the First Amendment in this area.

So any power that the Government possesses must come from its "inherent power." . . .

The Government says that it has inherent powers to go into court and obtain an injunction to protect that national interest, which in this case is alleged to be national security.

Near v. Minnesota [1931] repudiated that expansive doctrine in no uncertain terms.

The dominant purpose of the First Amendment was to prohibit the widespread practice of governmental suppression of embarrassing information. It is common knowledge that the First Amendment was adopted against the widespread use of the common law of seditious libel to punish the dissemination of material that is embarrassing to the powers-that-be. . . . The present cases will, I think, go down in history as the most dramatic illustration of that principle. A debate of large proportions goes on in the Nation over our posture in Vietnam. That debate antedated the disclosure of the contents of the present documents. The latter are highly relevant to the debate in progress.

Secrecy in government is fundamentally anti-democratic, perpetuating bureaucratic errors. Open debate and discussion of public issues are vital to our national health. On public questions there should be "open and robust debate." New York Times, Inc. v. Sullivan [1964].

I would affirm the judgment of the Court of Appeals in the Post case, vacate the stay of the Court of Appeals in the Times case and direct that it affirm the District Court. . . .

Mr. Justice **Brennan,** concurring, said in part:

I write separately in these cases only to emphasize what should be apparent: that our judgment in the present cases may not be taken to indicate the propriety, in the future, of issuing temporary stays and restraining orders to block the publication of material sought to be suppressed by the Government. So far as I can determine, never before has the United States sought to enjoin a newspaper from publishing information in its possession. . . .

II.

The error which has pervaded these cases from the outset was the granting of any injunctive relief whatsoever, interim or otherwise. The entire thrust of the Government's claim throughout these cases has been that publication of the material sought to be enjoined "could," or "might," or "may" prejudice the national interest in various ways. But the First Amendment tolerates absolutely no prior judicial restraints of the press predicated upon surmise or conjecture that untoward consequences may result. . . . Our cases, it is true, have indicated that there is a single, extremely narrow class of cases in which the First Amendment's ban on prior judicial restraint may be overridden. Our cases have thus far indicated that such cases may arise only when the Nation "is at war," Schenck v. United States (1919), during which times "no one would question but that a Government might prevent actual obstruction to its recruiting service or the publication of the sailing dates of transports or the number and location of troops." Near v. Minnesota (1931). Even if the present world situation were assumed to be tantamount to a time of war, or if the power of presently available armaments would justify even in peacetime the suppression of information that would set in motion a nuclear holocaust, in neither of these actions has the Government presented or even alleged that publication of items from or based upon the material at issue would cause the happening of an event of that nature. "The chief purpose of [the First Amendment's] guarantee [is] to prevent previous restraints upon publication." Near v. Minnesota. Thus, only governmental allegation and proof that publication must inevitably, directly and immediately cause the occurrence of an event kindred to imperiling the safety of a transport already at sea can support even the issuance of an interim restraining order. In no event may mere conclusions be sufficient: for if the Executive Branch seeks judicial aid in preventing the publication, it must inevitably submit the basis upon which that aid is sought to scrutiny by the judiciary. And therefore, every restraint issued in this case, whatever its form, has violated the First Amendment—and none the less so because that restraint was justified as necessary to afford the court an opportunity to examine the claim more thoroughly. Unless and until the Government has clearly made out its case, the First Amendment commands that no injunction may issue.

Mr. Justice **Stewart,** with whom Mr. Justice **White** joins, concurring, said in part:

In the absence of the governmental checks and balances present in other areas of our national life, the only effective restraint upon executive policy and power in the areas of national defense and international affairs may lie in an enlightened citizenry—in an informed and critical public opinion which alone can here protect the values of democratic government. For this reason, it is perhaps here that a press that is alert, aware, and free most vitally serves the basic purpose of the First Amendment. For without an informed and free press there cannot be an enlightened people.

Yet it is elementary that the successful conduct of international diplomacy and the maintenance of an effective national defense require both confidentiality and secrecy. Other nations can hardly deal with this Nation in an atmosphere of mutual trust unless they can be assured that their confidences will be kept. And within our own executive departments, the development of considered and intelligent international policies would be impossible if those charged with their formulation could not communicate with each other freely, frankly, and in confidence. In the area of basic national defense the frequent need for absolute secrecy is, of course, self-evident.

I think there can be but one answer to this dilemma, if dilemma it be. The responsibility must be where the power is. If the Constitution gives the Executive a large degree of unshared power in the conduct of foreign affairs and the maintenance of our national defense, then under the Constitution the Executive must have the largely unshared duty to determine and preserve the degree of internal security necessary to exercise that power successfully. It is an awesome responsibility, requiring judgment and wisdom of a high order. I should suppose that moral, political, and practical considerations would dictate that a very first principle of that wisdom would be an insistence upon avoiding secrecy for its own sake. For when everything is classified, then nothing is classified, and the system becomes one to be disregarded by the cynical or the careless, and to be manipulated by those intent on self-protection or self-promotion. I should suppose, in short, that the hallmark of a truly effective internal security system would be the maximum possible disclosure, recognizing that secrecy can best be preserved only when credibility is truly maintained. But be that as it may, it is clear to me that it is the constitutional duty of the Executive—as a matter of sovereign prerogative and not as a matter of law as the courts know law—through the promulgation and enforcement of executive regulations, to protect the confidentiality necessary to carry out its responsibilities in the fields of international relations and national defense.

This is not to say that Congress and the courts have no role to play. Undoubtedly Congress has the power to enact specific and appropriate criminal laws to protect government property and preserve government secrets. Congress has passed such laws, and several of them are of very colorable relevance to the apparent circumstances of these cases. And if a criminal prosecution is instituted, it will be the responsibility of the courts to decide the applicability of the criminal law under which the charge is brought. Moreover, if Congress should pass a specific law authorizing civil proceedings in this field, the courts would likewise have the duty to decide the constitutionality of such a law as well as its applicability to the facts proved.

But in the cases before us we are asked neither to construe specific regulations nor to apply specific laws. We are asked, instead, to perform a function that the Constitution gave to the Executive, not the Judiciary. We are asked, quite simply, to prevent the publication by two newspapers of material that the Executive Branch insists should not, in the national interest, be published. I am convinced that the Executive is correct with respect to some of the documents involved. But I cannot say that disclosure of any of them will surely result in direct, immediate, and irreparable damage to our Nation or its people. That being so, there can under the First Amendment be but one judicial resolution of the issues before us. I join the judgments of the Court.

Mr. Justice **White,** with whom Mr. Justice **Stewart** joins, concurring, said in part:

I concur in today's judgments, but only because of the concededly extraordinary protection against prior restraints enjoyed by the press under our constitutional system. I do not say that in no circumstances would the First Amendment permit an injunction against publishing information about government plans or operations. Nor, after examining the materials the Government characterizes as the most sensitive and destructive, can I deny that revelation of these documents will do substantial damage to public interests. Indeed, I am confident that their disclosure will have that result. But I nevertheless agree that the United States has not satisfied the very heavy burden which it must meet to warrant an injunction against publication in these cases, at least in the absence of express and appropriately limited congressional authorization for prior restraints in circumstances such as these.

The Government's position is simply stated: The responsibility of the Executive for the conduct of the foreign affairs and for the security of the Nation is so basic that the President is entitled to an injunction against publication of a newspaper story whenever he can convince a court that the information to be revealed threatens "grave and irreparable" injury to the public interest; and the injunction should issue whether or not the material to be published is classified, whether or not publication would be lawful under relevant criminal statutes enacted by Congress and regardless of the circumstances by which the newspaper came into possession of the information.

At least in the absence of legislation by Congress, based on its own investigations and findings, I am quite unable to agree that the inherent powers of the Executive and the courts reach so far as to authorize remedies having such sweeping potential for inhibiting publications by the press. . . .

What is more, terminating the ban on publication of the relatively few sensitive documents the Government now seeks to suppress does not mean that the law either requires or invites newspapers or others to publish them or that they would be immune from criminal action if they do. Prior restraints require an unusually heavy justification under the First Amendment; but failure by the Government to justify prior restraints does not measure its constitutional entitlement to a conviction for criminal publication. That the Government mistakenly chose to proceed by injunction does not mean that it could not successfully proceed in another way.

When the Espionage Act was under consideration in 1917, Congress eliminated from the bill a provision that would have given the President broad powers in time of war to proscribe, under threat of criminal penalty, the publication of various categories of information related to the national defense. Congress at that time was unwilling to clothe the President with such far-reaching powers to monitor the press, and those opposed to this part of the legislation assumed that a necessary concomitant of such power was the power to "filter out the news to the people through some man." . . . However, these same members of Congress appeared to have little doubt that newspapers would be subject to criminal prosecution if they insisted on publishing information of the type Congress had itself determined should not be revealed. . . .

. . . If any of the material here at issue is of this nature, the newspapers are presumably now on full notice of the position of the United States and must face the consequences if they publish. I would have no difficulty in sustaining convictions under these sections on facts that would not justify the intervention of equity and the imposition of a prior restraint. . . .

It is thus clear that Congress has addressed itself to the problems of protecting the security of the country and the national defense from unauthorized disclosure of potentially damaging information. . . . It has not, however, authorized the injunctive remedy against threatened publication. It has apparently been satisfied to rely on criminal sanctions and their deterrent effect on the responsible as well as the irresponsible press. I am not, of course, saying that either of these newspapers has yet committed a crime or that either would commit a crime if they published all the material now in their possession. That matter must await resolution in the context of a criminal proceeding if one is instituted by the United States. In that event, the issue of guilt or innocence would be determined by procedures and standards quite different from those that have purported to govern these injunctive proceedings.

Mr. Justice **Marshall,** concurring, said in part:

It would, however, be utterly inconsistent with the concept of separation of power for this Court to use its power of contempt to prevent behavior that Congress has specifically declined to prohibit. There would be a similar damage to the basic concept of these coequal branches of Government if when the Executive has adequate authority granted by Congress to protect "national security" it can choose instead to invoke the contempt power of a court to enjoin the threatened conduct. The Constitution provides that Congress shall make laws, the President execute laws, and courts interpret law. . . . It did not provide for government by injunction in which the courts and the Executive can "make law" without regard to the action of Congress. It may be more convenient for the Executive if it need only convince a judge to prohibit conduct rather than to ask the Congress to pass a law and it may be more convenient to enforce a contempt order than seek a criminal conviction in a jury trial. Moreover, it may be considered politically wise to get a court to share the responsibility for arresting those who the Executive has probable cause to believe are violating the law. But convenience and political considerations of the moment do not justify a basic departure from the principles of our system of government. . . .

Even if it is determined that the Government could not in good faith bring criminal prosecutions against the New York Times and the Washington Post, it is clear that Congress has specifically rejected passing legislation that would have clearly given the President the power he seeks here and made the current activity of the newspapers unlawful. When Congress specifically declines to make conduct unlawful it is not for this Court to redecide those issues—to overrule Congress. . . .

Mr. Chief Justice **Burger,** dissenting.

So clear are the constitutional limitations on prior restraint against expression, that from the time of Near v. Minnesota (1931) until recently in Organization for a Better Austin v. Keefe (1971), we have had little occasion to be concerned with cases involving prior restraints against news reporting on matters of public interest. There is, therefore, little variation among the members of the Court in terms of resistance to prior restraints against publication. Adherence to this basic constitutional principle, however, does not make this case a simple one. In this case, the imperative of a free and unfettered press comes into collision with another imperative, the effective functioning of a complex modern government and specifically the effective exercise of certain constitutional powers of the Executive. Only those who view the First Amendment as an absolute in all circumstances—a view I respect, but reject—can find such a case as this to be simple or easy.

This case is not simple for another and more immediate reason. We do not know the facts of the case. No District Judge knew all the facts. No Court of Appeals judge knew all the facts. No member of this Court knows all the facts.

Why are we in this posture, in which only those judges to whom the First Amendment is absolute and permits of no restraint in any circumstances or for any reason, are really in a position to act?

I suggest we are in this posture because these cases have been conducted in unseemly haste. Mr. Justice Harlan covers the chronology of events demonstrating the hectic pressures under which these cases have been processed and I need not restate them. The prompt setting of these cases reflects our universal abhorrence of prior restraint. But prompt judicial actions does not mean unjudicial haste.

Here, moreover, the frenetic haste is due in large part to the manner in which the Times proceeded from the date it obtained the purloined documents. It seems reasonably clear now that the haste precluded reasonable and deliberate judicial treatment of these cases and was not warranted. The precipitous action of this Court aborting a trial not yet completed is not the kind of judicial conduct which ought to attend the disposition of a great issue.

The newspapers make a derivative claim under the First Amendment; they denominate this right as the public right-to-know; by implication, the Times asserts a sole trusteeship of that right by virtue of its journalistic "scoop." The right is asserted as an absolute. Of course, the First Amendment right itself is not an absolute, as Justice Holmes so long ago pointed out in his aphorism concerning the right to shout fire in a crowded theater. There are other exceptions, some of which Chief Justice Hughes mentioned by way of example in Near v. Minnesota. There are no doubt other exceptions no one has had the occasion to describe or discuss. Conceivably such exceptions may be lurking in these cases and would have been flushed had they been properly considered in the trial courts, free from unwarranted deadlines and frenetic pressures. A great issue of this kind should be tried in a judicial atmosphere conducive to thoughtful, reflective deliberation, especially when haste, in terms of hours, is unwarranted in light of the long period the Times, by its own choice, deferred publication.

It is not disputed that the Times has had unauthorized possession of the documents for three to four months, during which it has had its expert analysts studying them, presumably digesting them and preparing the material for publication. During all of this time, the Times, presumably in its capacity as trustee of the public's "right to know," has held up publication for purposes it considered proper and thus public knowledge was delayed. No doubt this was for a good reason; the analysis of 7,000 pages of complex material drawn from a vastly greater volume of material would inevitably take time and the writing of good news stories takes time. But why should the United States Government, from whom this information was illegally acquired by someone, along with all the counsel, trial judges, and appellate judges be placed under needless pressure? After these months of deferral, the alleged right-to-know has somehow and suddenly become a right that must be vindicated instanter.

Would it have been unreasonable, since the newspaper could anticipate the government's objections to release of secret material, to give the government an opportunity to review the entire collection and determine whether agreement could be reached on publication? Stolen or not, if security was not in fact jeopardized, much of the material could no doubt have been declassified, since it spans a period ending in 1968. With such an approach—one that great newspapers have in the past practiced and stated editorially to be the duty of an honorable press—the newspapers and government might well have narrowed the area of disagreement as to what was and was not publishable, leaving the remainder to be resolved in orderly litigation if necessary. To me it is hardly believable that a newspaper long regarded as a

great institution in American life would fail to perform one of the basic and simple duties of every citizen with respect to the discovery or possession of stolen property or secret government documents. That duty, I had thought—perhaps naively—was to report forthwith, to responsible public officers. This duty rests on taxi drivers, Justices and the New York Times. The course followed by the Times, whether so calculated or not, removed any possibility of orderly litigation of the issues. If the action of the judges up to now has been correct, that result is sheer happenstance.*

Our grant of the writ before final judgment in the Times case aborted the trial in the District Court before it had made a complete record pursuant to the mandate of the Court of Appeals, Second Circuit.

The consequence of all this melancholy series of events is that we literally do not know what we are acting on. As I see it we have been forced to deal with litigation concerning rights of great magnitude without an adequate record, and surely without time for adequate treatment either in the prior proceedings or in this Court. It is interesting to note that counsel in oral argument before this Court were frequently unable to respond to questions on factual points. Not surprisingly they pointed out that they had been working literally "around the clock" and simply were unable to review the documents that give rise to these cases and were not familiar with them. This Court is in no better posture. I agree with Mr. Justice Harlan and Mr. Justice Blackmun but I am not prepared to reach the merits.†

I would affirm the Court of Appeals for the Second Circuit and allow the District Court to complete the trial aborted by our grant of certiorari meanwhile preserving the status quo in the Post case. I would direct that the District Court on remand give priority to the Times case to the exclusion of all other business of that court but I would not set arbitrary deadlines.

I should add that I am in general agreement with much of what Mr. Justice White has expressed with respect to penal sanctions concerning communication or retention of documents or information relating to the national defense.

We all crave speedier judicial processes but when judges are pressured as in these cases the result is a parody of the judicial process.

Mr. Justice **Harlan**, with whom **the Chief Justice** and Mr. Justice **Blackmun** join, dissenting, said in part:

---

*Interestingly the Times explained its refusal to allow the government to examine its own purloined documents by saying in substance this might compromise *their* sources and informants! The Times thus asserts a right to guard the secrecy of its sources while denying that the Government of the United States has that power.

†With respect to the question of inherent power of the Executive to classify papers, records and documents as secret, or otherwise unavailable for public exposure, and to secure aid of the courts for enforcement, there may be an analogy with respect to this Court. No statute gives this Court express power to establish and enforce the utmost security measures for the secrecy of our deliberations and records. Yet I have little doubt as to the inherent power of the Court to protect the confidentiality of its internal operations by whatever judicial measures may be required.

These cases forcefully call to mind the wise admonition of Mr. Justice Holmes, dissenting in Northern Securities Co. v. United States (1904):

"Great cases like hard cases make bad law. For great cases are called great, not by reason of their real importance in shaping the law of the future, but because of some accident of immediate overwhelming interest which appeals to the feelings and distorts the judgment. These immediate interests exercise a kind of hydraulic pressure which makes what previously was clear seem doubtful, and before which even well settled principles of law will bend."

With all respect, I consider that the Court has been almost irresponsibly feverish in dealing with these cases. . . .

Forced as I am to reach the merits of these cases, I dissent from the opinion and judgments of the Court. Within the severe limitations imposed by the time constraints under which I have been required to operate, I can only state my reasons in telescoped form. . . .

It is a sufficient basis for affirming the Court of Appeals for the Second Circuit in the Times litigation to observe that its order must rest on the conclusion that because of the time elements the Government had not been given an adequate opportunity to present its case to the District Court. At least this conclusion was not an abuse of discretion.

In the Post litigation the Government had more time to prepare; this was apparently the basis for the refusal of the Court of Appeals for the District of Columbia Circuit on rehearing to conform its judgment to that of the Second Circuit. But I think there is another and more fundamental reason why this judgment cannot stand—a reason which also furnishes an additional ground for not reinstating the judgment of the District Court in the Times litigation, set aside by the Court of Appeals. It is plain to me that the scope of the judicial function in passing upon the activities of the Executive Branch of the Government in the field of foreign affairs is very narrowly restricted. This view is, I think, dictated by the concept of separation of powers upon which our constitutional system rests.

In a speech on the floor of the House of Representatives, Chief Justice John Marshall, then a member of that body, stated: "The President is the sole organ of the nation in its external relations, and its sole representative with foreign nations." . . .

From that time, shortly after the founding of the Nation, to this, there has been no substantial challenge to this description of the scope of executive power. See United States v. Curtiss-Wright Export Corp. (1936), collecting authorities. . . .

The power to evaluate the "pernicious influence" of premature disclosure is not, however, lodged in the Executive alone. I agree that, in performance of its duty to protect the values of the First Amendment against political pressures, the judiciary must review the initial Executive determination to the point of satisfying itself that the subject matter of the dispute does lie within the proper compass of the President's foreign relations power. Constitutional considerations forbid "a complete abandonment of judicial control." Moreover, the judiciary may properly insist that the determination that disclosure of the subject matter would irreparably impair the national security be made by the head of the Executive Department concerned—here the Secretary of State or the Secretary of Defense—after actual personal consideration by that officer. This safeguard is required in the analogous area of executive claims of privilege for secrets of state. See United States v. Reynolds [1953]. . . . But in my judgment the judiciary may not properly go beyond these two inquiries and redetermine for itself the probable impact of disclosure on the national security. "[T]he very nature of executive decisions as to foreign policy is political, not judicial. Such decisions are wholly confided by our Constitution to the political departments of the government, Executive and Legislative. They are delicate, complex, and involve large elements of prophecy. They are and should be undertaken only by those directly responsible to the people whose welfare they advance or imperil. They are decisions of a kind for which the Judiciary has neither aptitude, facilities nor responsibility and which has long been held to belong in the domain of political power not subject to judicial intrusion or inquiry." Chicago & Southern Air Lines v. Waterman Steamship Corp. (1948) (Jackson, J.). . . . Pending further hearings in each case conducted under the appropriate ground rules, I would continue the restraints on publication. I cannot believe that the doctrine prohibiting prior restraints reaches to the point of preventing courts from maintaining the status quo long enough to act responsibly in matters of such national importance as those involved here.

Mr. Justice **Blackmun**, said in part:

I join Mr. Justice Harlan in his dissent. I also am in substantial accord with much that Mr. Justice White says, by way of admonition, in the latter part of his opinion. . . .

Two federal district courts, two United States courts of appeals, and this Court—within a period of less than three weeks from inception until today—have been pressed into hurried decision of profound constitutional issues on inadequately developed and largely assumed facts without the careful deliberation that, hopefully, should characterize the American judicial process. There has been much writing about the law and little knowledge and less digestion of the facts. In the New York case the judges, both trial and appellate, had not yet examined the basic material when the case was brought here. In the District of Columbia case, little more was done, and what was accomplished in this respect was only on required remand, with the Washington Post, on the excuse that it was trying to protect its source of information, initially refusing to reveal what material it actually possessed, and with the district court forced to make assumptions as to that possession.

With such respect as may be due to the contrary view, this, in my opinion, is not the way to try a lawsuit of this magnitude and asserted importance. It is not the way for federal courts to adjudicate, and to be required to adjudicate, issues that allegedly concern the Nation's vital welfare. The country would be none the worse off were the cases tried quickly, to be sure, but in the customary and properly deliberative manner. The most recent of the material, it is said, dates no later than 1968, already about three years ago, and the Times itself took three months to formulate its plan of procedure and, thus, deprived its public for that period.

The First Amendment, after all, is only one part of an entire Constitution. Article II of the great document vests in the Executive Branch primary power over the conduct of foreign affairs and places in that branch the responsibility for the Nation's safety. Each provision of the Constitution is important, and I cannot subscribe to a doctrine of unlimited absolutism for the First Amendment at the cost of downgrading other provisions. First Amendment absolutism has never commanded a majority of this Court. . . .

FREE PRESS - FAIR TRIAL

RICHMOND NEWSPAPERS, INC. v. VIRGINIA

488 U. S. 555; 100 S. Ct. 2814; 65 L. Ed. 2d 973
(1980)

Although it has always been assumed that libelous utterances were beyond constitutional protection, it was not until 1952, in Beauharnais v. Illinois, that the Court first passed on the validity of a state libel law. There it upheld Beauharnais' conviction under a so-called "group libel" statute, a criminal libel law designed to punish defamation of racial or religious groups, for publishing a bitterly anti-Negro leaflet in Chicago. The Court found the adoption of this law was justified by the "tendency [of such statements] to cause a breach of the peace"; and since libelous utterances themselves were beyond First Amendment protection, there was no need to show they created a clear and present danger of actually bringing about such a breach of the peace.

In a landmark case in 1964, however, the Court sharply restricted the power of a state to punish libels directed at public officials. A full-page advertisement in The New York Times *accused the police of Montgomery, Alabama, of abuse of power in connection with Negro demonstrations; and some of the statements in the ad were conceded to be false. Sullivan, the commissioner of police, claimed that the charges were directed at him and sued the* Times *for a half million dollars. The judge instructed the jury that under the law the statements were libelous, and hence falsity, malice, and injury could all be inferred from the fact of publication if they were found to apply to Sullivan. The jury awarded the full amount of damages claimed, and in New York Times v. Sullivan (1964) the Supreme Court reversed the judgment. Affirming a "profound national commitment to the principle that debate on public issues should be uninhibited, robust, and wide-open," the Court ruled that in order to be exempt from First Amendment protection, a statement*

about public officials must be made with "'actual malice'—that is, with knowledge that it was false or with reckless disregard of whether it was false or not." Any rule requiring a critic of official conduct to guarantee the truth of his statements "on pain of libel judgments virtually unlimited in amount" would result in self-censorship and dampen the vigor of public debate by deterring criticism "even though it is believed to be true and even though it is in fact true, because of the doubt whether it can be proved in court."

In Garrison v. Louisiana (1964) the Court used the new test to reverse the criminal contempt conviction of a New Orleans district attorney who publicly charged local judges with "inefficiency, laziness, and excessive vacations," and with hampering his efforts to enforce the vice laws. The Supreme Court emphasized that the New York Times rule gave absolute protection to truthful criticism of public officials, regardless of motive, and even protected false criticism not made with "actual malice."

In two cases in 1971 the Court extended the rule to cover candidates for public office in regard to any matter bearing on their fitness for office (Monitor Patriot v. Roy), but in Gertz v. Welch in 1974 it made clear that it did not extend to persons who were neither public officials nor public persons. In the latter case Gertz was an attorney who was falsely accused in a John Birch Society publication of being a Communist.

The cardinal value which we attach to freedom of speech and press in a democratic society sometimes tends to obscure the fact that the use of these freedoms may jeopardize other civil liberties of the individual. One of these is the right of a litigant in a court of law to have the case tried by an impartial judge or jury. The conflict arises when unrestrained newspaper comment on a pending or current trial threatens the impartiality of any jury which could be drawn, or brings pressure upon judge or jury to reach a particular decision. An essential phase of judicial power has always been the power of a judge to protect the administration of justice in court by punishing for contempt those who would interfere with it. In England, this power has always been very sternly used, and as recently as 1949 the Lord Chief Justice fined the London Daily Mirror *£s10,000 and sentenced the editor to three months in jail for the paper's lurid comments on the crimes of the so-called "English Bluebeard" who was then on trial for murder.*

In dealing with this conflict, courts in the United States have been far more lenient to questionable newspaper comment than have courts in England. While a motion for a new trial was pending in a case involving a dispute between an AF of L union and a CIO union of which Harry Bridges was an officer, Bridges sent to the Secretary of Labor, and also released to the press, a telegram which described the judge's decision as "outrageous," and further stated: "Attempted enforcement of . . . decision will tie up port of Los Angeles and involve entire Pacific Coast. . . . [CIO union] does not intend to allow state courts to override the majority vote of members in choosing its officers and representatives and to override the National Labor Relations Board." Bridges was cited for contempt of court on the ground that this telegram was an attempt to interfere by threats with the fair and orderly administration of justice. The Court reversed the contempt in Bridges v. California (1941), holding there was no clear and present danger of influencing the court, since the telegram told the judge nothing he did not already know.

Two important cases which followed the Bridges case make it clear that to spell out contempt of court there must be a clear and present danger of subverting justice, and this danger must be proved by solid evidence and not by mere conjectures or worries. In Pennekamp v. Florida (1946) the publisher of the Miami Herald was fined for contempt for publishing a cartoon and editorials charging that a local trial judge was playing into the hands of criminal elements and thwarting the efforts of the district attorney to enforce the law. In setting aside the conviction, the Supreme Court conceded that some of the comment was directed at cases then pending in court, and that some of it was not truthful. Nevertheless, "in the borderline instances where it is difficult to say upon which side the alleged offense falls, we think the specific freedom of public comment should weigh heavily against a possible tendency to influence pending cases. Freedom of discussion should be given the widest range compatible with the essential requirement of the fair and orderly administration of justice."

Craig v. Harney (1947) involved an intemperate and inaccurate newspaper attack on a lay judge who had directed a verdict in a civil suit. Three times the jury ignored the judge's direction, and finally capitulated with the announcement that it had acted under coercion of the court and against its conscience. The newspaper characterized the judge's order as "arbitrary action" and a "gross miscarriage of justice," and reported public demands for a new trial. The publisher was convicted in a criminal trial of contempt of court for attempting to force the judge to alter his decision. The Supreme Court, in reversing the contempt conviction, admitted that the "news articles were by any standard an unfair report of what transpired," but added that "it takes more imagination than we possess to find in this rather sketchy and one-sided report of a case any imminent or serious threat to a judge of reasonable fortitude. . . . The vehemence of the language used is not alone the measure of the power to punish for contempt. The fires which it kindles must constitute an imminent, not merely a likely, threat to the administration of justice. The danger must not be remote or even probable; it must immediately imperil. . . . A judge who is part of such a dramatic episode can hardly help but know that his decision is apt to be unpopular. But the law of contempt is not made for the protection of judges who may be sensitive to the winds of public opinion. Judges are supposed to be men of fortitude, able to thrive in a hardy climate. . . . Nor can we assume that the trial judge was not a man of fortitude."

The balance struck by the Supreme Court between free speech and fair trial has not gone unchallenged by members of the Court itself. In Shepherd v. Florida (1951) the Court reversed the conviction of four Negroes because discrimination had been practiced in the selection of the grand jury. Justices Frankfurter and Jackson,

who with Chief Justice Vinson had dissented in Craig v. Harney, emphasized that inflammatory newspaper comment made a fair trial in the community impossible. And in 1949 a trial court in Maryland punished for contempt a broadcasting company which had allowed on the air extremely prejudicial comment upon a pending murder trial. The broadcast stated that the man charged with the murder had confessed, had a long criminal record, and upon being taken to the scene of the crime, had reenacted it. The Maryland court of appeals reversed the contempt conviction on the basis of Bridges, Pennekamp, and Craig. While the Supreme Court of the United States denied certiorari, Justice Frankfurter felt called upon to explain at length that this did not necessarily signify approval of the lower court decision. See Maryland v. Baltimore Radio Show (1950).

While the Court has been unwilling to permit the punishment of newspapers for trying to influence the course of justice, it has not hesitated to reverse the conviction of persons whose trials were clearly so influenced. In Irvin v. Dowd (1961) the police issued a press release stating that Irvin had confessed to six murders. The one change of venue allowed by the state law merely took him into the next county—a county so blanketed by the adverse publicity that nearly 90 percent of the prospective jurors, and eight of the twelve members of the actual jury, believed the defendant was guilty before the trial even started. And in Rideau v. Louisiana (1963) police permitted the filming of a twenty-minute interview between Rideau and the sheriff, in which Rideau confessed to robbery, kidnapping, and murder. He was denied a change of venue despite the fact that three television broadcasts had carried the "interview," and three members of the jury had seen it. The Supreme Court reversed both convictions. In Beck v. Washington (1962), however, the Court (voting four to three) found that despite adverse publicity Teamster president David Beck had been indicted by an impartial grand jury and convicted by an impartial petit jury on charges of embezzling union funds. "A study of the voir dire indicates clearly that each juror's qualifications as to impartiality far exceeded the minimum standards this Court established in its earlier cases as well as in Irvin v. Dowd, on which petitioner depends."

The cooperation between police and the news media following President Kennedy's assassination, which culminated in the murder of Lee Harvey Oswald before a nationwide television audience, brought public demand for reform even before the Sheppard case. In 1964 the New Jersey supreme court ordered a ban on pretrial statements to newsmen by prosecutors, police, and defense attorneys, while the Judicial Conference of the United States recommended to Congress the passage of a bill prohibiting the release of information to the press which had not previously been filed with the trial court. And in 1966 a committee of the American Bar Association recommended strong limits on pretrial reporting by both prosecutors and defense attorneys. While official moves of this kind met considerable opposition from the organized press, informal codes of conduct, such as those adopted in Nebraska in the case below, have been worked out in conference among the industry, the bar associations, and the courts.

Strong impetus was given the reform movement by the decision in Sheppard v. Maxwell (1966) overturning the conviction of Dr. Sam Sheppard for the murder of his wife. "Doctor Sam," a prominent Cleveland physician, was tried in a suburban court in what the Supreme Court described as a "carnival atmosphere." The press, convinced of his guilt, demanded his conviction and inundated the community with highly inflammatory, prejudicial statements which the judge, who refused to sequester the jury or grant a change of venue, was unable to keep from reaching the jury. The Court noted that "every court that has considered this case, save the court that tried it, has deplored the manner in which the news media inflamed and prejudiced the public." As for the trial itself, "the fact is that bedlam reigned at the courthouse during the trial, and newsmen took over practically the entire courtroom hounding most of the participants in the trial, especially Sheppard." After a careful review of the authority of a trial court to control the conduct of the trials before it, the Court concluded that they were adequate to protect the fairness of the trial. Strict rules of press behavior were enforced when Dr. Sheppard was retried by Ohio in 1966. An unspectacular trial resulted in his acquittal.

The result of the efforts at reform has been to shift the constitutional battle between the courts and the press to new ground as courts have tried to devise ways of preventing the publication of prejudicial news comments. In 1975, Erwin Simants was arrested and prosecuted for the brutal murder of six members of the Henry Kellie family in their home in Sutherland, Nebraska, a town of about 850 people. The crime attracted nationwide attention, and both Simant's attorney and the county attorney, fearing the "reasonable likelihood of prejudicial news which would make difficult, if not impossible, the impaneling of an impartial jury and tend to prevent a fair trial," obtained from the county court an order restricting press coverage. The news media asked the United States district court to vacate the order, but that court issued an order of its own prohibiting reporting on five subjects: "(1) the existence or contents of a confession Simants had made to law enforcement officers, which had been introduced in open court at arraignment; (2) the fact or nature of statements Simants had made to other persons; (3) the contents of a note he had written the night of the crime; (4) certain aspects of the medical testimony at the preliminary hearing; (5) the identity of the victims of the alleged sexual assault and the nature of the assault."

In Nebraska Press Asso. v. Stuart (1976), the Supreme Court unanimously held the court's order void. While conceding that the trial judge was justified in concluding there would be intense pretrial publicity, it found no evidence that the restraining order, on its face a serious limit on freedom of the press, was the only or even an effective way of guaranteeing an impartial jury. Not only did the trial court not explore other alternatives open to it, but in a town of 850 there was no reason to suppose the press accounts would be any more damaging than the rumors that were bound to circulate. As far as the material that had been introduced in open court, the Court reiterated its statement in Sheppard v. Maxwell (1966) that "there is nothing that proscribes the press from reporting events that transpire in the courtroom." In 1979, this latter point was reaffirmed and extended to information obtained by normal reporting techniques—in this case the name of a juvenile killer obtained by merely querying witnesses. The Court held the state's interest in protecting the privacy of juveniles insufficient to justify punishing the paper for publishing the name, especially since the law did not apply to either radio or television. See Smith v. Daily Mail Publishing Co. (1979).

To what extent does the news media, as the eyes and ears of a public that can rarely if ever witness events and conditions first hand, have a right of access to information not available to the public at large? In Branzburg v. Hayes (1972) the Supreme Court refused to create a constitutional privilege under the First Amendment for journalists to withhold confidential sources of information from a grand jury investigating crime. The case involved newspaper reporters who had won the confidence of drug users and of the Black Panther Party and had written behind-the-scenes stories about them. Grand juries investigating these matters subpoenaed the reporters to testify and they refused on the ground that to do so would dry up their news sources and obstruct the free flow of news protected by the First Amendment. A five-man majority rejected their claim, holding that "the First Amendment does not guarantee the press a constitutional right of special access to information not available to the public generally."

In a series of cases the Supreme Court used this statement to justify forbidding the press access to prison facilities not available to the public at large. In Pell v. Procunier (1974), it upheld rules adopted by a California prison forbidding interviews with selected inmates on the ground that the inmates so selected became celebrities and posed a disciplinary problem. The Court noted that the rules reflected no intention to conceal conditions within the prison and that the press was free to visit the prison and speak with prisoners they happened to meet. In Saxbe v. Washington Post Co. (1974), the Court extended the same rule to federal prisons, and in Houchins v. KQED, Inc. (1978), in a four-to-three decision, it extended it to a California jail where it seemed apparent that the authorities were trying to conceal conditions within the jail from public scrutiny.

The first suggestion that the Court might be rethinking the question of access came in Gannett v. DePasquale (1979). Following the apparent murder of an upstate New York man, three suspects were apprehended in Michigan with the victim's pickup truck and gun. They were returned to New York for trial, and following their arraignment asked for a pretrial hearing to argue the inadmissibility in evidence of the gun and certain statements made to the Michigan police that they claimed were involuntary. Arguing that the "unabated buildup of adverse publicity had jeopardized the ability of the defendants to receive a fair trial," they moved that *the hearings be closed to the public and the press. Without objection from the press the hearing was closed but the trial judge later held a full hearing on whether or not the transcript of the hearing should be released. The trial judge presumed a constitutional right of access on the part of the press but after finding on the record that an open suppression hearing would pose a "reasonable probability of prejudice to these defendants," he refused to release the transcript.*

In a five-to-four decision, the Court upheld the trial judge. Justice Stewart's opinion reviewed the commentaries and precedents and concluded that the Sixth Amendment guarantee of a public trial was for the benefit of the accused, not the public. While he conceded the importance of open trials to the public, he made clear that "recognition of an independent public interest in the enforcement of Sixth Amendment guarantees is a far cry . . . from the creation of a constitutional right on the part of the public." Furthermore, while "there is no question that the Sixth Amendment permits and even assumes open trials as a norm," historically the public had no right to attend pretrial proceedings. In addition, even assuming a constitutional right of access on the part of the press, it had not been violated in this case because the trial court had properly "balanced the 'constitutional rights of the press and public' against the 'defendants' right to a fair trial.'" In 1965 in Estes v. Texas the Court had held that televising a sensational trial had denied the defendant due process of law, noting that the "public trial" guaranteed by the Sixth Amendment was not the equivalent of a day in a "stadium . . . or nationwide arena." In 1981, however, the Court in Chandler v. Florida construed Estes as not banning all television coverage, although a defendant clearly had a right (which had not been exercised in this case) to try to show that media coverage had an adverse affect upon the fairness of his trial.

In the present case, the state's prosecution of the defendant for murder had resulted in three mistrials, at least one of which was apparently the result of a prospective juror reading about inadmissible evidence. At the start of the fourth trial, the defendant asked that the trial be closed. A hearing was held from which the press was excluded and the judge ruled that the press and public be excluded from the trial.

Mr. Chief Justice **Burger** announced the judgment of the Court and delivered an opinion in which Mr. Justice **White** and Mr. Justice **Stevens** joined, saying in part:

II.

We begin consideration of this case by noting that the precise issue presented here has not previously been before this Court for decision. In Gannett Co., Inc. v. DePasquale (1979), the Court was not required to decide whether a right of access to *trials*, as distinguished from hearings on *pre*trial motions, was constitutionally guaranteed. The Court held that the Sixth Amendment's guarantee to the accused of a public trial gave neither the public nor the press an enforceable right of access to a *pre*trial suppression hearing. One concurring opinion specifically emphasized that "a hearing on a motion before trial to suppress evidence is not a *trial*. . . ." (Burger, C.J., concurring). Moreover, the Court did not decide whether the First and Fourteenth Amendments guarantee a right of the public to attend trials: nor did the dissenting opinion reach this issue.

In prior cases the Court has treated questions involving conflicts between publicity and a defendant's right to a fair trial; as we observed in Nebraska Press Assn. v. Stuart (1976), "[t]he problems presented by this [conflict] are almost as old as the Republic." . . . But here for the first time the Court is asked to decide whether a criminal trial itself may be closed to the public upon the unopposed request of a defendant, without any demonstration that closure is required to protect the defendant's superior right to a fair trial, or that some other overriding consideration requires closure.

A.

The origins of the proceeding which has become the modern criminal trial in Anglo-American justice can be traced back beyond reliable historical records. We need not here review all details of its development, but a summary of that history is instructive. What is significant for present purposes is that throughout its evolution, the trial has been open to all who cared to observe. . . .

[The Court here traced the development of the English court system from the days before the Norman Conquest down to the sixteenth century, noting the uniform openness of the criminal trial.] Three centuries later, Sir Frederic Pollock was able to state of the "rule of publicity" that, "[h]ere we have one tradition, at any rate, which has persisted through all changes." . . . See also E. Jenks, The Book of English Law 73-74 (6th ed. 1967): "[O]ne of the most conspicuous features of English justice, that all judicial trials are held in open court, to which the public have free access, . . . appears to have been the rule in England from time immemorial."

We have found nothing to suggest that the presumptive openness of the trial, which English courts were later to call "one of the essential qualities of a court of justice," . . . was not also an attribute of the judicial systems of colonial America. In Virginia, for example, such records as there are of early criminal trials indicate that they were open, and nothing to the contrary has been cited. . . . Indeed, when in the mid-1600's the Virginia Assembly felt that the respect due the courts was "by the clamorous unmannerlyness of the people lost, and order, gravity and decoram which should manifest the authority of a court in the court it selfe neglicted," the response was not to restrict the openness of the trials to the public, but instead to prescribe rules for the conduct of those attending them. . . .

In some instances, the openness of trials was explicitly recognized as part of the fundamental law of the colony. . . .

B.

As we have shown, and as was shown in both the Court's opinion and the dissent in Gannett, the historical evidence demonstrates conclusively that at the time when our organic laws were adopted, criminal trials both here and in England had long been presumptively open. This is no quirk of history; rather, it has long been recognized as an indispensible attribute of an Anglo-American trial. Both Hale in the 17th century and Blackstone in the 18th saw the importance of openness to the proper functioning of a trial; it gave assurance that the proceedings were conducted fairly to all concerned, and it discouraged perjury, the misconduct of participants, and decisions based on secret bias or partiality. . . . The nexus between openness, fairness, and the perception of fairness was not lost on [foreign observers]: "[T]he judge, the counsel, and the jury, are constantly exposed to public animadversion; and this greatly tends to augment the extraordinary confidence, which the English repose in the administration of justice."

This observation raises the important point that "[t]he publicity of a judicial proceeding is a requirement of much broader bearing than its mere effect on the quality of testimony." . . . The early history of open trials in part reflects the widespread acknowledgement, long before there were behavioral scientists, that public trials had significant community therapeutic value. Even without such experts to frame the concept in words, people sensed from experience and observation that, especially in the administration of criminal justice, the means used to achieve justice must have the support derived from public acceptance of both the process and its results.

When a shocking crime occurs, a community reaction of outrage and public protest often follows. . . . Thereafter the open processes of justice serve an important prophylactic purpose, providing an outlet for community concern, hostility, and emotion. Without an awareness that society's responses to criminal conduct are underway, natural human reactions of outrage and protest are frustrated and may manifest themselves in some form of vengeful "self-help," as indeed they did regularly in the activities of vigilante "committees" on our frontiers. . . .

Civilized societies withdraw both from the victim and the vigilante the enforcement of criminal laws, but they cannot erase from people's consciousness the fundamental, natural yearning to see justice done—or even the urge for retribution. The crucial prophylactic aspects of the administration of justice cannot function in the dark; no community catharsis can occur if justice is "done in a corner [or] in any covert manner." It is not enough to say that results alone will satiate the natural community desire for "satisfaction." A result considered untoward may undermine public confidence, and where the trial has been concealed from public view an unexpected outcome can cause a reaction that the system at best has failed and at worst has been corrupted. To work effectively, it is important that society's criminal process "satisfy the appearance of justice," . . . and the appearance of justice can best be provided by allowing people to observe it.

Looking back, we see that when the ancient "town meeting" form of trial became too cumbersome, twelve members of the community were delegated to act as its surrogates, but the community did not surrender its right to observe the conduct of trials. The people retained a "right of visitation" which enabled them to satisfy themselves that justice was in fact being done. . . .

In earlier times, both in England and America, attendance at court was a common mode of "passing the time." . . . With the press, cinema, and electronic media now supplying the representations or reality of the real life drama once available only in the courtroom, attendance at court is no longer a widespread pastime. Yet "[i]t is not unrealistic even in this day to believe that public inclusion affords citizens a form of legal education and hopefully promotes confidence in the fair administration of justice." . . . Instead of acquiring information about trials by firsthand observation or by word of mouth from those who attended, people now acquire it chiefly through the print and electronic media. In a sense, this validates the media claim of functioning as surrogates for the public. While media representatives enjoy the same right of access as the public, they often are provided special seating and priority of entry so that they may report what people in attendance have seen and heard. This "contributes[s] to public understanding of the rule of law and to comprehension of the functioning of the entire criminal justice system. . . ." Nebraska Press Assn. v. Stuart (Brennan, J., concurring).

C.

From this unbroken, uncontradicted history, supported by reasons as valid today as in centuries past, we are bound to conclude that a presumption of openness inheres in the very nature of a criminal trial under our system of justice. This conclusion is hardly novel; without a direct holding on the issue, the Court has voiced its recognition of it in a variety of contexts over the years. . . . Recently in Gannett Co. Inc. v. DePasquale (1979), both the majority and dissenting opinions agreed that open trials were part of the common law tradition.

Despite the history of criminal trials being presumptively open since long before the Constitution, the State presses its contention that neither the Constitution nor the Bill of Rights contains any provision which by its terms guarantees to the public the right to attend criminal trials. Standing alone, this is correct, but there remains the question whether, absent an explicit provision, the Constitution affords protection against exclusion of the public from criminal trials.

III.

A.

The First Amendment, in conjunction with the Fourteenth, prohibits governments from "abridging the freedom of speech, or of the press; or the right of the people peaceably to assemble, and to Petition the Government for a redress of grievances.'' These expressly guaranteed freedoms share a common core purpose of assuring freedom of communication on matters relating to the functioning of government. Plainly it would be difficult to single out any aspect of government of higher concern and importance to the people than the manner in which criminal trials are conducted; as we have shown, recognition of this pervades the centuries-old history of open trials and the opinions of this Court.

The Bill of Rights was enacted against the backdrop of the long history of trials being presumptively open. Public access to trials was then regarded as an important aspect of the process itself; the conduct of trials ''before as many of the people as chuse to attend'' was regarded as one of ''the inestimable advantages of a free English constitution of government.'' . . . In guaranteeing freedoms such as those of speech and press, the First Amendment can be read as protecting the right of everyone to attend trials so as to give meaning to those explicit guarantees. ''[T]he First Amendment goes beyond protection of the press and the self-expression of individuals to prohibit government from limiting the stock of information from which members of the public may draw.'' First National Bank of Boston v. Bellotti (1978). Free speech carries with it some freedom to listen. ''In a variety of contexts this Court has referred to a First Amendment right to 'receive information and ideas.' '' Kleindienst v. Mandel (1972). What this means in the context of trials is that the First Amendment guarantees of speech and press, standing alone, prohibit government from summarily closing courtroom doors which had long been open to the public at the time that amendment was adopted. ''For the First Amendment does not speak equivocally. . . . It must be taken as a command of the broadest scope that explicit language, read in the context of a liberty-loving society, will allow.'' Bridges v. California (1941).

It is not crucial whether we describe this right to attend criminal trials to hear, see, and communicate observations concerning them as a ''right of access,'' cf. Gannett (Powell, J., concurring); Saxbe v. Washington Post Co. (1974); Pell v. Procunier (1974)* or a ''right to gather information,'' for we have recognized that ''without some protection for seeking out the news, freedom of the press could be eviscerated.'' Branzburg v. Hayes (1972). The explicit, guaranteed rights to speak and to publish concerning what takes place at a trial would lose much meaning if access to observe the trial could, as it was here, be foreclosed arbitrarily.

B.

The right of access to places traditionally open to the public, as criminal trials have long been, may be seen as assured by the amalgam of the First Amendment guarantees of speech and press; and their affinity to the right of assembly is not without relevance. From the outset, the right of assembly was regarded not only as an independent right but also as a catalyst to augment the free exercise of the other First Amendment rights with which it was deliberately linked by the draftsmen. ''The right of peaceable assembly is a right cognate to those of free speech and free press and is equally fundamental.'' DeJonge v. Oregon (1937). People assemble in public places not only to speak or to take action, but also to listen, observe, and learn; indeed, they may ''assembl[e] for any lawful purpose,'' Hague v. C.I.O. (1939) (opinion of Stone, J.). Subject to the traditional time, place and manner restrictions, . . . streets, sidewalks, and parks are places traditionally open, where First Amendment rights may be exercised . . . ; a trial courtroom also is a public place where the people generally—and representatives of the media—have a right to be present, and where their presence historically has been thought to enhance the integrity and quality of what takes place.

C.

The State argues that the Constitution nowhere spells out a guarantee for the right of the public to attend trials, and that accordingly no such right is protected. The possibility that such a contention could be made did not escape the notice of the Constitution's draftsmen; they were concerned that some important rights might be thought disparaged because not specifically guaranteed. . . .

But arguments such as the State makes have not precluded recognition of important rights not enumerated. Notwithstanding the appropriate caution against reading into the Constitution rights not explicitly defined, the Court has acknowledged that certain unarticulated rights are implicit in enumerated guarantees. For example, the rights of association and of privacy, the right to be presumed innocent and the right to be judged by a standard of proof beyond a reasonable doubt in a criminal trial, as well as the right to travel, appear nowhere in the Constitution or Bill of Rights. Yet these important, but unarticulated rights have nonetheless been found to share constitutional protection in common with explicit guarantees. The concerns expressed by Madison and others have thus been resolved; fundamental rights, even though not expressly guaranteed, have been recognized by the Court as indispensable to the enjoyment of rights explicitly defined.

We hold that the right to attend criminal trials is implicit in the guarantees of the First Amendment; without the freedom to attend such trials, which people have exercised for centuries, important aspects of freedom of speech and ''of the press could be eviscerated.'' . . .

D.

. . . Despite the fact that this was the fourth trial of the accused, the trial judge made no findings to support

---

*Procunier and Saxbe, supra, are distinguishable in the sense that they were concerned with penal institutions which, by definition, are not ''open'' or public places. Penal institutions do not share the long tradition of openness. . . .

closure; no inquiry was made as to whether alternative solutions would have met the need to ensure fairness; there was no recognition of any right under the Constitution for the public or press to attend the trial. In contrast to the proceeding dealt with in Gannett, there exist in the context of the trial itself various tested alternatives to satisfy the constitutional demands of fairness. See, e.g., Nebraska Press Association v. Stuart, Sheppard v. Maxwell. There was no suggestion that any problems with witnesses could not have been dealt with by their exclusion from the courtroom or their sequestration during the trial. Nor is there anything to indicate that sequestration of the jurors would not have guarded against their being subjected to any improper information. All of the alternatives admittedly present difficulties for trial courts, but none of the factors relied on here was beyond the realm of the manageable. Absent an overriding interest articulated in findings, the trial of a criminal case must be open to the public. Accordingly, the judgment under review is reversed.

Reversed.

Mr. Justice **Powell** took no part in the consideration or decision of this case.

Mr. Justice **White** wrote a short concurring opinion.

Mr. Justice **Stevens,** concurring, said in part:

This is a watershed case. Until today the Court has accorded virtually absolute protection to the dissemination of ideas, but never before has it squarely held that the acquisition of newsworthy matter is entitled to any constitutional protection whatsoever. An additional word of emphasis is therefore appropriate. . . .

. . . In Houchins v. KQED, Inc. [1978], I explained at length why Mr. Justice Brennan, Mr. Justice Powell, and I were convinced that "[a]n official prison policy of concealing . . . knowledge from the public by arbitrarily cutting off the flow of information at its source abridges the freedom of speech and of the press protected by the First and Fourteenth Amendments to the Constitution." . . .

It is somewhat ironic that the Court should find more reason to recognize a right of access today than it did in Houchins. For Houchins involved the plight of a segment of society least able to protect itself, an attack on a longstanding policy of concealment, and an absence of any legitimate justification for abridging public access to information about how government operates. In this case we are protecting the interests of the most powerful voices in the community, we are concerned with an almost unique exception to an established tradition of openness in the conduct of criminal trials, and it is likely that the closure order was motivated by the judge's desire to protect the individual defendant from the burden of a fourth criminal trial.

Mr. Justice **Brennan,** with whom Mr. Justice **Marshall** joins, concurring in the judgment, said in part:

Gannett Co. v. DePasquale (1979), held that the Sixth Amendment right to a public trial was personal to the accused, conferring no right of access to pretrial proceedings that is separately enforceable by the public or the press. The instant case raises the question whether the First Amendment, of its own force and as applied to the States through the Fourteenth Amendment, secures the public an independent right of access to trial proceedings. Because I believe that the First Amendment—of itself and as applied to the States through the Fourteenth Amendment—secures such a public right of access, I agree with those of my Brethren who hold that, without more agreement of the trial judge and the parties cannot constitutionally close a trial to the public.

Mr. Justice **Blackmun,** concurring in the judgment, said in part:

II.

The Court's ultimate ruling in Gannett, with such clarification as is provided by the opinions in this case today, apparently is now to the effect that there is no *Sixth* Amendment right on the part of the public—or the press—to an open hearing on a motion to suppress. I, of course, continue to believe that Gannett was in error, both in its interpretation of the Sixth Amendment generally, and in its application to the suppression hearing, for I remain convinced that the right to a public trial is to be found where the constitution explicitly placed it—in the Sixth Amendment.

The Court, however, has eschewed the Sixth Amendment route. The plurality turns to other possible constitutional sources and invokes a veritable potpourri of them—the speech clause of the First Amendment, the press clause, the assembly clause, the Ninth Amendment, and a cluster of penumbral guarantees recognized in past decisions. This course is troublesome, but it is the route that has been selected, and, at least for now, we must live with it. . . .

Having said all this, and with the Sixth Amendment set to one side in this case, I am driven to conclude, as a secondary position, that the First Amendment must provide some measure of protection for public access to the trial. The opinion in partial dissent in Gannett explained that the public has an intense need and a deserved right to know about the administration of justice in general; about the prosecution of local crimes in particular; about the conduct of the judge, the prosecutor, defense counsel, police officers, other public servants, and all the actors in the judicial arena; and about the trial itself. . . . It is clear and obvious to me, on the approach the Court has chosen to take, that, by closing this criminal trial, the trial judge abridged these First Amendment interests of the public.

I also would reverse, and I join the judgment of the Court.

Mr. Justice **Rehnquist,** dissenting, said in part:

For the reasons stated in my separate concurrence

in Gannett Co., Inc. v. DePasquale, I do not believe that either the First or Sixth Amendments as made applicable to the States by the Fourteenth, require that a State's reasons for denying public access to a trial, where both the prosecuting attorney and the defendant have consented to an order of closure approved by the judge, are subject to any additional constitutional review at our hands. And I most certainly do not believe that the Ninth Amendment confers upon us any such power to review orders of state trial judges closing trials in such situations. . . .

The proper administration of justice in any nation is bound to be a matter of the highest concern to all thinking citizens. But to gradually rein in, as this Court has done over the past generation, all of the ultimate decision-making power over how justice shall be administered, not merely in the federal system but in each of the 50 States, is a task that no Court consisting of nine persons, however gifted, is equal to. Nor is it desirable that such authority be exercised by such a tiny numerical fragment of the 220 million people who compose the population of this country.

FREEDOM OF RELIGION

MURDOCK v. PENNSYLVANIA

319 U. S. 105; 63 S. Ct. 870; 87 L. Ed. 1292
(1943)

In its first 150 years the Supreme Court decided but one important case which dealt with freedom of religion. In 1879 the case of Reynolds v. United States reached the conclusion that the religious liberty protected by the First Amendment does not include the right to commit immoral or criminal acts, even though these are sanctioned by religious doctrine. Thus Reynolds, a Mormon in the Territory of Utah, was held properly convicted of the crime of polygamy in spite of the fact that the Mormon religion held polygamy to be proper and desirable. In Cleveland v. United States (1946) Cleveland, a polygamist, had transported his plural wife across state lines; he was convicted of violating the Mann Act, which forbids the interstate transportation of "any woman or girl for the purpose of prostitution or debauchery, or for any other immoral purpose." Supreme Court cases involving religious liberty were rare because the First Amendment, which protects freedom of religion, applies only to Congress and not to the states; see Barron v. Baltimore (1833). Congress had little opportunity and less inclination to violate the First Amendment, and what the states did by way of dealing with religious matters was their own business so far as the federal Constitution was concerned.

By the 1930s this situation had begun to change. As we have seen in Near v. Minnesota (1931), the Court had by this time held that certain of the civil liberties (freedom of speech and press) which are protected by the First Amendment against invasion by the federal government are also part of the liberty which the due process

clause of the Fourteenth Amendment forbids the states to abridge. This suggested that state action dealing with religious matters could also be attacked on constitutional grounds in the Supreme Court. Thus in 1934 the Court passed upon the question whether a student who had religious scruples against bearing arms could be compelled, under penalty of expulsion, to take military drill in the University of California. It held in Hamilton v. Regents of University of California (1934) that while the religious beliefs of Hamilton were protected by due process of law, he was not being compelled to attend the university and could assert no constitutional right to do so without complying with the state's requirement of military training.

In the early 1930s a religious group called Jehovah's Witnesses began a militant nationwide campaign to spread their religious doctrines. In this enterprise all Witnesses regard themselves as ministers of the gospel. The doctrines themselves are grounded on calculations as to the second coming of Christ and the battle of Armageddon, but they also include virulent condemnation of all organized religion and churches, especially the Roman Catholic Church. These are denounced as the works of Satan. The Jehovah's Witnesses spread their teachings by personal appeals, by the sale or free distribution of literature, and by canvassing house to house asking permission to play phonograph records, one of which, called "Enemies," is a bitter attack on religious organizations. Community resentment against the Witnesses and their methods was often intense; it expressed itself at first in a good deal of mob violence, and later in resort to a variety of legal measures designed to discourage the Witnesses and curb their more unpopular activities. With fanatical zeal the Witnesses fought every legal attempt to restrict their freedom of action. As a result they have brought to the Supreme Court since 1938 some thirty major cases involving religious liberty issues. In a majority of these they have been successful. These decisions have done much to clarify our constitutional law relating to freedom of religion.

The first of these cases was Lovell v. Griffin (1938), which held that a municipal ordinance forbidding the distribution within the city of all literature, including circular and handbills, without the written consent of the city manager established "a censorship of the press" and was therefore a denial of due process of law. "Liberty of the press is not confined to newspapers and periodicals. . . . [It] comprehends every sort of publication which affords a vehicle of information and opinion." This constitutional right to distribute literature without prior permission was held to exist in a company-owned town (see Marsh v. Alabama, 1946), and also in a town established by a federal housing authority (see Tucker v. Texas, 1946.) In Martin v. Struthers (1943) the Court decided that freedom of speech and press was violated by a city ordinance which made it unlawful to knock on doors or ring doorbells to summon the occupant of a residence in order to give him handbills, circulars, or other literature. In Cantwell v. Connecticut (1940) a state statute was held void which made it a crime for any person to solicit or canvass from house to house for any religious, charitable, or philanthropic cause without securing the prior approval of the secretary of the public welfare council, who was authorized to determine whether the cause was a religious one, was bona fide, and conformed to reasonable standards of efficiency and integrity. The Court found that, as applied to Jehovah's Witnesses or other religious groups, this requirement constituted a "censorship of religion as a means of determining its right to survive" and denied due process of law. The same case held that Cantwell could not be punished for a breach of the peace for playing phonograph records on the street, even though they were offensive to those who heard them. The right to do so is part of the religious liberty protected by the Constitution.

The most serious threat to the Jehovah's Witnesses was the widespread attempt of towns and cities to collect from them the usual license taxes or fees imposed on those who peddle, sell, or canvass. There was no discrimination against those religious pamphlets or books; the tax was the same regardless of what was sold. Some of the taxes were, however, substantial; and since in many parts of the country the Jehovah's Witnesses traveled from town to town in their religious crusade, the sum total of the taxes collected in all the towns visited might well be prohibitive. The Supreme Court found great difficulty in deciding whether such taxes could validly be collected on the sale of religious literature. In Jones v. Opelika (1942) it held, by a five-to-four vote, that since the taxes were nondiscriminatory and placed no special burdens on those who sold religious literature, they did not invalidly restrict freedom of religion. In the following year the Court, in Murdock v. Pennsylvania, printed below, reversed the Opelika decision, again by a vote of five to four. The new majority on the Court declared that the activities of the Witnesses in selling their literature constitute an exercise of religion, not a commercial enterprise. It is not enough that religious activities are not taxed higher than other activities. They may not be taxed at all. This complete immunity from taxation was later sustained in Follett v. McCormick (1944), in which a Jehovah's Witness was shown to make his entire living from the sale of religious literature.

The opinion in the Murdock case strongly indicates that religious speech and press enjoy a protection against restraint and regulation which may be denied to secular or commercial speech and press. This doctrine finds support in Breard v. Alexandria (1951), in which the Supreme Court held valid a city ordinance which forbade door-to-door solicitations (without the prior consent of those solicited) as applied to subscriptions to nationally known magazines. The Court distinguished this from Martin v. Struthers (1943) on the ground that in the earlier case "no element of the commercial entered into this free solicitation and the opinion was narrowly limited to the precise fact of the free distribution of an invitation to religious services. . . ." Secular books enjoy a broad range of freedom of the press; but it is not as broad as that enjoyed by religious literature.

Mr. Justice **Douglas** delivered the opinion of the Court, saying in part:

The City of Jeanette, Pennsylvania, has an ordinance, some forty years old, which provides in part:

"That all persons canvassing for or soliciting within said Borough, orders for goods, paintings, pictures, wares, or merchandise of any kind, or persons delivering such articles under orders so obtained or solicited, shall be required to procure from the Burgess a license to transact said business and shall pay to the Treasurer of said Borough therefore the following sums according to the time for which said license shall be granted.

"For one day $1.50, for one week seven dollars ($7.00), for two weeks twelve dollars ($12.00), for three weeks twenty dollars ($20.00), provided that the provisions of this ordinance shall not apply to persons selling by sample to manufacturers or licensed merchants or dealers doing business in said Borough of Jeanette."

Petitioners are "Jehovah's Witnesses." They went about from door to door in the City of Jeanette distributing literature and soliciting people to "purchase" certain religious books and pamphlets, all published by the Watch Tower Bible & Tract Society. The "price" of the books was twenty-five cents each, the "price" of the pamphlets five cents each. In connection with these activities petitioners used a phonograph on which they played a record expounding certain of their views on religion. None of them obtained a license under the ordinance. Before they were arrested each had made "sales" of books. There was evidence that it was their practice in making these solicitations to request a "contribution" of twenty-five cents each for the books and five cents each for the pamphlets but to accept lesser sums or even to donate the volumes in case an interested person was without funds. In the present case some donations of pamphlets were made when books were purchased. Petitioners were convicted and fined for violation of the ordinance. . . .

The First Amendment, which the Fourteenth makes applicable to the states, declares that "Congress shall make no law respecting an establishment of religion, or prohibiting the free exercise thereof; or abridging the freedom of speech, or of the press. . . ." It could hardly be denied that a tax laid specifically on the exercise of those freedoms would be unconstitutional. Yet the license tax imposed by this ordinance is in substance just that.

Petitioners spread their interpretations of the Bible and their religious beliefs largely through the hand distribution of literature by full or part time workers. They claim to follow the example of Paul, teaching "publickly, and from house to house." Acts 20:20. They take literally the mandate of the Scriptures, "Go ye into all the world, and preach the gospel to every creature." Mark 16:15. In doing so they believe that they are obeying a commandment of God.

The hand distribution of religious tracts is an age-old form of missionary evangelism—as old as the history of printing presses. It has been a potent force in various religious movements down through the years. This form of evangelism is utilized today on a large scale by various religious sects whose colporteurs carry the Gospel to thousands upon thousands of homes and seek through personal visitations to win adherents to their faith. It is more than preaching; it is more than distribution of religious literature. It is a combination of both. Its purpose is as evangelical as the revival meeting. This form of religious activity occupies the same high estate under the First Amendment as do worship in the churches and preaching from the pulpits. It has the same claim to protection as the more orthodox and conventional exercises of religion. It also has the same claim as the others to the guarantees of freedom of speech and freedom of the press.

The integrity of this conduct or behavior as a religious practice has not been challenged. Nor do we have presented any question as to the sincerity of petitioners in their religious beliefs and practices, however misguided they may be thought to be. Moreover, we do not intimate or suggest in respecting their sincerity that any conduct can be made a religious rite and by the zeal of the practitioners swept into the First Amendment. Reynolds v. United States [1879] denied any such claim to the practice of polygamy and bigamy. Other claims may well arise which deserve the same fate. We only hold that spreading one's religious beliefs or preaching the Gospel through distribution of religious literature and through personal visitations is an age-old type of evangelism with as high a claim to constitutional protection as the more orthodox types. The manner in which it is practiced at times gives rise to special problems with which the police power of the states is competent to deal. See for example Cox v. New Hampshire [1941] and Chaplinsky v. New Hampshire [1942]. But that merely illustrates that the rights with which we are dealing are not absolutes. . . . We are concerned, however, in these cases merely with one narrow issue. There is presented for decision no question whatsoever concerning punishment for any alleged unlawful acts during the solicitation. Nor is there involved here any question as to the validity of a registration system for colporteurs and other solicitors. The cases present a single issue—the constitutionality of an ordinance which as construed and applied requires religious colporteurs to pay a license tax as a condition to the pursuit of their activities.

The alleged justification for the exaction of this license tax is the fact that the religious literature is distributed with a solicitation of funds. Thus it was stated in Jones v. Opelika [1942] that when a religious sect uses "ordinary commercial methods of sales of articles to raise propaganda funds," it is proper for the state to charge "reasonable fees for the privilege of canvassing." . . . But the mere fact that the religious literature is "sold" by itinerant preachers rather than "donated" does not transform evangelism into a commercial enterprise. If it did, then the passing of the collection plate in church would make the church service a commercial project. The constitutional rights of those spreading their religious beliefs through the spoken and printed word are not to be gauged by standards governing retailers or wholesalers of books. The right to use the press for expressing one's views is not to be measured by the protection afforded commercial handbills. It should be remembered that the pamphlets of Thomas Paine were not distributed free of charge. It is plain that a religious organization needs funds to remain a going concern. But an itinerant evangelist however misguided or intolerant he may be, does not become a mere book agent by selling the Bible or religious tracts to help defray his expenses or to sustain him. Freedom of speech, freedom of the press, freedom of religion are available to all, not merely to those who can pay their own way. As we have said, the problem of drawing the line between a purely commercial activity and a religious one will at times be difficult. On this record it plainly cannot be said that petitioners were engaged in a commercial rather than a religious venture. It is a distortion of the facts of record to describe their activities as the occupation of selling books and pamphlets. . . .

We do not mean to say that religious groups and the press are free from all financial burdens of government. . . . We have here something quite different, for example, from a tax on the income of one who engages in religious activities or a tax on property used or employed in connection with those activities. It is one thing to impose a tax on the income or property of a preacher. It is quite another thing to exact a tax from him for the privilege of delivering a sermon. . . . Those who can tax the exercise of this religious practice can make its exercise so costly as to deprive it of the resources necessary for its maintenance. Those who can tax the privilege of engaging in this form of missionary evangelism can close its doors to all those who do not have a full purse. Spreading religious beliefs in this ancient and honorable manner would thus be denied the needy. Those who can deprive religious groups of their colporteurs can take from them a part of the vital power of the press which has survived from the Reformation.

It is contended, however, that the fact that the license tax can suppress or control this activity is unimportant if it does not do so. But that is to disregard the nature of this tax. It is a license tax—a flat tax imposed on the exercise of a privilege granted by the Bill of Rights. A state may not impose a charge for the enjoyment of a right granted by the federal constitution. Thus, it may not exact a license tax for the privilege of carrying on interstate commerce. . . . A license tax applied to activities guaranteed by the First Amendment would have the same destructive effect. It is true that the First Amendment, like the commerce clause, draws no distinction between license taxes, fixed sum taxes, and other kinds of taxes. But that is no reason why we should shut our eyes to the nature of the tax and its destructive influence. The power to impose a license tax on the exercise of these freedoms is indeed as potent as the power of censorship which this Court has repeatedly struck down. . . . In all of these cases the issuance of the permit or license is dependent on the payment of a license tax. And the license tax is fixed in amount and unrelated to the scope of the activities of petitioners or to their realized revenues. It is not a nominal fee imposed as a regulatory measure to defray the expenses of policing the activities in question. . . .

The taxes imposed by this ordinance can hardly help but be as severe and telling in their impact on the freedom of the press and religion as the ''taxes on knowledge'' at which the First Amendment was partly aimed. . . . They may indeed operate even more subtly. Itinerant evangelists moving throughout a state or from state to state would feel immediately the cumulative effect of such ordinances as they become fashionable. The way of the religious dissenter has long been hard. But if the formula of this type of ordinance is approved, a new device for the suppression of religious minorities will have been found. This method of disseminating religious beliefs can be crushed and closed out by the sheer weight of the toll or tribute which is exacted town by town, village by village. The spread of religious ideas through personal visitations by the literature ministry of numerous religious groups would be stopped.

The fact that the ordinance is ''nondiscriminatory'' is immaterial. The protection afforded by the First Amendment is not so restricted. A license tax certainly does not acquire constitutional validity because it classifies the privileges protected by the First Amendment along with the wares and merchandise of hucksters and peddlers and treats them all alike. Such equality in treatment does not save the ordinance. Freedom of press, freedom of speech, freedom of religion are in a preferred position.

It is claimed, however, that the ultimate question in determining the constitutionality of this license tax is whether the state has given something for which it can ask a return. That principle has wide applicability. . . . But it is quite irrelevant here. This tax is not a charge for the enjoyment of a privilege or benefit bestowed by the state. The privilege in question exists apart from state authority. It is guaranteed the people by the Federal constitution.

Considerable emphasis is placed on the kind of literature which petitioners were distributing—its provocative, abusive, and ill-mannered character and the assault which it makes on our established churches and the cherished faiths of many of us. . . . But those considerations are no justification for the license tax which the ordinance imposes. Plainly a community may not suppress, or the state tax, the dissemination of views because they are unpopular, annoying or distasteful. If that device were ever sanctioned, there would have been forged a ready instrument for the suppression of the faith which any minority cherishes but which does not happen to be in favor. That would be a complete repudiation of the philosophy of the Bill of Rights.

Jehovah's Witnesses are not ''above the law.'' But the present ordinance is not directed to the problems with which the police power of the state is free to deal. It does not cover, and petitioners are not charged with breaches of the peace. They are pursuing their solicitations peacefully and quietly. . . .

The judgment in Jones v. Opelika has this day been vacated. Freed from that controlling precedent, we can restore to their high, constitutional position the liberties of itinerant evangelists who disseminate their religious beliefs and the tenets of their faith through distribution of literature. The judgments are reversed and the causes are remanded to the Pennsylvania Superior Court for proceedings not inconsistent with this opinion.

Reversed.

Mr. Justice **Reed** dissented and Justices **Roberts, Frankfurter,** and **Jackson** concurred.

Mr. Justice **Frankfurter** also wrote a dissenting opinion.

WEST VIRGINIA STATE BOARD OF EDUCATION v. BARNETTE

319 U. S. 624; 63 S. Ct. 1178; 87 L. Ed. 1628 (1943)

The most spectacular issue of religious liberty to be raised by the Jehovah's Witnesses was that of the compulsory flag salute. The Witnesses refuse to salute the flag or permit their children to do so, because they believe that this violates the First Commandment. This refusal caused bitter resentment, and some seventeen states passed statutes requiring all school children to salute the flag and providing for the expulsion of those who refused. The question of whether these acts unconstitutionally restricted freedom of religion came to the Court in Minersville School District v. Gobitis (1940). With one judge dissenting, the Court held that it did not. In an opinion by Justice Frankfurter it was stated that freedom of religion is not absolute, and that some compromises may be necessary in order to secure the national unity, which is the basis of national security. The flag salute contributes to that national unity, or at least the question of whether it does or not is ''an issue of educational policy for which the courtroom is not the proper arena.'' For the Court to hold the requirement void as abridging religious liberty ''would amount to no less than the pronouncement of a pedagogical and psychological dogma in a field where courts possess no marked and certainly no controlling competence.'' The Court seemed content to assume that the Minersville school board was more competent to settle the flag salute issue than the Supreme Court, and it allowed the board's judgment to prevail. Justice Stone wrote a powerful dissenting opinion. The decision came as a shock and was widely and sharply criticized. Members of the Court who had participated in it began to have misgivings. When Jones v. Opelika was decided in 1942, Justices Black, Douglas, and Murphy dissented, and went further to state that they had become convinced that the Gobitis case was ''wrongly decided.'' With Justice Stone, this made four members of the Court who no longer supported the Gobitis decision. When, in February, 1943, Justice Rutledge replaced Justice

Byrnes on the bench, he joined with these four to overrule the Gobitis case by the decision in the case below.

These cases suggest that the Supreme Court, in dealing with questions of religious freedom, seeks to find a sound balance between the competing interests of the individual and of the society in which he or she lives. Society's interest is upheld where the disadvantage to the religious interest of the individual is relatively slight. Thus Cox v. New Hampshire (1941) held that a reasonable, nondiscriminatory fee, suitable to cover the cost of extra police service, may be charged for the privilege of holding public parades or processions, even though they be for religious purposes. And Prince v. Massachusetts (1944) held that a state child labor law may be validly enforced against those who allow young children under their care to sell religious literature on the streets.

In Sherbert v. Verner (1963), however, the free exercise clause was held violated where unemployment compensation was denied a Seventh Day Adventist who refused "suitable" work which required her to work on Saturday. Such a rule, the Court held, "forces her to choose between following the precepts of her religion and forfeiting benefits, on the one hand, and abandoning one of the precepts of her religion in order to accept work on the other hand. Governmental imposition of such a choice puts the same kind of burden upon the free exercise of religion as would a fine imposed against appellant for her Saturday worship." The holding was reaffirmed in Thomas v. Review Board (1981) where a Jehovah's Witness was held entitled to unemployment insurance after quitting for religious reasons a job which involved making weapons. The steel company for which he worked had closed the roll foundry where he worked and transferred him to a department making gun turrets.

In two cases the Court dealt with the unusual demands of the Old Order Amish, a plain people who lead a simple, rural farm life in cohesive, self-supporting religious communities, stressing "a life of 'goodness,' rather than a life of intellect; wisdom, rather than technical knowledge; community welfare rather than competition; and separation from, rather than integration with, contemporary worldly society." They dress plainly, do not use machinery or electricity and their transportation consists of horse-drawn wagons and buggies lighted at night with a lantern. In Wisconsin v. Yoder (1972) they resisted the efforts of the state to make their children attend school past the eighth grade. They argued that by sending their children to high school "they would not only expose themselves to the danger of the censure of the church community, but . . . endanger their own salvation and that of their children." The Court held that in view of the kind of life for which the Amish children were being trained and the unquestioned success of the Amish society, the state did not have sufficiently compelling interest in the additional years of schooling to warrant interfering with the free exercise of their religion. In United States v. Lee (1982), however, the Court held that Amish employers and employees had to pay into the social security system despite the self-sufficiency of the Amish and the fact "that both payment and receipt of social security benefits is forbidden by the Amish faith."

The Court found mandatory participation essential to the fiscal vitality of the system and noted the lack of difference in principle between this and the payment of income taxes which any number of religious groups might object to paying through religious objection to the purposes for which the money was spent.

Bob Jones University v. United States (1983) brought to the Court the unusual issue whether the IRS could validly withhold the normally available tax exemption from a private educational institution simply because it discriminated against blacks. The case, which turned primarily on the intent of Congress in adopting the statute, was given a bizarre twist when President Reagan ordered the government to change sides after certiorari had been granted. The case was kept from becoming moot when the court of appeals enjoined the government's grant of tax immunity, and since the Attorney General was now on the side of Bob Jones, the Court appointed outside counsel to defend the government's position. It found the IRS interpretation to be correct and held that it did not violate Bob Jones' religious freedom. It noted that freedom of religion was not an absolute but had to yield to "an overriding, governmental interest" and here "the Government has a fundamental, overriding interest in eradicating racial discrimination in education—discrimination that prevailed, with official approval, for the first 165 years of this Nation's history."

Mr. Justice **Jackson** delivered the opinion of the Court, saying in part:

Following the decision by this Court on June 3, 1940, in Minersville School Dist. v. Gobitis the West Virginia legislature amended its statutes to require all schools therein to conduct courses of instruction in history, civics, and in the Constitutions of the United States and of the State "for the purpose of teaching, fostering and perpetuating the ideals, principles and spirit of Americanism, and increasing the knowledge of the organization and machinery of the government." . . .

The Board of Education on January 9, 1942, adopted a resolution containing recitals taken largely from the Court's Gobitis opinion and ordering that the salute to the flag become "a regular part of the program of activities in the public schools," that all teachers and pupils "shall be required to participate in the salute honoring the Nation represented by the Flag; provided, however, that refusal to salute the Flag be regarded as an Act of insubordination, and shall be dealt with accordingly."

The resolution originally required the "commonly accepted salute to the Flag" which it defined. Objections to the salute as "being too much like Hitler's" were raised by the Parent and Teachers Association, the Boy and Girl Scouts, the Red Cross, and the Federation of Women's Clubs. Some modification appears to have been made in deference to these objections, but no concession was made to Jehovah's Witnesses. What is now required is the "stiff-arm" salute, the saluter to keep the right hand raised with palm turned up while the following is repeated: "I pledge allegiance to the Flag of the United States of America and to the Republic for which it stands; one Nation, indivisible, with liberty and justice for all."

Failure to conform is "insubordination" dealt with by expulsion. Readmissions is denied by statute until compliance. Meanwhile the expelled child is "unlawfully absent" and may be proceeded against as a delinquent. His parents or guardians are liable to prosecution, and if convicted are subject to fine not exceeding $50 and jail terms not exceeding thirty days.

Appellees, citizens of the United States and of West Virginia, brought suit in the United States District Court for themselves and others similarly situated asking its injunction to restrain enforcement of these laws and regulations against Jehovah's Witnesses. The Witnesses are an unincorporated body teaching that the obligation imposed by law of God is superior to that of laws enacted by temporal government. Their religious beliefs include a literal version of Exodus, Chapter 20, verses 4 and 5, which says: "Thou shalt not make unto thee any graven image, or any likeness of anything that is in heaven above, or that is in the earth beneath or that is in the water under the earth; thou shalt not bow down thyself to them, nor serve them." They consider that the flag is an "image" within this command. For this reason they refuse to salute it.

Children of this faith have been expelled from school and are threatened with exclusion for no other cause. Officials threaten to send them to reformatories maintained for criminally inclined juveniles. Parents of such children have been prosecuted and are threatened with prosecutions for causing delinquency. . . .

This case calls upon us to reconsider a precedent decision, as the Court throughout its history often has been required to do. Before turning to the Gobitis Case, however, it is desirable to notice certain characteristics by which this controversy is distinguished.

The freedom asserted by these appellees does not bring them into collision with rights asserted by any other individual. It is such conflicts which most frequently require intervention of the State to determine where the rights of one end and those of another begin. But the refusal of these persons to participate in the ceremony does not interfere with or deny rights of others to do so. Nor is there any question in this case that their behavior is peaceable and orderly. The sole conflict is between authority and rights of the individual. The State asserts power to condition access to public education on making a prescribed sign and profession and at the same time to coerce attendance by punishing both parent and child. The latter stand on a right of self-determination in matters that touch individual opinion and personal attitude.

As the present Chief Justice said in dissent in the Gobitis Case, the State may "require teaching by instruction and study of all in our history and in the structure and organization of our government, including the guaranties of civil liberty, which tend to inspire patriotism and love of country." Here, however, we are dealing with a compulsion of students to declare a belief. They are not merely made acquainted with the flag salute so that they may be informed as to what it is or even

what it means. The issue here is whether this slow and easily neglected route to aroused loyalties constitutionally may be short-cut by substituting a compulsory salute and slogan. . . .

There is no doubt that, in connection with the pledges, the flag salute is a form of utterance. Symbolism is a primitive but effective way of communicating ideas. The use of an emblem or flag to symbolize some system, idea, institution, or personality, is a short cut from mind to mind. Causes and nations, political parties, lodges and ecclesiastical groups seek to knit the loyalty of their followings to a flag or banner, a color or design. The State announces rank, function, and authority through crowns and maces, uniforms and black robes; the church speaks through the Cross, the Crucifix, the altar and shrine, and clerical raiment. Symbols of State often convey political ideas just as religious symbols come to convey theological ones. Associated with many of these symbols are appropriate gestures of acceptance or respect: a salute, a bowed or bared head, a bended knee. A person gets from a symbol the meaning he puts into it, and what is one man's comfort and inspiration is another's jest and scorn.

Over a decade ago Chief Justice Hughes led this Court in holding that the display of a red flag as a symbol of opposition by peaceful and legal means to organized government was protected by the free speech guaranties of the Constitution. Stromberg v. California [1931]. Here it is the State that employs a flag as a symbol of adherence to government as presently organized. It requires the individual to communicate by word and sign his acceptance of the political ideas it thus bespeaks. Objection to this form of communication when coerced is an old one, well known to the framers of the Bill of Rights.

It is also to be noted that the compulsory flag salute and pledge requires affirmation of a belief and an attitude of mind. It is not clear whether the regulation contemplates that pupils forego any contrary convictions of their own and become unwilling converts to the prescribed ceremony or whether it will be acceptable if they simulate assent by words without belief and by a gesture barren of meaning. It is now a commonplace that censorship or suppression of expression of opinion is tolerated by our Constitution only when the expression presents a clear and present danger of action of a kind the State is empowered to prevent and punish. It would seem that involuntary affirmation could be commanded only on even more immediate and urgent grounds than silence. But here the power of compulsion is invoked without any allegation that remaining passive during a flag salute ritual creates a clear and present danger that would justify an effort even to muffle expression. To sustain the compulsory flag salute we are required to say that a Bill of Rights which guards the individual's right to speak his own mind, left it open to public authorities to compel him to utter what is not in his mind.

Whether the First Amendment to the Constitution will permit officials to order observance of ritual of this nature does not depend upon whether as a voluntary exercise we would think it to be good, bad or merely innocuous. Any credo of nationalism is likely to include what some disapprove or to omit what others think essential, and to give off different overtones as it takes on different accents or interpretations. If official power exists to coerce acceptance of any patriotic creed, what it shall contain cannot be decided by courts, but must be largely discretionary with the ordaining authority, whose power to prescribe would no doubt include power to amend. Hence validity of the asserted power to force an American citizen publicly to profess any statement of belief or to engage in any ceremony of assent to one, presents questions of power that must be considered independently of any idea we may have as to the utility of the ceremony in question.

Nor does the issue as we see it turn on one's possession of particular religious views or the sincerity with which they are held. While religion supplies appellees' motive for enduring the discomforts of making the issue in this case, many citizens who do not share these religious views hold such a compulsory rite to infringe constitutional liberty of the individual. It is not necessary to inquire whether non-conformist beliefs will exempt from the duty to salute unless we first find power to make the salute a legal duty.

The Gobitis decision, however, *assumed,* as did the argument in that case and in this, that power exists in the State to impose the flag salute discipline upon school children in general. The Court only examined and rejected a claim based on religious beliefs of immunity from an unquestioned general rule. The question which underlies the flag salute controversy is whether such a ceremony so touching matters of opinion and political attitude may be imposed upon the individual by official authority under powers committed to any political organization under our Constitution. We examine rather than assume existence of this power and, against this broader definition of issues in this case, re-examine specific grounds assigned for the Gobitis decision.

1. It was said that the flag-salute controversy confronted the Court with "the problem which Lincoln cast in memorable dilemma: 'Must a government of necessity be too *strong* for the liberties of its people, or too *weak* to maintain its own existence?'" and that the answer must be in favor of strength. Minersville School District v. Gobitis.

We think these issues may be examined free of pressure or restraint growing out of such considerations.

It may be doubted whether Mr. Lincoln would have thought that the strength of government to maintain itself would be impressively vindicated by our confirming power of the state to expel a handful of children from school. Such oversimplification, so handy in political debate, often lacks the precision necessary to postulates of judicial reasoning. If validly applied to this problem, the utterance cited would resolve every issue of power in favor of those in authority and would require us to override every liberty thought to weaken or delay execution of their policies.

Government of limited power need not be anemic government. Assurance that rights are secure tends to diminish fear and jealousy of strong government, and by making us feel safe to live under it makes for its better support. Without promise of a limiting Bill of Rights it is doubtful if our Constitution could have mustered enough strength to enable its ratification. To enforce those rights today is not to choose weak government over strong government. It is only to adhere as a means of strength to individual freedom of mind in preference to officially disciplined uniformity for which history indicates a disappointing and disastrous end.

The subject now before us exemplifies this principle. Free public education, if faithful to the ideal of secular instruction and political neutrality, will not be partisan or enemy of any class, creed, party, or faction. If it is to impose any ideological discipline, however, each party or denomination must seek to control, or failing that, to weaken the influence of the educational system. Observance of the limitations of the Constitution will not weaken government in the field appropriate for its exercise.

2. It was also considered in the Gobitis Case that functions of educational officers in states, counties and school districts were such that to interfere with their authority "would in effect make us the school board for the country."

The Fourteenth Amendment, as now applied to the States, protects the citizen against the State itself and all of its creatures—Boards of Education not excepted. These have, of course, important, delicate, and highly discretionary functions, but none that they may not perform within the limits of the Bill of Rights. That they are educating the young for citizenship is reason for scrupulous protection of Constitutional freedoms of the individual, if we are not to strangle the free mind at its source and teach youth to discount important principles of our government as mere platitudes.

Such Boards are numerous and their territorial jurisdiction often small. But small and local authority may feel less sense of responsibility to the Constitution, and agencies of publicity may be less vigilant in calling it to account. The action of Congress in making flag observance voluntary and respecting the conscience of the objector in a matter so vital as raising the Army contrasts sharply with these local regulations in matters relatively trivial to the welfare of the nation. There are village tyrants as well as village Hampdens, but none who acts under color of law is beyond reach of the Constitution.

3. The Gobitis opinion reasoned that this is a field "where courts possess no marked and certainly no controlling competence," that it is committed to the legislatures as well as the courts to guard cherished liberties and that it is constitutionally appropriate to "fight out the wise use of legislative authority in the forum of public opinion and before legislative assemblies rather than to transfer such a contest to the judicial arena," since all the "effective means of inducing political changes are left free."

The very purpose of a Bill of Rights was to withdraw certain subjects from the vicissitudes of political controversy, to place them beyond the reach of majorities and officials and to establish them as legal principles to be applied by the courts. One's rights to life, liberty, and property, to free speech, a free press, freedom of worship and assembly, and other fundamental rights may not be submitted to vote; they depend on the outcome of no elections.

In weighing arguments of the parties it is important to distinguish between the due process clause of the Fourteenth Amendment as an instrument for transmitting the principles of the First Amendment and those cases in which it is applied for its own sake. The test of legislation which collides with the Fourteenth Amendment, because it also collides with the principles of the First, is much more definite than the test when only the Fourteenth is involved. Much of the vagueness of the due process clause disappears when the specific prohibitions of the First become its standard. The right of a State to regulate, for example, a public utility may well include, so far as the due process test is concerned, power to impose all of the restrictions which a legislature may have a "rational basis" for adopting. But freedoms of speech and of press, of assembly, and of worship may not be infringed on such slender grounds. They are susceptible of restriction only to prevent grave and immediate danger to interests which the state may lawfully protect. It is important to note that while it is the Fourteenth Amendment which bears directly upon the State it is the more specific limiting principles of the First Amendment that finally govern this case.

Nor does our duty to apply the Bill of Rights to assertions of official authority depend upon our possession of marked competence in the field where the invasion of rights occurs. True, the task of translating the majestic generalities of the Bill of Rights, conceived as part of the pattern of liberal government in the eighteenth century, into concrete restraints on officials dealing with the problems of the twentieth century, is one to disturb self-confidence. These principles grew in soil which also produced a philosophy that the individual was the center of society, that his liberty was attainable through mere absence of governmental restraints, and that government should be entrusted with few controls and only the mildest supervision over men's affairs. We must transplant these rights to a soil in which the laissez-faire concept or principle of non-interference has withered at least as to economic affairs, and social advancements are increasingly sought through closer integration of society and through expanded and strengthened governmental controls. These changed conditions often deprive precedents of reliability and cast us more than we would choose upon our own judgment. But we act in these matters not by authority of our competence but by force of our commissions. We cannot, because of modest estimates of our competence in such specialities as public education, withhold the judgment that history authenticates as the function of this Court when liberty is infringed.

4. Lastly, and this is the very heart of the Gobitis opinion, it reasons that "national unity is the basis of national security," that the authorities have "the right to select appropriate means for its attainment," and hence reaches the conclusion that such compulsory measures toward "national unity" are constitutional. Upon the verity of this assumption depends our answer in this case.

National unity as an end which officials may foster by persuasion and example is not in question. The problem is whether under our Constitution compulsion as here employed is a permissible means for its achievement.

Struggles to coerce uniformity of sentiment in support of some end thought essential to their time and country have been waged by many good as well as by evil men. Nationalism is a relatively recent phenomenon but at other times and places the ends have been racial or territorial security, support of a dynasty or regime, and particular plans for saving souls. As first and moderate methods to attain unity have failed, those bent on its accomplishment must resort to an ever increasing severity. As governmental pressure toward unity becomes greater, so strife becomes more bitter as to whose unity it shall be. Probably no deeper division of our people could proceed from any provocation than from finding it necessary to choose what doctrine and whose program public educational officials shall compel youth to unite in embracing. Ultimate futility of such attempts to compel coherence is the lesson of every such effort from the Roman drive to stamp out Christianity as a disturber of its pagan unity, the Inquisition, as a means to religious and dynastic unity, the Siberian exiles as a means to Russian unity, down to the fast-failing efforts of our present totalitarian enemies. Those who begin coercive elimination of dissent soon find themselves exterminating dissenters. Compulsory unification of opinion achieves only the unanimity of the graveyard.

It seems trite but necessary to say that the First Amendment to our Constitution was designed to avoid these ends by avoiding these beginnings. There is no mysticism in the American concept of the State or of the nature or origin of its authority. We set up government by consent of the governed, and the Bill of Rights denies those in power any legal opportunity to coerce that consent. Authority here is to be controlled by public opinion, not public opinion by authority.

The case is made difficult not because the principles of its decision are obscure but because the flag involved is our own. Nevertheless, we apply the limitations of the Constitution with no fear that freedom to be intellectually and spiritually diverse or even contrary will disintegrate the social organization. To believe that patriotism will not flourish if patriotic ceremonies are voluntary and spontaneous instead of a compulsory routine is to make an unflattering estimate of the appeal of our institutions to free minds. We can have intellectual individualism and the rich cultural diversities that we owe to exceptional minds only at the price of occasional eccentricity and abnormal attitudes. When they are so harmless to others or to the State as those we deal with here, the price is not too great. But freedom to differ is not limited to things that do not matter much. That would be a mere shadow of freedom. The test of its substance is the right to differ as to things that touch the heart of the existing order.

If there is any fixed star in our constitutional constellation, it is that no official, high or petty, can prescribe what shall be orthodox in politics, nationalism, religion, or other matters of opinion or force citizens to confess by word or act their faith therein. If there are any circumstances which permit an exception, they do not now occur to us.

We think the action of the local authorities in compelling the flag salute and pledge transcends constitutional limitations on their power and invades the sphere of intellect and spirit which it is the purpose of the First Amendment to our Constitution to reserve from all official control.

The decision of this Court in Minersville School District v. Gobitis . . . [is] overruled, and the judgment enjoining enforcement of the West Virginia Regulation is affirmed.

Justices **Black** and **Douglas** joined in a concurring opinion.

Mr. Justice **Murphy** wrote a concurring opinion.

Justices **Roberts** and **Reed** dissented.

Mr. Justice **Frankfurter,** in dissenting, said in part:

. . . As a member of this Court I am not justified in writing my private notions of policy into the Constitution, no matter how deeply I may cherish them or how mischievous I may deem their disregard. The duty of a judge who must decide which of two claims before the Court shall prevail, that of a State to enact and enforce laws within its general competence or that of an individual to refuse obedience because of the demands of his conscience, is not that of the ordinary person. It can never be emphasized too much that one's own opinion about the wisdom or evil of a law should be excluded altogether when one is doing one's duty on the bench. The only opinion of our own even looking in that direction that is material is our opinion whether legislators could in reason have enacted such a law. In the light of all the circumstances, including the history of this question in this Court, it would require more daring than I possess to deny that reasonable legislators could have taken the action which is before us for review. Most unwillingly, therefore, I must differ from my brethren with regard to legislation like this, I cannot bring my mind to believe that the 'liberty' secured by the Due Process Clause gives this Court authority to deny to the State of West Virginia the attainment of that which we all recognize as a legitimate legislative end, namely, the promotion of good citizenship, by employment of the means here chosen. . . .

ESTABLISHMENT OF RELIGION

ZORACH v. CLAUSON

343 U. S. 306; 72 S. Ct. 679; 96 L. Ed. 954
(1952)

In the Jehovah's Witnesses cases just presented the Supreme Court had to decide whether the government had violated the freedom of religion protected by the First and Fourteenth Amendments. The cases concerned directly a small militant group. In the cases below the Court faced highly complex problems affecting the interests of all citizens: namely, the problems of public aid to religion in connection with our nationwide system of compulsory education.

Early education in America was religious education, supported by the civil government in the Bible-commonwealth of Massachusetts, and by the various church groups in the middle and southern colonies. In the early nineteenth century the demand for free public education resulted in a system of public schools free from religious control and largely free from sectarian influence, a situation wholly satisfactory to an overwhelmingly Protestant nation. Waves of Catholic immigration injected a new element into the picture. The Catholic Church regards the teaching of religion as a primary function of education. Unwilling to send their children to the public schools, which they regarded as either devoid of all religious influence or tainted with Protestantism, the Catholics felt obliged to build and maintain a system of parochial schools at their own expense. When these parochial schools met the state's educational standards they were accredited as schools in which the requirements of the compulsory education laws could be satisfied. In 1922 the state of Oregon passed a law requiring all parents to send their children to the public schools of the state. The Supreme Court, in Pierce v. Society of Sisters (1925), held that the statute denied due process of law by taking from parents their freedom to "direct the upbringing and education" of their children by sending them either to parochial or to private nonsectarian schools of approved educational standards.

It is not surprising that Catholic citizens, who paid taxes to support public schools which they did not use, should try to secure some public aid for the parochial schools; and they exerted a good deal of pressure to bring this about. Opposition to this was, however, bitter and widespread; and by the end of the nineteenth century practically every state had adopted some kind of prohibition against the use of state funds for the support of religious education. In numerous cases the state courts held void attempts to extend direct or indirect aid to parochial schools.

Since the 1930s new and varied services and benefits have been offered by the states to pupils in the public schools. These include free textbooks, free bus transportation, free lunches, and free medical service. Can the state, if it desires, also give these benefits to children attending parochial or private schools? It was argued on the one hand that to do so would not only violate the constitutional clauses which forbid the use of public money in aid of religion or religious education, but would violate also the clause of the First Amendment which forbids "an establishment of religion," a clause now carried over into the Fourteenth Amendment as a limitation on the states. It was argued on the other side that in providing these services and benefits the state was aiding the child and not the school. Most state courts accepted this latter reasoning, which came to be known as the "child benefit theory''; and the Supreme Court, in *Cochran v. Louisiana State Board of Education* (1930), held valid a state law authorizing the use of public funds to supply ''school books to the school children of the state,'' including children in parochial and private nonsectarian schools. The Court agreed that ''the school children and the state alone are beneficiaries'' of these appropriations, and not the schools which the children attend. The Supreme Court again applied the theory in *Everson v. Board of Education* (1947) to hold valid the provision of free bus transportation to children attending parochial schools.

Unfortunately, the child benefit theory, while giving a plausible explanation for the results reached, does not provide any real test for reaching those results in the first place. If the fact that a child is benefited makes an expenditure valid, it is hard to see why the state cannot build and support religious schools. On the other hand, if anything that aids religion is forbidden by the First Amendment, why are not fire and police protection for churches unconstitutional? What the Constitution demands is state neutrality toward religion, but what constitutes neutrality in a society where governmental aid and supervision are almost ubiquitous? How is the line to be drawn between neutrality and impermissible state aid to religion?

While the Everson case held valid certain kinds of aid to children attending religious schools (discussed further in the note to *Mueller v. Allen* (1983), below) it did not answer the needs of parents whose children were getting what was viewed as a ''Godless'' education in the public schools. Two lines of attack were used in an effort to solve this problem. One was a series of efforts to introduce religious materials directly into the public schools; see the note to *Edwards v. Aguillard* (1987). The other, discussed below, was the use of what came to be known as ''released time.''

Churches, whose success in competing for the time and interest of children has never been outstanding, and parents who wanted their children to have religious training but could no longer get them to go to Sunday School finally devised a scheme whereby children could get such religious training during their ''working day'' rather than after school or on weekends. One such program was set up in Champaign, Illinois. Public school pupils whose parents signed ''request cards'' attended religious-instruction classes conducted during regular school hours in the school building, but taught by outside teachers (chosen by a religious council representing the various faiths) who were subject to the approval and supervision of the superintendent of schools. These teachers were not paid from public funds. Records of attendance at these classes were kept and reported to the school authorities, and pupils who did not attend them spent their time on their ordinary studies. The Supreme Court held the plan void in *Illinois ex rel. McCollum v. Board of Education* (1948). The facts stated, the Court said, ''show the use of tax-supported property for religious instruction and the close cooperation between the school authorities and the religious council in promoting religious education. The operation of the State's compulsory education system thus assists and is integrated with the program of religious instruction carried on by separate religious sects. Pupils compelled by law to go to school for secular education are released in part from their legal duty upon the condition that they attend the religious classes. This is beyond all question a utilization of the tax-established and tax-supported public school system to aid religious groups to spread their faith.'' The Court reaffirmed its statement in Everson that the First Amendment sets up a complete separation of church and state, and any government aid to religion violates this principle.

Although the justices in both Everson and McCollum agreed unanimously that the First Amendment set up a complete separation of church and state, they differed sharply in each case on whether aid to religion was in fact shown. They did not question that if it had been, it would have been bad. Religious leaders, both Catholic and Protestant, together with some lay critics, have challenged the basic rule which the Court has announced. They urge that the framers did not intend by the First Amendment to forbid completely all government aid to religion, but only such aid as favors one religion over another.

They argue, first, that there is no really persuasive historical ground for holding that the framers had in mind an absolute separation of church and state; the ''establishment'' clause was intended merely to prevent the establishment of a state church, such as the Church of England. Second, the historical material mustered by Justice Black in the Everson case to show that what the framers intended was, in Jefferson's phrase, a wall of separation between church and state has been sharply criticized by a number of historical scholars as presenting an incomplete and distorted picture. Third, the Supreme Court had itself recognized some aid to religion. In *Bradfield v. Roberts* (1899) it had held valid federal aid to a Roman Catholic hospital, although on the technical ground that the hospital corporation was a secular body which served patients without regard to denomination. Also, weight has been attached to the fact that in 1844 in the Girard will case, *Vidal v. Girard's Executors*, Justice Story had announced (though by way of dictum) that the ''Christian religion is part of the common law.''

In *Widmar v. Vincent* (1981) the problems of McCollum and Zorach came back to haunt the Court in a different form. Here a group of students at the University of Missouri at Kansas City wanted to use for a meeting of ''evangelical Christian students'' one of the rooms assigned for the use of the one-hundred-odd student organizations on the campus. The University denied the request on the ground that it would constitute aid to religion while the students argued that their freedom of speech was being abridged on account of its content. The Supreme Court upheld the students. It agreed that two of the three tests for establishment were easily met. A nondiscriminatory open-forum policy, including nondiscrimination against religious speech, would have a secular purpose and would avoid entanglement with religion. Nor was it persuaded that ''the primary effect of the pub-

lic forum, open to all forms of discourse, would be to advance religion. . . . This Court has explained that a religious organization's enjoyment of merely "incidental" benefits does not violate the prohibition against the "primary advancement" of religion. Here, any religious benefits would be "incidental."〉

One of the main difficulties encountered in challenging alleged aid to religious schools has been a rule of the Supreme Court dating back to 1923 that a person could not contest in federal court the expenditure of tax money solely on the ground that he was a taxpayer and had an interest in how the money was spent. See Frothingham v. Mellon (1923). Not only was the share of the interested taxpayer in the money too small to deserve judicial notice, but the Court clearly viewed with concern the specter of millions of taxpayers in a position to challenge in the courts every expenditure of federal funds. The result of this ruling was to make virtually impregnable to judicial attack any distribution of federal funds to religious groups. With the passage of Titles I and II of the Elementary and Secondary Education Act of 1965, under which funds could be used to finance secular education in religious schools, the attack on the "no taxpayer suits" rule was reopened. In Flast v. Cohen (1968) the Court eased the rule as applied to challenges brought under the establishment clause of the First Amendment. The Court held that "the taxpayer must show that the challenged enactment exceeds specific constitutional limitations imposed upon the exercise of the congressional taxing and spending power and not simply that the enactment is generally beyond the powers delegated to Congress by Art. I, § 8." Since one of the reasons for adopting the establishment clause was to prevent using the tax power to aid religion, this clause was such a "specific limitation." In Valley Forge Christian College v. Americans United (1982), however, the Court made clear that this restriction applied only to the taxing power. There the government had given to a religious school the land and buildings of a former veterans hospital valued at about $3 million. Since no money had changed hands no taxpayer had standing, as a taxpayer, to bring suit to contest the misuse of tax moneys.

Mr. Justice **Douglas** delivered the opinion of the Court, saying in part:

〈New York City has a program which permits its public schools to release students during the school day so that they may leave the school buildings and school grounds and go to religious centers for religious instruction or devotional exercises. A student is released on written request of his parents. Those not released stay in the classrooms. The churches make weekly reports to the schools, sending a list of children who have been released from public school but who have not reported for religious instruction.

This "released time" program involves neither religious instruction in public school classrooms nor the expenditure of public funds. All costs, including the application blanks, are paid by the religious organizations. The case is therefore unlike McCollum v. Board of Education [1948] which involved a "released time" program from Illinois. In that case the classrooms were turned over to religious instructors. We accordingly held that the program violated the First Amendment which (by reason of the Fourteenth Amendment) prohibits the states from establishing religion or prohibiting its free exercise.〉

Appellants, who are taxpayers and residents of New York City and whose children attend its public schools, challenge the present law, contending it is in essence not different from the one involved in the McCollum Case. Their argument, stated elaborately in various ways, reduces itself to this: the weight and influence of the school is put behind a program for religious instruction; public school teachers police it, keeping tab on students who are released; the classroom activities come to a halt while the students who are released for religious instruction are on leave; the school is a crutch on which the churches are leaning for support in their religious training; without the cooperation of the schools this "released time" program, like the one in the McCollum Case, would be futile and ineffective. The New York Court of Appeals sustained the law against this claim of unconstitutionality. . . . The case is here on appeal. . . .

〈 It takes obtuse reasoning to inject any issue of the "free exercise" of religion into the present case. No one is forced to go to the religious classroom and no religious exercise or instruction is brought to the classrooms of the public schools. A student need not take religious instruction. He is left to his own desires as to the manner or time of his religious devotions, if any.

There is a suggestion that the system involves the use of coercion to get public school students into religious classrooms. There is no evidence in the record before us that supports that conclusion. The present record indeed tells us that the school authorities are neutral in this regard and do no more than release students whose parents so request. If in fact coercion were used, if it were established that any one or more teachers were using their office to persuade or force students to take the religious instruction, a wholly different case would be presented. Hence we put aside that claim of coercion both as respects the "free exercise" of religion and "an establishment of religion" within the meaning of the First Amendment.〉

Moreover, apart from that claim of coercion, we do not see how New York by this type of "released time" program has made a law respecting an establishment of religion within the meaning of the First Amendment. There is much talk of the separation of Church and State in the history of the Bill of Rights and in the decisions clustering around the First Amendment. See Everson v. Board of Education [1947]; McCollum v. Board of Education. There cannot be the slightest doubt that the First Amendment reflects the philosophy that Church and State should be separated. And so far as interference with the "free exercise" of religion and an "establishment" of religion are concerned, the separation must be complete and unequivocal. The First Amendment within the scope of its coverage permits no exception; the prohibition is absolute. The First Amendment, however, does not say that in every and all respects there shall be a separation of Church and State. Rather, it studiously defines the manner, the specific ways, in which there shall be no concert or union or dependency one on the other. That is the common sense of the matter. Otherwise, the state and religion would be aliens to each other—hostile, suspicious, and even unfriendly. Churches could not be required to pay even property taxes. Municipalities would not be permitted to render police or fire protection to religious groups. Policemen who helped parishioners into their places of worship would violate the Constitution. Prayers in our legislative halls; the appeals to the Almighty in the messages of the Chief Executive; the proclamations making Thanksgiving Day a holiday; ''so help me God'' in our courtroom oaths—these and all other references to the Almighty that run through our laws, our public rituals, our ceremonies would be flouting the First Amendment. A fastidious atheist or agnostic could even object to the supplication with which the Court opens each session: ''God save the United States and this Honorable Court.''

We would have to press the concept of separation of Church and State to these extremes to condemn the present law on constitutional grounds. The nullification of this law would have wide and profound effects. A Catholic student applies to his teacher for permission to leave the school during hours on a Holy Day of Obligation to attend a mass. A Jewish student asks his teacher for permission to be excused for Yom Kippur. A Protestant wants the afternoon off for a family baptismal ceremony. In each case the teacher requires parental consent in writing. In each case the teacher, in order to make sure the student is not a truant, goes further and requires a report from the priest, the rabbi, or the minister. The teacher in other words cooperates in a religious program to the extent of making it possible for her students to participate in it. Whether she does it occasionally for a few students, regularly for one, or pursuant to a systematized program designed to further the religious needs of all the students does not alter the character of the act.

We are a religious people whose institutions presuppose a Supreme Being. We guarantee the freedom to worship as one chooses. We make room for as wide a variety of beliefs and creeds as the spiritual needs of man deem necessary. We sponsor an attitude on the part of government that shows no partiality to any one group and that lets each flourish according to the zeal of its adherents and the appeal of its dogma. When the state encourages religious instruction or cooperates with religious authorities by adjusting the schedule of public events to sectarian needs, it follows the best of our traditions. For it then respects the religious nature of our people and accommodates the public service to their spiritual needs. To hold that it may not would be to find in the Constitution a requirement that the government show a callous indifference to religious groups. That would be preferring those who believe in no religion over those who do believe. Government may not finance religious groups nor undertake religious instruction nor blend sec-

ular and sectarian education nor use secular institutions to force one or some religion on any person. But we find no constitutional requirement which makes it necessary for government to be hostile to religion and to throw its weight against efforts to widen the effective scope of religious influence. The government must be neutral when it comes to competition between sects. It may not thrust any sect on any person. It may not make a religious observance compulsory. It may not coerce anyone to attend church, to observe a religious holiday, or to take religious instruction. But it can close its doors or suspend its operations as to those who want to repair to their religious sanctuary for worship or instruction. No more than that is undertaken here. . . .

In the McCollum case the classrooms were used for religious instruction and the force of the public school was used to promote that instruction. Here, as we have said, the public schools do no more than accommodate their schedules to a program of outside religious instruction. We follow the McCollum case. But we cannot expand it to cover the present released time program unless separation of Church and State means that public institutions can make no adjustments of their schedules to accommodate the religious needs of the people. We cannot read into the Bill of Rights such a philosophy of hostility to religion.

Affirmed.

Justices **Black** and **Frankfurter** wrote dissenting opinions.

Mr. Justice **Jackson**, dissenting, said in part:

This released time program is founded upon a use of the State's power of coercion, which, for me, determines its unconstitutionality. Stripped to its essentials, the plan has two stages, first, that the State compel each student to yield a large part of his time for public secular education and, second, that some of it be ''released'' to him on condition that he devote it to sectarian religious purposes.

No one suggests that the Constitution would permit the State directly to require this ''released'' time to be spent ''under the control of a duly constituted religious body.'' This program accomplishes that forbidden result by indirection. If public education were taking so much of the pupils' time as to injure the public or the students' welfare by encroaching upon their religious opportunity, simply shortening everyone's school day would facilitate voluntary and optional attendance at Church classes. But that suggestion is rejected upon the ground that if they are made free many students will not go to the Church. Hence, they must be deprived of freedom for this period, with Church attendance put to them as one of the two permissible ways of using it.

The greater effectiveness of this system over voluntary attendance after school hours is due to the truant officer who, if the youngster fails to go to the Church school, dogs him back to the public schoolroom. Here schooling is more or less suspended during the ''released time'' so the nonreligious attendants will not forge ahead of the churchgoing absentees. But it serves as a temporary jail for a pupil who will not go to Church. It takes more subtlety of mind than I possess to deny that this is governmental constraint in support of religion. It is as unconstitutional, in my view, when exerted by indirection as when exercised forthrightly.

As one whose children, as a matter of free choice, have been sent to privately supported Church schools, I may challenge the Court's suggestion that opposition to this plan can only be antireligious, atheistic, or agnostic. My evangelistic brethren confuse an objection to compulsion with an objection to religion. It is possible to hold a faith with enough confidence to believe that what should be rendered to God does not need to be decided and collected by Caesar.

The day that this country ceases to be free from irreligion it will cease to be free for religion—except for the sect that can win political power. The same epithetical jurisprudence used by the Court today to beat down those who oppose pressuring children into some religion can devise as good epithets tomorrow against those who object to pressuring them into a favored religion. And, after all, if we concede to the State power and wisdom to single out "duly constituted religious" bodies as exclusive alternatives for compulsory secular instruction, it would be logical to also uphold the power and wisdom to choose the true faith among those "duly constituted." We start down a rough road when we begin to mix compulsory public education with compulsory godliness.

A number of Justices just short of a majority of the majority that promulgates today's passionate dialectics joined in answering them in Illinois ex rel. McCollum v. Board of Education. The distinction attempted between that case and this is trivial, almost to the point of cynicism, magnifying its nonessential details and disparaging compulsion which was the underlying reason for invalidity. A reading of the Court's opinion in that case along with its opinion in this case will show such difference of overtones and undertones as to make clear that the McCollum case has passed like a storm in a teacup. The wall which the Court was professing to erect between Church and State has become even more warped and twisted than I expected. Today's judgment will be more interesting to students of psychology and of the judicial processes than to students of constitutional law.

MUELLER v. ALLEN

463 U. S. 388; 103 S. Ct. 3062; 77 L. Ed. 2d (1983)

"Well, in our country," said Alice, still panting a little, *"You'd generally get to somewhere else—if you ran very fast for a long time as we've been doing."*

"A slow sort of country!" said the Queen. *"Now, here, you see, it takes all the running you can do, to keep in the same place."*

—*Lewis Carroll*, Through the Looking Glass

❮This sums up the plight of religious education in the United States. Born in an era when school teachers were poorly paid, school facilities simple and inexpensive, and extracurricular activities virtually nonexistent, the religious school had little difficulty keeping up with its public counterpart. But time has seen marked changes in the public schools. The curriculum, once limited to the three "R's," now includes a wide and sophisticated group of "cultural" subjects; organized athletics has replaced the simple playground games; pupils are transported to school, fed lunch in school, and transported home again; expensive electronic teaching devices have replaced or supplemented the traditional classroom teacher, and even that teacher comes to the job more completely and expensively educated, asking and receiving more money. The religious school must compete with all this if it is to "keep in the same place." An additional difficulty for the Roman Catholic Church, which operates most religious schools, is the falling enrollment in those religious orders whose members were called to teaching and who received no personal compensation.

In Board of Education v. Allen (1968) the Court held valid the provision by the state of New York of secular textbooks to religious schools. Noting the "significant and valuable role" played by private education in this country, it found that both the "purpose and primary effect" of providing such aid was to advance secular education and hence was not a violation of the establishment clause. In the years that followed, other states provided such aid as buses, textbooks, health services, and school lunches. But helpful as such services were they did not solve the problem of the rising cost of labor, and a number of states undertook to provide direct financial help for the secular segment of the religious school curriculum by paying part of the teachers' salaries.

In Lemon v. Kurtzman (1971) the plans adopted by Pennsylvania and Rhode Island were held void. In addition to the tests devised in Allen regarding purpose and primary effect, the Court added a test adopted in Walz v. Tax Commission (1970) holding that a statute must not foster "an excessive entanglement with religion." It was the last of these tests which the Court found to be violated by the teacher payment plans. Since the money was to be used to pay only for secular teaching, "a comprehensive, discriminating, and continuing state surveillance will inevitably be required to ensure that these restrictions are obeyed and the First Amendment otherwise respected. Unlike a book, a teacher cannot be inspected once so as to determine the extent and intent of his or her personal beliefs and subjective acceptance of the limitations imposed by the First Amendment. These prophylactic contacts will involve excessive and enduring entanglement between state and church. . . ." In Pennsylvania the entanglement was increased by a system of post-audit of school records "to determine which expenditures are religious and which are secular."

The Court found an even "broader base of entanglement . . . presented by the divisive political potential of these state programs." "Political division along religious lines was one of the principal evils against which the First Amendment was intended to protect," and in this case the inevitable religious divisiveness would be aggravated by "the need for continuing annual appropriations and the likelihood of larger and larger demands as costs and populations grow."

In the wake of the Lemon decision the states turned their efforts to finding ways of aiding religious schools that did not involve such entanglement. The revised New York law made a three-pronged attack on the problem. First, lump-sum payments to nonpublic schools on a per-pupil basis were given to reimburse the school for the cost of carrying out state-mandated functions, such as the maintenance and recording of pupil enrollment, health records, and the "administration, grading and the compiling and reporting of the results of tests and examinations." Second, the state provided as a safety measure grants to nonpublic schools serving low-income areas for the "maintenance and repair" of school facilities. Third, the parents of children in nonpublic schools were given financial help—those in low income brackets getting tuition reimbursement and those in higher brackets getting a tax credit.

In Levitt v. Committee for Public Education (1973) and Committee for Public Education v. Nyquist (1973) the Court held void all these plans and in Sloan v. Lemon (1973) it held void a Pennsylvania tuition plan similar to New York's, but passed after the Lemon decision. In this latter case a nonreligious private school argued that the aid statute was valid as to it, and a Catholic parochial school contended that if that were the case, then it was entitled to aid under the equal protection clause. The Court found the aid statute void in its entirety but noted that even if the state had decided to aid only nonreligious private schools, the equal protection clause could still not be invoked to get similar (but otherwise unconstitutional) aid for religious schools. It was not until the decision in the case below that the Court found valid a state plan which provided financial assistance to the parents of children attending religious elementary and secondary schools.

In 1963, in response to a demand for federal help for higher education, Congress passed the Higher Education Facilities Act, which provided building grants and loans to colleges and universities. The act expressly excluded "any facility used or to be used for sectarian instructions or as a place of worship . . ." or "any part of the program of a school or department of divinity," but did not otherwise rule out denominational schools. The interest of the government was to last only twenty years, after which the school was allowed to do what it pleased with the buildings.

In Tilton v. Richardson (1971), decided the same day as the Lemon case, the Court upheld the validity of the grants to religious colleges, except that the interest of the United States could not end at the end of twenty years. Chief Justice Burger, speaking for himself and Justices Harlan, Stewart, and Blackmun, found that the purpose of the act was to aid education, not religion; that the schools in this case had apparently quite separable secular and religious activities, and the buildings were devoted solely to the former. He refused to deal with the case in terms of a "composite profile" of sectarian institutions, which "imposes religious restrictions on admissions, requires attendance at religious activities, compels obedience to the doctrines and dogmas of the faith . . . and does everything it can to propagate a particular religion." He noted that a number of institutions had been denied aid, and at least one had had its funds withdrawn. "Individual projects can be properly evaluated if and when challenges arise with respect to particular recipients and some evidence is then presented to show that the institution does in fact possess these characteristics. We cannot, however, strike down an Act of Congress on the basis of a hypothetical profile." He agreed, however, that unless the restriction on the use of the buildings were maintained, the grant might become an aid to religion and hence violate the First Amendment.

The four justices found that the Tilton case did not violate the "excessive entanglement" test under which the aid in Lemon had been stricken down. First, it was not the dominant purpose of these colleges, as it was the secondary schools, to inculcate religious values in their students "to assure future adherents to a particular faith." Not only were the courses taught with the normal internal self-discipline and academic freedom, but "the skepticism of the college student is not an inconsiderable barrier to any attempt or tendency to subvert the congressional objectives and limitations." In addition, both the one-shot nature of the aid and the fact it was in the form of buildings rather than teachers tended to reduce the entanglement.

Mr. Justice White, the fifth member of the majority, concurred with the Chief Justice on the theory that since the purpose of all the aid was secular, the fact it aided religion did not make it unconstitutional.

Justices Douglas, Black, and Marshall agreed that the twenty-year limit to federal interest was void, but dissented from the rest on the ground that the "entanglement" was as great here as in the state case ("How can the Government know what is taught in the federally financed building without a continuous auditing of classroom instruction?") and that it is aid to religion ("Money saved from one item in the budget is free to be used elsewhere. By conducting religious services in another building, the school has—rent free—a building for nonsectarian use.")

The precedents the Supreme Court sets in solving one set of problems occasionally rise up to haunt it in wholly unforeseen circumstances, and the conflicts between justice and the demands of logical consistency pose some of the Court's stickiest legal wickets. In Board of Education v. Allen (1968) the Court had held that providing free textbooks to all pupils in the state did not constitute aid to the schools the pupils attended, so that a child attending a religious school could receive such books without its being an unconstitutional aid to the religious school. In Norwood v. Harrison (1973), the Court confronted a Mississippi law under which free textbooks were being given to pupils attending racially segregated schools. The Court held that such textbooks were an aid to the school and could not constitutionally *be given to private schools which discriminated on the basis of race.*

"This Court has consistently affirmed decisions enjoining state tuition grants to students attending racially discriminatory private schools. A textbook lending program is not legally distinguishable from the forms of state assistance foreclosed by the prior cases. Free textbooks, like tuition grants directed to private school students, are a form of financial assistance inuring to the benefit of the private schools themselves." In a footnote it distinguished the Allen case; "Plainly, religion benefits indirectly from governmental aid to parents and children; nevertheless, 'that religion may indirectly benefit from governmental aid . . . does not convert that aid into an impermissible establishment of religion.' . . . The leeway for indirect aid to sectarian schools has no place in defining the permissible scope of state aid to private racially discriminatory schools." In Bob Jones University v. United States (1983) the Court upheld the refusal of the IRS to grant tax exemption to segregated private schools.

While the preceding cases were not particularly encouraging to those who sought aid to religious schools, the fact that some kinds of aid were held permissible encouraged increasing experimentation on the part of the states. Each case involved a broad spectrum of aid, and in general the Court upheld those features that closely resembled such things as secular textbooks which could not be put to religious use, but held void those which either could be so used, or where the policing necessary to ensure proper use resulted in undue "entanglement."

Thus in Meek v. Pittenger (1975) the Court struck down the loan of instructional material made to the school and not the pupil, and a provision for professional personnel was held bad because it involved both an "entangling" degree of supervision and a potential for political entanglement and divisiveness. A similar result was reached in Wolman v. Walter (1977) in which items like tape recorders and projectors and the cost of field trips was involved, since all were susceptible of conversion to religious use. In Committee for Public Education v. Regan (1980), however, the Court in a five-to-four decision held that a revised New York law providing for state reimbursement to cover the costs of administering standardized tests and keeping attendance and other required records did not "foster an excessive government entanglement with religion." Meanwhile efforts to find a formula that would permit tuition aid to private school pupils persisted, and it is Minnesota's statue, passed in 1982, that is involved in the case below.

Justice **Rehnquist** delivered the opinion of the Court, saying in part:

Minnesota allows taxpayers, in computing their state income tax, to deduct certain expenses incurred in providing for the education of their children. . .

Minnesota, like every other state, provides its citizens with free elementary and secondary schooling. It seems to be agreed that about 820,000 students attended this school system in the most recent school year. During the same year, approximately 91,000 elementary and secondary students attended some 500 privately supported schools located in Minnesota, and about 95% of these students attended schools considering themselves to be sectarian.

Minnesota, by a law originally enacted in 1955 and revised in 1976 and again in 1978, permits state taxpayers to claim a deduction from gross income for certain expenses incurred in educating their children. The deduction is limited to actual expenses incurred for the "tuition, textbooks and transportation" of dependents attending elementary or secondary schools. A deduction may not exceed $500 per dependent in grades K through six and $700 per dependent in grades seven through twelve. . . .

Today's case is no exception to our oft-repeated statement that the Establishment Clause presents especially difficult questions of interpretation and application. It is easy enough to quote the few words comprising that clause—"Congress shall make no law respecting an establishment of religion." It is not at all easy, however, to apply this Court's various decisions construing the Clause to governmental programs of financial assistance to sectarian schools and the parents of children attending those schools. Indeed, in many of these decisions "we have expressly or implicitly acknowledged that 'we can only dimly perceive the lines of demarcation in this extraordinarily sensitive area of constitutional law.' " Lemon v. Kurtzman (1971), quoted with approval in Nyquist.

One fixed principle in this field is our consistent rejection of the argument that "any program which in some manner aids an institution with a religious affiliation" violates the Establishment Clause. . . . For example, it is now well-established that a state may reimburse parents for expenses incurred in transporting their children to school, Everson v. Board of Education (1947), and that it may loan secular textbooks to all schoolchildren within the state, Board of Education v. Allen (1968).

Notwithstanding the repeated approval given programs such as those in Allen and Everson, our decisions also have struck down arrangements resembling, in many respects, these forms of assistance. . . . In this case we are asked to decide whether Minnesota's tax deduction bears greater resemblance to those types of assistance to parochial schools we have approved, or to those we have struck down. Petitioners place particular reliance on our decision in Committee for Public Education v. Nyquist where we held invalid a New York statute providing public funds for the maintenance and repair of the physical facilities of private schools and granting thinly disguised "tax benefits," actually amounting to tuition grants, to the parents of children attending private schools. As explained below, we conclude that § 290.09(22) bears less resemblance to the arrangement struck down in Nyquist than it does to assistance programs upheld in our prior decisions and those discussed with approval in Nyquist.

The general nature of our inquiry in this area has

been guided, since the decision in Lemon v. Kurtzman (1971), by the "three-part" test laid down in that case: "First, the statute must have a secular legislative purpose; second, its principle or primary effect must be one that neither advances nor inhibits religion . . . ; finally, the statute must not foster 'an excessive government entanglement with religion.' " . . .

Little time need be spent on the question of whether the Minnesota tax deduction has a secular purpose. Under our prior decisions, governmental assistance programs have consistently survived this inquiry even when they have run afoul of other aspects of the Lemon framework. . . . This reflects, at least in part, our reluctance to attribute unconstitutional motives to the states, particularly when a plausible secular purpose for the state's program may be discerned from the face of the statute.

A state's decision to defray the cost of educational expenses incurred by parents—regardless of the type of schools their children attend—evidences a purpose that is both secular and understandable. An educated populace is essential to the political and economic health of any community, and a state's efforts to assist parents in meeting the rising cost of educational expenses plainly serves this secular purpose of ensuring that the state's citizenry is well-educated. Similarly, Minnesota, like other states, could conclude that there is a strong public interest in assuring the continued financial health of private schools, both sectarian and non-sectarian. By educating a substantial number of students such schools relieve public schools of a correspondingly great burden—to the benefit of all taxpayers. In addition, private schools may serve as a benchmark for public schools, in a manner analogous to the "TVA yardstick" for private power companies. . . . All these justifications are readily available to support § 290.09(22), and each is sufficient to satisfy the secular purpose inquiry of Lemon.

We turn therefore to the more difficult but related question whether the Minnesota statute has "the primary effect of advancing the sectarian aims of the nonpublic schools." . . . In concluding that it does not, we find several features of the Minnesota tax deduction particularly significant. . . . Under our prior decisions, the Minnesota legislature's judgment that a deduction for educational expenses fairly equalizes the tax burden of its citizens and encourages desirable expenditures for educational purposes is entitled to substantial deference.

Other characteristics of § 290.09(22) argue equally strongly for the provision's constitutionality. Most importantly, the deduction is available for educational expenses incurred by all parents, including those whose children attend non-sectarian private schools or sectarian private schools. Just as in Widmar v. Vincent (1981) where we concluded that the state's provision of a forum neutrally "open to a broad class of nonreligious as well as religious speakers" does not "confer any imprimatur of State approval," so here: "the provision of benefits to so broad a spectrum of groups is an important index of secular effect."

In this respect, as well as others, this case is vitally different from the scheme struck down in Nyquist.

There, public assistance amounting to tuition grants, was provided only to parents of children in nonpublic schools. This fact had considerable bearing on our decision striking down the New York statute at issue; we explicitly distinguished both Allen and Everson on the grounds that "In both cases the class of beneficiaries included all schoolchildren, those in public as well as those in private schools." . . . We think the tax deduction adopted by Minnesota is more similar to this latter type of program than it is to the arrangement struck down in Nyquist. Unlike the assistance at issue in Nyquist, § 290.09(22) permits all parents—whether their children attend public school or private—to deduct their children's educational expenses. As Widmar and our other decisions indicate, a program, like § 290.09(22), that neutrally provides state assistance to a broad spectrum of citizens is not readily subject to challenge under the Establishment Clause. . . .

We find it useful, in the light of the foregoing characteristics of § 290.09(22), to compare the attenuated financial benefits flowing to parochial schools from the section to the evils against which the Establishment Clause was designed to protect. These dangers are well-described by our statement that "what is at stake as a matter of policy [in Establishment Clause cases] is preventing that kind and degree of government involvement in religious life that, as history teaches us, is apt to lead to strife and frequently strain a political system to the breaking point." . . . The Establishment Clause of course extends beyond prohibition of a state church or payment of state funds to one or more churches. We do not think, however, that its prohibition extends to the type of tax deduction established by Minnesota. The historic purposes of the clause simply do not encompass the sort of attenuated financial benefit, ultimately controlled by the private choices of individual parents, that eventually flows to parochial schools from the neutrally available tax benefit at issue in this case.

Petitioners argue that, notwithstanding the facial neutrality of § 290.09(22), in application the statute primarily benefits religious institutions. Petitioners rely, as they did below, on a statistical analysis of the type of persons claiming the tax deduction. They contend that most parents of public school children incur no tuition expenses and that other expenses deductible under § 290.09(22) are negligible in value; moreover, they claim that 96% of the children in private schools in 1978-79 attended religiously-affiliated institutions. Because of all this, they reason, the bulk of deductions taken under § 290.09(22) will be claimed by parents of children in sectarian schools. Respondents reply that petitioners have failed to consider the impact of deductions for items such as transportation, summer school tuition, tuition paid by parents whose children attended schools outside the school districts in which they resided, rental or purchase costs for a variety of equipment, and tuition for certain types of instruction not ordinarily provided in public schools.

We need not consider these contentions in detail. We would be loath to adopt a rule grounding the constitutionality of a facially neutral law on annual reports reciting the extent to which various classes of private citizens claimed benefits under the law. Such an approach would scarcely provide the certainty that this field stands in need of, nor can we perceive principled standards by which such statistical evidence might be evaluated. Moreover, the fact that private persons fail in a particular year to claim the tax relief to which they are entitled—under a facially neutral statute—should be of little importance in determining the constitutionality of the statute permitting such relief.

Finally, private educational institutions, and parents paying for their children to attend these schools, make special contributions to the areas in which they operate. "Parochial schools, quite apart from their sectarian purpose, have provided an educational alternative for millions of young Americans; they often afford wholesome competition with our public schools; and in some States they relieve substantially the tax burden incident to the operation of public schools." Wolman (Powell, J., concurring and dissenting). If parents of children in private schools choose to take especial advantage of the relief provided by § 290.09(22), it is no doubt due to the fact that they bear a particularly great financial burden in educating their children. More fundamentally, whatever unequal effect may be attributed to the statutory classification can fairly be regarded as a rough return for the benefits, discussed above, provided to the state and all taxpayers by parents sending their children to parochial schools. In the light of all this, we believe it wiser to decline to engage in the type of empirical inquiry into those persons benefited by state law which petitioners urge.

Thus, we hold that the Minnesota tax deduction for educational expenses satisfies the primary effect inquiry of our Establishment Clause cases.

Turning to the third part of the Lemon inquiry, we have no difficulty in concluding that the Minnesota statute does not "excessively entangle" the state in religion. The only plausible source of the "comprehensive, discriminating, and continuing state surveillance" necessary to run afoul of this standard would lie in the fact that state officials must determine whether particular textbooks qualify for a deduction. In making this decision, state officials must disallow deductions taken from "instructional books and materials used in the teaching of religious tenets, doctrines or worship, the purpose of which is to inculcate such tenets, doctrines or worship" Minn. Stat. § 290.09(22). Making decisions such as this does not differ substantially from making the types of decisions approved in earlier opinions of this Court. In Board of Education v. Allen (1968), for example, the Court upheld the loan of secular textbooks to parents or children attending nonpublic schools; though state officials were required to determine whether particular books were or were not secular, the system was held not to violate the Establishment Clause. . . . The same result follows in this case.

Justice **Marshall**, with whom Justice **Brennan**, Justice **Blackmun** and Justice **Stevens** join, dissenting, said in part:

The Establishment Clause of the First Amendment prohibits a State from subsidizing religious education, whether it does so directly or indirectly. In my view, this principle of neutrality forbids not only the tax benefits struck down in Committee for Public Education v. Nyquist (1973), but any tax benefit, including the tax deduction at issue here, which subsidizes tuition payments to sectarian schools. I also believe that the Establishment Clause prohibits the tax deductions that Minnesota authorizes for the cost of books and other instructional materials used for sectarian purposes.

I.

The majority today does not question the continuing vitality of this Court's decision in Nyquist. That decision established that a State may not support religious education either through direct grants to parochial schools or through financial aid to parents of parochial school students. Nyquist also established that financial aid to parents of students attending parochial schools is no more permissible if it is provided in the form of a tax credit than if provided in the form of cash payments. Notwithstanding these accepted principles, the Court today upholds a statute that provides a tax deduction for the tuition charged by religious schools. The Court concludes that the Minnesota statute is "vitally different" from the New York statute at issue in Nyquist. As demonstrated below, there is no significant difference between the two schemes. The Minnesota tax statute violates the Establishment Clause for precisely the same reason as the statute struck down in Nyquist: it has a direct and immediate effect of advancing religion. . . .

B.

The majority attempts to distinguish Nyquist by pointing to two differences between the Minnesota tuition-assistance program and the program struck down in Nyquist. Neither of these distinctions can withstand scrutiny.

1.

The majority first attempts to distinguish Nyquist on the ground that Minnesota makes all parents eligible to deduct up to $500 or $700 for each dependent, whereas the New York law allowed a deduction only for parents whose children attended nonpublic schools. Although Minnesota taxpayers who send their children to local public schools may not deduct tuition expenses because they incur none, they may deduct other expenses, such as the cost of gym clothes, pencils, and notebooks, which are shared by all parents of school-age children. This, in the majority's view, distinguishes the Minnesota scheme from the law at issue in Nyquist.

That the Minnesota statute makes some small benefit available to all parents cannot alter the fact that the most substantial benefit provided by the statute is available only to those parents who send their children to schools that charge tuition. It is simply undeniable that the single largest expense that may be deducted under the Minnesota statute is tuition. The statute is little more than a subsidy of tuition masquerading as a subsidy of general educational expenses. The other deductible expenses are de minimis in comparison to tuition expenses.

Contrary to the majority's suggestion, the bulk of the tax benefits afforded by the Minnesota scheme are enjoyed by parents of parochial school children not because parents of public school children fail to claim deductions to which they are entitled, but because the latter are simply *unable* to claim the largest tax deduction that Minnesota authorizes. Fewer than 100 of more than 900,000 school-age children in Minnesota attend public schools that charge a general tuition. Of the total number of taxpayers who are eligible for the tuition deduction, approximately 96% send their children to religious schools. Parents who send their children to free public schools are simply ineligible to obtain the full benefit of the deduction except in the unlikely event that they buy $700 worth of pencils, notebooks, and bus rides for their school-age children. Yet parents who pay at least $700 in tuition to nonpublic, sectarian schools can claim the full deduction even if they incur no other educational expenses.

That this deduction has a primary effect of promoting religion can easily be determined without resort to the type of "statistical evidence" that the majority fears would lead to constitutional uncertainty. The only factual inquiry necessary is the same as that employed in Nyquist and Sloan v. Lemon (1973): whether the deduction permitted for tuition expenses primarily benefits those who send their children to religious schools. In Nyquist we unequivocally rejected any suggestion that, in determining the effect of a tax statute, this Court should look exclusively to what the statute on its face purports to do and ignore the actual operation of the challenged provision. In determining the effect of the New York statute, we emphasized that "virtually all" of the schools receiving direct grants for maintenance and repair were Roman Catholic schools, that reimbursements were given to parents "who send their children to nonpublic schools, the bulk of which is concededly sectarian in orientation," that "it is precisely the function of New York's law to provide assistance to private schools, the great majority of which are sectarian," and that "tax reductions authorized by this law flow primarily to the parents of children attending sectarian, nonpublic schools." . . .

In this case, it is undisputed that well over 90% of the children attending tuition-charging schools in Minnesota are enrolled in sectarian schools. History and experience likewise instruct us that any generally available financial assistance for elementary and secondary school tuition expenses mainly will further religious education because the majority of the schools which charge tuition are sectarian. . . . Because Minnesota, like every other State, is committed to providing free public education, tax assistance for tuition payments inevitably redounds to the benefit of nonpublic, sectarian schools and parents who send their children to those schools. . . .

C.

The majority incorrectly asserts that Minnesota's tax deduction for tuition expenses "bears less resemblance to the arrangement struck down in Nyquist than it does to assistance programs upheld in our prior decisions and discussed with approval in Nyquist." One might as well say that a tangerine bears less resemblance to an orange than to an apple. The two cases relied on by the majority, Board of Education v. Allen (1968) and Everson v. Board of Education (1947), are inapposite today for precisely the same reasons that they were inapposite in Nyquist.

We distinguished these cases in Nyquist and again in Sloan v. Lemon. Financial assistance for tuition payments has a consequence that "is quite unlike the sort of 'indirect' and 'incidental' benefits that flowed to sectarian schools from programs aiding *all* parents by supplying bus transportation and secular textbooks for their children. *Such benefits were carefully restricted to the purely secular side of church-affiliated institutions* and provided no special aid for those who had chosen to support religious schools. Yet such aid approached the 'verge' of the constitutionally impermissible." Sloan v. Lemon (emphasis added in part.) As previously noted, the Minnesota tuition tax deduction is not available to *all* parents, but only to parents whose children attend schools that charge tuition, which are comprised almost entirely of sectarian schools. More importantly, the assistance that flows to parochial schools as a result of the tax benefit is not restricted, and cannot be restricted, to the secular functions of those schools.

EDWARDS v. AGUILLARD

96 L. Ed. 2d 510 (1987)

⟨ *Those who felt that the public schools were becoming "Godless," and for whom released time was not an available or desirable solution, undertook a campaign to retain some religion in the public schools. In most public schools it was long the custom to begin the day with a short religious exercise. This usually consisted of reading excerpts from the Protestant Bible and sometimes of singing hymns and repeating the Lord's Prayer. Usually those children whose parents objected were excused from these exercises, although this was not always the case. State court decisions on the validity of these exercises were in sharp conflict, and this specific question never reached the Supreme Court.*

In 1962 in Engel v. Vitale, the Supreme Court held void the following prayer composed by the New York Board of Regents for use in the public schools. "Almighty God, we acknowledge our dependence upon Thee, and we beg Thy blessings upon us, our parents, our teachers and our Country." The Court conceded that no issue of religious freedom was involved, since no one was forced to hear or say the prayer. It emphasized, however, that under the establishment clause, "govern-

ment in this country, be it state or federal, is without power to prescribe by law any particular form of prayer which is to be used as an official prayer in carrying on any program of governmentally sponsored religious activity.''

The decision aroused a storm of protest. Members in both Houses of Congress began work on a constitutional amendment which would nullify the decision, while school boards throughout the country sought ways of avoiding the impact of the decision. Some required students to recite stanzas of ''America'' and ''The Star Spangled Banner'' in which there is reference to God; while others, evidently assuming that it was official participation that made the Regents' Prayer bad, merely authorized children to bring prayers to school and take turns reciting them ''voluntarily.'' One common solution was the adoption of a ''moment of silence,'' which a student could use for silent prayer or not, as he wished.

By 1965 the storm had largely abated. The proposed constitutional amendment had been opposed by most religious groups and was conceded to be dead; legal attempts to reverse New York's prohibition on ''voluntary'' prayers and the singing of the fourth stanza of ''America'' as a devotional (rather than a patriotic) exercise had failed; Chief Justice Warren had successfully opposed a House proposal to inscribe ''In God We Trust'' above the Supreme Court bench. On the other hand, a legal attack on the inclusion of ''under God'' in the pledge of allegiance had also failed, and the Supreme Court continued to open its sessions with the marshal asking that ''God save the United States and this honorable Court.''

In Abington School District v. Schempp (1963) the Court for the first time held the use of the Bible in morning devotionals to be in violation of the First Amendment. The state of Pennsylvania required by law that ''at least ten verses from the Holy Bible shall be read, without comment, at the opening of each public school on each school day. Any child shall be excused from such Bible reading . . . upon the written request of his parent or guardian.'' The Schempps were Unitarians who objected to some doctrines purveyed by a literal reading of the Bible, but who declined to ask that their children be excused because they would not only have to stand out in the hall during the exercise but would probably miss the school announcements which followed immediately after. A three-judge federal district court held the practice void on the basis of the Vitale case, and enjoined its continuance. In 1980 the doctrine was applied to hold void a Kentucky law requiring the posting in every classroom of a copy of the Ten Commandments. The Court found the document had ''no secular legislative purpose.'' See Stone v. Graham.

Many religious leaders, together with some lay critics, have challenged the basic rule which the Court has announced. They urge that the framers did not intend by the First Amendment to forbid all government aid to religion, but only such aid as favors one religion over another. They argue, first, that there is no really persuasive historical ground for holding that the framers had in mind an absolute separation of church and state; the ''establishment'' clause was intended merely to prevent the establishment of a state church, such as the Church of England. Second, the historical material mustered by Justice Black in the Everson case to show that what the framers intended was, in Jefferson's phrase, a wall of separation between church and state has been sharply criticized by a number of historical scholars as presenting an incomplete and distorted picture. Third, the Supreme Court had itself recognized some aid to religion. In Bradfield v. Roberts (1899) it had held valid federal aid to a Roman Catholic hospital, although on the technical ground that the hospital corporation was a secular body which served patients without regard to denomination. Also, some cite Justice Storey in the Girard will case, Vidal v. Girard's Executors (1844), where he said the ''Christian religion is part of the common law.''

In Wallace v. Jaffree (1985) the state of Alabama had sequentially adopted three statutes apparently designed to get as much prayer in the public schools as possible. The first statute, passed in 1978, merely authorized a one-minute period of silence in all public schools ''for meditation.'' The second, passed in 1981, authorized a period of silence ''for meditation or voluntary prayer,'' while the third, passed the following year, authorized teachers to lead ''willing students'' in a prescribed prayer to ''Almighty God . . . the Creator and Supreme Judge of the world.''

At trial the district judge found all three statutes valid. Relying on what he perceived to be newly discovered historical evidence, he held that, in his opinion, ''Alabama has the power to establish a state religion if it chooses to do so.'' The court of appeals rejected this approach and the Supreme Court found it ''unnecessary to comment at length on the District Court's remarkable conclusion that the Federal Constitution imposes no obstacle to Alabama's establishment of a state religion.'' The court of appeals also found the last two statutes void under the establishment clause, but no argument was made that the statute merely requiring ''meditation'' was in any way invalid.

A number of religions rely upon a literal interpretation of the Bible as the word of God. In their view the Darwinian theory that humans, like the earth and all forms of life upon it, have evolved over hundreds of thousands of years, is a contradiction of the Book of Genesis which states that God created the world and all its creatures in six days in the forms in which they appear today.

The year after the decision of the Tennessee courts upholding that state's so-called ''monkey law'' which banned the teaching of evolution (see Scopes v. State, 154 Tenn. 105 (1927)), members of these religious groups secured the enactment of a similar law in Arkansas. In Epperson v. Arkansas (1968) the Supreme Court struck down the Arkansas statute as an establishment of religion. ''There can be no doubt that Arkansas has sought to prevent its teachers from discussing the theory of evolution because it is contrary to the belief of some that the Book of Genesis must be the exclusive *source of doctrine as to the origin of man. No suggestion has been made that Arkansas' law may be justified by considerations of state policy other than the religious views of some of its citizens. It is clear that fundamentalist sectarian conviction was and is the law's reason for existence. Its antecedent, Tennessee's 'monkey law,' candidly stated its purpose: to make it unlawful 'to teach any theory that denies the story of the Divine Creation of man as taught in the Bible, and to teach instead that man has descended from a lower order of animals.' Perhaps the sensational publicity attendant upon the Scopes trial induced Arkansas to adopt less explicit language. It eliminated Tennessee's reference to 'the story of the Divine Creation of man' as taught in the Bible, but there is no doubt that the motivation for the law was the same: to suppress the teaching of a theory which, it was thought, 'denied' the divine creation of man."*

Justice **Brennan** delivered the opinion of the Court, saying in part:

The question for decision is whether Louisiana's "Balanced Treatment for Creation-Science and Evolution-Science in Public School Instruction" Act (Creationism Act), is facially invalid as violative of the Establishment Clause of the First Amendment.

I.

The Creationism Act forbids the teaching of the theory of evolution in public schools unless accompanied by instruction in "creation science." No school is required to teach evolution or creation science. If either is taught, however, the other must also be taught. The theories of evolution and creation science are statutorily defined as "the scientific evidences for [creation or evolution] and inferences from those scientific evidences.

Appellees, who include parents of children attending Louisiana public schools, Louisiana teachers, and religious leaders, challenged the constitutionality of the Act in District Court, seeking an injunction and declaratory relief. Appellants, Louisiana officials charged with implementing the Act, defended on the ground that the purpose of the Act is to protect a legitimate secular interest, namely, academic freedom. Appellees attacked the Act as facially invalid because it violated the Establishment Clause and made a motion for summary judgment. . . .

II.

The Establishment Clause forbids the enactment of any law "respecting an establishment of religion." The Court has applied a three-pronged test to determine whether legislation comports with the Establishment Clause. First, the legislature must have adopted the law with a secular purpose. Second, the statute's principal or primary effect must be one that neither advances nor inhibits religion. Third, the statute must not result in an excessive entanglement of government with religion. Lemon v. Kurtzman [1971]. State action violates the Establishment Clause if it fails to satisfy any of these prongs. . . .

The Court has been particularly vigilant in monitoring compliance with the Establishment Clause in elementary and secondary schools. Families entrust public schools with the education of their children, but condition their trust on the understanding that the classroom will not purposely be used to advance religious views that may conflict with the private beliefs of the student and his or her family. Students in such institutions are impressionable and their attendance is involuntary. . . . The State exerts great authority and coercive power through mandatory attendance requirements, and because of the students' emulation of teachers as role models and the children's susceptibility to peer pressure. . . .

Therefore, in employing the three-pronged Lemon test, we must do so mindful of the particular concerns that arise in the context of public elementary and secondary schools. We now turn to the evaluation of the Act under the Lemon test.

III.

Lemon's first prong focuses on the purpose that animated adoption of the Act. "The purpose prong of the Lemon test asks whether government's actual purpose is to endorse or disapprove of religion." Lynch v. Donnelly [1984] (O'Connor, J., concurring.) A governmental intention to promote religion is clear when the State enacts a law to serve a religious purpose. This intention may be evidenced by promotion of religion in general, see Wallace v. Jaffree [1985] (Establishment Clause protects individual freedom of conscience "to select any religious faith or none at all"), or by advancement of a particular religious belief. e.g., Stone v. Graham [1980] (invalidating requirement to post Ten Commandments, which are "undeniably a sacred text in the Jewish and Christian faiths"); Epperson v. Arkansas [1968] (holding that banning the teaching of evolution in public schools violates the First Amendment since "teaching and learning" must not be tailored to the principles or prohibitions of any religious sect or dogma.") If the law was enacted for the purpose of endorsing religion, "no consideration of the second or third criteria [of Lemon] is necessary. . . . In this case, the petitioners have identified no clear secular purpose for the Louisiana Act.

True, the Act's stated purpose is to protect academic freedom. This phrase might, in common parlance, be understood as referring to enhancing the freedom of teachers to teach what they will. The Court of Appeals, however, correctly concluded that the Act was not designed to further that goal. We find no merit in the State's argument that the "legislature may not [have] use[d] the terms 'academic freedom' in the correct legal sense. They might have [had] in mind, instead, a basic concept of fairness; teaching all of the evidence." Even if "academic freedom" is read to mean "teaching all of the evidence" with respect to the origin of human beings, the Act does not further this purpose. The goal of providing a more comprehensive science curriculum is not furthered either by outlawing the teaching of evolution or by requiring the teaching of creation science.

A.

While the Court is normally deferential to a State's articulation of a secular purpose, it is required that the statement of such purpose be sincere and not a sham. . . . As Justice O'Connor stated in Wallace: It is not a trivial mater, however, to require that the legislature manifest a secular purpose and omit all sectarian endorsements from its laws. That requirement is precisely tailored to the Establishment Clause's purpose of assuring that Government not intentionally endorse religion or a religious practice.''

It is clear from the legislative history that the purpose of the legislative sponsor, Senator Bill Keith, was to narrow the science curriculum. During the legislative hearings, Senator Keith stated: ''My preference would be that neither [creationism nor evolution] be taught.'' Such a ban on teaching does not promote—indeed, it undermines—the provision of a comprehensive scientific education.

It is equally clear that requiring schools to teach creation science with evolution does not advance academic freedom. The Act does not grant teachers a flexibility that they did not already possess to supplant the present science curriculum with the presentation of theories, besides evolution, about the origin of life. Indeed, the Court of Appeals found that no law prohibited Louisiana public schoolteachers from teaching any scientific theory. As the president of the Louisiana Science Teachers Association testified, ''[a]ny scientific concept that's based on established fact can be included in our curriculum already and no legislation allowing this is necessary.'' The Act provides Louisiana schoolteachers with no new authority. Thus the stated purpose is not furthered by it.

The Alabama statute held unconstitutional in Wallace v. Jaffree [1985] is analogous. In Wallace, the State characterized its new law as one designed to provide a one-minute period for meditation. We rejected that stated purpose as insufficient, because a previously adopted Alabama law already provided for such a one-minute period. Thus, in this case, as in Wallace, ''[a]ppellants have not identified any secular purpose that was not fully served by [existing state law] before the enactment of [the statute in question].''

Furthermore, the goal of basic ''fairness'' is hardly furthered by the Act's discriminatory preference for the teaching of creation science and against the teaching of evolution. While requiring that curriculum guides be developed for creation science, the Act says nothing of comparable guides for evolution. Similarly, research services are supplied for creation science but not for evolution. Only ''creation scientists'' can serve on the panel that supplies the resource services. The Act forbids school boards to discriminate against anyone who ''chooses to be a creation-scientist'' or to teach ''creationism,'' but fails to protect those who choose to teach evolution or any other non-creation science theory, or refuse to teach creation science.

If the Louisiana legislature's purpose was solely to maximize the comprehensiveness and effectiveness of science instruction, it would have encouraged the teaching of all scientific theories about the origins of humankind. But under the Act's requirements, teachers who were once free to teach any and all facts of this subject are now unable to do so. Moreover, the Act fails even to ensure that creation science will be taught, but instead requires the teaching of this theory only when the theory of evolution is taught. Thus we agree with the Court of Appeals' conclusion that the Act does not serve to protect academic freedom, but has the distinctly different purpose of discrediting ''evolution by counterbalancing its teaching at every turn with the teaching of creation science. . . .''

B.

Stone v. Graham invalidated the State's requirement that the Ten Commandments be posted in public classrooms. ''The Ten Commandments are undeniably a sacred text in the Jewish and Christian faiths, and no legislative recitation of a supposed secular purpose can blind us to that fact.'' As a result, the contention that the law was designed to provide instruction on a ''fundamental legal code'' was ''not sufficient to avoid conflict with the First Amendment.'' Similarly Abington School District v. Schempp [1963] held unconstitutional a statute ''requiring the selection and reading at the opening of the school day of verses from the Holy Bible and the recitation of the Lord's Prayer by the students in unison,'' despite the proffer of such secular purposes as the ''promotion of moral values, the contradiction to the materialistic trends of our times, the perpetuation of our institutions and the teaching of literature.''

As in Stone and Abington, we need not be blind in this case to the legislature's preeminent religious purpose in enacting this statute. There is a historic and contemporaneous link between the teachings of certain religious denominations and the teaching of evolution. It was this link that concerned the court in Epperson v. Arkansas which also involved a facial challenge to a statute regulating the teaching of evolution. In that case, the Court reviewed an Arkansas statute that made it unlawful for an instructor to teach evolution or to use a textbook that referred to this scientific theory. Although the Arkansas anti-evolution law did not explicitly state its predominate religious purpose, the Court could not ignore that ''[t]he statute was a product of the upsurge of 'fundamentalist' religious fervor'' that has long viewed this particular scientific theory as contradicting the literal interpretation of the Bible. After reviewing the history of anti-evolution statutes, the Court determined that ''there can be no doubt that the motivation for the [Arkansas] law was the same [as other anti-evolution statutes]: to suppress the teaching of a theory which, it was thought, 'denied' the divine creation of man.'' The Court found that there can be no legitimate state interest in protecting particular religions from scientific views ''distasteful to them,'' and concluded ''that the First Amendment does not permit the State to require that teaching and learning must be tailored to the principles or prohibitions of any religious sect or dogma.''

These same historic and contemporaneous antagonisms between the teachings of certain religious denominations and the teaching of evolution are present in this case. The preeminent purpose of the Louisiana legislature was clearly to advance the religious viewpoint that a supernatural being created humankind.

Furthermore, it is not happenstance that the legislature required the teaching of a theory that coincided with religious view. The legislative history documents that the Act's primary purpose was to change the science curriculum of public schools in order to provide persuasive advantage to a particular religious doctrine that rejects the factual basis of evolution in its entirety. The sponsor of the Creationism Act, Senator Keith, explained during the legislative hearings that his disdain for the theory of evolution resulted from the support that evolution supplied to views contrary to his own religious beliefs. According to Senator Keith, the theory of evolution was consonant with the ''cardinal principle[s] of religious humanism, secular humanism, theological liberalism, aetheistism [sic].'' The state senator repeatedly stated that scientific evidence supporting his religious views should be included in the public school curriculum to redress the fact that the theory of evolution incidentally coincided with what he characterized as religious beliefs antithetical to his own. The legislation therefore sought to alter the science curriculum to reflect endorsement of a religious view that is antagonistic to the theory of evolution.

In this case, the purpose of the Creationism Act was to restructure the science curriculum to conform with a particular religious viewpoint. Out of many possible science subjects taught in the public schools, the legislature chose to affect the teaching of the one scientific theory that historically has been opposed by certain religious sects. As in Epperson, the legislature passed the Act to give preference to those religious groups which have as one of their tenets the creation of humankind by a divine creator. The ''overriding fact'' that confronted the Court in Epperson was ''that Arkansas' law selects from the body of knowledge a particular segment which it proscribes for the sole reason that it is deemed to conflict with . . . a particular interpretation of the Book of Genesis by a particular religious group.'' Similarly, the Creationism Act is designed *either* to promote the theory of creation science which embodies a particular religious tenet by requiring that creation science be taught whenever evolution is taught *or* to prohibit the teaching of a scientific theory disfavored by certain religious sects by forbidding the teaching of evolution when creation science is not also taught. The Establishment Clause, however, ''forbids *alike* the preference of a religious doctrine *or* the prohibition of a theory which is deemed antagonistic to a particular dogma.'' (Emphasis added). Because the primary purpose of the Creationism Act is to advance a particular religious belief, the Act endorses religion in violation of the First Amendment. . . .

V.

The Louisiana Creationism Act advances a religious doctrine by requiring either the banishment of the theory of evolution from public school classrooms or the presentation of a religious viewpoint that rejects evolution in its entirety. The Act violates the Establishment Clause of the First Amendment because it seeks to employ the symbolic and financial support of government to achieve a religious purpose. The judgment of the Court of Appeals therefore is

Affirmed.

Justice **Powell**, with whom Justice **O'Connor** joins, concurring, said in part:

I write separately to note certain aspects of the legislative history, and to emphasize that nothing in the Court's opinion diminishes the traditionally broad discretion accorded state and local school officials in the selection of the public school curriculum. . . .

B.

In June 1980, Senator Bill Keith introduced Senate Bill 956 in the Louisiana legislature. The stated purpose of the bill was to ''assure academic freedom by requiring the teaching of the theory of creation ex nihilo in all public schools where the theory of evolution is taught.'' The bill defined the ''theory of creation ex nihilo'' as ''the belief that the origin of the elements, the galaxy, the solar system, of life, of all the species of plants and animals, the origin of man, and the origin of all things and their processes and relationships were created ex nihilo and fixed by God.'' This theory was referred to by Senator Keith as ''scientific creationism.''

While a Senate committee was studying scientific creationism, Senator Keith introduced a second draft of the bill, requiring balanced treatment of ''evolution-science'' and ''creation-science.'' Although the Keith bill prohibited ''instruction in any religious doctrine or materials,'' it defined ''creation-science'' to include ''the scientific evidences and related inferences that indicate (a) sudden creation of the universe, energy, and life from nothing; (b) the insufficiency of mutation and natural selection in bringing about development of all living kinds from a single organism; (c) changes only within fixed limits or originally created kinds of plants and animals; (d) separate ancestry for man and apes; (e) explanation of the earth's geology by catastrophism, including the occurrence of a worldwide flood; and (f) a relatively recent inception of the earth and living kinds.''

Significantly, the model act on which the Keith bill relied was also the basis for a similar statute in Arkansas. See McLean v. Arkansas Board of Education, 529 F. Supp. 1255 (1982). The District Court in McLean carefully examined this model act, particularly the section defining creation-science, and concluded that ''[b]oth [its] concepts and wording . . . convey an inescapable religiosity.'' The court found that ''[t]he ideas of [this section] are not merely similar to the literal interpretation of Genesis; they are identical and parallel to no other story of creation.''

The complaint in McLean was filed on May 27, 1981. On May 28, the Louisiana Senate committee amended the Keith bill to delete the illustrative list of scientific evidences. According to the legislator who proposed the amendment, it was "not intended to try to gut [the bill] in any way, or defeat the purpose [for] which Senator Keith introduced [it]," and was not viewed as working "any violence to the bill." Instead, the concern was "whether this should be an all inclusive list."

The legislature then held hearings on the amended bill, that became the Balanced Treatment Act under review. The principal creation-scientist to testify in support of the Act was Dr. Edward Boudreaux. He did not elaborate on the nature of creation-science except to indicate that the "scientific evidences" of the theory are "the objective information of science [that] point[s] to conditions of a creator." He further testified that the recognized creation-scientists in the United States, who "numbe[r] something like a thousand [and] who hold doctorate and masters degrees in all areas of science," are affiliated with either or both the Institute for Creation Research and the Creation Research Society. Information on both these organizations is part of the legislative history, and a review of their goals and activities sheds light on the nature of creation-science as it was presented to, and understood by, the Louisiana legislature.

The Institute for Creation Research is an affiliate of the Christian Heritage College in San Diego, California. The Institute was established to address the "urgent need for our nation to return to belief in a personal, omnipotent Creator, who has a purpose for His creation and to whom all people must eventually give account." A goal of the Institute is "a revival of belief in special creation as the true explanation of the origin of the world." Therefore, the Institute currently is working on the "development of new methods for teaching scientific creationism in public schools." The Creation Research Society (CRS) is located in Ann Arbor, Michigan. A member must subscribe to the following statement of belief: "The Bible is the written word of God, and because it is inspired throughout, all of its assertions are historically and scientifically true." To study creation-science at the CRS, a member must accept "that the account of origins in Genesis is a factual presentation of simple historical truth."

C.

When, as here, "both courts below are unable to discern an arguably valid secular purpose, this Court normally should hesitate to find one. . . . My examination of the language and the legislative history of the Balanced Treatment Act confirms that the intent of the Louisiana legislature was to promote a particular religious belief. . . .

Justice **White,** concurring in the judgment, said in part:

As it comes to us, this is not a difficult case. Based on the historical setting and plain language of the act both courts construed the statutory words "creation-science" to refer to a religious belief, which the act required to be taught if evolution was taught. In other words, the teaching of evolution was conditioned on the teaching of a religious belief. Both courts concluded that the state legislature's primary purpose was to advance religion and that the statute was therefore unconstitutional under the Establishment Clause.

. . . Unless . . . we are to reconsider the Court's decisions interpreting the Establishment Clause, I agree that the judgment of the Court of Appeals must be affirmed.

Justice **Scalia,** with whom Chief Justice **Rehnquist** joined, dissented, saying in part:

Even if I agreed with the questionable premise that legislation can be invalidated under the Establishment Clause on the basis of its motivation alone, without regard to its effects, I would still find no justification for today's decision. The Louisiana legislators who passed the "Balanced Treatment for Creation-Science and Evolution-Science Act," each of whom had sworn to support the Constitution, were well aware of the potential Establishment Clause problems and considered that aspect of the legislation with great care. After seven hearings and several months of study, resulting in substantial revision of the original proposal, they approved the Act overwhelmingly and specifically articulated the secular purpose they meant it to serve. Although the records contains abundant evidence of the sincerity of that purpose (the only issue pertinent to this case), the Court today holds, essentially on the basis of "its visceral knowledge regarding what *must* have motivated the legislators" that the members of the Louisiana Legislature knowingly violated their oaths and then lied about it. I dissent. . . .

I.

. . . The only evidence in the record of the "received meaning and acceptation" of "creation science" is found in five affidavits filed by appellants. In those affidavits, two scientists, a philosopher, a theologian, and an educator, all of whom claim extensive knowledge of creation science, swear that it is essentially a collection of scientific data supporting the theory that the physical universe and life within it appeared suddenly and have not changed substantially since appearing. These experts insist that creation science is a strictly scientific concept that can be presented without religious references. At this point, then, we must assume that the Balanced Treatment Act does *not* require the presentation of religious doctrine.

Nothing in today's opinion is plainly to the contrary, but what the statute means and what it requires are of rather little concern to the Court. Like the Court of Appeals, the Court finds it necessary to consider only the motives of the legislators who supported the Balanced Treatment Act. After examining the statute, its legislative history, and its historical and social context, the Court holds that the Louisiana Legislature acted without "a secular legislative purpose" and that the Act therefore fails the "purpose" prong of the three-part test set forth in Lemon v. Kurtzman (1971). As I explain below, I doubt whether that "purpose" requirement of Lemon is a proper interpretation of the Constitution; but even if it were, I could not agree with the Court's assessment that the requirement was not satisfied here.

This Court has said little about the first component of the Lemon test. Almost invariably, we have effortlessly discovered a secular purpose for measures challenged under the Establishment Clause. . . . [Justice Scalia here lists a dozen cases, most of which turned on the "entanglement" prong of Lemon.] In fact, only once before deciding Lemon, and twice since, have we invalidated a law for lack of a secular purpose. See Wallace v. Jaffree (1985); Stone v. Graham (1980) (per curiam); Epperson v. Arkansas (1968).

Nevertheless, a few principles have emerged from our cases, principles which should, but to an unfortunately large extent do not, guide the Court's application of Lemon today. It is clear, first of all, that regardless of what "legislative purpose" may mean in other contexts, for the purpose of the Lemon test it means the "actual" motives of those responsible for the challenged action. . . . Thus, if those legislators who supported the Balanced Treatment Act *in fact* acted with a "sincere" secular purpose, the Act survives the first component of the Lemon test, regardless of whether that purpose is likely to be achieved by the provisions they enacted.

Our cases have also confirmed that when the Lemon Court referred to "a secular . . . purpose," it meant "*a* secular purpose." The author of Lemon, writing for the Court, has said that invalidation under the purpose prong is appropriate when "there [is] *no question* that the statute or activity was motivated *wholly* by religious considerations." Lynch v. Donnelly (1984) (Burger, C.J.)(emphasis added); see also Wallace v. Jaffree ("the First Amendment requires that a statute must be invalidated if it is *entirely* motivated by a purpose to advance religion") (emphasis added). In all three cases in which we struck down laws under the Establishment Clause for lack of a secular purpose, we found that the legislature's sole motive was to promote religion. . . . Thus, the majority's invalidation of the Balanced Treatment Act is defensible only if the record indicates that the Louisiana Legislature had *no* secular purpose.

It is important to stress that the purpose forbidden by Lemon is the purpose of "advance religion." . . . Our cases in no way imply that the Establishment Clause forbids legislators merely to act upon their religious convictions. We surely would not strike down a law providing money to feed the hungry or shelter the homeless if it could be demonstrated that, but for the religious beliefs of the legislators, the funds would not have been approved. Also, political activism by the religiously motivated is part of our heritage. Notwithstanding the majority's implication to the contrary, we do not presume that the sole purpose of a law is to advance religion merely because it was supported strongly by organized religions or by adherents of particular faiths. . . . To do so would deprive religious men and women of their right to participate in the political process. Today's religious activism may give us the Balanced Treatment Act, but yesterday's

resulted in the abolition of slavery, and tomorrow's may bring relief for famine victims.

Similarly, we will not presume that a law's purpose is to advance religion merely because it " 'happens to coincide or harmonize with the tenets of some or all religions,' " . . . or because it benefits religion, even substantially. We have, for example, turned back Establishment Clause challenges to restrictions on abortion funding, Harris v. McRae [1980], and to Sunday closing laws, McGowan v. Maryland [1961], despite the fact that both "agre[e] with the dictates of [some] Judaeo-Christian religions." "In many instances, the Congress or state legislatures conclude that the general welfare of society, wholly apart from any religious considerations, demands such regulation." Ibid. On many occasions we have had no difficulty finding a secular purpose for governmental action far more likely to advance religion than the Balanced Treatment Act. See, e.g., Mueller v. Allen [1983]. . . . Thus, the fact that creation science coincides with the beliefs of certain religions, a fact upon which the majority relies heavily, does not itself justify invalidation of the Act.

Finally, our cases indicate that even certain kinds of governmental actions undertaken with the specific intention of improving the position of religion do not "advance religion" as that term is used in Lemon. Rather, we have said that in at least two circumstances government *must* act to advance religion, and that in a third it *may* do so.

First, since we have consistently described the Establishment Clause as forbidding not only state action motivated by the desire to *advance* religion, but also intended to "disapprove," "inhibit," or evince "hostility" toward religion, . . . and since we have said that governmental "neutrality" toward religion is the preeminent goal of the First Amendment, . . . a State which discovers that its employees are inhibiting religion must take steps to prevent them from doing so, even though its purpose would clearly be to advance religion. . . . Thus, if the Louisiana Legislature sincerely believed that the State's science teachers were being hostile to religion, our cases indicate that it could act to eliminate that hostility without running afoul of Lemon's purpose test.

Second, we have held that intentional governmental advancement of religion is sometimes required by the Free Exercise Clause. For example, in . . . Wisconsin v. Yoder (1972) . . . we held that in some circumstances States must accommodate the beliefs of religious citizens by exempting them from generally applicable regulations. We have not yet come close to reconciling Lemon and our Free Exercise cases, and typically we do not really try. . . . It is clear, however, that members of the Louisiana Legislature were not impermissibly motivated for purpose of the Lemon test if they believed that approval of the Balanced Treatment Act was *required* by the Free Exercise Clause.

We have also held that in some circumstances government may act to accommodate religion, even if that action is not required by the First Amendment. . . . We have implied that voluntary governmental accommodation of religion is not only permissible, but desirable.

Thus, few would contend that Title VII of the Civil Rights Act of 1964, which both forbids religious discrimination by private-sector employers and requires them reasonably to accommodate the religious practices of their employees, violates the Establishment Clause, even though its "purpose" is, of course, to advance religion, and even though it is almost certainly not required by the Free Exercise Clause. . . . It is possible, then, that even if the sole motive of those voting for the Balanced Treatment Act was to advance religion, and its passage was not actually required, or even believed to be required, by either the Free Exercise or Establishment Clauses, the Act would nonetheless survive scrutiny under Lemon's purpose test.

One final observation about the application of that test: Although the Court's opinion gives no hint of it, in the past we have repeatedly affirmed "our reluctance to attribute unconstitutional motives to the States." . . . Whenever we are called upon to judge the constitutionality of an act of a state legislature, "we must have 'due regard to the fact that this Court is not exercising a primary judgment but is sitting in judgment upon those who also have taken the oath to observe the Constitution and who have the responsibility for carrying on government.' " . . . This is particularly true, we have said, where the legislature has specifically considered the question of a law's constitutionality.

With the foregoing in mind, I now turn to the purposes underlying adoption of the Balanced Treatment Act.

II.

A.

We have relatively little information upon which to judge the motives of those who supported the Act. About the only direct evidence is the statute itself and transcripts of the seven committee hearings at which it was considered. . . . Nevertheless, there is ample evidence that the majority is wrong in holding that the Balanced Treatment Act is without secular purpose. . . .

. . . The Act had its genesis (so to speak) in legislation introduced by Senator Bill Keith in June 1980. . . .

Before summarizing the testimony of Senator Keith and his supporters, I wish to make clear that I by no means intended to endorse its accuracy. But my views (and the views of this Court) about creation science and evolution are (or should be) beside the point. Our task is not to judge the debate about teaching the origins of life, but to ascertain what the members of the Louisiana Legislature believed. The vast majority of them voted to approve a bill which explicitly stated a secular purpose; what is crucial is not their *wisdom* in believing that purpose would be achieved by the bill, but their *sincerity* in believing it would be.

Most of the testimony in support of Senator Keith's bill came from the Senator himself and from scientists and educators he presented, many of whom enjoyed academic credentials that may have been regarded as quite impressive by members of the Louisiana Legislature. To a substantial extent, their testimony was devoted to lengthy, and, to the layman, seemingly expert scientific expositions on the origin of life. . . . These scientific lectures touched upon, inter alia, biology, paleontology, genetics, astronomy, astrophysics, probability analysis, and biochemistry. The witnesses repeatedly assured committee members that "hundreds and hundreds" of highly respected, internationally renowned scientists believed in creation science and would support their testimony. . . .

Senator Keith and his witnesses testified essentially as set forth in the following numbered paragraphs:

(1) There are two and only two scientific explanations for the beginning of life—evolution and creation science. . . . Evolution posits that life arose out of inanimate chemical compounds and has gradually evolved over millions of years. Creation science posits that all life forms now on earth appeared suddenly and relatively recently and have changed little. . . .

(2) The body of scientific evidence supporting creation science is as strong as that supporting evolution. In fact, it may be *stronger*. . . . The evidence for evolution is far less compelling than we have been led to believe. Evolution is not a scientific "fact," since it cannot actually be observed in a laboratory. Rather, evolution is merely a scientific theory or "guess." . . .

(3) Creation science is educationally valuable. Students exposed to it better understand the current state of scientific evidence about the origin of life. . . . Those students even have a better understanding of evolution. . . .

(4) Although creation science is educationally valuable and strictly scientific, it is now being censored from or misrepresented in the public schools. . . . Teachers have been brainwashed by an entrenched scientific establishment composed almost exclusively of scientists to whom evolution is like a "religion." These scientists discriminate against creation scientists so as to prevent evolution's weaknesses from being exposed. . . .

(5) The censorship of creation science has at least two harmful effects. First, it deprives students of knowledge of one of the two scientific explanations for the origin of life and leads them to believe that evolution is a proven fact; thus, their education suffers and they are wrongly taught that science has proven their religious beliefs false. Second, it violates the Establishment Clause. The United States Supreme Court has held that secular humanism is a religion. [Sen. Keith, referring to Torcaso v. Watkins (1961)]. . . . Belief in evolution is a central tenet of that religion. . . . Thus, by censoring creation science and instructing students that evolution is fact, public school teachers are *now* advancing religion in violation of the Establishment Clause. . . .

We have no way of knowing, of course, how many legislators believed the testimony of Senator Keith and his witnesses. But the absence of evidence to the contrary, we have to assume that many of them did. Given that assumption, the Court today plainly errs in holding that the Louisiana Legislature passed the Balanced Treatment Act for exclusively religious purposes.

B.

. . . Even if the legislative history were silent or ambiguous about the existence of a secular purpose—and here it is not—the statute should survive Lemon's purpose test. But even more validation than mere legislative history is present here. The Louisiana Legislature explicitly set forth its secular purpose (''protecting academic freedom'') in the very test of the Act. . . .

The Court seeks to evade the force of this expression of purpose by stubbornly misinterpreting it, and then finding that the provisions of the Act do not advance that misinterpreted purpose, thereby showing it to be a sham. The Court first surmises that ''academic freedom'' means ''enhancing the freedom of teachers to teach what they will,'' even though ''academic freedom'' in that sense has little scope in the structured elementary and secondary curriculums with which the Act is concerned. Alternatively, the Court suggests that it might mean ''maximiz[ing] the comprehensiveness and effectiveness of science instruction,'' though that is an exceedingly strange interpretation of the words, and one that is refuted on the very face of the statute. Had the Court devoted to this central question of the meaning of the legislatively expressed purpose a small fraction of the research into legislative history that produced its quotations of religiously motivated statements by individual legislators, it would have discerned quite readily what ''academic freedom'' meant: *students'* freedom from *indoctrination*. The legislature wanted to ensure that students would be free to decide for themselves how life began, based upon a fair and balanced presentation of the scientific evidence—that is, to protect ''the right of each [student] voluntarily to determine what to believe (and what not to believe) free of any coercive pressures from the State.'' . . .

It is undoubtedly true that what prompted the Legislature to direct its attention to the misrepresentation of evolution in the schools (rather than the inaccurate presentation of other topics) was its awareness of the tension between evolution and the religious beliefs of many children. But even appellees concede that a valid secular purpose is not rendered impermissible simply because its pursuits prompted by concern for religious sensitivities. If a history teacher falsely told her students that the bones of Jesus Christ had been discovered, or a physics teacher that the Shroud of Turin had been conclusively established to be inexplicable on the basis of natural causes, I cannot believe (despite the majority's implication to the contrary) that legislators or school board members would be constitutionally prohibited from taking corrective action, simply because that action was prompted by concern for the religious beliefs of the misinstructed students.

In sum, even if one concedes, for the sake of argument, that a majority of the Louisiana Legislature voted for the Balanced Treatment Act partly in order to foster (rather than merely eliminate discrimination against) Christian fundamentalist beliefs, our cases establish that

that alone would not suffice to invalidate the Act, so long as there was a genuine secular purpose as well. We have, moreover, no adequate basis for disbelieving the secular purpose set forth in the Act itself, or for concluding that it is a sham enacted to conceal the legislators' violation of their oaths of office. I am astonished by the Court's unprecedented readiness to reach such a conclusion, which I can only attribute to an intellectual predisposition created by the facts and the legend of Scopes v. State, 154 Tenn. 105 (1927)—an instinctive reaction that any governmentally imposed requirements bearing upon the teaching of evolution must be a manifestation of Christian fundamentalist repression. In this case, however, it seems to me the Court's position is the repressive one. The people of Louisiana, including those who are Christian fundamentalists, are quite entitled, as a secular matter, to have whatever scientific evidence there may be against evolution presented in their schools, just as Mr. Scopes was entitled to present whatever scientific evidence there was for it. Perhaps what the Louisiana Legislature has done is unconstitutional because there *is* no such evidence, and the scheme they have established will amount to no more than a presentation of the Book of Genesis. But we cannot say that on the evidence before using this summary judgment context, which includes ample uncontradicted testimony that ''creation science'' is a body of scientific knowledge rather than revealed belief. *Infinitely less* can we say (or should we say) that the scientific evidence for evolution is so conclusive that no one could be gullible enough to believe that there is any real scientific evidence to the contrary, so that the legislation's stated purpose must be a lie. Yet that illiberal judgment, that Scopes-in-reverse, is ultimately the basis on which the Court's facile rejection of the Louisiana Legislature's purpose must rest. . . .

III.

I have to this point assumed the validity of the Lemon ''purpose'' test. In fact, however, I think the pessimistic evaluation that the Chief Justice [Rehnquist] made of the totality of Lemon is particularly applicable to the ''purpose'' prong: it is ''a constitutional theory [that] has no basis in the history of the amendment it seeks to interpret, is difficult to apply and yields unprincipled results.'' Wallace v. Jaffree (Rehnquist, J., dissenting). . . .

Given the many hazards involved in assessing the subjective intent of governmental decisionmakers, the first prong of Lemon is defensible, I think, only if the text of the Establishment Clause demands it. That is surely not the case. . . .

LYNCH v. DONNELLY

465 U. S. 668; 104 S. Ct. 1355; 79 L. Ed. 2d 604
(1984)

⟨*It seems apparent that while the early governments in this country tended to let the individual fend for himself as far as his economic welfare went, they did not take* any such hands-off policy with regard to his spiritual welfare. Even those that did not have established religions tended to encourage religion, usually a Protestant Christianity. Among the most common forms of such encouragement were the so-called Sunday Blue Laws, or Sunday Closing Laws, adopted to advance "the true and sincere worship of God according to his holy will" (New York) or "to the end that the Sabbath may be celebrated in a religious manner" (Massachusetts Bay Colony). Such laws, now present in every state but Alaska, forbid to a greater or lesser extent various forms of physical or economic activity on Sunday. Some merely forbid the selling of liquor, while others forbid all economic activity and then set up elaborate exceptions to the rule. In four cases in 1961 the Court held valid the Sunday closing laws of Maryland and Pennsylvania. In two of the cases the defendants did not allege that their religious freedom was involved, but merely that they were denied equal protection and that the laws constituted an establishment of religion. The Court rejected both these contentions. It held that the laws did not deny equal protection by the varied exceptions they permitted, since these were not shown to be completely irrational and unjustifiable. Nor did they constitute an establishment of religion. Conceding that the origin of such laws was undoubtedly religious and that the day chosen favored the dominant Christian sects, the Court pointed out that such laws had long since ceased to be religiously inspired and were merely an exercise of the police power of the state to provide the community a day of rest, amusement, and family togetherness. The state, the Court held, could reasonably decide that everyone should rest on the same day (rather than let each individual choose his own day) and it was not an establishment of religion to pick the day that most people thought of as a "day off," even though it had a religious origin. See McGowan v. Maryland (1961) and Two Guys from Harrison-Allentown, Inc. v. McGinley (1961). In two of the cases the Court faced the additional question of the free exercise of religion. Gallagher v. Crown Kosher Super Market (1961) and Braunfeld v. Brown (1961) involved Orthodox Jews who closed their businesses on Saturday, the Jewish Sabbath, and claimed that forcing them to close on Sunday, too, was in effect to place an economic burden upon them because of their religion. Although the six members of the majority could not agree on an opinion, they did agree that since the laws were valid under the police power and were not intended to discriminate against persons on religious grounds, the indirect economic disadvantage visited on persons because of their religious beliefs did not render the law a violation of their religious liberties. In illustration they pointed to the validity of laws against polygamy, held valid in Reynolds v. United States (1879). In 1964 New York City replaced its Sunday closing law with a Fair Sabbath Law, which permitted family-run businesses to stay open on Sunday if they were closed on Saturday.

In 1977 Connecticut amended its Sunday-closing law to provide that "no person who states that a particular day of the week is observed as his Sabbath may be required by his employer to work on such day. An employee's refusal to work on his Sabbath shall not consti-

tute grounds for dismissal." In Thornton v. Caldor (1985) the Court held the statute a violation of the establishment clause because it had no secular purpose. "The State . . . commands that Sabbath religious concerns automatically control over all secular interests at the work place; the statute takes no account of the convenience or interests of the employer or those of other employees who do not observe a Sabbath. . . . There is no exception under the statute for special circumstances, such as the Friday Sabbath observer employed in an occupation with a Monday through Friday schedule—a school teacher, for example. . . . This unyielding weighting in favor of Sabbath observers over all other interests contravenes a fundamental principle of the Religion Clauses. . . ."

While Article VI of the Constitution contains the provision that "no religious test shall ever be required as a qualification to any office or public trust under the United States," most of the early state constitutions did require such tests and some of those have survived. The constitution of Maryland provides that no religious test for public office shall be required "other than a declaration of belief in the existence of God." Torcaso was appointed to the office of notary public in Maryland but was refused his commission to the office because he would not declare his belief in God. In a unanimous decision the Court held that "this Maryland religious test for public office unconstitutionally invades the appellant's freedom of belief and religion and therefore cannot be enforced against him." The Court expressly rejected any suggestion that Zorach v. Clauson (1952) had weakened the holding of the Everson case (1947). "We repeat and again reaffirm that neither a State nor the Federal Government can constitutionally force a person 'to profess a belief or disbelief in any religion.' Neither can constitutionally pass laws or impose requirements which aid all religions as against non-believers, and neither can aid those religions based on a belief in the existence of God as against those religions founded on different beliefs." See Torcaso v. Watkins (1961)

The free exercise and no establishment clauses of the First Amendment were the framers' answer to the place of religion in the highly pluralistic social structures of the time. Religion was to be a private affair; the heavy thumb of the government was to be used neither to aid nor hinder, lest man's freedom to worship as he chose and the right to support only the church of his choice be jeopardized. But even as the framers wrote, many of the practices of the time made clear that the "separation of church and state" would not entail the government ignoring the existence of religion. Both houses of the Congress employed a chaplain; "In God We Trust" was embossed on our coins; and the help and understanding of God were exhorted on all public occasions. In general the people thought of themselves as religious, mostly Christian, and a government recognition of that fact did not seem in any way inconsistent with the doctrines of the First Amendment.

With the gradual diversification of religious beliefs many well-accepted religious practices and manifestations were challenged in the courts, and with the application to the states of the religion clauses of the First

Amendment, these challenges raised potential federal questions.

The Supreme Court has shown considerable reluctance to review many activities that have been part of our historical heritage. In November 1964, it left untouched a New York decision upholding the words "under God" in the pledge of allegiance; in 1966 (Murray v. Goldstein) it declined to review a Maryland case upholding the validity of tax exemption for church buildings, and as recently as 1971 it let stand the rejection by a district court of an effort to stop the astronauts from praying over television on their way to the moon (O'Hair v. Paine, 1971).

But the issue of tax exemption for churches could not stay buried forever, and in Walz v. Tax Commission the Supreme Court took a case involving a Staten Island resident who owned a 22 × 29 foot piece of land on which he owed the state $5.24 in property taxes. He refused to pay on the ground he was being forced to support churches and synagogues, which pay no taxes. The Court recognized its past struggles to "find a neutral course between the two Religion Clauses, both of which are cast in absolute terms, and either of which, if expanded to a logical extreme, would tend to clash with the other." It concluded that "no perfect or absolute separation is really possible," that both had to coexist, and the real function of the Court was to prevent "excessive entanglement" between the two. Since tax exemption for churches had been in existence since the formation of the Union, it posed no real threat to the separation of church and state. "The exemption creates only a minimal and remote involvement between church and state and far less than the taxation of churches. It restricts the fiscal relationship between church and state, and tends to complement and reinforce the desired separation insulating each from the other."

In Marsh v. Chambers (1983) the Court held valid the employment of a chaplain for the state legislature noting that the framers had employed one for Congress at the same time they were proposing the First Amendment, and "the practice of opening legislative sessions with prayer has become part of the fabric of our society."

The present case involves a challenge to the inclusion of a crèche in a city-owned Christmas display on the ground that "the erection of the crèche has the real and substantial effect of affiliating the City with the Christian beliefs that the crèche represents."

Chief Justice **Burger** delivered the opinion of the Court, saying in part:

We granted certiorari to decide whether the Establishment Clause of the First Amendment prohibits a municipality from including a crèche, or Nativity scene, in its annual Christmas display.

I.

Each year, in cooperation with the downtown retail merchants' association, the city of Pawtucket, R. I.,

erects a Christmas display as part of its observance of the Christmas holiday season. The display is situated in a park owned by a nonprofit organization and located in the heart of the shopping district. The display is essentially like those to be found in hundreds of towns or cities across the Nation—often on public grounds—during the Christmas season. The Pawtucket display comprises many of the figures and decorations traditionally associated with Christmas, including, among other things, a Santa Claus house, reindeer pulling Santa's sleigh, candy-striped poles, a Christmas tree, carolers, cutout figures representing such characters as a clown, an elephant, and a teddy bear, hundreds of colored lights, a large banner that reads "SEASONS GREETINGS," and the crèche at issue here. All components of this display are owned by the city.

The crèche, which has been included in the display for 40 or more years, consists of the traditional figures, including the Infant Jesus, Mary and Joseph, angels, shepherds, kings, and animals, all ranging in height from 5" to 5'. In 1973, when the present crèche was acquired, it cost the city $1365; it now is valued at $200. The erection and dismantling of the crèche costs the city about $20 per year; nominal expenses are incurred in lighting the crèche. No money has been expended on its maintenance for the past 10 years. . . .

II.

A.

This Court has explained that the purpose of the Establishment and Free Exercise Clauses of the First Amendment is "to prevent, as far as possible, the intrusion of either [the church or the state] into the precincts of the other." Lemon v. Kurtzman (1971). At the same time, however, the Court has recognized that "total separation is not possible in an absolute sense. Some relationship between government and religious organizations is inevitable." In every Establishment Clause case, we must reconcile the inescapable tension between the objective of preventing unnecessary intrusion of either the church or the state upon the other, and the reality that, as the Court has so often noted, total separation of the two is not possible.

The Court has sometimes described the Religion Clauses as erecting a "wall" between church and state, see, e.g., Everson v. Board of Education (1947). The concept of a "wall" of separation is a useful figure of speech probably deriving from views of Thomas Jefferson. The metaphor has served as a reminder that the Establishment Clause forbids an established church or anything approaching it. But the metaphor itself is not a wholly accurate description of the practical aspects of the relationship that in fact exists between church and state.

No significant segment of our society and no institution within it can exist in a vacuum or in total or absolute isolation from all the other parts, much less from government. "It has never been thought either possible or desirable to enforce a regime of total separation. . . ." . . . Nor does the Constitution require complete separation of church and state; it affirmatively mandates accommodation, not merely tolerance, of all religions, and forbids hostility toward any. . . . Anything less would require the "callous indifference" we have said was never intended by the Establishment Clause. Zorach [v. Clauson (1952)]. Indeed, we have observed, such hostility would bring us into "war with our national tradition as embodied in the First Amendment's guaranty of the free exercise of religion." . . .

B.

The Court's interpretation of the Establishment Clause has comported with what history reveals was the contemporaneous understanding of its guarantees. A significant example of the contemporaneous understanding of that Clause is found in the events of the first week of the First Session of the First Congress in 1789. In the very week that Congress approved the Establishment Clause as part of the Bill of Rights for submission to the states, it enacted legislation providing for paid chaplains for the House and Senate. . . .

The interpretation of the Establishment Clause by Congress in 1789 takes on special significance in light of the Court's emphasis that the First Congress "was a Congress whose constitutional decisions have always been regarded, as they should be regarded, as of the greatest weight in the interpretation of that fundamental instrument," Myers v. United States (1926).

It is clear that neither the 17 draftsmen of the Constitution who were Members of the First Congress, nor the Congress of 1789, saw any establishment problem in the employment of congressional Chaplains to offer daily prayers in the Congress, a practice that has continued for nearly two centuries. It would be difficult to identify a more striking example of the accommodation of religious belief intended by the Framers.

C. . . .

Other examples of reference to our religious heritage are found in the statutorily prescribed national motto "In God We Trust," which Congress and the President mandated for our currency, and in the language "One nation under God," as part of the Pledge of Allegiance to the American flag. That pledge is recited by many thousands of public school children—and adults—every year.

Art galleries supported by public revenues display religious paintings of the 15th and 16th centuries, predominantly inspired by one religious faith. . . . The very chamber in which oral arguments on this case were heard is decorated with a notable and permanent—not seasonal—symbol of religion: Moses with the Ten Commandments. Congress has long provided chapels in the Capitol for religious worship and meditation. . . .

III.

This history may help explain why the Court consistently has declined to take a rigid, absolutist view of the Establishment Clause. We have refused "to construe the Religion Clauses with a literalness that would undermine the ultimate constitutional objective *as illuminated by history*." Walz v. Tax Commission (1970) (Emphasis added). In our modern, complex society, whose traditions and constitutional underpinnings rest on and encourage diversity and pluralism in all areas, an absolutist approach in applying the Establishment Clause is simplistic and has been uniformly rejected by the Court.

Rather than mechanically invalidating all governmental conduct or statutes that confer benefits or give special recognition to religion in general or to one faith—as an absolutist approach would dictate—the Court has scrutinized challenged legislation or official conduct to determine whether, in reality, it establishes a religion or religious faith, or tends to do so. . . .

In the line-drawing process we have often found it useful to inquire whether the challenged law or conduct has a secular purpose, whether its principal or primary effect is to advance or inhibit religion, and whether it creates an excessive entanglement of government with religion. But, we have repeatedly emphasized our unwillingness to be confined to any single test or criterion in this sensitive area. . . .

In this case, the focus of our inquiry must be on the crèche in the context of the Christmas season. . . . Focus exclusively on the religious component of any activity would inevitably lead to its invalidation under the Establishment Clause.

The Court has invalidated legislation or governmental action on the ground that a secular purpose was lacking, but only when it has concluded there was no question that the statute or activity was motivated wholly by religious considerations. . . .

The District Court inferred from the religious nature of the crèche that the city has no secular purpose for the display. In so doing, it rejected the city's claim that its reasons for including the crèche are essentially the same as its reasons for sponsoring the display as a whole. . . . The city, like the Congresses and Presidents, . . . has principally taken note of a significant historical religious event long celebrated in the Western World. The crèche in the display depicts the historical origins of this traditional event long recognized as a National Holiday. . . .

The narrow question is whether there is a secular purpose for Pawtucket's display of the crèche. The display is sponsored by the city to celebrate the Holiday and to depict the origins of that Holiday. These are legitimate secular purposes. The District Court's inference, drawn from the religious nature of the crèche, that the city has no secular purpose was, on this record, clearly erroneous. . . .

The dissent asserts some observers may perceive that the city has aligned itself with the Christian faith by including a Christian symbol in its display and that this serves to advance religion. We can assume, arguendo, that the display advances religion in a sense; but our precedents plainly contemplate that on occasion some advancement of religion will result from governmental action. The Court has made it abundantly clear, however, that "not every law that confers an 'indirect,' 'remote,' or 'incidental' benefit upon [religion] is, for that reason alone, constitutionally invalid." [Committee for Public Education v.] Nyquist [1973]. . . .

The District Court found that there had been no administrative entanglement between religion and state resulting from the city's ownership and use of the crèche. But it went on to hold that some political divisiveness was engendered by this litigation. Coupled with its finding of an impermissible sectarian purpose and effect, this persuaded the court that there was "excessive entanglement." . . .

The Court of Appeals correctly observed that this Court has not held that political divisiveness alone can serve to invalidate otherwise permissible conduct. And we decline to so hold today. . . . In any event, apart from this litigation there is no evidence of political friction or divisiveness over the crèche in the 40-year history of Pawtucket's Christmas celebration. . . . A litigant cannot, by the very act of commencing a lawsuit . . . create the appearance of divisiveness and then exploit it as evidence of entanglement.

We are satisfied that the city has a secular purpose for including the crèche, that the city has not impermissibly advanced religion, and that including the crèche does not create excessive entanglement between religion and government. . . .

Justice **O'Connor,** concurring, said in part:

I concur in the opinion of the Court. I write separately to suggest a clarification of our Establishment Clause doctrine. . . .

I.

The Establishment Clause prohibits government from making adherence to a religion relevant in any way to a person's standing in the political community. Government can run afoul of that prohibition in two principal ways. One is excessive entanglement with religious institutions, which may interfere with the independence of the institutions, give the institutions access to government or governmental powers not fully shared by nonadherents of the religion, and foster the creation of political constituencies defined along religious lines. . . . The second and more direct infringement is government endorsement or disapproval of religion. Endorsement sends a message to nonadherents that they are outsiders, not full members of the political community, and an accompanying message to adherents that they are insiders, favored members of the political community. Disapproval sends the opposite message. . . .

III. . . .

B. . . .

Pawtucket's display of its crèche, I believe, does not communicate a message that the government intends to endorse the Christian beliefs represented by the crèche. Although the religious and indeed sectarian significance of the crèche, as the district court found, is not neutralized by the setting, the overall holiday setting changes what viewers may fairly understand to be the purpose of the display—as a typical museum setting, though not neutralizing the religious content of a religious painting, negates any message of endorsement of that content. The display celebrates a public holiday, and no one contends that declaration of that holiday is understood to be an endorsement of religion. . . .

Justice **Brennan,** with whom Justice **Marshall,** Justice **Blackmun** and Justice **Stevens** join, dissenting, said in part:

The principles announced in the compact phrases of the Religion Clauses have, as the Court today reminds us, proved difficult to apply. Faced with that uncertainty, the Court properly looks for guidance to the settled test announced in Lemon v. Kurtzman (1971). . . .

I. . . .

A. . . .

This well-defined three-part test expresses the essential concerns animating the Establishment Clause. Thus, the test is designed to ensure that the organs of government remain strictly separate and apart from religious affairs, for "a union of government and religion tends to destroy government and degrade religion." . . .

Applying the three-part test to Pawtucket's crèche, I am persuaded that the city's inclusion of the crèche in its Christmas display simply does not reflect a "clearly . . . secular purpose." . . . Here we have no explicit statement of purpose by Pawtucket's municipal government accompanying its decision to purchase, display, and maintain the crèche. Governmental purpose may nevertheless be inferred. . . . In the present case, the city claims that its purposes were exclusively secular. Pawtucket sought, according to this view, only to participate in the celebration of a national holiday and to attract people to the downtown area in order to promote pre-Christmas retail sales and to help engender the spirit of goodwill and neighborliness commonly associated with the Christmas season.

Despite these assertions, two compelling aspects of this case indicate that our generally prudent "reluctance to attribute unconstitutional motives" to a governmental body . . . should be overcome. First, . . . all of Pawtucket's "valid secular objectives can be readily accomplished by other means." Plainly, the city's interest in celebrating the holiday and in promoting both retail sales and goodwill are fully served by the elaborate display of Santa Claus, reindeer, and wishing wells that are already a part of Pawtucket's annual Christmas display. More importantly, the nativity scene, unlike every other element of the Hodgson Park display, reflects a sectarian exclusivity that the avowed purposes of celebrating the holiday season and promoting retail commerce simply do not encompass. To be found constitutional, Pawtucket's seasonal celebration must at least be nondenominational and not serve to promote religion. The inclusion of a distinctively religious element like the crèche, however, demonstrates that a narrower sectarian purpose lay behind the decision to include a nativity scene. That the crèche retained this religious character for the people and municipal government of Pawtucket is suggested by the Mayor's testimony at trial in which he stated that for him, as well as others in the city, the effort to eliminate the nativity scene from Pawtucket's Christmas celebration "is a step towards establishing another religion, non-religion that it may be." Plainly, the city and its leaders understood that the inclusion of the crèche in its display would serve the wholly religious purpose of "keep[ing] 'Christ in Christmas.'" From this record, therefore, it is impossible to say with the kind of confidence that was possible in McGowan v. Maryland (1961) that a wholly secular goal predominates.

The "primary effect" of including a nativity scene in the city's display is, as the District Court found, to place the government's imprimatur of approval on the particular religious beliefs exemplified by the crèche. Those who believe in the message of the nativity receive the unique and exclusive benefit of public recognition and approval of their views. For many, the city's decision to include the crèche as part of its extensive and costly efforts to celebrate Christmas can only mean that the prestige of the government has been conferred on the beliefs associated with the crèche, thereby providing "a significant symbolic benefit to religion. . . ." . . . The effect on minority religious groups, as well as on those who may reject all religion, is to convey the message that their views are not similarly worthy of public recognition nor entitled to public support. It was precisely this sort of religious chauvinism that the Establishment Clause was intended forever to prohibit. . . .

Finally, it is evident that Pawtucket's inclusion of a crèche as part of its annual Christmas display does pose a significant threat of fostering "excessive entanglement." . . . It is worth noting that after today's decision, administrative entanglements may well develop. Jews and other non-Christian groups, prompted perhaps by the Mayor's remark that he will include a Menorah in future displays, can be expected to press government for inclusion of their symbols, and faced with such requests, government will have to become involved in accommodating the various demands. . . . More importantly, although no political divisiveness was apparent in Pawtucket prior to the filing of respondents' lawsuit, that act, as the District Court found, unleashed powerful emotional reactions which divided the city along religious lines. The fact that calm had prevailed prior to this suit does not immediately suggest the absence of any division on the point for, as the District Court observed, the quiescence of those opposed to the crèche may have reflected nothing more than their sense of futility in opposing the majority. Of course, the Court is correct to note that we have never held that the potential for divisiveness alone is sufficient to invalidate a challenged governmental practice; we have, nevertheless, repeatedly emphasized that "too close a proximity" between religious and civil authorities . . . may represent a "warning signal" that the values embodied in the Establishment Clause are at risk. . . .

B. . . .

. . . I refuse to accept the notion implicit in today's decision that non-Christians would find that the religious content of the crèche is eliminated by the fact that it appears as part of the city's otherwise secular celebration of the Christmas holiday. The nativity scene is clearly distinct in its purpose and effect from the rest of the Hodgson Park display for the simple reason that it is the only one rooted in a biblical account of Christ's birth. It is the chief symbol of the characteristically Christian belief that a divine Savior was brought into the world and that the purpose of this miraculous birth was to illuminate a path toward salvation and redemption. For Christians, that path is exclusive, precious, and holy. But for those who do not share these beliefs, the symbolic reenactment of the birth of a divine being who has been miraculously incarnated as a man stands as a dramatic reminder of their differences with Christian faith. When government appears to sponsor such religiously inspired views, we cannot say that the practice is " 'so separate and so indisputably marked off from the religious function,' . . . that [it] may fairly be viewed as reflect[ing] a neutral posture toward religious institutions." . . . To be so excluded on religious grounds by one's elected government is an insult and an injury that, until today, could not be countenanced by the Establishment Clause.

Second. . . . The Court apparently believes that once it finds that the designation of Christmas as a public holiday is constitutionally acceptable, it is then free to conclude that virtually every form of governmental association with the celebration of the holiday is also constitutional. The vice of this dangerously superficial argument is that it overlooks the fact that the Christmas holiday in our national culture contains both secular and sectarian elements. To say that government may recognize the holiday's traditional, secular elements of gift-giving, public festivities, and community spirit, does not mean that government may indiscriminately embrace the distinctively sectarian aspects of the holiday. Indeed, in its eagerness to approve the crèche, the Court has advanced a rationale so simplistic that it would appear to allow the Mayor of Pawtucket to participate in the celebration of a Christmas Mass, since this would be just another unobjectionable way for the city to "celebrate the holiday." As is demonstrated below, the Court's logic is fundamentally flawed both because it obscures the reason why public designation of Christmas Day as a holiday is constitutionally acceptable, and blurs the distinction between the secular aspects of Christmas and its distinctively religious character, as exemplified by the crèche. . . .

III.

The American historical experience concerning the public celebration of Christmas, if carefully examined, provides no support for the Court's decision. The opening sections of the Court's opinion, while seeking to rely on historical evidence, do no more than recognize the obvious: because of the strong religious currents that run through our history, an inflexible or absolutistic enforcement of the Establishment Clause would be both imprudent and impossible. This observation is at once uncontroversial and unilluminating. Simply enumerating the various ways in which the Federal Government has recognized the vital role religion plays in our society does nothing to help decide the question presented in *this* case.

Indeed, the Court's approach suggests a fundamental misapprehension of the proper uses of history in constitutional interpretation. Certainly, our decisions reflect the fact that an awareness of historical practice often can provide a useful guide in interpreting the abstract language of the Establishment Clause. . . . But historical acceptance of a particular practice alone is never sufficient to justify a challenged governmental action, since, as the Court has rightly observed, "no one acquires a vested or protected right in violation of the Constitution by long use, even when that span of time covers our entire national existence and indeed predates it." . . .

In McGowan, for instance, the Court carefully canvassed the entire history of Sunday Closing Laws from the colonial period up to modern times. On the basis of this analysis, we concluded that while such laws were rooted in religious motivations, the current purpose was to serve the wholly secular goal of providing a uniform day of rest for all citizens. Our inquiry in Walz was similarly confined to the special history of the practice under review. There the Court found a pattern of "undeviating acceptance" over the entire course of the Nation's history of according property-tax exemptions to religious organizations, a pattern which supported our finding that the practice did not violate the Religion Clauses. Finally, where direct inquiry into the Framer's intent reveals that the First Amendment was not understood to prohibit a particular practice, we have found such an understanding compelling. Thus, in Marsh v. Chambers, after marshaling the historical evidence which indicated that the First Congress had authorized the appointment of paid chaplains for its own proceedings only three days before it reached agreement on the final wording of the Bill of Rights, the Court concluded on the basis of this "unique history" that the modern-day practice of opening legislative sessions with prayer was constitutional.

Although invoking these decisions in support of its result, the Court wholly fails to discuss the history of the public celebration of Christmas or the use of publicly displayed nativity scenes. The Court, instead, simply asserts, without any historical analysis or support whatsoever, that the now familiar celebration of Christmas springs from an unbroken history of acknowledgement "by the people, by the Executive Branch, by the Congress, and the courts for two centuries. . . ." The Court's complete failure to offer any explanation of its assertion is perhaps understandable, however, because the historical record points in precisely the opposite direction. Two features of this history are worth noting. First, at the time of the adoption of the Constitution and the Bill of Rights, there was no settled pattern of celebrating Christmas, either as a purely religious holiday or as a public event. Second, the historical evidence, such as it is, offers no uniform pattern of widespread acceptance of the holiday and indeed suggests that the development of Christmas as a public holiday is a comparatively recent phenomenon.* . . .

Furthermore, unlike the religious tax exemptions upheld in Walz, the public display of nativity scenes as part of governmental celebrations of Christmas does not come to us supported by an unbroken history of widespread acceptance. It was not until 1836 that a State first granted legal recognition to Christmas as a public holiday. This was followed in the period between 1845 and 1865, by 28 jurisdictions which included Christmas Day as a legal holiday. Congress did not follow the States' lead until 1870 when it established December 25th, along with the Fourth of July, New Year's Day, and Thanksgiving, as a legal holiday in the District of Columbia. This pattern of legal recognition tells us only that public acceptance of the holiday was gradual and that the practice—in stark contrast to the record presented in either Walz or Marsh—did not take on the character of a widely recognized holiday until the middle of the nineteenth century. . . .

In sum, there is no evidence whatsoever that the Framers would have expressly approved a federal celebration of the Christmas holiday including public displays of a nativity scene; accordingly, the Court's repeated invocation of the decision in Marsh is not only baffling, it is utterly irrelevant. Nor is there any suggestion that publicly financed and supported displays of Christmas crèches are supported by a record of widespread, undeviating acceptance that extends throughout our history. Therefore, our prior decisions which relied upon concrete, specific historical evidence to support a particular practice simply have no bearing on the question presented in this case. Contrary to today's careless decision, those prior cases have all recognized that the "illumination" provided by history must always be focused on the particular practice at issue in a given case. Without that guiding principle and the intellectual discipline it imposes, the Court is at sea, free to select random elements of America's varied history solely to suit the views of five Members of this Court.

Justice **Blackmun,** with whom Justice **Stevens** joins, dissenting, said in part:

Not only does the Court's resolution of this controversy make light of our precedents, but also, ironically, the majority does an injustice to the crèche and the message it manifests. While certain persons, including

---

*The Court's insistence upon pursuing this vague historical analysis is especially baffling since even the petitioners and their supporting amici concede that no historical evidence equivalent to that relied upon in Marsh, McGowan, or Walz supports publicly sponsored Christmas displays. . . .

the Mayor of Pawtucket, undertook a crusade to "keep 'Christ' in Christmas," the Court today has declared that presence virtually irrelevant. The majority urges that the display, "with or without a crèche," "recall[s] the religious nature of the Holiday," and "engenders a friendly community spirit of good will in keeping with the season." Before the District Court, an expert witness for the city made a similar, though perhaps more candid, point,

stating that Pawtucket's display invites people "to participate in the Christmas spirit, brotherhood, peace, and let loose with their money." The crèche has been relegated to the role of a neutral harbinger of the holiday season, useful for commercial purposes, but devoid of any inherent meaning and incapable of enhancing the religious tenor of a display of which it is an integral part. The city has its victory—but it is a Pyrrhic one indeed.

11

Equal Protection of the Laws

HOW EQUAL IS EQUAL— THE TRADITIONAL TEST

GOESAERT v. CLEARY

335 U. S. 464; 69 S. Ct. 198; 93 L. Ed. 163 (1948)

At the time the Fourteenth Amendment was being considered, it was obvious that the Southern states, left to their own devices, would subject newly freed blacks to numerous and drastic discriminatory laws and regulations designed to prevent them from achieving anything like a status of legal equality with the white citizens of the Southern states. Accordingly the Fourteenth Amendment contains the explicit statement that no state shall "deny to any person within its jurisdiction the equal protection of the law," a clause much clearer in its meaning than its companion clauses in the amendment relating to "due process of law" and "the privileges and immunities of citizens of the United States." The equal protection clause does not mention race, but when it first came before the Supreme Court for interpretation in the Slaughter-House Cases, in 1873, Justice Miller, with contemporary history and conditions in mind, observed: "We doubt very much whether any action of a state not directed by way of discrimination against the negroes as a class, or on account of their race, will ever be held to come within the purview of this provision." Justice Miller's appraisal of current history may have been correct,

but his prophecy as to the limited use of the equal protection clause was very bad. Over the years equal protection of the law has come to afford broad and general relief against all forms of arbitrary classification and discrimination, regardless of the persons affected or the character of the rights involved. In fact, blacks would probably constitute a minority of those who have invoked the equal protection clause against discriminatory treatment.

The equal protection clause does not, of course, forbid all legal classification. Classification in the law is not only constitutional but desirable and necessary; it is almost impossible to conceive of a law which does not in some way employ it. But however necessary such classification and grouping is, it is a function which lends itself to abuse; and it is this abuse which the equal protection clause seeks to prevent.

When does classification become discrimination? How equal is equal? Over the years the Court's approach to these questions has evolved from a laissez-faire attitude that upheld almost all legislative classifications to a more searching review that barred almost all use of certain classifications. But like the natural evolution of any organism, the evolution of the equal protection clause has been a gradual one. Just as in nature where the older systems survive alongside more recent adaptations, so in equal protection the first test used by the Court to determine the legitimacy of legislative classification still exists to judge certain classifications while newer tests have evolved to judge others.

The first, or traditional test, is often referred to as the "rational basis" test. It requires that the government have a rational basis for treating people or activities differently [and] that that basis must be related to a constitutionally permissible objective. Thus it is rational to demand of automobile drivers that they be able to meet certain standards of vision, and the highway safety it promotes is a constitutional goal. On the other hand, if the government were seeking to oppress blacks it would be perfectly rational to forbid them to go to school. But the oppression of people is not a constitutionally permissible goal and the government's action would not survive even the traditional test. Nevertheless, "mere rationality," as the Court sometimes calls it, is an easy standard to meet because governments can usually find a plausible constitutional objective to put forth no matter how constitutionally questionable the real objective may be.

The first appearance of the rational basis test in *F. S. Royster Guano Co. v. Virginia* (1920) suggested a good deal more rigorous requirement of equality than in fact developed. "The classification must be reasonable, not arbitrary, and must rest upon some ground of difference having a fair and substantial relation to the object of the legislation, so that all persons similarly circumstanced shall be treated alike." The words "fair and substantial" defining the relationship between the classification and the government's objective suggest that the Court would examine the fit between means and ends with considerable care. This did not happen, and today when the Court invokes the rational basis test it first asks whether the government's objective is constitutional. If it is, it then asks merely if there is some connection between that objective and the classification that divides people or things into categories for differential treatment. The Court does not concern itself with how tight a fit exists between the means and the end; the merits of the classification, or whether there ought to be any classification at all, are simply not considered. The right to treat people differently is simply assumed.

The words "fair and substantial" and the ideas they suggest have long ago been dropped from the formula. For example, in *McGowan v. Maryland* (1961), the Court stated that under this test the equal protection clause is "offended only if the classification rests on grounds wholly irrelevant to the achievement of the State's objective," and in *Dandridge v. Williams* (1970) the Court said that "a State does not violate the Equal Protection Clause merely because the classifications are imperfect. If the classification has some 'reasonable basis,' it does not offend the Constitution simply because the classification 'is not made with mathematical nicety or because in practice it results in some inequality.'" Thus, where the law undertakes to classify on a numerical basis, as with regard to money earned, hours worked, workers employed, etc., the choice by the legislature of a maximum or minimum number will not be considered arbitrary merely because those who are just over the line do not differ much from those who are not. To apply the original Social Security Act solely to those who employed eight or more persons was held not to discriminate invalidly despite the fact that those employing seven persons were not significantly different.

In addition, the Court has repeatedly held that in enacting remedial legislation the state is under no constitutional obligation to cure all evils merely because it undertakes to cure some of them. Thus a law forbidding the sale of obscene pictures is not invalid because it does not also apply to obscene phonograph records. As Justice Holmes expressed it in *Keokee Consolidated Coke Co. v. Taylor* (1914), "it is established by repeated decisions that a statute aimed at what is deemed an evil, and hitting it presumably where experience shows it to be most felt, is not to be upset by thinking up and enumerating other instances to which it might have been applied equally well, so far as the Court can see." (It should be noted that the requirement of a fair and substantial relationship between the classification and the objective has resurfaced as part of the new "intermediate" test—proof that it had long ceased to be part of the traditional test.)

The rational basis test assumes that the legislature had a valid, nondiscriminatory reason for passing the law and anyone challenging its validity bears the burden of proving the legislature's irrationality. This has proved to be an almost impossible burden to meet. Currently the rational basis test is most often used in challenges to laws regulating economic activities, but whenever it is invoked the result is almost certain to be a holding that the law is constitutional. In the past the rational basis test was used to uphold many laws that would be struck down today because a more demanding test would be used. This is particularly true of laws that discriminate on the basis of sex, such as the law at issue in the case below. See *Mississippi v. Hogan* (1983).

In *Goesaert v. Cleary* a Michigan law prohibited women from working as bartenders, with an exception for women who were married to, or the daughters of, men who owned bars. The law was challenged as unconstitutional under the Equal Protection Clause. Note the difference in the Court's justification of Michigan's right to prohibit all women to tend bar and its right to draw the distinction used here.

Mr. Justice **Frankfurter** delivered the opinion of the court:

. . . Beguiling as the subject is, it need not detain us long. To ask whether or not the Equal Protection of the Laws Clause of the Fourteenth Amendment barred Michigan from making the classification the State has made between wives and daughters of owners of liquor places and wives and daughters of non-owners, is one of those rare instances where to state the question is in effect to answer it.

We are, to be sure, dealing with a historic calling. We meet the ale-wife sprightly and ribald, in Shakespeare, but centuries before him she played a role in the social life of England. . . . The Fourteenth Amendment did not tear history up by the roots, and the regulation of the liquor traffic is one of the oldest and most untrammeled of legislative powers. Michigan could, beyond question, forbid all women from working behind a bar. This is so despite the vast changes in the social and legal position of women. The fact that women may now have achieved the virtues that men have long claimed as their prerogatives and now indulge in vices that men have long practiced, does not preclude the States from drawing a sharp line between the sexes, certainly in such matters as the regulation of the liquor traffic. . . . The Constitution does not require legislatures to reflect sociological insight, or shifting social standards, any more than it requires them to keep abreast of the latest scientific standards.

While Michigan may deny to all women opportunities for bartending, Michigan cannot play favorites among women without rhyme or reason. The Constitution in enjoining the equal protection of the laws upon States precludes irrational discrimination as between persons or groups of persons in the incidence of a law. But the Constitution does not require situations "which are different in fact or opinion to be treated in law as though they were the same." . . . Since bartending by women may, in the allowable legislative judgment, give rise to moral and social problems against which it may devise preventive measures, the legislature need not go to the full length of prohibition if it believes that as to a defined group of females other factors are operating which either eliminate or reduce the moral and social problems otherwise calling for prohibition. Michigan evidently believes that the oversight assured through ownership of a bar by a barmaid's husband or father minimizes hazards that may confront a barmaid without such protecting oversight. This Court is certainly not in a position to gainsay such a belief by the Michigan legislature. If it is entertainable, as we think it is, Michigan has not violated its duty to afford equal protection of its laws. We cannot cross-examine either actually or argumentatively the mind of Michigan legislators nor question their motives. Since the line they have drawn is not without a basis in reason, we cannot give ear to the suggestion that the real impulse behind this legislation was an unchivalrous desire of male bartenders to try to monopolize the calling. . . .

Nor is it unconstitutional for Michigan to withdraw from women the occupation of bartending because it allows women to serve as waitresses where liquor is dispensed. The District Court has sufficiently indicated the reasons that may have influenced the legislature in allowing women to be waitresses in a liquor establishment over which a man's ownership provides control. Nothing need be added to what was said below as to the other grounds on which the Michigan law was assailed.

Judgment affirmed.

Mr. Justice **Rutledge,** with whom Mr. Justice **Douglas** and Mr. Justice **Murphy** join, dissenting.

While the equal protection clause does not require a legislature to achieve "abstract symmetry" or to classify with "mathematical nicety," that clause does require lawmakers to refrain from invidious distinctions of the sort drawn by the statute challenged in this case.

The statute arbitrarily discriminates between male and female owners of liquor establishments. A male owner, although he himself is always absent from his bar, may employ his wife and daughter as barmaids. A female owner may neither work as a barmaid herself nor employ her daughter in that position, even if a man is always present in the establishment to keep order. This inevitable result of the classification belies the assumption that the statute was motivated by a legislative solicitude for the moral well-being of women who, but for the law, would be employed as barmaids. Since there could be no other conceivable justification for such discrimination against women owners of liquor establishments, the statute should be held invalid as a denial of equal protection.

STRICT SCRUTINY

KOREMATSU v. UNITED STATES

323 U. S. 214; 65 S. Ct. 193; 89 L. Ed. 194 (1944)

While the Fourteenth Amendment does not mention race, the Court has always recognized that racial discrimination against blacks was the primary concern of its framers and has therefore examined racial classifications with particular care. In 1880 in Strauder v. West Virginia the Court held that a black man had a right to be tried by a jury on which blacks had been eligible to sit. Laws that discriminate against other racial minorities were similarly treated. In Yick Wo v. Hopkins (1886) the Court struck down a San Francisco ordinance that prohibited anyone from operating a laundry in a wooden building without a permit issued by the Board of Supervisors. The Court found that the law as administered discriminated against Chinese applicants; non-Chinese applicants were routinely granted permits while almost all Chinese applications were denied.

As a greater variety of laws began to be challenged under the equal protection clause and the rational basis test began to take on its present form, it became clear that that test was an insufficient guard against racial discrimination. Allowing a state to discriminate on the basis of race any time it could show a rational relationship to a legitimate governmental purpose would provide too little protection for racial minorities. There was little question that states were being held to a higher standard when they attempted to treat people differently based on their race; decisions as early as Yick Wo in (1886) demonstrated that. The higher standard was, however, not spelled out until the decision in the present case in which the Court identifies race as a "suspect" classification for the first time. Justice Black, writing for the majority, states that because it is a suspect classification it must be subjected to the "most rigid scrutiny." Herein lies the genesis of what is usually called the "strict scrutiny" test.

Unlike the rational basis test, the strict scrutiny test assumes that the law is unconstitutional when it includes a suspect classification. Those defending the law bear the burden of proving that the government's objec-

tives are not only legitimate but are compelling. Even more difficult, the law's defenders must show that the suspect classification is necessary to accomplish the government's purpose—that it cannot be accomplished in any other way. The fit between the suspect classification and the compelling government objective must be nearly perfect.

The strict scrutiny test is used whenever a law employs a suspect classification. In addition to race, the prime examples of this are religion and national origin. A classification is more apt to be treated as suspect if its characteristics are immutable, so that a person born into it can never escape it. Generally, a suspect classification is also one that has been used historically to oppress a particular group, and one that discriminates against a "discrete and insular" minority—a phrase taken from Justice Stone's now famous footnote 4 in United States v. Carolene Products Co. (1938) in which he suggested that prejudice against such groups might tend "seriously to curtail the operation of those political processes ordinarily to be relied upon to protect minorities, and which may call for a correspondingly more searching judicial inquiry." See University of California v. Bakke (1978).

The rational basis test and the strict scrutiny test are functional opposites: Laws usually pass the rational basis test while they almost always fail the strict scrutiny test. It is therefore ironic that the strict scrutiny test was first articulated in one of the only cases to uphold the use of a racial classification.

The present case involved perhaps the most alarming use of executive military authority in our nation's history. Following the bombing of Pearl Harbor in December, 1941, the anti-Japanese sentiment on the West Coast brought the residents of that area to a state of near hysteria; and in February, 1942, President Roosevelt issued an executive order authorizing the creation of military areas from which any or all persons might be excluded as the military authorities might decide. On March 2, the entire West Coast to a depth of about forty miles was designated by the commanding general as Military Area No. 1, and he thereupon proclaimed a curfew in that area for all persons of Japanese ancestry. Later he ordered the compulsory evacuation from the area of all persons of Japanese ancestry, and by the middle of the summer most of these people had been moved inland to "war relocation centers," the American equivalent of concentration camps. Congress subsequently made it a crime to violate these military orders. Of the 112,000 persons of Japanese ancestry involved, about seventy thousand were native-born American citizens, none of whom had been specifically accused of disloyalty. Three cases were brought to the Supreme Court challenging the right of the government to override in this manner the customary civil rights of these citizens. In Hirabayashi v. United States (1943) the Court upheld the curfew regulations as a valid military measure to prevent espionage and sabotage. "Whatever views we may entertain regarding the loyalty to this country of the citizens of Japanese ancestry, we cannot reject as unfounded the judgment of the military authorities and of Congress that there were disloyal members of that population, whose

number and strength could not be precisely and quickly ascertained. We cannot say that the war-making branches of the Government did not have ground for believing that in a critical hour such persons could not readily be isolated and separately dealt with, and constituted a menace to the national defense and safety. . . ." While emphasizing that distinctions based on ancestry were "by their very nature odious to a free people" the Court nonetheless felt "that in time of war residents having ethnic affiliations with an invading enemy may be a greater source of danger than those of a different ancestry."

While the Court, in the present case, held valid the discriminatory mass evacuation of all persons of Japanese descent, it also held in Ex parte Endo (1944), that an American citizen of Japanese ancestry whose loyalty to this country had been established could not constitutionally be held in a war relocation center but must be unconditionally released. The government had allowed persons to leave the relocation centers under conditions and restrictions which aimed to guarantee that there should not be "a dangerously disorderly migration of unwanted people to unprepared communities." Permission to leave was granted only if the applicant had the assurance of a job and a place to live, and wanted to go to a place "approved" by the War Relocation Authority. The Court held that the sole purpose of the evacuation and detention program was to protect the war effort against sabotage and espionage. "A person who is concededly loyal presents no problem of espionage or sabotage . . . He who is loyal is by definition not a spy or a saboteur." It therefore follows that the authority to detain a citizen of Japanese ancestry ends when loyalty is established. To hold otherwise would be to justify a person's detention not on grounds of military necessity but purely on grounds of race. Although no case reached the Court squarely challenging the right of the government to incarcerate citizens of Japanese ancestry pending a determination of their loyalty, the tenor of the opinions leaves little doubt that such action would have been sustained. The present case involved only the right of the military to evacuate such persons from the West Coast.

In the years following World War II evidence accumulated suggesting that the demand for the evacuation was either the result of racism, encouraged by the local press, or the result of the deliberate efforts of persons who stood to gain financially if the Japanese had to abandon their property on short notice. A congressional commission set up in 1980 reported after a two-year study that the only responsible intelligence report, made by Naval Intelligence, rejected outright the justifications for incarceration advanced by the military. The existence of these reports was deliberately withheld by the Justice Department when it argued both Hirabayashi and Korematsu. See Hohri v. United States, 782 F. 2d 227 (1986). While Congress ultimately authorized a payment as restitution to each Japanese-American who was held in a relocation center, a number of damage suits were later filed. The government, while admitting in oral argument withholding evidence in the cases, argued that the statute of limitations against further suits should

*have started running with the decision in Korematsu. See
United States v. Hohri (1987).*

*An unusual tourist attraction is a bronze plaque,
installed by the government of the state on the main entry
gate of the Manzanar camp located in the desert near
Bishop, California. The text is as follows:*

* MANZANAR *

IN THE EARLY PART OF WORLD WAR II 110,000 PERSONS
OF JAPANESE ANCESTRY WERE INTERNED IN RELOCATION
CENTERS BY EXECUTIVE ORDER No. 9066, ISSUED ON
FEBRUARY 19, 1942.

MANZANAR, THE FIRST OF TEN SUCH CONCENTRATION
CAMPS, WAS BOUNDED BY BARBED WIRE AND GUARD
TOWERS, CONFINING 10,000 PERSONS, THE MAJORITY
BEING AMERICAN CITIZENS.

MAY THE INJUSTICE AND HUMILIATION SUFFERED HERE
AS A RESULT OF HYSTERIA, RACISM AND ECONOMIC
EXPLOITATION NEVER EMERGE AGAIN.

CALIFORNIA REGISTERED HISTORICAL LAND-
MARK NO. 850

Mr. Justice **Black** delivered the opinion of the Court,
saying in part:

The petitioner, an American citizen of Japanese
descent, was convicted in a federal district court for remaining in San Leandro, California, a "Military Area,"
contrary to Civilian Exclusion Order No. 34 of the Commanding General of the Western Command, U. S.
Army, which directed that after May 9, 1942, all persons
of Japanese ancestry should be excluded from that area.
No question was raised as to petitioner's loyalty to the
United States. The Circuit Court of Appeals affirmed,
and the importance of the constitutional question involved caused us to grant certiorari.

It should be noted, to begin with, that all legal restrictions which curtail the civil rights of a single racial
group are immediately suspect. That is not to say that all
such restrictions are unconstitutional. It is to say that
courts must subject them to the most rigid scrutiny.
Pressing public necessity may sometimes justify the existence of such restrictions; racial antagonism never can.

In the instant case prosecution of the petitioner was
begun by information charging violation of an Act of
Congress, of March 21, 1942, which provides that ". . .
whoever shall enter, remain in, leave, or commit any act
in any military area or military zone prescribed, under
the authority of an Executive order of the President, by
the Secretary of War, or by any military commander designated by the Secretary of War, contrary to the restrictions applicable to any such area or zone or contrary to
the order of the Secretary of War or any such military
commander, shall, if it appears that he knew or should
have known of the existence and extent of the restrictions
or order and that his act was in violation thereof, be
guilty of a misdemeanor and upon conviction shall be liable to a fine of not to exceed $5,000 or to imprisonment
for not more than one year, or both, for each offense."

Exclusion Order No. 34, which the petitioner
knowingly and admittedly violated was one of a number
of military orders and proclamations, all of which were
substantially based upon Executive Order No. 9066.
That order, issued after we were at war with Japan, declared that "the successful prosecution of the war requires every possible protection against espionage and
against sabotage to national-defense material, national-
defense premises, and national-defense utilities. . . ."

One of the series of orders and proclamations, a
curfew order, which like the exclusion order here was
promulgated pursuant to Executive Order 9066, subjected all persons of Japanese ancestry in prescribed
West Coast military areas to remain in their residences
from 8 p.m. to 6 a.m. As is the case with the exclusion
order here, that prior curfew order was designed as a
"protection against espionage and against sabotage." In
Kiyoshi Hirabayashi v. United States [1943], we sustained a conviction obtained for violation of the curfew
order. The Hirabayashi conviction and this one thus rest
on the same 1942 Congressional Act and the same basic
executive and military orders, all of which orders were
aimed at the twin dangers of espionage and sabotage.

The 1942 Act was attacked in the Hirabayashi case
as an unconstitutional delegation of power; it was contended that the curfew order and other orders on which it
rested were beyond the war powers of the Congress, the
military authorities and of the President, as Commander
in Chief of the Army; and finally that to apply the order
against none but citizens of Japanese ancestry amounted
to a constitutionally prohibited discrimination solely on
account of race. To these questions, we gave the serious
consideration which their importance justified. We
upheld the curfew order as an exercise of the power of
the government to take steps necessary to prevent espionage and sabotage in an area threatened by Japanese attack.

In the light of the principles we announced in the
Hirabayashi case, we are unable to conclude that it was
beyond the war power of Congress and the Executive to
exclude those of Japanese ancestry from the West Coast
war area at the time they did. True, exclusion from the
area in which one's home is located is a far greater deprivation than constant confinement to the home from 8
p.m. to 6 a.m. Nothing short of apprehension by the
proper military authorities of the gravest imminent danger to the public safety can constitutionally justify either.
But exclusion from a threatened area, no less than curfew, has a definite and close relationship to the prevention of espionage and sabotage. The military authorities,
charged with the primary responsibility of defending our
shores, concluded that curfew provided inadequate protection and ordered exclusion. They did so, as pointed
out in our Hirabayashi opinion, in accordance with Congressional authority to the military to say who should,
and who should not, remain in the threatened areas.

In this case the petitioner challenges the assumptions upon which we rested our conclusions in the Hirabayashi case. He also urges that by May 1942, when Or-

der No. 34 was promulgated, all danger of Japanese invasion of the West Coast had disappeared. After careful consideration of these contentions we are compelled to reject them.

Here, as in the Hirabayashi case, ". . . we cannot reject as unfounded the judgment of the military authorities and of Congress that there were disloyal members of that population, whose number and strength could not be precisely and quickly ascertained. We cannot say that the war-making branches of the Government did not have ground for believing that in a critical hour such persons could not readily be isolated and separately dealt with, and constituted a menace to the national defense and safety, which demanded that prompt and adequate measures be taken to guard against it.''

Like curfew, exclusion of those of Japanese origin was deemed necessary because of the presence of an unascertained number of disloyal members of the group, most of whom we have no doubt were loyal to this country. It was because we could not reject the finding of the military authorities that it was impossible to bring about an immediate segregation of the disloyal from the loyal that we sustained the validity of the curfew order as applying to the whole group. In the instant case, temporary exclusion of the entire group was rested by the military on the same ground. The judgment that exclusion of the whole group was for the same reason a military imperative answers the contention that the exclusion was in the nature of group punishment based on antagonism to those of Japanese origin. That there were members of the group who retained loyalties to Japan has been confirmed by investigations made subsequent to the exclusion. Approximately five thousand American citizens of Japanese ancestry refused to swear unqualified allegiance to the United States and to renounce allegiance to the Japanese Emperor, and several thousand evacuees requested repatriation to Japan.

We uphold the exclusion order as of the time it was made and when the petitioner violated it. . . . In doing so, we are not unmindful of the hardships imposed by it upon a large group of American citizens. . . . But hardships are part of war, and war is an aggregation of hardships. All citizens alike, both in and out of uniform, feel the impact of war in greater or lesser measure. Citizenship has its responsibilities as well as its privileges, and in time of war the burden is always heavier. Compulsory exclusion of large groups of citizens from their homes, except under circumstances of direst emergency and peril, is inconsistent with our basic governmental institution. But when under conditions of modern warfare our shores are threatened by hostile forces, the power to protect must be commensurate with the threatened danger. . . .

[The Court dealt at some length with a technical complication which arose in the case. On May 30, the date on which Korematsu was charged with remaining unlawfully in the prohibited area, there were two conflicting military orders outstanding, one forbidding him to remain in the area, the other forbidding him to leave but ordering him to report to an assembly center. Thus, he alleged, he was punished for doing what it was made a crime to fail to do. The Court held the orders not to be contradictory, since the requirement to report to the assembly center was merely a step in an orderly program of compulsory evacuation from the area.]

It is said that we are dealing here with the case of imprisonment of a citizen in a concentration camp solely because of his ancestry, without evidence or inquiry concerning his loyalty and good disposition towards the United States. Our task would be simple, our duty clear, were this a case involving the imprisonment of a loyal citizen in a concentration camp because of racial prejudice. Regardless of the true nature of the assembly and relocation centers—and we deem it unjustifiable to call them concentration camps with all the ugly connotations that term implies—we are dealing specifically with nothing but an exclusion order. To cast this case into outlines of racial prejudice, without reference to the real military dangers which were presented, merely confuses the issue. Korematsu was not excluded from the Military Area because of hostility to him or his race. He was excluded because we are at war with the Japanese Empire, because the properly constituted military authorities feared an invasion of our West Coast and felt constrained to take proper security measures, because they decided that the military urgency of the situation demanded that all citizens of Japanese ancestry be segregated from the West Coast temporarily, and finally, because Congress, reposing its confidence in this time of war in our military leaders—as inevitably it must—determined that they should have the power to do just this. There was evidence of disloyalty on the part of some, the military authorities considered that the need for action was great, and time was short. We cannot—by availing ourselves of the calm perspective of hindsight—now say that at that time these actions were unjustified.

Affirmed.

Mr. Justice **Frankfurter** wrote a concurring opinion.

Mr. Justice **Roberts,** dissenting, said in part:

I dissent, because I think the indisputable facts exhibit a clear violation of Constitutional rights.

This is not a case of keeping people off the streets at night as was Hirabayashi v. United States (1943), nor a case of temporary exclusion of a citizen from an area for his own safety or that of the community, nor a case of offering him an opportunity to go temporarily out of an area where his presence might cause danger to himself or to his fellows. On the contrary, it is the case of convicting a citizen as a punishment for not submitting to imprisonment in a concentration camp, based on his ancestry, and solely because of his ancestry, without evidence or inquiry concerning his loyalty and good disposition towards the United States. If this be a correct statement of the facts disclosed by this record, and facts of which we take judicial notice, I need hardly labor the conclusion that constitutional rights have been violated.

Mr. Justice **Murphy,** dissenting, said in part:

This exclusion of "all persons of Japanese ancestry, both alien and non-alien," from the Pacific Coast area on a plea of military necessity in the absence of martial law ought not to be approved. Such exclusion goes over "the very brink of constitutional power" and falls into the ugly abyss of racism.

In dealing with matters relating to the prosecution and progress of a war, we must accord great respect and consideration to the judgments of the military authorities who are on the scene and who have full knowledge of the military facts. The scope of their discretion must, as a matter of necessity and common sense, be wide. And their judgments ought not to be overruled lightly by those whose training and duties ill-equip them to deal intelligently with matters so vital to the physical security of the nation.

At the same time, however, it is essential that there be definite limits to military discretion especially where martial law has not been declared. Individuals must not be left impoverished of their constitutional rights on a plea of military necessity that has neither substance nor support. Thus, like other claims conflicting with the asserted constitutional rights of the individual, the military claim must subject itself to the judicial process of having its reasonableness determined and its conflicts with other interests reconciled. . . .

. . . Being an obvious racial discrimination, the order deprives all those within its scope of the equal protection of the laws as guaranteed by the Fifth Amendment. It further deprives these individuals of their constitutional rights to live and work where they will, to establish a home where they choose and to move about freely. In excommunicating them without benefit of hearings, this order also deprives them of all their constitutional rights to procedural due process. Yet no reasonable relation to an "immediate, imminent, and impending" public danger is evident to support this racial restriction which is one of the most sweeping and complete deprivations of constitutional rights in the history of this nation in the absence of martial law.

It must be conceded that the military and naval situation in the spring of 1942 was such as to generate a very real fear of invasion of the Pacific Coast, accompanied by fears of sabotage and espionage in that area. The military command was therefore justified in adopting all reasonable means necessary to combat these dangers. In adjudging the military action taken in light of the then apparent dangers, we must not erect too high or too meticulous standards; it is necessary only that the action have some reasonable relation to the removal of the dangers of invasion, sabotage and espionage. But the exclusion, either temporarily or permanently, of all persons with Japanese blood in their veins has no such reasonable relation. And that relation is lacking because the exclusion order necessarily must rely for its reasonableness upon the assumption that *all* persons of Japanese ancestry may have a dangerous tendency to commit sabotage and espionage and to aid our Japanese enemy in other ways. It is difficult to believe that reason, logic or experience could be marshalled in support of such an assumption.

That this forced exclusion was the result in good measure of this erroneous assumption of racial guilt rather than bona fide military necessity is evidenced by the Commanding General's Final Report on the evacuation from the Pacific Coast area. In it he refers to all individuals of Japanese descent as "subversive," as belonging to "an enemy race" whose "racial strains are undiluted," and as constituting "over 112,000 potential enemies . . . at large today" along the Pacific Coast. In support of this blanket condemnation of all persons of Japanese descent, however, no reliable evidence is cited to show that such individuals were generally disloyal, or had generally so conducted themselves in this area as to constitute a special menace to defense installations or war industries, or had otherwise by their behavior furnished reasonable ground for their exclusion as a group.

Justification for the exclusion is sought, instead, mainly upon questionable racial and sociological grounds not ordinarily within the realm of expert military judgment. . . . [Justice Murphy here reviews and refutes the sociological evidence.]

The main reasons relied upon by those responsible for the forced evacuation, therefore, do not prove a reasonable relation between the group characteristics of Japanese Americans and the dangers of invasion, sabotage and espionage. The reasons appear, instead, to be largely an accumulation of much of the misinformation, half-truths and insinuations that for years have been directed against Japanese Americans by people with racial and economic prejudices—the same people who have been among the foremost advocates of the evacuation. A military judgment based upon such racial and sociological considerations is not entitled to the great weight ordinarily given the judgments based upon strictly military considerations. Especially is this so when every charge relative to race, religion, culture, geographical location, and legal and economic status has been substantially discredited by independent studies made by experts in these matters.

The military necessity which is essential to the validity of the evacuation order thus resolves itself into a few intimations that certain individuals actively aided the enemy, from which it is inferred that the entire group of Japanese Americans could not be trusted to be or remain loyal to the United States. No one denies, of course, that there were some disloyal persons of Japanese descent on the Pacific Coast who did all in their power to aid their ancestral land. Similar disloyal activities have been engaged in by many persons of German, Italian and even more pioneer stock in our country. But to infer that examples of individual disloyalty prove group disloyalty and justify discriminatory action against the entire group is to deny that under our system of law individual guilt is the sole basis for deprivation of rights. Moreover, this inference, which is at the very heart of the evacuation orders, has been used in support of the abhorrent and despicable treatment of minority groups by the dictatorial tyrannies which this nation is now pledged to destroy. To give constitutional sanction to that inference in this case, however well-intentioned may have been the military command on the Pacific Coast, is to adopt one of the cruelest of the rationales used by our enemies to destroy the dignity of the individual and to encourage and open the door to discriminatory actions against other minority groups in the passions of tomorrow.

No adequate reason is given for the failure to treat these Japanese Americans on an individual basis by holding investigations and hearings to separate the loyal from the disloyal, as was done in the case of persons of German and Italian ancestry. . . . It is asserted merely that the loyalties of this group "were unknown and time was of the essence." Yet nearly four months elapsed after Pearl Harbor before the first exclusion order was issued; nearly eight months went by until the last order was issued; and the last of these "subversive" persons was not actually removed until almost eleven months had elapsed. Leisure and deliberation seem to have been more of the essence than speed. And the fact that conditions were not such as to warrant a declaration of martial law adds strength to the belief that the factors of time and military necessity were not as urgent as they have been represented to be.

Mr. Justice **Jackson,** dissenting, said in part:

It would be impracticable and dangerous idealism to expect or insist that each specific military command in an area of probable operations will conform to conventional tests of constitutionality. When an area is so beset that it must be put under military control at all, the paramount consideration is that its measures be successful, rather than legal. The armed services must protect a society, not merely its Constitution. . . .

But if we cannot confine military expedients by the Constitution, neither would I distort the Constitution to approve all that the military may deem expedient. That is what the Court appears to be doing, whether consciously or not. I cannot say, from any evidence before me, that the orders of General DeWitt were not reasonably expedient military precautions, nor could I say that they were. But even if they were permissible military procedures, I deny that it follows that they are constitutional. If, as the Court holds, it does follow, then we may as well say that any military order will be constitutional and have done with it. . . .

Much is said of the danger to liberty from the Army program for deporting and detaining these citizens of Japanese extraction. But a judicial construction of the due process clause that will sustain this order is a far more subtle blow to liberty than the promulgation of the order itself. A military order, however unconstitutional, is not apt to last longer than the military emergency. Even during that period a succeeding commander may revoke it all. But once a judicial opinion rationalizes such an order to show that it conforms to the Constitution, or rather rationalizes the Constitution to show that the Constitution sanctions such an order, the Court for all time has validated the principle of racial discrimination in criminal procedure and of transplanting American citizens. The principle then lies about like a loaded weapon ready for the hand of any authority that can bring forward a plausible claim of an urgent need. . . .

My duties as a justice as I see them do not require me to make a military judgment as to whether General DeWitt's evacuation and detention program was a reasonable military necessity. I do not suggest that the courts should have attempted to interfere with the Army in carrying out its task. But I do not think they may be asked to execute a military expedient that has no place in law under the Constitution. I would reverse the judgment and discharge the prisoner.

KRAMER v. UNION FREE SCHOOL DIST.

393 U. S. 818; 89 S. Ct. 1886; 23 L. Ed. 2d 583
(1969)

The strict scrutiny test developed in Korematsu to deal with suspect classification has been applied to another category of cases brought under the equal protection clause. This second category includes cases challenging laws that affect "fundamental rights or interests." There are at least two different concepts underlying the fundamental interest branch of strict scrutiny. The first involves rights, such as the right to appeal a conviction, that are so basic that even though there is no absolute right to them, once a state chooses to grant them it must allocate them equally—unless the state can show a compelling state interest for doing otherwise. Administrative convenience or added expense to the state do not rank as "compelling" in this context.

The second concept is that there are some fundamental rights implicit in the Constitution, such as the right to travel interstate, the exercise of which cannot be made the basis of differential treatment without a compelling governmental interest that cannot be satisfied in some other way. While this latter concept has been attacked on the ground that it should not require an equal protection clause to protect a right already guaranteed in the Constitution, it is apparent that equal protection does serve to prevent actions which may discourage *the exercise of a such a right but which do not rise to the level of a violation of the right itself. Thus, while it is clear a state could not directly forbid a person to travel interstate, only the equal protection clause might prevent laws against limiting access to welfare benefits or jobs which would have a discouraging effect on such travel. Criticism of the use of the strict scrutiny test in this area as judicial law-making has perhaps been influential in keeping the list a short one: voting, access to the judicial process and interstate travel.*

Some of the criticism of the fundamental interest branch of the strict scrutiny test may be due to the nature of the test itself. Whether it is applied to suspect classifications or fundamental interests, the strict scrutiny test is an exception to the rule of constitutional interpretation that presumes that laws and acts of government are constitutional, and in this sense the rational basis test reflects the Court's traditional approach. From earliest times the Court has regularly expressed the greatest respect for the constitutional interpretations necessarily made by Congress in the passing of legislation. While making clear that it is "the duty of the Court to say what the law is," it recognizes Congress as a coequal branch whose members "take the same oath as we do to uphold the Constitution.'' While the Court is probably right in attributing considered wisdom to a coequal branch, it is enlightening to consider that in 1981 Senator Moynihan of New York felt called upon to introduce a resolution prohibiting the Senate from voting on any bill unless a specified number of Senators could attest to the fact that they had read it.

The difference between the strict scrutiny test and the rational basis test is no more strikingly illustrated than by contrasting the Kramer case, printed below, with McDonald v. Board of Election (1969). McDonald was an inmate of the Cook County jail who was being held for trial without bail on a charge of murder. At election time he made timely request for an absentee ballot, backed by an affidavit from the warden that he was unable to attend the polls. Such ballots were available to those who were medically incapacitated, absent from the county, attending a religious holiday that precluded their voting, or who were serving as poll watchers in a precinct other than their own. Since McDonald did not fit any of these categories, the absentee ballot was refused.

McDonald argued that, since voting rights were involved, the burden lay on the state to produce a ''compelling state interest'' to justify its denial of the ballot. The Supreme Court rejected his argument. ''Such an exacting approach is not necessary here, however, for two readily apparent reasons. First, the distinctions made by Illinois' absentee provisions are not drawn on the basis of wealth or race [classifications which are highly suspect]. Secondly, there is nothing in the record to indicate that the Illinois statutory scheme has an impact on appellants' ability to exercise the fundamental right to vote. It is thus not the right to vote that is at stake here but a claimed right to receive absentee ballots. Despite appellants' claim to the contrary, the absentee statutes, which are designed to make voting more available to some groups who cannot easily get to the polls, do not themselves deny appellants the exercise of the franchise; nor, indeed, does Illinois' Election Code so operate as a whole, for the State's statutes specifically disenfranchise only those who have been convicted and sentenced, and not those similarly situated to appellants. Faced as we are with a constitutional question, we cannot lightly assume, with nothing in the record to support such an assumption, that Illinois has in fact precluded appellants from voting. We are then left with the more traditional standards for evaluating appellant's equal protection claims.'' Under these traditional standards the Court found that Illinois' absentee ballot law was among the most liberal, and the state was not required to solve all problems because it had attempted to solve some of them, so long as the distinctions were not arbitrary— which these were not.

Mr. Chief Justice **Warren** delivered the opinion of the Court, saying in part:

In this case we are called on to determine whether § 2012 of the New York Education Law is constitutional. The legislation provides that in certain New York school districts residents who are otherwise eligible to vote in state and federal elections may vote in the school district election only if they (1) own (or lease) taxable real property within the district, or (2) are parents (or have custody of) children enrolled in the local public schools. Appellant, a bachelor who neither owns nor leases taxable real property, filed suit in federal court claiming that § 2012 denied him equal protection of the law in violation of the Fourteenth Amendment. With one judge dissenting, a three-judge District Court dismissed appellant's complaint. Finding that § 2012 does violate the Equal Protection Clause of the Fourteenth Amendment, we reverse.

I.

New York law provides basically three methods of school board selection. In some large city districts, the school board is appointed by the mayor or city council. . . . On the other hand, in some cities, primarily those with less than 125,000 residents, the school board is elected at general or municipal elections in which all qualified city voters may participate. . . . Finally, in other districts such as the one involved in this case, which are primarily rural and suburban, the school board is elected at an annual meeting of qualified school district voters.

The challenged statute is applicable only in districts which hold annual meetings. To be eligible to vote at an annual district meeting, an otherwise qualified district resident must either (1) be the owner or lessee of taxable real property located in the district, (2) be the spouse of one who owns or leases qualifying property, or (3) be the parent or guardian of a child enrolled for a specified time during the preceding year in a local district school.

Although the New York State Department of Education has substantial responsibility for education in the State, the local school districts maintain significant control over the administration of local school district affairs. Generally, the board of education has the basic responsibility for local school operation, including prescribing the courses of study, determining the textbooks to be used, and even altering and equipping a former schoolhouse for use as a public library. . . . Additionally, in districts selecting members of the board of education at annual meetings, the local voters also pass directly on other district matters. For example, they must approve the school budget submitted by the school board. . . . Moreover, once the budget is approved, the governing body of the villages within the school district must raise the money which has been declared ''necessary for teachers' salaries and the ordinary contingent expenses [of the schools].'' . . . The voters also may ''authorize such acts and vote such taxes as they shall deem expedient . . . for . . . equipping for library use any former schoolhouse, . . . [and] for the purchase of land and buildings for agricultural, athletic, playground or social center purposes. . . .'' . . .

Appellant is a 31-year-old college-educated stockbroker who lives in his parents' home in the Union Free

School District No. 15, a district to which § 2012 applies. He is a citizen of the United States and has voted in federal and state elections since 1959. However, since he has no children and neither owns nor leases taxable real property, appellant's attempts to register for and vote in the local school district elections have been unsuccessful. After the school district rejected his 1965 application, appellant instituted the present class action challenging the constitutionality of the voter eligibility requirements.

II.

At the outset, it is important to note what is *not* at issue in this case. The requirements of § 2012 that school district voters must (1) be citizens of the United States, (2) be bona fide residents of the school district, and (3) be at least 21 years of age are not challenged. Appellant agrees that the States have the power to impose reasonable citizenship, age and residency requirements on the availability of the ballot. . . . The sole issue in this case is whether the *additional* requirements of § 2012—requirements which prohibit some district residents who are otherwise qualified by age and citizenship from participating in district meetings and school board elections—violate the Fourteenth Amendment's command that no State shall deny persons equal protection of the laws.

"In determining whether or not a state law violates the Equal Protection Clause, we must consider the facts and circumstances of the law, the interests which the State claims to be protecting, and the interests of those who are disadvantaged by the classification." Williams v. Rhodes (1968). And, in this case, we must give the statute a close and exacting examination. "[S]ince the right to exercise the franchise in a free and unimpaired manner is preservative of other basic civil and political rights, any alleged infringement of the right of citizens to vote must be carefully and meticulously scrutinized." Reynolds v. Sims (1964). . . . This careful examination is necessary because statutes distributing the franchise constitute the foundation of our representative society. Any unjustified discrimination in determining who may participate in political affairs or in the selection of public officials undermines the legitimacy of representative government.

Thus, state apportionment statutes, which may *dilute* the effectiveness of some citizens' votes, receive close scrutiny from this Court. Reynolds v. Sims. . . . No less rigid an examination is applicable to statutes *denying* the franchise to citizens who are otherwise qualified by residence and age.* Statutes granting the franchise to residents on a selective basis always pose the danger of denying some citizens any effective voice in the governmental affairs which substantially affect their lives. Therefore, if a challenged state statute grants the right to vote to some bona fide residents of requisite age and citizenship and denies the franchise to others, the Court must determine whether the exclusions are necessary to promote a compelling state interest. . . .

And, for these reasons, the deference usually given to the judgment of legislators does not extend to decisions concerning which resident citizens may participate in the election of legislators and other public officials. Those decisions must be carefully scrutinized by the Court to determine whether each resident citizen has, as far as is possible, an equal voice in the selections. Accordingly, when we are reviewing statutes which deny some residents the right to vote, the general presumption of constitutionality afforded state statutes and the traditional approval given state classifications if the Court can conceive of a "rational basis" for the distinctions made are not applicable. . . . The presumption of constitutionality and the approval given "rational" classifications in other types of enactments† are based on an assumption that the institutions of state government are structured so as to represent fairly all the people. However, when the challenge to the statute is in effect a challenge of this basic assumption, the assumption can no longer serve as the basis for presuming constitutionality. And, the assumption is no less under attack because the legislature which decides who may participate at the various levels of political choice is fairly elected. Legislation which delegates decision-making to bodies elected by only a portion of those eligible to vote for the legislature can cause unfair representation. Such legislation can exclude a minority of voters from any voice in the decisions just as effectively as if the decisions were made by legislators the minority had no voice in selecting.

The need for exacting judicial scrutiny of statutes distributing the franchise is undiminished simply because, under a different statutory scheme, the offices subject to election might have been filled through appointment. States do have latitude in determining whether certain public officials shall be selected by election or chosen by appointment and whether various questions shall be submitted to the voters. In fact, we have held that where a county school board is an administrative, not legislative, body, its members need not be elected. Sailors v. Kent Bd. of Education (1967). However, "once the franchise is granted to the electorate, lines may not be drawn which are inconsistent with the Equal Protection Clause of the Fourteenth Amendment." Harper v. Virginia Bd. of Elections [1966].

Nor is the need for close judicial examination affected because the district meetings and the school board do not have "general" legislative powers. Our exacting examination is necessitated not by the subject of the elec-

---

*This case presents an issue different from the one we faced in McDonald v. Board of Election Comm'rs of Chicago (1969). The present appeal involves an absolute denial of the franchise. In McDonald, on the other hand, we were reviewing a statute which made casting a ballot easier for some who were unable to come to the polls. As we noted, there was no evidence that the statute absolutely prohibited anyone from exercising the franchise; at issue was not a claimed right to vote but a claimed right to an absentee ballot.

---

†Of course, we have long held that if the basis of classification is inherently suspect, such as race, the statute must be subjected to an exacting scrutiny, regardless of the subject matter of the legislation. . . .

tion; rather, it is required because some resident citizens are permitted to participate and some are not. For example, a city charter might well provide that the elected city council appoint a mayor who would have broad administrative powers. Assuming the council were elected consistent with the commands of the Equal Protection Clause, the delegation of power to the mayor would not call for this Court's exacting review. On the other hand, if the city charter made the office of mayor subject to an election in which only some resident citizens were entitled to vote, there would be presented a situation calling for our close review.

III.

Besides appellant and others who similarly live in their parents' homes, the statute also disenfranchises the following persons (unless they are parents or guardians of children enrolled in the district public school): senior citizens and others living with children or relatives; clergy, military personnel and others who live on tax-exempt property; boarders and lodgers; parents who neither own nor lease qualifying property and whose children are too young to attend school; parents who neither own nor lease qualifying property and whose children attend private schools.

Appellant asserts that excluding him from participation in the district elections denies him equal protection of the law. He contends that he and others of his class are substantially interested in and significantly affected by the school meeting decisions. All members of the community have an interest in the quality and structure of public education, appellant says, and he urges that "the decisions taken by local boards . . . may have grave consequences to the entire population." Appellant also argues that the level of property taxation affects him, even though he does not own property, as property tax levels affect the price of goods and services in the community.

We turn therefore to question whether the exclusion is necessary to promote a compelling state interest. First, appellees argue that the State has a legitimate interest in limiting the franchise in school district elections to "members of the community of interest"—those "primarily interested in such elections." Second, appellees urge that the State may reasonably and permissibly conclude that "property taxpayers" (including lessees of taxable property who share the tax burden through rent payments) and parents of the children enrolled in the district's schools are those "primarily interested" in school affairs.

We do not understand appellees to argue that the State is attempting to limit the franchise to those "subjectively concerned" about school matters. Rather, they appear to argue that the State's legitimate interest is in restricting a voice in school matters to those "directly affected" by such decisions. The State apparently reasons that since the schools are financed in part by local property taxes, persons whose out-of-pocket expenses are "directly" affected by property tax changes should be allowed to vote. Similarly, parents of children in school

are thought to have a "direct" stake in school affairs and are given a vote.

Appellees argue that it is necessary to limit the franchise to those "primarily interested" in school affairs because "the very increasing complexity of the many interacting phases of the school system and structure make it extremely difficult for the electorate fully to understand the whys and wherefores of the detailed operations of the school system." Appellees say that many communications of school boards and school administrations are sent home to the parents through the district pupils and are "not broadcast to the general public"; thus, nonparents will be less informed than parents. Further, appellees argue, those who are assessed for local property taxes (either directly or indirectly through rent) will have enough of an interest "through the burden on their pocket books to acquire such information as they may need."

We need express no opinion as to whether the State in some circumstances might limit the exercise of the franchise to those "primarily interested" or "primarily affected." Of course, we therefore do not reach the issue of whether these particular elections are of the type in which the franchise may be so limited. For, assuming arguendo that New York legitimately might limit the franchise in these school district elections to those "primarily interested in school affairs," close scrutiny of the § 2012 classifications demonstrates that they do not accomplish this purpose with sufficient precision to justify denying appellant the franchise.

Whether classifications allegedly limiting the franchise to those resident citizens "primarily interested" deny those excluded equal protection of the law depends, inter alia, on whether all those excluded are in fact substantially less interested or affected than those the statute includes. In other words, the classifications must be tailored so that the exclusion of appellant and members of his class is necessary to achieve the articulated state goal.* Section 2012 does not meet the exacting standard of precision we require of statutes which selectively distribute the franchise. The classifications in § 2012 permit inclusion of many persons who have, at best, a remote and indirect interest in school affairs and on the other hand, exclude others who have a distinct and direct interest in the school meeting decisions.†

Nor do appellees offer any justification for the exclusion of seemingly interested and informed residents—other than to argue that the § 2012 classifications include those "whom the State could understandably deem to be the most intimately interested in actions taken by the

---

*Of course, if the exclusions are necessary to promote the articulated state interest, we must then determine whether the interest promoted by limiting the franchise constitutes a compelling state interest. We do not reach that issue in this case.

†For example, appellant resides with his parents in the school district, pays state and federal taxes and is interested in and affected by school board decisions; however, he has no vote. On the other hand, an uninterested unemployed young man who pays no state or federal taxes, but who rents an apartment in the district, can participate in the election.

school board," and urge that "the task of . . . balancing the interest of the community in the maintenance of orderly school district elections against the interest of any individual in voting in such elections should clearly remain with the legislature." But the issue is not whether the legislative judgments are rational. A more exacting standard obtains. The issue is whether the § 2012 requirements do in fact sufficiently further a compelling state interest to justify denying the franchise to appellant and members of his class. The requirements of § 2012 are not sufficiently tailored to limiting the franchise to those "primarily interested" in school affairs to justify the denial of the franchise to appellant and members of his class.

The judgment of the United States District Court for the Eastern District of New York is therefore reversed. The case is remanded for further proceedings consistent with this opinion.

It is so ordered.

Mr. Justice **Stewart,** with whom Mr. Justice **Black** and Mr. Justice **Harlan** join, dissenting, said in part:

In Lassiter v. Northampton Election Bd. [1959], this Court upheld against constitutional attack a literacy requirement, applicable to voters in all state and federal elections, imposed by the State of North Carolina. Writing for a unanimous Court, Mr. Justice Douglas said:

"The States have long been held to have broad powers to determine the conditions under which the right of suffrage may be exercised, . . . absent of course the discrimination which the Constitution condemns." Believing that the appellant in this case is not the victim of any "discrimination which the Constitution condemns," I would affirm the judgment of the District Court. . . .

Although at times variously phrased, the traditional test of a statute's validity under the equal protection clause is a familiar one: a legislative classification is invalid only "if it rest[s] on grounds wholly irrelevant to achievement of the regulation's objectives." Kotch v. Board of River Port Pilot Comm'rs [1947]. It was under just such a test that the literacy requirement involved in Lassiter was upheld. The premise of our decision in that case was that a State may constitutionally impose upon its citizens voting requirements reasonably "designed to promote intelligent use of the ballot." A similar premise underlies the proposition, consistently endorsed by this Court, that a State may exclude nonresidents from participation in its elections. Such residence requirements, designed to help ensure that voters have a substantial stake in the outcome of elections and an opportunity to become familiar with the candidates and issues voted upon, are entirely permissible exercises of state authority. Indeed, the appellant explicitly concedes, as he must, the validity of voting requirements relating to residence, literacy, and age. Yet he argues—and the Court accepts the argument—that the voting qualifications involved here somehow have a different constitutional status. I am unable to see the distinction.

Clearly a State may reasonably assume that its res-

idents have a greater stake in the outcome of elections held within its boundaries than do other persons. Likewise, it is entirely rational for a state legislature to suppose that residents, being generally better informed regarding state affairs than are nonresidents, will be more likely than nonresidents to vote responsibly. And the same may be said of legislative assumptions regarding the electoral competence of adults and literate persons on the one hand, and of minors and illiterates on the other. It is clear, of course, that lines thus drawn cannot infallibly perform their intended legislative function. Just as "[i]lliterate people may be intelligent voters," nonresidents or minors might also in some instances be interested, informed, and intelligent participants in the electoral process. Persons who commute across a state line to work may well have a great stake in the affairs of the State in which they are employed; some college students under 21 may be both better informed and more passionately interested in political affairs than many adults. But such discrepancies are the inevitable concomitant of the line-drawing that is essential to lawmaking. So long as the classification is rationally related to a permissible legislative end, therefore—as are residence, literacy, and age requirements imposed with respect to voting—there is no denial of equal protection.

Thus judged, the statutory classification involved here seems to me clearly to be valid. New York has made the judgment that local educational policy is best left to those persons who have certain direct and definable interests in that policy: those who are either immediately involved as parents of school children or who, as owners or lessees of taxable property, are burdened with the local cost of funding school district operations. True, persons outside those classes may be genuinely interested in the conduct of a school district's business—just as commuters from New Jersey may be genuinely interested in the outcome of a New York City election. But unless this Court is to claim a monopoly of wisdom regarding the sound operation of school systems in the 50 States, I see no way to justify the conclusion that the legislative classification involved here is not rationally related to a legitimate legislative purpose. "There is no group more interested in the operation and management of the public schools than the taxpayers who support them and the parents whose children attend them." Doremus v. Board of Educ. [1952] (Douglas, J., dissenting).

With good reason, the Court does not really argue the contrary. Instead, it strikes down New York's statute by asserting that the traditional equal protection standard is inapt in this case, and that a considerably stricter standard—under which classifications relating to "the franchise" are to be subjected to "exacting judicial scrutiny"—should be applied. But the asserted justification for applying such a standard cannot withstand analysis.

The Court is quite explicit in explaining why it believes this statute should be given "close scrutiny":

"The presumption of constitutionality and the approval given 'rational' classifications in other types of enactments are based on an assumption that the institutions of state government are structured so as to represent fairly all the people. However, when the challenge to the statute is in effect a challenge of this basic assumption, the assumption can no longer serve as the basis for presuming constitutionality.'' (Footnote omitted.)

I am at a loss to understand how such reasoning is at all relevant to the present case. The voting qualifications at issue have been promulgated not by Union Free School District No. 15, but by the New York State Legislature, and the appellant is of course fully able to participate in the election of representatives in that body. There is simply no claim whatever here that the state government is not ''structured so as to represent fairly all the people,'' including the appellant.

Nor is there any other justification for imposing the Court's ''exacting'' equal protection test. This case does not involve racial classifications, which in light of the genesis of the Fourteenth Amendment have traditionally been viewed as inherently ''suspect.'' And this statute is not one that impinges upon a constitutionally protected right, and that consequently can be justified only by a ''compelling'' state interest. For ''the Constitution of the United States does not confer the right of suffrage upon any one. . . .'' Minor v. Happersett [1875]. . . .

INTERMEDIATE TEST

SAN ANTONIO v. RODRIGUEZ

411 U. S. 1; 93 S. Ct. 1278; 36 L. Ed. 2d 16
(1973)

With two tests for judging cases brought under the equal protection clause, the Court entered the 1970s and found itself facing an increasing number of equal protection claims. The proliferation of government benefits, collectively referred to as the "welfare state" and the growing awareness of the disadvantages of the poor and of women generated new and complex equality questions for which the two tests seemed scarcely adequate. Nevertheless, as the Court took up each of these new questions it recited the formula for one of its two tests and proceeded to decide accordingly. It ultimately became apparent even to the Court, however, that the two-tiered approach was straining at the seams. The case below is an example. It raises the question of whether the equal protection clause requires the state to equalize the amounts spent on education throughout the districts of the state. The importance of the question to public education would be difficult to overestimate.

The city of San Antonio, Texas, finances its schools with a combination of state aid and local property taxes, the latter being divided between an amount which a district is required to raise and which is roughly proportional to its taxing power, and an additional amount which it may raise if it wishes to do so. Two districts are contrasted in this litigation. The first, the Edgewood Independent School District, which is 96 per-

cent Mexican-American and black, with an average property value of $5,960 (the lowest in the metropolitan area) and a tax rate of $1.05 per $100 (the highest in the metropolitan area), contributed $26 per pupil above its legal requirements. In contrast, Alamo Heights District is 81 percent white, its assessed value is $49,000 per pupil, and with a local tax rate of $.85 per $100 it raised $333 per pupil above the required minimum. In the 1970-1971 school year the state made marked increases in the state aid given to the poorer schools.

Mr. Justice **Powell** delivered the opinion of the Court, saying in part:

Despite these recent increases, substantial interdistrict disparities in school expenditures found by the District Court to prevail in San Antonio and in varying degrees throughout the State still exist. And it was these disparities, largely attributable to differences in the amounts of money collected through local property taxation, that led the District Court to conclude that Texas' dual system of public school finance violated the Equal Protection Clause. The District Court held that the Texas system discriminates on the basis of wealth in the manner in which education is provided for its people. Finding that wealth is a ''suspect'' classification and that education is a ''fundamental'' interest, the District Court held that the Texas system could be sustained only if the State could show that it was premised upon some compelling state interest. On this issue the court concluded that ''[n]ot only are defendants unable to demonstrate compelling state interests . . . they fail even to establish a reasonable basis for these classifications.''

This, then, establishes the framework for our analysis. We must decide, first, whether the Texas system of financing public education operates to the disadvantage of some suspect class or impinges upon a fundamental right explicitly or implicitly protected by the Constitution, thereby requiring strict judicial scrutiny. If so, the judgment of the District Court should be affirmed. If not, the Texas scheme must still be examined to determine whether it rationally furthers some legitimate, articulated state purpose and therefore does not constitute an invidious discrimination in violation of the Equal Protection Clause of the Fourteenth Amendment.

II. . . .

A.

The wealth discrimination discovered by the District Court in this case, and by several other courts that have recently struck down school financing laws in other States, is quite unlike any of the forms of wealth discrimination heretofore reviewed by this Court. Rather than focusing on the unique features of the alleged discrimination, the courts in these cases have virtually assumed their findings of a suspect classification through a simplistic process of analysis: since, under the traditional systems of financing public schools, some poorer people receive less expensive educations than other more affluent people, these systems discriminate on the basis of wealth. This approach largely ignores the hard threshold questions, including whether it makes a difference for purposes of consideration under the Constitution that the class of disadvantaged "poor" cannot be identified or defined in customary equal protection terms, and whether the relative—rather than absolute—nature of the asserted deprivation is of significant consequence. Before a State's laws and the justifications for the classifications they create are subjected to strict judicial scrutiny, we think these threshold considerations must be analyzed more closely than they were in the court below.

The case comes to us with no definitive description of the classifying facts or delineation of the disfavored class. Examination of the District Court's opinion and of appellees' complaint, briefs, and contentions at oral argument suggests, however, at least three ways in which the discrimination claimed here might be described. The Texas system of school finance might be regarded as discriminating (1) against "poor" persons whose incomes fall below some identifiable level of poverty or who might be characterized as functionally "indigent," or (2) against those who are relatively poorer than others, or (3) against all those who, irrespective of their personal incomes, happen to reside in relatively poorer school districts. Our task must be to ascertain whether, in fact, the Texas system has been shown to discriminate on any of these possible bases and, if so, whether the resulting classification may be regarded as suspect.

The precedents of this Court provide the proper starting point. The individuals or groups of individuals who constituted the class discriminated against in our prior cases shared two distinguishing characteristics: because of their impecunity they were completely unable to pay for some desired benefit, and as a consequence, they sustained an absolute deprivation of a meaningful opportunity to enjoy that benefit. In Griffin v. Illinois (1956) and its progeny, the Court invalidated state laws that prevented an indigent criminal defendant from acquiring a transcript, or an adequate substitute for a transcript, for use at several stages of the trial and appeal process. The payment requirements in each case were found to occasion de facto discrimination against those who, because of their indigency, were totally unable to pay for transcripts. . . .

Likewise, in Douglas v. California (1963), a decision establishing an indigent defendant's right to court-appointed counsel on direct appeal, the Court dealt only with defendants who could not pay for counsel from their own resources and who had no other way of gaining representation. . . .

Williams v. Illinois (1970) struck down criminal penalties that subjected indigents to incarceration simply because of their inability to pay a fine. Again, the disadvantaged class was composed only of persons who were totally unable to pay the demanded sum. . . .

Finally, in Bullock v. Carter (1972), the Court invalidated the Texas filing fee requirement for primary elections. Both of the relevant classifying facts found in the previous cases were present there. The size of the fee, often running into thousands of dollars and, in at least one case, as high as $8,900, effectively barred all potential candidates who were unable to pay the required fee. As the system provided "no reasonable alternative means of access to the ballot" inability to pay occasioned an absolute denial of a position on the primary ballot.

Only appellees' first possible basis for describing the class disadvantaged by the Texas school finance system—discrimination against a class of definably "poor" persons—might arguably meet the criteria established in these prior cases. Even a cursory examination, however, demonstrates that neither of the two distinguishing characteristics of wealth classifications can be found here. First, in support of their charge that the system discriminates against the "poor," appellees have made no effort to demonstrate that it operates to the peculiar disadvantage of any class fairly definable as indigent, or as composed of persons whose incomes are beneath any designated poverty level. Indeed, there is no reason to believe that the poorest families are not necessarily clustered in the poorest property districts. A recent and exhaustive study of school districts in Connecticut concluded that "[i]t is clearly incorrect . . . to contend that the 'poor' live in 'poor' districts. . . . Thus, the major factual assumption . . . —that the educational finance system discriminates against the 'poor'—is simply false in Connecticut." Defining "poor" families as those below the Bureau of the Census "poverty level," the Connecticut study found, not surprisingly, that the poor were clustered around commercial and industrial areas—those same areas that provide the most attractive sources of property tax income for school districts. Whether a similar pattern would be discovered in Texas is not known, but there is no basis on the record in this case for assuming that the poorest people—defined by reference to any level of absolute impecunity—are concentrated in the poorest districts.

Second, neither appellees nor the District Court addressed the fact that, unlike each of the foregoing cases, lack of personal resources has not occasioned an absolute deprivation of the desired benefit. The argument here is not that the children in districts having relatively low assessable property values are receiving no public education; rather, it is that they are receiving a poorer quality education than that available to children in districts having more assessable wealth. Apart from the unsettled and disputed question whether the quality of education may be determined by the amount of money expended for it,* a sufficient answer to appellees' argument is that at least where wealth is involved the Equal Protection Clause does not require absolute equality of precisely equal advantages. . . . The State repeatedly asserted in its briefs in this Court that . . . it now assures "every child in every school district an adequate educa-

---

*Each of appellees' possible theories of wealth discrimination is founded on the assumption that the quality of education varies directly with the amount of funds expended on it and that, therefore, the difference in quality between two schools can be determined simplistically by looking at the difference in per pupil expenditures. This is a matter of considerable dispute among educators and commentators.

tion.'' No proof was offered at trial persuasively discrediting or refuting the State's assertion.

For these two reasons—the absence of any evidence that the financing system discriminates against any definable category of ''poor'' people or that it results in the absolute deprivation of education—the disadvantaged class is not susceptible to identification in traditional terms. . . .

[The Court here reviews the evidence and rejects the argument that there is a direct correlation between the family income in a district and the amount it spends for education.]

This brings us, then, to the third way in which the classification scheme might be defined—*district* wealth discrimination. Since the only correlation indicated by the evidence is between district property wealth and expenditures, it may be argued that discrimination might be found without regard to the individual income characteristics of district residents. Assuming a perfect correlation between district property wealth and expenditures from top to bottom, the disadvantaged class might be viewed as encompassing every child in every district except the district that has the most assessable wealth and spends the most on education. . . .

However described, it is clear that appellees' suit asks this Court to extend its most exacting scrutiny to review a system that allegedly discriminates against a large, diverse, and amorphous class, unified only by the common factor of residence in districts that happen to have less taxable wealth than other districts. The system of alleged discrimination and the class it defines have none of the traditional indicia of suspectness: the class is not saddled with such disabilities, or subjected to such history of purposeful unequal treatment, or relegated to such a position of political powerlessness as to command extraordinary protection from the majoritarian political process.

We thus conclude that the Texas system does not operate to the peculiar disadvantage of any suspect class. But in recognition of the fact that this Court has never heretofore held that wealth discrimination alone provides an adequate basis for invoking strict scrutiny, appellees have not relied solely on this contention. They also assert that the State's system impermissibly interferes with the exercise of a ''fundamental'' right and that accordingly the prior decisions of this Court require the application of the strict standard of judicial review. It is this question—whether education is a fundamental right, in the sense that it is among the rights and liberties protected by the Constitution—which has so consumed the attention of courts and commentators in recent years.

B.

Nothing this Court holds today in any way detracts from our historic dedication to public education. We are in complete agreement with the conclusion of the three-judge panel below that ''the grave significance of education both to the individual and to our society'' cannot be doubted. But the importance of a service performed by the State does not determine whether it must be regarded as fundamental for purposes of examination under the Equal Protection Clause. Mr. Justice Harlan, dissenting from the Court's application of strict scrutiny to a law impinging upon the right of interstate travel, admonished that ''[v]irtually every state statute affects important rights.'' Shapiro v. Thompson (1969). In his view, if the degree of judicial scrutiny of state legislation fluctuated depending on a majority's view of the importance of the interest affected, we would have gone ''far toward making this Court a 'super-legislature.' '' We would indeed then be assuming a legislative role and one for which the Court lacks both authority and competence. But Mr. Justice Stewart's response in Shapiro to Mr. Justice Harlan's concern correctly articulates the limits of the fundamental rights rationale employed in the Court's equal protection decisions:

''The Court today does *not* 'pick out particular human activities, characterize them as ''fundamental,'' and give them added protection. . . .' To the contrary, the Court simply recognizes, as it must, an established constitutional right, and gives to that right no less protection than the Constitution itself demands.'' (Emphasis from original.)

Mr. Justice Stewart's statement serves to underline what the opinion of the Court in Shapiro makes clear. . . . The right to interstate travel had long been recognized as a right of constitutional significance, and the Court's decision therefore did not require an ad hoc determination as to the social or economic importance of that right.

Lindsey v. Normet (1972) decided only last Term, firmly reiterates that social importance is not the critical determinant for subjecting state legislation to strict scrutiny. . . . Mr. Justice White's analysis, in his opinion for the Court, is instructive:

''We do not denigrate the importance of decent, safe, and sanitary housing. But the Constitution does not provide judicial remedies for every social and economic ill. We are unable to perceive in that document any constitutional guarantee of access to dwellings of a particular quality or any recognition of the right of a tenant to occupy the real property of his landlord beyond the term of his lease, without the payment of rent. . . . *Absent constitutional mandate,* the assurance of adequate housing and the definition of landlord-tenant relationships are legislative, not judicial, functions.'' . . .

The lesson of these cases in addressing the question now before the Court is plain. It is not the province of this Court to create substantive constitutional rights in the name of guaranteeing equal protection of the laws. Thus the key to discovering whether education is ''fundamental'' is not to be found in comparisons of the relative societal significance of education as opposed to subsistence or housing. Nor is it to be found by weighing whether education is as important as the right to travel. Rather, the answer lies in assessing whether there is a right to education explicitly or implicitly guaranteed by the Constitution. . . .

Education, of course, is not among the rights afforded explicit protection under our Federal Constitution. Nor do we find any basis for saying it is implicitly so protected. It is appellees' contention, however, that education . . . is itself a fundamental personal right because it is essential to the effective exercise of First Amendment freedoms and to intelligent utilization of the right to vote. . . .

We need not dispute any of these propositions. The Court has long afforded zealous protection against unjustifiable governmental interference with the individual's rights to speak and to vote. Yet we have never presumed to possess either the ability or the authority to guarantee to the citizenry the most *effective* speech or the most *informed* electoral choice. . . .

Even if it were conceded that some identifiable quantum of education is a constitutionally protected prerequisite to the meaningful exercise of either right, we have no indication that the present levels of educational expenditure in Texas provide an education that falls short. . . .

We have carefully considered each of the arguments supportive of the District Court's finding that education is a fundamental right or liberty and have found those arguments unpersuasive. In one further respect we find this a particularly inappropriate case in which to subject state action to strict judicial scrutiny. The present case, in another basic sense, is significantly different from any of the cases in which the Court has applied strict scrutiny to state or federal legislation touching upon constitutionally protected rights. Each of our prior cases involved legislation which "deprived," "infringed," or "interfered" with the free exercise of some such fundamental personal right or liberty. . . . A critical distinction between those cases and the one now before us lies in what Texas is endeavoring to do with respect to education. Every step leading to the establishment of the system Texas utilizes today—including the decisions permitting localities to tax and expand locally, and creating and continuously expanding state aid—was implemented in an effort to *extend* public education and to improve its quality. Of course, every reform that benefits some more than others may be criticized for what it fails to accomplish. But we think it plain that, in substance, the thrust of the Texas system is affirmative and reformatory and, therefore, should be scrutinized under judicial principles sensitive to the nature of the State's efforts and to the rights reserved to the States under the Constitution.

C.

It should be clear, for the reasons stated above and in accord with the prior decisions of this Court, that this is not a case in which the challenged state action must be subjected to the searching judicial scrutiny reserved for laws that created suspect classification or impinge upon constitutionally protected rights.

We need not rest our decision, however, solely on the inappropriateness of the strict scrutiny test. A century of Supreme Court adjudication under the Equal Protection Clause affirmatively supports the application of the traditional standard of review, which requires only that the State's system be shown to bear some rational rela-

tionship to legitimate state purposes. This case represents far more than a challenge to the manner in which Texas provides for the education of its children. We have here nothing less than a direct attack on the way in which Texas has chosen to raise and disburse state and local tax revenues. . . .

[The Court here defends the appropriateness of the traditional standards in the field of taxation.]

The foregoing considerations buttress our conclusion that Texas' system of public school finance is an inappropriate candidate for strict judicial scrutiny. These same considerations are relevant to the determination whether that system, with its conceded imperfections, nevertheless bears some rational relationship to a legitimate state purpose. It is to this question that we next turn our attention. . . .

The Texas system of school finance is responsive to these two forces. While assuring a basic education for every child in the State, it permits and encourages a large measure of participation in and control of each district's schools at the local level. In an era that has witnessed a consistent trend toward centralization of the functions of government, local sharing of responsibility for public education has survived. . . .

The persistence of attachment to government at the lowest level where education is concerned reflects the depth of commitment of its supporters. In part, local control means . . . the freedom to devote more money to the education of one's children. Equally important, however, is the opportunity it offers for participation in the decision-making process that determines how those local tax dollars will be spent. Each locality is free to tailor local programs to local needs. Pluralism also affords some opportunity for experimentation, innovation, and a healthy competition for educational excellence. An analogy to the Nation-State relationship in our federal system seems uniquely appropriate. Mr. Justice Brandeis identified as one of the peculiar strengths of our form of government each State's freedom to "serve as a laboratory . . . and try novel social and economic experiments." No area of social concern stands to profit more from a multiplicity of viewpoints and from a diversity of approaches than does public education. . . .

. . . Appellees suggest that local control could be preserved and promoted under other financing systems that resulted in more equality in educational expenditures. While it is no doubt true that reliance on local property taxation for school revenues provides less freedom of choice with respect to expenditures for some districts than for others, the existence of "some inequality" in the manner in which the State's rationale is achieved is not alone a sufficient basis for striking down the entire system. . . . Only where state action impinges on the exercise of fundamental constitutional rights or liberties must it be found to have chosen the least restrictive alternative. . . . It is also well to remember that even those districts that have reduced ability to make free decisions with respect to how much they spend on education still retain under the present system a large measure of authority as to how available funds will be allocated. They further enjoy the power to make numerous other decisions with respect to the operation of the schools. The people of Texas may be justified in believing that other systems of school finance, which place more of the financial responsibility in the hands of the State, will result in a comparable lessening of desired local autonomy. That is, they may believe that along with increased control of the purse strings at the state level will go increased control over local policies. . . .

. . . One also must remember that the system here challenged is not peculiar to Texas or to any other State. In its essential characteristics the Texas plan for financing public education reflects what many educators for a half century have thought was an enlightened approach to a problem for which there is no perfect solution. We are unwilling to assume for ourselves a level of wisdom superior to that of legislators, scholars, and educational authorities in 49 States, especially where the alternatives proposed are only recently conceived and nowhere yet tested. The constitutional standard under the Equal Protection Clause is whether the challenged state action rationally furthers a legitimate state purpose or interest. . . . We hold that the Texas plan abundantly satisfies this standard.

Mr. Justice **Brennan,** dissenting, said in part:

Although I agree with my Brother White that the Texas statutory scheme is devoid of any rational basis, and for that reason is violative of the Equal Protection Clause, I also record my disagreement with the Court's rather distressing assertion that a right may be deemed "fundamental" for the purposes of equal protection analysis only if it is "explicitly or implicitly guaranteed by the Constitution." As my Brother Marshall convincingly demonstrates, our prior cases stand for the proposition that "fundamentality" is, in large measure, a function of the right's importance in terms of the effectuation of those rights which are in fact constitutionally guaranteed. Thus, "[a]s the nexus between the specific constitutional guarantee and the nonconstitutional interest draws closer, the nonconstitutional interest becomes more fundamental and the degree of judicial scrutiny applied when the interest is infringed on a discriminatory basis must be adjusted accordingly."

Here, there can be no doubt that education is inextricably linked to the right to participate in the electoral process and to the rights of free speech and association guaranteed by the First Amendment. This being so, any classification affecting education must be subjected to strict judicial scrutiny, and since even the State concedes that the statutory scheme now before us cannot pass constitutional muster under this stricter standard of review, I can only conclude that the Texas school financing scheme is constitutionally invalid.

Mr. Justice **White,** with whom Mr. Justice **Douglas** and Mr. Justice **Brennan** join, dissenting, said in part:

The Texas public schools are financed through a combination of state funding, local property tax revenue, and some federal funds. Concededly, the system yields wide disparity in per-pupil revenue among the various districts. In a typical year, for example, the Alamo Heights district had total revenues of $594 per pupil, while the Edgewood district had only $356 per student. The majority and the State concede, as they must, the existence of major disparities in spendable funds. But the State contends that the disparities do not invidiously discriminate against children and families in districts such as Edgewood, because the Texas scheme is designed "to provide an adequate education for all, with local autonomy to go beyond that as individual school districts desire and are able. . . . It leaves to the people of each district the choice whether to go beyond the minimum and, if so, by how much. The majority advances this rationalization: "While assuring a basic education for every child in the State, it permits and encourages a large measure of participation and control of each district's schools at the local level."

I cannot disagree with the proposition that local control and local decision making play an important part in our democratic system of government. . . .

The difficulty with the Texas system, however, is that it provides a meaningful option to Alamo Heights and like school districts but almost none to Edgewood and those other districts with a low per-pupil real estate tax base. In these latter districts, no matter how desirous parents are of supporting their schools with greater revenues, it is impossible to do so through the use of the real estate property tax. In these districts the Texas system utterly fails to extend a realistic choice to parents, because the property tax, which is the only revenue-raising mechanism extended to school districts, is practically and legally unavailable. That this is a situation may be readily demonstrated. . . .

In order to equal the highest yield in any other Bexar County district, Alamo Heights would be required to tax at the rate of 68¢ per $100 of assessed valuation. Edgewood would be required to tax at the prohibitive rate of $5.76 per $100. But state law places a $1.50 per $100 ceiling on the maintenance tax rate, a limit that would surely be reached long before Edgewood attained an equal yield. Edgewood is thus precluded in law, as well as in fact, from achieving a yield even close to that of some other districts.

The Equal Protection Clause permits discriminations between classes but requires that the classification bear some rational relationship to a permissible object sought to be attained by the statute. It is not enough that the Texas system before us seeks to achieve the valid, rational purpose of maximizing local initiative; the means chosen by the State must also be rationally related to the end sought to be achieved. . . .

Neither Texas nor the majority heeds this rule. If the State aims at maximizing local initiative and local choice, by permitting schools to resort to the real property tax if they choose to do so, it utterly fails in achieving its purpose in districts with property tax bases so low that there is little if any opportunity for interested parents, rich or poor, to augment school district revenues. Requiring the State to establish only that unequal treatment is in furtherance of a permissible goal, without also requiring the State to show that the means chosen to effectuate that goal are rationally related to its achievement, makes equal protection analysis no more than an empty gesture. In my view, the parents and children in Edgewood, and in like districts, suffer from an invidious discrimination violative of the Equal Protection Clause. . . .

There is no difficulty in identifying the class that is subject to the alleged discrimination and that is entitled to the benefits of the Equal Protection Clause. I need go no farther than the parents and children in the Edgewood district, who are plaintiffs here and who assert that they are entitled to the same choice as Alamo Heights to augment local expenditures for schools but are denied that choice by state law. This group constitutes a class sufficiently definite to invoke the protection of the Constitution. They are as entitled to the protection of the Equal Protection Clause as were the voters in allegedly unrepresented counties in the reapportionment cases. See, e. g., Baker v. Carr (1962). And in Bullock v. Carter (1972), where a challenge to the Texas candidate filing fee on equal protection grounds was upheld, we noted that the victims of alleged discrimination wrought by the filing fee "cannot be described by reference to discrete and precisely defined segments of the community as is typical of inequities challenged under the Equal Protection Clause," but concluded that "we would ignore reality were we not to recognize that this system falls with unequal weight on voters, as well as candidates, according to economic status." Similarly, in the present case we would blink reality to ignore the fact that school districts, and students in the end, are differentially affected by the Texas school financing scheme with respect to their capability to supplement the Minimum Foundation School Program. At the very least, the law discriminates against those children and their parents who live in districts where the per-pupil tax base is sufficiently low to make impossible the provision of comparable school revenues by resort to the real property tax which is the only device the State extends for this purpose.

Mr. Justice **Marshall,** with whom Mr. Justice **Douglas** concurs, dissenting, said in part:

I. . . .

B.

The appellants do not deny the disparities in educational funding caused by variations in taxable district property wealth. They do contend, however, that whatever the differences in per pupil spending among Texas districts, there are no discriminatory consequences for the children of the disadvantaged districts. They recognize that what is at stake in this case is the quality of the public education provided Texas children in the districts in which they live. But appellants reject the suggestion that the quality of education in any particular district is determined by money—beyond some minimal level of funding which they believe to be assured every Texas district by the Minimum Foundation School Program. In

their view, there is simply no denial of equal educational opportunity to any Texas school children as a result of the widely varying per pupil spending power provided districts under the current financing scheme.

In my view, though, even an unadorned restatement of this contention is sufficient to reveal its absurdity. Authorities concerned with educational quality no doubt disagree as to the significance of variations in per pupil spending. Indeed, conflicting expert testimony was presented to the District Court in this case concerning the effect of spending variations on educational achievement. We sit, however, not to resolve disputes over educational theory but to enforce our Constitution. It is an inescapable fact that if one district has more funds available per pupil than another district, the former will have greater choice in educational planning than will the latter. In this regard, I believe the question of discrimination in educational quality must be deemed to be an objective one that looks to what the State provides its children, not to what the children are able to do with what they receive. That a child is forced to attend an underfunded school with poorer physical facilities, less experienced teachers, larger classes, and a narrower range of courses than a school with substantially more funds—and thus with greater choice in educational planning—may nevertheless excel is to the credit of the child, not the State, cf. Missouri ex rel. Gaines v. Canada (1938). Indeed, who can ever measure for such a child the opportunities lost and the talents wasted for want of a broader, more enriched education? Discrimination in the opportunity to learn that is afforded a child must be our standard. . . .

II.

To avoid having the Texas financing scheme struck down because of the interdistrict variations in taxable property wealth, the District Court determined that it was insufficient for appellants to show merely that the State's scheme was rationally related to some legitimate state purpose; rather, the discrimination inherent in the scheme had to be shown necessary to promote a "compelling state interest" in order to withstand constitutional scrutiny. The basis for this determination was twofold: first, the financing scheme divides citizens on a wealth basis, a classification which the District Court viewed as highly suspect; and second, the discriminatory scheme directly affects what it considered to be a "fundamental interest," namely, education.

This Court has repeatedly held that state discrimination which either adversely affects a "fundamental interest," see, e.g., Dunn v. Blumstein, (1972); Shapiro v. Thompson, (1969), or is based on a distinction of a suspect character, . . . must be carefully scrutinized to ensure that the scheme is necessary to promote a substantial legitimate state interest. . . . The majority today concludes, however, that the Texas scheme is not subject to such a strict standard of review under the Equal Protection Clause. Instead, in its view, the Texas scheme must be tested by nothing more than that lenient standard of rationality which we have traditionally applied to discriminatory state action in the context of economic and commercial matters. . . . By so doing the Court avoids the telling task of searching for a substantial state interest which the Texas financing scheme, with its variations in taxable district property wealth, is necessary to further. I cannot accept such an emasculation of the Equal Protection Clause in the context of this case.

A.

To begin, I must once more voice my disagreement with the Court's rigidified approach to equal protection analysis. . . . The Court apparently seeks to establish today that equal protection cases fall into one of two neat categories which dictate the appropriate standard of review—strict scrutiny or mere rationality. But this Court's decisions in the field of equal protection defy such easy categorization. A principled reading of what this Court has done reveals that it has applied a spectrum of standards in reviewing discrimination allegedly violative of the Equal Protection Clause. This spectrum clearly comprehends variations in the degree of care with which the Court will scrutinize particular classifications, depending, I believe, on the constitutional and societal importance of the interest adversely affected and the recognized invidiousness of the basis upon which the particular classification is drawn. I find in fact that many of the Court's recent decisions embody the very sort of reasoned approach to equal protection analysis for which I previously argued—that is, an approach in which "concentration [is] placed upon the character of the classification in question, the relative importance to individuals in the class discriminated against of the governmental benefits that they do not receive, and the asserted state interests in support of the classification." Dandridge v. Williams (1970)

[Marshall here summarizes a long series of equal protection cases weighing the fundamentalness of the right and the "invidiousness" of the classification in each.]

In summary, it seems to me inescapably clear that this Court has consistently adjusted the care with which it will review state discrimination in light of the constitutional significance of the interests affected and the invidiousness of the particular classification. In the context of economic interests, we find that discriminatory state action is almost always sustained, for such interests are generally far removed from constitutional guarantees. Moreover, "[t]he extremes to which the Court has gone in dreaming up rational bases for state regulation in that area may in many instances be ascribed to a healthy revulsion from the Court's earlier excesses in using the Constitution to protect interests that have more than enough power to protect themselves in the legislative halls." Dandridge v. Williams. But the situation differs markedly when discrimination against important individual interests with constitutional implications and against particularly disadvantaged or powerless classes is involved. The majority suggests, however, that a variable standard of review would give this Court the appearance of a "super-legislature." Such an approach seems to me

a part of the guarantees of our Constitution and of the historic experiences with oppression of and discrimination against discrete, powerless minorities which underlie that document. In truth, the Court itself will be open to the criticism raised by the majority so long as it continues on its present course of effectively selecting in private which cases will be afforded special consideration without acknowledging the true basis of its action. . . .

Nevertheless, the majority today attempts to force this case into the same category for purposes of equal protection analysis as decisions involving discrimination affecting commercial interests. By so doing, the majority singles this case out for analytic treatment at odds with what seems to me to be the clear trend of recent decisions in this Court, and thereby ignores the constitutional importance of the interests at stake and the invidiousness of the particular classification, factors that call for far more than the lenient scrutiny of the Texas financing scheme which the majority pursues. Yet if the discrimination inherent in the Texas scheme is scrutinized with the care demanded by the interest and classification present in this case, the unconstitutionality of that scheme is unmistakable. . . .

D.

The nature of our inquiry into the justifications for state discrimination is essentially the same in all equal protection cases: We must consider the substantiality of the state interests sought to be served, and we must scrutinize the reasonableness of the means by which the State has sought to advance its interests. . . . Differences in the application of this test are, in my view, a function of the constitutional importance of the interests at stake and the invidiousness of the particular classification. In terms of the asserted state interests, the Court has indicated that it will require, for instance, a "compelling," Shapiro v. Thompson, [1969], or a "substantial" or "important", Dunn v. Blumstein, [1972], state interest to justify discrimination affecting individual interests of constitutional significance. Whatever the differences, if any, in these descriptions of the character of the state interest necessary to sustain such discrimination, basic to each is, I believe, a concern with the legitimacy and the reality of the asserted state interests. Thus, when interests of constitutional importance are at stake, the Court does not stand ready to credit the State's classification with any conceivable legitimate purpose, but demands a clear showing that there are legitimate state interests which the classification was in fact intended to serve. Beyond the question of the adequacy of the State's purpose for the classification, the Court traditionally has become increasingly sensitive to the means by which a State chooses to act as its action affects more directly interests of constitutional significance. . . . Thus, by now, "less restrictive alternatives" analysis is firmly established in equal protection jurisprudence. See Dunn v. Blumstein, [1972]; Kramer v. Union School District [1969]. It seems to me that the range of choice we are willing to accord the State in selecting the means by which it will act, and the care with which we scrutinize the effectiveness of the means which the State selects, also must reflect the constitutional importance of the interest affected and the invidiousness of the particular classification. Here both the nature of the interest and the classification dictate close judicial scrutiny of the purposes which Texas seeks to serve with its present educational financing scheme and of the means it has selected to serve that purpose.

The only justification offered by appellants to sustain the discrimination in educational opportunity caused by the Texas financing scheme is local educational control. Presented with this justification, the District Court concluded that "[n]ot only are defendants unable to demonstrate compelling state interests for their classifications based upon wealth, they fail even to establish a reasonable basis for these classifications." I must agree with this conclusion.

PLYLER v. DOE

457 U. S. 202; 102 S. Ct. 2382; 72 L. Ed. 2d 786 (1982)

In his dissent in Rodriguez, Justice Marshall argued that two tests for equal protection cases were not enough. The tests had become not tests, but answers: under the strict scrutiny test, the law is struck down; under the rational basis test the law is upheld. Justice Marshall not only criticized the two-tiered approach, he asserted that the Court had abandoned it and had, in its stead, been applying a "spectrum of standards" to analyze equal protection claims. He urged the Court to give up the pretense of two tests and begin articulating the real underpinnings of its more sophisticated equal protection analysis.

To decide what standard to apply under the equal protection clause, Justice Marshall said the Court was asking two questions. First, how important is the interest that is being adversely affected by the alleged discrimination. Second, how invidious is the classification that is being used. According to Justice Marshall, the answer to these questions determines the level of scrutiny to be applied.

The difference between this approach and the two-tiered approach is demonstrated by Rodriguez and the case below. In Rodriguez, the two-tiered approach can be outlined as follows: education is not a fundamental right, and wealth is not a suspect classification; strict scrutiny cannot therefore be applied; thus the rational basis test must be used. Justice Marshall's approach would be that education, even if not fundamental, is important; wealth, even if not a suspect classification, is questionable. Strict scrutiny does not apply, but neither is the rational basis test appropriate here: an intermediate test should be applied.

Gradually, the Court has come to accept the need for such an intermediate test and has formulated one. Under this test, the challenged classification must serve "important governmental objectives and the discrimina-

tory means employed" must be " substantially related to the achievement of those objectives;" see Mississippi v. Hogan (1982). This test is often referred to as the "substantial interest test" because an alternate and simple formulation of it is that the classification must serve a substantial governmental interest.

The intermediate test originated in sex discrimination cases. In Craig v. Boren (1976) the Court held void a law that set the legal age for drinking at a different point for men than for women. The test used to determine whether this law violated the equal protection test was the long formulation of the substantial interest test given above and was described by the Court in Craig as a midlevel test. Craig was one of the first explicit instances of the Court's use of this intermediate test and is often cited by the Court as the precedent for using the test.

Sex discrimination cases were fertile ground for the development of the new test for a number of reasons. The sheer number of sex discrimination cases in the 1970s, the growing women's rights movement, the political debate over the Equal Rights Amendment and the greater statutory protection afforded women by the Civil Rights Act and other laws, all contributed to the Court's reluctance to continue its casual scrutiny under the rational basis test. On the other hand, the Court was even less inclined to raise sex to the level of a suspect classification because that would, in effect, outlaw almost all use of sex as a legislative classification. The heated political debate over the Equal Rights Amendment, with opponents raising the specter of unisex bathrooms and women fighting wars on the front lines, provided no inducement for the Court to preempt the political process by declaring sex a suspect classification. The answer was an intermediate test by which the Court could legitimately consider the invidious nature of sexual discrimination without outlawing all use of sexual classifications.

At the same time that the Court was struggling with an increased number of sex discrimination cases, the existence of the welfare state raised a number of other recurring equal protection problems. Specifically, the Court found itself confronted with equal protection claims alleging discrimination against the poor and discrimination affecting access to education. Some argued that the poor, like blacks, were historically the subjects of the most invidious discrimination and that wealth, therefore, should be treated as a suspect classification. While it is true that the poor have been subjected to some of the cruelest discrimination, wealth, unlike race, is not an immutable characteristic and more important, a capitalist society is one that assumes differential treatment based on wealth as a reward for ability and an incentive to greater productivity. The Court is not on the verge of restructuring the economic basis of the nation.

Nevertheless, when discrimination against the poor, or another group not treated as a suspect class such as aliens, is combined with an adverse effect on an important, although not fundamental right such as education, the Court has apparently abandoned the casual scrutiny of the rational basis test and opted instead for the intermediate test used in the case below.

Plyler v. Doe was a suit brought on behalf of all school-age children of Mexican origin residing in Texas as illegal aliens. The suit challenged a provision of the Texas Education Code that denied free public education to illegal alien children. One year after the decision in Plyler the Court considered a challenge to another provision of the Texas education law in Martinez v. Bynum (1983). The provision challenged in Martinez denied free public education to any minor, living apart from his natural parents or legal guardian, who resided in the school district for the primary purpose of attending school. It was argued that the law was intended to and did discriminate against children of Mexican heritage. If an illegal alien gives birth to a child while in this country, that child is an American citizen. Some of these illegal aliens later return to Mexico but send their American children to live with friends or relatives in the United States so they may receive a free public education. These Mexican-American children, living apart from their parents, were denied a free education by the Texas law.

With only Justice Marshall dissenting, the Court in Martinez held that this Texas law was constitutional because it was a bona fide residence requirement designed to further the "substantial state interest in assuring that services provided for its residents are enjoyed only by residents." While the Court did not discuss the standard it was applying, the use of the word "substantial" suggests that the intermediate test was used just as it had been in Plyler—although with a different result. The majority in Martinez also held that the law did not unconstitutionally impede the right to travel interstate. Justice Marshall dissented on a number of grounds, including his continuing belief that education is a fundamental right, which requires the Court to exercise strict scrutiny, striking down any law that is not necessary to further a compelling governmental interest.

Justice **Brennan** delivered the opinion of the Court, saying in part:

The question presented by these cases is whether, consistent with the Equal Protection Clause of the Fourteenth Amendment, Texas may deny to undocumented school-age children the free public education that it provides to children who are citizens of the United States or legally admitted aliens.

I.

Since the late nineteenth century, the United States has restricted immigration into this country. Unsanctioned entry into the United States is a crime, and those who have entered unlawfully are subject to deportation. But despite the existence of these legal restrictions, a substantial number of persons have succeeded in unlawfully entering the United States, and now live within various States, including the State of Texas.

In May 1975, the Texas legislature revised its education laws to withhold from local school districts any state funds for the education of children who were not "legally admitted" into the United States. The 1975 revision also authorized local school districts to deny enrollment in their public schools to children not "legally admitted" to the country. These cases involve constitutional challenges to those provisions. . . .

III.

The Equal Protection Clause directs that "all persons similarly circumstanced shall be treated alike." F. S. Royster Guano Co. v. Virginia (1920). But so too, "[t]he Constitution does not require things which are different in fact or opinion to be treated in law as though they were the same." . . . The initial discretion to determine what is "different" and what is "the same" resides in the legislatures of the States. A legislature must have substantial latitude to establish classifications that roughly approximate the nature of the problem perceived, that accommodate competing concerns both public and private, and that account for limitations on the practical ability of the State to remedy every ill. In applying the Equal Protection Clause to most forms of state action, we thus seek only the assurance that the classification at issue bears some fair relationship to a legitimate public purpose.

But we would not be faithful to our obligations under the Fourteenth Amendment if we applied so deferential a standard to every classification. The Equal Protection Clause was intended as a restriction on state legislative action inconsistent with elemental constitutional premises. Thus we have treated as presumptively invidious those classifications that disadvantage a "suspect class,"* or that impinge upon the exercise of a "fundamental right."† With respect to such classifications, it is appropriate to enforce the mandate of equal

---

*Several formulations might explain our treatment of certain classifications as "suspect." Some classifications are more likely than others to reflect deep-seated prejudice rather than legislative rationality in pursuit of some legitimate objective. Legislation predicted on such prejudice is easily recognized as incompatible with the constitutional understanding that each person is to be judged individually and is entitled to equal justice under the law. Classifications treated as suspect tend to be irrelevant to any proper legislative goal. . . . Finally, certain groups, indeed largely the same groups, have historically been "relegated to such a position of political powerlessness as to command extraordinary protection from the majoritarian political process." . . . The experience of our Nation has shown that prejudice may manifest itself in the treatment of some groups. Our response to that experience is reflected in the Equal Protection Clause of the Fourteenth Amendment. Legislation imposing special disabilities upon groups disfavored by virtue of circumstances beyond their control suggests the kind of "class or caste" treatment that the Fourteenth Amendment was designed to abolish.

†In determining whether a class-based denial of a particular right is deserving of strict scrutiny under the Equal Protection Clause, we look to the Constitution to see if the right infringed has its source, explicitly or implicitly, therein. But we have also recognized the fundamentality of participation in state "elections on an equal basis with other citizens in the jurisdiction," Dunn v. Blumstein [1972], even though "the right to vote, per se, is not a constitutionally protected right." San Antonio [v. Rodriguez, 1973]. . . . With respect to suffrage, we have explained the need for strict scrutiny as arising from the significance of the franchise as the guardian of all other rights. . . .

protection by requiring the State to demonstrate that its classification has been precisely tailored to serve a compelling governmental interest. In addition, we have recognized that certain forms of legislative classification, while not facially invidious, nonetheless give rise to recurring constitutional difficulties; in these limited circumstances we have sought the assurance that the classification reflects a reasoned judgment consistent with the ideal of equal protection by inquiring whether it may fairly be viewed as furthering a substantial interest of the State. We turn to a consideration of the standard appropriate for the evaluation of § 21.031.

A.

Sheer incapability or lax enforcement of the laws barring entry into this country, coupled with the failure to establish an effective bar to the employment of undocumented aliens has resulted in the creation of a substantial "shadow population" of illegal migrants—numbering in the millions—within our borders. This situation raises the specter of a permanent caste of undocumented resident aliens, encouraged by some to remain here as a source of cheap labor, but nevertheless denied the benefits that our society makes available to citizens and lawful residents. The existence of such an underclass presents most difficult problems for a Nation that prides itself on adherence to principles of equality under law.

The children who are plaintiffs in these cases are special members of this underclass. Persuasive arguments support the view that a State may withhold its beneficence from those whose very presence within the United States is the product of their own unlawful conduct. These arguments do not apply with the same force to classifications imposing disabilities on the minor *children* of such illegal entrants. At the least, those who enter our territory by stealth and in violation of our law should be prepared to bear the consequences, including, but not limited to deportation. But the children of those illegal entrants are not comparably situated. Their "parents have the ability to conform their conduct to societal norms," and presumably the ability to remove themselves from the State's jurisdiction; but the children who are plaintiffs in these cases "can affect neither their parents' conduct nor their own status." . . . Even if the State found it expedient to control the conduct of adults by acting against their children, legislation directing the onus of a parent's misconduct against his children does not comport with fundamental conceptions of justice. . . .

Of course, undocumented status is not irrelevant to any proper legislative goal. Nor is undocumented status an absolutely immutable characteristic since it is the product of conscious, indeed unlawful, action. But § 21.031 is directed against children, and imposes its discriminatory burden on the basis of a legal characteristic over which children can have little control. It is thus difficult to conceive of a rational justification for penalizing these children for their presence within the United States. Yet that appears to be precisely the effect of § 21.031.

Public education is not a "right" granted to individuals by the Constitution. . . . But neither is it merely some governmental "benefit" indistinguishable from other forms of social welfare legislation. Both the importance of education in maintaining our basic institutions, and the lasting impact of its deprivation on the life of the child, mark the distinction. The "American people have always regarded education [and] the acquisition of knowledge as matters of supreme importance." . . . We have recognized "the public schools as a most vital civic institution for the preservation of a democratic system of government," Abington School District v. Schempp (1963), and as the primary vehicle for transmitting "the values on which our society rests." . . . [A]s . . . pointed out early in our history, "some degree of education is necessary to prepare citizens to participate effectively and intelligently in our open political system if we are to preserve freedom and independence." Wisconsin v. Yoder (1972). And these historic "perceptions of the public schools as inculcating fundamental values necessary to the maintenance of a democratic political system have been confirmed by the observations of social scientists." . . . In addition, education provides the basic tools by which individuals might lead economically productive lives to the benefit of us all. In sum, education has a fundamental role in maintaining the fabric of our society. We cannot ignore the significant social costs borne by our Nation when select groups are denied the means to absorb the values and skills upon which our social order rests.

In addition to the pivotal role of education in sustaining our political and cultural heritage, denial of education to some isolated group of children poses an affront to one of the goals of the Equal Protection Clause: the abolition of governmental barriers presenting unreasonable obstacles to advancement on the basis of individual merit. Paradoxically, by depriving the children of any disfavored group of an education, we foreclose the means by which that group might raise the level of esteem in which it is held by the majority. But more directly, "education prepares individuals to be self-reliant and self-sufficient participants in society." . . . Illiteracy is an enduring disability. The inability to read and write will handicap the individual deprived of a basic education each and every day of his life. The inestimable toll of that deprivation on the social, economic, intellectual and psychological well-being of the individual, and the obstacle it poses to individual achievement, make it most difficult to reconcile the cost or the principle of a status-based denial of basic education with the framework of equality embodied in the Equal Protection Clause. . . .

B.

These well-settled principles allow us to determine the proper level of deference to be afforded § 21.031. Undocumented aliens cannot be treated as a suspect class because their presence in this country in violation of federal law is not a "constitutional irrelevancy." Nor is education a fundamental right; a State need not justify by compelling necessity every variation in the manner in which education is provided to its population. . . . But more is involved in these cases than the abstract question whether § 21.031 discriminates against a suspect class, or whether education is a fundamental right. Section 21.031 imposes a lifetime hardship on a discrete class of children not accountable for their disabling status. The stigma of illiteracy will mark them for the rest of their lives. By denying these children a basic education, we deny them the ability to live within the structure of our civic institutions, and foreclose any realistic possibility that they will contribute in even the smallest way to the progress of our Nation. In determining the rationality of § 21.031, we may appropriately take into account its costs to the Nation and to the innocent children who are its victims. In light of these countervailing costs, the discrimination contained in § 21.031 can hardly be considered rational unless it furthers some substantial goal of the State.

IV.

It is the State's principal argument, and apparently the view of the dissenting Justices, that the undocumented status of these children vel non establishes a sufficient rational basis for denying them benefits that a State might choose to afford other residents. The State notes that while other aliens are admitted ''on an equality of legal privileges with all citizens under non-discriminatory laws,'' Takahashi v. Fish & Game Comm'n (1948), the asserted right of these children to an education can claim no implicit imprimatur. Indeed, in the State's view, Congress' apparent disapproval of the presence of these children within the United States, and the evasion of the federal regulatory program that is the mark of undocumented status, provides authority for its decision to impose upon them special disabilities. Faced with an equal protection challenge respecting the treatment of aliens, we agree that the courts must be attentive to congressional policy; the exercise of congressional power might well affect the State's prerogatives to afford differential treatment to a particular class of aliens. But we are unable to find in the congressional immigration scheme any statement of policy that might weigh significantly in arriving at an equal protection balance concerning the State's authority to deprive these children of an education. . . .

As we recognized in De Canas v. Bica (1976), the States do have some authority to act with respect to illegal aliens, at least where such action mirrors federal objectives and furthers a legitimate state goal. In De Canas, the State's program reflected Congress' intention to bar from employment all aliens except those possessing a grant of permission to work in this country. In contrast, there is no indication that the disability imposed by § 21.031 corresponds to any identifiable congressional policy. The State does not claim that the conservation of state educational resources was ever a congressional concern in restricting immigration. More importantly, the classification reflected in § 21.031 does not operate harmoniously within the federal program.

To be sure, like all persons who have entered the United States unlawfully, these children are subject to deportation. But there is no assurance that a child subject to deportation will ever be deported. An illegal entrant might be granted federal permission to continue to reside in this country, or even to become a citizen. In light of the discretionary federal power to grant relief from deportation, a State cannot realistically determine that any particular undocumented child will in fact be deported until after deportation proceedings have been completed. It would of course be most difficult for the State to justify a denial of education to a child enjoying an inchoate federal permission to remain.

We are reluctant to impute to Congress the intention to withhold from these children, for so long as they are present in this country through no fault of their own, access to a basic education. . . . The State may borrow the federal classification. But to justify its use as a criterion for its own discriminatory policy, the State must demonstrate that the classification is reasonably adapted to *"the purposes for which the state desires to use it."* Oyama v. California (1948) (Murphy, J., concurring) (emphasis added). We therefore turn to the state objectives that are said to support § 21.031.

V.

Appellants argue that the classification at issue furthers an interest in the "preservation of the state's limited resources for the education of its lawful residents." Of course, a concern for the preservation of resources standing alone can hardly justify the classification used in allocating those resources. . . . The State must do more than justify its classification with a concise expression of an intention to discriminate. . . . Apart from the asserted state prerogative to act against undocumented children solely on the basis of their undocumented status—an asserted prerogative that carries only minimal force in the circumstances of these cases—we discern three colorable state interests that might support § 21.031.

First, appellants appear to suggest that the State may seek to protect itself from an influx of illegal immigrants. While a State might have an interest in mitigating the potentially harsh economic effects of sudden shifts in population, § 21.031 hardly offers an effective method of dealing with an urgent demographic or economic problem. There is no evidence in the record suggesting that illegal entrants impose any significant burden on the State's economy. To the contrary, the available evidence suggests that illegal aliens underutilize public services, while contributing their labor to the local economy and tax money to the state. The dominant incentive for illegal entry into the State of Texas is the availability of employment; few if any illegal immigrants come to this country, or presumably to the State of Texas, in order to avail themselves of a free education. Thus, even making the doubtful assumption that the net impact of illegal aliens on the economy is negative, we think it clear that ''[c]harging tuition to undocumented children constitutes a ludicrously ineffectual attempt to stem the tide of illegal immigration," at least when compared with the alternative of prohibiting the employment of illegal aliens.

Second, while it is apparent that a State may "not . . . reduce expenditures for education by barring [some arbitrarily chosen class of] children from its schools," Shapiro v. Thompson (1969), appellants suggest that undocumented children are appropriately singled out for exclusion because of the special burdens they impose on the State's ability to provide high quality public education. But the record in no way supports the claim that exclusion of undocumented children is likely to improve the overall quality of education in the State. . . . And, after reviewing the State's school financing mechanism, the District Court concluded that barring undocumented children from local schools would not necessarily improve the quality of education provided in those schools. Of course, even if improvement in the quality of education were a likely result of barring some *number* of children from the schools of the State, the State must support its selection of *this* group as the appropriate target for exclusion. In terms of educational cost and need, however, undocumented children are "basically indistinguishable" from legally resident alien children.

Finally, appellants suggest that undocumented children are appropriately singled out because their unlawful presence within the United States renders them less likely than other children to remain within the boundaries of the State, and to put their education to productive social or political use within the State. Even assuming that such an interest is legitimate, it is an interest that is most difficult to quantify. The State has no assurance that any child, citizen or not, will employ the education provided by the State within the confines of the State's borders. . . . It is difficult to understand precisely what the State hopes to achieve by promoting the creation and perpetuation of a subclass of illiterates within our boundaries, surely adding to the problems and costs of unemployment, welfare, and crime. It is thus clear that whatever savings might be achieved by denying these children an education, they are wholly insubstantial in light of the costs involved to those children, the State, and the Nation.

VI.

If the State is to deny a discrete group of innocent children the free public education that it offers to other children residing within its borders, that denial must be justified by a showing that it furthers some substantial state interest. No such showing was made here. . . .

Justice **Marshall,** concurring.

While I join the Court opinion, I do so without in any way retreating from my opinion in San Antonio Independent School District v. Rodriguez (1973) (dissenting opinion). I continue to believe that an individual's interest in education is fundamental, and that this view is amply supported "by the unique status accorded public education by our society, and by the close relationship between education and some of our most basic

constitutional values." Furthermore, I believe that the facts of these cases demonstrate the wisdom of rejecting a rigidified approach to equal protection analysis, and of employing an approach that allows for varying levels of scrutiny depending upon "the constitutional and societal importance of the interest adversely affected and the recognized invidiousness of the basis upon which the particular classification is drawn." See also Dandridge v. Williams (1970) (Marshall, J., dissenting). It continues to be my view that a class-based denial of public education is utterly incompatible with the Equal Protection Clause of the Fourteenth Amendment.

Justice **Blackmun,** concurring, said in part:

I join the opinion and judgment of the Court. . . .

The "fundamental rights" aspect of the Court's equal protection analysis—the now-familiar concept that governmental classifications bearing on certain interests must be closely scrutinized—has been the subject of some controversy. Justice Harlan, for example, warned that "[v]irtually every state statute affects important rights. . . . [T]o extend the 'compelling interest' rule to all cases in which such rights are affected would go far toward making this Court a 'super-legislature.' " Shapiro v. Thompson (1969) (dissenting opinion). . . . Still others have suggested that fundamental rights are not properly a part of equal protection analysis at all, because they are unrelated to any defined principle of equality.

These considerations, combined with doubts about the judiciary's ability to make fine distinctions in assessing the effects of complex social policies, led the Court in Rodriguez to articulate a firm rule: fundamental rights are those that "explicitly or implicitly [are] guaranteed by the Constitution." It therefore squarely rejected the notion that "an ad hoc determination as to the social or economic importance" of a given interest is relevant to the level of scrutiny accorded classifications involving that interest, and made clear that "[i]t is not the province of the Court to create substantive constitutional rights in the name of guaranteeing equal protection of the laws."

I joined Justice Powell's opinion for the Court in Rodriguez, and I continue to believe that it provides the appropriate model for resolving most equal protection disputes. . . .

With all this said, however, I believe the Court's experience has demonstrated that the Rodriguez formulation does not settle every issue of "fundamental rights" arising under the Equal Protection Clause. Only a pedant would insist that there are no meaningful distinctions among the multitude of social and political interests regulated by the States, and Rodriguez does not stand for quite so absolute a proposition. To the contrary, Rodriguez implicitly acknowledged that certain interests, though not constitutionally guaranteed, must be accorded a special place in equal protection analysis. Thus, the Court's decisions long have accorded strict scrutiny to classifications bearing on the right to vote in state elections, and Rodriguez confirmed the "constitutional underpinnings of the right to equal treatment in the voting process." Yet "the right to vote, per se, is not a constitutionally protected right." . . . Instead, regulation of the electoral process receives unusual scrutiny because "the right to exercise the franchise in a free and unimpaired manner is preservative of other basic civil and political rights." . . .

In my view, when the State provides an education to some and denies it to others, it immediately and inevitably creates class distinctions of a type fundamentally inconsistent with those purposes, mentioned above, of the Equal Protection Clause. Children denied an education are placed at a permanent and insurmountable competitive disadvantage, for an uneducated child is denied even the opportunity to achieve. And when those children are members of an identifiable group, that group—through the State's action—will have been converted into a discrete underclass. . . . In a sense, then, denial of an education is the analogue of denial of the right to vote: the former relegates the individual to second-class social status; the latter places him at a permanent political disadvantage.

This conclusion is fully consistent with Rodriguez. The Court there reserved judgment on the constitutionality of a state system that "occasioned an absolute denial of educational opportunities to any of its children," noting that "no charge fairly could be made that the system [at issue in Rodriguez] fails to provide each child with an opportunity to acquire . . . basic minimal skills." . . . Similarly, it is undeniable that education is not a "fundamental right" in the sense that it is constitutionally guaranteed. Here, however, the State has undertaken to provide an education to most of the children residing within its borders. And, in contrast to the situation in Rodriguez, it does not take an advanced degree to predict the effects of a complete denial of education upon those children targeted by the State's classification. In such circumstances, the voting decisions suggest that the State must offer something more than a rational basis for its classification. . . .

Justice **Powell**, concurring, said in part:

I join the opinion of the Court, and write separately to emphasize the unique character of the cases before us. . . .

Although the analogy is not perfect, our holding today does find support in decisions of this Court with respect to the status of illegitimates. In Weber v. Aetna Casualty & Surety Co. (1972) we said: "[V]isiting . . . condemnation on the head of an infant" for the misdeeds of the parents is illogical, unjust, and "contrary to the basic concept of our system that legal burdens should bear some relationship to individual responsibility or wrongdoing." . . .

In my view, the State's denial of education to these children bears no substantial relation to any substantial state interest. Both of the District Courts found that an uncertain but significant percentage of illegal alien children will remain in Texas as residents and many eventually will become citizens. The discussion by the Court,

at Part V., of the State's purported interests demonstrates that they are poorly served by the educational exclusion. Indeed, the interests relied upon by the State would seem to be insubstantial in view of the consequences to the State itself of wholly uneducated persons living indefinitely within its borders. . . .

Chief Justice **Burger,** with whom Justice **White,** Justice **Rehnquist,** and Justice **O'Connor** join, dissenting, said in part:

The Court makes no attempt to disguise that it is acting to make up for Congress' lack of "effective leadership" in dealing with the serious national problems caused by the influx of uncountable millions of illegal aliens across our borders. . . .

The Court's holding today manifests the justly criticized judicial tendency to attempt speedy and wholesale formulation of "remedies" for the failures—or simply the laggard pace—of the political process of our system of government. The Court employs, and in my view abuses, the Fourteenth Amendment in an effort to become an omnipotent and omniscient problem solver. That the motives for doing so are noble and compassionate does not alter the fact that the Court distorts our constitutional function to make amends for the defaults of others.

I. . . .

A.

The Court acknowledges that, except in those cases when state classifications disadvantage a "suspect class" or impinge upon a "fundamental right," the Equal Protection Clause permits a state "substantial latitude" in distinguishing between different groups of persons. Moreover, the Court expressly—and correctly—rejects any suggestion that illegal aliens are a suspect class, or that education is a fundamental right. Yet by patching together bits and pieces of what might be termed quasi-suspect-class and quasi-fundamental-rights analysis, the Court spins out a theory custom-tailored to the facts of these cases.

In the end, we are told little more than that the level of scrutiny employed to strike down the Texas law applies only when illegal alien children are deprived of a public education. If ever a court was guilty of an unabashedly result-oriented approach, this case is a prime example. . . .

B.

Once it is conceded—as the Court does—that illegal aliens are not a suspect class, and that education is not a fundamental right, our inquiry should focus on and be limited to whether the legislative classification at issue bears a rational relationship to a legitimate state purpose. . . .

The State contends primarily that § 21.031 serves to prevent undue depletion of its limited revenues available for education, and to preserve the fiscal integrity of the State's school-financing system against an ever-increasing flood of illegal aliens—aliens over whose entry or continued presence it has no control. Of course such fiscal concerns alone could not justify discrimination against a suspect class or an arbitrary and irrational denial of benefits to a particular group of persons. Yet I assume no Member of this Court would argue that prudent conservation of finite state revenues is per se an illegitimate goal. Indeed, the numerous classifications this Court has sustained in social welfare legislation were invariably related to the limited amount of revenues available to spend on any given program or set of programs. . . . The significant question here is whether the requirement of tuition from illegal aliens who attend the public schools—as well as from residents of other states, for example—is a rational and reasonable means of furthering the State's legitimate fiscal ends. . . .

RACE DISCRIMINATION

BATSON v. KENTUCKY

476 U.S. 79; 106 S. Ct. 1712; 90 L Ed. 2d 69
(1986)

Despite a strong tendency to water down the guarantees of the Fourteenth Amendment in order to preserve the pre-Civil War balance between nation and state, evidenced by the Slaughter-House Cases (1873) and similar decisions, the Supreme Court did, in the same period, give meaning to the equal protection clause, particularly in the area of the administration of justice. Ex parte Virginia (1880) upheld the conviction of a county court judge for excluding blacks, because of their race, from jury lists made out by him, in violation of a federal statute forbidding such racial discrimination in the selection of jurors. The statute was held valid. In the same year, the Court held that a black was entitled to be tried by a jury from which blacks had not been excluded because of their race, Strauder v. West Virginia (1880). At the same time, however, it was decided that the black is not entitled to have any blacks on the jury; see Virginia v. Rives (1880). The Southern states adjusted themselves to these two judicial rules by the simple process of avoiding any open discrimination against blacks in the calling of grand or petit juries; and yet no names of blacks found their way on to the jury lists and no black was ever called for jury service.

This situation was tacitly acquiesced in until the famous Scottsboro cases—Powell v. Alabama (1932) and Norris v. Alabama—were brought to the Supreme Court. In Norris the Court examined with care the procedure by which the juries which had indicted and tried the blacks had been chosen, found that blacks had been excluded from them because of their race, and held that their rights under the Fourteenth Amendment had been
violated. Since it is so difficult to prove either that a particular act of discrimination did occur or that it did not occur, the party who bears the burden of proof in this matter is at a marked disadvantage. In Hill v. Texas (1942) the Supreme Court made it clear that this burden of proof is not borne by the black defendant who alleges discrimination in the matter of jury service. In this case no black had served on a grand jury in the county for at least sixteen years, although there were hundreds of blacks presumably qualified to serve as grand jurors. This, the Court held, amounted to a prima facie case of discrimination which the state must rebut if it could. But such rebuttal was not made merely by showing that the jury commissioners had chosen as jurors personal acquaintances whom they knew to be qualified and that they did not happen to know any qualified blacks; they were constitutionally obligated to acquaint themselves with the qualifications of potential black jurors.

In Avery v. Georgia (1953) the Court set aside the conviction of a black by a petit jury selected from a panel on which no blacks were present. The jury panel was selected as follows: names of prospective jurors were chosen from the tax rolls and printed on tickets, the names of white persons being printed on white tickets and the names of blacks on yellow tickets. These tickets were placed in a box. They were drawn out by a judge, handed to the sheriff, who in turn entrusted them to the clerk who typed up the final list. The Supreme Court held that equal protection had been denied. "Even if the white and yellow tickets were drawn from the jury box without discrimination, opportunity was available to resort to it at other stages in the selection process. And, in view of the case before us, where not a single black was selected to serve on a panel of sixty—though many were available—we think that petitioner has certainly established a prima facie case of discrimination. . . . When a prima facie case of discrimination is presented, the burden falls, forthwith, upon the state to overcome it. The State has failed to meet this test." In Hernandez v. Texas (1954) the Court applied the rule to another racial group. They reversed the conviction of Hernandez by a jury where it was shown that no person with a Mexican or Latin-American name had served on a jury in that county for twenty-five years.

In 1965 a new problem in jury discrimination was presented to the Court. Alabama, instead of using the common-law system of peremptory challenges of individual jurors, employs what is called the "struck jury" system. In a capital case about 100 prospective jurors are assembled and after excusals and removals for cause about seventy-five remain. The prosecutor then strikes one and the defense two, taking turns, until only the necessary twelve remain as the jury. In a trial of a black for rape there had been six blacks in the original venire, but the prosecutor had struck all of them. The Supreme Court, voting five to four in Swain v. Alabama (1965), held that the resulting jury trial did not deny equal protection of the laws, despite the fact there had never been a black on a jury in this particular county. The Court held that the system of peremptory challenges was designed to produce a fair jury, and the motives of a par-

ticular prosecutor in striking a particular venireman could not be questioned without destroying that system. It did concede that a long, uninterrupted, and systematic pattern of the state striking blacks would raise a presumption that equal protection was being denied, but there was no evidence in the record of this case that the all-white juries of the past were not, at least in part, attributable to the defendants.

In cases where blacks actually do appear on the grand or petit jury in a case, it is considerably more difficult to make out a prima facie case of discrimination. In Akins v. Texas (1944) a black was indicted and tried by juries on each of which only one black served. Each jury commissioner testified, "I did not have any intention of placing more than one black on the panel." The Court said that no race or group is entitled to proportional representation on juries, and the presence of only one black did not deny equal protection of the laws. In Cassell v. Texas (1950), however, the Court held there had been discrimination despite the appearance of blacks on the jury lists. As in Hill v. Texas, the commissioners chose jurors from personal acquaintances, and had failed to acquaint themselves with the qualifications of prospective black jurors. However, where the names of jurors are selected from the tax rolls and those with the most property are chosen first, no racial discrimination is shown by the fact that more whites than blacks appear on the jury lists; see Brown v. Allen (1953).

In Peters v. Kiff (1972) the Supreme Court for the first time heard and upheld the complaint of a white man that he had been denied a fair trial because blacks were excluded from the grand jury that indicted him and the petit jury that tried him. Justice Marshall, speaking for Justices Douglas and Stewart, argued that a segregated jury, illegal in itself, failed to provide a cross section of the community and could injure a defendant, regardless of his race, by excluding "from the jury room qualities of human nature and varieties of human experience, the range of which is unknown and perhaps unknowable." Justices White, Brennan, and Powell agreed with the result on the ground that the "majestic generalities of the Fourteenth Amendment" had been given meaning by the federal statute forbidding race discrimination in the selection of juries, while Justices Burger, Blackmun and Rehnquist dissented because there was no showing of jury prejudice.

Justice **Powell** delivered the opinion of the Court, saying in part:

This case requires us to reexamine that portion of Swain v. Alabama (1965) concerning the evidentiary burden placed on a criminal defendant who claims that he has been denied equal protection through the State's use of peremptory challenges to exclude members of his race from the petit jury.

III.

The principles announced in Strauder [v. West Virginia (1880)] never have been questioned in any sub-

sequent decision of this Court. Rather, the Court has been called upon repeatedly to review the application of those principles to particular facts. A recurring question in these cases, as in any case alleging a violation of the Equal Protection Clause, was whether the defendant had met his burden of proving purposeful discrimination on the part of the State. . . . That question also was at the heart of the portion of Swain v. Alabama we reexamine today.

A.

Swain required the Court to decide, among other issues, whether a black defendant was denied equal protection by the State's exercise of peremptory challenges to exclude members of his own race from the petit jury. . . . The record in Swain showed that the prosecutor had used the State's peremptory challenges to strike the six black persons included on the petit jury venire. While rejecting the defendant's claim for failure to prove purposeful discrimination, the Court nonetheless indicated that the Equal Protection Clause placed some limits on the State's exercise of peremptory challenges.

The Court sought to accommodate the prosecutor's historical privilege of peremptory challenge free of judicial control and the constitutional prohibition on exclusion of persons from jury service on account of race. While the Constitution does not confer a right to peremptory challenges . . . , those challenges traditionally have been viewed as one means of assuring the selection of a qualified and unbiased jury. To preserve the peremptory nature of the prosecutor's challenge, the Court in Swain declined to scrutinize his actions in a particular case by relying on a presumption that he properly exercised the State's challenges.

The Court went on to observe, however, that a state may not exercise its challenges in contravention of the Equal Protection Clause. It was impermissible for a prosecutor to use his challenges to exclude blacks from the jury "for reasons wholly unrelated to the outcome of the particular case on trial" or to deny to blacks "the same right and opportunity to participate in the administration of justice enjoyed by the white population." Accordingly, a black defendant could make out a prima facie case of purposeful discrimination on proof that the peremptory challenge system was "being perverted" in that manner. For example, an inference of purposeful discrimination would be raised on evidence that a prosecutor, "in case after case, whatever the circumstances, whatever the crime and whoever the defendant or the victim may be, is responsible for the removal of Negroes who have been selected as qualified jurors by the jury commissioners and who have survived challenges for cause, with the result that no Negroes ever serve on petit juries." Evidence offered by the defendant in Swain did not meet that standard. While the defendant showed that prosecutors in the jurisdiction had exercised their strikes to exclude blacks from the jury, he offered no proof of the circumstances under which prosecutors were responsible for striking black jurors beyond the facts of his own case. . . .

B.

Since the decision in Swain, we have explained that our cases concerning selection of the venire reflect the general equal protection principle that the "invidious quality" of governmental action claimed to be racially discriminatory "must ultimately be traced to a racially discriminatory purpose." Washington v. Davis (1976). As in any equal protection case, the "burden is, of course," on the defendant who alleges discriminatory selection of the venire "to prove the existence of purposeful discrimination." Whitus v. Georgia [1967]. . . . In deciding if the defendant has carried his burden of persuasion, a court must undertake "a sensitive inquiry into such circumstantial and direct evidence of intent as may be available." . . . Circumstantial evidence of invidious intent may include proof of disproportionate impact. . . . We have observed that under some circumstances proof of discriminatory impact "may for all practical purposes demonstrate unconstitutionality because in various circumstances the discrimination is very difficult to explain on nonracial grounds." For example, "total or seriously disproportionate exclusion of Negroes from jury venires," . . . "is itself such an 'unequal application of the law . . . as to show intentional discrimination,' " . . .

Moreover, since Swain, we have recognized that a black defendant alleging that members of his race have been impermissibly excluded from the venire may make out a prima facie case of purposeful discrimination by showing that the totality of the relevant facts gives rise to an inference of discrimination. Washington v. Davis. Once the defendant makes the requisite showing, the burden shifts to the State to explain adequately the racial exclusion. . . . The State cannot meet this burden on mere general assertions that its officials did not discriminate or that they properly performed their official duties. . . . Rather, the State must demonstrate that "permissible racially neutral selection criteria and procedures have produced the monochromatic result." . . .

The showing necessary to establish a prima facie case of purposeful discrimination in selection of the venire may be discerned in this Court's decisions. . . . The defendant initially must show that he is a member of a racial group capable of being singled out for differential treatment. . . . In combination with the evidence, a defendant may then make a prima facie case by proving that in the particular jurisdiction members of his race have not been summoned for jury service over an extended period of time. Proof of systematic exclusion from the venire raises an inference of purposeful discrimination because the "result bespeaks discrimination." . . .

Since the ultimate issue is whether the State has discriminated in selecting the defendant's venire, however, the defendant may establish a prima facie case "in other ways than by evidence of long-continued unexplained absence" of members of his race "from many panels." . . . In cases involving the venire, this Court has found a prima facie case on proof that members of the defendant's race were substantially underrepresented on the venire from which his jury was drawn, and that the venire was selected under a practice providing "the opportunity for discrimination." Whitus v. Georgia. . . . This combination of factors raises the necessary inference of purposeful discrimination because the Court has declined to attribute to chance the absence of black citizens on a particular jury array where the selection mechanism is subject to abuse. When circumstances suggest the need, the trial court must undertake a "factual inquiry" that "takes into account all possible explanatory factors" in the particular case. . . .

Thus, since the decision in Swain, this Court has recognized that a defendant may make a prima facie showing of purposeful racial discrimination in selection of the venire by relying solely on the facts concerning its selection in his case. These decisions are in accordance with the proposition . . . that "a consistent pattern of official racial discrimination" is not "a necessary predicate to a violation of the Equal Protection Clause. A single invidiously discriminatory governmental act" is not "immunized by the absence of such discrimination in the making of other comparable decisions." . . .

C.

The standards for assessing a prima facie case in the context of discriminatory selection of the venire have been fully articulated since Swain. . . . These principles support our conclusion that a defendant may establish a prima facie case of purposeful discrimination in selection of the petit jury solely on evidence concerning the prosecutor's exercise of peremptory challenges at the defendant's trial. To establish such a case, the defendant must first show that he is a member of a cognizable racial group . . . and that the prosecutor has exercised peremptory challenges to remove from the venire members of the defendant's race. Second, the defendant is entitled to rely on the fact, as to which there can be no dispute, that peremptory challenges constitute a jury selection practice that permits "those to discriminate who are of a mind to discriminate." Avery v. Georgia. Finally, the defendant must show that these facts and any other relevant circumstances raise an inference that the prosecutor used that practice to exclude the veniremen from the petit jury on account of their race. This combination of factors in the empaneling of the petit jury, as in the selection of the venire, raises the necessary inference of purposeful discrimination.

SHELLEY v. KRAEMER

334 U. S. 1; 68 S. Ct. 836; 92 L. Ed. 1161 (1948)

The Bill of Rights forbids the federal government to invade the civil liberties of the citizen; the Fourteenth Amendment forbids the state governments to do so. A private citizen cannot violate either the Bill of Rights or the Fourteenth Amendment, because neither forbids him to do anything. This fact has particular significance for the black American. In the Civil Rights Cases (1883) the Supreme Court held that the Fourteenth Amendment does not protect the black against racial discrimination practiced by private individuals. Much later this rule was sharply emphasized in decisions holding that private landowners may lawfully agree with one another not to sell or lease their land to blacks. Such agreements, known as restrictive covenants, became increasingly important after the Supreme Court in Buchanan v. Warley (1917) held that an ordinance of Louisville, Kentucky, establishing exclusive residential zones for whites and blacks violated the due process clause of the Fourteenth Amendment. What the city had tried unsuccessfully to do by law could still be done on a limited scale by private contract. In thousands of communities land in residential areas was sold by deeds which contained "covenants running with the land," by which the successive purchasers bound themselves not to sell or lease the property to blacks. The validity of such a covenant was challenged in the Supreme Court in 1926 in Corrigan v. Buckley. Here thirty white persons, owning twenty-five parcels of land in the District of Columbia, had entered into a mutually restrictive covenant barring the sale or use of the land by blacks for a period of twenty-one years. Buckley, one of the owners, sought to enjoin Corrigan, another owner, from breaching the covenant by selling one of the parcels of land to a black. It was argued that the covenant violated the due process clause of the Fifth Amendment since it discriminated against blacks. (Had the case arisen in a state, the argument would have been grounded on the Fourteenth Amendment.) The Court unanimously held the covenant valid. In a brief opinion it declared: "The Fifth Amendment is a limitation only upon the powers of the general government, and is not directed against the action of individuals."

The Court in the opinion printed below did not deny that a contract between private parties to discriminate against blacks is entirely valid, as Corrigan v. Buckley had held. What was argued, and what the Court decided, was that the judicial enforcement of such a contract by the state courts makes the government a guilty partner in the racial discrimination and thereby violates the Fourteenth Amendment. The companion case of Hurd v. Hodge (1948) held that the enforcement by the federal courts of restrictive covenants in the District of Columbia was a denial of due process of law guaranteed by the Fifth Amendment.

If a state cannot discriminate on the basis of race in its property ownership and housing policies, neither can the people, by using their law-making power, undo government efforts to abolish private discrimination. In the general election of 1964 the voters of California, by a two-to-one vote, approved a constitutional amendment forbidding either state or local governments to "limit or abridge, directly or indirectly, the right of any person, who is willing or desires to sell, lease or rent any part or all of his real property, to decline to sell, lease or rent such property to such person or persons as he, in his ab-

solute discretion, chooses." The amendment, sponsored by the real estate interests of California, had the effect of nullifying the open-housing provisions of the Unruh Act of 1959 and the Rumford Fair Housing Act of 1963 and prohibiting the enactment of such provisions in the future. The supreme court of California held the amendment void as a violation of the Fourteenth Amendment, and in Reitman v. Mulkey (1967) the Supreme Court affirmed. Although the Court did not deny the right of California to repeal its open housing laws, it agreed with the finding of the California court that the amendment "would encourage and significantly involve the State in private racial discrimination contrary to the Fourteenth Amendment. . . . The right to discriminate, including the right to discriminate on racial grounds, was now embodied in the State's basic charter, immune from legislative, executive, or judicial regulation at any level of the state government. Those practicing racial discriminations need no longer rely solely on their personal choice. They could now invoke express constitutional authority, free from censure or interference of any kind from official sources." Justices Harlan, Black, Clark, and Stewart dissented on the ground that the amendment merely left the state as "neutral" with respect to private discrimination as it would have been had it not passed the open housing law in the first place.

In Hunter v. Erickson (1969), involving a very similar situation, the Court held void an amendment to the Akron, Ohio, city charter requiring all fair housing laws (including the one already in existence) to be submitted to a popular referendum at a city election. The Court held the amendment void, pointing out that (1) "only laws to end housing discrimination based on 'race, color, religion, national origin or ancestry'" had to run this difficult gauntlet, (2) "racial classification" bore a " 'far heavier burden of justification' than other classifications," and (3) they were "unimpressed with any of the State's justifications for its discrimination." A similar result was reached when a Seattle, Washington, school district passed by initiative and referendum a prohibition against busing students for purposes of desegregating the schools, while permitting busing for other purposes; see Washington v. Seattle School Dist. No. 1 (1982). The Court did hold valid, however, an amendment to the California constitution forbidding the state courts to order busing unless the federal courts would do so to remedy violations of the Fourteenth Amendment; see Crawford v. Los Angeles Board of Education (1982).

Where, however, discrimination is not based on race a different standard applies, and in James v. Valtierra (1971) the Court upheld, voting five to three, a California constitutional requirement that "low-rent" housing projects be submitted to the voters in the community for approval, while those designed for other groups, including middle-income groups, need pass no such hurdle. The Court stressed that the "distinctions" were not "based on race," and observed that "provisions for referendums demonstrate devotion to democracy, not to bias, discrimination, or prejudice."

The Court has been slow to lay down guides as to how much state participation was necessary to convert clearly discriminatory private action into "state" action under the equal protection clause. While the Court in the present case answered the question with regard to court enforcement, in none of the "sit-in" cases of the 1960s did the Court say whether state enforcement of its trespass laws to back up private discrimination amounted to such action or not.

In Moose Lodge No. 107 v. Iris (1972) the Court held that the mere granting of a liquor license to a private club that discriminated against blacks did not normally involve the state in discrimination. To hold that any state aid, such as fire or police protection, made a private club an agent of the state would be to destroy entirely the distinction between state and private action. "The State must have 'significantly involved itself with invidious discriminations,' Reitman v. Mulkey (1967), in order for the discriminatory action to fall within the ambit of the constitutional prohibition." In this case, however, state regulations required the club to adhere to its bylaws, and to the extent that these required discrimination, the regulations were unconstitutional since this "would be to invoke the sanctions of the State to enforce a concededly discriminatory private rule."

Mr. Chief Justice **Vinson** delivered the opinion of the Court, saying in part:

These cases present for our consideration questions relating to the validity of court enforcement of private agreements, generally described as restrictive covenants, which have as their purpose the exclusion of persons of designated race or color from the ownership or occupancy of real property. Basic constitutional issues of obvious importance have been raised.

The first of these cases comes to this Court on certiorari to the Supreme Court of Missouri. On February 16, 1911, thirty out of a total of thirty-nine owners of property fronting both sides of Labadie Avenue between Taylor Avenue and Cora Avenue in the city of St. Louis, signed an agreement, which was subsequently recorded, providing in part:

". . . The said property is hereby restricted to the use and occupancy for the term of Fifty (50) years from this date, so that it shall be a condition all the time and whether recited and referred to as [sic] not in subsequent conveyances and shall attach to the land, as a condition precedent to the sale of the same, that hereafter no part of said property or any portion thereof shall be, for said term of Fifty years, occupied by any person not of the Caucasian race, it being intended hereby to restrict the use of said property for said period of time against the occupancy as owners or tenants of any portion of said property for resident or other purpose by people of the Negro or Mongolian Race." . . .

On August 11, 1945, pursuant to a contract of sale, petitioners Shelley, who are Negroes, for valuable consideration received from one Fitzgerald a warranty deed to the parcel in question. The trial court found that peti-

tioners had no actual knowledge of the restrictive agreement at the time of the purchase.

On October 9, 1945, respondents, as owners of other property subject to the terms of the restrictive covenant, brought suit in the Circuit Court of the city of St. Louis praying that petitioners Shelley be restrained from taking possession of the property and that judgment be entered divesting title out of petitioners Shelley and revesting title in the immediate grantor or in such other person as the court should direct. The trial court denied the requested relief on the ground that the restrictive agreement, upon which respondents based their action, had never become final and complete because it was the intention of the parties to that agreement that it was not to become effective until signed by all property owners in the district, and signatures of all the owners had never been obtained.

The Supreme Court of Missouri sitting en banc reversed and directed the trial court to grant the relief for which respondents had prayed. That court held the agreement effective and concluded that enforcement of its provisions violated no rights guaranteed to petitioners by the Federal Constitution. At the time the court rendered its decision, petitioners were occupying the property in question. . . .

Petitioners have placed primary reliance on their contentions, first raised in the state courts, that judicial enforcement of the restrictive agreements in these cases has violated rights guaranteed to petitioners by the Fourteenth Amendment of the Federal Constitution and Acts of Congress passed pursuant to that Amendment. Specifically, petitioners urge that they have been denied the equal protection of the laws, deprived of property without due process of law, and have been denied privileges and immunities of citizens of the United States. We pass to a consideration of those issues.

I.

Whether the equal protection clause of the Fourteenth Amendment inhibits judicial enforcement by state courts of restrictive covenants based on race or color is a question which this Court has not heretofore been called upon to consider. . . .

It is well, at the outset, to scrutinize the terms of the restrictive agreements involved in these cases. In the Missouri case, the covenant declares that no part of the affected property shall be "occupied by any person not of the Caucasian race, it being intended hereby to restrict the use of said property . . . against the occupancy as owners or tenants of any portion of said property for resident or other purpose by people of the Negro or Mongolian Race." Not only does the restriction seek to proscribe use and occupancy of the affected properties by members of the excluded class, but as construed by the Missouri courts, the agreement requires that title of any person who uses his property in violation of the restriction shall be divested. . . .

It cannot be doubted that among the civil rights intended to be protected from discriminatory state action by the Fourteenth Amendment are the rights to acquire, enjoy, own and dispose of property. Equality in the enjoyment of property rights was regarded by the framers of that Amendment as an essential pre-condition to the realization of other basic civil rights and liberties which the Amendment was intended to guarantee. Thus, § 1978 of the Revised Statutes, derived from § 1 of the Civil Rights Act of 1866 which was enacted by Congress while the Fourteenth Amendment was also under consideration provides:

"All citizens of the United States shall have the same right, in every State and Territory, as is enjoyed by white citizens thereof to inherit, purchase, lease, sell, hold, and convey real and personal property." This Court has given specific recognition to the same principle. Buchanan v. Warley (1917).

It is likewise clear that restrictions on the right of occupancy of the sort sought to be created by the private agreements in these cases could not be squared with the requirements of the Fourteenth Amendment if imposed by state statute or local ordinance. . . .

But the present cases, unlike those just discussed, do not involve action by state legislatures or city councils. Here the particular patterns of discrimination and the areas in which the restrictions are to operate, are determined, in the first instance, by the terms of agreements among private individuals. Participation of the State consists in the enforcement of the restrictions so defined. The crucial issue with which we are here confronted is whether this distinction removes these cases from the operation of the prohibitory provisions of the Fourteenth Amendment.

Since the decision of this Court in the Civil Rights Cases (1883) the principle has become firmly embedded in our constitutional law that the action inhibited by the first section of the Fourteenth Amendment is only such action as may fairly be said to be that of the States. That Amendment erects no shield against merely private conduct, however discriminatory or wrongful.

We conclude, therefore, that the restrictive agreements standing alone cannot be regarded as violative of any rights guaranteed to petitioners by the Fourteenth Amendment. So long as the purposes of those agreements are effectuated by voluntary adherence to their terms, it would appear clear that there has been no action by the State and the provisions of the Amendment have not been violated. Cf. Corrigan v. Buckley.

But here there was more. These are cases in which the purposes of the agreements were secured only by judicial enforcement by state courts of the restrictive terms of the agreements. The respondents urge that judicial enforcement of private agreements does not amount to state action; or, in any event, the participation of the States is so attenuated in character as not to amount to state action within the meaning of the Fourteenth Amendment. Finally, it is suggested, even if the States in these cases may be deemed to have acted in the constitutional sense, their action did not deprive petitioners of rights guaranteed by the Fourteenth Amendment. We move to a consideration of these matters.

II.

That the action of state courts and of judicial officers in their official capacities is to be regarded as action of the State within the meaning of the Fourteenth Amendment, is a proposition which has long been established by decisions of this Court. That principle was given expression in the earliest cases involving the construction of the terms of the Fourteenth Amendment. . . . [The Court here discusses several cases in which state judicial action was held to be discriminatory and therefore a violation of the Fourteenth Amendment.]

But the examples of state judicial action which have been held by this Court to violate the Amendment's commands are not restricted to situations in which the judicial proceedings were found in some manner to be procedurally unfair. It has been recognized that the action of state courts in enforcing a substantive common-law rule formulated by those courts, may result in the denial of rights guaranteed by the Fourteenth Amendment, even though the judicial proceedings in such cases may have been in complete accord with the most rigorous conceptions of procedural due process. . . .

The short of the matter is that from the time of the adoption of the Fourteenth Amendment until the present, it has been the consistent ruling of this Court that the action of the States to which the Amendment has reference, includes action of state courts and state judicial officials. Although, in construing the terms of the Fourteenth Amendment, differences have from time to time been expressed as to whether particular types of state action may be said to offend the Amendment's prohibitory provisions, it has never been suggested that state court action is immunized from the operation of those provisions simply because the act is that of the judicial branch of the state government.

III.

Against this background of judicial construction, extending over a period of some three-quarters of a century, we are called upon to consider whether enforcement by state courts of the restrictive agreements in these cases may be deemed to be the acts of those States; and, if so, whether that action has denied these petitioners the equal protection of the laws which the Amendment was intended to insure.

We have no doubt that there has been state action in these cases in the full and complete sense of the phrase. The undisputed facts disclose that petitioners were willing purchasers of properties upon which they desired to establish homes. The owners of the properties were willing sellers; and contracts of sale were accordingly consummated. It is clear that but for the active intervention of the state courts, supported by the full panoply of state power, petitioners would have been free to occupy the properties in question without restraint.

These are not cases, as has been suggested, in which the States have merely abstained from action, leaving private individuals free to impose such discriminations as they see fit. Rather, these are cases in which the States have made available to such individuals the full coercive power of government to deny to petitioners, on the grounds of race or color, the enjoyment of property rights in premises which petitioners are willing and financially able to acquire and which the grantors are willing to sell. The difference between judicial enforcement and non-enforcement of the restrictive covenants is the difference to petitioners between being denied rights of property available to other members of the community and being accorded full enjoyment of those rights on an equal footing. . . .

We hold that in granting judicial enforcement of the restrictive agreements in these cases, the States have denied petitioners the equal protection of the laws and that, therefore, the action of the state courts cannot stand. We have noted that freedom from discrimination by the States in the enjoyment of property rights was among the basic objectives sought to be effectuated by the framers of the Fourteenth Amendment. That such discrimination has occurred in these cases is clear. Because of the race or color of these petitioners they have been denied rights of ownership or occupancy enjoyed as a matter of course by other citizens of different race or color. . . .

Respondents urge, however, that since the state courts stand ready to enforce restrictive covenants excluding white persons from the ownership or occupancy of property covered by such agreements, enforcement of covenants excluding colored persons may not be deemed a denial of equal protection of the laws to the colored persons who are thereby affected. This contention does not bear scrutiny. The parties have directed our attention to no case in which a court, state or federal, has been called upon to enforce a covenant excluding members of the white majority from ownership or occupancy of real property on grounds of race or color. But there are more fundamental considerations. The rights created by the first section of the Fourteenth Amendment are, by its terms, guaranteed to the individual. The rights established are personal rights. It is, therefore, no answer to these petitioners to say that the courts may also be induced to deny white persons rights of ownership and occupancy on grounds of race or color. Equal protection of the laws is not achieved through indiscriminate imposition of inequalities. . . .

The historical context in which the Fourteenth Amendment became a part of the Constitution should not be forgotten. Whatever else the framers sought to achieve, it is clear that the matter of primary concern was the establishment of equality in the enjoyment of basic civil and political rights and the preservation of those rights from discriminatory action on the part of the States based on considerations of race or color. Seventy-five years ago this Court announced that the provisions of the Amendment are to be construed with this fundamental purpose in mind. Upon full consideration, we have concluded that in these cases the States have acted to deny petitioners the equal protection of the laws guaranteed by the Fourteenth Amendment. Having so decided, we find it unnecessary to consider whether petitioners have also been deprived of property without due process of law or denied privileges and immunities of citizens of the United States. . . .

Reversed.

Justices **Reed, Jackson,** and **Rutledge** took no part in the consideration or decision of these cases.

PLESSY v. FERGUSON

163 U. S. 537; 16 S. Ct. 1138; 41 L. Ed. 256
(1896)

With the passing of the Reconstruction era and the return of "white man's government" to the Southern states, state laws were again adopted reminiscent of the "Black Codes" which had been passed right after the Civil War to "keep the Negro in his place." These laws established, and enforced by criminal penalties, a system of racial segregation under which members of the black and white races were required to be separated in the enjoyment of public and semi-public facilities. Separate schools, parks, waiting rooms, bus and railroad accommodations were required by law to be furnished each race; and where completely separate facilities later on proved to be not feasible, as in a dining car, a curtained partition served to separate the races.

Where racial segregation was effected by private action, as in the case of stores or clubs, no constitutional issue could be raised after the decision in the Civil Rights Cases in 1883. Where the segregation was required by law, however, the question arose whether it violated the rights guaranteed to the newly freed black by the Fourteenth Amendment. This problem came to the Court for the first time in the present case, twenty-eight years after the Amendment had been adopted. The legislature of Louisiana had passed in 1890 a statute providing "that all railway companies carrying passengers in their coaches in this state shall provide equal but separate accommodations for the white and colored races, by providing two or more passenger coaches for each passenger train, or by dividing the passenger coaches by a partition so as to secure separate accommodations. . . ." A fine of $25 or twenty days in jail was the penalty for sitting in the wrong compartment. Plessy, a person who was one-eighth black, refused to vacate a seat in the white compartment of a railway car and was arrested for violating the statute.

The Plessy case made lawful for nearly sixty years the doctrine that blacks are not denied the equal protection of the laws by compelling them to accept "separate but equal" accommodations. There is a bit of irony in the fact that the majority opinion in the Plessy case was written by Justice Brown, a Yale man from the state of Michigan, while the eloquent protest against racial discrimination is found in the dissenting opinion of Justice Harlan, a Southerner from Kentucky.

Query: Does it raise an equal protection question that the Court accepted the state's determination that Plessy, who was seven-eighths white, was black? What would have been the impact of a ruling that permitted segregation but held that a person was to be considered white if he were more than 50 percent white, and black if he were more than 50 percent black?

Mr. Justice **Brown** delivered the opinion of the Court, saying in part:

The object of the [Fourteenth] amendment was undoubtedly to enforce the absolute equality of the two races before the law, but in the nature of things it could not have been intended to abolish distinctions based upon color, or to enforce social, as distinguished from political, equality, or a commingling of the two races upon terms unsatisfactory to either. Laws permitting, and even requiring their separation in places where they are liable to be brought into contact do not necessarily imply the inferiority of either race to the other, and have been generally, if not universally, recognized as within the competency of the state legislatures in the exercise of their police power. The most common instance of this is connected with the establishment of separate schools for white and colored children, which [has] been held to be a valid exercise of the legislative power even by courts of states where the political rights of the colored race have been longest and most earnestly enforced.

One of the earliest of these cases is that of Roberts v. Boston, 5 Cush. (Mass.) 198 [1849] in which the supreme judicial court of Massachusetts held that the general school committee of Boston had power to make provision for the instruction of colored children in separate schools established exclusively for them, and to prohibit their attendance upon the other schools. . . . Similar laws have been enacted by Congress under its general power of legislation over the District of Columbia, as well as by the legislatures of many of the states, and have been generally, if not uniformly, sustained by the courts. . . .

Laws forbidding the intermarriage of the two races may be said in a technical sense to interfere with the freedom of contract, and yet have been universally recognized as within the police power of the state. . . .

The distinction between laws interfering with the political equality of the negro and those requiring the separation of the two races in schools, theatres, and railway carriages, has been frequently drawn by this court. . . .

In this connection, it is also suggested by the learned counsel for the plaintiff in error that the same argument that will justify the state legislature in requiring railways to provide separate accommodations for the two races will also authorize them to require separate cars to be provided for people whose hair is of a certain color, or who are aliens, or who belong to certain nationalities, or to enact laws requiring colored people to walk upon one side of the street, and white people upon the other, or requiring white men's houses to be painted white, and colored men's black, or their vehicles or business signs to be of different colors, upon the theory that one side of the street is as good as the other, or that a house or vehicle of one color is as good as one of another color. The reply to all this is that every exercise of the police power must be reasonable, and extend only to such laws as are enacted in good faith for the promotion of the public good, and not for the annoyance or oppression of a particular class. . . .

So far, then, as a conflict with the 14th Amendment is concerned, the case reduces itself to the question whether the statute of Louisiana is a reasonable regulation, and with respect to this there must necessarily be a large discretion on the part of the legislature. In determining the question of reasonableness it is at liberty to act with reference to the established usages, customs, and traditions of the people, and with a view to the promotion of their comfort, and the preservation of the public peace and good order. Gauged by this standard, we cannot say that a law which authorizes or even requires the separation of the two races in public conveyances is unreasonable, or more obnoxious to the 14th Amendment than the acts of Congress requiring separate schools for colored children in the District of Columbia, the constitutionality of which does not seem to have been questioned, or the corresponding acts of state legislatures.

We consider the underlying fallacy of the plaintiff's argument to consist in the assumption that the enforced separation of the two races stamps the colored race with a badge of inferiority. If this be so, it is not by reason of anything found in the act, but solely because the colored race chooses to put that construction upon it. The argument necessarily assumes that if, as has been more than once the case, and is not unlikely to be so again, the colored race should become the dominant power in the state legislature, and should enact a law in precisely similar terms, it would thereby relegate the white race to an inferior position. We imagine that the white race, at least, would not acquiesce in this assumption. The argument also assumes that social prejudices may be overcome by legislation, and that equal rights cannot be secured to the negro except by an enforced commingling of the two races. We cannot accept this proposition. If the two races are to meet on terms of social equality, it must be the result of natural affinities, a mutual appreciation of each other's merits and a voluntary consent of individuals. . . . Legislation is powerless to eradicate racial instincts or to abolish distinctions based upon physical differences, and the attempt to do so can only result in accentuating the difficulties of the present situation. If the civil and political rights of both races be equal, one cannot be inferior to the other civilly or politically. If one race be inferior to the other socially, the Constitution of the United States cannot put them upon the same plane. . . .

The judgment of the court below is therefore affirmed.

Mr. Justice **Brewer** took no part in the decision of this case.

Mr. Justice **Harlan** wrote a dissenting opinion, saying in part:

While there may be in Louisiana persons of different races who are not citizens of the United States, the words in the act, "white and colored races," necessarily include all citizens of the United States of both races residing in that state. So that we have before us a state enactment that compels, under penalties, the separation of the two races in railroad passenger coaches, and makes it a crime for a citizen of either race to enter a coach that has been assigned to citizens of the other race.

Thus the state regulates the use of a public highway by citizens of the United States solely upon the basis of race.

However apparent the injustice of such legislation may be, we have only to consider whether it is consistent with the Constitution of the United States. . . .

In respect of civil rights, common to all citizens, the Constitution of the United States does not, I think, permit any public authority to know the race of those entitled to be protected in the enjoyment of such rights. Every true man has pride of race, and under appropriate circumstances, when the rights of others, his equals before the law, are not to be affected, it is his privilege to express such pride and to take such action based upon it as to him seems proper. But I deny that any legislative body or judicial tribunal may have regard to the race of citizens when the civil rights of those citizens are involved. Indeed such legislation as that here in question is inconsistent, not only with that equality of rights which pertains to citizenship, national and state, but with the personal liberty enjoyed by every one within the United States. . . .

The white race deems itself to be the dominant race in this country. And so it is, in prestige, in achievements, in education, in wealth and in power. So, I doubt not that it will continue to be for all time, if it remains true to its great heritage and holds fast to the principles of constitutional liberty. But in view of the Constitution, in the eye of the law, there is in this country no superior, dominant, ruling class of citizens. There is no caste here. Our Constitution is color-blind, and neither knows nor tolerates classes among citizens. In respect of civil rights, all citizens are equal before the law. The humblest is the peer of the most powerful. The law regards man as man, and takes no account of his surroundings or of his color when his civil rights as guaranteed by the supreme law of the land are involved. It is therefore to be regretted that this high tribunal, the final expositor of the fundamental law of the land, has reached the conclusion that it is competent for a state to regulate the enjoyment by citizens of their civil rights solely upon the basis of race.

In my opinion, the judgment this day rendered will, in time, prove to be quite as pernicious as the decision made by this tribunal in the Dred Scott Case. It was adjudged in that case that the descendants of Africans who were imported into this country and sold as slaves were not included nor intended to be included under the word "citizens" in the Constitution, and could not claim any of the rights and privileges which that instrument provided for and secured to citizens of the United States; that at the time of the adoption of the Constitution they were "considered as a subordinate and inferior class of beings, who had been subjugated by the dominant race, and, whether emancipated or not, yet remained subject to their authority, and had no rights or privileges but such as those who held the power and the government might choose to grant them." The recent amendments of the Constitution, it was supposed, had eradicated these principles from our institutions. But it seems that we have yet, in some of the states, a dominant race, a superior class of citizens, which assumes to regulate the enjoyment of civil rights, common to all citizens, upon the basis of race. The present decision, it may well be apprehended, will not [only] stimulate aggressions, more or less brutal and irritating, upon the admitted rights of colored citizens, but will encourage the belief that it is possible, by means of state enactments, to defeat the beneficent purposes which the people of the United States had in view when they adopted the recent amendments of the Constitution, by one of which the blacks of this country were made citizens of the United States and of the states in which they respectively reside and whose privileges and immunities, as citizens, the states are forbidden to abridge. Sixty millions of whites are in no danger from the presence here of eight millions of blacks. The destinies of the two races in this country are indissolubly linked together, and the interests of both require that the common government of all shall not permit the seeds of race hate to be planted under the sanction of law. What can more certainly arouse race hate, what more certainly create and perpetuate a feeling of distrust between these races, than State enactments which in fact proceed on the ground that colored citizens are so inferior and degraded that they cannot be allowed to sit in public coaches occupied by white citizens? That, as all will admit, is the real meaning of such legislation as was enacted in Louisiana.

The sure guarantee of the peace and security of each race is the clear, distinct, unconditional recognition by our governments, national and state, of every right that inheres in civil freedom, and of the equality before the law of all citizens of the United States without regard to race. State enactments, regulating the enjoyment of civil rights, upon the basis of race, and cunningly devised to defeat legitimate results of the war, under the pretense of recognizing equality of rights, can have no other result than to render permanent peace impossible and to keep alive a conflict of races, the continuance of which must do harm to all concerned. This question is not met by the suggestion that social equality cannot exist between the white and black races in this country. That argument, if it can be properly regarded as one, is scarcely worthy of consideration, for social equality no more exists between two races when travelling in a passenger coach or a public highway than when members of the same races sit by each other in a street car or in the jury box, or stand or sit with each other in a political assembly, or when they use in common the streets of a city or town, or when they are in the same room for the purpose of having their names placed on the registry of voters, or when they approach the ballot-box in order to exercise the high privilege of voting. . . .

The arbitrary separation of citizens, on the basis of race, while they are on a public highway, is a badge of servitude wholly inconsistent with the civil freedom and the equality before the law established by the Constitution. It cannot be justified upon any legal grounds.

If evils will result from the commingling of the two races upon public highways established for the benefit of all, they will be infinitely less than those that will surely come from state legislation regulating the enjoyment of civil rights upon the basis of race. We boast of the freedom enjoyed by our people above all other peoples. But it is difficult to reconcile that boast with a state of the law which, practically, puts the brand of servitude and degradation upon a large class of our fellow citizens, our equals before the law. The thin disguise of "equal" accommodations for passengers in railroad coaches will not mislead any one, or atone for the wrong this day done. . . .

I am of opinion that the statute of Louisiana is inconsistent with the personal liberty of citizens, white and black, in that state, and hostile to both the spirit and letter of the Constitution of the United States. If laws of like character should be enacted in the several states of the Union, the effect would be in the highest degree mischievous. Slavery as an institution tolerated by law would, it is true, have disappeared from our country, but there would remain a power in the states, by sinister legislation, to interfere with the full enjoyment of the blessings of freedom; to regulate civil rights, common to all citizens, upon the basis of race; and to place in a condition of legal inferiority a large body of American citizens, now constituting a part of the political community, called the people of the United States, for whom and by whom, through representatives, our government is administered. Such a system is inconsistent with the guarantee given by the Constitution to each state of a republican form of government, and may be stricken down by congressional action, or by the courts in the discharge of their solemn duty to maintain the supreme law of the land, anything in the Constitution or laws of any state to the contrary notwithstanding.

For the reasons stated, I am constrained to withhold my assent from the opinion and judgment of the majority.

SWEATT v. PAINTER

339 U. S. 629; 70 S. Ct. 848; 94 L. Ed. 1114
(1950)

Although Plessy v. Ferguson (1896) involved segregation only in the use of railroad facilities, there was no reason to doubt that the Court would uphold segregation in other areas as well, especially education. This be-

came clear when the Court, in Berea College v. Kentucky (1908), held that the state could validly forbid a college, even though a private institution, to teach whites and blacks at the same time and place. This left no doubt of the validity of the Southern laws requiring the education of white and black children in separate tax-supported schools.

While the segregation of whites and blacks was valid, it was valid only on the theory that the facilities offered were equal, since it is the "equal" protection of the laws that is guaranteed by the Fourteenth Amendment. In common usage there are no degrees of equality; things or conditions are either equal or they are not equal. But the Supreme Court has not taken this view. It has held, rather, that equality in accommodations means not exact or mathematical equality, but only "substantial" equality. In earlier cases the Court was extremely lenient in construing what "equality" required in the segregated school systems of the South. In Cumming v. County Board of Education (1899) it found no denial of equal protection of the laws in the failure of a Southern county to provide a high school for sixty black children, although it maintained a high school for white children. The Court seemed satisfied with the county's defense that it could not afford to build a high school for black children. In Gong Lum v. Rice (1927) the Court held that a Chinese girl could validly be required to attend a school for black children in a neighboring school district, rather than be allowed to attend the nearby school for white children.

In 1914 the Supreme Court began to show signs of requiring a much closer approach to equality under segregation. In McCabe v. Atchison, T. & S. F. Ry. Co. (1914) an Oklahoma law was held not to accord equal accommodations to blacks and whites when it allowed railroads to haul sleeping, dining, and chair cars for the exclusive use of whites without providing such cars on demand for the use of blacks.

The tougher attitude of the Court toward what equality under segregation means was made abundantly clear in 1938 in the leading case of Missouri ex rel. Gaines v. Canada. Gaines, a black graduate of Lincoln University and a citizen of Missouri, applied for admission to the University of Missouri law school. He was refused solely upon the ground that he was black, but the state agreed to pay his tuition in the law school of any adjacent state which would accept him, pending such time as Missouri should itself build a black law school. Kansas, Nebraska, Iowa, and Illinois had law schools which admitted nonresident blacks. The Supreme Court found that Gaines had been denied equal protection of the laws, and ruled that ". . . petitioner was entitled to be admitted to the law school of the State University in the absence of other and proper provision for his legal training within the State." The Court said, "The basic consideration is not as to what sort of opportunities other States provide, or whether they are as good as those in Missouri, but as to what opportunities Missouri itself furnishes to white students and denies to negroes solely upon the ground of color. . . . Manifestly, the obligation of the State to give the protection of equal laws can be performed only where its laws operate, that is, within its own jurisdiction.''

In 1948 a case almost identical with the Gaines case came to the Court from Oklahoma. A young black woman applied for admission to the law school of the University of Oklahoma and was refused. In Sipuel v. University of Oklahoma (1948) the Court in a one-page opinion reaffirmed the ruling in the Gaines case. It said: "The petitioner is entitled to secure legal education afforded by a state institution. To this time it has been denied her although during the same period many white applicants have been afforded legal education by the State. The State must provide it for her in conformity with the equal protection clause of the Fourteenth Amendment and provide it as soon as it does for applicants of any other group.''

A black graduate student was admitted to the University of Oklahoma, but was required to sit in a row in the classroom specified for black students, at a designated table in the library, and at a special table in the cafeteria. In McLaurin v. Oklahoma State Regents (1950) the Supreme Court held that under the equal protection clause the black student must be given the same treatment by the state as students of other races.

While Congress has full power to regulate interstate commerce, it had never abolished racial segregation on interstate trains. All it had done was to forbid any interstate common carrier to give any person or group any "unreasonable preference or advantage," or subject them to "any undue or unreasonable prejudice or disadvantage." In practice these restrictions had been interpreted in the light of the "separate but equal" doctrine of Plessy v. Ferguson. The Southern Railway Company segregated blacks in dining cars by reserving ten tables exclusively for white passengers, and one table exclusively for blacks. A curtain or partition cut the black table off from the others. In Henderson v. United States (1950) the Court held that such segregation subjected black passengers to undue prejudice and disadvantage, and in 1961 the Interstate Commerce Commission issued a regulation forbidding interstate motor carriers of passengers to discriminate on grounds of race, color, creed, or national origin in the seating of such passengers, or in the terminal facilities provided for them, such as "waiting room, restroom, eating, drinking, and ticket sales facilities," or to display signs indicating such discrimination.

In Allston v. School Board (1940) the circuit court of appeals held that in the segregated school system of Norfolk, Virginia, black teachers must be paid the same salaries as white teachers if they did the same work. The Supreme Court refused to review the case on certiorari, thereby affirming the decision of the lower court. The small salaries paid to black teachers had contributed directly to the low standard of black education in the South.

Mr. Chief Justice **Vinson** delivered the opinion of the Court:

This case and McLaurin v. Oklahoma State Regents [1950] present different aspects of this general question: To what extent does the Equal Protection Clause of the Fourteenth Amendment limit the power of a state to distinguish between students of different races in professional and graduate education in a state university? Broader issues have been urged for our consideration, but we adhere to the principle of deciding constitutional questions only in the context of the particular case before the Court. We have frequently reiterated that this Court will decide constitutional questions only when necessary to the disposition of the case at hand, and that such decisions will be drawn as narrowly as possible. . . . Because of this traditional reluctance to extend constitutional interpretations to situations or facts which are not before the Court, much of the excellent research and detailed argument presented in these cases is unnecessary to their disposition.

In the instant case, petitioner filed an application for admission to the University of Texas Law School for the February, 1946 term. His application was rejected solely because he is a Negro. Petitioner thereupon brought this suit for mandamus against the appropriate school officials, respondents here, to compel his admission. At that time, there was no law school in Texas which admitted Negroes.

The state trial court recognized that the action of the State in denying petitioner the opportunity to gain a legal education while granting it to others deprived him of the equal protection of the laws guaranteed by the Fourteenth Amendment. The court did not grant the relief requested, however, but continued the case for six months to allow the State to supply substantially equal facilities. At the expiration of the six months, in December, 1946, the court denied the writ on the showing that the authorized university officials had adopted an order calling for the opening of a law school for Negroes the following February. While petitioner's appeal was pending, such a school was made available, but petitioner refused to register therein. The Texas Court of Civil Appeals set aside the trial court's judgment and ordered the cause "remanded generally to the trial court for further proceedings without prejudice to the rights of any party to this suit.''

On remand, a hearing was held on the issue of the equality of the educational facilities at the newly established school as compared with the University of Texas Law School. Finding that the new school offered petitioner "privileges, advantages, and opportunities for the study of law substantially equivalent to those offered by the State to white students at the University of Texas," the trial court denied mandamus. The Court of Civil Appeals affirmed. . . . Petitioner's application for a writ of error was denied by the Texas Supreme Court. We granted certiorari because of the manifest importance of the constitutional issues involved.

The University of Texas Law School, from which petitioner was excluded, was staffed by a faculty of sixteen full-time and three part-time professors, some of whom are nationally recognized authorities in their field. Its student body numbered 850. The library contained over 65,000 volumes. Among the other facilities available to the students were a law review, moot court facilities, scholarship funds, and Order of the Coif affiliation.

The school's alumni occupy the most distinguished positions in the private practice of the law and in the public life of the State. It may properly be considered one of the nation's ranking law schools.

The law school for Negroes which was to have opened in February, 1947, would have had no independent faculty or library. The teaching was to be carried on by four members of the University of Texas Law School faculty, who were to maintain their offices at the University of Texas while teaching at both institutions. Few of the 10,000 volumes ordered for the library had arrived; nor was there any full-time librarian. The school lacked accreditation.

Since the trial of this case, respondents report the opening of a law school at the Texas State University for Negroes. It is apparently on the road to full accreditation. It has a faculty of five full-time professors; a student body of 23; a library of some 16,500 volumes serviced by a full-time staff; a practice court and legal aid association; and one alumnus who has become a member of the Texas Bar.

Whether the University of Texas Law School is compared with the original or the new law school for Negroes, we cannot find substantial equality in the educational opportunities offered white and Negro law students by the State. In terms of number of the faculty, variety of courses and opportunity for specialization, size of the student body, scope of the library, availability of law review and similar activities, the University of Texas Law School is superior. What is more important, the University of Texas Law School possesses to a far greater degree those qualities which are incapable of objective measurement but which make for greatness in a law school. Such qualities, to name but a few, include reputation of the faculty, experience of the administration, position and influence of the alumni, standing in the community, traditions and prestige. It is difficult to believe that one who had a free choice between these law schools would consider the question close.

Moreover, although the law is a highly learned profession, we are well aware that it is an intensely practical one. The law school, the proving ground for legal learning and practice, cannot be effective in isolation from the individuals and institutions with which the law interacts. Few students and no one who has practiced law would choose to study in an academic vacuum, removed from the interplay of ideas and the exchange of views with which the law is concerned. The law school to which Texas is willing to admit petitioner excludes from its student body members of the racial groups which number 85% of the population of the State and include most of the lawyers, witnesses, jurors, judges and other officials with whom petitioner will inevitably be dealing when he becomes a member of the Texas Bar. With such a substantial and significant segment of society excluded, we cannot conclude that the education offered petitioner is substantially equal to that which he would receive if admitted to the University of Texas Law School.

It may be argued that excluding petitioner from that school is no different from excluding white students from the new law school. This contention overlooks realities. It is unlikely that a member of a group so decisively in the majority, attending a school with rich traditions and prestige which only a history of consistently maintained excellence could command, would claim that the opportunities afforded him for legal education were unequal to those held open to petitioner. That such a claim, if made, would be dishonored by the State, is no answer. "Equal protection of the laws is not achieved through indiscriminate imposition of inequalities." . . .

It is fundamental that these cases concern rights which are personal and present. This Court has stated unanimously that "The State must provide [legal education] for [petitioner] in conformity with the equal protection clause of the Fourteenth Amendment and provide it as soon as it does for applicants of any other group." Sipuel v. Board of Regents (1948). That case "did not present the issue whether a state might not satisfy the equal protection clause of the Fourteenth Amendment by establishing a separate law school for Negroes." Fisher v. Hurst (1948). In Missouri ex rel. Gaines v. Canada (1938), the Court, speaking through Chief Justice Hughes, declared that "petitioner's right was a personal one. It was as an individual that he was entitled to the equal protection of the laws, and the State was bound to furnish him within its borders facilities for legal education substantially equal to those which the State there afforded for persons of the white race, whether or not other negroes sought the same opportunity." These are the only cases in this Court which present the issue of the constitutional validity of race distinctions in state-supported graduate and professional education.

In accordance with these cases, petitioner may claim his full constitutional right: legal education equivalent to that offered by the State to students of other races. Such education is not available to him in a separate law school as offered by the State. We cannot, therefore, agree with respondents that the doctrine of Plessy v. Ferguson (1896) requires affirmance of the judgment below. Nor need we reach petitioner's contention that Plessy v. Ferguson should be reexamined in the light of contemporary knowledge respecting the purposes of the Fourteenth Amendment and the effects of racial segregation.

We hold that the Equal Protection Clause of the Fourteenth Amendment requires that petitioner be admitted to the University of Texas Law School. The judgment is reversed and the cause is remanded for proceedings not inconsistent with this opinion.

Reversed.

BROWN v. BOARD OF EDUCATION OF TOPEKA

347 U. S. 483; 74 S. Ct. 686; 98 L. Ed. 873
(1954)

In the cases dealing with black segregation which reached the Supreme Court after Plessy v. Ferguson (1896) the doctrine of that case was followed and never reexamined. The Court seemed content with the "separate but equal" rule of that case, which, as someone aptly put it, guaranteed to the black "the equal, but different, protection of the laws." During the forty-year period beginning with the McCabe case in 1914, the Court, applying ever more rigid standards of equality under segregation, found that black plaintiffs in each case had in fact been denied equality of treatment; and so the Court, following the rule that it will not decide constitutional issues if it can avoid doing so, continued to grant relief to blacks not because they were segregated but because they were unequally treated under segregation. While in the Texas Law School case and the dining car case the Court virtually stated that there were circumstances in which segregation in itself resulted in inequality of treatment, the rule of Plessy v. Ferguson remained intact.

In the fall of 1952, however, the Supreme Court had on its docket cases from four states (Kansas, South Carolina, Virginia, and Delaware), and from the District of Columbia, challenging the constitutionality of racial segregation in public schools. In all these cases the facts showed that "the Negro and white schools involved have been equalized, or are being equalized, with respect to buildings, curricula, qualifications and salaries of teachers, and other 'tangible' factors." After nearly sixty years the Court again had squarely before it the question of the constitutionality of segregation per se—the question of whether the doctrine of Plessy v. Ferguson should be affirmed or reversed.

The five cases were argued together in December, 1952, and the country waited with tense interest for the Court's decision. On June 8, 1953, the Court restored the cases to the docket for reargument in the fall and issued a list of questions upon which it wished that argument to turn. The Court asked for enlightenment on two main points. First, is there historical evidence which shows the intentions of those who framed and ratified the Fourteenth Amendment with respect to the impact of that amendment upon racial segregation in the public school? Second, if the Court finds racial segregation violates the Fourteenth Amendment, what kind of decree could and should be issued to bring about an end of segregation?

The cases were reargued in December 1953. Elaborate briefs set forth in great detail the background of the Fourteenth Amendment and the intentions of its framers and ratifiers. The negative result of this historical research is commented on in the opinion below. Some of the briefs, including the one filed by the Attorney General, presented suggestions on the form of the court decree by which segregation might best be ended should the Court hold it to be invalid. Counsel for the National Association for the Advancement of Colored People, which had played a major part in the instigation of these cases, declined to deal with this point. In their counsel's view, segregation, if held invalid, should be abolished completely and without delay.

Again the Court moved with deliberation, and its decision was not handed down until May 17, 1954. It is doubtful if the Supreme Court in its entire history has rendered a decision of greater social and ideological significance than this one. Three things in the present case indicate the high sense of responsibility felt by the justices of the Supreme Court in deciding a case of such vital national importance. First, the Court was unanimous. Second, one opinion was written, and not half a dozen. Third, the Court set for argument in the fall of 1954 the problem of the nature of the decree by which its decision that segregation is invalid might best be given effect. Disagreement in the Court on the decision, or disagreement on the reasons for the decision, would have aided those who resented the Court's ruling and have sought to thwart it. There was wisdom in announcing the constitutional ruling and then allowing a breathing spell during which ways and means of implementing the decision might be carefully and deliberately studied.

Because the Supreme Court wanted a full bench to hear argument on the nature of the decrees necessary to implement its May 17 decision and the Senate marked time on the confirmation of John Marshall Harlan to succeed Justice Robert Jackson on the Court, the argument set for the fall of 1954 was postponed until the spring of 1955. The Court allowed an almost unprecedented fourteen hours of oral argument. On May 31, the Court handed down its decision remanding the cases back to the lower courts, which were directed to fashion decrees in accordance with "equitable principles." While recognizing that to abolish segregation "may call for the elimination of a variety of obstacles in making the transition," the Court declared that the district "courts will require that the defendants make a prompt and reasonable start toward full compliance with our May 17, 1954, ruling. Once such a start has been made, the courts may find that additional time is necessary to carry out the ruling in an effective manner. The burden rests upon the defendants to establish that such time is necessary in the public interest and is consistent with good faith compliance at the earliest practicable date. . . . The cases are remanded to the District Courts to take such proceedings and enter such orders and decrees consistent with this opinion as are necessary and proper to admit to public schools on a racially nondiscriminatory basis with all deliberate speed the parties to these cases."

The only persons directly bound by the decision in Brown v. Topeka were the five school boards actually parties to the suit, and the only laws specifically held unconstitutional were those involved in those cases. Normally, and in less controversial cases, a rule of constitutional law announced by the Court in a particular case will be accepted and complied with by all those across the country to whom the rule clearly applies. But this compliance is technically voluntary, since only the parties to the case are immediately bound by the Court's decree. It follows, therefore, that obstinate school boards can be compelled to desegregate their schools only as cases are brought against them in the courts and those courts apply to them the rule of the Brown case.

Thus the progress of desegregation has been and will continue to be uneven throughout the country. While in some areas it came quickly and easily, in others it is still coming with painful slowness which reflects community hostility to any program of racial integration in the schools. For example, one of the five districts ordered to desegregate its public schools "with all deliberate speed" was Prince Edward County, Virginia. The response of the Virginia legislature was a program of "massive resistance," which included closing integrated schools, cutting off their funds, paying tuition grants to students in private, nonsectarian schools, and providing state and local financial aid (including teacher retirement benefits) for such schools. In 1959 the supreme court of Virginia held the program void under the Virginia constitution, so the legislature repealed it and enacted instead a program under which school attendance was a matter of local option.

Faced with the desegregation order, Prince Edward County closed its public schools and provided various kinds of financial support for privately operated segregated schools. In Griffin v. School Board of Prince Edward County (1964) the Court held that the plan denied equal protection of the law. Noting that "the case has been delayed since 1951 by resistance at the state and county level, by legislation, and by law suits," it emphasized that "there has been entirely too much deliberation and not enough speed." The Court conceded to the state a "wide discretion" in deciding whether state laws should operate statewide or only in some counties, "but the record in the present case could not be clearer that Prince Edward's public schools were closed and private schools operated in their place with state and county assistance, for one reason, and one reason only: to ensure, through measures taken by the county and the State, that white and colored children in Prince Edward County would not, under any circumstances, go to the same school. Whatever nonracial grounds might support a State's allowing a county to abandon public schools, the object must be a constitutional one, and grounds of race and opposition to desegregation do not qualify as constitutional." The district court was told to "enter a decree which will guarantee that these petitioners will get the kind of education that is given in the State's public schools" even if it had to order the Board of Supervisors to levy taxes to do it. After trying in vain to discover what the penalties for refusal would be, the supervisors finally decided to obey, and in the fall of 1964 Prince Edward County reopened its schools on an integrated basis.

The county did not, however, abandon its aid to private segregated schools, and in what Negroes termed "a midnight raid on the treasury," the Board of Supervisors hurriedly paid out $180,000 in tuition grants to white pupils while the issue of the constitutionality of such payments was still being litigated in the United States court of appeals. That court subsequently barred such tuition grants as long as the schools remained segregated, and in 1966, it found the Board in contempt and ordered it to repay the grants. The Supreme Court refused to upset this contempt ruling, and in the summer of 1967 the Board finally returned the money to the county treasury.

Meanwhile the political branches of government had taken a hand in speeding integration, and threats by the Department of Health, Education and Welfare (HEW) to withhold federal aid to segregated schools under the Civil Rights Act of 1964 resulted in widespread token compliance, largely by offering blacks "freedom of choice" among schools. Yet with the start of the 1965-66 school year fewer than 10 percent of the South's blacks were attending desegregated schools. In March of 1966 HEW announced new guidelines designed to desegregate all twelve grades by the fall of 1967; and in December 1966 the United States Court of Appeals for the Fifth Circuit ordered the six states within its jurisdiction—Alabama, Florida, Georgia, Louisiana, Mississippi, and Texas—to desegregate according to the HEW timetable. In April 1967 the Supreme Court refused to delay the effect of the court of appeals order to establish "no Negro schools, and no white schools—just schools." Finally, in May 1968 the Court rejected as inadequate a "freedom of choice" plan under which no desegregation had actually taken place. "The burden on a school board today is to come forward with a plan that promises realistically to work, and promises realistically to work now." See Green v. County School Board (1968). That December the United States court of appeals in a Georgia case ordered that all schools in the states of the fifth circuit—Alabama, Florida, Louisiana, Mississippi, and Texas—be integrated by the fall of 1969 or abandoned.

In July 1969 it became apparent that some thirty schools in Mississippi would not be ready for integration with the opening of the fall term, and the government suddenly announced that it would no longer try to hold the South to "arbitrary" deadlines for desegregation. At the same time the United States Court of Appeals for the Fifth Circuit reaffirmed its policy and ordered full integration, by September, and the justice department replied by asking for a delay until December 1.

The announced change in policy came as a shock to the lawyers of the NAACP Legal Defense Fund who, after working for many years in partnership with government attorneys for full integration suddenly found themselves carrying on the fight alone. Even the government attorneys themselves had trouble accepting the sudden switch, and a large number of them signed a statement of protest against the new policy. In spite of this the court of appeals granted the requested delay, and the Legal Defense Fund appealed to the Supreme Court. In a brief per curiam opinion, one of the first in which Chief Justice Burger participated, the Court unanimously rejected the government's request for a delay. The "continued operation of segregated schools under a standard of allowing 'all deliberate speed' for desegregation" said the Court, "is no longer constitutionally permissible. Under explicit holdings of this Court the obligation of every school district is to terminate dual school systems at once and to operate now and hereafter only unitary schools." See Alexander v. Holmes County Board of Education (1969).

The extension of the Brown doctrine to other areas of segregation was done by the Court largely through the technique of affirming lower court decisions without opinion. In Baltimore v. Dawson (1955) the desegregation ruling was held applicable to public beaches, and in

Holmes v. Atlanta (1955), to public golf courses. In 1963, in deciding Watson v. Memphis, the Court held that recreation facilities, like universities, must be desegregated at once. On the strength of this rule, the city of Jackson, Mississippi, desegregated its parks and golf links but decided instead to close its five swimming pools. In Palmer v. Thompson (1971) the Court upheld the move, noting that a statute could not be held void because of the motivations of the legislature which adopted it, and there was no evidence that the city was "now covertly aiding the maintenance and operation of pools which are private in name only. It shows no state action affecting blacks differently from whites." Three of the four dissenting justices argued that the city action was a public stand against desegregating public facilities and the forbidding of blacks to swim because of their color— both denials of equal protection.

A separate opinion was necessary to invalidate segregation in the schools of the District of Columbia, which is under congressional authority. In Bolling v. Sharpe, the Court held that the due process clause of the Fifth Amendment forbade racial segregation by the federal government.

Mr. Chief Justice **Warren**, delivering the opinion of the Court in the Brown case, said in part:

These cases come to us from the States of Kansas, South Carolina, Virginia, and Delaware. They are premised on different facts and different local conditions, but a common legal question justifies their consideration together in this consolidated opinion.

In each of the cases, minors of the Negro race, through their legal representatives, seek the aid of the courts in obtaining admission to the public schools of their community on a nonsegregated basis. In each instance, they had been denied admission to schools attended by white children under laws requiring or permitting segregation according to race. This segregation was alleged to deprive the plaintiffs of the equal protection of the laws under the Fourteenth Amendment. . . .

The plaintiffs contend that segregated public schools are not "equal" and cannot be made "equal," and that hence they are deprived of the equal protection of the laws. Because of the obvious importance of the question presented, the Court took jurisdiction. Argument was heard in the 1952 Term, and reargument was heard this Term on certain questions propounded by the Court.

Reargument was largely devoted to the circumstances surrounding the adoption of the Fourteenth Amendment in 1868. It covered exhaustively consideration of the Amendment in Congress, ratification by the states, then existing practices in racial segregation, and the views of proponents and opponents of the Amendment. This discussion and our own investigation convince us that, although these sources cast some light, it is not enough to resolve the problem with which we are faced. At best, they are inconclusive. The most avid proponents of the post-War Amendments undoubtedly intended them to remove all legal distinctions among "all

persons born or naturalized in the United States." Their opponents, just as certainly, were antagonistic to both the letter and the spirit of the Amendments and wished them to have the most limited effect. What others in Congress and the state legislatures had in mind cannot be determined with any degree of certainty.

An additional reason for the inconclusive nature of the Amendment's history, with respect to segregated schools, is the status of public education at that time. In the South, the movement toward free common schools, supported by general taxation, had not yet taken hold. Education of white children was largely in the hands of private groups. Education of Negroes was almost nonexistent, and practically all of the race were illiterate. In fact, any education of Negroes was forbidden by law in some states. Today, in contrast, many Negroes have achieved outstanding success in the arts and sciences as well as in the business and professional world. It is true that public school education at the time of the Amendment had advanced further in the North, but the effect of the Amendment on Northern States was generally ignored in the congressional debates. Even in the North, the conditions of public education did not approximate those existing today. The curriculum was usually rudimentary; ungraded schools were common in rural areas; the school term was but three months a year in many states; and compulsory school attendance was virtually unknown. As a consequence, it is not surprising that there should be so little in the history of the Fourteenth Amendment relating to its intended effect on public education.

In the first cases in this Court construing the Fourteenth Amendment, decided shortly after its adoption the Court interpreted it as proscribing all state-imposed discriminations against the Negro race. The doctrine of "separate but equal" did not make its appearance in this Court until 1896 in the case of Plessy v. Ferguson, involving not education but transportation. American courts have since labored with the doctrine for over half a century. In this Court, there have been six cases involving the "separate but equal" doctrine in the field of public education. In Cumming v. Board of Education of Richmond County [1899] and Gong Lum v. Rice [1927] the validity of the doctrine itself was not challenged. In more recent cases, all on the graduate school level, inequality was found in that specific benefits enjoyed by white students were denied to Negro students of the same educational qualifications. State of Missouri ex rel. Gaines v. Canada [1938], Sipuel v. Board of Regents of University of Oklahoma [1948], Sweatt v. Painter [1950], McLaurin v. Oklahoma State Regents [1950]. In none of these cases was it necessary to reexamine the doctrine to grant relief to the Negro plaintiff. And in Sweatt v. Painter the Court expressly reserved decision on the question whether Plessy v. Ferguson should be held inapplicable to public education.

In the instant cases, that question is directly presented. Here, unlike Sweatt v. Painter, there are findings below that the Negro and white schools involved have been equalized, or are being equalized, with respect to buildings, curricula, qualifications and salaries of teachers, and other "tangible" factors. Our decision, therefore, cannot turn on merely a comparison of these tangible factors in the Negro and white schools involved in each of the cases. We must look instead to the effect of segregation itself on public education.

In approaching this problem, we cannot turn the clock back to 1868 when the Amendment was adopted, or even to 1896 when Plessy v. Ferguson was written. We must consider public education in the light of its full development and its present place in American life throughout the Nation. Only in this way can it be determined if segregation in public schools deprives these plaintiffs of the equal protection of the laws.

Today, education is perhaps the most important function of state and local governments. Compulsory school attendance laws and the great expenditures for education both demonstrate our recognition of the importance of education to our democratic society. It is required in the performance of our most basic public responsibilities, even service in the armed forces. It is the very foundation of good citizenship. Today it is a principal instrument in awakening the child to cultural values, in preparing him for later professional training, and in helping him to adjust normally to his environment. In these days, it is doubtful that any child may reasonably be expected to succeed in life if he is denied the opportunity of an education. Such an opportunity, where the state has undertaken to provide it, is a right which must be made available to all on equal terms.

We come then to the question presented: Does segregation of children in public schools solely on the basis of race, even though the physical facilities and other "tangible" factors may be equal, deprive the children of the minority group of equal educational opportunities? We believe that it does.

In Sweatt v. Painter, in finding that a segregated law school for Negroes could not provide them equal educational opportunities, this Court relied in large part on "those qualities which are incapable of objective measurement but which make for greatness in a law school." In McLaurin v. Oklahoma State Regents, the Court, in requiring that a Negro admitted to a white graduate school be treated like all other students, again resorted to intangible considerations: ". . . his ability to study, to engage in discussions and exchange views with other students, and, in general, to learn his profession." Such considerations apply with added force to children in grade and high schools. To separate them from others of similar age and qualifications solely because of their race generates a feeling of inferiority as to their status in the community that may effect their hearts and minds in a way unlikely ever to be undone. The effect of this separation on their educational opportunities was well stated by a finding in the Kansas case by a court which nevertheless felt compelled to rule against the Negro plaintiffs:

"Segregation of white and colored children in public schools has a detrimental effect upon the colored children. The impact is greater when it has the sanction of the law; for the policy of separating the races is usually interpreted as denoting the inferiority of the Negro group. A sense of inferiority affects the motivation of a child to learn. Segregation with the sanction of law, therefore, has a tendency to [retard] the educational and mental development of Negro children and to deprive them of some of the benefits they would receive in a racial[ly] integrated school system." Whatever may have been the extent of psychological knowledge at the time of Plessy v. Ferguson, this finding is amply supported by modern authority.* Any language in Plessy v. Ferguson contrary to this finding is rejected.

We conclude that in the field of public education the doctrine of "separate but equal" has no place. Separate educational facilities are inherently unequal. Therefore, we hold that the plaintiffs and others similarly situated for whom the actions have been brought are, by reason of the segregation complained of, deprived of the equal protection of the laws guaranteed by the Fourteenth Amendment. This disposition makes unnecessary any discussion whether such segregation also violates the Due Process Clause of the Fourteenth Amendment.

Because these are class actions, because of the wide applicability of this decision, and because of the great variety of local conditions, the formulation of decrees in these cases presents problems of considerable complexity. On reargument, the consideration of appropriate relief was necessarily subordinated to the primary question—the constitutionality of segregation in public education. We have now announced that such segregation is a denial of the equal protection of the laws. In order that we may have the full assistance of the parties in formulating decrees, the cases will be restored to the docket, and the parties are requested to present further argument on Questions 4 and 5 previously propounded by the Court for the reargument this Term.† The Attorney General of the United States is again invited to participate. The Attorneys General of the states requiring or permitting segregation in public education will also be permitted to appear as amici curiae upon request to do so by September 15, 1954, and submission of briefs by October 1, 1954.

It is so ordered.

---

*K. B. Clark, Effect of Prejudice and Discrimination on Personality Development (Midcentury White House Conference on Children and Youth, 1950); Witmer and Kotinsky, Personality in the Making (1952), ch VI; Deutscher and Chein, The Psychological Effects of Enforced Segregation: A Survey of Social Science Opinion, 26 J Psychol 259 (1948); Chein, What are the Psychological Effects of Segregation Under Conditions of Equal Facilities?, 3 Int J Opinion and Attitude Res 229 (1949); Brameld, Educational Costs, in Discrimination and National Welfare (MacIver, ed, 1949), 44–48; Frazier, The Negro in the United States (1949), 674–681. And see generally Myrdal, An American Dilemma (1944).

†"4. Assuming it is decided that segregation in public schools violates the Fourteenth Amendment

"(a) would a decree necessarily follow providing that, within the limits set by normal geographic school districting, Negro children should forthwith be admitted to schools of their choice, or

"(b) may this Court, in the exercise of its equity powers, permit an effective gradual adjustment to be brought about from existing segregated systems to a system not based on color distinctions?

"5. On the assumption on which questions 4(a) and (b) are based, and

SWANN v. CHARLOTTE-MECKLENBURG BOARD OF EDUCATION

402 U. S. 1; 9 S. Ct. 1267; 28 L. Ed. 2d 554
(1971)

*With the refusal of the Supreme Court to delay integra-
tion in thirty Mississippi school districts (see Alexander
v. Holmes County Board of Education, 1968), the Justice Department promptly announced that it would no
longer push for more rapid desegregation in over 100
schools in the Deep South. It did not matter much because the Department of Health, Education, and Welfare
(HEW) with its authority to withhold funds from schools
that were not desegregating effectively had become the
principle administrative support for the courts' orders.
The Mississippi school districts did integrate, but many
whites in heavily black areas transferred to hastily created all white "private academies." HEW promptly
urged the Internal Revenue Service (IRS) to withhold tax
exemption from such schools, and in July 1970 the IRS
complied.*

*While apparently most rural and small town
school districts moved rapidly and peacefully toward integration in 1970, in big cities a new cry was heard. To
desegregate urban schools located in the center of black
or white neighborhoods, it was necessary to transport
students out of their home neighborhoods by school bus.
As district courts prepared plans calling for busing between pairs of black and white schools, community
voices rose in defense of their "neighborhood schools."
In Florida, Governor Claude Kirk seized physically the
Bradenton schools to prevent busing and relinquished
them only when faced with a $10,000-a-day fine. In both
the House and Senate, amendments passed to prevent
HEW guidelines from requiring busing, only to have
them fail when the act finally passed.*

*And in Charlotte-Mecklenburg, the country's
forty-third largest school district, an "antibusing"
school board was elected. The district court rejected a
plan devised by the Board as not producing sufficient integration at the elementary level and accepted in its
place a plan prepared by an outside expert which called
for the pairing and grouping of elementary schools and
the busing of pupils between them. In upholding the validity of the district court's plan, the Supreme Court in
the present case and in the companion case of Davis v.
Board of Commissioners (1971) spelled out the lengths
to which district courts can go to achieve an integrated
school system. In Nyquist v. Lee (1971) the Court held*

---

assuming further that this Court will exercise its equity powers to the
end described in question 4(b),

"(a) should this Court formulate detailed decrees in these cases;
"(b) if so, what specific issues should the decrees reach;
"(c) should this Court appoint a special master to hear evidence with
a view to recommending specific terms for such decrees;
"(d) should this Court remand to the courts of first instance with directions to frame decrees in these cases, and if so, what general directions should the decrees of this Court include and what procedures
should the courts of first instance follow in arriving at the specific terms
of more detailed decrees?"

*void without opinion New York's 1969 antibusing statute
upon which most of the Southern antibusing statutes had
been based.*

Mr. Chief Justice **Burger** delivered the opinion of the
Court, saying in part:

V.

The central issue in this case is that of student assignment, and there are essentially four problem areas:
(1) to what extent racial balance or racial quotas may be
used as an implement in a remedial order to correct a previously segregated system; (2) whether every all-Negro
and all-white school must be eliminated as an indispensable part of a remedial process of desegregation; (3) what
are the limits, if any, on the rearrangement of school districts and attendance zones, as a remedial measure; and
(4) what are the limits, if any, on the use of transportation facilities to correct state-enforced racial school segregation.

(1) *Racial Balances or Racial Quotas.*

The constant theme and thrust of every holding
from Brown I [1954] to date is that state-enforced separation of races in public schools is discrimination that violates the Equal Protection Clause. The remedy commanded was to dismantle dual school systems.

We are concerned in these cases with the elimination of the discrimination inherent in the dual school systems, not with myriad factors of human existence which
can cause discrimination in a multitude of ways on racial, religious, or ethnic grounds. The target of the cases
from Brown I to the present was the dual school system.
The elimination of racial discrimination in public schools
is a large task and one that should not be retarded by efforts to achieve broader purposes lying beyond the jurisdiction of school authorities. One vehicle can carry only
a limited amount of baggage. . . .

Our objective in dealing with the issues presented
by these cases is to see that school authorities exclude no
pupil of a racial minority from any school, directly or indirectly, on account of race; it does not and cannot embrace all the problems of racial prejudice, even when
those problems contribute to disproportionate racial con-
centrations in some schools.

In this case it is urged that the District Court has
imposed a racial balance requirement of 71%–29% on
individual schools. . . . If we were to read the holding of
the District Court to require, as a matter of substantive
constitutional right, any particular degree of racial balance or mixing, that approach would be disapproved and
we would be obliged to reverse. The constitutional command to desegregate schools does not mean that every
school in every community must always reflect the racial
composition of the school system as a whole. . . .

. . . The use made of mathematical ratios was no
more than a starting point in the process of shaping a
remedy, rather than an inflexible requirement. From that
starting point the District Court proceeded to frame a de-

cree that was within its discretionary powers, an equitable remedy for the particular circumstances. As we said in Green [v. County School Board, 1968], a school authority's remedial plan or a district court's remedial decree is to be judged by its effectiveness. Awareness of the racial composition of the whole school system is likely to be a useful starting point in shaping a remedy to correct past constitutional violations. In sum, the very limited use made of mathematical ratios was within the equitable remedial discretion of the District Court.

(2) One-Race Schools.

The record in this case reveals the familiar phenomenon that in metropolitan areas minority groups are often found concentrated in one part of the city. In some circumstances certain schools may remain all or largely of one race until new schools can be provided or neighborhood patterns change. Schools all or predominately of one race in a district of mixed population will require close scrutiny to determine that school assignments are not part of state-enforced segregation.

In light of the above, it should be clear that the existence of some small number of one-race, or virtually one-race, schools within a district is not in and of itself the mark of a system which still practices segregation by a law. . . . Where the school authority's proposed plan for conversion from a dual to a unitary system contemplates the continued existence of some schools that are all or predominately of one race, they have the burden of showing that such school assignments are genuinely nondiscriminatory. The court should scrutinize such schools, and the burden upon the school authorities will be to satisfy the court that their racial composition is not the result of present or past discriminatory action on their part.

An optional majority-to-minority transfer provision has long been recognized as a useful part of every desegregation plan. Provision for optional transfer of those in the majority racial group of a particular school to other schools where they will be in the minority is an indispensable remedy for those students willing to transfer to other schools in order to lessen the impact on them of the state-imposed stigma of segregation. In order to be effective, such a transfer arrangement must grant the transferring student free transportation and space must be made available in the school to which he desires to move. . . . The court orders in this and the companion Davis case now provide such an option.

(3) Remedial Altering of Attendance Zones.

The maps submitted in these cases graphically demonstrate that one of the principal tools employed by school planners and by courts to break up the dual school system has been a frank—and sometimes drastic—gerrymandering of school districts and attendance zones. An additional step was pairing, "clustering," or "grouping" of schools with attendance assignments made deliberately to accomplish the transfer of Negro students out of formerly segregated Negro schools and transfer of white students to formerly all-Negro schools. More often than not, these zones are neither compact nor contiguous; indeed they may be on opposite ends of the city. As an interim corrective measure, this cannot be said to be beyond the broad remedial powers of a court.

Absent a constitutional violation there would be no basis for judicially ordering assignment of students on a racial basis. All things being equal, with no history of discrimination, it might well be desirable to assign pupils to schools nearest their homes. But all things are not equal in a system that has been deliberately constructed and maintained to enforce racial segregation. . . .

No fixed or even substantially fixed guidelines can be established as to how far a court can go, but it must be recognized that there are limits. The objective is to dismantle the dual school system. "Racially neutral" assignment plans proposed by school authorities to a district court may be inadequate; such plans may fail to counteract the continuing effects of past school segregation resulting from discriminatory location of school sites or distortion of school size in order to achieve or maintain an artificial racial separation. When school authorities present a district court with a "loaded game board," affirmative action in the form of remedial altering of attendance zones is proper to achieve truly nondiscriminatory assignments. In short, an assignment plan is not acceptable simply because it appears to be neutral. . . .

We hold that the pairing and grouping of noncontiguous school zones is a permissible tool and such action is to be considered in light of the objectives sought. . . .

(4) Transportation of Students.

The scope of permissible transportation of students as an implement of a remedial decree has never been defined by this Court and by the very nature of the problem it cannot be defined with precision. . . .

The importance of bus transportation as a normal and accepted tool of educational policy is readily discernible in this and the companion case. The Charlotte school authorities did not purport to assign students on the basis of geographically drawn zones until 1965 and then they allowed almost unlimited transfer privileges. The District Court's conclusion that assignment of children to the school nearest their home serving their grade would not produce an effective dismantling of the dual system is supported by the record.

Thus the remedial techniques used in the District Court's order were within that court's power to provide equitable relief; implementation of the decree is well within the capacity of the school authority.

The decree provided that the buses used to implement the plan would operate on direct routes. Students would be picked up at schools near their homes and transported to the schools they were to attend. The trips for elementary school pupils average about seven miles and the District Court found that they would take "not over 35 minutes at the most." This system compares favorably with the transportation plan previously operated in Charlotte under which each day 23,600 students on all grade levels were transported an average of 15 miles one way for an average trip requiring over an hour. In these circumstances, we find no basis for holding that the local school authorities may not be required to employ bus transportation as one tool of school desegregation. Desegregation plans cannot be limited to the walk-in school. . . .

VI.

. . . At some point, these school authorities and others like them should have achieved full compliance with this Court's decision in Brown I. The systems will then be "unitary" in the sense required by our decisions in Green and Alexander [v. Holmes County Board of Education, 1968].

It does not follow that the communities served by such systems will remain demographically stable, for in a growing, mobile society, few will do so. Neither school authorities nor district courts are constitutionally required to make year-by-year adjustments of the racial composition of student bodies once the affirmative duty to desegregate has been accomplished and racial discrimination through official action is eliminated from the system. This does not mean that federal courts are without power to deal with future problems; but in the absence of a showing that either the school authorities or some other agency of the State has deliberately attempted to fix or alter demographic patterns to affect the racial composition of the schools, further intervention by a district court should not be necessary. . . .

It is so ordered.

MILLIKEN v. BRADLEY

418 U. S. 717 94 S. Ct. 3112; 41 L. Ed. 2d 1069
(1974)

As the long fight to integrate Southern schools achieved increasing success, attention was turned to Northern cities in which segregation was as complete in many cases as it had ever been in the South. While segregation in the South had its genesis in laws providing separate facilities for the two races (de jure), in the big cities of the North an equally effective segregation (de facto) came about as a by-product of the development of single-race neighborhoods. The creation of these neighborhoods, while in part probably the result of personal preferences, has been fostered by both a tacit unwillingness of whites to sell to blacks and a system of economic zoning that puts the cost of homes in middle-class white communities beyond the financial reach of blacks whose economic opportunities are in turn restricted by both the inferior "ghetto" education afforded them and the hiring policies of business which reserves the best-paid jobs for whites. Thus, while in Charlotte-Mecklenburg only two-thirds of the black pupils were in schools that were 99 percent black and a quarter of them attended schools more than half white, in Chicago three-quarters

of the black children went to all-black schools and only three percent went to schools that were mostly white.

Even systematic desegregation, however, does not always provide a permanent solution to the segregation problem. Experience has shown that the migration that tends to follow desegregation orders in big cities merely converts de jure patterns into de facto ones. The most striking illustration is the District of Columbia school system, which integrated in 1956; in subsequent years so many whites with school-age children left the District that only 3.6 percent of the pupils in the system are white [as of 1988].

This situation faced the cities of Detroit, Michigan, and Richmond, Virginia. The school districts in those cities had such a high concentration of blacks that no amount of line-drawing or busing could change their racial composition. In contrast, the school districts in the surrounding suburban counties were almost entirely white. Despite the fact that the segregated schools were not the product of school board action, the district courts in both cases ordered the black inner-city districts merged with the white suburban districts and pupils bused across county lines to produce integrated schools in both communities. On appeal, the Justice Department sided with the white counties and the court of appeals for the Fourth Circuit, in June 1972, reversed the district court in the Richmond case, while the court of appeals for the Sixth Circuit upheld the district court in the Detroit case. In Richmond School Board v. Virginia Board of Education (1973) the decision of the court of appeals was affirmed by an equally divided Court. Justice Powell, who had been a member of both boards involved in the suit, disqualified himself. Meanwhile the Detroit case was delayed in its efforts to reach the Supreme Court, and in July 1973, a district judge in Indianapolis ordered inter-county transportation of pupils to achieve desegregation.

In contrast to the Detroit and Richmond cases, a number of communities were found to be supporting segregated schools by their deliberate actions and inactions, despite the absence of state laws requiring such segregation. In Pontiac, Michigan, and Denver, Colorado, for instance, district courts found that the school boards, by their power to locate new schools and draw attendance lines, had encouraged segregation. In dealing with this problem in Keyes v. School District (1973), the Court held that such conduct constituted de jure segregative action, and the fact that the board had acted to segregate the Park Hill section of the city created a presumption that heavily segregated parts of the core city were also the product of board action, rather than merely of community social patterns. Justice Powell, in a powerful concurrence, had attacked the de facto-de jure distinction and urged its abolition, pointing out that in the large metropolitan districts, both north and south, the causes of segregation were largely unrelated to government policy, that a pupil has a right not to be compelled by the state to attend a segregated school, and the state has an obligation to operate only integrated schools. Was he, the only southerner on the Court, suggesting the state responsibility for providing desegre-

gated schools made school district lines no more sacred than attendance zones?

In the present case, unlike the Richmond case, both the district court and the court of appeals had found that local school board action in the core city and state action both there and to a limited extent in the suburbs, had contributed to segregation and ordered a plan worked out which would involve both the core city and fifty-three suburban school districts. That the suburban districts as such might not be engaged in segregation was found immaterial. "[T]he State," said the Court, "has committed de jure acts of segregation and . . . the State controls the instrumentalities whose action is necessary to remedy the harmful effects of the State acts." The decision in the present case raises interesting questions regarding state responsibility for desegregation, as opposed to school board responsibility. If a state's obligation to stop segregating can be compartmentalized by district lines, what are its obligations when it decides to alter the size or shape of a district?

Following the remand of the present case the district court, after extensive hearings, ordered the school board to establish a remedial education program designed "to restore the victims of discriminatory conduct to the position they would have occupied in the absence of such conduct." The program was to include remedial reading, special in-service teacher training, the construction of bias-free testing procedures, and improved career guidance and counseling. The cost was to be shared equally by the district and the state. In Milliken v. Bradley (1977) (Milliken II) the Supreme Court unanimously held the plan valid.

Mr. Chief Justice **Burger** delivered the opinion of the Court, saying in part:

II.

Ever since Brown v. Board of Education (1954), judicial consideration of school desegregation cases has begun with the standard: "[I]n the field of public education the doctrine of 'separate but equal' has no place. Separate educational facilities are inherently unequal." This has been reaffirmed time and again as the meaning of the Constitution and the controlling rule of law.

The target of the Brown holding was clear and forthright: the elimination of state-mandated or deliberately maintained dual school systems with certain schools for Negro pupils and others for white pupils. This duality and racial segregation were held to violate the Constitution in the cases subsequent to 1954, including particularly Green v. County School Board of New Kent County (1968); . . . Swann v. Charlotte-Mecklenburg Board of Education (1971). . . .

The Swann case, of course, dealt "with the problem of defining in more precise terms than heretofore the scope of the duty of school authorities and district courts in implementing Brown I and the mandate to eliminate dual systems and establish unitary systems at once." In Brown v. Board of Education (1955) (Brown II), the

Court's first encounter with the problem of remedies in school desegregation cases, the Court noted:

"In fashioning and effectuating the decrees, the courts will be guided by equitable principles. Traditionally, equity has been characterized by a practical flexibility in shaping its remedies and by a facility for adjusting and reconciling public and private needs." Brown v. Board of Education. In further refining the remedial process, Swann held, the task is to correct, by balancing of the individual and collective interests, "the condition that offends the Constitution." A federal remedial power may be exercised "only on the basis of a constitutional violation" and, "[a]s with any equity case, the nature of the violation determines the scope of the remedy."

Proceeding from these basic principles, we first note that in the District Court the complainants sought a remedy aimed at the *condition* alleged to offend the Constitution—the segregation within the Detroit City School District. The court acted on this theory of the case and in its initial ruling on the "Desegregation Area" stated:

"The task before this court, therefore, is now, and . . . has always been, how to desegregate the Detroit public schools." Thereafter, however, the District Court abruptly rejected the proposed Detroit-only plans on the ground that "while [they] would provide a racial mix more in keeping with the Black-White proportions of the student population [they] would accentuate the racial identifiability of the [Detroit] district as a Black school system, and would not accomplish desegregation." "[T]he racial composition of the student body is such," said the court, "that the plan's implementation would clearly make the entire Detroit public school system racially identifiable." "leav[ing] many of its schools 75 to 90 percent Black." Consequently, the court reasoned, it was imperative to "look beyond the limits of the Detroit school district for a solution to the problem of segregation in the Detroit public schools . . ." since "[s]chool district lines are simply matters of political convenience and may not be used to deny constitutional rights." Accordingly, the District Court proceeded to redefine the relevant area to include areas of predominantly white pupil population in order to ensure that "upon implementation, no school, grade or classroom [would be] substantially disproportionate to the overall pupil racial composition" of the entire metropolitan area.

While specifically acknowledging that the District Court's findings of a condition of segregation were limited to Detroit, the Court of Appeals approved the use of a metropolitan remedy largely on the grounds that it is "impossible to declare 'clearly erroneous' the District Judge's conclusion that any Detroit only segregation plan will lead directly to a single segregated Detroit school district overwhelmingly black in all of its schools, surrounded by a ring of suburbs and suburban school districts overwhelmingly white in composition in a State in which the racial composition is 87 percent white and 13 percent black."

Viewing the record as a whole, it seems clear that the District Court and the Court of Appeals shifted the primary focus from a Detroit remedy to the metropolitan area only because of their conclusion that total desegregation of Detroit would not produce the racial balance which they perceived as desirable. Both courts proceeded on an assumption that the Detroit schools could not be truly desegregated—in their view of what constituted desegregation—unless the racial composition of the student body of each school substantially reflected the racial composition of the population of the metropolitan area as a whole. The metropolitan area was then defined as Detroit plus 53 of the outlying school districts. . . .

In Swann, which arose in the context of a single independent school district, the Court held: ''If we were to read the holding of the District Court to require, as a matter of substantive constitutional right, any particular degree of racial balance or mixing, that approach would be disapproved and we would be obliged to reverse.'' The clear import of this language from Swann is that desegregation, in the sense of dismantling a dual school system, does not require any particular racial balance in each ''school, grade or classroom.'' . . .

Here the District Court's approach to what constituted ''actual desegregation'' raises the fundamental question, not presented in Swann, as to the circumstances in which a federal court may order desegregation relief that embraces more than a single school district. The court's analytical starting point was its conclusion that school district lines are no more than arbitrary lines on a map drawn ''for political convenience.'' Boundary lines may be bridged where there has been a constitutional violation calling for interdistrict relief, but the notion that school district lines may be casually ignored or treated as a mere administrative convenience is contrary to the history of public education in our country. No single tradition in public education is more deeply rooted than local control over the operation of schools; local autonomy has long been thought essential both to the maintenance of community concern and support for public schools and to the quality of the educational process. . . .

Of course, no state law is above the Constitution. School district lines and the present laws with respect to local control, are not sacrosanct and if they conflict with the Fourteenth Amendment federal courts have a duty to prescribe appropriate remedies. . . . But our prior holdings have been confined to violations and remedies within a single school district. We therefore turn to address, for the first time, the validity of a remedy mandating cross-district or interdistrict consolidation to remedy a condition of segregation found to exist in only one district.

The controlling principle consistently expounded in our holdings is that the scope of the remedy is determined by the nature and extent of the constitutional violation. Swann. Before the boundaries of separate and autonomous school districts may be set aside by consolidating the separate units for remedial purposes or by imposing a cross-district remedy, it must first be shown that there has been a constitutional violation within one district that produces a significant segregative effect in another district. Specifically, it must be shown that racially discriminatory acts of the state or local school districts, or of a single school district have been a substantial cause of interdistrict segregation. Thus an interdistrict remedy might be in order where the racially discriminatory acts of one or more school districts caused racial segregation in an adjacent district, or where district lines have been deliberately drawn on the basis of race. In such circumstances an interdistrict remedy would be appropriate to eliminate the interdistrict segregation directly caused by the constitutional violation. Conversely, without an interdistrict violation and interdistrict effect, there is no constitutional wrong calling for an interdistrict remedy. . . .

. . . With no showing of significant violation by the 53 outlying school districts and no evidence of any interdistrict violation or effect, the court went beyond the original theory of the case as framed by the pleadings and mandated a metropolitan area remedy. To approve the remedy ordered by the court would impose on the outlying districts, not shown to have committed any constitutional violation, a wholly impermissible remedy based on a standard not hinted at in Brown I and II or any holding of this Court. . . .

III.

We recognize that the six-volume record presently under consideration contains language and some specific incidental findings thought by the District Court to afford a basis for interdistrict relief. However, these comparatively isolated findings and brief comments concern only one possible interdistrict violation and are found in the context of a proceeding that, as the District Court conceded, included no proof of segregation practiced by any of the 85 suburban school districts surrounding Detroit. . . .

According to the Court of Appeals, the arrangement during the late 1950's which allowed Carver students to be educated within the Detroit District was dependent upon the ''tacit or express'' approval of the State Board of Education and was the result of the refusal of the white suburban districts to accept the Carver students. Although there is nothing in the record supporting the Court of Appeals' supposition that suburban white schools refused to accept the Carver students, it appears that this situation, whether with or without the State's consent, may have had a segregative effect on the school populations of the two districts involved. However, since ''the nature of the violation determines the scope of the remedy'' this isolated instance affecting two of the school districts would not justify the broad metropolitan-wide remedy contemplated by the District Court, particularly since it embraced potentially 52 districts having no responsibility for the arrangement and involved 503,000 pupils in addition to Detroit's 276,000 students. . . .

Mr. Justice **Stewart,** concurring, said in part:

The opinion of the Court convincingly demonstrates, that traditions of local control of schools, together with the difficulty of a judicially supervised restructuring of local administration of schools, render improper and inequitable such an interdistrict response to a constitutional violation found to have occurred only within a single school district.

This is not to say, however, that an interdistrict remedy of the sort approved by the Court of Appeals would not be proper, or even necessary, in other factual situations. Were it to be shown, for example, that state officials had contributed to the separation of the races by drawing or redrawing school district lines . . . by transfer of school units between districts, . . . or by purposeful, racially discriminatory use of state housing or zoning laws, then a decree calling for transfer of pupils across district lines or for restructuring of district lines might well be appropriate. . . .

Mr. Justice **Douglas,** dissenting, said in part:

When we rule against the metropolitan area remedy we take a step that will likely put the problem of the blacks and our society back to the period that antedated the "separate but equal" regime of Plessy v. Ferguson [1896]. The reason is simple.

The inner core of Detroit is now rather solidly black; and the blacks, we know, in many instances are likely to be poorer, just as were the Chicanos in San Antonio School District v. Rodriguez [1973]. By that decision the poorer school districts must pay their own way. It is therefore a foregone conclusion that we have now given the States a formula whereby the poor must pay their own way.

Today's decision, given Rodriguez, means that there is no violation of the Equal Protection Clause though the schools are segregated by race and though the black schools are not only "separate" but "inferior."

So far as equal protection is concerned we are now in a dramatic retreat from the 7-to-1 decision in 1896 that blacks could be segregated in public facilities, provided they received equal treatment.

. . . Given the State's control over the educational system in Michigan, the fact that the black schools are in one district and the white schools are in another is not controlling—either constitutionally or equitably. No specific plan has yet been adopted. We are still at an interlocutory stage of a long drawn-out judicial effort at school desegregation. It is conceivable that ghettos develop on their own without any hint of state action. But since Michigan by one device or another has over the years created black school districts and white school districts, the task of equity is to provide a unitary system for the affected area where, as here, the State washes its hands of its own creations.

Mr. Justice **White,** with whom Mr. Justice **Douglas,** Mr. Justice **Brennan,** and Mr. Justice **Marshall** join, dissenting, said in part:

The District Court and the Court of Appeals found that over a long period of years those in charge of the Michigan public schools engaged in various practices calculated to effect the segregation of the Detroit school system. The Court does not question these findings, nor could it reasonably do so. Neither does it question the obligation of the federal courts to devise a feasible and effective remedy. But it promptly cripples the ability of the judiciary to perform this task, which is of fundamental importance to our constitutional system, by fashioning a strict rule that remedies in school cases must stop at the school district line unless certain other conditions are met. As applied here, the remedy for unquestioned violations of the equal protection rights of Detroit's Negroes by the Detroit School Board and the State of Michigan must be totally confined to the limits of the school district and may not reach into adjoining or surrounding districts unless and until it is proved there has been some sort of "interdistrict violation"—unless unconstitutional actions of the Detroit School Board have had segregative impact on other districts, or unless the segregated condition of the Detroit schools has itself been influenced by segregative practices in those surrounding districts into which it is proposed to extend the remedy. . . .

. . . The result is that the State of Michigan, the entity at which the Fourteenth Amendment is directed, has successfully insulated itself from its duty to provide effective desegregation remedies by vesting sufficient power over its public schools in its local school districts. If this is the case in Michigan, it will be the case in most States.

There are undoubted practical as well as legal limits to the remedial powers of federal courts in school desegregation cases. The Court has made it clear that the achievement of any particular degree of racial balance in the school system is not required by the Constitution; nor may it be the primary focus of a court in devising an acceptable remedy for de jure segregation. A variety of procedures and techniques are available to a district court engrossed in fashioning remedies in a case such as this; but the courts must keep in mind that they are dealing with the process of *educating* the young, including the very young. The task is not to devise a system of pains and penalties to punish constitutional violations brought to light. Rather, it is to desegregate an *educational* system in which the races have been kept apart, without, at the same time, losing sight of the central *educational* function of the schools.

Viewed in this light, remedies calling for school zoning, pairing, and pupil assignments, become more and more suspect as they require that school children spend more and more time in buses going to and from school and that more and more educational dollars be diverted to transportation systems. . . .

Despite the fact that a metropolitan remedy, if the findings of the District Court accepted by the Court of Appeals are to be credited, would more effectively desegregate the Detroit schools, would prevent resegregation, and would be easier and more feasible from many standpoints, the Court fashions out of whole cloth an arbitrary rule that remedies for constitutional violations occurring in a single Michigan school district must stop at the school district line. Apparently, no matter how much less burdensome or more effective and efficient in many respects, such as transportation, the metropolitan plan might be, the school district line may not be crossed. Otherwise, it seems, there would be too much disruption of the Michigan scheme for managing its educational system, too much confusion, and too much administrative burden. . . .

I am surprised that the Court, sitting at this distance from the State of Michigan, claims better insight than the Court of Appeals and the District Court as to whether an inter-district remedy for equal protection violations practiced by the State of Michigan would involve undue difficulties for the State in the management of its public schools. . . .

I am even more mystified as to how the Court can ignore the legal reality that the constitutional violations, even if occurring locally, were committed by governmental entities for which the State is responsible and that it is the State that must respond to the command of the Fourteenth Amendment. An inter-district remedy for the infringements that occurred in this case is well within the confines and powers of the State, which is the governmental entity ultimately responsible for desegregating its schools. . . .

It is unnecessary to catalogue at length the various public misdeeds found by the District Court and the Court of Appeals to have contributed to the present segregation of the Detroit public schools. The legislature contributed directly by enacting a statute overriding a partial high school desegregation plan voluntarily adopted by the Detroit Board of Education. Indirectly, the trial court found the State was accountable for the thinly disguised, pervasive acts of segregation committed by the Detroit Board, for Detroit's school construction plans that would promote segregation, and for the Detroit school district's not having funds for pupil transportation within the district. The State was also chargeable with responsibility for the transportation of Negro high school students in the late 1950's from the suburban Ferndale School District, past closer suburban and Detroit high schools with predominantly white student bodies, to a predominantly Negro high school within Detroit. . . .

The unwavering decisions of this Court over the past 20 years support the assumption of the Court of Appeals that the District Court's remedial power does not cease at the school district line. The Court's first formulation of the remedial principles to be followed in disestablishing racially discriminatory school systems recognized the variety of problems arising from different local school conditions and the necessity for that "practical flexibility" traditionally associated with courts of equity. . . . Indeed, the district courts to which the Brown cases were remanded for the formulation of remedial decrees were specifically instructed that they might consider, inter alia, "revision of school districts and attendance areas into compact units to achieve a system of determining admission to the public schools on a nonracial basis. . . ." The malady addressed in Brown II was the state-wide policy of requiring or permitting school segregation on the basis of race, while the record here concerns segregated schools only in the city of Detroit. The obliga-

tion to rectify the unlawful condition nevertheless rests on the State. The permissible revision of school districts contemplated in Brown II rested on the State's responsibility for desegregating its unlawfully segregated schools, not on any segregative effect which the condition of segregation in one school district might have had on the schools of a neighboring district. The same situation obtains here and the same remedial power is available to the District court. . . .

. . . There are indeed limitations on the equity powers of the federal judiciary, but until now the Court has not accepted the proposition that effective enforcement of the Fourteenth Amendment could be limited by political or administrative boundary lines demarcated by the very State responsible for the constitutional violation and for the disestablishment of the dual system. . . .

Mr. Justice **Marshall**, with whom Mr. Justice **Douglas**, Mr. Justice **Brennan**, and Mr. Justice **White** join, dissenting, said in part:

After 20 years of small, often difficult steps toward that great end, the Court today takes a giant step backwards. Notwithstanding a record showing widespread and pervasive racial segregation in the educational system provided by the State of Michigan for children in Detroit, this Court holds that the District Court was powerless to require the State to remedy its constitutional violation in any meaningful fashion. Ironically purporting to base its result on the principle that the scope of the remedy in a desegregation case should be determined by the nature and the extent of the constitutional violation, the Court's answer is to provide no remedy at all for the violation proved in this case, thereby guaranteeing that Negro children in Detroit will receive the same separate and inherently unequal education in the future as they have been unconstitutionally afforded in the past.

I cannot subscribe to this emasculation of our constitutional guarantee of equal protection of the laws and must respectively dissent. Our precedents, in my view, firmly establish that where, as here, state-imposed segregation has been demonstrated, it becomes the duty of the State to eliminate root and branch all vestiges of racial discrimination and to achieve the greatest possible degree of actual desegregation. . . .

II. . . .

Under a Detroit-only decree, Detroit's schools will clearly remain racially identifiable in comparison with neighboring schools in the metropolitan community. Schools with 65% and more Negro students will stand in sharp and obvious contrast to schools in neighboring districts with less than 2% Negro enrollment. Negro students will continue to perceive their schools as segregated educational facilities and this perception will only be increased when whites react to a Detroit-only decree by fleeing to the suburbs to avoid integration. School district lines, however innocently drawn, will surely be perceived as fences to separate the races when under a

Detroit-only decree, white parents withdraw their children from the Detroit city schools and move to the suburbs in order to continue them in all-white schools. The message of this action will not escape the Negro children in the city of Detroit. . . . It will be of scant significance to Negro children who have for years been confined by de jure acts of segregation to a growing core of all-Negro schools surrounded by a ring of all-white schools that the new dividing line between the races is the school district boundary. . . .

UNIVERSITY OF CALIFORNIA v. BAKKE

438 U. S. 265; 98 S. Ct. 2733; 57 L. Ed. 2d 750
(1978)

A major factor in maintaining the intellectual and cultural disadvantage of blacks has been an almost universal discrimination against them economically. White small businesses and professionals simply did not hire blacks, however well qualified. Large employers hired some, but they were systematically left in the servile or menial positions represented by Pullman porters in the railroad industry and the janitorial staff of industry generally. Labor unions of skilled workers ordinarily discriminated against blacks. Even where whites and blacks could compete for the same jobs, whites were better paid for the same work and their chances for promotion were better. And when technological advances displaced workers, it was the unskilled black workers who most often were out of jobs.

During most of our constitutional history Congress and the Court have left this problem to the states, and only a handful of states forbade discrimination in private employment. During World War II the President's Fair Employment Practices Committee achieved significant results, but with the return to a peace-time economy and the abolition of the Committee, much of the progress was lost. It was not until the Civil Rights Act of 1964, held valid in Heart of Atlanta Motel v. United States (1964), that a systematic national attack on the problem was made. Title VII of the act forbade race discrimination in hiring and the classification of employees in such a way as to "adversely affect" their status because of their race, color, sex, religion, or national origin.

Although the act permitted the use of professionally constructed ability tests provided they were not used to discriminate, In Griggs v. Duke Power Co. (1971) the Court found that the company had violated the act by using a high school diploma and an intelligence test to qualify workers for all but manual labor jobs. The Court noted that the tests bore no demonstrable relationship to the jobs for which they were required, and since blacks had long received an inferior education, the tests could be presumed to, and did in fact, discriminate against them. Speaking for a unanimous Court, Chief Justice Burger emphasized that "Congress has not commanded that the less qualified be preferred over the better qualified simply because of minority origins. Far from dis-paraging job qualifications as such, Congress had made such qualifications the controlling factor, so that race, religion, nationality and sex become irrelevant."

In Washington v. Davis (1976), however, the Court increased substantially the difficulty of showing that an employer's job qualification tests were discriminatory. It conceded that under Title VII, a job test or other qualification could be invalid even though it was not adopted with the intent to discriminate. Merely showing that a test had a discriminatory effect was enough to switch the burden to the employer to show that the test was valid under Title VII. However, the court made it relatively easy for the employer to meet this burden. Under the statute a test was valid if it was "job-related," but the Court said "job related" did not mean mere ability to perform the job. It also could also include the ability to enter a required training program, even though some of that program was unrelated to the job. Washington v. Davis itself, however, involved a test required by the government and thus raised constitutional issues. In this situation, what the Court described as the "more rigorous standard" for tests under Title VII was one which the Court was "not disposed to adopt . . . for the purposes of applying the Fifth and Fourteenth Amendments. . . .

The case involved two blacks who had failed to pass a verbal ability test required as a condition of admission to the Washington, D.C., police department. There was neither evidence nor claim of purposeful discrimination, and the Court declined to hold the test void despite the fact that four times as many blacks as whites failed it. Noting that in both jury cases and in de jure school segregation cases there had been purposeful discrimination, the Court said: "As an initial matter, we have difficulty understanding how a law establishing a racially neutral qualification for employment is nevertheless racially discriminatory and denies 'any person . . . equal protection of the law' simply because a greater proportion of Negroes fail to qualify than members of other racial or ethnic groups. . . . Test 21, which is administered generally to prospective Government employees, concededly seeks to ascertain whether those who take it have acquired a particular level of verbal skill; and it is untenable that the Constitution prevents the Government from seeking modestly to upgrade the communicative abilities of its employees rather than to be satisfied with some lower level of competence, particularly where the job requires special ability to communicate orally and in writing. Respondents, as Negroes, could no more successfully claim that the test denied them equal protection than could white applicants who also failed."

Where both the Constitution and the law look to a policy of nondiscrimination and desegregation, what steps may be taken to bring about the desired result? Can blacks be identified and considered as blacks? And if so, for what purposes? May an employer who has always hired whites now consider only black applicants until the balance is redressed? If he may not, and due to educational background white applicants are better qualified, how is the balance ever to be redressed? If he may, is he not illegally discriminating in favor of blacks over whites? The question is the difficult one of defining equality of racial treatment in the context of a society in which nearly every institution is structured to favor whites.

In the present case the University of California Medical School at Davis had set aside sixteen of its 100 entering seats for minority and disadvantaged applicants. The medical school was created in 1968, had no history of purposeful discrimination and adopted this minority program to increase the number of minority students attending the school. Allan Bakke, a 37-year-old white engineer was denied admission and brought suit against the University claiming he was better qualified than some of the sixteen minority students and was being discriminated against because of his race. The California Supreme Court, noting that the University could not show that Bakke would not have been admitted had there been no quota, found the program denied him equal protection of the laws and ordered him admitted. The University appealed to the Supreme Court.

In the years following the Bakke decision a divided Court whose membership was changing struggled with interpretations both of the Constitution and of §§ 703 (a) and (d) of Title VII of the Civil Rights Act of 1964, all of which, to some ill- defined extent, forbade race discrimination in employment. The question raised by the cases was the extent to which various employers, public and private, could undertake "affirmative action" or "reverse discrimination" to bring more minority personnel into what were largely all-white or all-male work forces.

While the mixture of constitutional and statutory issues and the wide variations among the facts of the cases make generalization virtually impossible, the cases appear to fall into three roughly defined categories:

First, where the group, whether public or private, had a long established record of discrimination and had defied court orders to desegregate, the Court held valid the court-ordered affirmative action. In Sheet Metal Workers v. EEOC (1976) a labor union with a long record of deliberate race discrimination was ordered to mend its ways and fined for contempt when it failed to do so. And in United States v. Paradise (1987) the Court found that Alabama state troopers had ignored for over a dozen years court orders to appoint or promote blacks to the force and upheld a court-devised affirmative action plan. With Justices O'Connor, White, Rehnquist and Burger dissenting, Justice Powell cast the deciding vote.

A second pair of cases involved firefighting organizations in two cities. In both cases, to avoid going to trial and risking a court order requiring the adoption of an affirmative action plan, the city fire departments settled by means of a "consent decree"—an official settlement whose terms are approved by the court. In Firefighters v. Stotts (1984), the city of Memphis agreed in the consent decree to hire more blacks, but denied having engaged in discrimination. Since there was no showing of deliberate discrimination, and since the consent decree made no mention of a union contract providing "first on, last off" in case of layoffs, the majority upheld the laying off of the last hired, most of whom were black.

On the other hand, in Firefighters v. Cleveland (1986), the city admitted to a long and serious record of race discrimination and in a six-to-three decision the Court upheld the consent decree, which provided a quota of minority promotions. The court further held that the decree was not a court "order" and hence not limited by the sections of Title VII limiting certain race-conscious relief after trial.

In the third category are four cases in which affirmative action was taken voluntarily, rather than as a result of a court finding of discrimination or a consent decree agreed to in order to avoid a finding of such discrimination. Two of these case involved public agencies, and both held the affirmative action void. The first, of course, was the Bakke decision printed below. The second was Wygant v. Jackson Board of Education (1986) in which a Union-School Board agreement gave probationary blacks preference over tenured whites at lay-off time in order to maintain a black quota. The presence of a state agency brought the equal protection clause into play and a four-member plurality applied the "strict scrutiny" test. "Societal discrimination, without more, is too amorphous a basis for imposing a racially classified remedy. The role model theory announced by the District Court and the resultant holding typify this indefiniteness."

Also in the third category are two cases involving voluntary affirmative action plans that the court considered solely under Title VII, not the equal protection clause. In both of these the Court upheld the affirmative action. The language of § 703 (a) made it illegal "to fail or refuse to hire or to discharge any individual, or otherwise to discriminate against any individual with respect to his compensation, terms, conditions, or privileges of employment, because of such individual's race, color, religion, sex, or national origin. . . ." In Steelworkers v. Weber (1979) a majority of the Court found that the intent of Title VII was to improve the lot of blacks and "we cannot agree with respondent that Congress intended to prohibit the private sector from taking effective steps to accomplish the goal that Congress designed Title VII to achieve."

It reached the same result in Johnson v. Transportation Agency (1987). Diane Joyce was appointed to the position of road dispatcher despite the fact a man had scored slightly higher on one of the tests. Prior to her appointment, none of the 238 Skilled Craft Worker positions in the Agency was held by a woman, although the Court conceded that this was a result of societal discrimination and not the deliberate policy of the Agency and that in promoting qualified applicants sex was only one of the factors to be considered. The dissenting justices in both cases argued that the language of . . . 703 forbade discriminating in favor of minorities as well as against them. [While one party in the Johnson case was a government agency, no constitutional issue was raised or considered.]

In Fullilove v. Klutznick (1980), a case raising a different constitutional issue, a badly divided Court held valid a Congressional statute requiring that ten percent of money granted to the states for public works be set *aside for minority contractors. Justices White, Burger, and Powell agreed that the law's purpose was to prevent the perpetuation of discriminatory practices, and that Congress could act both under its spending power and under Section 5 of the Fourteenth Amendment, while Justice Powell, speaking for himself, argued that because an appropriate governmental authority had identified the need for such affirmative action the law met the strict scrutiny test he had relied on in Bakke.*

Mr. Justice **Powell** announced the judgment of the Court and wrote an opinion, saying in part:

For the reasons stated in the following opinion, I believe that so much of the judgment of the California court as holds petitioner's special admissions program unlawful and directs that respondent be admitted to the Medical School must be affirmed. For the reasons expressed in a separate opinion, my Brothers The Chief Justice, Mr. Justice Stewart, Mr. Justice Rehnquist, and Mr. Justice Stevens concur in this judgment.

I also conclude for the reasons stated in the following opinion that the portion of the court's judgment enjoining petitioner from according any consideration to race in its admissions process must be reversed. For reasons expressed in separate opinions, my Brothers Mr. Justice Brennan, Mr. Justice White, Mr. Justice Marshall, and Mr. Justice Blackmun concur in this judgment. Affirmed in part and reversed in part.

III.

A.

Petitioner does not deny that decisions based on race or ethnic origin by faculties and administrations of state universities are reviewable under the Fourteenth Amendment. . . . For his part, respondent does not argue that all racial or ethnic classifications are per se invalid. . . . The parties do disagree as to the level of judicial scrutiny to be applied to the special admissions program. Petitioner argues that the court below erred in applying strict scrutiny, as this inexact term has been applied in our cases. . . .

En route to this crucial battle over the scope of judicial review, the parties fight a sharp preliminary action over the proper characterization of the special admissions program. Petitioner prefers to view it as establishing a "goal" of minority representation in the medical school. Respondent, echoing the courts below, labels it a racial quota.

This semantic distinction is beside the point: The special admissions program is undeniably a classification based on race and ethnic background. To the extent that there existed a pool of at least minimally qualified minority applicants to fill the 16 special admissions seats, white applicants could compete only for 84 seats in the entering class, rather than the 100 open to minority applicants. Whether this limitation is described as a quota or a goal, it is a line drawn on the basis of race and ethnic status.

. . . The guarantee of equal protection cannot mean one thing when applied to one individual and something else when applied to a person of another color. If both are not accorded the same protection, then it is not equal.

Nevertheless, petitioner argues that the court below erred in applying strict scrutiny to the special admissions program because white males, such as respondent, are not a "discrete and insular minority" requiring extraordinary protection from the majoritarian political process. . . . This rationale, however, has never been invoked in our decisions as a prerequisite to subjecting racial or ethnic distinctions to strict scrutiny. Nor has this Court held that discreteness and insularity constitute necessary preconditions to a holding that a particular classification is invidious. . . . These characteristics may be relevant in deciding whether or not to add new types of classifications to the list of "suspect" categories or whether a particular classification survives close examination. . . . Racial and ethnic classifications, however, are subject to stringent examination without regard to these additional characteristics. . . .

B. . . .

Over the past 30 years, this Court has embarked upon the crucial mission of interpreting the Equal Protection Clause with the view of assuring to all persons "the protection of equal laws" . . . in a Nation confronting a legacy of slavery and racial discrimination. . . . Because the landmark decisions in this area arose in response to the continued exclusion of Negroes from the mainstream of American society, they could be characterized as involving discrimination of the "majority" white race against the Negro minority. But they need not be read as depending upon that characterization for their results. It suffices to say that "[o]ver the years, this Court has consistently repudiated '[d]istinctions between citizens solely because of their ancestry' as being 'odious to a free people whose institutions are founded upon the doctrine of equality.' " . . .

Petitioner urges us to adopt for the first time a more restrictive view of the Equal Protection Clause and hold that discrimination against members of the white "majority" cannot be suspect if its purpose can be characterized as "benign." The clock of our liberties, however, cannot be turned back to 1868. . . . It is far too late to argue that the guarantee of equal protection to *all* persons permits the recognition of special wards entitled to a degree of protection greater than that accorded to others. "The Fourteenth Amendment is not directed solely against discrimination due to a 'two-class theory'— that is, based upon differences between 'white' and Negro." . . .

Once the artificial line of a "two-class theory" of the Fourteenth Amendment is put aside, the difficulties entailed in varying the level of judicial review according to a perceived "preferred" status of a particular racial or ethnic minority are intractable. The concepts of "majority" and "minority" necessarily reflect temporary arrangements and political judgments. As observed above, the white "majority" itself is composed of various minority groups, most of which can lay claim to a history of prior discrimination at the hands of the state and private individuals. Not all these groups can receive preferential treatment and corresponding judicial tolerance of distinctions drawn in terms of race and nationality, for then the only "majority" left would be a new minority of White Anglo-Saxon Protestants. There is no principled basis for deciding which groups would merit "heightened judicial solicitude" and which would not. Courts would be asked to evaluate the extent of the prejudice and consequent harm suffered by various minority groups. Those whose societal injury is thought to exceed some arbitrary level of tolerability then would be entitled to preferential classifications at the expense of individuals belonging to other groups. Those classifications would be free from exacting judicial scrutiny. As these preferences began to have their desired effect, and the consequences of past discrimination were undone, new judicial rankings would be necessary. The kind of variable sociological and political analysis necessary to produce such rankings simply does not lie within the judicial competence—even if they otherwise were politically feasible and socially desirable.

Moreover, there are serious problems of justice connected with the idea of preference itself. First, it may not always be clear that a so-called preference is in fact benign. . . . Second, preferential programs may only reinforce common stereotypes holding that certain groups are unable to achieve success without special protection based on a factor having no relationship to individual worth. . . . Third, there is a measure of inequity in forcing innocent persons in respondent's position to bear the burdens of redressing grievances not of their making. . . .

If it is the individual who is entitled to judicial protection against classifications based upon his racial or ethnic background because such distinctions impinge upon personal rights, rather than the individual only because of his membership in a particular group, then constitutional standards may be applied consistently. Political judgments regarding the necessity for the particular classification may be weighed in the constitutional balance, *Korematsu v. United States* (1944), but the standard of justification will remain constant. This is as it should be, since those political judgments are the product of rough compromise struck by contending groups within the democratic process. When they touch upon an individual's race or ethnic background, he is entitled to a judicial determination that the burden he is asked to bear on that basis is precisely tailored to serve a compelling governmental interest. The Constitution guarantees that right to every person regardless of his background. . . .

IV.

We have held that in "order to justify the use of a suspect classification, a State must show that its purpose or interest is both constitutionally permissible and substantial, and that its use of the classification is 'necessary . . . to the accomplishment' of its purpose or the safeguarding of its interest," . . . The special admissions

program purports to serve the purposes of: (i) "reducing the historic deficit of traditionally disfavored minorities in medical schools and the medical profession,"; (ii) countering the effects of societal discrimination; (iii) increasing the number of physicians who will practice in communities currently underserved; and (iv) obtaining the educational benefits that flow from an ethnically diverse student body. It is necessary to decide which, if any, of these purposes is substantial enough to support the use of a suspect classification.

A.

If petitioner's purpose is to assure within its student body some specified percentage of a particular group merely because of its race or ethnic origin, such a preferential purpose must be rejected not as insubstantial but as facially invalid. Preferring members of any one group for no reason other than race or ethnic origin is discrimination for its own sake. This the Constitution forbids. . . .

B.

The State certainly has a legitimate and substantial interest in ameliorating, or eliminating where feasible, the disabling effects of identified discrimination. The line of school desegregation cases, commencing with Brown, attests to the importance of this state goal and the commitment of the judiciary to affirm all lawful means towards its attainment. In the school cases, the States were required by court order to redress the wrongs worked by specific instances of racial discrimination. That goal was far more focused than the remedying of the effects of "societal discrimination," an amorphous concept of injury that may be ageless in its reach into the past.

We have never approved a classification that aids persons perceived as members of relatively victimized groups at the expense of other innocent individuals in the absence of judicial, legislative, or administrative findings of constitutional or statutory violations. . . . After such findings have been made, the governmental interest in preferring members of the injured groups at the expense of others is substantial, since the legal rights of the victims must be vindicated. In such a case, the extent of the injury and the consequent remedy will have been judicially, legislatively, or administratively defined. Also, the remedial action usually remains subject to continuing oversight to assure that it will work the least harm possible to other innocent persons competing for the benefit. Without such findings of constitutional or statutory violations, it cannot be said that the government has any greater interest in helping one individual than in refraining from harming another. Thus, the government has no compelling justification for inflicting such harm.

Petitioner does not purport to have made, and is in no position to make, such findings. Its broad mission is education, not the formulation of any legislative policy or the adjudication of particular claims of illegality. . . .

Hence, the purpose of helping certain groups

whom the faculty of the Davis Medical School perceived as victims of "societal discrimination" does not justify a classification that imposes disadvantages upon persons like respondent, who bear no responsibility for whatever harm the beneficiaries of the special admissions program are thought to have suffered. To hold otherwise would be to convert a remedy heretofore reserved for violations of legal rights into a privilege that all institutions throughout the Nation could grant at their pleasure to whatever groups are perceived as victims of societal discrimination. That is a step we have never approved. . . .

C.

Petitioner identifies, as another purpose of its program, improving the delivery of health-care services to communities currently underserved. It may be assumed that in some situations a State's interest in facilitating the health care of its citizens is sufficiently compelling to support the use of a suspect classification. But there is virtually no evidence in the record indicating that petitioner's special admissions program is either needed or geared to promote that goal. . . . "There are more precise and reliable ways to identify applicants who are genuinely interested in the medical problems of minorities than by race. An applicant of whatever race who has demonstrated his concern for disadvantaged minorities in the past and who declares that practice in such a community is his primary professional goal would be more likely to contribute to alleviation of the medical shortage than one who is chosen entirely on the basis of race and disadvantage. . . ."

Petitioner simply has not carried its burden of demonstrating that it must prefer members of particular ethnic groups over all other individuals in order to promote better health-care delivery to deprived citizens. Indeed, petitioner has not shown that its preferential classification is likely to have any significant effect on the problem.

D.

The fourth goal asserted by petitioner is the attainment of a diverse student body. This clearly is a constitutionally permissible goal for an institution of higher education. Academic freedom, though not a specifically enumerated constitutional right, long has been viewed as a special concern of the First Amendment. . . . The atmosphere of "speculation, experiment and creation"—so essential to the quality of higher education—is widely believed to be promoted by a diverse student body. . . .

It may be argued that there is greater force to these views at the undergraduate level than in a medical school where the training is centered primarily on professional competency. But even at the graduate level, our tradition and experience lend support to the view that the contribution of diversity is substantial. . . . Physicians serve a heterogeneous population. An otherwise qualified medical student with a particular background—whether it be ethnic, geographic, culturally advantaged or disadvantaged—may bring to a professional school of medicine

experiences, outlooks and ideas that enrich the training of its student body and better equip its graduates to render with understanding their vital service to humanity. . . .

. . . As the interest of diversity is compelling in the context of a university's admissions program, the question remains whether the program's racial classification is necessary to promote this interest. . . .

V.

A.

It may be assumed that the reservation of a specified number of seats in each class for individuals from the preferred ethnic groups would contribute to the attainment of considerable ethnic diversity in the student body. But petitioner's argument that this is the only effective means of serving the interest of diversity is seriously flawed. In a most fundamental sense the argument misconceives the nature of the state interest that would justify consideration of race or ethnic background. It is not an interest in simple ethnic diversity, in which a specified percentage of the student body is in effect guaranteed to be members of selected ethnic groups, with the remaining percentage an undifferentiated aggregation of students. The diversity that furthers a compelling state interest encompasses a far broader array of qualifications and characteristics of which racial or ethnic origin is but a single though important element. Petitioner's special admissions program, focused *solely* on ethnic diversity, would hinder rather than further attainment of genuine diversity. . . .

The experience of other university admissions programs, which take race into account in achieving the educational diversity valued by the First Amendment, demonstrates that the assignment of a fixed number of places to a minority group is not a necessary means toward that end. An illuminating example is found in the Harvard College program:

"In recent years Harvard College has expanded the concept of diversity to include students from disadvantaged economic, racial and ethnic groups. Harvard College now recruits not only Californians or Louisianans but also blacks and Chicanos and other minority students. . . .

"In practice, this new definition of diversity has meant that race has been a factor in some admissions decisions. When the Committee on Admissions review the large middle group of applicants who are 'admissible' and deemed capable of doing good work in their courses, the race of an applicant may tip the balance in his favor just as geographic origin or a life spent on a farm may tip the balance in other candidates' cases. A farm boy from Idaho can bring something to Harvard College that a Bostonian cannot offer. Similarly, a black student can usually bring something that a white person cannot offer. . . ." . . .

This kind of program treats each applicant as an individual in the admissions process. The applicant who loses out on the last available seat to another candidate receiving a "plus" on the basis of ethnic background will not have been foreclosed from all consideration for that seat simply because he was not the right color or had the wrong surname. It would mean only that his combined qualifications, which may have included similar nonobjective factors, did not outweigh those of the other applicant. His qualifications would have been weighed fairly and competitively, and he would have no basis to complain of unequal treatment under the Fourteenth Amendment.

It has been suggested that an admissions program which considers race only as one factor is simply a subtle and more sophisticated—but no less effective—means of according racial preference than the Davis program. A facial intent to discriminate, however, is evident in petitioner's preference program and not denied in this case. No such facial infirmity exists in an admissions program where race or ethnic background is simply one element—to be weighed fairly against other elements—in the selection process. . . .

B.

In summary, it is evident that the Davis special admission program involves the use of an explicit racial classification never before countenanced by this Court. . . .

The fatal flaw in petitioner's preferential program is its disregard of individual rights as guaranteed by the Fourteenth Amendment. . . . Such rights are not absolute. But when a State's distribution of benefits or imposition of burdens hinges on the color of a person's skin or ancestry, that individual is entitled to a demonstration that the challenged classification is necessary to promote a substantial state interest. Petitioner has failed to carry this burden. For this reason, that portion of the California court's judgment holding petitioner's special admissions program invalid under the Fourteenth Amendment must be affirmed.

C.

In enjoining petitioner from ever considering the race of any applicant, however, the courts below failed to recognize that the State has a substantial interest that legitimately may be served by a properly devised admissions program involving the competitive consideration of race and ethnic origin. For this reason, so much of the California court's judgment as enjoins petitioner from any consideration of the race of any applicant must be reversed. . . .

Opinion of Mr. Justice **Brennan,** Mr. Justice **White,** Mr. Justice **Marshall,** and Mr. Justice **Blackmun,** concurring in the judgment in part and dissenting in part, saying in part:

The Court today, in reversing in part the judgment of the Supreme Court of California, affirms the constitutional power of Federal and State Government to act affirmatively to achieve equal opportunity for all. The difficulty of the issue presented—whether Government may use race-conscious programs to redress the continuing effects of past discrimination—and the mature consideration which each of our Brethren has brought to it have resulted in many opinions, no single one speaking for the Court. But this should not and must not mask the central meaning of today's opinions: Government may take race into account when it acts not to demean or insult any racial group, but to remedy disadvantages cast on minorities by past racial prejudice, at least when appropriate findings have been made by judicial, legislative, or administrative bodies with competence to act in this area.

The Chief Justice and our Brothers Stewart, Rehnquist, and Stevens have concluded that Title VI of the Civil Rights Act of 1964, as amended, prohibits programs such as that at the Davis Medical School. On this statutory theory alone, they would hold that respondent Allan Bakke's rights have been violated and that he must, therefore, be admitted to the Medical School. Our Brother Powell, reaching the Constitution, concludes that, although race may be taken into account in university admissions, the particular special admissions program used by petitioner, which resulted in the exclusion of respondent Bakke, was not shown to be necessary to achieve petitioner's stated goals. Accordingly, these Members of the Court form a majority of five affirming the judgment of the Supreme Court of California insofar as it holds that respondent Bakke "is entitled to an order that he be admitted to the University."

We agree with Mr. Justice Powell that, as applied to the case before us, Title VI goes no further in prohibiting the use of race than the Equal Protection Clause of the Fourteenth Amendment itself. We also agree that the effect of the California Supreme Court's affirmance of the judgment of the Superior Court of California would be to prohibit the University from establishing in the future affirmative action programs that take race into account. Since we conclude that the affirmative admissions program at the Davis Medical School is constitutional, we would reverse the judgment below in all respects. Mr. Justice Powell agrees that some uses of race in university admissions are permissible, and, therefore, he joins with us to make five votes reversing the judgment below insofar as it prohibits the University from establishing race-conscious programs in the future. . . .

III.

A.

The assertion of human equality is closely associated with the proposition that differences in color or creed, birth or status, are neither significant nor relevant to the way in which persons should be treated. Nonetheless, the position that such factors must be "constitutionally an irrelevance," Edwards v. California (1941) (Jackson J., concurring), summed up by the shorthand phrase "[o]ur Constitution is color-blind," Plessy v. Ferguson (1896) (Harlan, J., dissenting), has never been adopted by this Court as the proper meaning of the Equal Protection Clause. Indeed, we have expressly rejected this proposition on a number of occasions.

Our cases have always implied that an "overriding statutory purpose," . . . could be found that would justify racial classifications. See, e.g., . . . Korematsu v. United States (1944); Hirabayashi v. United States (1943). . . .

We conclude, therefore, that racial classifications are not per se invalid under the Fourteenth Amendment. Accordingly, we turn to the problem of articulating what our role should be in reviewing state action that expressly classifies by race.

B.

Respondent argues that racial classifications are always suspect and, consequently, that this Court should weigh the importance of the objectives served by Davis' special admissions program to see if they are compelling. . . .

Unquestionably we have held that a government practice or statute which restricts "fundamental rights" or which contains "suspect classifications" is to be subjected to "strict scrutiny" and can be justified only if it furthers a compelling government purpose and, even then, only if no less restrictive alternative is available. . . . But no fundamental right is involved here. . . . Nor do whites as a class have any of the "traditional indicia of suspectness: the class is not saddled with such disabilities, or subjected to such a history of purposeful unequal treatment, or relegated to such a position of political powerlessness as to command extraordinary protection from the majoritarian political process." . . .

On the other hand, the fact that this case does not fit neatly into our prior analytic framework for race cases does not mean that it should be analyzed by applying the very loose rational-basis standard of review that is the very least that is always applied in equal protection cases. " '[T]he mere recitation of a benign, compensatory purpose is not an automatic shield which protects against any inquiry into the actual purposes underlying a statutory scheme.' " . . . Instead, a number of considerations—developed in gender-discrimination cases but which carry even more force when applied to racial classifications—lead us to conclude that racial classifications designed to further remedial purposes " 'must serve important governmental objectives and must be substantially related to achievement of those objectives.' " . . .

First, race, like "gender-based classifications too often [has] been inexcusably utilized to stereotype and stigmatize politically powerless segments of society." . . . State programs designed ostensibly to ameliorate the effects of past racial discrimination obviously create the same hazard of stigma, since they may promote racial separatism and reinforce the views of those who believe that members of racial minorities are inherently incapable of succeeding on their own. . . .

Second, race, like gender and illegitimacy, . . . is an immutable characteristic which its possessors are powerless to escape or set aside. While a classification is not per se invalid because it divides classes on the basis of an immutable characteristic, it is nevertheless true that such divisions are contrary to our deep belief that "legal

burdens should bear some relationship to individual responsibility or wrongdoing," . . . and that advancement sanctioned, sponsored, or approved by the State should ideally be based on individual merit or achievement, or at the least on factors within the control of an individual. . . .

In sum, because of the significant risk that racial classifications established for ostensibly benign purposes can be misused, causing effects not unlike those created by invidious classifications, it is inappropriate to inquire only whether there is any conceivable basis that might sustain such a classification. Instead, to justify such a classification an important and articulated purpose for its use must be shown. In addition, any statute must be stricken that stigmatizes any group or that singles out those least well represented in the political process to bear the brunt of a benign program. Thus, our review under the Fourteenth Amendment should be strict—not " 'strict' in theory and fatal in fact," because it is stigma that causes fatality—but strict and searching nonetheless.

IV.

Davis' articulated purpose of remedying the effects of past societal discrimination is, under our cases, sufficiently important to justify the use of race-conscious admissions programs where there is a sound basis for concluding that minority underrepresentation is substantial and chronic, and that the handicap of past discrimination is impeding access of minorities to the Medical School.

A.

At least since Green v. County School Board (1968), it has been clear that a public body which has itself been adjudged to have engaged in racial discrimination cannot bring itself into compliance with the Equal Protection Clause simply by ending its unlawful acts and adopting a neutral stance. . . . The creation of unitary school systems, in which the effects of past discrimination had been "eliminated root and branch," was recognized as a compelling social goal justifying the overt use of race.

Finally, the conclusion that state educational institutions may constitutionally adopt admissions programs designed to avoid exclusion of historically disadvantaged minorities, even when such programs explicitly take race into account, finds direct support in our cases construing congressional legislation designed to overcome the present effects of past discrimination. Congress can and has outlawed actions which have a disproportionately adverse and unjustified impact upon members of racial minorities and has required or authorized race-conscious action to put individuals disadvantaged by such impact in the position they otherwise might have enjoyed. . . . Such relief does not require as a predicate proof that recipients of preferential advancement have been individually discriminated against; it is enough that each recipient is within a general class of persons likely to have been the victims of discrimination. . . .

B. . . .

. . . Davis had very good reason to believe that the national pattern of underrepresentation of minorities in medicine would be perpetuated if it retained a single admissions standard. For example, the entering classes in 1968 and 1969, the years in which such a standard was used, included only 1 Chicano and 2 Negroes out of 50 admittees for each year. Nor is there any relief from this pattern of underrepresentation in the statistics for the regular admissions program in later years.

Davis clearly could conclude that the serious and persistent underrepresentation of minorities in medicine depicted by these statistics is the result of handicaps under which minority applicants labor as a consequence of a background of deliberate, purposeful discrimination against minorities in education and in society generally, as well as in the medical profession. . . .

. . . The generation of minority students applying to Davis Medical School since it opened in 1968—most of whom were born before or about the time Brown I was decided—clearly have been victims of this discrimination. Judicial decrees recognizing discrimination in public education in California testify to the fact of widespread discrimination suffered by California-born minority applicants; many minority group members living in California, moreover, were born and reared in school districts in southern States segregated by law. Since separation of school children by race "generates a feeling of inferiority as to their status in the community that may affect their hearts and minds in a way unlikely ever to be undone," Brown I, the conclusion is inescapable that applicants to medical school must be few indeed who endured the effects of de jure segregation, the resistance to Brown I, or the equally debilitating pervasive private discrimination fostered by our long history of official discrimination, and yet come to the starting line with an education equal to whites. . . .

C.

The second prong of our test—whether the Davis program stigmatizes any discrete group or individual and whether race is reasonably used in light of the program's objectives—is clearly satisfied by the Davis program.

It is not even claimed that Davis' program in any way operates to stigmatize or single out any discrete and insular, or even any identifiable, non-minority group. Nor will harm comparable to that imposed upon racial minorities by exclusion or separation on grounds of race be the likely result of the program. It does not, for example, establish an exclusive preserve for minority students apart from and exclusive of whites. Rather, its purpose is to overcome the effects of segregation by bringing the races together. True, whites are excluded from participation in the special admissions program, but this fact only operates to reduce the number of whites to be admitted in the regular admissions program in order to permit admission of a reasonable percentage—less than their proportion of the California population—of otherwise underrepresented qualified minority applicants.

Nor was Bakke in any sense stamped as inferior by the Medical School's rejection of him. Indeed, it is conceded by all that he satisfied those criteria regarded by the school as generally relevant to academic performance better than most of the minority members who were admitted. Moreover, there is absolutely no basis for concluding that Bakke's rejection as a result of Davis' use of racial preference will affect him throughout his life in the same way as the segregation of the Negro school children in Brown I would have affected them. Unlike discrimination against racial minorities, the use of racial preferences for remedial purposes does not inflict a pervasive injury upon individual whites in the sense that wherever they go or whatever they do there is a significant likelihood that they will be treated as second-class citizens because of their color. . . .

In addition, there is simply no evidence that the Davis program discriminates intentionally or unintentionally against any minority group which it purports to benefit. . . . The Davis program does not simply advance less qualified applicants; rather, it compensates applicants, who it is uncontested are fully qualified to study medicine, for educational disadvantages which it was reasonable to conclude were a product of state-fostered discrimination. Once admitted, these students must satisfy the same degree requirements as regularly admitted students; they are taught by the same faculty in the same classes; and their performance is evaluated by the same standards by which regularly admitted students are judged. Under these circumstances, their performance and degrees must be regarded equally with the regularly admitted students with whom they compete for standing. Since minority graduates cannot justifiably be regarded as less well qualified than non-minority graduates by virtue of the special admissions program, there is no reasonable basis to conclude that minority graduates at schools using such programs would be stigmatized as inferior by the existence of such programs.

D.

We disagree with the lower courts' conclusion that the Davis program's use of race was unreasonable in light of its objectives. First, as petitioner argues, there are no practical means by which it could achieve its ends in the foreseeable future without the use of race-conscious measures. With respect to any factor (such as poverty or family educational background) that may be used as a substitute for race as an indicator of past discrimination, whites greatly outnumber racial minorities simply because whites make up a far larger percentage of the total population and therefore far outnumber minorities in absolute terms at every socioeconomic level. . . . Moreover, while race is positively correlated with differences in GPA and MCAT scores, economic disadvantage is not. Thus, it appears that economically disadvantaged whites do not score less well than economically advantaged whites, while economically advantaged blacks score less well than do disadvantaged whites. These statistics graphically illustrate that the University's purpose to integrate its classes by compensating for past discrimination could not be achieved by a general preference for the economically disadvantaged or the children of parents of limited education unless such groups were to make up the entire class. . . .

E. . . .

Finally, Davis' special admissions program cannot be said to violate the Constitution simply because it has set aside a predetermined number of places for qualified minority applicants rather than using minority status as a positive factor to be considered in evaluating the applications of disadvantaged minority applicants. For purposes of constitutional adjudication, there is no difference between the two approaches. In any admissions program which accords special consideration to disadvantaged racial minorities, a determination of the degree of preference to be given is unavoidable, and any given preference that results in the exclusion of a white candidate is no more or less constitutionally acceptable than a program such as that at Davis. . . .

The "Harvard" program as those employing it readily concede, openly and successfully employs a racial criterion for the purpose of ensuring that some of the scarce places in institutions of higher education are allocated to disadvantaged minority students. That the Harvard approach does not also make public the extent of the preference and the precise workings of the system while the Davis program employs a specific, openly stated number, does not condemn the latter plan for purposes of the Fourteenth Amendment adjudication. . . .

V.

Accordingly, we would reverse the judgment of the Supreme Court of California holding the Medical School's special admissions program unconstitutional and directing respondent's admission, as well as that portion of the judgment enjoining the Medical School from according any consideration to race in the admissions process.

[Mr. Justice White filed a separate opinion in which he argued that Title VI did not authorize a private cause of action by an aggrieved applicant. His views regarding the merits of the Title VI issue and the equal protection issue were included in the opinion of Justices Brennan, White, Marshall and Blackmun. He also joined in Parts I, III-A and V-C of Mr. Justice Powell's opinion.]

Mr. Justice **Marshall** said in part:

I agree with the judgment of the Court only insofar as it permits a university to consider the race of an applicant in making admissions decisions. I do not agree that petitioner's admissions program violates the Constitution. . . .

[Mr. Justice Marshall traces the history of the Negro in American society from slavery to the present.]

II.

The position of the Negro today in America is the tragic but inevitable consequence of centuries of unequal treatment. Measured by any benchmark of comfort or achievement, meaningful equality remains a distant dream for the Negro.

A Negro child today has a life expectancy which is shorter by more than five years than that of a white child. The Negro child's mother is over three times more likely to die of complications in childbirth, and the infant mortality rate for Negroes is nearly twice that for whites. The median income of the Negro family is only 60% that of the median of a white family, and the percentage of Negroes who live in families with incomes below the poverty line is nearly four times greater than that of whites.

When the Negro child reaches working age, he finds that America offers him significantly less than it offers his white counterpart. For Negro adults, the unemployment rate is twice that of whites, and the unemployment rate for Negro teenagers is nearly three times that of white teenagers. A Negro male who completes four years of college can expect a median annual income of merely $110 more than a white male who has only a high school diploma. Although Negroes represent 11.5 % of the population, they are only 1.2% of the lawyers and judges, 2% of the physicians, 2.3% of the dentists, 1.1% of the engineers and 2.6% of the college and university professors.

The relationship between those figures and the history of unequal treatment afforded to the Negro cannot be denied. At every point from birth to death the impact of the past is reflected in the still disfavored position of the Negro.

In light of the sorry history of discrimination and its devastating impact on the lives of Negroes, bringing the Negro into the mainstream of American life should be a state interest of the highest order. To fail to do so is to ensure that America will forever remain a divided society.

III.

I do not believe that the Fourteenth Amendment requires us to accept that fate. Neither its history nor our past cases lend any support to the conclusion that a university may not remedy the cumulative effects of society's discrimination by giving consideration to race in an effort to increase the number and percentage of Negro doctors. . . .

IV.

While I applaud the judgment of the Court that a university may consider race in its admissions process, it is more than a little ironic that, after several hundred years of class-based discrimination against Negroes, the Court is unwilling to hold that a class-based remedy for that discrimination is permissible. In declining to so hold, today's judgment ignores the fact that for several hundred years Negroes have been discriminated against, not as individuals, but rather solely because of the color of their skins. It is unnecessary in 20th century America to have individual Negroes demonstrate that they have been victims of racial discrimination; the racism of our society has been so pervasive that none, regardless of wealth or position, has managed to escape its impact. The experience of Negroes in America has been different in kind, not just in degree, from that of other ethnic groups. It is not merely the history of slavery alone but also that a whole people were marked as inferior by the law. And that mark has endured. The dream of America as the great melting pot has not been realized for the Negro; because of his skin color he never even made it into the pot. . . .

It is because of a legacy of unequal treatment that we now must permit the institutions of this society to give consideration to race in making decisions about who will hold the positions of influence, affluence, and prestige in America. For far too long, the doors to those positions have been shut to Negroes. If we are ever to become a fully integrated society, one in which the color of a person's skin will not determine the opportunities available to him or her, we must be willing to take steps to open those doors. I do not believe that anyone can truly look into America's past and still find that a remedy for the effects of that past is impermissible. . . .

I fear that we have come full circle. After the Civil War our Government started several "affirmative action" programs. This Court in the Civil Rights Cases and Plessy v. Ferguson destroyed the movement toward complete equality. For almost a century no action was taken, and this nonaction was with the tacit approval of the courts. Then we had Brown v. Board of Education and the Civil Rights Acts of Congress, followed by numerous affirmative action programs. *Now,* we have this Court again stepping in, this time to stop affirmative action programs of the type used by the University of California.

Mr. Justice **Blackmun,** said in part:

I am not convinced, as Mr. Justice Powell seems to be, that the difference between the Davis program and the one employed by Harvard is very profound or constitutionally significant. The line between the two is a thin and indistinct one. In each, subjective application is at work. . . .

I suspect that it would be impossible to arrange an affirmative action program in a racially neutral way and have it successful. To ask that this be so is to demand the impossible. In order to get beyond racism, we must first take account of race. There is no other way. And in order to treat some persons equally, we must treat them differently. We cannot—we dare not—let the Equal Protection Clause perpetuate racial supremacy.

Mr. Justice **Stevens,** with whom The **Chief Justice,** Mr. Justice **Stewart,** and Mr. Justice **Rehnquist** join, concurring in the judgment in part and dissenting in part, said in part:

II.

Both petitioner and respondent have asked us to determine the legality of the University's special admissions program by reference to the Constitution. Our settled practice, however, is to avoid the decision of a constitutional issue if a case can be fairly decided on a statutory ground. "If there is one doctrine more deeply rooted than any other in the process of constitutional adjudication, it is that we ought not to pass on questions of constitutionality . . . unless such adjudication is unavoidable." . . .

III.

. . . In unmistakable terms the [Civil Rights Act of 1964] prohibits the exclusion of individuals from federally funded programs because of their race. As succinctly phrased during the Senate debate, under Title VI it is not "permissible to say 'yes' to one person; but to say 'no' to another person, only because of the color of his skin." . . .

The University's special admissions program violated Title VI of the Civil Rights Act of 1964 by excluding Bakke from the Medical School because of his race. It is therefore our duty to affirm the judgment ordering Bakke admitted to the University.

Accordingly, I concur in the Court's judgment insofar as it affirms the judgment of the Supreme Court of California. To the extent that it purports to do anything else, I respectfully dissent.

DISCRIMINATION AGAINST WOMEN

GEDULDIG v. AIELLO

417 U. S. 484; 94 S. Ct. 2485; 41 L. Ed. 2d 256
(1974)

Probably no group in the country is subject to a more pervasive, firmly established and staunchly defended system of discrimination than are women. Relying on such varied arguments as biblical authority, the woman's lack of muscular strength, her child-bearing function with its attendant incapacities, and the natural capacity for motherhood, male members of society have undertaken to protect "their women" from having to compete against men by assuring them, insofar as possible, a role of their own in society. States have, at one time or another, forbidden women to work at certain jobs, to engage publicly in certain sports, to work while pregnant or to collect unemployment benefits when on maternity leave. Until 1968, a Connecticut statute provided that a woman serve a three-year indeterminant sentence at the "State Farm" for a crime for which a man could be sentenced to only eighteen months in jail, and until 1982 a state could still establish a one-sex school, while one-race schools were held to deny equal protection of the laws. Even greater is the private discrimination against women. As with blacks, some employers simply refuse to hire women, hire them only for secretarial or clerical jobs, or pay them only about 60 percent of what they would pay a man for comparable work. Section 703(a) of the Civil Rights Act of 1964 provided the first nationwide prohibition against discriminatory hiring practices affecting women and in Phillips v. Marietta Corp. (1971) the Supreme Court held that the act forbade the corporation to refuse to hire a woman with pre-school-age children when it hired men with such children.

On the few occasions when the Court dealt with the rights of women under the equal protection clause, it treated sex as a legitimate basis of classification and as early as 1904 it held, in Cronin v. Adams, that a state could by law not only prevent women from working in saloons, but could even prevent their entering as customers. See the note to Goesaert v. Cleary. Nor was there any constitutional objection to treating men and women differently in regard to jury service. In Strauder v. West Virginia (1880) the Court suggested that a state could "confine the selection to males," and in Hoyt v. Florida (1961) it refused to review the "continuing validity of this dictum . . . which has gone unquestioned for more than eighty years in the decisions of this Court." The Court upheld a state law exempting women from jury service, noting that "despite the enlightened emancipation of women from the restrictions and protections of bygone years, and their entry into many parts of community life formerly considered to be reserved to men, woman is still regarded as the center of home and family life."

With the woman's rights amendment (ERA) a few votes short of ratification, the attitude of the Supreme Court began to reflect the changed status of women in society. When, in Taylor v. Louisiana (1975), it effectively overruled the Hoyt case, it acknowledged that "if at one time it could be held that Sixth Amendment juries must be drawn from a fair cross section of the community but that this requirement permitted the almost total exclusion of women, this is not the case today. Communities differ at different times and places. What is a fair cross section at one time or place is not necessarily a fair cross section at another time or a different place." The Court noted that 53 percent of the community were women, and added that the fact that 54 percent of all women between eighteen and sixty-four were part of the labor force "certainly put to rest the suggestion that all women should be exempt from jury service based solely on their sex and the presumed role in the home."

But while the Court seemed prepared to accept the new role of women and viewed state laws treating them differently from men more critically than equal protection standards traditionally required, it was apparently not so convinced of their equality as to consider sex, like race, a "suspect" or "invidious" classification which can be used by the state only to achieve some compelling state interest which it cannot achieve in any other way. See the note to Plyler v. Doe.

In deciding Reed v. Reed in 1971, the first case ever to hold void a state classification based on sex, the Court held that women were as entitled as men to serve as administrators of estates. While it conceded that "the objective of reducing the work load on probate courts by eliminating one class of contests is not without some legitimacy," it found that preferring one sex over another "merely to accomplish the elimination of hearings on the merits, is to make the very kind of arbitrary legislative choice forbidden by the Equal Protection Clause."

Although Reed was unanimous, it gave no clue as to the philosophy of the justices, and it was not until 1973 with the decision in Frontiero v. Richardson that their attitudes began to emerge. A divided Court held that a female member of the armed forces could claim her spouse as a dependent in the same way a male member could claim his, without having to prove actual dependency. In a plurality opinion, Justices Brennan, Douglas, White, and Marshall reasoned that "classifications based on sex, like classifications based upon race, alienage, or national origin, are inherently suspect, and must therefore be subjected to strict judicial scrutiny." Applying these standards, the four justices, quoting from Reed, found that "any statutory scheme which draws a sharp line between the sexes, solely for the purpose of achieving administrative convenience, necessarily commands 'dissimilar treatment for men and women who are . . . similarly situated,' and therefore involves the 'very kind of arbitrary legislative choice forbidden by the [Constitution].' " While Justice Rehnquist dissented and Justice Stewart concurred on the basis of Reed, Justices Powell, Burger, and Blackmun expressly rejected the idea "that all classifications based upon sex" are inherently suspect.

Despite this division on the nature of woman's equality, where the Court has been able to view a law favoring women as an affirmative action program to offset the economic disadvantages to which women are subjected, it has found there was no denial of equal protection or due process of law. Thus, in 1974 in Kahn v. Shevin, the Court upheld a Florida property tax exemption for widows but not widowers on the ground that "the financial difficulties confronting the lone woman in Florida or in another State exceed those facing the man. Whether from overt discrimination or from the socialization process or a male-dominated culture, the job market is inhospitable to the woman seeking any but the lowest paid jobs." Noting that this was a tax statute, Justice Douglas for a six-man majority applied the traditional rules regarding classification. "A state tax law is not arbitrary although it 'discriminates in favor of a certain class . . . if the discrimination is founded upon a reasonable distinction, or difference in state policy,' not in conflict with the Federal Constitution." And in Schlesinger v. Ballard (1975) a regulation allowing women to stay thirteen years in the Navy although twice passed over for promotion did not discriminate against men who could only stay nine years since the opportunity for promotion among men was greater than among women.

In contrast, in Weinberger v. Wiesenfeld (1975) the Court struck down a provision of the Social Security Act providing that a widow with minor children was entitled to benefit from the earnings of her husband, while a widower with minor children was not entitled to benefit from the earnings of his wife. The government argued that, like Kahn v. Shevin, the scheme was designed to *"offset the adverse economic situation of women," but the Court found the legislative purpose was to enable the surviving parent to stay home with the child and, as in Reed, this was not a purpose which justified discrimination on the basis of sex.*

While a majority of the Court refused to hold that classifications based on sex were "invidious" in the same way as those based on race, it was clearly tightening the reins on the "rational basis" test where the challenged classification was sex. In Stanton v. Stanton (1975) it held void a Utah law setting different ages at which males and females became legal adults, and in Craig v. Boren (1976) it struck down an Oklahoma law setting the age for drinking 3.2 beer at eighteen for females and twenty-one for males. In neither case was the Court willing to accept the state's argument that a legitimate state interest was being advanced, and in the latter case it rejected as unpersuasive the state's statistical evidence purporting to justify the law.

In General Electric v. Gilbert (1976) the Court extended the reasoning of the present case to cases arising under Title VII of the Civil Rights Act of 1964 forbidding sex discrimination by private employers. Noting the similarity of language used in the act with that appearing in equal protection decisions, the Court concluded that its decision in Geduldig was "quite relevant in determining whether or not the pregnancy exclusion did discriminate on the basis of sex." Justice Brennan's dissent pointed out that G.E. had a long history of discrimination against women and that its medical coverage included voluntary male-only disabilities such as prostatectomies, vasectomies, and circumcisions. "Pregnancy affords the only disability, sex-specific or otherwise, that is excluded from coverage." In 1978 Congress passed the Pregnancy Discrimination Act to nullify this interpretation.

Two cases in the 1980s broke the sex barrier of two of the nations largest businessmen's organizations, the Junior Chamber of Commerce and Rotary International. In both cases a state law forbade the organizations to discriminate against women and both argued their First Amendment right of "intimate" and "private" association was being abridged. In neither case were women excluded from meetings, membership in the associations offered important professional contacts and economic advantages and in both cases the organizations size and structure tended to refute the "intimacy" claim. See Roberts v. United States Jaycees (1984) and Board of Directors of Rotary International v. Rotary Club (1987).

Mr. Justice **Stewart** delivered the opinion of the Court, saying in part:

For almost 30 years California has administered a disability insurance system that pays benefits to persons in private employment who are temporarily unable to work because of disability not covered by workmen's compensation. The appellees brought this action to challenge the constitutionality of a provision of the California program that, in defining "disability," excludes from coverage certain disabilities resulting from pregnancy. Because the appellees sought to enjoin the enforcement of this state statute, a three-judge court was convened. . . . On the appellees' motion for summary judgment, the District Court, by a divided vote, held that this provision of the disability insurance program violates the Equal Protection Clause of the Fourteenth Amendment, and therefore enjoined its continued enforcement. . . .

I.

California's disability insurance system is funded entirely from contributions deducted from the wages of participating employees. Participation in the program is mandatory unless the employees are protected by a voluntary private plan approved by the State. Each employee is required to contribute one percent of his salary, up to an annual maximum of $85. These contributions are placed in the Unemployment Compensation Disability Fund, which is established and administered as a special trust fund within the state treasury. . . .

In return for his one-percent contribution to the Disability Fund, the individual employee is insured against the risk of disability stemming from a substantial number of "mental or physical illness[es] and mental or physical injur[ies]." It is not every disabling condition, however, that triggers the obligation to pay benefits under the program. . . .

At all times relevant to this case, § 2626 of the Unemployment Insurance Code provided:

" 'Disability' or 'disabled' includes both mental or physical illness and mental or physical injury. An individual shall be deemed disabled in any day in which, because of mental or physical condition, he is unable to perform his regular or customary work. *In no case shall the term 'disability' or 'disabled' include any injury or illness caused by or arising in connection with pregnancy up to the termination of such pregnancy and for a period of 28 days thereafter."* (Emphasis added.) . . .

. . . The state court construed the statute to preclude only the payment of benefits for disability accompanying normal pregnancy. The appellant acquiesced in this construction and issued administrative guidelines that exclude only the payment of "maternity benefits"—i.e., hospitalization and disability benefits for normal delivery and recuperation. . . .

. . . Thus, the issue before the Court on this appeal is whether the California disability insurance program invidiously discriminates against [Aiello] and others similarly situated by not paying insurance benefits for disability that accompanies normal pregnancy and childbirth.

II.

It is clear that California intended to establish this benefit system as an insurance program that was to function essentially in accordance with insurance concepts. Since the program was instituted in 1946, it has been totally self-supporting, never drawing on general state revenues to finance disability or hospital benefits. The Disability Fund is wholly supported by the one percent of wages annually contributed by participating employees. At oral argument, counsel for the appellant informed us that in recent years between 90% and 103% of the revenue to the Disability Fund has been paid out in disability and hospital benefits. This history strongly suggests that the one-percent contribution rate, in addition to being easily computable, bears a close and substantial relationship to the level of benefits payable and to the disability risks insured under the program.

Over the years California has demonstrated a strong commitment not to increase the contribution rate above the one-percent level. The State has sought to provide the broadest possible disability protection that would be affordable by all employees, including those with very low incomes. Because any larger percentage or any flat dollar-amount rate of contribution would impose an increasingly regressive levy bearing most heavily upon those with the lowest incomes, the State has resisted any attempt to change the required contribution from the one-percent level. The program is thus structured, in terms of the level of benefits and the risks insured, to maintain the solvency of the Disability Fund at a one-percent annual level of contribution.

In ordering the State to pay benefits for disability accompanying normal pregnancy and delivery, the District Court acknowledged the State's contention "that coverage of these disabilities is so extraordinarily expensive that it would be impossible to maintain a program supported by employee contributions if these disabilities are included." There is considerable disagreement between the parties with respect to how great the increased costs would actually be, but they would clearly be substantial. For purposes of analysis the District Court accepted the State's estimate, which was in excess of $100 million annually, and stated that "it is clear that including these disabilities would not destroy the program. The increased costs could be accommodated quite easily by making reasonable changes in the contribution rate, the maximum benefits allowable, and the other variables affecting the solvency of the program."

Each of these "variables"—the benefit level deemed appropriate to compensate employee disability, the risks selected to be insured under the program, and the contribution rate chosen to maintain the solvency of the program and at the same time to permit low-income employees to participate with minimal personal sacrifice—represents a policy determination by the State. The essential issue in this case is whether the Equal Protection Clause requires such policies to be sacrificed or compromised in order to finance the payment of benefits to those whose disability is attributable to normal pregnancy and delivery.

We cannot agree that the exclusion of this disability from coverage amounts to invidious discrimination under the Equal Protection Clause. California does not discriminate with respect to the persons or groups which are eligible for disability insurance protection under the program. The classification challenged in this case relates to the asserted underinclusiveness of the set of risks that the State has selected to insure. Although California has created a program to insure most risks of employment disability, it has not chosen to insure all such risks, and this decision is reflected in the level of annual contributions exacted from participating employees. This Court has held that, consistently with the Equal Protection Clause, a State "may take one step at a time, addressing itself to the phase of the problem which seems most acute to the legislative mind. . . . The legislature may select one phase of one field and apply a remedy there, neglecting the others. . . ." . . . Particularly with respect to social welfare programs, so long as the line drawn by the State is rationally supportable, the courts will not interpose their judgment as to the appropriate stopping point. "[T]he Equal Protection Clause does not require a State must choose between attacking every aspect of a problem or not attacking the problem at all." . . .

The State has a legitimate interest in maintaining the self-supporting nature of its insurance program. Similarly, it has an interest in distributing the available resources in such a way as to keep benefit payments at an adequate level for disabilities that are covered, rather than to cover all disabilities inadequately. Finally, California has a legitimate concern in maintaining the contribution rate at a level that will not unduly burden participating employees, particularly low-income employees who may be most in need of the disability insurance.

These policies provide an objective and wholly noninvidious basis for the State's decision not to create a more comprehensive insurance program than it has. There is no evidence in the record that the selection of the risks insured by the program worked to discriminate against any definable group or class in terms of the aggregate risk protection derived by that group or class from the program.* There is no risk from which men are protected and women are not. Likewise, there is no risk from which women are protected and men are not.

The appellee simply contends that, although she has received insurance protection equivalent to that pro-

---

*The dissenting opinion to the contrary, this case is thus a far cry from cases like Reed v. Reed (1971) and Frontiero v. Richardson (1973) involving discrimination based upon gender as such. The California insurance program does not exclude anyone from benefit eligibility because of gender but merely removes one physical condition—pregnancy—from the list of compensable disabilities. While it is true that only women can become pregnant, it does not follow that every legislative classification concerning pregnancy is a sex-based classification like those considered in Reed and Frontiero. Normal pregnancy is an objectively identifiable physical condition with unique characteristics. Absent a showing that distinctions involving pregnancy are mere pretexts designed to effect an invidious discrimination against the members of one sex or the other, lawmakers are constitutionally free to include or exclude pregnancy from the coverage of legislation such as this on any reasonable basis, just as with respect to any other physical condition.

The lack of identity between the excluded disability and gender as such under this insurance program becomes clear upon the most cursory analysis. The program divides potential recipients into two groups—pregnant women and non-pregnant persons. While the first group is exclusively female, the second includes members of both sexes. The fiscal and actuarial benefits of the program thus accrue to members of both sexes.

vided all other participating employees, she has suffered discrimination because she encountered a risk that was outside the program's protection. For the reasons we have stated, we hold that this contention is not a valid one under the Equal Protection Clause of the Fourteenth Amendment.

Mr. Justice **Brennan,** with whom Mr. Justice **Douglas** and Mr. Justice **Marshall** join, dissenting, said in part:

. . . The Court today rejects appellees' equal protection claim and upholds the exclusion of normal pregnancy-related disabilities from coverage under California's disability insurance program on the ground that the legislative classification rationally promotes the State's legitimate cost-saving interests in "maintaining the self-supporting nature of its insurance program[,] . . . distributing the available resources in such a way as to keep benefit payments at an adequate level for disabilities that are covered, . . . [and]maintaining the contribution rate at a level that will not unduly burden participating employees. . . ." Because I believe that Reed v. Reed (1971) and Frontiero v. Richardson (1973) mandate a stricter standard of scrutiny which the State's classification fails to satisfy, I respectfully dissent. . . .

Despite the Act's broad goals and scope of coverage, compensation is denied for disabilities suffered in connection with a "normal" pregnancy—disabilities suffered only by women. Disabilities caused by pregnancy, however, like other physically disabling conditions covered by the Act, require medical care, often include hospitalization, anesthesia and surgical procedures, and may involve genuine risk to life. Moreover, the economic effects caused by pregnancy-related disabilities are functionally indistinguishable from the effects caused by any other disability: wages are lost due to a physical inability to work, and medical expenses are incurred for the delivery of the child and for postpartum care. In my view, by singling out for less favorable treatment a gender-linked disability peculiar to women, the State has created a double standard for disability compensation: a limitation is imposed upon the disabilities for which women workers may recover, while men receive full compensation for all disabilities suffered, including those that effect only or primarily their sex, such as prostatectomies, circumcision, hemophilia, and gout. In effect, one set of rules is applied to females and another to males. Such dissimilar treatment of men and women, on the basis of physical characteristics inextricably linked to one sex, inevitably constitutes sex discrimination. . . .

In the past, when a legislative classification has turned on gender, the Court has justifiably applied a standard of judicial scrutiny more strict than that generally accorded economic or social welfare programs. . . . Yet, by its decision today, the Court appears willing to abandon that higher standard of review without satisfactorily explaining what differentiates the gender-based classification employed in this case from those found unconstitutional in Reed and Frontiero. The Court's decision threatens to return men and women to a time when "traditional" equal protection analysis sustained legislative classifications that treated differently members of a particular sex solely because of their sex. See, e.g., Muller v. Oregon; Goesaert v. Cleary; Hoyt v. Florida (1961).

I cannot join the Court's apparent retreat. I continue to adhere to my view that "classifications based upon sex, like classifications based upon race, alienage, or national origin, are inherently suspect, and must therefore be subjected to strict judicial scrutiny." Frontiero v. Richardson. When, as in this case, the State employs a legislative classification that distinguishes between beneficiaries solely by reference to gender-linked disability risks, "[t]he Court is not . . . free to sustain the statute on the ground that it rationally promotes legitimate governmental interests; rather, such suspect classifications can be sustained only when the State bears the burden of demonstrating that the challenged legislation serves overriding or compelling interests that cannot be achieved either by a more carefully tailored legislative classification or by the use of feasible, less drastic means." Kahn v. Shevin (1974) (Brennan, J., dissenting).

MISSISSIPPI UNIVERSITY FOR WOMEN v. HOGAN

458 U. S. 718; 102 S. Ct. 3331; 73 L.Ed. 2d 1090 (1982)

While the failure of the Equal Rights Amendment (ERA) to achieve ratification was a blow to its supporters there are perhaps a number of lessons to be learned from the struggle itself. In the first place, the very fact of the struggle publicized the legitimate and long overlooked claims of women to a status of legal and professional equality. Never again will it be easy to get laws passed denying a wife the right to own property or to enter the business or professional world. In the second place, it became apparent that some women identified with the role they were used to playing, and they both resented and were made to feel insecure by what they viewed as a threat to this role. They saw no reason for shame if they wanted to be housewives and mothers and felt threatened by a movement that seemed to make it hard for them to pursue that role with pride. Third, and this is the point that is most often overlooked, if the ERA had passed there is little assurance that much if any change would have accompanied it. The amending power is touted as the way to make the Constitution say what the people want it to say, but in the long run it is the Supreme Court that decides what the amendments themselves actually mean. One need only view the complete destruction of the "privileges and immunities" clause of the Fourteenth Amendment at the hands of the Court in the Slaughter-House Cases (1873), or the limitations on the right of Congress to tax following the adoption of the Income Tax Amendment to realize that the ERA would have granted women only those rights which the Court was prepared to see them have.

The difficulties of defining an "intermediate" test and knowing when to apply it are illustrated in Michael M. v. Sonoma County (1981). Five members of the Court upheld a state statutory rape law against the challenge that it punished the male participant to a consensual sex act (in this case a minor) but not his minor female partner. The Court gave "great deference" to California's assertion that the purpose of the law was to prevent teenage pregnancies and agreed that this was certainly a legitimate state purpose. Moreover, punishing just the male was sufficiently related to the purpose of the law because the female was already sufficiently deterred from the act by the fear of pregnancy, and were she to become pregnant and have to deal with the consequences she would be further punished while the male would not.

Justices Brennan, White and Marshall dissented, arguing that while ostensibly applying the same test, the majority had failed to carry the burden of showing that a sex-neutral law punishing both parties to the act would not be as effective a deterrent in preventing pregnancy as one punishing only the male. Justice Stevens dissented separately, pointing out that it was "totally irrational to exempt from punishment the one most likely to be injured by the dangerous act. In contrast to the Michael M. case, the Court in Kirchberg v. Feenstra (1981) found no important governmental interest was served by a Louisiana law allowing a husband to mortgage without his wife's consent their jointly owned home.

The Military Selective Service Act authorizes the President, by proclamation, to require the registration of "every male citizen" and male resident alien between the ages of eighteen and twenty-six. The purpose of the act, of course, is to provide a manpower pool should conscription become necessary, although Congress by statute in 1973 forbade any actual conscription under the act. At the time of the Soviet invasion of Afghanistan President Carter invoked the provisions of the act and asked Congress to allocate the necessary funds and to amend the MSSA to permit the registration of women. After prolonged debate Congress declined to amend the act and allocated only sufficient funds to register males.

In Rostker v. Goldberg (1981) the Supreme Court upheld the registration of males against the claim that by failing to register both sexes the act denied a male registrant the equal protection of the laws. Applying the test of Craig v. Boren (1976), the Court agreed that raising and supporting armies was "an important governmental interest," and that these were circumstances under which judicial deference to the congressional judgment was at its highest. It noted the extensive debates on the issue and found that Congress, in reaching its decision, had not acted "unthinkingly" or "reflexively and not for any considered reason," which might have suggested a mere response to prejudices about women in the armed forces. "The fact that Congress and the Executive have decided that women should not serve in combat fully justifies Congress in not authorizing their registration, since the purpose of registration is to develop a pool of potential combat troops. . . . The Constitution requires that Congress treat similarly situated persons similarly, not that it engage in gestures of superficial equality."

Justice **O'Connor** delivered the opinion of the Court, saying in part:

This case presents the narrow issue of whether a state statute that excludes males from enrolling in a state-supported professional nursing school violates the Equal Protection Clause of the Fourteenth Amendment.

I.

The facts are not in dispute. In 1884, the Mississippi legislature created the Mississippi Industrial Institute and College for the Education of White Girls of the State of Mississippi, now the oldest state-supported all-female college in the United States. The school, known today as Mississippi University (MUW), has from its inception limited its enrollment to women.

In 1971, MUW established a School of Nursing, initially offering a two-year associate degree. Three years later, the school instituted a four-year baccalaureate program in nursing and today also offers a graduate program. The School of Nursing has its own faculty and administers it own criteria for admission.

Respondent, Joe Hogan, is a registered nurse but does not hold a baccalaureate degree in nursing. Since 1974, he has worked as a nursing supervisor in a medical center in Columbus, the city in which MUW is located. In 1979, Hogan applied for admission to the MUW School of Nursing's baccalaureate program. Although he was otherwise qualified, he was denied admission solely because of his sex. School officials informed him that he could audit the courses in which he was interested, but could not enroll for credit. . . .

II.

We begin our analysis aided by several firmly-established principles. Because the challenged policy expressly discriminates among applicants on the basis of gender, it is subject to scrutiny under the Equal Protection Clause. . . . That this statute discriminates against males rather than against females does not exempt it from scrutiny or reduce the standard of review,* . . . Our decisions also establish that the party seeking to uphold a statute that classifies individuals on the basis of their gender must carry the burden of showing an "exceedingly persuasive justification" for the classification. Kirchberg v. Feenstra (1981). . . . The burden is met only by showing at least that the classification serves

---

*Without question, MUW's admission policy worked to Hogan's disadvantage. Although Hogan could have attended classes and received credit in one of Mississippi's state-supported coeducational nursing programs, none of which was located in Columbus, he could attend only by driving a considerable distance from his home. A similarly situated female would not have been required to choose between foregoing credit and bearing that inconvenience. Moreover, since many students enrolled in the School of Nursing hold full-time jobs, Hogan's female colleagues had available an opportunity, not open to Hogan, to obtain credit for additional training. The policy of denying males the right to obtain credit toward a baccalaureate degree thus imposed upon Hogan "a burden he would not bear were he female." Orr v. Orr (1979).

"important governmental objectives and that the discriminatory means employed" are "substantially related to the achievement of those objectives." . . .*

Although the test for determining the validity of a gender-based classification is straightforward, it must be applied free of fixed notions concerning the roles and abilities of males and females. Care must be taken in ascertaining whether the statutory objective itself reflects archaic and stereotypic notions. Thus, if the statutory objective is to exclude or "protect" members of one gender because they are presumed to suffer from an inherent handicap or to be innately inferior, the objective itself is illegitimate. See Frontiero v. Richardson (1973) (plurality opinion).†

If the State's objective is legitimate and important, we next determine whether the requisite direct, substantial relationship between objective and means is present. The purpose of requiring that close relationship is to assure that the validity of a classification is determined through reasoned analysis rather than through the mechanical application of traditional, often inaccurate, assumptions about the proper roles of men and women. The need for the requirement is amply revealed by reference to the broad range of statutes already invalidated by this Court, statutes that relied upon the simplistic, outdated assumption that gender could be used as a "proxy for other, more germane bases of classification," Craig v. Boren (1976), to establish a link between objective and classification.

Applying this framework, we now analyze the arguments advanced by the State to justify its refusal to allow males to enroll for credit in MUW's School of Nursing.

---

*. . . Our past decisions establish, however, that when a classification expressly discriminates on the basis of gender, the analysis and level of scrutiny applied to determine the validity of the classification do not vary simply because the objective appears acceptable to individual members of the Court. While the validity and importance of the objective may affect the outcome of the analysis, the analysis itself does not change.

Thus, we apply the test previously relied upon by the Court to measure the constitutionality of gender-based discrimination. Because we conclude that the challenged statutory classification is not substantially related to an important objective, we need not decide whether classifications based upon gender are inherently suspect. . . .

†History provides numerous examples of legislative attempts to exclude women from particular areas simply because legislators believed women were less able than men to perform a particular function. In 1872, this Court remained unmoved by Myra Bradwell's argument that the Fourteenth Amendment prohibited a State from classifying her as unfit to practice law simply because she was female. Bradwell v. Illinois (1872). In his concurring opinion, Justice Brady described the reasons underlying the State's decision to determine which positions only men could fill: "It is the prerogative of the legislator to prescribe regulations founded on nature, reason, and experience for the due admission of qualified persons to professions and callings demanding special skill and confidence. This fairly belongs to the police power of the State; and, in my opinion, in view of the peculiar characteristics, destiny, and mission of woman, it is within the province of the legislature to ordain what offices, positions, and callings shall be filled and discharged by men, and shall receive the benefit of those energies and responsibilities, and that decision and firmness which are presumed to predominate in the sterner sex." . . .

III.

A.

The State's primary justification for maintaining the single-sex admissions policy of MUW's School of Nursing is that it compensates for discrimination against women and, therefore, constitutes educational affirmative action. As applied to the School of Nursing, we find the State's argument unpersuasive.

It is readily apparent that a State can evoke a compensatory purpose to justify an otherwise discriminatory classification only if members of the gender benefited by the classification actually suffer a disadvantage related to the classification. . . .

. . . Mississippi has made no showing that women lacked opportunities to obtain training in the field of nursing or to attain positions of leadership in that field when the MUW School of Nursing opened its doors or that women currently are deprived of such opportunities. In fact, in 1970, the year before the School of Nursing's first class enrolled, women earned 94 percent of the nursing baccalaureate degrees conferred in Mississippi and 98.6 percent of the degrees earned nationwide. . . . That year was not an aberration; one decade earlier, women had earned all the nursing degrees conferred in Mississippi and 98.9 percent of the degrees earned nationwide. . . .

Rather than compensate for discriminatory barriers faced by women, MUW's policy of excluding males from admission to the School of Nursing tends to perpetuate the stereotyped view of nursing as an exclusively woman's job. By assuring that Mississippi allots more openings in its state-supported nursing schools to women than it does to men, MUW's admissions policy lends credibility to the old view that women, not men, should become nurses, and makes the assumption that nursing is a field for women a self-fulfilling prophecy. . . .

The policy is invalid also because it fails the second part of the equal protection test, for the State has made no showing that the gender-based classification is substantially and directly related to its proposed compensatory objective. To the contrary, MUW's policy of permitting men to attend classes as auditors fatally undermines its claim that women, at least those in the School of Nursing, are adversely affected by the presence of men.

. . . The uncontroverted record reveals that admitting men to nursing classes does not affect teaching style, that the presence of men in the classroom would not affect the performance of the female nursing students, and that men in coeducational nursing schools do not dominate the classroom. In sum, the record in this case is flatly inconsistent with the claim that excluding men from the School of Nursing is necessary to reach any of MUW's educational goals.

Thus, considering both the asserted interest and the relationship between the interest and the methods used by the State, we conclude that the State has fallen far short of establishing the "exceedingly persuasive justification" needed to sustain the gender-based classification. Accordingly, we hold that MUW's policy of denying males the right to enroll for credit in its School of Nursing violates the Equal Protection Clause of the Fourteenth Amendment.*

B.

In an additional attempt to justify its exclusion of men from MUW's School of Nursing, the State contends that MUW is the direct beneficiary "of specific congressional legislation which, on its face, permits the institution to exist as it has in the past." The argument is based upon the language of § 901(a) in Title IX of the Education Amendments of 1972, 20 USC §1681(a) [20 USCS § 1681(a)]. Although § 901(a) prohibits gender discrimination in education programs that receive federal financial assistance, subsection 5 exempts the admissions policies of undergraduate institutions "that traditionally and continually from [their] establishment [have] had a policy of admitting only students of one sex" from the general prohibition. Arguing that Congress enacted Title IX in furtherance of its power to enforce the Fourteenth Amendment, a power granted by § 5 of that Amendment, the State would have us conclude that § 1681(a)(5) is but "a congressional limitation upon the broad prohibitions of the Equal Protection Clause of the Fourteenth Amendment."

The argument requires little comment. Initially, it is far from clear that Congress intended, through § 1681(a)(5), to exempt MUW from any constitutional obligation. Rather, Congress apparently intended, at most, to exempt MUW from the requirements of Title IX.

Even if Congress envisioned a constitutional exemption, the State's argument would fail. Section 5 of the Fourteenth Amendment gives Congress broad power indeed to enforce the command of the Amendment and "to secure to all persons the enjoyment of perfect equality of civil rights and the equal protection of the laws against State denial or invasion. . . ." Ex parte Virginia (1879). Congress' power under § 5 grants Congress no power to restrict, abrogate, or dilute these guarantees." Katzenbach v. Morgan (1966). Although we give deference to congressional decisions and classifications, neither Congress nor a State can validate a law that denies the rights guaranteed by the Fourteenth Amendment. . . .

Chief Justice **Burger,** dissenting.

I agree generally with Justice Powell's dissenting opinion. I write separately, however, to emphasize that the Court's holding today is limited to the context of a professional nursing school. Since the Court's opinion relies heavily on its finding that women have traditionally dominated the nursing profession, it suggests that a State might well be justified in maintaining, for example, the option of an all-women's business school or liberal arts program.

Justice **Blackmun** wrote a short dissenting opinion.

Justice **Powell,** with whom Justice **Rehnquist** joins, dissenting, said in part:

The Court's opinion bows deeply to conformity. Left without honor—indeed, held unconstitutional—is an element of diversity that has characterized much of American education and enriched much of American life. The Court in effect holds today that no State now may provide even a single institution of higher learning open only to women students. It gives no heed to the efforts of the State of Mississippi to provide abundant opportunities for young men and young women to attend coeducational institutions, and none to the preferences of the more than 40,000 young women who over the years have evidenced their approval of an all-women's college by choosing Mississippi University for Women (MUW) over seven coeducational universities within the State. The Court decides today that the Equal Protection Clause makes it unlawful for the State to provide women with a traditionally popular and respected choice of educational environment. It does so in a case instituted by one man, who represents no class, and whose primary concern is personal convenience.

. . . His constitutional complaint is based upon a single asserted harm: that he must *travel* to attend the state-supported nursing schools that concededly are available to him. The Court characterizes this injury as one of "inconvenience." This description is fair and accurate, though somewhat embarrassed by the fact that there is, of course, no constitutional right to attend a state-supported university in one's home town. . . .

I.

Coeducation, historically, is a novel educational theory. From grade school through high school, college, and graduate and professional training, much of the nation's population during much of our history has been educated in sexually segregated classrooms. At the college level, for instance, until recently some of the most prestigious colleges and universities—including most of the Ivy League—had long histories of single-sex education. As Harvard, Yale, and Princeton remained all-male colleges well into the second half of this century, the "Seven Sister" institutions established a parallel standard of excellence for women's colleges. Of the Seven Sisters, Mount Holyoke opened as a female seminary in 1837 and was chartered as a college in 1888. Vassar was founded in 1865, Smith and Wellesley in 1875, Radcliffe in 1879, Bryn Mawr in 1885, and Barnard in 1889. Mount Holyoke, Smith, and Wellesley recently have made con-

---

*Justice Powell's dissent suggests that a second objective is served by the gender-based classification in that Mississippi has elected to provide women a choice of educational environments. Since any gender-based classification provides one class a benefit or choice not available to the other class, however, that argument begs the question. The issue is not whether the benefited class profits from the classification, but whether the State's decision to confer a benefit only upon one class by means of a discriminatory classification is substantially related to achieving a legitimate and substantial goal.

sidered decisions to remain essentially single-sex institutions. . . .

The sexual segregation of students has been a reflection of, rather than an imposition upon, the preference of those subject to the policy. It cannot be disputed, for example, that the highly qualified women attending the leading women's colleges could have earned admission to virtually any college of their choice. Women attending such colleges have chosen to be there, usually expressing a preference for the special benefits of single-sex institutions. Similar decisions were made by the colleges that elected to remain open to women only.

The arguable benefits of single-sex colleges also continue to be recognized by students of higher education. The Carnegie Commission on Higher Education has reported that it "favor[s] the continuation of colleges for women. They provide an element of diversity . . . and [an environment in which women] generally . . . speak up more in their classes, . . . hold more positions of leadership on campus, . . . and have more role models and mentors among women teachers and administrators."* . . .

Despite the continuing expressions that single-sex institutions may offer singular advantages to their students, there is no doubt that coeducational institutions are far more numerous. But their numerical predominance does not establish—in any sense properly cognizable by a court—that individual preferences for single-sex education are misguided or illegitimate, or that a State may not provide its citizens with a choice.

II.

The issue in this case is whether a State transgresses the Constitution when—within the context of a public system that offers a diverse range of campuses, curricula, and educational alternatives—it seeks to accommodate the legitimate personal preferences of those desiring the advantages of an all-women's college. In my view, the Court errs seriously by assuming—without argument or discussion—that the equal protection standard generally applicable to sex discrimination is appropriate here. That standard was designed to free women from "archaic and overbroad generalizations. . . ." Schlesinger v. Ballard, (1975). In no previous case have we ap-

---

*In this Court the benefits of single-sex education have been asserted by the students and alumnae of MUW. One would expect the Court to regard their views as directly relevant to this case: "[I]n the aspect of life known as courtship or mate-pairing, the American female remains in the old role of the pursued sex, expected to adorn and groom herself to attract the male. Without comment on the equities of this social arrangement, it remains a sociological fact."An institution of collegiate higher learning maintained exclusively for women is uniquely able to provide the education atmosphere in which some, but not all, women can best attain maximum learning potential. It can serve to overcome the historic repression of the past and can orient a woman to function and achieve in the still male-dominated economy. It can free its students of the burden of playing the mating game while attending classes, thus giving academic rather than sexual emphasis. Consequently, many such institutions flourish and their graduates make significant contributions to the arts, professions and business." Brief for Mississippi University for Women Alumnae Assn. as Amicus Curiae.

plied it to invalidate state efforts to *expand* women's choices. Nor are there prior sex discrimination decisions by this Court in which a male plaintiff, as in this case, had the choice of an equal benefit.

The cases cited by the Court therefore do not control the issue now before us. In most of them women were given no opportunity for the same benefit as men. Cases involving male plaintiffs are equally inapplicable. In Craig v. Boren, (1976), a male under 21 was not permitted to buy beer anywhere in the State, and women were afforded no choice as to whether they would accept the "statistically measured but loose-fitting generalities concerning the drinking tendencies of aggregate groups." . . .

By applying heightened equal protection analysis to this case, the Court frustrates the liberating spirit of the Equal Protection Clause. It forbids the States from providing women with an opportunity to choose the type of university they prefer. And yet it is these women whom the Court regards as the *victims* of an illegal, stereotyped perception of the role of women in our society. The Court reasons this way in a case in which no woman has complained, and the only complainant is a man who advances no claims on behalf of anyone else. His claim, it should be recalled, is not that he is being denied a substantive educational opportunity, or even the right to attend an all-male or a coeducational college. It is *only* that the colleges open to him are located at inconvenient distances.

III.

The Court views this case as presenting a serious equal protection claim of sex discrimination. I do not and I would sustain Mississippi's right to continue MUW on a rational basis analysis. But I need not apply this "lowest tier" of scrutiny. I can accept for present purposes the standard applied by the Court: that there is a gender-based distinction that must serve an important governmental objective by means that are substantially related to its achievement. E.g., Wengler v. Druggists Mutual Ins. Co. (1980). The record in this case reflects that MUW has a historic position in the State's educational system dating back to 1884. More than 2,000 women presently evidence their preference for MUW by having enrolled there. The choice is one that discriminates invidiously against no one. And the State's purpose in preserving that choice is legitimate and substantial. Generations of our finest minds, both among educators and students, have believed that single-sex college-level institutions afford distinctive benefits. There are many persons, of course, who have different views. But simply because there are these differences is no reason—certainly none of constitutional dimension—to conclude that no substantial state interest is served when such a choice is made available.

In arguing to the contrary, the Court suggests that the MUW is so operated as to "perpetuate the stereotyped view of nursing as an exclusively women's job." But as the Court itself acknowledges, MUW's School of Nursing was not created until 1971—about 90 years after the single-sex campus itself was founded. This hardly supports a link between nursing as a woman's profession and MUW's single-sex admission policy. Indeed, MUW's School of Nursing was not instituted until more than a decade *after* a separate School of Nursing was established at the coeducational University of Mississippi at Jackson. The School of Nursing makes up only one part—a relatively small part—of MUW's diverse modern university campus and curriculum. The other departments on the MUW campus offer a typical range of degrees and a typical range of subjects. There is no indication that women suffer fewer opportunities at other Mississippi state campuses because of MUW's admission policy.

In sum, the practice of voluntarily chosen single-sex education is an honored tradition in our country, even if it now rarely exists in state colleges and universities. Mississippi's accommodation of such student choices is legitimate because it is completely consensual and is important because it permits students to decide for themselves the type of college education they think will benefit them most. Finally, Mississippi's policy is substantially related to its long-respected objective. . . .

DISCRIMINATION AGAINST THE POOR

MAHER v. ROE

432 U. S. 464; 97 S. Ct. 2376; 53 L. Ed. 2d 484
(1977)

One of the clearest ideological hallmarks of a capitalist society is its general acceptance of wide differences in wealth among its members. Most people assume wealth results from personal earning power, which in turn is a result of natural talents and hard work. The fact that nearly everyone can point to as many exceptions as examples does not shake their belief that poor people are poor because they are lazy—that if they would just get out and work, they would not be poor. Over the years our constitutional doctrines have reflected these attitudes. In 1837 in New York v. Miln the Supreme Court had characterized paupers as a "moral pestilence," and this attitude largely prevailed throughout the nineteenth century.

It was not until the devastating impact of the Great Depression of the 1930s struck rich and poor alike that this view began to change and the first recognition was given to the idea that the poor, the unemployed, the aged, and the handicapped were a national responsibility. Out of this came the Social Security Act and other assistance programs. In Edwards v. California (1941) the Court rejected the characterization of the Miln case and struck down a law designed to keep destitute dustbowl farmers out of California. "Whatever may have been the notion then prevailing, we do not think that it will now be seriously contended that because a person is without employment and without funds he constitutes a

'moral pestilence.' Poverty and immorality are not synonymous."

But the idea dies hard that it is somehow wrong that the money of the "hard-working" taxpayer should be spent to support those who are "too lazy to work." To some persons public welfare is "charity" or "the dole" and should be only sufficient to let the donor feel virtuous and keep the recipient alive without encouraging him in his slothful ways. Others view welfare as the just claim of the recipient to a decent living from a society which has favored some people far more than others and which has failed to provide him with a useful or productive role. It is the eternal conflict between the "survival of the fittest" and the "brotherhood of man."

This conflict in philosophy was highlighted by the Court in Wyman v. James (1971), which held valid the unwarranted inspection of a welfare recipient's home as a condition of receiving aid for her child. The Court justified the intrusion in part on the ground that the taxpayer, like "one who dispenses purely private charity naturally has an interest in and expects to know how his charitable funds are utilized." Justice Douglas in dissent argued that Mrs. James was being discriminated against because she was poor and that no such breach of privacy would be tolerated were the welfare recipient "a prominent, affluent cotton or wheat farmer receiving benefit payments for not growing crops."

Most private institutions and many public ones continue to favor those who can pay their way over those who cannot, but perhaps the most anomalous institutionalized discrimination against the poor lies in the administration of justice. Justice is expensive. In civil litigation every paper filed with a court, every paper written, form filled out, or action taken by a lawyer costs money. A person wishing to enjoin someone's injuring him or her illegally may have to post a bond in case the injury turns out not to be illegal. Even in a criminal case defendants must post bail unless they wish to languish in jail until they can establish their innocence, must hire a lawyer to defend themselves, and if they lose at trial, each level to which they take an appeal multiplies their expenses. Those wishing to protest the procedure of a traffic court that has fined them $10 may be out of pocket thousands of dollars before they reach the Supreme Court. Such costs have traditionally been borne by litigants and have been defended both on the ground that those who use the judicial system should pay for its upkeep, and that making the system easily accessible to all persons would result in its being overburdened to the point of complete collapse. No claim was made that it really was equally available to rich and poor alike.

It was during the Depression that the Supreme Court took the first halting steps to do away with the worst results of this discrimination, and it did it not through any desire to equalize the status of rich and poor before the courts but because the handicap of being poor in some cases was so great that the resulting trial was unfair. In Powell v. Alabama (1932) the Court held that illiterate blacks being tried for a capital offense were entitled to a lawyer at state expense if they could not afford to hire one. While it was made clear in Betts v. Brady

(1942) that this was available only to a person whom the Court felt really needed a lawyer, in 1963 in Gideon v. Wainwright it finally conceded that all persons need a lawyer in a felony trial. The same day it assured a lawyer to a convicted indigent so he could bring that "first appeal, granted as a matter of right to rich and poor alike"; see Douglas v. California (1963). And in Argersinger v. Hamlin (1972) the right to appointed trial counsel was extended to all persons, misdemeanants as well as felons, who are faced with the possibility of a jail sentence.

In 1956 in Griffin v. Illinois the Supreme Court made its first attack on the costs imposed by the state to defray the expenses of its judicial system, holding that an indigent could not be denied a right to appeal a noncapital felony conviction merely because he could not afford to purchase a transcript. In his plurality opinion Justice Black noted that both "the Due Process and Equal Protection Clauses protect persons like petitioners from invidious discrimination" and added "there can be no equal justice where the kind of trial a man gets depends on the amount of money he has. Destitute defendants must be afforded as adequate appellate review as defendants who have money enough to buy transcripts."

In 1971 the essence of this protection was extended to indigent misdemeanants; see Mayer v. Chicago.

In Williams v. Illinois (1970) the Court held void a state statute under which an indigent prisoner who could not pay the "fine" part of his sentence had to stay in jail and work it off at the rate of $5 a day. Despite the fact that the practice went back to medieval England and was in use in nearly every state, the Court held it a denial of equal protection of the laws. Chief Justice Burger, speaking for seven members of the Court, cited the progress made since Griffin in mitigating the "disparate treatment of indigents in the criminal process," and concluded that "the Equal Protection Clause of the Fourteenth Amendment requires that the statutory ceiling placed on imprisonment for any substantive offense be the same for all defendants irrespective of their economic status." The holding was reaffirmed in Tate v. Short (1971), in which the Court struck down a Texas statute under which an indigent who could not pay a traffic fine went to jail instead. Nor can a state automatically revoke a convict's probation and commit the person to jail for failing to come up with a sum agreed upon as a condition of probation. Here the probationer had made some payments but had lost his job and had been unsuccessful in his good-faith effort to find another. In Bearden v. Georgia (1983) a unanimous Court held it unfair to send him to jail without considering alternative methods of punishment that might meet the state's interest in punishment and deterrence.

The Supreme Court decision in Roe v. Wade (1973) that a state could not forbid abortions triggered a highly emotional nationwide political battle. Efforts were made to overturn the case by constitutional amendment, and when these failed, legislation was introduced at both state and national levels to limit as much as possible the availability of the new freedom. While direct limitations were generally unavailing (see the note to Roe v. Wade) an approach which struck at the public financing of such abortions was successful. In Beal v. Doe (1977), the Court held the Medicaid provisions of the Social Security Act did not require the financing of nontherapeutic abortions, although a state was free to provide such funding under Medicaid if it wished. And in Poelker v. Doe (1977), it held that a city hospital had no constitutional obligation to provide nontherapeutic abortions. "We merely hold, for the reasons stated in Maher, that the Constitution does not forbid a State or city, pursuant to democratic processes, from expressing a preference for normal childbirth as St. Louis has done."

So successful was the technique of withholding funding in the actual limitation of abortions that in 1976 Representative Hyde of Illinois introduced the first of the so-called "Hyde Amendments" to the appropriation acts providing funding for Medicaid, a scheme by which the federal government provides financial help to states that volunteer to provide to the needy certain medically necessary professional services. The 1980 version of the amendment forbids the use of federal funds to perform abortions except "where the life of the mother would be endangered if the fetus were carried to term" or the pregnancy was the result of rape or incest promptly reported to the proper authorities. The result was to forbid the financing of abortions even where these were deemed "medically necessary." In Harris v. McRae (1980) the Court held that the state's obligation to provide necessary medical services "does not require a participating State to pay for those medically necessary abortions for which federal reimbursement is unavailable under the Hyde Amendment." The Court held the law valid. Quoting with approval from the case below, the Court again stressed that "although Congress has opted to subsidize medically necessary services generally, but not certain medically necessary abortions, the fact remains that the Hyde Amendment leaves an indigent woman with at least the same range of choice in deciding whether to obtain a medically necessary abortion as she would have had if Congress had chosen to subsidize no health care costs at all."

Connecticut law limits medicaid benefits for first-trimester abortions to those that are medically necessary, and in the present case two indigent women sought nontherapeutic abortions. One, a sixteen-year-old high school junior, obtained an abortion and the hospital had been denied reimbursement. The other, the unwed mother of three children, was unable to obtain an abortion because her physician refused to certify that it was medically necessary.

Mr. Justice **Powell** delivered the opinion of the Court, saying in part:

In Beal v. Doe, we hold today that Title XIX of the Social Security Act does not require the funding of nontherapeutic abortions as a condition of participation in the joint federal-state medicaid program established by that statute. In this case, as a result of our decision in Beal, we must decide whether the Constitution requires a participating State to pay for nontherapeutic abortions when it pays for childbirth. . . .

II.

The Constitution imposes no obligation on the States to pay the pregnancy-related medical expenses of indigent women, or indeed to pay any of the medical expenses of indigents. But when a State decides to alleviate some of the hardships of poverty by providing medical care, the manner in which it dispenses benefits is subject to constitutional limitations. Appellees' claim is that Connecticut must accord equal treatment to both abortion and childbirth, and may not evidence a policy preference by funding only the medical expenses incident to childbirth. This challenge to the classifications established by the Connecticut regulation presents a question arising under the Equal Protection Clause of the Fourteenth Amendment. The basic framework of analysis of such a claim is well-settled: "We must decide, first, whether [state legislation] operates to the disadvantage of some suspect class or impinges upon a fundamental right explicitly or implicitly protected by the Constitution, thereby requiring strict judicial scrutiny. . . . If not, the [legislative] scheme must still be examined to determine whether it rationally furthers some legitimate, articulated state purpose and therefore does not constitute an invidious discrimination. . . ." San Antonio School District v. Rodriguez (1973). . . .

A.

This case involves no discrimination against a suspect class. An indigent woman desiring an abortion does not come within the limited category of disadvantaged classes so recognized by our cases. Nor does the fact that the impact of the regulation falls upon those who cannot pay lead to a different conclusion. In a sense, every denial of welfare to an indigent creates a wealth classification as compared to nonindigents who are able to pay for the desired goods or services. But this Court has never held that financial need alone identifies a suspect class for purposes of equal protection analysis. . . . Accordingly, the central question in this case is whether the regulation "impinges upon a fundamental right explicitly or implicitly protected by the Constitution." The District Court read our decisions in Roe v. Wade, (1973), and the subsequent cases applying it, as establishing a fundamental right to abortion and therefore concluded that nothing less than a compelling state interest would justify Connecticut's different treatment of abortion and childbirth. We think the District Court misconceived the nature and scope of the fundamental right recognized in Roe. . . .

The Texas law in Roe was a stark example of impermissible interference with the pregnant woman's decision to terminate her pregnancy. In subsequent cases, we have invalidated other types of restrictions, different in form but similar in effect, on the woman's freedom of choice. Thus, in Planned Parenthood of Central Missouri v. Danforth, (1976), we held that Missouri's require-

ment of spousal consent was unconstitutional because it "granted [the husband] the right to prevent unilaterally, and for whatever reason, the effectuation of his wife's and her physician's decision to terminate her pregnancy." Missouri had interposed an "*absolute obstacle* to a woman's decision that Roe held to be constitutionally protected from such interference." (Emphasis added.) . . .

. . . Roe did not declare an unqualified "constitutional right to an abortion," as the District Court seemed to think. Rather, the right protects the woman from unduly burdensome interference with her freedom to decide whether to terminate her pregnancy. It implies no limitation on the authority of a State to make a value judgment favoring childbirth over abortion, and to implement that judgment by the allocation of public funds.

The Connecticut regulation before us is different in kind from the laws invalidated in our previous abortion decisions. The Connecticut regulation places no obstacles—absolute or otherwise—in the pregnant woman's path to an abortion. An indigent woman who desires an abortion suffers no disadvantage as a consequence of Connecticut's decision to fund childbirth; she continues as before to be dependent on private sources for the service she desires. The State may have made childbirth a more attractive alternative, thereby influencing the woman's decision, but it has imposed no restriction on access to abortions that was not already there. The indigency that may make it difficult—and in some cases, perhaps, impossible—for some women to have abortions is neither created nor in any way affected by the Connecticut regulation. We conclude that the Connecticut regulation does not impinge upon the fundamental right recognized in Roe.

C.

Our conclusion signals no retreat from Roe or the cases applying it. There is a basic difference between direct state interference with a protected activity and state encouragement of an alternative activity consonant with legislative policy. Constitutional concerns are greatest when the State attempts to impose its will by force of law; the State's power to encourage actions deemed to be in the public interest is necessarily far broader.

The distinction is implicit in two cases cited in Roe in support of the pregnant woman's right under the Fourteenth Amendment. Meyer v. Nebraska (1923), involved a Nebraska law making it criminal to teach foreign languages to children who had not passed the eighth grade. Nebraska's imposition of a criminal sanction on the providers of desired services makes Meyer closely analogous to Roe. In sustaining the constitutional challenge brought by a teacher convicted under the law, the Court held that the teacher's "right thus to teach and the right of parents to engage him so to instruct their children" were "within the liberty of the Amendment." In Pierce v. Society of Sisters (1925), the Court relied on Meyer to invalidate an Oregon criminal law requiring the parent or guardian of a child to send him to a public school, thus precluding the choice of a private school. Reasoning that the Fourteenth Amendment's concept of liberty "excludes any general power of the State to standardize its children by forcing them to accept instruction from public teachers only," the Court held that the law "unreasonably interfere[d] with the liberty of parents and guardians to direct the upbringing and education of children under their control."

Both cases invalidated substantial restrictions on constitutionally protected liberty interests: in Meyer, the parent's right to have his child taught a particular foreign language; in Pierce, the parent's right to choose private rather than public school education. But either case denied to a State the policy choice of encouraging the preferred course of action. Indeed, in Meyer the Court was careful to state that the power of the State "to prescribe a curriculum" that included English and excluded German in its free public schools "is not questioned." Similarly, Pierce casts no shadow over a State's power to favor public education by funding it—a policy choice pursued in some States for more than a century. . . . Yet, were we to accept appellees' argument, an indigent parent could challenge the state policy of favoring public rather than private schools, or of preferring instruction in English rather than German, on grounds identical in principle to those advanced here. We think it abundantly clear that a State is not required to show a compelling interest for its policy choice to favor normal childbirth any more than a State must so justify its election to fund public but not private education.

D.

The question remains whether Connecticut's regulation can be sustained under the less demanding test of rationality that applies in the absence of a suspect classification or the impingement of a fundamental right. This test requires that the distinction drawn between childbirth and nontherapeutic abortion by the regulation be "rationally related" to a "constitutionally permissible" purpose. . . . We hold that the Connecticut funding scheme satisfies this standard.

Roe itself explicitly acknowledged the State's strong interest in protecting the potential life of the fetus. That interest exists throughout the pregnancy, "grow[ing] in substantiality as the woman approaches term." Because the pregnant woman carries a potential human being, she "cannot be isolated in her privacy. . . . [Her] privacy is no longer sole and any right of privacy she possesses must be measured accordingly." The State unquestionably has a "strong and legitimate interest in encouraging normal childbirth." Beal v. Doe, an interest honored over the centuries. Nor can there be any question that the Connecticut regulation rationally furthers that interest. The medical costs associated with childbirth are substantial, and have increased significantly in recent years. As recognized by the District Court in this case, such costs are significantly greater than those normally associated with elective abortions during the first trimester. The subsidizing of costs incident to childbirth is a rational means of encouraging childbirth.

We certainly are not unsympathetic to the plight of an indigent woman who desires an abortion, but "the Constitution does not provide judicial remedies for every social and economic ill." . . .

The decision whether to expend state funds for nontherapeutic abortion is fraught with judgments of policy and value over which opinions are sharply divided. Our conclusion that the Connecticut regulation is constitutional is not based on a weighing of its wisdom or social desirability, for this Court does not strike down state laws "because they be unwise, improvident, or out of harmony with a particular school of thought." . . . Indeed, when an issue involves policy choices as sensitive as those implicated by public funding of nontherapeutic abortions, the appropriate forum for their resolution in a democracy is the legislature. We should not forget that "legislatures are ultimate guardians of the liberties and welfare of the people in quite as great a degree as the Courts." . . .

In conclusion, we emphasize that our decision today does not proscribe government funding of nontherapeutic abortions. It is open to Congress to require provision of Medicaid benefits for such abortions as a condition of state participation in the Medicaid program. Also, under Title XIX as construed in Beal v. Doe, Connecticut is free—through normal democratic processes—to decide that such benefits should be provided. We hold only that the Constitution does not require a judicially imposed resolution of these difficult issues. . . .

Mr. Justice **Brennan,** with whom Mr. Justice **Marshall** and Mr. Justice **Blackmun** join, dissenting, said in part:

The District Court held: "When Connecticut refuses to fund elective abortions while funding therapeutic abortions and prenatal and postnatal care, it weights the choice of the pregnant mother against choosing to exercise her constitutionally protected right to an elective abortion. . . . Her choice is affected not simply by the absence of payment for the abortion, but by the availability of public funds for childbirth if she chooses not to have the abortion. When the state thus infringes upon a fundamental interest, it must assert a compelling state interest." This Court reverses on the ground that "the District Court misconceived the nature and scope of the fundamental right recognized in Roe [v. Wade (1973)]," and therefore that Connecticut was not required to meet the "compelling interest test to justify its discrimination against elective abortion but only "the less demanding test of rationality that applies in the absence of . . . the impingement of a fundamental right." This holding, the Court insists "places no obstacles—absolute or otherwise—in the pregnant woman's path to an abortion"; she is still at liberty to finance the abortion from "private sources." . . .

But a distressing insensitivity to the plight of impoverished pregnant women is inherent in the Court's analysis. The stark reality for too many, not just "some," indigent pregnant women is that indigency makes access to competent licensed physicians not merely "difficult" but "impossible." As a practical matter, many indigent women will feel they have no choice but to carry their pregnancies to term because the State will pay for the associated medical services, even though they would have chosen to have abortions if the State had also provided funds for that procedure, or indeed if the State had provided funds for neither procedure. This disparity in funding by the State clearly operates to coerce indigent pregnant women to bear children they would not otherwise choose to have, and just as clearly, this coercion can only operate upon the poor, who are uniquely the victims of this form of financial pressure. . . .

None can take seriously the Court's assurance that its "conclusion signals no retreat from Roe [v. Wade] or the cases applying it." That statement must occasion great surprise among the Courts of Appeals and District Courts that, relying upon Roe v. Wade and Doe v. Bolton (1973), have held that States are constitutionally required to fund elective abortions if they fund pregnancies carried to term. . . . Indeed, it cannot be gainsaid that today's decision seriously erodes the principles that Roe and Doe announced to guide the determination of what constitutes an unconstitutional infringement of the fundamental right of pregnant women to be free to decide whether to have an abortion. . . .

Finally, cases involving other fundamental rights also make clear that the Court's concept of what constitutes an impermissible infringement upon the fundamental rights of a pregnant woman to choose to have an abortion makes new law. We have repeatedly found that infringements of fundamental rights are not limited to outright denials of those rights. First Amendment decisions have consistently held in a wide variety of contexts that the compelling-state-interest test has been applied in voting cases, even where only relatively small infringements upon voting power, such as dilution of voting strength caused by malapportionment, have been involved. See, e.g., Reynolds v. Sims (1964). . . .

Until today, I had not thought the nature of the fundamental right established in Roe was open to question, let alone susceptible to the interpretation advanced by the Court. The fact that the Connecticut scheme may not operate as an absolute bar preventing all indigent women from having abortions is not critical. What is critical is that the State has inhibited their fundamental right to make that choice free from state interference.

Nor does the manner in which Connecticut has burdened the right freely to choose to have an abortion save its Medicaid program. The Connecticut scheme cannot be distinguished from other grants and withholdings of financial benefits that we have held unconstitutionally burdened a fundamental right. Sherbert v. Verner, struck down a South Carolina statute that denied unemployment compensation to a woman who for religious reasons could not work on Saturday, but that would have provided such compensation if her unemployment had stemmed from a number of other nonreligious causes. Even though there was no proof of indigency in that case, Sherbert held that "the pressure upon her to forgo [her religious] practice [was] unmistakable," and therefore held the effect was the same as a fine imposed for Saturday worship. Here, though the burden

is upon the right to privacy derived from the Due Process Clause and not upon freedom of religion under the Free Exercise Clause of the First Amendment, the governing principle is the same, for Connecticut grants and withholds financial benefits in a manner that discourages significantly the exercise of a fundamental constitutional right. Indeed, the case for application of the principle actually is stronger than in Verner since appellees are all indigents and therefore even more vulnerable to the financial pressures imposed by the Connecticut regulations.

Belotti v. Baird (1976), held, and the Court today agrees, that a state requirement is unconstitutional if it "unduly burdens the right to seek an abortion." Connecticut has "unduly" burdened the fundamental right of pregnant women to be free to choose to have an abortion because the State has advanced no compelling state interest to justify its interference in that choice.

Although appellant does not argue it as justification, the Court concludes that the State's interest "in protecting the potential life of the fetus" suffices. Since only the first trimester of pregnancy is involved in this case, that justification is totally foreclosed if the Court is not overruling the holding of Roe v. Wade that "[w]ith respect to the State's important and legitimate interest in potential life, the 'compelling' point is at viability," occurring at about the end of the second trimester. The appellant also argues a further justification not relied upon by the Court, namely, that the State needs "to control the amount of its limited public funds which will be allocated to its public welfare budget." The District Court correctly held, however, that the asserted interest was "wholly chimerical" because the "state's assertion that it saves money when it declines to pay the cost of a welfare mother's abortion is simply contrary to undisputed facts."

Mr. Justice **Blackmun,** with whom Mr. Justice **Brennan** and Mr. Justice **Marshall** join, dissenting.

The Court today by its decisions in these cases, allows the States, and such municipalities as chose to do so, to accomplish indirectly what the court in Roe v. Wade (1973), and Doe v. Bolton (1973)—by a substantial majority and with some emphasis, I had thought— said they could not do so directly. The Court concedes the existence of a constitutional right but denies the realization and enjoyment of that right on the ground that existence and realization are separate and distinct. For the individual woman concerned, indigent and financially helpless, as the Court's opinions in the three cases concede her to be, the result is punitive and tragic. Implicit in the Court's holdings is the condescension that she may go elsewhere for her abortion. I find that disingenuous and alarming, almost reminiscent of "let them eat cake."

The result the Court reaches is particularly distressing in Poelker v. Doe, where a presumed majority, in electing as mayor one whom the record shows campaigned on the issue of closing public hospitals to nontherapeutic abortions, punitively impresses upon a needy minority its own concepts of the socially desirable, the publicly acceptable and the morally sound, with a touch of the devil-take-the-hindmost. This is not the kind of thing for which our Constitution stands.

The Court's financial argument, of course, is specious. To be sure, welfare funds are limited and welfare must be spread perhaps as best meets the community's concept of its needs. But the cost of a nontherapeutic abortion is far less than the cost of maternity care and delivery, and holds no comparison whatsoever with the welfare costs that will burden the State for the new indigents and their support in the long, long years ahead.

Neither is it an acceptable answer, as the Court well knows, to say that the Congress and the States are free to authorize the use of funds for nontherapeutic abortions. Why should any politician incur the demonstrated wrath and noise of the abortion opponents when mere silence and nonactivity accomplish the results the opponents want?

There is another world "out there," the existence of which the Court, I suspect, either chooses to ignore or fears to recognize. And so the cancer of poverty will continue to grow. This is a sad day for those who regard the Constitution as a force that would serve justice to all evenhandedly and, in so doing, would better the lot of the poorest among us.

Mr. Justice **Marshall,** dissenting, said in part:

It is all too obvious that the governmental actions in these cases, ostensibly taken to "encourage women to carry pregnancies to term, are in reality intended to impose a moral viewpoint that no State may constitutionally enforce. . . . I am appalled at the ethical bankruptcy of those who preach a "right to life" that means, under present social policies, a bare existence in utter misery for so many poor women and their children.

I.

The Court's insensitivity to the human dimension of these decisions is particularly obvious in its cursory discussion of appellees' equal protection claims in Maher v. Roe. That case points up once again the need for this Court to repudiate its outdated and intellectually disingenuous "two-tier" equal protection analysis. . . . As I have suggested before, this "model's two fixed modes of analysis, strict scrutiny and mere rationality, simply do not describe the inquiry the Court has undertaken—or should undertake—in equal protection cases." In the present case, in its evident desire to avoid strict scrutiny—or indeed any meaningful scrutiny—of the challenged legislation, which would almost surely result in its invalidation, the Court pulls from thin air a distinction between laws that absolutely prevent exercise of the

fundamental right to abortion and those that "merely" make its exercise difficult for some people. . . . Mr. Justice Brennan demonstrates that our cases support no such distinction, and I have argued above that the challenged regulations are little different from a total prohibition from the viewpoint of the poor. But the Court's legal legerdemain has produced the desired result: A fundamental right is no longer at stake and mere rationality becomes the appropriate mode of analysis. To no one's surprise, application of that test—combined with misreading of Roe v. Wade to generate a "strong" state interest in "potential life" during the first trimester of pregnancy, "leaves little doubt about the outcome; the challenged legislation is [as] always, upheld." . . .

As I have argued before, an equal protection analysis far more in keeping with the actions rather than the words of the Court, carefully weighs three factors—"the importance of the governmental benefits denied, the character of the class, and the asserted state interests." Application of this standard would invalidate the challenged regulations.

The governmental benefits at issue here, while perhaps not representing large amounts of money for any individual, are nevertheless of absolutely vital importance in the lives of the recipients. . . .

It is no less disturbing that the effect of the challenged regulations will fall with great disparity upon women of minority races. Nonwhite women now obtain abortions at nearly twice the rate of whites, and it appears that almost 40 percent of minority women—more than five times the proportion of whites—are dependent upon Medicaid for their health care. Even if this strongly disparate racial impact does not alone violate the Equal Protection Clause, . . . "at some point a showing that state action has a devastating impact on the lives of minority racial groups must be relevant."

Against the brutal effect that the challenged laws will have must be weighed the asserted state interest. The Court describes this as a "strong interest in protecting the potential life of the fetus." Yet in Doe v. Bolton, the Court expressly held that any state interest during the first trimester of pregnancy, when 86 percent of all abortions occur, was wholly insufficient to justify state interference with the right to abortion. If a State's interest in potential human life before the point of viability is insufficient to justify requiring several physicians' concurrence for an abortion, I cannot comprehend how it magically becomes adequate to allow the present infringement on rights of disfavored classes. If there is any state interest in potential life before the point of viability, it certainly does not outweigh the deprivation or serious discouragement of a vital constitutional right of especial importance to poor and minority women.

Mr. Chief Justice **Burger** wrote a concurring opinion.

12

The Power to Protect Individuals

THE CIVIL RIGHTS CASES

109 U.S. 3; 3 S. Ct. 18; 27 L. Ed. 835 (1883)

In the closing days of the Reconstruction, with the white race rapidly resuming control of Southern state governments, Congress passed the Civil Rights Act of 1875 to ensure continued federal power to prevent racial discrimination in the South. This act made it both a crime and a civil wrong for any person to deny to any other person "the full and equal enjoyment of any of the accommodations, advantages, facilities and privileges of inns, public conveyances on land or water, theaters and other places of public amusement; subject only to the conditions and limitations established by law, and applicable alike to citizens of every race and color. . . ." In the Civil Rights Cases, printed below, the Supreme Court held the act unconstitutional. It held that the Thirteenth Amendment was not applicable, since racial discrimination is not involuntary servitude, and the Fourteenth Amendment gave Congress no authority to prevent racial discrimination by private individuals. The Court rested its decision upon the explicit language of the Fourteenth Amendment, which is that "no state" shall deny equal protection of the laws or due process of law; it does not say that "no person" shall do these things; and Congress, in passing laws to enforce the amendment, may not make it a crime to do what the amendment does not forbid. Thus the Civil Rights Cases prevented Congress from exercising disciplinary control

over private racial discrimination. For protection against such discrimination the citizen had to look to his state government, not to the federal government.

In a forceful forty-page dissenting opinion Justice Harlan directed a many-pronged attack at the Court's decision, most of which, with the passage of time, is no longer relevant. One of his points, however, deserves mention. He argued persuasively that common carriers and those who operate inns and places of amusement are not "private persons." On the contrary, they carry on businesses under state authority subject to public controls, and are in a very real sense agents of the state. This association with and dependence on the state brings them within the prohibiting language of the due process and equal protection clauses.

Mr. Justice **Bradley** delivered the opinion of the Court, saying in part:

These cases are all founded on the 1st and 2nd sections of the Act of Congress, known as the Civil Rights Act, passed March 1, 1875. . . . Two of the cases, those against Stanley and Nichols, are indictments for denying to persons of color the accommodations and privileges of an inn or hotel; two of them, those against Ryan and Singleton, are, one an information, the other an indictment, for denying to individuals the privileges and accommodations of a theatre, the information against Ryan being for refusing a colored person a seat in the dress circle of Maguire's theater in San Francisco; and the indictment against Singleton being for denying to another person, whose color is not stated, the full enjoyment of the accommodations of the theater known as the Grand Opera House in New York. . . . The case of Robinson and wife against the Memphis and Charleston R. R. Company was . . . the refusal by the conductor of the Railroad Company to allow the wife to ride in the ladies' car, for the reason . . . that she was a person of African descent. . . .

It is obvious that the primary and important question in all the cases, is the constitutionality of the law; for if the law is unconstitutional, none of the prosecutions can stand. . . .

[The Court here reviews the provisions of the law in detail.]

Has Congress constitutional power to make such a law? Of course, no one will contend that the power to pass it was contained in the Constitution before the adoption of the last three Amendments. The power is sought, first, in the 14th Amendment, and the views and arguments of distinguished Senators, advanced whilst the law was under consideration, claiming authority to pass it by virtue of that Amendment, are the principal arguments adduced in favor of the power. . . .

The 1st section of the 14th Amendment, which is the one relied on, after declaring who shall be citizens of the United States, and of the several States, is prohibitory in its character, and prohibitory upon the States. It declares that "No State shall make or enforce any law which shall abridge the privileges or immunities of citizens of the United States; nor shall any State deprive any person of life, liberty, or property without due process of law; nor deny to any person within its jurisdiction the equal protection of the laws." It is state action of a particular character that is prohibited. Individual invasion of individual rights is not the subject-matter of the Amendment. It has a deeper and broader scope. It nullifies and makes void all state legislation, and state action of every kind, which impairs the privileges and immunities of citizens of the United States, or which injures them in life, liberty or property without due process of law, or which denies to any of them the equal protection of the laws. It not only does this, but, in order that the national will, thus declared, may not be a mere brutum fulmen, the last section of the Amendment invests Congress with power to enforce it by appropriate legislation. To enforce what? To enforce the prohibition. To adopt appropriate legislation for correcting the effects of such prohibited state laws and state Acts, and thus to render them effectually null, void and innocuous. This is the legislative power conferred upon Congress, and this is the whole of it. It does not invest Congress with power to legislate upon subjects which are within the domain of state legislation; but to provide modes of relief against state legislation or state action, of the kind referred to. It does not authorize Congress to create a code of municipal law for the regulation of private rights; but to provide modes of redress against the operation of state laws, and the action of state officers executive or judicial, when these are subversive of the fundamental rights specified in the Amendment. Positive rights and privileges are undoubtedly secured by

the 14th Amendment; but they are secured by way of prohibition against state laws and state proceedings affecting those rights and privileges, and by power given to Congress to legislate for the purpose of carrying such prohibition into effect; and such legislation must, necessarily, be predicated upon such supposed state laws or state proceedings, and be directed to the correction of their operation and effect. . . .

An apt illustration of this distinction may be found in some of the provisions of the original Constitution. Take the subject of contracts, for example; the Constitution prohibited the States from passing any law impairing the obligation of contracts. This did not give to Congress power to provide laws for the general enforcement of contracts; nor power to invest the courts of the United States with jurisdiction over contracts, so as to enable parties to sue upon them in those courts. It did, however, give the power to provide remedies by which the impairment of contracts by state legislation might be counteracted and corrected; and this power was exercised. The remedy which Congress actually provided was that contained in the 25th section of the Judiciary Act of 1789, giving to the Supreme Court of the United States jurisdiction by writ of error to review the final decisions of state courts whenever they should sustain the validity of a state statute or authority alleged to be repugnant to the Constitution or laws of the United States. By this means, if a state law was passed impairing the obligation of a contract, and the state tribunals sustained the validity of the law, the mischief could be corrected in this court. The legislation of Congress, and the proceedings provided for under it, were corrective in their character. No attempt was made to draw into the United States courts the litigation of contracts generally; and no such attempt would have been sustained. . . .

And so in the present case, until some state law has been passed or some state action through its officers or agents has been taken, adverse to the rights of citizens sought to be protected by the 14th Amendment, no legislation of the United States under said Amendment, nor any proceeding under such legislation, can be called into activity; for the prohibitions of the Amendment are against state laws and acts done under state authority. Of course, legislation may and should be provided in advance to meet the exigency when it arises; but it should be adapted to the mischief and wrong which the Amendment was intended to provide against; and that is, state laws, or state action of some kind, adverse to the rights of the citizen secured by the Amendment. Such legislation cannot properly cover the whole domain of rights appertaining to life, liberty and property, defining them and providing for their vindication. That would be to establish a code of municipal law regulative of all private rights between man and man in society. It would be to make Congress take the place of the State Legislatures and to supersede them. It is absurd to affirm that, because the rights of life, liberty and property, which include all civil rights that men have, are, by the Amendment, sought to be protected against invasion on the part of the State without due process of law, Congress may, therefore, provide due process of law for their vindication in every case; and that, because the denial by a State to any persons, of the equal protection of the laws, is prohibited by the Amendment, therefore Congress may establish laws for their equal protection. In fine, the legislation which Congress is authorized to adopt in this behalf is not general legislation upon the rights of the citizen, but corrective legislation, that is, such as may be necessary and proper for counteracting such laws as the States may adopt or enforce, and which, by the Amendment, they are prohibited from making or enforcing, or such acts and proceedings as the States may commit or take, and which, by the Amendment, they are prohibited from committing or taking. It is not necessary for us to state, if we could, what legislation would be proper for Congress to adopt. It is sufficient for us to examine whether the law in question is of that character.

An inspection of the law shows that it makes no reference whatever to any supposed or apprehended violation of the 14th Amendment on the part of the States. It is not predicated on any such view. It proceeds ex directo to declare that certain acts committed by individuals shall be deemed offenses, and shall be prosecuted and punished by proceedings in the courts of the United States. It does not profess to be corrective of any constitutional wrong committed by the States; it does not make its operation to depend upon any such wrong committed. It applies only to cases arising in States which have the justest laws respecting the personal rights of citizens, and whose authorities are ever ready to enforce such laws, as to those which arise in States that may have violated the prohibition of the Amendment. In other words, it steps into the domain of local jurisprudence, and lays down rules for the conduct of individuals in society towards each other, and imposes sanctions for the enforcement of those rules, without referring in any manner to any supposed action of the State or its authorities.

If this legislation is appropriate for enforcing the prohibitions of the Amendment, it is difficult to see where it is to stop. Why may not Congress with equal show of authority enact a code of laws for the enforcement and vindication of all rights of life, liberty and property? If it is supposable that the States may deprive persons of life, liberty and property without due process of law, and the Amendment itself does not suppose this, why should not Congress proceed at once to prescribe due process of law for the protection of every one of these fundamental rights, in every possible case, as well as to prescribe equal privileges in inns, public conveyances and theatres? The truth is, that the implication of a power to legislate in this manner is based upon the assumption that if the States are forbidden to legislate or act in a particular way on a particular subject, and power is conferred upon Congress to enforce the prohibition, this gives Congress power to legislate generally upon that subject, and not merely power to provide modes of redress against such state legislation or action. The assumption is certainly unsound. It is repugnant to the 10th Amendment of the Constitution, which declares that powers not delegated to the United States by the Constitution, nor prohibited by it to the States, are reserved to the States respectively or to the people. . . .

In this connection it is proper to state that civil rights, such as are guaranteed by the Constitution against state aggression, cannot be impaired by the wrongful acts of individuals, unsupported by state authority in the shape of laws, customs or judicial or executive proceedings. The wrongful act of an individual, unsupported by any such authority, is simply a private wrong, or a crime of that individual; an invasion of the rights of the injured party, it is true, whether they affect his person, his property or his reputation; but if not sanctioned in some way by the State, or not done under state authority, his rights remain in full force and may presumably be vindicated by resort to the laws of the State for redress. An individual cannot deprive a man of his right to vote, to hold property, to buy and to sell, to sue in the courts or to be a witness or a juror; he may, by force or fraud, interfere with the enjoyment of the right in a particular case; he may commit an assault against the person, or commit murder, or use ruffian violence at the polls, or slander the good name of a fellow citizen; but, unless protected in these wrongful acts by some shield of state law or state authority, he cannot destroy or injure the right; he will only render himself amenable to satisfaction or punishment; and amenable therefore to the laws of the State where the wrongful acts are committed. Hence, in all those cases where the Constitution seeks to protect the rights of the citizen against discriminative and unjust laws of the State by prohibiting such laws, it is not individual offenses, but abrogation and denial of rights, which it denounces, and for which it clothes the Congress with power to provide a remedy. This abrogation and denial of rights, for which the States alone were or could be responsible, was the great seminal and fundamental wrong which was intended to be remedied. And the remedy to be provided must necessarily be predicated upon that wrong. It must assume that in the cases provided for, the evil or wrong actually committed rests upon some state law or state authority for its excuse and perpetration.

Of course, these remarks do not apply to those cases in which Congress is clothed with direct and plenary powers of legislation over the whole subject, accompanied with an express or implied denial of such power to the States, as in the regulation of commerce with foreign Nations, . . . the coining of money, the establishment of postoffices and post-roads, the declaring of war, etc. In these cases, Congress has power to pass laws for regulating the subjects specified in every detail, and the conduct and transactions of individuals in respect thereof. But where a subject is not submitted to the general legislative power of Congress, but is only submitted thereto for the purpose of rendering effective some prohibition against particular state legislation or state action in reference to that subject, the power given is limited by its object, and any legislation by Congress in the matter must necessarily be corrective in its character, adapted to counteract and redress the operation of such prohibited state laws or proceedings of state officers. . . .

But the power of Congress to adopt direct and primary, as distinguished from corrective, legislation on the subject in hand, is sought, in the second place, from the 13th Amendment, which abolishes slavery. . . .

This Amendment, as well as the 14th, is undoubtedly self-executing without any ancillary legislation, so far as its terms are applicable to any existing state of circumstances. By its own unaided force and effect, it abolished slavery and established universal freedom. . . .

The only question under the present head, therefore, is, whether the refusal to any persons of accommodations of an inn or a public conveyance or a place of public amusement, by an individual and without any sanction or support from any state law or regulation, does inflict upon such persons any manner of servitude, or form of slavery, as those terms are understood in this country?

. . . It would be running the slavery argument into the ground, to make it apply to every act of discrimination which a person may see fit to make as to the guests he will entertain, or as to the people he will take into his coach or cab or car, or admit to his concert or theater, or deal with in other matters of intercourse or business. . . .

On the whole we are of the opinion, that no countenance of authority for the passage of the law in question can be found in either the 13th or the 14th Amendment of the Constitution; and no other ground of authority for its passage being suggested, it must necessarily be declared void, at least so far as its operation in the several States is concerned.

Mr. Justice Harlan wrote a dissenting opinion.

UNITED STATES v. GUEST

383 U.S. 745; 86 S. Ct. 1170; 16 L. Ed. 2d 239 (1966)

While it is well settled that the Bill of Rights and the Fourteenth Amendment are not "directed against the action of individuals," it must not be assumed that the citizen enjoys no federal protection against the invasion of his civil rights. Until the 1960s such protection was measured by the scope of two federal statutes passed in the period following the Civil War. The first of these, directed at the actions of private individuals, was Sec. 6 of the Enforcement Act of 1870, which at various times has been known as § 19 of the Criminal Code of 1909, later as § 51 of the U.S. Code of 1926, and is presently known as § 241 of Title 18 of the U.S. Code. This section provides:

"If two or more persons conspire to injure, oppress, threaten or intimidate any citizen in the free exercise or enjoyment of any right or privilege secured to him by the Constitution or laws of the United States, or because of his having so exercised the same; or

"If two or more persons go in disguise on the highway, or on the premises of another, with intent to prevent or hinder his free exercise or enjoyment of any right or privilege so secured—

"They shall be fined not more than $5000 or imprisoned not more than ten years, or both."

Since § 241 is limited to the rights of citizens which come from the national Constitution or laws, it forbids private interference with exactly those things which are "privileges and immunities of citizens of the United States" within the meaning of the Fourteenth Amendment. In fact, it is in construing this statute rather than the Fourteenth Amendment itself that the scope of such "privileges and immunities" has been spelled out by the Court. In Ex parte Yarbrough (1884), § 19 was held applicable to the right to vote in federal elections if the voter is qualified under state law; and in Logan v. United States (1892) it was held to cover the right of a citizen not to be taken by a mob from the custody of a United States marshal and lynched.

If, on the other hand, a person is deprived of his constitutional or statutory rights by a state officer, a different statute comes into play. A state officer is the "state" against which the provisions of the Fourteenth Amendment are directed, and he may be punished not only for abridging the privileges and immunities of a United States citizen, but also for denying any person due process or equal protection of the laws. Congress first provided for the punishment of such acts of state officers in the Civil Rights Act of 1866, and one of the purposes of the Fourteenth Amendment was to provide a constitutional basis for this statute. Reenacted as Sec. 17 of the Enforcement Act of 1870, this statute has been known variously as § 20 of the Criminal Code, § 52 of the U. S. Code, and is presently called § 242 of Title 18 of the U. S. Code. This section provides that:

"Whoever, under color of any law, statute, ordinance, regulation, or custom, willfully subjects any inhabitant of any State, Territory, or District to the deprivation of any rights, privileges, or immunities secured or protected by the Constitution or laws of the United States, or to different punishments, pains, or penalties, on account of such inhabitant being an alien, or by reason of his color, or race, than are prescribed for the punishment of citizens, shall be fined not more than $1,000 or imprisoned not more than one year, or both."

It was not until the Civil Rights Section in the Department of Justice, created in 1939, decided to appeal the Classic case (1941) that the Supreme Court got its first opportunity to interpret § 242. There it held the statute applicable to Classic, a state election official, on the ground that "misuse of power, possessed by virtue of state law and made possible only because the wrongdoer is clothed with the authority of state law, is action taken 'under color of' state law."

In Screws v. United States (1945) the Civil Rights Section invoked the provisions of § 242 for a very different purpose. Screws was sheriff in a county in Georgia. Aided by a deputy and a policeman he arrested Hall, a Negro, late one night for the alleged theft of a tire. There was evidence that Screws had a grudge against Hall and had threatened to "get" him. The three officers hand-

cuffed Hall, brought him to the courthouse, and there proceeded to beat him to death. The state authorities failed to prosecute Screws, and he was thereupon indicted and convicted under the section of the federal statute. The indictment of Screws rested on the theory that the three officers had deprived Hall, under color of the law of Georgia, of rights guaranteed to him by the Fourteenth Amendment: namely, "the right not to be deprived of life without due process of law; the right to be tried upon the charge on which he was arrested, by due process of law and if found guilty to be punished in accordance with the laws of Georgia." The results reached by the Supreme Court in this case were rather confusing. Six justices agreed that the federal statute could validly be applied to the kind of conduct of which Screws was guilty. Five justices, however, ruled that Screws was entitled to a new trial because the trial court had not properly charged the jury that Screws's violation of the statute must be shown to have been "willful." At the new trial Screws was acquitted. The case did, however, extend the authority of the federal government to punish state officers for violations of civil rights which lie within the range of federal protection.

In two cases decided in 1951 (Williams v. United States and United States v. Williams) the Court held that §§ 241 and 242 were mutually exclusive, so that Williams, a police officer, could not be prosecuted under § 241 even though, as a state official, he had denied a person his rights by giving him the "third degree." Four members of the five-man majority agreed that even though Williams was acting under color of law, § 241 was intended to protect only the kind of rights "which Congress can beyond doubt constitutionally secure against interferences by private individuals," rights which can be classified as privileges and immunities of United States citizenship. It was not intended to protect those rights, like the right to be tried by due process of law, which are guaranteed solely against state abridgment. However, both state officers and private persons can be prosecuted under § 241 if, as in the Classic case, the right denied is a privilege of United States citizenship. The importance of this lies in the fact that § 241 carries a penalty of a ten-year prison sentence, while § 242 is limited to one year. The Court did, however, sustain Williams's indictment under § 242. There was no question that he was a state officer and had deprived a citizen, by extorting the confession, of his liberty without due process of law.

The present case grew out of the shotgun murder on a Georgia highway of Lemuel Penn, a Negro educator, who was driving back to Washington after summer duty as a reserve officer. Two of the six members of the alleged conspiracy were tried by the state for murder and acquitted. In October 1964, a federal grand jury returned an indictment charging them with conspiring to violate § 241. The district court dismissed the indictments, but the Supreme Court reversed. In 1966 they were tried for conspiracy, and the two who had been tried for murder and acquitted by the state were found guilty and sentenced to ten years in prison.

In the companion case of United States v. Price, 18 persons, three of them police officers, were indicted under § 241 and § 242 for the slaying of three civil rights workers near Philadelphia, Mississippi. The district court dismissed the indictments under § 242 of all but the three officers, and all the indictments under § 241. The Supreme Court reinstated the indictments. It conceded that § 242 dealt only with actions taken "under color" of law, but held that "private persons, jointly engaged with state officials in the prohibited action, are acting 'under color' of law for purposes of the statute. To act 'under color' of law does not require that the accused be an officer of the State. It is enough that he is a willful participant in joint activity with the State or its agents. . . . In effect, if the allegations are true, they were participants in official lawlessness, acting in willful concert with state officers and hence under color of law." In sustaining the charges under § 241 the Court reversed what the district court considered the holding in Williams I, that the section applied only to constitutional rights arising from the substantive powers of the federal government. Since Justice Black had concurred in the result of that case on different grounds, the Court considered the question open. "On the basis of an extensive reexamination of the question, we conclude . . . that § 241 must be read as it is written . . . ; that this language includes rights or privileges protected by the Fourteenth Amendment." The defendants were ultimately tried under the indictment and seven of them, including the three police officials, were convicted.

One other statute authorizing federal intervention to protect civil rights was Sec. 4 of the Civil Rights Act of 1875. This provided that "no citizen . . . shall be disqualified for service as grand or petit juror . . . on account of race . . ." and made it a crime for anyone concerned with the summoning of jurors to fail to summon any citizen because of his color. Although the bulk of this statute was held invalid in the Civil Rights Cases (1883), this provision applied to state officers rather than private individuals; and in Ex parte Virginia (1880) the Court held valid under this act the indictment of a county judge who had excluded Negroes from jury service on account of their race.

Mr. Justice **Stewart** delivered the opinion of the Court, saying in part:

II.

The second numbered paragraph of the indictment alleged that the defendants conspired to injure, oppress, threaten, and intimidate Negro citizens of the United States in the free exercise and enjoyment of:

"The right to the equal utilization, without discrimination upon the basis of race, of public facilities in the vicinity of Athens, Georgia, owned, operated or managed by or on behalf of the State of Georgia or any subdivision thereof."

Correctly characterizing this paragraph as embracing rights protected by the Equal Protection Clause of the

Fourteenth Amendment, the District Court held as a matter of statutory construction that 18 USC § 241 does not encompass any Fourteenth Amendment rights, and further held as a matter of constitutional law that "any broader construction of § 241 . . . would render it void for indefiniteness." In so holding, the District Court was in error, as our opinion in United States v. Price [1966] makes abundantly clear.

To be sure, Price involves rights under the Due Process Clause, whereas the present case involves rights under the Equal Protection Clause. But no possible reason suggests itself for concluding that § 241—if it protects Fourteenth Amendment rights—protects rights secured by the one Clause but not those secured by the other. We have made clear in Price that when § 241 speaks of "any right or privilege secured . . . by the Constitution or laws of the United States," it means precisely that. . . .

Unlike the indictment in Price, however, the indictment in the present case names no person alleged to have acted in any way under the color of state law. The argument is therefore made that, since there exist no Equal Protection Clause rights against wholly private action, the judgment of the District Court on this branch of the case must be affirmed. On its face, the argument is unexceptionable. The Equal Protection Clause speaks to the State or to those acting under the color of its authority. . . .

It is a commonplace that rights under the Equal Protection Clause itself arise only where there has been involvement of the State or of one acting under the color of its authority. The Equal Protection Clause "does not . . . add any thing to the rights which one citizen has under the Constitution against another." United States v. Cruikshank [1876]. As Mr. Justice Douglas more recently put it, "The Fourteenth Amendment protects the individual against *state action*, not against wrongs done by *individuals*." United States v. Williams [1951] (dissenting opinion). This has been the view of the Court from the beginning. United States v. Cruikshank. . . . It remains the Court's view today. . . .

This is not to say, however, that the involvement of the State need be either exclusive or direct. In a variety of situations the Court has found state action of a nature sufficient to create rights under the Equal Protection Clause even though the participation of the State was peripheral, or its action was only one of several co-operative forces leading to the constitutional violation. See, e.g., Shelley v. Kraemer [1948]. . . .

This case, however, requires no determination of the threshold level that state action must attain in order to create rights under the Equal Protection Clause. This is so because, contrary to the argument of the litigants, the indictment in fact contains an express allegation of state involvement sufficient at least to require the denial of a motion to dismiss. One of the means of accomplishing the object of the conspiracy, according to the indictment, was "By causing the arrest of Negroes by means of false reports that such Negroes had committed criminal acts."

In Bell v. Maryland [1964] three members of the Court expressed the view that a private businessman's invocation of state police and judicial action to carry out his own policy of racial discrimination was sufficient to create Equal Protection Clause rights in those against whom the racial discrimination was directed. Three other members of the Court strongly disagreed with that view, and three expressed no opinion on the question. The allegation of the extent of official involvement in the present case is not clear. It may charge no more than co-operative private and state action similar to that involved in Bell, but it may go considerably further. For example, the allegation is broad enough to cover a charge of active connivance by agents of the State in the making of the "false reports," or other conduct amounting to official discrimination clearly sufficient to constitute denial of rights protected by the Equal Protection Clause. Although it is possible that a bill of particulars, or the proof if the case goes to trial, would disclose no co-operative action of that kind by officials of the State, the allegation is enough to prevent dismissal of this branch of the indictment.

III.

The fourth numbered paragraph of the indictment alleged that the defendants conspired to injure, oppress, threaten, and intimidate Negro citizens of the United States in the free exercise and enjoyment of:

"The right to travel freely to and from the State of Georgia and to use highway facilities and other instrumentalities of interstate commerce within the State of Georgia."

The District Court was in error in dismissing the indictment as to this paragraph. The constitutional right to travel from one State to another, and necessarily to use the highways and other instrumentalities of interstate commerce in doing so, occupies a position fundamental to the concept of our Federal Union. It is a right that has been firmly established and repeatedly recognized. . . .

In Edwards v. California [1941] invalidating a California law which impeded the free interstate passage of the indigent, the Court based its reaffirmation of the federal right of interstate travel upon the Commerce Clause. This ground of decision was consistent with precedents firmly establishing that the federal commerce power surely encompasses the movement in interstate commerce of persons as well as commodities. . . . Hoke v. United States [1913]. . . . It is also well settled in our decisions that the federal commerce power authorizes Congress to legislate for the protection of individuals from violations of civil rights that impinge on their free movement in interstate commerce . . . [Heart of] Atlanta Motel v. United States [1964], Katzenbach v. McClung [1964].

Although there have been recurring differences in emphasis within the Court as to the source of the constitutional right of interstate travel, there is no need here to canvass those differences further. All have agreed that right exists. Its explicit recognition as one of the federal rights protected by what is now 18 USC § 241 goes back at least as far as 1904. . . . We reaffirm it now.

This does not mean, of course, that every criminal conspiracy affecting an individual's right of free interstate passage is within the sanction of 18 USC § 241. A specific intent to interfere with the federal right must be proved, and at a trial the defendants are entitled to a jury instruction phrased in those terms. Screws v. United States [1945]. Thus, for example, a conspiracy to rob an interstate traveler would not, of itself, violate § 241. But if the predominant purpose of the conspiracy is to impede or prevent the exercise of the right of interstate travel, or to oppress a person because of his exercise of that right, then, whether or not motivated by racial discrimination, the conspiracy becomes a proper object of the federal law under which the indictment in this case was brought. Accordingly, it was error to grant the motion to dismiss on this branch of the indictment.

For these reasons, the judgment of the District Court is reversed and the case is remanded to that court for further proceedings consistent with this opinion.

It is so ordered.

Mr. Justice **Clark**, with whom Mr. Justice **Black** and Mr. Justice **Fortas** joined, wrote a concurring opinion.

Mr. Justice **Harlan**, concurring in part and dissenting in part, said in part:

I join Parts I and II of the Court's opinion, but I cannot subscribe to Part III in its full sweep. To the extent that it is there held that 18 USC § 241 (1964 ed.) reaches conspiracies, embracing only the action of private persons, to obstruct or otherwise interfere with the right of citizens freely to engage in interstate travel, I am constrained to dissent. On the other hand, I agree that § 241 does embrace state interference with such interstate travel, and I therefore consider that this aspect of the indictment is sustainable on the reasoning of Part II of the Court's opinion. . . .

[Justice Harlan here considers, and rejects, several alternative arguments under which the right to travel could be protected from private interference.]

V.

If I have succeeded in showing anything in this constitutional exercise, it is that until today there was no federal right to be free from private interference with interstate transit, and very little reason for creating one. Although the Court has ostensibly only "discovered" this private right in the Constitution and then applied § 241 mechanically to punish those who conspire to threaten it, it should be recognized that what the Court has in effect done is to use this all-encompassing criminal statute to fashion federal common-law crimes, forbidden to the federal judiciary since the 1812 decision in United States v. Hudson. My Brother Douglas, dissenting in United States v. Classic [1941], noted well the dangers of the indiscriminate application of the predecessor of § 241: "It is not enough for us to find in the vague penumbra of a statute some offense about which Congress could have legislated, and then to particularize it as a crime because it is highly offensive."

Mr. Justice **Brennan**, with whom the **Chief Justice [Warren]** and Mr. Justice **Douglas** join, concurring in part and dissenting in part, said in part:

. . . I agree with so much of Part II as construes 18 USC § 241 (1964 ed.) to encompass conspiracies to injure, oppress, threaten or intimidate citizens in the free exercise or enjoyment of Fourteenth Amendment rights and holds that, as so construed, § 241 is not void for indefiniteness. I do not agree, however, with the remainder of Part II which holds, as I read the opinion, that a conspiracy to interfere with the exercise of the right to equal utilization of state facilities is not, within the meaning of § 241, a conspiracy to interfere with the exercise of a "right . . . secured . . . by the Constitution" unless discriminatory conduct by state officers is involved in the alleged conspiracy. . . .

I cannot agree with that construction of § 241. I am of the opinion that a conspiracy to interfere with the right to equal utilization of state facilities described in the second numbered paragraph of the indictment is a conspiracy to interfere with a "right . . . secured . . . by the Constitution" within the meaning of §241—without regard to whether state officers participated in the alleged conspiracy. I believe that § 241 reaches such a private conspiracy, not because the Fourteenth Amendment of its own force prohibits such a conspiracy, but because § 241, as an exercise of congressional power under § 5 of that Amendment, prohibits *all* conspiracies to interfere with the exercise of a "right . . . secured . . . by the Constitution" and because the right to equal utilization of state facilities is a "right . . . secured . . . by the Constitution" within the meaning of that phrase as used in § 241. . . .

SOUTH CAROLINA v. KATZENBACH—RN-1
SouthCarolina v. Katzenbach

383 U. S. 301; 86 S. Ct. 803; 15 L. Ed. 2d 769
(1966)

Within months after the states had ratified the Fifteenth Amendment, Congress passed the Enforcement Act of 1870, the first four sections of which undertook to enforce the right to vote guaranteed by that amendment. In the first two sections guaranteeing the right to vote and punishing interference with a person's registering to vote, the act explicitly forbade discrimination on account of race; but in the last two sections of the act, which punished actual interferences with the voting, these limiting words were omitted so that the law seemed to forbid voting interference even for reasons other than race. Since this was beyond the authority given by the amendment, the Court held these crucial sections void. See *United States v. Reese* (1876).

It was nearly ninety years before Congress tried again. The Civil Rights Act of 1965, held valid in the present case, is the result of nearly a decade of struggle. Timid and experimental, the early laws were limited to federal elections alone and relied almost entirely on the courts for their operation. The Civil Rights Act of 1957 forbade anyone to interfere with a person's right to vote and authorized the Attorney General to seek an injunction to prevent such interference where it was occurring or seemed likely to occur. In *United States v. Raines* (1960) the act was held valid as applied to voting registrars in Georgia who were discriminating on racial grounds.

Failure of these measures to increase black voting substantially led Congress to strengthen them in the Civil Rights Act of 1960, which made it a crime to obstruct the exercise of (voting) rights granted by court order and gave the Attorney General access to voting records for the purpose of determining if a pattern of discrimination existed. In addition, the district courts were authorized both to appoint voting referees to hear complaints and to qualify or to have the voting referees qualify persons to vote in areas where a pattern of discrimination resulted in disfranchising them. Failure to permit a person so qualified to vote was contempt of court.

Continued state resistance, abetted by a lack of aggressiveness on the part of local United States attorneys and district courts, still prevented any marked increase in black voter registration and led to still stronger voting legislation in the Civil Rights Act of 1964. In Title I of this omnibus measure Congress forbade applying different literacy tests to different applicants, prohibited disqualifying applicants for immaterial errors, and made a sixth-grade education in an English-language school prima facie evidence of literacy for purposes of voting in federal elections. Provision was made for getting quick decisions from federal courts in voter registration cases, some of which had dragged on for over a year. But again, state ingenuity in devising delaying tactics kept black registration to a trickle, and again Congress acted.

While the Voting Rights Act of 1965 falls short of providing complete federal election machinery, it harnesses federal power to prevent voting discrimination to a degree never before attempted. Singling out by the use of a "triggering" formula those areas in which voting discrimination is most flagrant, it abolishes literacy tests, waives accumulated poll taxes, and forbids the state to institute new voting requirements until the courts or the Attorney General has found them nondiscriminatory. Furthermore, federal examiners can be appointed to list qualified applicants and declare them eligible to vote in all elections, state as well as federal; and federal poll watchers can be assigned to see that their votes are actually counted. If a qualified person is denied access to the polls, United States officials may permit him to cast his ballot and include the vote in the official totals.

Even in areas not singled out by the triggering formula, the Attorney General may institute proceedings to guarantee voting rights, in which case federal examiners and poll watchers may be appointed, all voting tests and devices may be suspended, and the courts may retain jurisdiction of the proceedings to ensure that no new and discriminatory voting rules are adopted.

The only part of the act to be directed primarily at non-Southern voting practices is a section which outlaws forbidding a person to vote because he cannot read and write English. Directed primarily at New York's vast Spanish-speaking Puerto Rican population, the section was introduced by Senators Javits and Kennedy of New York and declares to be literate any person who, in any American flag school and regardless of the language of instruction, has completed the sixth grade, or such higher grade as is used by the state to qualify its voters. In the elections of 1965 Herman Badillo, a Puerto Rican, defeated incumbent Joseph F. Periconi for reelection as Bronx Borough President by a margin of 2,000 votes. Voting in this election were over 4,000 Spanish-speaking voters who had been enfranchised by this provision of the act. Following the election, a three-judge court in the District of Columbia held the section invalid on the ground that the power to set voting qualifications was reserved to the states. The Supreme Court held the restriction valid in *Katzenbach v. Morgan* (1966). It refused to decide whether a requirement of literacy in English, per se, would deny equal protection, but held that the statute was a valid exercise of congressional power under § 5 of the Fourteenth Amendment providing that "Congress shall have power to enforce, by appropriate legislation, the provisions of this article." Thus, while a restrictive state law must be tested against the equal protection clause with the presumption of validity in favor of the state, a federal statute enforcing equal protection is judged by its "appropriateness," with the burden of showing it to be unreasonable resting on its attackers. Clearly this opens up to Congress an almost wholly untried area of power to protect civil rights.

Mr. **Chief Justice Warren** delivered the opinion of the Court, saying in part:

By leave of the Court, South Carolina has filed a bill of complaint, seeking a declaration that selected provisions of the Voting Rights Act of 1965 violate the Federal Constitution, and asking for an injunction against enforcement of these provisions by the Attorney General. Original jurisdiction is founded on the presence of a controversy between a State and a citizen of another State under Art. III, § 2, of the Constitution. . . .

The Voting Rights Act was designed by Congress to banish the blight of racial discrimination in voting, which has infected the electoral process in parts of our country for nearly a century. The Act creates stringent new remedies for voting discrimination where it persists on a pervasive scale, and in addition the statute strengthens existing remedies for pockets of voting discrimination elsewhere in the country. Congress assumed the power to prescribe these remedies from § 2 of the Fifteenth Amendment, which authorizes the National Legislature to effectuate by ''appropriate'' measures the constitutional prohibition against racial discrimination in voting. We hold that the sections of the Act which are properly before us are an appropriate means for carrying out Congress' constitutional responsibilities and are consonant with all other provisions of the Constitution. We therefore deny South Carolina's request that enforcement of these sections of the Act be enjoined.

I.

The constitutional propriety of the Voting Rights Act of 1965 must be judged with reference to the historical experience which it reflects. Before enacting the measure, Congress explored with great care the problem of racial discrimination in voting. The House and Senate Committees on the Judiciary each held hearings for nine days and received testimony from a total of 67 witnesses. More than three full days were consumed discussing the bill on the floor of the House, while the debate in the Senate covered 26 days in all. At the close of these deliberations, the verdict of both chambers was overwhelming. The House approved the bill by a vote of 328-74, and the measure passed the Senate by a margin of 79-18.

Two points emerge vividly from the voluminous legislative history of the Act contained in the committee hearings and floor debates. First: Congress felt itself confronted by an insidious and pervasive evil which had been perpetuated in certain parts of our country through unremitting and ingenious defiance of the Constitution. Second: Congress concluded that the unsuccessful remedies which it had prescribed in the past would have to be replaced by sterner and more elaborate measures in order to satisfy the clear commands of the Fifteenth Amendment. We pause here to summarize the majority reports of the House and Senate Committees, which document in considerable detail the factual basis for these reactions by Congress. . . . [The Court here summarizes the systematic efforts of Southern states to disfranchise the Negro.]

According to the evidence in recent Justice Department voting suits, . . . [discriminatory application of voting tests is now the principal] method used to bar Negroes from the polls. Discriminatory administration of voting qualifications has been found in all eight Alabama cases, in all nine Louisiana cases, and in all nine Mississippi cases which have gone to final judgment. Moreover, in almost all of these cases, the courts have held that the discrimination was pursuant to a widespread ''pattern or practice.'' White applicants for registration have often been excused altogether from the literacy and understanding tests or have been given easy versions, have received extensive help from voting officials, and have been registered despite serious errors in their answers. Negroes, on the other hand, have typically been required to pass difficult versions of all the tests, without any outside assistance and without the slightest error. The good-morals requirement is so vague and subjective that it has constituted an open invitation to abuse at the hands of voting officials. Negroes obliged to obtain vouchers from registered voters have found it virtually impossible to comply in areas where almost no Negroes are on the rolls.

In recent years, Congress has repeatedly tried to cope with the problem by facilitating case-by-case litigation against voting discrimination. The Civil Rights Act of 1957 authorized the Attorney General to seek injunctions against public and private interference with the right to vote on racial grounds. Perfecting amendments in the Civil Rights Act of 1960 permitted the joinder of States as parties defendant, gave the Attorney General access to local voting records, and authorized courts to register voters in areas of systematic discrimination. Title I of the Civil Rights Act of 1964 expedited the hearing of voting cases before three-judge courts and outlawed some of the tactics used to disqualify Negroes from voting in federal elections.

Despite the earnest efforts of the Justice Department and of many federal judges, these new laws have done little to cure the problem of voting discrimination. According to estimates by the Attorney General during hearings on the Act, registration of voting-age Negroes in Alabama rose only from 14.2% to 19.4% between 1958 and 1964; in Louisiana it barely inched ahead from 31.7% to 31.8% between 1956 and 1965; and in Mississippi it increased only from 4.4% to 6.4% between 1954 and 1964. In each instance, registration of voting-age whites ran roughly 50 percentage points or more ahead of Negro registration.

The previous legislation has proved ineffective for a number of reasons. Voting suits are unusually onerous to prepare, sometimes requiring as many as 6,000 man-hours spent combing through registration records in preparation for trial. Litigation has been exceedingly slow, in part because of the ample opportunities for delay afforded voting officials and others involved in the proceedings. Even when favorable decisions have finally been obtained, some of the States affected have merely switched to discriminatory devices not covered by the federal decrees or have enacted difficult new tests designed to prolong the existing disparity between white and Negro registration. Alternatively, certain local officials have defied and evaded court orders or have simply closed their registration offices to freeze the voting rolls. The provision of the 1960 law authorizing registration by federal officers has had little impact on local maladministration because of its procedural complexities.

During the hearings and debates on the Act, Selma, Alabama, was repeatedly referred to as the preeminent example of the ineffectiveness of existing legislation. In Dallas County, of which Selma is the seat, there were four years of litigation by the Justice Department and two findings by the federal courts of widespread voting discrimination. Yet in those four years, Negro registration rose only from 156 to 383, although there are approximately 15,000 Negroes of voting age in the county. Any possibility that these figures were attributable to political apathy was dispelled by the protest demonstrations in Selma in the early months of 1965. . . .

II.

The Voting Rights Act of 1965 reflects Congress' firm intention to rid the country of racial discrimination in voting. The heart of the Act is a complex scheme of stringent remedies aimed at areas where voting discrimination has been most flagrant. . . .

At the outset, we emphasize that only some of the many portions of the Act are properly before us. . . .

Coverage Formula

The remedial sections of the Act assailed by South Carolina automatically apply to any State, or to any separate political subdivision such as a county or parish, for which two findings have been made: (1) the Attorney General has determined that on November 1, 1964, it maintained a "test or device," and (2) the Director of the Census has determined that less than 50% of its voting-age residents were registered on November 1, 1964, or voted in the presidential election of November 1964. . . . As used throughout the Act, the phrase "test or device" means any requirement that a registrant or voter must "(1) demonstrate the ability to read, write, understand, or interpret any matter, (2) demonstrate any educational achievement or his knowledge on any particular subject, (3) possess good moral character, or (4) prove his qualifications by the voucher of registered voters or members of any class." § 4 (c). . . .

South Carolina was brought within the coverage formula of the Act on August 7, 1965. . . .

Suspension of Tests

In a State or political subdivision covered by § 4 (b) of the Act, no person may be denied the right to vote in any election because of his failure to comply with a "test or device." § 4 (a).

On account of this provision, South Carolina is temporarily barred from enforcing the portion of its voting laws which requires every applicant for registration to show that he:

"Can both read and write any section of [the State] Constitution submitted to [him] by the registration officer or can show that he owns, and has paid all taxes collectable during the previous year on, property in this State assessed at three hundred dollars or more." . . .

Review of New Rules

In a State or political subdivision covered by § 4 (b) of the Act, no person may be denied the right to vote in any election because of his failure to comply with a voting qualification or procedure different from those in force on November 1, 1964. . . .

Federal Examiners

In any political subdivision covered by § 4 (b) of the Act, the Civil Service Commission shall appoint voting examiners whenever the Attorney General certifies either of the following facts: (1) that he has received meritorious written complaints from at least 20 residents alleging that they have been disenfranchised under color of law because of their race, or (2) that the appointment of examiners is otherwise necessary to effectuate the guarantees of the Fifteenth Amendment. In making the latter determination, the Attorney General must consider, among other factors, whether the registration ratio of non-whites to whites seems reasonably attributable to racial discrimination, or whether there is substantial evidence of good-faith efforts to comply with the Fifteenth Amendment § 6 (b). . . .

The examiners who have been appointed are to test the voting qualifications of applicants according to regulations of the Civil Service Commission prescribing times, places, procedures, and forms. §§ 7 (a) and 9 (b). Any person who meets the voting requirements of state law, insofar as these have not been suspended by the Act, must promptly be placed on a list of eligible voters. . . . Any person listed by an examiner is entitled to vote in all elections held more than 45 days after his name has been transmitted. § 7 (b). . . .

On October 30, 1965, the Attorney General certified the need for federal examiners in two South Carolina counties, and examiners appointed by the Civil Service Commission have been serving there since November 8, 1965. . . .

III.

These provisions of the Voting Rights Act of 1965 are challenged on the fundamental ground that they exceed the powers of Congress and encroach on an area reserved to the States by the Constitution. . . .

Has Congress exercised its powers under the Fifteenth Amendment in an appropriate manner with relation to the States?

The ground rules for resolving this question are clear. The language and purpose of the Fifteenth Amendment, the prior decisions construing its several provisions, and the general doctrines of constitutional interpretation, all point to one fundamental principle. As against the reserved powers of the States, Congress may use any rational means to effectuate the constitutional prohibition of racial discrimination in voting. Cf. our rulings last Term, sustaining Title II of the Civil Rights Act of 1964, in Heart of Atlanta Motel v. United States [1964], and Katzenbach v. McClung [1964]. We turn now to a more detailed description of the standards which govern our review of the Act.

Section 1 of the Fifteenth Amendment declares

that "[t]he right of citizens of the United States to vote shall not be denied or abridged by the United States or by any State on account of race, color, or previous condition of servitude." This declaration has always been treated as self-executing and has repeatedly been construed, without further legislative specification, to invalidate state voting qualifications or procedures which are discriminatory on their face or in practice. . . . Guinn v. United States [1915] . . . Smith v. Allwright [1944]. The gist of the matter is that the Fifteenth Amendment supersedes contrary exertions of state power. . . .

South Carolina contends that the cases cited above are precedents only for the authority of the judiciary to strike down state statutes and procedures—that to allow an exercise of this authority by Congress would be to rob the courts of their rightful constitutional role. On the contrary, § 2 of the Fifteenth Amendment expressly declares that "Congress shall have the power to enforce this article by appropriate legislation." By adding this authorization, the Framers indicated that Congress was to be chiefly responsible for implementing the rights created in § 1. . . .

Congress has repeatedly exercised these powers in the past, and its enactments have repeatedly been upheld. For recent examples, see the Civil Rights Act of 1957, which was sustained in United States v. Raines [1960]. . . .

The basic test to be applied in a case involving § 2 of the Fifteenth Amendment is the same as in all cases concerning the express powers of Congress with relation to the reserved powers of the States. Chief Justice Marshall laid down the classic formulation, 50 years before the Fifteenth Amendment was ratified:

"Let the end be legitimate, let it be within the scope of the constitution, and all means which are appropriate, which are plainly adapted to that end, which are not prohibited, but consist with the letter and spirit of the constitution, are constitutional." McCulloch v. Maryland [1819]. . . .

We therefore reject South Carolina's argument that Congress may appropriately do no more than to forbid violations of the Fifteenth Amendment in general terms—that the task of fashioning specific remedies or of applying them to particular localities must necessarily be left entirely to the courts. Congress is not circumscribed by any such artificial rules under § 2 of the Fifteenth Amendment. In the oft-repeated words of Chief Justice Marshall, referring to another specific legislative authorization in the Constitution, "This power, like all others vested in Congress, is complete in itself, may be exercised to its utmost extent, and acknowledges no limitations, other than are prescribed in the constitution." Gibbons v. Ogden [1824].

IV.

Congress exercised its authority under the Fifteenth Amendment in an inventive manner when it enacted the Voting Rights Act of 1965. First: The measure prescribes remedies for voting discrimination which go into effect without any need for prior adjudication. This was clearly a legitimate response to the problem, for which there is ample precedent under other constitutional provisions. . . . Congress had found that case-by-case litigation was inadequate to combat widespread and persistent discrimination in voting, because of the inordinate amount of time and energy required to overcome the obstructionist tactics invariably encountered in these lawsuits. After enduring nearly a century of systematic resistance to the Fifteenth Amendment, Congress might well decide to shift the advantage of time and inertia from the perpetrators of the evil to its victims. The question remains, of course, whether the specific remedies prescribed in the Act were an appropriate means of combating the evil, and to this question we shall presently address ourselves.

Second: The Act intentionally confines these remedies to a small number of States and political subdivisions which in most instances were familiar to Congress by name. This, too, was a permissible method of dealing with the problem. Congress had learned that substantial voting discrimination presently occurs in certain sections of the country, and it knew no way of accurately forecasting whether the evil might spread elsewhere in the future. In acceptable legislative fashion, Congress chose to limit its attention to the geographic areas where immediate action seemed necessary. . . . The doctrine of the equality of States, invoked by South Carolina, does not bar this approach, for that doctrine applies only to the terms upon which States are admitted to the Union, and not to the remedies for local evils which have subsequently appeared. See Coyle v. Smith [1911]. . . .

Coverage Formula

We now consider the related question of whether the specific States and political subdivisions within § 4 (b) of the Act were an appropriate target for the new remedies. . . . Congress began work with reliable evidence of actual voting discrimination in a great majority of the States and political subdivisions affected by the new remedies of the Act. The formula eventually evolved to describe these areas was relevant to the problem of voting discrimination. . . .

To be specific, the new remedies of the Act are imposed on three States—Alabama, Louisiana, and Mississippi—in which federal courts have repeatedly found substantial voting discrimination. . . .

The areas listed above, for which there was evidence of actual voting discrimination, share two characteristics incorporated by Congress into the coverage formula: the use of tests and devices for voter registration, and a voting rate in the 1964 presidential election at least 12 points below the national average. Tests and devices are relevant to voting discrimination because of their long history as a tool for perpetrating the evil; a low voting rate is pertinent for the obvious reason that widespread disenfranchisement must inevitably affect the number of actual voters. Accordingly, the coverage formula is rational in both practice and theory. It was therefore permissible to impose the new remedies on the few remaining States and political subdivisions covered by the formula, at least in the absence of proof that they have been free of substantial voting discrimination in recent years. . . .

Suspension of Tests

We now arrive at consideration of the specific remedies prescribed by the Act for areas included within the coverage formula. South Carolina assails the temporary suspension of existing voting qualification. . . . The record shows that in most of the States covered by the Act, including South Carolina, various tests and devices have been instituted with the purpose of disenfranchising Negroes, have been framed in such a way as to facilitate this aim, and have been administered in a discriminatory fashion for many years. Under these circumstances, the Fifteenth Amendment has clearly been violated. . . .

The Act suspends literacy tests and similar devices for a period of five years from the last occurrence of substantial voting discrimination. This was a legitimate response to the problem, for which there is ample precedent in Fifteenth Amendment cases. Underlying the response was the feeling that States and political subdivisions which had been allowing white illiterates to vote for years could not sincerely complain about "dilution" of their electorates through the registration of Negro illiterates. Congress knew that continuance of the tests and devices in use at the present time, no matter how fairly administered in the future, would freeze the effect of past discrimination in favor of unqualified white registrants. Congress permissibly rejected the alternative of requiring a complete re-registration of all voters, believing that this would be too harsh on many whites who had enjoyed the franchise for their entire adult lives.

Review of New Rules

The Act suspends new voting regulations pending scrutiny by federal authorities to determine whether their use would violate the Fifteenth Amendment. . . . Congress knew that some of the States covered by § 4 (b) of the Act had resorted to the extraordinary stratagem of contriving new rules of various kinds for the sole purpose of perpetuating voting discrimination in the face of adverse federal court decrees. Congress had reason to suppose that these States might try similar maneuvers in the future in order to evade the remedies for voting discrimination contained in the Act itself. Under the compulsion of these unique circumstances, Congress responded in a permissibly decisive manner. . . .

Federal Examiners

The Act authorizes the appointment of federal examiners to list qualified applicants who are thereafter en-

titled to vote, subject to an expeditious challenge procedure. This was clearly an appropriate response to the problem, closely related to remedies authorized in prior cases. . . . In many of the political subdivisions covered by § 4 (b) of the Act, voting officials have persistently employed a variety of procedural tactics to deny Negroes the franchise, often in direct defiance or evasion of federal court decrees. Congress realized that merely to suspend voting rules which have been misused or are subject to misuse might leave this localized evil undisturbed. As for the briskness of the challenge procedure, Congress knew that in some of the areas affected, challenges had been persistently employed to harass registered Negroes. It chose to forestall this abuse, at the same time providing alternative ways for removing persons listed through error or fraud. In addition to the judicial challenge procedure, § 7 (d) allows for the removal of names by the examiner himself, and § 11 (c) makes it a crime to obtain a listing through fraud. . . .

The bill of complaint is dismissed.

Mr. Justice **Black** concurred except as to the validity of § 5.

JONES v. ALFRED H. MAYER CO.

392 U. S. 409; 88 S. Ct. 2186; 20 L. Ed. 2d 1189
(1968)

It is one of the anomalies of our system of government that federal efforts to provide protection for human safety and dignity must be undertaken through what was once called "back-stairs legislation." Under our federal system Congress has no "police power" delegated to it. To provide such protection it must rely on using some power which has been delegated to it. Thus, Title II of the Civil Rights Act of 1964 (see Heart of Atlanta Motel v. United States, 1964) rests upon the commerce power, while the Fair Housing section of the Civil Rights Act of 1968 relies for its validity on the power of Congress to control those who receive its financial help.

During the bitter days of Reconstruction following the Civil War, the Radical Republicans, under the leadership of Thaddeus Stevens, made a serious if not wholly altruistic attempt to provide Congress with just such a police power to protect the newly freed Negro. Three constitutional amendments were passed, and to carry them out Congress passed, over the veto of President Johnson, a series of civil rights enforcement acts. The first of these, the Civil Rights Act of 1866, was passed to enforce the provisions of the Thirteenth Amendment abolishing slavery. Section 1 of this act, printed in the case below and now included in §§ 1981 and 1982 of Title 42 of the U. S. Code, declared that "all . . . citizens . . . without regard to any previous condition of slavery . . . shall have the same rights to . . . purchase, lease, sell, hold and convey real and personal property, as is enjoyed by white citizens. . . ." Whether one individual could sue another under the provisions of § 1 was not made explicit, but in § 2 of the act (now § 242 of Title 18 of the U. S. Code) violation of these rights was made a federal crime punishable, where the violator was "acting under color of" state law, by a $1,000 fine and one year in jail. Although the bill became law on April 9, 1866, there was doubt in the minds of many congressmen as to the constitutionality of § 2 punishing for the first time the conduct of state officers, and on June 13, Congress submitted to the states the Fourteenth Amendment to provide a constitutional underpinning for this provision.

The Fourteenth Amendment was ratified by the states in 1868 and the Fifteenth in 1870. Two months later Congress enacted a second civil rights bill known as the Enforcement Act of 1870. This was a catch-all measure which, among other things, provided federal protection for voting, reenacted §§ 1 and 2 of the act of 1866, and in what has become § 241 of Title 18 of the U.S. Code, made it a crime punishable by $5,000 or ten years in jail for "two or more persons" to "conspire together, or go in disguise upon the highway . . . with intent to violate any provision of this act, or to . . . intimidate any citizen with intent to . . . hinder his free exercise . . . of any right or privilege granted or secured to him by the Constitution or laws of the United States."

The result of these statutes was to make it a crime for either a private individual or a state officer to interfere with certain specified civil rights. Then in the Ku Klux Klan Act of 1871, Congress provided a private right of action against a private individual who conspired to deprive anyone of the "equal protection of the laws or of the equal privileges and immunities under the laws," as well as against a state officer who subjected any citizen "to the deprivation of any rights, privileges, or immunities secured by the Constitution. . . ." With the passage of the Revised Statutes of 1874, this privilege and immunities clause was also incorporated into § 242, so that not only rights mentioned in the statute but constitutional rights as well were protected from both state and private interference. Finally, with the end of the Reconstruction era in sight, Congress passed the Civil Rights Act of 1875, making it both a crime and a civil wrong to deny anyone, on account of race, the "full and equal enjoyment" of public accommodations.

The ensuing decade saw the Supreme Court systematically eviscerate both the newly passed constitutional amendments and the acts passed to enforce them. In a series of cases the Court spelled out its basic assumption that none of the Civil War amendments had been intended to give Congress any new power to enforce individual civil rights. Their only function was to forbid certain state actions. While Congress was given power to enforce the amendments, such enforcement was limited to preventing such state action, and since the amendments limited only states, under no circumstances could the actions of an individual be deemed to violate them. Thus, in the Slaughter-House Cases (1873) the "privileges and immunities" of United States citizenship protected by the Fourteenth Amendment and subsequent statutes were limited to those that Congress, under its delegated powers, had always had power to grant and protect. In United States v. Reese (1876) most of the voting protections of the Enforcement Act were struck down because they were not limited to racial discrimination, and in the Civil Rights Cases (1883), the Civil Rights Act of 1875, punishing discrimination in public accommodations, was held void because it forbade private rather than governmental action.

Only a handful of provisions survived the onslaught. Those forbidding discriminative action taken "under color of" state law were held to be directed to state action and hence were valid enforcement measures. Those provisions forbidding interference with rights by private individuals, on the other hand, were, like the privileges and immunities of the Fourteenth Amendment, limited to rights in those few areas, such as control over the manner of conducting federal elections, where Congress had power from the original Constitution; see Ex parte Yarbrough (1884).

The Thirteenth Amendment presented the Court with a slightly different problem. Worded to forbid involuntary servitude in any form, and since individuals rather than states had held slaves, the amendment could not reasonably be considered merely a limit upon state action. Two devices, however, permitted the Court to avoid unleashing the tremendous breadth of power latent in the amendment. The first was a refusal to extend the amendment to kinds of servitude "which have from time immemorial been treated as exceptional." Thus in Robertson v. Baldwin (1897), the Court held that seamen who had signed for a voyage aboard ship and deserted could be arrested and returned to the ship; while in the Selective Draft Law Cases (1918) it upheld the "servitude" involved in drafting a person into the armed forces of the United States. Butler v. Perry (1916) held valid on this ground a Florida law requiring that citizens work a specified number of days each year on the county roads and bridges in lieu of the payment of road taxes.

The second and most important was to interpret narrowly the word slavery. Conceding, in the Civil Rights Cases, that Congress had authority to outlaw the "badges of slavery," the Court nevertheless held it would be "running the slavery argument into the ground" to consider such badges as including the private discriminatory conduct of one man toward another. That this also applied to the "make and enforce contracts" guarantees of § 1 of the Civil Rights Act of 1866 was decided in 1906 in Hodges v. United States, discussed in the opinion below, where Negro workmen were intimidated by a group of whites into quitting their jobs.

In the 1960s the Supreme Court suggested subtly that the "back-stairs legislation" approach to civil rights may no longer be needed, and that an overt reliance on the enforcement power granted in the three amendments would be received more sympathetically than it had been before. In upholding the Voting Rights Act of 1965, the Court permitted Congress to substitute federal for state voting machinery where necessary to prevent discrimination, and to outlaw voting *qualifications which might not, of themselves, violate the Fourteenth Amendment. These provisions were upheld in South Carolina v. Katzenbach (1966) and Katzenbach v. Morgan (1966). In United States v. Guest (1966), six justices indicated that Congress could protect an individual right to use state facilities; and in the Civil Rights Act of 1968 Congress acted on this suggestion and outlawed interference with "any person because of his race . . . and because he is or has been . . . participating in or enjoying any benefit, service, privilege, program, facility or activity provided or administered by any State or subdivision thereof. . . .*

Following the decision in the present case the Court held that a cause of action existed under the old Ku Klux Klan Act of 1871 where a black mistakenly thought to be a civil rights worker was stopped on the highway and beaten up by two armed white men. The law forbids private individuals to deprive other private individuals of the "equal protection of the laws." The Court conceded that "a century of Fourteenth Amendment adjudication has . . . made it understandably difficult to conceive of what might constitute a deprivation of the equal protection of the laws by private persons. Yet there is nothing inherent in the phrase that requires the action working the deprivation to come from the State. . . . Indeed, the failure to mention any such requisite can be viewed as an important indication of congressional intent to speak in [the act] of all deprivation of 'equal protection of the laws' and 'equal privileges and immunities under the laws,' whatever their source." Nor is the power to control individual conduct limited to the kinds of things traditionally thought of as privileges and immunities of citizenship and hence subject to federal power. Citing Jones v. Alfred H. Mayer Co., the Court found that "Congress was wholly within its powers under § 2 of the Thirteenth Amendment in creating a statutory cause of action for Negro citizens who have been the victims of conspiratorial, racially discriminatory private action aimed at depriving them of the basic rights that the law secures to all free men." See Griffin v. Breckenridge (1971).

Mr. Justice **Stewart** delivered the opinion of the Court, saying in part:

In this case we are called upon to determine the scope and the constitutionality of an Act of Congress, 42 U. S. C. § 1982, which provides that:

"All citizens of the United States shall have the same right, in every State and Territory, as is enjoyed by white citizens thereof to inherit, purchase, lease, sell, hold, and convey real and personal property."

On September 2, 1965, the petitioners filed a complaint in the District Court for the Eastern District of Missouri, alleging that the respondents had refused to sell them a home in the Paddock Woods community of St. Louis County for the sole reason that petitioner Joseph Lee Jones is a Negro. Relying in part upon § 1982, the petitioners sought injunctive and other relief. The District Court sustained the respondents' motion to dis-

miss the complaint, and the Court of Appeals for the Eighth Circuit affirmed, concluding that § 1982 applies only to state action and does not reach private refusals to sell. We granted certiorari to consider the questions thus presented. For the reasons that follow, we reverse the judgment of the Court of Appeals. We hold that § 1982 bars *all* racial discrimination, private as well as public, in the sale or rental of property, and that the statute, thus construed, is a valid exercise of the power of Congress to enforce the Thirteenth Amendment.

I.

At the outset, it is important to make clear precisely what this case does *not* involve. Whatever else it may be, 42 U. S. C. § 1982 is not a comprehensive open housing law. In sharp contrast to the Fair Housing Title (Title VIII) of the Civil Rights Act of 1968, the statute in this case deals only with racial discrimination and does not address itself to discrimination on grounds of religion or national origin. It does not deal specifically with discrimination in the provision of services or facilities in connection with the sale or rental of a dwelling. It does not prohibit advertising or other representations that indicate discriminatory preferences. It does not refer explicitly to discrimination in financing arrangements or in the provision of brokerage services. It does not empower a federal administrative agency to assist aggrieved parties. It makes no provision for intervention by the Attorney General. And, although it can be enforced by injunction, it contains no provision expressly authorizing a federal court to order the payment of damages.

Thus, although § 1982 contains none of the exemptions that Congress included in the Civil Rights Act of 1968, it would be a serious mistake to suppose that § 1982 in any way diminishes the significance of the law recently enacted by Congress. Indeed, the Senate Subcommittee on Housing and Urban Affairs was informed in hearings held after the Court of Appeals had rendered its decision in this case that § 1982 might well be "a presently valid federal statutory ban against discrimination by private persons in the sale or lease of real property." The Subcommittee was told, however, that even if this Court should so construe § 1982, the existence of that statute would not "eliminate the need for congressional action" to spell out "responsibility on the part of the federal government to enforce the rights it protects." The point was made that, in light of the many difficulties confronted by private litigants seeking to enforce such rights on their own, "legislation is needed to establish federal machinery for enforcement of the rights guaranteed under Section 1982 of Title 42 even if the plaintiffs in Jones v. Alfred H. Mayer Company should prevail in the United States Supreme Court." . . .

. . . Having noted these differences, we turn to a consideration of § 1982 itself. . . .

III.

We begin with the language of the statute itself. In plain and unambiguous terms, § 1982 grants to all citizens, without regard to race or color, "the same right" to purchase and lease property "as is enjoyed by white citizens." As the Court of Appeals in this case evidently recognized, that right can be impaired as effectively by "those who place property on the market" as by the State itself. For, even if the State and its agents lend no support to those who wish to exclude persons from their communities on racial grounds, the fact remains that, whenever property "is placed on the market for whites only, whites have a right denied to Negroes." So long as a Negro citizen who wants to buy or rent a home can be turned away simply because he is not white, he cannot be said to enjoy "the *same* right . . . as is enjoyed by white citizens . . . to . . . purchase [and] lease . . . real and personal property." 42 U. S. C. § 1982. (Emphasis added.)

On its face, therefore, § 1982 appears to prohibit *all* discrimination against Negroes in the sale or rental of property—discrimination by private owners as well as discrimination by public authorities. Indeed, even the respondents seem to concede that, if § 1982 "means what it says"—to use the words of the respondents' brief—then it must encompass every racially motivated refusal to sell or rent and cannot be confined to officially sanctioned segregation in housing. Stressing what they consider to be the revolutionary implications of so literal a reading of § 1982, the respondents argue that Congress cannot possibly have intended any such result. Our examination of the relevant history, however, persuades us that Congress meant exactly what it said. . . .

V.

The remaining question is whether Congress has power under the Constitution to do what § 1982 purports to do: to prohibit all racial discrimination, private and public, in the sale and rental of property. Our starting point is the Thirteenth Amendment, for it was pursuant to that constitutional provision that Congress originally enacted what is now § 1982. The Amendment consists of two parts. Section 1 states:

"Neither slavery nor involuntary servitude except as a punishment for a crime whereof the party shall have been duly convicted, shall exist within the United States, or any place subject to their jurisdiction." Section 2 provides:

"Congress shall have power to enforce this article by appropriate legislation."

As its text reveals, the Thirteenth Amendment "is not a mere prohibition of State laws establishing or upholding slavery, but an absolute declaration that slavery or involuntary servitude shall not exist in any part of the United States." Civil Rights Cases [1883]. It has never been doubted, therefore, "that the power vested in Congress to enforce the article by appropriate legislation," includes the power to enact laws "direct and primary, operating upon the acts of individuals, whether sanctioned by State legislation or not."

Thus, the fact that § 1982 operates upon the unofficial acts of private individuals, whether or not sanctioned

by state law, presents no constitutional problem. If Congress has power under the Thirteenth Amendment to eradicate conditions that prevent Negroes from buying and renting property because of their race or color, then no federal statute calculated to achieve that objective can be thought to exceed the constitutional power of Congress simply because it reaches beyond state action to regulate the conduct of private individuals. The constitutional question in this case, therefore, comes to this: Does the authority of Congress to enforce the Thirteenth Amendment "by appropriate legislation" include the power to eliminate all racial barriers to the acquisition of real and personal property? We think the answer to that question is plainly yes. . . .

. . . Surely Congress has the power under the Thirteenth Amendment rationally to determine what are the badges and the incidents of slavery, and the authority to translate that determination into effective legislation. Nor can we say that the determination Congress has made is an irrational one. For this Court recognized long ago that, whatever else they may have encompassed, the badges and incidents of slavery—its "burdens and disabilities"—included restraints upon "those fundamental rights which are the essence of civil freedom, namely, the same right . . . to inherit, purchase, lease, sell and convey property, as is enjoyed by white citizens." Civil Rights Cases.* Just as the Black Codes, enacted after the

---

*The Court did conclude in the Civil Rights Cases that "the act of . . . the owner of the inn, the public conveyance or place of amusement, refusing . . . accommodation" cannot be "justly regarded as imposing any badge of slavery or servitude upon the applicant." "It would be running the slavery argument into the ground," the Court thought, "to make it apply to every act of discrimination which a person may see fit to make as to the guests he will entertain, or as to the people he will take into his coach or cab or car, or admit to his concert or theatre, or deal with in other matters of intercourse or business." Mr. Justice Harlan dissented, expressing the view that "such discrimination practiced by corporations and individuals in the exercise of their public or quasi-public functions is a badge of servitude the imposition of which Congress may prevent under its power, by appropriate legislation, to enforce the Thirteenth Amendment."

Whatever the present validity of the position taken by the majority on that issue—a question rendered largely academic by Title II of the Civil Rights Act of 1964 (see Heart of Atlanta Motel v. United States [1964]; Katzenbach v. McClung [1964])—we note that the entire Court agreed upon at least one proposition: The Thirteenth Amendment authorizes Congress not only to outlaw all forms of slavery and involuntary servitude but also to eradicate the last vestiges and incidents of a society half slave and half free, securing to all citizens, of every race and color, "the same right to make and enforce contracts, to sue, be parties, give evidence, and to inherit, purchase, lease, sell and convey property, as is enjoyed by white citizens."

In Hodges v. United States [1906], a group of white men had terrorized several Negroes to prevent them from working in a sawmill. The terrorizers were convicted under 18 U. S. C. § 241 . . . of conspiring to prevent the Negroes from exercising the right to contract for employment, a right . . . derived from § 1 of the Civil Rights Act of 1866. . . .

This court reversed the conviction. The majority recognized that "one of the disabilities of slavery, one of the indicia of its existence, was a lack of power to make or perform contracts." And there was no doubt that the defendants had deprived their Negro victims, on racial grounds, of the opportunity to dispose of their labor by contract. Yet the majority said that "no mere personal assault or trespass or appropri-

Civil War to restrict the free exercise of those rights, were substitutes for the slave system, so the exclusion of Negroes from white communities became a substitute for the Black Codes. And when racial discrimination herds men into ghettos and makes their ability to buy property turn on the color of their skin, then it too is a relic of slavery.

Negro citizens North and South, who saw in the Thirteenth Amendment a promise of freedom—freedom to "go and come at pleasure" and to "buy and sell when they please"— would be left with "a mere paper guarantee" if Congress were powerless to assure that a dollar in the hands of a Negro will purchase the same thing as a dollar in the hands of a white man. At the very least, the freedom that Congress is empowered to secure under the Thirteenth Amendment includes the freedom to buy whatever a white man can buy, the right to live wherever a white man can live. If Congress cannot say that being a free man means at least this much, then the Thirteenth Amendment made a promise the Nation cannot keep. . . .

We agree. The judgment is
Reversed.

Mr. Justice **Douglas** wrote a concurring opinion.

Mr. Justice **Harlan**, whom Mr. Justice **White** joins, dissenting, said in part:

The decision in this case appears to me to be most ill-considered and ill-advised.

The petitioners argue that the respondent's racially motivated refusal to sell them a house entitles them to judicial relief on two separate grounds. First, they claim that the respondent acted in violation of 42 U. S. C. § 1982; second, they assert that the respondent's conduct amounted in the circumstances to "state action" and was therefore forbidden by the Fourteenth Amendment even in the absence of any statute. The Court, without reaching the second alleged ground, holds that the petitioners are entitled to relief under 42 U. S. C. § 1982, and that § 1982 is constitutional as legislation appropriate to enforce the Thirteenth Amendment.

For reasons which follow, I believe that the Court's construction of § 1982 as applying to purely private action is almost surely wrong, and at least is open to serious doubt. The issue of the constitutionality of § 1982, as construed by the Court, and of liability under the Fourteenth Amendment alone, also present formidable difficulties. Moreover, the political processes of our own era have, since the date of oral argument in this case, given birth to a civil rights statute embodying "fair housing" provisions which would at the end of this year make available to others, though apparently not to the petitioners themselves, the type of relief which the petitioners now seek. It seems to me that this latter factor so diminishes the public importance of this case that by far the wisest course would be for this Court to refrain from decision and to dismiss the writ as improvidently granted. . . .

---

ation operates to reduce the individual to a condition of slavery," and asserted that only conduct which actually enslaves someone can be subjected to punishment under legislation enacted to enforce the Thirteenth Amendment. . . .

The conclusion of the majority in Hodges rested upon a concept of congressional power under the Thirteenth Amendment irreconcilable with the position taken by every member of this Court in the Civil Rights Cases and incompatible with the history and purpose of the Amendment itself. Insofar as Hodges is inconsistent with our holding today, it is hereby overruled.

13

1987-1988 Cases

MORRISON v. OLSON

101 L. Ed. 2d 569 (1988)

As the inquiry into the Watergate scandal began to suggest that President Nixon might be implicated, the President fired special prosecutor Archibald Cox for refusing to drop the investigation. See the note to United States v. Nixon. It was popularly assumed that the firing was done by the President to conceal his personal involvement in the conspiracy, and it was under the threat of impeachment that the President agreed to appoint a new special prosecutor.

While the government had used special prosecutors on an ad hoc basis in the past, the dramatic spectacle of the administration using its power over the office to conceal its own misdeeds brought a widespread demand for an investigative office less subject to pressure from those it was investigating. The result was the passage of the Ethics in Government Act of 1978 which made permanent provision for the appointment of special prosecutors (independent counsels, as they were renamed in the 1982 revision of the Act).

To reduce the possible misuse of the office as in the Watergate situation and to provide the special prosecutor with a greater measure of independence, a number of provisions were included in the law. First, a special division of the D.C. Circuit Court of Appeals was created, its members chosen by the Chief Justice of the United States from among sitting federal judges, and it was this court that selected the special prosecutors and spelled out their jurisdictions. Thus, while the special prosecutor was in the executive branch, he or she was appointed, not by the executive, but by the judiciary. Second, while the Attorney General has to be persuaded there is evidence warranting investigating an alleged violation of law, if he does so find he must conduct a preliminary investigation. Only if he is persuaded that "there are no reasonable grounds to believe further investigation is warranted" is he not required to request of the court the appointment of a special prosecutor. Third, once a special prosecutor has been appointed, the Justice Department must suspend all further investigations of its own regarding the matter.

It was not long before the independent counsel provisions of the 1978 law produced strong reactions from both supporters and critics. The proponents, citing the Watergate investigation and the "Saturday Night Massacre," rested their argument on political grounds. How could the Justice Department and the President himself be expected vigorously and impartially to investigate and prosecute alleged wrongdoing of their own administration's executive branch officials?

Critics, on the other hand, faced with these arguments, relied on constitutional arguments. They viewed the "independence" from presidential control which was the purpose of the act as one of its most objectionable features. They argued that criminal prosecution is an exclusive and "core executive function" that cannot be shared with the judicial branch to which the law delegated the appointment of the special prosecutors, and that such delegation constitutes a violation of the separation of powers doctrine. Second, opponents of the law charged that the appointment provisions of the law violated the appointments clause of Article II. Special prosecutors, they claimed, were "principal" officers of the United States and must be appointed by the president with the advice and consent of the Senate — not "inferior" officers whose appointment (through the succeeding phrase of the Appointments Clause known as the "excepting clause") Congress may vest in "the President alone, the courts or department heads." It was on this point that the lower courts disagreed, the court of appeals holding the office "superior."

Following the law's enactment in 1978 four special prosecutors were appointed to investigate various officials of the Carter and Reagan administrations. Two of President Carter's aides, Chief of Staff Hamilton Jordan and national campaign manager Tim Kraft, were the subject of special prosecutor investigation and, with the advent of the Republican administration, Reagan's first Secretary of Labor Raymond Donovan was investigated. In none of these cases did the prosecutor recommend criminal prosecution. After special prosecutor Leon Silverman declined to prosecute Donovan on federal charges of ties to organized crime because of "insufficient credible evidence" (in Silverman's own words, the witnesses against Donovan were "inherently incredible"), Donovan was subsequently prosecuted and acquitted in New York state on similar criminal charges.

At the time that the present case reached the Supreme Court a dramatic second round of investigations, stemming in part from testimony at the Iran-Contra hearings, was in various stages of progress. Five such investigations were going on simultaneously and all those being investigated were upper echelon administrators in the Reagan administration — the only group specified by the law as eligible for such attention. Perhaps the least well-known to the public was the investigation by special prosecutor Alexia Morrison of Theodore B. Olson, Assistant Attorney General for the Office of Legal Counsel (the President's lawyer), on charges of lying to Congress during a controversy over the Environmental Protection Agency. This was the case the Supreme Court chose for review.

Of far more significance and interest to the public (and to the President) were the investigations of (1) former White House Deputy Chief of Staff and Assistant to the President Michael Deaver, by special prosecutor Whitney North Seymour, Jr.; (2) former White House aide Lyn Nofziger by special prosecutor James McKay; and (3) several former executive branch officials alleged to have masterminded the Iran-Contra affair, including Lt. Colonel Oliver North and former National Security Adviser John Poindexter and three others, by special prosecutor Lawrence Walsh. By the time the present case reached the Court, Deaver and Nofziger had been the first officials to be convicted of federal ethics law violations by special prosecutors under the 1978 law. North and Poindexter et al. were indicted and were (in August 1988) awaiting federal trial on charges of conspiring to defraud the government.

None of the previous investigations, however, matched in dramatic impact the investigation of Edwin Meese III, Attorney General of the United States. Over a fourteen-month, $1.7 million dollar investigation, special prosecutor James McKay explored the charges that Meese was involved in the Wedtech and Iraqi- pipeline scandals. While McKay, in his 830-page report, exonerated Meese in the two scandals, he asserted that the Attorney General "probably" had violated conflict-of-interest and income tax laws but given the circumstances he declined to ask for an indictment. "It all came down really to the question:'If this were an ordinary person, would he be prosecuted?' " and "We concluded that he probably would not be." A little-known sidelight on the case is the fact that, while the constitutionality of the statute was still undecided, Attorney General Meese offered the four special prosecutors permanent jobs in the Justice Department. Walsh and McKay accepted these parallel appointments, so they would have had jobs whichever way the decision went.

In the few years prior to the present case the Court had ruled in three cases in favor of a strict interpretation of the separation of powers, thus raising serious doubts that the special prosecutor provisions of the law would be upheld. In Buckley v. Valeo (1976), the Court ruled that Congress could not appoint members of the Federal Election Commission whose functions included administering the law. In INS v. Chadha (1983), the Court ruled the legislative veto unconstitutional on the ground that the veto power was an executive power. In Bowsher v. Synar (1986), the Court struck down the provision in the Gramm-Rudman-Hollings Act which authorized the Comptroller General (an officer removable only by Congress) to make across-the-board spending cuts—a clearly executive function.

The voting behavior of the individual judges in Morrison was a surprise to most Court observers, in view of the fierce nomination battles, previous positions of the Justices, and the expectations of the Reagan administration that this was "their" hand-picked Court. This case followed the contentious and unsuccessful nomination by President Reagan of appeals court judge Robert Bork to the Supreme Court in the fall of 1987. Judge Bork, who, as Nixon's Solicitor General had removed Archibald Cox as special prosecutor in the "Saturday Night Massacre," had publicly made known his clear opposition to the special prosecutor provisions in the law. Judge Anthony Kennedy was confirmed to the vacant seat with ease, but did not participate in either the consideration or decision in Morrison, thereby leaving open the possibility for an evenly divided Court, thus leaving in place the Court of appeals decision striking down the law.

Chief Justice Rehnquist, elevated to the Chief's position by Reagan two years earlier, was widely known for his defense of broad executive authority in his opinions as Assistant Attorney General during the Nixon ad-

ministration and for his adherence to the doctrine of "original intent"— an interpretation of the Constitution which doubtless rejects the idea that a prosecuting attorney could be appointed by a court. Justice Scalia was a confirmed supporter of inherent executive power and a vigorous opponent of congressionally created "devices," as evidenced by his opinion in opposition to the legislative veto mechanism in the court of appeals decision of Chadha. Justice O'Connor was somewhat difficult to predict on the issue of executive power, but appeared to save her sharpest and most critical questions during oral argument of the case for special prosecutor Alexia Morrison, leading observers to speculate that she might side with Rehnquist and Scalia. Justice White, a Kennedy appointee, but one upon whom the Reagan administration could generally rely to vote with the conservative bloc, had strongly opposed the legislative veto in the Chadha case and appeared to be the swing vote here which could convert a five-to-three decision to uphold the law into a four-to-four decision to leave standing the court of appeals decision to hold the law void.

When the decision was announced on the last day of the Court's 1988 Spring term, few seasoned Court-watchers were prepared for the very lopsided 7-1 vote upholding the law, and even fewer could have anticipated Chief Justice Rehnquists's vote to sustain the law coupled with his opinion for the majority with its clear and unequivocal repudiation of a rigid concept of executive authority.

Chief Justice **Rehnquist** delivered the opinion of the Court, saying in part:

This case presents us with a challenge to the independent counsel provisions of the Ethics in Government Act of 1978. We hold today that these provisions of the Act do not violate the Appointments Clause of the Constitution, Art. II, § 2, cl. 2, or the limitations of Article III, nor do they impermissibly interfere with the President's authority under Article II in violation of the constitutional principle of separation of powers.

I.

Briefly stated, Title VI of the Ethics of Government Act allows for the appointment of an "independent counsel" to investigate and, if appropriate, prosecute certain high ranking government officials for violations of federal criminal laws. The Act requires the Attorney General, upon receipt of information that he determines is "sufficient to constitute grounds to investigate whether any person [covered by the Act] may have violated any Federal criminal law," to conduct a preliminary investigation of the matter. When the Attorney General has completed this investigation, or 90 days has elapsed, he is required to report to a special court (the Special Division) created by the Act "for the purpose of appointing independent counsels."* If the Attorney General determines that "there are no reasonable grounds to believe that further investigation is warranted," then he must notify the Special Division of this result. In such a case, "the division of the court shall have no power to appoint an independent counsel." If, however, the Attorney General has determined that there are "reasonable grounds to believe that further investigation or prosecution is warranted," then he "shall apply to the division of the court for the appointment of an independent counsel." The Attorney General's application to the court "shall contain sufficient information to assist the [court] in selecting an independent counsel and in defining that independent counsel's prosecutorial jurisdiction." Upon receiving this application, the Special Division "shall appoint an appropriate independent counsel and shall define that independent counsel's prosecutorial jurisdiction."

With respect to all matters within the independent counsel's jurisdiction, the Act grants the counsel "full power and independent authority to exercise all investigative and prosecutorial functions and powers of the Department of Justice, the Attorney General, and any other officer or employee of the Department of Justice." The functions of the independent counsel include conducting grand jury proceedings and other investigations, participating in civil and criminal court proceedings and litigation, and appealing any decision in any case in which the counsel participates in an official capacity. Under [the Act], the counsel's powers include "initiating and conducting prosecutions in any court of competent jurisdiction, framing and signing indictments, filing informations, and handling all aspects of any case, in the name of the United States." The counsel may appoint employees, may request and obtain assistance from the Department of Justice, and may accept referral of matters from the Attorney General if the matter falls within the counsel's jurisdiction as defined by the Special Division. The Act also states that an independent counsel "shall, except where not possible, comply with the written or other established policies of the Department of Justice respecting enforcement of the criminal laws." In addition, whenever a matter has been referred to an independent counsel under the Act, the Attorney General and the Justice Department are required to suspend all investigations and proceedings regarding the matter. An independent counsel has "full authority to dismiss matters within [his] prosecutorial jurisdiction without conducting an investigation or at any subsequent time before prosecution, if to do so would be consistent" with Department of Justice policy.

---

*The Special Division is a "division of the United States Court of Appeals for the District of Columbia." The court consists of three Circuit Court Judges or Justices appointed by the Chief Justice of the United States. One of the judges must be a judge of the United States Court of Appeals for the District of Columbia, and no two of the judges may be named to the Special Division from a particular court. The judges are appointed for 2-year terms, with any vacancy being filled only for the remainder of the 2-year period.

Two statutory provisions govern the length of an independent counsel's tenure in office. The first defines the procedure for removing an independent counsel. The Act provides: "An independent counsel appointed under this chapter may be removed from office, other than by impeachment and conviction, only by the personal action of the Attorney General and only for good cause, physical disability, mental incapacity, or any other condition that substantially impairs the performance of such independent counsel's duties." If an independent counsel is removed pursuant to this section, the Attorney General is required to submit a report to both the Special Division and the Judiciary Committees of the Senate and the House "specifying the facts found and the ultimate grounds for such removal." . . .

The other provision governing the tenure of the independent counsel defines the procedures for "terminating" the counsel's office. Under the statute the office of an independent counsel terminates when he notifies the Attorney General that he has completed or substantially completed any investigations or prosecutions undertaken pursuant to the Act. In addition, the Special Division, acting either on its own or on the suggestion of the Attorney General, may terminate the office of an independent counsel at any time if it finds that "the investigation of all matters within the prosecutorial jurisdiction of such independent counsel . . . have been completed or so substantially completed that it would be appropriate for the Department of Justice to complete such investigations and prosecutions."

Finally, the Act provides for Congressional oversight of the activities of independent counsels. An independent counsel may from time to time send Congress statements or reports on his activities. The "appropriate committees of the Congress" are given oversight jurisdiction in regard to the official conduct of an independent counsel, and the counsel is required by the Act to cooperate with Congress in the exercise of this jurisdiction. The counsel is required to inform the House of Representatives of "substantial and credible information which [the counsel] receives . . . that may constitute grounds for an impeachment." In addition, the Act gives certain Congressional Committee Members the power to "request in writing that the Attorney General apply for the appointment of an independent counsel." The Attorney General is required to respond to this request within a specified time but is not required to accede to the request.

The proceedings in this case provide an example of how the Act works in practice. In 1982, two subcommittees of the House of Representatives issued subpoenas directing the Environmental Protection Agency (EPA) to produce certain documents relating to the efforts of the EPA and the Land and Natural Resources Division of the Justice Department to enforce the "Superfund Law." At that time, appellee Olson was the Assistant Attorney General for the Office of Legal Counsel (OLC), appellee Schmults was Deputy Attorney General, and appellee Dinkins was the Assistant Attorney General for the Land and Natural Resources Division. Acting on the advice of the Justice Department, the President ordered the Administrator of EPA to invoke executive privilege to withhold certain of the documents on the ground that they contained "enforcement sensitive information." The Administrator obeyed this order and withheld the documents. In response, the House voted to hold the Administrator in contempt, after which the Administrator and the United States together filed a lawsuit against the House. The conflict abated in March 1983, when the Administration agreed to give the House committees limited access to the documents.

The following year, the House Judiciary Committee began an investigation into the Justice Department's role in the controversy over the EPA documents. During this investigation, appellee Olson testified before a House subcommittee on March 10, 1983. Both before and after that testimony, the Department complied with several Committee requests to produce certain documents. Other documents were at first withheld, although these documents were eventually disclosed by the Department after the Committee learned of their existence. In 1985, the majority members of the Judiciary Committee published a lengthy report on the Committee's investigation. . . . The report not only criticized various officials in the Department of Justice for their role in the EPA executive privilege dispute, but it also suggested that appellee Olson had given false and misleading testimony to the subcommittee on March 10, 1983, and that appellees Schmults and Dinkins had wrongfully withheld certain documents from the Committee, thus obstructing the Committee's investigation. The Chairman of the Judiciary Committee forwarded a copy of the report to the Attorney General with a request . . . that he seek the appointment of an independent counsel to investigate the allegations against Olson, Schmults, and Dinkins.

The Attorney General directed the Public Integrity Section of the Criminal Division to conduct a preliminary investigation. The Section's report concluded that the appointment of an independent counsel was warranted to investigate the Committee's allegations with respect to all three appellees. After consulting with other Department officials, however, the Attorney General chose to apply to the Special Division for the appointment of an independent counsel solely with respect to appellee Olson. The Attorney General accordingly requested appointment of an independent counsel to investigate whether Olson's March 10, 1983, testimony "regarding the completeness of [OLC's] response to the Judiciary Committee's request for OLC documents, and regarding his knowledge of EPA's willingness to turn over certain disputed documents to Congress, violated . . . any . . . provision of federal criminal law." The Attorney General also requested that the independent counsel have authority to investigate "any other matter related to that allegation."

On April 23, 1986, the Special Division appointed James C. McKay as independent counsel to investigate "whether the testimony of . . . Olson and his revision of such testimony on March 10, 1983, violated . . . any . . . provision of federal law." The court also ordered that the independent counsel "shall have jurisdiction to investigate any other allegation of evidence of violation of any Federal criminal law by Theodore Olson developed during investigations, by the Independent Counsel, referred to above, and connected with or arising out of that investigation, and Independent Counsel shall have jurisdiction to prosecute for any such violation."

McKay later resigned as independent counsel, and on May 29, 1986, the Division appointed appellant Morrison as his replacement, with the same jurisdiction.

In January 1987, appellant asked the Attorney General . . . to refer to her as "related matters" the Committee's allegations against appellees Schmults and Dinkins. The Attorney General refused to refer the matters, concluding that his decision not to request the appointment of an independent counsel in regard to those matters was final. . . . Appellant then asked the Special Division to order that the matters be referred to her. . . . On April 2, 1987, the Division ruled that the Attorney General's decision not to seek appointment of an independent counsel with respect to Schmults and Dinkins was final and unreviewable . . . and that therefore the court had no authority to make the requested referral. . . . The court ruled, however, that its original grant of jurisdiction to appellant was broad enough to permit inquiry into whether Olson may have conspired with others, including Schmults and Dinkins, to obstruct the Committee's investigation.

Following this ruling, in May and June 1987, appellant caused a grand jury to issue and serve subpoenas ad testificandum and duces tecum on appellees. All three appellees moved to quash the subpoenas, claiming, among other things, that the independent counsel provisions of the Act were unconstitutional and that appellant accordingly had no authority to proceed. On July 20, 1987, the District Court upheld the constitutionality of the Act and denied the motions to quash. . . . The court subsequently ordered that appellees be held in contempt . . . for continuing to refuse to comply with the subpoenas. . . . The court stayed the effect of its contempt orders pending expedited appeal.

A divided Court of Appeals reversed. . . . The majority ruled first that an independent counsel is not an "inferior Officer" of the United States for purposes of the Appointments Clause. Accordingly, the court found the Act invalid because it does not provide for the independent counsel to be nominated by the President and confirmed by the Senate, as the Clause requires for "principal" officers. The court then went on to consider several alternative grounds for its conclusion that the statute was unconstitutional. In the majority's view, the Act also violates the Appointments Clause insofar as it empowers a court of law to appoint an "inferior" officer who performs core executive functions; the Act's delegation of various powers to the Special Division violates the limitations of Article III; the Act's restrictions on the Attorney General's power to remove an independent counsel violate the separation of powers; and finally, the Act interferes with the Executive Branch's prerogative to "take care that the Laws be faithfully executed," Art. II,

§ 3. . . . Appellant then sought review by this Court, and we noted probable jurisdiction. We now reverse. . . .

III.

The Appointments Clause of Article II reads as follows: "[The President] shall nominate, and by and with the Advice and Consent of the Senate, shall appoint Ambassadors, other public Ministers and Consuls, Judges of the supreme Court, and all other Officers of the United States, whose Appointments are not herein otherwise provided for, and which shall be established by Law: but the Congress may by Law vest the Appointment of such inferior Officers, as they think proper, in the President alone, in the Courts of Law, or in the Heads of Departments." U. S. Const., Art. II, § 2, cl. 2. The parties do not dispute that "[t]he Constitution for purposes of appointment . . . divides all its officers into two classes." . . . As we stated in Buckley v. Valeo (1976), "[p]rincipal officers are selected by the President with the advice and consent of the Senate. Inferior officers Congress may allow to be appointed by the President alone, by the heads of departments, or by the Judiciary." The initial question is, accordingly, whether appellant is an "inferior" or a "principal" officer. If she is the latter, as the Court of Appeals concluded, then the Act is in violation of the Appointments Clause.

The line between "inferior" and "principal" officers is one that is far from clear, and the Framers provided little guidance into where it should be drawn. . . . We need not attempt here to decide exactly where the line falls between the two types of officers, because in our view appellant clearly falls on the "inferior officer" side of that line. Several factors lead to this conclusion.

First, appellant is subject to removal by a higher Executive Branch official. Although appellant may not be "subordinate" to the Attorney General (and the President) insofar as she possesses a degree of independent discretion to exercise the powers delegated to her under the Act, the fact that she can be removed by the Attorney General indicates that she is to some degree "inferior" in rank and authority. Second, appellant is empowered by the Act to perform only certain, limited duties. An independent counsel's role is restricted primarily to investigation and, if appropriate, prosecution for certain federal crimes. Admittedly, the Act delegates to appellant "full power and independent authority to exercise all investigative and prosecutorial functions and powers of the Department of Justice," but this grant of authority does not include any authority to formulate policy for the Government or the Executive Branch, nor does it give appellant any administrative duties outside of those necessary to operate her office. The Act specifically provides that in policy matters appellant is to comply to the extent possible with the policies of the Department.

Third, appellant's office is limited in jurisdiction. Not only is the Act itself restricted in applicability to certain federal officials suspected of certain serious federal crimes, but an independent counsel can only act within the scope of the jurisdiction that has been granted by the

Special Division pursuant to a request by the Attorney General. Finally, appellant's office is limited in tenure. There is concededly no time limit on the appointment of a particular counsel. Nonetheless, the office of independent counsel is "temporary" in the sense that an independent counsel is appointed essentially to accomplish a single task, and when that task is over the office is terminated, either by the counsel herself or by action of the Special Division. Unlike other prosecutors, appellant has no ongoing responsibilities that extend beyond the accomplishment of the mission that she was appointed for and authorized by the Special Division to undertake. In our view, these factors relating to the "ideas of tenure, duration . . . and duties" of the independent counsel . . . are sufficient to establish that appellant is an "inferior" officer in the constitutional sense.

This conclusion is consistent with our few previous decisions that considered the question of whether a particular government official is a "principal" or an "inferior" officer. In United States v. Eaton (1898), for example, we approved Department of State regulations that allowed executive officials to appoint a "vice-consul" during the temporary absence of the consul, terming the "vice-consul" a "subordinate officer" notwithstanding the Appointment Clause's specific reference to "Consuls" as principal officers. As we stated, "Because the subordinate officer is charged with the performance of the duty of the superior for a limited time and under special and temporary conditions he is not thereby transformed into the superior and permanent official." In Ex parte Siebold (1880) the Court found that federal "supervisor[s] of elections," who were charged with various duties involving oversight of local congressional elections, were inferior officers for purposes of the Clause. In Go-Bart Importing Co. v. United States (1931), we held that "United States commissioners are inferior officers." These commissioners had various judicial and prosecutorial powers, including the power to arrest and imprison for trial, to issue warrants, and to institute prosecutions under "laws relating to the elective franchise and civil rights." All of this is consistent with our reference in United States v. Nixon (1974) to the office of Watergate Special Prosecutor—whose authority was similar to that of appellant—as a "subordinate officer."

This does not, however, end our inquiry under the Appointments Clause. Appellees argue that even if appellant is an "inferior" officer, the Clause does not empower Congress to place the power to appoint such an officer outside the Executive Branch. They contend that the Clause does not contemplate congressional authorization of "interbranch appointments," in which an officer of one branch is appointed by officers of another branch. The relevant language of the Appointments Clause is worth repeating. It reads: " . . . but the Congress may by Law vest the Appointment of such inferior Officers, as they think proper, in the President alone, in the courts of Law, or in the Heads of Departments." On its face, the language of this "excepting clause" admits of no limitation on innerbranch appointments. Indeed, the inclusion of "as they think proper" seems clearly to give Congress significant discretion to determine whether it is "proper" to vest the appointment of, for example, executive officials in the "courts of Law." We recognized as much in one of our few decisions in this area, Ex parte Siebold, where we stated: "It is no doubt usual and proper to vest the appointment of inferior officers in that department of the government, executive or judicial, or in that particular executive department to which the duties of such officers appertain. But there is no absolute requirement to this effect in the Constitution; and, if there were, it would be difficult in many cases to determine to which department an office properly belonged. . . .

"But as the Constitution stands, the selection of the appointing power, as between the functionaries named, is a matter resting in the discretion of Congress. And, looking at the subject in a practical light, it is perhaps better that it should rest there, than that the country should be harassed by the endless controversies to which a more specific direction on this subject might have given rise." Our only decision to suggest otherwise, Ex parte Hennen (1839), from which the first sentence in the above quotation from Siebold was derived, was discussed in Siebold and distinguished as "not intended to define the constitutional power of Congress in this regard, but rather to express the law or rule by which it should be governed." Outside of these two cases, there is very little, if any, express discussion of the propriety of interbranch appointments in our decisions, and we see no reason now to depart from the holding of Siebold that such appointments are not proscribed by the excepting clause.

We also note that the history of the clause provides no support for appellees' position. Throughout most of the process of drafting the Constitution, the Convention concentrated on the problem of who should have the authority to appoint judges. At the suggestion of James Madison, the Convention adopted a proposal that the Senate should have this authority, . . . and several attempts to transfer the appointment power to the president were rejected. . . . The August 6, 1787, draft of the Constitution reported by the Committee of Detail retained Senate appointment of Supreme Court Judges, provided also for Senate appointment of ambassadors, and vested in the president the authority to "appoint officers in all cases not otherwise provided for by this Constitution." This scheme was maintained until September 4, when the Committee of Eleven reported its suggestions to the Convention. This Committee suggested that the Constitution be amended to state that the president "shall nominate and by and with the advice and consent of the Senate shall appoint ambassadors, and other public Ministers, Judges of the Supreme Court, and all other Officers of the [United States], whose appointments are not otherwise herein provided for." After the addition of "Consuls" to the list, the Committee's proposal was adopted and was subsequently reported to the Convention by the Committee of Style. It was at this point, on September 15, that Gouverneur Morris moved to add the Excepting Clause to Art. II, § 2. The one comment made on this motion was by Madison, who felt that the Clause did not go far enough in that it did not allow Congress to vest appointment powers in ''Superior Officers below Heads of Departments.'' The first vote on Morris's motion ended in tie. It was then put forward a second time, with the urging that ''some such provision [was] too necessary, to be omitted.'' This time the proposal was adopted. As this discussion shows, there was little or no debate on the question of whether the Clause empowers Congress to provide for interbranch appointments, and there is nothing to suggest that the Framers intended to prevent Congress from having that power.

We do not mean to say that Congress' power to provide for interbranch appointments of ''inferior officers'' is unlimited. In addition to separation of powers concerns, which would arise if such provisions for appointment had the potential to impair the constitutional functions assigned to one of the branches, Siebold itself suggested that Congress' decision to vest the appointment power in the courts would be improper if there was some ''incongruity'' between the functions normally performed by the courts and the performance of their duty to appoint. . . . In this case, however, we do not think it impermissible for Congress to vest the power to appoint independent counsels in a specially created federal court. We thus disagree with the Court of Appeals' conclusion that there is an inherent incongruity about a court having the power to appoint prosecutorial officers.* We have recognized that courts may appoint private attorneys to act as prosecutor for judicial contempt judgments. . . . In Go-Bart Importing Co. v. United States (1931), we approved court appointment of United States commissioners, who exercised certain limited prosecutorial powers. In Siebold, as well, we indicated that judicial appointment of federal marshals, who are ''executive officer[s],'' would not be inappropriate. . . . Congress of course was concerned when it created the office of independent counsel with the conflicts of interest that could arise in situations when the Executive Branch is called upon to investigate its own high-ranking officers. If it were to remove the appointing authority from the Executive Branch, the most logical place to put it was in the Judicial Branch. In the light of the Act's provision making the judges of the Special Division ineligible to participate in any matters relating to an independent counsel they have appointed, we do not think that appointment of the independent counsels by the court runs afoul of the constitutional limitation on ''incongruous'' interbranch appointments.

IV.

Appellees next contend that the powers vested in the Special Division by the Act conflict with Article III

of the Constitution. We have long recognized that by the express provision of Article III, the judicial power of the United States is limited to ''Cases'' and ''Controversies.'' See Muskrat v. United States (1911). As a general rule, we have broadly stated that ''executive or administrative duties of a nonjudicial nature may not be imposed on judges holding office under Art. III of the Constitution.'' Buckley, (citing United States v. Ferreira (1852); Hayburn's Case (1792)). The purpose of this limitation is to help ensure the independence of the Judicial Branch and to prevent the judiciary from encroaching into areas reserved for the other branches. . . . With this in mind, we address in turn the various duties given to the Special Division by the Act.

Most importantly, the Act vests in the Special Division the power to choose who will serve as independent counsel and the power to define his or her jurisdiction. Clearly, once it is accepted that the Appointments Clause gives Congress the power to vest the appointment of officials such as the independent counsel in the ''courts of Law,'' there can be no Article III objection to the Special Division's exercise of that power, as the power itself derives from the Appointments Clause, a source of authority for judicial action that is independent of Article III.† Appellees contend, however, that the Division's Appointments Clause powers do not encompass the power to define the independent counsel's jurisdiction. We disagree. In our view, Congress' power under the Clause to vest the ''Appointment'' of inferior officers in the courts may, in certain circumstances, allow Congress to give the courts some discretion in defining the nature and scope of the appointed official's authority. Particularly when, as here, Congress creates a temporary ''office'' the nature and duties of which will by necessity vary with the factual circumstances giving rise to the need for an appointment in the first place, it may vest the power to define the scope of the office in the court as an incident to the appointment of the officer pursuant to the Appointments Clause. This said, we do not think that Congress may give the Division *unlimited* discretion to determine the independent counsel's jurisdiction. In order for the Division's definition of the counsel's jurisdiction to be truly ''incidental'' to its power to appoint, the jurisdiction that the court decides upon must be demonstrably related to the factual circumstances that gave rise to the Attorney General's investigation and request for the appointment of the independent counsel in the particular case.

The Act also vests in the Special Division various powers and duties in relation to the independent counsel that, because they do not involve appointing the counsel or defining her jurisdiction, cannot be said to derive from

---

*Indeed, in light of judicial experience with prosecutors in criminal cases, it could be said that courts are especially well qualified to appoint prosecutors. This is not a case in which judges are given power to appoint an officer in an area in which they have no special knowledge or expertise, as in, for example, a statute authorizing the courts to appoint officials in the Department of Agriculture or the Federal Energy Regulatory Commission.

†We do not think that judicial exercise of the power to appoint, per se, is in any way inconsistent as a functional matter with the courts' exercise of their Article III powers. We note that courts have long participated in the appointment of court officials such as United States commissioners or magistrates . . . without disruption of normal judicial functions. And certainly the court in Ex parte Hennen (1839) deemed it entirely appropriate that a court should have the authority to appoint its own clerk.

the Division's Appointments Clause authority. These duties include granting extensions for the Attorney General's preliminary investigation; receiving the report of the Attorney General at the conclusion of his preliminary investigation; referring matters to the counsel upon request; receiving reports from the counsel regarding expenses incurred; receiving a report from the Attorney General following the removal of an independent counsel; granting attorney's fees upon request to individuals who were investigated but not indicted by an independent counsel; receiving a final report from the counsel; deciding whether to release the counsel's final report to Congress or the public and determining whether any protective orders should be issued; and terminating an independent counsel when his task is completed.

Leaving aside for the moment the Division's power to terminate an independent counsel, we do not think that Article III absolutely prevents Congress from vesting these other miscellaneous powers in the Special Division pursuant to the Act. As we observed above, one purpose of the broad prohibition upon the courts' exercise of "executive or administrative duties of a nonjudicial nature" is to maintain the separation between the judiciary and the other branches of the Federal Government by ensuring that judges do not encroach upon executive or legislative authority or undertake tasks that are more properly accomplished by those branches. In this case, the miscellaneous powers described above do not impermissibly trespass upon the authority of the Executive Branch. Some of these allegedly "supervisory" powers conferred on the court are passive: the Division merely "receives" reports from the counsel or the Attorney General, it is not entitled to act on them or to specifically approve or disapprove of their contents. Other provisions of the Act do require the court to exercise some judgment and discretion, but the powers granted by these provisions are themselves essentially ministerial. The Act simply does not give the Division the power to "supervise" the independent counsel in the exercise of her investigative or prosecutorial authority. And, the functions that the Special Division is empowered to perform are not inherently "Executive"; indeed, they are directly analogous to functions that federal judges perform in other contexts, such as deciding whether to allow disclosure of matters occurring before a grand jury, deciding to extend a grand jury investigation, or awarding attorney's fees.

We are more doubtful about the Special Division's power to terminate the office of the independent counsel. . . . As appellees suggest, the power to terminate, especially when exercised by the Division on its own motion, is "administrative" to the extent that it requires the Special Division to monitor the progress of proceedings of the independent counsel and come to a decision as to whether the counsel's job is "completed." It also is not a power that could be considered typically "judicial," as it has few analogues among the court's more traditional powers. Nonetheless, we do not, as did the Court of Appeals, view this provision as a significant judicial en-

croachment upon executive power or upon the prosecutorial discretion of the independent counsel.

We think that the Court of Appeals overstated the matter when it described the power to terminate as a "broadsword and . . . rapier" that enables the court to "control the pace and depth of the independent counsel's activities." The provision has not been tested in practice, and we do not mean to say that an adventurous special court could not reasonably construe the provision as did the Court of Appeals; but it is the duty of federal courts to construe a statute in order to save it from constitutional infirmities, . . . and to that end we think a narrow construction is appropriate here. The termination provisions of the Act do not give the Special Division anything approaching the power to remove the counsel while an investigation or court proceeding is still underway — this power is vested solely in the Attorney General. As we see it, "termination" may occur only when the duties of the counsel are truly "completed" or "so substantially completed" that there remains no need for any continuing action by the independent counsel. It is basically a device for removing from the public payroll an independent counsel who has served her purpose, but is unwilling to acknowledge the fact. So construed, the Special Division's power to terminate does not pose a sufficient threat of judicial intrusion into matters that are more properly within the Executive's authority to require that the Act be invalidated as inconsistent with Article III.

Nor do we believe, as appellees contend, that the Special Division's exercise of the various powers specifically granted to it under the Act poses any threat to the "impartial and independent federal adjudication of claims within the judicial power of the United States." . . . We reach this conclusion for two reasons. First, the Act as it currently stands gives the Special Division itself no power to review any of the actions of the independent counsel or any of the actions of the Attorney General with regard to the counsel. Accordingly, there is no risk of partisan or biased adjudication of claims regarding the independent counsel by that court. Second, the Act prevents members of the Special Division from participating in "*any* judicial proceeding concerning a matter which involves such independent counsel while such independent counsel is serving in that office or which involves the exercise of such independent counsel's official duties, regardless of whether such independent counsel is still serving in that office." . . . We think both the special court and its judges are sufficiently isolated by these statutory provisions from the review of the activities of the independent counsel so as to avoid any taint of the independence of the judiciary such as would render the Act invalid under Article III.

We emphasize, nevertheless, that the Special Division has *no* authority to take any action or undertake any duties that are not specifically authorized by the Act. The gradual expansion of the authority of the Special Division might in another context be a bureaucratic success story, but it would be one that would have serious constitutional ramifications. The record in other cases involving independent counsels indicates that the Special Division has at times given advisory opinions or issued orders that are not directly authorized by the Act. Two examples of this were cited by the Court of Appeals, which noted that the Special Division issued ''orders'' that ostensibly exempted the independent counsel from conflict of interest laws. . . . In another case, the Division reportedly ordered that a counsel postpone an investigation into certain allegations until the completion of related state criminal proceedings. . . . The propriety of the Special Division's actions in these instances is not before us as such, but we nonetheless think it appropriate to point out not only that there is no authorization for such actions in the Act itself, but that the division's exercise of unauthorized powers risks the transgression of the constitutional limitations of Article III that we have just discussed.

V.

We now turn to consider whether the Act is invalid under the constitutional principle of separation of powers. Two related issues must be addressed: The first is whether the provision of the Act restricting the Attorney General's power to remove the independent counsel to only those instances in which he can show ''good cause,'' taken by itself, impermissibly interferes with the President's exercise of his constitutionally appointed functions. The second is whether, taken as a whole, the Act violates the separation of powers by reducing the President's ability to control the prosecutorial powers wielded by the independent counsel.

A.

Two Terms ago we had occasion to consider whether it was consistent with the separation of powers for Congress to pass a statute that authorized a government official who is removable only by Congress to participate in what we found to be ''executive powers.'' Bowsher v. Synar (1986). We held in Bowsher that ''Congress cannot reserve for itself the power of removal of an officer charged with the execution of the laws except by impeachment.'' A primary antecedent for this ruling was our 1925 decision in Myers v. United States (1926). Myers had considered the propriety of a federal statute by which certain postmasters of the United States could be removed by the President only ''by and with the advice and consent of the Senate.'' There too, Congress' attempt to involve itself in the removal of an executive official was found to be sufficient grounds to render the statute invalid. As we observed in Bowsher, the essence of the decision in Myers was the judgment that the Constitution prevents Congress from ''draw[ing] to itself . . . the power to remove or the right to participate in the exercise of that power. To do this would be to go beyond the words and implications of the [Appointments Clause]

and to infringe the constitutional principle of the separation of governmental powers.''

Unlike both Bowsher and Myers, this case does not involve an attempt by Congress itself to gain a role in the removal of executive officials other than its established powers of impeachment and conviction. The Act instead puts the removal power squarely in the hands of the Executive Branch; an independent counsel may be removed from office, ''only by the personal action of the Attorney General, and only for good cause.'' There is no requirement of congressional approval of the Attorney General's removal decision, though the decision is subject to judicial review. In our view, the removal provisions of the Act make this case more analogous to Humphrey's Executor v. United States (1935) and Wiener v. United States (1958) than to Myers or Bowsher. In Humphrey's Executor, the issue was whether a statute restricting the President's power to remove the commissioners of the Federal Trade Commission only for ''inefficiency, neglect of duty, or malfeasance in office'' was consistent with the Constitution. We stated that whether Congress can ''condition the [President's power of removal] by fixing a definite term and precluding a removal except for cause, will depend upon the character of the office.'' Contrary to the implication of some dicta in Myers, the President's power to remove government officials simply was not ''all-inclusive in respect of civil officers with the exception of the judiciary provided for by the Constitution.'' At least in regard to ''quasi-legislative'' and ''quasi-judicial'' agencies such as the FTC, ''[t]he authority of Congress, in creating [such] agencies, to require them to act in discharge of their duties independently of executive control . . . includes, as an appropriate incident, power to fix the period during which they shall continue in office, and to forbid their removal except for cause in the meantime.'' In Humphrey's Executor, we found it ''plain'' that the Constitution did not give the President ''illimitable power of removal'' over the officers of independent agencies. Were the President to have the power to remove FTC commissioners at will, the ''coercive influence'' of the removal power would ''threate[n] the independence of [the] commission.''

Similarly, in Wiener we considered whether the President had unfettered discretion to remove a member of the War Claims Commission, which had been established by Congress in the War Claims Act of 1948. The Commission's function was to receive and adjudicate certain claims for compensation from those who had suffered personal injury or property damage at the hands of the enemy during World War II. Commissioners were appointed by the President, with the advice and consent of the Senate, but the statute made no provision for the removal of officers, perhaps because the Commission itself was to have a limited existence. As in Humphrey's Executor, however, the Commissioners were entrusted by Congress with adjudicatory powers that were to be exercised free from executive control. In this context, ''Congress did not wish to have hang over the Commission the Damocles' sword of removal by the President for no reason other than that he preferred to have on that Commission men of his own choosing.'' Accordingly, we rejected the President's attempt to remove a Commissioner ''merely because he wanted his own appointees on [the] Commission,'' stating that ''no such power is given to the President directly by the Constitution, and none is impliedly conferred upon him by statute.''

Appellees contend that Humphrey's Executor and Wiener are distinguishable from this case because they did not involve officials who performed a ''core executive function.'' They argue that our decision in Humphrey's Executor rests on a distinction between ''purely executive'' officials and officials who exercise ''quasi-legislative'' and ''quasi-judicial'' powers. In their view, when a ''purely executive'' official is involved, the governing precedent is Myers, not Humphrey's Executor. . . . And, under Myers, the President must have absolute discretion to discharge ''purely'' executive officials at will. . . .

We undoubtedly did rely on the terms ''quasi-legislative'' and ''quasi-judicial'' to distinguish the officials involved in Humphrey's Executor and Wiener from those in Myers, but our present considered view is that the determination of whether the Constitution allows Congress to impose a ''good cause''-type restriction on the President's power to remove an official cannot be made to turn on whether or not that official is classified as ''purely executive.''* The analysis contained in our removal cases is designed not to define rigid categories of those officials who may or may not be removed at will by the President, but to ensure that Congress does not interfere with the President's exercise of the ''executive power'' and his constitutionally appointed duty to ''take care that the laws be faithfully executed'' under Article II. Myers was undoubtedly correct in its holding, and in its broader suggestion that there are some ''purely executive'' officials who must be removable by the President at will if he is to be able to accomplish his constitutional role. But as the Court noted in Wiener, ''The assumption was short-lived that the Myers case recognized the President's inherent constitutional power to remove officials no matter what the relation of the executive to the discharge of their duties and no matter what restrictions Congress may have imposed regarding the nature of their

tenure.'' At the other end of the spectrum from Myers, the characterization of the agencies in Humphrey's Executor and Wiener as ''quasi-legislative'' or ''quasi-judicial'' in large part reflected our judgment that it was not essential to the President's proper execution of his Article II powers that these agencies be headed up by individuals who were removable at will. We do not mean to suggest that an analysis of the functions served by the officials at issue is irrelevant. But the real question is whether the removal restrictions are of such a nature that they impede the President's ability to perform his constitutional duty, and the functions of the officials in question must be analyzed in that light.

Considering for the moment the ''good cause'' removal provision in isolation from the other parts of the Act at issue in this case, we cannot say that the imposition of a ''good cause'' standard for removal by itself unduly trammels on executive authority. There is no real dispute that the functions performed by the independent counsel are ''executive'' in the sense that they are law enforcement functions that typically have been undertaken by officials within the Executive Branch. As we noted above, however, the independent counsel is an inferior officer under the Appointments Clause, with limited jurisdiction and tenure and lacking policymaking or significant administrative authority. Although the counsel exercises no small amount of discretion and judgment in deciding how to carry out her duties under the Act, we simply do not see how the President's need to control the exercise of that discretion is so central to the functioning of the Executive Branch as to require as a matter of constitutional law that the counsel be terminable at will by the President.

Nor do we think that the ''good cause'' removal provision at issue here impermissibly burdens the President's power to control or supervise the independent counsel, as an executive official, in the execution of her duties under the Act. This is not a case in which the power to remove an executive official has been completely stripped from the President, thus providing no means for the President to ensure the ''faithful execution'' of the laws. Rather, because the independent counsel may be terminated for ''good cause,'' the Executive, through the Attorney General, retains ample authority to assure that the counsel is competently performing her statutory responsibilities in a manner that comports with the provisions of the Act. Although we need not decide in this case exactly what is encompassed within the term ''good cause'' under the Act, the legislative history of the removal provision also makes clear that the Attorney General may remove an independent counsel for ''misconduct.'' . . . Here, as with the provision of the Act conferring the appointment authority of the independent counsel on the special court, the congressional determination to limit the removal power of the Attorney General was essential, in the view of Congress, to establish the necessary independence of the office. We do not think that this limitation as it presently stands sufficiently deprives the President of control over the independent

---

*Indeed, this Court has never held that the Constitution prevents Congress from imposing limitations on the President's power to remove all executive officials simply because they wield ''executive'' power. Myers itself expressly distinguished cases in which Congress had chosen to vest the appointment of ''inferior'' executive officials in the head of a department. In such a situation, we saw no specific constitutional impediment to congressionally imposed restrictions on the President's removal powers. See also United States v. Perkins (1886) ('' 'The constitutional authority in Congress to thus vest the appointment [of inferior officers in the heads of departments] implies authority to limit, restrict, and regulate the removal by such laws as Congress may enact in relation to the officers so appointed' '') (quoting the Court of Claims' decision in the case).

counsel to interfere impermissibly with his constitutional obligation to ensure the faithful execution of the laws.*

B.

The final question to be addressed is whether the Act, taken as a whole, violates the principle of separation of powers by unduly interfering with the role of the Executive Branch. Time and again we have reaffirmed the importance in our constitutional scheme of the separation of governmental powers into the three coordinate branches. . . . As we stated in Buckley v. Valeo (1976), the system of separated powers and checks and balances established in the Constitution was regarded by the Framers as "a self-executing safeguard against the encroachment or aggrandizement of one branch at the expense of the other." We have not hesitated to invalidate provisions of law which violate this principle. On the other hand, we have never held that the Constitution requires that the three Branches of Government "operate with absolute independence." . . . In the often-quoted words of Justice Jackson, "While the Constitution diffuses power the better to secure liberty, it also contemplates that practice will integrate the dispersed powers into a workable government. It enjoins upon its branches separateness but interdependence, autonomy but reciprocity." Youngstown Sheet & Tube Co. v. Sawyer (1952) (concurring opinion).

We observe first that this case does not involve an attempt by Congress to increase its own powers at the expense of the Executive Branch. . . . Unlike some of our previous cases, most recently Bowsher v. Synar, this case simply does not pose a "dange[r] of congressional usurpation of Executive Branch functions." Indeed, with the exception of the power of impeachment — which applies to all officers of the United States — Congress retained for itself no powers of control or supervision over an independent counsel. The Act does empower certain members of Congress to request the Attorney General to apply for the appointment of an independent counsel, but the Attorney General has no duty to comply with the request, although he must respond within a certain time limit. Other than that, Congress' role under the Act is limited to receiving reports or other information and oversight of the independent counsel's activities, functions that we have recognized generally as being incidental to the legislative function of Congress. See McGrain v. Daugherty (1927).

Similarly, we do not think that the Act works any *judicial* usurpation of properly executive functions. As should be apparent from our discussion of the Appoint-

ments Clause above, the power to appoint inferior officers such as independent counsels is not in itself an "executive" function in the constitutional sense, at least when Congress has exercised its power to vest the appointment of an inferior office in the "courts of Law." We note nonetheless that under the Act the Special Division has no power to appoint an independent counsel sua sponte; it may only do so upon the specific request of the Attorney General, and the courts are specifically prevented from reviewing the Attorney General's decision not to seek appointment. In addition, once the court has appointed a counsel and defined her jurisdiction, it has no power to supervise or control the activities of the counsel. As we pointed out in our discussion of the Special Division in relation to Article III, the various powers delegated by the statute to the Division are not supervisory or administrative, nor are they functions that the Constitution requires be performed by officials within the Executive Branch. The Act does give a federal court the power to review the Attorney General's decision to remove an independent counsel, but in our view this is a function that is well within the traditional power of the judiciary.

Finally, we do not think that the Act "impermissibly undermine[s]" the powers of the Executive Branch . . . or "disrupts the proper balance between the coordinate branches [by] prevent[ing] the Executive Branch from accomplishing its constitutionally assigned functions," . . . It is undeniable that the Act reduces the amount of control or supervision that the Attorney General and, through him, the President exercises over the investigation and prosecution of a certain class of alleged criminal activity. The Attorney General is not allowed to appoint the individual of his choice; he does not determine the counsel's jurisdiction; and his power to remove a counsel is limited. Nonetheless, the Act does give the Attorney General several means of supervising or controlling the prosecutorial powers that may be wielded by an independent counsel. Most importantly, the Attorney General retains the power to remove the counsel for "good cause," a power that we have already concluded provides the Executive with substantial ability to ensure that the laws are "faithfully executed" by an independent counsel. No independent counsel may be appointed without a specific request by the Attorney General, and the Attorney General's decision not to request appointment if he finds "no reasonable grounds to believe that further investigation is warranted" is committed to his unreviewable discretion. The Act thus gives the Executive a degree of control over the power to initiate an investigation by the independent counsel. In addition, the jurisdiction of the independent counsel is defined with reference to the facts submitted by the Attorney General, and once a counsel is appointed, the Act requires that the counsel abide by Justice Department policy unless it is not "possible" to do so. Notwithstanding the fact that the counsel is to some degree "independent" and free from Executive supervision to a greater extent than other federal prosecutors, in our view these features of the Act

---

*We see no constitutional problem in the fact that the Act provides for judicial review of the removal decision. The purpose of such review is to ensure that an independent counsel is removed only in accordance with the will of Congress as expressed in the Act. The possibility of judicial review does not inject the Judicial Branch into the removal decision, nor does it, by itself, put any additional burden on the President's exercise of executive authority. . . .

give the Executive Branch sufficient control over the independent counsel to ensure that the President is able to perform his constitutionally assigned duties.

VI.

In sum, we conclude today that it does not violate the Appointments Clause for Congress to vest the appointment of independent counsels in the Special Division; that the powers exercised by the Special Division under the Act do not violate Article III; and that the Act does not violate the separation of powers principle by impermissibly interfering with the functions of the Executive Branch. The decision of the Court of Appeals is therefore Reversed.

Justice **Kennedy** took no part in the consideration or decision of this case.

Justice **Scalia** dissenting, said in part:

I.

The present case began when the Legislative and Executive Branches became "embroiled in a dispute concerning the scope of the congressional investigatory power," . . . which — as is often the case with such interbranch conflicts — became quite acrimonious. In the course of oversight hearings into the administration of the Superfund by the Environmental Protection Agency (EPA), two subcommittees of the House of Representatives requested and then subpoenaed numerous internal EPA documents. The President responded by personally directing the EPA Administrator not to turn over certain of the documents, . . . and by having the Attorney General notify the congressional subcommittees of this assertion of executive privilege. . . . In his decision to assert executive privilege, the President was counseled by appellee Olson, who was then Assistant Attorney General of the Department of Justice for the Office of Legal Counsel, a post that has traditionally had responsibility for providing legal advice to the President (subject to approval of the Attorney General). The House's response was to pass a resolution citing the EPA Administrator, who had possession of the documents, for contempt. Contempt of Congress is a criminal offense. . . . The United States Attorney, however, a member of the Executive Branch, initially took no steps to prosecute the contempt citation. Instead, the Executive Branch sought the immediate assistance of the Third Branch by filing a civil action asking the District Court to declare that the EPA Administrator had acted lawfully in withholding the documents under a claim of executive privilege. The District Court declined (in my view correctly) to get involved in the controversy, and urged the other two Branches to try "[c]ompromise and cooperation, rather than confrontation." After further haggling, the two Branches eventually reached an agreement giving the House subcommittees limited access to the contested documents.

Congress did not, however, leave things there. Certain Members of the House remained angered by the confrontation, particularly by the role played by the Department of Justice. Specifically, the Committee remained disturbed by the possibility that the Department had persuaded the President to assert executive privilege despite reservations by the EPA; that the Department had "deliberately and unnecessarily precipitated a constitutional confrontation with Congress"; that the Department had not properly reviewed and selected the documents as to which executive privilege was asserted; that the Department had directed the U. S. Attorney not to present the contempt certification involving the EPA Administrator to a grand jury for prosecution; that the Department had made the decision to sue the House of Representatives; and that the Department had not adequately advised and represented the President, the EPA and the EPA Administrator. . . . Accordingly, staff counsel of the House Judiciary Committee were commissioned (apparently without the knowledge of many of the Committee's Members) to investigate the Justice Department's role in the controversy. That investigation lasted 2½ years, and produced a 3,000-page report issued by the Committee over the vigorous dissent of all but one of its minority-party members. That report, which among other charges questioned the truthfulness of certain statements made by Assistant Attorney General Olson during testimony in front of the Committee during the early stages of its investigation, was sent to the Attorney General along with a formal request that he appoint an independent counsel to investigate Mr. Olson and others.

As a general matter, the Act before us here requires the Attorney General to apply for the appointment of an independent counsel within 90 days after receiving a request to do so, unless he determines within that period that "there are no reasonable grounds to believe that further investigation or prosecution is warranted." . . . As a practical matter, it would be surprising if the Attorney General had any choice (assuming this statute is constitutional) but to seek appointment of an independent counsel to pursue the charges against the principal object of the congressional request, Mr. Olson. Merely the political consequences (to him and the President) of seeming to break the law by refusing to do so would have been substantial. How could it not be, the public would ask, that a 3,000-page indictment drawn by our representatives over 2½ years does not even establish "reasonable grounds to believe" that further investigation or prosecution is warranted with respect to at least the principal alleged culprit? But the Act establishes more than just practical compulsion. Although the Court's opinion asserts that the Attorney General had "no duty to comply with the [congressional] request," that is not entirely accurate. He *had* a duty to comply unless he could conclude that there were "*no reasonable grounds to believe*," not that prosecution was warranted, but merely that "*further investigation*" was warranted, . . . (emphasis added), after a 90-day investigation in which he was prohibited from using such routine investigative techniques as grand juries, plea bargaining, grants of immunity or even subpoenas. . . . The Court also makes much of the fact that "the courts are specifically prevented from reviewing the Attorney General's decision not to seek appointment. . . ." Yes, but *Congress* is not prevented from reviewing it. The context of this statute is acrid with the smell of threatened impeachment. Where, as here, a request for appointment of an independent counsel has come from the Judiciary Committee of either House of Congress, the Attorney General must, if he decides not to seek appointment, explain to that Committee why. . . .

Thus, by the application of this statute in the present case, Congress has effectively compelled a criminal investigation of a high-level appointee of the President in connection with his action arising out of a bitter power dispute between the President and the Legislative Branch. Mr. Olson may or may not be guilty of a crime; we do not know. But we do know that the investigation of him has been commenced, not necessarily because the President or his authorized subordinates believe it is in the interest of the United States, in the sense that it warrants the diversion of resources from other efforts, and is worth the cost in money and in possible damage to other governmental interests; and not even, leaving aside those normally considered factors, because the President or his authorized subordinates necessarily believe that an investigation is likely to unearth a violation worth prosecuting; but only because the Attorney General cannot affirm, as Congress demands, that there are *no reasonable grounds to believe* that further investigation is warranted. The decision regarding the scope of that further investigation, its duration, and, finally, whether or not prosecution should ensue, are likewise beyond the control of the President and his subordinates.

II.

If to describe this case is not to decide it, the concept of a government of separate and coordinate powers no longer has meaning. The Court devotes most of its attention to such relatively technical details as the Appointments Clause and the removal power, addressing briefly and only at the end of its opinion the separation of powers. As my prologue suggests, I think that has it backwards. Our opinions are full of the recognition that it is the principle of separation of powers, and the inseparable corollary that each department's "defense must . . . be made commensurate to the danger of attack," . . . which gives comprehensible content to the appointments clause, and determines the appropriate scope of the removal power. Thus, while I will subsequently discuss why our appointments and removal jurisprudence does not support today's holding, I begin with a consideration of the fountainhead of that jurisprudence, the separation and equilibration of powers. . . .

"The executive Power shall be vested in a President of the United States."

As I described at the outset of this opinion, this

does not mean *some of* the executive power, but *all of* the executive power. It seems to me, therefore, that the decision of the Court of Appeals invalidating the present statute must be upheld on fundamental separation-of-powers principles if the following two questions are answered affirmatively: (1) Is the conduct of a criminal prosecution (and of an investigation to decide whether to prosecute) the exercise of purely executive power? (2) Does the statute deprive the President of the United States of exclusive control over the exercise of that power? Surprising to say, the Court appears to concede an affirmative answer to both questions, but seeks to avoid the inevitable conclusion that since the statute vests some purely executive power in a person who is not the President of the United States it is void.

The Court concedes that "[t]here is no real dispute that the functions performed by the independent counsel are 'executive.' " . . . She is vested with the "full power and independent authority to exercise all *investigative and prosecutorial* function and powers of the Department of Justice [and] the Attorney General." . . . (emphasis added). Governmental investigation and prosecution of crimes is a quintessentially executive function. See . . . Buckley v. Valeo (1976); United States v. Nixon (1974).

As for the second question, whether the statute before us deprives the President of exclusive control over that quintessentially executive activity: The Court does not, and could not possibly, assert that it does not. That is indeed the whole object of the statute. Instead, the Court points out that the President, through his Attorney General, has at least *some* control. That concession is alone enough to invalidate the statute, but I cannot refrain from pointing out that the Court greatly exaggerates the extent of that "some" presidential control. "Most importan[t]" among these controls, the Court asserts, is the Attorney General's "power to remove the counsel for 'good cause.' " This is somewhat like referring to shackles as an effective means of locomotion. As we recognized in Humphrey's Executor v. United States (1935) — indeed, what Humphrey's Executor was all about — limiting removal power to "good cause" is an impediment to, not an effective grant of, presidential control. We said that limitation was necessary with respect to members of the Federal Trade Commission, which we found to be "an agency of the legislative and judicial departments," and "wholly disconnected from the executive department," because "it is quite evident that one who holds his office only during the pleasure of another, cannot be depended upon to maintain an attitude of independence against the latter's will." What we in Humphrey's Executor found to be a means of eliminating presidential control, the Court today considers the "most importan[t]" means of assuring presidential control. Congress, of course, operated under no such illusion when it enacted this statute, describing the "good cause" limitation as "protecting the independent counsel's ability to act independently of the President's direct control" since it permits removal only for "misconduct." . . .

Moving on to the presumably "less important" controls that the President retains, the Court notes that no independent counsel may be appointed without a specific request from the Attorney General. As I have discussed above, the condition that renders such a request mandatory (inability to find "no reasonable grounds to believe" that further investigation is warranted) is so insubstantial that the Attorney General's discretion is severely confined. And once the referral is made, it is for the Special Division to determine the scope and duration of the investigation. . . . And in any event, the limited power over referral is irrelevant to the question whether, *once appointed*, the independent counsel exercises executive power free from the President's control. Finally, the Court points out that the Act directs the independent counsel to abide by general Justice Department policy, except when not "possible." . . . The exception alone shows this to be an empty promise. Even without that, however, one would be hard put to come up with many investigative or prosecutorial "policies" (other than those imposed by the Constitution or by Congress through law) that are absolute. Almost all investigative and prosecutorial decisions — including the ultimate decision whether, after a technical violation of the law has been found, prosecution is warranted — involve the balancing of innumerable legal and practical considerations. Indeed, even political considerations (in the nonpartisan sense) must be considered, as exemplified by the recent decision of an independent counsel to subpoena the former Ambassador of Canada, producing considerable tension in our relations with that country. . . . Another preeminently political decision is whether getting a conviction in a particular case is worth the disclosure of national security information that would be necessary. The Justice Department and our intelligence agencies are often in disagreement on this point, and the Justice Department does not always win. The present Act even goes so far as specifically to take the resolution of that dispute away from the President and give it to the independent counsel. . . . In sum, the balancing of various legal, practical and political considerations, none of which is absolute, is the very essence of prosecutorial discretion. To take this away is to remove the core of the prosecutorial function, and not merely "some" presidential control.

As I have said, however, it is ultimately irrelevant *how much* the statute reduces presidential control. The case is over when the Court acknowledges, as it must, that "[i]t is undeniable that the Act reduces the amount of control or supervision that the Attorney General and, through him, the President exercises over the investigation and prosecution of a certain class of alleged criminal activity." It effects a revolution in our constitutional jurisprudence for the Court, once it has determined that (1) purely executive functions are at issue here, and (2) those functions have been given to a person whose actions are not fully within the supervision and control of the President, nonetheless to proceed further to sit in judgment of whether "the President's need to control the exercise of [the independent counsel's] discretion is *so*

central to the functioning of the Executive Branch" as to require complete control (emphasis added), whether the conferral of his powers upon someone else "*sufficiently* deprives the President of control over the independent counsel to interfere impermissibly with [his] constitutional obligation to ensure the faithful execution of the laws," (emphasis added), and whether "the Act give[s] the Executive Branch *sufficient* control over the independent counsel to ensure that the President is able to perform his constitutionally assigned duties," (emphasis added). It is not for us to determine, and we have never presumed to determine, how much of the purely executive powers of government must be within the full control of the President. The Constitution prescribes that they *all* are. . . .

The Court has, nonetheless, replaced the clear constitutional prescription that the executive power belongs to the President with a "balancing test." What are the standards to determine how the balance is to be struck, that is, how much removal of presidential power is too much? Many countries of the world get along with an Executive that is much weaker than ours — in fact, entirely dependent upon the continued support of the legislature. Once we depart from the text of the Constitution, just where short of that do we stop? The most amazing feature of the Court's opinion is that it does not even purport to give an answer. It simply *announces*, with no analysis, that the ability to control the decision whether to investigate and prosecute the President's closest advisors, and indeed the President himself, is not "so central to the functioning of the Executive Branch" as to be constitutionally required to be within the President's control. Apparently that is so because we say it is so. Having abandoned as the basis for our decision-making the text of Article II that "the executive Power" must be vested in the President, the Court does not even attempt to craft a *substitute* criterion — a "justiciable standard," see, e.g., Baker v. Carr (1962); Coleman v. Miller (1939), however remote from the Constitution — that today governs, and in the future will govern, the decision of such questions. Evidently, the governing standard is to be what might be called the unfettered wisdom of a majority of this Court, revealed to an obedient people on a case-by-case basis. This is not only not the government of laws that the Constitution established; it is not a government of laws at all. . . .

III.

As I indicated earlier, the basic separation-of-powers principles I have discussed are what give life and content to our jurisprudence concerning the President's power to appoint and remove officers. The same result of unconstitutionality is therefore plainly indicated by our caselaw in these areas. Article II, § 2, cl. 2 of the Constitution provides as follows: "[The President] shall nominate, and by and with the Advice and Consent of the Senate, shall appoint Ambassadors, other public Ministers and Consuls, Judges of the supreme Court, and all other Officers of the United States, whose Appointments are not herein otherwise provided for, and which shall be established by Law: but the Congress may by Law vest the Appointment of such inferior Officers, as they think proper, in the President alone, in the Courts of Law, or in the Heads of Departments." Because appellant (who all parties and the Court agree is an officer of the United States) was not appointed by the President with the advice and consent of the Senate, but rather by the Special Division of the United States Court of Appeals, her appointment is constitutional only if (1) she is an "inferior" officer within the meaning of the above clause, and (2) Congress may vest her appointment in a court of law.

As to the first of these inquiries, the Court does not attempt to "decide exactly" what establishes the line between principal and "inferior" officers, but is confident that, whatever the line may be, appellant "clearly falls on the 'inferior officer' side" of it. The Court gives three reasons: *First*, she "is subject to removal by a higher Executive branch official," namely the Attorney General. *Second*, she is "empowered by the Act to perform only certain, limited duties." *Third*, her office is "limited in jurisdiction" and "limited in tenure."

The first of these lends no support to the view that appellant is an inferior officer. Appellant is removable only for "good cause" or physical or mental incapacity. . . . By contrast, most (if not all) *principal* officers in the Executive Branch may be removed by the President *at will*. I fail to see how the fact that appellant is more difficult to remove than most principal officers helps to establish that she is an inferior officer. And I do not see how it could possibly make any difference to her superior or inferior status that the President's limited power to remove her must be exercised through the Attorney General. If she were removable at will by the Attorney General, then she would be subordinate to him and thus properly designated as inferior; but the Court essentially admits that she is not subordinate. If it were common usage to refer to someone as "inferior" who is subject to removal for cause by another, then one would say that the President is "inferior" to Congress.

The second reason offered by the Court — that appellant performs only certain, limited duties — may be relevant to whether she is an inferior officer, but it mischaracterizes the extent of her powers. As the Court states: "Admittedly, the Act delegates to appellant [the] '*full power and independent authority to exercise all investigative and prosecutorial functions and powers of the department of justice.*' ". . . (emphasis added). Moreover, in addition to this general grant of power she is given a broad range of specifically enumerated powers, including a power not even the Attorney General possesses: to "contes[t] in court . . . any claim of privilege or attempt to withhold evidence on grounds of national security." . . . Once all of this is "admitted," it seems to me impossible to maintain that appellant's authority is so "limited" as to render her an inferior officer. The Court seeks to brush this away by asserting that the independent counsel's power does not include any authority to "formulate policy for the Government or the Executive Branch." But the same could be said for all officers

of the Government, with the single exception of the President. All of them only formulate policy within their respective spheres of responsibility — as does the independent counsel, who must comply with the policies of the Department of Justice only "to the extent possible." . . .

The final set of reasons given by the Court for why the independent counsel clearly is an inferior officer emphasizes the limited nature of her jurisdiction and tenure. Taking the latter first, I find nothing unusually limited about the independent counsel's tenure. To the contrary, unlike most high-ranking Executive Branch officials, she continues to serve until she (or the Special Division) decides that her work is substantially completed. . . . This particular independent prosecutor has already served more than two years, which is at least as long as many cabinet officials. As to the scope of her jurisdiction, there can be no doubt that is small (though far from unimportant). But within it she exercises more than the full power of the Attorney General. The Ambassador to Luxembourg is not anything less than a principal officer, simply because Luxembourg is small. And the federal judge who sits in a small district is not for that reason "inferior in rank and authority." If the mere fragmentation of Executive responsibilities into small compartments suffices to render the heads of each of those compartments inferior officers, then Congress could deprive the President of the right to appoint his chief law-enforcement officer by dividing up the Attorney General's responsibilities among a number of "lesser" functionaries. . . .

IV.

I will not discuss at any length why the restrictions upon the removal of the independent counsel also violate our established precedent dealing with that specific subject. . . . I cannot avoid commenting, however, about the essence of what the Court has done to our removal jurisprudence today.

There is of course no provision in the Constitution stating who may remove executive officers, except the provisions for removal by impeachment. Before the present decision it was established, however, (1) that the President's power to remove principal officers who exercise purely executive powers could not be restricted, see Myers v. United States (1926); and (2) that his power to remove inferior officers who exercise purely executive powers, and whose appointment Congress had removed from the usual procedure of presidential appointment with Senate consent, could be restricted, at least where the appointment had been made by an officer of the Executive Branch; United States v. Perkins (1886).

The Court could have resolved the removal power issue in this case by simply relying upon its erroneous conclusion that the independent counsel was an inferior officer, and then extending our holding that the removal of inferior officers appointed by the Executive can be restricted, to a new holding that even the removal of inferior officers appointed by the courts can be restricted.

That would in my view be a considerable and unjustified extension, giving the Executive full discretion in *neither* the selection *nor* the removal of a purely executive officer. The course the Court has chosen, however, is even worse.

Since our 1935 decision in Humphrey's Executor v. United States — which was considered by many at the time the product of an activist, anti-New Deal court bent on reducing the power of President Franklin Roosevelt — it has been established that the line of permissible restriction upon removal of principal officers lies at the point at which the powers exercised by those officers are no longer purely executive. Thus, removal restrictions have been generally regarded as lawful for so-called "independent regulatory agencies," such as the Federal Trade Commission, . . . the Interstate Commerce Commission, . . . and the Consumer Products Safety Commission, . . . which engage substantially in what has been called the "quasi-legislative activity" of rulemaking, and for members of Article I courts, such as the Court of Military Appeals, . . . who engage in the "quasi-judicial" function of adjudication. It has often been observed, correctly in my view, that the line between "purely executive" functions and "quasi-legislative" or "quasi judicial" functions is not a clear one or even a rational one. . . . Bowsher v. Synar (1986) (White, J., dissenting). . . . But at least it permitted the identification of certain officers, and certain agencies, whose functions were entirely within the control of the President. Congress had to be aware of that restriction in its legislation. Today, however, Humphrey's Executor is swept into the dustbin of repudiated constitutional principles. "[O]ur present considered view," the Court says, "is that the determination of whether the Constitution allows Congress to impose a 'good cause' type restriction on the President's power to remove an official cannot be made to turn on whether or not that official is classified as 'purely executive.' " What Humphrey's Executor (and presumably Myers) really means, we are now told, is not that there are any "rigid categories of those officials who may or may not be removed at will by the President," but simply that Congress cannot "interfere with the President's exercise of the 'executive power' and his constitutionally appointed duty to 'take care that the laws be faithfully executed.' "

One can hardly grieve for the shoddy treatment given today to Humphrey's Executor, which, after all, accorded the same indignity (with much less justification) to Chief Justice Taft's opinion 10 years earlier in Myers v. United States, — gutting, in six quick pages devoid of textual or historical precedent for the novel principle it set forth, a carefully researched and reasoned 70-page opinion. It is in fact comforting to witness the reality that he who lives by the ipse dixit dies by the ipse dixit. But one must grieve for the Constitution. Humphrey's Executor at least had the decency formally to observe the constitutional principle that the President had to be the repository of *all* executive power, which, as Myers carefully explained, necessarily means that he must be able to discharge those who do not perform ex-

ecutive functions according to his liking. As we noted in Bowsher, once an officer is appointed " 'it is only the authority that can remove him, and not the authority that appointed him, that he must fear and, in the performance of his functions, obey.' " . . . By contrast, "our present considered view" is simply that *any* Executive officer's removal can be restricted, so long as the President remains "able to accomplish his constitutional role." There are now no lines. If the removal of a prosecutor, the virtual embodiment of the power to "take care that the laws be faithfully executed," can be restricted, what officer's removal cannot? This is an open invitation for Congress to experiment. What about a special Assistant Secretary of State, with responsibility for one very narrow area of foreign policy, who would not only have to be confirmed by the Senate but could also be removed only pursuant to certain carefully designed restrictions? Could this possibly render the President "[un]able to accomplish his constitutional role"? Or a special Assistant Secretary of Defense for Procurement? The possibilities are endless, and the Court does not understand what the separation of powers, what "[a]mbition . . . counteract[ing] ambition," . . . is all about, if it does not expect Congress to try them. As far as I can discern from the Court's opinion, it is now open season upon the President's removal power for all executive officers, with not even the superficially principled restriction of Humphrey's Executor as cover. The Court essentially says to the President "Trust us. We will make sure that you are able to accomplish your constitutional role." I think the Constitution gives the President — and the people — more protection than that.

V.

The purpose of the separation and equilibration of powers in general, and of the unitary Executive in particular, was not merely to assure effective government but to preserve individual freedom. Those who hold or have held offices covered by the Ethics in Government Act are entitled to that protection as much as the rest of us, and I conclude my discussion by considering the effect of the Act upon the fairness of the process they receive. Only someone who has worked in the field of law enforcement can fully appreciate the vast power and the immense discretion that are placed in the hands of a prosecutor with respect to the objects of his investigation. Justice Robert Jackson, when he was Attorney General under President Franklin Roosevelt, described it in a memorable speech to United States Attorneys, as follows:

"There is a most important reason why the prosecutor should have, as nearly as possible, a detached and impartial view of all groups in his community. Law enforcement is not automatic. It isn't blind. One of the greatest difficulties of the position of prosecutor is that he must pick his cases, because no prosecutor can even investigate all of the cases in which he receives complaints. If the Department of Justice were to make even a pretense of reaching every probable violation of federal law, ten times its present staff will be inadequate. We know that no local police force can strictly enforce the traffic laws, or it would arrest half the driving population on any given morning. What every prosecutor is practically required to do is to select the cases for prosecution and to select those in which the offense is the most flagrant, the public harm the greatest, and the proof the most certain.

"If the prosecutor is obliged to choose his case, it follows that he can choose his defendants. Therein is the most dangerous power of the prosecutor: that he will pick people that he thinks he should get, rather than cases that need to be prosecuted. With the law books filled with a great assortment of crimes, a prosecutor stands a fair chance of finding at least a technical violation of some act on the part of almost anyone. In such a case, it is not a question of discovering the commission of a crime and then looking for the man who has committed it, it is a question of picking the man and then searching the law books, or putting investigators to work, to pin some offense on him. It is in this realm — in which the prosecutor picks some person whom he dislikes or desires to embarrass, or selects some group of unpopular persons and then looks for an offense, that the greatest danger of abuse of prosecuting power lies. It is here that law enforcement becomes personal, and the real crime becomes that of being unpopular with the predominant or governing group, being attached to the wrong political views, or being personally obnoxious to or in the way of the prosecutor himself." R. Jackson, The Federal Prosecutor, Address Delivered at the Second Annual Conference of United States Attorneys, April 1, 1940.

Under our system of government, the primary check against prosecutorial abuse is a political one. The prosecutors who exercise this awesome discretion are selected and can be removed by a President, whom the people have trusted enough to elect. Moreover, when crimes are not investigated and prosecuted fairly, nonselectively, with a reasonable sense of proportion, the President pays the cost in political damage to his administration. If federal prosecutors "pick people that [they] thin[k] [they] should get, rather than cases that need to be prosecuted," if they amass many more resources against a particular prominent individual, or against a particular class of political protesters, or against members of a particular political party, than the gravity of the alleged offenses or the record of successful prosecutions seems to warrant, the unfairness will come home to roost in the Oval Office. I leave it to the reader to recall the examples of this in recent years. That result, of course, was precisely what the Founders had in mind when they provided that all executive powers would be exercised by a *single* Executive. As Hamilton put it, "[t]he ingredients which constitute safety in the republican sense are a due dependence on the people, and a due responsibility." . . . The President is directly dependent on the people, and since there is only *one* President, *he* is responsible. The people know whom to blame, whereas "one of the weightiest objections to a plurality in the executive . . . is that it tends to conceal faults and destroy responsibility."

That is the system of justice the rest of us are entitled to, but what of that select class consisting of present or former high-level executive-branch officials? If an allegation is made against them of any violation of any federal criminal law (except Class B or C misdemeanors or infractions) the Attorney General must give it his attention. That in itself is not objectionable. But if, after a 90-day investigation without the benefit of normal investigatory tools, the Attorney General is unable to say that there are "no reasonable grounds to believe" that further investigation is warranted, a process is set in motion that is *not* in the full control of persons "dependent on the people," and whose flaws cannot be blamed on the President. An independent counsel is selected, and the scope of her authority prescribed, by a panel of judges. What if they are politically partisan, as judges have been known to be, and select a prosecutor antagonistic to the administration, or even to the particular individual who has been selected for this special treatment? There is no remedy for that, not even a political one. Judges, after all, have life tenure, and appointing a sure-fire enthusiastic prosecutor could hardly be considered an impeachable offense. So if there is anything wrong with the selection, there is effectively no one to blame. The independent counsel thus selected proceeds to assemble a staff. As I observed earlier, in the nature of things this has to be done by finding lawyers who are willing to lay aside their current careers for an indeterminate amount of time, to take on a job that has no prospect of permanence and little prospect for promotion. One thing is certain, however: it involves investigating and perhaps prosecuting a particular individual. Can one imagine a less equitable manner of fulfilling the Executive responsibility to investigate and prosecute? What would be the reaction if, in an area not covered by this statute, the Justice Department posted a public notice inviting applicants to assist in an investigation and possible prosecution of a certain prominent person. Does this not invite what Justice Jackson described as "picking the man and then searching the law books, or putting investigators to work, to pin some offense on him"? To be sure, the investigation must relate to the area of criminal offense specified by the life-tenured judges. But that has often been (and nothing prevents it from being) very broad — and should the independent counsel or her staff come up with something beyond that scope, nothing prevents her from asking the judges to expand her authority or, if that does not work, referring it to the Attorney General, whereupon the whole process would recommence and, if there was "reasonable basis to believe" that further investigation was warranted, that new offense would be referred to the Special Tribunal, which would in all likelihood assign it to the same independent counsel. It seems to me not conducive to fairness. But even if it were entirely evident that unfairness was in fact the result — the judges hostile to the administration, the independent counsel an old foe of the President, the staff refugees from the recently defeated administration — *there would be no one account-*

able to the public to whom the blame could be assigned.

I do not mean to suggest that anything of this sort (other than the inevitable self-selection of the prosecutory staff) occurred in the present case. I know and have the highest regard for the judges on the Special Division, and the independent counsel herself is a woman of accomplishment, impartiality and integrity. But the fairness of a process must be adjudged on the basis of what it permits to happen, not what it produced in a particular case. It is true, of course, that a similar list of horribles could be attributed to an ordinary Justice Department prosecution — a vindictive prosecutor, an antagonistic staff, etc. But the difference is the difference that the Founders envisioned when they established a single Chief Executive accountable to the people: the blame can be assigned to someone who can be punished.

THOMPSON v. OKLAHOMA

101 L. Ed. 2d 702 (1988)

When the Supreme Court in Furman v. Georgia (1972) struck down the death penalty as a cruel and unusual punishment, only two justices felt that the country's standard of decency and humanity had progressed to the point where it would no longer tolerate the execution of persons for crime. The three justices who joined them to form the majority concentrated instead on the procedures by which very few of those convicted were selected for execution instead of life imprisonment. Justice Stewart characterized the unpredictable imposition of the penalty as "cruel and unusual in the same way that being struck by lightning is cruel and unusual." The fact that seven members of the Court were willing to accept the death penalty, provided it was done right, prompted many state legislatures to rewrite their laws in an effort to meet these objections. Finally, in Gregg v. Georgia (1976), the Court held valid an execution carried out under a charge to a jury which the Court held made a serious effort to identify those murders as serious enough to warrant the death penalty. To impose the penalty the jury had to find one or more of a series of aggravating circumstances: (1) that the murder was committed during the commission of two other capital felonies, (2) that the murder was committed for money, or (3) that it was "outrageously and wantonly vile, horrible and inhuman." The jury found the first and second of these circumstances and returned a verdict of death.

Once the Court decided that execution did not constitute a cruel and unusual punishment, two kinds of problems arose to plague it. One involved the culpability of persons who had conspired to commit the murder but had not actually done the killing. In 1978 in Lockett v. Ohio the Court had held that the death penalty could not be inflicted on the driver of a get-away car where the victim of an attempted robbery had been shot. See note to Gregg v. Georgia. In 1982 in Enmund v. Florida, a case almost identical in facts to the Lockett case, the Court in

a five-to-four decision reaffirmed its holding in Lockett. Noting that only eight states allow the death penalty to be imposed "solely because the defendant somehow participated in a robbery in the course of which a murder was committed" and a survey showed "only 6 cases out of 362 where a nontriggerman felony murderer was executed," the Court concluded that society had rejected "the death penalty for accomplice liability in felony murders." Relying on its conclusion that "cruel and unusual" is to be judged in terms of present standards, the Court held that "the Eighth Amendment [forbids] imposition of the death penalty on one . . . who aids and abets a felony in the course of which a murder is committed by others but who does not himself kill, attempt to kill, or intend that a killing will take place or that lethal force will be employed."

Cabana v. Bullock (1986) involved a new facet of the problem. Here the accused had held the victim's head while the murderer had hit him first with a whisky bottle and then with a cement block. The issue was which court should decide if the test of Enmund had been met, and Justices White, Burger, Powell, Rehnquist and O'Connor concluded that the Mississippi state courts should make the initial determination, rather than a federal court on a writ of habeas corpus.

Another problem that arose out of the Gregg decision was how horrible a murder must be before the death penalty could be invoked, and how this degree of horror was to be determined. Furman had struck down the death penalty because a sentencing jury was free to impose death without any guidance or restriction whatever. In Gregg the Court upheld the death penalty because the Georgia legislature had devised a method of limiting jury discretion. It narrowed the "class of murderers subject to capital punishment by specifying 10 statutory aggravating circumstances, one of which must be found by the jury to exist beyond a reasonable doubt before a death sentence can ever be imposed." The Court was satisfied that the jury could no longer "reach a finding of the defendant's guilt, and then, without guidance or direction, decide whether he should live or die."

However, Georgia law does not require that the jury give any special weight to the aggravating circumstance which it finds; this was attacked in Zant v. Stephens (1983) on the ground that once a murderer was found to belong in a class which made him eligible for the death penalty, the sentencing jury was free from all restriction. The Supreme Court rejected this argument. "Respondent argues that the mandate of Furman is violated by a scheme that permits the jury to exercise unbridled discretion in determining whether the death penalty should be imposed after it has found that the defendant is a member of the class made eligible for that penalty by statute. But that argument could not be accepted without overruling our specific holding in Gregg." There was no suggestion that Gregg should be reconsidered.

In Lowenfield v. Phelps (1988) the Court moved to merge the "aggravating circumstances" needed to justify the death penalty with the definition of the crime of murder. In Louisiana the definition of first degree mur-

der includes (among others) *"when the offender has a specific intent to kill or to inflict great bodily harm upon more than one persons"* and the same language is used to define one of the ten aggravating circumstances from which the jury could find ground to recommend execution. In Lowenfield's case this was the only aggravating circumstance found, and she argued that by merely finding her guilty she was automatically placed among those eligible for the death penalty. The Court rejected her argument. *"The use of 'aggravating circumstances,' is not an end in itself, but a means of genuinely narrowing the class of death-eligible persons and thereby channeling the jury's discretion. We see no reason why this narrowing function may not be performed by jury findings at either the sentencing phase of the trial or the guilt phase."*

The Court has made clear that the aggravating circumstances must have some real narrowing effect. In Godfrey v. Georgia (1980) the Court had held void an execution based on the finding that the murder was "outrageously or wantonly vile, horrible and inhuman." The statute included the words "in that it involved torture, depravity of mind, or an aggravated battery to the victim," but despite the charge to the jury these words had been omitted from the jury's verdict. Godfrey was reaffirmed in Maynard v. Cartwright (1988) where the aggravating circumstance was that the murder was "especially heinous, atrocious, or cruel." In this case the jury had found a second, valid, aggravating circumstance; but since such circumstances are weighed by the jury against any mitigating factors, the presence of the invalid circumstance rendered the death verdict void.

Query: *Could a state, by defining first degree murder entirely in terms of aggravating circumstances, make automatically eligible for the death penalty all those convicted and thus enable a sentencing jury to act with unfettered discretion?*

The present case raises moral and philosophical questions similar to those raised by Furman. All of the arguments in favor of executing adult murderers would appear to apply equally to children, as would all the arguments against such executions. It is difficult to apply Justice Marshall's argument that the rejection of the death penalty is a sign of evolving standards of decency in a maturing civilization to a distinction based on age. On what basis does one conclude that it is inhumane and uncivilized to execute a six-year-old for murder while considering it all right to execute a twenty-year-old? And assuming there is a difference, at what age should the line be drawn? Is there an age below which a child cannot become a "street-wise, hardened criminal" subject to no greater consideration than any adult? The Court clearly has one more difficult problem to wrestle with in the area of cruel and unusual punishments.

Justice **Stevens** announced the judgment of the Court, and delivered an opinion in which Justice **Brennan**, Justice —**Marshall**, and Justice **Blackmun** joined, saying in part:

Petitioner was convicted of first-degree murder and sentenced to death. The principal question presented is whether the execution of that sentence would violate the constitutional prohibition against the infliction of "cruel and unusual punishments" because petitioner was only 15 years old at the time of his offense.

I.

Because there is no claim that the punishment would be excessive if the crime had been committed by an adult, only a brief statement of facts is necessary. In concert with three older persons, petitioner actively participated in the brutal murder of his former brother-in-law in the early morning hours of January 23, 1983. The evidence disclosed that the victim had been shot twice, and that his throat, chest, and abdomen had been cut. He also had multiple bruises and a broken leg. His body had been chained to a concrete block and thrown into a river where it remained for almost four weeks. Each of the four participants was tried separately and each was sentenced to death.

Because petitioner was a "child" as a matter of Oklahoma law, the district attorney filed a statutory petition . . . seeking an order finding "that said child is competent and had the mental capacity to know and appreciate the wrongfulness of his [conduct]." After a hearing, the trial court concluded "that there are virtually no *reasonable* prospects for rehabilitation of William Wayne Thompson within the juvenile system and that William Wayne Thompson should be held accountable for his acts as if he were an adult and should be certified to stand trial as an adult." (emphasis in original). . . .

At the penalty phase of the trial, the prosecutor asked the jury to find two aggravating circumstances: that the murder was especially heinous, atrocious, or cruel; and that there was a probability that the defendant would commit criminal acts of violence that would constitute a continuing threat to society. The jury found the first, but not the second, and fixed petitioner's punishment at death.

The Court of Criminal Appeals affirmed the conviction and sentence. . . . We granted certiorari to consider whether a sentence of death is cruel and unusual punishment for a crime committed by a 15-year-old child. . . .

II.

The authors of the Eighth Amendment drafted a categorical prohibition against the infliction of cruel and unusual punishments, but they made no attempt to define the contours of that category. They delegated that task to future generations of judges who have been guided by the "evolving standards of decency that mark the progress of a maturing society." Trop v. Dulles (1958) (plurality opinion) (Warren, C. J.). In performing that task the Court has reviewed the work product of state legislatures and sentencing juries, and has carefully considered the reasons why a civilized society may accept or reject the death penalty in certain types of cases. Thus, in confronting the question whether the youth of the defendant — more specifically, the fact that he was less than 16 years old at the time of his offense — is a sufficient reason for denying the state the power to sentence him to death, we first review relevant legislative enactments, then refer to jury determinations, and finally explain why these indicators of contemporary standards of decency confirm our judgment that such a young person is not capable of acting with the degree of culpability that can justify the ultimate penalty.

III.

Justice Powell has repeatedly reminded us of the importance of "the experience of mankind, as well as the long history of our law, recognizing that there *are* differences which must be accommodated in determining the rights and duties of children as compared with those of adults. Examples of this distinction abound in our law: in contracts, in torts, in criminal law and procedure, in criminal sanctions and rehabilitation, and in the right to vote and to hold office." . . . Oklahoma recognizes this basic distinction in a number of its statutes. Thus, a minor is not eligible to vote, to sit on a jury, to marry without parental consent, or to purchase alcohol or cigarettes. Like all other States, Oklahoma has developed a juvenile justice system in which most offenders under the age of 18 are not held criminally responsible. Its statutes do provide, however, that a 16- or 17-year-old charged with murder and other serious felonies shall be considered an adult. Other than the special certification procedure that was used to authorize petitioner's trial in this case "as an adult," apparently there are no Oklahoma statutes, either civil or criminal, that treat a person under 16 years of age as anything but a "child."

The line between childhood and adulthood is drawn in different ways by various States. There is, however, complete or near unanimity among all 50 States and the District of Columbia in treating a person under 16 as a minor for several important purposes. In no State may a 15-year-old vote or serve on a jury. Further, in all but one State a 15-year-old may not drive without parental consent, and in all but four States a 15-year-old may not marry without parental consent. Additionally, in those States that have legislated on the subject, no one under age 16 may purchase pornographic materials (50 States), and in most States that have some form of legalized gambling, minors are not permitted to participate without parental consent (42 States). Most relevant, however, is the fact that all States have enacted legislation designating the maximum age for juvenile court jurisdiction at no less than 16. All of this legislation is consistent with the experience of mankind, as well as the long history of our law, that the normal 15-year-old is not prepared to assume the full responsibilities of an adult.

Most state legislatures have not expressly confronted the question of establishing a minimum age for imposition of the death penalty.* In 14 States, capital punishment is not authorized at all, and in 19 others capital punishment is authorized but no minimum age is expressly stated in the death penalty statute. One might argue on the basis of this body of legislation that there is no chronological age at which the imposition of the death penalty is unconstitutional and that our current standards of decency would still tolerate the execution of 10-year-old children.† We think it self-evident that such an argument is unacceptable; indeed, no such argument has been advanced in this case. If, therefore, we accept the premise that some offenders are simply too young to be put to death, it is reasonable to put this group of statutes to one side because they do not focus on the question of where the chronological age line should be drawn. When we confine our attention to the 18 States that have expressly established a minimum age in their death-penalty statutes, we find that all of them require that the defendant have attained at least the age of 16 at the time of the capital offense.

The conclusion that it would offend civilized standards of decency to execute a person who was less than 16 years old at the time of his or her offense is consistent with the views that have been expressed by respected professional organizations, by other nations that share our Anglo-American heritage, and by the leading members of the Western European community. Thus, the American Bar Association and the American Law Institute have formally expressed their opposition to the death penalty for juveniles. Although the death penalty has not been entirely abolished in the United Kingdom or New

---

*Almost every State, and the federal government, has set a minimum age at which juveniles accused of committing serious crimes can be waived from juvenile court into criminal court. . . . The dissent's focus on the presence of these waiver ages in jurisdictions that retain the death penalty but that have not expressly set a minimum age for the death sentence distorts what is truly at issue in this case. Consider the following example: The States of Michigan, Oregon, and Virginia have all determined that a 15-year-old may be waived from juvenile to criminal court when charged with first-degree murder. . . . However, in Michigan, that 15-year-old may not be executed — because the State has abolished the death penalty — in Oregon; that 15-year-old may not be executed — because the State has expressly set a minimum age of 18 for executions — and in Virginia that 15-year-old may be executed — because the State has a death penalty and has not expressly addressed the issue of minimum age for execution. That these three States have all set a 15-year-old waiver floor for first-degree murder tells us that the States consider 15-year-olds to be old enough to be tried in criminal court for serious crimes (or too old to be dealt with effectively in juvenile court), *but tells us nothing about the judgment these states have made regarding the appropriate punishment for such youthful offenders.* As a matter of fact, many States in the Union have waiver ages below 16, including many of the States that have either abolished the death penalty or that have set an express minimum age for the death penalty at 16 or higher. . . .

†It is reported that a 10-year-old black child was hanged in Louisiana in 1855 and a Cherokee Indian child of the same age was hanged in Arkansas in 1885. . . .

Zealand (it has been abolished in Australia, except in the State of New South Wales, where it is available for treason and piracy), in neither of those countries may a juvenile be executed. The death penalty has been abolished in West Germany, France, Portugal, The Netherlands, and all of the Scandanavian countries, and is available only for exceptional crimes such as treason in Canada, Italy, Spain, and Switzerland. Juvenile executions are also prohibited in the Soviet Union.

IV.

The second societal factor the Court has examined in determining the acceptability of capital punishment to the American sensibility is the behavior of juries. In fact, the infrequent and haphazard handing out of death sentences by capital juries was a prime factor underlying our judgment in Furman v. Georgia (1972), that the death penalty, as then administered in unguided fashion, was unconstitutional.

While it is not known precisely how many persons have been executed during the 20th century for crimes committed under the age of 16, a scholar has recently compiled a table revealing this number to be between 18 and 20. All of these occurred during the first half of the century, with the last such execution taking place apparently in 1948. In the following year this Court observed that this "whole country has traveled far from the period in which the death sentence was an automatic and commonplace result of convictions. . . ." Williams v. New York (1949). The road we have traveled during the past four decades — in which thousands of juries have tried murder cases — leads to the unambiguous conclusion that the imposition of the death penalty on a 15-year-old offender is now generally abhorrent to the conscience of the community.

Department of Justice statistics indicate that during the years 1982 through 1986 an average of over 16,000 persons were arrested for willful criminal homicide (murder and non-negligent manslaughter) each year. Of that group of 82,094 persons, 1,393 were sentenced to death. Only five of them, including the petitioner in this case, were less than 16 years old at the time of the offense. Statistics of this kind can, of course, be interpreted in different ways, but they do suggest that these five young offenders have received sentences that are "cruel and unusual in the same way that being struck by lightning is cruel and unusual." Furman v. Georgia (Stewart, J., concurring).

V.

"Although the judgments of legislatures, juries, and prosecutors weigh heavily in the balance, it is for us ultimately to judge whether the Eighth Amendment permits imposition of the death penalty" on one such as petitioner who committed a heinous murder when he was only 15 years old. Enmund v. Florida (1982). In making that judgment, we first ask whether the juvenile's culpability should be measured by the same standard as that of an adult, and then consider whether the application of the death penalty to this class of offenders "measurably contributes" to the social purposes that are served by the death penalty.

It is generally agreed "that punishment should be directly related to the personal culpability of the criminal defendant." California v. Brown (1987) (O'Connor, J., concurring). There is also broad agreement on the proposition that adolescents as a class are less mature and responsible than adults. We stressed this difference in explaining the importance of treating the defendant's youth as a mitigating factor in capital cases: "But youth is more than a chronological fact. It is a time and condition of life when a person may be most susceptible to influence and to psychological damage. Our history is replete with laws and judicial recognition that minors, especially in their earlier years, generally are less mature and responsible than adults. Particularly 'during the formative years of childhood and adolescence, minors often lack the experience, perspective, and judgment' expected of adults. Bellotti v. Baird (1979)." Eddings v. Oklahoma [1982].

To add further emphasis to the special mitigating force of youth, Justice Powell quoted the following passage from the 1978 Report of the Twentieth Century Fund Task Force on Sentencing Policy Toward Young Offenders: "Adolescents, particularly in the early and middle teen years, are more vulnerable, more impulsive, and less self-disciplined than adults. Crimes committed by youths may be just as harmful to victims as those committed by older persons, but they deserve less punishment because adolescents may have less capacity to control their conduct and to think in long-range terms than adults. Moreover, youth crime as such is not exclusively the offender's fault; offenses by the young also represent a failure of family, school, and the social system, which share responsibility for the development of America's youth." Thus, the Court has already endorsed the proposition that less culpability should attach to a crime committed by a juvenile than to a comparable crime committed by an adult. The basis for this conclusion is too obvious to require extended explanation. Inexperience, less education, and less intelligence make the teenager less able to evaluate the consequences of his or her conduct while at the same time he or she is much more apt to be motivated by mere emotion or peer pressure than is an adult. The reasons why juveniles are not trusted with the privileges and responsibilities of an adult also explain why their irresponsible conduct is not as morally reprehensible as that of an adult.

"The death penalty is said to serve two principal social purposes: retribution and deterrence of capital crimes by prospective offenders." Gregg v. Georgia (1976) (joint opinion of Stewart, Powell, and Stevens, JJ.). In Gregg we concluded that as "an expression of society's moral outrage at particularly offensive conduct," retribution was not "inconsistent with our respect for the dignity of men." Given the lesser culpability of the juvenile offender, the teenager's capacity for growth, and society's fiduciary obligations to its children, this conclusion is simply inapplicable to the execution of a 15-year-old offender.

For such a young offender, the deterrence rationale is equally unacceptable. The Department of Justice statistics indicate that about 98 percent of the arrests for willful homicide involved persons who were over 16 at the time of the offense. Thus, excluding younger persons from the class that is eligible for the death penalty will not diminish the deterrent value of capital punishment for the vast majority of potential offenders. And even with respect to those under 16 years of age, it is obvious that the potential deterrent value of the death sentence is insignificant for two reasons. The likelihood that the teenage offender has made the kind of cost-benefit analysis that attaches any weight to the possibility of execution is so remote as to be virtually nonexistent. And, even if one posits such a cold-blooded calculation by a 15-year-old, it is fanciful to believe that he would be deterred by the knowledge that a small number of persons his age have been executed during the 20th century. In short, we are not persuaded that the imposition of the death penalty for offenses committed by persons under 16 years of age has made, or can be expected to make, any measurable contribution to the goals that capital punishment is intended to achieve. It is, therefore, ''nothing more than the purposeless and needless imposition of pain and suffering,'' Coker v. Georgia [1977], and thus an unconstitutional punishment.

VI. . . .

The judgment of the Court of Criminal Appeals is vacated and the case is remanded with instructions to enter an appropriate order vacating petitioner's death sentence.

· It is so ordered.

Justice **Kennedy** took no part in the consideration or decision of this case.

Justice **O'Connor**, concurring in the judgment, said in part:

The plurality and dissent agree on two fundamental propositions: that there is some age below which a juvenile's crimes can never be constitutionally punished by death, and that our precedents require us to locate this age in light of the '' 'evolving standards of decency that mark the progress of maturing society.' '' . . . I accept both principles. The disagreements between the plurality and the dissent rest on their different evaluations of the evidence available to us about the relevant social consensus. Although I believe that a national consensus forbidding the execution of any person for a crime committed before the age of 16 very likely does exist, I am reluctant to adopt this conclusion as a matter of constitutional law without better evidence than we now possess. Because I conclude that the sentence in this case can and should be set aside on narrower grounds than those adopted by the plurality, and because the grounds on which I rest should allow us to face the more general question when better evidence is available, I concur only in the judgment of the Court.

I.

Both the plurality and the dissent look initially to the decisions of American legislatures for signs of a national consensus about the minimum age at which a juvenile's crimes may lead to capital punishment. Although I agree with the dissent's contention that these decisions should provide the most reliable signs of a society-wide consensus on this issue, I cannot agree with the dissent's interpretation of the evidence.

The most salient statistic that bears on this case is that every single American legislature that has expressly set a minimum age for capital punishment has set that age at 16 or above. When one adds these 18 States to the 14 that have rejected capital punishment completely it appears that almost two-thirds of the state legislatures have definitely concluded that no 15-year-old should be exposed to the threat of execution. . . . [(Also,] an additional two States with death penalty statutes on their books seem to have abandoned capital punishment in practice). Where such a large majority of the state legislatures have unambiguously outlawed capital punishment for 15-year-olds, and where no legislature in this country has affirmatively and unequivocally endorsed such a practice, strong counterevidence would be required to persuade me that a national consensus against this practice does not exist.

The dissent argues that it has found such counterevidence in the laws of the 19 States that authorize capital punishment without setting any statutory minimum age. If we could be sure that each of these 19 state legislatures had deliberately chosen to authorize capital punishment for crimes committed at the age of 15, one could hardly suppose that there is a settled national consensus opposing such a practice. In fact, however, the statistics relied on by the dissent may be quite misleading. When a legislature provides for some 15-year olds to be processed through the adult criminal justice system, and capital punishment is available for adults in that jurisdiction, the death penalty becomes at least theoretically applicable to such defendants. This is how petitioner was rendered death-eligible, and the same possibility appears to exist in 18 other States. As the plurality points out, however, it does not necessarily follow that the legislatures in those jurisdictions have deliberately concluded that it would be appropriate to impose capital punishment on 15-year-olds (or on even younger defendants who may be tried as adults in some jurisdictions).

There are many reasons, having nothing whatsoever to do with capital punishment, that might motivate a legislature to provide as a general matter for some 15-year-olds to be channeled into the adult criminal justice process. The length or conditions of confinement available in the juvenile system, for example, might be considered inappropriate for serious crimes or for some recidivists. Similarly, a state legislature might conclude that very dangerous individuals, whatever their age, should not be confined in the same facility with more vulnerable juvenile offenders. Such reasons would suggest nothing about the appropriateness of capital punishment for 15-year-olds. The absence of any such implication is illustrated by the very States that the dissent cites as evidence of a trend toward lowering the age at which juveniles may be punished as adults. New York, which recently adopted legislation allowing juveniles as young as 13 to be tried as adults, does not authorize capital punishment under any circumstances. In New Jersey, which now permits some 14- year-olds to be tried as adults, the minimum age for capital punishment is 18. In both cases, therefore, the decisions to lower the age at which some juveniles may be treated as adults must have been based on reasons quite separate from the legislatures' views about the minimum age at which a crime should render a juvenile eligible for the death penalty.

Nor have we been shown evidence that other legislatures directly considered the fact that the interaction between their capital punishment statutes and their juvenile offender statutes could in theory lead to executions for crimes committed before the age of 16. The very real possibility that this result was not considered is illustrated by the recent federal legislation, cited by the dissent, which lowers to 15 the age at which a defendant may be tried as an adult. . . . Because a number of federal statutes have long provided for capital punishment, this legislation appears to imply that 15-year-olds may now be rendered death-eligible under federal law. The dissent does not point to any legislative history suggesting that Congress considered this implication when it enacted the Comprehensive Crime Control Act. The apparent absence of such legislative history is especially striking in light of the fact that the United States has agreed by treaty to set a minimum age of 18 for capital punishment in certain circumstances. . . . Perhaps even more striking is the fact that the United States Senate recently passed a bill authorizing capital punishment for certain drug offenses, but prohibiting application of this penalty to persons below the age of 18 at the time of the crime. . . . Whatever other implications the ratification of Article 68 of the Geneva Convention may have, and whatever effects the Senate's recent action may eventually have, both tend to undercut any assumption that the Comprehensive Crime Control Act signals a decision by Congress to authorize the death penalty for some 15-year-old felons.

Thus, there is no indication that any legislative body in this country has rendered a considered judgment approving the imposition of capital punishment on juveniles who were below the age of 16 at the time of the offense. It nonetheless is true, although I think the dissent has overstated its significance, that the Federal Government and 19 States have adopted statutes that appear to have the legal effect of rendering some of these juveniles death-eligible. That fact is a real obstacle in the way of concluding that a national consensus forbids this

practice. It is appropriate, therefore, to examine other evidence that might indicate whether or not these statutes are inconsistent with settled notions of decency in our society.

In previous cases, we have examined execution statistics, as well as data about jury determinations, in an effort to discern whether the application of capital punishment to certain classes of defendants has been so aberrational that it can be considered unacceptable in our society. See, e.g., Coker v. Georgia (1977) (plurality opinion); Enmund v. Florida (1982) (O'Connor, J., dissenting). In this case, the plurality emphasize that four decades have gone by since the last execution of a defendant who was younger than 16 at the time of the offense, and that only 5 out of 1,393 death sentences during a recent 5-year period involved such defendants. Like the statistics about the behavior of legislatures, these execution and sentencing statistics support the inference of a national consensus opposing the death penalty for 15-year-olds, but they are not dispositive.

A variety of factors, having little or nothing to do with any individual's blameworthiness, may cause some groups in our population to commit capital crimes at a much lower rate than other groups. The statistics relied on by the plurality, moreover, do not indicate how many juries have been asked to impose the death penalty for crimes committed below the age of 16, or how many times prosecutors have exercised their discretion to refrain from seeking the death penalty in cases where the statutory prerequisites might have been proved. Without such data, raw execution and sentencing statistics cannot allow us reliably to infer that juries are or would be significantly more reluctant to impose the death penalty on 15-year-olds than on similarly situated older defendants.

Nor, finally, do I believe that this case can be resolved through the kind of disproportionality analysis employed in Part V. of the plurality opinion. I agree that "proportionality requires a nexus between the punishment imposed and the defendant's blameworthiness." . . . Granting the plurality's other premise — that adolescents are generally less blameworthy than adults who commit similar crimes — it does not necessarily follow that all 15-year-olds are incapable of the moral culpability that would justify the imposition of capital punishment. Nor has the plurality reduced evidence demonstrating that 15-year-olds as a class are inherently incapable of being deterred from major crimes by the prospect of the death penalty.

Legislatures recognize the relative immaturity of adolescents, and we have often permitted them to define age-based classes that take account of this qualitative difference between juveniles and adults. . . . The special qualitative characteristics of juveniles that justify legislatures in treating them differently from adults for many other purposes are also relevant to Eighth Amendment proportionality analysis. These characteristics, however, vary widely among different individuals of the same age, and I would not substitute our inevitably subjective judgment about the best age at which to draw a line in the capital punishment context for the judgments of the nation's legislatures. . . .

The history of the death penalty instructs that there is danger in inferring a settled societal consensus from statistics like those relied on in this case. In 1846, Michigan became the first State to abolish the death penalty for all crimes except treason, and Rhode Island soon thereafter became the first jurisdiction to abolish capital punishment completely. . . . In succeeding decades, other American States continued the trend towards abolition, especially during the years just before and during World War I. . . .

In 1972, when this Court heard arguments on the constitutionality of the death penalty, such statistics might have suggested that the practice had become a relic, implicitly rejected by a new societal consensus. Indeed, counsel urged the Court to conclude ''that the number of cases in which the death penalty is imposed, as compared with the number of cases in which it is statutorily available, reflects a general revulsion toward the penalty that would lead to its repeal if only it were more generally and widely enforced.'' Furman v. Georgia (1972) (Burger, C. J., dissenting). We now know that any inference of a societal consensus rejecting the death penalty would have been mistaken. But had this Court then declared the existence of such a consensus, and outlawed capital punishment, legislatures would very likely not have been able to revive it. The mistaken premise of the decision would have been frozen into constitutional law, making it difficult to refute and even more difficult to reject.

The step that the plurality would take today is much narrower in scope, but it could conceivably reflect an error similar to the one we were urged to make in Furman. The day may come when we must decide whether a legislature may deliberately and unequivocally resolve upon a policy authorizing capital punishment for crimes committed at the age of 15. In that event, we shall have to decide the Eighth Amendment issue that divides the plurality and the dissent in this case, and we shall have to evaluate the evidence of societal standards of decency that is available to us at that time. In my view, however, we need not and should not decide the question today.

II.

Under the Eighth Amendment, the death penalty has been treated differently from all other punishments. . . . Among the most important and consistent themes in this Court's death penalty jurisprudence is the need for special care and deliberation in decisions that may lead to the imposition of that sanction. The Court has accordingly imposed a series of unique substantive and procedural restrictions designed to ensure that capital punishment is not imposed without the serious and calm reflection that ought to precede any decision of such gravity and finality.

The restrictions that we have required under the Eighth Amendment affect both legislatures and the sentencing authorities responsible for decisions in individual cases. Neither automatic death sentences for certain crimes, for example, nor statutes committing the sentencing decision to the unguided discretion of judges or juries, have been upheld. . . .

The case before us today raises some of the same concerns that have led us to erect barriers to the imposition of capital punishment in other contexts. Oklahoma has enacted a statute that authorizes capital punishment for murder, without setting any minimum age at which the commission of murder may lead to the imposition of that penalty. The State has also, but quite separately, provided that 15-year-old murder defendants may be treated as adults in some circumstances. Because it proceeded in this manner, there is a considerable risk that the Oklahoma legislature either did not realize that its actions would have the effect of rendering 15-year-old defendants death-eligible or did not give the question the serious consideration that would have been reflected in the explicit choice of some minimum age for death-eligibility. Were it clear that no national consensus forbids the imposition of capital punishment for crimes committed before the age of 16, the implicit nature of the Oklahoma legislature's decision would not be constitutionally problematic. In the peculiar circumstances we face today, however, the Oklahoma statutes have presented this Court with a result that is of very dubious constitutionality, and they have done so without the earmarks of careful consideration that we have required for other kinds of decisions leading to the death penalty. In this unique situation, I am prepared to conclude that petitioner and others who were below the age of 16 at the time of their offense may not be executed under the authority of a capital punishment statute that specifies no minimum age at which the commission of a capital crime can lead to the offender's execution. . . .

For the reasons stated in this opinion, I agree that petitioner's death sentence should be vacated, and I therefore concur in the judgment of the Court.

Justice **Scalia**, with whom Chief Justice **Rehnquist** and Justice **White** join, dissenting, said in part:

If the issue before us today were whether an automatic death penalty for conviction of certain crimes could be extended to individuals younger than 16 when they commit the crimes, thereby preventing individualized consideration of their maturity and moral responsibility, I would accept the plurality's conclusion that such a practice is opposed by a national consensus, sufficiently uniform and of sufficiently long standing, to render it cruel and usual punishment within the meaning of the Eighth Amendment. We have already decided as much, and more, in Lockett v. Ohio (1978). I might even agree with the plurality's conclusion if the question were whether a person under 16 when he commits a crime can be deprived of the benefit of a rebuttable presumption that he is not mature and responsible enough to be punished as an adult. The question posed here, however, is radically different from both of these. It is whether there is a national consensus that no criminal so much as one day under 16, after individuated consideration of his circumstances, including the overcoming of a presumption that he should not be tried as an adult, can possibly be deemed mature and responsible enough to be punished with death for any crime. Because there seems to me no plausible basis for answering this last question in the affirmative, I respectfully dissent.

I.

I begin by restating the facts since I think that a fuller account of William Wayne Thompson's participation in the murder, and of his certification to stand trial as an adult, is helpful in understanding the case. . . .

[Justice Scalia here introduces a detailed description including the defendant's previous criminal record, the brutality of the crime, and the justice system's conclusion that he was incorrigible.]

II.

A.

As the foregoing history of this case demonstrates, William Wayne Thompson is not a juvenile caught up in a legislative scheme that unthinkingly lumped him together with adults for purposes of determining that death was an appropriate penalty for him, and for his crime. To the contrary, Oklahoma first gave careful consideration to whether, in light of his young age, he should be subjected to the normal criminal system at all. That question having been answered affirmatively, a jury then considered whether, despite his young age, his maturity and moral responsibility were sufficiently developed to justify the sentence of death. In upsetting this particularized judgment on the basis of a constitutional absolute, the plurality pronounces it to be a fundamental principle of our society that no one who is as little as one day short of his 16th birthday can have sufficient maturity and moral responsibility to be subjected to capital punishment for any crime. As a sociological and moral conclusion that is implausible; and it is doubly implausible as an interpretation of the United States Constitution.

The text of the Eighth Amendment, made applicable to the states by the Fourteenth, prohibits the imposition of "cruel and unusual punishments." The plurality does not attempt to maintain that this was originally understood to prohibit capital punishment for crimes committed by persons under the age of 16; the evidence is unusually clear and unequivocal that it was not. The age at which juveniles could be subjected to capital punishment was explicitly addressed in Blackstone's Commentaries on the Laws of England, published in 1769 and widely accepted at the time the Eighth Amendment was adopted as an accurate description of the common law. According to Blackstone, not only was 15 above the age (viz., 7) at which capital punishment could theoretically be imposed; it was even above the age (14) up to which there was a rebuttable presumption of incapacity to commit a capital (or any other) felony. . . . The historical practice in this country conformed with the common-law understanding that 15-year-olds were not categorically immune from commission of capital crimes. One scholar has documented 22 executions, between 1642 and 1899, for crimes committed under the age of 16. . . .

Necessarily, therefore, the plurality seeks to rest its holding on the conclusion that Thompson's punishment as an adult is contrary to the "evolving standards of decency that mark the progress of a maturing society." Trop v. Dulles (1958) (plurality opinion) (Warren, C. J.). Of course the risk of assessing evolving standards is that it is all too easy to believe that evolution has culminated in one's own views. To avoid the danger we have, when making such an assessment in prior cases, looked for objective signs of how today's society views a particular punishment. Furman v. Georgia (1972) (Brennan, J., concurring). . . . The most reliable objective signs consist of the legislation that the society has enacted. It will rarely if ever be the case that the members of this Court will have a better sense of the evolution in views of the American people than do their elected representatives.

It is thus significant that, only four years ago, in the Comprehensive Crime Control Act of 1984, Congress expressly addressed the effect of youth upon the imposition of criminal punishment, and changed the law in precisely the opposite direction from that which the plurality's perceived evolution in social attitudes would suggest: It lowered from 16 to 15 the age at which a juvenile's case can, "in the interest of justice," be transferred from juvenile court to federal District Court, enabling him to be tried and punished as an adult. . . . This legislation was passed in light of Justice Department testimony that many juvenile delinquents were "cynical, street-wise, repeat offenders, indistinguishable, except for their age, from their adult criminal counterparts," . . . and that in 1979 alone juveniles under the age of fifteen, i.e., almost a year *younger* than Thompson, had committed a total of 206 homicides nationwide, more than 1,000 forcible rapes, 10,000 robberies and 10,000 aggravated assaults. Since there are federal death-penalty statutes which have not been determined to be unconstitutional, adoption of this new legislation could at least theoretically result in the imposition of the death penalty upon a 15-year-old. There is, to be sure, no reason to believe that the Members of Congress had the death penalty specifically in mind; but that does not alter the reality of what federal law now on its face permits. Moreover, if it is appropriate to go behind the face of the statutes to the subjective intentions of those who enacted them, it would be strange to find the consensus regarding criminal liability of juveniles to be moving in the direction the plurality perceives for capital punishment, while moving in precisely the opposite direction for all other penalties.*

Turning to legislation at the state level, one observes the same trend of *lowering* rather than raising the age of juvenile criminal liability. As for the state status quo with respect to the death penalty in particular: The plurality chooses to "confine [its] attention" to the fact that all 18 of the States that establish a minimum age for capital punishment have chosen at least 16. But it is beyond me why an accurate analysis would not include within the computation the larger number of States (19) that have determined that no minimum age for capital punishment is appropriate, leaving that to be governed by their general rules for the age at which juveniles can be criminally responsible. A survey of state laws shows, in other words, that a majority of the States for which the issue exists (the rest do not have capital punishment) are of the view that death is not different insofar as the age of juvenile criminal responsibility is concerned. And the latter age, while presumed to be 16 in all the States, can, in virtually all the States, be less than 16 when individuated consideration of the particular case warrants it. Thus, what Oklahoma has done here is precisely what the majority of capital-punishment States would do.

When the Federal Government, and almost 40% of the States, including a majority of the States that include capital punishment as a permissible sanction, allow for the imposition of the death penalty on any juvenile who has been tried as an adult, which category can include juveniles under 16 at the time of the offense, it is obviously impossible for the plurality to rely upon any evolved societal consensus discernible in legislation—or at least discernible in the legislation of *this* society, which is assuredly all that is relevant. Thus, the plurality falls back upon what it promises will be an examination of "the behavior of juries." It turns out not to be that, perhaps because of the inconvenient fact that no fewer than 5 murderers who committed their crimes under the age of 16 were sentenced to death, in five different States, between the years 1984 and 1986. . . . Instead, the plurality examines the statistics on capital executions, which are of course substantially lower than those for capital sentences because of various factors, most notably the exercise of executive clemency. . . . Those statistics show, unsurprisingly, that capital punishment for persons who committed crimes under the age of 16 is rare. We are not discussing whether the Constitution requires such procedures as will continue to cause it to be rare, but whether the Constitution prohibits it entirely. The plurality takes it to be persuasive evidence that social attitudes have changed to embrace such a prohibition

— changed so clearly and permanently as to be irrevocably enshrined in the Constitution — that in this century all of the 18 to 20 executions of persons below 16 when they committed crimes occurred before 1948.

. . . A society less ready to impose the death penalty, and entirely unwilling to impose it without individualized consideration, will of course pronounce death for a crime committed by a person under 16 very rarely. There is absolutely no basis, however, for attributing that phenomenon to a modern consensus that such an execution should never occur — any more than it would have been accurate to discern such a consensus in 1927 when, despite a level of total executions almost five times higher than that of the post-1950 period, there had been no execution for crime committed by juveniles under the age of 16 for almost 17 years. That that did not reflect a new societal absolute was demonstrated by the fact that in approximately the next 17 years there were 10 such executions.

In sum, the statistics of executions demonstrate nothing except the fact that our society has always agreed that executions of 15-year-old criminals should be rare, and in more modern times has agreed that they (like all other executions) should be even rarer still. . . .

B.

Having avoided any attempt to justify its holding on the basis of the original understanding of what was "cruel and unusual punishment," and having utterly failed in justifying its holding on the basis of "evolving standards of decency" evidenced by "the work product of state legislatures and sentencing juries," the plurality proceeds, in Part V of the opinion, to set forth its views regarding the desirability of ever imposing capital punishment for a murder committed by a 15-year-old. That discussion begins with the recitation of propositions upon which there is "broad agreement" within our society, namely, that "punishment should be directly related to the personal culpability of the criminal defendant," and that "adolescents as a class are less mature and responsible than adults." It soon proceeds, however, to the conclusion that "[g]iven the lesser culpability of the juvenile offender, the teenager's capacity for growth, and society's fiduciary obligations to its children," none of the rationales for the death penalty can apply to the execution of a 15-year-old criminal, so that it is " 'nothing more than the purposeless and needless imposition of pain and suffering.' " . . . On this, as we have seen, there is assuredly no general agreement. Nonetheless, the plurality would make it one of the fundamental laws governing our society solely because they have an " 'abiding conviction' " that it is so. . . .

Because I think the views of this Court on the policy questions discussed in Part V. of the plurality opinion to be irrelevant, I make no attempt to refute them. It suffices to say that there is another point of view, suggested in the following passage written by our esteemed former colleague Justice Powell, whose views the plurality several times invokes for support: "Minors who be-

---

*The concurrence disputes the significance of Congress' lowering of the federal waiver age by pointing to a recently approved Senate bill that would set a minimum age of 18 before capital punishment could be imposed for certain narcotics related offenses. This bill has not, however, been passed by the House of Representatives and signed into law by the President. Even if it eventually were, it would not result in the setting of a minimum age of 18 for any of the other federal death penalty statutes. . . . It would simply reflect a judgment by Congress that the death penalty is inappropriate for juvenile narcotics offenders.

come embroiled with the law range from the very young up to those on the brink of majority. Some of the older minors become fully 'street-wise,' hardened criminals, deserving no greater consideration than that properly accorded all persons suspected of crime." Fare v. Michael C. (1979) (Powell, J., dissenting). The view that it is possible for a 15-year-old to come within this category uncontestably prevailed when the Eighth and Fourteenth Amendments were adopted, and, judging from the actions of the society's democratically elected representatives, still persuades a substantial segment of the people whose "evolving standards of decency" we have been appointed to discern rather than decree. It is not necessary, as the plurality's opinion suggests, that "we [be] persuaded" of the correctness of the people's views.

III.

If I understand Justice O'Connor's separate concurrence correctly, it agrees (1) that we have no constitutional authority to set aside this death penalty unless we can find it contrary to a firm national consensus that persons younger than 16 at the time of their crime cannot be executed, and (2) that we cannot make such a finding. It does not, however, reach the seemingly inevitable conclusion that (3) we therefore have no constitutional authority to set aside this death penalty. Rather, it proceeds (in Part II) to state that since (a) we have treated the death penalty "differently from all other punishments," imposing special procedural and substantive protections not required in other contexts, and (b) although we cannot actually *find* any national consensus forbidding execution for crimes committed under 16, there may *perhaps* be such a consensus, therefore (c) the Oklahoma statutes plainly authorizing the present execution by treating 15-year-old felons (after individuated findings) as adults, and authorizing execution of adults, are not adequate, and what is needed is a statute explicitly stating that "15-year-olds can be guilty of capital crimes."

First, of course, I do not agree with (b) — that there is any doubt about the nonexistence of a national consensus. The concurrence produces the doubt only by arbitrarily refusing to believe that what the laws of the Federal Government and 19 States clearly provide for represents a "considered judgment." Second, I do not see how (c) follows from (b) — how the problem of doubt about whether what the Oklahoma laws permit is contrary to a firm national consensus and therefore unconstitutional is solved by making *absolutely sure* that the citizens of Oklahoma really want to take this unconstitutional action. And finally, I do not see how the procedural and substantive protections referred to in (a) provide any precedent for what is done in (c). Those special protections for capital cases, such as the prohibition of unguided discretion, Gregg v. Georgia (1976) (opinion of Stewart, Powell, and Stevens, JJ.) and the prohibition of automatic death sentences for certain crimes, Woodson v. North Carolina (1976) (opinion of Stewart, Powell, and Stevens, JJ.), were not drawn from a hat, but were thought to be (once again) what a national con-

sensus required. I am unaware of any national consensus, and the concurrence does not suggest the existence of any, that the death penalty for felons under 16 can only be imposed by a single statute that explicitly addresses that subject. . . .

It could not possibly be the concurrence's concern that this death sentence is a fluke — a punishment not really contemplated by Oklahoma law but produced as an accidental result of its interlocking statutes governing capital punishment and the age for treating juveniles as adults. The statutes, and their consequences, are quite clear. The present case, moreover, is of such prominence that it has received extensive coverage not only in the Oklahoma press but nationally. It would not even have been necessary for the Oklahoma legislature to act in order to remedy the miscarriage of its intent, if that is what this sentence was. The Governor of Oklahoma, who can certainly recognize a frustration of the will of the citizens of Oklahoma more readily than we, would certainly have used his pardon power if there was some mistake here. What the concurrence proposes is obviously designed to nullify rather than effectuate the will of the people of Oklahoma, even though the concurrence cannot find that will to be unconstitutional.

ARIZONA v. ROBERSON

100 L. Ed. 2d 704 (1988)

Miranda v. Arizona was decided in 1966 by a Court headed by Chief Justice Earl Warren. Its purpose was to ensure that the underprivileged, uneasy in the presence of the police and unfamiliar with their rights under the law, would be told of their right to legal counsel and assured that they did not need to answer questions until such counsel was provided. Police and prosecutors alike viewed this class of people as providing the bulk of the "criminal element" and were concerned that providing them with lawyers would make it exceedingly difficult if not impossible to get them to confess to their crimes and would thus reduce the number of convictions. The political pressure provided by the law enforcement agencies, abetted by those who viewed themselves as possible victims of crime, has resulted over the years in a watering down of the protections afforded by the Miranda rule. (See the note to the Miranda case.)

In New York v. Quarles (1984) the Court held the Miranda warnings unnecessary in cases in which the public safety was at stake. The police had cornered a suspected criminal in a supermarket at about 12:30 A.M., handcuffed him and frisked him and found an empty shoulder holster under his arm. They asked him where the gun was and he nodded in the direction of some empty cartons and said, "The gun is over there." The police retrieved the gun and then read the defendant his Miranda rights. He waived right to counsel, answered the questions asked, and was convicted with the use of the statements given both before and after the Miranda warnings were given.

In holding valid the use of the statements the Court announced and justified what it called a "public safety" exception to the Miranda rule. "In such a situation, if the police are required to recite the familiar Miranda warnings before asking the whereabouts of the gun, suspects in Quarles' position might well be deterred from responding. Procedural safeguards that deter a suspect from responding were deemed acceptable in Miranda in order to protect the Fifth Amendment privilege; when the primary social cost of those added protections is the possibility of fewer convictions, the Miranda majority was willing to bear that cost. Here, had Miranda warnings deterred Quarles from responding . . . the cost would have been something more than merely the failure to obtain evidence. . . . Officer Kraft needed an answer to his question not simply to make his case against Quarles but to ensure that additional danger to the public did not result from the concealment of the gun in a public area. We conclude that the need for answers to questions in a situation posing a threat to the public safety outweighs the need for the prophylactic rule protecting the Fifth Amendment's privilege against self-incrimination."

In Oregon v. Elstad (1985) the Court refused to hold that a confession given without Miranda warnings made invalid later confessions made after Miranda warnings. When an 18-year old boy was asked by police about his involvement in a burglary and admitted his involvement, the Court rejected his contention that this made inadmissible later statements made after Miranda warnings. "Respondent's contention that his confession was tainted by the earlier failure of the police to provide Miranda warnings and must be excluded as 'fruit of the poisonous tree' assumes the existence of a constitutional violation. This figure of speech is drawn from Wong Sun v. United States (1963), in which the Court held that evidence and witnesses discovered as a result of a search in violation of the Fourth Amendment must be excluded from evidence. The Wong Sun doctrine applies as well when the fruit of the Fourth Amendment violation is a confession. It is settled law that "a confession obtained through custodial interrogation after an illegal arrest should be excluded unless intervening events break the causal connection between the illegal arrest and the confession so that the confession is 'sufficiently an act of free will to purge the primary taint.' Taylor v. Alabama (1982). . . .'' The Court rejected the belief of the Oregon court "that the unwarned remark compromised the voluntariness of respondent's later confession. It was the court's view that the prior answer and not the unwarned questioning impaired respondent's ability to give a valid waiver and that only lapse of time and change of place could dissipate what it termed the 'coercive impact' of the inadmissible statement."

A rigid, technical approach to the Miranda rule is another way in which the purpose of the rule to provide legal help for a defendant can be defeated. There is no better illustration of this than the case of Moran v. Burbine (1986). Burbine had been picked up by the Cranston, Rhode Island, police for breaking and entering, and while he was in their custody they learned that he might be implicated in a recent murder in Providence. The Providence police immediately sent over three men to question him. About two hours later Burbine's sister, not knowing anything about the murder charge, obtained a public defender to represent him in the breaking and entering inquiry. She phoned the Cranston police and notified them that she would represent Burbine if the police intended to put him in a lineup or question him. The police informed her that he would not be questioned until the next day. Burbine was not notified that his sister had obtained counsel or the substance of the phone conversation.

Less than an hour later the police began a series of interrogations, following properly administered Miranda warnings, which ultimately produced three signed confessions admitting the murder. The trial court ruled that the constitutional right to request a lawyer was personal to the defendant and could not be exercised by the lawyer. Since Burbine had never requested a lawyer, the phone call was irrelevant.

Justice O'Connor, joined by justices Burger, White, Blackmun, Powell and Rehnquist, upheld Burbine's conviction. They concluded that whatever the motives or conduct of the police, the freely signed confessions following valid Miranda warnings made the conviction constitutional. "Events occurring outside of the presence of the suspect and entirely unknown to him surely can have no bearing on the capacity to comprehend and knowingly relinquish a constitutional right. Under the analysis of the Court of Appeals, the same defendant, armed with the same information and confronted with precisely the same police conduct, would have knowingly waived his Miranda rights had a lawyer not telephoned the police station to inquire about his status. Nothing in any of our waiver decisions or in our understanding of the essential components of a valid waiver requires so incongruous a result. No doubt the additional information would have been useful to respondent; perhaps even it might have affected his decision to confess. But we have never read the Constitution to require that the police supply a suspect with a flow of information to help him calibrate his self-interest in deciding whether to speak or stand by his rights."

Justices Stevens, Brennan and Marshall addressed the moral aspects of the case in their dissent. "The Court concludes that the police may deceive an attorney by giving her false information about whether her client will be questioned, and that the police may deceive a suspect by failing to inform him of his attorney's communications and efforts to represent him. For the majority, this conclusion, though "distaste[ful]," is not even debatable. The deception of the attorney is irrelevant because the attorney has no right to information, accuracy, honesty, or fairness in the police response to her questions about her client. The deception of the client is acceptable, because, although the information would affect the client's assertion of his rights, the client's actions in ignorance of the availability of his attorney are voluntary, knowing, and intelligent; additionally, society's interest in apprehending, prosecuting, and punishing *criminals outweighs the suspect's interest in information regarding his attorney's efforts to communicate with him. Finally, even mendacious police interference in the communications between a suspect and his lawyer does not violate any notion of fundamental fairness because it does not shock the conscience of the majority.''*

In Patterson v. Illinois (1988) the Court faced directly for the first time the question of whether a Miranda warning of the right to counsel at the questioning stage to avoid possible self-incrimination also met the requirements of the Sixth Amendment that a person charged with crime "have the assistance of counsel for his defense." In the course of a gang war Patterson had participated in the murder of a member of the opposing gang. He was arrested, fully informed of his Miranda rights (even to the point of initialing each requirement and signing the waiver) and agreed to answer questions. The following day he was indicted for murder and again asked to sign a Miranda warning form. Each time another member of the prosecutor's office questioned him, he was again read his Miranda rights. The Court found that waiver of his Miranda rights constituted an informed waiver of his right to counsel at trial.

"In this case, we are convinced that by admonishing petitioner with the Miranda warnings, respondent has met this burden and that petitioner's waiver of his right to counsel at the questioning was valid.

"First, the Miranda warnings given petitioner made him aware of his right to have counsel present during the questioning. By telling petitioner that he had a right to consult with an attorney, to have a lawyer present while he was questioned, and even to have a lawyer appointed for him if he could not afford to retain one on his own, Officer Gresham and ASA Smith conveyed to petitioner the sum and substance of the rights that the Sixth Amendment provided him. . . .

"Second, the Miranda warnings also served to make petitioner aware of the consequences of a decision by him to waive his Sixth Amendment rights during postindictment questioning. Petitioner knew that any statement that he made could be used against him in subsequent criminal proceedings. . . .

"Our conclusion is supported by petitioner's inability, in the proceedings before this Court, to articulate with precision what additional information should have been provided to him before he would have been competent to waive his right to counsel. All that petitioner's brief and reply brief suggest is petitioner should have been made aware of his 'right under the Sixth Amendment to the broad protection of counsel'—a rather nebulous suggestion — and the 'gravity of [his] situation.' . . .''

Justices Blackmun, Stevens, Brennan and Marshall dissented, Justice Stevens making clear that "it is well settled that there is a strong presumption against waiver of Sixth Amendment protections, see . . . Von Moltke v. Gillies (1948) (plurality opinion); Johnson v. Zerbst (1938), and that a waiver may only be accepted if made with full awareness of 'the dangers and disadvantages of self-representation,' . . .

"The majority premises its conclusion that Miranda warnings lay a sufficient basis for accepting a waiver of the right to counsel on the assumption that those warnings make clear to an accused "what a lawyer could 'do for him' during the postindictment questioning: namely, advise [him] to refrain from making any [incriminating] statements." Yet, this is surely a gross understatement of the disadvantage of proceeding without a lawyer and an understatement of what a defendant must understand to make a knowing waiver. The Miranda warnings do not, for example, inform the accused that a lawyer might examine the indictment for legal sufficiency before submitting his or her client to interrogation or that a lawyer is likely to be considerably more skillful at negotiating a plea bargain and that such negotiations may be most fruitful if initiated prior to any interrogation. Rather, the warnings do not even go so far as to explain to the accused the nature of the charges pending against him — advice that a court would insist upon before allowing a defendant to enter a guilty plea with or without the presence of an attorney. . . . Without defining precisely the nature of the inquiry required to establish a valid waiver of the Sixth Amendment right to counsel, it must be conceded that at least minimal advice is necessary — the accused must be told of the 'dangers and disadvantages of self-representation.'

"Yet, once it is conceded that certain advice is required and that after indictment the adversary relationship between the state and the accused has solidified, it inescapably follows that a prosecutor may not conduct private interviews with a charged defendant. As at least one Court of Appeals has recognized, there are ethical constraints that prevent a prosecutor from giving legal advice to an uncounseled adversary. Thus, neither the prosecutor nor his or her agents can ethically provide the unrepresented defendant with the kind of advice that should precede an evidence-gathering interview after formal proceedings have been commenced. Indeed, in my opinion even the Miranda warnings themselves are a species of legal advice that is improper when given by the prosecutor after indictment.''

Justice **Stevens** delivered the opinion of the Court, saying in part:

In Edwards v. Arizona (1981), we held that a suspect who has "expressed his desire to deal with the police only through counsel is not subject to further interrogation by the authorities until counsel has been made available to him, unless the accused himself initiates further communication, exchanges, or conversations with the police." In this case Arizona asks us to craft an exception to that rule for cases in which the police want to interrogate a suspect about an offense that is unrelated to the subject of their initial interrogation. Several years ago the Arizona Supreme Court considered, and rejected, a similar argument, stating:

"The only difference between Edwards and the appellant is that Edwards was questioned about the same offense after a request for counsel while the appellant was reinterrogated about an unrelated offense. We do not believe that this factual distinction holds any legal significance for fifth amendment purposes.'' State v. Routhier, 137 Ariz. 90 (1983). We agree with the Arizona Supreme Court's conclusion.

I.

On April 16, 1985, respondent was arrested at the scene of a just-completed burglary. The arresting officer advised him that he had a constitutional right to remain silent and also the right to have an attorney present during any interrogation. See Miranda v. Arizona (1966). Respondent replied that he ''wanted a lawyer before answering any questions.'' This fact was duly recorded in the officer's written report of the incident. In due course, respondent was convicted of the April 16, 1985, burglary.

On April 19, 1985, while respondent was still in custody pursuant to the arrest three days earlier, a different officer interrogated him about a different burglary that had occurred on April 15. That officer was not aware of the fact that respondent had requested the assistance of counsel three days earlier. After advising respondent of his rights, the officer obtained an incriminating statement concerning the April 15 burglary. In the prosecution for that offense, the trial court suppressed that statement. In explaining his ruling, the trial judge relied squarely on the Arizona Supreme Court's opinion in State v. Routhier, characterizing the rule of the Edwards case as ''clear and unequivocal.''*

The Arizona Court of Appeals affirmed the suppression order in a brief opinion, stating: ''In Routhier, as in the instant case, the accused was continuously in police custody from the time of asserting his Fifth Amendment right through the time of the impermissible questioning. The coercive environment never dissipated.'' . . . We granted certiorari to resolve a conflict with certain other state court decisions.

We now affirm.

II.

A major purpose of the Court's opinion in Miranda v. Arizona was ''to give concrete constitutional guidelines for law enforcement agencies and courts to follow.'' ''As we have stressed on numerous occasions,

---

*''Routhier was based on Edwards versus Arizona, which held that once the defendant has invoked his right to counsel, he may not be re-interrogated unless counsel has been made available to him or he initiates the conversation.

''The Routhier court states that whether the defendant is re-interrogated about the same offense or an unrelated offense makes no difference for Fifth Amendment purposes.

''The Routhier court further stated that Edwards is clear and unequivocal, there is to be no further interrogation by authorities once the right to counsel is invoked, the Court in that case finding that the assertion of the right to counsel is an assertion by the accused that he is not competent to deal with authorities without legal advice, and that the resumption of questioning by the police without the requested attorney being provided strongly suggests to the accused that he has no choice but to answer.''

'[o]ne of the principal advantages' of Miranda is the ease and clarity of its application. . . .''

The rule of the Edwards case came as a corollary to Miranda's admonition that ''[i]f the individual states that he wants an attorney, the interrogation must cease until an attorney is present.'' In such an instance, we had concluded in Miranda, ''[i]f the interrogation continues without the presence of an attorney and a statement is taken, a heavy burden rests on the government to demonstrate that the defendant knowingly and intelligently waived his privilege against self-incrimination and his right to retained or appointed counsel.'' In Edwards we ''reconfirm[ed] these views and, to lend them substance, emphasize[d] that it is inconsistent with Miranda and its progeny for the authorities, at their instance, to reinterrogate an accused in custody if he has clearly asserted his right to counsel.'' We concluded that re-interrogation may only occur if ''the accused himself initiates further communication, exchanges, or conversations with the police.'' Thus, the prophylactic protections that the Miranda warnings provide to counteract the ''inherently compelling pressures'' of custodial interrogation and to ''permit a full opportunity to exercise the privilege against self-incrimination'' are implemented by the application of the Edwards corollary that if a suspect believes that he is not capable of undergoing such questioning without advice of counsel, then it is presumed that any subsequent waiver that has come at the authorities' behest, and not at the suspect's own instigation, is itself the product of the ''inherently compelling pressures'' and not the purely voluntary choice of the suspect. As Justice White has explained, ''the accused having expressed his own view that he is not competent to deal with the authorities without legal advice, a later decision at the authorities' insistence to make a statement without counsel's presence may properly be viewed with skepticism.'' . . .

We have repeatedly emphasized the virtues of a bright-line rule in cases following Edwards as well as Miranda. . . . In Fare v. Michael C. (1979), we explained that the ''relatively rigid requirement that interrogation must cease upon the accused's request for an attorney . . . has the virtue of informing police and prosecutors with specificity as to what they may do in conducting custodial interrogation, and of informing courts under what circumstances statements obtained during such interrogation are not admissible. This gain in specificity, which benefits the accused and the State alike, has been thought to outweigh the burdens that the decision in Miranda imposes on law enforcement agencies and the courts by requiring the suppression of trustworthy and highly probative evidence even though the confession might be voluntary under traditional Fifth Amendment analysis.''* The Edwards rule thus serves

---

*It is significant that our explanation of the basis for the ''per se aspect of Miranda'' in Fare v. Michael C. applies to the application of the Edwards rule in a case such as this. As we stated in Fare:

''The rule in Miranda . . . was based on this Court's perception that the lawyer occupies a critical position in our legal system because of his unique ability to protect the Fifth Amendment rights of a client undergoing custodial interrogation. Because of this special ability of the law-the purpose of providing "clear and unequivocal" guidelines to the law enforcement profession. Surely there is nothing ambiguous about the requirement that after a person in custody has expressed his desire to deal with the police only through counsel, he "is not subject to further interrogation by the authorities until counsel has been made available to him, unless the accused himself initiates further communication, exchanges, or conversations with the police."

III.

Petitioner contends that the bright-line, prophylactic Edwards rule should not apply when the police-initiated interrogation following a suspect's request for counsel occurs in the context of a separate investigation. According to petitioner, both our cases and the nature of the factual setting compel this distinction. We are unpersuaded.

Petitioner points to our holding in Michigan v. Mosley [1975] (quoting Miranda v. Arizona, that when a suspect asserts his right to cut off questioning, the police may " 'scrupulously honor' " that right by "immediately ceas[ing] the interrogation, resum[ing] questioning only after the passage of a significant period of time and the provision of a fresh set of warnings, and restrict[ing] the second interrogation to a crime that had not been a subject of the earlier interrogation." The police in this case followed precisely that course, claims the State. However, as Mosley made clear, a suspect's decision to cut off questioning, unlike his request for counsel, does not raise the presumption that he is unable to proceed without a lawyer's advice.

Petitioner points as well to Connecticut v. Barrett (1987), which concerned a suspect who had "told the officers that he would not give a written statement unless his attorney was present but had 'no problem' talking about the incident." We held that this was a limited request for counsel, that Barrett himself had drawn a distinction between oral and written statements and thus that the officers could continue to question him. Petitioner argues that Roberson's request for counsel was similarly limited, this time to the investigation pursuant to which the request was made. This argument is flawed both factually and legally. As a matter of fact, according to the initial police report, respondent stated "that he wanted a lawyer before answering any questions." As a matter of law, the presumption raised by a suspect's request for counsel—that he considers himself unable to deal with the pressures of custodial interrogation without legal assistance—does not disappear simply because the

yer to help the client preserve his Fifth Amendment rights once the client becomes enmeshed in the adversary process, the Court found that 'the right to have counsel present at the interrogation is indispensable to the protection of the Fifth Amendment privilege under the system' established by the Court. Moreover, the lawyer's presence helps guard against overreaching by the police and ensures that any statements actually obtained are accurately transcribed for presentation into evidence.

"The per se aspect of Miranda was thus based on the unique role the lawyer plays in the adversary system of criminal justice in this country."

police have approached the suspect, still in custody, still without counsel, about a separate investigation.

That a suspect's request for counsel should apply to any questions the police wish to pose follows, we think, not only from Edwards and Miranda, but also from a case decided the same day as Barrett. In Colorado v. Spring (1987), we held that "a suspect's awareness of all the possible subjects of questioning in advance of interrogation is not relevant to determining whether the suspect voluntarily, knowingly, and intelligently waived his Fifth Amendment privilege." In the face of the warning that anything he said could be used as evidence against him, Spring's willingness to answer questions, without limiting such a waiver, see Connecticut v. Barrett, [1987] indicated that he felt comfortable enough with the pressures of custodial interrogation both to answer questions and to do so without an attorney. Since there is "no qualification of [the] broad and explicit warning" that "*anything* [a suspect] says may be used against him" (emphasis in original), Spring's decision to talk was properly considered to be equally unqualified. Conversely, Roberson's unwillingness to answer any questions without the advice of counsel, without limiting his request for counsel, indicated that he did not feel sufficiently comfortable with the pressures of custodial interrogation to answer questions without an attorney. This discomfort is precisely the state of mind that Edwards presumes to persist unless the suspect himself initiates further conversation about the investigation; unless he otherwise states, see Connecticut v. Barrett, there is no reason to assume that a suspect's state of mind is in any way investigation-specific. . . .

Finally, petitioner raises the case of Maine v. Moulton (1985), which held that Moulton's "Sixth Amendment right to the assistance of counsel was violated by the admission at trial of incriminating statements made by him to his codefendant, a secret government informant, after indictment and at a meeting of the two to plan defense strategy for the upcoming trial." That case did not involve any Miranda issue because Moulton was not in custody. In our opinion, we rejected an argument that the statements should be admissible because the police were seeking information regarding both the crime for which Moulton had already been indicted, and a separate, inchoate scheme. Following Massiah v. United States (1964), we recognized, though, that the continuing investigation of uncharged offenses did not violate the defendant's Sixth Amendment right to the assistance of counsel. Our recognition of that fact, however, surely lends no support to petitioner's argument that in the Fifth Amendment context, "statements about different offenses, developed at different times, by different investigators, in the course of two wholly independent investigations, should not be treated the same." This argument overlooks the difference between the Sixth Amendment right to counsel and the Fifth Amendment right against self-incrimination. The former arises from the fact that the suspect has been formally charged with a particular crime and thus is facing a State apparatus that has been geared up to prosecute him. The latter is protected by the prophylaxis of having an attorney present to counteract the inherent pressures of custodial interrogation, which arise from the fact of such interrogation and exist regardless of the number of crimes under investigation or whether those crimes have resulted in formal charges.

In sum, our cases do not support petitioner's position.

IV.

Petitioner's attempts at distinguishing the factual setting here from that in Edwards are equally unavailing. Petitioner first relies on the plurality opinion in Oregon v. Bradshaw [1983] (Rehnquist, J.), which stated that Edwards laid down "a prophylactic rule, designed to protect an accused in police custody from being badgered by police officers in the manner in which the defendant in Edwards was." Petitioner reasons that "the chances that an accused will be questioned so repeatedly and in such quick succession that it will 'undermine the will' of the person questioned, or will constitute 'badger[ing],' are so minute as not to warrant consideration, if the officers are truly pursuing separate investigations." It is by no means clear, though, that police engaged in separate investigations will be any less eager than police involved in only one inquiry to question a suspect in custody. Further, to a suspect who has indicated his inability to cope with the pressures of custodial interrogation by requesting counsel, any further interrogation without counsel having been provided will surely exacerbate whatever compulsion to speak the suspect may be feeling. Thus, we also disagree with petitioner's contention that fresh sets of Miranda warnings will "reassure" a suspect who has been denied the counsel he has clearly requested that his rights have remained untrammeled. Especially in a case such as this, in which a period of three days elapsed between the unsatisfied request for counsel and the interrogation about a second offense, there is a serious risk that the mere repetition of the Miranda warnings would not overcome the presumption of coercion that is created by prolonged police custody.*

The United States, as amicus curiae supporting petitioner, suggests that a suspect in custody might have "good reasons for wanting to speak with the police about the offenses involved in the new investigation, or at least to learn from the police what the new investigation is about so that he can decide whether it is in his interest to

make a statement about that matter without the assistance of counsel." The simple answer is that the suspect, having requested counsel, can determine how to deal with the separate investigations with counsel's advice. Further, even if the police have decided temporarily not to provide counsel, they are free to inform the suspect of the facts of the second investigation as long as such communication does not constitute interrogation, see Rhode Island v. Innis (1980). As we have made clear, any "further communication, exchanges, or conversations with the police" that the suspect himself initiates, Edwards v. Arizona, are perfectly valid.

Finally, we attach no significance to the fact that the officer who conducted the second interrogation did not know that respondent had made a request for counsel. In addition to the fact that Edwards focuses on the state of mind of the suspect and not of the police, custodial interrogation must be conducted pursuant to established procedures, and those procedures in turn must enable an officer who proposes to initiate an interrogation to determine whether the suspect has previously requested counsel. In this case respondent's request had been properly memorialized in a written report but the officer who conducted the interrogation simply failed to examine that report. Whether a contemplated reinterrogation concerns the same or a different offense, or whether the same or different law enforcement authorities are involved in the second investigation, the same need to determine whether the suspect has requested counsel exists.* The police department's failure to honor that request cannot be justified by the lack of diligence of a particular officer. . . .

The judgment of the Arizona Court of Appeals is Affirmed.

Justice **O'Connor** took no part in the consideration or decision of this case.

Justice **Kennedy**, with whom the **Chief Justice [Rehnquist]** joins, dissenting, said in part:

The majority frames the case as one in which we are asked to "craft an exception" to Edwards v. Arizona (1981). The implication from this, it would seem, is that the burden of proof falls on those who say no constitutional or preventative purpose is served by prohibiting the police from asking a suspect, once he has requested counsel, if he chooses to waive that right in a new and independent investigation of a different crime. But the rule of Edwards is our rule, not a constitutional command; and it is our obligation to justify its expansion. Our justification must be consistent with the practical realities of suspects' rights and police investigations. With all respect, I suggest the majority does not have a con-

---

*The United States, as *amicus curiae* supporting petitioner, suggests similarly that "respondent's failure to reiterate his request for counsel to [the officer involved in the second investigation], even after [that officer] gave respondent complete Miranda warnings, could not have been the result of any doubt on respondent's part that the police would honor a request for counsel if one were made." This conclusion is surprising, considering that respondent had not been provided with the attorney he had already requested, despite having been subjected to police-initiated interrogation with respect to the first investigation as well. We reiterate here, though, that the "right" to counsel to protect the Fifth Amendment right against self-incrimination is not absolute; that is, "[i]f authorities conclude that they will not provide counsel during a reasonable period of time in which investigation in the field is carried out, they may refrain from doing so without violating the person's Fifth Amendment privilege so long as they do not question him during that time." Miranda v. Arizona.

---

*Indeed, the facts of this case indicate that different officers investigating the same offense are just as likely to bypass proper procedures as an officer investigating a different offense, inasmuch as the record discloses no less than five violations of the Edwards rule, four concerning the April 16 burglary and only one concerning the April 15 burglary. It is only the last violation that is at issue in this case.

vincing case. The majority's rule is not necessary to protect the rights of suspects, and it will in many instances deprive our nationwide law enforcement network of a legitimate investigative technique now routinely used to resolve major crimes.

When a suspect is in custody for even the most minor offense, his name and fingerprints are checked against master files. It is a frequent occurrence that the suspect is wanted for questioning with respect to crimes unrelated to the one for which he has been apprehended. The rule announced today will bar law enforcement officials, even those from some other city or other jurisdiction, from questioning a suspect about an unrelated matter if he is in custody and has requested counsel to assist in answering questions put to him about the crime for which he was arrested.

This is the first case in which we are asked to apply Edwards to separate and independent investigations. The statements deemed inadmissible in Edwards and in our later cases applying its doctrine were statements relating to the same investigation in which the right to counsel was invoked. See Connecticut v. Barrett (1987); . . . Oregon v. Bradshaw (1983). . . . The majority's extension of the Edwards rule to separate and independent investigations is unwarranted.

The petitioner in Edwards, arrested on serious charges, first submitted to interrogation but then requested an attorney. Questions ceased for a while, but when two detectives came to the jail the next morning, a guard advised him that he must talk with them. The petitioner in Edwards waived his right to silence and implicated himself in the crime. We reversed the conviction, holding that an accused who expresses his desire to face further questioning with counsel present will not be subject to further interrogation until counsel is made available, unless the accused initiates the exchange himself.

Our ultimate concern in Edwards, and in the cases which follow it, is whether the suspect knows and understands his rights and is willing to waive them, and whether courts can be assured that coercion did not induce the waiver. That concern does not dictate the result reached by the Court today, for the dangers present in Edwards and later cases are insubstantial here.

The rule in Edwards "was in effect a prophylactic rule, designed to protect an accused in police custody from being badgered by police officers in the manner in which the defendant in Edwards was." Oregon v. Bradshaw (plurality opinion). Where the subsequent questioning is confined to an entirely independent investigation, there is little risk that the suspect will be badgered into submission.

The Court reasons that it is "by no means clear" that "police engaged in separate investigations will be any less eager than police involved in only one inquiry to question a suspect in custody." That misses the point. Unless there are so many separate investigations that fresh teams of police are regularly turning up to question the suspect, the danger of badgering is minimal, and insufficient to justify a rigid per se rule. Whatever their eagerness, the police in a separate investigation may not commence any questioning unless the suspect is read-

vised of his Miranda rights and consents to the interrogation, and they are required by Edwards to cease questioning him if he invokes his right to counsel. Consequently, the legitimate interest of the suspect in not being subjected to coercive badgering is already protected. The reason for the Edwards rule is not that confessions are disfavored but that coercion is feared. The rule announced today, however, prohibits the police from resuming questions, after a second Miranda warning, when there is no more likelihood of coercion than when the first interrogation began. The Court suggests that the suspect may believe his rights are fictitious if he must assert them a second time, but the support for this suggestion is weak. The suspect, having observed that his earlier invocation of rights was effective in terminating questioning and having been advised that further questioning may not relate to that crime, would understand that he may invoke his rights again with respect to the new investigation, and so terminate questioning regarding that investigation as well. Indeed, the new warnings and explanations will reinforce his comprehension of a suspect's rights.

I note that the conduct of the police in this case was hardly exemplary; they reinitiated questioning of respondent regarding the first investigation after he had asserted his right to counsel in that investigation. The statements he gave in response, however, properly were excluded at trial for all purposes except impeachment. Any sense of coercion generated by this violation which carried over into the questioning on the second offense would of course be taken into account by a court reviewing whether the waiver of Miranda rights in the second investigation was voluntary, and the per se rule announced today is therefore not necessary to respond to such misconduct.

Allowing authorities who conduct a separate investigation to read the suspect his Miranda rights and ask him whether he wishes to invoke them strikes an appropriate balance, which protects the suspect's freedom from coercion without unnecessarily disrupting legitimate law enforcement efforts. Balance is essential when the Court fashions rules which are preventative and do not themselves stem from violations of a constitutional right. Michigan v. Tucker (1974). By contrast with the Fourth Amendment exclusionary rule, for instance, the rule here operates even absent constitutional violation, see Oregon v. Elstad (1985), and we should be cautious in extending it. The Court expresses a preference for bright lines, but the line it draws here is far more restrictive than necessary to protect the interests at stake.

By prohibiting the police from questioning the suspect regarding a separate investigation, the Court chooses to presume that a suspect has made the decision that he does not wish to talk about that investigation without counsel present, although that decision was made when the suspect was unaware of even the existence of a separate investigation. The underlying premise seems to be that there are two types of people: those who never talk without a lawyer and those who always talk without a lawyer. The more realistic view of human nature suggests that a suspect will want the opportunity, when he learns of the separate investigations, to decide whether he wishes to speak to the authorities in a particular investigation with or without representation. In other contexts, we have taken a more realistic approach to separate and independent investigations. In Maine v. Moulton (1985), we held that the Sixth Amendment right to counsel barred admission of statements elicited from a criminal defendant by a government informant when the statements related to the charge on which the defendant had been indicted. We were careful to note, however, that the rule would have been otherwise had the statements related to a different charge. ''[T]o exclude evidence pertaining to charges as to which the Sixth Amendment right to counsel had not attached at the time the evidence was obtained, simply because other charges were pending at that time, would unnecessarily frustrate the public's interest in the investigation of criminal activities.'' Similarly, we held in Michigan v. Mosley that a suspect who had been arrested on charges of committing robbery and who had invoked his right to silence could be questioned later about an unrelated murder, if first read his Miranda rights. The Court correctly points out that neither of these cases necessarily control the one before us; Moulton involved the Sixth Amendment right to counsel and Mosley involved the Fifth Amendment right to silence, while this case involves the Fifth Amendment right to counsel. Moulton and Mosley nevertheless reflected an understanding that the invocation of a criminal suspect's constitutional rights could be respected, and the opportunities for unfair coercion restricted, without the establishment of a broad-brush rule by which the assertion of a right in one investigation is automatically applied to a separate and independent one.

In considering whether to extend the Edwards rule to this case, the choice is not between holding, as the Court does, that such statements will never be admissible, and holding that such statements will always be admissible. The choice is between the Court's absolute rule establishing an irrebuttable presumption of coercion, and one which relies upon known and tested warnings, applied to each investigation as required by Edwards and Miranda v. Arizona (1966), to insure that a waiver is voluntary. The problems to which Edwards was addressed are not present here in any substantial degree. Today's rule will neither serve the interest of law enforcement nor give necessary protection to the rights of those suspected of crime. I respectfully dissent.

Appendix

Constitution
of
the United States

WE THE PEOPLE of the United States, in order to form a more perfect union, establish justice, insure domestic tranquillity, provide for the common defense, promote the general welfare, and secure the blessings of liberty to ourselves and our posterity, do ordain and establish this Constitution for the United States of America.

ARTICLE I

SECTION 1. All legislative powers herein granted shall be vested in a Congress of the United States, which shall consist of a Senate and House of Representatives.

SECTION 2. (1) The House of Representatives shall be composed of members chosen every second year by the people of the several States, and the electors in each State shall have the qualifications requisite for electors of the most numerous branch of the State legislature.

(2) No person shall be a Representative who shall not have attained to the age of twenty-five years, and been seven years a citizen of the United States, and who shall not, when elected, be an inhabitant of that State in which he shall be chosen.

(3) Representatives and direct taxes[1] shall be apportioned among the several States which may be included within this Union, according to their respective numbers, which shall be determined by adding to the whole number of free persons, including those bound to service for a term of years, and excluding Indians not taxed, three fifths of all other persons.[2] The actual enumeration shall be made within three years after the first meeting of the Congress of the United States, and within every subsequent term of ten years, in such manner as they shall by law direct. The number of Representatives shall not exceed one for every thirty thousand, but each State shall have at least one Representative; and until such enumeration shall be made, the State of New Hampshire shall be entitled to choose three, Massachusetts eight, Rhode Island and Providence Plantations one, Connecticut five, New York six, New Jersey four, Pennsylvania eight, Delaware one, Maryland six, Virginia ten, North Carolina five, South Carolina five, and Georgia three.

(4) When vacancies happen in the representation from any State, the executive authority thereof shall issue writs of election to fill such vacancies.

(5) The House of Representatives shall choose their Speaker and other officers; and shall have the sole power of impeachment.

SECTION 3. (1) The Senate of the United States shall be composed of two Senators from each State, chosen by the Legislature thereof,[3] for six years; and each Senator shall have one vote.

---

[1]Modified as to income taxes by the 16th Amendment.
[2]Replaced by the 14th Amendment.
[3]Modified by the 17th Amendment.

(2) Immediately after they shall be assembled in consequence of the first election, they shall be divided as equally as may be into three classes. The seats of the Senators of the first class shall be vacated at the expiration of the second year, of the second class at the expiration of the fourth year, and of the third class at the expiration of the sixth year, so that one third may be chosen every second year; and if vacancies happen by resignation, or otherwise, during the recess of the legislature of any State, the executive thereof may make temporary appointments until the next meeting of the legislature, which[3] shall then fill such vacancies.

(3) No person shall be a Senator who shall not have attained to the age of thirty years, and been nine years a citizen of the United States, and who shall not, when elected, be an inhabitant of that State for which he shall be chosen.

(4) The Vice President of the United States shall be president of the Senate, but shall have no vote, unless they be equally divided.

(5) The Senate shall choose their other officers, and also a president pro tempore, in the absence of the Vice President, or when he shall exercise the office of President of the United States.

(6) The Senate shall have the sole power to try all impeachments. When sitting for that purpose, they shall be on oath or affirmation. When the President of the United States is tried, the Chief Justice shall preside: and no person shall be convicted without the concurrence of two-thirds of the members present.

(7) Judgment in cases of impeachment shall not extend further than to removal from office, and disqualification to hold and enjoy any office of honor, trust or profit under the United States: but the party convicted shall nevertheless be liable and subject to indictment, trial, judgment and punishment, according to law.

SECTION 4. (1) The times, places and manner of holding elections for Senators and Representatives, shall be prescribed in each State by the legislature thereof; but the Congress may at any time by law make or alter such regulations, except as to the places of choosing Senators.

(2) The Congress shall assemble at least once in every year, and such meeting shall be on the first Monday in December, unless they shall by law appoint a different day.

SECTION 5. (1) Each House shall be the judge of the elections, returns and qualifications of its own members, and a majority of each shall constitute a quorum to do business; but a smaller number may adjourn from day to day, and may be authorized to compel the attendance of absent members, in such manner, and under such penalties as each House may provide.

(2) Each House may determine the rules of its proceedings, punish its members for disorderly behavior, and, with the concurrence of two thirds, expel a member.

(3) Each House shall keep a journal of its proceedings, and from time to time publish the same, excepting such parts as may in their judgement require secrecy; and the yeas and nays of the members of either House on any question shall, at the desire of one fifth of those present, be entered on the journal.

(4) Neither House, during the session of Congress, shall, without the consent of the other, adjourn for more than three days, nor to any other place than that in which the two Houses shall be sitting.

SECTION 6. (1) The Senators and Representatives shall receive a compensation for their services, to be ascertained by law, and paid out of the Treasury of the United States. They shall in all cases, except treason, felony and breach of the peace, be privileged from arrest during their attendance at the session of their respective Houses, and in going to and returning from the same; and for any speech or debate in either House, they shall not be questioned in any other place.

(2) No Senator or Representative shall, during the time for which he was elected, be appointed to any civil office under the authority of the United States, which shall have been created, or the emoluments whereof shall have been increased during such time; and no person holding any office under the United States, shall be a member of either House during his continuance in office.

SECTION 7. (1) All bills for raising revenue shall originate in the House of Representatives; but the Senate may propose or concur with amendments as on other bills.

(2) Every bill which shall have passed the House of Representatives and the Senate, shall, before it become a law, be presented to the President of the United States; if he approve he shall sign it, but if not he shall return it, with his objections to that House in which it shall have originated, who shall enter the objections at large on their journal, and proceed to reconsider it. If after such reconsideration two thirds of that House shall agree to pass the bill, it shall be sent, together with the objections, to the other House, by which it shall likewise be reconsidered, and if approved by two thirds of that House, it shall become a law. But in all such cases the votes of both Houses shall be determined by yeas and nays, and the names of the persons voting for and against the bill shall be entered on the journal of each House respectively. If any bill shall not be returned by the President within ten days (Sundays excepted) after it shall have been presented to him, the same shall be a law, in like manner as if he had signed it, unless the Congress by their adjournment prevent its return, in which case it shall not be a law.

(3) Every order, resolution, or vote to which the concurrence of the Senate and House of Representatives may be necessary (except on a question of adjournment) shall be presented to the President of the United States; and before the same shall take effect, shall be approved by him, or being disapproved by him, shall be repassed by two thirds of the Senate and House of Representatives, according to the rules and limitations prescribed in the case of a bill.

SECTION 8. (1) The Congress shall have power to lay and collect taxes, duties, imposts and excises, to pay the debts and provide for the common defense and general welfare of the United States; but all duties, imposts and excises shall be uniform throughout the United States;

(2) To borrow money on the credit of the United States.

(3) To regulate commerce with foreign nations, and among the several States, and with the Indian tribes;

(4) To establish an uniform rule of naturalization, and uniform laws on the subject of bankruptcies throughout the United States;

(5) To coin money, regulate the value thereof, and of foreign coin, and fix the standard of weights and measures;

(6) To provide for the punishment of counterfeiting the securities and current coin of the United States;

(7) To establish post offices and post roads;

(8) To promote the progress of science and useful arts, by securing for limited times to authors and inventors the exclusive right to their respective writings and discoveries;

(9) To constitute tribunals inferior to the Supreme Court;

(10) To define and punish piracies and felonies committed on the high seas, and offenses against the law of nations;

(11) To declare war, grant letters of marque and reprisal, and make rules concerning captures on land and water;

(12) To raise and support armies, but no appropriation of money to that use shall be for a longer term than two years;

(13) To provide and maintain a navy;

(14) To make rules for the government and regulation of the land and naval forces;

(15) To provide for calling forth the militia to execute the laws of the Union, suppress insurrections and repel invasions;

(16) To provide for organizing, arming, and disciplining the militia, and for governing such part of them as may be employed in the service of the United States,

reserving to the States respectively, the appointment of the officers, and the authority of training the militia according to the discipline prescribed by Congress;

(17) To exercise exclusive legislation in all cases whatsoever, over such district (not exceeding ten miles square) as may, by cession of particular States, and the acceptance of Congress, become the seat of the government of the United States,[4] and to exercise like authority over all places purchased by the consent of the legislature of the State in which the same shall be, for the erection of forts, magazines, arsenals, dockyards, and other needful buildings; and

(18) To make all laws which shall be necessary and proper for carrying into execution the foregoing powers, and all other powers vested by this Constitution in the government of the United States, or in any department or officer thereof.

SECTION 9. (1) The migration or importation of such persons as any of the States now existing shall think proper to admit, shall not be prohibited by the Congress prior to the year one thousand eight hundred and eight, but a tax or duty may be imposed on such importation, not exceeding ten dollars for each person.

(2) The privilege of the writ of habeas corpus shall not be suspended, unless when in cases of rebellion or invasion the public safety may require it.

(3) No bill of attainder or ex post facto law shall be passed.

(4) No capitation, or other direct, tax shall be laid, unless in proportion to the census or enumeration herein before directed to be taken.[5]

(5) No tax or duty shall be laid on articles exported from any State.

(6) No preference shall be given by any regulation of commerce or revenue to the ports of one State over those of another: nor shall vessels bound to, or from, one State, be obliged to enter, clear, or pay duties in another.

(7) No money shall be drawn from the Treasury, but in consequence of appropriations made by law; and a regular statement and account of the receipts and expenditures of all public money shall be published from time to time.

(8) No title of nobility shall be granted by the United States: and no person holding any office of profit or trust under them, shall, without the consent of the Congress, accept of any present, emolument, office, or title, of any kind whatever, from any king, prince, or foreign State.

---

[4]Modified by the 23rd Amendment.

[5]Modified by the 16th Amendment.

SECTION 10. (1) No State shall enter into any treaty, alliance, or confederation; grant letters of marque and reprisal; coin money; emit bills of credit; make anything but gold and silver coin a tender in payment of debts; pass any bill of attainder, ex post facto law, or law impairing the obligation of contracts, or grant any title of nobility.

(2) No State shall, without the consent of the Congress, lay any imposts or duties on imports or exports, except what may be absolutely necessary for executing its inspection laws; and the net produce of all duties and imposts, laid by any State on imports or exports, shall be for the use of the Treasury of the United States; and all such laws shall be subject to the revision and control of the Congress.

(3) No State shall, without the consent of Congress, lay any duty of tonnage, keep troops, or ships of war in time of peace, enter into any agreement or compact with another State, or with a foreign power, or engage in war, unless actually invaded, or in such imminent danger as will not admit of delay.

ARTICLE II

SECTION 1. (1) The executive power shall be vested in a President of the United States of America. He shall hold his office during the term of four years,[6] and, together with the Vice President, chosen for the same term, be elected, as follows:

(2) Each State shall appoint, in such manner as the legislature thereof may direct, a number of electors, equal to the whole number of Senators and Representatives to which the State may be entitled in the Congress: but no Senator or Representative, or person holding an office of trust or profit under the United States, shall be appointed an elector.

The electors[7] shall meet in their respective States, and vote by ballot for two persons, of whom one at least shall not be an inhabitant of the same State with themselves. And they shall make a list of all the persons voted for, and of the number of votes for each; which list they shall sign and certify, and transmit sealed to the seat of the government of the United States, directed to the president of the Senate. The president of the Senate shall, in the presence of the Senate and House of Representatives, open all the certificates, and the votes shall then be counted. The person having the greatest number of votes shall be the President, if such number be a majority of the whole number of electors appointed; and if there be more than one who have such majority, and have an equal number of votes, then the House of Representatives shall immediately choose by ballot one of them for President; and if no person have a majority, then from the five highest on the list the said House

shall in like manner choose the President. But in choosing the President, the votes shall be taken by States, the representation from each State having one vote; a quorum for this purpose shall consist of a member or members from two thirds of the States, and a majority of all the States shall be necessary to a choice. In every case, after the choice of the President, the person having the greatest number of votes of the electors shall be the Vice President. But if there should remain two or more who have equal votes, the Senate shall choose from them by ballot the Vice President.

(3) The Congress may determine the time of choosing the electors, and the day on which they shall give their votes; which day shall be the same throughout the United States.

(4) No person except a natural born citizen, or a citizen of the United States, at the time of the adoption of this Constitution, shall be eligible to the office of President; neither shall any person be eligible to that office who shall not have attained to the age of thirty five years, and been fourteen years a resident within the United States.

(5) In the case of the removal of the President from office, or of his death, resignation, or inability to discharge the powers and duties of the said office, the same shall devolve on the Vice President, and the Congress may by law provide for the case of removal, death, resignation, or inability, both of the President and Vice President, declaring what officer shall then act as President, and such officer shall act accordingly, until the disability be removed, or a President shall be elected.[8]

(6) The President shall, at stated times, receive for his services, a compensation, which shall neither be increased nor diminished during the period for which he shall have been elected, and he shall not receive within that period any other emolument from the United States, or any of them.

(7) Before he enter on the execution of his office, he shall take the following oath or affirmation:—"I do solemnly swear (or affirm) that I will faithfully execute the office of President of the United States, and will to the best of my ability, preserve, protect and defend the Constitution of the United States."

SECTION 2. (1) The President shall be commander in chief of the army and navy of the United States, and of the militia of the several States, when called into the actual service of the United States; he may require the opinion, in writing, of the principal officer in each of the executive departments, upon any subject relating to the duties of their respective offices, and he shall have power to grant reprieves and pardons for offenses against the United States, except in cases of impeachment.

---

[6]Modified by the 22nd Amendment.

[7]Replaced in 1804 by the 12th Amendment.

---

[8]Replaced by the 25th Amendment.

(2) He shall have power, by and with the advice and consent of the Senate, to make treaties, provided two thirds of the Senators present concur; and he shall nominate, and by and with the advice and consent of the Senate, shall appoint ambassadors, other public ministers and consuls, judges of the Supreme Court, and all other officers of the United States, whose appointments are not herein otherwise provided for, and which shall be established by law: but the Congress may by law vest the appointment of such inferior officers, as they think proper, in the President alone, in the courts of law, or in the heads of departments.

(3) The President shall have power to fill up all vacancies that may happen during the recess of the Senate, by granting commissions which shall expire at the end of their next session.

SECTION 3. He shall from time to time give to the Congress information of the state of the Union, and recommend to their consideration such measures as he shall judge necessary and expedient; he may, on extraordinary occasions, convene both Houses, or either of them, and in case of disagreement between them, with respect to the time of adjournment, he may adjourn them to such time as he shall think proper; he shall receive ambassadors and other public ministers; he shall take care that the laws be faithfully executed, and shall commission all the officers of the United States.

SECTION 4. The President, Vice President and all civil officers of the United States, shall be removed from office on impeachment for, and conviction of, treason, bribery, or other high crimes and misdemeanors.

ARTICLE III

SECTION 1. The judicial power of the United States, shall be vested in one Supreme Court, and in such inferior courts as the Congress may from time to time ordain and establish. The judges, both of the Supreme and inferior courts, shall hold their offices during good behavior, and shall, at stated times, receive for their services, a compensation, which shall not be diminished during their continuance in office.

SECTION 2. (1) The judicial power shall extend to all cases, in law and equity, arising under this Constitution, the laws of the United States, and treaties made, or which shall be made, under their authority;—to all cases affecting ambassadors, other public ministers and consuls;—to all cases of admiralty and maritime jurisdiction;—to controversies to which the United States shall be a party;—to controversies between two or more States;—between a State and citizens of another State;[9]—between citizens of different States;—between citizens of the same State

---

[9]Restricted by the 11th Amendment.

claiming lands under grants of different States, and between a State, or the citizens thereof, and foreign States, citizens or subjects.

(2) In all cases affecting ambassadors, other public ministers and consuls, and those in which a State shall be party, the Supreme Court shall have original jurisdiction. In all the other cases before mentioned, the Supreme Court shall have appellate jurisdiction, both as to law and fact, with such exceptions, and under such regulations as the Congress shall make.

(3) The trial of all crimes, except in cases of impeachment, shall be by jury; and such trial shall be held in the State where the said crimes shall have been committed; but when not committed within any State, the trial shall be at such place or places as the Congress may by law have directed.

SECTION 3. (1) Treason against the United States, shall consist only in levying war against them, or in adhering to their enemies, giving them aid and comfort. No person shall be convicted of treason unless on the testimony of two witnesses to the same overt act, or on confession in open court.

(2) The Congress shall have power to declare the punishment of treason, but no attainder of treason shall work corruption of blood, or forfeiture except during the life of the person attainted.

ARTICLE IV

SECTION 1. Full faith and credit shall be given in each State to the public acts, records, and judicial proceedings of every other State. And the Congress may by general laws prescribe the manner in which such acts, records and proceedings shall be proved, and the effect thereof.

SECTION 2. (1) The citizens of each State shall be entitled to all privileges and immunities of citizens in the several States.

(2) A person charged in any State with treason, felony, or other crime, who shall flee from justice, and be found in another State, shall on demand of the executive authority of the State from which he fled, be delivered up, to be removed to the State having jurisdiction of the crime.

(3) No person held to service or labor in one State, under the laws thereof, escaping into another, shall, in consequence of any law or regulation therein, be discharged from such service or labor, but shall be delivered up on claim of the party to whom such service or labor may be due.

SECTION 3. (1) New States may be admitted by the Congress into this Union; but no new State shall be formed or erected within the jurisdiction of any other State; nor any State be formed by the junction of two or more States, or parts of States, without the consent of the legislatures of the States concerned as well as of the Congress.

(2) The Congress shall have power to dispose of and make all needful rules and regulations respecting the territory or other property belonging to the United States; and nothing in this Constitution shall be so construed as to prejudice any claims of the United States, or of any particular State.

SECTION 4. The United States shall guarantee to every State in this Union a republican form of government, and shall protect each of them against invasion; and on application of the legislature, or of the executive (when the legislature cannot be convened) against domestic violence.

ARTICLE V

The Congress, whenever two thirds of both Houses shall deem it necessary, shall propose amendments to this Constitution, or, on the application of the legislatures of two thirds of the several States, shall call a convention for proposing amendments, which, in either case, shall be valid to all intents and purposes, as part of this Constitution, when ratified by the legislatures of three fourths of the several States, or by conventions in three fourths thereof, as the one or the other mode of ratification may be proposed by the Congress; Provided that no amendment which may be made prior to the year one thousand eight hundred and eight shall in any manner affect the first and fourth clauses in the ninth section of the first article; and that no State, without its consent, shall be deprived of its equal suffrage in the Senate.

ARTICLE VI

SECTION 1. All debts contracted and engagements entered into, before the adoption of this Constitution, shall be as valid against the United States under this Constitution, as under the Confederation.

SECTION 2. This Constitution, and the laws of the United States which shall be made in pursuance thereof; and all treaties made, or which shall be made, under the authority of the United States, shall be the supreme law of the land; and the judges in every State shall be bound thereby, anything in the constitution or laws of any State to the contrary notwithstanding.

SECTION 3. The Senators and Representatives before mentioned, and the members of the several State legislatures, and all executive and judicial officers, both of the United States and of the several States, shall be bound by oath or affirmation to support this Constitution; but no religious test shall ever be required as a qualification to any office or public trust under the United States.

ARTICLE VII

The ratification of the conventions of nine States, shall be sufficient for the establishment of this Constitution between the States so ratifying the same.

done in Convention by the unanimous consent of the States present the seventeenth day of September in the year of our Lord one thousand seven hundred and eighty-seven, and of the independence of the United States of America the twelfth. In witness whereof we have hereunto subscribed our names.
Go Washington—
Presidt. and Deputy from Virginia

Articles in addition to and amendment of the Constitution of the United States of America, proposed by Congress, and ratified by the legislatures of the several States, pursuant to the fifth article of the original Constitution.

ARTICLE I[10]

Congress shall make no law respecting an establishment of religion, or prohibiting the free exercise thereof; or abridging the freedom of speech, or of the press; or the right of the people peaceably to assemble, and to petition the government for a redress of grievances.

ARTICLE II

A well regulated militia, being necessary to the security of a free State, the right of the people to keep and bear arms, shall not be infringed.

ARTICLE III

No soldier shall, in time of peace be quartered in any house, without the consent of the owner, nor in time of war, but in a manner to be prescribed by law.

ARTICLE IV

The right of the people to be secure in their persons, houses, papers, and effects, against unreasonable searches and seizures, shall not be violated, and no warrants shall issue, but upon probable cause, supported by oath or affirmation, and particularly describing the place to be searched, and the persons or things to be seized.

ARTICLE V

No person shall be held to answer for a capital, or otherwise infamous crime, unless on a presentment or indictment of a grand jury, except in cases arising in the land or naval forces, or in the militia, when in actual service in time of war or public danger; nor shall any person be subject for the same offense to be twice put in jeopardy of life or limb; nor shall be compelled in any criminal case to be a witness against himself, nor be deprived of life, liberty, or property, without due process of law; nor shall private property be taken for public use, without just compensation.

---

[10]The first ten Amendments were adopted in 1791.

ARTICLE VI

In all criminal prosecutions the accused shall enjoy the right to a speedy and public trial, by an impartial jury of the State and district wherein the crime shall have been committed, which district shall have been previously ascertained by law, and to be informed of the nature and cause of the accusation; to be confronted with the witnesses against him; to have compulsory process for obtaining witnesses in his favor, and to have the assistance of counsel for his defense.

ARTICLE VII

In suits at common law, where the value in controversy shall exceed twenty dollars, the right of trial by jury shall be preserved, and no fact tried by a jury shall be otherwise reexamined in any court of the United States, than according to the rules of the common law.

ARTICLE VIII

Excessive bail shall not be required, nor excessive fines imposed, nor cruel and unusual punishments inflicted.

ARTICLE IX

The enumeration in the Constitution, of certain rights, shall not be construed to deny or disparage others retained by the people.

ARTICLE X

The powers not delegated to the United States by the Constitution, nor prohibited by it to the States, are reserved to the States respectively, or to the people.

ARTICLE XI[11]

The judicial power of the United States shall not be construed to extend to any suit in law or equity, commenced or prosecuted against one of the United States by citizens of another State, or by citizens or subjects of any foreign State.

ARTICLE XII[12]

The electors shall meet in their respective States and vote by ballot for President and Vice-President, one of whom, at least, shall not be an inhabitant of the same State with themselves; they shall name in their ballots the person voted for as President, and in distinct ballots the person voted for as Vice-President, and they shall make distinct lists of all persons voted for as President, and of all persons voted for as Vice-President, and of the number of votes for each, which lists they shall sign and certify,

[11]Ratified in 1795; proclaimed in 1798.

[12]Adopted in 1804.

and transmit sealed to the seat of the government of the United States, directed to the president of the Senate;—The president of the Senate shall, in the presence of the Senate and House of Representatives, open all the certificates and the votes shall then be counted;—The person having the greatest number of votes for President, shall be the President, if such number be a majority of the whole number of electors appointed; and if no person have such majority, then from the persons having the highest numbers not exceeding three on the list of those voted for as President, the House of Representatives shall choose immediately, by ballot, the President. But in choosing the President, the votes shall be taken by States, the representation from each State having one vote; a quorum for this purpose shall consist of a member or members from two thirds of the States, and a majority of all the States shall be necessary to a choice. And if the House of Representatives shall not choose a President whenever the right of choice shall devolve upon them, before the fourth day of March next following, then the Vice-President shall act as President, as in the case of the death or other constitutional disability of the President.—The person having the greatest number of votes as Vice-President, shall be the Vice-President, if such number be a majority of the whole number of electors appointed, and if no person have a majority, then from the two highest numbers on the list, the Senate shall choose the Vice-President; a quorum for the purpose shall consist of two thirds of the whole number of Senators, and a majority of the whole number shall be necessary to a choice. But no person constitutionally ineligible to the office of President shall be eligible to that of Vice-President of the United States.

ARTICLE XIII[13]

SECTION 1. Neither slavery nor involuntary servitude, except as a punishment for crime whereof the party shall have been duly convicted, shall exist within the United States, or any place subject to their jurisdiction.

SECTION 2. Congress shall have power to enforce this article by appropriate legislation.

ARTICLE XIV[14]

SECTION 1. All persons born or naturalized in the United States, and subject to the jurisdiction thereof, are citizens of the United States and of the State wherein they reside. No State shall make or enforce any law which shall abridge the privileges or immunities of citizens of the United States; nor shall any State deprive any person of life, liberty, or prop-

[13]Adopted in 1865.

[14]Adopted in 1868.

erty, without due process of law; nor deny to any person within its jurisdiction the equal protection of the laws.

SECTION 2. Representatives shall be apportioned among the several States according to their respective numbers, counting the whole number of persons in each State, excluding Indians not taxed. But when the right to vote at any election for the choice of electors for President and Vice President of the United States, Representatives in Congress, the executive and judicial offices of a State, or the members of the legislature thereof, is denied to any of the male inhabitants of such State, being twentyone years of age, and citizens of the United States, or in any way abridged, except for participation in rebellion, or other crime, the basis of representation therein shall be reduced in the proportion which the number of such male citizens shall bear to the whole number of male citizens twentyone years of age in such State.

SECTION 3. No person shall be a Senator or Representative in Congress, or elector of President and Vice President, or hold any office, civil or military, under the United States, or under any State, who, having previously taken an oath, as a member of Congress, or as an officer of the United States, or as a member of any State legislature, or as an executive or judicial officer of any State, to support the Constitution of the United States, shall have engaged in insurrection or rebellion against the same, or given aid or comfort to the enemies thereof. But Congress may by a vote of two thirds of each House, remove such disability.

SECTION 4. The validity of the public debt of the United States, authorized by law, including debts incurred for payment of pensions and bounties for services in suppressing insurrection or rebellion, shall not be questioned. But neither the United States nor any State shall assume or pay any debt or obligation incurred in aid of insurrection or rebellion against the United States, or any claim for the loss or emancipation of any slave; but all such debts, obligations and claims shall be held illegal and void.

SECTION 5. The Congress shall have power to enforce, by appropriate legislation, the provisions of this article.

ARTICLE XV[15]

SECTION 1. The right of citizens of the United States to vote shall not be denied or abridged by the United States or by any State on account of race, color, or previous condition of servitude.

SECTION 2. The Congress shall have power to enforce this article by appropriate legislation.

ARTICLE XVI[16]

The Congress shall have power to lay and collect taxes on incomes, from whatever source derived,

without apportionment among the several States, and without regard to census or enumeration.

ARTICLE XVII

The Senate of the United States shall be composed of two Senators from each State, elected by the people thereof, for six years; and each Senator shall have one vote. The electors in each State shall have the qualifications requisite for electors of the most numerous branch of the State legislatures.

When vacancies happen in the representation of any State in the Senate, the executive authority of such State shall issue writs of election to fill such vacancies: *Provided,* That the legislature of any State may empower the executive thereof to make temporary appointments until the people fill the vacancies by election as the legislature may direct.

This amendment shall not be so construed as to affect the election or term of any Senator chosen before it becomes valid as part of the Constitution.

ARTICLE XVIII[17]

SECTION 1. After one year from the ratification of this article the manufacture, sale, or transportation of intoxicating liquors within, the importation thereof into, or the exportation thereof from the United States and all territory subject to the jurisdiction thereof for beverage purposes is hereby prohibited.

SECTION 2. The Congress and the several States shall have concurrent power to enforce this article by appropriate legislation.

SECTION 3. This article shall be inoperative unless it shall have been ratified as an amendment to the Constitution by the legislatures of the several States, as provided in the Constitution, within seven years from the date of the submission hereof to the States by the Congress.

ARTICLE XIX[18]

The right of citizens of the United States to vote shall not be denied or abridged by the United States or by any State on account of sex.

The Congress shall have power to enforce this article by appropriate legislation.

ARTICLE XX[19]

SECTION 1. The terms of the President and Vice President shall end at noon on the 20th day of Janu-

---

[15]Adopted in 1870.
[16]Adopted in 1913.
[17]Adopted in 1919. Repealed by Article XXI.
[18]Adopted in 1920.
[19]Adopted in 1933.

ary, and the terms of Senators and Representatives at noon on the 3rd day of January, of the years in which such terms would have ended if this article had not been ratified; and the terms of their successors shall then begin.

SECTION 2. The Congress shall assemble at least once in every year, and such meeting shall begin at noon on the 3rd day of January, unless they shall by law appoint a different day.

SECTION 3. If, at the time fixed for the beginning of the term of the President, the President elect shall have died, the Vice President elect shall become President. If a President shall not have been chosen before the time fixed for the beginning of his term, or if the President elect shall have failed to qualify, then the Vice President elect shall act as President until a President shall have qualified; and the Congress may by law provide for the case wherein neither a President elect nor a Vice President elect shall have qualified, declaring who shall then act as President, or the manner in which one who is to act shall be selected, and such person shall act accordingly until a President or Vice President shall have qualified.

SECTION 4. The Congress may by law provide for the case of the death of any of the persons from whom the House of Representatives may choose a President whenever the right of choice shall have devolved upon them, and for the case of the death of any of the persons from whom the Senate may choose a Vice President whenever the right of choice shall have devolved upon them.

SECTION 5. Sections 1 and 2 shall take effect on the 15th day of October following the ratification of this article.

SECTION 6. This article shall be inoperative unless it shall have been ratified as an amendment to the Constitution by the legislatures of three-fourths of the several States within seven years from the date of its submission.

ARTICLE XXI[20]

SECTION 1. The eighteenth article of amendment to the Constitution of the United States is hereby repealed.

SECTION 2. The transportation or importation into any State, Territory or Possession of the United States for delivery or use therein of intoxicating liquors in violation of the laws thereof is hereby prohibited.

SECTION 3. This article shall be inoperative unless it shall have been ratified as an amendment to the Constitution by conventions in the several States, as provided in the Constitution, within seven years from the date of submission hereof to the States by the Congress.

ARTICLE XXII[21]

SECTION 1. No person shall be elected to the office of the President more than twice, and no person who has held the office of President, or acted as President for more than two years of a term to which some other person was elected President shall be elected to the office of the President more than once. But this Article shall not apply to any person holding the office of President when this Article was proposed by the Congress, and shall not prevent any person who may be holding the office of President, or acting as President, during the term within which this Article becomes operative from holding the office of President or acting as President during the remainder of such term.

SECTION 2. This Article shall be inoperative unless it shall have been ratified as an amendment to the Constitution by the legislatures of three-fourths of the several States within seven years from the date of its submission to the States by the Congress.

ARTICLE XXIII[22]

SECTION 1. The District constituting the seat of Government of the United States shall appoint in such manner as the Congress may direct:

A number of electors of President and Vice-President equal to the whole number of Senators and Representatives in Congress to which the District would be entitled if it were a State, but in no event more than the least populous state; they shall be in addition to those appointed by the states, but they shall be considered, for the purposes of the election of President and Vice-President, to be electors appointed by a state; and they shall meet in the District and perform such duties as provided by the twelfth article of amendment.

SECTION 2. The Congress shall have power to enforce this article by appropriate legislation.

ARTICLE XXIV[23]

SECTION 1. The right of citizens of the United States to vote in any primary or other election for President or Vice-President, for electors for President or Vice-President, or for Senator or Representative in Congress, shall not be denied or abridged by the United States or any state by reason of failure to pay any poll tax or other tax.

SECTION 2. The Congress shall have power to enforce this article by appropriate legislation.

---

[20]Adopted in 1933.
[21]Adopted in 1951.
[22]Adopted in 1961.
[23]Adopted in 1964.

ARTICLE XXV[24]

SECTION 1. In case of the removal of the President from office or his death or resignation, the Vice President shall become President.

SECTION 2. Whenever there is a vacancy in the office of the Vice President, the President shall nominate a Vice President who shall take the office upon confirmation by a majority vote of both houses of Congress.

SECTION 3. Whenever the President transmits to the President pro tempore of the Senate and the Speaker of the House of Representatives his written declaration that he is unable to discharge the powers and duties of his office, and until he transmits to them a written declaration to the contrary, such powers and duties shall be discharged by the Vice President as Acting President.

SECTION 4. Whenever the Vice President and a majority of either the principal officers of the executive departments, or of such other body as Congress may by law provide, transmit to the President pro tempore of the Senate and the Speaker of the House of Representatives their written declaration that the President is unable to discharge the powers and duties of his office, the Vice President shall immediately assume the powers and duties of the office as Acting President.

Thereafter, when the President transmits to the Pres-

ident pro tempore of the Senate and the Speaker of the House of Representatives his written declaration that no inability exists, he shall resume the powers and duties of his office unless the Vice President and a majority of either the principal officers of the executive department, or of such other body as Congress may by law provide, transmit within four days to the President pro tempore of the Senate and the Speaker of the House of Representatives their written declaration that the President is unable to discharge the powers and duties of his office. Thereupon Congress shall decide the issue, assembling within 48 hours for that purpose if not in session. If the Congress, within 21 days after receipt of the latter written declaration, or, if Congress is not in session, within 21 days after Congress is required to assemble, determines by two-thirds vote of both houses that the President is unable to discharge the powers and duties of his office, the Vice President shall continue to discharge the same as Acting President; otherwise, the President shall resume the powers and duties of his office.

ARTICLE XXVI[25]

SECTION 1. The right of citizens of the United States, who are eighteen years of age, or older, to vote shall not be denied or abridged by the United States or by any state on account of age.

SECTION 2. The Congress shall have the power to enforce this article by appropriate legislation.

---

[24]Adopted in 1967.

[25]Adopted in 1971.

Table of Cases

Boldface type and page numbers indicate the cases reprinted in this volume; italics indicate cases commented on in the editor's notes; ordinary type indicates cases quoted or discussed in the opinions. For convenience, all cases in which the United States is plaintiff are also indexed under the name of the defendant.

Arizona v. Roberson, 100 L. Ed. 2d 704, **573**
Arkansas v. Sanders, 442 U. S. 753 (1979) 327f.
Arver v. United States, 245 U. S. 366 (1918) 224
Ashcraft v. Tennessee, 322 U. S. 143 (1944) 279
Ashton v. Cameron County Water Improvement Dist., 298 U. S. 513 (1936) 159
Avery v. Alabama, 308 U. S. 444 (1940) 277
Avery v. Georgia, 345 U. S. 559 (1953) 484, 486
Avery v. Midland County, 390 U. S. 474 (1968) 139

Bailey v. Drexel Furniture Co. 259 U. S. 20 (1922) 182, *184, 205*
Bailey v. Richardson, 182 Fed 2d 46 (1950) 234
Baker v. Carr, 369 U. S. 186 (1962), 22, 31, *33,* 37, 81, *138,* 140, 142ff., 476, 560
Baldwin v. New York, 399 U. S. 66 (1970) 352, 354
Baldwin v. Seelig, 294 U. S. 511 (1935) 195
Baltimore v. Dawson, 350 U. S. 877 (1955) 497
Baltimore & O. R. Co. v. Interstate Commerce Commission, 221 U. S. 612 (1911) 16, 213
Bank of the United States v. Halstead, 10 Wheat. 51 (1825) 42
Bantam Books v. Sullivan, 372 U. S. 58 (1963) 394, 399, 411
Barenblatt v. United States, 360 U. S. 109 (1959) 51
Barr v. Columbia, 378 U. S. 146 (1964) 379
Barron v. Baltimore, 7 Pet. 243 (1833) 247, *272, 425*
Barry v. United States ex rel. Cunningham, 279 U. S. 597 (1929) 47
Bates v. Little Rock, 361 U. S. 516 (1960) 291
Batson v. Kentucky, 476 U. S. 79 (1986) 484
Bayard v. Singleton, 1 Martin (N. C.) 42 (1787) 8
Beal v. Doe, 432 U. S. 438 (1977) 526, 526, 528
Bearden v. Georgia, 461 U. S. 660 (1983) 526
Beauharnais v. Illinois, 343 U. S. 250 (1952) 418
Beck v. Ohio, 379 U. S. 89 (1964) 319
Beck v. Washington, 369 U. S. 541 (1962) 419
Beilan v. Board of Public Education, 357 U. S. 299 (1958) 276
Bell v. Maryland, 378 U. S. 226 (1964) 218, 379, 536
Bellotti v. Baird, 428 U. S. 132 (1976) 529, 567
Belmont, United States v.
Benanti v. United States, 355 U. S. 96 (1957) 300
Benton v. Maryland, 395 U. S. 784 (1969) 359
Berea College v. Kentucky, 211 U. S. 45 (1908) 493
Berger v. New York, 388 U. S. 1941 (1967) 323
Berger v. United States, 295 U.S. 78 (1935) 82
Bethea, In re, 215 Pa. Super. 75 (1969) 284
Betts v. Brady, 316 U. S. 455 (1942) 274, 303, 335, 336ff., *525*
Blackburn v. Alabama, 361 U. S. 199 (1960) 311
Blackledge v. Perry, 417 U. S. 21 (1974) 366f.
Blair v. United States, 250 U.S. 273 (1919) 36
Block v. Hirsh, 256 U. S. 135 (1921) 225
Blodgett v. Holden, 275 U. S. 142 (1928) 125
Board of Education v. Allen, 392 U. S. 236 (1968) 406, 437f., 439, 441f.
Board of Governors v. Agnew, 329 U. S. 441 (1947) 237, 240
Board of Rotary Int'l. v. Rotary Club, 95 L. Ed. 2d 474 (1987) 518
Board of Trade v. Olsen, 262 U. S. 1 (1923) 210
Bob Jones University v. United States, 461 U. S. 574 (1983) 429, 439
Bob-Lo Excursion Co. v. Michigan, 333 U. S. 28 (1948) 192
Bolling v. Sharpe, 347 U. S. 497 (1954) 498
Bordenkircher v. Hayes, 434 U. S. 357 (1978) 365
Bouie v. Columbia, 378 U. S. 374 (1964) 379
Bowles v. Willingham, 321 U. S. 503 (1944) 225
Bowsher v. Synar, 478 U. S. 714 (1986) 108, 548, 555, 557, 562
Boyd v. United States, 116 U. S. 616 (1886) 304, 306, *321, 360*
Braden v. United States, 365 U. S. 431 (1961) 51
Bradfield v. Roberts, 175 U. S. 291 (1899) 28, 434, 443

Bradwell v. Illinois, 16 Wall. 130 (1872) 522
Bram v. United States, 168 U. S. 532 (1897) 305, 313
Brandenburg v. Ohio, 395 U. S. 444 (1969) 376
Branzburg v. Hayes, 408 U. S. 665 (1972) 411, 420, 423
Braunfeld v. Brown, 366 U. S. 599 (1961) 451
Breard v. Alexandria, 341 U. S. 622 (1951) 426
Breithaupt v. Abram, 352 U. S. 432 (1957) 279
Bridges v. California, 314 U. S. 252 (1941) 419, 423
Brig Aurora, The, v. United States, 7 Cr. 382 (1813) 56
Brignoni-Ponce, United States v.
Brinegar v. United States, 388 U. S. 160 (1949) 316
Brooks v. United States, 267 U. S. 432 (1925) 202, 205, 221f.
Brown v. Allen, 344 U. S. 443 (1953) 485
Brown v. Board of Education of Topeka, 347 U. S. 483 (1954) *46, 192,* **495,** 503
Brown v. Board of Education of Topeka, 349 U. S. 294 (1955) 503
Brown v. Illinois, 422 U. S. 590 (1975) 310
Brown v. Maryland, 12 Wheat. 419 (1827) 206
Brown v. Mississippi, 297 U. S. 278 (1936) 278, 281, 309, 347
Brown v. Texas, 443 U.S. 47 (1979) 330
Brown v. Walker, 161 U. S. 591 (1896) 42
Brown, United States v.
Brushaber v. Union Pacific Railroad Co., 240 U. S. 1 (1916) 180
Buchanan v. Warley, 245 U. S. 60 (1917) 487, 489
Buck v. Bell, 274 U. S. 200 (1927) 294
Buckley v. Valeo, 424 U. S. 1 (1976) *80,* **98,** *103,* 105, *108,* 110, *548, 551, 557, 559*
Bullock v. Carter, 405 U. S. 134 (1972) *472, 476*
Bunting v. Oregon, 243 U. S. 427 (1917) 261
Burnet v. Coronado Oil & Gas Co., 285 U. S. 393 (1932) 162
Burr, United States v.
Burroughs v. United States, 290 U. S. 534 (1934) 131
Burstyn v. Wilson, 343 U. S. 495 (1952) 397, 399
Butler v. Michigan, 352 U. S. 380 (1957) 394, 409
Butler v. Perry, 240 U. S. 328 (1916) 543
Butler, United States v.
Butz v. Economou, 438 U. S. 478 (1978) 85ff.

Cabana v. Bullock, 474 U.S. 376 (1986) 564
Calandra, United States v.
Calder v. Bull, 3 Dall. 387 (1798) 231, *249*
California v. Brown, 479 U. 538 (1987) 567
California v. Central Pacific R. Co., 127 U. S. 1 (1888) 162
California, United States v.
Callan v. Wilson, 127 U.S. 540 (1888) 351
Camara v. Municipal Court, 387 U. S. 523 (1967) 319, 360, 362
Caminetti v. United States, 242 U. S. 470 (1917) 198, 216
Cantwell v. Connecticut, 310 U. S. 296 (1940) 381, 425
Cappaert v. United States,' 426 U. S. 128 (1976) 198
Cardwell v. Lewis, 417 U. S. 483 (1974) 325f.
Carolene Products Co., United States v.
Carriage Tax Case. *See* **Hylton v. United States**
Carrington v. Rash, 380 U. S. 89 (1965) 136
Carroll v. United States, 267 U. S. 132 (1925) 325, 326ff.
Carter v. Carter Coal Co., 298 U. S. 238 (1936) 61, 170, 208, 210, 212, 223
Case v. Bowles, 327 U. S. 92 (1946) 152, 170
Cassell v. Texas, 339 U. S. 282 (1950) 485
Chadwick, United States
Chambers v. Florida, 309 U.S. 227 (1940) 279, 311
Chambers v. Maroney, 399 U. S. 42 (1970) 325, 328f.
Champion v. Ames, 188 U. S. 321 (1903) 202, 204f., 221
Chae Chan Ping v. United States, 130 U. S. 581 (1889) 227

Gitlow v. New York, 268 U.S. 652 (1925) *268,* 270, *291, 370,* **371,** 377
Gladstone, Realtors v. Village of Bellwood, 441 U. S. 91 (1979) 35
Gober v. Birmingham, 373 U. S. 374 (1963) 388
Godfrey v. Georgia, 446 U. S. 420 (1980) 341, 565
Goesaert v. Cleary, 335 U. S. 464 (1948) 459, *517,* 520
Go-Bart Importing Co. v. United States, 282 U. S. 344 (1931) 552f.
Gojack v. United States, 384 U. S. 702 (1966) 51
Goldberg v. Kelly, 397 U. S. 254 (1970) 365
Goldman v. United States, 316 U. S. 129 (1942) 322, 323
Goldstein v. United States, 316 U.S. 114 (1942) 300
Gomillion v. Lightfoot, 364 U. S. 339 (1960) 22
Gompers v. Buck's Stove & Range Co., 221 U. S. 418 (1911) 371
Gong Lum v. Rice, 275 U. S. 78 (1927) 493, 498
Gooch v. United States, 297 U. S. 124 (1936) 202, 221
Gordon v. United States, 2 Wall. 561 (1865) 16
Gould v. United States, 255 U. S. 298 (1921) 321f.
Grace, United States v.
Granger Cases. *See* **Munn v. Illinois**
Gravel v. United States, 408 U. S. 606 (1972) 81
Graves v. New York ex rel. O'Keefe, 306 U. S. 466 (1939) 163, 167
Gray v. Sanders, 372 U. S. 368 (1963) 138, 140
Green v. County School Board, 391 U. S. 430 (1968) 497, 501ff.
Gregg v. Georgia, 428 U. S. 153 (1976) 338, *564,* 567, 573
Griffin v. Breckenridge, 403 U. S. 88 (1971) 214, 544
Griffin v. Illinois, 351 U. S. 12 (1956) 276, 472, 526
Griffin v. Maryland, 378 U. S. 130 (1964) 379
Griffin v. School Board of Prince Edward County, 377 U. S. 218 (1964) 46, 497
Griggs v. Duke Power Co., 401 U. S. 424 (1971) 507
Grisham v. Hagan, 361 U. S. 278 (1960) 348
Griswold v. Connecticut, 381 U. S. 479 (1965) 288, 293ff.
Groppi v. Wisconsin, 400 U. S. 505 (1971) 347
Grosjean v. American Press Co., 297 U. S. 233 (1936) 277, 337
Grossman, Ex parte, 267 U. S. 87 (1925) 44
Grovey v. Townsend, 295 U. S. 45 (1935) 134f., 137f.
Guinn v. United States, 238 U. S. 347 (1915) 134, 541
Gutknecht v. United States, 396 U. S. 295 (1970) 224

Hague v. CIO, 307 U. S. 496 (1939) 118, 423
Haig v. Agee, 453 U. S. 280 (1981) 124
Hall v. De Cuir, 95 U. S. 485 (1878) 192, 216
Hamilton v. Alabama, 368 U. S. 52 (1961) 309
Hamilton v. Kentucky Distilleries Co., 251 U. S. 146 (1919) 226
Hamilton v. Regents of the U. of California, 293 U. S. 245 (1934) 268, 273, 425
Hamm v. Rock Hill, 379 U. S. 306 (1964) 217, 379, 381
Hammer v. Dagenhart, 247 U. S. 251 (1918) 159, 170, *182, 184,* **202,** *205, 220, 222*
Hampton, J. W., Jr. & Co. v. United States, 276 U. S. 394 (1928) 42, 56, 108
Hannegan v. Esquire, 327 U. S. 146 (1946) 363
Hannibal & St. J. R. Co. v. Husen, 95 U. S. 465 (1878) 193
Harlow v. Fitzgerald, 457 U. S. 800 (1982) 83
Harman v. Forssenius, 380 U. S. 528 (1965) 131
Harper v. Virginia Bd. of Elections, 383 U. S. 663 (1966) 131, 135, 468
Harris v. McRae, 448 U. S. 297 (1980) 448, 526
Harris v. New York, 401 U. S. 222 (1971) 300, 310
Harris v. United States, 331 U. S. 145 (1947) 315
Hart, United States v.
Hartzel v. United States, 322 U.S. 680 (1944) 370
Hauenstein v. Lynham, 100 U. S. 483 (1880) 227
Hawaii v. Mankichi, 190 U. S. 197 (1903) 357
Hawke v. Smith, 253 U. S. 221 (1920) 1

Hawker v. New York, 170 U. S. 189 (1898) 231, 239f.
Hayburn's Case, 2 Dall. 409 (1792) 553
Haynes v. Washington, 373 U. S. 503 (1963) 309, 312
Head Money Cases, 112 U. S. 580 (1884) 165
Heart of Atlanta Motel v. United States, 379 U.S. 241 (1964) 172, **213,** 218, *379, 507, 536,* 540, 542, 545
Hebert v. Louisiana, 272 U. S. 312 (1926) 271
Heller v. New York, 413 U. S. 483 (1973) 394
Helvering v. Davis, 301 U.S. 619 (1937) 185, 186
Henderson v. United States, 339 U. S. 816 (1950) 494
Hennen, Ex parte, 13 Pet. 230 (1839) 552
Henry, United States v.
Henry v. United States, 361 U. S. 98 (1959) 328
Hernandez v. Texas, 347 U. S. 475 (1954) 484
Hester v. United States, 265 U. S. 57 (1924) 321, 325
Hiatt v. Brown, 339 U. S. 103 (1950) 347
Hill v. Texas, 316 U. S. 400 (1942) 484f.
Hill v. Wallace, 259 U. S. 44 (1922) 182
Hipolite Egg Co., 220 U. S. 45 (1911) 205
Hirabayashi v. United States, 320 U. S. 81 (1943) 462, 463f.
Hodel v. Virginia Surface Mining & Recl. Assn., 452 U. S. 264 (1981) 172
Hodges v. United States, 203 U. S. 1 (1906) 543, 545f.
Hoffa v. United States, 385 U.S. 293 (1966) 322
Hohri, United States v.
Hohri v. United States, 782 F. 2d 227 (1986) 462
Hoke v. United States, 227 U. S. 308 (1913) 202, 216, 536
Holden v. Hardy, 169 U. S. 366 (1898) 260, 263
Hollingworth v. Virginia, 3 Dall. 378 (1798) 1, 4
Holmes v. Atlanta, 350 U. S. 879 (1955) 498
Home Building & Loan Ass'n. v. Blaisdell, 290 U. S. 398 (1934) 224, 241
Houchins v. KQED, 438 U. S. 1 (1978) 420, 424
Howatt v. Kansas, 258 U. S. 181 (1922) 387
Hoyt v. Florida, 368 U. S. 57 (1961) 517, 520
Humphrey's Executor v. United States, 295 U. S. 602 (1935) 81, 89, **94,** 101f., *103,* 106, *109,* 110, 555f., 559, 562
Hunter v. Erickson, 393 U. S. 385 (1969) 487
Hunter v. Pittsburgh, 297 U. S. 161 (1907) 142
Hurd v. Hodge, 334 U. S. 24 (1948) 487
Hurtado v. California, 110 U. S. 516 (1884) 264, *268,* 270, 272, 273, 337
Hutto v. Davis, 454 U. S. 370 (1982) 339
Hylton v. United States, 3 Dall. 171 (1796) *8, 15,* **177,** *180*

Illinois v. Gates, 462 U. S. 213 (1983) 331
Illinois ex rel. McCollum v. Board of Education. See McCollum v. Board of Education
Illinois v. Allen, 397 U. S. 337 (1970) 352
Immigration and Naturalization Service v. Chadha, 462 U. S. 919 (1983) 103, 110, 112, *548*
Immigration and Naturalization Service v. Lopez-Mendoza, 468 U. S. 1032 (1984) 334
Income Tax Cases. See Pollock v. Farmers' Loan & Trust Co.
Indian Motocycle Co. v. United States, 283 U. S. 570 (1931) 162
Indian Territory Illuminating Oil Co. v. Oklahoma, 240 U. S. 522 (1916) 162
Insurance Company v. Ritchie, 5 Wall. 541 (1867) 46
Intermountain Rate Cases, 234 U. S. 476 (1914) 42
International Boxing Club of New York, United States v.
Interstate Commerce Commission v. Brimson, 144 U. S. 477 (1894) 47
Interstate Circuit, Inc. v. Dallas, 390 U. S. 676 (1968) 402f.
Irvin v. Dowd, 366 U. S. 717 (1961) 419
Irvine v. California, 347 U. S. 128 (1954) 281

Jackson, Ex parte, 96 U. S. 727 (1878) 323
Jacobellis v. Ohio, 378 U. S. 184 (1964) 400, 402f., 406f.

McCray v. United States, 195 U. S. 27 (1904) 55, 182, 184, 205
McCulloch v. Maryland, 4 Wheat. 316 (1819) *8, 12, 71,* 81, **145,** *152, 159,* 161, *162,* 170, 184, *187,* 217, 541
McCullagh, United States v.
McDonald v. Board of Election Comm'rs, 394 U. S. 801 (1969) 467, 468
McDonald v. United States, 335 U. S. 451 (1948) 315
McElroy v. United States ex rel. Guagliardo, 361 U. S. 281 (1960) 348
McGautha v. California, 402 U. S. 183 (1971) 340, 343
McGowan v. Maryland, 366 U. S. 420 (1961) 448, 451, 455f., 460
McGrain v. Daugherty, 273 U. S. 135 (1927) *23,* **46,** 52, 102, 557
McKeiver v. Pennsylvania, 403 U. S. 528 (1971) 283, *352*
McLaurin v. Oklahoma State Regents, 339 U. S. 637 (1950) 494, 494, 498f.
McLean v. Arkansas Board of Education, 529 F. Supp. 1255 (1982) 446
McNabb v. United States, 318 U. S. 332 (1943) 274
Meek v. Pittenger, 421 U. S. 349 (1975) 439
Meese v. Keene, 95 L. Ed 2d 415 (1987) 376
Memoirs v. Massachusetts, 383 U. S. 413 (1966) 401, 402f., 408
Merryman, Ex parte, 17 Fed. Cas. 9487 (1861) 65
Metcalf & Eddy v. Mitchell, 269 U. S. 514 (1926) 162, 168
Meyer v. Nebraska, 262 U. S. 390 (1923) 268, 289, 294, 296, 527
Michael M. v. Sonoma County, 450 U. S. 464 (1981) 521
Michaelson v. United States, 291 Fed. 940 (1923) 44
Michigan v. DeFillippo, 443 U. S. 31 (1979) 330
Michigan v. Mosley, 423 U. S. 96 (1975) 577, 579f.
Michigan v. Tucker, 417 U. S. 433 (1974) 579
Milk Control Board v. Eisenberg Farm Products, 306 U. S. 345 (1639) 195
Miller v. California, 413 U. S. 15 (1973) 405
Milligan, Ex parte, 4 Wall. 2 (1866) *43,* **65,** 126, *348*
Milliken v. Bradley, 418 U. S. 717 (1974) 502
Milliken v. Bradley, 433 U. S. 267 (1977) 503
Minersville School District v. Gobitis, 310 U. S. 586 (1940) 428, 429ff.
Minnesota v. Barber, 136 U. S. 313 (1890) 194
Minnesota v. Blasius, 290 U. S. 1 (1933) 200
Minor v. Happersett, 21 Wall. 162 (1875) 128, 130, 471
Mintz v. Baldwin, 289 U. S. 346 (1933) 194
Miranda v. Arizona, 384 U. S. 436 (1966) *300,* **308,** *342, 573,* 576f., 580
Mishkin v. New York, 383 U. S. 502 (1966) 403f.
Mississippi University for Women v. Hogan, 458 U. S. 718 (1982) *460, 478,* **520**
Mississippi v. Johnson, 4 Wall. 475 (1867) 22, 79
Missouri v. Holland, 252 U. S. 416 (1920) 227
Missouri v. Lewis, 101 U. S. 22 (1880) 266
Missouri ex rel. Gaines v. Canada, 305 U. S. 337 (1938) 476, 493, 495, 498
Monitor Patriot Co. v. Ray, 401 U. S. 265 (1971) 418
Monroe v. Pape, 365 U. S. 167 (1961) 301
Mooney v. Holohan, 294 U. S. 103 (1935) 276
Moore v. Dempsey, 261 U. S. 86 (1923) 273, 275
Moore v. Ogilvie, 394 U. S. 814 (1969) 135
Moose Lodge No. 107 v. Irvis, 407 U. S. 163 (1972) 488
Moran v. Burbine, 475 U. S. 412 (1986) 574
Morehead v. New York ex rel. Tipaldo, 298 U. S. 587 (1936) 262, 262
Morgan v. Tennessee Valley Authority, 312 U.S. 701 (1941) 95
Morgan v. Tennessee Valley Authority, 115 Fed. 2d 990 (1940) 95
Morgan v. Virginia, 328 U. S. 373 (1946) 192, 216
Morrison v. Olson, 101 L. Ed. 2d 569 (1988) 547
Mosley, United States
Motor Coach Employees v. Missouri, 374 U. S. 74 (1963) 152
Mueller v. Allen, 463 U. S. 388 (1983) 434, **437,** 448
Mugler v. Kansas, 123 U. S. 623 (1887) 257
Mulford v. Smith, 307 U.S. 38 (1939) 170, 209, 222
Muller v. Oregon, 208 U. S. 412 (1908) 261, 263, 520

Munn v. Illinois, 94 U. S. 113 (1877) 249, *253ff., 257, 267*
Murdock v. Pennsylvania, 319 U. S. 104 (1943) *291,* **425**
Murray v. Goldstein, 385 U. S. 816 (1966) 452
Murray's Lessee v. Hoboken Land & Improvement Co., 18 How. 272 (1856) 264f.
Muskrat v. United States, 219 U. S. 346 (1911) 14, *33, 44, 553*
Mutual Film Corp. v. Industrial Comm. of Ohio, 236 U. S. 230 (1915) 397
Myers v. United States, 272 U. S. 52 (1926) *41,* 75f., **89,** *97f.,* 102, 105, *109,* 110, 453, 555f., 561f.

NAACP v. Alabama, 357 U. S. 449 (1958) 289, 380
NAACP v. Alabama, 377 U.S. 288 (1964) 289, 380
NAACP v. Button, 371 U. S. 415 (1963) 289, 380, 398
Nardone v. United States, 302 U. S. 379 (1937) 274
National Prohibition Cases, 253 U. S. 350 (1920) 1
National League of Cities v. Usery, 426 U.S. 833 (1976) *160,* **167,** *171,* 171, 175
Neagle, In re, 135 U. S. 1 (1890) 71
Near v. Minnesota, 283 U. S. 697 (1931) 268, 273, *384,* **389,** 395f., *397,* 398, 411, 413, 415f., *425*
Nebbia v. New York, 291 U. S. 502 (1934) 253
Nebraska Press Asso. v. Stuart, 427 U. S. 539 (1976) 420, 421ff.
New Jersey v. Portash, 440 U. S. 450 (1979) 310
New Orleans Waterworks Co. v. New Orleans, 164 U. S. 471 (1896) 46
New State Ice Company v. Liebmann, 285 U. S. 262 (1932) 254
New York ex rel. Pennsylvania R. Co. v. Knight, 192 U. S. 21 (1904) 206
New York Times Co. v. United States, 403 U. S. 713 (1971) 410
New York Times v. Sullivan, 376 U. S. 254 (1964) 413, 418
New York Trust Co. v. Eisner, 256 U. S. 345 (1921) 127
New York v. Belton, 453 U. S. 454 (1981) 316
New York v. Miln, 11 Pet. 102 (1837) 195, 525
New York v. Quarles, 467 U. S. 649 (1984) 573
New York v. United States, 257 U.S. 591 (1922) 166
Newberry v. United States, 256 U. S. 232 (1921) 47, 131, 137
Ng Fung Ho v. White, 259 U. S. 276 (1922) 126
Nixon, United States
Nixon v. Condon, 286 U. S. 73 (1927) 134, 137
Nixon v. Fitzgerald, 457 U. S. 731 (1982) 83
Nixon v. Herndon, 273 U. S. 536 (1927) 134, 137
Nixon v. Sirica, 487 Fed. 2d 700 (1973) 79, 82
NLRB v. Jones & Laughlin Steel Corp., 301 U. S. 1 (1937) 170, **208,** 222
Norris v. Alabama, 294 U. S. 587 (1935) 484
Norris v. Clymer, 2 Pa. St. 277 (1845) 12
Norris v. Crocker, 13 How. 429 (1852) 46
North Carolina v. Pearce, 395 U. S. 711 (1969) 366f.
Northern Securities Co. v. United States, 193 U. S. 197 (1904) 260
Norwood v. Harrison, 413 U. S. 455 (1973) 438
Nyquist v. Lee, 402 U. S. 935 (1971) 500

O'Brien, United States v.
O'Callahan v. Parker, 395 U. S. 258 (1969) 348
O'Hair v. Paine, 401 U. S. 955 (1971) 452
O'Neil v. Vermont, 144 U. S. 323 (1892) 339
Oceanic Steam Navigation Co. v. Stranahan, 214 U. S. 320 (1909) 42
Ogden v. Saunders, 12 Wheat. 213 (1827) 240
Ohio Oil Co., United States
Ohio ex rel. Davis v. Hildebrant, 241 U. S. 565 (1916) 24
Oklahoma v. Civil Service Comm'n, 330 U.S. 127 (1947) 186
Oliver, In re, 333 U. S. 257 (1948) 349
Oliver Iron Mining Co. v. Lord, 262 U. S. 172 (1923) 197
Olmstead v. United States, 277 U. S. 438 (1928) 300, 304, 314, *321f.,* 323, 364

On Lee v. United States, 343 U. S. 747 (1952) 322
Oregon v. Bradshaw, 462 U. S. 1039 (1983) 577ff.
Oregon v. Elstad, 470 U. S. 298 (1985) 574
Oregon v. Hass, 420 U. S. 714 (1975) 310
Oregon v. Mitchell, 400 U. S. 112 (1970) 2, 136
Organization for a Better Austin v. Keefe, 402 U. S. 415 (1971) 411, 411, 415
Orito, United States v.
Orr v. Orr, 440 U. S. 268 (1979) 521
Osborn v. Bank of the United States, 9 Wheat. 738 (1824) 17, 146
Oyama v. California, 332 U. S. 633 (1948) 481

Pacific Railway Comm., In re, 32 Fed 241 (1887) 16
Pacific States Tel. & Teleg. Co. v. Oregon, 223 U. S. 118 (1912) 19, 22
Palko v. Connecticut, 302 U. S. 319 (1937) 272, 276, 278, 280, 290, 294, 301, *335,* 337f., *349f.,* 395, 406
Palmer v. Thompson, 403 U. S. 217 (1971) 498
Panama Refining Co. v Ryan, 293 U. S. 388 (1935) 57
Panhandle Oil Co. v. Mississippi, 277 U.S. 218 (1928) 162
Papachristou v. Jacksonville, 405 U. S. 156 (1972) 275
Paramount Pictures, United States v.
Paris Adult Theater I v. Slaton, 413 U. S. 49 (1973) 404f., **405**
Parker v. Gladden, 385 U.S. 363 (1966) 347
Patterson v. Colorado, 205 U.S. 454 (1907) 268, 371
Patterson v. Illinois, 101 L. Ed. 2d 261 (1988) 575
Patton v. United States, 281 U. S. 276 (1930) 347, 353, 357
Peik v. Chicago & N. W. R. Co., 94 U. S. 164 (1877) 191
Pell v. Procunier, 417 U. S. 817 (1974) 420, 423
Peltier, United States v.
Pennekamp v. Florida, 328 U. S. 331 (1946) 419
Pennsylvania Hospital v. Philadelphia, 245 U. S. 20 (1917) 241
Pennsylvania v. Wheeling & Belmont Bridge Co., 18 How. 421 (1856) 42
Pensacola Teleg. Co. v. Western Union Teleg. Co., 96 U. S. 1 (1878) 198
People v. Defore, 242 N. Y. 13 (1926) 303, 305, *315,* 333
Perez, United States v.
Perez v. Brownell, 356 U. S. 44 (1958) 123f., 125ff.
Perkins, United States v.
Perkins v. Elg, 307 U. S. 325 (1939) 123
Peters v. Kiff, 407 U. S. 493 (1972) 485
Phillips v. Marietta Corp., 400 U. S. 542 (1971) 517
Pierce v. Society of Sisters, 268 U. S. 510 (1925) 289, 296, 433, 527
Pierce v. United States, 252 U. S. 239 (1920) 370
Place, United States v.
Planned Parenthood Assn. v. Ashcroft, 462 U. S. 467 (1983) 292
Planned Parenthood of Missouri v. Danforth, 428 U. S. 52 (1976) 292, 527
Plessy v. Ferguson, 163 U. S. 537 (1896) 490, *493f.,* 495, *495f.,* 498f., 505
Plyler v. Doe, 457 U. S. 202 (1982) 478, *517*
Poe v. Ullman, 367 U. S. 497 (1961) 30, 288
Poelker v. Doe, 432 U. S. 519 (1977) 526, 529
Pointer v. Texas, 380 U. S. 400 (1965) 347
Pollard v. Hagan, 3 How. 212 (1845) 157
Pollock v. Farmers' Loan & Trust Co., 158 U. S. 601 (1895) *2, 15, 44,* **180,** *208*
Pope v. Williams, 193 U. S. 621 (1904) 135
Poulos v. New Hampshire, 345 U. S. 395 (1953) 385, 387
Powell v. Alabama, 287 U. S. 45 (1932) 267, *272, 273, 276, 277f., 335,* 336ff., *349, 390, 484, 525*
Powell v. Hart, 396 U. S. 1055 (1970) 47
Powell v. McCormack, 395 U. S. 486 (1969) 23, 47, 81
Powell v. Texas, 392 U. S. 514 (1968) 339
Preston v. United States, 376 U. S. 364 (1964) 319
Price, United States v.

Prince v. Massachusetts, 321 U. S. 158 (1944) 409, 429
Prize Cases, 2 Black 635 (1863) 73
Prudential Insurance Co. v. Cheek, 259 U. S. 530 (1922) 268

Quirin, Ex parte, 317 U. S. 1 (1942) 66

Rabinowitz, United States v.
Radovich v. National Football League, 352 U. S. 445 (1957) 197
Railroad Commission v. Chicago, B. & Q. R. Co., 257 U. S. 563 (1922) 200
Raines, United States v.
Rankin v. McPherson, 97 L. Ed. 2d 315 (1987) 360
Rassmussen v. United States, 197 U. S. 516 (1900) 353
Ray v. Blair, 343 U. S. 214 (1952) 131
Rea v. United States, 350 U. S. 214 (1956) 301
Redrup v. New York, 386 U. S. 767 (1967) 404f., 409
Reed v. Reed, 401 U. S. 71 (1971) 517, 519f.
Reid v. Covert, 354 U. S. 1 (1957) 228, 348
Reidel, United States v.
Reitman v. Mulkey, 387 U. S. 369 (1967) 487f.
Relford v. Commandant, 401 U. S. 355 (1971) 348
Reynolds, United States v.
Reynolds v. Sims, 377 U. S. 533 (1964) 46, **138,** 468 , 529
Reynolds v. United States, 98 U. S. 145 (1879) 425, 427, 451
Rhode Island v. Innis, 446 U.S. 291 (1980) 330, 578
Ribnik v. McBride, 277 U. S. 350 (1928) 254
Rice v. Elmore, 333 U. S. 875 (1948) 135
Richardson, United States v.
Richmond School Bd. v. Virginia School Bd., 412 U. S. 92 (1973) 502
Richmond Newspapers, Inc. v. Virginia, 448 U. S. 555 (1980) 418
Rideau v. Louisiana, 373 U. S. 723 (1963) 419
Roaden v. Kentucky, 413 U. S. 496 (1973) 394
Robbins v. California, 453 U. S. 420 (1981) 327, 329
Roberts v. Boston, 5 Cush. (Mass.) 198 (1849) 491
Roberts v. Louisiana, 428 U. S. 325 (1976) 341
Roberts v. United States Jaycees, 468 U. S. 609 (1984) 518
Robertson v. Baldwin, 165 U. S. 275 (1897) 543
Robinson, United States v.
Robinson v. California, 370 U. S. 660 (1962) 303, 339
Robinson v. Florida, 378 U. S. 153 (1964) 379
Rochin v. California, 342 U. S. 165 (1952) 278, *281, 282f., 309*
Rock Royal Co-operative, United States v.
Roe v. Wade, 410 U. S. 113 (1973) *2,* **291,** *406, 409, 526, 527ff.*
Rogers v. Bellei, 401 U. S. 815 (1970) 124
Rogers v. Richmond, 365 U. S. 534 (1961) 279, 309
Ross, United States v.
Rostker v. Goldberg, 453 U. S. 57 (1981) 225, 521
Roth v. United States, 354 U. S. 476 (1957) 393f., 400f., 402ff., 406f.
Rowan v. United States Post Office, 397 U. S. 728 (1970) 401
Rowold v. Perfetto, 355 U. S. 115 (1957) 232
Royster Guano Co. v. Virginia, 253 U. S. 412 (1920) 460, 479
Rummel v. Estelle, 445 U. S. 263 (1980) 339
Ruppert v. Caffey, 251 U. S. 264 (1920) 226
Russell v. United States, 369 U. S. 749 (1962) 51

Saia v. New York, 334 U. S. 558 (1948) 384
Sailors v. Kent Board of Education, 387 U. S. 105 (1967) 468
San Antonio v. Rodriguez, 411 U. S. 1 (1973) *291,* **471,** *479, 482, 505*

United States v. Ohio Oil Co., 234 U. S. 548 (1914) 198
United States v. Orito, 413 U. S. 139 (1973) 401
United States v. Paramount Pictures, 334 U. S. 131 (1948) 397
United States v. Peltier, 442 U. S. 531 (1975) 329
United States v. Perez, 9 Wheat. 579 (1824) 359
United States v. Perkins, 116 U. S. 483 (1886) 91, 93, 561
United States v. Place, 462 U. S. 696 (1983) 317
United States v. Price, 383 U. S. 787 (1966) 535, 536
United States v. Reese, 92 U. S. 214 (1876) 538, 543
United States v. Rabinowitz, 339 U. S. 56 (1950) 316
United States v. Raines, 362 U. S. 17 (1960) 583, 585
United States v. Reidel, 402 U. S. 351 (1971) 401
United States v. Reynolds, 234 U. S. 1 (1953) 82, 417
United States v. Richardson, 418 U. S. 166 (1974) 34, 37, 39
United States v. Robinson, 414 U. S. 218 (1973) 317
United States v. Rock Royal Co-operative, 307 U. S. 533 (1939) 222
United States v. Ross, 456 U. S. 798 (1982) 325
United States v. SCRAP, 412 U. S. 669 (1973) 33f., 35, 37
United States v. Seeger, 380 U. S. 163 (1965) 224
United States v. Shipp, 203 U. S. 563 (1906) 44
United States v. Shauver, 214 Fed. 154 (1914) 227, 228
United States v. Shubert, 348 U. S. 222 (1955) 197
United States v. Simpson, 252 U. S. 465 (1920) 198
United States v. Sisson, 297 Fed. Supp. 902 (1969) 224
United States v. Smith, 286 U. S. 6 (1932) 95
United States v. Sprague, 282 U. S. 716 (1931) 1
United States v. Texas, 339 U. S. 707 (1950) 157
United States ex rel. Toth v. Quarles, 350 U. S. 11 (1955) 348
United States v. Twelve 200-foot Reels, 413 U. S. 123 (1973) 401
United States v. United Mine Workers, 330 U. S. 258 (1947) 44
United States v. Wade, 388 U. S. 218 (1967) 279, 309
United States v. Williams, 341 U. S. 70 (1951) 535, 536
United States v. Wong Kim Ark, 169 U. S. 649 (1898) 123
University of California v. Bakke, 438 U. S. 265 (1978) 462, 507
University of Illinois v. United States, 289 U. S. 48 (1933) 164, 166, *184*

Vallandigham, Ex parte, 1 Wall. 243 (1864) 65
Valley Forge Christian College v. Americans United, 454 U. S. 464 (1982) 33, *435*
Veazie Bank v. Fenno, 8 Wall. 533 (1869) 165, 184, 205, 222
Vidal v. Girard's Executors, 2 How. 127 (1884) 434 443
Virginia, Ex parte, 100 U. S. 339 (1880) 484, 523
Virginia v. Rives, 100 U. S. 313 (1880) 484
Virginian Ry. Co. v. System Federation No. 40, 300 U. S. 515 (1937) 208, 211
Von Moltke v. Gillies, 332 U. S. 708 (1948) 335

Wabash, St. L. & P. Ry Co. v. Illinois, 118 U. S. 557 (1886) 191
Walder v. United States, 374 U. S. 62 (1954) 300, 310
Walker v. Birmingham, 388 U. S. 307 (1967) *83,* **384**
Walker v. Sauvinet, 92 U. S. 90 (1876) 273, 347
Wallace v. Jaffree, 472 U. S. 38 (1985) 443, 444f., 448 450
Walz v. Tax Commission, 397 U. S. 664 (1970) 437, 452, 453, 456
Ward v. Maryland, 12 Wall. 418 (1871) 120
Warden v. Hayden, 387 U. S. 294 (1967) 318ff., 321, 323
Ware v. Hylton, 3 Dall. 199 (1796) 227
Washington v. Davis, 426 U. S. 229 (1976) 486, 507
Washington v. Seattle School Dist., 458 U. S. 457 (1982) 487
Washington v. Texas, 388 U. S. 14 (1967) 347
Watkins v. United States, 354 U. S. 178 (1957) 51, 52ff.
Watson v. Memphis, 373 U. S. 526 (1963) 498